Fundamentals of Federal Tax Procedure and Enforcement

ASPEN SELECT SERIES

FUNDAMENTALS OF FEDERAL TAX PROCEDURE AND ENFORCEMENT

Allen D. Madison
Professor of Law
University of South Dakota School of Law

 Wolters Kluwer

To contact Customer Service, e-mail customer.service@wolterskluwer.com, call 1-800-234-1660, fax 1-800-901-9075, or mail correspondence to:

Wolters Kluwer
Attn: Order Department
PO Box 990
Frederick, MD 21705

Printed in the United States of America.

1 2 3 4 5 6 7 8 9 0

ISBN 978-1-5438-1005-9

Library of Congress Cataloging-in-Publication Data application is in process.

FSC

MIX

FSC® C103993

About Wolters Kluwer Legal & Regulatory U.S.

Wolters Kluwer Legal & Regulatory U.S. delivers expert content and solutions in the areas of law, corporate compliance, health compliance, reimbursement, and legal education. Its practical solutions help customers successfully navigate the demands of a changing environment to drive their daily activities, enhance decision quality and inspire confident outcomes.

Serving customers worldwide, its legal and regulatory portfolio includes products under the Aspen Publishers, CCH Incorporated, Kluwer Law International, ftwilliam.com and MediRegs names. They are regarded as exceptional and trusted resources for general legal and practice-specific knowledge, compliance and risk management, dynamic workflow solutions, and expert commentary.

To Dad

Summary of Contents

Table of Contents

Preface

A tax system is integral to civilization and is one of democracy's greatest accomplishments. It is important for any tax professional to learn how the federal tax system works. The system, however, does not present a welcoming structure.

Any course on federal tax procedure and enforcement should illuminate a simple path through the thicket of rules and procedures that comprise the federal tax system, giving the students the tools to venture into the thicket when called upon to do so. After taking a course from these materials, students often find themselves surprised that the IRS—along with the rest of the tax system—is not as scary and oppressive as they thought. The thicket is no longer an opaque black box to be avoided.

This book makes sense of a seemingly random collection of dense rules and seemingly inaccessible entities governing federal tax procedure and enforcement. For ease of understanding, the rules and concepts can be broken down into four distinct parts based on the decisions and determinations the parties to a tax dispute must make as well as the rules affecting those decisions, as follows:

1. The taxpayer's determination whether to comply with the tax laws (Unit 1). This decision must consider the negative consequences imposed for noncompliance with the tax laws. This stage of tax enforcement is referred to here as noncompliance as the taxpayer has not yet decided to comply.

2. The taxpayer's determination on how to comply with the tax laws (Unit 2). The taxpayer must translate the government's communications regarding its expectations on how to file, how much to pay, and how long the parties have to catch an error and then act accordingly. This stage of enforcement is referred to as compliance because the taxpayer has decided to comply and has to figure out how.

3. The IRS reviews returns to determine whether a taxpayer owes more tax (Unit 3). If on investigation the IRS decides the taxpayer underreported tax, the IRS will make a preliminary determination, negotiate most cases, and then issue a final determination if no settlement is reached. This stage of enforcement is referred to as the IRS's tax determination authority because the IRS, after investigation and negotiation, reaches a final determination.

4. Taxpayers may seek judicial review of the IRS's determinations (Unit 4). The taxpayer must decide on the forum in which to sue, sue, and then appeal if the result is unacceptable. This stage of enforcement is referred to as judicial review for reasons that are self-evident.

Broken down into a table, the course proceeds sequentially through these stages, as follows:

Noncompliance	Compliance	IRS Determination Authority	Judicial Review
• Criminal liability • Civil penalties • Enforced collection	• Self-assess • Report tax • Pay tax • Consider changes	• Return review • Negotiation • Final determination	• Choose forum • Sue • Appeal

A three-credit hour J.D. or LL.M course should proceed through all four of the above stages in this book. In a two-credit hour course, an instructor may want to pick and choose the chapters that fit with the intended focus. For example, a two-credit hour course focused solely on tax controversies should cover Units 3 and 4 along with Chapter 10 on statutes of limitations.

A clinic course could proceed sequentially as set forth above. The problem in a clinic, however, is that a clinic professor may want the students to learn it all immediately so that case work may begin. The best way to deal with this inclination is to change the order and focus on the topics immediately impacting the bulk of the clinic's cases. Thus, a clinical professor may want to start with collection, return review, negotiation, or Tax Court and then revert back to the beginning to proceed through the other chapters after acquiring the tools to deal with the clinic's immediate caseload.

Like other casebooks, this book is not a treatise. It is designed as a teaching tool to uncover the most important parts of the tax system without delving so deep that students fail to get a full overview. For a deep dive into IRS procedure and tax litigation, students may benefit from SALTZMAN & BOOK, IRS PRACTICE AND PROCEDURE and KAFKA & CAVANAUGH, LITIGATION OF FEDERAL CIVIL TAX CONTROVERSIES respectively.

Acknowledgments

This book draws on previously published articles of mine in *The Tax Lawyer*. Unit 1 draws on *The Legal Consequences of Noncompliance with Federal Tax Laws*, 70 TAX LAW. 367 (2016); Unit 2 on *The Legal Framework for Tax Compliance*, 70 TAX LAW. 497 (2017); and Unit 3 on *The IRS's Tax Determination Authority*, 71 TAX LAW. 143 (2017).

So many people influenced this book in so many ways that it is impossible to thank everyone. Micah Levy has managed to provide valuable advice and counsel at every stage in my career along with his incredible tax procedure insight. Judge Lawrence Whalen initiated me into the system. Ken Clark, Jim Fuller, Ron Schrotenboer, Bill Colgin, Andy Kim, and Adam Halpern were involved with my development regarding how to challenge the IRS in court and in internal appeals. After I had a stint at the IRS Chief Counsel Office, Bill Curry, Don Maher, Craig Jones, Hal Heltzer, Alex Sadler, Robert Willmore, John Magee, Sonya Miller, Nikki McCain, and Ramon Ortiz all contributed to my learning on self-determining tax liabilities and dealing with the IRS's return reviews. Sonya Miller, Nikki McCain, Micah Levy, and Andy Grewal have all engaged me on the academic aspects of tax procedure.

This book also would not have been possible without a grant allocated by the IRS Taxpayer Advocate Service to establish a Low-Income Taxpayer Clinic at the University of South Dakota School of Law.

My wife, DaVida, and my son, Lazer, have put up with me through the development of these materials, and I am eternally grateful. The University of South Dakota School of Law has supported and inspired me to develop these materials. Thanks, also, to Sam Sharpe, Nick Koontz, Mallory Schulte, and Emily Lessin for their research assistance; Julia Wessel, Emily Posthumus, and Christina Schroeder for their administrative support; and Sarah Kammer and Eric Young for their library support.

There are so many more who have helped—academics, practitioners, students, government officials, etc. I thank you all.

CHAPTER 1

INTRODUCTION

A. The Field

The U.S. government, like any civilized sovereign entity, needs revenue to survive. Some sovereigns do not need to generate revenue from taxpayer contributions to survive because the country, state, city, or tribe has sufficient natural resources to operate. For example, some countries have oil reserves that make contributions unnecessary. Most sovereigns, however, are in the uncomfortable position in which they must depend on revenue from residents or citizens who are reluctant to contribute. The process occurs through interaction between the government and taxpayers through a system of procedure and enforcement.

The federal tax system acts as an intermediary between the government and taxpayers. The government cannot function without taxpayers. Taxpayers need the government to provide infrastructure for a civilized society.

This relationship is complex, as are the procedures that moderate it. This book breaks tax procedure and enforcement down to the four primary components of a typical dispute in the relationship: (1) the imposition of negative consequences for tax noncompliance, (2) the legal framework for tax compliance, (3) the IRS's tax determination authority, and (4) judicial review of the IRS's final determinations. The determinations tied to these components occur chronologically. First, a taxpayer must decide whether to comply with the tax laws. Next, the taxpayer must determine how to comply with the tax laws. Once the taxpayer complies by filing a return, the IRS may determine whether the taxpayer's return is correct. Once the IRS makes a final determination, if there is still an ongoing dispute then the taxpayer may seek a judicial determination.

The first decision is whether to comply with the tax laws. To influence the taxpayer's decision, the government imposes negative consequences for noncompliance. In the case of tax noncompliance, the government is authorized to impose penalties, collect the tax owed through administrative or judicial enforcement, and, if the noncompliance is criminal, jail the taxpayer.

Once the taxpayer decides to comply with the tax laws, the taxpayer must work within the legal framework for tax compliance to determine her own tax liability, report that liability on a timely return, and timely pay the liability. Once the return is filed, the IRS has three years to determine whether the taxpayer owes more tax and, if so, assess it. Conversely, the taxpayer has three years to determine if the amount she reported and paid was actually an overpayment, in which case the taxpayer can request a refund by amending the return.

Once the IRS receives a return, the IRS must determine whether the taxpayer has properly reported and paid the amount owed. Accordingly, the IRS has procedures for verifying the return, adjusting it, and notifying the taxpayer of the adjustment. During the verification process, the IRS may require the taxpayer to turn over additional information necessary to verify the correctness of the return. If the taxpayer disagrees with the IRS's initial determination, he or she may generally negotiate with the IRS through internal appeals procedures. If negotiations fail, the IRS then sends a final determination notice to the taxpayer that more tax is owed or that a refund request is denied.

If the taxpayer still disagrees with the IRS's determination, he may sue in court to resolve the disagreement through judicial review. Unlike many other law enforcement contexts, the taxpayer may choose the forum in which to sue depending on the characteristics of litigation in that particular forum. If the final determination from the IRS provided that the taxpayer owed more money, i.e., the IRS determined there is a deficiency in the amount the taxpayer paid compared to what he owes, the taxpayer may sue in U.S. Tax Court. If the notification from the IRS disallowed the taxpayer's refund claim, the taxpayer may sue in the federal district court or the U.S. Court of Federal Claims to obtain the refund. In the former case where the taxpayer receives a deficiency notice permitting a suit in Tax Court, the taxpayer may instead sue in a refund forum by paying the deficiency amount and then filing an amended return or refund claim. The taxpayer may then sue in federal district court or the U.S. Court of Federal Claims upon receipt of the refund disallowance.

B.   Government Employees

The tax system has many players. There are different types of taxpayers and different types of government actors. The taxpayers range from people who put a great deal of effort into reporting their tax items correctly according to the current tax laws to people who expend great amounts of effort toward denying the tax system exists. This latter type of taxpayer is known as a tax protester or tax denier.

Although the IRS and the courts have little patience for the tax protesters and the arguments they make, tax protesters serve as useful examples to introduce the various contexts, characters, and concepts presented throughout this book. The taxpayer that has had the most public and the broadest exposure to tax enforcement personnel was Mr. Irwin Schiff. His story is hopefully one that will not be repeated.

1. Noncompliance

As discussed, the first phase of tax procedure and enforcement is weighing the negative legal consequences of noncompliance with the tax laws, consequences that our Mr. Schiff never fully appreciated. Mr. Schiff first experienced these negative consequences following appearances on *The Tomorrow Show*, a television show starring Tom Snyder. Mr. Schiff left his income tax returns from 1974 and 1975 mostly blank. He did, however, claim on the returns that he was not required to fill out his tax returns according to the Fifth Amendment.[1] On two occasions in 1978, Mr. Schiff appeared on *The Tomorrow Show* to brag about how he paid no taxes and that no one is required to do so. Less than a week after his second appearance, Mr. Schiff had his first of many meetings with IRS enforcement personnel.

After Mr. Schiff's second appearance on *The Tomorrow Show*, the government sent IRS criminal investigators, known as special agents, to Mr. Schiff's office to investigate his 1974 and 1975 tax returns. Eventually the government charged him with criminal failure to file income tax returns. At the end of 2016, the IRS had over 2,200 special agents in its employ. The IRS special agents from the Criminal Investigation Division investigate tax crimes and refer cases to the Department of Justice for prosecution. Many issues that arise in a tax prosecution are not much different from prosecutions in other areas of the law, so this book will not cover them in detail. For this first offense, Mr. Schiff was convicted, sentenced to six months in prison, and fined $20,000.

In addition to criminally failing to file his tax returns, Mr. Schiff failed to pay the tax owed for his 1976, 1977, and 1978 tax years as well. This failure exposed him to another category of IRS tax enforcement employee known as a revenue officer. A revenue officer handles the collection side of negative consequences imposed on noncompliant taxpayers. Where a taxpayer has decided not to pay an established tax liability, the IRS will institute a collection action. The point of contact will be a revenue officer and supporting personnel. At the end of 2016, the IRS reported that it had over 3,500 revenue officers. In Mr. Schiff's case, a revenue officer was responsible for levying on $200,000 in tax liability presumably including interest and penalties. In other words, the IRS collected $200,000 from Mr. Schiff involuntarily. Nevertheless, Schiff persisted. He sued the IRS attempting to recover what he still believed to be his money.

Although the outcome would have been the same, Mr. Schiff's experience with revenue officers regarding civil liability for his 1976 through 1978 tax returns would have been different had the encounter occurred today. There would

---

[1] This, of course, is incorrect for many reasons including that the forms on which taxpayers report income does not require the disclosure of criminal activity.

have been an additional step in the process. In the late 1990s, Congress enacted a statute providing taxpayers the opportunity to request a Collection Due Process (CDP) hearing to review the collection action. An IRS employee who has remained independent of the revenue officer's actions conducts the hearing. These IRS personnel are known as hearing officers. The hearing officers are the same individuals that serve as appeals officers in the examination context to be discussed later. The IRS reported it had over 700 appeals officers at the end of 2016.

2. Compliance

Rather than defy the federal government like Mr. Schiff, most taxpayers report and pay their tax liabilities without any assistance from the IRS. Taxpayers are able to report and pay their liabilities on their own because the government communicates its expectations through tax laws. Congress is constitutionally tasked with determining how much tax to impose, communicating to taxpayers their tax obligations by defining various tax bases (income, estate, excise, etc.), and enacting further legislation to enable the government to receive and collect the taxes.

Mr. Schiff claimed he did not appreciate this process. In *The Federal Mafia*, Mr. Schiff wrote (while in jail for tax evasion and other tax crimes):

> It would be important for this nation, I suggest, to track down those responsible for writing the Internal Revenue Code, since it is clear that it was deliberately written to deceive us. It would be extremely enlightening, I suggest, to discover under whose direction it was done, and who and how many were involved.

Id. at 46. At other parts of *The Federal Mafia*, Mr. Schiff makes statements that reveal he understood that Congress enacts the laws, including the tax laws. On page 42, Mr. Schiff wrote: "I do not see how Congress can legally pass a tax bill without clearly defining that which it seeks to tax." In other words, Mr. Schiff acknowledged that Congress enacts the laws, but Congress didn't live up to Mr. Schiff's expectation that all terms must be defined. This expectation reflects a misunderstanding of how the law works. It is not uncommon for statutes to leave important terms left undefined. Otherwise, people will find some tortured way to interpret the definition in order to avoid it. Neither securities statutes nor securities regulations, for example, define what a security is. Similarly, the key term in antitrust law, contracts in restraint of trade, is not defined in the statute or regulations.

The legislative process, however, permits taxpayers to become involved in determining how much taxpayers should pay and other tax policy issues. Although a taxpayer may call their Representative or Senator about these issues, tax law knowledge is not a requirement for obtaining a job as a congressperson. Congress, however, employs tax professionals that do know about tax laws. These are boots on the ground policy people. The Senate Finance Committee staff has between 15 and 20 tax professionals, and the House Ways and Means Committee staff also has between 15 and 20 tax professionals. The congressional tax experts with both the broadest and deepest knowledge, however, serve on the staff of a nonpartisan committee called the Joint Committee on Taxation, which has between 45 and 50 tax professionals.

In general, congressional members and their staffs are careful about communications with taxpayers in order to prevent misinformation that could support tax protester arguments. Mr. Schiff apparently found one of these communications from a congressional staffer to a consultant about the tax laws. It is clear, however, that the staff person was not one of the staffers that advises congresspeople on the tax laws. The letter from Mr. Mark Forman, a legislative correspondent acting on behalf of Senator Daniel Inouye in 1989, reads as follows:

> Based on the research performed by the Congressional Research Service, there is no provision which specifically and unequivocally requires an individual to pay income taxes.

This is an unfortunate letter because Mr. Schiff used it to support his theory that there is a vast conspiracy in the federal government to collect taxes that no one owes. The letter is wrong. Section 1 of the Internal Revenue Code imposes an income tax. The government collects income taxes lawfully, and needs the revenue to exist. The legislative correspondent that wrote it should not have asked the Congressional Research Service (CRS) to research a tax issue. The Staff of the Joint Committee on Taxation is assigned the task of explaining how the tax laws work to members of Congress as well as their legislative correspondents.

Taxpayers are permitted to participate in the tax regulation drafting process during the notice and comment phase. These regulations are issued jointly by the IRS and the Department of Treasury. Accordingly, a taxpayer participating in the regulation drafting process may come into contact with attorneys from either agency. The Treasury Department personnel that work on regulations includes only a small cadre of attorneys in the Treasury Office of Tax Policy. The Office of Tax Policy does not have a large staff. They rely on the IRS Chief Counsel National Office for institutional knowledge on virtually every Internal Revenue Code section and for drafting the regulations.

A taxpayer participating in the regulation process might also contact the IRS. The taxpayer would contact the IRS Chief Counsel National Office attorneys working on the regulation project. The IRS Chief Counsel Office has over 1,500 attorneys. Attorneys are located in the field offices and in the National Office. The National Office (which houses the attorneys that draft regulations) is divided by substantive areas as follows:

- Corporate (approximately 60 attorneys)
- Financial Institutions and Products (FIP) (approximately 50 attorneys)
- International (approximately 90 attorneys)
- Income Tax Accounting (ITA) (approximately 100 attorneys)

- Passthroughs and Special Industries (PSI) (approximately 80 attorneys)
- Procedure and Administration (P&A) (approximately 100 attorneys)
- General Legal Services (approximately 70 attorneys)
- Criminal (CT) (approximately 70 attorneys)
- Tax Exempt/Government Entities (TEGE) (approximately 115 attorneys)

It appears Mr. Schiff never contacted the IRS Chief Counsel National Office attorneys or Treasury Tax Policy Office attorneys. He makes no mention of them in his book nor in any of his court cases. This lack of contact is understandable because Mr. Schiff believed the Internal Revenue Code, the IRS, and the IRS's collection procedures were all illegal. Thus, he would have no reason to participate in the legislative or regulation process.

3. IRS Tax Determinations

If the IRS decides to review a tax return, there are two levels of personnel that may have contact with the taxpayer who filed it. The personnel that audit tax returns are the revenue agents. At the end of 2016, the IRS reported having over 10,000 of these revenue agents. If the taxpayer disagrees with the outcome of an audit, the taxpayer might have the opportunity to appeal the decision. The personnel that hear the appeals are called Appeals Officers. As discussed with respect to collections, there were over 900 of these Appeals Officers as of year-end 2016.

Revenue agents likely contacted Mr. Schiff regarding his 1976-1978 tax returns. In *The Federal Mafia*, Mr. Schiff wrote that the IRS computed his tax liability from his bank statements. It is the IRS's revenue agents that seek out bank statements and other documents to determine a taxpayer's liability. Thus, revenue agents likely are the ones that obtained Mr. Schiff's bank statements.

It appears that Mr. Schiff had no contact with any appeals officers. Taxpayers generally may appeal an adverse audit decision. There is, however, an exception for tax protester cases. Accordingly, Mr. Schiff probably did not have the opportunity to appeal his audit through the IRS's internal appeal procedures. Moreover, Mr. Schiff's discussion of his cases in *The Federal Mafia* has no references to the Appeals Office or appeals officers.

Taxpayers going through an audit and deficiency determination usually have more contact with revenue officers and appeals officers than did Mr. Schiff. It appears, however, that Mr. Schiff thought he could win in court by arguing to a judge that the Internal Revenue Code, the IRS, and IRS's collection procedures are all illegal. This line of thinking is consistent with avoiding revenue agent contacts as much as possible.

Field attorneys support the IRS's examination and appeals efforts with general tax advice. The Large Business and International Division (LB&I) field offices have approximately 290 attorneys, the Small Business/Self-Employed Division (SB/SE) field offices have approximately 450 attorneys, and the Tax Exempt/Government Entities Division (TEGE) field offices have approximately 45 attorneys. These attorneys rarely have taxpayer contact unless the taxpayer has petitioned the Tax Court. Accordingly, Mr. Schiff probably had no contact with these attorneys at the examination or appeals stage.

4. Judicial Review

If a taxpayer does not agree with the IRS's final determination regarding her tax liability, the taxpayer may go to court. IRS Chief Counsel field attorneys from SB/SE and LB&I also handle cases in Tax Court. Department of Justice attorneys from the Tax Division handle the cases in district court and the Court of Federal Claims. Mr. Schiff had one Tax Court case where he had contact with IRS Chief Counsel field attorneys. In Tax Court, he made nonsensical arguments (no statute imposes a tax on income, the IRS may not compel filing a return under the Fifth Amendment, etc.).

Most cases are heard by Tax Court judges. As of 2017, there are 32 in the following positions:
- 16 President-appointed judges (maximum 19 by law)
- 11 Senior Judges
- 5 Special Trial Judges

The President-appointed judges are assigned two law clerks, while Senior Judges and Special Trial Judges are assigned one law clerk. That means that the Tax Court in general has about 50 law clerks, nearly all of which are in the same building. Other courts don't have tax professionals.

In Mr. Schiff's Tax Court case, he argued in front of a Tax Court judge. The judge likely had a law clerk draft an opinion after the trial. It is also likely that the law clerk and the other law clerks had a good laugh about the case. Of course, the IRS's deficiency notice was sustained.

C. Government Leaders

In some ways, it appears that Mr. Schiff preferred to go to court than to talk to revenue agents, revenue officers, or appeals officers because he did not believe they were official decision-makers. Nor does it appear he thought that if he prevailed at audit, in collection, or in the Appeals Office with his crazy arguments that he would get any recognition when the weight of his arguments would supposedly bring down the entire tax system. In court, however, as was the case in the Tax Court, Mr. Schiff could make his argument to an official decision-maker rather than dealing with a lower-level employee. Mr. Schiff failed to recognize, however, that revenue agents, revenue officers, and appeals officers were all authorized to decide his fate. The government employees with whom he likely dealt during his disputes with the IRS were actually more important than the government leaders we are about to discuss because government leaders overseeing the tax enforcement process rarely have direct contact with taxpayers.

Many people are aware of the IRS, and some are aware that the IRS Commissioner runs it. He (currently a he) is one of many executive branch leaders working for the President of United States. The IRS Commissioner reports to the Deputy Treasury Secretary of the United States, as does the Assistant Treasury Secretary for Tax Policy. Generally, the IRS Commissioner handles return processing, investigations, and enforcement while the Assistant Treasury Secretary for Tax Policy handles tax policy matters.

The IRS Commissioner has other leaders working with him. The IRS Chief Counsel, for example, reports to both the IRS Commissioner and the Treasury General Counsel. The Chief Counsel's office advises the IRS Commissioner on all legal issues the IRS encounters. In addition, Chief Counsel attorneys represent the IRS before the United States Tax Court.

Another important leader is the National Taxpayer Advocate. The National Taxpayer Advocate reports to the IRS Commissioner but also reports on the IRS Commissioner to Congress. Every year she (currently a she) compiles a report telling Congress about everything at the IRS that needs improvement of which she is aware.

At the Department of Justice, the Assistant Attorney General for the Tax Division is involved in enforcing the tax laws as well. Tax Division attorneys represent the IRS in courts other than the U.S. Tax Court, such as federal district court, the Court of Federal Claims, circuit courts of appeals, and, along with the Solicitor General, in the U.S. Supreme Court.

Inside the IRS, there is a Director of the Office of Professional Responsibility (OPR). The OPR regulates representatives who practice before the IRS. The Office's salience is often dependent on the Director. Some OPR directors take a strong public stance regarding regulating practitioners and have an expanded view of who is subject to OPR regulation, while other directors are less vocal.[2]

Another government leader in the tax system is the Director of the IRS's Whistleblower Office. The Whistleblower Office investigates claims by confidential informants. If the IRS obtains money through a whistleblower claim, the Whistleblower Office determines the amount of the obtained proceeds the informant will receive.

Important tax system leaders work in the legislative branch as well. Every taxpayer in the United States lives in a congressional district with a representative from the House of Representatives. Taxpayers may call their representative about potential improvements in the tax laws. If the representative finds some merit to the taxpayer's suggestion, he or she may call a member of the House Ways and Means Committee, one of Congress's tax law–writing committees.

---

[2] *See* Loving v. IRS, 742 F.3d 1013 (D.C. Cir. 2014) (holding that OPR's asserted authority over tax preparers exceeded the authority granted OPR by statute); Karen Hawkins, *2017 Erwin Griswold Lecture Before the American College of Tax Counsel: A (Not So) Modest Proposal*, 70 TAX LAW. 647, 650 (2017) (former OPR Director suggesting that the current OPR Director should be more assertive).

All taxpayers live in states represented by two senators as well. Taxpayers may also call their Senator. If the senator finds some merit to the taxpayer's suggestion, he or she may call a member of the Senate Finance Committee, the Congress's other tax law–writing committee.

The judicial branch's leaders are the judges. There are Tax Court judges, federal district court judges that hear tax cases when they fail to avoid it, Court of Federal Claims judges, and Bankruptcy Court judges. Courts of Appeals judges and Supreme Court justices also hear many tax cases.

D. Taxpayer Representation

Taxpayers themselves can hire tax professionals. Taxpayers may seek advice about criminal sanctions from a tax attorney. Audits and Collections cases can be handled by tax controversy attorneys, CPAs, or enrolled agents. These practitioners are regulated by the Office of Professional Responsibility (OPR).

Taxpayers may seek assistance in tax planning and reporting. Tax planning may legitimately involve attempting to change the law. It is often difficult to meet directly with the government leaders who write the laws, so taxpayers with resources to do so may choose to hire professional lobbyists. When reporting a tax liability, a taxpayer may choose from a number of different providers depending on the complexity of the tax returns. To file a simple return, a taxpayer may consult a CPA, enrolled agent, or, if simple enough, software. Attorneys can help, too, but for a simple return, it is not necessary. For more complicated returns and planning, tax lawyers specializing in certain issues are indispensable.

In audits and Appeals, taxpayers can be represented by law firms, major accounting firms, or CPAs. These practitioners are also subject to OPR regulation.

In court, a taxpayer can be represented by a tax litigation attorney or a CPA who has passed the Tax Court bar. In federal district court or Court of Federal Claims, a taxpayer will likely be represented by an attorney.

E. Anatomy of a Tax Dispute

The following opinion involves a dispute between the IRS and a taxpayer. Following the case, there will be a breakdown of the procedures underlying the case. In other words, read this case differently than the rest of the cases in the book. For purposes of this exercise, the concern is more the underlying procedures than the substance of the case. You might be thankful that this is so.

PPL CORPORATION v. COMMISSIONER
569 U.S. 329 (2013)
Supreme Court of the United States

Justice THOMAS delivered the opinion of the Court.

In 1997, the United Kingdom (U.K.) imposed a one-time "windfall tax" on 32 U.K. companies privatized between 1984 and 1996. This case addresses whether that tax is creditable for U.S. tax purposes. Internal Revenue Code § 901(b)(1) states that any "income, war profits, and excess profits taxes" paid overseas are creditable against U.S. income taxes. 26 U.S.C. § 901(b)(1). Treasury Regulations interpret this section to mean that a foreign tax is creditable if its "predominant character" "is that of an income tax in the U.S. sense." Treas. Reg. § 1.901–2(a)(1)(ii), 26 C.F.R. § 1.901–2(a)(1) (1992). Consistent with precedent and the Tax Court's analysis below, we apply the predominant character test using a commonsense approach that considers the substantive effect of the tax. Under this approach, we hold that the U.K. tax is creditable under § 901 and reverse the judgment of the Court of Appeals for the Third Circuit.

I

A

During the 1980's and 1990's, the U.K.'s Conservative Party controlled Parliament and privatized a number of government-owned companies. These companies were sold to private parties through an initial sale of shares, known as a "flotation." As part of privatization, many companies were required to continue providing services at the same rates they had offered under government control for a fixed period, typically their first four years of private operation. As a result, the companies could only increase profits during this period by operating more efficiently. Responding to market incentives, many of the companies became dramatically more efficient and earned substantial profits in the process.

The U.K.'s Labour Party, which had unsuccessfully opposed privatization, used the companies' profitability as a campaign issue against the Conservative Party. In part because of campaign promises to tax what it characterized as undue profits, the Labour Party defeated the Conservative Party at the polls in 1997. Prior to coming to power, Labour Party leaders hired accounting firm Arthur Andersen to structure a tax that would capture excess, or "windfall," profits earned during the initial years in which the companies were prohibited from increasing rates. Parliament eventually adopted the tax, which applied only to the regulated companies that were prohibited from raising their rates. See Finance (No. 2) Act, 1997, ch. 58, pt. I, cls. 1 and 2(5) (Eng.) (U.K. Windfall Tax Act). It imposed a 23 percent tax on any "windfall" earned by such companies. *Id.,* cl. 1(2). A separate schedule "se[t] out how to quantify the windfall from which a company was benefitting." *Id.,* cl. 1(3). See *id.,* sched. 1.

In the proceedings below, the parties stipulated [to a] formula [that] summarizes the tax imposed by the Labour Party. . . .

B

Petitioner PPL Corporation (PPL) was an owner, through a number of subsidiaries, of 25 percent of South Western Electricity plc, 1 of 12 government-owned electric companies that were privatized in 1990 and that were subject to the tax. See 135 T.C. 304, 307, App. (2010) (diagram of PPL corporate structure in 1997). South Western Electricity's total U.K. windfall tax burden was £90,419,265. In its 1997 federal income-tax return, PPL claimed a credit under § 901 for its share of the bill. The Commissioner of Internal Revenue (Commissioner) rejected the claim, but the Tax Court held that the U.K. windfall tax was creditable for U.S. tax purposes under § 901. See *id.,* at 342. The Third Circuit reversed. 665 F.3d 60, 68 (2011). We granted certiorari, 568 U.S. —, 133 S.Ct. 571, 184 L.Ed.2d 338 (2012), to resolve a Circuit split concerning the windfall tax's creditability under § 901. Compare 665 F.3d, at 68, with *Entergy Corp. & Affiliated Subsidiaries v. Commissioner,* 683 F.3d 233, 239 (C.A.5 2012).

II

Internal Revenue Code § 901(b)(1) provides that "[i]n the case of . . . a domestic corporation, the amount of any income, war profits, and excess profits taxes paid or accrued during the taxable year to any foreign country or to any possession of the United States" shall be creditable.[3] Under relevant Treasury Regulations, "[a] foreign levy is an income tax if and only if . . . [t]he predominant character of that tax is that of an income tax in the U.S. sense." 26 C.F.R. § 1.901–2(a)(1). The parties agree that Treasury Regulation § 1.901–2 applies to this case. That regulation codifies longstanding doctrine dating back to *Biddle v. Commissioner,* 302 U.S. 573, 578–579, 58 S.Ct. 379, 82 L.Ed. 431 (1938), and provides the relevant legal standard.

The regulation establishes several principles relevant to our inquiry. First, the "predominant character" of a tax, or the normal manner in which a tax applies, is controlling. See *id.,* at 579, 58 S.Ct. 379 ("We are here concerned only with the 'standard' or normal tax"). Under this principle, a foreign tax that operates as an income, war profits, or excess profits tax in most instances is creditable, even if it may affect a handful of taxpayers differently. Creditability is an all or nothing proposition. As the Treasury Regulations confirm, "a tax either is or is not an income tax, in its entirety, for all persons subject to the tax." 26 C.F.R. § 1.901–2(a)(1).

Second, the way a foreign government characterizes its tax is not dispositive with respect to the U.S. creditability analysis. See § 1.901–2(a)(1)(ii) (foreign tax creditable if predominantly "an income tax in the U.S. sense"). In *Biddle,* the Court considered the creditability of certain U.K. taxes on stock dividends under the substantively identical predecessor to § 901. The Court recognized that "there is nothing in [the statute's] language to suggest that in allowing the credit for foreign tax payments, a shifting standard was adopted by reference to foreign characterizations and classifications of tax legislation." 302 U.S., at 578–579, 58

---

[3] [fn 2] Prior to enactment of what is now § 901, income earned overseas was subject to taxes not only in the foreign country but also in the United States. See *Burnet v. Chicago Portrait Co.,* 285 U.S. 1, 7, 52 S.Ct. 275, 76 L.Ed. 587 (1932). The relevant text making "income, war-profits and excess-profits taxes" creditable has not changed since 1918. See Revenue Act of 1918, §§ 222(a)(1), 238(a), 40 Stat. 1073, 1080.

S.Ct. 379. See also *United States v. Goodyear Tire & Rubber Co.,* 493 U.S. 132, 145, 110 S.Ct. 462, 107 L.Ed.2d 449 (1989) (noting in interpreting 26 U.S.C. § 902 that *Biddle* is particularly applicable "where a contrary interpretation would leave" tax interpretation "to the varying tax policies of foreign tax authorities"); *Heiner v. Mellon,* 304 U.S. 271, 279, and n. 7, 58 S.Ct. 926, 82 L.Ed. 1337 (1938) (state-law definitions generally not controlling in federal tax context). Instead of the foreign government's characterization of the tax, the crucial inquiry is the tax's economic effect. See *Biddle, supra,* at 579, 58 S.Ct. 379 (inquiry is "whether [a tax] is the substantial equivalent of payment of the tax as those terms are used in our own statute"). In other words, foreign tax creditability depends on whether the tax, if enacted in the U.S., would be an income, war profits, or excess profits tax.

Giving further form to these principles, Treasury Regulation § 1.901–2(a)(3)(i) explains that a foreign tax's predominant character is that of a U.S. income tax "[i]f . . . the foreign tax is likely to reach net gain in the normal circumstances in which it applies." The regulation then sets forth three tests for assessing whether a foreign tax reaches net gain. A tax does so if, "judged on the basis of its predominant character, [it] satisfies each of the realization, gross receipts, and net income requirements set forth in paragraphs (b)(2), (b)(3) and (b)(4), respectively, of this section." § 1.901–2(b)(1).[4] The tests indicate that net gain (also referred to as net income) consists of realized gross receipts reduced by significant costs and expenses attributable to such gross receipts. A foreign tax that reaches net income, or profits, is creditable.

---

[4] [fn 3] The relevant provisions provide as follows:

"A foreign tax satisfies the realization requirement if, judged on the basis of its predominant character, it is imposed—(A) Upon or subsequent to the occurrence of events ('realization events') that would result in the realization of income under the income tax provisions of the Internal Revenue Code." 26 C.F.R. § 1.901–2(b)(2)(i).

"A foreign tax satisfies the gross receipts requirement if, judged on the basis of its predominant character, it is imposed on the basis of—(A) Gross receipts; or (B) Gross receipts computed under a method that is likely to produce an amount that is not greater than fair market value." § 1.901–2(b)(3)(i).

"A foreign tax satisfies the net income requirement if, judged on the basis of its predominant character, the base of the tax is computed by reducing gross receipts . . . to permit—(A) Recovery of the significant costs and expenses (including significant capital expenditures) attributable, under reasonable principles, to such gross receipts; or (B) Recovery of such significant costs and expenses computed under a method that is likely to produce an amount that approximates, or is greater than, recovery of such significant costs and expenses." § 1.901–2(b)(4)(i).

III

A

It is undisputed that net income is a component of the U.K.'s "windfall tax" formula. See Brief for Respondent 23 ("The windfall tax takes into account a company's profits during its four-year initial period"). Indeed, annual profit is a variable in the tax formula. U.K. Windfall Tax Act, sched. 1, § 1, cls. 2(2) and 5. It is also undisputed that there is no meaningful difference for our purposes in the accounting principles by which the U.K. and the U.S. calculate profits. See Brief for Petitioners 47. The disagreement instead centers on how to characterize the tax formula the Labour Party adopted.

The Third Circuit, following the Commissioner's lead, believed it could look no further than the tax formula that the Parliament enacted and the way in which the Labour government characterized it. Under that view, the windfall tax must be considered a tax on the difference between a company's flotation value (the total amount investors paid for the company when the government sold it) and an imputed "profit-making value," defined as a company's "average annual profit during its 'initial period' . . . times 9, the assumed price-to-earnings ratio." 665 F.3d, at 65. So characterized, the tax captures a portion of the difference between the price at which each company was sold and the price at which the Labour government believed each company *should have been* sold given the actual profits earned during the initial period. Relying on this characterization, the Third Circuit believed the windfall tax failed at least the Treasury Regulation's realization and gross receipts tests because it reached some artificial form of valuation instead of profits. See *id.,* at 67, and n. 3.

In contrast, PPL's position is that the substance of the windfall tax is that of an income tax in the U.S. sense. While recognizing that the tax ostensibly is based on the difference between two values, it argues that every "variable" in the windfall tax formula except for profits and flotation value is fixed (at least with regard to 27 of the 32 companies). PPL emphasizes that the only way the Labour government was able to calculate the imputed "profit-making value" at which it claimed companies should have been privatized was by looking after the fact at the *actual profits* earned by each company. In PPL's view, it matters not how the U.K. chose to arrange the formula or what it *claimed* to be taxing, because a tax based on profits above some threshold is an excess profits tax, regardless of how it is mathematically arranged or what labels foreign law places on it. PPL, thus, contends that the windfall taxes it paid meet the Treasury Regulation's tests and are creditable under § 901.

We agree with PPL and conclude that the predominant character of the windfall tax is that of an excess profits tax, a category of income tax in the U.S. sense. It is important to note that the Labour government's conception of "profit-making value" as a backward-looking analysis of historic profits is not a recognized valuation method; instead, it is a fictitious value calculated using an imputed price-to-earnings ratio. At trial, one of PPL's expert witnesses explained that " '9 is not an accurate P/E multiple, and it is not applied to current or expected future earnings.' " 135 T. C., at 326, n. 17 (quoting testimony). Instead, the windfall tax is a tax on realized net income disguised as a tax on the difference between two values, one of which is completely fictitious. See App. 251, Report ¶ 1.7 ("[T]he *value in profit making terms* described in the wording of the act . . . is not a real value: it is rather a construct based on realised profits that would not have been known at the date of privatisation").

The substance of the windfall tax confirms the accuracy of this observation. As already noted, the parties stipulated that the windfall tax could be calculated [the Court set forth agreed upon formulas].

Of course, other algebraic reformulations of the windfall tax equation are possible. See 665 F.3d, at 66; Brief for Anne Alstott et al. as *Amici Curiae* 21–23 (Alstott Brief). The point of the reformulation is not that it yields a particular percentage (51.75 percent for most of the companies). Rather, the algebraic reformulations illustrate the economic substance of the tax and its interrelationship with net income.

The Commissioner argues that any algebraic rearrangement is improper, asserting that U.S. courts must take the foreign tax rate as written and accept whatever tax base the foreign tax purports to adopt. Brief for Respondent 28. As a result, the Commissioner claims that the analysis begins and ends with the Labour government's choice to characterize its tax base as the difference between "profit-making value" and flotation value. Such a rigid construction is unwarranted. It cannot be squared with the black-letter principle that "tax law deals in economic realities, not legal abstractions." *Commissioner v. Southwest Exploration Co.,* 350 U.S. 308, 315, 76 S.Ct. 395, 100 L.Ed. 347 (1956). Given the artificiality of the U.K.'s method of calculating purported "value," we follow substance over form and recognize that the windfall tax is nothing more than a tax on actual profits above a threshold.

B

We find the Commissioner's other arguments unpersuasive as well. First, the Commissioner attempts to buttress the argument that the windfall tax is a tax on value by noting that some U.S. gift and estate taxes use actual, past profits to estimate value. Brief for Respondent 17–18 (citing 26 C.F.R. § 20.2031–3 (2012) and 26 U.S.C. § 2032A). This argument misses the point. In the case of valuation for gift and estate taxes, past income may be used to estimate future income streams. But, it is *future* revenue-earning potential, reduced to market value, that is subject to taxation. The windfall profits tax, by contrast, undisputedly taxed *past,* realized net income alone.

The Commissioner contends that the U.K. was not trying to establish valuation as of the 1997 date on which the windfall tax was enacted but instead was attempting to derive a proper flotation valuation as of each company's flotation date. Brief for Respondent 21. The Commissioner asserts that there was no need to estimate future income (as in the case of the gift or estate recipient) because actual revenue numbers for the privatized companies were available. *Ibid.* That argument also misses the mark. It is true, of course, that the companies might have been privatized at higher flotation values had the government recognized how efficient—and thus how profitable—the companies would become. But, the windfall tax requires an underlying concept of value (based on actual *ex post* earnings) that would be alien to any valuer. Taxing actual, realized net income in hindsight is not the same as considering past income for purposes of estimating future earning potential.

The Commissioner's reliance on Example 3 to the Treasury Regulation's gross receipts test is also misplaced. *Id.,* at 37–38; 26 C.F.R. § 1.901–2(b)(3)(ii), Ex. 3. That example posits a petroleum tax in which "gross receipts from extraction income are deemed to equal 105 percent of the fair market value of petroleum extracted. This computation is designed to produce an amount that is greater than the fair market value of actual gross receipts." *Ibid.* Under the example, a tax based on inflated gross receipts is not creditable.

The Third Circuit believed that the same type of algebraic rearrangement used above could also be used to rearrange a tax imposed on Example 3. It hypothesized:

> "Say that the tax rate on the hypothetical extraction tax is 20%. It is true that a 20% tax on 105% of receipts is mathematically equivalent to a 21% tax on 100% of receipts, the latter of which would satisfy the gross receipts requirement. PPL proposes that we make the same move here, increasing the tax rate from 23% to 51.75% so that there is no multiple of receipts in the tax base. But if the regulation allowed us to do that, the example would be a nullity. Any tax on a multiple of receipts or profits could satisfy the gross receipts requirement, because we could reduce the starting point of its tax base to 100% of gross receipts by imagining a higher tax rate." 665 F.3d, at 67.

The Commissioner reiterates the Third Circuit's argument. Brief for Respondent 37–38.

There are three basic problems with this approach. As the Fifth Circuit correctly recognized, there is a difference between imputed and actual receipts. "Example 3 hypothesizes a tax on the extraction of petroleum where the income value of the petroleum is deemed to be . . . deliberately greater than actual gross receipts." *Entergy Corp.,* 683 F.3d, at 238. In contrast, the windfall tax depends on *actual* figures. *Ibid.* ("There was no need to calculate imputed gross receipts; gross receipts were actually known"). Example 3 simply addresses a different foreign taxation issue.

The argument also incorrectly equates imputed *gross receipts* under Example 3 with *net income.* See 665 F.3d, at 67 ("*[a]ny* tax on a multiple of receipts or profits"). As noted, a tax is creditable only if it applies to realized gross receipts *reduced by significant costs and expenses attributable to such gross receipts.* 26 C.F.R. § 1.901–2(b)(4)(i). A tax based solely on gross receipts (like the Third Circuit's analysis) would be noncreditable because it would fail the Treasury Regulation's *net income* requirement.

Finally, even if expenses were subtracted from imputed gross receipts before a tax was imposed, the effect of inflating only gross receipts would be to inflate revenue while holding expenses (the other component of net income) constant. A tax imposed on inflated income minus actual expenses is not the same as a tax on net income.[5]

For these reasons, a tax based on imputed gross receipts is not creditable. But, as the Fifth Circuit explained in rejecting the Third Circuit's analysis, Example 3 is "facially irrelevant" to the analysis of the U.K. windfall tax, which is based on true net income. *Entergy Corp., supra,* at 238.[6]

The economic substance of the U.K. windfall tax is that of a U.S. income tax. The tax is based on net income, and the fact that the Labour government chose to characterize it as a tax on the difference between two values is not dispositive under Treasury Regulation § 1.901–2. Therefore, the tax is creditable under § 901.

The judgment of the Third Circuit is reversed.

It is so ordered.

Justice SOTOMAYOR, concurring. [omitted]

NOTES AND QUESTIONS

1. PPL Corporation decided to comply with its tax obligations. In making its decision to comply, the corporation likely considered potential negative consequences to not complying. Section 7201 imposes a fine on a corporation for tax evasion of $500,000. Criminal liability is probably sufficient to deter most corporations from attempting to evade taxes because securities laws would require disclosure of the fraud to its investors, the number of which would likely dwindle upon such a disclosure. The tax laws also provide negative consequences in the form of civil penalties and judicially enforced collection of unpaid taxes. The procedural aspect of the negative consequences generally does not appear in the case itself because the consideration takes place off the

---

[5] [fn 5] Mathematically, the Third Circuit's hypothetical was incomplete. It should have been:

20% [105% (Gross Receipts) − Expenses] = Tax

But 105% of gross receipts minus expenses is *not* net income. Thus, the 20% tax is not a tax on net income and is not creditable.

[6] [fn 6] An amici brief argues that because two companies had initial periods substantially shorter than four years, the predominant character of the U.K. windfall tax was not a tax on income in the U.S. sense. See Alstott Brief 29 (discussing Railtrack Group plc and British Energy plc). The argument amounts to a claim that two outliers changed the predominant character of the U.K. tax. See 135 T.C. 304, 340, n. 33 (2010) (rejecting this view).

The Commissioner admitted at oral argument that it did not preserve this argument, a fact reflected in its briefing before this Court and in the Third Circuit. See Tr. of Oral Arg. 35–36; Opening Brief for Appellant and Reply Brief for Appellant in No. 11–1069(CA3). We therefore express no view on its merits.

* * *

record. The negative consequences imposed for noncompliance with federal tax laws comprise the first unit of this casebook. Chapter 2 covers criminal liability, Chapter 3 discusses assessment of tax liabilities, Chapter 4 examines penalties, and Chapters 5 and 6 consider tax collection actions.

2. In this case, the taxpayer paid an excess profits tax in England, which resulted from its ownership in a privatized energy corporation. The Internal Revenue provides a foreign tax credit for taxes paid to foreign governments. The taxpayer filed a return, but to comply with the federal tax laws as well as possible, the taxpayer had to determine what the government expected. Congress believed that United States taxpayers, such as PPL, should not be taxed twice on income earned in foreign countries. Otherwise the taxes would make it too costly for United States taxpayers to expand their businesses into foreign countries.

3. To reduce the double income taxation, Congress decided to permit taxpayers to claim a foreign tax credit in certain circumstances, which Congress communicated by enacting legislation saying so. In order to clarify the law Congress communicated by statute, Treasury and the IRS promulgated a regulation to assist taxpayers in determining whether a tax is creditable. The foreign tax credit is a credit against income tax, so the regulation assists taxpayers in determining whether a tax imposed by a foreign government looks sufficiently like an income tax that it can be creditable against the foreign tax.

4. The taxpayer, after reviewing Congress's and the administration's communications of the law, determined that it was entitled to the foreign tax credit and filed its tax returns consistent with this decision. Taxpayers in the United States all have to file their tax returns and base the amount on a self-determination of their liability based on the current law at the time. They self-determine their liability, report the tax liability determined, and pay it. Once the taxpayer has reported and paid the liability, the taxpayer and the IRS each have three years to determine whether to change the amount originally reported. The second unit of this casebook discusses this compliance framework. Chapter 7 covers self-determination of tax liabilities, Chapter 8 discusses reporting tax liabilities, Chapter 9 discusses paying tax liabilities, and Chapter 10 discusses the compliance limitations periods.

5. After a taxpayer files a return, the IRS may review or "audit" it. When the audit is complete, typically the taxpayer may seek review by the IRS's Appeals Office. Most individuals that seek an opportunity to discuss their cases with the Appeals Office are permitted to do so. After Appeals consideration, if the case is not settled, the IRS issues a notice of deficiency, which can be challenged in court.

6. The reviews that take place after the return filing and before the deficiency notice do not appear in most tax cases. This is because a tax case is based on the IRS's determination, and the taxpayer must sue to

show the determination is wrong. In the suit, the taxpayer presents evidence based on the transactions that occurred prior to filing the return rather than what happened in the IRS's investigation.

7. We can presume what happened prior to the deficiency notice based on the typical case. The IRS audits most tax returns filed by large taxpayers like PPL, so the fact that there was an audit is not controversial. After the IRS reviewed PPL's position on the foreign tax credit, the taxpayer might have had an opportunity to try to settle the case with the IRS Appeals Office. It is possible, however, that PPL might not have had that opportunity to go to Appeals because Appeals is not required to consider all cases. After the internal appeal, if there was one, the IRS disallowed the taxpayer's foreign tax credit claim. The IRS generally does this in a statutory notice of deficiency, which presumably gave rise to litigation in this case. Unit 3 discusses these internal procedures and processes. Chapter 11 covers administrative return reviews, Chapters 12 and 13 discuss the summons process, Chapter 14 considers Appeals Office review of audit findings, and Chapter 15 discusses final determinations like the notice of deficiency in this case.

8. PPL petitioned the Tax Court to review the IRS's determination that PPL was not entitled to the foreign tax credit it claimed on its tax return. We can tell the trial below was in Tax Court by the case's caption—the taxpayer is the petitioner and the "Commissioner" is designated as the respondent. Tax cases in other courts bear a caption with the "United States" as the defendant.

9. At trial the Tax Court held for the taxpayer, PPL. Often, students find it hard to believe that the IRS would ever lose a case. Our legal system, however, including our tax system, does not like tyranny. Taxpayers may challenge the IRS in a neutral forum, and if this were not the case then tyranny would prevail. Sometimes the IRS is wrong about the law or the facts, and sometimes oversteps its authority.

10. In this case, the Third Circuit Court of Appeals reversed the Tax Court based on the regulation promulgated by the administration. The Supreme Court, however, reversed the Sixth Circuit interpreting the same regulation in favor of the taxpayer. The IRS was wrong in its interpretation of the law according to the Supreme Court. Unit 4 covers judicial review of IRS determinations. Chapter 16 provides an overview of tax litigation, Chapter 17 takes a closer look at litigation in Tax Court, and Chapter 18 focuses on tax refund litigation.

UNIT 1

TAX NONCOMPLIANCE

This unit addresses the legal consequences a taxpayer should consider when deciding whether to comply with the basic requirements of the federal income tax laws. A taxpayer considering noncompliance should consider the government's authority to assert criminal liability, impose civil tax penalties, and forcibly collect any unpaid tax. Although there are numerous criminal tax offenses, the potential offenses that may affect a taxpayer's decision whether to comply are the failure to file and failure to pay misdemeanors, tax perjury felony, and attempted tax evasion felony. Similarly, the civil tax penalties that are intended to deter basic noncompliance are the failure to file addition to tax, failure to pay addition to tax, and civil fraud penalty. The remaining penalties (over 100 of them) target various types of behavior engaged in by people other than the taxpayer or that occur after a taxpayer has already decided to file a tax return. Thus, a taxpayer deciding whether to file a tax return or attempt to defraud the government need only consider these three. A taxpayer must also consider that the government is authorized, after satisfying certain procedural requirements, to forcibly collect the tax the taxpayer owes.

In the study of tax controversy, it is unusual to group these topics—collection, penalties, and criminal liability—together under the umbrella of noncompliance. The Code disperses these topics throughout its procedural subtitle. Treasury Regulations are organized by Code provision, so they are of no help either. Although tax controversy events rarely flow chronologically, the decisions and determinations that taxpayers and the government make flow sequentially. The first decision a taxpayer makes is whether to comply with the tax laws. Thus, it makes sense to discuss criminal liability, penalties, and collection before the discussing the decision to file a return or the procedures for determining a deficiency.

UNIT 9

TAX NONCOMPLIANCE

CHAPTER 2

CRIMINAL TAX LIABILITY

Criminal tax liability is the first of the three major consequences of tax noncompliance. In addition to the seizure of assets and the imposition of civil penalties, the government ultimately is authorized to criminally prosecute a taxpayer for tax crimes, which can result in fines and imprisonment. Potential jail time is an important consideration in the decision whether to comply with the tax laws. Both Wesley Snipes and former U.S. Tax Court Judge Diane Kroupa—who have both served time for tax crimes—can confirm the importance of considering criminal liability.[1]

A. Criminal Tax Enforcement

The process of investigating a tax crime is different than in other areas of the law. In other areas of criminal law, a crime is committed and authorities investigate to figure out who did it. For example, when a bank reports a robbery, the police investigate to determine who robbed it. Where a tax crime has taken place, the victim is a collective group—the people of the United States. An individual member of the collective group is unlikely to have any way of knowing the crime occurred. Thus, a criminal tax investigation must start with a taxpayer to determine whether he committed a crime.

Although IRS criminal investigators—special agents—and IRS civil investigators—revenue agents—have some overlapping tools, their investigations ideally stay separate. The main tool that special agents and revenue agents have in common is the summons power to compel the production of documents, records, and testimony. However, special agents should not rely heavily on information from an ongoing audit or discovery in a tax prosecution as it may appear that the criminal investigator obtained information in circumvention of Miranda v. Arizona, 384 U.S. 436 (1966). If a crime is suspected and the case

---

[1] Mr. Snipes' sentence was three years. *See* United States v. Snipes, 611 F.3d 855, 871-72 (11th Cir. 2010). Judge Kroupa's sentence is 34 months. *See* Department of Justice News Release, 2017 WL 8808776 (June 22, 2017).

referred to the Criminal Investigation Division (CID), usually the civil audit halts until CID can complete the criminal investigation.

UNITED STATES v. RUTHERFORD
555 F.3d 190 (6th Cir. 2009)
United States Court of Appeals, Sixth Circuit

BOGGS, Chief Judge.

Defendants Jon Rutherford and Judith Bugaiski were charged with numerous tax violations and conspiracy to defraud investigators from the Internal Revenue Service (IRS). The United States appeals the district court's suppression of certain statements and documents obtained pursuant to an allegedly improper civil investigation. The IRS civil examiners who interviewed Rutherford and Bugaiski were required under an IRS manual to suspend their investigation when a "firm indication of fraud on the part of the taxpayer[s]" surfaced and refer the case to the criminal division. Internal Revenue Manual § 4565.21(1). Despite the fact such indications had emerged, civil examiners continued their investigation, conducting further interviews with the defendants and requesting additional documents.

In the criminal proceedings that followed, the IRS sought admission of their incriminating statements. The district court held the statements had to be suppressed, initially citing *United States v. McKee,* 192 F.3d 535 (6th Cir.1999), for the proposition that any continuation of discussions under a civil audit after firm indications of fraud have emerged would violate the Due Process Clause of the Fifth Amendment.; JA 81. At a later hearing, the court narrowed its explanation orally, remarking that not every "violation of the [IRS] manual [creates] a per se constitutional violation," but that this case did establish a violation. The United States now appeals, contending that the district court misread the Sixth Circuit's [precedent.]

Because the defendants' constitutional rights were not violated by the IRS's negligent violation of its manual, we reverse the district court. Despite the district court's reliance on *McKee,* in that case the Sixth Circuit explicitly reserved the issue now before us. Whether the government violates a person's due process rights in the course of taking his statement is assessed under a voluntariness standard, and the Constitution does not demand a bright-line rule whereby every breach of federal administrative policy also violates the Due Process Clause. The Fifth Amendment is implicated only when a federal agent's conduct actually compels a person to speak against his will. With respect to Rutherford and Bugaiski, there is no credible basis for concluding that their statements were coerced.

Although the civil examiners may have been negligent in failing to refer the case to the IRS's Criminal Division, the district court found no evidence that they deliberately disregarded the manual in order to mislead the defendants. Nor is there evidence in the record that suggests Rutherford and Bugaiski were familiar with the manual, or that they were lulled into a false sense of security about the nature of the charges they might face. In short, their statements were given voluntarily and may be properly admitted into evidence without infringing upon their constitutional rights.

I

Rutherford and Bugaiski were both officers of Metro Emergency Services (MES), a non-profit tax exempt organization operating a homeless shelter for women in Highland Park, Michigan. Rutherford served as the organization's president, and Bugaiski served as its controller. The IRS first became interested in MES when a newspaper article reported on political contributions made by the group. As a non-profit organization, such disbursements could affect the group's tax status. In the course of reviewing the IRS filings, agent Wesley Tagami of the Tax Exempt and Government Entities Division discovered that MES had not filed several forms related to tax withholding from employee salaries. At this point, no direct evidence of fraud had surfaced, as there was no indication that Rutherford or any other employee had not reported all income. But Tagami's findings suggested there was the potential for fraud and, noting the irregularity, he referred the case to a fraud specialist. Soon thereafter, several other agents were assigned to work on this case, including Suzanne Carene, a revenue agent, who was tasked with examining the organization's tax returns, and another agent who was charged with collecting any unpaid taxes from MES.

Some indications of fraud began to emerge. Agents discovered that Rutherford's personal tax return showed that taxes had been withheld from his pay, even though MES never remitted the money to the IRS. Still, agents believed no firm indications of fraud were yet apparent, because certain elements of criminal fraud remained unsupported by the records. As the government notes, "there could be innocent explanations for the problem with the returns, such as Rutherford's lack of knowledge about the non-filings of 941s or the fact that the funds had not been remitted to the IRS." Since a taxpayer's intent is crucial to the distinction between criminal and civil fraud, agents could not determine whether there was an innocent explanation for the discrepancy or if the omission was intentional and therefore potentially criminal until they interviewed Rutherford and Bugaiski.

Agent Carene met with the defendants and their CPA for the first time on December 16, 2003. Rutherford and Bugaiski stated that their failure to remit taxes was unintentional, and that funds owed to them had come in late. Rutherford thereafter abruptly ended the interview. Agent Carene attempted to continue the interview, but the defendants refused to answer any more questions. She then made several requests to meet with the defendants again for further questioning, and when they declined, she caused a summons to be served on the defendants.[2] Pursuant to the summons, Carene met with defendants on June 17,

---

[2] [fn 1] Rutherford and Bugaiski were not served as officers of MES. Rather, they were summoned for their involvement with DPR Management, Inc. Rutherford was a controlling owner of DPR, and Bugaiski was DPR's custodian

2004. At that time, Bugaiski turned over various documents, but no interviews were conducted. On June 21 and June 25, 2004, Carene interviewed Rutherford for a second and third time. In the course of these interviews, he answered some questions and declined to answer others. On June 23, 2004, she interviewed Bugaiski.

IRS agents involved in the case held a conference call on July 20, 2004, and finally determined that a criminal referral should be made. Explaining the decision later, one investigator said, "I believe we had enough, or we had affirmative acts that showed intent and willfulness by the taxpayer to fail to collect and turn over the employment taxes, not report substantial amounts of income, not file tax returns. . .." On April 21, 2006, defendants were charged in a 22–count indictment alleging various violations of the tax code, including tax evasion, failure to pay taxes that were withheld from employees, making false returns, and conspiracy to defraud IRS investigators. In a pretrial motion to suppress evidence and dismiss the indictment, the defendants claimed that the IRS agents improperly continued the civil examination after firm indications of fraud had emerged. By doing so, the defendants argued, their rights under the Due Process Clause had been violated. The district court agreed that statements made in the later stage of the investigation had to be suppressed as violating the Constitution.

II

The district court found that firm indications had emerged by the time the IRS conducted its second round of interviews in June 2004. Although the United States did not concede this point on appeal, the government paid little attention to this issue in its brief and at oral argument—perhaps in recognition of the standard of review. Whether firm indications of fraud had emerged is a question of fact, and this court reviews such findings for clear error. *McKee,* 192 F.3d at 543. Nothing in the record suggests the district court's finding was clearly erroneous, and therefore we proceed on the assumption that the IRS civil investigation was improperly continued.

The Sixth Circuit has once before considered the issue now before this court, and this case has proven a source of some confusion. . . . Only in dicta did the lead opinion in *McKee* touch on the issue we are now asked to resolve. After affirming the district court's finding that the IRS manual had not been violated, the opinion departed from the well-established rule, elaborating, "[The defendant] can satisfy her burden, as a practical matter, by showing that [the revenue agent] knowingly failed to comply with the Manual's suspension-of-investigation rules." 192 F.3d at 542. Judge Jones also added a footnote, explicitly stating: "If the revenue agent continues the civil audit even after she has developed 'firm indications of fraud,' then she is, in fact, making affirmative misrepresentations

---

of records. DPR purchased the MES building for $1,000 in late 1998, and in turn, MES paid hundreds of thousands of dollars a year in rent to DPR. With this money, DPR made a number of political contributions. A separate investigation of DPR's dealings was already underway.

to the constitutional detriment of the taxpayer because she is gathering criminal evidence against the taxpayer under the guise of a civil proceeding." *Id.* at 542 n. 5.

Although Judge Jones's analysis may serve as a persuasive authority, it does not bind this panel in resolving this issue today. *See Williams v. Anderson,* 460 F.3d 789, 796 (6th Cir.2006) (holding that dicta is not binding precedent). . . . Now that the issue is before us, we are free to reach a contrary conclusion. And a different result is warranted, because merely failing to refer a case to the Criminal Division pursuant to the IRS's internal policy is not alone sufficient to establish a violation of the defendants' right to due process.

The Due Process Clause of the Fifth Amendment provides that "No person shall . . . be deprived of life, liberty, or property, without due process of law. . . ." Violating this right entails government conduct that "shocks the sensibilities of civilized society." *Moran v. Burbine,* 475 U.S. 412, 433–34, 106 S.Ct. 1135, 89 L.Ed.2d 410 (1986). The sort of conduct at issue may be proscribed by internal government policy, or in certain cases, the government may even have a policy of engaging in the objectionable behavior. Whether a person's due process rights were violated in the course of taking his statement hinges on the voluntariness of the statement. *Colorado v. Connelly,* 479 U.S. 157, 166, 107 S.Ct. 515, 93 L.Ed.2d 473 (1986); *United States v. Johnson,* 351 F.3d 254, 260 (6th Cir.2003). So the effect of the government misconduct on the defendants, not its mere existence, is what must guide our analysis. Consequently, the IRS's failure to refer a case cannot *of its own force* violate the Due Process Clause, and to find otherwise would radically overstate the protections afforded by the Fifth Amendment. In this case, the district court said that the IRS agents were "perhaps" negligent in failing to refer the matter to the Criminal Division, but that there was insufficient evidence of intentionality to find that the failure to refer was deliberate. The record reveals that the agents knew of the manual and were sensitive to its requirements well before their first interview with the defendants. But whether the agents were acting deliberately or merely negligently, the failure to refer a case, standing alone, does not demonstrate a lack of voluntariness in the defendants' statements, absent evidence that the defendants were in fact compelled to talk by the government's affirmative misrepresentations.

There is no bright-line rule for determining whether a suspect's statements were given voluntarily. Voluntariness is instead judged by the "totality of the circumstances" in which the person made the statement. *United States v. Greene,* 250 F.3d 471, 479 (6th Cir.2001). To frame this analysis, the Sixth Circuit has set forth three factors for courts to consider: "(i) the police activity was objectively coercive; (ii) the coercion in question was sufficient to overbear the defendant's will; and (iii) the alleged police misconduct was the crucial motivating factor in the defendant's decision to offer the statement." *United States v. Mahan,* 190 F.3d 416, 422 (6th Cir.1999). Nothing in the record of this case suggests that IRS agents made affirmative misrepresentations to Rutherford and Bugaiski, or that defendants' will was overcome by the circumstances of these interviews. That a summons was issued cannot on its own mean that their later statements were involuntarily given, because the statements of persons who are subpoenaed by grand juries are routinely admitted in criminal proceedings against them.[3]

The tenor of the IRS's interviews does not in any way suggest that the suspects were either in custody or that their statements were compelled. The trial court's review of the record uncovered no indicia of coercion. "[The IRS agent] did not threaten, force, or trick the defendants." Indeed, the defendants declined to answer questions on numerous occasions, suggesting they felt free when they answered those questions that they did. At one point, Rutherford even laughed in explaining one of the deductions he was asked about. There is no evidence that the suspects relied on, or even knew of, the provisions of the manual in making the incriminating statements, which strongly suggests they were made voluntarily. Although defendants could argue the improper use of a civil examiner acted as a silent misrepresentation, lulling them into a false sense of security such that their statements were compelled, this argument is not persuasive for two reasons. First, the defendants bear the burden of proof here, and they do not claim, let alone put forward any evidence indicating, that the use of a civil examiner played a "crucial motivating factor" in their decision to answer questions in June 2004. Second, even if the defendants had believed there was only a civil investigation underway, the regulation does not stipulate that a civil investigation cannot later become a criminal investigation. As a result, the potential repercussions of making incriminating statements remained the same, and the defendants had no basis for concluding that a criminal investigation would not be undertaken in the future. Perhaps the defendants could argue they would have exercised greater caution if the agents questioning them had represented the investigation as criminal in nature, but notes of the conversations suggest the defendants were already guarded in their dealings with the IRS. . . .

To affirm the district court's decision notwithstanding this record would be to embrace openly a double standard for the incriminating statements of white-collar criminals, making it much more likely their statements will be considered involuntary and thus excluded from criminal proceedings. Such a rule would not only be hypocritical, it would be contrary to the Supreme Court's Fifth Amendment jurisprudence, which recognizes that statements made while under arrest, during a custodial interrogation with the prospect of imprisonment, are much more likely to involve coercion. *See Miranda v. Arizona*, 384 U.S. 436, 468, 86 S.Ct. 1602, 16 L.Ed.2d 694 (1966) ("[A *Miranda*] warning is an absolute prerequisite in overcoming the inherent pressures of the interrogation

---

[3] [fn 2] Indeed, the district court properly recognized the authority of grand juries to gather evidence, noting that if a grand jury separately gathered the documents handed over to civil examiners, there would be no need to suppress them. In this appeal, neither party has focused on the documents produced by the defendants after firm indications of fraud emerged. For the sake of clarity, we note explicitly that we reach the same result with respect to them as we do with respect to the defendant's statements.

atmosphere."). To increase the standard for voluntariness in a noncustodial context moves in the exact opposite direction of recent Supreme Court cases.

III

The Due Process Clause is not violated here where there was no deception or trickery and where defendants' statements were clearly voluntary. IRS agents did not engage in any affirmative misrepresentation, and to the extent that the very use of civil examiners silently misrepresented the nature of the government's investigation, the defendants have presented no evidence indicating that they relied upon the regulation so that their statements were not voluntary. In short, though government misconduct is regrettable, whether engaged in deliberately or, as here, merely negligently, the misconduct at issue in this case simply does not "shock[ ] the conscience." *Rochin v. California,* 342 U.S. 165, 172, 72 S.Ct. 205, 96 L.Ed. 183 (1952). If a remedy does exist, it is not one this court may impose by application of the exclusionary rule. We therefore REVERSE the district court's pre-trial motion suppressing statements and documents and REMAND for further proceedings consistent with this opinion.

[Concurring opinion omitted.]

NOTES AND QUESTIONS

1. May the IRS trick a taxpayer into admitting to the commission of a crime?
2. What is the test for when a revenue agent turns a case over to CID for a criminal investigation?

The IRS does not have sufficient resources to find, prosecute, and extinguish all criminal tax activity. Therefore, the IRS has to make the most of the resources it has. When it pursues a criminal case, there is usually a publicity angle to it. The IRS will make examples out of high-profile taxpayers. One example category is celebrity taxpayers. When a celebrity gets caught, the IRS gets free publicity for its enforcement efforts. Another high impact category is tax protesters. When tax protesters get caught, their prosecution sends a message to other tax protesters that their arguments have no merit. The IRS gets double the value for its money when it prosecutes a celebrity tax protester. To the IRS, Wesley Snipes was both a tax protester and a celebrity. He was prosecuted for tax evasion and failure to file tax returns. Although he was acquitted of the evasion charges, he went to jail for three years for failing to file a tax return for three years. *See* United States v. Snipes, 611 F.3d 855, 863 (11th Cir. 2010).

There is also a heightened impact to prosecuting a high-ranking tax official or or former government tax employee. Judge Diane Kroupa served on the United States Tax Court for 11 years and had served as the chief judge of the Minnesota Tax Court. Judge Kroupa and her husband at the time tried to maintain the lifestyle they had before she was appointed to the Tax Court, but that meant maintaining homes in both Minnesota and the Washington, D.C. area. They tried to finance this lifestyle through aggressive tax deduction claims. Eventually, however, their tax deduction claims went beyond aggressive into criminally fraudulent claims. Her sentence is 34 months. *See* Department of Justice News Release, 2017 WL 8808776 (June 22, 2017).

B. Tax Crimes

The Code creates a number of tax crimes. For purposes of this book, the concern is with the tax crimes that constitute basic noncompliance that a taxpayer would consider in deciding whether to comply with the tax laws. The basic tax crimes are (1) willful failure to file a tax return, (2) attempted tax evasion, and (3) false statement. *See* IRC §§ 7201-7203.

The criminal failure to file a tax return is a misdemeanor. With respect to failure to file a return, section 7203 provides:

> Any person required . . . to make a return . . . who willfully fails to . . . make such return . . . shall, in addition to other penalties provided by law, be guilty of a misdemeanor . . . .

Thus, the elements of criminal failure to file a return are: (1) an obligation to file a tax return, (2) failure to file, and (3) willfulness. It is punishable by a fine of $25,000 for individuals. The government may also imprison the perpetrator for up to one year. It should be noted that taking affirmative steps beyond merely not filing a tax return—such as requesting cash payments, holding deposits under a pseudonym, or keeping misleading records—could elevate the offense to tax evasion, the next topic.

The tax crime carrying the highest punishment is attempted tax evasion under section 7201. Section 7201 provides as follows:

> Any person who willfully attempts in any manner to evade or defeat any tax imposed by this title or the payment thereof shall, in addition to other penalties provided by law, be guilty of a felony. . . .

The elements of tax evasion are as follows: (1) a tax deficiency, (2) an attempt to evade or defeat the tax, and (3) willfulness. *See* Sansone v. United States, 380 U.S. 343, 351 (1965). Tax evasion is a felony. The government may impose a fine up to a $100,000 for an individual or $500,000 for a corporation. In addition, the government may imprison a taxpayer for up to five years per violation. The five-year maximum can be misleading. Most often, the government prosecutes alleged tax evaders for more than one violation, which can lead to longer sentences. *See, e.g.,* United States v. Cohen, 510 F.3d 1114, 1117 & n.2 (9th Cir. 2007) (convicting infamous tax protester Irwin Schiff on multiple counts leading to a 13-year sentence).

Although felony evasion and misdemeanor failure to file a tax return have the same willfulness element, an element of evasion is an affirmative act rather than a mere omission. The affirmative act is the differentiating factor between a misdemeanor tax crime and a felony tax crime.

SPIES v. UNITED STATES
317 U.S. 492 (1943)
Supreme Court of the United States

Mr. Justice JACKSON delivered the opinion of the Court.

Petitioner has been convicted of attempting to defeat and evade income tax in violation of § 145(b) of the . . . Internal Revenue Code [now codified at 26 U.S.C. § 7201]. As the construction of the section raises an important question of federal law not passed on by this Court, we granted certiorari.

Petitioner admitted at the opening of the trial that he had sufficient income during the year in question to place him under a statutory duty to file a return and to pay a tax, and that he failed to do either. The evidence during nearly two weeks of trial was directed principally toward establishing the exact amount of the tax and the manner of receiving and handling income and accounting, which the Government contends shows an intent to evade and defeat tax. Petitioner's testimony related to his good character, his physical illness at the time the return became due, and lack of willfulness in his defaults, chiefly because of a psychological disturbance, amounting to something more than worry but something less than insanity.

Section 145(a) [now codified at 26 U.S.C. § 7203] makes, among other things, willful failure to pay a tax or make a return by one having petitioner's income at the time or times required by law a misdemeanor.[4] Section 145(b) makes a willful attempt in any manner to evade or defeat any tax such as his a felony.[5] Petitioner was not indicted for either misdemeanor. The indictment contained a single count setting forth the felony charge of willfully attempting to defeat and evade the tax, and recited willful failure to file a return and willful failure to pay the tax as the means to the felonious end.

---

[4] "Any person required under this title (chapter) to pay any tax, or required by law or regulations made under authority thereof to make a return, keep any records, or supply any information, for the purposes of the computation, assessment, or collection of any tax imposed by this title (chapter), who willfully fails to pay such tax, make such return, keep such records, or supply such information, at the time or times required by law or regulations, shall, in addition to other penalties provided by law, be guilty of a misdemeanor and, upon conviction thereof, be fined not more than $10,000, or imprisoned for not more than one year, or both, together with the costs of prosecution."

[5] "Any person required under this title (chapter) to collect, account for, and pay over any tax imposed by this title (chapter), who willfully fails to collect or truthfully account for and pay over such tax, and any person who willfully attempts in any manner to evade or defeat any tax imposed by this title (chapter) or the payment thereof, shall, in addition to other penalties provided by law, be guilty of a felony and, upon conviction thereof, be fined not more than $10,000, or imprisoned for not more than five years, or both, together with the costs of prosecution."

The petitioner requested an instruction that 'You may not find the defendant guilty of a willful attempt to defeat and evade the income tax, if you find only that he had willfully failed to make a return of taxable income and has willfully failed to pay the tax on that income.' This was refused, and the Court charged that 'If you find that the defendant had a net income for 1936 upon which some income tax was due, and I believe that is conceded, if you find that the defendant willfully failed to file an income tax return for that year, if you find that the defendant willfully failed to pay the tax due on his income for that year, you may, if you find that the facts and circumstances warrant it find that the defendant willfully attempted to evade or defeat the tax.' The Court refused a request to instruct that an affirmative act was necessary to constitute a willful attempt and charged that 'Attempt means to try to do or accomplish. In order to find an attempt it is not necessary to find affirmative steps to accomplish the prohibited purpose. An attempt may be found on the basis of inactivity or on refraining to act, as well.'

It is the Government's contention that a willful failure to file a return together with a willful failure to pay the tax may, without more, constitute an attempt to defeat or evade a tax within § 145(b). Petitioner claims that such proof establishes only two misdemeanors under § 145(a) and that it takes more than the sum of two such misdemeanors to make the felony under § 145(b). The legislative history of the section contains nothing helpful on the question here at issue, and we must find the answer from the section itself and its context in the revenue laws.

The United States has relied for the collection of its income tax largely upon the taxpayer's own disclosures rather than upon a system of withholding the tax from him by those from whom income may be received. This system can function successfully only if those within and near taxable income keep and render true accounts. In many ways taxpayers' neglect or deceit may prejudice the orderly and punctual administration of the system as well as the revenues themselves. Congress has imposed a variety of sanctions for the protection of the system and the revenues. The relation of the offense of which this petitioner has been convicted to other and lesser revenue offenses appears more clearly from its position in this structure of sanctions.

The penalties imposed by Congress to enforce the tax laws embrace both civil and criminal sanctions. The former consist of additions to the tax upon determinations of fact made by an administrative agency and with no burden on the Government to prove its case beyond a reasonable doubt. The latter consist of penal offenses enforced by the criminal process in the familiar manner. Invocation of one does not exclude resort to the other. Helvering v. Mitchell, 303 U.S. 391.

The failure in a duty to make a timely return, unless it is shown that such failure is due to reasonable cause and not due to willful neglect, is punishable by an addition to the tax of 5 to 25 per cent thereof, depending on the duration of the default. But a duty may exist even when there is no tax liability to serve as a base for application of a percentage delinquency penalty; the default may relate to matters not identifiable with tax for a particular period; and the offense may be more grievous than a case for civil penalty. Hence the willful failure to make a return, keep records, or supply information when required, is made a misdemeanor, without regard to existence of a tax liability. § 145(a). Punctuality is important to the fiscal system, and these are sanctions to assure punctual as well as faithful performance of these duties.

Sanctions to insure payment of the tax are even more varied to meet the variety of causes of default. It is the right as well as the interest of the taxpayer to limit his admission of liability to the amount he actually owes. But the law is complicated, accounting treatment of various items raises problems of great complexity, and innocent errors are numerous, as appear from the number who make overpayments.[63] It is not the purpose of the law to penalize frank difference of opinion of innocent errors made despite the exercise of reasonable care. Such errors are corrected by the assessment of the deficiency of tax and its collection with interest for the delay. If any part of the deficiency is due to negligence or intentional disregard of rules and regulations, but without intent to defraud, five per cent of such deficiency is added thereto; and if any part of any deficiency is due to fraud with intent to evade tax, the addition is 50 per cent thereof. Willful failure to pay the tax when due is punishable as a misdemeanor. The climax of this variety of sanctions is the serious and inclusive felony defined to consist of willful attempt in any manner to evade or defeat the tax. The question here is whether there is a distinction between the acts necessary to make out the felony and those which may make out the misdemeanor.

A felony may, and frequently does, include lesser offenses in combination either with each other or with other elements. We think it clear that this felony may include one or several of the other offenses against the revenue laws. But it would be unusual and we would not readily assume that Congress by the felony defined in § 145(b) meant no more than the same derelictions it had just defined in § 145(a) as a misdemeanor. Such an interpretation becomes even more difficult to accept when we consider this felony as the capstone of a system of sanctions which singly or in combination were calculated to induce prompt and forthright fulfillment of every duty under the income tax law and to provide a penalty suitable to every degree of delinquency.

The difference between willful failure to pay a tax when due, which is made a misdemeanor, and willful attempt to defeat and evade one, which is made a

---

[6] The following statistics are given by the Commissioner of Internal Revenue for the fiscal year 1941: 73,627 certificates of overassessment of income tax issued, for 39,730 of which no claims had been filed; 236,610 assessments of additional income taxes made; 871 investigations made of alleged evasion of income and miscellaneous taxes, with recommendation for prosecution in 239 cases involving 446 individuals, of whom 192 were tried and 156 convicted. The total number of income tax returns filed was 16,052,007, of which number 7,867,319 reported a tax. Annual Report of the Commissioner of Internal Revenue (1941), pp. 17, 20, 21, 22, 52, 108.

felony, is not easy to detect or define. Both must be willful, and willful, as we have said, is a word of many meanings, its construction often being influenced by its context. United States v. Murdock, 290 U.S. 389, 54 S.Ct. 223, 78 L.Ed. 381. It may well mean something more as applied to nonpayment of a tax than when applied to failure to make a return. Mere voluntary and purposeful, as distinguished from accidental, omission to make a timely return might meet the test of willfulness. But in view of our traditional aversion to imprisonment for debt, we would not without the clearest manifestation of Congressional intent assume that mere knowing and intentional default in payment of a tax where there had been no willful failure to disclose the liability is intended to constitute a criminal offense of any degree. We would expect willfulness in such a case to include some element of evil motive and want of justification in view of all the financial circumstances of the taxpayer.

Had § 145(a) not included willful failure to pay a tax, it would have defined as misdemeanors generally a failure to observe statutory duties to make timely returns, keep records, or supply information—duties imposed to facilitate administration of the Act even if, because of insufficient net income, there were no duty to pay a tax. It would then be a permissible and perhaps an appropriate construction of § 145(b) that it made felonies of the same willful omissions when there was the added element of duty to pay a tax. The definition of such nonpayment as a misdemeanor we think argues strongly against such an interpretation.

The difference between the two offenses, it seems to us, is found in the affirmative action implied from the term 'attempt,' as used in the felony subsection. It is not necessary to involve this subject with the complexities of the common-law 'attempt'.[7] The attempt made criminal by this statute does not consist of conduct that would culminate in a more serious crime but for some impossibility of completion or interruption or frustration. This is an independent crime, complete in its most serious form when the attempt is complete and nothing is added to its criminality by success or consummation, as would be the case, say, of attempted murder. Although the attempt succeed in evading tax, there is no criminal offense of that kind, and the prosecution can be only for the attempt. We think that in employing the terminology of attempt to embrace the gravest of offenses against the revenues Congress intended some willful commission in addition to the willful omissions that make up the list of misdemeanors. Willful but passive neglect of the statutory duty may constitute the lesser offense, but to combine with it a willful and positive attempt to evade tax in any manner or to defeat it by any means lifts the offense to the degree of felony.

---

[7] Holmes, THE COMMON LAW, pp. 65—Foundations of Criminal Liability, 49 70; Hall, Criminal Attempt—A Study of Yale Law Journal 789; Arnold, *Criminal Attempts—The Rise and Fall of an Abstraction*, 40 YALE LAW JOURNAL 53.

Congress did not define or limit the methods by which a willful attempt to defeat and evade might be accomplished and perhaps did not define lest its effort to do so result in some unexpected limitation. Nor would we by definition constrict the scope of the Congressional provision that it may be accomplished 'in any manner'. By way of illustration, and not by way of limitation, we would think affirmative willful attempt may be inferred from conduct such as keeping a double set of books, making false entries of alterations, or false invoices or documents, destruction of books or records, concealment of assets or covering up sources of income, handling of one's affairs to avoid making the records usual in transactions of the kind, and any conduct, the likely effect of which would be to mislead or to conceal. If the tax-evasion motive plays any part in such conduct the offense may be made out even though the conduct may also serve other purposes such as concealment of other crime.

In this case there are several items of evidence apart from the default in filing the return and paying the tax which the Government claims will support an inference of willful attempt to evade or defeat the tax. These go to establish that petitioner insisted that certain income be paid to him in cash, transferred it to his own bank by armored car, deposited it, not in his own name but in the names of others of his family, and kept inadequate and misleading records. Petitioner claims other motives animated him in these matters. We intimate no opinion. Such inferences are for the jury. If on proper submission the jury found these acts, taken together with willful failure to file a return and willful failure to pay the tax, to constitute a willful attempt to defeat and evade tax, we would consider conviction of a felony sustainable. But we think a defendant is entitled to a charge which will point out the necessity for such an inference of willful attempt to defeat or evade tax from some proof in the case other than that necessary to make out the misdemeanors; and if the evidence fails to afford such an inference, the defendant should be acquitted.

The Government argues against this construction, contending that the milder punishment of a misdemeanor and the benefits of a short statute of limitation should not be extended to violators of the income tax laws such as political grafters, gamblers, racketeers, and gangsters. We doubt that this construction will handicap prosecution for felony of such flagrant violators. Few of them, we think, in their efforts to escape tax stop with mere omission of the duties put upon them by the statute, but if such there be, they are entitled to be convicted only of the offense which they have committed.

Reversed.

NOTES AND QUESTIONS

1. On what charge was Mr. Spies convicted?
2. What were the elements of the crime?
3. How were the defendant's actions different from those of a criminal failure to file misdemeanor under section 7203?

4. What does attempted tax evasion under section 7201 require beyond criminal failure to file under section 7203?

Another basic tax crime is tax perjury under section 7206. The primary provisions of section 7206 are as follows:

Any person who

(1) Willfully makes and subscribes any return, statement, or other document, which contains or is verified by a written declaration that it is made under the penalties of perjury, and which he does not believe to be true and correct as to every material matter . . . .

shall be guilty of a felony and, upon conviction thereof, shall be fined not more than $100,000 ($500,000 in the case of a corporation), or imprisoned not more than 3 years, or both, together with the costs of prosecution.

The elements of a false statement crime are: (1) the making of a false return, statement, or other document, (2) a declaration under penalty of perjury, (3) the taxpayer's belief that the return was not true and correct to every material matter, and (4) willfulness. *See* United States v. Bishop, 412 U.S. 346, 350 (1973). No affirmative act other than filing a return is required for a violation to occur.

It should be noted that if the return is not false then no violation of section 7206(1) occurs, even if the other elements are satisfied. In *United States v. Borman*, the taxpayers filed a Form 1040A for each of the years in issue that was technically correct. 992 F.2d 124 (7th Cir. 1993). The couple had earned income from manufacturing and selling seasonal wreaths, but Form 1040A did not inquire about income earned from a business. Rather, the form inquires only about wages, salaries, tips, etc. Accordingly, the taxpayers argued, each return was true and correct. The court agreed.

C. Willfulness

A component each punishable criminal tax violation discussed here shares is willfulness. Willful in the criminal tax context means: "[a] voluntary, intentional violation of a known legal duty." United States v. Pomponio, 429 U.S. 10, 12 (1976). A taxpayer has not committed a crime, however, if he was unaware of his tax obligations when the act occurred. This is an exception to the rule that ignorance of the law is no defense. If a taxpayer subjectively believes, as Mr. John L. Cheek did, his actions are legal, his actions are not willful.

CHEEK v. UNITED STATES
498 U.S. 192 (1991)
Supreme Court of the United States

Justice WHITE delivered the opinion of the Court.

Title 26, § 7201 of the United States Code provides that any person "who willfully attempts in any manner to evade or defeat any tax imposed by this title or the payment thereof" shall be guilty of a felony. Under 26 U.S.C. § 7203, "[a]ny person required under this title . . . or by regulations made under authority thereof to make a return . . . who willfully fails to . . . make such return" shall be guilty of a misdemeanor. This case turns on the meaning of the word "willfully" as used in §§ 7201 and 7203.

I.

Petitioner John L. Cheek has been a pilot for American Airlines since 1973. He filed federal income tax returns through 1979 but thereafter ceased to file returns.[8] He also claimed an increasing number of withholding allowances—eventually claiming 60 allowances by mid-1980—and for the years 1981 to 1984 indicated on his W-4 forms that he was exempt from federal income taxes. In 1983, petitioner unsuccessfully sought a refund of all tax withheld by his employer in 1982. Petitioner's income during this period at all times far exceeded the minimum necessary to trigger the statutory filing requirement.

As a result of his activities, petitioner was indicted for 10 violations of federal law. He was charged with six counts of willfully failing to file a federal income tax return for the years 1980, 1981, and 1983 through 1986, in violation of § 7203. He was further charged with three counts of willfully attempting to evade his income taxes for the years 1980, 1981, and 1983 in violation of 26 U.S.C. § 7201. In those years, American Airlines withheld substantially less than the amount of tax petitioner owed because of the numerous allowances and exempt status he claimed on his W-4 forms.[9] The tax offenses with which petitioner was charged are specific intent crimes that require the defendant to have acted willfully.

At trial, the evidence established that between 1982 and 1986, petitioner was involved in at least four civil cases that challenged various aspects of the federal income tax system.[10] In all four of those cases, the plaintiffs were informed by

---

[8] [fn 1] Cheek did file what the Court of Appeals described as a frivolous return in 1982.

[9] [fn 2] Because petitioner filed a refund claim for the entire amount withheld by his employer in 1982, petitioner was also charged under 18 U.S.C. § 287 with one count of presenting a claim to an agency of the United States knowing the claim to be false and fraudulent.

[10] [fn 3] In March 1982, Cheek and another employee of the company sued American Airlines to challenge the withholding of federal income taxes. In April 1982, Cheek sued the Internal Revenue Service (IRS) in the United States Tax Court, asserting that he was not a taxpayer or a person for purposes of the Internal Revenue Code and that his wages were not income, and making several other related claims. Cheek and four others also filed an action against the United States and the Commissioner of Internal Revenue in Federal District Court, claiming that withholding taxes from their wages violated the Sixteenth Amendment. Finally, in 1985 Cheek filed claims with the IRS seeking to have

the courts that many of their arguments, including that they were not taxpayers within the meaning of the tax laws, that wages are not income, that the Sixteenth Amendment does not authorize the imposition of an income tax on individuals, and that the Sixteenth Amendment is unenforceable, were frivolous or had been repeatedly rejected by the courts. During this time period, petitioner also attended at least two criminal trials of persons charged with tax offenses. In addition, there was evidence that in 1980 or 1981 an attorney had advised Cheek that the courts had rejected as frivolous the claim that wages are not income.[11]

Cheek represented himself at trial and testified in his defense. He admitted that he had not filed personal income tax returns during the years in question. He testified that as early as 1978, he had begun attending seminars sponsored by, and following the advice of, a group that believes, among other things, that the federal tax system is unconstitutional. Some of the speakers at these meetings were lawyers who purported to give professional opinions about the invalidity of the federal income tax laws. Cheek produced a letter from an attorney stating that the Sixteenth Amendment did not authorize a tax on wages and salaries but only on gain or profit. Petitioner's defense was that, based on the indoctrination he received from this group and from his own study, he sincerely believed that the tax laws were being unconstitutionally enforced and that his actions during the 1980-1986 period were lawful. He therefore argued that he had acted without the willfulness required for conviction of the various offenses with which he was charged.

In the course of its instructions, the trial court advised the jury that to prove "willfulness" the Government must prove the voluntary and intentional violation of a known legal duty, a burden that could not be proved by showing mistake, ignorance, or negligence. The court further advised the jury that an objectively reasonable good-faith misunderstanding of the law would negate willfulness, but mere disagreement with the law would not. The court described Cheek's beliefs about the income tax system[12] and instructed the jury that if it found that Cheek

---

refunded the taxes withheld from his wages in 1983 and 1984. When these claims were not allowed, he brought suit in the District Court claiming that the withholding was an unconstitutional taking of his property and that his wages were not income. In dismissing this action as frivolous, the District Court imposed costs and attorneys fees of $1,500 and a sanction under Federal Rule of Civil Procedure 11 in the amount of $10,000. The Court of Appeals agreed that Cheek's claims were frivolous, reduced the District Court sanction to $5,000, and imposed an additional sanction of $1,500 for bringing a frivolous appeal.

[11] [fn 4] The attorney also advised that despite the Fifth Amendment, the filing of a tax return was required and that a person could challenge the constitutionality of the system by suing for a refund after the taxes had been withheld, or by putting himself "at risk of criminal prosecution."

[12] [fn 5] "The defendant has testified as to what he states are his interpretations of the United States Constitution, court opinions, common law and other materials he has reviewed. ... He has also introduced materials which

"honestly and reasonably believed that he was not required to pay income taxes or to file tax returns," App. 81, a not guilty verdict should be returned.

After several hours of deliberation, the jury sent a note to the judge that stated in part:

> "'We have a basic disagreement between some of us as to if Mr. Cheek honestly & reasonably believed that he was not required to pay income taxes.
>
> . . .
>
> "'Page 32 [the relevant jury instruction] discusses good faith misunderstanding & disagreement. Is there any additional clarification you can give us on this point?' " *Id.*, at 85.

The District Judge responded with a supplemental instruction containing the following statements:

> "[A] person's opinion that the tax laws violate his constitutional rights does not constitute a good faith misunderstanding of the law. Furthermore, a person's disagreement with the government's tax collection systems and policies does not constitute a good faith misunderstanding of the law." *Id.*, at 86.

At the end of the first day of deliberation, the jury sent out another note saying that it still could not reach a verdict because " '[w]e are divided on the issue as to if Mr. Cheek honestly & reasonably believed that he was not required to pay income tax.' " *Id.*, at 87. When the jury resumed its deliberations, the District Judge gave the jury an additional instruction. This instruction stated in part that "[a]n honest but unreasonable belief is not a defense and does not negate willfulness," *id.*, at 88, and that "[a]dvice or research resulting in the conclusion that wages of a privately employed person are not income or that the tax laws are unconstitutional is not objectively reasonable and cannot serve as the basis for a good faith misunderstanding of the law defense." *Ibid.* The court also instructed the jury that "[p]ersistent refusal to acknowledge the law does not constitute a

---

contain references to quotations from the United States Constitution, court opinions, statutes, and other sources.

"He testified he relied on his interpretations and on these materials in concluding that he was not a person required to file income tax returns for the year or years charged, was not required to pay income taxes and that he could claim exempt status on his W-4 forms, and that he could claim refunds of all moneys withheld." App. 75-76.

"Among other things, Mr. Cheek contends that his wages from a private employer, American Airlines, does [*sic*] not constitute income under the Internal Revenue Service laws." *Id.*, at 81.

good faith misunderstanding of the law." *Ibid.* Approximately two hours later, the jury returned a verdict finding petitioner guilty on all counts.[13]

Petitioner appealed his convictions, arguing that the District Court erred by instructing the jury that only an objectively reasonable misunderstanding of the law negates the statutory willfulness requirement. The United States Court of Appeals for the Seventh Circuit rejected that contention and affirmed the convictions. 882 F.2d 1263 (1989). In prior cases, the Seventh Circuit had made clear that good-faith misunderstanding of the law negates willfulness only if the defendant's beliefs are objectively reasonable; in the Seventh Circuit, even actual ignorance is not a defense unless the defendant's ignorance was itself objectively reasonable. See, e.g., United States v. Buckner, 830 F.2d 102 (1987). In its opinion in this case, the court noted that several specified beliefs, including the beliefs that the tax laws are unconstitutional and that wages are not income, would not be objectively reasonable. [14] Because the Seventh Circuit's interpretation of "willfully" as used in these statutes conflicts with the decisions of several other Courts of Appeals, see, e.g., United States v. Whiteside, 810 F.2d 1306, 1310-1311 (CA5 1987); United States v. Phillips, 775 F.2d 262, 263-264

---

[13] [fn 6] A note signed by all 12 jurors also informed the judge that although the jury found petitioner guilty, several jurors wanted to express their personal opinions of the case and that notes from these individual jurors to the court were "a complaint against the narrow & hard expression under the constraints of the law." *Id.*, at 90. At least two notes from individual jurors expressed the opinion that petitioner sincerely believed in his cause even though his beliefs might have been unreasonable.

[14] [fn 7] The opinion stated, 882 F.2d 1263, 1268-1269, n. 2 (CA7 1989), as follows:

"For the record, we note that the following beliefs, which are stock arguments of the tax protester movement, have not been, nor ever will be, considered 'objectively reasonable' in this circuit:

"(1) the belief that the sixteenth amendment to the constitution was improperly ratified and therefore never came into being;

"(2) the belief that the sixteenth amendment is unconstitutional generally;

"(3) the belief that the income tax violates the takings clause of the fifth amendment;

"(4) the belief that the tax laws are unconstitutional;

"(5) the belief that wages are not income and therefore are not subject to federal income tax laws;

"(6) the belief that filing a tax return violates the privilege against self-incrimination; and

"(7) the belief that Federal Reserve Notes do not constitute cash or income.

"Miller v. United States, 868 F.2d 236, 239-41 (7th Cir.1989); *Buckner*, 830 F.2d at 102; *United States v. Dube*, 820 F.2d 886, 891 (7th Cir.1987); *Coleman v. Comm'r*, 791 F.2d 68, 70-71 (7th Cir.1986); *Moore*, 627 F.2d at 833. We have no doubt that this list will increase with time."

CHAPTER 2—CRIMINAL TAX LIABILITY

(CA10 1985); United States v. Aitken, 755 F.2d 188, 191-193 (CA1 1985), we granted certiorari, 493 U.S. 1068, 110 S.Ct. 1108, 107 L.Ed.2d 1016 (1990).

II

The general rule that ignorance of the law or a mistake of law is no defense to criminal prosecution is deeply rooted in the American legal system. Based on the notion that the law is definite and knowable, the common law presumed that every person knew the law. This common-law rule has been applied by the Court in numerous cases construing criminal statutes.

The proliferation of statutes and regulations has sometimes made it difficult for the average citizen to know and comprehend the extent of the duties and obligations imposed by the tax laws. Congress has accordingly softened the impact of the common-law presumption by making specific intent to violate the law an element of certain federal criminal tax offenses. Thus, the Court almost 60 years ago interpreted the statutory term "willfully" as used in the federal criminal tax statutes as carving out an exception to the traditional rule. This special treatment of criminal tax offenses is largely due to the complexity of the tax laws. In United States v. Murdock, 290 U.S. 389 (1933), the Court recognized that:

> "Congress did not intend that a person, by reason of a bona fide misunderstanding as to his liability for the tax, as to his duty to make a return, or as to the adequacy of the records he maintained, should become a criminal by his mere failure to measure up to the prescribed standard of conduct." *Id.*, at 396.

The Court held that the defendant was entitled to an instruction with respect to whether he acted in good faith based on his actual belief. In *Murdock,* the Court interpreted the term "willfully" as used in the criminal tax statutes generally to mean "an act done with a bad purpose," *id.,* at 394, or with "an evil motive," *id.,* at 395.

Subsequent decisions have refined this proposition. In *United States v. Bishop,* 412 U.S. 346 (1973), we described the term "willfully" as connoting "a voluntary, intentional violation of a known legal duty," *id.,* at 360, and did so with specific reference to the "bad faith or evil intent" language employed in *Murdock.* Still later, *United States v. Pomponio,* 429 U.S. 10, 97 S.Ct. 22, 50 L.Ed.2d 12 (1976) (*per curiam*), addressed a situation in which several defendants had been charged with willfully filing false tax returns. The jury was given an instruction on willfulness similar to the standard set forth in *Bishop.* In addition, it was instructed that " '[g]ood motive alone is never a defense where the act done or omitted is a crime.' " *Id.,* at 11, 97 S. Ct., at 23. The defendants were convicted but the Court of Appeals reversed, concluding that the latter instruction was improper because the statute required a finding of bad purpose or evil motive. *Ibid.*

We reversed the Court of Appeals, stating that "the Court of Appeals incorrectly assumed that the reference to an 'evil motive' in *United States v. Bishop, supra,* and prior cases," *ibid,* "requires proof of any motive other than an intentional violation of a known legal duty." *Id.,* at 12, 97 S.Ct., at 23. As "the other Courts of Appeals that have considered the question have recognized, willfulness in this context simply means a voluntary, intentional violation of a known legal duty." *Ibid.* We concluded that after instructing the jury on willfulness, "[a]n additional instruction on good faith was unnecessary." *Id.,* at 13, 97 S.Ct., at 24. Taken together, *Bishop* and *Pomponio* conclusively establish that the standard for the statutory willfulness requirement is the "voluntary, intentional violation of a known legal duty."

III

Cheek accepts the *Pomponio* definition of willfulness, Brief for Petitioner 5, and n. 4, 13, 36; Reply Brief for Petitioner 4, 6-7, 11, 13, but asserts that the District Court's instructions and the Court of Appeals' opinion departed from that definition. In particular, he challenges the ruling that a good-faith misunderstanding of the law or a good-faith belief that one is not violating the law, if it is to negate willfulness, must be objectively reasonable. We agree that the Court of Appeals and the District Court erred in this respect.

A

Willfulness, as construed by our prior decisions in criminal tax cases, requires the Government to prove that the law imposed a duty on the defendant, that the defendant knew of this duty, and that he voluntarily and intentionally violated that duty. We deal first with the case where the issue is whether the defendant knew of the duty purportedly imposed by the provision of the statute or regulation he is accused of violating, a case in which there is no claim that the provision at issue is invalid. In such a case, if the Government proves actual knowledge of the pertinent legal duty, the prosecution, without more, has satisfied the knowledge component of the willfulness requirement. But carrying this burden requires negating a defendant's claim of ignorance of the law or a claim that because of a misunderstanding of the law, he had a good-faith belief that he was not violating any of the provisions of the tax laws. This is so because one cannot be aware that the law imposes a duty upon him and yet be ignorant of it, misunderstand the law, or believe that the duty does not exist. In the end, the issue is whether, based on all the evidence, the Government has proved that the defendant was aware of the duty at issue, which cannot be true if the jury credits a good-faith misunderstanding and belief submission, whether or not the claimed belief or misunderstanding is objectively reasonable.

In this case, if Cheek asserted that he truly believed that the Internal Revenue Code did not purport to treat wages as income, and the jury believed him, the Government would not have carried its burden to prove willfulness, however unreasonable a court might deem such a belief. Of course, in deciding whether to credit Cheek's good-faith belief claim, the jury would be free to consider any admissible evidence from any source showing that Cheek was aware of his duty to file a return and to treat wages as income, including evidence showing his awareness of the relevant provisions of the Code or regulations, of court decisions rejecting his interpretation of the tax law, of authoritative rulings of the Internal Revenue Service, or of any contents of the personal income tax return forms and accompanying instructions that made it plain that wages should be returned as income.[15]

We thus disagree with the Court of Appeals' requirement that a claimed good-faith belief must be objectively reasonable if it is to be considered as possibly negating the Government's evidence purporting to show a defendant's awareness of the legal duty at issue. Knowledge and belief are characteristically questions for the factfinder, in this case the jury. Characterizing a particular belief as not objectively reasonable transforms the inquiry into a legal one and would prevent the jury from considering it. It would of course be proper to exclude evidence having no relevance or probative value with respect to willfulness; but it is not contrary to common sense, let alone impossible, for a defendant to be ignorant of his duty based on an irrational belief that he has no duty, and forbidding the jury to consider evidence that might negate willfulness would raise a serious question under the Sixth Amendment's jury trial provision. It is common ground that this Court, where possible, interprets congressional enactments so as to avoid raising serious constitutional questions.

It was therefore error to instruct the jury to disregard evidence of Cheek's understanding that, within the meaning of the tax laws, he was not a person required to file a return or to pay income taxes and that wages are not taxable income, as incredible as such misunderstandings of and beliefs about the law might be. Of course, the more unreasonable the asserted beliefs or misunderstandings are, the more likely the jury will consider them to be nothing more than simple disagreement with known legal duties imposed by the tax laws and will find that the Government has carried its burden of proving knowledge.

B

Cheek asserted in the trial court that he should be acquitted because he believed in good faith that the income tax law is unconstitutional as applied to him and thus could not legally impose any duty upon him of which he should have been aware.[16] Such a submission is unsound, not because Cheek's

---

[15] [fn 8] Cheek recognizes that a "defendant who knows what the law is and who disagrees with it . . . does not have a bona fide misunderstanding defense," but asserts that "a defendant who has a bona fide misunderstanding of [the law] does not 'know' his legal duty and lacks willfulness." Brief for Petitioner 29, and n. 13. The Reply Brief for Petitioner, at 13, states: "We are in no way suggesting that Cheek or anyone else is immune from criminal prosecution if he knows what the law is, but believes it should be otherwise, and therefore violates it." See also Tr. of Oral Arg. 9, 11, 12, 15, 17.

[16] [fn 9] In his opening and reply briefs and at oral argument, Cheek asserts that this case does not present the issue whether a claim of unconstitutionality would serve to negate willfulness and that we need not address the issue. Brief for Petitioner 13; Reply Brief for Petitioner 5, 11, 12; Tr. of Oral Arg. 6, 13. Cheek testified at trial, however, that "[i]t is my belief that the law is being enforced unconstitutionally." App. 60. He also produced a letter from counsel advising him that " 'Finally you make a valid contention . . . that Congress'

constitutional arguments are not objectively reasonable or frivolous, which they surely are, but because the *Murdock-Pomponio* line of cases does not support such a position. Those cases construed the willfulness requirement in the criminal provisions of the Internal Revenue Code to require proof of knowledge of the law. This was because in "our complex tax system, uncertainty often arises even among taxpayers who earnestly wish to follow the law," and " '[i]t is not the purpose of the law to penalize frank difference of opinion or innocent errors made despite the exercise of reasonable care.' " *United States v. Bishop,* 412 U.S. 346, 360-361, 93 S.Ct. 2008, 2017-2018, 36 L.Ed.2d 941 (1973) (quoting *Spies v. United States,* 317 U.S. 492, 496, 63 S.Ct. 364, 367, 87 L.Ed. 418 (1943)).

Claims that some of the provisions of the tax code are unconstitutional are submissions of a different order.[17] They do not arise from innocent mistakes

---

power to tax comes from Article I, Section 8, Clause 1 of the U.S. Constitution, and not from the Sixteenth Amendment and that the [latter], construed with Article I, Section 2, Clause 3, never authorized a tax on wages and salaries, but only on gain and profit." *Id.,* at 57. We note also that the jury asked for "the portion [of the transcript] wherein Mr. Cheek stated he was attempting to test the constitutionality of the income tax laws," Tr. 1704, and that the trial judge later instructed the jury that an opinion that the tax laws violate a person's constitutional rights does not constitute a good-faith misunderstanding of the law. We also note that at oral argument Cheek's counsel observed that "personal belief that a known statute is unconstitutional smacks of knowledge with existing law, but disagreement with it." Tr. of Oral Arg. 5. He also opined:

> "If the person believes as a personal belief that known-law known to them *[sic]* is unconstitutional, I submit that that would not be a defense, because what the person is really saying is I know what the law is, for constitutional reasons I have made my own determination that it is invalid. I am not suggesting that that is a defense.

> "However, if the person was told by a lawyer or by an accountant erroneously that the statute is unconstitutional, and it's my professional advice to you that you don't have to follow it, then you have got a little different situation. This is not that case." *Id.,* at 6.

Given this posture of the case, we perceive no reason not to address the significance of Cheek's constitutional claims to the issue of willfulness.

[17] [fn 10] In United States v. Murdock, 290 U.S. 389, 54 S.Ct. 223, 78 L.Ed. 381 (1933), discussed supra, at 609-610, the defendant Murdock was summoned to appear before a revenue agent for examination. Questions were put to him, which he refused to answer for fear of self-incrimination under state law. He was indicted for refusing to give testimony and supply information contrary to the pertinent provisions of the Internal Revenue Code. This Court affirmed the reversal of Murdock's conviction, holding that the trial court erred in refusing to give an instruction directing the jury to consider Murdock's asserted claim of a

caused by the complexity of the Internal Revenue Code. Rather, they reveal full knowledge of the provisions at issue and a studied conclusion, however wrong, that those provisions are invalid and unenforceable. Thus in this case, Cheek paid his taxes for years, but after attending various seminars and based on his own study, he concluded that the income tax laws could not constitutionally require him to pay a tax.

We do not believe that Congress contemplated that such a taxpayer, without risking criminal prosecution, could ignore the duties imposed upon him by the Internal Revenue Code and refuse to utilize the mechanisms provided by Congress to present his claims of invalidity to the courts and to abide by their decisions. There is no doubt that Cheek, from year to year, was free to pay the tax that the law purported to require, file for a refund and, if denied, present his claims of invalidity, constitutional or otherwise, to the courts. See 26 U.S.C. § 7422. Also, without paying the tax, he could have challenged claims of tax deficiencies in the Tax Court, § 6213, with the right to appeal to a higher court if unsuccessful. § 7482(a)(1). Cheek took neither course in some years, and when he did was unwilling to accept the outcome. As we see it, he is in no position to claim that his good-faith belief about the validity of the Internal Revenue Code negates willfulness or provides a defense to criminal prosecution under §§ 7201 and 7203. Of course, Cheek was free in this very case to present his claims of invalidity and have them adjudicated, but like defendants in criminal cases in other contexts, who "willfully" refuse to comply with the duties placed upon them by the law, he must take the risk of being wrong.

We thus hold that in a case like this, a defendant's views about the validity of the tax statutes are irrelevant to the issue of willfulness and need not be heard by the jury, and, if they are, an instruction to disregard them would be proper. For this purpose, it makes no difference whether the claims of invalidity are frivolous or have substance. It was therefore not error in this case for the District Judge to instruct the jury not to consider Cheek's claims that the tax laws were unconstitutional. However, it was error for the court to instruct the jury that petitioner's asserted beliefs that wages are not income and that he was not a taxpayer within the meaning of the Internal Revenue Code should not be considered by the jury in determining whether Cheek had acted willfully.[18]

---

good-faith, actual belief that because of the Fifth Amendment he was privileged not to answer the questions put to him. It is thus the case that Murdock's asserted belief was grounded in the Constitution, but it was a claim of privilege not to answer, not a claim that any provision of the tax laws were unconstitutional, and not a claim for which the tax laws provided procedures to entertain and resolve. Cheek's position at trial, in contrast, was that the tax laws were unconstitutional as applied to him.

[18] [fn 11] Cheek argues that applying to him the Court of Appeals' standard of objective reasonableness violates his rights under the First, Fifth, and Sixth Amendments of the Constitution. Since we have invalidated the challenged standard on statutory grounds, we need not address these submissions.

IV

For the reasons set forth in the opinion above, the judgment of the Court of Appeals is vacated, and the case is remanded for further proceedings consistent with this opinion.

It is so ordered.

[Concurring opinion omitted.]

NOTES AND QUESTIONS

1. Did the defendant reasonably believe that his actions—failing to file tax returns for a number of years—were lawful? Did it matter?
2. Although ignorance of the law is a defense in tax cases, the ignorance may itself not be willful. The defendant was retried and convicted under this theory. *See* United States v. Cheek, 3 F.3d 1057 (3d Cir. 1993).
3. If a taxpayer failed to file tax returns for a number of years and then files all of the tax returns at once, will the IRS be able to prove that the failures to file for all those years was willful?

D. The IRS's Voluntary Disclosure Policy

The government generally will not prosecute a taxpayer who has failed to file a tax return and voluntarily disclosed that fact to the IRS. This is a surprisingly common issue. Tax attorneys are often approached by people who have not filed their tax returns for a number of years. Although ultimately the taxpayer below was not successful, he was able to convince the district court that he should not be prosecuted.

UNITED STATES v. TENZER
950 F. Supp. 554 (S.D.N.Y. 1996)
United States District Court, Southern District of New York

MEMORANDUM AND ORDER

BRIEANT, District Judge.

By motion docketed March 4, 1996, James L. Tenzer, the single defendant in a four count misdemeanor Information filed November 30, 1995, charging failure to file income tax returns, seeks to dismiss the Information on grounds that his Constitutional rights were violated by the filing of the charges, and that he is entitled to immunity granted by the Internal Revenue Service ("IRS"). Alternatively, Mr. Tenzer seeks to dismiss Count One on the ground that it is time barred and to suppress certain statements and documents received by the Government from Mr. Tenzer prior to the filing of the criminal Information and all leads and other derivative evidence derived therefrom.

For the most part, the motion is based on the IRS Voluntary Disclosure Policy (the "Policy") discussed below, and the so-called "*Caceres* doctrine" which holds that once an agency adopts regulations they are duty bound to obey them, even if the agency was not required by the Constitution to adopt them in the first instance. The doctrine was set forth in *United States v. Caceres,* 440 U.S. 741, 99 S.Ct. 1465, 59 L.Ed.2d 733 (1979), where the Supreme Court noted that:

> "Our decisions in Lopez [v. United States, 373 U.S. 427, 83 S.Ct. 1381, 10 L.Ed.2d 462 (1963)] and [United States v.] White [401 U.S. 745, 91 S.Ct. 1122, 28 L.Ed.2d 453 (1971)] demonstrate that the IRS was not required by the Constitution to adopt these regulations.14

[Footnote 14 reads as follows:]

> It does not necessarily follow, however, as a matter of either logic or law, that the Agency had no duty to obey them. 'Where the rights of individuals are affected, it is incumbent upon agencies to follow their own procedures. This is so even where the internal procedures are possibly more rigorous than otherwise would be required.' (Citations omitted.)

Id. at 751, n. 14, 99 S.Ct. at 1471, n. 14.

The misdemeanor Information charges defendant Tenzer with having unlawfully, willingly and knowingly failed to make income tax returns for the calendar years 1987, 1988, 1989 and 1990. The Information charges that during each of those years the gross income of the defendant ranged between $261,488.00 and $717,344.00.

The following facts were developed at an evidentiary hearing or are presumed to be true for purposes of the motion. Defendant himself did not testify at the hearing.

Mr. Tenzer is an experienced tax attorney and one of the principals of Margolin, Winer and Evens, described as a large accounting firm located in Long Island New York. It is clear that defendant received substantial income during the four years charged and paid little or no estimated tax. The primary source of his income was from approximately six partnerships. The fact of his existence and his receipt of funds from the partnerships was fully known at all times to the IRS. During the period 1976 through 1991, Mr. Tenzer filed his tax returns timely only for the years 1983, 1984, and 1985. Mr. Tenzer never filed any tax return at all, nor did he pay any tax for the years 1978 and 1979. During this period, the IRS treated the repeated incidents of late filing only as a civil, not a criminal matter, and did nothing about 1978 and 1979.

On February 29, 1988, the IRS sent Mr. Tenzer a computer generated notice stating "we have not received your tax return" for 1986, and requesting that a return be filed. (Gov.Ex. 2.) Additional notices were sent on April 25, 1988, (Gov.Ex. 3.) and June 6, 1988. (Gov.Ex. 4.) On July 18, 1988, the IRS sent another warning that "we may have to . . . [b]egin criminal proceedings . . . if you willfully fail to file a tax return." (Gov.Ex. 5.)

Despite these notices, the first evidence of Mr. Tenzer's intent to comply with IRS filing requirements did not occur until March 29, 1991, when he retained Steven Solomon, Esq., also an experienced tax practitioner, to assist him in filing his returns.

For many years, the Margolin firm, through Mr. Tenzer, acted as the tax accountants for a major real estate enterprise in Westchester County known as "JRD". JRD, its principals and several of its employees were under Grand Jury investigation, not only for income tax violations but for other crimes, including violations of the Taft Hartley law, making false statements and similar activities. This was a lengthy and elaborate investigation.

In July of 1991, the Margolin firm was notified by JRD that JRD had been served with a Federal Grand Jury subpoena seeking records in connection with a Title 26 tax investigation of JRD. In November 1991, the Margolin firm was itself served with a Federal Grand Jury subpoena calling for the production of the accounting firm's documents relating to JRD. This service was effected on Mr. Tenzer by Special Agent Trezza of the IRS, who testified before me. Mr. Trezza recalled that upon the service of the subpoena upon Mr. Tenzer, which showed on its face that it was in connection with an investigation of JRD under Section 7201 of Title 26, Mr. Tenzer displayed considerable nervousness and inquired whether "his personal taxes were the subject of the investigation." (Transcript, 394.) This was an unusual reaction for a tax accountant in the experience of Agent Trezza. While the Court finds Mr. Trezza's testimony credible in all respects, I decline to find the weight and significance which the Government attributes to this event. The Government now argues that this service of process (unrelated to Tenzer's own records) was a triggering event which constituted a "contact" by the IRS "notifying" the taxpayer that he was under criminal investigation for failure to file, a relevant issue under the Policy. This Court rejects this inference.

There is a high level of suspicion attached to Tenzer's activities as a possible aider and abettor of JRD's tax frauds. His nervousness, and inquiry about his own taxes may merely reflect a consciousness of guilt concerning JRD. Reading the Policy literally, service of a subpoena to produce the records of a crooked client does not, as a matter of law, arise to a level of notification that the record custodian's own failure to file was known, or under criminal investigation, and indeed, at that point in time it was not. This "triggering event" is also discounted by this Court's finding that by the spring of 1991, prior to the service of the JRD subpoena, Mr. Tenzer had retained Mr. Solomon to assist him in becoming current on his obligations to the IRS. (Transcript, 310.)

On October 7, 1991, by another computer generated notice as a result of activity unrelated to Mr. Trezza or the JRD investigation, the IRS notified Tenzer and his wife that due to their continued failure to respond to repeated inquiries, their accounts had been referred to enforcement action. The letter noted that Tenzer could still avoid enforcement action if he filed all delinquent returns and paid all outstanding taxes within ten days or if he immediately contacted the IRS by telephone.

Following receipt of this letter, Myron Weinberg, Esq., a law partner of Steven Solomon, called the IRS to pledge that the returns would soon be filed, and requested additional time to do so. The IRS granted a series of extensions, through January 31, 1992. On February 10, 1992, Mr. Tenzer filed his tax returns for 1986, 1987, 1988, and 1989. The truthfulness of these returns was not questioned by the IRS at the time and they were "cleared for assessment." The returns were not accompanied with payment for his tax liabilities. Despite filing the returns, Mr. Tenzer failed to make any estimated tax payments throughout the year and thus did not remain current on his 1992 accruing taxes.

In September of 1992, Revenue Officer Elizabeth Kishlansky was assigned to collect the tax deficiency resulting from the returns as filed. On October 15, 1992, Revenue Officer Kishlansky met with Attorney Weinberg regarding the Tenzer matter. Weinberg advised Kishlansky that Tenzer was unable to make full payment, but instead wanted to enter into an Installment Agreement with the IRS whereby he would be allowed to make full payment to the IRS over time. Revenue Officer Kishlansky informed Weinberg that Tenzer would only be given 30 days, until November 16, 1992, to resolve the collection situation. Kishlansky also informed Weinberg that Tenzer would have to submit a financial statement to evaluate this proposed Installment Agreement, and if the situation was not resolved by that time, the IRS would take enforcement action by levy, seizure and/or administrative action.

On October 16, 1992, Revenue Officer Kishlansky filed liens in New York County and Nassau County to protect the IRS' interest. On October 22, 1992, Kishlansky learned that Tenzer had not filed his 1990 or 1991 tax returns. She then "demanded" that those returns be filed. (GX C; Tr. 446.) This was a "solicitation" of the 1990 return, which is the subject of Count Four of the Information. The effect of this is discussed below.

On November 13, 1992, Tenzer filed his tax returns for the years 1990 and 1991.

On January 8, 1993, Ms. Kishlansky attended a meeting with Tenzer's tax counsel Myron Weinberg, Steven Solomon, and newcomer Ernest Honecker, an attorney who formerly was employed with the IRS in the Chief Counsel's office. Mr. Honecker testified, and I find, that he asked Ms. Kishlansky at the start of the meeting for assurances that Mr. Tenzer's voluntary disclosure was being handled as a civil matter. Kishlansky assured Honecker that it was a civil matter and that she was there only for collection. Revenue Officer Kishlansky was informed that rather than enter into an Installment Agreement, Mr. Tenzer wished to submit an Offer in Compromise. Kishlansky advised the representatives that if Tenzer wanted an Offer in Compromise to be considered by the IRS, he would have to start becoming current on accruing taxes and make all required current estimated tax payments. Tenzer's representatives indicated that the Offer would be approximately $250,000. Because a financial statement submitted at that time indicated that Tenzer had substantial assets and significant earnings potential, Kishlansky estimated that a reasonable Offer would be closer to $600,000.

After the meeting, but on that same day, Kishlansky called Weinberg and demanded that Tenzer sell several assets and begin making monthly payments of $7,000 towards his tax liability. No such payments were never made by Mr. Tenzer.

In February, 1993, Tenzer submitted an Offer in Compromise to Revenue Officer Kishlansky, which covered the tax years 1986 through 1991. This document was prepared by Tenzer's team of lawyers led by IRS alumnus Honecker, pursuant to a practice commonly followed by persons who owe large amounts of unpaid income taxes. Kishlansky reviewed the Offer, and advised Mr. Honecker that the Offer would most likely be rejected due to its failure to take into consideration Tenzer's future earning potential and his ability to liquidate assets to generate available cash to pay the IRS, and also that the Offer failed to include 1992. However, Ms. Kishlansky determined that the Offer was not facially inadequate or made in bad faith, and forwarded the Offer to a service center in Maine for processing and review.

In early April of 1993, attorney Honecker learned that the Offer in Compromise had been rejected. The Offer was rejected according to Honecker because of the Service's failure to discount Tenzer's non-liquid assets to their "forced sale" value. With news of the Offer's rejection, Honecker informed Kishlansky that he would be re-submitting the Offer, with whatever amendments were necessary to reflect Mr. Tenzer's current financial status.

Shortly after April 22, 1993, after having discussions with her Group Manager, Revenue Officer Kishlansky transferred the collections case to the Brooklyn office of the IRS, because Tenzer and his assets upon which to levy were located in Long Island. There the file became dormant.

The records of JRD called for in the subpoena issued in 1991 were produced in April, 1993. Special Agent Anthony Trezza of the Internal Revenue Service testified, and I find, that about May 14, 1993 he and others working with him found documents among records produced by the Margolin firm which supported an inference that Mr. Tenzer "may have been a party to back-dating some [tax related corporate] documents" involved in the JRD investigation. This was the first occasion when Agent Trezza had reason to believe that Mr. Tenzer may have engaged in criminal conduct, essentially as an aider and abettor of tax evasion by JRD or its principals. Mr. Trezza, almost immediately thereafter, discussed his conclusions with AUSA Dunne of this District, who in turn informed Mr. William Wachtel, who was then representing the Margolin firm, that Mr. Tenzer along with another Margolin partner, was now a "subject" of a criminal investigation in connection with JRD. (Transcript 8.) Mr. Wachtel was not affiliated with the Solomon, Weinberg, Honecker group of lawyers who were dealing with the civil tax matter. Apparently his representation of Mr. Tenzer began in connection with Tenzer's status as a JRD subject.

Mr. Trezza testified that probably around June of 1993, he, or Special Agent Walter Gross, with whom he was working on the matter, obtained from a computer terminal, a transcript of Mr. Tenzer's account as to his personal taxes. At the time the transcript was obtained, the witness Trezza and his fellow agents regarded Tenzer only as a subject for assisting JRD or its principals in committing fraud as to JRD's tax obligations or those of its principals and affiliates. He sought the transcript "in order to get a tax Grand Jury approved" through the Department of Justice to consider this aiding and abetting charge. Special Agent Trezza testified that the IRS required that tax background on the individual be obtained and submitted with any request to enlarge an existing tax Grand Jury. Mr. Trezza explained (Transcript, 14), "where it is an accountant aiding and assisting somebody else we always request transcripts, because the attorneys that review our work want to see the IRS file on it." He testified that it was "required that when we submit the information pertaining to any individual tax crime, even if it doesn't pertain to his own taxes, we always have to get a transcript of their filing record." Thus, Mr. Trezza ascertained that Mr. Tenzer had been a late filer for the years included in this prosecution, but that his returns had been filed, and desultory efforts to collect the taxes due had begun.

In June 1993, Mr. Trezza spoke to the Civil Collection Officer. Finding from that discussion that there was a file showing collection efforts, he asked for that file. The civil file was requested from the Collections Office on June 14, 1993 by Special Agent Gross. Special Agent Gross notified the collections officer not to take any action on the account until a decision was made to put a "914" freeze on the account. On June 23, Gross notified the collections officer that steps were being taken to put such a freeze on the collection efforts. Collection remains frozen to this day.

On June 24, 1993, the office of the United States Attorney requested from IRS District Counsel authorization to expand the Title 26 Grand Jury investigation of JRD to include James Tenzer as a named subject in his role in the preparation of JRD's tax returns. By letter dated July 8, 1993 the United States Attorney received authorization to investigate Tenzer for Title 26 offenses, without limit. The following day, July 9, 1993, Special Agents Trezza and Gross notified Myron Weinberg that Tenzer was now a subject of a Grand Jury investigation into his personal tax matters.

On September 28, 1994, Special Agents Trezza and Gross attended a pre-referral conference with James Biaggi, an attorney with the IRS' District Counsel's Office. As a result of that meeting, by a memorandum authored by Robert B. Marino, Assistant District Counsel, the IRS concluded that it would be appropriate for the United States Attorney's Office to proceed with a prosecution for failure to timely file tax returns as Tenzer did not meet the criteria for the Voluntary Disclosure Policy.

As will be understood, this was unusual. Most prosecutions for failure to file originate with the IRS and are sent to the Department of Justice which may decline. In this case the request to proceed against Tenzer as a non-filer originated with the DOJ, or more correctly, the local United States Attorney's Office, after it had exhausted its ability to make a case against Tenzer for his likely complicity in the JRD tax fraud. An understandable desire to make some charge of some sort stick against Tenzer appears to have influenced subsequent consideration of his case in light of the Voluntary Disclosure Policy.

The Special Agent's Report dated November 15, 1994, recommending that charges be brought for failure to timely file, was forwarded by the IRS to the Department of Justice. Thereafter, Tenzer's counsel attended a meeting at the DOJ where they argued that Tenzer should not be prosecuted because he fell within the provision of the IRS' Voluntary Disclosure Policy. Rejecting this contention, the DOJ subsequently authorized this prosecution of Tenzer for failure to timely file tax returns for the years 1987–1990, as four separate counts.

THE VOLUNTARY DISCLOSURE PROGRAM

Since about 1961, the IRS has had a publicly announced Policy, changed from time to time, which is to encourage taxpayers who have failed to file returns, to do so and in effect come, or be brought back into the system for past and future returns. There are many such non-filers, some of whom are entitled to refunds, and some of whom fail to file for a variety of reasons which do not include the intent to evade income taxes. The goal of the agency is not to procure misdemeanor convictions against these non-filers as a general deterrent to others, as authorized by Congress, but rather, to collect their taxes and welcome them back to the largest voluntary tax assessment system in the world.

To lure these non-filers into a state of grace with their taxes, offers and promises were made from time to time with much public fanfare, couched, unfortunately, in language not always precise as a penal statute, and written without much consideration of possible application of the rule of the *Caceres* footnote.

While the applicability and scope of the Voluntary Disclosure Policy are a matter of law for this Court to determine, there is some dispute as to what the actual publicly stated Policy of the IRS was at the relevant times in this case, and how it was imparted to the public. In this regard, the testimony of Assistant District Counsel Robert Marino and former Acting Assistant Attorney General James Bruton during the evidentiary hearing is relevant.

Mr. Robert Marino testified that the Voluntary Disclosure Policy (the "Policy") governs how the IRS reviews its cases when considering a referral for prosecution, and that it is not intended to create any substantive rights. Marino testified that it was the IRS' view that Tenzer did not make a true voluntary disclosure, and that even if he had, prosecution was warranted due to his egregious circumstances. (Transcript, 170.) We note that there is no exception stated in the Policy for egregious circumstances, whatever that means. Marino testified that the voluntary disclosure did not apply to Tenzer because (1) it was "triggered" by Mr. Trezza's service of the JRD subpoena on Mr. Tenzer; (2) that he did not believe that the Offer and Compromise was legitimate; and (3) that "[t]he amount of money involved; the amount of years involved; no withholding paid; taxpayers sophistication; being an attorney: All of these matters, I think, make this an egregious case." (Transcript, 171.) This Court agrees that the misconduct of Tenzer is egregious by any definition of the word; that is besides the point under the IRS Policy.

The Internal Revenue Manual ("I.R.M.") at Section 342.142 (promulgated April 5, 1993) set forth the Service's Voluntary Disclosure Policy as effective when this prosecution commenced. Subsection (3) lays out the conditions under which a non-filer may qualify for relief under the Voluntary Disclosure Policy. The person must have:

1) informed the Service that he or she has not filed returns for one or more taxable years;

2) had only legal-source income;

3) made the disclosure *prior to being contacted by the Service notifying the taxpayer* or his/her representative by letter, the phone or personal visit *that the taxpayer is under criminal investigation*;

4) either filed true and correct tax returns or cooperated with the Service in ascertaining his/her correct tax liability; and

5) either made full payment of the amounts due or in those situations where the taxpayer was unable to make full payment, made a bona fide arrangement to pay.

(Emphasis added)

Subsection (5) provides that the IRS' voluntary disclosure practice creates no substantive or procedural rights for taxpayers, but rather is a matter of internal IRS practice, provided solely for guidance to IRS personnel. The validity of this reservation is challenged in light of *Caceres,* discussed below.

The Government's position is that the proper Voluntary Disclosure Policy to apply is not that which was in force when the decision was made to prosecute, in clear derogation of the express terms of the Policy, but rather that Policy which was in effect in February of 1992, when Tenzer's tax returns were filed. This Court rejects this argument. The Policy in effect when the decision to prosecute is made is the Policy which under *Caceres* must control the decision making.

The critical distinction between the Policy when the returns were filed, and the Policy as effective at the initiation of this prosecution is the definition of when a Voluntary Disclosure is timely made. Section 342.14, as effective when the defendant was initially contacted by the IRS regarding his non-filing status, required the disclosure to be made prior to the taxpayer's awareness of an IRS inquiry. Unlike the April 5, 1993 "Policy", the provision did not limit itself to "criminal" inquiries. Specifically, the Voluntary Disclosure Policy as effective in February, 1992, considered a disclosure to be timely when it is received before:

(a) The IRS has initiated an inquiry that is likely to lead to the taxpayer, and the taxpayer is reasonably thought to be aware of that investigative activity; or

(b) some event known to the taxpayer occurred, which event is likely to cause an audit into the taxpayer's liabilities, e.g., a newspaper article highlighting commercial bribery in a particular industry or corruption in a government office.

The Policy as in effect during 1993 was first announced in an IRS press release issued in December of 1992 by then IRS Commissioner Shirley Peterson. In April of 1993, the IRS Manual was updated to conform to the Policy announced in the press release. During the evidentiary hearing, Robert Marino attempted to minimize the importance of this change by suggesting that the

December 1992 press release did not accurately reflect Ms. Peterson's intent, and that what she really meant was only that out of 147 million returns that are filed in a year only 2,500 are actually prosecuted. "[W]hat [Peterson is] really saying, as a practical matter, is that most people who don't file returns probably don't get prosecuted, and I think that's what she was saying there." (Transcript, 134.) While it is not uncommon for press releases to reflect inaccurately the drafter's intent, any notion that the press release quoted *infra,* was inaccurate is belied by the fact that in April of 1993 the IRS Manual was updated to reflect the change.

In 1995 the IRS switched back to the Policy in effect prior to April 5, 1993 and amended its Manual provisions accordingly.

The Government argues that the service upon Mr. Tenzer of the subpoena directed at JRD documents was enough to put him on inquiry of investigative activity into his own return and make any subsequent disclosures untimely. However, under either standard, pre or post 1993, this Court concludes that the Voluntary Disclosure Policy standards were met by Mr. Tenzer. Under the "Peterson" Policy, Tenzer filed prior to being notified of a pending "criminal" investigation into his personal taxes. And under the prior and now current Policy, Tenzer began good faith efforts through Attorney Weinberg to file his returns and become current on his obligations prior to a sufficient "triggering" to alert him that he was under investigation.

An October 5, 1994 memorandum to Peter Persampieri, Manager of CID Group C–21, from District Counsel Manhattan signed by Robert B. Marino, Assistant District Counsel which was examined by this Court as *in camera* exhibit, summarized the tax filing history of Mr. Tenzer noting that he had filed his 1987, 1988 and 1989 tax returns delinquently on February 10, 1992 and his 1990 return was filed on November 13, 1992. "Tenzer has a long history of delinquent filing. Since 1976 he has filed only one timely return." The report notices that on November 13, 1992, when Tenzer filed his 1990 return upon the request of a revenue officer "he was aware that he was a potential target of the JRD investigation." This report continues:

> The Internal Revenue Manual at Section 342.142 (promulgated April 5, 1993) sets forth the Service's voluntary disclosure Policy regarding a tax payer who come [sic] forward to report his/her tax crime. According to Sub-section (2), a voluntary disclosure occurs when a taxpayer's communication is truthful, timely, complete, and he/she shows a willingness to cooperate. Subsection (3) lays out the condition under which a non-filer may qualify for relief under the voluntary disclosure Policy.

The memorandum then listed the five elements required to be satisfied and concluded that elements 1, 2 and 4 were in fact satisfied by Mr. Tenzer in that he had informed the service he had not filed for one or more years, had only legal-source income and filed correct tax returns. Accordingly, Mr. Marino concluded that the only issues to be addressed were whether Mr. Tenzer had met elements 3 and 5. The attorney concluded in his authoritative interpretation of IRS Policy that the 1990 return was not within the Voluntary Disclosure Policy because the tax payer had been "contacted by CID prior to filing."

As noted earlier, this conclusion is not supported by the facts. There was nothing in the service of the subpoena for JRD papers which would reasonably be regarded as a triggering event or contact by CID which notified Tenzer he was under criminal investigation for failure to file his own returns. Such contact was at most notice with regard to criminality in connection with his activities as accountant for JRD and its affiliates.

Recognizing that Mr. Tenzer, "may meet the literal meaning of the third element" counsel rendered the opinion that "treating Tenzer's filing as a timely disclosure" would pervert application of the Service's Voluntary Disclosure Policy. Counsel concluded that in light of Tenzer's involvement with JRD, his expertise in taxation and the fact that he may have assisted in JRD's tax evasion scheme:

> [I]t is reasonable to conclude that Tenzer's notification of the JRD investigation was adequate to alert him that he was a potential target of a criminal investigation thereby prompting his delinquent filings. As such it is this Office's opinion that Tenzer did not make timely disclosure.

Counsel also took the position with respect to the amendment of Section 342.142 that the prior provision should be applied to determine whether Tenzer made a timely disclosure. Under the previous version, counsel argued, disclosure was timely if it was received before the Service had initiated an inquiry that was likely to lead to the taxpayer and the taxpayer was reasonably thought to be aware of the investigative activity, or some event known by the taxpayer occurred which was likely to cause an audit into the taxpayer's liabilities. However, as noted above, this limitation was not applicable after December 1992 when the voluntary disclosure program was loosened so as to permit a taxpayer to qualify if he/she made disclosure prior to CID contact. The Assistant District Counsel also concluded that the application of the Voluntary Disclosure Policy was unwarranted because of Tenzer's refusal to pay the tax that was due and because there were no bona fide arrangements to pay. The opinion remarked upon Tenzer's "extravagant lifestyle, spending substantially all of his large income on expensive cars and homes."

The Policy then in effect does not allow for these conclusions to affect its administration. Insofar as concerns the inadequacy or claimed bad faith in the offer to Compromise (1.3 Million in taxes for $250,000,) this Court concludes that the filing of the Offer (the work of experienced IRS alumnus Honecker and two other tax specialists) laughable as it may be, was not sufficient to disqualify Tenzer form the benefits of Voluntary Disclosure. Tenzer acted on the advice of experienced counsel, intending fully to comply with and get the benefit of the Policy. The attorneys were following their customary practice, in effect opening negotiations with a low-ball offer. The Service could have and did reject the Offer, and was free to have assessed, liened, restrained, and otherwise collected the tax from Tenzer at any time.

Having concluded that Tenzer met the requirements of the IRS' Voluntary Disclosure Policy, this Court must now determine the consequences of the IRS' failure to follow its own Policy.

The doctrine expressed in footnote 14 of *Caceres* has its origins well prior to that case. As our Court of Appeals explained in *Montilla v. I.N.S.,* 926 F.2d 162, 166 (2nd Cir.1991), the seeds of the doctrine "are found in the long settled principal that rules promulgated by a federal agency, which regulate the rights and interests of others, are controlling upon the agency." Citing *Columbia Broadcasting System, Inc. v. United States,* 316 U.S. 407, 422, 62 S.Ct. 1194, 1202–03, 86 L.Ed. 1563 (1942) (agency regulations on which individuals are entitled to rely bind agency.) In *Smith v. Resor,* 406 F.2d 141, 145 (2nd Cir.1969), our Court of Appeals recognized that "[a]lthough the courts have declined to review the merits of decisions made within the area of discretion delegated to administrative agencies they have insisted that where the agencies have laid down their own procedures and regulations, those procedures and regulations cannot be ignored by the agencies themselves even where discretionary decisions are involved." In *Montilla v. I.N.S.,* our Court of Appeals concluded that the rule requiring an agency to abide by its own policies and regulations as being "premised on fundamental notions of fair play underlying the concept of due process," and that "[i]ts ambit is not limited to rules attaining the status of formal regulations." 926 F.2d at 167.

The Government argues that the IRS' Voluntary Disclosure Policy governs only "internal agency procedures" and thus affords Mr. Tenzer no Due Process rights. As the evidentiary hearing made clear however, the Voluntary Disclosure Policy was disseminated to the public through grandiloquent press releases, and materials made available at IRS offices which tend to omit the fine print. For example, Defendant's Exhibit D is IRS publication 1715 (Rev. 7–93) entitled "It's Never Too Late!" The brochure explains the benefits of the Voluntary Disclosure Policy. Under the subheading "Will I go to jail?" it provides:

> Our long-standing practice has been not to recommend criminal prosecution of individuals for failure to file tax returns—provided they voluntarily file, or make arrangements to file before being notified that they are under criminal investigation. (Emphasis added)
>
> * * *
>
> . . . We want to get people back into the system, not prosecute ordinary people who made a mistake. However, we will continue to investigate flagrant cases involving criminal violations of the tax laws.

Under the totality of the circumstances, any reservation by which the Government may nevertheless prosecute individuals regardless of compliance with the Policy must be ineffective if the *Caceres* doctrine is to be given any weight. Indeed it is fair to say that Tenzer's case is unique in the regular day to day administration of the Policy.

The Government argues that even were the Voluntary Disclosure Policy applicable to Mr. Tenzer, as this Court concludes that it is, the Information should not be dismissed because Tenzer has failed to demonstrate that he relied on the Policy or suffered any prejudice because of the IRS' noncompliance with the Policy. There can be little doubt however that Tenzer's experienced counsel were familiar with the Policy and were advising him in light thereof. Tenzer's counsel informed Revenue Officer Kishlansky that it was Tenzer's intent to make such a Voluntary Disclosure, and she informed them that the case was being handled as a civil and not a criminal matter. The same notions of fairness which require an agency to abide by its own regulations require that Tenzer, who met the requirements of the Policy, be afforded its benefits even were he not relying on it. Insofar as concerns prejudice, we doubt this needs to be proved to rely on the *Caceres* doctrine. If Tenzer is being prosecuted because of a failure to apply the Policy because of mistake of fact or law, he is prejudiced. If, as appears highly likely, the Policy would have been applied to him but for the justifiable conclusion on the part of the authorities that he lived an extravagant lifestyle and probably aided and abetted JRD in criminality, the case represents a denial of Constitutionally protected due process.

An issue that arose during the evidentiary hearing was whether Count Four of the Information against Mr. Tenzer should also be dismissed because his prosecution violates the Non–Solicitation Policy of the IRS. Section (31)3600 of the Internal Revenue Manual entitled "Solicitation of Returns" provides that prosecution should not be recommended when a return is solicited and received prior to the taxpayer being contacted by the Criminal Investigation Division. Because the Non–Solicitation Policy expressly excludes "Computer generated inquiries" from solicitations, and because the returns for the years 1987, 1988 and 1989 were filed in response to computer generated notices the solicitation policy would not seem to apply to those years. However, the 1990 return, which was personally demanded by the Revenue Officer, would seem to fit squarely within the Non–Solicitation Policy and should not have been prosecuted. This presents an additional ground to bar prosecution under Count Four of the Information.

The Government argues that the Non–Solicitation Policy is not applicable because (1) the returns were only demanded so that Tenzer's Offer in Compromise could be processed, and (2) Tenzer did not rely upon the Policy. Both arguments are without merit. The Government argues that in essence the 1990 return was not solicited because it would not have been demanded by the Revenue Officer had it not been for Tenzer's desire to file an Offer in Compromise. The rights protected by the Non–Solicitation Policy however are not concerned with *why* a return was solicited, but only that it was solicited. The Non–Solicitation Policy is premised upon the concerns protected by the Fifth Amendment protections against self incrimination. The concerns protected by the Non–Solicitation Policy involve situations where an individual has not filed a return, the IRS subsequently demands the return, the return is filed by the individual, and then the IRS turns around and prosecutes the individual based upon the information supplied in the return. Such a situation is no less egregious when the taxpayer is unaware of the Non–Solicitation Policy and does not rely upon it in filing the return.

As a final matter, Mr. Tenzer moves to dismiss Count One of the Information as it relates to 1987 on the basis that prosecution for that year is time barred. The uncontested evidence indicates the following: Tenzer's 1987 tax return was originally due on April 15, 1988. He sought and received two extensions for filing, extending his filing date through October 17, 1988. Accordingly, absent a tolling agreement, the statute of limitations for the 1987 tax return would have run on October 17, 1994, six years from his extended date of filing. Tenzer however entered into a series of tolling agreements with the Government and agreed to toll the limitations periods for all charges that could have been brought on August 31, 1994, until and including November 30, 1995, the date on which the Information was filed. Title 26 of the United States Code at Section 6513(a) provides a uniform expiration date by providing that returns filed before the deadline date are to be considered as having been filed on the deadline date. In *United States v. Habig,* 390 U.S. 222, 88 S.Ct. 926, 19 L.Ed.2d 1055 (1968), the United States Supreme Court concluded that the provision is limited to cases in which the return is filed or payment is made prior to the statutory deadline. As such, the provision is inapplicable to this case and Count One was timely brought.

Accordingly, the defendant's motion is granted and the Information is dismissed as to all Counts on the ground that defendant complied with and is protected by the Internal Revenue Service's Voluntary Disclosure Policy. Count Four relating to the tax year 1990 must also be dismissed for the independent reason that the return was actively solicited in violation of the IRS' published Non–Solicitation Policy.

SO ORDERED.

NOTES AND QUESTIONS

1. The Second Circuit reversed *Tenzer. See* United States v. Tenzer, 127 F.3d 222 (2d Cir. 1997). The Second Circuit concluded that the voluntary disclosure policy did not apply to Mr. Tenzer's circumstances because even though he filed his returns before the criminal investigation into his taxes began, he did not pay the liability before the criminal investigation began.
2. Why is the government willing to forgive criminal activity when a taxpayer makes a voluntary disclosure?
3. If there is technically no voluntary disclosure policy in place, does that mean that the government will prosecute a taxpayer that meets the requirements of the voluntary disclosure policy? Why or why not?

There is more than one way to go about making a voluntary disclosure. One way—referred to as a quiet voluntary disclosure—is to file an amended return without contacting the government.[19] Another way—referred to as a noisy voluntary disclosure—is to contact the IRS or the Department of Justice to confirm that there is no current investigation of the taxpayer going on.[20] This inquiry is important for timeliness. If a taxpayer is making a disclosure because he has been notified of an investigation, there is no negation of willfulness.

---

[19] *See* MICHAEL I. SALTZMAN & LESLIE BOOK, IRS PRAC. & PROC. ¶ 12.06[2][b] (2016) ("Still another approach followed where there is no examination or investigation pending is preparing and filing delinquent or amended returns without drawing attention to them. The advantage of these 'quiet disclosures' is that the Service may not examine the returns after receipt.").

[20] *See* Scott D. Michel, *Developments in Offshore Tax Compliance in* INTERNATIONAL TRUST AND ESTATE PLANNING, ALI-ABA COURSE OF STUDY 801, 835 (2010) ("Noisy Disclosures. A second method is to contact [CID] in the appropriate district. . . . In some districts, the CID agent will accept the name of the taxpayer and confirm the taxpayer's eligibility for a voluntary disclosure without seeking much more additional information.").

CHAPTER 3

ASSESSMENT

Although criminal liability could be the most powerful deterrent of tax noncompliance, the meat of the government's tax enforcement efforts is on the civil side. Accordingly, the remainder of this book will concentrate on the government's civil enforcement procedures.

At bottom, the assessment is merely the recording of a tax liability. *See* IRC § 6201. It is much more than that, however. In fact, it is often the single most important event in a collection action's life. In a civil tax dispute, the assessment is a critical focal point. Prior to an assessment, the IRS is in investigation mode. To go from investigation mode to collection mode, the IRS must assess the tax, which unleashes the IRS's administration collection procedures. In addition, an assessment is a prerequisite for the IRS to impose certain civil tax penalties.

An income tax liability arises by operation of law on the close of the taxable year. Before the IRS may begin collecting a tax liability, it still must establish the existence and amount of the liability. Although the Code does not define an assessment, the most descriptive reference there is section 6502, which provides as follows:

> Where the assessment of any tax imposed by this title has been made within the period of limitation properly applicable thereto, such tax may be collected by levy or by a proceeding in court . . . .

The assessment occurs when the assessment officer signs the assessment record in accordance with the IRS's rules and regulations. *See* Treas. Reg. § 301.6203-1. The summary record and supporting documents identify the taxpayer, the amount owed, the character of the liability, and period at issue if applicable.

A taxpayer may argue that he or she must be named in an assessment for the assessment to have legal effect. *United States v. Galletti* held, however, that according to "the function and nature of an assessment," it is *the tax* that is assessed, not the taxpayer." 541 U.S. 114, 123 (2004). An assessment, the Court held, is "identical to the initiation of a formal collection action against any person or entity who might be liable for payment of a debt." In that case, the IRS assessed a tax liability explicitly naming a partnership but not its partners. The partners attempted to escape collection by claiming that the IRS could not collect the tax from the partners because they were not named in the assessment. The taxpayers lost because a tax assessment need not name the specific person who owes the tax being assessed.

There are various types of assessments. The first is the summary assessment. This type of assessment can take place without an investigation. The IRS invokes its summary assessment authority to assess tax liabilities reported on tax returns as well as assess additional amounts resulting from math or clerical errors. *See* section 6213(b). Under the summary assessment procedures, the IRS assesses the liabilities and then sends a notice to the taxpayer if the liability is not fully paid. The summary assessment is considered the general rule, while the other types of assessments are exceptions to the IRS's summary assessment authority. *See* Bryan T. Camp, *The Mysteries of Erroneous Refunds*, 114 TAX NOTES (TA) 231, 234 (Jan. 15, 2007).

The second type is the deficiency assessment. *See* section 6212. This type of assessment occurs after the IRS has investigated a tax return and determined the taxpayer owes more tax. Prior to a deficiency assessment, the taxpayer has the opportunity to dispute the IRS's determination of a deficiency in the Tax Court. *See* section 6213. The IRS must first send the taxpayer a statutory notice of deficiency giving the taxpayer 90 days to file a Tax Court petition. The IRS may not assess until the taxpayer either fails to file a petition in Tax Court or the Tax Court proceeding has come to a final decision.

The third type of assessment is a penalty assessment. The IRS may immediately assess certain penalties without going through its deficiency procedures. One example of an immediately assessable penalty is the delinquency penalty under certain circumstances. The Code also imposes immediately assessable penalties on taxes held in trust for the IRS. These are called assessable penalties because the imposition of the penalty constitutes an independent assessment of a taxpayer's liability for the penalty with no restrictions.

Two rare types of assessments are the jeopardy assessment and termination assessment. *See* IRC §§ 6861, 6851 (2015). The IRS may rely on the authority under these provisions where it suspects the taxpayer may hide himself, his assets, or in some other way substantially decrease his ability to pay a tax due. *See* IRC §§ 6861, 6851.

If certain conditions are satisfied, the assessment gives rise to the lien that facilitates the IRS's collection process. If the IRS fails to assess a tax, no lien arises. Accordingly, if the IRS asserts it has a lien on which to collect, and the IRS failed to assess the taxpayer, the IRS may not institute a collection action. The following case is an example.

COSON v. UNITED STATES
169 F. Supp. 671 (S.D. Cal. 1958), aff'd, 286 F.2d 453 (1961)
United States District Court, Southern District of California

CLARKE, District Judge.

This action is one to quiet title to specific parcels of real property owned by plaintiff, against which the United States claims a lien for unpaid withholding, employment, and cabaret taxes. Viewed in the light of the pleadings and the evidence adduced at trial, plaintiff's main contention is that the United States has no lien because these taxes never have been assessed against him.

Between March and August of 1955, plaintiff invested $31,000 in a newly organized Las Vegas, Nevada, hotel and gambling establishment known as the 'Moulin Rouge,' and obtained a 1.70 per cent interest therein. He reasonably and in good faith thought he was investing as a limited partner in a limited partnership. The Moulin Rouge was not, however, a limited partnership. Upon first ascertaining this, plaintiff promptly mailed notices of renunciation.

On November 15, 1955, there was filed with the County Recorder of Los Angeles County, California, a Notice of Federal Tax Lien for unpaid withholding, employment, and cabaret taxes in the sum of over $133,000 against the 'Moulin Rouge Partnership,' and many individuals, including the plaintiff, James R. Coson.

Notice and demand for the payment of these taxes was first individually given James R. Coson subsequent to the commencement of this action.

Plaintiff asserts this court has jurisdiction over the subject matter of this action under section 1340 of Title 28 U.S.C.[1] * * *

In the instant case, plaintiff asserts the invalidity of the Government's claim of lien against his property under the Internal Revenue Code of 1954. The basic question raised is whether or not such a lien exists. This court concludes that this is a controversy arising under an internal revenue law . . . and that it has jurisdiction of the action by virtue of 1340.

This action is one to quiet title. It is not one for declaratory judgment, forbidden by section 2201 of Title 28 U.S.C.7[2] It does not seek to restrain the assessment or collection of any tax; rather, its purpose is to quiet plaintiff's title

---

[1] [fn 1] '§ 1340. Internal revenue; customs duties. The district courts shall have original jurisdiction of any civil action arising under any Act of Congress providing for internal revenue, * * *'.

[2] [fn 7] '§ 2201. Creation of remedy. In a case of actual controversy within its jurisdiction, except with respect to Federal taxes, any court of the United States (and the District Court for the Territory of Alaska), upon the filing of an appropriate pleading, may declare the rights and other legal relations of any interested party seeking such declaration, whether or not further relief is or could be sought. Any such declaration shall have the force and effect of a final judgment or decree and shall be reviewable as such.'

to certain real property against a claimed lien for taxes by the United States. Thus, it is not within the prohibition of section 7421 of Title 26 U.S.C.[3]

Plaintiff relies upon section 2410 of Title 28 U.S.C. as authorizing this action against the United States. As noted above, § 2410 is a waiver of sovereign immunity, and is not limited to actions seeking to foreclose and obtain a judicial sale, but extends to actions to quiet title. United States v. Morrison, 5 Cir., 1957, 247 F.2d 285; Seattle Ass'n of Credit Men v. United States, supra, 240 F.2d at page 908.

The critical question is whether § 2410(a) authorizes an action to quiet title against a lien asserted by the Government for taxes allegedly owed by the plaintiff.

In Commercial Credit Corp. v. Schwartz, D.C.E.D.Ark.1954, 126 F. Supp. 728, a mortgagee brought a foreclosure action in a state court. He named as a defendant the United States, which claimed a lien against the property for unpaid taxes of the mortgagor. The Government removed the case to the federal district court pursuant to § 1444. The mortgagees, defendants in the action, sought leave to file an amended answer, whereby they might 'attack the validity of the assessment upon which the Government's lien is based on the ground that the Commissioner of Internal Revenue in computing their income tax for that year erroneously treated as income certain moneys which were not in fact such.' at page 729. In denying the motion, the court observed 'it should be kept in mind that the movants are not seeking merely to remove a lien from the fund which now stands in the place of their property; the Government's lien for unpaid taxes is one thing, and the assessment upon which such lien is based is quite a different thing. * * *' at page 729.

In Sanders v. Andrews, D.C.W.D.Okl.1954, 121 F.Supp. 584, rev'd sub nom Sanders v. Commissioner, 10 Cir., 1955, 225 F.2d 629, another case involving a taxpayer's action to quiet title against a federal tax lien, the court observed: 'The defendants contend that it is an attempt on the part of the plaintiffs to have this court determine their tax liability. This court would have no jurisdiction in a purely income tax controversy, but this is not an income tax case. The mere fact that the liens claimed are for a tax lien does not deprive this court of jurisdiction. Under the statutes this court has jurisdiction in this character of case to quiet title against liens asserted if under the record it is disclosed to the satisfaction of the court that the liens are invalid or the result of arbitrary and capricious conduct.' 121 F.Supp. at page 593....

§ 2410(a), as first enacted in 1931 . . . was limited to foreclosure actions. In 1942 . . . it was amended to include actions to quiet title. The Reports by the Committees on the Judiciary of both Houses of Congress are identical. . . . One stated purpose of the bill was 'to provide a method to clear real-estate titles of

---

[3] [fn 8] '§ 7421. Prohibition of suits to restrain assessment or collection (a) Tax. Except as provided in sections 6212(a) and (c), and 6213(a), no suit for the purpose of restraining the assessment or collection of any tax shall be maintained in any court. * * *'.

questionable or valueless Government liens.' The Committee Reports then printed a letter from the Attorney General of the United States pertaining to certain suggestions concerning a previous bill, which had been incorporated in the bill then before the committees. That letter stated:

'It should be observed * * * that under existing law there is no provision whereby the owner of real estate may clear his title to such real estate of the cloud of a Government mortgage or lien. Welch v. Hamilton, (D.C.) (S.D.Cal.), 33 F.2d 224, and United States v. Turner (8 Cir.), 47 F.2d 86.

'In many instances persons acting in good faith have purchased real estate without knowledge of the Government lien or in the belief that the lien had been extinguished. In other instances, mortgagees have foreclosed on property and have failed to join the United States. It appears that justice and fair dealing would require that a method be provided to clear real estate titles of questionable or valueless Government liens. Accordingly, I suggest that the bill be amended by inserting the phrase 'to quiet title' between the words 'matter' and 'for the foreclosure of' * * *.'

Clearly, the bringing of a quiet title action solely against the United States was contemplated. Although the examples discussed by the Attorney General in his letter both dealt with situations where one other than a taxpayer might seek to quiet title to his property against liens asserted by the Government, the statute contains no language precluding such an action by a taxpayer.

In this case, plaintiff does not seek to contest the correctness of an assessment; instead, he contends there just never was any assessment of the taxes in question against him. Since the taxes were not income, estate, or gift taxes, he did not have the alternative of filing a petition with the Tax Court. . . . This court concludes this action may be maintained pursuant to § 2410(a).

Section 6203 of Title 26 U.S.C.[4] and section 301.6203-1 of Title 26 C.F.R. (1955)[5] set forth, as one of the requirements for an assessment, that the taxpayer be identified.

The Government offered and introduced in evidence five Assessment Certificates (Forms 23C) and eight unit ledger cards as 'showing the actual assessment of the taxes against the Moulin Rouge' in 1955. . . . Each Assessment Certificate is merely a summary record of current and deficiency assessments, for many types of federal taxes, against an unknown number of unidentified taxpayers for a particular period of time by the District Director's Office for

---

[4] [fn 15] '§ 6203. *Method of assessment.* The *assessment* shall be *made* by *recording* the *liability* of the taxpayer in the office of the Secretary or his delegate in accordance with rules or *regulations prescribed* by the Secretary or his delegate. * * *'' (Emphasis added.)

[5] [fn 16] '§301.6203-1 *Method of assessment.* The district director shall appoint one or more assessment officers, and the assessment shall be made by an assessment officer signing the summary record of assessment. The *summary record*, through *supporting records*, shall provide *identification of the taxpayer*, * * *' (Emphasis added.)

Nevada. Although these Assessment Certificates contain symbols indicating the accounting abstracts or journals from which they were prepared, these abstracts or journals were not offered in evidence. The Government apparently proceeded on the theory that the eight ledger cards showed the same information as would have been disclosed by the pertinent abstracts or journals. Only five of the eight ledger cards appear relevant to this action, and all five are, with small variations in the order of names or abbreviations thereof, in the name of Alexander Bisno, Louis Rubin, and the Moulin Rouge.

In addition, counsel for defendant introduced a Certificate of Assessments and Payments (Form 899), pertaining to Alexander Bisno, Louis Rubin, and the Moulin Rouge. The Certificate of Assessments and Payments, the five Assessment Certificates, and the five ledger cards referred only to Alexander Bisno, Louis Rubin, and the Moulin Rouge. They neither labeled Bisno or Rubin as partners, nor the Moulin Rouge as a partnership. They did not name the plaintiff, James R. Coson.

No case has been discovered which deals with the required identification of an individual in order for there to be an assessment of taxes against him. . . . However, on the facts of this case, it is concluded that the plaintiff herein never was assessed for these taxes.

Section 6322 of Title 26 U.S.C.19[6] provides that a lien, of the type asserted by the Government in this case, arises at the time of assessment. Although there is an apparent inconsistency between § 632120[7] and § 6322 . . . and 6321 contains no requirement of an assessment . . . this court is of the opinion that such a lien does not exist against a particular individual's property pursuant to § 6321 and 6322 unless the underlying tax obligation has been assessed against him under § 6203. . . .

Since plaintiff never was assessed and no lien exists without such an assessment, it follows that the Government does not have any lien.

Judgment will be entered for plaintiff, wherein it will be declared that the Government has no lien for the taxes asserted in the Notice of Tax Lien filed with the County Recorder of Los Angeles County against the specific real property involved herein, and it will be ordered that the United States refrain from any further assertion of such a lien based upon the 1955 assessment of Bisno, Rubin, and the Moulin Rouge. Such judgment will not, however, in any

---

[6] [fn 19] '§ 6322. Period of lien. Unless another date is specifically fixed by law, the lien imposed by section 6321 shall arise at the time the assessment is made and shall continue until the liability for the amount so assessed is satisfied or becomes unenforceable by reason of lapse of time.'

[7] [fn 20] '§ 6321. Lien for taxes. If any person liable to pay any tax neglects or refuses to pay the same after demand, the amount (including any interest, additional amount, addition to tax, or assessable penalty, together with any costs that may accrue in addition thereto) shall be a lien in favor of the United States upon all property and rights to property, whether real or personal, belonging to such person.'

way purport to restrain any subsequent assessment of these same taxes or any action by the United States to collect the alleged underlying tax obligation.

NOTES AND QUESTIONS

1. Did the IRS assess a tax owed by the taxpayer in this case?
2. Did the court invalidate the lien with respect to all taxpayers involved in this case?

Except in limited circumstances, the IRS assesses a tax only with respect to a filed tax return. This general rule, however, does not require that the taxpayer have filed the return. The IRS may file a return for a taxpayer that has not filed one. *See* IRC § 6020(b). Otherwise, it would be easy to bypass the tax system completely. The country's revenue is too important to permit such a loophole. The importance of the government's collection tools, including assessment, is illustrated by *Bull v. United States*.

BULL v. UNITED STATES
295 U.S. 247 (1935)
Supreme Court of the United States

Mr. Justice ROBERTS delivered the opinion of the Court.

Archibald H. Bull died February 13, 1920. He had been a member of a partnership engaged in the business of ship-brokers. . . . Bull's share of profits from January 1, 1920, to the date of his death, February 13, 1920, was $24,124.20; he had no other accumulated profits and no interest in any tangible property belonging to the firm. Profits accruing to the estate for the period from the decedent's death to the end of 1920 were $212,718.79; $200,117.90 being paid during the year, and $12,601.70 during the first two months of 1921.

[The executor filed an estate tax return and an income tax return after the taxpayer's death. Neither return included the taxpayer's allocation of partnership profits after his death nor the amount the estate actually received from the partnership after his death. The IRS required that the profits accrued after death, the $212,718.79 amount, be included in the gross estate. In addition, the IRS required that the amount received from the partnership in 1921 after the taxpayer's death, the $200,117.90 amount, be included in the taxpayer's gross income without a deduction for the amount included in the gross estate.]

[On] July 11, 1928, the executor filed a claim for refund of this amount, setting forth that the $200,117.99, by reason of which the additional tax was assessed and paid, was corpus; that it was so originally determined by the Commissioner and the estate tax assessed thereon was paid by the executor; and that the subsequent assessment of an income tax against the estate for the receipt of the same sum was erroneous. The claim was rejected May 8, 1929. September 16, 1930, the executor brought suit in the Court of Claims . . . . [In addition to suing for an income tax refund, the lawsuit requested an alternative judgment refunding the estate tax paid on the taxpayer's partnership allocation after death.]

The Court of Claims held that the item was income and properly so taxed. With respect to the alternative relief sought, it said: "We cannot consider whether the Commissioner correctly included the total amount received from the business in the net estate of the decedent subject to estate tax for the reason that the suit was not timely instituted." Judgment went for the United States.[8] Because of the novelty and importance of the question presented we granted certiorari.[9]

[The Supreme Court concluded that the taxpayer was not entitled to a refund for his timely income tax claim, but would have been entitled to a refund of estate tax on the merits had it been timely. The remainder of the opinion considers whether the taxpayer should have prevailed on his untimely estate tax refund suit as part of the relief in the taxpayer's timely filed refund suit for income tax.]

The fact that the petitioner relied on the Commissioner's assessment for estate tax, and believed the inconsistent claim of deficiency of income tax was of no force, cannot avail to toll the statute of limitations, which forbade the bringing of any action in 1930 for refund of the estate tax payments made in 1921. As the income tax was properly collected, suit for the recovery of any part of the amount paid on that account was futile. Upon what theory, then, may the petitioner obtain redress in the present action for the unlawful retention of the money of the estate? Before an answer can be given the system of enforcing the government's claims for taxes must be considered in its relation to the problem.

A tax is an exaction by the sovereign, and necessarily the sovereign has an enforceable claim against every one within the taxable class for the amount lawfully due from him. The statute prescribes the rule of taxation. Some machinery must be provided for applying the rule to the facts in each taxpayer's case, in order to ascertain the amount due. The chosen instrumentality for the purpose is an administrative agency whose action is called an assessment. The assessment may be a valuation of property subject to taxation, which valuation is to be multiplied by the statutory rate to ascertain the amount of tax. Or it may include the calculation and fix the amount of tax payable, and assessments of federal estate and income taxes are of this type. Once the tax is assessed, the taxpayer will owe the sovereign the amount when the date fixed by law for payment arrives. Default in meeting the obligation calls for some procedure whereby payment can be enforced. The statute might remit the government to an action at law wherein the taxpayer could offer such defense as he had. A judgment against him might be collected by the levy of an execution. But taxes are the lifeblood of government, and their prompt and certain availability an imperious need. Time out of mind, therefore, the sovereign has resorted to more drastic means of collection. The assessment is given the force of a judgment, and

---

[8] [fn 4] 6 F. Supp. 141.
[9] [fn 5] 294 U.S. 704, 55 S. Ct. 544, 79 L.Ed. 1239.

if the amount assessed is not paid when due, administrative officials may seize the debtor's property to satisfy the debt.

In recognition of the fact that erroneous determinations and assessments will inevitably occur, the statutes, in a spirit of fairness, invariably afford the taxpayer an opportunity at some stage to have mistakes rectified. Often an administrative hearing is afforded before the assessment becomes final; or administrative machinery is provided whereby an erroneous collection may be refunded; in some instances both administrative relief and redress by an action against the sovereign in one of its courts are permitted methods of restitution of excessive or illegal exaction. Thus, the usual procedure for the recovery of debts is reversed in the field of taxation. Payment precedes defense, and the burden of proof, normally on the claimant, is shifted to the taxpayer. The assessment supersedes the pleading, proof, and judgment necessary in an action at law, and has the force of such a judgment. The ordinary defendant stands in judgment only after a hearing. The taxpayer often is afforded his hearing after judgment and after payment, and his only redress for unjust administrative action is the right to claim restitution. But these reversals of the normal process of collecting a claim cannot obscure the fact that after all what is being accomplished is the recovery of a just debt owed the sovereign. If that which the sovereign retains was unjustly taken in violation of its own statute, the withholding is wrongful. Restitution is owed the taxpayer. Nevertheless he may be without a remedy. But we think this is not true here.

In a proceeding for the collection of estate tax, the United States through a palpable mistake took more than it was entitled to. Retention of the money was against morality and conscience. But claim for refund or credit was not presented or action instituted for restitution within the period fixed by the statute of limitations. If nothing further had occurred, congressional action would have been the sole avenue of redress. . . .

If the claim for income tax deficiency had been the subject of a suit, any counter demand for recoupment of the overpayment of estate tax could have been asserted by way of defense and credit obtained, notwithstanding the statute of limitations had barred an independent suit against the government therefor. This is because recoupment is in the nature of a defense arising out of some feature of the transaction upon which the plaintiff's action is grounded. Such a defense is never barred by the statute of limitations so long as the main action itself is timely. . . .

To the objection that the sovereign is not liable to respond to the petitioner the answer is that it has given him a right of credit or refund, which, though he could not assert it in an action brought by him in 1930, had accrued and was available to him, since it was actionable and not barred in 1925 when the government proceeded against him for the collection of income tax.

The pleading was sufficient to put in issue the right to recoupment. The Court of Claims is not bound by any special rules of pleading;[10] all that is required is that the petition shall contain a plain and concise statement of the facts relied on and give the United States reasonable notice of the matters it is called upon to meet.[11] And a prayer for alternative relief, based upon the facts set out in the petition, may be the basis of the judgment rendered.[12]

We are of opinion that the petitioner was entitled to have credited against the deficiency of income tax the amount of his overpayment of estate tax with interest, and that he should have been given judgment accordingly. The judgment must be reversed, and the cause remanded for further proceedings in conformity with this opinion.

So ordered.

NOTES AND QUESTIONS

1. This case is important because of the language the Court uses to describe the tax assessment system.
2. What is equitable recoupment?
3. It should be noted that whether equitable recoupment was available in the Tax Court was unclear for a decade until Congress resolved the controversy by enacting statutory authorization for the Tax Court to apply such a remedy.

---

[10] [fn 11] United States v. Burns, 12 Wall. 246, 254, 20 L.Ed. 388; District of Columbia v. Barnes, 197 U.S. 146, 153, 154, 25 S.Ct. 401, 49 L.Ed. 699.

[11] [fn 12] Merritt v. United States, 267 U.S. 338, 341, 45 S.Ct. 278, 69 L.Ed. 643.

[12] [fn 13] United States v. Behan, 110 U.S. 338, 347, 4 S.Ct. 81, 28 L.Ed. 168.

CHAPTER 4

CIVIL PENALTIES

A. Penalties Generally

One of the potential consequences of noncompliance with the tax laws is the imposition of civil penalties. Since 1955, the number of civil penalties imposed by the Code has grown from 14 to over 100. In the federal tax system—which relies on voluntary compliance—penalties are important. Some question whether taxpayers would ever voluntarily comply without them.

Although there are over 100 civil tax penalties, only a few of them are in place to deter the average taxpayer from noncompliance. This chapter focuses on the basic deterrence penalties a typical taxpayer considers in the process of deciding whether to comply with the laws. In deciding whether to comply, average taxpayers need concern themselves only with the basic penalties such as the civil tax filing, paying, and fraud penalties.

Although there are only three penalties to be examined in this chapter, there are other concepts that are important as well. This chapter will discuss penalty assessability, reasonable cause, return sufficiency, and civil versus criminal fraud. A later chapter will cover incidental and administrative penalties with a broad brush. Incidental penalties are those that are imposed to make inaccuracy and feigned compliance more expensive and thus less attractive to a taxpayer. Administrative penalties are those imposed on accessories to the tax system. An accessory can be a person aiding the IRS in collecting tax like an employer that pays the IRS with taxes it withheld from an employee. An accessory can also be a person who is advising a taxpayer on planning or promoting nefarious tax schemes.

To summarize, deterrence penalties keep taxpayers from taking a completely different path, incidental penalties ensure taxpayers stay on the road once taken, and administrative penalties make sure the road is properly maintained for taxpayers to get through. With respect to these latter two types of penalties, it is important for law students to be aware of their existence, but the focus for this casebook is enforcement efforts that have a direct effect on taxpayers. The effect of incidental penalties, such as negligence penalties,[1] is not direct because they closely follow the underlying tax liability. Administrative penalties have an indirect effect on taxpayers because they are imposed on other people or entities, such as withholding agents.

In examining penalties, it is important to distinguish between penalties that are assessable and those that are not assessable. Assessable penalties are those imposed on acts or omissions rather than imposed as a function of a tax liability. Penalties arising from a tax liability are not independently assessable. Rather, they are imposed along with the underlying tax liability. Thus, these penalties are included in a proposed liability in audit and a final determination when no settlement has been reached after an audit. Often these penalties are considered not assessable because the IRS may not impose them separate from an assessment following an audit and notice of deficiency. Conversely, the IRS may impose assessable penalties without going through the audit and deficiency determination process. Imposition of an assessable penalty is in and of itself an assessment.

B. Basic Penalties

1. Failure to File

The most important penalties for deterring noncompliance are the delinquency penalties. Typical taxpayers are aware that if they do not file a required tax return or pay a tax owed to the government that penalties will apply. The Code's delinquency penalties coincide with a typical taxpayer's general awareness. The Code imposes a penalty for two failures to act: (1) the failure to file a required tax return and (2) the failure to pay a tax owed. Section 6651(a)(1), which imposes the penalty for failing to file a required tax return, provides as follows:

> In case of failure . . . to file any [tax] return . . . on the date prescribed therefor . . . there shall be added to the amount required to be shown as tax on such return 5 percent of the amount of such tax . . . .

This penalty starts at a rate of 5% of the correct tax liability and then increases by 5% every month up to 25%. The penalty amount is based on the taxpayer's actual net tax liability arising out of operation of law. For income tax

---

[1] Negligence penalties appear in the vast majority of the IRS's final tax liability determinations (see Chapter 15 — IRS Final Tax Determinations). The Code and the IRS refer to these penalties as "accuracy-related" penalties, perhaps to sound less accusatory than alleging negligence on so many occasions. *See* IRC § 6662.

returns (*i.e.*, not estate, gift, excise, or other taxes) filed more than 60 days late, the penalty cannot be less than $205 or 100% of the correct tax liability.

Generally a taxpayer must file a prescribed tax return to avoid the failure to file penalty, but there is an exception. A taxpayer may file an informal statement as a tentative return. *See* Treas. Reg. § 1.6011-1(b). If a taxpayer files a tentative return, a proper return must follow; otherwise the IRS will impose the filing penalty.

A taxpayer may not avoid the filing penalty by filing a "return" with insufficient information or on an altered form that masks the information relevant to determining the return's accuracy. A tax return must satisfy the requirements of Beard v. Commissioner, 82 T.C. 766 (1984), *aff'd*, 793 F.2d 139 (6th Cir. 1986), discussed in Chapter 8. In that case, the Tax Court held that for a document filed with the IRS to constitute a return for purposes of the "failure to file" penalty, the document must contain enough information for the Service to determine the amount of tax owed, purport to be a tax return, represent a sincere effort to comply with the tax laws, and reflect a signature made under penalty of perjury.

The IRS asserts the failure to file penalty in two fundamentally different ways. The most common way is in a notice of deficiency, the IRS's final determination of a tax liability after reviewing a tax return. It would be paradoxical if the IRS had to wait until a taxpayer filed a return to assert a penalty for failing to file a return. Avoiding this paradox, the failure to file penalty is also asserted as an assessable penalty, which means the IRS may assess the penalty independent from a notice of deficiency arising from reviewing a return. In the following case, the failure to file penalty was asserted both as an independent assessment and in the notice of deficiency.

Estate of FORGEY v. COMMISSIONER
115 T.C. 142 (2000)
United States Tax Court

VASQUEZ, J.

A Form 706, United States Estate (and Generation–Skipping Transfer) Tax Return, was delinquently filed on behalf of the Estate of Glenn G. Forgey (the estate). Respondent assessed the estate tax reported on the return and a section 6651(a)(1)[2] addition to tax for late filing. Respondent subsequently determined a deficiency in estate tax of $866,434 and an additional section 6651(a)(1) addition to tax of $216,609 based on such deficiency.

The parties reached an agreement as to all issues raised in the notice of deficiency except for the section 6651(a)(1) addition to tax. The agreement, when

---

[2] [fn 1] Unless otherwise indicated, section references are to the Internal Revenue Code as in effect on the date of the decedent's death, and all Rule references are to the Tax Court Rules of Practice and Procedure.

taken together with the concessions[3] made by respondent in the notice of deficiency, produced an overassessment.

The estate requests the Court to review the late-filing addition to tax assessed by respondent prior to the issuance of the notice of deficiency (the assessed addition to tax). In response to respondent's argument that we lack jurisdiction to do so, the estate contends that, despite the resulting overassessment in tax, a portion of the assessed addition to tax is attributable to a deficiency. Therefore, the issues for decision are whether the Court has jurisdiction to review any portion of the assessed addition to tax, and if so, whether the estate is liable for such addition.

FINDINGS OF FACT

Some of the facts have been stipulated and are so found. The stipulated facts and the related exhibits are incorporated herein by reference.

Glenn G. Forgey (decedent) died testate on October 14, 1993. At the time of his death, decedent resided in Keya Paha County, Nebraska. Decedent's son, Lyle A. Forgey (Mr. Forgey), was appointed as the personal representative of decedent's estate. At the time the petition was filed, Mr. Forgey resided in Springview, Nebraska.

The Federal estate tax return for the estate was originally due on July 14, 1994.[4] A day prior to the due date, Mr. Forgey filed a Form 4768, Application for Extension of Time to File a Return and/or Pay U.S. Estate Taxes, requesting an extension of time to file the estate tax return until January 14, 1995, and an extension of time to pay the estate tax until July 14, 1995. The requested extensions were granted by the Commissioner.

The January 14, 1995 extended due date for filing the estate tax return expired with no return having been filed. Following respondent's written inquiry as to the status of the estate tax return in late May 1995, Mr. Forgey signed the return and mailed it to the Internal Revenue Service Center in Ogden, Utah. The Commissioner received the estate tax return on June 2, 1995. The return reflected an estate tax liability of $2,165,565 and a balance due of $1,683,565.[5]

On July 17, 1995, respondent assessed the estate tax liability and a section 6651(a)(1) addition to tax for late filing in the amount of $378,802.[6] The addition to tax was based on the tax reported as due on the return.

---

[3] [fn 2] Respondent allowed a deduction for interest expense, discussed in detail *infra*.

[4] [fn 3] Form 706, United States Estate (and Generation–Skipping Transfer) Tax Return, must be filed within 9 months of the decedent's date of death. See sec. 6075(a).

[5] [fn 4] The estate submitted a payment of $482,000 with the Form 4768, Application for Extension of Time to File a Return and/or Pay U.S. Estate Taxes.

[6] [fn 5] Respondent also assessed interest and an addition to tax for late payment under sec. 6651(a)(2). These amounts are not in dispute.

By notice of deficiency dated April 23, 1998, respondent determined a deficiency in estate tax of $866,434. Based on this deficiency, respondent determined an additional section 6651(a)(1) addition to tax in the amount of $216,609.

In the notice of deficiency, respondent determined a $1,580,433 net increase in the amount of the taxable estate. This net adjustment, in turn, was based on the following: (1) A $2,040,249 increase in the value of items included in the gross estate; (2) a $28,373 reduction in the allowable deductions claimed on the estate tax return; and (3) the allowance of a $488,190 deduction for interest accrued on the deferred estate tax obligation (the interest expense deduction).[7]

The parties reached an agreement on the correct amount of the taxable estate, as evidenced by a stipulation of settled issues (the settlement). Apart from the interest expense deduction, the settlement resulted in a $332,352 increase in the taxable estate.[8] However, when the $488,190 interest expense deduction is taken into account, the net adjustment to the taxable estate is negative. Thus, the settlement produced an estate tax liability that was lower than that reported on the return.[9] Consequently, any addition to tax under section 6651(a)(1) that remains relates to the amount assessed by respondent prior to the issuance of the notice of deficiency.[10]

OPINION

By way of a motion for entry of decision, respondent contends that this Court does not have jurisdiction to review the assessed addition to tax. The question of the Court's jurisdiction is fundamental and must be addressed when raised by a party or on the Court's own motion. See Naftel v. Commissioner, 85 T.C. 527, 530, 1985 WL 15396 (1985); Estate of Young v. Commissioner, 81 T.C. 879, 880–881, 1983 WL 14898 (1983).

---

[7] [fn 6] The estate made an election under sec. 6166 to pay the estate tax liability on a deferred basis. The estate of a decedent dying prior to 1998 is entitled to deduct interest expense on a deferred estate tax obligation as an administrative expense under sec. 2053(a)(2). See Estate of Bahr v. Commissioner, 68 T.C. 74, 1977 WL 3655 (1977); Rev. Rul. 78–125, 1978–1 C.B. 292. This deduction is expressly disallowed by sec. 2053(c)(1)(D) with respect to estates of a decedent dying after 1997.

[8] [fn 7] The estate conceded $303,979 of the $2,040,249 valuation increase sought by respondent, and the estate further conceded respondent's $28,373 reduction in allowable deductions claimed on the return.

[9] [fn 8] The statement of account dated Feb. 29, 2000, which the parties have stipulated, provides for a revised estate tax liability of $2,003,524. This figure is $162,041 less than the estate tax liability of $2,165,565 shown on the estate tax return.

[10] [fn 9] The statement of account provides for a revised sec. 6651(a)(1) addition to tax of $342,343. This figure is $36,459 less than the addition to tax previously assessed by respondent of $378,802.

This Court is a court of limited jurisdiction. See Judge v. Commissioner, 88 T.C. 1175, 1180, 1987 WL 49322 (1987); Estate of Young v. Commissioner, supra at 881; Medeiros v. Commissioner, 77 T.C. 1255, 1259, 1981 WL 11307 (1981). We may exercise jurisdiction only to the extent expressly provided by Congress. See sec. 7442; Breman v. Commissioner, 66 T.C. 61, 66, 1976 WL 3667 (1976). Section 6213 confers jurisdiction on this Court to redetermine deficiencies in income, estate, gift, and certain excise taxes. See also secs. 6211–6212, 6214–6215; Rule 13. The provision which confers jurisdiction on this Court to review an addition to tax for late filing is section 6665.

Section 6665(a) sets forth the general rule that the deficiency procedures applicable to income, estate, gift, and certain excise taxes are equally applicable to additions to tax. See sec. 301.6659–1(a) and (b), Proced. & Admin. Regs. Section 6665(b) excludes from this general rule additions to tax under section 6651. As further provided in paragraph (1) of section 6665(b), however, the exclusion is not applicable "to that portion of such addition which is attributable to a deficiency in tax described in section 6211". Thus, the determination of whether we have jurisdiction over any portion of the assessed addition to tax turns on whether a deficiency within the meaning of section 6211 exists in this case. See Estate of Young v. Commissioner, supra at 882; Estate of DiRezza v. Commissioner, 78 T.C. 19, 26, 1982 WL 11060 (1982); sec. 301.6659–1(c)(1), Proced. & Admin. Regs.

Respondent contends that no statutory deficiency exists, given that the deficiency procedures and the parties' settlement resulted in an overassessment. The estate contends otherwise. The estate's argument is essentially that, but for the "fortuitous accrual of interest", the taxable estate would have increased by $333,919[11] as a result of the deficiency procedures and the parties' settlement. The estate treats the tax attributable to this figure as the deficiency, ignoring the interest expense deduction in this context on grounds that the interest accrual occurred "independent of the deficiency process".

The estate's argument as to the existence of a deficiency must be rejected as it ignores the statutory definition. Section 6211(a) defines a deficiency as:

the amount by which the tax imposed * * * exceeds the excess of—

(1) the sum of

(A) the amount shown as tax by the taxpayer upon his return * * * plus

(B) the amounts previously assessed * * * as a deficiency, over—

(2) the amount of rebates * * * made.

This case involves no rebates. Furthermore, respondent has not previously assessed any amounts as a deficiency. Accordingly, the definition of a deficiency

---

[11] [fn 11] The $333,919 figure ignores an increase of $1,567 in deductions claimed by the estate on the estate tax return that was allowed by respondent in the notice of deficiency. The proper figure therefore should be $332,352.

for present purposes is reduced to the excess of the estate tax imposed over the amount of estate tax shown on the return.

The parties' settlement in this case produced an overassessment in tax. This somewhat anomalous result (particularly in light of the concessions made by the estate) is attributable to the interest expense deduction, which the estate was prohibited from claiming prospectively on the estate tax return.[12] Yet, despite the unique circumstances of this case, it remains that the tax imposed on the estate does not exceed the amount of the tax shown on the estate tax return. A deficiency in tax, as defined by section 6211, therefore does not exist.

Having decided that there is no statutory deficiency, it follows that no portion of the assessed addition to tax is attributable to a deficiency. In other words, the requirements of paragraph (1) of section 6665(b) have not been met. Accordingly, pursuant to section 6665(b), we lack jurisdiction over the addition to tax at issue.[13] We therefore may not reach the estate's claim that the failure to timely file was due to reasonable cause and not due to willful neglect, or the estate's alternative argument that the assessed addition to tax constitutes an excessive fine in violation of the Eighth Amendment of the United States Constitution.

We have considered the estate's other arguments for a contrary holding[14] and, to the extent not discussed herein, find them to be without merit.

Accordingly, respondent's motion for entry of decision will be granted.

An appropriate order and decision will be entered.

---

[12] [fn 12] The procedure for claiming a deduction for interest expense attributable to a deferred estate tax obligation is to file a supplemental estate tax return after the interest has accrued and been paid. See Rev. Proc. 81–27, 1981–2 C.B. 548. Therefore, a taxpayer may not take a deduction on the original estate tax return for interest which is estimated to accrue on the deferred estate tax obligation. See Bailly v. Commissioner, 81 T.C. 246, 1983 WL 14862 (1983), supplemented by 81 T.C. 949, 1983 WL 14903 (1983).

[13] [fn 13] That we lack jurisdiction to decide the issue is confined to the facts of this case. We do not hold, for example, that this Court lacks jurisdiction under sec. 6512(b)(1) to decide the same issue in the case of an overpayment. See, e.g., Judge v. Commissioner, 88 T.C. 1175, 1180–1187, 1987 WL 49322 (1987). In this regard, the estate does not claim that it overpaid this addition, and we are unable to find that it did.

[14] [fn 14] In support of its argument that we have jurisdiction over the assessed addition to tax, the estate cites our opinion in Hannan v. Commissioner, 52 T.C. 787, 791, 1969 WL 1549 (1969), in which we stated that "it is not the existence of a deficiency but the Commissioner's determination of a deficiency that provides a predicate for Tax Court jurisdiction." However, in Estate of Young v. Commissioner, 81 T.C. 879, 886–887, 1983 WL 14898 (1983), we held that *Hannan* was inapposite to the case where the addition to tax is attributable to the amount shown as tax by the taxpayer on the return. Our opinion in *Hannan* therefore does not support the estates argument.

NOTES AND QUESTIONS

1. Why did the Tax Court have no jurisdiction over the failure to file penalty assessment at issue in the case?
2. What should the taxpayer have done instead of suing in Tax Court regarding the penalty assessment at issue?

2. Failure to Pay

The government would cease to function if taxpayers did not actually pay their taxes. To encourage taxpayers to pay tax, section 6651(a)(2) imposes a penalty for failure to pay a tax due as follows:

> In case of failure . . . to pay the amount shown as tax on any [tax] return . . . on or before the [due] date . . . there shall be added to the amount shown as tax on such return 0.5 percent . . . .

The penalty applies at a rate of .5% percent of the correct tax liability and increases, like the filing penalty, by .5% percent every month up to 25%. *See* IRC § 6651(a)(2). It is notable that the penalty rate for a failure to pay a tax is substantially lower than the penalty for failure to file a tax return. One can infer from the difference in penalty rates that legislators place more importance on filing a return for penalty purposes. Perhaps legislators accord more importance to the filing penalty because, if no return is filed, the IRS has to spend time and resources to find the taxpayer, determine the amount that the taxpayer should have reported without any information, and collect the tax. Where a taxpayer has filed a return, the taxpayer has made himself known, provided income information to verify, and all that remains is collection.

3. Reasonable Cause

Reasonable cause may excuse a taxpayer from the delinquency penalties. A penalty will not be imposed if it is shown that the failure to file or pay is "due to reasonable cause and not due to willful neglect." *See* IRC § 6651(a). There are ways to show the delinquency is due to reasonable cause. First, a taxpayer might show reasonable cause by showing that he was unable to comply with his disclosure obligation due to factors beyond his control. Treasury Regulation § 301.6651-1(c)(1) provides as follows:

> If the taxpayer exercised ordinary business care and prudence and was nevertheless unable to file the return within the prescribed time, then the delay is due to a reasonable cause.

An example would be the loss of records due to an accidental fire.

Second, a taxpayer might establish reasonable cause by showing he made reasonable efforts to comply with the law. Treasury Regulation § 1.6664-4(b) provides as follows:

[T]he most important factor [to show reasonable cause under this subsection] is the extent of the taxpayer's effort to assess the taxpayer's proper tax liability. Circumstances that may indicate reasonable cause . . . include an honest misunderstanding of fact or law . . . .

On occasion, taxpayers have taken the "misunderstanding" rule too far. In *Unites States v. Boyle*, the question was whether reliance on an attorney or advisor constitutes reasonable cause for a failure to file in a timely manner.

UNITED STATES v. BOYLE
469 U.S. 241 (1985)
Supreme Court of the United States

Chief Justice BURGER delivered the opinion of the Court.

We granted certiorari to resolve a conflict among the Circuits on whether a taxpayer's reliance on an attorney to prepare and file a tax return constitutes "reasonable cause" under § 6651(a)(1) of the Internal Revenue Code, so as to defeat a statutory penalty incurred because of a late filing.

I

A

Respondent, Robert W. Boyle, was appointed executor of the will of his mother, Myra Boyle, who died on September 14, 1978; respondent retained Ronald Keyser to serve as attorney for the estate. Keyser informed respondent that the estate must file a federal estate tax return, but he did not mention the deadline for filing this return. Under 26 U.S.C. § 6075(a), the return was due within nine months of the decedent's death, *i.e.,* not later than June 14, 1979.

Although a businessman, respondent was not experienced in the field of federal estate taxation, other than having been executor of his father's will 20 years earlier. It is undisputed that he relied on Keyser for instruction and guidance. He cooperated fully with his attorney and provided Keyser with all relevant information and records. Respondent and his wife contacted Keyser a number of times during the spring and summer of 1979 to inquire about the progress of the proceedings and the preparation of the tax return; they were assured that they would be notified when the return was due and that the return would be filed "in plenty of time." App. 39. When respondent called Keyser on September 6, 1979, he learned for the first time that the return was by then overdue. Apparently, Keyser had overlooked the matter because of a clerical oversight in omitting the filing date from Keyser's master calendar. Respondent met with Keyser on September 11, and the return was filed on September 13, three months late.

B

Acting pursuant to 26 U.S.C. § 6651(a)(1), the Internal Revenue Service assessed against the estate an additional tax of $17,124.45 as a penalty for the late filing, with $1,326.56 in interest. Section 6651(a)(1) reads in pertinent part:

"In case of failure . . . to file any return . . . on the date prescribed therefor . . . , *unless it is shown that such failure is due to reasonable cause and not due to willful neglect,* there shall be added to the amount required to be shown as tax on such return 5 percent of the amount of such tax if the failure is for not more than 1 month, with an additional 5 percent for each additional month or fraction thereof during which such failure continues, not exceeding 25 percent in the aggregate. . . ." (Emphasis added.)

A Treasury Regulation provides that, to demonstrate "reasonable cause," a taxpayer filing a late return must show that he "exercised ordinary business care and prudence and was nevertheless unable to file the return within the prescribed time." 26 CFR § 301.6651-1(c)(1) (1984).[15]

Respondent paid the penalty and filed a claim for a refund. He conceded that the assessment for interest was proper, but contended that the penalty was unjustified because his failure to file the return on time was "due to reasonable cause," *i.e.,* reliance on his attorney. Respondent brought suit in the United States District Court, which concluded that the claim was controlled by the Court of Appeals' holding in *Rohrabaugh v. United States,* 611 F.2d 211 (CA7 1979). In *Rohrabaugh,* the United States Court of Appeals for the Seventh Circuit held that reliance upon counsel constitutes "reasonable cause" under § 6651(a)(1) when: (1) the taxpayer is unfamiliar with the tax law; (2) the taxpayer makes full disclosure of all relevant facts to the attorney that he relies upon, and maintains contact with the attorney from time to time during the administration of the estate; and (3) the taxpayer has otherwise exercised ordinary business care and prudence. 611 F.2d, at 215, 219. The District Court held that, under *Rohrabaugh,* respondent had established "reasonable cause" for the late filing of his tax return; accordingly, it granted summary judgment for respondent and ordered refund of the penalty. A

---

[15] [fn 1] The Internal Revenue Service has articulated eight reasons for a late filing that it considers to constitute "reasonable cause." These reasons include unavoidable postal delays, the taxpayer's timely filing of a return with the wrong IRS office, the taxpayer's reliance on the erroneous advice of an IRS officer or employee, the death or serious illness of the taxpayer or a member of his immediate family, the taxpayer's unavoidable absence, destruction by casualty of the taxpayer's records or place of business, failure of the IRS to furnish the taxpayer with the necessary forms in a timely fashion, and the inability of an IRS representative to meet with the taxpayer when the taxpayer makes a timely visit to an IRS office in an attempt to secure information or aid in the preparation of a return. Internal Revenue Manual (CCH) § 4350, (24) ¶ 22.2(2) (Mar. 20, 1980) (Audit Technique Manual for Estate Tax Examiners). If the cause asserted by the taxpayer does not implicate any of these eight reasons, the district director determines whether the asserted cause is reasonable. "A cause for delinquency which appears to a person of ordinary prudence and intelligence as a reasonable cause for delay in filing a return and which clearly negatives willful neglect will be accepted as reasonable." Id., ¶ 22.2(3).

divided panel of the Seventh Circuit, with three opinions, affirmed. 710 F.2d 1251 (1983).

We granted certiorari, 466 U.S. 903, 104 S.Ct. 1676, 80 L.Ed.2d 152 (1984), and we reverse.

II

A

Congress' purpose in the prescribed civil penalty was to ensure timely filing of tax returns to the end that tax liability will be ascertained and paid promptly. The relevant statutory deadline provision is clear; it mandates that all federal estate tax returns be filed within nine months from the decedent's death, 26 U.S.C. 6075(a).[16] Failure to comply incurs a penalty of 5 percent of the ultimately determined tax for each month the return is late, with a maximum of 25 percent of the base tax. To escape the penalty, the taxpayer bears the heavy burden of proving both (1) that the failure did not result from "willful neglect," and (2) that the failure was "due to reasonable cause." 26 U.S.C. § 6651(a)(1).

The meaning of these two standards has become clear over the near-70 years of their presence in the statutes.[17] As used here, the term "willful neglect" may be read as meaning a conscious, intentional failure or reckless indifference. See *Orient Investment & Finance Co. v. Commissioner,* 83 U.S.App.D.C. 74, 75, 166 F.2d 601, 602 (1948); *Hatfried, Inc. v. Commissioner,* 162 F.2d 628, 634 (CA3 1947); *Janice Leather Imports Ltd. v. United States,* 391 F.Supp. 1235, 1237 (SDNY 1974); *Gemological Institute of America, Inc. v. Riddell,* 149 F.Supp. 128, 131-132 (SD Cal.1957). Like "willful neglect," the term "reasonable cause" is not defined in the Code, but the relevant Treasury Regulation calls on the taxpayer to demonstrate that he exercised "ordinary business care and prudence"

---

[16] [fn 2] Section 6081(a) of the Internal Revenue Code authorizes the IRS to grant "a reasonable extension of time," generally no longer than six months, for filing any return.

[17] [fn 3] Congress added the relevant language to the tax statutes in 1916. For many years before that, § 3176 mandated a 50 percent penalty "in case of a *refusal* or *neglect,* except in cases of sickness or absence, to make a list or return, or to verify the same. . . ." Rev.Stat. § 3176 (emphasis added). The Revenue Act of 1916 amended this provision to require the 50 percent penalty for failure to file a return within the prescribed time, "except that, when a return is voluntarily and without notice from the collector filed after such time and it is shown that the failure to file it was *due to a reasonable cause and not due to willful neglect,* no such addition shall be made to the tax." Revenue Act of 1916, ch. 463, § 16, 39 Stat. 756, 775 (emphasis added). No committee reports or congressional hearings or debates discuss the change in language. It would be logical to assume that Congress intended "willful neglect" to replace "refusal"—both expressions implying intentional failure—and "[absence of] reasonable cause" to replace "neglect"—both expressions implying carelessness.

but nevertheless was "unable to file the return within the prescribed time."[18] 26 CFR § 301.6651(c)(1) (1984); accord, *e.g.*, *Fleming v. United States*, 648 F.2d 1122, 1124 (CA7 1981); *Ferrando v. United States*, 245 F.2d 582, 587 (CA9 1957); *Haywood Lumber & Mining Co. v. Commissioner*, 178 F.2d 769, 770 (CA2 1950); *Southeastern Finance Co. v. Commissioner*, 153 F.2d 205 (CA5 1946); *Girard Investment Co. v. Commissioner*, 122 F.2d 843, 848 (CA3 1941); see also n. 1, *supra*. The Commissioner does not contend that respondent's failure to file the estate tax return on time was willful or reckless. The question to be resolved is whether, under the statute, reliance on an attorney in the instant circumstances is a "reasonable cause" for failure to meet the deadline.

B

In affirming the District Court, the Court of Appeals recognized the difficulties presented by its formulation but concluded that it was bound by *Rohrabaugh v. United States*, 611 F.2d 211 (CA7 1979). The Court of Appeals placed great importance on the fact that respondent engaged the services of an experienced attorney specializing in probate matters and that he duly inquired from time to time as to the progress of the proceedings. As in *Rohrabaugh*, see *id.*, at 219, the Court of Appeals in this case emphasized that its holding was narrowly drawn and closely tailored to the facts before it. The court stressed that the question of "reasonable cause" was an issue to be determined on a case-by-case basis. See 710 F.2d, at 1253-1254; *id.*, at 1254 (Coffey, J., concurring).

Other Courts of Appeals have dealt with the issue of "reasonable cause" for a late filing and reached contrary conclusions.[19] In *Ferrando v. United States*, 245

---

[18] [fn 4] Respondent contends that the statute must be construed to apply a standard of willfulness only, and that the Treasury Regulation is incompatible with this construction of the statute. He argues that the Regulation converts the statute into a test of "ordinary business care," because a taxpayer who demonstrates ordinary business care can never be guilty of "willful neglect." By construing "reasonable cause" as the equivalent of "ordinary business care," respondent urges, the IRS has removed from consideration any question of willfulness.

We cannot accept this reasoning. Congress obviously intended to make absence of fault a prerequisite to avoidance of the late-filing penalty. See n. 3, supra. A taxpayer seeking a refund must therefore prove that his failure to file on time was the result neither of carelessness, reckless indifference, nor intentional failure. Thus, the Service's correlation of "reasonable cause" with "ordinary business care and prudence" is consistent with Congress' intent, and over 40 years of case law as well. That interpretation merits deference. See, e.g., Chevron U.S.A. Inc. v. Natural Resources Defense Council, Inc., 467 U.S. 837, 844, and n. 14, 104 S.Ct. 2778, 2782, and n. 14, 81 L.Ed.2d 694 (1984).

[19] [fn 5] Although at one point the Court of Appeals for the Sixth Circuit held that reliance on counsel could constitute reasonable cause, see In re Fisk's Estate, 203 F.2d 358, 360 (1953), the Sixth Circuit appears now to be following those courts that have held that the taxpayer has a nondelegable duty to ascertain the

F.2d 582 (CA9 1957), the court held that taxpayers have a personal and nondelegable duty to file a return on time, and that reliance on an attorney to fulfill this obligation does not constitute "reasonable cause" for a tardy filing. *Id.,* at 589. The Fifth Circuit has similarly held that the responsibility for ensuring a timely filing is the taxpayer's alone, and that the taxpayer's reliance on his tax advisers—accountants or attorneys—is not a "reasonable cause." *Millette & Associates v. Commissioner,* 594 F.2d 121, 124-125 *(per curiam),* cert. denied, 444 U.S. 899, 100 S.Ct. 207, 62 L.Ed.2d 135 (1979); *Logan Lumber Co. v. Commissioner,* 365 F.2d 846, 854 (1966). The Eighth Circuit also has concluded that reliance on counsel does not constitute "reasonable cause." *Smith v. United States,* 702 F.2d 741, 743 (1983) *(per curiam); Boeving v. United States,* 650 F.2d 493, 495 (1981); *Estate of Lillehei v. Commissioner,* 638 F.2d 65, 66 (1981) *(per curiam).*

III

We need not dwell on the similarities or differences in the facts presented by the conflicting holdings. The time has come for a rule with as "bright" a line as can be drawn consistent with the statute and implementing regulations.[20]

---

deadline for a return and ensure that the return is filed by that deadline. See Estate of Geraci v. Commissioner, 32 TCM 424, 425 (1973), aff'd, 502 F.2d 1148 (CA6 1974), cert. denied, 420 U.S. 992, 95 S.Ct. 1428, 43 L.Ed.2d 673 (1975); Estate of Duttenhofer v. Commissioner, 49 T.C. 200, 205 (1967), aff'd, 410 F.2d 302 (CA6 1969) (per curiam).

[20] [fn 6] The administrative regulations and practices exempt late filings from the penalty when the tardiness results from postal delays, illness, and other factors largely beyond the taxpayer's control. See supra, at 689, and n. 1. The principle underlying the IRS regulations and practices—that a taxpayer should not be penalized for circumstances beyond his control—already recognizes a range of exceptions which there is no reason for us to pass on today. This principle might well cover a filing default by a taxpayer who relied on an attorney or accountant because the taxpayer was, for some reason, incapable by objective standards of meeting the criteria of "ordinary business care and prudence." In that situation, however, the disability alone could well be an acceptable excuse for a late filing.

But this case does not involve the effect of a taxpayer's disability; it involves the effect of a taxpayer's reliance on an agent employed by the taxpayer, and our holding necessarily is limited to that issue rather than the wide range of issues that might arise in future cases under the statute and regulations. Those potential future cases are purely hypothetical at the moment and simply have no bearing on the issue now before us. The concurring opinion seems to agree in part. After four pages of discussion, it concludes:

"Because the respondent here was fully capable of meeting the required standard of ordinary business care and prudence, we need not decide the issue of whether and under what circumstances a taxpayer who presents evidence that he

Deadlines are inherently arbitrary; fixed dates, however, are often essential to accomplish necessary results. The Government has millions of taxpayers to monitor, and our system of self-assessment in the initial calculation of a tax simply cannot work on any basis other than one of strict filing standards. Any less rigid standard would risk encouraging a lax attitude toward filing dates.[21] Prompt payment of taxes is imperative to the Government, which should not have to assume the burden of unnecessary ad hoc determinations.[22]

Congress has placed the burden of prompt filing on the executor, not on some agent or employee of the executor. The duty is fixed and clear; Congress intended to place upon the taxpayer an obligation to ascertain the statutory deadline and then to meet that deadline, except in a very narrow range of situations. Engaging an attorney to assist in the probate proceedings is plainly an exercise of the "ordinary business care and prudence" prescribed by the regulations, 26 CFR § 301.6651-1(c)(1) (1984), but that does not provide an answer to the question we face here. To say that it was "reasonable" for the executor to *assume* that the attorney would comply with the statute may resolve the matter as between them, but not with respect to the executor's obligations under the statute. Congress has charged the executor with an unambiguous, precisely defined duty to file the return within nine months; extensions are

---

was unable to adhere to the required standard might be entitled to relief from the penalty." Post, at 695.

This conclusion is unquestionably correct. See also, e.g., Reed v. Ross, 468 U.S. 1, 8, n. 5, 104 S.Ct. 2901, 2906, n. 5, 82 L.Ed.2d 1 (1984); Heckler v. Day, 467 U.S. 104, 119, nn. 33 and 34, 104 S.Ct. 2249, 2257-2258, nn. 33 and 34 (1984); Kosak v. United States, 465 U.S. 848, 853, n. 8, 104 S.Ct. 1519, 1523, n. 8, 79 L.Ed.2d 860 (1984); Bell v. New Jersey, 461 U.S. 773, 779, n. 4, 103 S.Ct. 2187, 2191, n. 4, 76 L.Ed.2d 312 (1983).

[21] [fn 7] Many systems that do not collect taxes on a self-assessment basis have experienced difficulties in administering tax collection. See J. Wagner, France's Soak-the-Rich Tax, Congressional Quarterly (Editorial Research Reports), Oct. 12, 1982; Dodging Taxes in the Old World, Time, Mar. 28, 1983, p. 32.

[22] [fn 8] A number of courts have indicated that "reasonable cause" is a question of fact, to be determined only from the particular situation presented in each particular case. See, e.g., Estate of Mayer v. Commissioner, 351 F.2d 617 (CA2 1965) (per curiam), cert. denied, 383 U.S. 935, 86 S.Ct. 1065, 15 L.Ed.2d 852 (1966); Coates v. Commissioner, 234 F.2d 459, 462 (CA8 1956). This view is not entirely correct. Whether the elements that constitute "reasonable cause" are present in a given situation is a question of fact, but what elements must be present to constitute "reasonable cause" is a question of law. See, e.g., Haywood Lumber & Mining Co. v. Commissioner, 178 F.2d 769, 772 (CA2 1950); Daley v. United States, 480 F.Supp. 808, 811 (ND 1979). When faced with a recurring situation, such as that presented by the instant case, the courts of appeals should not be reluctant to formulate a clear rule of law to deal with that situation.

granted fairly routinely. That the attorney, as the executor's agent, was expected to attend to the matter does not relieve the principal of his duty to comply with the statute.

This case is not one in which a taxpayer has relied on the erroneous advice of counsel concerning a question of law. Courts have frequently held that "reasonable cause" is established when a taxpayer shows that he reasonably relied on the advice of an accountant or attorney that it was unnecessary to file a return, even when such advice turned out to have been mistaken. See, *e.g., United States v. Kroll,* 547 F.2d 393, 395-396 (CA7 1977); *Commissioner v. American Assn. of Engineers Employment, Inc.,* 204 F.2d 19, 21 (CA7 1953); *Burton Swartz Land Corp. v. Commissioner,* 198 F.2d 558, 560 (CA5 1952); *Haywood Lumber & Mining Co. v. Commissioner,* 178 F.2d, at 771; *Orient Investment & Finance Co. v. Commissioner,* 83 U.S.App.D.C., at 75, 166 F.2d, at 603; *Hatfried, Inc. v. Commissioner,* 162 F.2d, at 633-635; *Girard Investment Co. v. Commissioner,* 122 F.2d, at 848; *Dayton Bronze Bearing Co. v. Gilligan,* 281 Fed. 709, 712 (CA6 1922). This Court also has implied that, in such a situation, reliance on the opinion of a tax adviser may constitute reasonable cause for failure to file a return. See *Commissioner v. Lane-Wells Co.,* 321 U.S. 219, 64 S.Ct. 511, 88 L.Ed. 684 (1944) (remanding for determination whether failure to file return was due to reasonable cause, when taxpayer was advised that filing was not required).[23]

When an accountant or attorney *advises* a taxpayer on a matter of tax law, such as whether a liability exists, it is reasonable for the taxpayer to rely on that advice. Most taxpayers are not competent to discern error in the substantive advice of an accountant or attorney. To require the taxpayer to challenge the attorney, to seek a "second opinion," or to try to monitor counsel on the provisions of the Code himself would nullify the very purpose of seeking the advice of a presumed expert in the first place. See *Haywood Lumber, supra,* at 771. "Ordinary business care and prudence" do not demand such actions.

By contrast, one does not have to be a tax expert to know that tax returns have fixed filing dates and that taxes must be paid when they are due. In short,

---

[23] [fn 9] Courts have differed over whether a taxpayer demonstrates "reasonable cause" when, in reliance on the advice of his accountant or attorney, the taxpayer files a return after the actual due date but within the time the adviser erroneously told him was available. Compare Sanderling, Inc. v. Commissioner, 571 F.2d 174, 178-179 (CA3 1978) (finding "reasonable cause" in such a situation); Estate of Rapelje v. Commissioner, 73 T.C. 82, 90, n. 9 (1979) (same); Estate of DiPalma v. Commissioner, 71 T.C. 324, 327 (1978) (same), acq., 1979-1 Cum.Bull. 1; Estate of Bradley v. Commissioner, 33 TCM 70, 72-73 (1974) (same), aff'd, 511 F.2d 527 (CA6 1975), with Estate of Kerber v. United States, 717 F.2d 454, 454-455, and n. 1 (CA8 1983) (per curiam) (no "reasonable cause"), cert. pending, No. 83-1038; Smith v. United States, 702 F.2d 741, 742 (CA8 1983) (same); Sarto v. United States, 563 F.Supp. 476, 478 (ND Cal.1983) (same). We need not and do not address ourselves to this issue.

tax returns imply deadlines. Reliance by a lay person on a lawyer is of course common; but that reliance cannot function as a substitute for compliance with an unambiguous statute. Among the first duties of the representative of a decedent's estate is to identify and assemble the assets of the decedent and to ascertain tax obligations. Although it is common practice for an executor to engage a professional to prepare and file an estate tax return, a person experienced in business matters can perform that task personally. It is not unknown for an executor to prepare tax returns, take inventories, and carry out other significant steps in the probate of an estate. It is even not uncommon for an executor to conduct probate proceedings without counsel.

It requires no special training or effort to ascertain a deadline and make sure that it is met. The failure to make a timely filing of a tax return is not excused by the taxpayer's reliance on an agent, and such reliance is not "reasonable cause" for a late filing under § 6651(a)(1). The judgment of the Court of Appeals is reversed.

It is so ordered.

Justice BRENNAN, with whom Justice MARSHALL, Justice POWELL, and Justice O'CONNOR join, concurring.

I concur that the judgment must be reversed. Although the standard of taxpayer liability found in 26 U.S.C. § 6651(a)(1) might plausibly be characterized as ambiguous,[24] courts and the Internal Revenue Service have for almost 70 years interpreted the statute as imposing a standard of "ordinary business care and prudence." *Ante,* at 690-691. I agree with the Court that we should defer to this long-standing construction. *Ante,* at 690, n. 4. I also agree that taxpayers in the exercise of ordinary business care and prudence must ascertain relevant filing deadlines and ensure that those deadlines are met. As the Court correctly holds, a taxpayer cannot avoid the reach of § 6651(a)(1) merely by delegating this duty to an attorney, accountant, or other individual. *Ante,* at 693-694.[25]

I write separately, however, to underscore the importance of an issue that the Court expressly leaves open. Specifically, I believe there is a substantial argument that the "ordinary business care and prudence" standard is applicable only to the "ordinary person"—namely, one who is physically and mentally

---

[24] [fn 1] For each month or fraction of a month that a tax return is overdue, 26 U.S.C. § 6651(a)(1) provides for a mandatory penalty of 5% of the tax (up to a maximum of 25%) "unless it is shown that [the failure to file on time] is due to reasonable cause and not due to willful neglect." As Judge Posner observed in his dissent below, "in making 'willful neglect' the opposite of 'reasonable cause' the statute might seem to have modified the ordinary meaning of 'reasonable' . . .." 710 F.2d 1251, 1256 (CA7 1983).

[25] [fn 2] As the Court emphasizes, this principle of non-delegation does not extend to situations in which a taxpayer reasonably relies on expert advice concerning substantive questions of tax law, such as whether a liability exists in the first instance. *Ante,* at 693.

capable of knowing, remembering, and complying with a filing deadline. In the instant case, there is no question that the respondent not only failed to exercise ordinary business care in monitoring the progress of his mother's estate, but also made no showing that he was *unable* to exercise the usual care and diligence required of an executor. The outcome could be different if a taxpayer were able to demonstrate that, for reasons of incompetence or infirmity, he understandably was unable to meet the standard of ordinary business care and prudence. In such circumstances, there might well be no good reason for imposing the harsh penalty of § 6651(a)(1) over and above the prescribed statutory interest penalty. See 26 U.S.C. §§ 6601(a), 6621(b).

The Court proclaims the need "for a rule with as 'bright' a line as can be drawn," and it stresses that the Government "should not have to assume the burden of unnecessary ad hoc determinations." *Ante,* at 692. On the other hand, it notes that the "bright line" might not cover a taxpayer who is "incapable by objective standards of meeting the criteria of 'ordinary business care and prudence,' " reasoning that "the disability alone could well be an acceptable excuse for a late filing." *Ante,* at 692, n. 6.

I share the Court's reservations about the sweep of its "bright line" rule. If the Government were determined to draw a "bright line" and to avoid the "burden" of "ad hoc determinations," it would not provide for *any* exemptions from the penalty provision. Congress has emphasized, however, that exemptions *must* be made where a taxpayer demonstrates "reasonable cause." 26 U.S.C. § 6651(a)(1). Accordingly, the IRS already allows dispensations where, for example, a taxpayer or a member of his family has been seriously ill, the taxpayer has been unavoidably absent, or the taxpayer's records have been destroyed. Internal Revenue Manual (CCH) § 4350, (24) ¶ 22.2(2) (Mar. 20, 1980) (Audit Technique Manual for Estate Tax Examiners). Thus the Government itself has eschewed a bright-line rule and committed itself to *necessarily* case-by-case decision-making. The gravamen of the IRS's exemptions seems to be that a taxpayer will not be penalized where he reasonably was *unable* to exercise ordinary business care and prudence. The IRS does not appear to interpret its enumerated exemptions as being exclusive, see *id.,* ¶ 22.2(3), and it might well act arbitrarily if it purported to do otherwise.[26] Thus a substantial argument can be made that the draconian penalty provision should not apply where a taxpayer convincingly demonstrates that, for whatever reason, he reasonably was unable to exercise ordinary business care.

---

[26] [fn 3] It is difficult to perceive a material distinction, for example, between a filing delay that results from a serious illness in the taxpayer's immediate family or a taxpayer's unavoidable absence—situations in which the IRS excuses the delay—and a filing delay that comes about because the taxpayer is infirm or incompetent. The common thread running through all these unfortunate situations is that the taxpayer, for reasons beyond his control, has been unable to exercise ordinary business care and prudence.

Many executors are widows or widowers well along in years, and a penalty against the "estate" usually will be a penalty against their inheritance. Moreover, the principles we announce today will apply with full force to the personal income tax returns required of every individual who receives an annual gross income of $1,000 or more. See 26 U.S.C. § 6651(a)(1); see also § 6012. Although the overwhelming majority of taxpayers are fully capable of understanding and complying with the prescribed filing deadlines, exceptional cases necessarily will arise where taxpayers, by virtue of senility, mental retardation, or other causes, are understandably unable to attain society's norm. The Court today properly emphasizes the need for efficient tax collection and stern incentives. *Ante*, at 691-692. But it seems to me that Congress and the IRS already have made the decision that efficiency should yield to other values in appropriate circumstances.

Because the respondent here was fully capable of meeting the required standard of ordinary business care and prudence, we need not decide the issue of whether and under what circumstances a taxpayer who presents evidence that he was *unable* to adhere to the required standard might be entitled to relief from the penalty. As the Court has expressly left this issue open for another day, I join the Court's opinion.

NOTES AND QUESTIONS

1. The reasonable cause provision in section 6664 specifically permits the IRS to apply a reasonable cause exception to a penalty imposed under section 6663, which is civil fraud. How many times has the IRS likely applied reasonable cause to civil fraud?
2. Are the IRS's regulations imposing essentially a negligence standard consistent with the statutory language that the neglect to file a return must not be willful?

4. Civil Fraud

Another basic penalty is imposed for civil fraud. Section 6663(a) provides as follows:

> If any part of any underpayment of tax required to be shown on a return is due to fraud, there shall be added to the tax an amount equal to 75 percent of the portion of the underpayment which is attributable to fraud.

This penalty is imposed on the portion of the underpayment due to fraud. The penalty rate is high. It is imposed on 75% of the underpayment. However, the taxpayer may show that only a portion of the underpayment occurred due to fraud. *See* IRC § 6663(b). If the taxpayer fails to make such a showing, the penalty applies to the entire underpayment.

Civil fraud is not defined in the Code. In general, civil tax fraud is an intentional act to evade underpaid taxes through deceptive conduct. In deciding whether fraud is present, courts consider a number of factors or "badges" of fraud, as discussed in the following case.

NELON v. COMMISSIONER
73 T.C.M. (CCH) 1843 (1997)
United State Tax Court

MEMORANDUM FINDINGS OF FACT AND OPINION

GERBER, Judge:

In a notice of deficiency dated October 21, 1993, respondent determined . . . income tax deficiencies and additions with respect to petitioner Richard Nelon's Federal income taxes . . . :

Respondent also determined a deficiency and additions to tax against petitioners, jointly, for the 1987 taxable year. . . .

Finally, as an alternative position, respondent determined that if the Court does not find liability for sections 6651(f) and/or 6653(b), then the delinquency addition to tax should apply in each year and the negligence addition should also be applied for 1986, 1987, and 1988.

After concessions, the remaining issues for our consideration are: (1) Whether petitioner Richard Nelon is liable for additions to tax for fraud under section 6653(b)(1)(A)[27] and (B) for the taxable years 1986 and 1987 and under section 6653(b)(1) for the taxable year 1988; (2) whether petitioner Richard Nelon is liable for additions to tax for fraudulent failure to file income tax returns under section 6651(f) for the taxable years 1989 through 1991; (3) whether petitioner Richard Nelon is liable, in the alternative, for a 25-percent addition to tax under section 6651(a)(1); and (4) whether petitioner Richard Nelon is liable, in the alternative, for a 5-percent addition to tax under section 6653(a)(1)(A) and (B) for 1986 and 1987 and section 6653(a)(1) for 1988.

FINDINGS OF FACT[28]

Petitioners Richard and Brenda Nelon resided in Rutherfordton, North Carolina, at the time the petition in this case was filed.[29] Richard Nelon (petitioner) left high school when he was 16 years old, and he is inexperienced in bookkeeping and financial matters. Petitioner operated a logging business in the area around Rutherfordton as a sole proprietorship. This activity was his primary source of income during the years 1986 through 1991. The activity in question was physically demanding and dangerous work. In practice, petitioner would have to cut the standing timber, put it on the truck, and deliver the logs to the yard.

---

[27] [fn 1] Section references are to the Internal Revenue Code in effect for the taxable years at issue. Rule references are to this Court's Rules of Practice and Procedure.

[28] [fn 2] The stipulations of facts and the exhibits are incorporated by this reference.

[29] [fn 3] Brenda Nelon is a party only with respect to the 1987 tax year.

Petitioner received compensation in the amounts and years at issue. . . .

The payers supplied Forms 1099 to respondent and petitioner reflecting the above-listed payments. During the aforementioned years, petitioner did not make any estimated payments of income tax. Petitioner also did not file any income tax returns for the years at issue. Petitioner maintained some records of his expenses for his logging business in the form of receipts, which he could not locate for purposes of trial.

Sometime in 1985, petitioner hired Larry R. Melton (Melton) to paint his residence. Melton, who was not a qualified tax adviser, was involved in a tax protester group. The primary precept of members of the protester group was that they were not subject to Federal income taxes. Consonant with that belief, Melton advised that petitioner was not required to pay taxes to the U.S. Government. Petitioner accepted Melton's advice, and he joined the protester group, attended meetings, and paid dues during 1987 and 1988. Beginning with his 1986 taxable year, petitioner did not file a Federal income tax return in accord with his belief that he was not subject to the Federal income tax.

An accountant prepared petitioner's 1985 Federal income tax return. In 1989, respondent audited petitioner's 1985 return. Petitioner represented himself in the audit process and did not agree with the adjustments respondent's agent proposed or that he owed additional tax for his 1985 tax year. Petitioner believed that his income and deductions for 1985 had been correctly reported. Petitioner took no further action, the additional tax was assessed, and respondent seized petitioner's bank account for satisfaction of the assessed deficiency. The results of his 1985 audit during 1989 made petitioner angry and frustrated. Because of that experience and following the seizure of the proceeds of his bank account in 1989, petitioner chose to no longer maintain a bank account.

On June 15, 1992, respondent's agent, David Walden (Walden), advised petitioner by letter that his 1986 through 1991 tax years were being subjected to examination. Brenda Nelon's 1987 taxable year was also under examination by Walden. By a June 25, 1992, letter, Walden was advised that petitioner was under no obligation to communicate with respondent's agents and that petitioner was not subject to the Federal income tax. The letter also acknowledged that petitioner did not file Federal income tax returns for the years in question. The letter was written by another person but was signed by petitioner. Petitioner did not meet with Walden or produce requested records or documents.

On October 21, 1993, respondent issued a statutory notice of deficiency to petitioner, determining deficiencies in income tax for the 1986, 1988, 1989, 1990, and 1991 tax years and related additions to tax. On the same date, respondent also issued a statutory notice of deficiency to both Richard Nelon and Brenda Nelon for the taxable year 1987, determining a deficiency in income tax and related additions to tax.

At trial, petitioner acknowledged that he did not file income tax returns for 1986 through 1991 and that he followed the advice of Melton and the protester group that he did not have to pay income taxes. After trial, the parties filed a stipulation of settled issues. Among the issues settled, respondent conceded that there was no deficiency in income tax due from, nor overpayment due to, petitioner Brenda Nelon for the taxable year 1987. The parties also stipulated that petitioner was entitled to deductions in connection with his logging business. . . .

OPINION

The parties have agreed that petitioner earned income and incurred deductions for the 1986 through 1991 taxable years. The only remaining controversy is whether petitioner is liable for the addition to tax for fraud or, in the alternative, negligence and failure to file. For 1986 and 1987, section 6653(b)(1)(A) and for 1988 section 6653(b)(1) provide for an addition to tax in an amount equal to 75 percent of the underpayment that is attributable to fraud. For 1986 and 1987, section 6653(b)(1)(B) provides for an additional amount equal to 50 percent of the interest due on any part of the underpayment attributable to fraud. Section 6653(b)(2) provides that if any portion of an underpayment is due to fraud, the entire underpayment is treated as fraudulent, unless the taxpayer proves some portion of the underpayment is not due to fraud.

For 1989, 1990, and 1991, section 6651(f) provides for a maximum addition to tax of 75 percent if any failure to file is fraudulent. If the failure to file is not due to reasonable cause and it is not fraudulent, section 6651(a) provides for a maximum addition to tax of 25 percent.

The addition to tax in the case of fraud is a civil sanction provided primarily as a safeguard for the protection of the revenue and to reimburse the Government for the heavy expense of investigation and the loss resulting from the taxpayer's fraud. *Helvering v. Mitchell,* 303 U.S. 391, 401 (1938).

Respondent bears the burden of proving fraud by clear and convincing evidence. Sec. 7454(a); Rule 142(b). Respondent's burden is met if it is shown that petitioner intended to evade taxes known to be due and owing by conduct intended to conceal, mislead, or otherwise prevent the collection of taxes, and that there is an underpayment of tax. *Stoltzfus v. United States,* 398 F.2d 1002, 1004 (3d Cir. 1968); *Rowlee v. Commissioner,* 80 T.C. 1111, 1123 (1983); *Acker v. Commissioner,* 26 T.C. 107, 112 (1956).

The existence of fraud is a question of fact to be resolved upon consideration of the entire record. DiLeo v. Commissioner, 96 T.C. 858, 874 (1991), affd. 959 F.2d 16 (2d Cir. 1992). Fraud is never presumed but, rather, must be established by affirmative evidence. Edelson v. Commissioner, 829 F.2d 828 (9th Cir. 1987), affg. T.C. Memo. 1986-223. Direct evidence of the requisite fraudulent intent is seldom available, but fraud may be proved by circumstantial evidence. Spies v. United States, 317 U.S. 492, 499 (1943); Rowlee v. Commissioner, supra at 1123. The taxpayer's entire course of conduct may establish the requisite intent. Otsuki v. Commissioner, 53 T.C. 96, 105-106 (1969).

Over the years, courts have developed various factors, or "badges", which tend to establish fraud. Recklitis v. Commissioner, 91 T.C. 874, 910 (1988). These include: (1) A pattern of understatement of income; (2) inadequate books and records; (3) failure to file tax returns; (4) concealment of assets; (5) failure to cooperate with tax authorities; (6) income from illegal activities; (7) implausible or inconsistent explanations of behavior; (8) an intent to mislead which may be inferred from a pattern of conduct; (9) lack of credibility of the taxpayer's testimony; (10) dealings in cash. Laurins v. Commissioner, 889 F.2d 910, 913 (9th Cir. 1989), affg. Norman v. Commissioner, T.C. Memo. 1987-265; Edelson v. Commissioner, supra at 832; Bradford v. Commissioner, 796 F.2d 303, 307 (9th Cir. 1986), affg. T.C. Memo. 1984-601; Petzoldt v. Commissioner, 92 T.C. 661, 699 (1989); Rowlee v. Commissioner, supra at 1125. These badges of fraud are nonexclusive. Miller v. Commissioner, 94 T.C. 316, 334 (1990).

The list of the badges of fraud, however, is illustrative. We consider the totality of the facts and circumstances of each case to determine whether there is fraudulent intent. *King's Court Mobile Home Park, Inc. v. Commissioner*, 98 T.C. 511, 516 (1992); *Recklitis v. Commissioner, supra.*

Respondent contends that the following facts, taken as a whole, prove that petitioner had the intent to fraudulently evade paying income tax on at least some part of the underpayment for the years in issue: (1) His failure to file income tax returns for the years 1986 through 1991; (2) through that failure to file, a corresponding consistent failure to report substantial amounts of income from the logging business; (3) the failure to maintain books and records of the amounts derived from the logging business; (4) his failure to pay estimated income taxes for the years in question; and (5) the cashing, rather than depositing, of checks derived from the logging business.

In the instant case, petitioner did not file income tax returns for the taxable years 1986 through 1991. The parties have stipulated this fact. It is also without dispute that petitioner did not report relatively large amounts of income and expenses in connection with his logging business.

An initial analysis reveals that some of the badges of fraud are present. Petitioner earned substantial amounts of income that were not reported, did not keep adequate records, and failed to provide records to or meet with respondent's agent. Due to the 1989 audit of his 1985 Federal income tax return and the seizure of his bank account, petitioner decided to close his bank account and, to some extent, deal in cash. Petitioner, however, did not misrepresent, secrete, or attempt to deceive. Although we do not approve of petitioner's reasons for failing to file returns and failing to submit to respondent's examination, those events, on this record, do not satisfy respondent's burden to clearly and convincingly prove fraud.

On this record, we do not find that petitioner's underpayment was due to an intent to evade taxes known to be due and owing by conduct intended to conceal, mislead, or otherwise prevent the collection of taxes. *Stoltzfus v. United States, supra* at 1004; *Rowlee v. Commissioner, supra* at 1123; *Acker v. Commissioner, supra* at 112.

Respondent places great emphasis on the fact that petitioner had an accountant for the 1985 taxable year, contending that this reflects a history of filing timely tax returns, and thus petitioner knew of the filing requirements. Petitioner, however, did not set out to evade tax he thought to be due. Instead, he came to believe that he was not obligated to file a Federal tax return and that he had no obligation to pay Federal tax. On this record, we find that his belief was not an intentional attempt to fraudulently evade the payment of tax.

Respondent also argues that petitioner attempted to conceal assets by dealing in cash. Petitioner's resolve to close his bank account and, therefore, use cash was not coupled with his belief that he was not obligated to pay tax. Petitioner, based on his belief, failed to file his 1986 and later years' returns. It was only after his bank account was seized in 1989 in connection with the audit of his 1985 tax return that petitioner closed his bank account. By 1989, petitioner had failed to file several Federal income tax returns. Petitioner believed that he had correctly reported his income and deductions for 1985 by using a professional return preparer (accountant). Petitioner, who is not well educated or versed in business and tax matters, represented himself in the 1985 audit. From his perspective he had properly filed his 1985 return, and the resulting seizure of his bank account caused him to react by closing the bank account. There is no indication that the 1989 audit of petitioner's 1985 return involved the so-called protester arguments or that he failed to cooperate with respondent's agent.

Petitioner did not cooperate with the revenue agent in the determination of his tax liability for 1986 through 1991. On occasion, this has been found to be an indicium of fraud. See *Rowlee v. Commissioner*, 80 T.C. at 1125; *Grosshandler v. Commissioner*, 75 T.C. 1, 20 (1980); *Gajewski v. Commissioner*, 67 T.C. 181, 200 (1976), affd. without published opinion 578 F.2d 1383 (8th Cir. 1978). Here, however, petitioner did not attempt to deceive or mislead the revenue agent. Instead, he acknowledged that he did not file any Federal income tax returns and provided his reasons for not meeting with the agent or filing returns. In this regard, tax protester arguments, even though meritless and frivolous, without more, do not necessarily amount to fraud. *Kotmair v. Commissioner*, 86 T.C. 1253, 1262 (1986).[30] Petitioner's failure to cooperate here was to his own detriment. Respondent had received Forms 1099 from the company(ies) that had paid petitioner for harvested timber in each year. Petitioner, by his failure to come forward, however, did not obtain the benefit of the deductions to which he was entitled in connection with the harvesting of timber. His failure to cooperate did not keep respondent from being able to determine his income or receipts.

At trial, petitioner admitted that he knew Melton was not an accountant or an attorney experienced in tax matters, but he believed Melton's advice that he did not owe tax. Petitioner is not well versed in tax and financial matters and has only limited formal education. We cannot say that his holding to so-called protester tenets was with intent to defraud or misrepresent. In general, a taxpayer's negligence, whether slight or gross, is not enough to prove fraud. *Kellett v. Commissioner*, 5 T.C. 608, 616 (1945).

---

[30] [fn 4] We stated in Kotmair v. Commissioner, 86 T.C. 1253, 1262 (1986) that the taxpayer's protester arguments "may have been meritless, frivolous, wrongheaded, and even stupid, but we cannot hold that they amounted to fraud, without something more. Were we to do so, every failure-to-file protester case would be automatically converted into a fraud case."

Respondent maintains that petitioner's failure to file timely income tax returns was part of a pattern of fraud. Although a taxpayer's failure to file is prima facie evidence of negligence for purposes of section 6653(a), see *Emmons v. Commissioner*, 92 T.C. 342, 350 (1989), affd. 898 F.2d 50 (5th Cir. 1990), it is insufficient in and of itself to prove fraud. *Rowlee v. Commissioner, supra* at 1123.

The record here simply does not show any *affirmative* acts of concealment or misrepresentation so as to constitute fraud, such as filing false information or attempting to mislead respondent. *Zell v. Commissioner*, 763 F.2d 1139, 1146 (10th Cir. 1985), affg. T.C. Memo. 1984-152. For respondent to sustain her position as to the fraud addition to tax, it is not enough that respondent can show the taxpayer to be devious. See *Kreps v. Commissioner*, 351 F.2d 1, 7 (2d Cir. 1965), affg. 42 T.C. 660 (1964); *Shaw v. Commissioner*, 27 T.C. 561, 569-570 (1956), affd. 252 F.2d 681 (6th Cir. 1958); *Gano v. Commissioner*, 19 B.T.A. 518, 532-533 (1930). The evidence must be clear and convincing. In the instant case, we find that the evidence falls short of being clear and convincing. Accordingly, we find that petitioner is not liable for additions to tax or penalties based on fraud.

In the alternative, respondent determined that petitioner is liable for the additions to tax for failure to timely file for all the years in issue. Section 6651(a)(1) imposes an addition to tax for a taxpayer's failure to file timely returns required to be filed (including income tax returns), unless the taxpayer can establish that such failure "is due to reasonable cause and not due to willful neglect". The addition to tax is 5 percent of the amount required to be shown on the return for each month beyond the return's due date, not exceeding 25 percent. Sec. 6651(a)(1). Petitioner bears the burden of showing respondent's determination to be in error and that there was reasonable cause for his failure to timely file. Rule 142(a).

Respondent, in the alternative, also determined a 5-percent addition to tax for each of the years 1986 through 1988 for negligence or intentional disregard of rules or regulations. Section 6653(a)(1)(A) for 1986 and 1987 and section 6653(a)(1) for 1988 provide for a 5-percent addition to tax if any part of the underpayment is due to negligence or intentional disregard of rules and regulations. If section 6653(a)(1)(A) applies for 1986 and 1987, then section 6653(a)(1)(B) provides for a further addition to tax equal to 50 percent of the interest attributable to that portion of the underpayment resulting from negligence or intentional disregard of rules and regulations. Negligence is defined as a lack of due care or failure to do what a reasonable and prudent person would do under the circumstances. *Neely v. Commissioner*, 85 T.C. 934, 947 (1985). Petitioner bears the burden of showing that he was not negligent. Rule 142(a); *Bixby v. Commissioner*, 58 T.C. 757, 791-792 (1972).

Petitioner did not contend, either at trial or on brief, that his failure to file returns was due to reasonable cause or that his actions were reasonable. On this record, we find that petitioner is liable for additions to tax for failure to file and negligence for the years indicated above. In addition, we find that petitioner is liable for additions to tax under section 6654 as determined by respondent.

To reflect the foregoing,

Decision will be entered under Rule 155.

NOTES AND QUESTIONS

1. Why is the court lenient on Mr. Nelon even though he made frivolous arguments?
2. What other badges of fraud might there be?

In a Tax Court proceeding, the IRS has the burden of presenting clear and convincing evidence of fraud. *See* IRC § 7454(a); U.S. TAX CT. R. PRAC. & P. PROC. 142(b). Taxpayers often fail to respond to the fraud penalty in pleadings thus essentially conceding the fraud penalty if they lose the case. In these instances, the IRS has no requirement to present any evidence. If the IRS introduces some evidence, the taxpayer will concede if he does not respond.

The IRS may rely on a taxpayer's conviction for criminal fraud under section 7201 to establish liability for civil fraud. This is because section 6663 is essentially the civil version of section 7201. In contrast, liability for civil fraud under section 6663 does not establish a violation of section 7201 because the burden of proof is much higher in a criminal case.

WRIGHT v. COMMISSIONER
84 T.C. 636 (1985)
United States Tax Court

OPINION

TANNENWALD, Judge:

Deficiencies in petitioners' Federal income taxes having been agreed to and the resultant tax assessed, respondent determined . . . additions to petitioners' Federal income taxes. . . .

The case is before this Court on respondent's motion for partial summary judgment under Rule 121(b) on the issues of petitioners' understatement of income for the years in issue, petitioners' underpayments of tax for the years in issue, and the addition to tax for 1978. After concessions,[31] the sole issue for our decision is whether petitioner John T. Wright's[32] conviction under section 7206(1)

---

[31] [fn 2] Respondent has conceded that the additions to tax as to petitioner Susan L. Wright were erroneously determined; petitioners have conceded the existence and amounts of the understatements of income and underpayments of tax for the years in issue.

[32] [fn 3] As this case concerns the addition to tax only as to John T. Wright, see supra note 2, we will hereinafter refer to Mr. Wright as 'petitioner,'' and Mr. and Mrs. Wright as 'petitioners.''

collaterally estops petitioners from denying, for purposes of section 6653(b), that part of their underpayment for 1978 was due to fraud.

At the time they filed their petition in this case, petitioners maintained their residence in Illiopolis, Illinois. Petitioners filed joint Federal income tax returns for 1976, 1977, and 1978.

Petitioners, in their response to respondent's motion, claim the following: In June 1975, petitioner's father died suddenly, leaving petitioner's mother to run the family farm. Petitioner was asked by his mother to assume responsibility for the farming operation. Prior to June 1975, petitioner had no business or farming experience, and had no training in bookkeeping, accounting, or business management. Petitioner managed the farm through the years in issue, and for purposes of income tax return preparation, turned his records of the farm's receipts and disbursements over to a local accountant skilled in farming bookkeeping methods. Petitioner's wife did not participate in either the farming business or the preparation of petitioners' income tax returns.

On their Federal income tax returns for the years in issue, petitioners understated their taxable income for 1976 by $8,824.46 and their tax table income for 1977 and 1978 by $24,167.18 and $29,904.82, respectively. Petitioners underpaid their Federal income taxes for the years 1976, 1977, and 1978 by $1,487.95, $4,599.72, and $13,810.05, respectively.

Petitioner was indicted in the United States District Court, Central District of Illinois, Springfield Division, on March 22, 1982 on two counts of violation of section 7206(1) and two counts of violation of section 7201, one of each of the counts relating to the taxable year 1977 and one of each of the counts relating to the taxable year 1978. On June 15, 1982, that court, based on petitioner's guilty plea, entered a finding of guilty for 'the offense(s) of subscribing to a false income tax return as charged in Count 3 of the Indictment, in violation of Title 26, USC sec. 7206(1). Counts 1, 2, & 4 dismissed upon Government Motion.'

Count 3 of the indictment charged:

That on or about the 10th day of January 1979, in the Central District of Illinois,

John T. Wright

a resident of Illiopolis, Illinois, did willfully and knowingly make and subscribe to a United States Individual Tax Return (form 1040) for John T. and Susan L. Wright, which was verified by a written declaration that it was made under the penalties of perjury, and was filed with the Internal Revenue Service, when he did not believe said Income Tax Return to be true and correct as to every material matter in that the Income Tax Return stated that the grain sale and other income of John T. and Susan L. Wright was $84,665.69 whereas, as he then and there well knew and believed, he had received substantial income in addition to that here before stated.

All in violation of Title 26, United States Code, Section 7206(1).

Respondent issued the deficiency notice on which the instant case is based on September 26, 1983.

Rule 121(a) provides that '(e)ither party may move, with or without supporting affidavits, for a summary adjudication in his favor upon all or any part of the legal issues in controversy.' Decision is to be entered for the moving party

> if the pleadings, answers to interrogatories, depositions, admissions, and any other acceptable materials, together with the affidavits, if any, show that there is no genuine issue as to any material fact and that a decision may be rendered as a matter of law. A partial summary adjudication may be made which does not dispose of all the issues in the case.

Rule 121(b). While we must view the facts and inferences to be drawn therefrom in the light most favorable to the party opposing the motion, such party has the burden of setting forth 'specific facts showing that there is a genuine issue for trial.' Rule 121(d); Jacklin v. Commissioner, 79 T.C. 340, 344 (1982).

Respondent bases his motion on the allegedly preclusive effect of petitioner's conviction under section 7206(1)[33] upon the issue of fraud under section 6653(b).[34] Respondent contends that our opinions in Goodwin v. Commissioner, 73 T.C. 215 (1979), and Considine v. Commissioner, 68 T.C. 52 (1977), compel the conclusion that petitioner's conviction establishes as a matter of law that the underpayment for 1978 was 'due to fraud,' for purposes of section 6653(b), and thus that respondent's motion should be granted. Petitioners contend that petitioner's lack of business acumen raises a genuine issue as to a material fact, and that respondent's motion should thus be denied. For the reasons hereinafter stated, we agree with petitioners.

The doctrine of collateral estoppel precludes relitigation of any issue of fact or law that is actually litigated and necessarily determined by a valid and final judgment. Montana v. United States, 440 U.S. 147, 153 (1979); see Restatement (Second) of Judgments sec. 27 (1982). Its purpose is to avoid repetitious litigation of issues between the same parties or their privies. See Jaggard v. Commissioner, 76 T.C. 222, 223 (1981). The doctrine, however, 'must be confined to situations where the matter raised in the second suit is identical in all

---

[33] [fn 4] Sec. 7206 provides, in relevant part,

Any person who,

(1) DECLARATION UNDER PENALTIES OF PERJURY. Willfully makes and subscribes any return, statement, or other document, which contains or is verified by a written declaration that it is made under the penalties of perjury, and which he does not believe to be true and correct as to every material matter; * * * * * *

shall be guilty of a felony * * *.

[34] [fn 5] Sec. 6653(b)(1) provides: 'If any part of any underpayment (as defined in subsection (c)) of tax required to be shown on a return is due to fraud, there shall be added to the tax an amount equal to 50 percent of the underpayment.''

respects with that decided in the first proceeding and where the controlling facts and applicable legal rules remain unchanged.' Commissioner v. Sunnen, 333 U.S. 591, 599-600 (1948); see Cromwell v. County of Sac, 94 U.S. 351, 353 (1876). Thus, the question is whether the issue under section 6653(b) is 'identical in all respects' to that decided under section 7206(1).

Under section 6653(b), respondent has the burden of proving, by clear and convincing evidence, that 'any part of any underpayment * * * is due to fraud.' See sec. 7454(a); Rule 142(b). The 'due to fraud' language has been consistently interpreted to require proof of specific intent to evade a tax believed to be owing. See, e.g., Hebrank v. Commissioner, 81 T.C. 640, 642 (1983).[35] Section 7206(1) makes it a crime for one willfully to make and submit any return verified by a written declaration that it is made under the penalties of perjury which he or she does not believe to be true and correct as to every material matter. The indictment on which petitioner's conviction was based charged that he willfully filed a verified return that 'he did not believe * * * to be true and correct as to every material matter' in that petitioner 'well knew and believed (that) he had received substantial income in addition to' that which he reported.

In Considine v. Commissioner, 68 T.C. 52, a case in which the taxpayer had been convicted under section 7206(1) and was disputing the addition to tax under section 6653(b), we held that 'a conviction under section 7206(1) for "willfully" making a return which the taxpayer does not believe to be true and correct is proof that the return is fraudulent,' and that the taxpayer was thus 'collaterally estopped to deny that he willfully filed a false and fraudulent return.' Considine v. Commissioner, supra at 61, 68.

Our reasoning in *Considine* was as follows: (1) this Court, in Amos v. Commissioner, 43 T.C. 50, 55 (1964), affd. 360 F.2d 358 (4th Cir. 1965), had held that 'the term "willfully" as used in section 7201[36] has authoritatively been defined in prior judicial decisions to encompass all of the elements of fraud which are envisioned by the civil penalty described in section 6653(b)'; (2) the Supreme Court, in United States v. Bishop, 412 U.S. 346, 356-361 (1973), had held that 'willfully' has the same meaning in each of sections 7201, 7202, 7203, 7204, 7205, 7206, and 7207; therefore, (3) a conviction under section 7206(1) actually and necessarily determined that there was, for purposes of section 6653(b), a specific intention to evade tax. Considine v. Commissioner, supra at 59-60. Our opinion in *Considine* and the rationale upon which it was predicated were followed in the Court-reviewed opinion in Goodwin v. Commissioner, 73 T.C. 215, 224 (1979), with six Judges dissenting.

Subsequent to our opinions in Considine v. Commissioner, supra, and Goodwin v. Commissioner, supra, the Court of Appeals for the Ninth Circuit had

---

[35] [fn 6] See also Gersh v. Commissioner, T.C. Memo. 1984-522.

[36] [fn 7] Sec. 7201 provides, in relevant part,

'Any person who willfully attempts in any manner to evade or defeat any tax imposed by this title or the payment thereof shall, in addition to other penalties provided by law, be guilty of a felony.''

occasion, in Considine v. United States, 683 F.2d 1285, 1287 (9th Cir. 1982), to review the imposition of the addition to tax for fraud on the Considines for the taxable year 1965[37] by the United States District Court on the ground that Mr. Considine's conviction of a violation of section 7206(1) for that year collaterally estopped him from contesting the fraud element of the addition to tax for that year under section 6653(b). The Ninth Circuit disagreed with the District Court's application of collateral estoppel, and, in so doing, stated flatly that they believed that our opinion in Considine v. Commissioner, supra, was incorrect. See 683 F.2d at 1287.[38] Beyond the Ninth Circuit's criticism of our opinion in Considine v. Commissioner, supra, it has been held on numerous occasions, both before and after *Considine*, although not in the context of the issue of collateral estoppel, that the intent to evade taxes is not an element of the crime covered by section 7206(1). United States v. Tsanas, 572 F.2d 340, 343 (2d Cir. 1978); United States v. Beasley, 519 F.2d 233, 245 (5th Cir. 1975); United States v. DiVarco, 484 F.2d 670, 673-674 (7th Cir. 1973); Siravo v. United States, 377 F.2d 469, 472 n.4 (1st Cir. 1967); United States v. Hans, 548 F. Supp. 1119, 1124 (S.D. Ohio 1982); United States v. Anderson, 254 F. Supp. 177, 183-185 (W.D. Ark. 1966); see also United States v. Whyte, 699 F.2d 375, 381 (7th Cir. 1983).[39] TEXT Against

---

[37] [fn 8] The interplay between the criminal and civil phases of the Considines' liability for Federal income taxes for the taxable years 1965-67 and 1969 has had the attention of the courts on several occasions. Mr. Considine was convicted under sec. 7206(1) as to his returns for 1965-67 and 1969, United States v. Considine, an unreported case (S.D. Cal. 1973, 34 AFTR 2d 74-5412, 74-2 USTC par. 9639), affd. 502 F.2d 246 (9th Cir. 1973), and brought three separate actions challenging respondent's subsequent imposition of the additions to tax under sec. 6653(b). Considine v. Commissioner, 68 T.C. 52 (1977), concerned the addition for 1969; Considine v. United States, 645 F.2d 925 (Ct. Cl. 1981), concerned the additions for 1966 and 1967; and Considine v. United States, 683 F.2d 1285 (9th Cir. 1982), concerned the addition for 1965.

[38] [fn 9] The District Court was nevertheless affirmed on the ground that the Government had in fact carried its burden of proof on the fraud issue under section 6653(b) with respect to both Mr. and Mrs. Considine. In Considine v. United States, 645 F.2d 925, 928-931 (Ct. Cl. 1981), which involved the Considines' taxable years 1966 and 1967, the Government contended only that the issue of knowing falsification as to the amount of income and deductions should be disposed of on the basis of collateral estoppel, and did not claim that collateral estoppel applied to the issues of intent to evade or existence of an underpayment. See 645 F.2d at 928. The Court of Claims was thus not required to reach the issue which was the fulcrum of our opinions in Considine and Goodwin. It sustained the Government's limited contention and, like the Court of Appeals for the Ninth Circuit, went on to hold that the Government had in fact carried its burden of proof as to fraud.

[39] [fn 10] We note that respondent has not cited, and our research has not revealed, any authority, other than our opinions in Considine and Goodwin, that

this background, we have reexamined our opinions in Goodwin v. Commissioner, supra, and Considine v. Commissioner, supra, and have concluded that they should no longer be followed to the extent that they hold that a conviction under section 7206(1) is equated by way of collateral estoppel with the existence of fraud within the meaning of section 6653(b).

We begin our analysis in support of our conclusion with the word 'willfully,' as used in section 7206(1). In United States v. Pomponio, 429 U.S. 10 (1976), the Supreme Court held that, for purposes of sections 7201-7207, 'willfully' 'simply means a voluntary, intentional violation of a known legal duty.' 429 U.S. at 12; see United States v. Bishop, supra at 360. This definition says nothing about fraud, and requires nothing more than a specific intention to violate the law. United States v. Pomponio, supra at 11-13; see also United States v. Koliboski, buttressed its conclusion that 'willfully' has this uniform meaning in sections 7201-7207 by noting those statutes' differences from one another, specifically in the express designation of the specific elements of each offense. United States v. Bishop, supra at 357-360. For example, the Court described the specific element of the offense under section 7201 as the 'attempt to evade.' United States v. Bishop, supra at 359. The Court went on explicitly to caution against interpreting the word 'willfully,' as used in sections 7201-7207, to include this section 7201 element,

> Semantic confusion sometimes has been created when courts discuss the express requirement of an 'attempt to evade' in section 7201 as if it were implicit in the word 'willfully' in that statute. * * * Greater clarity might well result from an analysis that distinguishes the express elements, such as an 'attempt to evade,' prescribed by section 7201, from the uniform requirement of willfulness.

United States v. Bishop, supra at 360 n.8.

In Amos v. Commissioner, supra, we equated the element necessary for conviction under section 7201 (i.e., an 'attempt to evade') with that essential for the imposition of the civil penalty under section 6653(b) (i.e., an 'underpayment * * * due to fraud'). Amos v. Commissioner, supra at 55. Because the attempt to evade tax is the gravamen of fraud, see, e.g., Hebrank v. Commissioner, supra at 642, we concluded in Amos that a taxpayer convicted under section 7201 of having attempted to evade or defeat a tax for a taxable year is collaterally estopped from denying under section 6653(b) that part of his underpayment for the same year was 'due to fraud.' Such identity of criminal tax evasion and civil tax fraud for purposes of collateral estoppel has been repeatedly sustained by the courts. See Gray v. Commissioner, 708 F.2d 243, 246 (6th Cir. 1983), affg. a Memorandum Opinion of this Court, and cases cited threat; see also Plunkett v. Commissioner, 465 F.2d 299, 305 (7th Cir. 1972), affg. a Memorandum Opinion of this Court. However, to have held, as we did in Considine v. Commissioner,

---

fraud, i.e., intent to evade taxes, is an element of the offense under section 7206(1).

supra, and Goodwin v. Commissioner, supra, that a conviction for 'willfully' making a false statement in an income tax return within the meaning of section 7206(1) estops a taxpayer from denying that any underpayment made for the year of the return was 'due to fraud' misapplies the principle of collateral estoppel and creates the semantic confusion warned against in United States v. Bishop, supra.

In a criminal action under section 7206(1), the issue actually litigated and necessarily determined is whether the taxpayer voluntarily and intentionally violated his or her known legal duty not to make a false statement as to any material matter on a return. See United States v. Pomponio, supra at 12; United States v. Bishop, supra at 360. The purpose of section 7206(1) is to facilitate the carrying out of respondent's proper functions by punishing those who intentionally falsify their Federal income tax returns (United States v. Greenberg, 735 F.2d 29, 31 (2d Cir. 1984); United States v. DiVarco, supra at 673), and the penalty for such perjury is imposed irrespective of the tax consequences of the falsification (Gaunt v. United States, 184 F.2d 284, 288 (1st Cir. 1950); United States v. DiVarco, 343 F. Supp. 101, 103 (N.D. Ill. 1972), affd. 484 F.2d 670 (7th Cir. 1973)). As noted above, the intent to evade taxes is not an element of the crime charged under section 7206(1). See cases cited supra p. 10. Thus, the crime is complete with the knowing, material falsification, and a conviction under section 7206(1) does not establish as a matter of law that the taxpayer violated the legal duty with an intent, or in an attempt, to evade taxes.

In short, it cannot be said that the combined effect of the Supreme Court's opinions in United States v. Pomponio, supra, and United States v. Bishop, supra, and our opinion in Amos v. Commissioner, supra, is to equate the standards under section 7206(1) with those under section 6653(b); the Supreme Court simply did not engraft the 'attempt to evade' language from section 7201 into section 7206(1) by holding that 'willfully' has a uniform meaning in sections 7201-7207. See Considine v. United States, supra, 683 F.2d at 1287.[40] Thus, to the extent that they give collateral estoppel effect to a conviction under section 7206(1) on the issue of intent to evade tax under section 6653(b), Considine v. Commissioner, supra, and Goodwin v. Commissioner, supra, are overruled. Of course, a conviction for willful falsification, under section 7206(1), while not dispositive, will be one of the facts to be considered in a trial on the merits.

In the instant case, petitioners argue that we should deny respondent's motion for partial summary judgment because petitioner's lack of business acumen, and not an attempt to evade taxes, was the reason for the underpayments in question, and the factual issue thus raised is a 'genuine issue as to any material fact' under Rule 121(b). We agree. The issue of intent, adequately raised by petitioners herein, is clearly one requiring a trial on the merits. See Oakland Hills Country Club v. Commissioner, 74 T.C. 35, 39-40 (1980); Hoeme v. Commissioner, 63 T.C. 18, 20 (1974); cf. Considine v. United States, supra, 683

---

[40] [fn 11] See also Rinehart v. Commissioner, T.C. Memo. 1983-184; Schmitz v. Commissioner, T.C. Memo. 1983-482; cf. Buras v. Commissioner, T.C. Memo. 1985-26 (sec. 7203).

F.2d at 1288 (intent to evade is 'natural inference' from willful underpayment by sophisticated, knowledgeable taxpayer).[41] Thus, on the sole issue before us, i.e., the addition to tax for 1978, respondent's motion for partial summary judgment will be denied.

An appropriate order will be entered.

Reviewed by the Court.

DAWSON, FAY, SIMPSON, STERRETT, GOFFE, CHABOT, NIMS, PARKER, WHITAKER, SHIELDS, HAMBLEN, COHEN, CLAPP, SWIFT, and WRIGHT, JJ., agee with the majority opinion.

WILBUR, JACOBS, and GERBER, JJ., did not participate in the consideration of this case.

KORNER, J., dissenting: I respectfully disagree with the conclusion of the majority in this case that petitioner, John T. Wright, is not estopped by his conviction under section 7206(1) to deny that his Federal income tax return for 1978 was false in that he willfully and knowingly omitted income therefrom which he knew should have been reported. That fact was conclusively established by his guilty plea to the indictment under section 7206(1), which contains the specific allegation of willfully and intentionally failing to report income which petitioner knew he should have done. He is thus collaterally estopped to deny that fact in the instant case. Nell v. Commissioner, T.C. Memo. 1982-228. His guilty plea is as much a conviction as a conviction following a jury trial. Gray v. Commissioner, 708 F.2d 243, (6th Cir. 1983), affg. T.C. Memo. 1981-1, cert. denied 466 U.S. ___ (1984).

For this reason, I would conclude that there is no issue of material fact in this case as to whether petitioner's failure to report all his income on his 1978 return was an innocent mistake due to his lack of business acumen. A conviction under section 7206(1) of filing a false return from which income is omitted does not, standing alone, establish the fraudulent intent to evade tax required to support the addition to tax under section 6653(b). However, here the parties have stipulated that petitioner's willful and knowing omission of income from his 1978 return resulted in an underpayment of tax. In my view, petitioner's willfully and knowingly filing a false return for the year 1978, combined with the stipulation of the parties that the willful omission of income from that return resulted in an underpayment of tax, establishes the intent to evade necessary to a determination of the addition to tax under section 6653(b). Based on the holdings and discussions in Considine v. United States, 683 F.2d 1285 (9th Cir. 1982); Considine v. United States, 645 F.2d 925 (Ct. Cl. 1981); and Goodwin v.

---

[41] [fn 12] We do not have a sufficient factual foundation in the moving papers to determine that no material issue of fact exists as to the fraud, as the Court of Appeals for the Ninth Circuit and the Court of Claims were able to do in the Considine cases before them.

Commissioner, 73 T.C. 215 (1979), I would grant respondent's Motion for Summary Judgment in this case.

NOTES AND QUESTIONS

1. What reasons can you give for why the number of civil penalties has grown over the years?
2. Which of the following would constitute reasonable cause?
   a. Amber relies on her lawyer to file her tax return on time, but her lawyer fails to file the return in a timely manner.
   b. Brian does not file a return because his lawyer advised him he was not required to because he did not meet the income threshold amount that triggers the obligation to file a return.
   c. Cathy's house burns down, destroying the records she needs to file a timely tax return, and, accordingly, she fails to do so.
   d. David burns down his own house where he stored tax documents necessary for filing his returns in order to avoid paying tax.
   e. Eleanor's son commits suicide leaving a gruesome scene, and Eleanor finds him. Eleanor was unable to file her tax returns for two years.
   f. Frank's son commits suicide leaving a gruesome scene, and Frank finds him. Frank was unable to file his tax returns for 15 years.

CHAPTER 5

ENFORCED COLLECTION

One of the negative consequences of tax noncompliance is the enforced collection of unpaid tax. This authority is rooted in sections 6301 and 6331. Section 6301 provides: "The [IRS] shall collect the taxes imposed by the internal revenue laws." Further, section 6331(a) provides:

> If any person liable to pay any tax [fails to pay] within 10 days after notice and demand, it shall be lawful for the [IRS] to collect such tax . . . by levy upon all property and rights to property . . . belonging to such person.

These provisions demonstrate the force inherent in IRS's administrative collection authority. When the IRS's administrative authority is unavailable, the IRS may also rely on judicial collection procedures as well.

Although the IRS's collection tools have the potential to do serious financial damage to a taxpayer, both the taxpayer and the IRS have an interest in working together to resolve collection issues. A collection action with a noncompliant taxpayer can ruin the taxpayer's credit rating, which, ironically, can impair the taxpayer's ability to obtain proceeds to pay the IRS. In such a case, neither the taxpayer nor the IRS come out ahead. Chapter 6 discusses how these situations arise and the taxpayer's options in collection.

A. Overview of the Administrative Collection Process

Taxpayers have a number of opportunities to become current with their tax liabilities even during the collection process. If the taxpayer continues to refuse to pay, the IRS may take the following steps:

- Assessment — the IRS establishes the amount to be collected by assessing the tax (section 6201).
- Notice and demand — the IRS issues a notice of the amount due and demand for payment (section 6303(a)).
- Federal tax lien — a lien arises by operation of law if no payment is made within ten days of the notice and demand (section 6321)).

- Notice of federal tax lien — the IRS files a notice of the lien if necessary to gain priority over certain creditors (section 6320(a)(1)).
- Levy — the IRS takes possession of the taxpayer's assets if all else has failed (section 6331(b)).
- Sale — the IRS sells the levied property to satisfy the tax liability (section 6331(b)).

Throughout the collection process, the IRS attempts to contact the taxpayer to make arrangements to pay the liability. Some of the statutory notices the IRS sends to a taxpayer notify him of the right to a Collection Due Process (CDP) hearing. *See* sections 6330(a)(3)(B), 6320(a)(3)(B). Both the correspondence with the taxpayer and the CDP hearings provide the opportunity for a taxpayer to discuss payment alternatives that would end the collection process.

Once the IRS assesses a tax, the Code provides the IRS a ten-year period to collect the tax by levy or judicial proceeding. *See* section 6502(a)(1). The collection statute extends in a few circumstances. An installment agreement between the IRS and the taxpayer, for example, can extend the statutory period. *See* IRC § 6502(a)(2)(A). In addition, the IRS and the taxpayer may agree on a period of collection in an installment agreement, after which the IRS has another 90 days to continue collection efforts. *See* IRC § 6502(a)(2)(B).The IRS may also complete a judicial proceeding that starts prior to the expiration of the statutory period.

B. Lien and Levy Procedures

The IRS's administrative collection authority permits the IRS to collect tax without judicial action. In contrast, state law generally requires ordinary creditors to go to court to collect on a judgment. The IRS is no ordinary creditor—the Code provides powerful administrative procedures that make judicial action unnecessary for collection. A federal tax lien attaches to a taxpayer's assets if the IRS receives no payment after the IRS has informed the taxpayer of the tax due and demanded payment. Everything is in place at that point for the IRS to take the taxpayer's assets to satisfy the tax. Technically, the IRS could just wait the statutory length of time and issue a levy. But if an investigation shows there are competing creditors, the IRS may issue a Notice of Federal Tax Lien (NFTL) before initiating a levy action to take the taxpayer's assets.

1. Notice and Demand

Collection begins with an assessment, but the IRS's contact with the taxpayer begins with a notice of liability and demand for payment, referred to as "notice and demand." *See* section 6331(a). The IRS has 60 days after assessment to send the taxpayer a notice and demand letter. *See* section 6303(a). Included in the letter is a notification of how much the taxpayer owes for a particular tax year.

After the notice and demand, the taxpayer has ten days to pay the tax. In addition, failure to respond within 21 days of the notice triggers a penalty for failing to pay the tax demanded. *See* section 6651(a)(3). Although not required by statute, the IRS's practice after the notice and demand is to send a number of follow-up letters, make multiple phone calls, and, if possible, see the taxpayer in person prior to taking the next step in collecting the liability.

The failure of the IRS to issue a notice and demand within 60 days does not invalidate the underlying tax assessment. The IRS may still collect the tax. After the 60-day period, the IRS loses its "awesome" administrative summary collection authority. But while the assessment remains, the IRS retains the option to institute a judicial collection proceeding to collect the liability.

BLACKSTON v. UNITED STATES
778 F. Supp. 244 (D. Md. 1991)
United States District Court, District of Maryland

GARBIS, District Judge.

Plaintiffs Linwood Blackston and Barbara Blackston ("the taxpayers") are, and were at all times relevant to this case, citizens of the United States residing in Baltimore, Maryland. The taxpayers filed timely Joint Federal Income Tax Returns for the years 1979, 1980, and 1981. On or about April 15, 1983, the Internal Revenue Service issued a statutory notice of deficiency for the years 1977 through 1981. The taxpayers contested the proposed deficiencies in the United States Tax Court. Ultimately, the Tax Court case was resolved by a settlement (stipulated decision) in which the parties agreed to . . . deficiencies in tax and penalties (plus interest thereon in accordance with law). . . .

The above-noted deficiencies for 1979, 1980, and 1981 were assessed on January 28, 1985, pursuant to § 6503(a)(1).

The issues presented are whether the Internal Revenue Service has complied with § 6303(a) of the Internal Revenue Code by giving notice to the taxpayers stating the amount due and demanding payment within 60 days after the making of the subject assessments and, if not, what is the effect of the Service's failure.

JURISDICTIONAL PREREQUISITES

The substantive issues concern the validity of assessments of deficiencies in income tax, penalties and interest for the years 1979, 1980 and 1981. As to the year 1979, the taxpayers made full payment on or about March 18, 1988 and timely filed a claim for refund on or about the same date. On May 4, 1988 the claim for refund was denied. The taxpayers timely commenced this action, seeking a refund with regard to the year 1979. § 6532(a). Thus, the jurisdictional prerequisites have been met for the taxpayers to sue for a refund for 1979. See, generally, M. Garbis, P. Junghans, S. Struntz, Federal Tax Litigation, Para. 15.01 et seq. (1985).

As to 1980 and 1981, the Government filed a Counterclaim to reduce to judgment the balance due on the assessments for those years. By virtue of the

Government's counterclaim, the Court has jurisdiction to determine the validity of the 1980 and 1981 assessments. *See Id.* Par. 15.02[6]

NONCOMPLIANCE WITH SECTION 6303(A)
Section 6303(a) provides in relevant part that:

> . . . [The IRS] shall, as soon as practicable, and within 60 days after the making of an assessment of a tax . . . give notice to each person liable for the unpaid tax, stating the amount and demanding payment thereof. Said notice shall . . . be sent by mail to such person's last known address.

The I.R.S. records reflect that a first notice of assessment and demand for payment ("Notice and Demand") was mailed to the taxpayers at their current address on or about January 28, 1985, within 60 days of the assessments. It is stipulated, however, that the first notice which the taxpayers actually received relating to the subject deficiencies was dated May 31, 1985—more than 60 days after the assessments. The question presented is whether the Service in fact properly mailed a notice and demand on or about January 28, 1985 as reflected in its computer generated records.[1]

It is the Government's position that the mere fact that the Internal Revenue Service is able to present a computer generated printout reflecting that a Notice of Demand had been sent on January 28, 1988 establishes an *irrebuttable presumption* that the notice was in fact sent. This Court rejects this position. A similar contention had been rejected by the district court in the case of *United States v. Berman*, 825 F.2d 1053, 1056–57 (6th Cir.1987). As found by the trial court in the *Berman* case, and as this Court finds from the evidence presented here, there are sufficient irregularities presented in the IRS computer evidence to cause this Court to doubt its reliability. Therefore, the Court refuses to accept the records as conclusive. In particular, the Court notes that the I.R.S. records reflect the mailing of a first notice on January 28, 1985 and the mailing of a second notice some four months later on May 31, 1985. However, the IRS Service Center computer is programmed to send the second notice five weeks after the first notice. M. Saltzman, IRS Practice and Procedure Para. 14.03(3) (2nd ed. 1991) and Para. 14.03 (1st ed. 1981); *See also* Salchow, *IRS Practice & Policy,* Para. 1010.A.2.a (1991).

This Court was sufficiently concerned about the matter to ask the Government at argument, and in a post trial Order, the following:

The I.R.S. records reflect the mailing of a first notice on January 28, 1985 and a second notice on May 31, 1985 (a four month period) while the I.R.S. manual allegedly indicates that there would be a much shorter period between a

---

[1] [fn 2] The Government, quite correctly, notes that the fact that the taxpayers did not receive the alleged January 28, 1985 first notice is not determinative. So long as the notice was timely mailed to the taxpayers' last known address, the IRS has complied with § 6303(a) even absent receipt.

CHAPTER 5—ENFORCED COLLECTION | 107

first and second notice. How can this inconsistency be explained without resulting in uncertainty as to the accuracy of either the January or May date, or both?

In response the Government stated:

[A]fter consultation with the appropriate IRS representative, the United States does not intend to proffer any further evidence on this particular point.

The Court interprets this response to mean that the Government cannot provide any satisfactory answer to the Court's question. Therefore, on the record in this case, which includes the Government's refusal (or inability) to provide an explanation of the inconsistency of its computer generated records as to the date of the first notice,[2] the Court finds as a fact that the IRS did not comply with § 6303(a) by sending a Notice and Demand within 60 days of the subject assessments. This finding requires the Court to address the question of the effect of such a failure.

EFFECT OF NONCOMPLIANCE WITH SECTION 6303(A)

Having found that the IRS failed to comply with § 6303(a) by not sending a notice and demand within 60 days of the subject assessments, the Court must determine the effect of such a failure. In this case, the issue arises in both a refund context[3] and in a collection context.[4] In both contexts the issue presented is whether the failure to send a timely notice and demand renders the January 28, 1985 assessment void altogether or whether it leaves the assessment valid but bars the Internal Revenue Service from utilizing its lien and levy collection powers.

There is no Fourth Circuit precedent addressing the issue presented. The decisions in other circuits addressing the absence of a timely notice and demand do not answer all of the questions presented in this case. *See United States v. Chila,* 871 F.2d 1015 (11th Cir.1989); *United States v. Berman,* 825 F.2d 1053 (6th Cir.1987) *on remand* U.S.T.C. 88–2 Para. 9550, 1988 WL 126557 (S.D.Ohio 1988) *after remand* 884 F.2d 916 (6th Cir.1989); *Marvel v. United States,* 719 F.2d 1507 (10th Cir.1983). Nevertheless, this Court concludes, consistent with the views expressed in *Berman, Marvel,* and *Chila* that the appropriate "sanction" against the I.R.S. for its failure to comply the § 6303(a) notice and demand requirement is to take away its awesome nonjudicial collection powers. It would be irrational to conclude that an assessment becomes

---

[2] [fn 3] If the first and second notices were, in fact, mailed 5 weeks apart then the computer records are erroneous as to the January 28, 1985 date for the first notice and/or the May 31, 1985 date for the second notice.

[3] [fn 4] *I.e.* for 1979 as to which the taxpayers have made full payment and seek recovery of what they have paid.

[4] [fn 5] For 1980 and 1981 the IRS has filed suit to reduce an assessment of judgment.

void after 60 days if there is no notice and demand. Such a rule of law would serve only to provide a windfall to permit taxpayers to avoid paying valid assessments of determined tax liabilities because of an I.R.S. clerical error in failing to mail a notice and demand to the taxpayer's last known address.

The Court's decision is in accord with the views of leading publications on federal tax procedures. As stated in M. Saltzman, IRS Practice and Procedure, Para. 14.05(2) (2nd ed. 1991):

> Under the collection mechanism established by the Code, once tax has been assessed, a taxpayer is subject to the summary nonjudicial procedures (lien and levy) available to the Service to collect the assessed tax. The notice and demand provided by Section 6303 gives the taxpayer warning that the taxpayer must take some action to resolve the delinquent account if these summary collection procedures are to be avoided. Thus, preseizure notice serves an important practical, and possibly a due process, purpose in the statutory scheme. A taxpayer's liability is recorded by the official act of assessment, but where no Section 6303 notice is given, or an invalid notice is given, a statutory prerequisite is missing and, absent compliance with the Code, any collection action that follows is invalid. No lien can arise, nor can a levy be effective, absent a notice and demand. Where the government elects to collect tax by a civil suit, the complaint gives the taxpayer notice, and collection cannot be taken without court approval. A Section 6303 notice does not appear to be required where liability is asserted in a judicial proceeding. [Footnotes in original omitted.]

And, as stated in Salchow, *IRS Practice & Policy,* Para. 1010.A.2.d (1991):

> Since the administrative collection remedies require a timely and properly issued notice and demand, it is in the taxpayer's interest initially to determine whether the IRS made such notice and demand. The general rule is that no tax lien arises until the IRS makes a demand for payment. *Myrick v. United States,* 296 F.2d 312 (5th Cir.1961). Without a valid notice and demand, there can be no tax lien; without a tax lien, the IRS cannot levy against the taxpayer's property. The IRS' failure to serve a timely notice and demand, however, does not prevent the government from instituting a judicial proceeding to collect the tax liability. *United States v. Chila,* 871 F.2d 1015 (11th Cir.1989); *United States v. Berman,* 825 F.2d 1053 (6th Cir.1983); *Marvel v. United States,* 719 F.2d [1507] 1513 (10th Cir.1983).

THE 1979 REFUND CLAIM

As to the year 1979, the outcome depends upon the manner in which the taxes were collected. That is, was collection effected by the illegal use of liens and levies in the absence of a notice and demand. If so, the taxpayers would be entitled to a refund.[5] Here, the 1979 taxes were paid by the taxpayers' check and not through the use of the lien or levy power. Accordingly, there can be no refund for 1979.

The Court has considered the argument that the taxpayers here paid by check only because of the threat of nonjudicial collection action. Hence, it could be argued that the I.R.S., as a practical matter, did utilize its nonjudicial collection powers. However, it is fair to say that many, if not virtually all, tax payments are made because the taxpayer realizes that a failure to pay what is owed will result in I.R.S. collection activity. Accordingly, the effect of the taxpayer's argument would be to provide a windfall to all taxpayers who do not receive a timely notice and demand but pay their tax liability anyhow. Thus, in a not uncommon situation, the I.R.S. might innocently misaddress a notice and demand but the taxpayer would nevertheless become aware of the assessment more than 60 days after it is made. At that point the taxpayer could (and should) pay the I.R.S. (resulting in a closing of the account) without any reason for the IRS to be aware that it had made a clerical error in issuing a notice and demand. It would be strange indeed if this would result in giving the taxpayer the ability to get a refund of the payment and avoid entirely his determined liability.

It should further be noted that a § 6303(a) "violation" occurs 60 days after the assessment. Therefore, if the taxpayer's position were correct, a valid assessment would become invalid on the 61st day after assessment because of the nonoccurrence of an event, i.e. a properly addressed notice and demand. There is nothing to indicate to this Court that such retroactive invalidation was intended or makes any sense at all.

This Court concludes that § 6303(a) was placed in the Code to insure that taxpayers received notice of tax liability so that they could make "voluntary" payment before the I.R.S. could use its lien and levy collection powers. Therefore, the purpose of the statute would be served by preventing the I.R.S. from the exercise of this power where it has not complied with § 6303(a). To go further and eliminate a taxpayer's duly determined liability would be neither consistent with the statutory scheme nor sensible.

THE 1980 AND 1981 COUNTERCLAIM

As to 1980 and 1981, the Government has sued to reduce to judgment the assessments made on January 28, 1985. The taxpayers have defended in reliance

---

[5] [fn 6] In the case of *Sasscer v. United States*, MJG–91–158 (D.Md.) the Government stated:

"This letter is in response to your order dated May 8, 1991, in which you requested the United States' position as to whether a taxpayer is entitled to a refund on the sole ground that the liability was collected by administrative levy in the absence of a notice and demand. The United States' position is that the taxpayer would be entitled to a refund, as long as he filed his claim for refund with the Internal Revenue Service within two years from the time the funds were administratively collected."

on the statute of limitations. In essence, the taxpayers contend that the January 28, 1985 assessments were rendered invalid once 60 days passed without notice and demand. Therefore, they say, the Government could only sue on the underlying tax liability and not on the assessment. Accordingly, since the Counterclaim was filed after the running of limitations for a suit on the liability itself and not the assessment, the taxpayers would be entitled to judgment.[6]

It is the Government's position, with which the Court agrees, that the January 28, 1985 assessment was, and remains, valid and that the Counterclaim was timely filed to reduce the assessment to judgment pursuant to § 6502(a).[7] The Counterclaim is, in effect, a collection suit, which is permitted even though there had been no notice and demand. *Chila, supra, Berman, supra, Marvel, supra.* Thus, the Counterclaim was timely filed and, there being no debate as to the substantive merit of the assessments, the Government is entitled to judgment.

CONCLUSION

For the foregoing reasons, the Court holds in favor of the Government on the Plaintiff's suit for refund for 1979 and on the Government's Counterclaim to reduce its assessments to judgment for 1980 and 1981.

NOTES AND QUESTIONS

1. For purposes of the IRS's compliance with sending the taxpayer a notice and demand, which controls, the delivery of the notice and demand, or the receipt of the notice and demand?
2. Why does the court permit the IRS to proceed with judicial collection in this case?

2. Federal Tax Lien

The failure to pay the amount owed after notice and demand triggers a federal tax lien by operation of law. Section 6321 provides as follows:

> If any person liable to pay any tax neglects . . . to pay the same after demand, the amount . . . shall be a lien in favor of the United States upon all property and rights to property, whether real or personal, belonging to such person.

---

[6] [fn 7] § 6502(a)(1). A suit on the tax liability (*sans* assessment) would be timely if brought within three years from the date the return was filed plus the period of time during which the running of limitations was extended by virtue of the Tax Court litigation. § 6503(a). It appears that this period of limitations would have expired prior to the 1988 filing of the Government's counterclaim in this case.

[7] [fn 8] The period of limitations for suit on the January 25, 1985 assessments was originally six years and was, in 1990, extended to ten years. Omnibus Budget Reconciliation Act of 1990, § 11317(a)(1), amending IRC § 6502(a).

The lien relates back to the date of the assessment and stays in place until paid or the statutory collection period expires. Section 6322 provides as follows:

[T]he lien imposed by section 6321 shall arise at the time the assessment is made and shall continue until the liability for the amount so assessed . . . is satisfied or becomes unenforceable by reason of lapse of time.

The lien attaches to all property and rights to property of the taxpayer, including certain property acquired after the lien. The IRS may enforce this lien by seizing the property subject to the lien.

The federal tax lien can attach to property that state law would protect from other creditors. This rule has been tested twice in the Supreme Court. In Drye v. United States, 528 U.S. 49 (1999), the question was whether the federal tax lien attached to a disclaimed inheritance. Three years later in United States v. Craft, 535 U.S. 274 (2002), the issue was whether the federal tax lien attached to jointly held real estate. This was a new issue at the time, and many were surprised at the result.

UNITED STATES v. CRAFT
535 U.S. 274 (2002)
Supreme Court of the United States

Justice O'CONNOR delivered the opinion of the Court.

This case raises the question whether a tenant by the entirety possesses "property" or "rights to property" to which a federal tax lien may attach. 26 U.S.C. § 6321. Relying on the state law fiction that a tenant by the entirety has no separate interest in entireties property, the United States Court of Appeals for the Sixth Circuit held that such property is exempt from the tax lien. We conclude that, despite the fiction, each tenant possesses individual rights in the estate sufficient to constitute "property" or "rights to property" for the purposes of the lien, and reverse the judgment of the Court of Appeals.

I

In 1988, the Internal Revenue Service (IRS) assessed $482,446 in unpaid income tax liabilities against Don Craft, the husband of respondent Sandra L. Craft, for failure to file federal income tax returns for the years 1979 through 1986. App. to Pet. for Cert. 45a, 72a. When he failed to pay, a federal tax lien attached to "all property and rights to property, whether real or personal, belonging to" him. 26 U.S.C. § 6321.

At the time the lien attached, respondent and her husband owned a piece of real property in Grand Rapids, Michigan, as tenants by the entirety. App. to Pet. for Cert. 45a. After notice of the lien was filed, they jointly executed a quitclaim deed purporting to transfer the husband's interest in the property to respondent for one dollar. *Ibid.* When respondent attempted to sell the property a few years later, a title search revealed the lien. The IRS agreed to release the lien and allow the sale with the stipulation that half of the net proceeds be held in escrow pending determination of the Government's interest in the property. *Ibid.*

Respondent brought this action to quiet title to the escrowed proceeds. The Government claimed that its lien had attached to the husband's interest in the tenancy by the entirety. It further asserted that the transfer of the property to respondent was invalid as a fraud on creditors. *Id.,* at 46a–47a. The District Court granted the Government's motion for summary judgment, holding that the federal tax lien attached at the moment of the transfer to respondent, which terminated the tenancy by the entirety and entitled the Government to one-half of the value of the property. No. 1:93-CV-306, 1994 WL 669680, *3 (W.D. Mich., Sept. 12, 1994).

Both parties appealed. The Sixth Circuit held that the tax lien did not attach to the property because under Michigan state law, the husband had no separate interest in property held as a tenant by the entirety. 140 F.3d 638, 643 (C.A.6 1998). It remanded to the District Court to consider the Government's alternative claim that the conveyance should be set aside as fraudulent. *Id.,* at 644.

On remand, the District Court concluded that where, as here, state law makes property exempt from the claims of creditors, no fraudulent conveyance can occur. 65 F.Supp.2d 651, 657–658 (W.D.Mich.1999). It found, however, that respondent's husband's use of nonexempt funds to pay the mortgage on the entireties property, which placed them beyond the reach of creditors, constituted a fraudulent act under state law, and the court awarded the IRS a share of the proceeds of the sale of the property equal to that amount. *Id.,* at 659.

Both parties appealed the District Court's decision, the Government again claiming that its lien attached to the husband's interest in the entireties property. The Court of Appeals held that the prior panel's opinion was law of the case on that issue. 233 F.3d 358, 363–369 (C.A.6 2000). It also affirmed the District Court's determination that the husband's mortgage payments were fraudulent. *Id.,* at 369–375.

We granted certiorari to consider the Government's claim that respondent's husband had a separate interest in the entireties property to which the federal tax lien attached. 533 U.S. 976, 122 S.Ct. 23, 150 L.Ed.2d 804 (2001).

II

Whether the interests of respondent's husband in the property he held as a tenant by the entirety constitutes "property and rights to property" for the purposes of the federal tax lien statute, 26 U.S.C. § 6321, is ultimately a question of federal law. The answer to this federal question, however, largely depends upon state law. The federal tax lien statute itself "creates no property rights but merely attaches consequences, federally defined, to rights created under state law." *United States v. Bess,* 357 U.S. 51, 55, 78 S.Ct. 1054, 2 L.Ed.2d 1135 (1958); see also *United States v. National Bank of Commerce,* 472 U.S. 713, 722, 105 S.Ct. 2919, 86 L.Ed.2d 565 (1985). Accordingly, "[w]e look initially to state law to determine what rights the taxpayer has in the property the Government seeks to reach, then to federal law to determine whether the taxpayer's state-delineated rights qualify as 'property' or 'rights to property' within the compass of the federal tax lien legislation." *Drye v. United States,* 528 U.S. 49, 58, 120 S.Ct. 474, 145 L.Ed.2d 466 (1999).

A common idiom describes property as a "bundle of sticks"—a collection of individual rights which, in certain combinations, constitute property. See B. Cardozo, Paradoxes of Legal Science 129 (1928) (reprint 2000); see also *Dickman v. Commissioner,* 465 U.S. 330, 336, 104 S.Ct. 1086, 79 L.Ed.2d 343 (1984). State law determines only which sticks are in a person's bundle. Whether those sticks qualify as "property" for purposes of the federal tax lien statute is a question of federal law.

In looking to state law, we must be careful to consider the substance of the rights state law provides, not merely the labels the State gives these rights or the conclusions it draws from them. Such state law labels are irrelevant to the federal question of which bundles of rights constitute property that may be attached by a federal tax lien. In *Drye v. United States, supra,* we considered a situation where state law allowed an heir subject to a federal tax lien to disclaim his interest in the estate. The state law also provided that such a disclaimer would "creat[e] the legal fiction" that the heir had predeceased the decedent and would correspondingly be deemed to have had no property interest in the estate. *Id.,* at 53, 120 S.Ct. 474. We unanimously held that this state law fiction did not control the federal question and looked instead to the realities of the heir's interest. We concluded that, despite the State's characterization, the heir possessed a "right to property" in the estate—the right to accept the inheritance or pass it along to another—to which the federal lien could attach. *Id.,* at 59–61, 120 S.Ct. 474.

III

We turn first to the question of what rights respondent's husband had in the entireties property by virtue of state law. In order to understand these rights, the tenancy by the entirety must first be placed in some context.

English common law provided three legal structures for the concurrent ownership of property that have survived into modern times: tenancy in common, joint tenancy, and tenancy by the entirety. 1 G. Thompson, Real Property § 4.06(g) (D. Thomas ed. 1994) (hereinafter Thompson). The tenancy in common is now the most common form of concurrent ownership. 7 R. Powell & P. Rohan, Real Property §51.01[3] (M. Wolf ed. 2001) (hereinafter Powell). The common law characterized tenants in common as each owning a separate fractional share in undivided property. *Id.,* § 50.01[1]. Tenants in common may each unilaterally alienate their shares through sale or gift or place encumbrances upon these shares. They also have the power to pass these shares to their heirs upon death. Tenants in common have many other rights in the property, including the right to use the property, to exclude third parties from it, and to receive a portion of any income produced from it. *Id.,* §§ 50.03-50.06.

Joint tenancies were the predominant form of concurrent ownership at common law, and still persist in some States today. 4 Thompson § 31.05. The common law characterized each joint tenant as possessing the entire estate, rather than a fractional share: "[J]oint-tenants have one and the same interest . . . held by one and the same undivided possession." 2 W. Blackstone, Commentaries on the Laws of England 180 (1766). Joint tenants possess many of the rights enjoyed by tenants in common: the right to use, to exclude, and to enjoy a share of the property's income. The main difference between a joint tenancy and a tenancy in common is that a joint tenant also has a right of automatic inheritance known as "survivorship." Upon the death of one joint tenant, that tenant's share in the property does not pass through will or the rules of intestate succession; rather, the remaining tenant or tenants automatically inherit it. *Id.,* at 183; 7 Powell § 51.01[3]. Joint tenants' right to alienate their individual shares is also somewhat different. In order for one tenant to alienate his or her individual interest in the tenancy, the estate must first be severed—that is, converted to a tenancy in common with each tenant possessing an equal fractional share. *Id.,* § 51.04[1]. Most States allowing joint tenancies facilitate alienation, however, by allowing severance to automatically accompany a conveyance of that interest or any other overt act indicating an intent to sever. *Ibid.*

A tenancy by the entirety is a unique sort of concurrent ownership that can only exist between married persons. 4 Thompson § 33.02. Because of the common-law fiction that the husband and wife were one person at law (that person, practically speaking, was the husband, see J. Cribbet et al., Cases and Materials on Property 329 (6th ed. 1990)), Blackstone did not characterize the tenancy by the entirety as a form of concurrent ownership at all. Instead, he thought that entireties property was a form of single ownership by the marital unity. Orth, Tenancy by the Entirety: The Strange Career of the Common-Law Marital Estate, 1997 B.Y.U.L. Rev. 35, 38–39. Neither spouse was considered to own any individual interest in the estate; rather, it belonged to the couple.

Like joint tenants, tenants by the entirety enjoy the right of survivorship. Also like a joint tenancy, unilateral alienation of a spouse's interest in entireties property is typically not possible without severance. Unlike joint tenancies, however, tenancies by the entirety cannot easily be severed unilaterally. 4 Thompson § 33.08(b). Typically, severance requires the consent of both spouses, *id.,* § 33.08(a), or the ending of the marriage in divorce, *id.,* § 33.08(d). At common law, all of the other rights associated with the entireties property belonged to the husband: as the head of the household, he could control the use of the property and the exclusion of others from it and enjoy all of the income produced from it. *Id.,* § 33.05. The husband's control of the property was so extensive that, despite the rules on alienation, the common law eventually provided that he could unilaterally alienate entireties property without severance subject only to the wife's survivorship interest. Orth, *supra,* at 40–41.

With the passage of the Married Women's Property Acts in the late 19th century granting women distinct rights with respect to marital property, most States either abolished the tenancy by the entirety or altered it significantly. 7 Powell § 52.01[2]. Michigan's version of the estate is typical of the modern tenancy by the entirety. Following Blackstone, Michigan characterizes its tenancy by the entirety as creating no individual rights whatsoever: "It is well settled under the law of this State that one tenant by the entirety has no interest separable from that of the other . . .. Each is vested with an entire title." *Long v. Earle*, 277 Mich. 505, 517, 269 N.W. 577, 581 (1936). And yet, in Michigan, each tenant by the entirety possesses the right of survivorship. Mich. Comp. Laws Ann. § 554.872(g) (West Supp. 1997), recodified at § 700.2901(2)(g) (West Supp. Pamphlet 2001). Each spouse—the wife as well as the husband—may also use the property, exclude third parties from it, and receive an equal share of the income produced by it. See § 557.71 (West 1988). Neither spouse may unilaterally alienate or encumber the property, *Long v. Earle, supra*, at 517, 269 N.W., at 581; *Rogers v. Rogers*, 136 Mich.App. 125, 134, 356 N.W.2d 288, 292 (1984), although this may be accomplished with mutual consent, *Eadus v. Hunter*, 249 Mich. 190, 228 N.W. 782 (1930). Divorce ends the tenancy by the entirety, generally giving each spouse an equal interest in the property as a tenant in common, unless the divorce decree specifies otherwise. Mich. Comp. Laws Ann. § 552.102 (West 1988).

In determining whether respondent's husband possessed "property" or "rights to property" within the meaning of 26 U.S.C. § 6321, we look to the individual rights created by these state law rules. According to Michigan law, respondent's husband had, among other rights, the following rights with respect to the entireties property: the right to use the property, the right to exclude third parties from it, the right to a share of income produced from it, the right of survivorship, the right to become a tenant in common with equal shares upon divorce, the right to sell the property with the respondent's consent and to receive half the proceeds from such a sale, the right to place an encumbrance on the property with the respondent's consent, and the right to block respondent from selling or encumbering the property unilaterally.

IV

We turn now to the federal question of whether the rights Michigan law granted to respondent's husband as a tenant by the entirety qualify as "property" or "rights to property" under § 6321. The statutory language authorizing the tax lien "is broad and reveals on its face that Congress meant to reach every interest in property that a taxpayer might have." *United States v. National Bank of Commerce*, 472 U.S., at 719–720, 105 S.Ct. 2919. "Stronger language could hardly have been selected to reveal a purpose to assure the collection of taxes." *Glass City Bank v. United States*, 326 U.S. 265, 267, 66 S.Ct. 108, 90 L.Ed. 56 (1945). We conclude that the husband's rights in the entireties property fall within this broad statutory language.

Michigan law grants a tenant by the entirety some of the most essential property rights: the right to use the property, to receive income produced by it, and to exclude others from it. See *Dolan v. City of Tigard*, 512 U.S. 374, 384, 114 S.Ct. 2309, 129 L.Ed.2d 304 (1994) ("[T]he right to exclude others" is " 'one of the most essential sticks in the bundle of rights that are commonly characterized as property' " (quoting *Kaiser Aetna v. United States*, 444 U.S. 164, 176, 100 S.Ct. 383, 62 L.Ed.2d 332 (1979))); *Loretto v. Teleprompter Manhattan*

CATV Corp., 458 U.S. 419, 435, 102 S.Ct. 3164, 73 L.Ed.2d 868 (1982) (including "use" as one of the "[p]roperty rights in a physical thing"). These rights alone may be sufficient to subject the husband's interest in the entireties property to the federal tax lien. They gave him a substantial degree of control over the entireties property, and, as we noted in *Drye*, "in determining whether a federal taxpayer's state-law rights constitute 'property' or 'rights to property,' [t]he important consideration is the breadth of the control the [taxpayer] could exercise over the property." 528 U.S., at 61, 120 S.Ct. 474 (some internal quotation marks omitted).

The husband's rights in the estate, however, went beyond use, exclusion, and income. He also possessed the right to alienate (or otherwise encumber) the property with the consent of respondent, his wife. *Loretto, supra,* at 435, 102 S.Ct. 3164 (the right to "dispose" of an item is a property right). It is true, as respondent notes, that he lacked the right to unilaterally alienate the property, a right that is often in the bundle of property rights. See also *post,* at 1429–1430 (THOMAS, J., dissenting). There is no reason to believe, however, that this one stick—the right of unilateral alienation—is essential to the category of "property."

This Court has already stated that federal tax liens may attach to property that cannot be unilaterally alienated. In United States v. Rodgers, 461 U.S. 677, 103 S.Ct. 2132, 76 L.Ed.2d 236 (1983), we considered the Federal Government's power to foreclose homestead property attached by a federal tax lien. Texas law provided that " 'the owner or claimant of the property claimed as homestead [may not], if married, sell or abandon the homestead without the consent of the other spouse.' " Id., at 684–685, 103 S.Ct. 2132 (quoting Tex. Const., Art. 16, § 50). We nonetheless stated that "[i]n the homestead context . . ., there is no doubt . . . that not only do both spouses (rather than neither) have an independent interest in the homestead property, but that a federal tax lien can at least attach to each of those interests." 461 U.S., at 703, n. 31, 103 S.Ct. 2132; cf. *Drye, supra,* at 60, n. 7, 120 S.Ct. 474 (noting that "an interest in a spendthrift trust has been held to constitute ' "property" for purposes of § 6321' even though the beneficiary may not transfer that interest to third parties").

Excluding property from a federal tax lien simply because the taxpayer does not have the power to unilaterally alienate it would, moreover, exempt a rather large amount of what is commonly thought of as property. It would exempt not only the type of property discussed in *Rodgers,* but also some community property. Community property States often provide that real community property cannot be alienated without the consent of both spouses. See, *e.g.,* Ariz. Rev. Stat. Ann. § 25–214(C) (2000); Cal. Fam. Code Ann. § 1102 (West 1994); Idaho Code § 32–912 (1996); La. Civ. Code Ann., Art. 2347 (West Supp. 2002); Nev. Rev. Stat. Ann. § 123.230(3) (Supp. 2001); N.M. Stat. Ann. § 40–3–13 (1999); Wash. Rev. Code § 26.16.030(3) (1994). Accordingly, the fact that respondent's husband could not unilaterally alienate the property does not preclude him from possessing "property and rights to property" for the purposes of § 6321.

Respondent's husband also possessed the right of survivorship—the right to automatically inherit the whole of the estate should his wife predecease him.

Respondent argues that this interest was merely an expectancy, which we suggested in *Drye* would not constitute "property" for the purposes of a federal tax lien. 528 U.S., at 60, n. 7, 120 S.Ct. 474 ("[We do not mean to suggest] that an expectancy that has pecuniary value . . . would fall within § 6321 prior to the time it ripens into a present estate"). *Drye* did not decide this question, however, nor do we need to do so here. As we have discussed above, a number of the sticks in respondent's husband's bundle were presently existing. It is therefore not necessary to decide whether the right to survivorship alone would qualify as "property" or "rights to property" under § 6321.

That the rights of respondent's husband in the entireties property constitute "property" or "rights to property" "belonging to" him is further underscored by the fact that, if the conclusion were otherwise, the entireties property would belong to no one for the purposes of § 6321. Respondent had no more interest in the property than her husband; if neither of them had a property interest in the entireties property, who did? This result not only seems absurd, but would also allow spouses to shield their property from federal taxation by classifying it as entireties property, facilitating abuse of the federal tax system. Johnson, After *Drye:* The Likely Attachment of the Federal Tax Lien to Tenancy-by-the-Entireties Interests, 75 Ind. L. J. 1163, 1171 (2000).

Justice SCALIA's and Justice THOMAS' dissents claim that the conclusion that the husband possessed an interest in the entireties property to which the federal tax lien could attach is in conflict with the rules for tax liens relating to partnership property. See *post,* at 1426 (opinion of SCALIA, J.); see also *post,* at 1429, n. 4. This is not so. As the authorities cited by Justice THOMAS reflect, the federal tax lien does attach to an individual partner's interest in the partnership, that is, to the fair market value of his or her share in the partnership assets. *Ibid.* (citing B. Bittker & M. McMahon, Federal Income Taxation of Individuals ¶ 44.5[4][a] (2d ed. 1995 and 2000 Cum. Supp.)); see also 1 A. Bromberg & L. Ribstein, Partnership § 3.05(d) (2002-1 Supp.) (hereinafter Bromberg & Ribstein) citing Uniform Partnership Act § 28, 6 U.L.A. 744 (1995). As a holder of this lien, the Federal Government is entitled to "receive . . . the profits to which the assigning partner would otherwise be entitled," including predissolution distributions and the proceeds from dissolution. Uniform Partnership Act § 27(1), *id.,* at 736.

There is, however, a difference between the treatment of entireties property and partnership assets. The Federal Government may not compel the sale of partnership assets (although it may foreclose on the partner's interest, 1 Bromberg & Ribstein § 3.05(d)(3)(iv)). It is this difference that is reflected in Justice SCALIA's assertion that partnership property cannot be encumbered by an individual partner's debts. See *post,* at 1426. This disparity in treatment between the two forms of ownership, however, arises from our decision in *United States v. Rodgers, supra* (holding that the Government may foreclose on property even where the co-owners lack the right of unilateral alienation), and not our holding today. In this case, it is instead the dissenters' theory that departs from partnership law, as it would hold that the Federal Government's lien does not attach to the husband's interest in the entireties property at all, whereas the lien may attach to an individual's interest in partnership property.

Respondent argues that, whether or not we would conclude that respondent's husband had an interest in the entireties property, legislative history indicates that Congress did not intend that a federal tax lien should attach to such an interest. In 1954, the Senate rejected a proposed amendment to the tax lien statute that would have provided that the lien attach to "property or rights to property (including the interest of such person as tenant by the entirety)." S. Rep. No. 1622, 83d Cong., 2d Sess., 575 (1954). We have elsewhere held, however, that failed legislative proposals are "a particularly dangerous ground on which to rest an interpretation of a prior statute," *Pension Benefit Guaranty Corporation v. LTV Corp.*, 496 U.S. 633, 650, 110 S.Ct. 2668, 110 L.Ed.2d 579 (1990), reasoning that " '[c]ongressional inaction lacks persuasive significance because several equally tenable inferences may be drawn from such inaction, including the inference that the existing legislation already incorporated the offered change'." *Central Bank of Denver, N.A. v. First Interstate Bank of Denver, N.A.*, 511 U.S. 164, 187, 114 S.Ct. 1439, 128 L.Ed.2d 119 (1994). This case exemplifies the risk of relying on such legislative history. As we noted in *United States v. Rodgers*, 461 U.S., at 704, n. 31, 103 S.Ct. 2132, some legislative history surrounding the 1954 amendment indicates that the House intended the amendment to be nothing more than a "clarification" of existing law, and that the Senate rejected the amendment only because it found it "superfluous." See H. R. Rep. No. 1337, 83d Cong., 2d Sess., A406 (1954) (noting that the amendment would "clarif[y] the term 'property and rights to property' by expressly including therein the interest of the delinquent taxpayer in an estate by the entirety"); S. Rep. No. 1622, at 575 ("It is not clear what change in existing law would be made by the parenthetical phrase. The deletion of the phrase is intended to continue the existing law").

The same ambiguity that plagues the legislative history accompanies the common-law background of Congress' enactment of the tax lien statute. Respondent argues that Congress could not have intended the passage of the federal tax lien statute to alter the generally accepted rule that liens could not attach to entireties property. See *Astoria Fed. Sav. & Loan Assn. v. Solimino*, 501 U.S. 104, 108, 111 S.Ct. 2166, 115 L.Ed.2d 96 (1991) ("[W]here a common-law principle is well established . . . the courts may take it as given that Congress has legislated with an expectation that the principle will apply except 'when a statutory purpose to the contrary is evident' "). The common-law rule was not so well established with respect to the application of a federal tax lien that we must assume that Congress considered the impact of its enactment on the question now before us. There was not much of a common-law background on the question of the application of federal tax liens, as the first court of appeals cases dealing with the application of such a lien did not arise until the 1950's. *United States v. Hutcherson*, 188 F.2d 326 (C.A.8 1951); *Raffaele v. Granger*, 196 F.2d 620 (C.A.3 1952). This background is not sufficient to overcome the broad statutory language Congress did enact, authorizing the lien to attach to "all property and rights to property" a taxpayer might have.

We therefore conclude that respondent's husband's interest in the entireties property constituted "property" or "rights to property" for the purposes of the federal tax lien statute. We recognize that Michigan makes a different choice with respect to state law creditors: "[L]and held by husband and wife as tenants by entirety is not subject to levy under execution on judgment rendered against either husband or wife alone." *Sanford v. Bertrau*, 204 Mich. 244, 247, 169 N.W. 880, 881 (1918). But that by no means dictates our choice. The interpretation of 26 U.S.C. § 6321 is a federal question, and in answering that question we are in no way bound by state courts' answers to similar questions involving state law. As we elsewhere have held, " 'exempt status under state law does not bind the federal collector.' " *Drye v. United States,* 528 U.S., at 59, 120 S.Ct. 474. See also *Rodgers, supra,* at 701, 103 S.Ct. 2132 (clarifying that the Supremacy Clause "provides the underpinning for the Federal Government's right to sweep aside state-created exemptions").

V

We express no view as to the proper valuation of respondent's husband's interest in the entireties property, leaving this for the Sixth Circuit to determine on remand. We note, however, that insofar as the amount is dependent upon whether the 1989 conveyance was fraudulent, see *post*, at 1426, n. 1 (THOMAS, J., dissenting), this case is somewhat anomalous. The Sixth Circuit affirmed the District Court's judgment that this conveyance was not fraudulent, and the Government has not sought certiorari review of that determination. Since the District Court's judgment was based on the notion that, because the federal tax lien could not attach to the property, transferring it could not constitute an attempt to evade the Government creditor, 65 F.Supp.2d, at 657–659, in future cases, the fraudulent conveyance question will no doubt be answered differently.

The judgment of the United States Court of Appeals for the Sixth Circuit is accordingly reversed, and the case is remanded for proceedings consistent with this opinion.

It is so ordered.

[Dissenting opinions omitted.]

NOTES AND QUESTIONS

1. How are state property laws relevant in a tax case in light of *Craft*?
2. May taxpayers defeat tax collection merely by characterizing their property rights a certain way?
3. The Supreme Court has also held that a taxpayer may not avoid tax collection by disclaiming an inheritance. *See* Drye v. United States, 528 U.S. 49 (1999).

The federal tax lien encumbers all property and rights to property of the taxpayer without the government recording the lien in the state and local recording offices. *See* section 6321. This means that other creditors and credit reporting agencies receive no notice that the government has a lien on the property. Because these stakeholders receive no notice, a federal tax lien is sometimes referred to as a "secret lien." Even without notice, the lien gives the government priority over unsecured creditors. However, the federal tax lien does not give the government priority over subsequent purchasers, mechanics lienors, or judgment creditors. *See* section 6323(a) ("The lien imposed by section 6321 shall not be valid as against any purchaser, holder of a security interest, mechanic's lienor, or judgment lien creditor . . . ."). To take priority over these creditors, the IRS must file an NFTL.

3. Notice of Federal Tax Lien

Although the IRS may enforce the federal tax lien by levy without notifying any creditors beforehand, the IRS will not have priority over certain creditors without filing an NFTL. To obtain priority over subsequent purchasers, mechanics lienors, or judgment creditors, the IRS must file an NFTL in the relevant state and local recording offices. *See* sections 6321(a) and 6323(a), (f). The act of filing the NFTL announces to the public—including other creditors and credit reporting agencies—that the IRS has a lien on the taxpayer's property. The post-Notice lien still does not take priority over certain third parties' interests who had no knowledge of the NFTL. Section 6323(b) provides the following:

> Even though notice of a lien imposed by section 6321 has been filed, such lien shall not be valid . . . [w]ith respect to [the purchaser unaware of the NFTL] of a security, . . . a motor vehicle, . . . property purchased at retail, . . . household goods . . . in a casual sale, . . . tangible personal property subject to a [repair] lien . . . . This provision also cedes priority to state tax liens, certain types of mechanic liens, and attorney liens.

The IRS may defer the filing of the NFTL where filing it would impair the taxpayer's ability to pay the tax. The IRS's Internal Revenue Manual states:

> A decision may be made to defer the filing of an NFTL when the revenue officer can substantiate with reasonable certainty and supported with documentation from the taxpayer, that filing the NFTL will hamper collection. (emphasis omitted).

I.R.M. 5.12.2.3(3) (January 1, 2015). Filing the NFTL may make it difficult for the taxpayer to get a loan to pay the debt because the NFTL becomes a public record. Revenue officers often wait to file the NFTL until they have given a taxpayer the opportunity to work out a plan to pay.

A taxpayer who believes the IRS filed an erroneous NFTL has a vested interest in filing an administrative appeal because the NFTL has serious consequences. Section 6326 provides such an appeal as follows:

> [A]ny person shall be allowed to appeal to the Secretary after the filing of a notice of a lien under this subchapter on the property or the rights to property of such person for a release of such lien alleging an error in the filing of the notice of such lien.

In such an appeal, the taxpayer may not challenge a deficiency determination. *See* Treas. Reg. § 301.6326-1(a) (2015). If the taxpayer prevails, the IRS will release the lien. This kind of appeal is especially helpful where the IRS filed an NFTL for the wrong taxpayer.

Withdrawal of an IRS lien is better for a taxpayer than the mere release of an IRS lien. In a lien withdrawal, the IRS will alert the credit reporting agencies of the withdrawal and treat the lien as though it never happened. *See* section 6323(j)(1). In other words, the lien is removed from the taxpayer's credit report. In contrast, a tax lien release—which occurs automatically 30 days after the debt is paid—does not remove the prior existence of the lien from the taxpayer's credit history.

4. Levy

If the bill, notice and demand for payment, lien, notice of lien, and phone calls from the IRS fail to motivate the taxpayer to act, the IRS may institute a levy action. Section 6331(a) authorizes the levy as follows:

> If any person . . . neglects or refuses to pay [a tax owed] within 10 days after notice and demand, it shall be lawful for the Secretary to collect such tax . . . by levy upon all property and rights to property . . . belonging to such person or on which there is a lien provided in this chapter for the payment of such tax.

In a levy action, the IRS may seize the taxpayer's property and rights to property as well as property encumbered by the federal tax lien. Once the IRS has possession of the property, the IRS may sell it to cover the taxpayer's unpaid liabilities.

Nonetheless, the IRS must execute various steps before instituting the levy. First, the IRS must wait for ten days after it sends the taxpayer a notice and demand for payment. Second, the IRS must wait for 30 days after it has issued a notice of intent to levy. *See* section 6331(d)(2). The notice of intent to levy must describe the statutory and administrative procedures relating to levy and sale alternatives that might be available to prevent the levy. *See* section 6331(d)(4). Third, the IRS must inform the taxpayer of the right to a pre-levy hearing. *See* IRC § 6330(a)(1).

Two of the most common items the IRS levies are bank accounts and wages. A taxpayer who has ignored or not received the notice and demand, the notice of lien, and the notice of intent to levy might not be aware of a tax liability until the IRS levies on the taxpayer's bank account or wages. The IRS levies on these assets by serving a notice of levy. The IRS's regulations require banks to hold onto deposits subject to levy for a certain amount of time to give the taxpayer an opportunity to seek a release. *See* Treas. Reg. § 301.6331-1(a)(1).

The IRS is authorized to levy nonexempt property that exists at the time it issues the notice of levy. *See* IRC § 6331(b). Many life necessities are exempt from the IRS's levy authority. These exemptions protect a taxpayer from, among other things, being stripped of clothing and crucial household items, means to carry on a business, and the ability to support family members. *See* IRC § 6334(a). As shown by the following case, tax laws restrain the IRS from levying on the assets of a taxpayer who is suffering a serious hardship.

VINATIERI v. COMMISSIONER
133 T.C. 392 (2009)
United States Tax Court

DAWSON, Judge.

This matter is before the Court on respondent's motion for summary judgment filed pursuant to Rule 121.[8] Petitioner timely filed a petition pursuant to section 6330(d) appealing respondent's determination to proceed with collection by levy of petitioner's 2002 income tax liability. The issue to be decided is whether respondent's determination was an abuse of discretion.

BACKGROUND

Petitioner resided in Tennessee when she filed the petition. Her residence is an apartment that she rents for $600 per month.

On September 13, 2007, respondent sent petitioner a Final Notice of Intent to Levy and Notice of Your Right to a Hearing (levy notice). The underlying tax liability was attributable to unpaid self-assessed tax reported on her 2002 return. Petitioner timely requested a hearing on September 24, 2007, and the hearing was conducted through correspondence and by telephone with the settlement officer.

Petitioner first learned of the collection activity when her employer notified her about the proposed levy on her wages. When the settlement officer asked petitioner whether she wanted to enter into an installment agreement, petitioner said "she has nothing."[9] Petitioner told the settlement officer that she has pulmonary fibrosis and is dying. Because of her health she can only find part-time employment.

The settlement officer could not find a record that petitioner had filed a return for 2005. Petitioner explained to the settlement officer that the payroll company responsible for completing her 2005 Form W–2, Wage and Tax Statement, was no longer in business. She had attempted to get the tax information from the Internal Revenue Service (IRS), but the IRS had no information regarding her income for 2005.

The settlement officer told petitioner that she might be able to have her account placed in currently not collectible status. The settlement officer asked petitioner to submit a Form 433–A, Collection Information Statement for Wage

---

[8] [fn 1] All Rule references are to the Tax Court Rules of Practice and Procedure, and all section references are to the Internal Revenue Code

[9] [fn 2] Petitioner explained to the settlement officer that she had previously agreed to pay in installments and that she was told she would be sent envelopes for each payment, but she never received the envelopes or monthly bills.

Earners and Self–Employed Individuals, and a diagnosis regarding her current health condition.

Petitioner sent a completed Form 433–A, indicating she had monthly income of $800 and expenses of $800, had $14 cash on hand, and owned a 1996 Toyota Corolla four-door sedan with 243,000 miles and a value of $300. The Form 433–A reported that petitioner did not own any other assets. Verification received by the settlement officer was consistent with the information petitioner provided in the Form 433–A. Petitioner was unable to obtain a written diagnosis of her medical condition from her physician because her physician would provide a diagnosis only in a claim for worker's compensation.

The settlement officer's log entry dated May 15, 2008, states:

> TP [petitioner] meets the criteria to have account placed in CNC [currently not collectible] status per IRM 5.16.[1.] 2.9 Hardship. The balance due is less than 10K and the TP has stated she has a terminal illness. CIS verification is not required. The TP has stated she has nothing and is not able to full pay or make payments. However, the TP is not in compliance. The TP has not filed a 2005 return and there is no record of the 2007 tax return being filed. The TP stated she does not have income information for 2005 and company that did payroll is no longer in business. TP stated she contacted IRS and they advised her they have no income information. There is no information per IRTRL. S/O [the settlement officer] contacted TP regarding filing of the 2007 return. The TP stated the return was filed late. The S/O requested the TP fax a copy of the return with the W–2. TP to fax information by 5–19–08. S/O asked TP if she obtained health diagnosis and the TP stated the doctor would only give her something if she is applying for diability. S/O requested income information for 2005 per IRPTRE.

The settlement officer's log entry dated May 20, 2008, states:

> TP did not provide a copy of 2007 return and there is no record that the return has been filed per IDRS research. The TP was employed in 2007 and is currently employed. The 2005 return has not been filed. Since the TP is not in compliance, collection alternative cannot be considered. S/O will issue determination letter. If the 2005 income information is received, the S/O will forward it to the TP.

Respondent issued petitioner a Notice of Determination Concerning Collection Action(s) Under Section 6320 and/or 6330 (notice of determination) dated June 2, 2008, sustaining the proposed levy action and stating that, because petitioner was not in compliance with filing the required tax returns, a collection alternative could not be considered. The notice of determination was reviewed and signed by the Appeals team manager. The attachment to the notice of determination stated:

> The settlement officer inquired about a collection alternative and you stated you could not make payments. You stated you had pulmonary fibrosis and can only work part-time hours due to your heath condition. The Settlement

officer [who] advised you of the collection alternative however explained a collection alternative could not be considered because you were not in compliance with filing required tax returns. * * *

The attachment explained the balancing of efficient tax collection with concern regarding intrusiveness as follows:

Appeals has verified, or received verification, that applicable laws and administrative procedures have been met; has considered the issues raised; and has balanced the proposed collection with the legitimate concern that such action be no more intrusive than necessary by IRC Section 6330(c)(3).

Collection alternatives include full payment, installment agreement, offer in compromise and currently-not-collectible. However, since unfiled tax returns exist, the only alternative at present is to take enforced action by levying your assets. It is Appeals decision that the proposed levy action is appropriate. The proposed levy action balances the need for the efficient collection of the taxes with the legitimate concern that any collection action be no more intrusive than necessary.

Neither the notice of determination nor the attachment reflect any consideration of the fact that the levy would create an economic hardship as stated by the settlement officer in her daily log and supported by the Form 433–A petitioner submitted.

Petitioner timely filed a petition in this Court challenging respondent's determination. Respondent filed the motion for summary judgment, and the Court ordered petitioner to file a response.[10] Petitioner filed a response to respondent's motion for summary judgment but did not file a cross-motion for summary judgment.[11] In her response petitioner describes her situation as follows:

To Whom It May Concern,

---

[10] [fn 3] In the order we observed that our preliminary review of the record indicated that the proposed levy action involved a hardship situation and that petitioner needed the assistance of an attorney. We urged petitioner to contact the legal aid society or the local bar association pro bono services and provided their addresses and phone numbers.

[11] [fn 4] After petitioner filed her response to respondent's motion for summary judgment, respondent filed a motion to continue the case wherein respondent stated that petitioner was in the process of submitting a collection alternative to the IRS and that, if the alternative is accepted by the IRS, a trial in this case would not be necessary. The Court granted respondent's motion and directed the parties to file a status report on or before July 27, 2009. In a status report filed on July 17, 2009, respondent reported that respondent has not received any communication from petitioner and requested the Court to grant respondent's motion for summary judgment.

I don't know what you want to know cause I don't understand all the legal stuff you sent me. I can't afford a lawyer. And the closest legal aid is in Knoxville 30 miles away. My poor car will not go that far. So I will start at the beginning of my story and see if you can help me.

I was in an unhealthy relationship for many years. During a great deal of that time my husband was doing alcohol and drugs. I had 2 children plus his 3 to take care of. I had been doing janitorial work at a strip mall * * *. It was the only place that I could work that I could take my [then] 3 year old daughter with me. I could not support my family and pay day care. * * * My husband took care of bills and such cause he demanded that I turn over my money. We even got a divorce during that time cause I was not obeying him. * * *

Now I am not looking for sympathy just understanding. Do you know how hard it is to be a single parent? * * * I have a high school education and nothing else.

It was nearly five years before I was notified of a problem by the I.R.S. Danny [petitioner's former spouse] was suppose to be doing taxes. He even made me sign a form that because he made more money he could claim my kids on his taxes cause we were no longer legally married.

I got all the W–2's from the I.R.S. except 2005 that they still have not sent me. That is why they are not done. I did all those taxes and forfeited the refunds. I do not remember what that total came to. But it was enough to pay I would say most of back taxes. The 2007 taxes were late and I don't know why they didn't arrive. I sent a second copy in as soon as my son gave me my copy. He had my copy for college financial aid and he lost them for a bit of time.

I am not a rich person. I work in a job so I can be home with my daughter. I left my husband in July after he threatened to beat my daughter with a baseball bat. Beating me is one thing but I could not have him beating my girl. So I am a single parent again. Right now we have not had much work in nearly a year. I have rent of 600 a mo. Utilities of 150 and get food stamps or I wouldn't eat. I make about 700–800 [per] month. There are no better jobs in our town. My daughter is only 11 so its not like I can leave her alone at night or on weekends. D.H.S. says it's not even legal. She is too young. There is no child care and I have no family here. I have pulmonary fibrosis that makes me sick all the time and the diagnosis says I have about 10 yrs to live. Right now I can work thank God.

I did my taxes this year [for 2008] and you are getting a little over $4,700. I'm not asking for much just a break. You can have my tax returns [refunds?] I don't care. Well I do that is a tremendous loss but oh well. I don't have any money to send you on a monthly basis. Can we stop all the penalties. They are killing me. I will never be able to pay it off. * * * I let a relationship screw me up. I am truly sorry for that and am begging for a lifeline here. You can come to my home and see for yourself. I don't have fancy t.v.'s or even cable except for internet. I can't afford a phone. My clothes have holes in them. I even cut my own hair. If I could pay this off faster I would just to stop the nightmares it gives me.

DISCUSSION

A. Summary Judgment

Summary judgment is used to expedite litigation and avoid unnecessary and expensive trials. The Court will render a decision on a motion for summary judgment if the pleadings, answers to interrogatories, depositions, admissions, and other acceptable materials, together with the affidavits, if any, show that there is no genuine issue as to any material fact and that a decision may be rendered as a matter of law. Rule 121(b). Because the effect of granting a motion for summary judgment is to decide the case against a party without allowing that party an opportunity for a trial, the Court should grant the motion only after a careful consideration of the case. *Associated Press v. United States,* 326 U.S. 1, 6, 65 S.Ct. 1416, 89 L.Ed. 2013 (1945); *Kroh v. Commissioner,* 98 T.C. 383, 390, 1992 WL 64746 (1992).

For purposes of respondent's motion for summary judgment, respondent has the burden of showing the absence of a genuine issue as to any material fact. Petitioner is afforded the benefit of all reasonable doubt, and the material submitted by both sides is viewed in the light most favorable to petitioner. See, e.g., *Adickes v. S.H. Kress & Co.,* 398 U.S. 144, 157, 90 S.Ct. 1598, 26 L.Ed.2d 142 (1970); *Kroh v. Commissioner, supra* at 390.

Respondent moves the Court for summary judgment on the ground that the settlement officer did not abuse her discretion in rejecting collection alternatives and determining to proceed with levy because petitioner was not in compliance with the filing requirements. Petitioner asks that the levy not be sustained because, if her wages are taken, she will be unable to pay her basic living expenses; and, if her car is taken, she will not be able to work.

B. Collection of Federal Taxes by Levy

If a taxpayer liable for Federal taxes fails to pay the taxes within 10 days after notice and demand, section 6331 authorizes the Secretary to collect the tax by levy upon all property and rights to property (except any property that is exempt under section 6334) belonging to the taxpayer or on which there is a lien for the payment of the tax.

Section 6343(a)(1) provides that, under regulations prescribed by the Secretary, if the Secretary has determined that the levy is creating an economic hardship due to the financial condition of the taxpayer, the Secretary must release a levy upon all, or part of, a taxpayer's property or rights to property.[12] Sec.

---

[12] [fn 5] The regulations provide a method whereby a taxpayer may inform the Secretary that a levy is creating an economic hardship and request that the levy be released. See sec. 301.6343–1(c), Proced. & Admin. Regs. "A taxpayer

6343(a)(1)(D). The regulations provide that a levy is creating an economic hardship due to the financial condition of an individual taxpayer and must be released "if satisfaction of the levy in whole or in part will cause an individual taxpayer to be unable to pay his or her reasonable basic living expenses." Sec. 301.6343–1(b)(4), Proced. & Admin. Regs.

A taxpayer alleging that collection of the liability would create undue hardship must submit complete and current financial data to enable the Commissioner to evaluate the taxpayer's qualification for collection alternatives or other relief. *Picchiottino v. Commissioner,* T.C. Memo.2004–231. The regulations provide that, for purposes of determining the taxpayer's reasonable amount of living expenses, any information that is provided by the taxpayer is to be considered, including the following:

(A) The taxpayer's age, employment status and history, ability to earn, number of dependents, and status as a dependent of someone else;

(B) The amount reasonably necessary for food, clothing, housing * * *, medical expenses * * *, transportation, current tax payments * * *, alimony, child support, or other court-ordered payments, and expenses necessary to the taxpayer's production of income * * *;

(C) The cost of living in the geographic area in which the taxpayer resides;

(D) The amount of property exempt from levy which is available to pay the taxpayer's expenses;

(E) Any extraordinary circumstances such as special education expenses, a medical catastrophe, or natural disaster; and

(F) Any other factor that the taxpayer claims bears on economic hardship and brings to the attention of the director.

Sec. 301.6343–1(b)(4)(ii), Proced. & Admin. Regs.

C. Section 6330 Procedures

Section 6330(a) provides the general rule that no levy may be made on any property or right to property of any taxpayer unless the Secretary has provided 30 days' notice to the taxpayer of the right to an administrative hearing before the levy is carried out. If the taxpayer makes a timely request for an administrative hearing, the hearing is conducted by the IRS Office of Appeals (Appeals Office) before an impartial officer. Sec. 6330(b)(1), (3).

---

who wishes to obtain a release of a levy must submit a request for release in writing or by telephone to the district director for the Internal Revenue district in which the levy was made." *Id.* However, service center directors and compliance center directors (to whom requests by taxpayers are not made) who have determined that a levy is creating an economic hardship must also release the levy and promptly notify the taxpayer of the release pursuant to sec. 301.6343–1(a), Proced. & Admin. Regs.

The taxpayer may raise any relevant issue during the hearing, including appropriate spousal defenses and challenges to "the appropriateness of collection actions", and may make "offers of collection alternatives, which may include the posting of a bond, the substitution of other assets, an installment agreement, or an offer-in-compromise." Sec. 6330(c)(2)(A). The taxpayer also may raise challenges to the existence or amount of the underlying tax liability if he/she did not receive a notice of deficiency for that liability or did not otherwise have an opportunity to dispute it. Sec. 6330(c)(2)(B).

During the hearing the Appeals officer must verify that the requirements of applicable law and administrative procedure have been met, consider issues properly raised by the taxpayer, and consider whether any proposed collection action balances the need for the efficient collection of taxes with the taxpayer's legitimate concern that any collection action be no more intrusive than necessary. Sec. 6330(c)(3). The Appeals Office then issues a notice of determination indicating whether the proposed levy may proceed.

Under section 6330(d)(1) the taxpayer may petition this Court to review the determination made by the Appeals Office. See sec. 301.6330–1(f)(1), Proced. & Admin. Regs. Where, as in this case, the underlying tax liability is not at issue, we review the Appeals Office's determinations regarding the collection action for abuse of discretion. *Goza v. Commissioner,* 114 T.C. 176, 2000 WL 283864 (2000). An abuse of discretion occurs if the Appeals Office exercises its discretion "arbitrarily, capriciously, or without sound basis in fact or law." *Woodral v. Commissioner,* 112 T.C. 19, 23, 1999 WL 9947 (1999).

When a taxpayer establishes in a pre-levy collection hearing under section 6330 that the proposed levy would create an economic hardship, it is unreasonable for the settlement officer to determine to proceed with the levy which section 6343(a)(1)(D) would require the IRS to immediately release. Rather than proceed with the levy, the settlement officer should consider alternatives to the levy.

Respondent argues under the holdings of Rodriguez v. Commissioner, T.C. Memo.2003–153, and McCorkle v. Commissioner, T.C. Memo.2003–34, that there is no abuse of discretion if a settlement officer rejects collection alternatives because the taxpayer was not in compliance with the filing requirements for all required tax returns.[13]

Generally, we have found the Commissioner's policy requiring individuals seeking collection alternatives to be current with filing their returns to be

---

[13] [fn 6] Generally, the IRS will not grant an installment agreement, accept an offer-in-compromise, or report an account as currently not collectible if any tax return for which the taxpayer has a filing requirement has not been filed. See Internal Revenue Manual pts. 5.14.1.4.1(4)-(6) (Sept. 26, 2008) (installment agreements); 5.8.3.13(1), (2), (4) (Sept. 23, 2008) (offers-in-compromise); 5.16.1.1(5) and (6), 5.16.1.2.9(8) (May 5, 2009) (currently not collectible), 5.1.11.2.3 (June 2, 2004) (general collection procedures).

reasonable.[14] However, taxpayers in those cases have had sufficient income to meet basic living expenses. See, e.g., *Speltz v. Commissioner,* 124 T.C. 165, 178, 2005 WL 668404 (2005) (taxpayers claimed hardship because the tax liability was disproportionate to the value that they received from initial stock offerings and because they had already been forced to change their lifestyle), affd. 454 F.3d 782 (8th Cir.2006); *Peterson v. Commissioner,* T.C. Memo.2009–46 (the Court upheld rejection of taxpayers' offer of $20,000 to compromise $70,000 liability where, although they had minimal income from Social Security retirement and disability payments, they had reasonable collection potential of $68,000 from two parcels of real property valued at $80,000); *Fangonilo v. Commissioner,* T.C. Memo.2008–75 (Commissioner's refusal to treat taxpayer's tax liability as currently not collectible was not an abuse of discretion where although taxpayer's income was not sufficient to meet his stated monthly living expenses, he had a liquid asset worth more than his tax liability); *Willis v. Commissioner,* T.C. Memo.2003–302 (taxpayers' ability to make some payments toward their cumulative liability made them ineligible to have the cumulative liability classified as currently not collectible); *Rodriguez v. Commissioner,* T.C. Memo.2003–153 (taxpayer had not filed returns for 12 years and did not submit all of the financial information supporting her offer-in-compromise that the settlement officer requested); *Ashley v. Commissioner,* T.C. Memo.2002–286 (taxpayer had income in excess of expenses and sufficient equity in his real property to pay his tax liability in full).

We have found no cases addressing the requirement that the taxpayer be current with filing returns in a levy case involving economic hardship under section 6343(a)(1)(D) and section 301.6343–1(b)(4), Proced. & Admin. Regs. Neither section 6343 nor the regulations condition a release of a levy that is creating an economic hardship on the taxpayer's compliance with filing and payment requirements. The purpose of section 6330 is to "afford taxpayers adequate notice of collection activity and a meaningful hearing *before* the IRS deprives them of their property." S. Rept. 105–174, at 67 (1998), 1998–3 C.B. 537, 603 (emphasis added). A determination in a hardship case to proceed with a levy that must immediately be released is unreasonable and undermines public confidence that tax laws are being administered fairly. In a section 6330 pre-levy hearing, if the taxpayer has provided information that establishes the proposed levy will create an economic hardship, the settlement officer cannot go forward with the levy and must consider an alternative.

---

[14] [fn 7] In Estate of Atkinson v. Commissioner, T.C. Memo.2007–89, we found reasonable requirements that an entity seeking collection alternatives to full payment, including reporting an account as currently not collectible, filing any outstanding tax returns and submitting a full financial statement and verification information for analysis. Mandatory release of levy creating an economic hardship applies only to individuals. Sec. 301.6343–1(b)(4), Proced. & Admin. Regs.

D. Appeals Office's Determination to Proceed with Levy of Petitioner's Assets

The financial information petitioner submitted on the Form 433–A, which was consistent with other information the settlement officer obtained, showed that if petitioner's wages are levied on, she will be unable to pay her basic living expenses; and, if her car is levied on, she will not be able to work. After analyzing petitioner's financial information, the settlement officer concluded that the levy would create an economic hardship and so stated in her log. However, the settlement officer determined collection alternatives to the levy, including an installment agreement, an offer-in-compromise, and reporting the account as currently not collectible, were not available because petitioner had not filed her 2005 and 2007 returns. The settlement officer's determination to proceed with the levy was reviewed and approved by the Appeals team manager who signed the notice of determination. Although the attachment to the notice of determination shows that the Appeals team manager was aware of petitioner's financial situation and health problems, the Appeals team manager signed the notice of determination to proceed with the levy because petitioner had not filed her 2005 and 2007 returns. Proceeding with the levy would be unreasonable because section 6343 would require its immediate release, and the determination to do so was arbitrary. The determination to proceed with the levy was wrong as a matter of law and, therefore, was an abuse of discretion. Respondent is not entitled to summary judgment, and respondent's motion will be denied.

An order denying respondent's motion will be issued.

NOTES AND QUESTIONS

1. The IRS has acted with more compassion since this case.
2. What could Ms. Vinatieri done to interact better with the IRS?

After instituting a proper levy, the IRS may take the levied property from the taxpayer in possession of it. *See* Section 6331(b). The IRS can also take the taxpayer's property or property subject to the federal tax lien held by a third party. Section 6331(a) provides as follows:

> If any person . . . neglects or refuses to pay [a tax owed] within 10 days after notice and demand, it shall be lawful for the Secretary to collect such tax . . . by levy upon all property and rights to property . . . belonging to such person or on which there is a lien provided in this chapter for the payment of such tax.

The Code imposes steep penalties and personal liability for the value of the property for failing to surrender levied property on demand. *See* IRC § 6332(d).

5. Sale of Levied Property

When all else has failed, the IRS may sell levied property to satisfy the taxpayer's tax liability. Before selling a taxpayer's property, the IRS must issue a notice of sale. Section 6331(b) provides as follows:

> The term "levy" as used in this title includes the power of distraint and seizure by any means. . . . In any case in which the Secretary may levy upon property or rights to property, he may seize and sell such property or rights to property . . . .

The IRS must also investigate the facts and circumstances surrounding the taxpayer's account and the value of the property. *See* section 6335(e). The sale must take place no sooner than ten days after the notice and no later than 40 days. *See* section 6335(d). If the proceeds exceed the liability and costs, the excess is returned to the taxpayer or another party who can prove he owns an interest in the property. *See* IRC § 6342(b). Once real estate is sold, the taxpayer still has 180 days to redeem the property. *See* IRC § 6337(b)(1).

The Code provides taxpayers an opportunity to be heard at certain points in the collection process. When the taxpayer receives a notification letter—the taxpayer is entitled to at least one for the lien and another for the levy—the IRS includes information on the right to a CDP hearing. The CDP hearing provides, among other things, the opportunity for the taxpayer to negotiate settlement options of the debt or enter into a payment plan.

C. Judicial Collection

As an alternative to the IRS's "awesome administrative collection authority," the IRS may proceed with judicial collection. An alternative to administrative collection may become necessary where there is a defect in the IRS's administrative lien. If the administrative lien is defective, the IRS has no authority to levy the property to which the lien failed to attach. In a case where the lien is defective, the underlying tax assessment may still be valid. With the underlying assessment in place, the IRS may sue in court like any other creditor because the lien is tantamount to a court judgment. The following case began as an administrative collection proceeding but turned into judicial collection proceeding.

AMERICAN TRUST v. UNITED STATES
142 F.3d 920 (6th Cir. 1998)
United States Court of Appeals, Sixth Circuit

KENNEDY, Circuit Judge.

Defendant Edgar F. Bradley, II, appeals the District Court's order granting summary judgment in favor of the United States in these consolidated breach of contract and interpleader actions. In its complaint in the interpleader action, the

United States sought enforcement of tax liens against insurance sales commissions attributable to defendant. The District Court held that the Government had valid tax liens under 26 U.S.C. § 6321 and that these liens gave the United States the first priority claim to the commissions. On appeal, defendant contends he is entitled to the exemptions allowed taxpayers during administrative levy proceedings under 26 U.S.C. § 6331. For the following reasons, we affirm the District Court.

I. FACTS

The facts underlying this case are undisputed. Between 1988 and 1992 Bradley, an agent authorized to sell insurance policies for American Community Mutual Insurance Company (hereinafter, "American Community"), entered into agreements with three other American Community insurance agents. Under these agreements, the three other agents assigned to Bradley their rights to the commissions that resulted from their sales of American Community policies. On December 4, 1992, Bradley assigned the rights to all of the commissions, including his own, to a trust identified as "American AMB 06044 Irrevocable Trust" (the "Trust"). From this date, American Community paid all monthly commissions directly to the Trust.[15]

On August 9, 1993, the Internal Revenue Service ("IRS") issued assessments against Bradley for deficiencies in income tax for his 1987, 1988, and 1989 taxable years. In October of 1993, the IRS, claiming a lien for tax deficiencies, penalties, and statutory additions totaling $85,617.55, issued a Notice of Levy to American Community. Through this notice, the IRS asked American Community to pay over to the IRS all property or rights to property belonging to Bradley. American Community responded by stating that it had no funds in its possession payable to Bradley, and that all commissions had been assigned to the Trust. In April of 1994, the IRS issued a second Notice of Levy to American Community, claiming a lien for taxes and statutory additions owed by Bradley in the amount of $90,406.74. American Community continued to pay Bradley's commissions, as well as the commissions assigned to him by the other agents, to the Trust, until June of 1994, when the IRS issued a Final Demand to American Community for payment of all "property, rights to property, money, credits, and bank deposits . . . to the credit of, belonging to, or owned by [Bradley]" and in American Community's possession or owed to Bradley as of the first Notice of Levy.

The final payment to the Trust represented commissions earned through March 31, 1994. Upon receiving this Final Demand, American Community withheld payment of additional commissions to the Trust. The insurance agents and representatives of the Trust told American Community that the liens asserted by the IRS were invalid. Rather than comply with the Final Demand to pay the commissions to the IRS, American Community withheld the commissions from both claimants, and eventually deposited them, along with interest earned thereon,

---

[15] [fn 1] The District Court found that the Trust, which named the four agents as its beneficiaries, was created to evade income taxation.

in the registry of the Clerk of the Court of Common Pleas in Hamilton County, Ohio.

This case embodies two separate actions that were filed in the Court of Common Pleas in Hamilton County, Ohio. First, the Trust brought a breach of contract claim against American Community, asserting that American Community had a contractual obligation to pay the commissions to the Trust. Second, American Community filed an action in interpleader to determine ownership of accumulated commissions. The defendants named in the second action included the Trust, the IRS, Bradley, and the other agents. The Court of Common Pleas consolidated the cases, and the United States removed the consolidated case to the United States District Court for the Southern District of Ohio. The funds in question were transferred to the registry of the Clerk of the District Court.

In the District Court, American Community moved for summary judgment on the breach of contract claim, and the United States moved for summary judgment in the interpleader action, asserting that, by virtue of its tax lien, the United States had a superior claim to the funds in dispute. On March 11, 1997, the District Court granted summary judgment in favor of American Community on the contract claim and the United States on the interpleader action.

II. DISCUSSION

We review de novo the District Court's grant of summary judgment in favor of the Government. E.g., Roush v. Weastec, Inc., 96 F.3d 840, 843 (6th Cir.1996). The facts underlying this case are undisputed and Bradley's appeal raises a single question of law: whether an exemption from levy that is listed in Internal Revenue Code ("I.R.C.") § 6334, 26 U.S.C. § 6334, applies when the IRS seeks enforcement of a tax lien in an interpleader action.

To answer this question we look to the relationship of several sections of the Internal Revenue Code. Section 6321 of the I.R.C. provides that the amount of unpaid taxes, interest, and penalties that any person neglects or refuses to pay "shall be a lien in favor of the United States upon all property and rights to property, whether real or personal, belonging to such person." 26 U.S.C. § 6321. The Supreme Court has stated that "[t]he statutory language 'all property and rights to property,' appearing in § 6321 . . . is broad and reveals on its face that Congress meant to reach every interest in property that a taxpayer might have." *United States v. National Bank of Commerce,* 472 U.S. 713, 719-20, 105 S.Ct. 2919, 2923-24, 86 L.Ed.2d 565 (1985). This tax lien arises at the time the unpaid taxes are assessed and persists until the liability for the amount assessed is satisfied. 26 U.S.C. § 6322.

The Government has several separate procedures through which it can recover the tax deficiency. As the Supreme Court explained in *United States v. Rodgers,* 461 U.S. 677, 682, 103 S.Ct. 2132, 2136-37, 76 L.Ed.2d 236 (1983), the Government is authorized under 26 U.S.C. § 7403 to file a lien-foreclosure suit in a district court of the United States to enforce the tax lien. In other cases, the Government may decide simply to sue for the amount of unpaid taxes, "and, on getting a judgment, exercise the usual rights of a judgment creditor." 461 U.S. at 682, 103 S.Ct. at 2136-37 (citing 26 U.S.C. §§ 6502(a), 7401, 7402(a)). Section 6331 of the I.R.C., 26 U.S.C. § 6331, provides an additional, administrative avenue for recovery:

> If any person liable to pay any tax neglects or refuses to pay same within 10 days after notice and demand, it shall be lawful for the Secretary to collect such tax (and such further sum as shall be sufficient to cover the expenses of the levy) by levy upon all property and rights to property (except such property as is exempt under section 6334) belonging to such person or on which there is a lien provided in this chapter for the payment of such tax.

26 U.S.C. § 6331(a). As the Court explained, "[t]he common purpose of this formidable arsenal of collection tools is to ensure the prompt and certain enforcement of the tax laws in a system relying primarily on self-reporting." 461 U.S. at 683, 103 S.Ct. at 2137.

The "[a]dministrative levy, unlike an ordinary lawsuit, and unlike the procedure described in § 7403, does not require any judicial intervention, and it is up to the taxpayer, if he so chooses, to go to court if he claims that the assessed amount was not legally owing." *Rodgers,* 461 U.S. at 682-83, 103 S.Ct. at 2136-37. Third parties who may have been aggrieved by an administrative levy against a recalcitrant taxpayer also must wait until a post-seizure proceeding to assert their rights to disputed property. *See National Bank of Commerce,* 472 U.S. at 731, 105 S.Ct. at 2930. "In contrast to the lien-foreclosure suit, the levy does not determine whether the Government's rights to the seized property are superior to those of other claimants; it, however, does protect the government against diversion or loss while such claims are being resolved." *Id.* at 721, 105 S.Ct. at 2924-25. In sum, § 6331 provides the Government with a mechanism to secure expeditiously property that might satisfy tax deficiencies and postpones the resolution of property rights until after the seizure. *See id.*

Although the Code authorizes the IRS to execute an administrative levy without prior judicial approval, it also provides some protection to the taxpayer. Internal Revenue Code § 6334, 26 U.S.C. § 6334, exempts specific types of property from attachment by levy. Most relevant to the instant case, § 6334(a)(9) provides that the following income is exempt from levy:

> Any amount payable to or received by an individual as wages or salary for personal services, or as income derived from other sources, during any period, to the extent that the total of such amounts payable to or received by him during such period does not exceed the amount determined under subsection (d).

This exemption prevents the IRS from seizing all of a taxpayer's paycheck through a purely administrative proceeding, and allows the taxpayer to retain from his wages or salary an amount that is determined in relation to the sum of the standard personal income tax deduction and the taxpayer's aggregate number of personal income tax exemptions. *See* 26 U.S.C. § 6334(d).

In the instant case, the IRS first selected the administrative levy from its arsenal of collection tools and demanded that American Community pay over any of Bradley's property or rights to property that it had in its possession. Instead of complying, American Community filed an interpleader action to resolve the competing claims to the withheld commissions. After removing the interpleader to the District Court, the Government successfully filed a claim for enforcement of its tax lien against the accumulated commissions. Bradley now contends that the judgment in favor of the United States should have been reduced by the amount of money that, pursuant to § 6334(a)(9), he would have been entitled to claim as exempt from the original levy. In response, the United States argues that the judicial enforcement of a lien is independent of and distinct from an administrative levy, and that a valid tax lien may attach property that is exempted from levy.

We have yet to decide whether the Government may enforce a tax lien created by 26 U.S.C. § 6321 against property that § 6334 would exempt from levy.[16] The United States Courts of Appeals that have considered the relationship between administrative levies and tax liens have recognized that a tax lien under § 6321 can attach to property that would be exempt from a § 6331 administrative levy. In *United States v. Barbier,* 896 F.2d 377 (9th Cir.1990), the Ninth Circuit considered an appeal from a bankruptcy proceeding in which debtor-taxpayers argued that § 6334 prohibited the attachment of a federal tax lien on property that was exempt from an administrative levy. The court rejected the taxpayers' argument, holding that "for the purposes of the Barbiers' Chapter 13 plan, the IRS's claim against the Barbiers for their income tax deficiencies, including interest and penalties, may be secured by a lien on property exempt under section 6334(a)." 896 F.2d at 378. It reasoned that restricting the scope of a tax lien's reach would be inconsistent with both Supreme Court precedent and the statutory purpose of promoting tax collection. *Id.* at 378-79 (citing *National Bank of Commerce,* 472 U.S. at 720-21, 105 S.Ct. at 2924-25). It also reasoned that "[t]he IRS's levying power is limited because a levy is an immediate seizure not requiring judicial intervention." *Id.* at 379. The court, however, confined its opinion to the determination of the scope of a tax lien in a bankruptcy proceeding, stating in a footnote that they "need not consider here whether exempt assets are

---

[16] [fn 2] In Woods v. Simpson, 46 F.3d 21 (6th Cir.1995), we considered a case with the same procedural history as the instant case: the IRS sought to enforce a tax lien against interpleaded funds that the taxpayer inherited, and the taxpayer's former wife argued that her child support claims were exempted under § 6334(a)(8) from the federal tax lien. In considering their claims, we explicitly declined to reach the question before us today: "Given our conclusion that 26 U.S.C. § 6334(a)(8) does not exempt an inheritance from levy, we need not decide whether 26 U.S.C. § 6334 also operates to exempt certain property from a 26 U.S.C. § 6321 federal lien for taxes." 46 F.3d at 24. Thus, despite his assertions to the contrary, Woods does not provide any support for Bradley's argument that exemptions under § 6334 should provide him some protection from federal tax liens.

subject to judicial foreclosure and express no view on that question." *Id.* at 380 n. 3.

The Seventh Circuit has also considered, in a case arising out of bankruptcy, whether a tax lien can reach property exempt from levy. *See In re Voelker,* 42 F.3d 1050 (7th Cir.1994). Relying heavily on the Ninth Circuit's analysis in *Barbier,* the Seventh Circuit held that "[t]he language of the statute unambiguously shows that the federal tax lien attaches to all of a debtor's property, without exception. Thus, we agree with the district court, and the majority of the other courts addressing the issue, that the lien attached to Voelker's [exempt personal property]." 42 F.3d at 1051.

Finally, the Fifth Circuit has considered this issue, again in the context of a bankruptcy proceedings, in Sills v. United States (In re Sills), 82 F.3d 111 (5th Cir.1996). In *Sills,* the taxpayers purchased a house with workers' compensation proceeds. In the bankruptcy proceeding, they sought to insulate that house from a tax lien, arguing that property purchased with workers' compensation benefits is exempt from levy under 26 U.S.C. § 6334(a)(7). The Fifth Circuit rejected their arguments and held that tax liens may reach property exempt from levy. Although the court did not decide if the taxpayers' house actually qualified under § 6334(a)(7), it reasoned as follows:

> Even if the Sills' house were exempt from levy, the tax lien still may be valid and enforceable. For example, the IRS may enforce the lien by foreclosure action under I.R.C. § 7403; it may seek to have its lien satisfied in proceeding brought by third parties, in which the IRS is brought pursuant to 28 U.S.C. § 2410; or it may exercise redemption rights provided by I.R.C. § 7425(d) if another party forecloses on the property.

82 F.3d at 114. This reasoning emphasizes the myriad of mechanisms that the IRS can employ to collect taxes through the enforcement of tax liens that reach property that would be exempt from attachment by levy.

Bradley relies heavily on Don King Productions, Inc. v. Thomas, 749 F.Supp. 79 (S.D.N.Y.1990), rev'd in part, 945 F.2d 529 (2d Cir.1991), a case in which the court reached the opposite conclusion. There, the District Court held, in an interpleader action, that "a lien cannot attach to child support monies that are exempt from levy." 749 F.Supp. at 84. The court based its decision purely on policy grounds, reasoning that "exemption allows the delinquent taxpayer to fulfil his court ordered obligation to support his children." Id.

Although Bradley acknowledges that exemptions under § 6334 would not apply if the United States had sought enforcement of its tax lien by instituting judicial proceedings under § 7403, he argues that this case is different because the United States was responding to an interpleader action that resulted from its levies. He asserts that it is unfair to allow third parties to negate taxpayers' claims to exemptions from levy under § 6334 whenever third parties refuse to surrender property that is the object of an IRS levy and then bring an interpleader action to determine the priority of rights to that property. Appellant's argument can be distilled to the claim that once the IRS files a levy, the taxpayer is entitled to claim exemptions under § 6334, unless it is the IRS that initiates the action for judgment on its lien under § 7304.

Bradley's argument conflicts with the statutory scheme of the Internal Revenue Code, which has created a "number of distinct enforcement tools available to the United States for the collection of delinquent taxes." *Rodgers,* 461 U.S. at 682, 103 S.Ct. at 2136-37. An administrative levy, one such tool, is a "provisional remedy," without judicial intervention, in which the Government seeks to secure quickly and inexpensively property to satisfy a tax deficiency. *See National Bank of Commerce,* 472 U.S. at 720-21, 105 S.Ct. at 2924-25. Although administrative recovery may be relatively quick and inexpensive, the IRS's powers to levy are limited by the exceptions in 26 U.S.C. § 6334. These exemptions make sense in an administrative proceeding, where no court has found that taxes are even due. Enforcement of a tax lien is another distinct mechanism for tax collection. Such a proceeding has different characteristics: it requires judicial intervention, but the lien created by 26 U.S.C. § 6321 "is broad and reveals on its face that Congress meant to reach every interest in property that a taxpayer might have." *National Bank of Commerce,* 472 U.S. at 719-20, 105 S.Ct. at 2923-24. The statute exempts certain property from a levy but not from a lien, and we decline to alter this allocation.

Bradley's argument also relies heavily on the order in which the Government uses its distinct enforcement tools. In this case, although the Government first sought to recover tax deficiencies by administrative levy, the interpleader action changed the nature of the proceedings. The parties were then in court, and the remedy the United States sought was no longer "provisional" in nature. Bradley fails to explain why it should make a difference whether the United States seeks to enforce a tax lien in a proceeding that it initiated or whether it seeks enforcement of the lien in an action that was initiated by another party. The scope of the lien remains the same in either instance. If we were to adopt Bradley's arguments, we would create the odd situation where a tax lien created under § 6321 would reach all of Bradley's commissions if the Government had immediately sought enforcement by filing suit under § 7403, but the same lien would be subject to certain exemptions if the Government sought judicial enforcement of the lien after the quicker and less expensive levy procedure had failed and led to an interpleader. To do so would not only re-write the broad language of § 6321, it would also lessen the incentive of taxpayers to comply with an administrative levy. This would conflict with "the policy inherent in the tax statutes in favor of the prompt and certain collection of delinquent taxes." *Id.* at 694, 103 S.Ct. at 2142-43.

III. CONCLUSION

For the foregoing reasons we affirm the District Court's order granting summary judgment in favor of the United States.

NOTES AND QUESTIONS

1. What did the court mean when it described the IRS's administrative collection authority as "awesome"?

2. Why were wages not exempted from levy under section 6334(a)(9)?

CHAPTER 6

TAXPAYER COLLECTION OPTIONS

Previous chapters have discussed criminal liability, penalties, and enforced collection—negative consequences the government imposes on noncompliant taxpayers. One of the noncompliant omissions a taxpayer can make is the failure to pay tax. The failure to pay tax is one among many acts that draws criminal sanctions and civil penalties. If the government seeks criminal sanctions against a taxpayer for failing to pay tax, the taxpayer must either plead guilty to the omission or defend himself in court much like any other crime. If the government proposes a civil penalty for failing to pay tax, the taxpayer may negotiate the penalty during the collection process or pay the penalty and pursue a refund action.

In responding to the IRS's collection efforts, a taxpayer has a broad array of options. As discussed in the previous chapter, once the IRS begins collecting, the IRS contacts the the taxpayer on many occasions to provide the opportunity to pay or settle the tax liability. The taxpayer's options depend on the taxpayer's resources. In general, taxpayers fall into one of four categories with respect to taxpayer resources to pay or settle with the government. First, some taxpayers in collection have sufficient resources to pay the entire amount owed immediately. Second, some taxpayers have the resources to pay the entire amount owed as long as the IRS permits payment over time. Third, some taxpayers have the resources to pay only part of the liability, but insufficient resources to ever pay the full amount owed. Fourth, some taxpayers have insufficient resources to pay any of the amount owed due to hardship.

A. Payment and Settlement Mechanisms

Each of the above taxpayers has negotiation options. The Code and the IRS's guidance refer to these options as "collection alternatives." A taxpayer who can pay his tax liability all at once should do so. If the taxpayer has paid or the IRS has collected the payment in full, the collection actions will stop. Next, a taxpayer with steady income but scarce liquid resources, *i.e.*, someone who cannot pay right away, can enter into an installment agreement with the IRS. A taxpayer who cannot pay an entire liability without undue hardship can enter into an "offer in compromise," or "OIC." *See* IRC § 7122(a) ("The Secretary may compromise any civil . . . case arising under the internal revenue laws . . . ."). Finally, a taxpayer with little or no income as well as a lack of other resources, *i.e.*, someone who cannot pay the IRS anything at all and may already be suffering hardship, can request that the IRS remove the account from its collection inventory and reclassify the liability as "currently not collectible," or "CNC." Taxpayers have other options as well—Taxpayer Assistance Orders, audit reconsideration, or bankruptcy.

1. Installment Agreements

A taxpayer that does not have a sufficient amount of money on hand to pay a tax debt, but can pay soon or over time may enter into an installment agreement. Section 6159(a) provides as follows:

> The Secretary is authorized to enter into written agreements with any taxpayer under which such taxpayer is allowed to make payment on any tax in installment payments if the Secretary determines that such agreement will facilitate full or partial collection of such liability.

The Code authorizes the IRS to enter into installment agreements. Thus, generally the IRS has discretion, but is not required, to accept an installment agreement proposal. In some cases, however, the Code requires the IRS to accept proposals that meet certain statutory requirements. *See* IRC § 6159(c).

The IRS refers to installment agreement proposals it is required to accept as "Guaranteed Installment Agreements." Section 5.14.5.2 (May 23, 2014) of the IRS's Internal Revenue Manual provides as follows:

> Guaranteed Installment Agreements—Internal Revenue Code (IRC) section 6159(c) requires the Service to accept proposals of installment agreements under certain circumstances.

A proposal is "guaranteed" acceptance if the individual owes less than $10,000 (excluding penalties and interest), demonstrates to the IRS the inability to pay at the time, has remained in compliance for the last five years, agrees to pay within three years, and agrees to remain in compliance while the payment plan is in effect. *See* IRC § 6159.

The IRS has automated or "streamlined" its discretion in some cases. The IRS's policies for streamlined installment agreements provide for acceptance of a proposal where the taxpayer's liability is $50,000 or less (including unpaid penalties and interest) and the taxpayer agrees to complete payments in six years. I.R.M. 5.14.5.2. (May 23, 2014). A streamlined installment agreement proposal requires no management approval and no financial statements for acceptance.

For proposals involving a liability over $50,000, the IRS exercises its discretion on the basis of the taxpayer's circumstances. The IRS ascertains the taxpayer's circumstances from the financial statements the taxpayer must include with the proposal. The IRS carefully considers the taxpayer's financial statements when deciding whether to accept a proposal.

Although the IRS lacks authority to reject proposals that qualify as guaranteed or streamlined, the IRS has the discretion to reject any installment agreement proposal that does not qualify. A taxpayer may file for an administrative appeal of the proposal rejection within 30 days of notice. *See* Treas. Reg. § 301.6159-1(d)(3). The Appeals Office considers the appeal, and the taxpayer may further appeal that decision to the Tax Court. *See* IRC § 6330(b) & (d).

The IRS has had procedures for considering and enforcing installment agreements for a long time. Prior to 1998, the IRS was not always fair in how it went about enforcing these installment plans. The following case both illustrates how important installment agreements are to the IRS and provides some history of the 1998 IRS Restructuring and Reform Act. As a result of cases like this and the lack of any review procedures during the collection process at the time, taxpayers in collection are now entitled to a hearing with the IRS appealable to the United States Tax Court.

ROSENBLOOM v. COMMISSIONER
T.C. Memo. 2011-140
United States Tax Court

HOLMES, Judge:

In the summer of 1997 an IRS agent visited the office of a down-on-his-luck Chicago lawyer named Mark Rosenbloom. Rosenbloom knew he owed back taxes—he had signed installment agreements with the IRS in 1988 and 1993. But his severe personal problems had caused him to delay sending in updated financial information and to miss a couple months' payments. The agent squeezed hard, threatening to shut down Rosenbloom's office and put him out of business unless he consented to waive the statute of limitations until 2009 for overdue taxes dating back to 1981. A month later, the agent returned to try to seize Rosenbloom's office furniture, and a few weeks after that tried to seal the elevator to Rosenbloom's office.

In 1998 Congress put an end to such aggressive collection tactics.[1] The Commissioner announced that he would no longer rely on long-term waivers of the statute of limitations obtained (some might say coerced) while an installment agreement was in effect. He also promised to cancel any such waivers that he had already obtained and refund or credit any payments that he had received. The

---

[1] [fn 2] See the Internal Revenue Service Restructuring and Reform Act of 1998 (RRA 1998), Pub.L. 105–206, secs. 3401–68, 112 Stat. 746–770.

question in this case is whether Rosenbloom had an installment agreement in place when he signed that waiver of the statute of limitations back in 1997. Rosenbloom and the Commissioner agree that the IRS had sent him a notice of default before getting the waiver. The Commissioner argues that this means there was no longer a valid installment agreement. Rosenbloom argues that the notice of default wasn't by itself enough to terminate his installment agreement. Both parties agree that if an installment agreement was in effect when the Commissioner persuaded Rosenbloom to sign the waiver, the Commissioner may no longer collect.

FINDINGS OF FACT

Rosenbloom practiced law in Chicago for more than two decades and recognizes now that he was an alcoholic for most of that time, especially after 1980 when his stepson died from a long and painful illness. He nevertheless managed for a while to make a good living from his practice, where he did a little of everything from real-estate closings to criminal defense to tax. By the late '90s he had even become a bit of a rainmaker, but as his drinking grew worse he started to rely more heavily on several of his employees to do most of the work. Leaning on them, he was able to try, and partly win, a case in our Court as late as 1996.

Throughout much of this time, Rosenbloom was haunted by tax trouble. Many, many years ago, he had incurred an enormous tax debt—$1,748,248.37 in unpaid income tax, interest, and penalties from 1977–87 plus two quarters of trust-fund-recovery penalties[2] from 1984 which he has never been able to pay.[3] Rosenbloom signed two installment agreements to deal with this problem: the first in 1988, which covered tax debts from 1977–79 and 1982–84; and the second in 1993 which increased his monthly payment and added his debts for tax

---

[2] [fn 3] Taxes that employers withhold from their employees' wages are known as "trust fund taxes" because they are held by the employer essentially in trust for the United States under section 7501(a). *Slodov v. United States,* 436 U.S. 238, 243, 98 S.Ct. 1778, 56 L.Ed.2d 251 (1978). The Commissioner may collect unpaid employment taxes from a "responsible person" within the company; i.e., someone who was required to pay over the tax. The money that's assessed and collected this way is called trust-fund-recovery penalties. Sec. 6672. (Unless otherwise indicated, references to sections in this opinion are to the Internal Revenue Code, and all references to Rules are to the Tax Court's Rules of Practice and Procedure.)

[3] [fn 4] Rosenbloom testified that he vastly overreported his income some years—because "he was in a fog" before he became sober. Far too much time has passed to challenge any of these liabilities, of course, but this part of his story does seem to be borne out. Account transcripts for some of the years show exceptionally high adjusted gross income nearly equal to taxable income, an unusual result for high-income taxpayers who typically have personal deductions and exemptions in excess of those Rosenbloom seems to have claimed.

years 1980–81 and 1985–87. It's the second agreement that concerns us here: It called on him to pay $406 per month to shave down his debt. One of the important terms of these agreements was Rosenbloom's promise to provide updated financial information whenever the IRS asked for it. Rosenbloom knew he had a good deal. And the IRS's agreement to accept payments so small relative to the total tax debt would get even better for him over time, as the statute of limitations for collecting each year's debt expired.[4] Rosenbloom nevertheless acquiesced when an agent visited him in 1996 and got him to extend until the end of 2006 the statute of limitations for tax years 1977–79 and 1982–83. No one disputes that the installment agreement covered these years and was in effect when Rosenbloom signed this waiver. The Commissioner long ago revoked this waiver and stopped trying to collect these taxes.

This case focuses on 1997. It was a terrible time for Rosenbloom: Drinking led to his divorce that year, and he credibly testified that a brief reconciliation with his wife ended when his tax troubles erupted with the appearance in his life of Revenue Officer H. (as we'll call him, since he was not present at trial) in July. But the trend had been downhill for some time: He was losing clients, referrals were drying up, and he had been hit by several malpractice cases. To add to his woes, he received a Letter 1064(DO) (or "Defaulted Installment Agreement—Notice of Intent to Levy") dated May 5. The letter threatened to cancel the installment agreement if he didn't provide updated financial information within 30 days. Rosenbloom panicked, misconstrued the letter more as a notice that his giant tax debt was crashing back on him than a warning that it might if he didn't update his financial information, and stopped making his installment payments.

About a week after Rosenbloom got the letter, he was referred to an attorney, Alan Segal. Segal called Revenue Officer H. and asked for a very brief extension to get him the updated financial information. Segal said he needed more time because he had three trials on our Court's trial calendar in Chicago for the week that the information was due.[5] Review Officer H. extended the deadline to

---

[4] [fn 5] Where the assessment of Federal income tax is made within the prescribed time under the Code (i.e., section 6501), the IRS in general has ten years to collect the assessed tax by levy. Sec. 6502. See also sec. 6503 (tolling of the statute of limitations under secs. 6501 and 6502); *Jordan v. Commissioner,* 134 T.C. 1, 7 n. 5, 2010 WL 92479 (2010) (discussing the 1990 change to the statute of limitations under sec. 6502). The government, however, cannot levy on property for a debt covered by an installment agreement that is still in effect. E.g., sec. 301.6159–1(d), Proceed. & Admin. Regs., 59 Fed.Reg. 66192, 66193 (as in effect Dec. 23, 1994); sec. 6331(k). Because the statute of limitations continues to run while a taxpayer is making payments under the agreement, once the time for levying has run out for a particular year, he is off the hook for that year's tax liability.

[5] [fn 6] We found Segal to be an entirely credible witness, but checked our records on this minor point and found they corroborated his testimony. See *Drnovsek v. Commissioner,* docket No. 14712–96 (hearing held June 2, 1997;

provide the updated financial information,[6] and it was sent to him on June 19, 1997. Segal's June 19 letter obliquely refers to the oral agreement to extend the 30–day deadline: "[e]nclosed *as promised,* are the [financial information forms]." (Emphasis added.) Segal also credibly testified that he always followed up on his promises to revenue officers to comply with deadlines,[7] because "when you're dealing with a Revenue Officer, the only thing you have primarily is your credibility." It's worth noting that other than objecting to Segal's testimony, the Commissioner provided no evidence, not even a cross-examination of Segal, to show that H. did not extend the 30–day deadline. Having found Segal credible, we find that H. did extend the deadline for Rosenbloom to provide updated financial information.

Rosenbloom by then had missed a couple of his $406 monthly payments. Officer H. did not send another letter, but instead showed up at Rosenbloom's office on July 29, 1997. By this time H. had Segal's name on file as being Rosenbloom's attorney and so should have contacted Segal instead. See sec. 601.506(b), Statement of Procedural Rules.[8] Rosenbloom, though inebriated at the time, still had enough wit to ask to speak to his lawyer. H., however, told him that the IRS would "close him down" and "put him out of business" if he didn't

---

stipulated decision entered July 9, 1997); *Karnatz v. Commissioner,* docket Nos. 15296–96 and 23667–96 (set for trial June 2, 1997; stipulated decision entered June 18, 1997); *Weiner v. Commissioner,* docket No. 15229–96 (set for trial June 2, 1997; stipulated decision entered June 18, 1997).

[6] [fn 7] The Commissioner objected to Segal's testimony (on which we largely base this finding) as hearsay. On reflection, we regard it as evidence of a verbal act, or proof of an act of independent legal significance—here the agreement between H. and Segal to extend the 30–day period to provide updated financial information. See 2 McCormick on Evidence, sec. 249 (6th ed.2000 & supp.2009); *United States v. Montana,* 199 F.3d 947, 950 (7th Cir.1999) (treating "performative utterances", illustrated by promise, offer, or demand, as nonhearsay because they do not make any truth claims); *United States v. Feldman,* 825 F.2d 124 (7th Cir.1987) (testimony of investors as to statements by salesmen admissible to show existence of fraudulent scheme).

[7] [fn 8] The Commissioner often extends nonstatutory deadlines, so there is nothing extraordinary about Segal's explanation. See, e.g., Dinino v. Commissioner, T.C. Memo.2009–284 (policy of Office of Appeals to consider financial information submitted past the deadline, and up until a notice of determination is issued); Judge v. Commissioner, T.C. Memo.2009–135 (settlement officer abused his discretion in denying taxpayer a brief extension to correct his financial information); Mills v. Commissioner, T.C. Memo.2004–164 (revenue officer grants deadline extension to submit financial information for an offer in compromise).

[8] [fn 9] In the RRA 1998 Congress added section 6304 to the Code, prohibiting the IRS from communicating directly with a taxpayer known to be represented by an attorney. See Pub.L. 105–206, sec. 3566(a), 112 stat. 768.

extend the statute. Rosenbloom called Segal. We believe Segal's testimony that Rosenbloom's words were slurred. We also believe Segal when he said that he told Rosenbloom to just sign the waiver that H. presented. This second waiver—giving the IRS until January 2, 2009, to collect Rosenbloom's 1981, and 1985–87 tax debts—is the waiver on which this case turns.[9]

Rosenbloom's signature on the waiver form isn't the end of this part of the story. Sometime in August 1997, Rosenbloom again called Segal in a panic because H. had again visited his office, this time to try to seize the furniture. (He also levied on Rosenbloom's bank account that month.) Segal took Rosenbloom to meet with H. in late August or early September to try to work things out. They gave him a check for the four missed installment payments and one for September (which wasn't yet due). Rosenbloom resumed his payments for October, November, and December of 1997. Segal also sent in a check for $3,412.50—150 percent of the supposed forced-sale value of the office furniture (which he noted was generous given the state of the furniture) to forestall a levy that would have shut down what was left of Rosenbloom's practice.

H. nevertheless continued to seek a writ of entry to seize the furniture. And on the morning of September 30, 1997, Rosenbloom got a call from his office building's landlord telling him that someone from the IRS was trying to get permission to seal off his elevator. Believing that H. seemed more interested in retribution than collection (the office furniture he was trying to seize had already been preredeemed), Segal filed an application for Taxpayer Assistance (on the appropriately named Form 911) with the IRS Problem Resolution Office in Chicago.

This form requires a description of the hardship that will occur if the Office doesn't intervene. Segal described Rosenbloom's history of alcoholism, his recent breakdown and entry into an eight-week outpatient program, and even his trichotillomania (a compulsive disorder whose victims pull out their hair). Segal appealed to the Commissioner's reason: Rosenbloom had already more than made up the missed payments, as well as tendered a check for more than the forced-sale value of the office furniture. Rosenbloom was trying to recover from alcoholism, Segal wrote, and trying simultaneously to settle several malpractice suits. If the Commissioner "closed him down," the debt would likely become completely uncollectible. The IRS Problem Resolution Office intervened and stopped the seizure.

But Rosenbloom was getting worse. In November 1997 he was hospitalized at the Mayo Clinic, which recommended that he detox at the Hazelden Addiction Treatment Center. Segal oversaw Rosenbloom's purchase of money orders for

[9] [fn 10] As a result of RRA 1998, sec. 3461(a), 112 Stat. 764, waivers executed after 1999 are invalid if not agreed to at the time the installment agreement is entered into. See sec. 6502. But because Rosenbloom's waiver was given in 1997, that limitation does not apply. See *Joy v. Commissioner*, T.C. Memo.2008–197.

the November and December installment payments, but then things completely fell apart. Rosenbloom ended up checking into more than six rehabilitation centers in the next few years. While in treatment, Rosenbloom abandoned his law practice and stopped making installment payments. The Commissioner moved the tax debts into currently-not-collectible status.

Cases like Rosenbloom's led to the Internal Revenue Service Restructuring and Reform Act of 1998 (RRA 1998), Pub.L. 105–206, 112 Stat. 685, which created the system of pre-levy hearing and judicial review that we have today. But by then many abusive IRS policies and procedures had come to light. The Commissioner had learned about a particularly bad one: If there was an installment agreement in which the tax liability would not be paid off before the expiration of the statute of limitations, some IRS Service Centers would terminate or default the installment agreement (or threaten to do so) if the taxpayer didn't agree to extend the statute.[10]

This was a problem—no Code section, regulation, or Internal Revenue Manual (IRM) provision allows the IRS to terminate an installment agreement (and then presumably proceed with a levy) solely because the taxpayer refused to extend the collection statute. See generally sec. 6159. Therefore the IRS was exposed to potential civil liability, as well as negative press. See sec. 7433; Service Center Advice 1998–003 (Feb. 17, 1998) (discussing the problem). Statute-of-limitations waivers that the IRS procured this way were also possibly invalid as a product of duress, or otherwise unenforceable on equitable grounds.[11]

It came as no surprise, then, when on June 5, 1998, the IRS publicly apologized and said that it had implemented a recovery program to provide relief to taxpayers who were harmed by the improper terminations of installment agreements or improper requests for a waiver of the statute of limitations. See IRS News Release IR–98–44 (June 5, 1998). This is what the parties call the Collection Statute Expiration Date (CSED) Recovery Project. They claim that the Commissioner established the project to correct IRS records, identify unreasonably extended statutes of limitation, and either refund or credit payments made. The parties also claim that the Commissioner implemented a new policy

---

[10] [fn 11] In the RRA 1998, secs. 3401, 3433, 3461, and 3467, 112 Stat. 750, 759–60, 764, 769–70, Congress amended sections 6159, 6331, 6502, 7443, etc., to make sure that the IRS stopped these offensive practices, as well as some others.

[11] [fn 12] See, e.g., Fredericks v. Commissioner, 126 F.3d 433 (3d Cir.1997) (equitable estoppel overcomes waiver of statute), revg. T.C. Memo.1996–222; Zapara v. Commissioner, 124 T.C. 223, 228–29, 2005 WL 1398695 (2005); Shireman v. Commissioner, T.C. Memo.2004–155 (waiver signed under duress invalid, but threats to take legally authorized action if taxpayer doesn't sign generally not duress); Robertson v. Commissioner, T.C. Memo.1973–205 (taxpayer's consent to extend the statute under duress).

where he would no longer rely on waivers solicited from taxpayers who had an installment agreement in place.[12]

The Taxpayer Advocate Service (successor to the IRS Problem Resolution Office), as part of this CSED Project, got the job of figuring out which waivers the IRS had unreasonably obtained. The taxpayer advocate sent Rosenbloom three letters. The first, sent in June 1998, told Rosenbloom that the Commissioner "may have made a mistake in handling [his] installment agreement." It stated "[t]he law permits the IRS to ask for an extension of the collection time limit before, not after, the installment plan begins. Our records indicate that * * * we may have improperly asked you to extend the legal time limit for collection of the taxes covered by this installment agreement." It even went on to tell him that he might be entitled to a refund of amounts improperly collected.

A couple of months later, the Commissioner fully abated Rosenbloom's taxes for 1977–80 and 1982–84 (i.e., years not at issue in this case).[13] Some of the installment payments that the IRS credited to the earlier years' tax liabilities were credited instead to 1986.

The second letter sent in August 1998, told Rosenbloom that the IRS needed more time to research his case. It seemed to acknowledge that the installment agreement was still in effect, telling him that "if you are making monthly payments to the Internal Revenue Service (IRS) under your installment agreement, you should continue."

---

[12] [fn 13] The parties fail to cite to any source documenting the existence of such a policy (as they describe it). And even though we looked long and hard, we couldn't find one either. Enforcing "policy" rather than "law" is also problematic—some courts have ruled that policies contained in the IRM (and the like) do not have the force of law and aren't binding on the Commissioner. E.g., *Fargo v. Commissioner,* 447 F.3d 706, 713 (9th Cir.2006), affg. T.C. Memo.2004–13; *Carlson v. United States,* 126 F.3d 915, 922 (7th Cir.1997). But see sec. 6330(c)(1) ("The appeals officer shall at the hearing obtain verification from the Secretary that the requirements of any applicable law or administrative procedure have been met."). The Commissioner made our job a bit easier by initially taking the position that although the Code did not foreclose his actions at the time, if "the consent was obtained by a threatened termination of an installment agreement, [he] would agree that the statute has expired in this case." This position was not refuted at trial or on brief. Instead, the parties chose to focus on the validity of the installment agreement: "[The Commissioner's] position is that the decision was not an abuse of discretion, because the policy did not apply; the installment agreement was terminated before the waiver was signed."

[13] [fn 14] Rosenbloom's first installment agreement covered 1977–79 and 1982–84; his second covered 1977–87. The tax debts that the IRS abated did not match the years covered by either.

The last letter, dated November 4, 1998, told Rosenbloom that "[w]e have determined that we did make a mistake." According to this letter, the Commissioner admitted that the IRS should not have asked Rosenbloom to extend the statute of limitations for collection of the taxes covered by "this installment agreement." He concluded that "the time limit for collecting the taxes you were paying under your installment agreement has expired. You are no longer required to make payments for these taxes and the IRS will take no further action to collect them. *You may consider this matter closed.*" (Emphasis is in the original). In contrast to the first letter, nothing happened administratively—either a refund or credit—after this last letter.

The ambiguity in these letters is obvious: Rosenbloom had signed two waivers covering two different sets of tax years. The letters from the Taxpayer Advocate were imprecise in describing which waiver—and thus which tax debts—they were referring to. The Commissioner argues that they refer only to Rosenbloom's waiver of the statute for 1977–79 and 1982–83. Rosenbloom argues that the letters referred to a single installment agreement and draw no distinction between the tax debts covered by each waiver. He does admit to being confused, and wrote the Service asking which years were involved.

He never heard back. And Segal contacted the Philadelphia Service Center, which told him that their review showed only the year 1989 was still open though neither Rosenbloom nor Segal received anything in writing to confirm this.

More time passed. When Rosenbloom had recovered enough to get back to work, the IRS noticed and sent him an unexpected letter in April 2002—a Final Notice of Intent to Levy to collect his still unpaid 1981 and 1985–87 taxes (plus a couple later years that became moot or that Rosenbloom does not challenge). Rosenbloom timely asked for a collection-due-process (CDP) hearing. He claimed that the assessments are barred by the expiration of the statute of limitations under the Commissioner's own CSED policy.

Revenue Officer H. died in 2003, and the Commissioner has either lost or destroyed the IRS collection files, the Problem Resolution files, and the Taxpayer Advocate files for this case. After Settlement Officer Ursula Wastian pondered the resulting mess (she was in charge of the CDP hearing), the IRS Appeals Office issued a notice of determination rejecting Rosenbloom's challenge and sustaining the proposed levy. Officer Wastian concluded without explanation that the statute had expired only for tax years 1977–80 and 1982–83, but not for 1981 and 1985–1987 because the letter from the Taxpayer Advocate "regarding the collection statutes related to earlier assessments and an agreement taken in the year 1988." She looked into IRS records and concluded that "the signed waiver for the [extension for 1981, and 1985–87] did not coincide with the dates installment agreements were entered into with the Service."

The notice of determination upheld the levy for the . . . unpaid tax liabilities. . . .

OPINION

Section 6502(a) generally gives the IRS ten years from the date of assessment to collect unpaid taxes. But there are exceptions, and one is for taxpayers who voluntarily consent to extend the statute. Sec. 6502(a)(2). The CSED Recovery Project rested on the IRS leadership's conclusion that some revenue officers were systematically engaging in unfair collection and in some districts these practices were routine, entrenched, and condoned by management. In this case, the Commissioner is arguing that the CSED Recovery Project's policy doesn't apply to Rosenbloom's second installment agreement because that agreement was lawfully terminated before he signed the July 29, 1997 waiver.

Section 6159(b)(4) states that the Commissioner may terminate an agreement if the taxpayer fails to provide financial information as requested:

> The Secretary may alter, modify, or terminate an agreement entered into by the Secretary under subsection (a) in the case of the failure of the taxpayer—
>
> (A) to pay any installment at the time such installment payment is due under such agreement,
>
> (B) to pay any other tax liability at the time such liability is due, or
>
> (C) to provide a financial condition update as requested by the Secretary.

Section 6159(b)(5), however, requires the Commissioner to send a notice and explanation 30 days before he terminates an agreement:

> (5) Notice requirements.—The Secretary may not take any action under paragraph (2), (3), or (4) unless—
>
> (A) a notice of such action is provided to the taxpayer not later than the day 30 days before the date of such action, and
>
> (B) such notice includes an explanation why the Secretary intends to take such action.
>
> The preceding sentence shall not apply in any case in which the Secretary believes that collection of any tax to which an agreement under this section relates is in jeopardy.

None of this made it into the notice of determination. Instead, Officer Wastian noted that she secured Rosenbloom's case history which, according to her, began in December 1999. She acknowledged that the relevant facts all occurred before then, but concluded that "[t]here is no way to validate the statements made * * * by the now-deceased field representative." She also undertook to examine the relevant tax transcripts, but found nothing in them to upset her decision to sustain the notice of levy.

We review her decision for abuse of discretion, since Rosenbloom isn't challenging his underlying tax liabilities. A decisionmaker abuses his discretion "when * * * [he] makes an error of law * * * or rests [his] determination on a clearly erroneous finding of fact. * * * [Or] 'applies the correct law to facts which are not clearly erroneous but rules in an irrational manner.'" *United States v. Sherburne,* 249 F.3d 1121, 1125–26 (9th Cir.2001). And both parties agree that if the 1993 installment agreement was still in place when Rosenbloom signed the second waiver in 1997, the Commissioner's CSED policy dictates a conclusion that the statute has expired for the years at issue.

As to the scope of our review, we held in Robinette v. Commissioner, 123 T.C. 85, 101, 2004 WL 1616381 (2004), revd. 439 F.3d 455 (8th Cir.2006), that we are not limited to the administrative record in reviewing CDP determinations. . . .

The settlement officer based her determination at least in part by concluding that Rosenbloom had only one installment agreement, the one signed in 1988.

The taxpayer had entered into a payment agreement in 1988 * * *. The agreement * * * was for taxes that were assessed, due and owing at that time. The settlement Officer[14] conducted research and determined the Collection Statutes had expired for the years 1977, 1978, 1979, 1980, 1982, and 1983. She discovered that full abatements of all taxes due for these years was made in the sum of $432,078.40.

The letter regarding the collection statutes related to earlier assessments and an agreement taken in the year 1988 not the tax periods and assessments listed on the Notice of Intent to Levy * * *.

This is an odd conclusion. As Segal pointed out to her in 2003, the Commissioner had assessed Rosenbloom's giant tax debts for 1985 and 1986 only in April 1988, and his debt for 1987 only in January 1989. Accumulating such debts would have defaulted the 1988 installment agreement, which required Rosenbloom to stay current on his taxes.[15]

This should have set off the settlement officer's internal alarm that she might be overlooking or misinterpreting relevant evidence, because Rosenbloom responded to Wastian's assertion that the years at issue weren't covered by an installment agreement by explaining that he had signed two installment agreements. The Commissioner says that Wastian didn't look at the 1993 installment agreement simply because she didn't have it—it was part of the files

---

[14] [fn 18] The Court notes that settlement officers, like judges, sometimes refer to themselves in the third person.

[15] [fn 19] Neither the IRS nor Rosenbloom still had a copy of the 1988 installment agreement. But under section 6159(b)(4) a failure to pay taxes on time would be considered a default of the installment agreement. Rosenbloom's 1993 agreement expressly states:

Conditions of this Agreement:

All Federal tax returns and Federal taxes that become due while this agreement is in effect must be filed and paid on time.

***

If the conditions of this agreement are not met, it will be terminated and the entire tax liability may be collected by levy ***.

that the Commissioner lost. And although she asked Rosenbloom for a copy of the agreement, he didn't give her one.

Rosenbloom and Segal finally found a copy of the missing installment agreement after the CDP hearing, and it was stipulated into evidence at trial. The agreement is on an IRS form, and has a box labeled "Tax Periods." The periods listed in the box include all the tax years from 1977 through 1987. The body of the agreement contains Rosenbloom's promise to pay $406 each month beginning on March 25, 1993. It is clear from this document that there was only one installment agreement in effect in 1997 and that it covered all the tax years covered by both waivers that Rosenbloom had signed. We have a definite and firm conviction that on this key point, the settlement officer clearly erred.

That might leave us with some tricky questions of whether it is legitimate for us to consider evidence outside the administrative record. But we don't think these questions need answering here. The settlement officer knew (or should have been able to tell) that the payments that Rosenbloom was making under some installment agreement were $406 each month. Even the surviving IRS records—accounts of Rosenbloom's tax debts organized by year—show that the IRS credited the $406 to several different tax years: mostly to 1977, but eighteen months' worth to 1980, four months' worth to 1984; and ten months' worth to 1986. The 1977 record also shows that Rosenbloom had been making monthly payments of $350 for years—right up to March 25, 1993, when they begin to show the start of $406 payments. There really is only one reasonable conclusion—whatever installment agreement Rosenbloom had been under since 1988 was superseded by the 1993 agreement, which covered all the years for which Rosenbloom owed back taxes as of the date he signed it.

The Taxpayer Advocate's November 4, 1998 letter admitted that the Commissioner made a mistake by referring to only one installment agreement, not two. But the IRS's abatement of Rosenbloom's tax debt for only some of the years covered by the installment agreement raises a serious question: Is there some reason to cancel the waivers of the statute of limitations for 1977–79 and 1982–84 and not the waivers for the years at issue in this case?

The Commissioner argues that there is—that the IRS must have terminated Rosenbloom's 1993 installment agreement between the time that he signed the first waiver in 1996, and the time that he signed the second waiver in July 1997. Why else, he argues, would even an aggressive revenue officer levy on a bank account or try to seize used office furniture, when he must have known that that would be contrary to the Code's prohibition on levies while an installment agreement is in effect? See sec. 301.6159–1(d), Proceed. & Admin. Regs., 59 Fed.Reg. 66193 (Dec. 23, 1994).

The solution to this puzzle lies in the tax transcripts that the parties produced at trial. These were the same tax transcripts that the settlement officer had access to before making her determination. These transcripts are troves of information, but they are also almost completely incomprehensible to one not skilled at interpreting the various numerical codes they use. See *Roberts v. Commissioner,* T.C. Memo.2004–100 (admitting evidence that helped identify entries in a transcript). Whether or not our scope of review is limited to the administrative record, taking testimony to explain that record is allowed.[16] And, after careful review, we conclude that the transcripts show no termination of the 1993 installment agreement.[17] At trial, even the Commissioner's expert witness conceded that "Code 64" (Defaulted Installment Agreement) is nowhere to be found in them. The Code "Status 26," dated May 6, 1996, is an entry for all the years covered by both sets of waivers. The Commissioner's expert wrote in his report that this indicates that the installment agreement was no longer in effect, but at trial he conceded that in this case "Code 26" meant that the case had been transferred to the local Chicago office. By itself, this would be an ambiguous bit of information—simply evidence that control over the installment agreement had passed into local hands, but evidence of neither its continuation nor its termination.[18]

His concession on this point ties into a distinction made in the IRM from that era that distinguishes between installment agreements monitored by the IRS computer system and those monitored manually. 2 Administration, IRM (CCH), pt. 5, sec. 5339, at 6546 (Dec. 11, 1992). According to the IRM, only taxpayers with manually monitored agreements would get the Letter 1064(DO) that set Rosenbloom off in May 1997. *Id.* The entries record Rosenbloom's continuing to make $406 monthly payments before and after he signed the July 1997 waiver. The IRS transcript of Rosenbloom's account for those years confirm this, and would make no sense if "Code 26" meant there was no installment agreement in place. The additional fact that there is no "Code 64" on any transcript for any year is consistent with Rosenbloom's story—that he received a notice of default, which stated that his installment agreement might be terminated, not that it *was* terminated. We therefore conclude that the settlement officer clearly erred in her

---

[16] [fn 20] E.g., Yale–New Haven Hosp. v. Leavitt, 470 F.3d 71, 82 (2d Cir.2006) (courts may consider extrarecord evidence to illuminate agency's record); Franklin Savings Association v. Director, Office of Thrift Supervision, 934 F.2d 1127, 1137 (10th Cir.1991) (discussing exceptions to record rule); Bunker Hill Co. v. EPA, 572 F.2d 1286, 1292 (9th Cir.1977) (courts can go beyond the administrative record to explain technical terms or complex subject matter).

[17] [fn 21] Because we find the installment agreement was still in effect at the time Rosenbloom signed the 1997 waivers, we also find that H.'s abusive tactics also constituted a clear threat to the continuance of the installment agreement when Rosenbloom gave the waivers.

[18] [fn 22] If the expert had stood by his report, he'd have been in the odd position of saying that something happened to default the installment agreement between March 6, 1996 (when Rosenbloom signed the first set of waivers) and May 6 of the same year. Yet the records show no correspondence, and no interruption of payments from Rosenbloom in that short time.

implicit conclusion that there was no installment agreement in effect when Rosenbloom signed the second set of waivers.

The Commissioner next argues that the Taxpayer Advocate's letter was "sent in error," or alternatively, that it refers to the "earlier years" rather than the later years (or the ones at issue in this case). He points to several clues. First, he says the letter suggests that Rosenbloom was still making payments on the installment agreement, when he hadn't made any payments for nine months. It does not. It is instead phrased in the conditional—"if you are making monthly payments". Second, he says the letter states that the time limits for collecting the taxes covered by the installment agreement had expired. But even without considering the waivers to extend the statute, he argues the statute hadn't expired for 1982 and 1987 because the IRS hadn't actually assessed the tax for those years until late 1988 or January 1989.

We acknowledge this point, but do note that the IRS letters appear to be forms, and do not think the Taxpayer Advocate put much effort into customizing them to Rosenbloom's situation. Correspondence in a case this complicated is likely to have some infelicities of phrase, but they can't obscure the fact that the IRS's own transcripts show that Rosenbloom and his lawyer both reacted in that summer as if the installment agreement were tottering on the edge of default, not that it had already toppled over.

The Commissioner's final argument relies on the flush language of section 6159(b)(5)—the language that authorizes the Commissioner to terminate an agreement without notice if he believes that tax collection is in jeopardy. He argues that this must have been what triggered the bank levy in August 1997, and is proof that the installment agreement was terminated by that time.

The actions referred to in this flush language, however, require notice to the taxpayer before the Commissioner terminates an installment agreement. The argument that the bank levy is evidence of a jeopardy termination might be convincing if the levy had occurred in June or July. But Segal had sent Rosenbloom's updated financial information to H. well before the levy. That the levy occurred close to two months after Rosenbloom sent the missing information to the IRS isn't consistent with a jeopardy termination. We find instead that the bank levy is better explained as another example of the heavy-handed manner in which that particular revenue officer was pursuing Rosenbloom. We conclude that the bank levy in August was not evidence that the installment agreement had been terminated.

We therefore conclude that the determination to sustain the levy was an abuse of discretion for the years included in the set of waivers that Rosenbloom signed in 1997.

An appropriate decision will be entered.

NOTES AND QUESTIONS

1. This case has striking facts. An IRS agent uses tactics that courts would be concerned about upon review if such review were to arise. No

provision provided for such review until after this case. Collection due process is discussed later in this chapter.

2. How long did this case take to reach resolution?

3. Prior to the RRA 1998, taxpayers had no opportunities to challenge collection actions until after the IRS obtained the amount it sought. At that point, the taxpayer could request a refund and then sue the IRS for a refund of the amounts collected. Taxpayers succeeded in convincing Congress that a lack of recourse permitted the IRS's collection organization to run amok. Congress provided for collection due process hearings to alleviate the problem.

Applying for an installment agreement suspends the IRS's collection statute while under consideration. *See* Treas. Reg. § 301.6159-1(g). The collection statute resumes 30 days after a rejection, default, or appeal. During an installment agreement, collection actions are also suspended, though the IRS does not revoke a lien if there is already one in place.

2. Offers in Compromise

A taxpayer with limited income and scarce liquid resources, *i.e.*, someone who cannot pay an entire liability without undue hardship, can submit an "offer in compromise," or "OIC." Section 7122 provides as follows:

> The Secretary may compromise any civil . . . case arising under the internal revenue laws . . . .

An offer in compromise is a taxpayer request for the IRS to accept less than the full tax liability and relieve the taxpayer of the remaining unpaid liability. Such settlements with the government help benefit both the government and the taxpayer. The government can collect the maximum amount possible without causing the taxpayer financial ruin.

The IRS considers offers in compromise on three bases: (1) collection potential, (2) liability, and (3) equity. Treasury regulations provide parameters for when the IRS may accept an offer on these bases. *See generally* Treas. Reg. § 301.7122-1. In general, however, the IRS will not accept an offer in compromise from a taxpayer who has not kept current with return filing and tax payments subsequent to the period covered by the offer. *See* Vinatieri v. Commissioner, 133 T.C. 392, 400 & n.6 (2009).

When considering collection potential, the IRS may accept an offer where there is "doubt as to collectibility." The IRS may accept an offer on these grounds where the taxpayer has neither sufficient income nor sufficient assets to pay the tax liability. "Doubt as to collectibility" means there is doubt as to "reasonable collection potential" of the taxpayer's full tax liability within the ten-year statute on collection. Essentially, doubt exists as to whether the taxpayer can pay. The taxpayer must fill out financial statements listing his assets, liabilities, and earning potential. The IRS makes its determination on the basis of these financial statements.

The IRS may also accept an offer where there is "doubt as to liability." The IRS may accept an offer on these grounds only where there is a legitimate dispute as to whether the taxpayer owes tax. The IRS does not accept offers on these grounds where the taxpayer has already had an opportunity to dispute the underlying tax liability. By the time the taxpayer is in collections and offering to compromise because of doubt as to liability, the taxpayer has usually had an audit, an administrative appeal of that audit, and the opportunity to petition the Tax Court. Because the liability is at issue rather than the taxpayer's finances, the taxpayer need not include a financial statement with this type of offer. *See* IRC § 7122(d)(3)(B)(ii).

When considering equity grounds for accepting an offer, the IRS looks for opportunities to promote "effective tax administration." *See* Treas. Reg. § 301.7122-1(b)(3). The IRS may accept an "effective tax administration" offer where a taxpayer technically has the ability to pay the tax liability, but rejecting the offer would make the taxpayer suffer economic hardship. Such a hardship situation may occur because the taxpayer has limited resources due to long-term illness, medical conditions, disabilities, or similar circumstances. Another hardship where the IRS might be inclined to accept an offer on grounds of effective tax administration occurs where paying the tax would prevent the taxpayer from meeting basic living expenses. Acceptance on this basis is only available where the taxpayer cannot qualify for an acceptance on the basis of doubt as to collectibility.

The taxpayer may appeal the rejection of an offer in compromise to the Tax Court. The Tax Court reviews OIC determinations under an abuse of discretion standard. In *Samuel*, the question was whether the IRS abused its discretion when it rejected the taxpayer's offer in compromise.

SAMUEL v. COMMISSIONER
T.C. Memo. 2007-312
United States Tax Court

NIMS, Judge.

This case arises from a petition for judicial review filed in response to a Notice of Determination Concerning Collection Action(s) Under Section 6320 and/or 6330. Unless otherwise indicated, all section references are to the Internal Revenue Code in effect for the years in issue as amended, and all Rule references are to the Tax Court Rules of Practice and Procedure. The issue for decision is whether respondent's rejection of petitioner's offer-in-compromise was an abuse of discretion.

BACKGROUND

This case was submitted fully stipulated pursuant to Rule 122, and the facts are so found. The stipulations of the parties, with accompanying exhibits, are incorporated herein by this reference. At the time he filed the petition, petitioner resided in Louisiana.

Petitioner is a practicing physician specializing in adult and pediatric urology. He operates his own medical practice, David L. Samuel, M.D., A Professional Medical Corporation. Petitioner is also a partner in Pontchartrain Lithotripsy, LLC. Prior to starting his own practice, petitioner practiced with another urologist until sometime in 2002.

Beginning on February 3, 2003, petitioner began filing delinquent individual income tax returns for 1996–2002. . . .

The so-called "TXMODA" computer transcripts of petitioner's IRS accounts for each of these years show adjusted gross income posted from petitioner's tax returns. . . .

Petitioner did not remit any payments for the amounts due on these returns when they were filed.

Respondent assessed the taxes shown on the above returns. Calculated as of January 1, 2005, petitioner owed in excess of $773,368 for the tax years 1996–2002, inclusive.

In October 2004, petitioner filed his 2003 individual income tax return. Withheld taxes for 2003 exceeded total tax by $8,016. The excess withheld taxes combined with an estimated tax payment of $15,600 resulted in a $23,616 overpayment of tax for 2003. This overpayment was applied to petitioner's 1996 unpaid tax liability.

Respondent sent the following collection notices to petitioner for unpaid Federal income taxes: Notice of Federal Tax Lien Filing and Your Right to a Hearing Under IRC 6320, dated October 2, 2003, for the 1997–2001 tax years; a Final Notice—Notice of Intent to Levy and Notice of Your Right to a Hearing, dated February 10, 2004, for 2002; a Final Notice—Notice of Intent to Levy and Notice of Your Right to a Hearing, dated March 8, 2004, for 1996; and a Notice of Federal Tax Lien Filing and Your Right to a Hearing Under IRC 6320, dated April 1, 2004, for 1996. (Neither party has explained this 1996 discrepancy.) Petitioner timely requested a hearing in response to each of these Notices. On each Form 12153, Request for a Collection Due Process Hearing, petitioner stated that he was preparing a Form 433–A, Collection Information Statement for Wage Earners and Self–Employed Individuals, and a Form 433–B, Collection Information Statement for Businesses, in order to submit an offer-in-compromise for his tax liabilities.

On July 8, 2004, petitioner submitted a Form 656, Offer in Compromise, along with two different Forms 433–A (both dated June 1, 2004) and a Form 433–B for his professional corporation. Petitioner submitted the offer on the basis of "doubt as to collectibility". Petitioner was not then, and is not now, contesting his 1996–2002 income tax liabilities. Petitioner offered to pay $30,000 to compromise his 1996–2002 tax liabilities. This was a short-term deferred payment offer payable in monthly installments of $1,250 for 24 months.

On one of the Forms 433–A, petitioner indicated that he operated David L. Samuel, M.D., P.C., and identified this corporation as his employer for the prior

4 years. Petitioner listed his assets as $1,409.89 in a checking account, a house valued at $330,000 (with a loan balance of $322,025), and furniture/personal effects worth $10,000. Petitioner indicated that he was the plaintiff in a $25,000 civil lawsuit for unpaid wages. Petitioner showed his only source of income as monthly wages of $7,963. Petitioner reported monthly expenses of: $976 for food, clothing, and miscellaneous (noted as the statutory allowance); $1,024 for housing and utilities (noted as the statutory allowance); $50 for health care; $2,470 for taxes; $2,750 for court-ordered payments (child support); and $250 for other expenses (later identified as attorney's fees for representation in the instant matter). The second Form 433–A contained the same information as the first, except that it reported gross monthly wages of $8,144.10 and monthly medical expenses of $41.20.

The Form 433–B for David L. Samuel, M.D., P.C., reflected that petitioner was the only shareholder. The total accounts/notes receivable of the medical corporation was shown as $87,388.73. The only other assets disclosed on the Form 433–B were $613.74 in a bank account, $200.22 of cash on hand, and office furniture valued at $4,000. In the "Investments" section, petitioner listed one share of Pontchartrain Lithotripsy, LLC, with a value of $10,000. Total monthly income for petitioner's professional corporation consisted of $26,435.20 in gross receipts and $4,416 in dividends for a total of $30,851.20. Petitioner reported monthly expenses totaling $33,523.93 for the professional corporation.

Petitioner's offer-in-compromise was accepted for processing and forwarded to respondent's New Orleans Compliance Office for investigation.

Petitioner requested a face-to-face hearing at the New Orleans Appeals Office, to which the IRS agreed. The face-to-face hearing was conducted in New Orleans on January 31, 2005. During the face-to-face hearing, petitioner disclosed that he sold an interest in Fairway Medical Center (FMC) in June 2003, for $108,000 and refinanced his home in September 2003, for a net cash payment to him of $25,158. Petitioner also discussed his ownership interest in Pontchartrain Lithotripsy, LLC, from which he reported $51,922 of income in 2003, but which he designated on the Form 433–B as a $10,000 investment held by his professional corporation. Petitioner explained that his $10,000 initial investment in Sabine Lithotripsy, LLC (which dissolved into four entities, one of which was Pontchartrain Lithotripsy, LLC) entitles him to access a medical mobile unit for use in his medical practice. He also receives monthly income receipts, which he said are deposited into his business account. After the hearing, petitioner provided a list of the monthly income received from Pontchartrain Lithotripsy. This income totaled $61,440 for 2004.

Petitioner clarified other issues at the hearing. He indicated that the lower of the two monthly income amounts on the different Forms 433–A, $7,963, should be used for consideration of the offer-in-compromise. Petitioner asserted that his interest in his professional corporation is limited to the value of the medical and office equipment (which he estimated to be $3,630) and that a patient list in the urology field has little or no value. Petitioner also gave details regarding the abovementioned lawsuit against his previous employer to collect back wages. He said that billings show that he is entitled to $60,000 plus interest.

On February 10, 2005, the settlement officer sent petitioner a letter with her preliminary determination. She stated her position that petitioner had "dissipated assets" with a disregard of his outstanding tax liabilities when he sold his interest in FMC and refinanced his home. She reasoned that at the time the transactions occurred, the outstanding assessed balances due to the IRS exceeded the amounts realized from the dissipated assets. In addition, she noted that none of the funds were remitted to the IRS, and she took the position that petitioner did not use any of the funds for necessary expenses. She said that unless petitioner increased his offer to $163,158 ($30,000 initial offer amount plus 100 percent of the dissipated asset values), she would assume that petitioner was not interested in pursuing the matter further, and that she would recommend that Appeals issue a notice of determination.

The settlement officer indicated that her preliminary determination did not represent a final amount determined to be an acceptable offer. She noted that she did not include in the reasonable collection potential calculation any amounts for petitioner's interest in his civil lawsuit, his ownership interest in his medical practice, or his interest in Pontchartrain Lithotripsy.

On March 2, 2005, petitioner responded to the preliminary determination letter. In his letter he said that when he "lost his job" practicing with another urologist in 2002, he accumulated substantial debt setting up his new medical practice and paying necessary living expenses and fell behind on his child support payments. The letter claimed that the payments made from the funds realized from the FMC sale in July and home refinancing in September 2003, were necessary to pay judgments rendered against him and to avoid additional legal proceedings. Petitioner provided details on the distribution of the proceeds of these two transactions. He alleged that he distributed the $108,000 from the sale of his interest in FMC. . . .

From the refinance of his residence petitioner received a net amount of $25,158. Petitioner used $11,000 to pay delinquent child support and transferred the remaining $14,158 to his professional corporation (which was used to pay a supplier, malpractice insurance, delinquent telephone charges, and payroll).

Also in his response to the preliminary determination, petitioner asserted that the attorney's fees were an allowable necessary expense because they were necessary for his representation before the IRS with respect to his current tax matters. He closed the letter by saying he thought negotiation of an offer-in-compromise was possible given his belief that he did not dissipate assets and that he is allowed to claim attorney's fees as an expense.

On March 8, 2005, the settlement officer sent a letter to petitioner stating that her positions on the dissipated assets and attorney's fees remained unchanged. Petitioner did not respond to this letter and never increased his offer.

On April 8, 2005, Appeals issued petitioner a notice of determination sustaining the proposed collection actions. The summary of determination concluded that petitioner's proposed collection alternative was not a viable option. The notice indicated Appeals' finding that the IRS could collect more than the $30,000 offer. The notice referred to the discovery of the dissipated assets during consideration of the offer-in-compromise. The notice acknowledged the $15,600 payment to the IRS but pointed out that the remaining $117,558 was distributed to other creditors. It noted that petitioner was given the opportunity to increase his offer but declined to do so. The notice also stated that

> The proposed levy action balances the need for efficient collection with the concern that it be no more intrusive than necessary because your offer-in-compromise does not outweigh the government's need for efficient collection of your tax liabilities. Your collection alternative was considered however we find that it is not a viable alternative given the facts and evidence raised.

The settlement officer's Appeals Case Determination (Case Determination) reflects that in recommending petitioner's offer based on doubt as to collectibility be rejected, she calculated petitioner's future income potential plus his net realizable equity (NRE) in assets to get the reasonable collection potential for the case.

In determining petitioner's NRE, the settlement officer decided that petitioner had dissipated assets in disregard of his tax liabilities when he sold his interest in FMC and when he refinanced his home. She considered the assets dissipated because petitioner realized the funds after his tax liabilities for 1996–2002 had accrued and after the amounts due for 1997–2001 were assessed, and he used all of the funds to pay other creditors, with the exception of the $15,600 payment to the IRS. She determined that 100 percent of the $133,158 received from the dissipated assets should be included in petitioner's NRE with the possible exception of the $15,600 paid to the IRS, the $5,000 legal fees incurred in the lawsuit against his former employer, and the $5,464 paid for child support. She reached this conclusion despite recognizing that the assets were dissipated before the offer-in-compromise was made. The settlement officer did not include any amount for the value of petitioner's residence in NRE, having determined that he had no equity. She also expressed doubt as to whether petitioner reported an accurate value for his interest in his medical corporation, noting the comparatively low value of equipment totaling $3,630 given that the business had gross income in excess of $300,000 in 2003. The settlement officer did not account for petitioner's interests in his medical corporation or Pontchartrain Lithotripsy in calculating NRE. The settlement officer determined petitioner's future income collection potential to be $946 per month, which, over 60 months (the multiplier for a short-term deferred payment offer) amounted to $56,760.

In response to the notice of determination, petitioner filed a petition with this Court.

DISCUSSION

Before a levy may be made on any property or right to property, a taxpayer is entitled to notice of the Commissioner's intent to levy and notice of the right to a fair hearing before an impartial officer of the IRS Appeals Office. Secs. 6330(a) and (b), 6331(d). Section 6320 provides that after the filing of a Federal tax lien under section 6323, the Secretary shall furnish written notice. This notice must advise the taxpayer of the opportunity for administrative review in the form of a hearing, which is generally conducted consistent with the procedures set forth in section 6330(c), (d), and (e). Sec. 6320(c).

Where, as here, the underlying tax liability is not at issue, our review of the notice of determination under section 6330 is for abuse of discretion. See *Sego v. Commissioner,* 114 T.C. 604, 610, 2000 WL 889754 (2000); *Goza v. Commissioner,* 114 T.C. 176, 182, 2000 WL 283864 (2000). This standard does not require us to decide what we think would be an acceptable offer-in-compromise. *Murphy v. Commissioner,* 125 T.C. 301, 320, 2005 WL 3555953 (2005), affd. 469 F.3d 27 (1st Cir.2006). Rather, our review is to determine whether respondent's rejection of petitioner's offer-in-compromise was arbitrary, capricious, or without sound basis in fact or law. *Id.*

At the hearing, taxpayers may raise challenges to "the appropriateness of collection actions" and may make "offers of collection alternatives, which may include the posting of a bond, the substitution of other assets, an installment agreement, or an offer-in-compromise." Sec. 6330(c)(2)(A). The Appeals officer must consider those issues, verify that the requirements of applicable law and administrative procedures have been met, and consider "whether any proposed collection action balances the need for the efficient collection of taxes with the legitimate concern of the person [involved] that any collection action be no more intrusive than necessary." Sec. 6330(c)(3)(C). As his collection alternative, petitioner chose to make an offer-in-compromise. In the case before us, petitioner disputes respondent's rejection of his offer-in-compromise.

Section 7122(a) authorizes the Secretary to compromise any civil or criminal case arising under the internal revenue laws. Section 7122(c) provides that the Secretary shall prescribe guidelines for evaluation of whether an offer-in-compromise should be accepted. The decision whether to accept or reject an offer-in-compromise is left to the Secretary's discretion. *Fargo v. Commissioner,* 447 F.3d 706, 712 (9th Cir.2006), affg. T.C. Memo.2004–13; sec. 301.7122–1(c)(1), Proced. & Admin. Regs.

The section 7122 regulations set forth three grounds for compromise of a taxpayer's liability. These grounds are doubt as to liability, doubt as to collectibility, and the promotion of effective tax administration. Sec. 301.7122–1(b), Proced. & Admin. Regs. Petitioner seeks a compromise based on doubt as to collectibility.

The Secretary may compromise a tax liability based on doubt as to collectibility where the taxpayer's assets and income are less than the full amount of the liability. Sec. 301.7122–1(b)(2), Proced. & Admin. Regs. Generally, under the Commissioner's administrative procedures, an offer-in-compromise based on doubt as to collectibility will be acceptable only if it reflects the taxpayer's "reasonable collection potential". Rev. Proc.2003–71, sec. 4.02(2), 2003–2 C.B. 517. Both parties appear to agree that petitioner's reasonable collection potential is substantially less than his tax liability which, as above noted, stood at more than $773,368, as of January 1, 2005. The parties obviously disagree as to petitioner's collection potential.

The IRS has developed guidelines and procedures for the submission and evaluation of offers to compromise under section 7122. Rev. Proc.2003–71, *supra.* In furtherance thereof, the Internal Revenue Manual (IRM) contains extensive guidelines for evaluating offers-in-compromise. 1 Administration, Internal Revenue Manual (CCH), sec. 5.8, at 16,253. Both petitioner and respondent focus substantial attention in their briefs to the issue of "Dissipation of Assets", discussed below.

The IRM provides in part, in "Dissipation of Assets", section 5.8.5.4, at 16,339–6, the following:

(1) During an offer investigation it may be discovered that assets (liquid or non-liquid) have been sold, gifted, transferred, or spent on non-priority items and/or debts and are *no longer available to pay the tax liability.* This section discusses treatment of the value of these assets when considering an offer in compromise.

(2) Once it is determined that a specific asset has been dissipated, the investigation should address whether the value of the asset, or a portion of the value, should be included in an acceptable offer amount.

(3) Inclusion of the value of dissipated assets must clearly be justified in the case file and documented on the ICS/AOIC history. * * *

(4) When the taxpayer can show that assets have been dissipated to provide for necessary living expenses, these amounts should not be included in the reasonable collection potential (RCP) calculation.

(5) If the investigation clearly reveals that assets have been dissipated with a disregard of the outstanding tax liability, *consider including the value in the reasonable collection potential (RCP) calculation.* [Emphasis added.]

It is not totally clear how dissipated assets can be "no longer available to pay the tax liability" (see (1), above) while at the same time included in the "reasonable collection potential (RCP) calculation" (see (5), above).

The settlement officer apparently considered herself required to apply this rather cryptic guideline, and under an abuse of discretion standard we are not at liberty to challenge her judgment that it should be used. However, under the abuse of discretion standard, we must assure that the guideline is correctly applied.

The Appeals Case Determination states that

Appeals preliminary determination of Dr. Samuel's net realizable equity (NRE) in his assets is that it should include 100% of his dissipated assets totaling $133,158 with the possible exception of the $15,600 paid for his 2003 estimated tax payment, his legal fees of $5,000 incurred in association with his civil law suit against his prior employer and $5,464 paid for child support. He has no net realizable equity in his personal residence given that quick sale value (QSV) is used and offset against his mortgage of $322,000. Since his mortgage exceeds the QSV of $320,000 (80% of FMV determined to be at $400,000), he has no equity to include in his NRE. Appeals believes that his interest in his medical corporation exceeds that which was reported at the face-to-face hearing to be the value of the equipment totaling $3,630. This is an on-going business that had gross income in excess of $300,000 in 2003.

The Appeals Case Determination goes on to state that

Dr. Samuel was provided the opportunity to increase his offered amount to at least include amounts he realized pursuant to his dissipated assets in order that his offer receive further consideration. He declined to so do.

The $15,600 which Dr. Samuel paid for his 2003 estimated tax payment should have been excluded from the dissipated assets category, and if Appeals was in doubt about the includability of the $5,000 incurred in association with Dr. Samuel's civil law suit and the $5,464 paid for child support, these amounts should have been excluded also. It was an abuse of discretion not to do so.

It is represented in his brief that petitioner has been current on all of the filings and payments of his taxes, starting with 2003. It appears from the Appeals Case Determination that petitioner has in fact minimal assets from which cash could be realized, but that he has a medical practice that produces a fairly substantial amount of income. Clearly, then, any IRS recovery from petitioner would have to come principally, if not entirely, from his medical practice income.

In connection with its consideration of petitioner's offer-in-compromise, Appeals prepared [a] table to illustrate petitioner's future income potential. The Case Determination states that the table is intended to show that petitioner's future income potential is more than his $30,000 offer. . . .

Petitioner points out that 2 Administration, Internal Revenue Manual (CCH), section 5.15.1.10(3), at 17,662, allows as a necessary expense accounting and legal fees if representation before the IRS is needed or meets the necessary expense tests. The costs must be related to solving the current controversy. In calculating petitioner's future income potential, the settlement officer failed to allow monthly payments of $250 which petitioner was making to his tax attorney in connection with the current controversy. The corrected income potential would thus be $41,760.

The Appeals Case Determination takes the position that Appeals was not required to counteroffer petitioner's offer-in-compromise, but petitioner points out that 1 Administration, Internal Revenue Manual (CCH), section 5.8.4.6., at 16,308, provides that in the course of processing the case, if the taxpayer's offer must be increased in order to be recommended for acceptance, the taxpayer must be contacted by letter or telephone advising the taxpayer "to amend the offer to the acceptable amount". In the present case, petitioner should have been advised that instead of 100 percent of the dissipated assets, totaling $133,158, an acceptable amount would be $133,158 less $26,064 ($15,600 plus $5,000 plus $5,464), or $107,094. Appeals' failure to do so was an abuse of discretion, and we so hold.

Petitioner should be given the opportunity to revise his offer-in-compromise to reflect the $107,094, referred to above. However, since petitioner appears to lack any substantial assets outside his medical practice which could provide a source for paying any compromise amount, it is obvious, as previously observed, that any payments would come from his medical earnings. The table prepared by Appeals, above, unquestionably reveals that petitioner has ample income in excess of his $30,000 offer payable over 24 months.

We shall remand this case to Appeals for a 60–day period within which petitioner may, if he so chooses, revise the amount of his offer-in-compromise and suggest new terms of payment in accordance herewith.

An appropriate order will be issued.

FOWLER v. COMMISSIONER
T.C. Memo. 2004-163
United States Tax Court

GERBER, Chief J.

Respondent, on February 21, 2002, sent Mark Fowler (petitioner) a Notice of Determination Concerning Collection Action(s) Under Section 6320 and/or 6330, in which respondent sustained the filing of a Federal tax lien for petitioner's 1990–92 tax liabilities. In that same notice respondent also rejected petitioner's offer in compromise. On that same date respondent sent Mark Fowler and Joylyn Souter–Fowler (petitioners) a second Notice of Determination Concerning Collection Action(s) Under Section 6320 and/or 6330. In this notice respondent sustained the filing of a Federal tax lien with respect to petitioners' 1994–96 tax liabilities, and respondent again rejected petitioners' offer in compromise.

Prior to these determinations, petitioners sought and were offered an Appeals hearing, but they did not attend due to personal reasons. One month after the scheduled hearing date, the Appeals officer issued the above determinations sustaining the filing of the Federal tax liens and rejecting petitioners' offers in compromise. With respect to both determinations, petitioners appealed to this Court.

The issue for consideration is whether respondent abused his discretion by rejecting petitioners' offers in compromise and by sustaining the filing of the Federal tax liens.

FINDINGS OF FACT

Petitioners resided in Garden Grove, California, when the petition in this case was filed.

Separate Liabilities

Petitioner filed his 1990 Federal income tax return late on September 6, 1991. On July 21, 1993, respondent mailed a statutory notice of deficiency to petitioner for his 1990 taxable year. Petitioner did not petition this Court to dispute the deficiency. On December 20, 1993, respondent assessed the $399 income tax deficiency and a $98.74 late-filing penalty under section 6651(a)(1). In addition, $104.40 of interest was assessed. Petitioner does not contest the 1990 tax liability.

Petitioner timely filed his 1991 Federal income tax return that contained several mathematical errors. Respondent corrected the mathematical errors in accord with section 6213(b)(1), and assessments were made to correct the errors. Respondent subsequently selected petitioner's 1991 return for an audit examination. On April 5, 1994, respondent mailed petitioner a statutory notice of deficiency for his 1991 taxable year determining a $545 income tax deficiency. Petitioner did not petition this Court with respect to the 1991 notice of deficiency. On September 5, 1994, respondent assessed the $545 deficiency and $103.37 of accrued interest.

Petitioner filed his 1992 Federal income tax return late on July 28, 1993. Respondent selected petitioner's 1992 return for an audit examination. On January 11, 1995, respondent mailed petitioner a statutory notice of deficiency for his 1992 taxable year determining a $1,193 income tax deficiency and a $189 penalty for late filing under section 6651(a)(1). On July 17, 1995, respondent assessed the deficiency, the late-filing penalty, and accrued interest in the amount of $265.92. On the same day, the late-filing penalty was abated leaving an unpaid balance of $1,458.92 for 1992.

Joint Liabilities

Petitioners were married in 1993. Under cover of a letter dated September 15, 1997, petitioners submitted their untimely 1994, 1995, and 1996 joint Federal income tax returns. These returns were filed by respondent on September 29, 1997. Petitioners reported tax due for 1994, 1995, and 1996 on their returns in the amounts of $402.04, $402.03, and $1,480.66, respectively.

On October 27, 1997, respondent assessed the 1994 income tax liability, a late-filing penalty in the amount of $100, a failure to pay tax penalty in the amount of $62.32, and accrued interest in the amount of $128.35, for a total assessment of $692.71. On that same date, respondent assessed the 1995 income tax liability, a late-filing penalty in the amount of $100, a failure to pay tax penalty in the amount of $38.19, and accrued interest in the amount of $73.03, for a total assessment of $613.25. On November 17, 1997, respondent assessed the 1996 income tax liability, a late-filing penalty in the amount of $333.15, a failure to pay tax penalty in the amount of $59.23, and accrued interest in the amount of $99.21, for a total assessment of $1,972.25.

Events Leading to the Issuance of the Notice of Determination

On December 21, 1999, respondent mailed two separate Notices of Intent to Levy and Notice of Your Right to a Hearing to petitioners. The notices reflected petitioners' unpaid Federal income tax liabilities for 1990 through 1992 and 1994 through 1996. On January 26, 2000, petitioners informed respondent of their desire to submit an offer in compromise to resolve all of their individual and joint liabilities. In response, respondent mailed petitioners a package of materials for the submission of offers in compromise for their outstanding individual and joint liabilities.

On April 19, 2000, respondent received petitioners' offer to compromise the 1994 through 1996 joint liabilities for $1,150. On that same date respondent received petitioner's offer to compromise the 1990 through 1992 liabilities for $360. Both offers in compromise were submitted on Form 656, Offer in Compromise. Petitioners' offer was to make monthly payments to satisfy the liabilities. Petitioners planned to pay a portion of the offer amount from their expected tax refund for 1999.

On May 19, 2000, respondent's revenue officer advised petitioners that their offers in compromise could not be processed until petitioners' 1999 Federal income tax return was filed. Under respondent's procedures, offers are not processed while taxpayers are not in compliance with the internal revenue laws.

Petitioners had already filed for an extension of time to file for 1999 because they were awaiting information from third parties to complete the return. On June 15, 2000, respondent filed two Notices of Federal Tax Lien (NFTL) at the county recorder's office in Orange County, California, with respect to the individual and joint tax liabilities. Respondent sent petitioners the filed NFTLs and Notices of Right to a Collection Due Process Hearing. On July 14, 2000, petitioners submitted Form 12153, Request for a Collection Due Process Hearing (administrative hearing), contesting the NFTLs filed by respondent and noting the pending offers in compromise.

Sometime in 2001, petitioners' claims were assigned to respondent's Appeals officer. On June 20, 2001, the Appeals officer and petitioners had a telephone conversation discussing petitioners' desire to compromise all of the liabilities. The Appeals officer requested more information from petitioners, which they timely provided with a copy of their filed 1999 Federal income tax return. At some time in the process, petitioners submitted an amended offer in compromise for $2,400, to be paid in $100–monthly installments. Under those terms, the $2,400–offer could be paid in full in 2 years.

On October 16, 2001, respondent's Appeals officer sent petitioners a letter informing them that he had reviewed the offers in compromise. The Appeals officer determined that the minimum offer to compromise both the individual and joint liabilities should be a total of $2,400. The Appeals officer used petitioners' estimate of their primary vehicle[19] to calculate a quick sale value of $2,400, which was determined to be the minimum acceptable offer. The Appeals officer then attempted to determine whether petitioners would be able to meet the monthly installment offer obligation. In calculating petitioners' financial capability, the Appeals officer used petitioners' submitted monthly gross income figure of $4,608, but did not use petitioners' submitted $3,989 monthly expense figure. Instead of using the $3,989 expense figure provided by petitioners, the Appeals officer used $4,644, an estimated amount based on national statistical averages. Using $4,644 resulted in petitioners' estimated monthly expenses

---

[19] [fn 3] Petitioners estimated the value of their primary vehicle to be $3,000. Respondent used this figure to calculate the $2,400 quick sale value.

exceeding their monthly income by $36 and rendering petitioners ineligible due to their projected inability to make the $100–monthly payments.

The Appeals officer rejected petitioners' offers in compromise. Petitioners requested an in person hearing, but a hearing was not held due to petitioners' unavailability. On February 21, 2002, respondent issued two separate notices of determination for the individual and joint liabilities sustaining the filing of the notices of Federal tax liens and rejecting petitioners' offers in compromise. Petitioners timely appealed to this Court for review of respondent's determinations.

OPINION

Petitioners contend that the Appeals officer abused his discretion by rejecting their offers in compromise and by sustaining the filing of the Federal tax liens.

Section 6320 provides that a taxpayer shall be notified in writing by the Secretary of the filing of a Federal tax lien and provided with an opportunity for an administrative hearing. Sec. 6320(b). Hearings under section 6320 are conducted in accordance with the procedural requirements set forth in section 6330. Sec. 6320(c).

When an Appeals officer issues a determination regarding a disputed collection action, section 6330(d) allows a taxpayer to seek judicial review with the Tax Court or a District Court. Where the validity of the underlying tax liability is properly at issue, the Court will review the matter on a de novo basis. *Sego v. Commissioner,* 114 T.C. 604, 610, 2000 WL 889754 (2000). However, when the validity of the underlying tax is not at issue, the Court will review the Commissioner's administrative determination for an abuse of discretion. *Id.* Petitioners do not dispute the validity of the underlying tax. Accordingly, our review is for an abuse of discretion.

We do not conduct an independent review of what would be acceptable offers in compromise. We review only whether the Appeals officer's refusal to accept the offers in compromise was arbitrary, capricious, or without sound basis in fact or law. See *Woodral v. Commissioner,* 112 T.C. 19, 23, 1999 WL 9947 (1999). The Court considers whether the Commissioner abused his discretion in rejecting a taxpayer's position with respect to any relevant issues, including challenges to the appropriateness of the collections action, and offers of collection alternatives. See sec. 6330(c)(2)(A). This case involves collection alternatives.

Section 7122(a) authorizes the Secretary to compromise any civil case arising under the internal revenue laws. There are three standards that the Secretary may use to compromise a liability. The first standard is doubt as to liability, the second being doubt as to ability to collect, and the third being promotion of effective tax administration. Sec. 301.7122–1T(b), Temporary Proced. & Admin. Regs., 64 Fed.Reg. 39024 (July 21, 1999); see sec. 7122(c)(1).

The record reflects that petitioners' offers are with respect to doubt as to collectibility.[20]

Section 7122(c) provides the standards for evaluation of such offers. Under section 7122(c)(2):

(A) * * * the Secretary shall develop and publish schedules of national and local allowances designed to provide that taxpayers entering into a compromise have an adequate means to provide for basic living expenses.

(B) Use of schedules.—The guidelines shall provide that officers and employees of the Internal Revenue Service shall determine, on the basis of the facts and circumstances of each taxpayer, whether the use of the schedules published under subparagraph (A) is appropriate and *shall not use the schedules to the extent such use would result in the taxpayer not having adequate means to provide for basic living expenses.* [Emphasis added.]

The Appeals officer chose to use the national averages and that use resulted in petitioners' being categorized as not having adequate means to provide for basic living expenses.

The national average statistics are published by the Internal Revenue Service, but use of the statistics by Appeals officers is not mandatory. The Appeals officer exercised discretion in ignoring petitioners' submitted expense amount and, instead, used the national statistical amount as an estimate of petitioners' expenses. The use of the national averages for petitioners' expenses resulted in petitioners' monthly expenses exceeding their monthly income by $36. Therefore, by using the average expense figure, petitioners' income was $136 short of producing the $100 per month needed to compromise their tax liabilities for $2,400. We note that, percentagewise, the shortfall is less than 3 percent of petitioners' gross income. The Appeals officer chose to use the national statistical averages rather than the expense figures provided by petitioners. If the Appeals officer had used petitioners' submitted expense figure of $3,989, petitioners would have had $619 monthly and would have been financially capable of satisfying the $100 installments.

The Appeals officer is allowed to use the national schedules when considering the facts and circumstances of this case. However, if use of the schedules results in petitioners' not having adequate means to provide for basic living expenses, as here when the Appeals officer determined a negative $36 amount for basic living expenses, an installment offer may not be appropriate. See sec. 7122(c)(2)(B).

Under the regulations for doubt as to collectibility cases:

A determination of doubt as to collectibility will include a determination of ability to pay. In determining ability to pay, the Secretary will permit

---

[20] [fn 4] Doubt as to collectibility exists in any case where the taxpayer's assets and income are less than the full amount of the assessed liability. Sec. 301.7122–1T(b)(3), Temporary Proced. & Admin. Regs., 64 Fed.Reg. 39024 (July 21, 1999).

taxpayers to retain sufficient funds to pay basic living expenses. The determination of the amount of such basic living expenses will be founded upon an evaluation of the individual facts and circumstances presented by the taxpayer's case. To guide this determination, guidelines published by the Secretary on national and local living expense standards will be taken into account. [Sec. 301.7122–1T(b)(3)(ii), Temporary Proced. & Admin. Regs., 64 Fed.Reg. 39024 (July 21, 1999).]

The regulation provides that the guidelines are to be taken into account. When the Appeals officer reviewed petitioners' offers, he decided to use the guidelines because he thought petitioners' actual figures were too low. In that regard, there is no specific explanation why the Appeals officer believed that petitioners' monthly expenses of $3,989 was too low or why the guideline figure of $4,644 was more accurate. The use of the guideline expense figure resulted in a $136 shortfall in petitioners' capability to meet the $100–monthly installment to satisfy the $2,400 compromise. If petitioners' submitted monthly expenses of $3,989 had been used, there would have been a $619 surplus of income over expenses that would have enabled petitioners to meet the $100–monthly installment to satisfy the compromise.

In essence, the Appeals officer decided that petitioners could not live less expensively than the national average (guidelines). We find it curious that the Appeals officer relied on petitioners' figures for their vehicle and for their income, but chose not to use petitioners' figures for their monthly expenses. Petitioners made an estimate of $3,000 for the value of their primary car and the Appeals officer used this figure to calculate the quick sale value of $2,400. Based on this premise, the Appeals officer determined that an offer of $2,400 would be an appropriate amount to settle the outstanding liabilities due for 1990–92 and 1994–96. The Appeals officer requested a lump-sum payment through the sale of petitioners' primary vehicle. Petitioners rejected this approach as this was their primary vehicle and to sell it would have caused great financial harm.

Petitioners submitted an amended offer in compromise for $2,400, to be paid in $100 monthly installments. Under those terms, the $2,400 compromise could be paid in full in 2 years. That offer was rejected due to the Appeals officer's determination that petitioners were financially unable to make the payments. We note that petitioners had cooperated with all requests from the Internal Revenue Service in an attempt to resolve this matter.

Appeals officers, in the consideration of an offer in compromise should verify that the requirements of applicable law and administrative procedures have been met, and "whether any proposed collection action balances the need for the efficient collection of taxes with the legitimate concern of the person that any collection action be no more intrusive than necessary." See sec. 6330(c)(3)(C). The verification of applicable law and administrative procedure was met in this case. However, it is questionable as to whether the proposed collection action balanced the need for efficient collection of taxes with the concern of petitioners that any collection action be no more intrusive than necessary.

Payment plans are one possible option for an offer in compromise. According to the instructions that accompany the Form 656, there are three possible payment plans under the short-term deferred payment offer. One plan requires full payment of the realizable value of assets within 90 days from the date the Internal Revenue Service accepts the offer, and payment, within 2 years of acceptance of the amount that they could collect over 60 months. A second plan permits a cash payment for a portion of the realizable value of petitioners' assets within 90 days of the offer being accepted, and the balance of the realizable value plus the remainder of the amount that could have been collected over 60 months within 2 years. The third plan permits monthly payments of the entire offer amount over a period not to exceed 2 years from the date of acceptance by the Internal Revenue Service. Petitioners offered $100 per month for 2 years or 24 months, which equals the $2,400–compromise amount.[21]

Under the various payment options, respondent would be able to file Federal tax liens to protect his interests until such time as the liability is satisfied. Accordingly, respondent's interest would be protected through the liens while respondent received monthly payments. The result of the Appeals officer's financial analysis, however, was to deny petitioners' offers in compromise. To use the national guidelines rather than actual figures in this instance was arbitrary, capricious, and without a sound basis in fact. Petitioners have stated that they are still willing to compromise their tax liabilities for $2,400, but through monthly payments rather than a lump-sum payment.[22]

Therefore, based on the facts and circumstances of this case, we hold that respondent abused his discretion in denying petitioners' offer to compromise their tax liabilities for $2,400. We further hold that respondent did not abuse his discretion in sustaining the filing of the Notices of Federal Tax Liens.[23]

An appropriate decision will be entered.

NOTES AND QUESTIONS

1. The offer in compromise program is an essential feature of the IRS's collection efforts. It presents a tradeoff. It helps taxpayers who otherwise

---

[21] [fn 5] Although not relevant to the facts of this case, there is also a deferred payment offer that provides for a plan similar to the short-term deferred plan (the third plan described above). The deferred payment plan allows the entire offer amount to be made in monthly payments over the life of the collection statute. The deferred plan could result in a longer payment period than 24 months.

[22] [fn 6] Petitioners and respondent agreed on the amount of the compromise. The only disagreement here is the method of payment. Based on the financial information submitted by petitioners, a payment plan is a reasonable option.

[23] [fn 7] Petitioners have made no argument of merit from which an abuse of discretion could be found with respect to respondent's determination that the filing of the Notices of Federal Tax Liens was appropriate.

would not be able to satisfy their tax obligations, but it is also strict in order to avoid taxpayer abuse.

2. Do the taxpayers in *Samuel* and *Fowler* have proper reasons for pursuing an offer in compromise?

3. Did the IRS have good reason to reject the offers in *Samuel* and *Fowler*?

The IRS is not required to accept an offer where doing so would be against public policy. In *Barnes*, the IRS rejected an offer of $32,000 to settle a $400,000 liability.[24] The grounds for the offer were doubt as to collectibility with special circumstances and effective tax administration.[25]

The IRS rejected the Barnes' "effective tax administration" offer because the regulations require that the taxpayer have a sufficient amount of assets to pay the offer.[26] The IRS also rejected the "doubt as to collectibility" offer, because the taxpayers could afford to pay more than their minimum offer.[27]

One of the arguments the taxpayers made was that the IRS should have accepted their offer on the grounds of effective tax administration because they were fraud victims.[28] The taxpayers had been involved in "Hoyt" tax shelter partnerships.[29] Mr. Hoyt was a tax shelter promoter who told investors he had 38,000 head of cattle for breeding, when in reality he had fewer than 5,000.[30] He

---

[24] *See* Barnes v. Commissioner, 92 T.C.M. (CCH) 31, 31 (2006 T.C.M. (RIA) ¶ 2006-150 at 1014) ("Petitioners argue that Appeals was required to accept their offer of $32,000 to compromise what they estimate is their approximately $400,000 Federal income tax liability.").

[25] *See id.* at 34, 2006 T.C.M. (RIA) ¶ 2006-150 at 1018 ("Petitioners made their offer-in-compromise due to doubt as to collectibility with special circumstances and to promote effective tax administration.").

[26] *See id.* at 34, 2006 T.C.M. (RIA) ¶ 2006-150 at 1018 ("Cochran [the IRS Appeals Officer] determined that petitioners' offer did not qualify as an offer-in-compromise to promote effective tax administration because petitioners were unable to pay their liability in full.").

[27] *See id.* at 34, 2006 T.C.M. (RIA) ¶ 2006-150 at 1018 ("Cochran [the IRS Appeals Officer] determined that petitioners' offer [on the grounds of doubtful collectibility] was unacceptable because they were able to pay more than the $32,000 that they offered to compromise their tax liability.").

[28] *See id.* at 36, 2006 T.C.M. (RIA) ¶ 2006-150 at 1021 ("[P]etitioners argue that public policy demands that their offer-in-compromise be accepted because they were victims of fraud.").

[29] *See id.* at 33, 2006 T.C.M. (RIA) ¶ 2006-150 at 1017 ("This case is one in a long list of cases brought in this Court involving respondent's proposal to levy on the assets of a partner in a Hoyt partnership to collect Federal income taxes attributable to the partner's participation in the partnership.").

[30] *See* Durham Farms No. 1 v. Commissioner, 79 T.C.M. (CCH) 2009, 2016, (2000 T.C.M. (RIA) ¶ 2000-159, at 887) ("In the cattle count he performed from

procured investments in this imaginary cattle herd for tax benefits.[31] Over 3,000 investors were defrauded.[32] He sold these cows with inflated values to limited partnerships, including a partnership with the taxpayer, and then managed the herd.[33] Taxpayers who invested claimed deductions for expenses allocated to them under the partnership agreements.[34] With respect to Barnes, the court determined it was against public policy to compromise tax liabilities for those who owe taxes due to attempts to hide their tax liabilities as Barnes did by investing in Hoyt partnerships.[35]

---

fall 1992 through spring 1993, Mr. Daily determined there were a total of . . . 4,764 . . . mature breeding cattle."), *aff'd*, 59 Fed. Appx. 952 (9th Cir. 2003); Press Release, Dep't of Justice Exec. Office for U.S. Trs. (2003); Indictment Charges 54 Counts of Fraud in Oregon "Phantom Cow" Investment Scheme; Grand Jury Alleges Investors Lost $100,000, Press Release, Department of Justice Executive Office for United States Trustees (June 7, 1999) ("[W]hile" 38,000 adult female breeding cows were sold to investors, the defendants knew that they never had more than approximately 5,000 of such cows on hand. "'In short,'" the indictment stated, "'Defendants sold thousands of cows they never had and which did not exist.') . . .").

[31] *See Durham Farms*, 79 T.C.M. (CCH) at 2029, 2000 T.C.M. (RIA) ¶ 2000-159 at 902 ("The Hoyt organization greatly inflated the stated purchase prices in order to increase the potential tax benefits for investors.")

[32] *See* Indictment Charges 54 Counts of Fraud in Oregon "Phantom Cow" Investment Scheme; Grand Jury Alleges Investors Lost $100,000, Press Release, Dep't of Justice Exec. Office for U.S. Trs. (June 7, 1999), *supra* note 30.

[33] *See Durham Farms*, 79 T.C.M (CCH) at 2029, 2000 T.C.M. (RIA) ¶ 2000-159 at 901-02 ("Jay Hoyt, as managing general partner, represented each partnership in these transactions and other Hoyt organization entities 'sold'"" and then 'managed'"" the "'breeding cattle'" that a partnership had purportedly purchased. The Hoyt organization greatly inflated the stated purchase prices in order to increase the potential tax benefits for investors.").

[34] *See* Indictment Charges 54 Counts of Fraud in Oregon "Phantom Cow" Investment Scheme; Grand Jury Alleges Investors Lost $100,000, Press Release, Dep't of Justice Exec. Office for U.S. Trs. (June 7, 1999), supra note 30 ("Investment returns were to come from tax deductions and profits on the herd sale.").

[35] *See Barnes*, 92 T.C.M. (CCH) at 36, 2006 T.C.M. (RIA) ¶ 2006-150 at 1021 ("Reducing the risks of participating in tax shelters [by compromising the liabilities arising from disallowing the benefits from the tax shelters] would encourage more taxpayers to run those risks, thus undermining rather than enhancing compliance with the tax laws.").

3. Currently Not Collectible

A taxpayer with little or no income as well as a lack of other resources, *i.e.*, someone who cannot pay the IRS anything at all and may already be suffering hardship, can request that the IRS suspend its collection efforts and reclassify the liability as "currently not collectible," or "CNC." *See* Willis v. Commissioner, 86 T.C.M. (CCH) 506 (2003). Classifying the account as CNC removes the liability from collection inventory. Section 5.16.1.1(1) of the IRS's Internal Revenue Manual provides as follows:

> Accounts can be removed from active inventory after taking the necessary steps in the collection process.

The IRS may also classify an account as CNC where it has lost track of the taxpayer. If the taxpayer does not make a financial recovery and the liability is not settled, the CNC status will remain in effect until the collection statute runs out.

4. Combined Alternatives

The above three alternatives—installment agreements, OICs, and reclassification as CNC—can apply separately or together. For example, an installment agreement and an offer in compromise can combine. As part of an offer in compromise, a taxpayer may enter into an installment agreement that will pay only part of the tax liability while the IRS compromises the rest.

Another example is the combination of reclassifying an account as CNC and submitting an offer in compromise. Such a combination works well where the IRS has placed an account in CNC, but the taxpayer anticipates or hopes that he will return to the workforce. Once the account is in CNC, the taxpayer may make an offer in compromise so that when the taxpayer does regain taxpaying ability, he has a truly fresh start. The OIC in such a case is important because the CNC reclassification does not clear the underlying tax liability. In some cases, the continued liability does not matter. If the IRS has reclassified a taxpayer's account as CNC because of a permanent injury, the possibility exists that the taxpayer will never regain the ability to pay the tax so the collection statute eventually expires.

5. Taxpayer Assistance Orders

Another settlement mechanism is the Taxpayer Assistance Order or TAO. A taxpayer who is currently suffering or will imminently suffer a "significant hardship" resulting from an IRS administrative action may apply for a TAO with the National Taxpayer Advocate. Section 7811(a)(1)(A) provides as follows:

> Upon application filed by a taxpayer with the Office of the Taxpayer Advocate . . . the National Taxpayer Advocate [(NTA)] may issue a [TAO] if . . . the [NTA] determines the taxpayer is suffering or about to suffer a

significant hardship as a result of the manner in which the internal revenue laws are being administered by the Secretary.

Hardship in this context means an adverse IRS action, an excessive IRS delay in handling a taxpayer's account issues, the likely incurrence of costly representation absent relief, or suffering of serious harm absent relief. The TAO can force the IRS to release levied property; cease, take, or refrain from any action in the collection, bankruptcy, or investigation process; or any other process as seen fit by the NTA. Applying for a TAO to prevent a collection action suspends the ten-year collection statute until the National Taxpayer Advocate issues the TAO.

6. Audit Reconsideration

A taxpayer who has not had the opportunity to dispute the underlying tax liability prior to a proposed collection action may request audit reconsideration. *See* Tucker v. Commissioner, 135 T.C. 114, 148 (2010) (citing IRC § 6404(a)). The IRS has the authority to reconsider an audit. In an audit reconsideration, the IRS conducts another review of the taxpayer's underlying tax liability. The IRS may reconsider the underlying tax liability on request for audit reconsideration where the taxpayer has discovered new documentation or the IRS has made an error in the process of assessing the taxpayer's liability. The process is somewhat informal for income tax issues because, although the IRS may abate any tax, taxpayers may not file a formal claim for abatement of income tax. IRC § 6404(b) ("No claim for abatement shall be filed by a taxpayer in respect of any assessment of any tax imposed under subtitle A [income taxes].").

B. Collection Due Process Proceedings

Before the IRS can levy on a taxpayer's property, it must give the taxpayer an opportunity for administrative review of the IRS's collection actions by the Appeals Office, also known as a CDP hearing. Section 6330(b)(1) provides as follows:

> If the person [who has received a Notice of Intent to Levy] requests a [CDP] hearing in writing . . . and states the grounds for the requested hearing, such hearing shall be held by the Internal Revenue Service Office of Appeals.

Once the Appeals Officer issues a notice of determination, the taxpayer may appeal to the Tax Court. *See* IRC § 6330(d)(1). These procedures provide the taxpayer an opportunity to resolve most concerns regarding the lien and levy process and to negotiate with the IRS over whether and how the collection action should proceed. *See* Treas. Reg. § 301.6330-1(e)(1).

The IRS is required to notify the taxpayer of the right to request a CDP hearing around the time the IRS files an NFTL and around the time it files a notice of intent to levy. Section 6320(a)(2) provides as follows:

The [CDP] notice . . . shall be [provided] not more than 5 business days after the day of the filing of the notice of lien.

For each tax period addressed in a CDP notice, a taxpayer is entitled to request one lien hearing and one levy hearing. *See* IRC § 6320(b)(2); IRC § 6330(b)(2). Although it is not uncommon for the IRS to file NFTLs and levy notices on multiple properties at different times, only the first lien and first levy trigger the right to a CDP hearing. The taxpayer must request the CDP hearing in writing within 35 days of the lien filing in the case of a lien and 30 days from the CDP notice in the case of a levy. *See* IRC § 6320(a)(3)(B); Treas. Reg. § 301.6320-1(c); Treas. Reg. § 301.6330-1(c)(1); *but cf.* IRC § 6330(a)(2)(C) (containing no reference to a time period in which a taxpayer must make a request for a CDP hearing with respect to a levy).

If the taxpayer makes an untimely request for a CDP hearing, the IRS generally permits an "equivalent hearing." *See* Treas. Reg. § 301.6330-1(i)(1). An equivalent hearing is, as the name suggests, equivalent to a CDP hearing, except there is no right to appeal the decision to the Tax Court. *See* Treas. Reg. § 301.6330-1(i)(1)(iv). The period to request an equivalent hearing with respect to an NFTL is one year and five days after the filing of the NFTL. *See* Treas. Reg. § 301.6320-1(i)(2)(i).

While the Appeals Office considers a CDP request, the IRS suspends its administrative collection activities. *See* IRC § 6330(e). At the same time, the collection statute stops running. *See* IRC § 6330(e); IRC § 6320(c). The tolling of the limitations period begins upon the request for a CDP hearing and extends through resolution.

In a CDP hearing, a taxpayer may dispute the underlying tax liability in only limited circumstances. *See* IRC § 6330(c)(2)(B). The taxpayer may challenge the IRS's determination only in situations where he or she did not actually receive a Statutory Notice of Deficiency or had no other chance to dispute the underlying tax liability. For example, the Tax Court permitted a taxpayer couple that had filed a tax return without full payment to dispute their underlying liability in a CDP hearing because the opportunity to dispute an underlying tax liability typically occurs in the audit and appeal of a tax return where the IRS suspected the taxpayer had misreported the liability. *See generally* Montgomery v. Commissioner, 122 T.C. 1 (2004) (reviewed opinion).

Quirky disputes can arise as to whether a hearing was a CDP hearing or equivalent hearing. The following is such a case.

CRAIG v. COMMISSIONER
119 T.C. 252 (2002)
United States Tax Court

LARO, J.

Petitioner, while residing in Scottsdale, Arizona, petitioned the Court under section 6330(d)(1) to review respondent's determination as to his proposed levy upon petitioner's property. Respondent proposed the levy to collect Federal income taxes of approximately $10,656.55 for 1990, $12,192.27 for 1991, $18,437.01 for 1992, and $307.63 for 1995.[36] Currently, the case is before the Court on respondent's motion for summary judgment under Rule 121 and to impose a penalty against petitioner under section 6673(a). Petitioner has filed with the Court a response to respondent's motion.

We decide as a matter of first impression whether the Court has jurisdiction under section 6330(d)(1), given that respondent has never issued to petitioner a notice of determination with respect to a hearing described in section 6330 (Hearing[37]). Respondent acknowledges that petitioner was entitled to and should have been given a Hearing. All the same, respondent argues, the Court has jurisdiction to decide this case. Respondent argues that respondent's failure to grant petitioner's timely request for a Hearing was harmless error because petitioner was offered and attended an "equivalent hearing" under section 301.6330–1(i), Proced. & Admin. Regs. (equivalent hearing), and received a decision letter (decision letter) as to the equivalent hearing.

We hold that we have jurisdiction. Also, we shall grant respondent's motion for summary judgment, and we shall impose a $2,500 penalty against petitioner. . . .

BACKGROUND

A. Income Tax Returns for 1990, 1991, and 1992

Petitioner and his wife, Lorraine Craig (Ms. Craig), did not file timely Federal income tax returns for 1990 and 1991. On February 18, 1993, respondent prepared and filed substitutes for returns for those years under section 6020. In preparing the substitutes for returns, respondent relied on information received from the Bureau of Labor Statistics. On October 27, 1994, and on December 14, 1994, petitioner and Ms. Craig filed joint 1990 and 1991 Federal income tax returns, respectively. Those returns were treated by respondent as amended returns. On February 3, 1995, petitioner and Ms. Craig filed a joint 1992 Federal income tax return.

On October 5, 1995, respondent issued a notice of deficiency to petitioner and Ms. Craig. The notice determined that petitioner and Ms. Craig were liable for deficiencies in their 1990, 1991, and 1992 Federal income taxes. . . .

---

[36] [fn 1] We use the term "approximately" because these amounts were computed before the present proceeding and have since increased on account of interest.

[37] [fn 2] The parties and the Treasury regulations refer to the hearing described in sec. 6330 as a "collection due process hearing" (or a "CDP hearing" for short). That term is not used in either sec. 6330 or the legislative history underlying the promulgation of that section. The legislative history refers to the hearing as a "pre-levy hearing". H. Conf. Rept. 105–599, at 266 (1998); 1998–3 C.B. 747, 1020. We refer to it as a "Hearing".

Petitioner and Ms. Craig petitioned the Court with respect to the notice on December 21, 1995. On February 24, 1997, petitioner and Ms. Craig signed a stipulated decision. This decision listed the deficiencies in Federal income tax due from petitioner and Ms. Craig in accordance with the notice of deficiency and provided that "effective upon the entry of the decision by the Court, petitioners [petitioner and Ms. Craig] waive the restriction contained in Internal Revenue Code § 6213(a) prohibiting assessment and collection of the deficiencies and additions to the tax (plus statutory interest) until the decision of the Tax Court has become final." That stipulated decision was entered by the Court on February 27, 1997.

On May 5, 1997, on the basis of the stipulated decision, respondent assessed the 1990, 1991, and 1992 Federal income tax liabilities of petitioner and Ms. Craig.

B. Income Tax Return for 1995

On December 4, 1997, petitioner filed a 1995 Federal income tax return. On the basis of this return, respondent assessed petitioner's tax liability for 1995 on January 12, 1998.

C. Request for a Hearing

On February 22, 2001, respondent mailed to petitioner and Ms. Craig a letter, "Final Notice—Notice of Intent to Levy and Notice of Your Right to a Hearing" (final notice), for 1990, 1991, and 1992. On the same day, respondent mailed to petitioner a final notice for 1995. Both final notices were signed by a chief of the IRS Automated Collection Branch in Ogden, Utah. These notices informed petitioner and Ms. Craig of (1) respondent's intent to levy upon their property pursuant to section 6331 and (2) their right under section 6330 to a Hearing with respondent's Office of Appeals (Appeals). Enclosed with the final notices were copies of Forms 12153, Request for a Collection Due Process Hearing. On March 17, 2001, petitioner requested timely the referenced Hearing for 1990, 1991, 1992, and 1995 by mailing to respondent a letter accompanied by two Forms 12153, the first for 1990, 1991, and 1992, and the second for 1995. Petitioner signed the letter, but he did not sign the Forms 12153. In that letter, petitioner requested a Hearing and stated the following disagreement with the proposed levy:

> this letter constitutes my request for a Collection Due Process Hearing, as provided for in Code Sections 6320 and 6330, with regards to the Final Notice—Notice of Intent to Levy at issue * * *

> Since Section 6330(c)(1) requires that "The appeals officer shall at the hearing obtain verification from the Secretary that the requirements of any applicable law or administrative procedure have been met," I am requesting that the appeals officer have such verification with him at the Collection Due Process Hearing and that he send me a copy such verification within 30 days from the date of this letter. In the absence of any such hearing, and if you fail to send me the requested Treasury Department Regulations and Delegation Orders within 30 days from the date of this letter, then I will consider this

entire matter closed. If you do attempt to take any enforcement action against me without according me the hearing requested, and without sending me the documentation requested, you will be violating numerous laws which I will identify in a 7433 lawsuit against you and the government.

On April 12, 2001, the Ogden Service Center returned the requests to petitioner and Ms. Craig because the Forms 12153 were not signed. Two identical letters with respect to 1990, 1991, 1992, and with respect to 1995, sent to petitioner with Forms 12153 stated:

> We are returning your Form 12153, Request for a Collection Due Process Hearing, because you did not sign it. If you have not been able to work out a solution to your tax liability and still want to request a hearing with the IRS Office of Appeals, you need to complete and sign the Form 12153.

> If we do not hear from you by May 3, 2001, we may take enforcement action without notifying you further.

On May 6, 2001, the Ogden Service Center received from petitioner two signed Forms 12153 for 1990, 1991, and 1992, and for 1995, respectively, which stated:

> This Form 12153 WAS NOT SIGNED VOLUNTARILY, but UNDER DURESS, not wishing to give the I.R.S. or it's agents any cause to deny or delay the Due Process Hearing guaranteed to me by law as per IRC Section 6330. My signature on this document DOES NOT give even TACIT AGREEMENT that the "statutory period of limitations for collection be suspended during the Collection Due Process Hearing and any subsequent judicial review".

On September 28, 2001, the Appeals officer held with petitioner an equivalent hearing. At the equivalent hearing, the Appeals officer explained to petitioner that it was an equivalent hearing and not a Hearing. The Appeals officer then reviewed and showed to petitioner Forms 4340, Certificate of Assessments, Payments and Other Specified Matters. The Forms 4340 were dated July 17, 2001, and were for 1990, 1991, 1992, and 1995. On September 28, 2001, after the equivalent hearing, the Appeals officer sent the Forms 4340 to petitioner.

On October 27, 2001, the Appeals officer issued to petitioner a "Decision Letter Concerning Equivalent Hearing Under Section 6320 and/or 6330" (i.e., the decision letter) for 1990, 1991, 1992, and 1995. The decision letter sustained the proposed collection action against petitioner. The decision letter stated that petitioner did not have the right to judicial review of the decision set forth in the decision letter. The decision letter stated:

> Your due process hearing request was not filed within the time prescribed under Section 6320 and/or 6330. However, you received a hearing equivalent to a due process hearing except that there is no right to dispute a decision by the Appeals Office in court under IRC Sections 6320 and/or 6330.

DISCUSSION

A. Jurisdiction Under Section 6330(d)(1)

We decide for the first time whether we have jurisdiction under section 6330(d)(1) in the setting at hand. We conclude that we do. We set forth the relevant text of section 6330 in an appendix.

Section 6330(d)(1) is the specific provision that governs our jurisdiction to review a proposed collection action. Our jurisdiction under that section depends upon the issuance of a valid notice of determination and a timely petition for review. E.g., *Goza v. Commissioner,* 114 T.C. 176, 182, 2000 WL 283864 (2000); see also *Lunsford v. Commissioner,* 117 T.C. 159, 161, 2001 WL 1521578 (2001). See generally *Offiler v. Commissioner,* 114 T.C. 492, 498, 2000 WL 777218 (2000) ("The notice of determination provided for in section 6330 is, from a jurisdictional perspective, the equivalent of a notice of deficiency."). Here, petitioner has timely filed a petition with this Court.[38] Thus, we are left to decide whether respondent has made a "determination" within the meaning of section 6330(d)(1) which we have jurisdiction to review.

Respondent acknowledges that petitioner did not have the Hearing described in section 6330. All the same, respondent argues, the decision letter issued to petitioner as to the equivalent hearing reflects a "determination" sufficient to invoke the Court's jurisdiction under section 6330(d)(1). We agree. The Treasury Department regulations interpreting section 6330 recognize specifically that there are two types of hearings which may be conducted by Appeals in connection with section 6330; i.e., Hearings and equivalent hearings. As explained below, the Treasury Department regulations state that an Appeals officer will consider at an equivalent hearing the same issues as at a Hearing, and that the contents of the decision letter that results from an equivalent hearing will generally be the same as in the notice of determination that results from a Hearing.

As to a Hearing, the statute provides that a taxpayer has a right to a Hearing with an Appeals officer before a levy may be made upon his or her property, if the Hearing is timely requested by the taxpayer. Sec. 6330(a)(1), (a)(2), (a)(3)(B), and (b)(1). The statute provides further that at the Hearing the taxpayer may raise any relevant matter set forth in section 6330(c) and that the Appeals officer shall make a "determination" as to those matters. Sec. 6330(c) and (d)(1); see also sec. 301.6330–1(f), Proced. & Admin. Regs. (regulations interpreting section 6330 provide that the Appeals officer must issue a "Notice of Determination" to any taxpayer who timely requests a Hearing).[39] The statute gives a taxpayer the right

---

[38] [fn 3] The decision letter was sent to petitioner on Oct. 27, 2001, and the petition was postmarked Nov. 21, 2001. Whereas the petition was actually filed by the Court when received on Dec. 28, 2001, the approximately 6–week delivery time was attributable to delays in the receipt of mail experienced by the Court because of anthrax.

[39] [fn 4] The regulations provide further that, in general, the notice of determination must set forth the Appeals officer's findings and decisions. Sec. 301.6330–1(e)(3), Q & A–E8, Proced. & Admin. Regs. More specifically, the

to contest the Appeals officer's determination in the appropriate judicial forum, sec. 6330(d)(1), and precludes respondent from proceeding with the proposed levy that is the subject of the Hearing while the Hearing and any appeals thereof are pending, sec. 6330(e)(1). The statute provides that the applicable periods of limitation under sections 6502, 6531, or 6532 are suspended for the same period. Sec. 6330(e)(1).

Whereas the above-stated rules for a Hearing are provided explicitly in the statute, the rules for an equivalent hearing have their genesis in the statute's legislative history and the regulations implementing Congressional intent as gleaned from that history. See H. Conf. Rept. 105–599, at 266 (1998); 1998–3 C.B. 1020 (in the event that a taxpayer does not timely request a Hearing, "The Secretary must provide a hearing equivalent to the hearing if later requested by the taxpayer"); cf. *Johnson v. Commissioner,* 86 AFTR 2d 2000–5225, 2000–2 USTC par. 50,591 (D.Or.2000) ("'equivalent hearing' is provided for only by regulation and is not mandated by Section 6330 itself"). The scheme of the regulations as they apply to equivalent hearings generally follows the statutory scheme for Hearings.

Under the regulations, any taxpayer who fails to timely request a Hearing may receive an equivalent hearing. Sec. 301.6330–1(i)(1), Proced. & Admin. Regs. The equivalent hearing (like the Hearing) is held with Appeals, and the Appeals officer considers the same issues which he or she would have considered had the equivalent hearing been a Hearing. *Id.* The Appeals officer also generally follows the same procedures at an equivalent hearing which he or she would have followed had the equivalent hearing been a Hearing. *Id.* Although the Appeals officer concludes an equivalent hearing by issuing a decision letter, as opposed to a notice of determination, the different names which are assigned to these documents are merely a distinction without a difference when it comes to our jurisdiction over this case, where a Hearing was timely requested. The decision letter contains all of the information required by section 301.6330–1(e)(3), Q & A–E8, Proced. & Admin. Regs., to be included in a notice of determination but for the fact that the decision letter ordinarily states in regard to most issues that a

---

notice of determination must: (1) State whether respondent met the requirements of any applicable law or administrative procedure; (2) resolve any issue appropriately raised by the taxpayer relating to the unpaid tax; (3) decide any appropriate spousal defenses raised by the taxpayer; (4) decide any challenge made by the taxpayer to the appropriateness of the collection action; (5) respond to any offers by the taxpayer for collection alternatives; (6) address whether the proposed collection action represents a balance between the need for the efficient collection of taxes and the legitimate concern of the taxpayer that any collection action be no more intrusive than necessary; (7) set forth any agreements that Appeals reached with the taxpayer, any relief given the taxpayer, and any actions which the taxpayer or respondent are required to take; and (8) advise the taxpayer of the right to seek judicial review within 30 days of the date of the notice of determination. Id.

taxpayer may not (as opposed to may) seek judicial review of the decision.[40] *Id.;* cf. sec. 301.6330–1(i)(2), Q & A–I5, Proced. & Admin. Regs. (taxpayer may in certain cases contest in court the Appeals officer's decision in an equivalent hearing to deny a claim for relief from joint liability under section 6015).

Under the facts herein, where Appeals issued the decision letter to petitioner in response to his timely request for a Hearing, we conclude that the "decision" reflected in the decision letter issued to petitioner is a "determination" for purposes of section 6330(d)(1). Cf. *Moorhous v. Commissioner,* 116 T.C. 263, 270, 2001 WL 406389 (2001) (decision reflected in a decision letter was not a "determination" under section 6330(d)(1) where the taxpayer's request for a Hearing was untimely); *Nelson v. Commissioner,* T.C. Memo.2002–264 (same); *Lopez v. Commissioner,* T.C. Memo.2001–228 (same). The fact that respondent held with petitioner a hearing labeled as an equivalent hearing, rather than a hearing labeled as a Hearing, and that respondent issued to petitioner a document labeled as a decision letter, rather than a document labeled as a notice of determination, does not erase the fact that petitioner received a "determination" within the meaning of section 6330(d)(1). We hold that we have jurisdiction to decide this case.

B. Respondent's Motion for Summary Judgment

Summary judgment is intended to expedite litigation and avoid unnecessary and expensive trials. Fla. Peach Corp. v. Commissioner, 90 T.C. 678, 681, 1988 WL 31439 (1988). Summary judgment may be granted with respect to all or any part of the legal issues in controversy "if the pleadings, answers to interrogatories, depositions, admissions, and any other acceptable materials, together with the affidavits, if any, show that there is no genuine issue as to any material fact and that a decision may be rendered as a matter of law." Rule 121(a) and (b); Sundstrand Corp. v. Commissioner, 98 T.C. 518, 520, 1992 WL 88529 (1992), affd. 17 F.3d 965 (7th Cir.1994). The moving party bears the burden of proving that there is no genuine issue of material fact, and factual inferences are drawn in a manner most favorable to the party opposing summary judgment. Dahlstrom v. Commissioner, 85 T.C. 812, 821, 1985 WL 15413 (1985); Jacklin v. Commissioner, 79 T.C. 340, 344, 1982 WL 11139 (1982).

Petitioner has raised no genuine issue as to any material fact. Accordingly, we conclude that this case is ripe for summary judgment.

Section 6331(a) provides that if any person liable to pay any tax neglects or refuses to pay such tax within 10 days after notice and demand for payment, the Secretary may collect such tax by levy on the person's property. Section 6331(d) provides that at least 30 days before enforcing collection by levy on the person's

---

[40] [fn 5] Nor do we find a distinction for purposes of our jurisdiction in the fact that the Treasury Department's regulations provide that a taxpayer's request for an equivalent hearing neither automatically suspends the levy actions which are subject of the Hearing nor the running of any period of limitations under secs. 6502, 6531, or 6532. Sec. 301.6330–1(i)(2), Q & A–I1 and 2, Proced. & Admin. Regs.

property, the Secretary must provide the person with a final notice of intent to levy, including notice of the administrative appeals available to the person.

Section 6330 generally provides that the Commissioner cannot proceed with collection by levy until the person has been provided with notice and the opportunity for an administrative review of the matter (in the form of a Hearing before Appeals) and, if dissatisfied, with judicial review of the administrative determination. *Davis v. Commissioner,* 115 T.C. 35, 37, 2000 WL 1048515 (2000); *Goza v. Commissioner,* 114 T.C. at 179. In the event of such a judicial review, the Court's standard of review depends on whether the underlying tax liability is at issue. The Court reviews a taxpayer's liability under the de novo standard where the validity of the underlying tax liability is at issue. The Court reviews the other administrative determinations for abuse of discretion. *Sego v. Commissioner,* 114 T.C. 604, 610, 2000 WL 889754 (2000). A taxpayer's underlying tax liability may be at issue only if he or she "did not receive any statutory notice of deficiency for such tax liability or did not otherwise have an opportunity to dispute such tax liability." Sec. 6330(c)(2)(B).

With respect to 1990, 1991, and 1992, petitioner received a notice of deficiency and petitioned the Court with respect thereto. It follows that petitioner's underlying tax liability for 1990, 1991, and 1992 is not at issue. Accordingly, we review respondent's determination for these years for abuse of discretion.

With respect to 1995, petitioner neither received a notice of deficiency nor had an opportunity to dispute the underlying tax liability. Whereas the Appeals officer did not allow petitioner to raise at the equivalent hearing the underlying tax liability for that year, respondent now recognizes that it was error to do so (i.e., to not allow petitioner to dispute the underlying tax liability for 1995). See *Hoffman v. Commissioner,* 119 T.C. 140 (2002). We review petitioner's underlying tax liability for 1995 on a de novo basis.

Petitioner asserts in his petition the following allegations of error as to 1990, 1991, 1992, and 1995:

a) * * * the appeals officer violated the law by not "presenting" petitioner with the "verification from the Secretary" as required by Code Sections 6330(c)(1) and 6330(c)(3)(A).

b) No statutory Notice and Demand for payment was ever sent to petitioner in accordance with the provisions and requirements of Code Sections 6303, 6321, and 6331.

c) No Regulation exists, as referred to in Code Sections 6001 and 6011, that requires petitioner to pay the tax at issue.

d) No valid statutory notice of deficiency was sent to petitioner.

e) No valid assessment showing an amount due could have been assessed from petitioner's returns.

f) No other returns exist from which an assessment could have complied with the provisions of section 26 USC 6201(a)(1).

g) No statute in the Internal Revenue Code establishes the "existence * * * of the underlying liability" as referred to in 6330(c)(2)(B), and the United States will not be able to identify for this Court any statute that refers to any such tax liability as for example Code sections 4401(c), 5005(a), and 5703(a) do with respect to Wagering, Distilled spirits, and Tobacco taxes.

h) No statute in the Internal Revenue code establishes a requirement "to pay" the income tax at issue, as for example code sections 4401(c), 5007(a) and 5703(b) do with respect to Federal Wagering, Alcohol, and Tobacco taxes.

i) The notice received by petitioner notifying him of his right to a hearing was not signed by the Secretary or his delegate as required by 26 USC 6330(a)(1).

We turn to address these allegations.

First, petitioner alleges that the Appeals officer failed to obtain verification from the Secretary that the requirements of all applicable laws and administrative procedures were met as required by section 6330(c)(1). We disagree. Section 6330(c)(1) does not require the Appeals officer to rely upon a particular document (e.g., the summary record itself rather than transcripts of account) in order to satisfy this verification requirement. *Kuglin v. Commissioner*, T.C. Memo.2002–51; see also *Weishan v. Commissioner*, T.C. Memo.2002–88. Nor does it mandate that the Appeals officer actually give a taxpayer a copy of the verification upon which the Appeals officer relied. Sec. 6330(c)(1); sec. 301.6330–1(e)(1), Proced. & Admin. Regs.; see also *Nestor v. Commissioner*, 118 T.C. 162, 2002 WL 236682 (2002). Given the additional fact that petitioner was actually given copies of the relevant Forms 4340,[41] which are a valid verification that the requirements of any applicable law or administrative procedure have been met, *Roberts v. Commissioner*, 118 T.C. 365, 2002 WL 844724 (2002); *Mudd v. Commissioner*, T.C. Memo.2002–204; *Howard v. Commissioner*, T.C. Memo.2002–81; *Mann v. Commissioner*, T.C. Memo.2002–48, we hold that: (1) The assessments were valid, *Kuglin v. Commissioner, supra;* see also *Duffield v. Commissioner*, T.C. Memo.2002–53; and (2) the Appeals officer satisfied the verification requirement of section 6330(c)(1), *Yacksyzn v. Commissioner*, T.C. Memo.2002–99; cf. *Nicklaus v. Commissioner*, 117 T.C. 117,

---

[41] [fn 6] Federal tax assessments are formally recorded on a record of assessment. Sec. 6203. The summary record of assessment must "provide identification of the taxpayer, the character of the liability assessed, the taxable period, if applicable, and the amount of the assessment." Sec. 301.6203–1, Proced. & Admin. Regs. The record shows that in addition to Forms 4340, petitioner received IMF MCC transcripts of account for 1990, 1991, 1992, and 1995. Those transcripts of petitioner's account for respective years also contained all the information required under section 301.6203–1, Proced. & Admin. Regs.

120–121, 2001 WL 1083721 (2001). Petitioner has not demonstrated in this proceeding any irregularity in the assessment procedure that would raise a question about the validity of the assessment or the information contained in Forms 4340.

Second, petitioner alleges that no statutory notice and demand for payment was sent to him. We disagree. "The Secretary shall, as soon as practicable, and within 60 days, after the making of an assessment of a tax pursuant to section 6203, give notice to each person liable for the unpaid tax, stating the amount and demanding payment thereof." Sec. 6303(a). If mailed, this notice and demand is required to be sent to the taxpayer's last known address. *Id.* Forms 4340 show that respondent sent petitioner notices of balance due on the same dates that respondent made assessments against petitioner for the subject years. A notice of balance due constitutes a notice and demand for payment under section 6303(a). *Schaper v. Commissioner,* T.C. Memo.2002–203. In addition, petitioner received numerous final notices (notices of intention to levy), as well as notices of deficiency, receipt of which petitioner does not dispute. These numerous notices were sufficient and met the requirements of section 6303(a). *Hansen v. United States,* 7 F.3d 137, 138 (9th Cir.1993); *Hughes v. United States,* 953 F.2d 531, 536 (9th Cir.1992); *Weishan v. Commissioner, supra.* "The form on which a notice of assessment and demand for payment is made is irrelevant as long as it provides the taxpayer with all the information required under 26 U.S.C. § 6303(a)." *Elias v. Connett,* 908 F.2d 521, 525 (9th Cir.1990).

Third, petitioner alleges that the final notice is invalid because it was not signed by the Secretary or his delegate as required by section 6330(a)(1). We disagree. For purposes of section 6330(a), either the Secretary or his delegate (e.g., the Commissioner) may issue a final notice of intent to levy. Secs. 7701(a)(11)(B) and (12)(A)(i), 7803(a)(2); see also sec. 301.6330–1(a)(1), Proced. & Admin. Regs. Here, the authority to levy on petitioner's property was delegated to the "Automated Collection Branch Chiefs pursuant to Delegation Order No. 191 (Rev. 2), effective October 1, 1999. Internal Revenue Manual, sec. 1.2.104, 102 (Nov. 24, 1999)." *Wilson v. Commissioner,* T.C. Memo.2002–242. Consistent with this delegation of authority, the final notice on intent to levy in this case, which was executed by the chief of the Automated Collection Branch in Ogden, Utah, was valid.

As to petitioner's remaining allegations, each allegation is a shop-worn, frivolous contention which "We perceive no need to refute * * * with somber reasoning and copious citation of precedent; to do so might suggest that these arguments have some colorable merit." *Crain v. Commissioner,* 737 F.2d 1417, 1417 (5th Cir.1984). Suffice it to say:

1. the Internal Revenue Code establishes the existence of his underlying tax liability and requires him to pay income tax, Tolotti v. Commissioner, T.C. Memo.2002–86;

2. petitioner is a taxpayer subject to the Federal income tax, see secs. 1(c), 7701(a)(1), (14);

3. compensation for labor or services rendered constitutes income subject to the Federal income tax, sec. 61(a)(1); *United States v. Romero,* 640 F.2d 1014, 1016 (9th Cir.1981);

4. petitioner is required to file an income tax return, sec. 6012(a)(1); and

5. petitioner's failure to report tax on a return does not prevent the Commissioner from determining a deficiency in his Federal income tax, secs. 6211(a), 6212(a); see *Monaco v. Commissioner,* T.C. Memo.1998–284.

Petitioner has failed to raise a spousal defense, make a valid challenge to the appropriateness of respondent's intended collection action, or offer alternative means of collection. These issues are now deemed conceded. Rule 331(b)(4).

For the foregoing reasons, we sustain respondent's determination as to the proposed levy as a permissible exercise of discretion.

C. Respondent's Motion to Impose a Penalty Against Petitioner

We now turn to the requested penalty under section 6673. Section 6673(a)(1) authorizes the Court to require a taxpayer to pay to the United States a penalty not in excess of $25,000 whenever it appears that proceedings have been instituted or maintained by the taxpayer primarily for delay or that the taxpayer's position in such proceeding is frivolous or groundless. We have repeatedly indicated our willingness to impose such penalties in lien and levy review proceedings. *Roberts v. Commissioner,* 118 T.C. 365, 2002 WL 844724 (2002); *Hoffman v. Commissioner,* T.C. Memo.2000–198. Moreover, we have imposed penalties in such proceedings when the taxpayer has raised frivolous and groundless arguments as to the legality of the Federal tax laws. *Yacksyzn v. Commissioner,* T.C. Memo.2002–99; *Watson v. Commissioner,* T.C. Memo.2001–213; *Davis v. Commissioner,* T.C. Memo.2001–87.

In accordance with the firmly established law set forth above, we conclude that petitioner's positions in this proceeding are frivolous and/or groundless.[42] We also conclude from the record that petitioner has instituted and maintained this proceeding primarily for delay. Accordingly, pursuant to section 6673, we require him to pay to the United States a penalty of $2,500.

We have considered all arguments and have found those arguments not discussed herein to be irrelevant and/or without merit. To reflect the foregoing,

An appropriate order and decision will be entered for respondent.

[Appendix omitted.]

---

[42] [fn 7] The Appeals officer directed petitioner's attention to our decision in Pierson v. Commissioner, 115 T.C. 576, 2000 WL 1840062 (2000), wherein taxpayers advancing frivolous and groundless claims and instituting proceedings under sec. 6330(d) for the purpose of delay were given an unequivocal warning that the Court would impose penalties. In addition, petitioner received a copy of our opinion in that case; that opinion was sent to him by the Appeals officer after the equivalent hearing.

NOTES AND QUESTIONS

1. What is the difference between a CDP hearing and an equivalent hearing?
2. Is a taxpayer entitled to an equivalent hearing?
3. If a taxpayer would have been entitled to a CDP hearing but fails to make a timely request, what is the likelihood the IRS will provide an equivalent hearing if requested?

UNIT 2

TAX COMPLIANCE

A taxpayer who has decided to comply with the tax laws must figure out how to navigate a complex tax compliance legal framework. Tax compliance means different things in different contexts to different people. Here, tax compliance has a broad meaning. The substantive and procedural tax compliance legal framework covers far more than merely filing a tax return. A taxpayer must self-determine her tax liability, timely report the liability on a return, and timely pay. In addition, the compliance framework provides both the government and the taxpayer a limited time period in which either may make changes to the taxpayer's reported liability.

CHAPTER 7

TAX LIABILITY SELF-DETERMINATION

A. Framework

The government has a reasonable expectation that each taxpayer pay her fair share to fund the government. As a guiding principle, the term "fair share" does not provide any direction as to what the government expects. Leaving it to taxpayers to contribute whatever they want has proven to be unsuccessful as a means to run the government. For example, the original constitution, the Articles of Confederation, permitted state governments to contribute whatever amounts they wanted to the federal government. The system predictably failed. *See* THE FEDERALIST NO. 30 (Alexander Hamilton).

When a taxpayer decides to comply with the tax laws, the first thing she has to do is figure out how much tax she owes. Intuitively, one would expect the government to determine how much tax a taxpayer owes and then require payment. In the United States, however, instead of determining how much income tax each taxpayer owes, the government tells taxpayers how to determine their own liability. Tax professionals refer to the process of self-determination and subsequent return filing as "self-assessment." Although the government does not tell taxpayers what precise amount to pay, the reporting and paying of income and other taxes is mandatory.

Taxpayers do not, however, intuitively know how to determine their fair share in the manner the government requires. Therefore, the government must communicate how it expects taxpayers to determine their own tax liabilities. The United States government communicates its expectations through statutes, administrative guidance, and judicial opinions. Taxpayers must interpret this guidance to determine their own liabilities. Interpreting each set of communications involves different legal issues. Taken together, these communications form the relevant tax law with which taxpayers comply.

To determine one's own tax liability, a taxpayer must understand the interplay of the communications the three government branches provide to taxpayers. This interpretation is both a science and an art. Three common challenges in interpreting the government's communications for purposes of tax compliance are the following: (1) interpreting statutes, (2) evaluating administrative guidance, and (3) weighing stare decisis and precedent. Understanding this interplay provides taxpayers with opportunities for tax planning.

B. Tax Statutes

The United States Constitution grants Congress the authority to enact statutes. The Internal Revenue Code is a grouping of tax statutes Congress has enacted that communicates to taxpayers how the government expects them to determine their own tax liabilities. Like much other statutory language, the Code's language is imprecise. A taxpayer, like a court, must figure out what the government wants her to do by interpreting the statute. If a dispute arises, and the taxpayer has the resources and the will to pursue a judicial remedy, a court will have the last word as to what the Code requires of the taxpayer. Therefore, it is important to anticipate how a court interprets statutes such as the Code.[1]

Despite its imprecision, statutory language cannot simply be anything the reader desires it to be. An individual who sees a sign that says, "Stop," yet fails to stop at the intersection where the sign stands, cannot reasonably expect a positive result after telling the police officer that he interprets "stop" to mean "go." Conversely, a police officer cannot reasonably expect a court to enforce a ticket given to a driver who did not stop at the "stop" sign indefinitely.

The Supreme Court is the ultimate interpreter of statutes, but it has given no formal guidance as to the correct interpretive theory.[2] There are a number of different theoretical methods espoused by judges and scholars. These theories take into account, among other things, the process of enacting legislation.

The legislative process begins with a proposal for a new law. The proposal can come from anywhere—federal agencies, taxpayers, members of Congress, or nonprofit organizations. If a member of the U.S. House of Representatives finds merit in the proposal, the member acts as its sponsor and submits it to the House

---

[1] As Justice Oliver Wendell Holmes once said, "The prophecies of what the courts will do in fact, and nothing more pretentious, are what I mean by the law." O. W. Holmes, *The Path of Law*, 10 HARV. L. REV. 457, 461 (1897).

[2] *See* HENRY M. HART, JR. & ALBERT M. SACKS, THE LEGAL PROCESS: BASIC PROBLEMS IN THE MAKING AND APPLICATION OF LAW 1169 (William N. Eskridge, Jr. & Philip P. Frickey eds., 1994) ("The hard truth of the matter is that American courts have no intelligible, generally accepted, and consistently applied theory of statutory interpretation.").

Clerk. Generally, either a Senator or a House member can introduce legislation, but tax legislation can be introduced only in the House. *See* U.S. CONST. art. I, § 7, cl. 1. Once the Clerk processes the proposal, converting it into an official bill, the Speaker of the House forwards the bill to the House Ways and Means Committee for consideration. The Ways and Means Committee then conducts hearings and markup sessions. If the committee supports the proposal, it drafts a report before sending it to the full House for all members to consider. If approved, the bill moves to the Senate Finance Committee for a similar committee review, reporting, and approval process. Usually, the bill approved in the Senate is not identical to the bill approved in the House. A conference committee generally convenes and works out the differences in the language of the two chambers. The revised bill and the Conference Report return to both the House and the Senate for approval. Upon both House and Senate approval, the President must act on the bill. Once the President signs the bill, it becomes a law.

During this process, there are opportunities for taxpayer involvement. As stated, a proposal can come from a taxpayer. Although most taxpayers do not have sufficient resources to develop viable tax proposals, some taxpayers have the resources to hire tax professionals and lobbyists to assist them in developing tax legislation proposals and facilitating congressional review of them. Research shows that compliance rates are higher when taxpayers have the opportunity to participate in the lawmaking process.[3]

As discussed, interpretive theories take the legislative process into account. Four of the leading interpretive theories are realism, purposivism, intentionalism, and textualism. All four theories agree that Congress's intent in enacting a statute is the relevant law, that there are clues to this intent in legislative process byproducts, and that the legislation's context can be considered. Thus, the three central debates regarding interpretation focus on: (1) the scope of Congress's intent to consider, (2) the breadth of the internal and external context to consider, and (3) which byproducts of the legislative process are important in examining intent and context.

If a statute is clear, and there are no countervailing reasons not to apply it as written, an interpreter who employs any of the above interpretive theories would have no doubts about giving effect to the statutory language. The problems arise when a statute is unclear or there are countervailing reasons for applying it as written. Perhaps the statute is ambiguous or the legislature had another obvious intention when it enacted the statutory words. This is the point where the leading interpretive theories become important.

1. Realism

---

[3] *See* Lars P. Feld & Bruno S. Frey, *Tax Compliance as the Result of a Psychological Tax Contract: The Role of Incentives and Responsive Regulation*, 29 LAW & POL'Y 102, 107 (2007); TOM R. TYLER, WHY PEOPLE OBEY THE LAW (2006).

Of the four leading theories of interpretation, realism is the broadest in scope. Realists view the judge's role as giving effect to Congress's intent in a broad sense.[4] Where a statute has not addressed a particular issue or has not addressed the issue coherently, a realist judge will fill in legislative gaps according to what Congress should have done if faced with the situation. Realists take on a legislative role in this process. A realist judge also considers the broad factual context of the statute at issue, including the consequences. The court considers the statute, the legal context, the economic impact of the statute or new rule, and any other adverse consequences of a new rule.

2. Intentionalism

Intentionalists take a slightly narrower view than realists of the interpreter's role. They see the judge's role as giving effect to Congress's intent as expressed in the statutory language as well as any clues to legislative intent as expressed in the statute's legislative history. Although intentionalists do not see themselves as legislators, they appear willing to piece together rules contrary to an enacted statute from a statute's unenacted legislative history. *See, e.g.*, Bob Jones Univ. v. United States, 461 U.S. 574, 590-91 (1983) (relying on legislative history to infer that section 501(c)(3) includes public policy requirement for organizations to maintain a tax exemption under that provision). Intentionalists also take a broad view of the context in which a rule is applied. Where it appears a statute has not considered a specific factual context, an intentionalist does not have a problem ignoring a statute's language. *See, e.g.*, Church of the Holy Trinity v. United States, 143 U.S. 457, 458-59 (1892) (exempting a foreign priest from a statutory prohibition on helping an alien immigrate to the United States to "perform . . . labor of any kind").

3. Purposivism

Purposivists take a slightly narrower view of their domain than intentionalists. The differences between a purposivist and an intentionalist are subtle. The purposivist sees the judge's role as giving effect to Congress's intent as expressed by a reasonable legislature as opposed to intentionalist's focus on the intent expressed by individual legislators involved in passing the legislation at issue. This focus on the reasonable legislature shows less reverence to legislative history as compared to intentionalists, but does not exclude it. When faced with an unclear statute, the purposivist may rely on the legislative history to determine the problem the legislature tried to resolve with the legislation.

---

[4] *See* RICHARD A. POSNER, REFLECTIONS ON JUDGING 121 (2013).

4. Textualism

Textualism is the most restrained of the four interpretive categories. Textualists see the court's role as limited to giving effect to the legislature's will as formally enacted in statutory language. Textualism is often referred to as formalism because of this focus on the formal enactments. The perspective the textualist interpreter takes is that of a reasonable person attempting to comply with the enacted language. Unlike an intentionalist, a textualist does not focus on the legislature's intent as determined by individual legislators. And unlike a purposivist, a textualist does not focus on the problems the legislature was trying to resolve. Rather, the textualist focuses on intent as determined by the language agreed upon by the legislature and actually enacted. Textualists, therefore, find legislative history of little use because its language is not the language put to popular vote. The legislative process involves negotiation through debate and political pressure. The words uttered on the debate floor that otherwise appear in the legislative history, however, are not the agreed upon enacted text.

5. "Stop" Sign Example

Suppose a legislative body receives a proposal to place a "stop" sign such that people traveling east and west on State Street will encounter the sign before crossing Michigan Avenue. Next, a legislator sponsors a bill to enact a statute for the sign's placement as proposed. In the floor debate over the sign, a legislator points out that many collisions occur at that corner because drivers going east and west on State Street travel too fast during rush hour to notice northbound or southbound traffic on Michigan Avenue. One of the legislators objected, saying, "making every car come to a complete stop at Michigan Avenue will impose a burden on those drivers—let's put in a 'yield' sign." Rejecting the "yield" sign proposal, the "stop" sign bill passes in the legislature and the executive signs the bill into law.

What is required of a driver encountering the new "stop" sign on a Saturday evening? Does the plain language of the sign tell the driver what to do? Initially, yes. The plain language suggests a driver should stop. The driver's next move is not necessarily clear. The driver cannot stay there forever.

A textualist interpreter will expect the driver to come to a complete stop. That is what the sign says. A reasonable driver, however, will know not to stay there indefinitely. No new sign is going to appear from the ground or the sky and tell the driver to go. Thus, the textualist interpreter will understand when the driver eventually drives through the intersection after a complete stop.

The purposivist interpreter might not expect the driver to come to a complete stop. The language says, "stop," but the problem the legislature resolved with the "stop" sign was the high rate of collisions. Thus, if a driver comes to a near halt, looks both ways, and proceeds with caution, a purposivist interpreter—perhaps a traffic officer in this instance—might not pull the driver over. The idea of staying at the "stop" sign indefinitely may never actually cross the purposivist's mind.

The intentionalist interpreter's expectations will depend more on the interpreter's view of "stop" signs generally. There is support in the sign's language suggesting that every driver should come to a complete stop. There is also evidence in the legislative history that coming to a complete stop is an undue burden on drivers crossing Michigan Avenue. Therefore, the intentionalist interpreter may draw his own conclusions as to whether or not a driver must come to a complete stop. A driver with the desire to predict what course an interpreter such as a police officer will take will have a difficult task.

The realist will look at the entire context of the situation. Clearly, if there is heavy traffic on Michigan Avenue, the driver should stop. In the middle of the night, however, perhaps there would be no point to coming to a complete stop. If every driver came to a complete stop at every "stop" sign all the time, the effect on society might be to hinder economic efficiency. On the other hand, "stop" signs exist for a reason. Perhaps drivers should not be ignoring them. Predicting a police officer's course of action here is difficult as well.

A police officer whose job is to enforce the "stop" sign has a broad range for interpreting the "stop" sign merely on the basis of these four leading interpretive theories, and might very well make choices among them depending on the factual context. For example, at closing time for the local bars, it might be reasonable for a police officer to take a textualist approach in hopes of catching a driver who is drunk beyond the legal limit. It might also be reasonable for the same police officer witnessing a rolling stop to take a more realist approach toward the end of a shift or when the driver of the car appears to be a fine, upstanding citizen.

It might be reasonable for the IRS and courts to operate in a similar fashion. An approach that casts the widest net might be reasonable when the IRS suspects a particular taxpayer or class of taxpayers is improperly reporting tax liabilities. This wide net could be textualism if the suspected activity is outside the bounds of the Code, or it could be realism if a suspected taxpayer is merely violating the "spirit" of the Code.

Examining an average taxpayer's return, especially a taxpayer's return where there are few opportunities to hide income, the IRS might use an interpretive methodology designed to look out only for major issues. As with a wide net, this narrow set of parameters could be textualism if the return positions are expected to be well within the bounds of the Code, or it could be realism if an IRS employee expects a particular type of activity that violates a literal reading of the Code but not its spirit.

In *Bob Jones University*, the majority opinion and the dissenting opinion exemplify the realist and textualist approaches to statutory interpretation, respectively.

BOB JONES UNIVERSITY v. UNITED STATES
461 U.S. 574 (1983)
Supreme Court of the United States

Chief Justice BURGER delivered the opinion of the Court.

We granted certiorari to decide whether petitioners, nonprofit private schools that prescribe and enforce racially discriminatory admissions standards on the basis of religious doctrine, qualify as tax-exempt organizations under § 501(c)(3) of the Internal Revenue Code of 1954. . . .

II

A

In Revenue Ruling 71–447, the IRS formalized the policy first announced in 1970, that § 170 and § 501(c)(3) embrace the common law "charity" concept. Under that view, to qualify for a tax exemption pursuant to § 501(c)(3), an institution must show, first, that it falls within one of the eight categories expressly set forth in that section, and second, that its activity is not contrary to settled public policy.

Section 501(c)(3) provides that "[c]orporations . . . organized and operated exclusively for religious, charitable . . . or educational purposes" are entitled to tax exemption. Petitioners argue that the plain language of the statute guarantees them tax-exempt status. They emphasize the absence of any language in the statute expressly requiring all exempt organizations to be "charitable" in the common law sense, and they contend that the disjunctive "or" separating the categories in § 501(c)(3) precludes such a reading. Instead, they argue that if an institution falls within one or more of the specified categories it is automatically entitled to exemption, without regard to whether it also qualifies as "charitable." The Court of Appeals rejected that contention and concluded that petitioners' interpretation of the statute "tears section 501(c)(3) from its roots." *United States v. Bob Jones University, supra,* 639 F.2d, at 151.

It is a well-established canon of statutory construction that a court should go beyond the literal language of a statute if reliance on that language would defeat the plain purpose of the statute:

> The general words used in the clause . . ., taken by themselves, and literally construed, without regard to the object in view, would seem to sanction the claim of the plaintiff. But this mode of expounding a statute has never been adopted by any enlightened tribunal—because it is evident that in many cases it would defeat the object which the Legislature intended to accomplish. And it is well settled that, in interpreting a statute, the court will not look merely to a particular clause in which general words may be used, *but will take in connection with it the whole statute . . . and the objects and policy of the law. . . .*

Brown v. Duchesne, 19 How. 183, 194, 15 L.Ed. 595 (1857) (emphasis added).

Section 501(c)(3) therefore must be analyzed and construed within the framework of the Internal Revenue Code and against the background of the Congressional purposes. Such an examination reveals unmistakable evidence that, underlying all relevant parts of the Code, is the intent that entitlement to tax exemption depends on meeting certain common law standards of charity— namely, that an institution seeking tax-exempt status must serve a public purpose and not be contrary to established public policy.

This "charitable" concept appears explicitly in § 170 of the Code. That section contains a list of organizations virtually identical to that contained in § 501(c)(3). It is apparent that Congress intended that list to have the same meaning in both sections.[5] In § 170, Congress used the list of organizations in defining the term "charitable contributions." On its face, therefore, § 170 reveals that Congress' intention was to provide tax benefits to organizations serving charitable purposes.[6] The form of § 170 simply makes plain what common sense and history tell us: in enacting both § 170 and § 501(c)(3), Congress sought to provide tax benefits to charitable organizations, to encourage the development of

---

[5] [fn 10] The predecessor of § 170 originally was enacted in 1917, as part of the War Revenue Act of 1917, ch. 63, § 1201(2), 40 Stat. 300, 330 (1917), whereas the predecessor of § 501(c)(3) dates back to the income tax law of 1894, Act of August 27, 1894, ch. 349, 28 Stat. 509, see n. 14, infra. There are minor differences between the lists of organizations in the two sections, see generally Liles & Blum, Development of the Federal Tax Treatment of Charities, 39 L. & Contemp. Prob. 6, 24–25 (No. 4, 1975) (hereinafter Liles & Blum). Nevertheless, the two sections are closely related; both seek to achieve the same basic goal of encouraging the development of certain organizations through the grant of tax benefits. The language of the two sections is in most respects identical, and the Commissioner and the courts consistently have applied many of the same standards in interpreting those sections. See 5 J. Mertens, The Law of Federal Income Taxation § 31.12 (1980); 6 id. §§ 34.01–34.13 (1975); B. Bittker & L. Stone, Federal Income Taxation 220–222 (5th ed. 1980). To the extent that § 170 "aids in ascertaining the meaning" of § 501(c)(3), therefore, it is "entitled to great weight," United States v. Stewart, 311 U.S. 60, 64–65, 61 S.Ct. 102, 105–106, 85 L.Ed. 40 (1940). See Harris v. Commissioner, 340 U.S. 106, 107, 71 S.Ct. 181, 182, 95 L.Ed. 111 (1950).

[6] [fn 11] The dissent suggests that the Court "quite adeptly avoids the statute it is construing," post, at 2039, and "seeks refuge . . . by turning to § 170," post, at 2040. This assertion dissolves when one sees that § 501(c)(3) and § 170 are construed together, as they must be. The dissent acknowledges that the two sections are "mirror" provisions; surely there can be no doubt that the Court properly looks to § 170 to determine the meaning of § 501(c)(3). It is also suggested that § 170 is "at best of little usefulness in finding the meaning of § 501(c)(3)," since "§ 170(c) simply tracks the requirements set forth in § 501(c)(3)," post, at 2040. That reading loses sight of the fact that § 170(c) defines the term "charitable contribution." The plain language of § 170 reveals that Congress' objective was to employ tax exemptions and deductions to promote certain charitable purposes. While the eight categories of institutions specified in the statute are indeed presumptively charitable in nature, the IRS properly considered principles of charitable trust law in determining whether the institutions in question may truly be considered "charitable," for purposes of entitlement to the tax benefits conferred by § 170 and § 501(c)(3).

private institutions that serve a useful public purpose or supplement or take the place of public institutions of the same kind.

Tax exemptions for certain institutions thought beneficial to the social order of the country as a whole, or to a particular community, are deeply rooted in our history, as in that of England. The origins of such exemptions lie in the special privileges that have long been extended to charitable trusts.

[The Court provided quotes from several nineteenth-century cases supporting the proposition that a trust that violates law or public policy is not "charitable."]

These statements clearly reveal the legal background against which Congress enacted the first charitable exemption statute in 1894: . . . charities were to be given preferential treatment because they provide a benefit to society. . . .

A corollary to the public benefit principle is the requirement, long recognized in the law of trusts, that the purpose of a charitable trust may not be illegal or violate established public policy. In 1861, this Court stated that a public charitable use must be "consistent with local laws and public policy. . . ."

When the Government grants exemptions or allows deductions all taxpayers are affected; the very fact of the exemption or deduction for the donor means that other taxpayers can be said to be indirect and vicarious "donors." Charitable exemptions are justified on the basis that the exempt entity confers a public benefit—a benefit which the society or the community may not itself choose or be able to provide, or which supplements and advances the work of public institutions already supported by tax revenues.[7] History buttresses logic to make

---

[7] [fn 18] The dissent acknowledges that "Congress intended . . . to offer a tax benefit to organizations . . . providing a public benefit," post, at 2040, but suggests that Congress itself fully defined what organizations provide a public benefit, through the list of eight categories of exempt organizations contained in § 170 and § 501(c)(3). Under that view, any nonprofit organization that falls within one of the specified categories is automatically entitled to the tax benefits, provided it does not engage in expressly prohibited lobbying or political activities. Post, at 2042. The dissent thus would have us conclude, for example, that any nonprofit organization that does not engage in prohibited lobbying activities is entitled to tax exemption as an "educational" institution if it is organized for the "instruction or training of the individual for the purpose of improving or developing his capabilities," 26 CFR § 1.501(c)(3)–1(d)(3). See post, at 2045. As Judge Leventhal noted in Green v. Connally, 330 F.Supp. 1150, 1160 (D.D.C.), aff'd sub nom. Coit v. Green, 404 U.S. 997, 92 S.Ct. 564, 30 L.Ed.2d 550 (1971) (per curiam), Fagin's school for educating English boys in the art of picking pockets would be an "educational" institution under that definition. Similarly, a band of former military personnel might well set up a school for intensive training of subversives for guerrilla warfare and terrorism in other countries; in the abstract, that "school" would qualify as an "educational" institution. Surely Congress had no thought of affording such an unthinking, wooden meaning to § 170 and § 501(c)(3) as to provide tax benefits to "educational" organizations that do not serve a public, charitable purpose.

clear that, to warrant exemption under § 501(c)(3), an institution must fall within a category specified in that section and must demonstrably serve and be in harmony with the public interest.[8] The institution's purpose must not be so at odds with the common community conscience as to undermine any public benefit that might otherwise be conferred.

B

We are bound to approach these questions with full awareness that determinations of public benefit and public policy are sensitive matters with serious implications for the institutions affected; a declaration that a given institution is not "charitable" should be made only where there can be no doubt that the activity involved is contrary to a fundamental public policy. But there can no longer be any doubt that racial discrimination in education violates deeply and widely accepted views of elementary justice. . . . Over the past quarter of a century, every pronouncement of this Court and myriad Acts of Congress and Executive Orders attest a firm national policy to prohibit racial segregation and discrimination in public education. . . .

There can thus be no question that the interpretation of § 170 and § 501(c)(3) announced by the IRS in 1970 was correct. That it may be seen as belated does not undermine its soundness. It would be wholly incompatible with the concepts underlying tax exemption to grant the benefit of tax-exempt status to racially discriminatory educational entities, which "exer[t] a pervasive influence on the entire educational process." *Norwood v. Harrison, supra,* 413 U.S., at 469, 93 S.Ct., at 2812. Whatever may be the rationale for such private schools' policies, and however sincere the rationale may be, racial discrimination in education is contrary to public policy. Racially discriminatory educational institutions cannot be viewed as conferring a public benefit within the "charitable" concept discussed earlier, or within the Congressional intent underlying § 170 and § 501(c)(3).[9]

C

Petitioners contend that, regardless of whether the IRS properly concluded that racially discriminatory private schools violate public policy, only Congress

---

[8] [fn 19] The Court's reading of § 501(c)(3) does not render meaningless Congress' action in specifying the eight categories of presumptively exempt organizations, as petitioners suggest. See Brief of Petitioner Goldsboro Christian Schools 18–24. To be entitled to tax-exempt status under § 501(c)(3), an organization must first fall within one of the categories specified by Congress, and in addition must serve a valid charitable purpose.

[9] [fn 21] In view of our conclusion that racially discriminatory private schools violate fundamental public policy and cannot be deemed to confer a benefit on the public, we need not decide whether an organization providing a public benefit and otherwise meeting the requirements of § 501(c)(3) could nevertheless be denied tax-exempt status if certain of its activities violated a law or public policy.

can alter the scope of § 170 and § 501(c)(3). Petitioners accordingly argue that the IRS overstepped its lawful bounds in issuing its 1970 and 1971 rulings.

Yet ever since the inception of the tax code, Congress has seen fit to vest in those administering the tax laws very broad authority to interpret those laws. In an area as complex as the tax system, the agency Congress vests with administrative responsibility must be able to exercise its authority to meet changing conditions and new problems. Indeed as early as 1918, Congress expressly authorized the Commissioner "to make all needful rules and regulations for the enforcement" of the tax laws. . . . The same provision, so essential to efficient and fair administration of the tax laws, has appeared in tax codes ever since, see 26 U.S.C. § 7805(a) (1976); and this Court has long recognized the primary authority of the IRS and its predecessors in construing the Internal Revenue Code. . . .

Congress, the source of IRS authority, can modify IRS rulings it considers improper; and courts exercise review over IRS actions. In the first instance, however, the responsibility for construing the Code falls to the IRS. Since Congress cannot be expected to anticipate every conceivable problem that can arise or to carry out day-to-day oversight, it relies on the administrators and on the courts to implement the legislative will. Administrators, like judges, are under oath to do so. . . .

Guided, of course, by the Code, the IRS has the responsibility, in the first instance, to determine whether a particular entity is "charitable" for purposes of § 170 and § 501(c)(3).[10] This in turn may necessitate later determinations of whether given activities so violate public policy that the entities involved cannot be deemed to provide a public benefit worthy of "charitable" status. We emphasize, however, that these sensitive determinations should be made only where there is no doubt that the organization's activities violate fundamental public policy.

On the record before us, there can be no doubt as to the national policy. In 1970, when the IRS first issued the ruling challenged here, the position of all three branches of the Federal Government was unmistakably clear. The correctness of the Commissioner's conclusion that a racially discriminatory private school "is not 'charitable' within the common law concepts reflected in . . . the Code," Rev.Rul. 71–447, 1972–2 Cum.Bull., at 231, is wholly consistent with what Congress, the Executive and the courts had repeatedly declared before 1970. Indeed, it would be anomalous for the Executive, Legislative and Judicial Branches to reach conclusions that add up to a firm public policy on racial discrimination, and at the same time have the IRS blissfully ignore what all three branches of the Federal Government had

---

[10] [fn 22] In the present case, the IRS issued its rulings denying exemptions to racially discriminatory schools only after a three-judge District Court had issued a preliminary injunction. See supra, at 2021–2022.

declared.[11] Clearly an educational institution engaging in practices affirmatively at odds with this declared position of the whole government cannot be seen as exercising a "beneficial and stabilizing influenc[e] in community life," *Walz v. Tax Comm'n, supra,* 397 U.S., at 673, 90 S.Ct., at 1413, and is not "charitable," within the meaning of § 170 and § 501(c)(3). We therefore hold that the IRS did not exceed its authority when it announced its interpretation of § 170 and § 501(c)(3) in 1970 and 1971.[12]

D

The actions of Congress since 1970 leave no doubt that the IRS reached the correct conclusion in exercising its authority. It is, of course, not unknown for independent agencies or the Executive Branch to misconstrue the intent of a statute; Congress can and often does correct such misconceptions, if the courts have not done so. Yet for a dozen years Congress has been made aware—acutely aware—of the IRS rulings of 1970 and 1971. . . .

Ordinarily, and quite appropriately, courts are slow to attribute significance to the failure of Congress to act on particular legislation. . . . We have observed that "unsuccessful attempts at legislation are not the best of guides to legislative intent . . . ." Here, however, we do not have an ordinary claim of legislative acquiescence. Only one month after the IRS announced its position in 1970, Congress held its first hearings on this precise issue. *Equal Educational Opportunity: Hearings Before the Senate Select Comm. on Equal Educational Opportunity,* 91st Cong., 2d Sess. 1991 (1970). Exhaustive hearings have been held on the issue at various times since then. . . .

Non-action by Congress is not often a useful guide, but the non-action here is significant. During the past 12 years there have been no fewer than 13 bills introduced to overturn the IRS interpretation of § 501(c)(3). . . . Not one of these

---

[11] [fn 23] Justice POWELL misreads the Court's opinion when he suggests that the Court implies that "the Internal Revenue Service is invested with authority to decide which public policies are sufficiently 'fundamental' to require denial of tax exemptions," post, at 2039. The Court's opinion does not warrant that interpretation. Justice POWELL concedes that "if any national policy is sufficiently fundamental to constitute such an overriding limitation on the availability of tax-exempt status under § 501(c)(3), it is the policy against racial discrimination in education." Post, at 2037. Since that policy is sufficiently clear to warrant Justice POWELL's concession and for him to support our finding of longstanding Congressional acquiescence, it should be apparent that his concerns about the Court's opinion are unfounded.

[12] [fn 24] Many of the amici curiae, including Amicus William T. Coleman, Jr. (appointed by the Court), argue that denial of tax-exempt status to racially discriminatory schools is independently required by the equal protection component of the Fifth Amendment. In light of our resolution of this case, we do not reach that issue. See, e.g., United States v. Clark, 445 U.S. 23, 27, 100 S.Ct. 895, 899, 63 L.Ed.2d 171 (1980); NLRB v. Catholic Bishop of Chicago, 440 U.S. 490, 504, 99 S.Ct. 1313, 1320, 59 L.Ed.2d 533 (1979).

bills has emerged from any committee, although Congress has enacted numerous other amendments to § 501 during this same period, including an amendment to § 501(c)(3) itself. Tax Reform Act of 1976, Pub.L. 94–455, § 1313(a), 90 Stat. 1520, 1730 (1976). It is hardly conceivable that Congress—and in this setting, any Member of Congress—was not abundantly aware of what was going on. In view of its prolonged and acute awareness of so important an issue, Congress' failure to act on the bills proposed on this subject provides added support for concluding that Congress acquiesced in the IRS rulings of 1970 and 1971. . . .

The evidence of Congressional approval of the policy embodied in Revenue Ruling 71–447 goes well beyond the failure of Congress to act on legislative proposals. Congress affirmatively manifested its acquiescence in the IRS policy when it enacted the present § 501(i) of the Code, Act of October 20, 1976, Pub.L. 94–568, 90 Stat. 2697 (1976). That provision denies tax-exempt status to social clubs whose charters or policy statements provide for "discrimination against any person on the basis of race, color, or religion."[13] Both the House and Senate committee reports on that bill articulated the national policy against granting tax exemptions to racially discriminatory private clubs. S.Rep. No. 1318, 94th Cong., 2d Sess., 8 (1976); H.R.Rep. No. 1353, 94th Cong., 2d Sess., 8 (1976), U.S.Code Cong. & Admin.News 1976, p. 6051.

Even more significant is the fact that both reports focus on this Court's affirmance of *Green v. Connally, supra,* as having established that "discrimination on account of race is inconsistent with an *educational institution's* tax exempt status." S.Rep. No. 1318, *supra,* at 7–8 and n. 5; H.R.Rep. No. 1353, *supra,* at 8 and n. 5 (emphasis added), U.S.Code Cong. & Admin.News, p. 6058. These references in Congressional committee reports on an enactment denying tax exemptions to racially discriminatory private social clubs cannot be read other than as indicating approval of the standards applied to racially discriminatory private schools by the IRS subsequent to 1970, and specifically of Revenue Ruling 71–447. . . .

III

Petitioners contend that, even if the Commissioner's policy is valid as to nonreligious private schools, that policy cannot constitutionally be applied to schools that engage in racial discrimination on the basis of sincerely held religious beliefs.[14] As to such schools, it is argued that the IRS construction of §

---

[13] [fn 26] Prior to the introduction of this legislation, a three-judge district court had held that segregated social clubs were entitled to tax exemptions. McGlotten v. Connally, 338 F.Supp. 448 (D.D.C.1972). Section 501(i) was enacted primarily in response to that decision. See S.Rep. No. 1318, 94th Cong., 2d Sess., 7–8 (1976); H.R.Rep. No. 1353, 94th Cong., 2d Sess., 8 (1976), U.S.Code Cong. & Admin.News 1976, p. 6051.

[14] [fn 28] The District Court found, on the basis of a full evidentiary record, that the challenged practices of petitioner Bob Jones University were based on a genuine belief that the Bible forbids interracial dating and marriage. 468 F.Supp.,

170 and § 501(c)(3) violates their free exercise rights under the Religion Clauses of the First Amendment. This contention presents claims not heretofore considered by this Court in precisely this context.

This Court has long held the Free Exercise Clause of the First Amendment an absolute prohibition against governmental regulation of religious beliefs . . . . As interpreted by this Court, moreover, the Free Exercise Clause provides substantial protection for lawful conduct grounded in religious belief . . . . However, "[n]ot all burdens on religion are unconstitutional. . .. The state may justify a limitation on religious liberty by showing that it is essential to accomplish an overriding governmental interest." *United States v. Lee,* 455 U.S. 252 (1982) (citations omitted), 257–258, 102 S.Ct. 1051, 1055, 71 L.Ed.2d 127 (1982) (citations omitted).

On occasion this Court has found certain governmental interests so compelling as to allow even regulations prohibiting religiously based conduct. . . . Denial of tax benefits will inevitably have a substantial impact on the operation of private religious schools, but will not prevent those schools from observing their religious tenets.

The governmental interest at stake here is compelling. As discussed in Part II(B), *supra,* the Government has a fundamental, overriding interest in eradicating racial discrimination in education[15]—discrimination that prevailed, with official approval, for the first 165 years of this Nation's history. That governmental interest substantially outweighs whatever burden denial of tax benefits places on petitioners' exercise of their religious beliefs. The interests asserted by petitioners cannot be accommodated with that compelling governmental interest . . . and no "less restrictive means" . . . are available to achieve the governmental interest.[16]

---

at 894. We assume, as did the District Court, that the same is true with respect to petitioner Goldsboro Christian Schools. See 436 F.Supp., at 1317.

[15] [fn 29] We deal here only with religious schools—not with churches or other purely religious institutions; here, the governmental interest is in denying public support to racial discrimination in education. As noted earlier, racially discriminatory schools "exer[t] a pervasive influence on the entire educational process," outweighing any public benefit that they might otherwise provide, Norwood v. Harrison, 413 U.S. 455, 469, 93 S.Ct. 2804, 2812, 37 L.Ed.2d 723 (1973). See generally *Simon* 495–496.

[16] [fn 30] Bob Jones University also contends that denial of tax exemption violates the Establishment Clause by preferring religions whose tenets do not require racial discrimination over those which believe racial intermixing is forbidden. It is well settled that neither a State nor the Federal Government may pass laws which "prefer one religion over another," Everson v. Board of Education, 330 U.S. 1, 15, 67 S.Ct. 504, 511, 91 L.Ed. 711 (1947), but "[i]t is equally true" that a regulation does not violate the Establishment Clause merely because it "happens to coincide or harmonize with the tenets of some or all religions." McGowan v. Maryland, 366 U.S. 420, 442, 81 S.Ct. 1101, 1113, 6

IV

The remaining issue is whether the IRS properly applied its policy to these petitioners. Petitioner Goldsboro Christian Schools admits that it "maintain[s] racially discriminatory policies," Brief of Petitioner, Goldsboro Christian Schools, No. 81–1, at 10, but seeks to justify those policies on grounds we have fully discussed. The IRS properly denied tax-exempt status to Goldsboro Christian Schools.

Petitioner Bob Jones University, however, contends that it is not racially discriminatory. It emphasizes that it now allows all races to enroll, subject only to its restrictions on the conduct of all students, including its prohibitions of association between men and women of different races, and of interracial marriage. . . . Although a ban on intermarriage or interracial dating applies to all races, decisions of this Court firmly establish that discrimination on the basis of racial affiliation and association is a form of racial discrimination. . . . We therefore find that the IRS properly applied Revenue Ruling 71–447 to Bob Jones University.[17]

The judgments of the Court of Appeals are, accordingly,

Affirmed.

[Concurrence in part and concurrence in the judgment by Justice POWELL omitted.]

Justice REHNQUIST, dissenting.

The Court points out that there is a strong national policy in this country against racial discrimination. To the extent that the Court states that Congress in furtherance of this policy could deny tax-exempt status to educational institutions that promote racial discrimination, I readily agree. But, unlike the Court, I am

---

L.Ed.2d 393 (1961). See Harris v. McRae, 448 U.S. 297, 319–320, 100 S.Ct. 2671, 2689, 65 L.Ed.2d 784 (1980). The IRS policy at issue here is founded on a "neutral, secular basis," Gillette v. United States, 401 U.S. 437, 452, 91 S.Ct. 828, 837, 28 L.Ed.2d 168 (1971), and does not violate the Establishment Clause. See generally U.S. Comm'n on Civil Rights, Discriminatory Religious Schools and Tax Exempt Status 10–17 (1982). In addition, as the Court of Appeals noted, "the uniform application of the rule to all religiously operated schools *avoids* the necessity for a potentially entangling inquiry into whether a racially restrictive practice is the result of sincere religious belief." United States v. Bob Jones Univ., 639 F.2d 147, 155 (CA4 1980) (emphasis in original). Cf. NLRB v. Catholic Bishop of Chicago, 440 U.S. 490, 99 S.Ct. 1313, 59 L.Ed.2d 533 (1979). But see generally Note, 90 Yale L.J. 350 (1980).

[17] [fn 32] Bob Jones University also argues that the IRS policy should not apply to it because it is entitled to exemption under § 501(c)(3) as a "religious" organization, rather than as an "educational" institution. The record in this case leaves no doubt, however, that Bob Jones University is both an educational institution and a religious institution. As discussed previously, the IRS policy properly extends to all private schools, including religious schools. See n. 29, supra. The IRS policy thus was properly applied to Bob Jones University.

convinced that Congress simply has failed to take this action and, as this Court has said over and over again, regardless of our view on the propriety of Congress' failure to legislate we are not constitutionally empowered to act for them.

In approaching this statutory construction question the Court quite adeptly avoids the statute it is construing. This I am sure is no accident, for there is nothing in the language of § 501(c)(3) that supports the result obtained by the Court. . . .

With undeniable clarity, Congress has explicitly defined the requirements for § 501(c)(3) status. An entity must be (1) a corporation, or community chest, fund, or foundation, (2) organized for one of the eight enumerated purposes, (3) operated on a nonprofit basis, and (4) free from involvement in lobbying activities and political campaigns. Nowhere is there to be found some additional, undefined public policy requirement.

The Court first seeks refuge from the obvious reading of § 501(c)(3) by turning to § 170 of the Internal Revenue Code which provides a tax deduction for contributions made to § 501(c)(3) organizations. . . . The Court seizes the words "charitable contribution" and with little discussion concludes that "[o]n its face, therefore, § 170 reveals that Congress' intention was to provide tax benefits to organizations serving charitable purposes," intimating that this implies some unspecified common law charitable trust requirement. . . .

The Court would have been well advised to look to subsection (c) where, as § 170(a)(1) indicates, Congress has defined a "charitable contribution." . . . Plainly, § 170(c) simply tracks the requirements set forth in § 501(c)(3). Since § 170 is no more than a mirror of § 501(c)(3) and, as the Court points out, § 170 followed § 501(c)(3) by more than two decades, *ante,* at 2026, n. 10, it is at best of little usefulness in finding the meaning of § 501(c)(3).

Making a more fruitful inquiry, the Court next turns to the legislative history of § 501(c)(3) and finds that Congress intended in that statute to offer a tax benefit to organizations that Congress believed were providing a public benefit. I certainly agree. But then the Court leaps to the conclusion that this history is proof Congress intended that an organization seeking § 501(c)(3) status "must fall within a category specified in that section *and must demonstrably serve and be in harmony with the public interest." Ante,* at 2029 (emphasis added). To the contrary, I think that the legislative history of § 501(c)(3) unmistakably makes clear that *Congress has decided* what organizations are serving a public purpose and providing a public benefit within the meaning of § 501(c)(3) and has clearly set forth in § 501(c)(3) the characteristics of such organizations. In fact, there are few examples which better illustrate Congress' effort to define and redefine the requirements of a legislative act. . . .

One way to read the opinion handed down by the Court today leads to the conclusion that this long and arduous refining process of § 501(c)(3) was certainly a waste of time, for when enacting the original 1894 statute Congress intended to adopt a common law term of art, and intended that this term of art carry with it all of the common law baggage which defines it. Such a view, however, leads also to the unsupportable idea that Congress has spent almost a century adding illustrations simply to clarify an already defined common law term.

Another way to read the Court's opinion leads to the conclusion that even though Congress has set forth *some* of the requirements of a § 501(c)(3) organization, it intended that the IRS additionally require that organizations meet a higher standard of public interest, not stated by Congress, but to be determined and defined by the IRS and the courts. This view I find equally unsupportable. Almost a century of statutory history proves that Congress itself intended to decide what § 501(c)(3) requires. Congress has expressed its decision in the plainest of terms in § 501(c)(3) by providing that tax-exempt status is to be given to any corporation, or community chest, fund, or foundation that is organized for one of the eight enumerated purposes, operated on a nonprofit basis, and uninvolved in lobbying activities or political campaigns. The IRS certainly is empowered to adopt regulations for the enforcement of these specified requirements, and the courts have authority to resolve challenges to the IRS's exercise of this power, but Congress has left it to neither the IRS nor the courts to select or add to the requirements of § 501(c)(3). . . .

But simply because I reject the Court's heavy-handed creation of the requirement that an organization seeking § 501(c)(3) status must "serve and be in harmony with the public interest," *ante,* at 2029, does not mean that I would deny to the IRS the usual authority to adopt regulations further explaining what Congress meant by the term "educational." The IRS has fully exercised that authority in 26 CFR § 1.501(c)(3)–1(d)(3) . . .

I have little doubt that neither the "Fagin School for Pickpockets" nor a school training students for guerrilla warfare and terrorism in other countries would meet the definitions contained in the regulations.

Prior to 1970, when the charted course was abruptly changed, the IRS had continuously interpreted § 501(c)(3) and its predecessors in accordance with the view I have expressed above. This, of course, is of considerable significance in determining the intended meaning of the statute. . . .

In 1970 the IRS was sued by parents of black public school children seeking to enjoin the IRS from according tax-exempt status under § 501(c)(3) to private schools in Mississippi that discriminated against blacks. The IRS answered, consistent with its long standing position, by maintaining a lack of authority to deny the tax-exemption if the schools met the specified requirements of § 501(c)(3). Then . . . in the face of a preliminary injunction, the IRS changed its position and adopted the view of the plaintiffs. . . .

Perhaps recognizing the lack of support in the statute itself, or in its history, for the 1970 IRS change in interpretation, the Court finds that "[t]he actions of Congress since 1970 leave no doubt that the IRS reached the correct conclusion in exercising its authority," concluding that there is "an unusually strong case of legislative acquiescence in and ratification by implication of the 1970 and 1971 rulings. . . ." The Court relies first on several bills introduced to overturn the IRS interpretation of § 501(c)(3). . . . But we have said before, and it is equally applicable here, that this type of congressional inaction is of virtually no weight in determining legislative intent. . . . These bills and related hearings indicate little more than that a vigorous debate has existed in Congress concerning the new IRS position.

This Court continuously has been hesitant to find ratification through inaction. . . . Few cases would call for more caution in finding ratification by acquiescence than the present one. The new IRS interpretation is not only far less than a long standing administrative policy, it is at odds with a position maintained by the IRS, and unquestioned by Congress, for several decades prior to 1970. The interpretation is unsupported by the statutory language, it is unsupported by legislative history, the interpretation has lead to considerable controversy in and out of Congress, and the interpretation gives to the IRS a broad power which until now Congress had kept for itself. Where in addition to these circumstances Congress has shown time and time again that it is ready to enact positive legislation to change the tax code when it desires, this Court has no business finding that Congress has adopted the new IRS position by failing to enact legislation to reverse it. . . .

I have no disagreement with the Court's finding that there is a strong national policy in this country opposed to racial discrimination. I agree with the Court that Congress has the power to further this policy by denying § 501(c)(3) status to organizations that practice racial discrimination.[18] But as of yet Congress has failed to do so. Whatever the reasons for the failure, this Court should not legislate for Congress.[19]

Petitioners are each organized for the "instruction or training of the individual for the purpose of improving or developing his capabilities," 26 CFR § 1.501(c)(3)–1(d)(3), and thus are organized for "educational purposes" within the meaning of § 501(c)(3). Petitioners' nonprofit status is uncontested. There is no indication that either petitioner has been involved in lobbying activities or political campaigns. Therefore, it is my view that unless and until Congress affirmatively amends § 501(c)(3) to require more, the IRS is without authority to deny petitioners § 501(c)(3) status. For this reason, I would reverse the Court of Appeals.

---

[18] [fn 3] I agree with the Court that such a requirement would not infringe on petitioners' First Amendment rights.

[19] [fn 4] Because of its holding, the Court does not have to decide whether it would violate the equal protection component of the Fifth Amendment for Congress to grant § 501(c)(3) status to organizations that practice racial discrimination. Ante, at 2032 n. 24. I would decide that it does not. The statute is facially neutral; absent a showing of a discriminatory purpose, no equal protection violation is established. Washington v. Davis, 426 U.S. 229, 241–244, 96 S.Ct. 2040, 2048–2049, 48 L.Ed.2d 597 (1976).

NOTES AND QUESTIONS

1. Describe the interpretive stance of the majority and the dissent. Which one is more compelling?
2. What would have been the result if Bob Jones University had not had a written policy?

C. Tax Law Administration

The federal government's executive branch has the authority to administer and enforce the nation's laws. *See* U.S. CONST. art. II, § 1, cl. 1. In detailed areas of the law, Congress has neither the time nor the expertise to draft statutes that cover the myriad of situations that arise in administration and enforcement. In these detailed areas of the law, the executive branch must bear some of the lawmaking responsibility. Like Congress, the President acting on his own lacks sufficient time to enforce all the laws that Congress has enacted. He also lacks sufficient time to develop and issue continuous guidance to the public necessary to administer the laws. Thus, the President conducts the bulk of his work through administrative agencies. The three primary agencies involved in administering and enforcing the tax laws are the Department of Treasury (through its Office of Tax Policy), the IRS, and the Department of Justice (through its Tax Division). Important issues in examining federal tax agencies involve the categories of guidance the agencies issue, judicial deference to guidance issued by federal tax agencies, interpretive methods that apply to regulations, and constraints on the federal tax agencies by their own administrative guidance.

1. Categories of Administrative Tax Guidance

The IRS and Treasury communicate with taxpayers through administrative tax guidance. In general, IRS and Treasury guidance fit into one of two main categories that can each be further subdivided into two subsidiary categories. The two main categories are public guidance and "private" guidance. Public guidance consists of formal and informal guidance. Generally, public guidance is more authoritative than private guidance. Further, courts tend to take guidance that has undergone formal publication procedures more seriously than less formal guidance. Private guidance, on the other hand, consists of taxpayer-specific guidance and internal guidance. Some private guidance can fit into both taxpayer-specific and internal categories.

The most formal and authoritative form of public guidance in the tax world—and the most important—is a Treasury regulation. Treasury uses the following process to issue a regulation. First, an attorney in the IRS's Chief Counsel Office drafts a regulation relying on the Office's institutional knowledge. Treasury and IRS personnel review the regulation. Generally, once the appropriate Treasury and IRS personnel approve the regulation, the IRS and Treasury issue a Notice of Proposed Rulemaking, which notifies taxpayers the

IRS plans on issuing a regulation and gives taxpayers the opportunity to provide comments. Sometimes the IRS issues a temporary regulation as well. A temporary regulation is treated as the applicable law while the proposed regulation goes through the promulgation process. During this process the proposed regulation is not in effect. The expectation is that by the time the temporary regulation expires, the proposed regulation will become an official final regulation.

Proposed, temporary, and current Treasury regulations are published in both the Internal Revenue Bulletin and the Federal Register. The Internal Revenue Bulletin is the official vehicle Treasury and the IRS use for communicating its administrative actions to the public. *See* Reg. § 601.601(d)(1). The Federal Register is the official publication through which the federal government communicates its administrative actions to the public. *See* 44 U.S.C. § 1505(a).

One might be skeptical of the extent to which Treasury and the IRS will consider comments from taxpayers. Generally, Treasury and the IRS address reasonable taxpayer concerns. On occasion, however, they ignore reasonable taxpayer comments. In *Altera v. Commissioner*, for example, Treasury and the IRS ignored comments in the proposal process. When the IRS enforced the regulations against Altera, Altera sued in Tax Court.

ALTERA CORP. v. COMMISSIONER
145 T.C. 91 (2015)
United States Tax Court

OPINION

MARVEL, Judge:

These consolidated cases are before the Court on the parties' cross-motions for partial summary judgment under Rule 121.[20] The issue presented by the parties' cross-motions is whether section 1.482–7(d)(2), Income Tax Regs. (the final rule)—which the Department of the Treasury (Treasury) issued in 2003 and which requires participants in qualified cost-sharing arrangements (QCSAs) to share stock-based compensation costs to achieve an arm's-length result—is arbitrary and capricious and therefore invalid.

BACKGROUND

Petitioner is an affiliated group of corporations that filed consolidated Federal income tax returns for the years at issue. During all relevant years, Altera Corp. (Altera U.S.), the parent company, was a Delaware corporation, and Altera International, a subsidiary of Altera U.S., was a Cayman Islands corporation.

---

[20] [fn 1] Unless otherwise indicated, all section references are to the Internal Revenue Code (Code) in effect at all relevant times, and all Rule references are to the Tax Court Rules of Practice and Procedure. All APA section references are to the Administrative Procedure Act (APA), 5 U.S.C. secs. 551–559, 701–706 (2012).

When petitioner filed its petitions with this Court, the principal place of business of Altera U.S. was in California.

I. PETITIONER'S R & D COST-SHARING AGREEMENT

Petitioner develops, manufactures, markets, and sells programmable logic devices (PLDs) and related hardware, software, and pre-defined design building blocks for use in programming the PLDs (programming tools). Altera U.S. and Altera International entered into concurrent agreements that became effective May 23, 1997: a master technology license agreement (technology license agreement) and a technology research and development cost-sharing agreement (R & D cost-sharing agreement).

Under the technology license agreement, Altera U.S. licensed to Altera International the right to use and exploit, everywhere except the United States and Canada, all of Altera U.S.'s intangible property relating to PLDs and programming tools that existed before the R & D cost-sharing agreement (pre-cost-sharing intangible property). In exchange for the rights granted under the technology license agreement, Altera International paid royalties to Altera U.S. in each year from 1997 through 2003. As of December 31, 2003, Altera International owned a fully paid-up license to use the pre-cost-sharing intangible property in its territory.

Under the R & D cost-sharing agreement, Altera U.S. and Altera International agreed to pool their respective resources to conduct research and development using the pre-cost-sharing intangible property. Under the R & D cost-sharing agreement, Altera U.S. and Altera International agreed to share the risks and costs of research and development activities they performed on or after May 23, 1997. The R & D cost-sharing agreement was in effect from May 23, 1997, through 2007.

During each of petitioner's taxable years ending December 31, 2004, December 30, 2005, December 29, 2006, and December 28, 2007 (2004–07 taxable years), Altera U.S. granted stock options and other stock-based compensation to certain of its employees. Certain of the employees of Altera U.S. who performed research and development activities subject to the R & D cost-sharing agreement received stock options or other stock-based compensation. The employees' cash compensation was included in the cost pool under the R & D cost-sharing agreement. Their stock-based compensation was not included. . . .

II. PETITIONER'S TAX REPORTING AND RESPONDENT'S SECTION 482 ALLOCATIONS

Petitioner timely filed its Forms 1120, U.S. Corporation Income Tax Return, for its 2004–07 taxable years. Respondent timely mailed notices of deficiency to petitioner with respect to its 2004–07 taxable years. The notices of deficiency allocated, pursuant to section 482, income from Altera International to Altera U.S. by increasing Altera International's cost-sharing payments for 2004–07 by [over $80 million.]

Bringing petitioner into compliance with the final rule was the sole purpose of the cost-sharing adjustments in the notice of deficiency.

III. SECTION 482

A. Arm's-Length Standard

Section 482 authorizes the Commissioner to allocate income and expenses among related entities to prevent tax evasion and to ensure that taxpayers clearly reflect income relating to transactions between related entities. The first sentence of section 482 provides, in relevant part, as follows:

> In any case of two or more organizations, trades, or businesses * * * owned or controlled directly or indirectly by the same interests, the Secretary[21] may distribute, apportion, or allocate gross income, deductions, credits, or allowances between or among such organizations, trades, or businesses, if he determines that such distribution, apportionment, or allocation is necessary in order to prevent evasion of taxes or clearly to reflect the income of any of such organizations, trades, or businesses. * * *

Section 1.482–1(a)(1), Income Tax Regs., explains the purpose of section 482 as follows:

> The purpose of section 482 is to ensure that taxpayers clearly reflect income attributable to controlled transactions and to prevent the avoidance of taxes with respect to such transactions. Section 482 places a controlled taxpayer[22] on a tax parity with an uncontrolled taxpayer by determining the true taxable income of the controlled taxpayer. * * *

Section 1.482–1(b)(1), Income Tax Regs., provides that

> [i]n determining the true taxable income of a controlled taxpayer, the standard to be applied in every case is that of a taxpayer dealing at arm's length with an uncontrolled taxpayer. A controlled transaction meets the arm's length standard if the results of the transaction are consistent with the results that would have been realized if uncontrolled taxpayers had engaged in the same transaction under the same circumstances (arm's length result). However, because identical transactions can rarely be located, whether a transaction produces an arm's length result generally will be determined by reference to the results of comparable transactions under comparable circumstances. * * *

---

[21] [fn 2] The term "Secretary" means the Secretary of the Treasury or his delegate. Sec. 7701(a)(11)(B).

[22] [fn 3] The term "controlled taxpayer" means "any one of two or more taxpayers owned or controlled directly or indirectly by the same interests, and includes the taxpayer that owns or controls the other taxpayers." Sec. 1.482–1(i)(5), Income Tax Regs.

V. 2003 COST-SHARING REGULATIONS

A. Notice of Proposed Rulemaking

In July 2002 Treasury issued a notice of proposed rulemaking and notice of a public hearing (NPRM) with respect to proposed amendments to the 1995 cost-sharing regulations. The NPRM set a public hearing on the proposed amendments for November 20, 2002. *See* 67 Fed.Reg. 48997 (July 29, 2002). The preamble to the NPRM states that the proposed amendments to the 1995 cost-sharing regulations sought to clarify that stock-based compensation must be taken into account in determining operating expenses under § 1.482–7(d)(1)[, Income Tax Regs.,] and to provide rules for measuring stock-based compensation costs * * * [, and] to include express provisions to coordinate the cost sharing rules of § 1.482–7[, Income Tax Regs.,] with the arm's length standard as set forth in § 1.482–1[, Income Tax Regs]. Id. at 48998.

B. Comments Submitted in Response to the Proposed Regulations

In response to the NPRM [numerous] organizations submitted written comments to Treasury. . . .

Several of the commentators informed Treasury that they knew of no transactions between unrelated parties, including any cost-sharing arrangement, service agreement, or other contract, that required one party to pay or reimburse the other party for amounts attributable to stock-based compensation. . . .

[T]he Baumol and Malkiel analysis concluded that there is no net economic cost to a corporation or its shareholders from the issuance of stock-based compensation. Similarly, Mr. Grundfest asserted that a company's "decision to grant options to employees * * * does not change its operating expenses" and does not factor into its pricing decisions.

C. Final Rule

1. Regulatory Provisions

In August 2003 Treasury issued the final rule. The final rule explicitly required parties to QCSAs to share stock-based compensation costs. *See* sec. 1.482–7(d)(2), Income Tax Regs. The final rule also added sections 1.482–1(b)(2)(i) through 1.482–7(a)(3), Income Tax Regs., to provide that a QCSA produces an arm's-length result only if the parties' costs are determined in accordance with the final rule. *See* T.D. 9088, 2003–2 C.B. 841, 847–848.

The final rule provides two methods for measuring the value of stock-based compensation: a default method and an elective method. Under the default method, "the costs attributable to stock-based compensation generally are included as intangible development costs upon the exercise of the option and measured by the spread between the option strike price and the price of the underlying stock." *Id., 2003–2 C.B. at 844. Under the elective method, "the costs attributable to stock options are taken into account in certain cases in accordance with the 'fair value' of the option, as reported for financial accounting purposes either as a charge against income or in footnoted disclosures." *Id.* The elective method, however, is available only with respect to options on stock that is publicly traded "on an established United States securities market and is issued by a company whose financial statements are prepared in accordance with United

States generally accepted accounting principles for the taxable year." Sec. 1.482–7(d)(3) (iii)(B)(2), Income Tax Regs.

2. Lack of Evidence from Uncontrolled Transactions

When it issued the final rule, the files maintained by Treasury relating to the final rule did not contain any expert opinions, empirical data, or published or unpublished articles, papers, surveys, or reports supporting a determination that the amounts attributable to stock-based compensation must be included in the cost pool of QCSAs to achieve an arm's-length result. Those files also did not contain any record that Treasury searched any database that could have contained agreements between unrelated parties relating to joint undertakings or the provision of services. Additionally, Treasury was unaware of any written contract between unrelated parties, whether in a cost-sharing arrangement or otherwise, that required one party to pay or reimburse the other party for amounts attributable to stock-based compensation; or any evidence of any actual transaction between unrelated parties, whether in a cost-sharing arrangement or otherwise, in which one party paid or reimbursed the other party for amounts attributable to stock-based compensation.

3. Response to Comments

The preamble to the final rule responded to comments that asserted that the proposed amendments to the 1995 cost-sharing regulations were inconsistent with the arm's-length standard, in relevant part, as follows:

> Treasury and the IRS continue to believe that requiring stock-based compensation to be taken into account for purposes of QCSAs is consistent with the legislative intent underlying section 482 and with the arm's length standard (and therefore with the obligations of the United States under its income tax treaties and with the OECD transfer pricing guidelines). The legislative history of the Tax Reform Act of 1986 expressed Congress's intent to respect cost sharing arrangements as consistent with the commensurate with income standard, and therefore consistent with the arm's length standard, if and to the extent that the participants' shares of income "reasonably reflect the actual economic activity undertaken by each." *See* H.R. Conf. Rep[t]. No. 99–481 [Vol. II], at II–638 (1986). * * * In order for the costs incurred by a participant to reasonably reflect its actual economic activity, the costs must be determined on a comprehensive basis. Therefore, in order for a QCSA to reach an arm's length result consistent with legislative intent, the QCSA must reflect all relevant costs, including such critical elements of cost as the cost of compensating employees for providing services related to the development of the intangibles pursuant to the QCSA. Treasury and the IRS do not believe that there is any basis for distinguishing between stock-based compensation and other forms of compensation in this context.

> Treasury and the IRS do not agree with the comments that assert that taking stock-based compensation into account in the QCSA context would be inconsistent with the arm's length standard in the absence of evidence that

parties at arm's length take stock-based compensation into account in similar circumstances. Section 1.482–1(b)(1)[, Income Tax Regs.,] provides that a "controlled transaction meets the arm's length standard if the results of the transaction are consistent with the results that *would have been realized* if uncontrolled taxpayers *had engaged* in the same transaction under the same circumstances." * * * While the results actually realized in similar transactions under similar circumstances ordinarily provide significant evidence in determining whether a controlled transaction meets the arm's length standard, in the case of QCSAs such data may not be available. As recognized in the legislative history of the Tax Reform Act of 1986, there is little, if any, public data regarding transactions involving high-profit intangibles. H.R. Rep[t]. No. 99–426, at 423–[4]25 (1985). The uncontrolled transactions cited by commentators do not share enough characteristics of QCSAs involving the development of high-profit intangibles to establish that parties at arm's length would not take stock options into account in the context of an arrangement similar to a QCSA. Government contractors that are entitled to reimbursement for services on a cost-plus basis under government procurement law assume substantially less entrepreneurial risk than that assumed by service providers that participate in QCSAs, and therefore the economic relationship between the parties to such an arrangement is very different from the economic relationship between participants in a QCSA. The other agreements highlighted by commentators establish arrangements that differ significantly from QCSAs in that they provide for the payment of markups on cost or of non-cost-based service fees to service providers within the arrangement or for the payment of royalties among participants in the arrangement. Such terms, which may have the effect of mitigating the impact of using a cost base to be shared or reimbursed that is less than comprehensive, would not be permitted by the QCSA regulations. * * *

The regulations relating to QCSAs have as their focus reaching results consistent with what parties at arm's length generally would do if they entered into cost sharing arrangements for the development of high-profit intangibles. These final regulations reflect that at arm's length the parties to an arrangement that is based on the sharing of costs to develop intangibles in order to obtain the benefit of an independent right to exploit such intangibles would ensure through bargaining that the arrangement reflected all relevant costs, including all costs of compensating employees for providing services related to the arrangement. Parties dealing at arm's length in such an arrangement based on the sharing of costs and benefits generally would not distinguish between stock-based compensation and other forms of compensation.

For example, assume that two parties are negotiating an arrangement similar to a QCSA in order to attempt to develop patentable pharmaceutical products, and that they anticipate that they will benefit equally from their exploitation of such patents in their respective geographic markets. Assume further that one party is considering the commitment of several employees to perform research with respect to the arrangement. That party would not agree to commit employees to an arrangement that is based on the sharing of costs in order to obtain the benefit of independent exploitation rights unless the other party agrees to reimburse its share of the compensation costs of the employees. Treasury and the IRS believe that if a significant element of that compensation consists of stock-based compensation, the party committing employees to the arrangement generally would not agree to do so on terms that ignore the stock-based compensation.

T.D. 9088, 2003–2 C.B. at 842–843.

The preamble to the final rule responded to comments that asserted that stock-based compensation does not constitute an economic cost, or relevant economic cost, as follows:

> Treasury and the IRS continue to believe that requiring stock-based compensation to be taken into account in the context of QCSAs is appropriate. The final regulations provide that stock-based compensation must be taken into account in the context of QCSAs because such a result is consistent with the arm's length standard. Treasury and the IRS agree that the disposition of financial reporting issues does not mandate a particular result under these regulations.

Id., 2003–2 C.B. at 843.

The preamble to the final rule responded to comments that asserted that parties at arm's length would not share either the exercise spread or grant date value of stock-based compensation because they would produce results that are too speculative or not sufficiently related to the employee services that are compensated, as follows:

> Treasury and the IRS believe that it is appropriate for regulations to prescribe guidance in this context that is consistent with the arm's length standard and that also is objective and administrable. As long as the measurement method is determined at or before grant date, either of the prescribed measurement methods can be expected to result in an appropriate allocation of costs among QCSA participants and therefore would be consistent with the arm's length standard.

Id., 2003–2 C.B. at 844.

Finally, the preamble to the final rule states that "[i]t has also been determined that [APA] section 553(b) * * * does not apply to these regulations." Id., 2003–2 C.B. at 847.

DISCUSSION
I. SUMMARY JUDGMENT

Rule 121(a) provides that either party may move for summary judgment upon all or any part of the legal issues in controversy. Full or partial summary judgment may be granted only if it is demonstrated that there is no genuine dispute as to any material fact and that a decision may be rendered as a matter of law. *See* Rule 121(b); *Sundstrand Corp. v. Commissioner,* 98 T.C. 518, 520, 1992 WL 88529 (1992), *aff'd,* 17 F.3d 965 (7th Cir.1994). We conclude that there is no genuine dispute as to any material fact relating to the issue presented by the parties' cross-motions for partial summary judgment and that the issue may be decided as a matter of law. . . .

II. APPLICABLE PRINCIPLES OF ADMINISTRATIVE LAW . . .

B. Judicial Review of Agency Decisionmaking—State Farm Review

Pursuant to APA sec. 706(2)(A), a court must "hold unlawful and set aside agency action, findings, and conclusions" that the court finds to be "arbitrary, capricious, an abuse of discretion, or otherwise not in accordance with law". A court's review under this "standard is narrow and a court is not to substitute its judgment for that of the agency." *Motor Vehicle Mfrs. Ass'n of the U.S. v. State Farm Mut. Auto. Ins. Co.,* 463 U.S. 29, 43, 103 S.Ct. 2856, 77 L.Ed.2d 443 (1983); *see also Judulang v. Holder,* 565 U.S. ——, ——, 132 S.Ct. 476, 483, 181 L.Ed.2d 449 (2011); *Citizens to Pres. Overton Park, Inc. v. Volpe,* 401 U.S. 402, 416, 91 S.Ct. 814, 28 L.Ed.2d 136 (1971), *abrogated on other grounds by Califano v. Sanders,* 430 U.S. 99, 97 S.Ct. 980, 51 L.Ed.2d 192 (1977). However, a reviewing court must ensure that the agency "engaged in reasoned decisionmaking." *Judulang,* 565 U.S. at ——, 132 S.Ct. at 484. To engage in reasoned decisionmaking, "the agency must examine the relevant data and articulate a satisfactory explanation for its action including a 'rational connection between the facts found and the choice made.'" *State Farm,* 463 U.S. at 43 (quoting *Burlington Truck Lines v. United States,* 371 U.S. 156, 168, 83 S.Ct. 239, 9 L.Ed.2d 207 (1962)).

In reviewing an agency action a court must determine " 'whether the decision was based on a consideration of the relevant factors and whether there has been a clear error of judgment.'" *Id.* (quoting *Bowman Transp., Inc. v. Arkansas–Best Freight Sys., Inc.,* 419 U.S. 281, 285, 95 S.Ct. 438, 42 L.Ed.2d 447 (1974)); *see also Judulang,* 565 U.S. at ——, 132 S.Ct. at 484. "Normally, an agency rule would be arbitrary and capricious if the agency has relied on factors which Congress has not intended it to consider, entirely failed to consider an important aspect of the problem, offered an explanation for its decision that runs counter to the evidence before the agency, or is so implausible that it could not be ascribed to a difference in view or the product of agency expertise." *State Farm,* 463 U.S. at 43.

In providing a reasoned explanation for agency action that departs from an agency's prior position the agency must "display awareness that it *is* changing position." *FCC v. Fox Television Stations, Inc.,* 556 U.S. 502, 515, 129 S.Ct. 1800, 173 L.Ed.2d 738 (2009) (citing *United States v. Nixon,* 418 U.S. 683, 696, 94 S.Ct. 3090, 41 L.Ed.2d 1039 (1974)). However, the agency need not demonstrate "that the reasons for the new policy are better than the reasons for the old one". *Id.*

In examining an agency's explanation for issuing a rule a reviewing court " 'may not supply a reasoned basis for the agency's action that the agency itself has not given.'" *State Farm*, 463 U.S. at 43 (quoting *SEC v. Chenery Corp.*, 332 U.S. 194, 196, 67 S.Ct. 1575, 91 L.Ed. 1995 (1947)); *see also Carpenter Family Invs., LLC v. Commissioner*, 136 T.C. 373, 380, 396 n. 30, 2011 WL 1627952 (2011). Similarly, when an agency "relie[s] on multiple rationales (and has not done so in the alternative), and * * * [a reviewing court] conclude[s] that at least one of the rationales is deficient," *Nat'l Fuel Gas Supply Corp. v. FERC*, 468 F.3d 831, 839 (D.C.Cir.2006) (citing *Allied–Signal, Inc. v. U.S. Nuclear Regulatory Comm'n*, 988 F.2d 146, 150–151 (D.C.Cir.1993), and *Consol. Edison Co. of N.Y. v. FERC*, 823 F.2d 630, 641–642 (D.C.Cir.1987)), the court cannot sustain the agency action on the basis of the sufficient rationale unless the court is certain that the agency would have taken the same action "even absent the flawed rationale", *id.* However, the reviewing court must " 'uphold a decision of less than ideal clarity if the agency's path may reasonably be discerned.'" *State Farm*, 463 U.S. at 43 (quoting *Bowman Transp.*, 419 U.S. at 286).

III. PRELIMINARY ADMINISTRATIVE LAW ISSUES

The parties disagree whether the final rule is a legislative rule or an interpretive rule. The parties also disagree regarding the standard of review that we should apply. We therefore address these issues before considering the validity of the final rule. . . .

B. The Final Rule Must Satisfy *State Farm*'s Reasoned Decisionmaking Standard

Petitioner contends that we should review the final rule under *State Farm*. Respondent contends that we should review the final rule under *Chevron*. For the reasons that follow, we conclude that—regardless of the ultimate standard of review—the final rule must satisfy *State Farm*'s reasoned decisionmaking standard.

Respondent contends that *State Farm* review is not appropriate because the interpretation and implementation of section 482 do not require empirical analysis. Similarly, respondent repeatedly argues that section 482 does not require allocations to be made with reference to uncontrolled party conduct. But " '[t]he purpose of section 482 is to place a controlled taxpayer on a tax parity with an uncontrolled taxpayer, by determining according to the standard of an uncontrolled taxpayer, the true taxable income from the property and business of a controlled taxpayer. * * * The standard to be applied in every case is that of an uncontrolled taxpayer dealing at arm's length with another uncontrolled taxpayer.'" *Commissioner v. First Sec. Bank of Utah*, 405 U.S. 394, 400, 92 S.Ct. 1085, 31 L.Ed.2d 318 (1972) (quoting section 1.482–1(b)(1) (1971), Income Tax Regs.); *accord* sec. 1.482–1(a)(1), (b)(1), Income Tax Regs.; Treasury Department Technical Explanation of the 2001 U.S.-U.K. Income Tax Convention, art. 9; Treasury Department Technical Explanation of the 1997 U.S.-Ir. Income Tax Convention and Protocol, art. 9, Tax Treaties (CCH) para. 4435, at 103,223; Treasury Department Technical Explanation of the 2006 U.S. Model Income Tax Convention, art. 9. For these reasons we have previously stated that "the determination under section 482 is essentially and intensely factual". *Procacci v. Commissioner,* 94 T.C. 397, 412, 1990 WL 25737 (1990).

Section 1.482–1(b)(1), Income Tax Regs., provides that "[i]n determining the true taxable income of a controlled taxpayer, the standard to be applied in every case is that of a taxpayer dealing at arm's length with an uncontrolled taxpayer." In *Xilinx Inc. v. Commissioner,* 125 T.C. at 53–55, we held that the arm's-length standard always requires an analysis of what unrelated entities do under comparable circumstances. Similarly, in promulgating the final rule Treasury explicitly considered whether unrelated parties would share stock-based compensation costs in the context of a QCSA. *See* T.D. 9088, 2003–2 C.B. at 843 ("Treasury and the IRS believe that if a significant element of that compensation consists of stock-based compensation, the party committing employees to the arrangement generally would not agree to do so on terms that ignore the stock-based compensation."). Treasury necessarily decided an empirical question when it concluded that the final rule was consistent with the arm's-length standard.

Respondent counters that Treasury should be permitted to issue regulations modifying—or even abandoning—the arm's-length standard. But the preamble to the final rule does not justify the final rule on the basis of any modification or abandonment of the arm's-length standard,[23] and respondent concedes that the purpose of section 482 is to achieve tax parity.[24] The preamble also did not dismiss any of the evidence submitted by commentators regarding unrelated party conduct as addressing an irrelevant or inconsequential factor. *See id.,* 2003–2 C.B. at 842–843. We therefore need not decide whether, under *Brand X,* 545 U.S. at 982–983, Treasury would be free to modify or abandon the arm's-length standard because it has not done so here. *See Chenery Corp.,* 332 U.S. at 196; *Carpenter Family Invs., LLC v. Commissioner,* 136 T.C. at 380, 396 n. 30.

The validity of the final rule therefore turns on whether Treasury reasonably concluded, see *State Farm,* 463 U.S. at 43, that it is consistent with the arm's-

---

[23] [fn 14] For example, the preamble does not say that controlled transactions can never be comparable to uncontrolled transactions because related and unrelated parties always occupy materially different circumstances. Cf. Xilinx Inc. v. Commissioner, 598 F.3d at 1197 (Fisher, J., concurring) ("The Commissioner * * * contends that analyzing comparable transactions is unhelpful in situations where related and unrelated parties always occupy materially different circumstances.").

[24] [fn 15] The preamble states that "Treasury and the IRS do not agree with the comments that assert that taking stock-based compensation into account in the QCSA context would be inconsistent with the arm's length standard in the absence of evidence that parties at arm's length take stock-based compensation into account in similar circumstances." T.D. 9088, 2003–2 C.B. 841, 842. However, the preamble never suggests that the final rule could be consistent with the arm's-length standard if evidence showed that unrelated parties would not share stock-based compensation costs or that an evidentiary inquiry was unnecessary. See id., 2003–2 C.B. at 842–843.

length standard, and that is necessarily an empirical determination. The reasonableness of Treasury's conclusion in no way depends on its interpretation of section 482 or any other statute. As the Supreme Court recently articulated, *State Farm* review is "the more apt analytic framework" where the challenged regulation does not rely on an agency's interpretation of a statute. *Judulang,* 565 U.S. at —n. 7, 132 S.Ct. at 483.

Nevertheless, respondent contends that we should not review the final rule under *State Farm* because the Supreme Court has never, and this Court has rarely, reviewed Treasury regulations under *State Farm.* However, respondent concedes that Treasury is subject to the APA, and respondent has not advanced any justification for exempting Treasury regulations from *State Farm* review. The Supreme Court has stated that "[i]n the absence of such justification, we are not inclined to carve out an approach to administrative review good for tax law only. To the contrary, we have expressly '[r]ecogniz[ed] the importance of maintaining a uniform approach to judicial review of administrative action.'" *Mayo Found.,* 562 U.S. at 55 (quoting *Dickinson v. Zurko,* 527 U.S. 150, 154, 119 S.Ct. 1816, 144 L.Ed.2d 143 (1999) (alteration in original)); *see also Dominion Res., Inc. v. United States,* 681 F.3d 1313, 1319 (Fed.Cir.2012) (invalidating the associated-property rule in section 1.263A–11(e)(1)(ii)(B), Income Tax Regs., under *State Farm*).

Ultimately, however, whether *State Farm* or *Chevron* supplies the standard of review is immaterial because *Chevron* step 2^{25} incorporates the reasoned decisionmaking standard of *State Farm.* . . . Accordingly, we will examine whether the final rule satisfies that standard without deciding whether *Chevron* or *State Farm* provides the ultimate standard of review.

IV. WHETHER THE FINAL RULE SATISFIES STATE FARM'S REASONED DECISIONMAKING STANDARD

Petitioner contends that the final rule is invalid because (A) it lacks a basis in fact, (B) Treasury failed to rationally connect the choice it made with the facts it found, (C) Treasury failed to respond to significant comments, and (D) the final rule is contrary to the evidence before Treasury. Respondent disagrees.

A. The Final Rule Lacks a Basis in Fact

Petitioner contends that the final rule lacks a basis in fact because Treasury issued the final rule without any evidence that unrelated parties would ever agree to share stock-based compensation costs. Respondent contends that (1) Treasury did not rely solely on its belief that unrelated parties entering into QCSAs would generally share stock-based compensation costs but also on the commensurate-with-income standard and (2) Treasury was sufficiently experienced with cost-sharing agreements to conclude that unrelated parties entering into QCSAs would generally share stock-based compensation costs. . . .

2. Treasury's Unsupported Assertion Cannot Justify the Final Rule

---

[25] [fn 16] The parties agree that sec. 482 is ambiguous. These cases would therefore be resolved at *Chevron* step 2.

A court will generally not override an agency's "reasoned judgment about what conclusions to draw from technical evidence or how to adjudicate between rival scientific [or economic] theories". *Tripoli Rocketry Ass'n v. Bureau of Alcohol, Tobacco, Firearms & Explosives*, 437 F.3d 75, 83 (D.C.Cir.2006). However, "where an agency has articulated no reasoned basis for its decision—where its action is founded on unsupported assertions or unstated inferences—* * * [a court] will not 'abdicate the judicial duty carefully to "review the record to ascertain that the agency has made a reasoned decision based on reasonable extrapolations from some reliable evidence."" *Id.* (quoting *Am. Mining Cong. v. EPA*, 907 F.2d 1179, 1187 (D.C.Cir.1990)).

Respondent concedes that (1) in adopting the final rule, Treasury took the position that it was not obligated to engage in fact finding or to follow evidence gathering procedures; (2) the files maintained by Treasury relating to the final rule did not contain any empirical or other evidence supporting Treasury's belief that unrelated parties entering into QCSAs would generally share stock-based compensation costs; (3) the files maintained by Treasury relating to the final rule did not have any record that Treasury searched any database that could have contained agreements between unrelated parties; and (4) Treasury was unaware of any written agreement—or of any transaction—between unrelated parties that required one party to pay or reimburse the other party for amounts attributable to stock-based compensation.[26]

The preamble to the final rule offered only Treasury's belief that unrelated parties entering into QCSAs would generally share stock-based compensation costs. Specifically, the preamble to the final rule states that, in the context of a hypothetical QCSA between unrelated parties to develop patentable pharmaceutical products, "Treasury and the IRS believe that if a significant element of that compensation consists of stock-based compensation, the party committing employees to the arrangement generally would not agree to do so on terms that ignore the stock-based compensation ." T.D. 9088, 2003–2 C.B. at 843. Treasury, however, failed to provide a reasoned basis for reaching this conclusion from any evidence in the administrative record. *See Tripoli Rocketry*, 437 F.3d at 83. Indeed, "every indication in the record points the other way", *State Farm*, 463 U.S. at 57 (internal quotation omitted). *See infra* part IV.C.

Respondent defends Treasury's failure to provide a reasoned basis for its conclusion from any evidence in the administrative record on the notion that "[t]here are some propositions for which scant empirical evidence can be marshaled". *See Fox Television*, 556 U.S. at 519. This may be true regarding certain propositions, *see id.* ("the harmful effect of broadcast profanity on

---

[26] [fn 20] Treasury's failure to conduct any factfinding before issuing the final rule is also evident in the preamble to the final rule. See T.D. 9088, 2003–2 C.B. at 842 ("While the results actually realized in similar transactions under similar circumstances ordinarily provide significant evidence in determining whether a controlled transaction meets the arm's length standard, in the case of QCSAs *such data may not be available.*" (Emphasis added.)).

children is one of them"), but we do not agree that the belief that unrelated parties would share stock-based compensation costs in the context of a QCSA is one of them. First, commentators submitted significant evidence regarding this proposition. *See infra* part IV.C. Second, we were able to reach a definitive factual determination on the basis of significant evidence regarding this very proposition in *Xilinx. See Xilinx Inc. v. Commissioner,* 125 T.C. at 58–62. Third, Treasury could not have rationally concluded that this is a proposition "for which scant empirical evidence can be marshaled", *see Fox Television,* 556 U.S. at 519, without attempting to marshal empirical evidence in the first instance, which respondent concedes it did not do. . . .

We conclude that (1) by failing to engage in any fact finding, Treasury failed to "examine the relevant data", *State Farm,* 463 U.S. at 43, and (2) Treasury failed to support its belief that unrelated parties would share stock-based compensation costs in the context of a QCSA with any evidence in the record. Accordingly, the final rule lacks a basis in fact.

B. Treasury Failed to Rationally Connect the Choice It Made with the Facts It Found

Petitioner contends that the preamble to the final rule fails to rationally connect the choice that Treasury made in issuing a uniform final rule with the facts on which it purported to rely. *See id.* The preamble to the final rule indicates that Treasury relied on its belief that unrelated parties entering into QCSAs to develop "high-profit intangibles" would share stock-based compensation if the stock-based compensation was a "significant element" of the compensation. T.D. 9088, 2003–2 C.B. at 842–843. However, petitioner alleges, and respondent does not dispute, that (1) many QCSAs do not deal with "high-profit intangibles" and (2) stock-based compensation is often not a "significant element" of the compensation of the employees of taxpayers that enter into QCSAs. Yet the final rule does not distinguish between QCSAs to develop "high-profit intangibles" in which stock-based compensation was a "significant element" of the compensation and QCSAs in which these elements are not present. Petitioner contends—and we agree—that the preamble's explanation for Treasury's decision is therefore inadequate. *See State Farm,* 463 U.S. at 43.

Indeed, respondent does not directly refute petitioner's contention. Instead, respondent defends the final rule's inflexibility by arguing that the final rule is reasonable because it eases administrative burdens.[27]

Improving administrability can be a reasonable basis for agency action. *See Mayo Found.,* 562 U.S. at 59 ("[Treasury] reasonably concluded that its full-time

---

[27] [fn 21] Respondent also argues that petitioner cannot complain if the final rule sometimes produces results that are inconsistent with the arm's-length standard because the QCSA regime provides an "elective assured treatment". However, Treasury rejected commentators' suggestion to issue the final rule as a safe harbor, *see* T.D. 9088, 2003–2 C.B. at 843–844, and we conclude that petitioner has not forfeited its right to challenge the validity of the final rule because it chose to structure the R & D cost-sharing agreement as a QCSA.

employee rule would 'improve administrability[.]'" (quoting T.D. 9167, 2005–1 C.B. 261, 262)). However, Treasury failed to give this—or any other—explanation for treating all QCSAs identically in the preamble to the final rule,[28] cf. id., and we cannot reasonably discern, see *State Farm*, 463 U.S. at 43, that this was Treasury's rationale for adopting a uniform final rule because the administrative benefits of a uniform final rule are entirely speculative.[29]

Moreover, even if we could discern that this was Treasury's intent, we would be unable to sustain the final rule on that basis because Treasury did not disclose its factual findings and we would therefore be unable to evaluate whether Treasury reasonably concluded that the purported administrative benefits of a uniform final rule can justify erroneously allocating income in some of those cases. We therefore conclude that, by treating all QCSAs identically, Treasury failed to articulate a " 'rational connection between the facts found and the choice made,'" *State Farm*, 463 U.S. at 43 (quoting *Burlington Truck Lines*, 371 U.S. at 168).

C. Treasury Failed to Respond to Significant Comments

Petitioner contends that Treasury failed to respond to significant comments submitted by commentators. Respondent contends that Treasury was not persuaded by the submitted comments.

Several commentators informed Treasury that they knew of no evidence of any transaction between unrelated parties that required one party to reimburse the other party for amounts attributable to stock-based compensation. Additionally, AeA informed Treasury that a survey of its member companies' arm's-length codevelopment and joint venture agreements found none in which the parties agreed to share stock-based compensation costs. We found similar evidence to be relevant in *Xilinx. See Xilinx Inc. v. Commissioner*, 125 T.C. at 59. Treasury never directly responded to this evidence. Instead, Treasury reasoned that the final rule would not be inconsistent with the arm's-length standard in the absence of evidence that unrelated parties share stock-based compensation costs because relevant data may not be available. *See* T.D. 9088, 2003–2 C.B. at 842.

---

[28] [fn 22] The preamble to the final rule discusses administrability only with respect to Treasury's selection of the exercise spread method and the elective grant date method as the only available valuation methods. See T.D. 9088, 2003–2 C.B. at 844.

[29] [fn 23] We also note that unlike the statutory provision at issue in *Mayo Found.*, sec. 482 purports only to empower the Secretary to allocate income among controlled entities but not to directly govern taxpayer conduct. See sec. 1.4821(a)(3), Income Tax Regs. ("If necessary to reflect an arm's length result, a controlled taxpayer *may* report * * * the results of its controlled transactions based upon prices different from those actually charged." (Emphasis added.)). It is accordingly unclear whether administrability concerns are relevant in the context of sec. 482. However, because we cannot reasonably discern that Treasury relied on administrability concerns here, we need not resolve this question.

Treasury's response, however, in no way refutes the commentators' evidence that unrelated parties never share such compensation. . . .

The Baumol and Malkiel analysis also concluded that there is no net economic cost to a corporation or its shareholders from the issuance of stock-based compensation. Treasury identified this evidence in the preamble to the final rule but did not directly respond to it. *See id.,* 2003–2 C.B. at 843. Instead, the preamble states that "[t]he final regulations provide that stock-based compensation must be taken into account in the context of QCSAs because such a result is consistent with the arm's length standard." *Id.* Treasury, however, never explained why unrelated parties would share stock-based compensation costs—or how the commensurate-with-income standard could justify the final rule—if stock-based compensation is not an economic cost to the issuing corporation or its shareholders. . . .[30]

Indeed, Treasury failed to respond directly to any of the evidence that unrelated parties would not share stock-based compensation costs, other than by asserting that the transactions cited by the commentators did not "share enough characteristics of QCSAs involving the development of high-profit intangibles" to be relevant. T.D. 9088, 2003–2 C.B. at 842. This was a mere assertion; Treasury offered no analysis addressing the extent of the supposed differences or explaining why any differences make the cited transactions irrelevant or unpersuasive. By contrast, in *Xilinx* we examined a broad array of evidence to determine whether unrelated parties would share such costs. *See Xilinx Inc. v. Commissioner,* 125 T.C. at 58–62. Tellingly, respondent does not even attempt to explain why Treasury failed to address similar evidence in the preamble to the final rule.

Although Treasury's failure to respond to an isolated comment or two would probably not be fatal to the final rule, Treasury's failure to meaningfully respond to numerous relevant and significant comments certainly is. *See Home Box Office,* 567 F.2d at 35–36. Meaningful judicial review and fair treatment of affected persons require "an exchange of views, information, and criticism between interested persons and the agency." *Id.* at 35. Treasury's failure to adequately respond to commentators frustrates our review of the final rule and was prejudicial to affected entities.

D. The Final Rule Is Contrary to the Evidence Before Treasury

Petitioner contends that the final rule is contrary to the evidence before Treasury when it issued the final rule. We agree.

---

[30] [fn 26] Respondent contends that the final rule is consistent with the commensurate-with-income standard because stock-based compensation is economic activity even if it is not an economic cost. However, Treasury never made this distinction in the preamble to the final rule, see SEC v. Chenery Corp., 332 U.S. 194, 196 (1947); Carpenter Family Invs., LLC v. Commissioner, 136 T.C. 373, 380, 396 n. 30, 2011 WL 1627952 (2011), and it did not explain why unrelated parties would share items that are not economic costs.

We have already discussed Treasury's failure to cite any evidence supporting its belief that unrelated parties to QCSAs would share stock-based compensation costs, *see supra* part IV.A; the significant evidence submitted by commentators showing that unrelated parties to QCSAs would not share stock-based compensation costs, *see supra* part IV.C; and Treasury's failure to respond to much of the submitted evidence, *see id.*

Significantly, Treasury never said that it found any of the submitted evidence incredible. Treasury also seemed to accept the commentators' economic analyses, which concluded that—and explained why—unrelated parties to a QCSA would be unwilling to share the exercise spread or grant date value of stock-based compensation. Finally, respondent has not identified any evidence in the administrative record that supports Treasury's belief that unrelated parties to QCSAs would generally share stock-based compensation costs.

Although we are mindful that "a court is not to substitute its judgment for that of the agency", *State Farm*, 463 U.S. at 43, we conclude that Treasury's "explanation for its decision * * * runs counter to the evidence before" it, see id.

VI. CONCLUSION

Because the final rule lacks a basis in fact, Treasury failed to rationally connect the choice it made with the facts found, Treasury failed to respond to significant comments when it issued the final rule, and Treasury's conclusion that the final rule is consistent with the arm's-length standard is contrary to all of the evidence before it, we conclude that the final rule fails to satisfy *State Farm*'s reasoned decisionmaking standard and therefore is invalid.[31] *See* APA sec. 706(2)(A); *State Farm*, 463 U.S. at 43. Indeed, Treasury's "*ipse dixit* conclusion, coupled with its failure to respond to contrary arguments resting on solid data, epitomizes arbitrary and capricious decisionmaking." *Ill. Pub. Telecomms. Ass'n v. FCC*, 117 F.3d 555, 564 (D.C.Cir.1997).

By reason of the above respondent erred in making the section 482 allocations at issue, and petitioner is therefore entitled to partial summary judgment. We will grant petitioner's motion and deny respondent's motion.

We have considered the parties' remaining arguments, and to the extent not discussed above, conclude those arguments are irrelevant, moot, or without merit.

To reflect the foregoing,

---

[31] [fn 29] Because we conclude that the final rule fails to satisfy *State Farm*'s reasoned decisionmaking standard, the final rule would be invalid even if we were to conclude that *Chevron* supplies the ultimate standard of review. See supra part III.B. The analysis under *Chevron* would proceed as follows: The parties agree that sec. 482 is ambiguous. We would therefore proceed to *Chevron* step 2. Under *Chevron* step 2, we would conclude the final rule is invalid because it is " 'arbitrary or capricious in substance'"", Judulang v. Holder, 565 U.S. ——, —— n. 7, 132 S.Ct. 476, 483, 181 L.Ed.2d 449 (2011) (quoting *Mayo Found.*, 562 U.S. at 53), and therefore cannot be justified as being a reasonable interpretation of what sec. 482 requires.

An appropriate order will be issued.

Reviewed by the Court.

THORNTON, COLVIN, HALPERN, FOLEY, VASQUEZ, GALE, GOEKE, HOLMES, PARIS, KERRIGAN, BUCH, LAUBER, NEGA, and ASHFORD, JJ., agree with this opinion of the Court.

MORRISON and PUGH, JJ., did not participate in the consideration of this opinion.

NOTES AND QUESTIONS

1. What obligation do Treasury and the IRS have to respond to comments in the process of issuing a regulation?
2. If there is an obligation to consider taxpayer comments, does it matter if the comments are unreasonable?
3. The Ninth Circuit initially reversed this Tax Court opinion on appeal. The Circuit Court withdrew the reversal, however, because one of the judges passed away. A new appellate panel member replaced the deceased judge.

An interesting outgrowth of the regulation writing process is the IRS Notice. The IRS issues a Notice when a time-sensitive issue arises. Rather than waiting for the regulation drafting process, the IRS uses the Notice to announce a substantive position that it expects taxpayers to follow immediately. Although the IRS appears to use Notices to take a position that will eventually appear in more formal regulations, not all Notices turn into Treasury regulations. Notices are published in the Internal Revenue Bulletin, but not in the Federal Register.

There are two additional types of guidance that are very important to tax administration, the revenue ruling and the revenue procedure. These two forms of guidance are slightly less formal and authoritative than a Treasury regulation. A revenue ruling represents the IRS's official position on a substantive tax issue. Reg. § 601.601(d)(2)(i)(a). Generally, a revenue ruling provides a set of generic hypothetical facts, a rule, and the IRS's reasoning for resolving the issue. Although the facts set forth in a revenue ruling are hypothetical rather than specific to a particular taxpayer, the issues are generally similar to those that many taxpayers are facing at the time. The IRS and the courts see this type of ruling as generally binding on the IRS. *See* Estate of McLendon v. Commissioner, 135 F.3d 1017, 1024 (5th Cir. 1998); Rauenhorst v. Commissioner, 119 T.C. 157, 173 (2002); Chief Counsel Notice CC-2002-043 (October 17, 2002), *superseded in part*, Chief Counsel Notice CC-2003-014 (May 8, 2003).

Similar to a revenue ruling, a revenue procedure (Rev. Proc.) provides the IRS's official position on a particular issue. The difference is that a Rev. Proc. applies to procedural issues rather than substantive issues. For example, a Rev. Proc. might state the IRS's position is that a 40% threshold is necessary to establish a continuing business interest in a specific type of reorganization. A taxpayer entering into the particular type of reorganization will feel some comfort that the IRS will not challenge a transaction that satisfies the 40% threshold. Both revenue rulings and revenue procedures are published in the Internal Revenue Bulletin, but generally not in the Federal Register.

One of the principal administrative roles of the IRS and the IRS's Chief Counsel Office is to make formal determinations on legal issues by providing private guidance to specific taxpayers upon request. There are three basic document types setting forth such determinations—the Private Letter Ruling (PLR); the Technical Advice Memoranda (TAM); and the Field Service Advice (FSA). They are less formal and less authoritative than revenue rulings and revenue procedures because they were traditionally private and unavailable to the public. *See, e.g.,* Tax Analysts and Advocates v. IRS, 505 F.2d 350 (D.C. Cir. 1974) (lawsuit to make PLRs public). For example, a PLR is a ruling the IRS issues at the request of a particular taxpayer based on facts presented by the taxpayer. Because PLRs were private, the IRS did not deem it necessary to come to a final conclusion for the entire agency to follow. Thus, originally and today, a PLR is binding only on the taxpayer for whom it is written. PLRs often contain a disclaimer providing that the position taken is not the IRS's official position. FSAs and TAMs contain similar disclaimers.

The remaining guidance forms are less authoritative or less formal, or both, than the above forms. They are still important because they reflect the IRS's thinking on various legal issues at specific points in time. Although the IRS might not consider itself bound by private guidance and these informal guidance formats, the IRS departs from them only in rare instances. When IRS personnel with taxpayer contact, like examiners, make determinations that depart from established IRS guidance, their superiors may require them to make changes to conform to the established guidance. These inferior guidance formats include IRS Announcements, Actions on Decision, Chief Counsel Advice, Internal Revenue Manual provisions, IRS products, and litigating positions.

2. Judicial Deference to Administrative Tax Guidance

Although the IRS and Treasury communicate with taxpayers through various forms of guidance, courts determine which administrative guidance has the force of law, persuasive value in determining the law, or no legal value. Thus, it is important for taxpayers and their advisors to be able to evaluate whether and to what extent a court will defer to an agency's administrative guidance for preparing tax returns.

i. *Deference to Administrative Guidance Generally*

Courts determine whether and to what extent an administrative interpretation deserves deference under a framework the Supreme Court set forth in *Chevron* and *Skidmore*. There are two categories of deference under this framework. The first is full deference. Under *Chevron*, a court faced with a qualifying interpretation treats the agency's interpretation as having the same force and effect of law as a statute. *See* Chevron, U.S.A. v. Natural Res. Def. Council, 467 U.S. 837, 865 (1984). This full deference is commonly referred to as *Chevron* deference. The second category of deference is persuasive deference. Under *Skidmore*, a court faced with an interpretation that does not merit the same force of law as a statute defers to the agency interpretation to the extent of its persuasiveness. This persuasive deference is commonly referred to as *Skidmore* deference. *See* Skidmore v. Swift & Co., 323 U.S. 134 (1944).

It is not easy to determine whether an interpretation deserves *Chevron* or *Skidmore* deference. Under the *Chevron-Skidmore* framework, the deference level depends on the scope of the legislature's delegation, the administering agency's intent, and the consistency of the guidance with the underlying statute. *See* United States v. Mead Corp., 533 U.S. 218, 226-27 (2001). *Chevron* deference applies to two different types of delegations with slightly different standards for consistency with the statute. An agency's interpretation issued in some form of guidance pursuant to an explicit delegation—whether the delegation is specific or general—is treated as having the force of law if it is not "arbitrary, capricious, or manifestly contrary to the statute." An agency interpretation issued in some form of guidance pursuant to an implicit delegation is treated as having the force of law if the interpretation is a "reasonable" construction of the statute.

Skidmore deference begins where *Chevron* deference ends. Under *Skidmore*, an agency interpretation that does not have the force of law is entitled to persuasive deference, the level of which "depend[s] upon the thoroughness evident in its consideration, the validity of its reasoning, its consistency with earlier and later pronouncements, and all those factors which give it power to persuade . . . ." In other words, if *Chevron* deference does not apply, the court will weigh the interpretation's persuasiveness.

Skidmore may apply to an agency interpretation for various reasons. For example, if *Chevron* does not apply because the interpretation is inconsistent with the statute, the interpretation might be entitled to deference under *Skidmore*, but not much deference. Although an agency is more familiar than a court with governing law, an agency may not overrule Congress.

Skidmore might also apply as a result of the agency's intent. Even when Congress has delegated authority to an agency, and the agency has issued an interpretation consistent with that authority, *Chevron* deference will still not apply if the agency does not intend the interpretation to have the force of law. An agency might not want to exercise its authority to make law every time it issues guidance. To exercise an agency's full legislative authority can be time consuming and may also hinder an agency's need for flexibility. Conversely, an agency might attempt to exercise full legislative authority and fail in the process by issuing guidance on a matter foreclosed by the underlying legislation. *See, e.g.,* United States v. Home Concrete & Supply Co., 566 U.S. 478, 485-89 (2012). Thus, *Chevron* deference applies where Congress has delegated authority to a federal agency and the agency has exercised that authority. Otherwise, *Skidmore* deference applies.

ii.   *Deference to Administrative Tax Guidance*

The level of deference to administrative tax guidance turns on Congress's delegation of authority and the administrative exercise of authority. In the tax realm, Congress delegates authority in two ways. Congress makes explicit lawmaking authority delegations to the IRS and Treasury with respect to specific statutory provisions. In the absence of a specific delegation, Treasury and the IRS may rely on a general delegation. *See* IRC § 7805(a). As an example of a specific delegation, Congress has enacted explicit language that delegates lawmaking authority to Treasury and the IRS to issue regulations governing how an affiliated corporate group files a consolidated tax return. Treasury and the IRS have exercised this authority by issuing over 100 Treasury regulations governing consolidated returns. More generally, Congress has delegated to Treasury and the IRS the authority to "prescribe all needful rules and regulations for the enforcement of [the Code]." IRC § 7805(a). Courts defer to the general delegation to the same extent as a specific delegation, but that was not always understood to be the case. The Supreme Court only recently confirmed that deference is the same for regulations issued under the general delegation as it is for regulations issued under specific delegations in *Mayo Foundation for Medical Education & Research v. United States.*

MAYO FOUND. FOR MED. EDUC. & RESEARCH v. UNITED STATES
562 U.S. 44 (2011)
Supreme Court of the United States

Chief Justice ROBERTS delivered the opinion of the Court.

Nearly all Americans who work for wages pay taxes on those wages under the Federal Insurance Contributions Act (FICA), which Congress enacted to collect funds for Social Security. The question presented in this case is whether doctors who serve as medical residents are properly viewed as "student[s]" whose service Congress has exempted from FICA taxes under 26 U.S.C. § 3121(b)(10).

I

A

Most doctors who graduate from medical school in the United States pursue additional education in a specialty to become board certified to practice in that field. Petitioners Mayo Foundation for Medical Education and Research, Mayo Clinic, and the Regents of the University of Minnesota (collectively Mayo) offer medical residency programs that provide such instruction. Mayo's residency programs, which usually last three to five years, train doctors primarily through hands-on experience. Residents often spend between 50 and 80 hours a week caring for patients, typically examining and diagnosing them, prescribing medication, recommending plans of care, and performing certain procedures. Residents are generally supervised in this work by more senior residents and by faculty members known as attending physicians. In 2005, Mayo paid its residents annual "stipends" ranging between $41,000 and $56,000 and provided them with health insurance, malpractice insurance, and paid vacation time.

Mayo residents also take part in "a formal and structured educational program." Brief for Petitioners 5 (internal quotation marks omitted). Residents are assigned textbooks and journal articles to read and are expected to attend weekly lectures and other conferences. Residents also take written exams and are evaluated by the attending faculty physicians. But the parties do not dispute that the bulk of residents' time is spent caring for patients.

B

Through the Social Security Act and related legislation, Congress has created a comprehensive national insurance system that provides benefits for retired workers, disabled workers, unemployed workers, and their families. See *United States v. Lee,* 455 U.S. 252, 254, 258, and nn. 1, 7, 102 S.Ct. 1051, 71 L.Ed.2d 127 (1982). Congress funds Social Security by taxing both employers and employees under FICA on the wages employees earn. See 26 U.S.C. § 3101(a) (tax on employees); § 3111(a) (tax on employers). Congress has defined "wages" broadly, to encompass "all remuneration for employment." § 3121(a) (2006 ed. and Supp. III). The term "employment" has a similarly broad reach, extending to "any service, of whatever nature, performed . . . by an employee for the person employing him." § 3121(b).

Congress has, however, exempted certain categories of service and individuals from FICA's demands. As relevant here, Congress has excluded from taxation "service performed in the employ of . . . a school, college, or university . . . if such service is performed by a student who is enrolled and regularly attending classes at such school, college, or university." § 3121(b)(10) (2006 ed.). The Social Security Act, which governs workers' eligibility for benefits, contains a corresponding student exception materially identical to § 3121(b)(10). 42 U.S.C. § 410(a)(10).

Since 1951, the Treasury Department has applied the student exception to exempt from taxation students who work for their schools "as an incident to and for the purpose of pursuing a course of study" there. 16 Fed.Reg. 12474 (adopting Treas. Regs. 127, § 408.219(c)); see Treas. Reg. § 31.3121(b)(10)–2(d), 26 CFR § 31.3121(b)(10)–2(d) (2010). Until 2005, the Department determined whether an individual's work was "incident to" his studies by performing a case-by-case analysis. The primary considerations in that analysis were the number of hours worked and the course load taken. See, *e.g.,* Rev. Rul. 78–17, 1978–1 Cum. Bull. 307 (services of individual "employed on a full-time basis" with a part-time course load are "not incident to and for the purpose of pursuing a course of study").

For its part, the Social Security Administration (SSA) also articulated in its regulations a case-by-case approach to the corresponding student exception in the Social Security Act. See 20 CFR § 404.1028(c) (1998). The SSA has, however, "always held that resident physicians are not students." SSR 78–3, Cum. Bull. 1978, pp. 55–56. In 1998, the Court of Appeals for the Eighth Circuit held that the SSA could not categorically exclude residents from student status, given that its regulations provided for a case-by-case approach. See *Minnesota v. Apfel*, 151 F.3d 742, 747–748. Following that decision, the Internal Revenue Service received more than 7,000 claims seeking FICA tax refunds on the ground that medical residents qualified as students under § 3121(b)(10) of the Internal Revenue Code. 568 F.3d 675, 677 (C.A.8 2009).

Facing that flood of claims, the Treasury Department "determined that it [wa]s necessary to provide additional clarification of the ter[m]" "student" as used in § 3121(b)(10), particularly with respect to individuals who perform "services that are in the nature of on the job training." 69 Fed.Reg. 8605 (2004). The Department proposed an amended rule for comment and held a public hearing on it. See *id.*, at 76405.

On December 21, 2004, the Department adopted an amended rule prescribing that an employee's service is "incident" to his studies only when "[t]he educational aspect of the relationship between the employer and the employee, as compared to the service aspect of the relationship, [is] predominant." *Id.*, at 76408; Treas. Reg. § 31.3121(b)(10)–2(d)(3)(i), 26 CFR § 31.3121(b)(10)–2(d)(3)(i) (2005). The rule categorically provides that "[t]he services of a full-time employee"—as defined by the employer's policies, but in any event including any employee normally scheduled to work 40 hours or more per week—"are not incident to and for the purpose of pursuing a course of study." 69 Fed.Reg. 76408; Treas. Reg. § 31.3121(b)(10)–2(d)(3)(iii), 26 CFR § 31.3121(b)(10)–2(d)(3)(iii) (the full-time employee rule). The amended provision clarifies that the Department's analysis "is not affected by the fact that the services performed . . . may have an educational, instructional, or training aspect." *Ibid.* The rule also includes as an example the case of "Employee E," who is employed by "University V" as a medical resident. 69 Fed.Reg. 76409; Treas. Reg. § 31.3121(b)(10)–2(e), 26 CFR § 31.3121(b)(10)–2(e) (Example 4). Because Employee E's "normal work schedule calls for [him] to perform services 40 or more hours per week," the rule provides that his service is "not incident to and for the purpose of pursuing a course of study," and he accordingly is not an exempt "student" under § 3121(b)(10). 69 Fed.Reg. 76409, 76410; Treas. Reg. § 31.3121(b)(10)–2(e), 26 CFR § 31.3121(b)(10)–2(e) (Example 4).

C

After the Department promulgated the full-time employee rule, Mayo filed suit seeking a refund of the money it had withheld and paid on its residents' stipends during the second quarter of 2005. 503 F.Supp.2d 1164, 1166–1167 (Minn.2007); *Regents of Univ. of Minn. v. United States*, No. 06–5084, 2008 WL 906799 (D.Minn., Apr. 1, 2008), App. to Pet. for Cert. Civ. 47a. Mayo asserted that its residents were exempt under § 3121(b)(10) and that the Treasury Department's full-time employee rule was invalid.

The District Court granted Mayo's motion for summary judgment. The court held that the full-time employee rule is inconsistent with the unambiguous text of § 3121, which the court understood to dictate that "an employee is a 'student' so long as the educational aspect of his service predominates over the service aspect of the relationship with his employer." 503 F.Supp.2d, at 1175. The court also determined that the factors governing this Court's analysis of regulations set forth in *National Muffler Dealers Assn., Inc. v. United States,* 440 U.S. 472, 99 S.Ct. 1304, 59 L.Ed.2d 519 (1979), "indicate that the full-time employee exception is invalid." 503 F.Supp.2d, at 1176; see App. to Pet. for Cert. 54a.

The Government appealed, and the Court of Appeals reversed. 568 F.3d 675. Applying our opinion in *Chevron U.S.A. Inc. v. Natural Resources Defense Council, Inc.,* 467 U.S. 837, 104 S.Ct. 2778, 81 L.Ed.2d 694 (1984), the Court of Appeals concluded that "the statute is silent or ambiguous on the question whether a medical resident working for the school full-time is a 'student' " for purposes of § 3121(b)(10), and that the Department's amended regulation "is a permissible interpretation of the statut[e]." 568 F.3d, at 679–680, 683.

We granted Mayo's petition for certiorari. 560 U.S. 938, 130 S.Ct. 3353, 176 L.Ed.2d 1244 (2010).

II

A

We begin our analysis with the first step of the two-part framework announced in *Chevron,* supra, at 842–843, and ask whether Congress has "directly addressed the precise question at issue." We agree with the Court of Appeals that Congress has not done so. The statute does not define the term "student," and does not otherwise attend to the precise question whether medical residents are subject to FICA. See 26 U.S.C. § 3121(b)(10).

Mayo nonetheless contends that the Treasury Department's full-time employee rule must be rejected under *Chevron* step one. Mayo argues that the dictionary definition of "student"—one "who engages in 'study' by applying the mind 'to the acquisition of learning, whether by means of books, observation, or experiment' "—plainly encompasses residents. Brief for Petitioners 22 (quoting Oxford Universal Dictionary 2049–2050 (3d ed.1955)). And, Mayo adds, residents are not excluded from that category by the only limitation on students Congress has imposed under the statute—that they "be 'enrolled and regularly attending classes at [a] school.' " Brief for Petitioners 22 (quoting § 3121(b)(10)).

Mayo's reading does not eliminate the statute's ambiguity as applied to working professionals. In its reply brief, Mayo acknowledges that a full-time professor taking evening classes—a person who presumably would satisfy the statute's class-enrollment requirement and apply his mind to learning—could be excluded from the exemption and taxed because he is not " 'predominant[ly]' " a student. Reply Brief for Petitioners 7. Medical residents might likewise be excluded on the same basis; the statute itself does not resolve the ambiguity.

The District Court interpreted § 3121(b)(10) as unambiguously foreclosing the Department's rule by mandating that an employee be deemed "a 'student' so long as the educational aspect of his service predominates over the service aspect of the relationship with his employer." 503 F.Supp.2d, at 1175. We do not think it possible to glean so much from the little that § 3121 provides. In any event, the statutory text still would offer no insight into how Congress intended predominance to be determined or whether Congress thought that medical residents would satisfy the requirement.

To the extent Congress has specifically addressed medical residents in § 3121, moreover, it has expressly excluded these doctors from exemptions they might otherwise invoke. See §§ 3121(b)(6)(B), (7)(C)(ii) (excluding medical residents from exemptions available to employees of the District of Columbia and the United States). That choice casts doubt on any claim that Congress specifically intended to insulate medical residents from FICA's reach in the first place.

In sum, neither the plain text of the statute nor the District Court's interpretation of the exemption "speak[s] with the precision necessary to say definitively whether [the statute] applies to" medical residents. *United States v. Eurodif S.A.,* 555 U.S. 305, 319, 129 S.Ct. 878, 881, 172 L.Ed.2d 679 (2009).

B

In the typical case, such an ambiguity would lead us inexorably to *Chevron* step two, under which we may not disturb an agency rule unless it is " 'arbitrary or capricious in substance, or manifestly contrary to the statute.' " *Household Credit Services, Inc. v. Pfennig,* 541 U.S. 232, 242, 124 S.Ct. 1741, 158 L.Ed.2d 450 (2004) (quoting *United States v. Mead Corp.,* 533 U.S. 218, 227, 121 S.Ct. 2164, 150 L.Ed.2d 292 (2001)). In this case, however, the parties disagree over the proper framework for evaluating an ambiguous provision of the Internal Revenue Code.

Mayo asks us to apply the multi-factor analysis we used to review a tax regulation in *National Muffler*, supra. There we explained:

"A regulation may have particular force if it is a substantially contemporaneous construction of the statute by those presumed to have been aware of congressional intent. If the regulation dates from a later period, the manner in which it evolved merits inquiry. Other relevant considerations are the length of time the regulation has been in effect, the reliance placed on it, the consistency of the Commissioner's interpretation, and the degree of scrutiny Congress has devoted to the regulation during subsequent re-enactments of the statute." *Id.,* at 477, 99 S.Ct. 1304.

The Government, on the other hand, contends that the *National Muffler* standard has been superseded by *Chevron*. The sole question for the Court at step two under the *Chevron* analysis is "whether the agency's answer is based on a permissible construction of the statute." 467 U.S., at 843, 104 S.Ct. 2778.

Since deciding *Chevron*, we have cited both *National Muffler* and *Chevron* in our review of Treasury Department regulations. See, e.g., United States v. Cleveland Indians Baseball Co., 532 U.S. 200, 219, 121 S.Ct. 1433, 149 L.Ed.2d 401 (2001) (citing *National Muffler*); Cottage Savings Assn. v. Commissioner, 499 U.S. 554, 560–561, 111 S.Ct. 1503, 113 L.Ed.2d 589 (1991) (same); United States v. Boyle, 469 U.S. 241, 246, n. 4, 105 S.Ct. 687, 83 L.Ed.2d 622 (1985) (citing *Chevron*); see also Atlantic Mut. Ins. Co. v. Commissioner, 523 U.S. 382, 387, 389, 118 S.Ct. 1413, 140 L.Ed.2d 542 (1998) (citing *Chevron* and *Cottage Savings*).

Although we have not thus far distinguished between *National Muffler* and *Chevron*, they call for different analyses of an ambiguous statute. Under *National Muffler*, for example, a court might view an agency's interpretation of a statute with heightened skepticism when it has not been consistent over time, when it was promulgated years after the relevant statute was enacted, or because of the way in which the regulation evolved. 440 U.S., at 477, 99 S.Ct. 1304. The District Court in this case cited each of these factors in rejecting the Treasury Department's rule, noting in particular that the regulation had been promulgated after an adverse judicial decision. See 503 F.Supp.2d, at 1176; see also Brief for Petitioners 41–44 (relying on the same considerations).

Under *Chevron*, in contrast, deference to an agency's interpretation of an ambiguous statute does not turn on such considerations. We have repeatedly held that "[a]gency inconsistency is not a basis for declining to analyze the agency's interpretation under the *Chevron* framework." *National Cable & Telecommunications Assn. v. Brand X Internet Services*, 545 U.S. 967, 981, 125 S.Ct. 2688, 162 L.Ed.2d 820 (2005); accord, *Eurodif S. A., supra*, at 316, 129 S.Ct., at 887. We have instructed that "neither antiquity nor contemporaneity with [a] statute is a condition of [a regulation's] validity." *Smiley v. Citibank (South Dakota), N. A.*, 517 U.S. 735, 740, 116 S.Ct. 1730, 135 L.Ed.2d 25 (1996). And we have found it immaterial to our analysis that a "regulation was prompted by litigation." Indeed, in *United Dominion Industries, Inc. v. United States*, 532 U.S. 822, 838, 121 S.Ct. 1934, 150 L.Ed.2d 45 (2001), we expressly invited the Treasury Department to "amend its regulations" if troubled by the consequences of our resolution of the case.

Aside from our past citation of *National Muffler*, Mayo has not advanced any justification for applying a less deferential standard of review to Treasury Department regulations than we apply to the rules of any other agency. In the absence of such justification, we are not inclined to carve out an approach to administrative review good for tax law only. To the contrary, we have expressly "[r]ecogniz[ed] the importance of maintaining a uniform approach to judicial review of administrative action." *Dickinson v. Zurko*, 527 U.S. 150, 154, 119 S.Ct. 1816, 144 L.Ed.2d 143 (1999). See, *e.g., Skinner v. Mid–America Pipeline Co.*, 490 U.S. 212, 222–223, 109 S.Ct. 1726, 104 L.Ed.2d 250 (1989) (declining to apply "a different and stricter nondelegation doctrine in cases where Congress delegates discretionary authority to the Executive under its taxing power").

The principles underlying our decision in *Chevron* apply with full force in the tax context. *Chevron* recognized that "[t]he power of an administrative agency to administer a congressionally created . . . program necessarily requires the formulation of policy and the making of rules to fill any gap left, implicitly or explicitly, by Congress." 467 U.S., at 843, 104 S.Ct. 2778 (internal quotation marks omitted). It acknowledged that the formulation of that policy might require "more than ordinary knowledge respecting the matters subjected to agency regulations." *Id.*, at 844, 104 S.Ct. 2778 (internal quotation marks omitted). Filling gaps in the Internal Revenue Code plainly requires the Treasury Department to make interpretive choices for statutory implementation at least as complex as the ones other agencies must make in administering their statutes. Cf. *Bob Jones Univ. v. United States,* 461 U.S. 574, 596, 103 S.Ct. 2017, 76 L.Ed.2d 157 (1983) ("In an area as complex as the tax system, the agency Congress vests with administrative responsibility must be able to exercise its authority to meet changing conditions and new problems"). We see no reason why our review of tax regulations should not be guided by agency expertise pursuant to *Chevron* to the same extent as our review of other regulations.

As one of Mayo's *amici* points out, however, both the full-time employee rule and the rule at issue in *National Muffler* were promulgated pursuant to the Treasury Department's general authority under 26 U.S.C. § 7805(a) to "prescribe all needful rules and regulations for the enforcement" of the Internal Revenue Code. See Brief for Carlton M. Smith 4–7. In two decisions predating *Chevron,* this Court stated that "we owe the [Treasury Department's] interpretation less deference" when it is contained in a rule adopted under that "general authority" than when it is "issued under a specific grant of authority to define a statutory term or prescribe a method of executing a statutory provision." *Rowan Cos. v. United States,* 452 U.S. 247, 253, 101 S.Ct. 2288, 68 L.Ed.2d 814 (1981); *United States v. Vogel Fertilizer Co.,* 455 U.S. 16, 24, 102 S.Ct. 821, 70 L.Ed.2d 792 (1982) (quoting *Rowan*).

Since *Rowan* and *Vogel* were decided, however, the administrative landscape has changed significantly. We have held that *Chevron* deference is appropriate "when it appears that Congress delegated authority to the agency generally to make rules carrying the force of law, and that the agency interpretation claiming deference was promulgated in the exercise of that authority." *Mead,* 533 U.S., at 226–227, 121 S.Ct. 2164. Our inquiry in that regard does not turn on whether Congress's delegation of authority was general or specific. For example, in *National Cable & Telecommunications Assn., supra,* we held that the Federal Communications Commission was delegated "the authority to promulgate binding legal rules" entitled to *Chevron* deference under statutes that gave the Commission "the authority to 'execute and enforce,'" and "to 'prescribe such rules and regulations as may be necessary in the public interest to carry out the provisions' of," the Communications Act of 1934. 545 U.S., at 980–981, 125 S.Ct. 2688 (quoting 47 U.S.C. §§ 151, 201(b)). See also *Sullivan v. Everhart,* 494 U.S. 83, 87, 88–89, 110 S.Ct. 960, 108 L.Ed.2d 72 (1990) (applying *Chevron* deference to rule promulgated pursuant to delegation of "general authority to 'make rules and regulations and to establish procedures, not inconsistent with the provisions of this subchapter, which are necessary or appropriate to carry out such provisions'" (quoting 42 U.S.C. § 405(a) (1982 ed.))).

We believe *Chevron* and *Mead,* rather than *National Muffler* and *Rowan,* provide the appropriate framework for evaluating the full-time employee rule. The Department issued the full-time employee rule pursuant to the explicit authorization to "prescribe all needful rules and regulations for the enforcement" of the Internal Revenue Code. 26 U.S.C. § 7805(a) (2006 ed.). We have found such "express congressional authorizations to engage in the process of rulemaking" to be "a very good indicator of delegation meriting *Chevron* treatment." *Mead, supra,* at 229, 121 S.Ct. 2164. The Department issued the full-time employee rule only after notice-and-comment procedures, 69 Fed.Reg. 76405, again a consideration identified in our precedents as a "significant" sign that a rule merits *Chevron* deference. *Mead, supra,* at 230–231, 121 S.Ct. 2164; see, *e.g., Long Island Care at Home, Ltd. v. Coke,* 551 U.S. 158, 173–174, 127 S.Ct. 2339, 168 L.Ed.2d 54 (2007).

We have explained that "the ultimate question is whether Congress would have intended, and expected, courts to treat [the regulation] as within, or outside, its delegation to the agency of 'gap-filling' authority." *Id.,* at 173, 127 S.Ct. 2339 (emphasis deleted). In the *Long Island Care* case, we found that *Chevron* provided the appropriate standard of review "[w]here an agency rule sets forth important individual rights and duties, where the agency focuses fully and directly upon the issue, where the agency uses full notice-and-comment procedures to promulgate a rule, [and] where the resulting rule falls within the statutory grant of authority." 551 U.S., at 173, 127 S.Ct. 2339. These same considerations point to the same result here. This case falls squarely within the bounds of, and is properly analyzed under, *Chevron* and *Mead.*

C

The full-time employee rule easily satisfies the second step of *Chevron,* which asks whether the Department's rule is a "reasonable interpretation" of the enacted text. 467 U.S., at 844, 104 S.Ct. 2778. To begin, Mayo accepts that "the 'educational aspect of the relationship between the employer and the employee, as compared to the service aspect of the relationship, [must] be predominant' " in order for an individual to qualify for the exemption. Reply Brief for Petitioners 6–7 (quoting Treas. Reg. § 31.3121(b)(10)–2(d)(3)(i), 26 CFR § 31.3121(b)(10)–2(d)(3)(i)). Mayo objects, however, to the Department's conclusion that residents who work more than 40 hours per week categorically cannot satisfy that requirement. Because residents' employment is itself educational, Mayo argues, the hours a resident spends working make him "more of a student, not less of one." Reply Brief for Petitioners 15, n. 3 (emphasis deleted). Mayo contends that the Treasury Department should be required to engage in a case-by-case inquiry into "*what* [each] employee does [in his service] and *why*" he does it. *Id.,* at 7. Mayo also objects that the Department has drawn an arbitrary distinction between "hands-on training" and "classroom instruction." Brief for Petitioners 35.

We disagree. Regulation, like legislation, often requires drawing lines. Mayo does not dispute that the Treasury Department reasonably sought a way to distinguish between workers who study and students who work, see IRS Letter Ruling 9332005 (May 3, 1993). Focusing on the hours an individual works and the hours he spends in studies is a perfectly sensible way of accomplishing that goal. The Department explained that an individual's service and his "course of study are separate and distinct activities" in "the vast majority of cases," and reasoned that "[e]mployees who are working enough hours to be considered full-time employees . . . have filled the conventional measure of available time with work, and not study." 69 Fed.Reg. 8607. The Department thus did not distinguish classroom education from clinical training but rather education from service. The

Department reasonably concluded that its full-time employee rule would "improve administrability," *id.,* at 76405, and it thereby "has avoided the wasteful litigation and continuing uncertainty that would inevitably accompany any purely case-by-case approach" like the one Mayo advocates, *United States v. Correll,* 389 U.S. 299, 302, 88 S.Ct. 445, 19 L.Ed.2d 537 (1967).

As the Treasury Department has explained, moreover, the full-time employee rule has more to recommend it than administrative convenience. The Department reasonably determined that taxing residents under FICA would further the purpose of the Social Security Act and comport with this Court's precedent. As the Treasury Department appreciated, this Court has understood the terms of the Social Security Act to " 'import a breadth of coverage,' " 69 Fed.Reg. 8605 (quoting *Social Security Bd. v. Nierotko,* 327 U.S. 358, 365, 66 S.Ct. 637, 90 L.Ed. 718 (1946)), and we have instructed that "exemptions from taxation are to be construed narrowly," *Bingler v. Johnson,* 394 U.S. 741, 752, 89 S.Ct. 1439, 22 L.Ed.2d 695 (1969). Although Mayo contends that medical residents have not yet begun their "working lives" because they are not "fully trained," Reply Brief for Petitioners 13 (internal quotation marks omitted), the Department certainly did not act irrationally in concluding that these doctors—"who work long hours, serve as highly skilled professionals, and typically share some or all of the terms of employment of career employees"—are the kind of workers that Congress intended to both contribute to and benefit from the Social Security system, 69 Fed.Reg. 8608.

The Department's rule takes into account the SSA's concern that exempting residents from FICA would deprive residents and their families of vital disability and survivorship benefits that Social Security provides. *Id.,* at 8605. Mayo wonders whether the full-time employee rule will result in residents being taxed under FICA but denied coverage by the SSA. The Government informs us, however, that the SSA continues to adhere to its longstanding position that medical residents are not students and thus remain eligible for coverage. Brief for United States 29–30; Tr. of Oral Arg. 33–34.

* * *

We do not doubt that Mayo's residents are engaged in a valuable educational pursuit or that they are students of their craft. The question whether they are "students" for purposes of § 3121, however, is a different matter. Because it is one to which Congress has not directly spoken, and because the Treasury Department's rule is a reasonable construction of what Congress has said, the judgment of the Court of Appeals must be affirmed.

It is so ordered.

Justice KAGAN took no part in the consideration or decision of this case.

NOTES AND QUESTIONS

1. According to *Chevron*, a court defers to the federal agency tasked with administering the statute at issue where Congress explicitly or implicitly

delegated lawmaking authority to the agency. The administrative guidance, however, deserves deference only as long as it is consistent with the underlying statute. *National Muffler* involved a determination of whether an agency determination was consistent with the underlying statute. How similar are the approaches to determining whether there is an explicit or implicit delegation of authority to determining whether a guidance is consistent with an underlying statute?

2. Do you agree that the term "student" is ambiguous? How certain must a statutory term be in order to be deemed unambiguous?

Despite having the authority to issue guidance with the force and effect of law in many situations, Treasury and the IRS do not always invoke the full authority. Some forms of guidance are not officially published, some are published on the IRS web site. Some, but not all, guidance forms published on the web site are also published in the Internal Revenue Bulletin. In turn some, but not all, guidance forms published in the Internal Revenue Bulletin are published in the Federal Register. Whether and where the IRS publishes a particular form of guidance serves as a gauge as to what level of deference, if any, the IRS expects.

The IRS often indicates the level of deference it expects by inserting qualifying language in the guidance or regulation. There are certain forms of guidance to which the IRS clearly does not want to feel bound. For example, certain unpublished guidance contains language saying that it cannot be cited as precedent.

Unless there is an inconsistency with the statute or a procedural defect, Treasury regulations are likely to yield the same force of law as a statute under *Chevron*. This near complete deference is because Treasury and the IRS publish the regulations in both the Federal Register and the Internal Revenue Bulletin, and the issuing process includes notice and comment procedures. Congress's intent to delegate authority—as in most of the IRS's rulemaking—can be inferred from a specific delegation or, in its absence, a general delegation. Whether Treasury and the IRS issued a particular regulation pursuant to Congress's delegation can be inferred by the fact that Treasury and the IRS chose to subject the rulemaking to publication in the federal register and notice and comment.

Whether courts would give full deference to a revenue ruling, a revenue procedure, or an IRS Notice is less certain. Under *Chevron*, courts defer to agency lawmaking that Congress has delegated to the agency explicitly or by leaving statutory gaps for an agency to fill. These three forms of guidance are the type that appear authorized by the general delegation, mandating that the IRS "shall prescribe all needful rules and regulations for the enforcement of [the Internal Revenue Code], including all rules and regulations as may be necessary by reason of any alteration of law in relation to internal revenue." *See* IRC § 7805(a). Thus, although these forms of guidance do not go through public comment procedures, Congress has delegated to the IRS authority to make this guidance binding. Also, the IRS commits to the positions taken in these guidance vehicles. It would appear, then, that these guidance forms could receive full deference under *Chevron*.

On the other hand, a reason for courts to accord less deference to these three forms of guidance is the IRS's intent. Under the framework described in *Chevron*, for full deference the rulemaking action must be carried out in furtherance of Congress's delegation. With respect to these three forms of guidance, the IRS routinely invokes neither a specific nor the general rulemaking delegation. With no language invoking Congress's explicit lawmaking authority delegations, courts might infer that the IRS does not intend to exercise such authority. Moreover, the IRS often states explicitly that these forms of guidance do not have the legislative authority entrusted to Treasury regulations.

The Supreme Court has refused to opine on the deference owed revenue rulings. *See* United States v. Cleveland Indians Baseball Co., 532 U.S. 200, 220 (2001) ("We need not decide whether the Revenue Rulings themselves are entitled to deference."). This refusal seems wise. An all-encompassing classification might not make sense because there is more than one type of revenue ruling. First, there is the revenue ruling that invokes section 7805, Congress's general delegation to the Treasury and the IRS for rulemaking. Although most revenue rulings do not invoke section 7805 because that section does not generally authorize retroactive rulemaking, the IRS invokes section 7805 in many cases when the revenue ruling is not intended to be retroactive. A revenue ruling that invokes section 7805 ought to merit *Chevron* deference as long as it is not "arbitrary, capricious, or manifestly contrary to the statute." Second, there is the revenue ruling where the IRS is acting on an implicit delegation from Congress to fill in a statutory gap. A revenue ruling issued under an implicit delegation probably ought to merit *Chevron* deference as long as it is a reasonable construction of the statute. Third, there is the revenue ruling that stands on neither implicit nor explicit rulemaking authority. A revenue ruling invoking no rulemaking authority probably should not merit *Chevron* deference, but should be entitled to *Skidmore* deference.

IRS Notices and revenue procedures are similar to revenue rulings. There are the same three types—the IRS acting on explicit, implicit, or no rulemaking authority. They should be accorded the same level of deference as revenue rulings, *Chevron* with respect to explicit and implicit rulemaking authority, and *Skidmore* with respect to interpretations standing on no rulemaking authority.

The IRS publishes two other types of guidance in the Internal Revenue Bulletin, Actions on Decision (AODs) and Announcements. These two forms of guidance, however, do not merit *Chevron* deference. An Announcement merits no deference under *Chevron* because the IRS does not take a position in it. Rather, Announcements merely disseminate information.

In an AOD, however, the IRS does take a position. An AOD generally announces the IRS's position on a recent court case holding, generally whether it will follow the case's holding or not. When the Tax Court publishes a case that the IRS disagrees with, the IRS announces its "nonacquiescence" in an AOD. Nonacquiescence means that the IRS will not follow the holding in a particular case. An AOD announcing a nonacquiescence, therefore, signals to taxpayers that the IRS may continue to litigate the particular issue. Although the IRS publishes its position formally in an AOD, the IRS makes clear that taxpayers may not cite an AOD as precedent. This position is a clear indication that the IRS does not intend these interpretations to have the force of law. Thus, AODs do not merit *Chevron* deference.

Another form of public guidance containing agency interpretations is the Internal Revenue Manual. The Internal Revenue Manual serves as the official internal IRS staff instruction manual. It used to be a loose leaf document, but became too cumbersome to maintain in physical form. The IRM now appears only in digital form. The IRS does not present the Internal Revenue Manual to the public as its official position on tax matters. On the other hand, the IRS does not disavow its precedential value. Courts generally apply *Skidmore* deference rather than *Chevron* deference to these types of manuals.

Field Service Advice memoranda (FSAs), PLRs, and TAMs are also not entitled to *Chevron* deference. Although these forms of guidance are internal and are published against the IRS's will, they do not merit *Chevron* deference for the same reason AODs do not receive deference under *Chevron*. The IRS disavows any precedential value, thus showing no intent for these interpretations to have the force of law.

3. Methods of Interpreting Administrative Guidance

Agency guidance with the force of law might still need interpretation. Courts interpret this type of agency guidance the same way they interpret statutes. Thus, one would expect the same interpretive methods that apply to statutes also apply to an agency interpretation to which a court accords *Chevron* deference. Textualists would focus on the meaning of the words, intentionalists and purposivists could consider the regulatory equivalents of legislative history, and realists would likely focus on the entire context and consequences of its interpretation.

The same cannot be said for agency guidance deferred to under *Skidmore*. *Skidmore* applies when an agency interpretation does not have the force of law. Further, under *Skidmore* a court defers to an agency interpretation only to the extent of its power to persuade. An agency interpretation without the force of law that needs further interpretation has already lost its persuasive power.

In contrast, an agency is considered highly authoritative when it interprets its own guidance. Agency guidance that would otherwise be entitled to only *Skidmore* deference is entitled to controlling weight when it interprets the agency's own regulations. *See* Auer v. Robbins, 519 U.S. 452, 461 (1997). Although the Tax Court has held that such deference is not due where the interpretation was not a matter of public record—such as in a Private Letter Ruling—the Supreme Court later applied this deference to an interpretation contained in a brief filed by the agency in the case. *See Auer*, 519 U.S. at 461.

4. Administrative Guidance Constraints on the IRS

Anticipating whether the IRS will be bound by its own guidance is difficult. In its guidance, the IRS communicates its expectations to the public to assist each taxpayer to self-determine his or her tax liability. Generally, the IRS sticks to its guidance. The reason the IRS issues guidance is to "promote a uniform application of the laws administered by the IRS." Reg. § 601.601(d)(1). Occasionally, an agent for the IRS attempts to take action against a taxpayer inconsistent with IRS guidance. Courts—and often senior IRS personnel—do not take kindly to these IRS employee actions.

Rauenhorst is an example of this sort of vengeful IRS claim. There, a husband and wife contributed warrants to various charities. The charities, although not obligated to do so, sold the warrants for a profit on which they paid no tax. To the IRS, this anticipatory contribution looked like an attempt on the taxpayers' part to avoid tax on imminent gains. This is exactly what the taxpayers were trying to do, and a revenue ruling gave taxpayers permission to escape tax in that very situation. Nevertheless, the IRS determined the taxpayers owed tax and issued a deficiency notice to the husband and wife notifying them they were liable.

The taxpayers argued that a revenue ruling shielded the taxpayers from paying tax in this situation. In response, the IRS tried to wiggle out of being bound by its revenue ruling. The Tax Court characterized the IRS's arguments as follows:

> [The Commissioner's] quotation from the *Blake* opinion makes his position patently clear. [The Commissioner] is disavowing Rev. Rul. 78–197 . . . in this case. When [the Commissioner's] arguments are boiled down to their essential elements, he argues against the validity of the bright-line test of Rev. Rul. 78–197.

Rauenhorst, 119 T.C. at 169.

The Tax Court also noted that the IRS continued to rely on the revenue ruling when dealing with other taxpayers. The Tax Court added:

> [W]e cannot agree that the Commissioner is not bound to follow his revenue rulings in Tax Court proceedings. Indeed, we have on several occasions treated revenue rulings as concessions by the Commissioner where those rulings are relevant to our disposition of the case.

See id. Thus, the Tax Court treated the revenue ruling on which the taxpayers relied as a concession, and held for the taxpayers.

Generally, the IRS also has a duty of consistency in issuing private rulings or decisions. In *IBM v. United States*, for example, the IRS issued a private letter ruling granting an exemption from tax to Remington Rand—IBM's only competitor—with respect to a particular equipment class. IBM learned of the ruling for Remington Rand and requested a similar ruling with respect to the tax on the same equipment class. The IRS declined to grant IBM's request. Two years later, the IRS revoked Remington Rand's ruling, but IBM had paid about $13 million in taxes that it would not have paid had the IRS treated IBM similarly. The Court of Claims held:

> Implicit . . . in the Congressional award of discretion to the Service, through Section 7805(b), is the power as well as the obligation to consider the totality of the circumstances surrounding the handing down of a ruling—including the comparative or differential effect on the other taxpayers in the same class. "The Commissioner cannot tax one and not tax another without some rational basis for the difference." This factor has come to be recognized as central to the administration of the section. Equality of treatment is so dominant in our understanding of justice that discretion, where it is allowed a role, must pay the strictest heed.

IBM v. United States, 343 F.2d 914, 920 (Ct. Cl. 1965) (quoting United States v. Kaiser, 363 U.S. 299, 308 (1960) (Frankfurter, J., concurring)). The court held for IBM because the IRS failed to treat IBM and Remington Rand consistently even though they were similarly situated.

D. Precedent

Legislators and administrative agencies are not the only ones who communicate to taxpayers the government's expectations for self-determining tax liabilities. The courts do so as well. A court interprets the statutes and regulations and applies them to disputes between the IRS and taxpayers litigating in court. Courts apply the interpretive methods above to statutes and regulations, give the IRS due deference where appropriate, and examine their own precedent to determine whether there is pre-existing law that governs.

There are some general principles courts apply in determining the governing law. A lower court follows the precedent in the court to which the case is appealable. Thus, a federal district court in Detroit, Michigan applies the precedent of the Sixth Circuit. Further, the Sixth Circuit in turn applies the precedent of the U.S. Supreme Court. But an interesting issue arises when the only existing precedent is the court's own. In other words, what does the court do if there is no precedent in the court to which appeal lies, or the deciding court is the Supreme Court beyond which no further appeal exists?

When the only existing precedent is the court's own, a court will apply its own precedent unless there is a good reason not to. *See* Hurst v. Florida, 136 S. Ct. 616, 623 (2012). Courts follow their own precedent to avoid instability and uncertainty in the law. But if a precedent turns out to be wrong due to developments in the law, a court can overturn its own precedent and take a different direction. *Miller v. Commissioner* is an example of a court overruling its own precedent. 733 F.2d 399 (6th Cir. 1984). There, the taxpayer before the Sixth Circuit had failed to make an insurance claim before taking a casualty loss deduction. That Circuit had previously held that section 165 required a taxpayer to have first made an insurance claim before properly claiming a casualty loss deduction. Another Circuit addressing the same issue came to a different conclusion—that a deduction under section 165 required no insurance claim. Despite having no legal duty to follow the other Circuit's precedent, the other Circuit's analysis persuaded the Sixth Circuit that the original precedent was incorrect and overruled it. Accordingly, the Sixth Circuit permitted the taxpayer's casualty loss deduction even though he had not made an insurance claim.

E. Tax Planning

Generally, taxpayers are entitled to make choices in their lives—taking into account the government's communications of its expectations for reporting—that minimize their taxes. Judge Learned Hand said that "there is nothing sinister in so arranging one's affairs as to keep taxes as low as possible . . . . [N]obody owes any public duty to pay more than the law demands: taxes are enforced exactions, not voluntary contributions."[32] Making choices and "arranging one's affairs" are the essence of tax planning.

There are numerous tax planning examples in everyday life: buying a house with a mortgage rather than renting or paying cash,[33] investing in tax-exempt municipal bonds,[34] timing a sale of a stock with a built-in loss to coincide with a stock sale for a gain. A taxpayer whose income subject to tax derives solely from wages has limited tax planning opportunities because there are few issues related to the timing, character, realization, or costs of wages. A taxpayer that owns all or part of a business, or is a business, has more planning opportunities. Businesses are taxed on net profit, which means gross receipts reduced by cost-related deductions and adjusted for investment-related timing issues. There are also more credits offered for inducing business activity than for personal activities. These issues and others involve choices that can make a business more tax efficient for itself and its owners.

Businesses also have more opportunities to do tax planning by lobbying Congress. A wage earner lobbying Congress will have trouble showing that a tax break would induce any activity to benefit society. A business lobbying Congress can validly suggest that a tax benefit may stimulate research, investment, or other activities leading to economic growth.

Tax planning, however, can go too far. Unfortunately, differentiating between appropriate tax planning and inappropriate planning is difficult, if not impossible. This likeness between legitimate and illegitimate tax planning puts the government in a bind. The government would like nothing better than to leave the gate open for legitimate tax planners and shut the gate when illegitimate planners try to get through. If they try to leave the gate closed, the government

---

[32] Commissioner v. Newman, 159 F.2d 848, 850-51 (2d Cir. 1947) (Hand, J., dissenting).

[33] See IRC § 163(h)(3) (providing a deduction for interest paid for acquiring a personal residence).

[34] See IRC § 103(a) (excluding interest from municipal bonds from tax).

obstructs good people from doing good things. If they leave the gate open, the government loses revenue to which it is legitimately entitled.

To overcome this discernment problem as between legitimate and illegitimate tax planning, the Code contains numerous provisions preventing abusive planning in certain situations. There are also some more overarching remedies for the government provided in the Code. The two most general are the alternative minimum tax and the economic substance doctrine.

The alternative minimum tax (AMT) is a tax that applies instead of the ordinary computation when a high-earning taxpayer plans too aggressively. When enacting the AMT in 1986, Congress provided the following comment:

> [T]he minimum tax should serve one overriding objective: to ensure that no taxpayer with substantial economic income can avoid significant tax liability by using exclusions, deductions, and credits. Although these provisions may provide incentives for worthy goals, they become counterproductive when taxpayers are allowed to use them to avoid virtually all tax liability.

S. Rep. No. 99-313 (1986), *reprinted* in 1986-3 C.B. 518-19.

The AMT operates by prohibiting or limiting certain deductions, exclusions, and credits for taxpayers that earn income beyond a designated threshold. Computation of the AMT is highly complex and far beyond the scope of this book. *See* IRC § 55. For a few decades, the AMT was not indexed to inflation. This flaw led to criticism because without inflation adjustments the AMT expanded from affecting only wealthy taxpayers to affecting middle-class earners. As of 2013, however, the AMT is indexed to inflation.

The economic substance doctrine is another weapon the IRS deploys to combat overzealous tax planning. Under the economic substance doctrine, the IRS may disallow tax benefits from a particular transaction where the taxpayer either experiences no meaningful economic effect other than tax benefits or the taxpayer lacked a business purpose other than tax savings. *See* IRC § 7701(o)(1). Although the doctrine is attributed to Judge Learned Hand's opinion in *Helvering v. Gregory*, there is no mention of economic effects or the requirement of a business purpose. Nevertheless, the opinion provides an example of legal realism. Over many decades, the economic substance doctrine lived as a pure judicial construction. Although it has attracted a great deal of criticism, Congress eventually incorporated it into the Code in 2010.

HELVERING v. GREGORY
69 F.2d 809 (2d Cir. 1934)
United States Court of Appeals, Second Circuit

Before L. HAND, SWAN, and AUGUSTUS N. HAND, Circuit Judges.
Opinion
L. HAND, Circuit Judge.

This is an appeal (petition to review), by the Commissioner of Internal Revenue from an order of the Board of Tax Appeals expunging a deficiency in income taxes for the year 1928. The facts were as follows: The taxpayer owned all the shares of the United Mortgage Corporation, among whose assets were some of the shares of another company, the Monitor Securities Corporation. In 1928 it became possible to sell the Monitor shares at a large profit, but if this had been done directly, the United Mortgage Corporation would have been obliged to pay a normal tax on the resulting gain, and the taxpayer, if she wished to touch her profit, must do so in the form of a dividend, on which a surtax would have been assessed against her personally. To reduce these taxes as much as possible, the following plan was conceived and put through: The taxpayer incorporated in Delaware a new company, organized ad hoc, and called the Averill Corporation, to which the United Mortgage Corporation transferred all its shares in the Monitor Securities Corporation, under an agreement by which the Averill Corporation issued all its shares to the taxpayer. Being so possessed of all the Averill shares, she would up the Averill company three days later, receiving as a liquidating dividend the Monitor shares, which she thereupon sold. It is not disputed that all these steps were part of one purpose to reduce taxes, and that the Averill Corporation, which was in existence for only a few days, conducted none, except to act as conduit for the Monitor shares in the way we have described. The taxpayer's return for the year 1928 was made on the theory that the transfer of the Monitor shares to the Averill Corporation was a 'reorganization' under section 112(i)(1)(B) of the Revenue Act of 1928 (26 USCA 2112(i)(1)(B), being 'a transfer by a corporation of * * * a part of its assets to another corporation' in such circumstances that immediately thereafter 'the transferor or its stockholders or both are in control of the corporation to which the assets are transferred.' Since the transfer was a reorganization, she claimed to come within section 112(g) of that act, 26 USCA 2112(g), and that her 'gain' should not be 'recognized,' because the Averill shares were 'distributed, in pursuance of a plan of reorganization.' The Monitor shares she asserted to have been received as a single liquidating dividend of the Averill Corporation, and that as such she was only taxable for them under section 115(c), 26 USCA 2115(c) and upon their value less the cost properly allocated to the Averill shares. That cost she determined as that proportion of the original cost of her shares in the United Mortgage Corporation, which the Monitor shares bore to the whole assets of the United Mortgage Corporation. This difference she returned, and paid the tax calculated upon it. The Commissioner assessed a deficiency taxed upon the theory that the transfer of the Monitor shares to the Averill Corporation was not a true 'reorganization' within section 112(i)(1)(B), 26 USCA 2112(i)(1)(B), being intended only to avoid taxes. He treated as nullities that transfer, the transfer of the Averill shares to the taxpayer, and the winding up of the Averill Corporation ending in the receipt by her of the Monitor shares; and he ruled that the whole transaction was merely the declaration of a dividend by the United Mortgage Corporation consisting of the Monitor shares in specie, on which the taxpayer must pay a surtax calculated at their full value. The taxpayer appealed and the Board held that the Averill Corporation had been in fact organized and was indubitably a corporation, that the United Mortgage Corporation had with equal certainty transferred to it the Monitor shares, and that the taxpayer had got the Averill shares as part of the transaction. All these transactions being real, their purpose was irrelevant, and section 112(i)(1)(B) was applicable, especially since it was part of a statute of such small mesh as the Revenue Act of 1928; the finer the reticulation, the less room for inference. The Board therefore expunged the deficiency, and the Commissioner appealed.

We agree with the Board and the taxpayer that a transaction, otherwise within an exception of the tax law, does not lose its immunity, because it is actuated by a desire to avoid, or, if one choose, to evade, taxation. Any one may so arrange his affairs that his taxes shall be as low as possible; he is not bound to choose that pattern which will best pay the Treasury; there is not even a patriotic duty to increase one's taxes. . . . Therefore, if what was done here, was what was intended by section 112(i)(1)(B), it is of no consequence that it was all an elaborate scheme to get rid of income taxes, as it certainly was. Nevertheless, it does not follow that Congress meant to cover such a transaction, not even though the facts answer the dictionary definitions of each term used in the statutory definition. It is quite true, as the Board has very well said, that as the articulation of a statute increases, the room for interpretation must contract; but the meaning of a sentence may be more than that of the separate words, as a melody is more than the notes, and no degree of particularity can ever obviate recourse to the setting in which all appear, and which all collectively create. The purpose of the section is plain enough; men engaged in enterprises—industrial, commercial, financial, or any other—might wish to consolidate, or divide, to add to, or subtract from, their holdings. Such transactions were not to be considered as 'realizing' any profit, because the collective interests still remained in solution. But the underlying presupposition is plain that the readjustment shall be undertaken for reasons germane to the conduct of the venture in hand, not as an ephemeral incident, egregious to its prosecution. To dodge the shareholders' taxes is not one of the transactions contemplated as corporate 'reorganizations.'

This accords both with the history of the section, and with its interpretation by the courts, though the exact point has not hitherto arisen. It first appeared in the Act of 1924, Sec. 203(h)(1)(B), 26 USCA 934(h)(1)(B), and as the committee reports show (Senate Reports 398), was intended as supplementary to section 112(g), 26 USCA 2112(g), then section 203(c), 26 USCA 934(c); both in combination changed the law as laid down in U.S. v. Phellis, 257 U.S. 156, 42 S.Ct. 63, 66 L.Ed. 180, and Rockefeller v. U.S., 257 U.S. 176, 42 S.Ct. 68, 66 L.Ed. 186. In the House Report (No. 179, 68th Congress 1st Sess.), and in the Senate Report (No. 398), the purpose was stated to be to exempt 'from tax the gain from exchanges made in connection with a reorganization in order that ordinary business transactions will not be prevented.' . . . Moreover, we regard Pinellas Ice & Cold Storage Co. v. Com'r, 287 U.S. 462, 53 S.Ct. 257, 77 L.Ed. 428, and our own decision in Cortland Specialty Co. v. Com'r, 60 F. (2d) 937, as pertinent, if not authoritative. In each the question was of the applicability of a precursor of section 112(i)(1)(A) of 1928, 26 USCA 2112(i)(1)(A), to the sale of all the assets of one company to another, which gave in exchange, cash and short time notes. The taxpayer's argument was that this was a 'merger or consolidation,' because the buyer acquired 'all the property of another corporation,' the seller, that being one statutory definition of 'merger or consolidation.' That assumed, the exemption was urged to fall within section 112(g) as here. It might have been enough to hold that short time notes were not 'securities,' within section 112(g); but both courts went further and declared that the transaction was not a 'merger or consolidation,' but a sale, though literally it fell within the words of section 112(i)(1)(A). This they did, because its plain purpose was to cover only a situation in which after the transaction there continued some community of interest between the companies, other than holding such notes. The violence done the literal interpretation of the words is no less than what we do here. Moreover, the act itself gives evidence that, on occasion anyway, the purpose of a transaction should be the guide; thus in section 115(g), 26 USCA 2115(g), the cancellation of shares is to be treated as a dividend—though otherwise it would not be such—if it is 'essentially equivalent to the distribution of a taxable dividend'; again in section 112(c)(2), 26 USCA 2112(c)(2), a distribution is in part taxable as a dividend, if it 'has the effect of the distribution of a taxable dividend.'

We do not indeed agree fully with the way in which the Commissioner treated the transaction; we cannot treat as inoperative the transfer of the Monitor shares by the United Mortgage Corporation, the issue by the Averill Corporation of its own shares to the taxpayer, and her acquisition of the Monitor shares by winding up that company. The Averill Corporation held a juristic personality, whatever the purpose of its organization; the transfer passed title to the Monitor shares and the taxpayer became a shareholder in the transferee. All these steps were real, and their only defect was that they were not what the statute means by a 'reorganization,' because the transactions were no part of the conduct of the business of either or both companies; so viewed they were a sham, though all the proceedings had their usual effect. But the result is the same whether the tax be calculated as the Commissioner calculated it, or upon the value of the Averill shares as a dividend, and the only question that can arise is whether the deficiency must be expunged, though right in result, if it was computed by a method, partly wrong. Although this is argued with some warmth, it is plain that the taxpayer may not avoid her just taxes because the reasoning of the assessing officials has not been entirely our own.

Order reversed; deficiency assessed.

NOTES AND QUESTIONS

1. The Supreme Court affirmed the Second Circuit opinion, but avoided using the word "sham."
2. This case's spirit is embodied in section 7701(o). Section 7701(o)(5)(A) provides as follows:

   The term "economic substance doctrine" means the common law doctrine under which tax benefits under [the income tax provisions of the

Internal Revenue Code] with respect to a transaction are not allowable if the transaction does not have economic substance or lacks a business purpose.

Section 7701(o)(1) provides as follows:

> (1) In the case of any transaction to which the economic substance doctrine is relevant, such transaction shall be treated as having economic substance only if—
>
> (A) the transaction changes in a meaningful way (apart from Federal income tax effects) the taxpayer's economic position, and
>
> (B) the taxpayer has a substantial purpose (apart from Federal income tax effects) for entering into such transaction.

3. The IRS is the defendant or the respondent in tax cases. In court, the IRS often raises *Gregory* and the economic substance doctrine to defend its actions. Either may apply when a taxpayer has complied with the technical language of the statute. Despite the fact that invoking *Gregory* or the economic substance doctrine involves asking a court to ignore the statute's language, courts often accept the IRS's defense and deny the taxpayer the benefits provided by statute.

4. Is it extraordinary that the IRS can defend itself by arguing that the statute does not apply?

Whether it is the AMT or the economic substance doctrine, a taxpayer that believes she has found an ingenious way to reduce income tax liabilities may receive a surprise when the IRS reviews the tax return. To an aggressive taxpayer, these occasional surprises seem unfair. In this respect, the AMT has an advantage over the economic substance doctrine in that it is somewhat objective. The AMT's objective rules give the taxpayer a fair warning even before filing the tax return that the AMT will apply. The economic substance doctrine factors are more subjective and vague. Thus, a taxpayer might not be able to arrive at a final amount owed until having engaged in years of litigation against the IRS.[35]

---

[35] *See, e.g.*, Frank Lyon Co. v. United States, 435 U.S. 561, 568 (1978) (concluding in 1978 that contracts entered into in 1968 had economic substance); Del Commercial Props. v. Commissioner, 251 F.3d 210, 214 (D.C. Cir. 2001) (concluding in 2001 that loans made in 1990 lacked economic substance).

CHAPTER 8

TAX LIABILITY REPORTING

Once a compliant taxpayer has determined how much tax she owes, she reports the amount by filing a proper and timely tax return. A taxpayer may also file an amended return if necessary. Reporting the tax liability and paying the tax liability are covered in separate chapters in this casebook because failing either obligation raises different enforcement issues for the IRS as well as different negative legal consequences for the taxpayer.

This chapter covers legal issues related to reporting a tax liability on a tax return. There are two types of tax returns, original returns and amended returns. Although they are both referred to as tax returns, each is distinct with respect to the legal duty to file the return, the content requirements, and timeliness. This chapter also covers underreporting in the context of original returns.

A. Original Tax Returns

1. Legal Duty to File a Tax Return

The attainment of a threshold amount of income triggers the obligation to file a tax return. Section 6012(a)(1) provides as follows:

> Returns with respect to income taxes . . . shall be made by . . . [e]very individual having for the taxable year gross income which equals or exceeds the exemption amount . . . .

The amount of income that creates the filing obligation is not fixed. Rather, it varies depending on the amount of the taxpayer's applicable personal exemption and standard deduction. Failure to file a tax return may lead to penalties, collection, or criminal liability. See Chapters 2-4.

2. Return Sufficiency

To comply with the tax laws, a taxpayer must file a proper return. There are legal guidelines as to what a return must contain for the IRS to consider it or reject it. When a taxpayer files a return using the form the IRS requires, provides all the requested information, and signs it under penalty of perjury, there is generally no problem. Problems arise when taxpayers modify the required form or submit a different document entirely as their tax return. *Beard v. Commissioner* illustrates the difficulties raised by a modified form.

BEARD v. COMMISSIONER
82 T.C. 766 (1984), aff'd, 793 F.2d 139 (6th Cir. 1986)
United States Tax Court

WHITAKER, Judge:

This case is before us on respondent's Motion for Summary Judgment.[1] Pursuant to Rule 121,[2] a response to the motion was filed by petitioner on February 13, 1984 (the Response). On February 22, 1984, the Motion for Summary Judgment was heard. Respondent was represented by counsel but there was no appearance by or on behalf of petitioner. The motion was taken under advisement.

In the notice of deficiency issued to petitioner, respondent determined a deficiency in petitioner's 1981 Federal income tax in the amount of $6,535. In the answer, respondent alleged that additions to tax were due under section 6651(a)(1) for failure to file a return and section 6653(a) for negligence or intentional disregard of the rules and regulations. Additionally, damages pursuant to section 6673 for instituting proceedings before the Tax Court merely for delay were requested.

The petition alleged as errors in the Notice of Deficiency that petitioner's wages are not taxable income and were wrongfully included in his gross income. He claims that his receipts are a product of the exchange of labor for wages. Since the fair market value of the labor transferred is equivalent to the amount of wages received, there is no excess gain to be reported as taxable income.[3] The "equal exchange" theory was also set forth in a memorandum signed by

---

[1] [fn 1] In accordance with Rule 121, Tax Court Rules of Practice and Procedure, such motion was filed on Jan. 17, 1984, and was submitted more than 30 days after the Reply was filed in this case.

[2] [fn 2] Unless otherwise indicated, all rule references are to the Tax Court Rules of Practice and Procedure and all statutory references are to the Internal Revenue Code of 1954, as amended and in effect during the years at issue.

[3] [fn 3] This theory hereinafter will sometimes be referred to as the "equal exchange" theory. He also argues that the Commissioner has erroneously implied that he is a tax protester, which may prejudice this Court against petitioner in this case. We find this is a rhetorical argument rather than an assignment of error.

petitioner and submitted to the Internal Revenue Service as part of the purported "return" for the 1981 year. A copy of the memorandum was attached to his petition.

In his Reply, petitioner alleges "* * * the petition contains specific justiciable errors of law and/or fact in relation to the recognition by the Respondent of the Petitioner's 'labor' to be 'property,' * * *."[4] Petitioner asserts that he has arrived at his conclusions by lengthy study and research of the rules and regulations. He contends that no additions to tax are due under sections 6653(a) and 6651(a)(1). Petitioner denies he was required to file a 1981 income tax return on or before April 15, 1982, in that he owed no tax liability for that year. He admits that the document in question in this case is the only submission he made to the Internal Revenue Service for the 1981 year, claiming that it is a return under section 6012 because it contains figures and numbers from which to compute a tax. Furthermore, he requests a trial by jury on all issues raised by the pleadings and alleges respondent has the burden of proof on all issues. Finally, he denies he has begun this proceeding before this Court merely for the purpose of delay.

We must first decide whether any genuine issue of material fact exists to prevent our summary adjudication of the legal issues in controversy. Rule 121. If summary judgment is warranted we must decide whether (1) petitioner or respondent has the burden of proof as to the issues raised in the pleadings; (2) the wages earned by petitioner are taxable; (3) petitioner is entitled to a trial by jury; (4) the purported "return" filed by petitioner was a return for the purposes of sections 6011, 6012, 6072 and 6651(a)(1); (5) the failure to include these wages in taxable income was due to negligence or intentional disregard of the rules and regulations for section 6653(a) purposes; and (6) under section 6673 an award of damages for instituting a proceeding before this Court merely for the purpose of delay is merited.

Certain facts are not disputed by the parties. Pursuant to Rule 121, respondent filed an affidavit with exhibits in connection with the instant motion.[5] Petitioner did not file any affidavits or exhibits. The undisputed documents

---

[4] [fn 4] This is the only justiciable error alleged by petitioner in the Reply in response to respondent's allegation that there was no justiciable error present. Rule 37(c) provides, "[w]here a reply is filed, every affirmative allegation set out in the answer and not expressly admitted or denied in the reply, shall be deemed to be admitted."

[5] [fn 5] An affidavit of Timothy S. Murphy, an attorney who has custody and control over the Commissioner of Internal Revenue's administrative file along with exhibits, was filed on Jan. 17, 1984. The attached exhibits include a copy of the statutory notice sent to petitioner for the 1981 year, a copy of Form W-2 issued to petitioner, a copy of the purported "return" and accompanying memorandums submitted by petitioner, a copy of petitioner's 1979 tax return (he filed a joint return) with accompanying Forms W-2, and a Form CSC 8–255-B letter sent to petitioner dated July 16, 1982.

supplied by respondent and the undisputed facts in the pleadings constitute the facts used for the purposes of this motion. Rule 121(c).

FINDINGS OF FACT

Petitioner resided in Carleton, Michigan, when the petition was filed in this case. During the 1981 taxable year petitioner was employed by and received wages from Guardian Industries totaling $24,401.89. Such amounts were actually received by petitioner during that year.[6]

He submitted to the Internal Revenue Service the below-described form and an accompanying memorandum dated February 22, 1982, as his 1981 return, thus indicating his protest to the Federal income tax laws. No other document alleged to be a return for the 1981 year was submitted.[7] This document (the tampered form) was prepared by or for petitioner by making changes to an official Treasury Form 1040 in such fashion (by printing or typing) that the changes may not be readily apparent to a casual reader.[8]

In that part of the first page of the official form intended to reflect income, petitioner deleted the word "income" from the item captions in lines 8a, 11, 18 and 20 and inserted in those spaces the word "gain." On line 21 of the form he obliterated the word "income" from the item caption. In addition, in the margin caption to this section, petitioner deleted the word "Income" and inserted the word "Receipts."

In that part of the first page of the form intended to reflect deductions from income, he deleted the words "Employee business expense (attach Form 2106)" from line 23 of the form and inserted "Non-taxable receipts." In addition, in the marginal caption to this section, petitioner deleted the word "Income" and inserted the word "Receipts," so that the caption reads "Adjustments to Receipts" instead of "Adjustments to Income."

Petitioner filled in his name, address, Social Security number, occupation, and filing status in addition to the name, occupation and Social Security number of his spouse. He claimed one exemption on the tampered form. The relevant information entries are as follows: On line 7 entitled "Wages, salaries, tips, etc." taxpayer inserted the amount of $24,401.89. On line 23, under the category of "Non-taxable receipts," petitioner claimed an adjustment to "Receipts" of $29,401.89. He therefore showed a tax liability of zero. On line 55, entitled "Total Federal income tax withheld," he showed an amount of $1,770.75. The total $1,770.75 that had been withheld from his wages was claimed as a refund. This tampered form was signed by petitioner and dated February 22, 1982. Petitioner's Form W-2 issued by Guardian Industries was attached.

---

[6] [fn 6] Petitioner admits in his petition that he actually received such amounts.

[7] [fn 7] Petitioner did not allege that an extension of time to file was requested.

[8] [fn 8] Since the Court records only contain copies of the tampered form, we cannot comment to what extent the tamperings are evident to the naked eye.

Petitioner's scheme in submitting this tampered form apparently was to conceal from the Service Center operators the fact that his inclusion of his wages on the tampered form was negated by his fabrication of "Non-taxable receipts" on line 23 thus simultaneously excluding the wages theoretically reported. The net effect of the two steps was to create a zero tax liability. Since his employer had withheld against the amounts paid to him for the 1981 year, this scheme allowed him to claim a refund for that year.

Petitioner has not always protested against his duty to pay taxes. For taxable year 1979 petitioner and his spouse, cash basis, calendar year taxpayers, reported jointly on an official Treasury Form 1040A wages they received as taxable income, and showed the appropriate tax on such income. Their taxes withheld exceeded their tax liability and they were due a small refund. The Treasury Form 1040A was fully completed and correctly reflected the wages shown on the Forms W-2 they received.

Petitioner has studied court cases, statutes, rules and regulations pertaining to income tax. He recognizes that this Court has on numerous occasions categorized the "equal exchange" theory that wages are not subject to income tax as frivolous and utterly without merit.[9]

The instant case is one of 23 cases that were on the March 5, 1984, trial calendar for Detroit, Michigan, in which tampered forms are at issue.[10] Many other similar cases are pending before this Court. All of these 23 cases contain a fabricated adjustment for "Non-taxable receipts." All were submitted to the Internal Revenue Service in the year 1980[11] or 1981.[12] All but two of the 23 were

---

[9] [fn 9] Petitioner's admissions in his Reply filed April 1, 1983, paragraphs 9(b) and 10(a).

[10] [fn 10] Although the facts in each case are not identical, they are sufficiently similar to be classified as parts of a single protester group.

[11] [fn 11] For the 1980 taxable year, nine of the 10 tampered forms had "Non-taxable receipts" inserted on line 24 and "Eisner v. Macomber, 252 U.S. 189" inserted on line 25. In two places in the left margin of these "forms" the word "receipts" replaced the word "income." On lines 9, 13, 19 and 21, the word "gain" replaced "income" and on line 22, the word "income" had been deleted. Five of the 1980 tampered forms had the same changes as above except that line 25 had not been changed. One tampered form for the 1980 year was a copyrighted 1980 Eugene J. May "form" that placed "Non-taxable receipts" on line 23 and inserted cases on lines 24 through 29. Numerous other changes were made by replacing the word "income" with "receipts."

[12] [fn 12] For the 1981 year, 11 of the 13 tampered forms had inserted "Non-taxable receipts" on line 23, replaced the word "income" in the left margin of the form with "receipts," replaced the word "income" on lines 8a, 11, 18 and 20 with the word "gain" and deleted the word "income" from line 21. The remaining two "forms" for the 1981 year placed "Non-taxable receipts" on line 22, were copyrighted Eugene J. May 1981 "forms," and had numerous other changes similar to those in the 1980 Eugene J. May "forms."

submitted with two- or three-page memorandums advocating that wages are not taxable income. Twenty-two of the petitions in these cases contained identical language except for entries relevant to the petitioners' personal data. The remaining case contained a handwritten, individually composed petition. In cases in which replies or responses to respondent's motion for summary judgment were filed, all but one were the same format and language with minor deviations to suit the petitioners in each case. It is abundantly clear that these docketed cases and documents represent a coordinated protest effort—an attempt to obtain refunds where employers had withheld against amounts paid, as well as to drain further the limited resources of this Court with these frivolous contentions.

The Internal Revenue Service has been forced to develop special procedures[13] to handle tampered forms like those in the group referred to above. The tampered forms are also referred to as "Eisner v. Macomber returns" because Eisner v. Macomber, 252 U.S. 189 (1920), is usually cited either in the form or in the literature attached.[14] From a cursory look, they appear to be official Forms 1040 but upon closer inspection definitively are not. Internal Revenue Service employees must identify and then withdraw these from the normal processing channels, and gather and deliver them to a special team for review. After such

---

[13] [fn 13] In the transcript of the hearing on Feb. 22, 1984, counsel for respondent brought to our attention information regarding these special procedures. Reference was made to affidavits filed in certain cases in the above-mentioned group. We take judicial notice of an affidavit of Marjorie A. Wyman, filed in Michael J. Blackwell, docket No. 26384–82.

[14] [fn 14] We note that a similar type of return was filed by a Robert D. Beard of Carleton, Mich., and in Beard v. United States, an unreported case (E.D. Mich. 1984, 84–1 USTC par. 9362, —— AFTR 2d ——), a sec. 6702 civil penalty of $500 was sustained. The court in that case granted a motion to dismiss without an oral argument on the basis of papers filed. Petitioner filed a tampered form and made these same arguments concerning "receipts," "non-taxable receipts," and the "equal exchange" theory. The purported "return" was found frivolous on its face and petitioner was found liable for the penalty pursuant to sec. 6702, a section that imposes a civil penalty for the filing of a frivolous "return."

A similar type of return as that used by petitioner was again at issue in the case of United States v. May, 555 F.Supp. 1008 (1983). The United States District Court for the Eastern District of Michigan has recently enjoined May from engaging in conduct which interferes with the proper administration of the Internal Revenue laws. Included was conduct by Mr. May relating to the Eisner v. Macomber returns.

We also note that the "Non-taxable receipts" deduction has been used by taxpayers in the Michigan area on other occasions. Cannon v. United States, an unreported case (E.D. Mich. 1983, 83–2 USTC par. 9699, 52 AFTR 2d 83–6348); Corcoran v. United States, an unreported case (E.D. Mich. 1983, 84–1 USTC par. 9148; Ervans v. United States, an unreported case (E.D. Mich. 1984, 53 AFTR 2d 84–772, 84–1 USTC par. 9300).

review, the person who submitted such a tampered return is often but not always informed that it is not acceptable as a return because it does not comply with the Internal Revenue Code. Petitioner was so informed by a letter dated July 16, 1982, stating that the tampered form was "not acceptable as an income tax return because it does not contain information required by law, and it does not comply with Internal Revenue Code requirements."

ULTIMATE FINDINGS OF FACT

Petitioner actually received $24,401.89 from his employer as wages during the 1981 taxable year. The only documents he submitted for the 1981 taxable year were the tampered form and its accompanying memorandum. Petitioner has extensively studied the rules and regulations regarding the income tax laws in addition to income tax cases and, thus, his actions were the product of informed deliberation.

OPINION

Summary Judgment Issue

The threshold issue is whether a motion for summary judgment is appropriate in this case. We conclude that it is. Rule 121 provides that a party may move for summary judgment upon all or any part of the legal issues in controversy "if the pleadings * * * and any other acceptable materials, together with the affidavits, if any, show that there is no genuine issue as to any material fact and that a decision may be rendered as a matter of law." Rule 121(b). The summary judgment procedure is available even though there is a dispute under the pleadings if it is shown through materials in the record outside the pleadings that no genuine issue of material fact exists.[15] In passing upon such a motion, the factual materials presented "must be viewed in the light most favorable to the party opposing the motion." Jacklin v. Commissioner, 79 T.C. 340, 344 (1982); Elkins v. Commissioner, 81 T.C. 669 (1983).

Since respondent is the movant with respect to this motion, he has the burden of proving there is no genuine dispute as to any material fact and that a decision may be rendered as a matter of law. There is no dispute among the parties as a factual matter that petitioner received his Form W-2 from his employer reflecting the $24,401.89 amount. The only justiciable error that petitioner alleges in his Reply and Response is that such amounts are not taxable, a legal issue. Petitioner does not question and thereby concedes to the authenticity of the respondent's evidence attached as exhibits to a submitted affidavit,[16] i.e.: the 1979 tax return and the tampered form at issue. He admits in his Reply that this is the only form filed for the 1981 taxable year. That petitioner is familiar with the Federal income tax statutes, regulations and case law is confirmed by the frequent citation of the Federal income tax cases, statutes, rules and regulations in the

---

[15] [fn 15] Such outside materials may consist of affidavits, interrogatories, admissions documents or other materials which demonstrate the absence of such an issue of fact despite the pleadings. See Note to Rule 121(a), 60 T.C. 1127 (1973).

[16] [fn 16] See footnote 5, supra.

documents filed by petitioner in this Court. The summary judgment pleadings, affidavits and exhibits establish that there is no genuine issue as to any material fact and that a decision may be rendered as a matter of law.

The burden of proof is upon the petitioner with respect to the deficiency set forth in the statutory notice and upon the respondent as to the issues raised in the answer. Welch v. Helvering, 290 U.S. 111 (1933); Nicholson v. Commissioner, 32 B.T.A. 977 (1935), affd. 90 F.2d 978 (8th Cir. 1937); Rule 142(a).

Frivolous Contentions

We first dispose of petitioner's two frivolous contentions. Respondent maintains that the amounts petitioner received for services performed as reflected in the 1981 Form W-2 are taxable as gross income to petitioner for the year in which he received such amounts. There is no doubt that such amounts are taxable as gross income. Section 61; Eisner v. Macomber, supra at 207; Commissioner v. Glenshaw Glass Co., 348 U.S. 426 (1955); Rowlee v. Commissioner, 80 T.C. 1111 (1983).

Petitioner received wages for the taxable year of $24,401.89 and thus was required to file a Federal income tax return for that year. Section 6012(a)(1)(A). Section 6072 provides that in the case of returns under section 6012, returns made on the basis of the calendar year shall be filed on or before the 15th day of April following the close of the calendar year. It is clear that petitioner had a duty to file a return. The crucial issue is whether respondent must accept this tampered form in satisfaction of that duty.

Petitioner in his Reply asserts that he is entitled to a trial by jury for all issues contained in this case. It is well settled that in a suit concerning Federal tax liability, no right to a jury trial exists under the Seventh Amendment guaranteeing a jury trial on common law actions. Cupp v. Commissioner, 65 T.C. 68 (1975), affd. without published opinion 559 F.2d 1207 (3d Cir. 1977). Thus, we find taxpayer is not entitled to a jury trial.

Failure to File

Respondent alleges an addition to tax under section 6651(a)(1) for failure to file a Federal income tax return for taxable year 1981. Section 6651(a)(1) provides for an addition to tax if a taxpayer fails to file a timely return unless such failure is due to reasonable cause and not due to willful neglect. Respondent maintains that the tampered form submitted by petitioner was not a return within the meaning of sections 6012, 6072 and 6651(a)(1), that it will not be accepted as such (and was not accepted in this case) and thus petitioner is liable for an addition under section 6651(a)(1). We agree.

The general requirements of a Federal income tax return are set forth in section 6011(a) in relevant part as follows:

> When required by regulations prescribed by the Secretary any person made liable for any tax * * * shall make a return or statement *according to the forms* and *regulations* prescribed by the Secretary. [Emphasis added.]

Regulations implementing this legislative mandate provide:

(a) General rule.—Every person subject to any tax, or required to collect any tax, under subtitle A of the Code, shall make such returns or statements as are required by the regulations in this chapter. The return or statement shall include therein the information required by the applicable regulations or forms.[17]

(b) Use of prescribed forms.—Copies of the prescribed return forms will so far as possible be furnished taxpayers by district directors. A taxpayer will not be excused from making a return, however, by the fact that no return form has been furnished to him. Taxpayers not supplied with the proper forms should make application therefor to the district director in ample time to have their returns prepared, verified, and filed on or before the due date with the internal revenue office where such returns are required to be filed. Each taxpayer should carefully prepare his return and set forth fully and clearly the information required to be included therein. Returns which have not been so prepared will not be accepted as meeting the requirements of the Code. * * *[18]

The statutory grant of authority to the Treasury requires that taxpayers make a return or statement according to the forms and regulations prescribed by the Secretary of the Treasury. These regulations mandate the use of the proper official form, except as noted below.[19] The United States Supreme Court in the case of Commissioner v. Lane-Wells Co., 321 U.S. 219 (1944), has recognized this mandate in stating:

Congress has given discretion to the Commissioner to prescribe by regulation forms of returns and has made it the duty of the taxpayer to comply. It thus implements the system of self assessment which is so largely the basis of our American scheme of income taxation. The purpose is not alone to get tax information in some form but also to get it with such *uniformity, completeness,* and *arrangement* that the physical task of handling and verifying returns may be readily accomplished. [Emphasis added.] [321 U.S. at 223.]

---

[17] [fn 17] Sec. 1.6011-1(a), Income Tax Regs. General requirement of return, statement, or list. These regulations specifically apply to persons subject to any tax under subtitle A of the Code.

[18] [fn 18] Sec. 1.6011-1(b), Income Tax Regs. Although not applicable to the facts of the instant case, the regulations also provide for the filing of a timely tentative return when the official form is not available, provided that without unnecessary delay such a tentative return is supplemented by a return made on the proper form.

[19] [fn 19] Respondent could have argued that the Commissioner's rejection of the tampered form as a return was a proper exercise of his discretion under these regulations. Since he did not, we do not address this argument.

This discretionary authority outlined in the regulations at section 1.6011–1, Income Tax Regs., has also been recognized in the case of Parker v. Commissioner, 365 F.2d 792 (8th Cir. 1966). Although the facts of that case are distinguishable from the instant case, the court did note that—

> Taxpayers are required to file timely returns on forms established by the Commissioner. * * * The Commissioner is certainly not required to accept any facsimile the taxpayer sees fit to submit. If the Commissioner were obligated to do so, the business of tax collecting would result in insurmountable confusion. * * * [365 F.2d at 800.]

For years, the only permissible exception to the use of the official form has been the permission, granted from time to time to tax return preparers by the Internal Revenue Service, to reproduce and vary very slightly the official form pursuant to the Commissioner's revenue procedures. These revenue procedures require advance approval of a specially designed form prior to use as well as following the guidelines for acceptable changes in the form. The philosophy of the revenue procedure is and has been to require forms to conform in material respects to the official form for the obvious reasons of convenience and processing facilitation but also to be clearly distinguishable from the official form, thereby removing the opportunity for deceit. Portions of the revenue procedure in effect and applicable to the facts of this case are printed in an appendix hereto.

On the tampered form various margin and item captions, in whole or in part, have been deleted and most replaced with language fabricated by petitioner. These changes were not in conformity with the Revenue Procedure[20] rules at section 5.01(2)(a)(1) requiring each substitute or privately designed form to follow the design of the official form as to format, arrangement, item caption, line numbers, line references and sequence. Also, section 3.04(1) and (2) prohibits any change of any Internal Revenue Service tax form, graphic or otherwise, or the use of a taxpayer's own (non-approved) version without prior approval from the Internal Revenue Service. Petitioner made no attempt to obtain such approval. Additionally, petitioner was required by section 6.01 to remove the Government Printing Office symbol and jacket numbers and in such space (using the same type size) print the Employer Identifying Number of the printer or the Social Security Number of the form designer. Petitioner did not remove the symbol and numbers and did not insert in their place his appropriate number. The tampered form deceptively bore the markings of an official form. Section 8.01 prohibits the filing of reproductions of official forms and substitute forms that do not meet the requirements of the procedure. The only filing made by petitioner for the 1981 taxable year was the non-conforming tampered form.

Petitioner's prohibited tampering with the official form, the net effect of which is the creation of a zero tax liability, adversely affects the form's useability

---

[20] [fn 20] Rev. Proc. 80–47, 1980–2 C.B. 782. The current version of this revenue procedure is Rev. Proc. 84–9, I.R.B. 1984–7, 14.

by respondent. The tampered form, because of these numerous irregularities, must be handled by special procedures and must be withdrawn from normal processing channels. There can be no doubt that due to its lack of conformity to the official form, it substantially impedes the Commissioner's physical task of handling and verifying tax returns. Under the facts of this case, taxpayer has not made a return according to the forms and regulations prescribed by the Secretary as required by section 6011(a). The rejection of the tampered form was authorized by the regulations for failure to conform to the revenue procedure. But whether or not rejected in this case, the question remains—is the Internal Revenue Service nevertheless required to accept and treat as a tax return this tampered form? We conclude that it is not.

There have been factual circumstances in which the courts have treated as returns for statute of limitations purposes documents which did not conform to the regulations as prescribed by section 6011(a). Since the instant case is one of first impression, we will consider these cases that were decided on the statute of limitations issue because a return that is sufficient to trigger the running of the statute of limitation must also be sufficient for the purpose of section 6651(a)(1).

The Supreme Court test to determine whether a document is sufficient for statute of limitations purposes has several elements: First, there must be sufficient data to calculate tax liability; second, the document must purport to be a return; third, there must be an honest and reasonable attempt to satisfy the requirements of the tax law; and fourth, the taxpayer must execute the return under penalties of perjury.

It is important to consider the factual circumstances under which this test has been applied. In Florsheim Bros. Drygoods Co. v. United States, 280 U.S. 453 (1930), at issue was whether the filing of a "tentative return" or the later filing of a "completed return" triggered the statute of limitations. A corporation had filed a tentative return along with a request for an extension of time to file a return which was later filed. The Court found that the filing of the tentative return was not in the nature of a "list," "schedule" or "return" required by tax statutes. It was designed to meet a peculiar exigency and "[i]ts purpose was to secure to the taxpayer a needed extension of time for filing the required return, without defeating the Government's right to prompt payment of the first installment [of tax]." The statute plainly manifested a purpose that the period of limitations was to commence only when the taxpayer supplied the required information in the prescribed manner—the completed return.

The Court recognized that the filing of a return that is defective or incomplete may under some circumstances be sufficient to start the running of the period of limitation. However, such a return must purport to be a specific statement of the items of income, deductions and credits in compliance with the statutory duty to report information and *"to have that effect it must honestly and reasonable be intended as such."* (Emphasis added.) Thus, the filing of the tentative return was not a return to start the period of limitation running.

This issue of whether the document was a return for the statute of limitation purposes was again before the Court in Zellerbach Paper Co. v. Helvering, 293 U.S. 172 (1934). Justice Cardozo, speaking for the Court, said:

> Perfect accuracy or completeness is not necessary to rescue a return from nullity, if it purports to be a return, is sworn to as such [citations omitted] and evinces an honest and genuine endeavor to satisfy the law. This is so even though at the time of filing the omissions or inaccuracies are such as to make amendment necessary. [Zellerbach Paper Co. v. Helvering, supra at 180.]

The most recent Supreme Court reaffirmation of the test articulated in *Florsheim* and *Zellerbach* is found in Badaracco, Sr. v. Commissioner, — U.S. — (January 17, 1984). The issue was whether the filing of a nonfraudulent amended return following a fraudulent original return started the running of the statute of limitations. One of the taxpayers' arguments was that their original return, to the extent it was fraudulent, was a nullity for purposes of the statute of limitations, relying upon *Zellerbach*. The Supreme Court noted that the Badaracco returns "purported to be returns, were sworn to as such and appeared on their faces to constitute endeavors to satisfy the law." Although fraudulent, these returns were not nullities under the *Zellerbach* test.

The tampered form before us may purport to be a return in that it may "convey, imply or profess outwardly" to be a return. Black's Law Dictionary, page 1112 (5th ed. 1979) It was also sworn to. But it does not reflect an endeavor to satisfy the law. It in fact makes a mockery of the requirements for a tax return, both as to form and content. Whether or not the form contains sufficient information to permit a tax to be calculated is not altogether clear. We have held that the attachment of a Form W-2 does not substitute for the disclosure on the return itself of information as to income, deductions, credits and tax liability. Reiff v. Commissioner, 77 T.C. 1169 (1981). Ignoring the Form W-2, the tampered form does show an amount of "Wages, salaries, tips, etc." but with the margin description altered from "Income" to "Receipts." Similarly, in place of a deduction, the form has an amount for "Non-taxable receipts." Thus, to compute a tax from this tampered form, one must effectively ignore the margin and line descriptions, imagining instead the correct ones from an official Form 1040 or one must simply select from the form, including the Form W-2, that information which appears to be applicable and correct, and from the information so selected, irrespective of its label, compute a tax. We do not believe such an exercise is what the United States Supreme Court had in mind in Commissioner v. Lane-Wells Co., supra at 222–223, and Germantown Trust Co. v. Commissioner, 309 U.S. 304, 309 (1940).

The tampered form here is a conspicuous protest against the payment of tax, intended to deceive respondent's return-processing personnel into refunding the withheld tax. Since such intentional tampering could go undetected in computer processing, respondent was forced to develop and institute special procedures for handling such submissions. The critical requirement that there must be an honest and reasonable attempt to satisfy the requirements of the Federal income tax law clearly is not met. As the Court of Appeals for the Seventh Circuit has said,

> In the tax protestor cases, it is obvious that there is no "honest and genuine" attempt to meet the requirements of the code. In our self-reporting tax system the government should not be forced to accept as a return a document which plainly is not intended to give the required information. [United States v. Moore, 627 F.2d 830, 835 (7th Cir. 1980).]

The tampered form is not in conformity with the requirements in section 6011(a) or section 1.6011–1(a) and (b), Income Tax Regs., and it is not a return under the judicial line of authority set forth above.

Section 6651(a)(1) provides that an addition to tax is due if a taxpayer fails to timely file a return unless such failure is due to reasonable cause and not due to willful neglect. The evidence is clear that petitioner's actions were deliberate, intentional and in complete disregard of the statute and respondent's regulations. Petitioner made no attempt to file an authentic tax return, as he did for 1979, and offers no excuse for his failure to do so. He must accept the consequences of actions knowingly taken. See Reiff v. Commissioner, supra at 1180. Respondent has met his burden of proving that petitioner did not file a return for sections 6011, 6012, 6072 and 6651(a)(1) purposes and thus an addition to tax is due.

Intentional Disregard of Rules and Regulations

Respondent, in the answer, alleged an addition to tax under section 6653(a) in that all or part of petitioner's underpayment of income tax was due to petitioner's negligence or intentional disregard of rules and regulations. It was alleged further that the tampered form filed by petitioner was not a return as required by section 6011 and without reasonable cause and due to willful neglect, petitioner failed to file a Federal income tax return for the year 1981 as required by section 6011.

When a taxpayer has not filed a return for the taxable year, the underpayment is defined as "[t]he amount of the tax imposed by subtitle A * * * if a return was not filed on or before the last date (determined with regard to any extension of time) prescribed for filing such return."[21] In this case we have found petitioner has willfully failed to file a return for the 1981 year. Additionally, we note petitioner is aware of the income statutes, regulations and relevant case law such as Eisner v. Macomber, 252 U.S. 189 (1920), as shown by his petition and the memorandum filed with the 1981 tampered form. Furthermore, petitioner has shown that he knows of his duty and how to properly report his income on his 1979 return. We conclude that petitioner's underpayment of tax was due to intentional disregard of rules and regulations.

Proceeding Instituted Merely for Delay

Respondent has requested that damages be awarded under section 6673 for instituting a proceeding before the Tax Court merely for delay. For cases

---

[21] [fn 21] Sec. 6653(c)(1) and sec. 301.6653–1(c)(1), Proced. & Admin. Regs. See Estate of Haseltine v. Commissioner, T.C. Memo 1976–278.

commenced in this Court before January 1, 1983, the maximum damages that may be awarded is an amount not in excess of $500.[22] Petitioner, in his Reply,[23] recognizes that this Court has on many occasions found the argument that wages are non-taxable, frivolous and groundless. We have warned taxpayers that if they continue to bring frivolous cases, serious consideration would be given to imposing damages under section 6673. See, e.g., Hatfield v. Commissioner, 68 T.C. 895, 899–900 (1977). Petitioner knowingly instituted a frivolous proceeding merely for the purposes of delay. Discussions of the reasons for awarding such damages are set forth in Grimes v. Commissioner, 82 T.C. 235 (1984); Abrams v. Commissioner, 82 T.C. 403 (1984); Perkins v. Commissioner, T.C. Memo. 1983–474. We see no reason to add to those discussions and hereby award the United States damages of $500.

Accordingly, we grant the motion for summary judgment.

An appropriate order and decision will be entered.

Reviewed by the Court.

DAWSON, FAY, SIMPSON, STERRETT, GOFFE, WILES, WILBUR, NIMS, PARKER, KORNER, SHIELDS, HAMBLEN, COHEN, CLAPP, and JACOBS, JJ., agree with the majority opinion.

[Appendix omitted.]

NIMS, J. concurring:

I write this concurring opinion only to expressly dissociate myself from the views expressed in a concurring and dissenting opinion in support of petitioner's travesty tax return. I find it impossible to suppose that the Supreme Court intended its reasoning in *Badaracco* to be applied so totally out of context as to give intellectual aid and comfort to petitioner and others like him, whose so-called returns on their face make clear a concerted effort to disrupt the tax system.

I fully agree with the reasoning and the result reached in the majority opinion.

STERRETT, WILES, HAMBLEN, COHEN, and CLAPP, JJ., agree with this concurring opinion.

CHABOT, J., concurring in part and dissenting in part: I agree with the majority's holdings as to the following issues:

(1) Petitioner's wages are income, subject to tax, and he is not entitled to an offsetting deduction for "Non-taxable receipts".

---

[22] [fn 22] Sec. 6673, as in effect prior to amendment by sec. 292(b), Tax Equity and Fiscal Responsibility Act of 1982, Pub. L. 97–248, 96 Stat. 574, provided as follows:

Whenever it appears to the Tax Court that proceedings before it have been instituted by the taxpayer merely for delay, damages in an amount not in excess of $500 shall be awarded to the United States by the Tax Court in its decision. Damages so awarded shall be assessed at the same time as the deficiency and shall be paid upon notice and demand from the Secretary and shall be collected as a part of the tax.

[23] [fn 23] See Reply at paragraph 9(b).

(2) Petitioner intentionally disregarded respondent's rules and regulations in claiming the unwarranted deduction for "Non-taxable receipts", and so is liable for an addition to tax under section 6653(a).

(3) Petitioner is liable for damages under section 6673, for instituting proceedings in the Court merely for delay. (When he filed the petition in the instant case, the only matter in dispute was the deficiency, no additions to tax or damages having yet been asserted. In the words attributable to a sports figure in the 1930's, petitioner "should of stood in bed".

(4) Petitioner is not entitled to a jury trial. From the majority's determination to grant summary judgment that the Form 1040 filed by petitioner was not a tax return, I respectfully dissent.

In Badaracco v. Commissioner, 464 U.S. ——, 52 USLW 4081, 4084 (1984), the Supreme Court confronted the contention of the taxpayers therein that the first documents they had filed "were 'nullities' for the statute of limitations purposes." In the course of its analysis, the Supreme Court stated as follows:

> * * * a document which on its face plausibly purports to be in compliance, and which is signed by the taxpayer, is a return despite its inaccuracies. * * *

Zellerbach Paper Co. v. Helvering, 293 U.S. 172 (1934), which petitioners cite, affords no support for their argument. The Court in *Zellerbach* held that an original return, despite its inaccuracy, was a "return" for limitations purposes, so that the filing of an amended return did not start a new period of limitations running. In the instant cases, the original returns similarly purported to be returns, were sworn to as such, and appeared on their faces to constitute endeavors to satisfy the law. Although those returns, in fact, were not honest, the holding in *Zellerbach* does not render them nullities.

An examination of the Form 1040 in question (see Appendix, infra) shows the following: (1) it is a document which on its face plausibly purports to be in compliance with the law; (2) it is signed by the taxpayer (under penalties of perjury); (3) it does not make believe that only gold and silver coins need be reported; (4) it is not chock-full of refusals to provide information (indeed, it provides all the information requested as to petitioner's "Wages, salaries, tips, etc." and respondent does not contend that petitioner had any other reportable income); (5) the income is reported on the correct line of the return; (6) an unwarranted deduction is reported on a line reserved for deductions; and (7) apparently the Form 1040 includes everything respondent needed in order to determine petitioner's income tax liability. Compare the instant case with Reiff v. Commissioner, 77 T.C. 1169, 1177–1179 (1981), and the cases cited therein. Nothing in the majority's opinion or on the face of the Form 1040 shows that respondent is led into error because of the change in the text of any line on the Form 1040.

I would hold that the document filed by petitioner constitutes a tax return under the standards adopted by the Supreme Court, as most recently articulated in Badaracco v. Commissioner, supra.

We deal with this matter in the context of respondent's motion for summary judgment, a context in which, as the majority concede (p. 772 supra), "the factual materials presented 'must be viewed in the light most favorable to the party opposing the motion.'" The majority fail to make a finding of fact that any problem described in their opinion results from any of the eight alterations petitioner made on his Form 1040, whether the alterations are taken singly or in combination.

The majority's opinion, at pages 776-777 supra, states that petitioner's alteration of the Form 1040 had "the net effect of * * * the creation of a zero tax liability" and that "because of these numerous irregularities, [it had to] be handled by special procedures and must be withdrawn from normal processing channels." This misdescribes the situation. Both the zero tax liability, and the requirement of special procedures, result from the unwarranted deduction. These problems would exist—because of the deduction—even if there were no alterations to the Form 1040.

On page 779 of their opinion, the majority state that

> to compute a tax from this tampered form, one must effectively ignore the margin and line descriptions, imagining instead the correct ones from an official Form 1040 or one must simply select from the form, including the Form W-2, that information which appears to be applicable and correct, and from the information so selected, irrespective of its label, compute a tax.

The Form 1040 in question shows the necessary income information, and does so on the correct line, and that line has not been altered. This information is in accord with the Form W-2 (and not in conflict with it, as was the case in Reiff v. Commissioner, supra, relied on by the majority). There is no need to imagine the correct margin and line descriptions from an official Form 1040 because respondent's problems are no different, with the altered Form 1040, than they would be with an official Form 1040.

The majority emphasize (p. 16, supra) the explanation by the Supreme Court in Commissioner v. Lane-Wells Co., 321 U.S. 219, 223 (1944), that "The purpose is not alone to get tax information in some form but also to get it with such uniformity, completeness, and arrangement that the physical task of handling and verifying returns may be readily accomplished." I agree that we must follow the Supreme Court's analysis in applying section 6651(a)(1). However, the record in the instant case does not show — and the majority have not found — that the alterations to the Form 1040 (as distinguished from the unwarranted deduction) interfered in any manner with the accomplishment of the physical task of handling and verifying income tax returns.

I understand and share the majority's frustration at having to deal with frivolous arguments such as the "equal exchange" theory. However, this Court should not confuse the law as to what is a tax return, just to punish a particular individual or even a class of individuals. The Congress has given the courts more effective tools. We have used these tools to impose damages of up to $5,000 for frivolous or groundless actions. (Sec. 6673.) The district courts have used these tools to uphold penalties of $500 for frivolous filings. (Sec. 6702.) As the majority note (p. 10, n. 14, supra), the injunction has been used to prevent conduct which interferes with proper administration of the Internal Revenue laws. (Secs. 7402(a), 7407.) When civil fraud is found, the sanction therefor now includes an additional amount under section 6653(b)(2). The criminal fraud fine has been increased from a maximum of $10,000 to a maximum of $100,000 ($500,000 in the case of a corporation). (Sec. 7201.)

I would hold that petitioner's Form 1040 is a tax return. Since there is no finding that it was filed late, I would not impose an addition to tax under section 6651(a)(1). From the majority's contrary holding, I respectfully dissent.

SWIFT, J., agrees with this concurring and dissenting opinion.

[Appendix omitted.]

NOTES AND QUESTIONS

1. Under the *Beard* test, to satisfy the requirements of a return for purposes of the "failure to file" penalty the document must contain enough information for the IRS to determine the amount of tax owed, purport to be a tax return, represent a sincere effort to comply with the tax laws, and reflect a signature made under penalty of perjury. The court held that the return at issue contained sufficient information for the IRS to determine the amount of tax owed, purported to be a tax return, and the return was signed under penalty of perjury. How instructive is the "sincere effort to comply with the tax laws" element?
2. In his dissent, Judge Chabot suggests that the majority confused the law as to what is a tax return, just to punish a particular individual or even a class of individuals. Do you agree?
3. In *Beard*, affirmed by the Sixth Circuit, the taxpayer altered a Form 1040, and included the actual amounts of income earned, but the majority concluded it was not a proper return on a different basis, that the return was not a sincere effort to comply with the law. Other taxpayers have tried using asterisks or zeroes where the income amount would appear on the return. For example, in the Ninth Circuit, a Form 1040 with asterisks where income amounts would appear is not considered a proper return for purposes of the failure to file misdemeanor statute. *See* United States v. Kimball, 925 F.2d 356 (9th Cir. 1991) (en banc). In contrast, the Ninth Circuit holds that a Form 1040 with zeros where income amounts would normally appear may satisfy the legal requirements for a return. *See* United States v. Long, 618 F.2d 74 (9th Cir. 1980).

Filing a proper tax return is important because it avoids the delinquency penalties imposed in *Beard*. It also triggers the running of the statute of limitations on assessment. *See* IRC § 6501. Until the taxpayer files the return, the assessment statute for the particular year remains open.

3. Timeliness

Failure to file a tax return on or before the due date can generate late-filing penalties. *See* IRC § 6651. Individual income tax returns are due on the fifteenth day of the fourth month after the tax year ends. *See* IRC § 6072(a). For calendar year taxpayers, this means the due date is generally on April 15 of the subsequent tax year. Corporate returns are due on the 15th of the fourth month after fiscal year end. For a calendar year corporation, this means the due date is April 15 of the following year. Other business returns are generally due by March 15 following the tax year.

The operative date in terms of legal consequences is the filing date. Generally, the filing date is the date delivered to the IRS. *See* United States v. Lombardo, 241 U.S. 73, 76 (1916). There are, however, some important exceptions. First, the mailbox rule provides that timely mailing is timely filing. Thus, a tax return postmarked before the due date is deemed filed on the due date even if the IRS receives it after the due date. Section 7502(a)(1) provides as follows:

> If any . . . document required to be filed . . . on or before a prescribed date under [the Code] is . . . delivered by United States mail, . . . the date of the United States postmark . . . shall be deemed to be the date of delivery. . . .

The filing date marks the beginning of the statutory period in which the IRS may assess tax as discussed in Chapter 10—Compliance Limitations Periods. For purposes of the compliance limitations periods (assessment and refund), a return filed before the due date is deemed filed on the due date. *See* IRC § 6501(b)(1). The mailbox rule does not apply where a tax return is received before the due date.

NATALIE HOLDINGS, LTD v. UNITED STATES
91 A.F.T.R.2d 2003-616 (W.D. Tex. 2003)
United States District Court, Western District of Texas

ORDER

Judge: EDWARD C. PRADO United States District Judge

On this date, the Court considered Plaintiff's motion for summary judgment, filed September 05, 2002, Defendant's response and partial motion for summary judgment and Plaintiff's reply. After careful consideration, the Court will DENY Plaintiff's motion for summary judgment and GRANT the Defendant's cross-motion for partial summary judgment based upon the following analysis.

NATURE OF THE CASE

Plaintiff DAVMY Corporation (DAVMY), as the tax matters partners of Natalie Holdings, Ltd. (Natalie), petitions Defendant United States of America acting through the Commissioner of Internal Revenue Service (IRS) for the readjustment of the partnership items set forth in a Notice of Final Partnership Administrative Adjustment (the FPAA). The FPAA was dated and mailed to Plaintiff on September 7, 2001, by the IRS pursuant to 26 U.S.C. 6226(a)(2).[24]

DAVMY is a Texas corporation owned by Amy and David Perez, who each own 50% of the corporation, Natalie is a Texas limited partnership. DAVMY holds a one percent interest in Natalie and is the sole general partner of NATALIE. NATALIE deposited its 1997 tax returns in the mail in an envelope, certified postage prepaid, and addressed to the IRS Service Center in Philadelphia, Pennsylvania on September 3, 1998.[25] The IRS received the NATALIE return on September 10, 1998.

In March 2001, the IRS alerted various IRS executives, agents and managers of an emerging potentially abusive tax shelter. In April 2001, the IRS requested a list of shelter investors from the Seattle based firm involved in the promotion of the shelter. This list was forwarded to the IRS, Office of Tax Shelter Analysis (OTSA), the focal point for IRS investigations of abusive corporate tax shelter issues. Using the list, OTSA retrieved information from the IRS's Integrated Document Retrieval System to order tax returns for the tax shelter participants. In July 2001, an IRS agent with OTSA, an IRS manager and a tax shelter coordinator for this tax shelter reviewed the information and prepared an investor list and determined that entities on the list were involved in a Foreign Leverage Investment Program (FLIP).

In July 2001, IRS agents, financial products specialists and an economist attended a training session in Washington D.C. regarding the examination of this tax shelter program. Using their expertise and training, upon analyzing the available information, the IRS decided to assign a group of experts to examine Natalie's tax liabilities. The group examined the tax returns for all entities involved in the FLIP except for Natalie's and one other entity's, which were unavailable. After hours of analysis, the group was able to develop an organizational chart showing the ownership of the various entities and the flow through of the various tax attributes of the shelter. Based upon this analysis and advice of IRS counsel, the IRS manager assigned to this case decided to issue an FPAA to Plaintiffs based upon the correct determination of Natalie's participation in the tax shelter under review.

---

[24] [fn 1] Plaintiff is a TEFRA partnership subject to the 26 U.S.C. §§ 6221–6234 which requires that the IRS to address proposed adjustments to partnership items in one proceeding by providing notice to tax matters partners as identified by the partnership.

[25] [fn 2] NATALIE received two valid extensions, one to August 15, 1998 and the second to October 15, 1998.

The IRS mailed the FPAA to Plaintiff on September 7, 2001 disallowing $5,002,941 in capital losses. Plaintiff filed a petition in this Court to contest the FPAA as provided in 26 U.S.C. § 6226(a)(2).[26]

SUMMARY JUDGMENT STANDARD

Federal Rule of Civil Procedure 12(b) provides that if, on a motion to dismiss for failure to state a claim, "matters outside the pleading are presented to and not excluded by the court, the motion shall be treated as one for summary judgment and disposed of as provided in Rule 56." Because the Court relied on the Defendant's documentary evidence to resolve this dispute, the Court treated Defendant's motion as one for summary judgment.

In the usual case, the party who seeks summary judgment must show by affidavit or other evidentiary materials that there is no genuine dispute as to any fact material to resolution of the motion. *See Celotex Corp. v. Catrett*, 477 U.S. 317, 325 (1986); *Anderson v. Liberty Lobby, Inc.*, 477 U.S. 242, 250 n.4 (1986); *Lavespere v. Niagra Machine & Tool Works, Inc.*, 910 F.2d 167, 178 (5th Cir. 1990); *Fontenot v. Upjohn Co.*, 780 F.2d 1190, 1194 (5th Cir. 1986). To satisfy this burden, the movant must either submit evidentiary documents that negate the existence of some material element of the nonmoving party's claim or defense or, if the crucial issue is one for which the nonmoving party will bear the burden of proof at trial, merely point out that the evidentiary documents in the record contain insufficient proof concerning an essential element of the nonmoving party's claim or defense. *See Celotex Corp.*, 477 U.S. at 325; *Lavespere*, 910 F.2d at 178.

Once the moving party has carried that burden, the burden shifts to the nonmoving party to show that summary judgment is not appropriate. *See Fields v. City of South Houston*, 922 F.2d 1183, 1187 (5th Cir. 1991). The nonmoving party cannot discharge this burden by referring to the mere allegations or denials of the nonmoving party's pleadings; rather, that party must, either by submitting opposing evidentiary documents or by referring to evidentiary documents already in the record, set out specific facts showing that a genuine issue exists. *See Celotex*, 477 U.S. at 324; *Fields*, 922 F.2d at 1187. In order for a court to find there are no genuine material factual issues, the court must be satisfied that no reasonable trier of fact could have found for the nonmoving party or, in other words, that the evidence favoring the nonmoving party is insufficient to enable a reasonable jury to return a verdict for the nonmovant. *See Liberty Lobby*, 477 U.S. at 249–50; Fed. R. Civ. P. 56(e).

---

[26] [fn 3] As a prerequisite to filing a petition disputing an FPAA, 26 U.S.C. § 6226(e)(1) requires the tax matters partner to deposit with the Secretary of the Treasury the amount by which the tax liability of the tax matters partner would be increased if the FPAA's adjustments to partnership tax returns were correct. Because the tax matters corporation, DAVMY, is an "S-Corporation," the shareholders, David and Amy Perez, are required to make tax deposits rather than the corporation pursuant to 26 U.S.C. §§ 1366–1368. The Perezes deposited $1,624,000 with the IRS's Secretary of the Treasury.

STATUTE OF LIMITATIONS

Plaintiff argues it is entitled to summary judgment because the IRS issued the FPAA after the governing statute of limitations expired. The statute of limitations for issuing an FPAA expires three years after the later of (i) the date on which the partnership return for such taxable year was filed or (ii) the last day for filing such return for such year, without regard to extensions. 26 U.S.C. § 6229(a). Here, the Natalie return was mailed on September 3, 1998 by certified mail and received by the IRS on September 10, 1998. Dep. David Perez, para 5 and Ex. G, stipulation No. 5. The resolution of this issue turns on whether the Natalie return was "filed" on the date it was postmarked or the date it was received where it was both timely mailed and timely received.

Normally, a return is considered "filed" with the IRS on the date that it is received by the appropriate office of the IRS. United States v. Lombardo, 241 U.S. 73, 76 (1916); Phinney v. Bank of Southwest Nat'l Ass'n, Houston, 335 F.2d 266, 268 [14 A.F.T.R.2d 6179] (5th Cir. 1964); Poynor v. Comm'r, 81 F.2d 521, 522 [17 A.F.T.R. 392] (5th Cir. 1936); Chasar v. Internal Revenue Serv., 733 F. Supp. 48, 49 [66 A.F.T.R.2d 90-5272] (N.D. Tex. 1990). Here, Plaintiff's returns were due on October 15, 1998. The returns were received by the IRS on September 10, 1998. The statute of limitations thus began to run on September 10, 1998. The FPAA was mailed on September 7, 2001, within the three-year statute of limitations under 26 U.S.C. § 6229(a).

Plaintiff argues that under 26 U.S.C. § 7502 the postage date of a timely mailed return is the date of filing and that here, the statute of limitations began to run on September 3, 1998 and thus the FPAA mailed on September 7, 2001 was timebarred by the three-year statute of limitations. Section 7502 states in relevant part:

(a) General rule.—

(1) Date of delivery.—If any return, claim, statement, or other document required to be filed, or any payment required to be made, within a prescribed period or on or before a prescribed date under authority of any provision of the internal revenue laws is, after such period or such date, delivered by United States mail to the agency, officer, or office with which such return, claim, statement, or other document is required to be filed, or to which such payment is required to be made, the date of the United States postmark stamped on the cover in which such return, claim, statement, or other document, or payment, is mailed shall be deemed to be the date of delivery or the date of payment, as the case may be.

(2) Mailing requirements.—This subsection shall apply only if—

(A) the postmark date falls within the prescribed period or on or before the prescribed date—

(i) for the filing (including any extension granted for such filing) of the return, claim, statement, or other document, or . . .

26 U.S.C. § 7502. The plain language of the statute states that § 7502 only applies to situations where a return is timely mailed but *delivered to the IRS after a prescribed date.* Interpreting this provision, the United States Court of Appeals for the Sixth Circuit has held:

> Section 7502 was enacted as a remedial provision to alleviate inequities arising from differences in mail delivery from one part of the country to another. . .. This "mailbox rule," both by its terms and as revealed in the legislative history, applies only in cases where the document is actually received by the I.R.S. after the statutory period.

Miller v. United States, 784 F.2d 728, 730 [57 A.F.T.R.2d 86-928]. In this case, Plaintiff wants to avail itself of the postage date equals filing date rule in § 7502. The problem is, however, that Plaintiff's return was timely mailed and timely received. There is no reason for the Court to depart from the general rule that delivery date equals filing date and apply the exceptions in § 7502 to the facts here. If timely mailing equals filing even when the return is timely delivered, there would be no need for § 7502 since all returns that were timely mailed would be considered timely filed on the date of postage, not delivery.

Plaintiff relies on Emmons v. Comm'r, 898 F.2d 50 [65 A.F.T.R.2d 90-997] (5th Cir. 1990), for the proposition that the filing date of a timely filed return is the date of mailing. Plaintiff cites the language, "We decline to ignore the statute's plain words. Thus, all timely [mailed] returns are considered filed as of the postmark date and all late [mailed] returns are considered filed as of the date of delivery." *Emmons,* 898 F.2d at 51. The facts in *Emmons,* however, involve returns that were mailed late and received late. Id. at 50. The issue in *Emmons* is on what date, post date or receipt date, did the statute of limitations run. The court simply noted that timely mailed and late received returns get the benefit of the mailing equals filing rule of § 7502 while late mailed and late received returns are determined by the general rule that delivery equals filing. In both instances the *Emmons* court referred to late received returns. This Court will not ignore the statute's plain words, ". . . after such period or date, delivered . . ." and finds that § 7502 is inapplicable to these facts since the FPAA in this case was timely delivered. The Court finds that the Natalie returns were delivered to the IRS on September 10, 1998, that they were due on October 15, 1998 and thus the filing date is September 10, 1998. As such, the FPAA mailed on September 7, 2001 was mailed within the three-year statute of limitations as prescribed by 26 U.S.C. § 6229(a). As a result, Plaintiff is not entitled to summary judgment on the grounds of limitations.

CONSIDERED DETERMINATION

Plaintiffs argue that the FPAA issued by the Defendant is invalid because it is not a "considered determination" as required by 26 U.S.C. § 6212(a). The United States Court of Appeals for the Fifth Circuit held that "courts have interpreted the term "determination" to mean, for purposes of Section 6212(a), a "thoughtful and considered determination that the United States is entitled to an amount not yet paid," *Sealy Power v. Comm'r*, 46 F.3d 382, 387–88 [75 A.F.T.R.2d 95-1213] (5th Cir. 1995) (citing *Portillo v. Commissioner*, 932 F.2d 1128, 1132 [67 A.F.T.R.2d 91-1149] (5th Cir. 1991) (quoting *Scar v. Comm'r*, 814 F.2d 1363, 1369 [59 A.F.T.R.2d 87-950] (9th Cir. 1987)). "The Internal Revenue Code does not specify the form or content of a valid notice of deficiency. Courts have held, however, that the notice generally must advise the taxpayer that the Commissioner has determined a deficiency for a particular year and must specify the amount of the deficiency or provide the information necessary to compute the deficiency." *Sealy*, 46 F.3d 386.[27] (citing *Portillo*, 932 F.2d at 1132) (citations omitted). The "notice of deficiency, which merely serves as a warning to the taxpayer that the Commissioner has assessed a deficiency and plans to hale the taxpayer into court, need not give any reasons for the assessment of a deficiency." *Sealy*, 46 F.3d at 388; *see Scar*, 814 F.2d at 1396.

There is a general rule that a determination of deficiency issued by the Commissioner is given a presumption of correctness. *Sealy*, 46 F.3d at 386 (citing U.S. v. Janis, 428 U.S. 433, 441 [38 A.F.T.R.2d 76-5378], 96 S. Ct. 3021, 3025 [38 A.F.T.R.2d 76-5378] 49 L.Ed.2d 1046, 1053 [38 A.F.T.R.2d 76-5378] (1976)). That is, courts will not look behind the notice of deficiency to determine whether it is arbitrary. *Sealy*, 46 F.3d at 387. "On rare occasions, as in *Scar*, however, the reason given on the face of the notice reveals that the Commissioner failed to make a determination." Id. at 387–88; See *Scar*, 814 F.2d at 1367; Clapp v. Comm'r, 875 F.2d 1396, 1403 [63 A.F.T.R.2d 89-1451] (9th Cir. 1989). The issue here is whether the FPAA is void on its face.

Plaintiff asserts that under *Scar*, the IRS must have in fact examined the taxpayer's return in order for an FPAA to be valid. Pl.'s Mot. for Summ. J. at 17, Pl.'s Reply to Def.'s Resp. in Opp'n to Pl.'s Mot. for Summ. J. at 8. *Scar* establishes no such requirement. *Clapp*, 875 F.2d 1396, 1402 [63 A.F.T.R.2d 89-1451] ("As the Tax Court has since pointed out, *Scar* did *not even require any affirmative showing* by the Commissioner that a determination set forth in an alleged notice of deficiency was made on the basis of the taxpayers' return."). In *Scar*, the notice had no relation to the taxpayers and on its face stated that because the taxpayers' return was not available, the Commissioner was imposing the maximum tax rate to the adjustment amount. *Scar*, 814 F.2d at 1364–65. Further, the notice referred to a tax shelter that had no connection to the taxpayers. *Id.* In this case, the notice properly identified tax shelters and related entities and explained why the adjustments were being made. Unlike in *Scar*, there was no language indicating that the Commissioner imposed the maximum tax rate until the proper rate could be determined. Although the notice contained mistakes, the notice clearly contained information that related to the taxpayer. Therefore, under *Scar*, the FPAA in this case is not void on its face.

---

[27] [fn 4] An FPAA issued in relation to a partnership's tax return is the functional equivalent of a notice of deficiency. *Sealy*, 46 F.3d at 382 [75 A.F.T.R.2d 95-1213] (5th Cir. 1995).

Plaintiffs assert that the FPAA in this case is void under *Sealy* because the Commissioner did not examine the Natalie returns. The Court disagrees. In *Sealy*, taxpayers challenged an FPAA disallowing several deductions and credits. *Sealy*, 46 F.3d at 385. The FPAA set out adjustments for each year involved and explained in an attachment the reasons for the adjustments. *Id.* at 388. The court concluded that the Commissioner did consider the taxpayer's return and that the FPAA on its face reflected that the Commissioner made a "determination" for purposes of the Tax Court's jurisdiction. *Id.* Nowhere, however, does the *Sealy* court state that there is an affirmative duty of the Commissioner to consider the taxpayer's tax return in order for a determination to be valid.[28] In *Sealy*, the Fifth Circuit found a FPAA that set out the adjustment items for each year involved and explained the adjustments in an attachment to be a considered determination. *Id.* Here, the Commissioner also set out adjustments and explained the adjustments in an attachment. The Commissioner considered Danmar's tax returns and traced the losses arising from the tax shelter from the partner's returns back up the chain to Natalie. The *Sealy* court focused on the substantive information contained in the underlying determination, not a bright line rule of whether the Commissioner had the partnership's tax returns. Therefore, the Court finds that under *Sealy*, the FPAA in this case is valid.

Plaintiff also relies on Estate of Weller v. United States, 58 F.Supp.2d 734 [83 A.F.T.R.2d 99-2118] (S.D. Tex. 1998) to support its position that the FPAA in this case is void. The Court disagrees. Two of the determinations in *Weller* stated, "we have been unable to determine the exact deficiency to which the proposed penalties for this adjustment apply. Since we are required to provide you with appeal rights for the proposed penalties, we have based our penalty computations on an estimated deficiency of $100,000." *Weller*, 58 F.Supp.2d at 736. The other determination, which did not contain the estimation language, was also invalidated. The court pointed out, however:

> Significantly, this is a case where the IRS had in its possession all the information it needed to make a determination of a tax deficiency as required by the Code, yet failed to do so within the limitations. Therefore, the present facts can be distinguished from cases in which the illegal source of income, or *lack of taxpayer records*, prevented the Commissioner from making an assessment with mathematical precision. . .. The August 20, 1992 assessments on the 1983 and 1985 tax years were made without any substantive basis, are arbitrary and erroneous, and are void.

Id. at 741–42. In *Weller*, the IRS had the returns and failed to look at them, sending a "Protective Manual Assessment" instead. *Id.* at 737. The IRS did not

---

[28] [fn 5] Logically, reviewing the taxpayer's return is the ideal way to make a determination because most of the relevant information would be contained in the return. It is conceivable, however, that in rare instances such as this one, the Commissioner could make a valid determination through an IRS, OTSA investigation, which examines sufficient information related to the taxpayer.

review *any* information related to the taxpayer. *Id.* Here, the IRS did not have the returns which would have allowed it to make a determination with mathematical precision. It did, however, act in good faith by analyzing all of the available information that related to the taxpayers in order to make a substantive determination. The Court therefore finds that the FPAA is valid under *Weller*.

Plaintiff relies on Abrams v. Commissioner, 787 F.2d 939, 941 [57 A.F.T.R.2d 86-1130] (4th Cir. 1986), for the proposition that the IRS must have in fact examined a return in order to be valid. The Court finds the facts of *Abrams* inapplicable to this case. In *Abrams*, the IRS sent the taxpayers a letter warning them that their claims would be denied if they attempted to utilize a specific tax shelter. *Abrams*, 787 F.2d at 940. The taxpayers later tried to claim that the letter was a notice of deficiency in order to receive a tax liability determination at a preferentially early date. Id. at 942. The court noted:

> The most important observation to be made about the letter is that it left no doubt that, as yet, there had been *no general review of any return, no computation of any deficiency nor any reduction in refunds* to which the taxpayers might otherwise be entitled to. It was in essence only fair warning of what the taxpayers sheltering income through . . . the tax shelter in question . . . "might expect."

Abrams, 787 F.2d 939 [57 A.F.T.R.2d 86-1130] at 941. Here, the IRS reviewed the partnership tax returns for Danmar, the individual tax returns for David Perez and Amy Perez, the partners involved in Natalie and other information related to the Plaintiff pursuant to the OTSA review of the tax shelter. Based upon the information it had, the IRS group was able to develop an organizational chart detailing the loss disallowance attributable to the Plaintiff. The Court therefore finds the facts of *Abrams* unpersuasive. Consequently, Plaintiff is not entitled to summary judgment on the grounds that the IRS failed to make a considered determination.

CONCLUSION

Accordingly, the Court DENIES Plaintiff's Motion for Summary Judgment (Docket entry #14) on each of Plaintiff's claims. And because Defendant has moved for partial summary judgment on the grounds that the FPAA was both timely mailed and a considered determination, the Court GRANTS Defendant's Cross Motion for Partial Summary Judgment (Docket entry #18).

SIGNED this 15th day of January, 2003.
EDWARD C. PRADO
UNITED STATES DISTRICT JUDGE

NOTES AND QUESTIONS

1. Does the mailbox rule apply to documents put in the mail after the due date?
2. To what documents does the mailbox rule not apply?

Another exception to the rule that a document is deemed filed when delivered applies when the due date falls on a weekend or legal holiday. If the last day for filing the return falls on a Saturday, Sunday, or legal holiday, the return is still considered timely filed on the next business day. *See* IRC § 7503. Private metering systems do not generally establish mailing date for the mailbox rule. *See* Reg. § 301.7502-1(c)(1)(iii)(B). Eventually, electronic filing will likely make the mailbox rule obsolete.

Registered mail and certified mail provide proof of postmark date. *See* IRC § 7502(c)(1)(B). The Code authorizes Treasury and the IRS to issue regulations that designate private delivery carriers for sending mail to the IRS or Tax Court. *See* IRC § 7502(f). Under this authority, the IRS has designated products from DHL, UPS, and FedEx as authorized carriers for purposes of the mailbox rule. *See* Notice 2016-30, 2016-18 I.R.B. 676.

The Code permits the IRS to grant extensions for filing a tax return. *See* IRC § 6081. Regulations issued in 2008 under this authority granted in section 6801 provide an automatic six-month extension for return filing. *See* Reg. § 1.6081-4(a). The automatic extension on filing a return does not extend the due date for tax payments. *See* Reg. § 1.6081-4(c).

4. Underreporting

Failing to report or underreporting a tax liability creates potential liability for civil penalties or criminal sanctions once the IRS detects or discovers the act or omission. The term "understatement" refers to a subset of acts and omissions described as underreporting. There are two different definitions relating to understatements in the Code. *See* IRC § 6662(d)(2) (defining substantial understatement for purposes of the negligence penalties); IRC § 6694(e) (defining understatement of liability for purposes of return preparer penalties). To detect underreporting and resolve underreporting issues, the IRS reviews returns, permits the taxpayer to dispute the asserted underreporting in an internal appeal, and provides a final determination to the taxpayer. These procedures are the topic of Unit 3, which covers the IRS's tax determination authority. A taxpayer may seek judicial review of the final determination arising from the IRS's tax determination authority.

B. Amended Returns/Refund Claims

1. Taxpayer Obligation to Amend a Return

There is no legal obligation to file an amended return even if an error is discovered. *See* Badaracco v. Commissioner, 464 U.S. 386, 397 (1984). Although there is no legal obligation to file an amended return where an error in the original return is discovered, it is likely to the taxpayer's advantage to do so. Amending an erroneous return will stop the accrual of penalties and interest. It is also advantageous to amend a return where the taxpayer has overpaid tax. Generally, the only way to obtain a refund after filing an original return is by filing an amended return claiming a refund.

2. IRS Obligation to Accept an Amended a Return

The IRS is not required to accept an amended return containing no inaccuracies. Taxpayers often have choices when filing a tax return to which they are bound. *See* Pacific National Co. v. Welch, 304 U.S. 191, 194 (1938). In *Pacific National*, a taxpayer had sold properties for which the buyers paid in installments. On his return, he reported the profits on the sales as though the buyers had paid in cash. He filed a refund claim, which the IRS rejected. The case made its way to the Supreme Court, which held that reporting the sale in cash was tantamount to making an election to which the taxpayer was bound.

Taxpayers often make elections in their tax returns. If a taxpayer makes a valid election, the election cannot be changed in an amended return as discussed in the following case.

GOLDSTONE v. COMMISSIONER
65 T.C. 113 (1975)
United States Tax Court

OPINION

STERRETT, Judge:

Respondent determined deficiencies in petitioners' Federal income taxes for the calendar years 1969 and 1970. . . .

Respondent also determined that, pursuant to section 6651(a),[29] petitioners were liable for an addition to tax in the amount of $208.79 for the year 1969. Due to concessions by the parties and the failure of petitioners to contest the section 6651(a) addition, the sole issue for decision is whether petitioners may, in an amended return for 1967, delete an investment credit properly claimed on their original return for that year in lieu of recapturing such credit in the year of disposition of the property for which the credit was claimed.

All of the facts have been stipulated and are so found. The stipulation of facts, together with the exhibits attached thereto, are incorporated herein by this reference.

Petitioners Jack R. and Ursula Goldstone, husband and wife, were residents of San Francisco, Calif., at the time they filed their petition herein. Petitioners filed joint Federal income tax returns for the calendar years 1967, 1969, and 1970 with the Director, Internal Revenue Service Center, Ogden, Utah.

---

[29] [fn 2] All statutory references are to the Internal Revenue Code of 1954, as amended.

On their return for 1967, petitioners properly claimed an investment credit under section 38 in the amount of $1,400 for certain property they purchased in that year. Hereinafter, this property will be referred to as the credit property.

On October 1, 1967, Golden Gate Fashions, Inc. (hereinafter Fashions) was incorporated under the laws of the State of California. During October 1967 petitioners transferred various assets of a gift shop business, including the credit property, to Fashions in exchange for all of the capital stock thereof. This transfer met the statutory requirements for nonrecognition of gain or loss under section 351.

Fashions disposed of the credit property during petitioners' 1970 taxable year. As a result of this disposition the parties have agreed that petitioners were required to recapture the investment credit of $1,400 claimed on their 1967 return.

On or about July 1, 1971, petitioners mailed an amended 1967 joint Federal income tax return to the Internal Revenue Service Center, Fresno, Calif.

On or about December 1, 1972, petitioners mailed an amendment to the aforementioned amended return. On both the amended return and amendment thereto, petitioners claimed a refund of $4,596.61 and attempted to delete the investment credit as claimed on their original 1967 return stating,

The $1,400 Investment Credit Claimed on the original return has not been considered in the preparation of the amended return.

This means that the credit is recaptured by the IRS through the 1967 Amended Tax Return Adjustment.

Respondent denied petitioners' refund claims for 1967 in two letters, both dated November 1, 1973, and made no direct comment in either letter on petitioners' statement on the investment credit. Implicit in his action on the refund claims was a nonacceptance of the purported changed treatment of the credit by petitioners. In a statutory notice of deficiency for 1970 respondent increased petitioners' 1970 tax liability as follows:

Investment credit in the amount of $1,400.00 which was deducted by you on your 1967 income tax return has been recaptured on your 1970 income tax return as the assets, from which the investment credit was computed in 1967 were disposed of during 1970.

We must decide the correctness of respondent's determination.

Respondent argues that the acceptance or rejection of an amended return is discretionary with the Internal Revenue Service. He contends that since both petitioners' amended returns were appropriately rejected, petitioners' initial return for 1967 on which the investment credit was claimed remains their effective return for that year. Consequently, the investment credit must be recaptured in 1970, the year of disposition of the credit property, pursuant to the express terms of section 47(a)(1).[30]

---

[30] [fn 3] SEC. 47. CERTAIN DISPOSITIONS, ETC., OF SECTION 38 PROPERTY.

Petitioners advance the argument that the Internal Revenue Code grants them the right to file an amended return. They argue that the effect of exercising this right and deleting the investment credit on their amended returns is the same as if the credit had never been claimed. They urge, therefore, that there is no credit to be recaptured in 1970 and that section 47(a)(1) is inapplicable in the present context.

Petitioners have cited no authority in support of their arguments and we have found none. Rather, we conclude that the instant case is within the ambit of the Supreme Court's decision in Pacific National Co. v. Welch, 304 U.S. 191 (1938). There the issue was whether the taxpayer, having filed a return on which he employed the deferred payment method, was entitled to file a claim for refund 2 years later utilizing the installment method to compute the profit on the sales. In holding that the taxpayer was bound by his original method of reporting the gain from the sales the Supreme Court stated:

> Change from one method to the other, as petitioner seeks, would require recomputation and readjustment of tax liability for subsequent years and impose burdensome uncertainties upon the administration of the revenue laws. It would operate to enlarge the statutory period for filing returns (sec. 53(a)) to include the period allowed for recovering overpayments (sec. 322(b)). There is nothing to suggest that Congress intended to permit a taxpayer, after expiration of the time within which return is to be made, to have his tax liability computed and settled according to the other method. * * * (Pacific National Co. v. Welch, supra at 194.)

See also Riley Co. v. Commissioner, 311 U.S. 55 (1940); Miskovsky v. United States, 414 F.2d 954 (3d Cir. 1969); Lord v. United States, 296 F.2d 333 (9th Cir. 1961).

The rationale of Pacific National Co. v. Welch, supra, is clearly applicable to the case before us. Petitioners correctly claimed an investment credit on their initial 1967 tax return. Should they be allowed to change their tax treatment of the credit both problems envisioned by the Supreme Court in Pacific National Co. would surface. Such change would obviously impose uncertainty in the administration of section 47 as a taxpayer would have at his disposal the option

---

(a) GENERAL RULE.—Under regulations prescribed by the Secretary or his delegate—(1) EARLY DISPOSITION, ETC.—IF during any taxable year any property is disposed of, or otherwise ceases to be section 38 property with respect to the taxpayer, before the close of the useful life which was taken into account in computing the credit under section 38, then the tax under this chapter for such taxable year shall be increased by an amount equal to the aggregate decrease in the credits allowed under section 38 for all prior taxable years which would have resulted solely from substituting, in determining qualified investment, for such useful life the period beginning with the time such property was placed in service by the taxpayer and ending with the time such property ceased to be section 38 property.

to file an amended return deleting an investment credit rather than have the recapture provisions of section 47 apply. As is clear in the instant case, such change would also bear on a taxpayer's liability for a subsequent year, the year of disposition. Hence, we hold that petitioners must recapture the investment credit in 1970, the year of disposition of the credit property.

In so holding we are aware that cases in a myriad of factual settings have upheld the validity of amended returns. See, e.g., Haggar Co. v. Helvering, 308 U.S. 389 (1940); Mamula v. Commissioner, 346 F.2d 1016 (9th Cir. 1965), revg. 41 T.C. 572 (1964); John P. Reaver, 42 T.C. 72 (1964); Robert M. Foley, 56 T.C. 765 (1971). However, such cases fall within one of the following factual contexts: (1) The amended return was filed prior to the date prescribed for filing a return; (2) the taxpayer's treatment of the contested item in the amended return was not inconsistent with his treatment of that item in his original return; or (3) the taxpayer's treatment of the item in the original return was improper and the taxpayer elected one of several allowable alternatives in the amended return.

It is obvious that the factual setting before us falls within none of the aforenoted contexts. Petitioners' treatment of the investment credit on their 1967 return was entirely correct, and the treatment accorded it on the amended returns, filed long after the period for filing a return for 1967 had expired, is manifestly inconsistent with the initial treatment thereof.

Furthermore, we note that the plain, unambiguous language of section 47(a) requires that the investment credit be recaptured in the year of disposition. To sanction the course of action petitioners seek to pursue would enable petitioners to contravene the clear statutory language and would constitute a usurpation of the legislative function by this Court. Petitioners must, pursuant to section 47, recapture the investment credit in 1970.

As noted at the outset petitioners have not contested the imposition of an addition to tax for late filing in the amount of $208.79 under section 6651(a). Therefore, the respondent's determination is this respect is also sustained.

Decision will be entered under Rule 155.

NOTES AND QUESTIONS

1. What is the IRS's obligation when an amended return is filed?
2. What types of amended returns does the IRS accept?

3. Requirements for a Refund Claim

When a taxpayer files an amended return owing tax along with a correct payment, the IRS processes the payment. The IRS has no reason to be picky about the form of the amended return. On the other hand, when a taxpayer files an amended return to make a refund claim, there are some requirements the taxpayer must satisfy to obtain the refund. If the IRS denies the claim, the taxpayer must sue for the refund.

A taxpayer may request a refund of tax paid to the IRS. To qualify for a refund, the taxpayer must have: (1) overpaid, (2) submitted a request on the proper form signed under penalty of perjury, and (3) detailed the grounds for the refund. Neither the Code nor the regulations provide a complete definition of the term "overpayment." Courts have held, however, that the term "overpayment" as used in the Code means overpayment in the usual sense. Thus, an overpayment is an amount paid beyond what the taxpayer owed. *See* Jones v. Liberty Glass Co., 382 U.S. 524, 531 (1947). Often a refund claim occurs where a taxpayer pays a tax the IRS has asserted is owed but with which the taxpayer disagrees. In such a case, the taxpayer must pay the full tax—thus making an alleged overpayment— before making the claim. If the IRS discovers new amounts owed beyond the refund claim—even if it makes the discovery after the refund claim is made— then no overpayment exists and the taxpayer is not entitled to a refund. *See, e.g.,* Lewis v. Reynolds, 284 U.S. 281 (1932).

Generally, a claim for a refund due to an error in the original return is made on an amended tax return. *See* Reg. § 301.6402-3(a). The return must be signed under penalty of perjury. There are forms, beyond the scope of this book, that can be used if the refund claim is based on actions other than an original return filing.

A refund claim must also detail each ground on which the taxpayer claims a credit or a refund and include sufficient facts to inform the IRS of the basis of the claim.[31] This requirement dovetails with the variance doctrine, which places limits on the arguments a taxpayer can make in a suit to recover the refund. Under the variance doctrine the taxpayer may not make claims outside the grounds in the original refund claim.[32] Thus it is in the taxpayer's interest to be thorough in setting forth grounds for requesting a refund.

Just as an original tax return can be filed without using the actual form, actions of a taxpayer may constitute an informal refund claim. A taxpayer's act may be treated as an informal refund claim if: (1) The court determines an informal refund claim was filed, (2) the claim is in writing or has a written component, and (3) the matters set forth in the writing are sufficient to apprise the IRS that a refund is sought and to focus the IRS on the merits of the dispute. This gives the IRS the opportunity to commence examination of the claim if it wants, as in the following case.

FISHER v. UNITED STATES
1990 U.S. Dist. LEXIS 15229
United States District Court, Northern District of California

---

[31] *See* Reg. § 301.6402-2(b) ("The claim must set forth in detail each ground upon which a credit or refund is claimed and facts sufficient to apprise the Commissioner of the exact basis thereof.").

[32] *See* Decker v. United States, 93-2 U.S.T.C. ¶50,408, 72 A.F.T.R.2d 93-5362 (D. Conn. 1993) ("The 'variance doctrine' holds that '[i]n an action for a refund . . . the law is clear that the district court is limited to those grounds which were raised in the claim for refund presented to the Commissioner.'").

PATEL, J.

MEMORANDUM AND ORDER

Plaintiffs husband and wife, residents of Contra Costa County, California, bring this action for recovery of taxes erroneously paid to the Internal Revenue Service for the taxable years 1977 and 1978. The parties are now before the court on defendant's motion to dismiss plaintiffs' complaint for lack of subject matter jurisdiction pursuant to *Federal Rule of Civil Procedure 12(b)(1)*. The United States argues that the court lacks jurisdiction because plaintiffs failed to timely file their claims for refund in accordance with *26 U.S.C. § 7422(a)*.

BACKGROUND

In connection with a series of commodities transactions on the London Metals Exchange, plaintiffs reported ordinary losses on their 1976 income tax return and capital gains on their 1977 and 1978 returns, and paid appropriate taxes for those years in full.

After being informed by the Commissioner of the Internal Revenue Service ("Commissioner") that the London Metals investments were under investigation, plaintiffs executed a series of Consents to Extend the Time to Assess Tax, the last of which extended the statute of limitations for 1976 and 1977 to December 31, 1981.

On December 31, 1981, the Commissioner mailed to plaintiffs a statutory notice of tax deficiency for 1976 and tax overassessments for 1977 and 1978, explaining that the series of London Metals transactions had been determined to be "fully integrated and constituted but a single transaction," and that the transactions were a sham. Compl. at 3-4. The statutory notice statement also provided that the overassessments would be scheduled for adjustment "provided that you protect yourself against the expiration of the statutory period of limitations by filing timely claims for refund for each year on the enclosed Forms 1040X with your District Director of Internal Revenue." Def. MTD at 7.

On March 29, 1982, plaintiffs filed a petition with the United States Tax Court challenging the deficiency in tax year 1976, to which they attached the notice of deficiency and overassessments and the explanation of adjustments. That matter is still pending before the Tax Court. On December 15, 1982, plaintiffs filed formal refund claims for the tax years 1977 and 1978.

Defendants assert that plaintiffs' Consent to Extend the Time to Assess Tax for 1977 extended the deadline for a refund claim for 1977 to June 30, 1982. They further assert that because no consent was signed for 1978, the deadline for filing a refund claim for 1978 was October 17, 1982. The United States moves to dismiss on the ground that plaintiffs did not file their claims for refund until December 1982.

Plaintiffs do not dispute these filing dates; nor do they deny that their formal refund claims were filed beyond the statute of limitations. However, they allege that by filing a petition with the Tax Court challenging the 1976 deficiency along with attachments concerning 1977 and 1978, they made an informal claim for refunds for 1977 and 1978, and that the Tax Court filing tolled the statute of limitations governing claims for the latter two years.

Plaintiffs further argue that they have a right to recover the overassessments for 1977 and 1978 under the doctrine of equitable recoupment. Here, plaintiffs argue, the doctrine would require that the deficiency judgment for 1976 take into account the overassessments for 1977 and 1978, which were based upon the same underlying transaction.

In addition, plaintiffs argue that the United States waived any objections it may have to plaintiffs' claims by its conduct during the audit and ongoing negotiations.

Finally, plaintiffs argue that the IRS should be estopped from denying the validity of plaintiffs' informal refund claims because the Service represented to plaintiffs that if the 1976 adjustments were upheld, plaintiffs would receive an offsetting reduction by the amounts of the 1977 and 1978 overassessments.

LEGAL STANDARD

A motion to dismiss will be denied unless it appears that the plaintiff can prove no set of facts which would entitle him or her to relief. *Conley v. Gibson,* 355 U.S. 41, 45-46 (1957); *Fidelity Fin. Corp. v. Federal Home Loan Bank of San Francisco,* 792 F.2d 1432, 1435 (9th Cir. 1986), *cert. denied,* 479 U.S. 1064 (1987). All material allegations in the complaint will be taken as true and construed in the light most favorable to the non-moving party. *NL Indus., Inc. v. Kaplan,* 792 F.2d 896, 898 (9th Cir. 1986). Although the court is generally confined to consideration of the allegations in the pleadings, when the complaint is accompanied by attached documents, such documents are deemed part of the complaint and may be considered in evaluating the merits of a motion to dismiss. *Durning v. First Boston Corp.,* 815 F.2d 1265, 1267 (9th Cir.), *cert. denied,* 484 U.S. 944 (1987).

DISCUSSION

I. Informal Claims for 1977 and 1978

Courts have routinely held that an informal claim for refund that is timely filed and later perfected may be treated as a valid claim. *Crocker v. United States,* 563 F. Supp. 496, 499-500 (S.D.N.Y. 1983); *American Radiator & Standard Sanitary Corp. v. United States,* 318 F.2d 915, 921-22 (Ct. Cl. 1963). Defendants contend that plaintiffs have not alleged facts sufficient to demonstrate that they filed an informal claim for refund of the overassessments for 1977 and 1978.

An informal claim must fairly advise the IRS of the nature and ground of the taxpayer's claim and intent to request a refund. *United States v. Kales,* 314 U.S. 186, 193-94 (1941). It must "set forth facts sufficient to enable the [IRS] to make an intelligent administrative review of the claim." *Crocker,* 563 F. Supp. at 500 (quoting *Scovill Mfg. Co. v. Fitzpatrick,* 215 F.2d 567, 569 (2d Cir. 1954)). Moreover, the claim must have a written component; oral claims alone are insufficient. *Gustin v. United States Internal Revenue Serv.,* 876 F.2d 485, 488 (5th Cir. 1989).

The general approach of the courts has been to examine each allegation of the informal claim on its own facts "with a view towards determining whether under those facts the Commissioner knew, or should have known, that a claim was being made." *Gustin,* 876 F.2d at 488-89 (quoting *Newton v. United States,*

163 F. Supp. 614, 619 (Ct. Cl. 1958)). Thus, although some form of written claim is required, it need not contain the entirety or every component of the claim. In addition to the written claim, the taxpayer may rely upon circumstances known to the Commissioner, or detailed knowledge of the agent investigating the claim, which would be sufficient to inform the IRS of the taxpayer's claim. *Id.* at 489.

Here, plaintiffs argue that by filing a Tax Court petition for 1976, and by attaching thereto a copy of the IRS's statutory notice statement setting forth the deficiency for 1976 and the overassessments for 1977 and 1978, they had put the IRS on notice of their intention to settle the overassessment. This settlement could have come about either by plaintiffs' receipt of an offsetting reduction in their 1976 liability based on the 1977 and 1978 overassessments, or by treating the circumstances, including the petition, attachments and ongoing negotiations with the IRS, as an informal claim for refunds for 1977 and 1978 should the deficiency for 1976 be upheld. This informal claim was perfected by plaintiffs' filing of a formal refund claim for those years on December 15, 1982.

The court agrees that, in the overall factual context of their dealings with the IRS, plaintiffs' filing of the petition and inclusion of the statutory notice statement with the Tax Court should be treated as an informal claim for refunds for 1977 and 1978. The IRS itself had determined that the series of 1976, 1977 and 1978 London Metals Exchange transactions were to be treated as a single, integrated transaction, so that disallowing the transaction would not only result in the 1976 deficiency that plaintiffs are challenging in Tax Court, but would entitle them to refunds for the 1977 and 1978 overassessments. To the extent that the basic issue in a taxpayer's assertion of an informal claim is whether the Commissioner was on notice of the taxpayer's intent, and whether that notice was sufficiently detailed in nature, there can be no question that the IRS had notice. They knew that the validity of the 1977 and 1978 overassessments would turn on the result of plaintiff's Tax Court challenge concerning 1976, and that plaintiffs intended to seek refunds for 1977 and 1978 should the deficiency for 1976 be upheld.

The court rejects the United States' overly formalistic argument that there can be no informal claim here because the only writing prepared by plaintiffs was the Tax Court petition pertaining only to 1976 and because the attached statutory notice concerning overassessments for 1977 and 1978 had been prepared by the IRS, not plaintiffs. The underlying inquiry in determining whether an informal claim was made is not whether the taxpayer authored a statement of claim in all its particulars, but whether the Government was on notice. As the court noted in *United States v. Commercial National Bank of Peoria*:

> the written component of an informal refund request need not contain magical words or contain every fact supporting that request. A taxpayer may rely upon other documents, conversations or correspondence to fulfill his notice obligations. Such is the case especially when taxpayers cannot claim an immediate refund because their right to a refund cannot vest until pending litigation is settled.

874 F.2d 1165, 1171 (7th Cir. 1989) (holding that informal claim had been made where IRS knew from ongoing negotiations to settle tax court litigation that taxpayers would have a right to and would request a refund pending the outcome of such negotiations).

Here, as in *Commercial National Bank,* plaintiffs are engaged in ongoing Tax Court litigation, and that litigation itself has a history of negotiations between plaintiffs and the IRS over the disputed transactions. The outcome of the Tax Court proceedings will determine the validity not only of the IRS's statutory notice of deficiency concerning 1976, but also of the overassessments concerning 1977 and 1978. Moreover, the Government was put on notice of plaintiffs' protest, and it was the IRS itself that asserted and provided the basis for the overassessments.

Because the court finds, viewing the facts and making inferences in the light most favorable to plaintiffs, that plaintiffs have asserted facts sufficient to show that informal claims had been made for refunds for the years 1977 and 1978 and that those claims were later perfected, defendant's motion to dismiss for lack of jurisdiction is DENIED.

Although the court's finding of a later-perfected informal claim for 1977 and 1978 suffices to deny the United States' motion to dismiss, plaintiffs' alternative arguments are considered below.

II. Equitable Recoupment

Plaintiffs have argued in the alternative that they are entitled to relief under the doctrine of equitable recoupment, which permits a taxpayer to litigate a time-barred tax claim for overassessment where the government has timely asserted a deficiency, and the deficiency and overassessment are part of a single transaction. *Kolom v. United States,* 791 F.2d 762, 766-67 (9th Cir. 1986). However, the Supreme Court has recently restricted that doctrine, holding that "a party litigating a tax claim in a timely proceeding may, in that proceeding, seek recoupment of a related, and inconsistent, but now time-barred tax claim relating to the same transaction." *United States v. Dalm, U.S.,* 110 S. Ct. 1361, 1368 (1990).

Because plaintiffs do not assert that their formal refund claims were timely made in this court, they are not entitled to invoke the doctrine of equitable recoupment in this proceeding. They may, however, seek to invoke the doctrine in their Tax Court proceeding, in which the petition concerning 1976 liability was timely filed.

III. Government Waiver of Objection to Plaintiffs' Claims

Plaintiffs assert that the Commissioner has waived any objection to plaintiffs' claims in this court through his conduct with respect to plaintiffs' claims during the audit period and thereafter.

As defendant properly notes, the Government may not waive a jurisdictional requirement. *Bender v. Williamsport Area School Dist.,* 475 U.S. 534, 541 (1986); *Latch v. United States,* 842 F.2d 1031, 1032 (9th Cir. 1988). Therefore, plaintiffs may not assert that the government's conduct constituted a waiver of the jurisdictional requirement of a timely filed claim.

IV. Equitable Estoppel

Finally, plaintiffs argue that the IRS led them to believe that the 1977 and 1978 overassessments were addressed by the statutory notice of deficiency, and that the issue of their validity would be preserved by plaintiffs' Tax Court petition concerning liability for 1976.

The parties agree that the statutory notice statement contained clear language providing that the overassessments would be scheduled for adjustment "provided that you protect yourself against the expiration of the statutory period of limitations by filing timely claims for refund for each year . . . ." Def. MTD at 2; Pl. Opp. to Def. MTD at 2-3.

Despite finding that the IRS had clear notice of plaintiffs' intention to seek a refund should the tax deficiency for 1976 be upheld, the court finds no facts suggesting that the IRS led plaintiffs to believe that they would not be subject to the express language of the statutory notice statement, nor that the overassessments would be used to offset any deficiency for 1976 upheld by the Tax Court. The court finds that the United States is not estopped from denying the validity of plaintiffs' informal refund claim by the doctrine of equitable estoppel.

CONCLUSION

Plaintiffs have pled facts, including a series of negotiations, writings and agreements, sufficient to show that the Commissioner was put on notice of the existence and basis of plaintiffs' claim for a refund for the years 1977 and 1978, conditioned upon the outcome of their Tax Court petition concerning 1976. The court finds that plaintiffs made an informal refund claim for the years 1977 and 1978, perfected by the formal claim made on December 15, 1982. Defendant's motion to dismiss for lack of jurisdiction is therefore DENIED.

IT IS SO ORDERED.

NOTES AND QUESTIONS

1. How likely is it that the IRS treats an informal refund claim like an actual refund claim?
2. What can a taxpayer do to increase the likelihood that an informal refund claim will be treated as an actual refund claim?

4. Timeliness of a Refund Claim

The taxpayer has a limited amount of time to make a refund claim. The taxpayer must file a refund claim "within 3 years from the time the return was filed." *See* IRC § 6511. This limitations period and others relating to refunds are discussed in Chapter 10.

5. Joint Committee Review of Refund Claims

An amended return making a refund claim goes through the same process as an original tax return. Thus, it goes through the same audit procedures. The IRS audits the claim and makes a determination. Before issuing a refund of over $2 million, however, a congressional committee, the Joint Committee on Taxation (JCT), performs a review. *See* IRC § 6405(a).

It may seem strange for the JCT to review a proposed grant of a refund. Generally, Congress writes laws rather than participating in their enforcement. The IRS and the JCT have worked out procedures that avoid the appearance of a problem with the separation of legislative and administrative powers. These procedures have not been challenged in the Supreme Court, but they have been called into question. *See generally* Amandeep S. Grewal, *The Congressional Revenue Service*, 2014 U. ILL. L. REV. 689.

CHAPTER 9

TAX PAYMENT

Although it would seem that the timely payment of tax would be a simple or boring topic, the topic raises more interesting issues than one would expect. An important aspect of tax compliance is timely payment of the tax. The payment of tax raises a few legal issues. Taxpayer and the IRS have to deal with issues regarding: (1) the obligation to pay, (2) the composition of a payment, and (3) the timeliness of a payment.

A. Obligation to Pay Tax

Taxpayers have a legal obligation to pay their self-determined taxes on the due date of their returns. This obligation arises from section 6151(a), which provides:

> [T]he person required to make such return shall, without assessment or notice and demand . . . pay such tax at the time and place fixed for filing the return (determined without regard to any extension of time for filing the return).

Failure to pay tax can give rise to penalties, collection actions (including wage garnishment and bank account levies), and criminal liability. The obligation to pay is tied to the obligation to file a tax return much less than one would expect. For example, the failure to file a tax return and the failure to pay tax have different penalty rates. *See* IRC § 6651(a). Although the penalty rate for failing to pay tax is more lenient than the penalty rate for failing to file a return, the government is less forgiving when it comes to extensions.

The obligation to pay tax continues even if a taxpayer has made a bona fide attempt to pay.

UNITED STATES v. ZARRA
810 F. Supp. 2d 758 (2011)
United States District Court, Western District of Pennsylvania

MEMORANDUM OPINION

CONTI, District Judge.

This is a suit for unpaid federal income taxes. On June 14, 2010, plaintiff the United States of America ("government" or "plaintiff"), filed a complaint against defendants John and Marsha Zarra (the "Zarras" or "defendants") pursuant to 26 U.S.C. § 7403(a) (the government may file a civil action where there has been a refusal or neglect to pay any tax). On August 11, 2010, the government filed an amended complaint (ECF No. 7), which is the subject of the instant memorandum opinion. On August 25, 2010, the Zarras filed a motion to dismiss the amended complaint (ECF No. 9). On September 15, 2010, the government filed a motion for summary judgment (ECF No. 15). On November 9, 2010, the court denied the motion to dismiss with prejudice and denied the motion for summary judgment without prejudice. On February 24, 2011, the Zarras filed a third party complaint against J.P. Morgan Chase & Co. and Citizens Financial Group, Inc. (ECF No. 34), which was dismissed. (ECF No. 73.)

Waiting the court's determination are cross-motions for summary judgment. The government's renewed motion for summary judgment (ECF No. 35), filed on February 25, 2011, requests the court grant summary judgment in its favor and award damages because the Zarras cannot properly assert any affirmative defenses, and no rational trier of fact could find that the Zarras satisfied their tax obligation. The Zarras' motion (ECF No. 63), filed on June 30, 2011, requests the court grant summary judgment in their favor with respect to the government's claim, relying on three alternative theories. First, the government did not demonstrate that a timely assessment was made against the Zarras for the 1999 tax year.[1] Second, the Zarras satisfied their obligation to the government because their check, which was written for the correct amount, was accepted by the banks involved in the transaction. Third, the doctrines of laches, waiver, and equitable estoppel preclude the government's claim at this juncture.

After considering these motions and the parties' briefs in opposition and other submissions, the government's motion will be granted and the Zarras' motion will be denied because the Zarras failed to pay fully their tax obligation, and no affirmative defenses shield them from liability under these circumstances.

I. FACTUAL BACKGROUND

In April 2000, the Zarras timely submitted a check to the Internal Revenue Service ("IRS") to pay their 1999 tax liability of $179,501. (Defs.' Concise

---

[1] [fn 1] Surprisingly, the Zarras continue to pursue this theory as a bar to the government's claim. During the hearing on the Zarras' motion to dismiss, the court denied the motion with prejudice because the court found that the assessment was timely made. As explained infra, the Zarras' argument on this point remains unavailing.

Statement of Material Facts ("D.C.S.") (ECF No. 64) ¶ 3; D.C.S. Ex. 4.) The check was written for the correct amount, presented, and accepted; however, the check was negotiated for $179.50. (D.C.S. ¶ 3.) The IRS subsequently received only $179.50 from the Zarras' account. (D.C.S. Ex. 5 at 2.)

The Zarras discovered this mistake when they received their monthly bank statement in May 2000. (*Id.*) Although Mrs. Zarra contacted the IRS twice seeking to rectify the error, the IRS sent notice to the Zarras in September 2000 demanding payment of the outstanding balance along with interest and penalties. (*Id.*) The Zarras contacted the IRS a third time, but they were unsuccessful in their attempt to fix the error. (*Id.* at 2–3.)

On July 3, 2000, a delegate of the Secretary of the Treasury made various assessments against the Zarras for income tax, penalties, and interest, relating to the 1999 tax year. (Pl. Concise Statement of Material Facts ("P.C.S.") (ECF No. 37) ¶ 1.) The government presented a Form 4340 and RACS 006 form as evidence of the assessment against the Zarras, and both documents list the assessment date as July 3, 2000. (P.C.S. Ex. B; D.C.S. Ex. 3.) Sandra Mikkelsen, a government representative, testified during her deposition that the Zarras' assessment is included in one of the three entries with cycle number 200025 on the RACS 006. (Pl.' Resp. to Defs.' Concise Statement of Material Facts ("P.R.D.C.S.") (ECF No.) ¶ 1.)

Although the Zarras had sufficient funds in their account when they submitted the check, their income and financial situation has since deteriorated. (P.R.D.C.S. Ex. E.) The government asserts that, as of March 7, 2011, $364,424 remains due including interest and penalties. (P.C.S. ¶ 3.)

II. STANDARD OF REVIEW

Federal Rule of Civil Procedure 56 provides in relevant part:

(a) Motion for Summary Judgment or Partial Summary Judgment. A party may move for summary judgment, identifying each claim or defense—or the part of each claim or defense—on which summary judgment is sought. The court shall grant summary judgment if the movant shows that there is no genuine dispute as to any material fact and the movant is entitled to judgment as a matter of law. The court should state on the record the reasons for granting or denying the motion. . . .

(c) Procedures.

(1) *Supporting Factual Positions.* A party asserting that a fact cannot be or is genuinely disputed must support the assertion by:

(A) citing to particular parts of materials in the record, including depositions, documents, electronically stored information, affidavits or declarations, stipulations (including those made for purposes of the motion only), admissions, interrogatory answers, or other materials; or

(B) showing that the materials cited do not establish the absence or presence of a genuine dispute, or that an adverse party cannot produce admissible evidence to support the fact.

FED. R. CIV. P. 56(a), (c)(1)(A), (B).

Rule 56 of the Federal Rules of Civil Procedure "mandates the entry of summary judgment, after adequate time for discovery and upon motion, against a party who fails to make a showing sufficient to establish the existence of an element essential to that party's case, and on which that party will bear the burden of proof at trial." Marten v. Godwin, 499 F.3d 290, 295 (3d Cir.2007) (quoting Celotex Corp. v. Catrett, 477 U.S. 317, 322–23, 106 S.Ct. 2548, 91 L.Ed.2d 265 (1986)).

An issue of material fact is in genuine dispute if the evidence is such that a reasonable jury could return a verdict for the nonmoving party. Anderson v. Liberty Lobby, Inc., 477 U.S. 242, 248, 106 S.Ct. 2505, 91 L.Ed.2d 202 (1986); see Doe v. Abington Friends Sch., 480 F.3d 252, 256 (3d Cir.2007) ("A genuine issue is present when a reasonable trier of fact, viewing all of the record evidence, could rationally find in favor of the non-moving party in light of his burden of proof.") (citing Anderson, 477 U.S. at 248, 106 S.Ct. 2505; Celotex Corp., 477 U.S. at 322–23, 106 S.Ct. 2548).

"[W]hen the moving party has carried its burden under Rule 56(c), its opponent must do more than simply show that there is some metaphysical doubt as to the material facts . . . .. Where the record taken as a whole could not lead a rational trier of fact to find for the nonmoving party, there is no genuine issue for trial." Scott v. Harris, 550 U.S. 372, 380, 127 S.Ct. 1769, 167 L.Ed.2d 686 (2007) (quoting Matsushita Elec. Indus. Co. v. Zenith Radio Corp., 475 U.S. 574, 586–87, 106 S.Ct. 1348, 89 L.Ed.2d 538 (1986)).

In deciding a summary judgment motion, a court must view the facts in the light most favorable to the nonmoving party and must draw all reasonable inferences, and resolve all doubts in favor of the nonmoving party. Woodside v. Sch. Dist. of Phila. Bd. of Educ., 248 F.3d 129, 130 (3d Cir.2001); Doe v. Cnty. of Centre, PA, 242 F.3d 437, 446 (3d Cir.2001); Heller v. Shaw Indus., Inc., 167 F.3d 146, 151 (3d Cir.1999). A court must not engage in credibility determinations at the summary judgment stage. Simpson v. Kay Jewelers, Div. of Sterling, Inc., 142 F.3d 639, 643 n. 3 (3d Cir.1998).

III. DISCUSSION

A. Whether a Timely IRS Assessment Occurred

The Zarras assert the government did not demonstrate that a timely assessment was made against them for the 1999 tax year. Pursuant to 26 U.S.C. § 6501(a), "the amount of any tax imposed by this title shall be assessed within 3 years after the return was filed." 26 U.S.C. § 6501(a). Because a tax claim must be brought within ten years after assessment, see 26 U.S.C. § 6502(a)(1), the government's complaint would be time barred if the Zarras' assessment occurred before June 14, 2000. The Zarras argue that the government is unable to establish the requisite connection between the RACS 006 and the Form 4340. The Form 4340, however, clearly states that the assessment date was July 3, 2000. "Courts have indicated that a Form 4340 is adequate to prove a valid assessment if it lists the [']23C date,' indicating the date on which the actual assessment was made." Huff v. United States, 10 F.3d 1440, 1446 (9th Cir.1993) (citations omitted). Moreover, the Form 4340 is admissible evidence. See, e.g., Hughes v. United

States, 953 F.2d 531, 539–40 (9th Cir.1992) (holding that a Form 4340 is admissible under both Federal Rule of Evidence 803(8) and Federal Rule of Evidence 902(1)). A Form 4340 is "valid evidence of a taxpayer's assessed liabilities and the IRS's notice thereof." *Perez v. United States,* 312 F.3d 191, 195 (5th Cir.2002). By submitting the Zarras' Form 4340, which confirms the assessment date, the government sufficiently demonstrated that a valid tax assessment occurred on July 3, 2000.

The Zarras contend that the court's March 1, 2011 minute entry ordered the government to prove a connection between the Zarras' unique Form 4340 and the RACS 006.[2] A court, however, speaks through its judgment and not through its minute entries. *See United States v. Penney,* 576 F.3d 297, 304–05 (6th Cir.2009). The court did not impose a greater burden on the government; the "order" merely enabled the Zarras to obtain discovery of information they sought to attain to challenge the Form 4340. The government provided a deponent who explained the connection between the Zarras' Form 4340 and the RACS 006. The deponent testified that the Zarras' assessment is included in one of three entries with cycle number 200025 on the RACS 006. It would be nonsensical to expect a summary report of over 100,000 assessments to individually identify taxpayers. "It is well established in the tax law that an assessment is entitled to a legal presumption of correctness." *United States v. Fior D'Italia, Inc.,* 536 U.S. 238, 242, 122 S.Ct. 2117, 153 L.Ed.2d 280 (2002). The government met its burden to establish the presumption that the assessment occurred on July 3, 2000;[3] the Zarras did not adduce any evidence to refute this assessment date.

B. Whether the Zarras' Payment Satisfied Their Obligation

The Zarras contend that they have no outstanding tax liability because they submitted a valid check in the correct amount with sufficient funds available before the relevant deadline, and the check was presented and accepted, thus constituting payment. The court disagrees. A taxpayer has a "positive obligation to the United States: a duty to pay its tax." *Manning v. Seeley Tube & Box Co. of New Jersey,* 338 U.S. 561, 565, 70 S.Ct. 386, 94 L.Ed. 346 (1950). Unlike typical commercial transactions involving check payments, where finality and liquidity are important concerns, "Congress has given the IRS an extraordinarily broad mandate to enforce the internal revenue laws." *Wheeler v. United States,* 459 F.Supp.2d 399, 403 (W.D.Pa.2006). "[T]axes are the lifeblood of government,

---

[2] [fn 2] The minute entry provided in relevant part: "The government will turn over the signed RACS 006 form as it relates to the assessment on July 3, 2000, and make available an individual for a deposition who can provide a connection between the particular 4340 in this case and the RACS 006, and the deposition will be limited to the relevant information on those two forms." (Minute Entry 3/1/2011.)

[3] [fn 3] The government provided additional evidence of the assessment including an IRS employee declaration (Decl. of William Charlton ("Charlton Decl.") ¶ 5) and IRS transcripts of the Zarras' account. (P.R.D.C.S. Exs. A, B, and E.)

and their prompt and certain availability an imperious need." *Bull v. United States,* 295 U.S. 247, 259, 55 S.Ct. 695, 79 L.Ed. 1421 (1935).

There is no genuine dispute over the fact that the face amount of the check was $179,501,[4] and there is no question that a payment was posted to the Treasury. A deficiency remains, however, because only $179.50 was actually paid. Accordingly, the Zarras have not satisfied their duty to the government because they did not provide full payment of their tax obligation.[5]

Proffering several theories, the Zarras contend that the final posting of the check shifted their obligation to pay over to the banks as intermediaries. First, the Zarras point to some courts having held that an underencoded check has been "finally paid." *See infra.* Moreover, they argue the language of 13 PA. CONS.STAT. § 3310, particularly in light of these holdings, could be interpreted as discharging the Zarras' liability for the full face amount of the check. Second, the Zarras assert that pursuant to 13 PA. CONS.STAT. § 4209, banks warranty that the encoded amount of a check is correct and are liable for any errors. Third, the Zarras argue that the IRS could have and should have recovered the rest of the funds directly from the bank.

The Zarras' theories lack merit, however, because they (1) rely on inapplicable state law, (2) are not supported by case law, and (3) directly contravene the clear language of 26 U.S.C. § 6311. It is doubtful that the Zarras' theories would prevail under circumstances involving a typical commercial transaction. Regardless, § 6311 and relevant case law eliminate any doubt that the Zarras remain liable to the government for the outstanding balance. Even if a bank assumed liability for the entire face amount of the check, the Zarras cannot satisfy their continuing tax obligation until the government receives full payment.

First, the Uniform Commercial Code ("UCC") does not apply to the extent that it conflicts with the Internal Revenue Code.[6] "We . . . state flatly that the

---

[4] [fn 4] The Zarras do not dispute the amount that they originally owed for the 1999 tax year.

[5] [fn 5] The government maintains that collateral estoppel bars the Zarras' claim that they fulfilled their obligation. Although the Court of Appeals for the Third Circuit noted that "the Zarras' underlying tax liability has not been discharged," Zarra v. United States, 254 Fed.Appx. 931, 934 (3d Cir.2007), this conclusion was unnecessary to the holding that the district court lacked subject-matter jurisdiction. The court of appeals held that the Zarras failed to satisfy the Enochs v. Williams Packing & Nav. Co., 370 U.S. 1, 82 S.Ct. 1125, 8 L.Ed.2d 292 (1962), exception to 26 U.S.C. § 7421, because the IRS could prevail " 'under the most liberal view of the law and the facts.' " Id. (quoting *Williams Packing,* 370 U.S. at 7, 82 S.Ct. 1125). Thus, whether the Zarras' fully paid their liabilities to the government is a question properly before this court.

[6] [fn 6] Under Pennsylvania's statutory adoption of the UCC, "[i]f a note or an uncertified check is taken for an obligation, the obligation is suspended to the same extent the obligation would be discharged if an amount of money equal to the amount of the instrument were taken." 13 PA. CONS.STAT. § 3310(a). "In

Uniform Commercial Code does not govern the power of [the plaintiff] to administer the Federal income taxation system with respect to [the defendants]." *Hunt v. C.I.R.*, No. 10272, 1990 WL 90951, at *3 (T.C.M. July 3, 1990). Even if the court accepts the Zarras' proposal that the check was fully paid according to 13 PA. CONS.STAT. § 3310 or if, instead, that the payment by check is still suspended because neither dishonor nor full payment has occurred, 26 U.S.C. § 6311 controls the present circumstances and supersedes any contrary state rules or regulations.[7] The Zarras have not cited any case law for the proposition that the UCC governs the payment of their federal tax obligation.

Second, there is a paucity of case law addressing whether an obligation is discharged once a misencoded check is accepted by a bank, and the one case on point refutes the Zarras' argument. In *France v. Ford Motor Credit Co.*, 323 Ark. 167, 913 S.W.2d 770 (1996), a purchaser of a used tractor made two unsuccessful attempts to prepay the full obligation because both checks were underencoded, leaving an unpaid balance of $7,992. The court interpreted the similar Arkansas version of UCC § 3-310: "[T]he language of the statute leaves us with little doubt as to the proper resolution of this case. It does no more than recognize the uncertainty attendant upon an uncertified and unpaid check and suspends the obligation until that uncertainty is resolved." *Id.* at 772. The court held that the remaining obligation was not discharged because "[t]he suspense is over, and all are aware of the amount . . . which has yet to be satisfied." *Id.*[8]

Finally, 26 U.S.C. § 6311 clearly requires full payment before a taxpayer is relieved of his liability. "If a check . . . is not duly paid, or is paid and subsequently charged back to the Secretary, the person . . . shall remain liable for the payment of the tax . . . and for all legal penalties and additions, to the same extent as if such check . . . had not been tendered." 26 U.S.C. § 6311(b). "[S]ection 6311 yields a plain, unambiguous meaning . . . it supplies two means of protecting the interests of the United States in the event the [check] is not duly

---

the case of an uncertified check, suspension of the obligation continues until dishonor of the check or until it is paid or certified." 13 PA. CONS.STAT. § 3310(b)(1). "In plain words, payment is conditionally made when the creditor . . . accepts payment by a check from the debtor. . . .. If the check is honored, the condition is removed and payment relates back to the date of acceptance (i.e., receipt)." Romaine v. W.C.A.B., 587 Pa. 471, 901 A.2d 477, 485 (2006).

[7] "Conflict preemption nullifies state law inasmuch as it conflicts with federal law, either where compliance with both laws is impossible or where state law erects an 'obstacle to the accomplishment and execution of the full purposes and objectives of Congress.'" Farina v. Nokia Inc., 625 F.3d 97, 115 (3d Cir.2010) (quoting Hillsborough Cnty. v. Automated Med. Labs., Inc., 471 U.S. 707, 713, 105 S.Ct. 2371, 85 L.Ed.2d 714 (1985)).

[8] The Zarras disagree with this analysis, however, because the suspense was not over when the bank accepted the check. At any moment, the bank could have been alerted to or discovered the mistake and debited the remaining funds from the Zarras' account.

paid: the taxpayer remains liable for the taxes; and the United States may also have a lien on the assets of the bank." *United States v. Second Nat'l Bank of North Miami*, 502 F.2d 535, 540 (5th Cir.1974).[9] The word "duly" is defined as "[i]n a proper manner; in accordance with legal requirements." *Black's Law Dictionary* 540 (8th ed. 2004). Because the IRS received only $179.50, the Zarras remain liable for the outstanding balance that was not duly, or properly, paid.

In the context of a taxpayer's certified check, where the bank becomes liable to the government, the taxpayer continues to be liable until the government receives full payment. *See* 26 U.S.C. § 6311(c) (the government has a lien against the bank "in addition to its right to exact payment from the party originally indebted therefor"). Section 6311(c) is directly contrary to the relevant UCC provision.[10] If a certified check, which requires the bank to pay the check in full, does not discharge the taxpayer's obligation, then an underencoded, uncertified check certainly does not release the Zarras from their tax liability.

The above reasoning must be applied to each of the Zarras' arguments in turn. First, in the context of assigning loss and liability *among banks* that participate in a misencoded transaction, some courts have held that an underencoded check has been "finally paid." *See, e.g., First Nat'l Bank of Boston v. Fidelity Bank*, 724 F.Supp. 1168, 1172 (E.D.Pa.1989) ("I reject the argument that the [']amount of the item' for § 4–213(1) purposes is the encoded amount, rather than the face amount, of the check.").[11] Important policies support these holdings. "[T]he Board [of Governors of the Federal Reserve System] believes that finality of payment and the discharge of the underlying obligation are fundamental and

---

[9] [fn 9] The panel in *Second National Bank* recognized that paying taxes with checks is an added convenience that in no way diminishes the government's right to collect taxes due and owing. *Second National Bank*, 502 F.2d at 543 ("[A]t the same time that taxpayers were offered increased convenience, the government was to receive increased protection of its interest in receiving the taxes owing not only by retaining the right to pursue the taxpayer, but also by gaining the right to hold the respective bank or trust company for negotiable instruments not duly paid.").

[10] [fn 10] "[I]f a certified check . . . is taken for an obligation, the obligation is discharged to the same extent discharge would result if an amount of money equal to the amount of the instrument were taken in payment of the obligation." 13 PA. CONS.STAT. § 3310(a).

[11] [fn 11] *See also Georgia R.R. Bank & Trust Co. v. First Nat'l Bank & Trust Co. of Augusta*, 139 Ga.App. 683, 229 S.E.2d 482, 484 (Ga.Ct.App.1976) (finding that "posting of the item, although in a smaller amount than the true amount of the item, was sufficient to constitute final payment . . . the payor bank became accountable for the amount of the item."); *Azalea City Motels, Inc. v. First Alabama Bank of Mobile*, 551 So.2d 967, 976 (Ala.1989) (holding that "partial payment . . . constituted final payment . . . so that the drawee bank was rendered accountable for the full and proper amount of the item").

valuable features of the check collection process." Collections of Checks and Other Items by Federal Reserve Banks, 70 Fed. Reg. 71218, 71221 (Nov. 28, 2005) (to be codified at 12 C.F.R. pts. 210 and 229). In the present circumstances, however, the court addresses the liability between the parties and not how the banks should respond to the encoding error by reallocating accountability amongst themselves.

The Zarras urge the court to extend the above reasoning to obligations outside the banking system. In the case of an uncertified check, "[p]ayment or certification of the check results in discharge of the obligation to the extent of the *amount of the check.*" 13 PA. CONS.STAT. § 3310(b)(1) (emphasis added). The Zarras construe the "amount" to be the face amount of the check. In fact, the UCC uses different language in reference to payment by note. "Payment of the note results in discharge of the obligation to the *extent of the payment.*" 13 PA. CONS.STAT. § 3310(b)(2) (emphasis added). Although important policy considerations may support treating posted checks as final *within* the banking system and although the government was entitled to enforce the instrument to collect the remaining balance, 26 U.S.C. § 6311 embodies a countervailing public interest favoring full and timely payment of taxes and rejects the notion that the Zarras' obligation was completely satisfied.

Second, banks warranty accurate check encoding. "A person who encodes information . . . warrants to any subsequent collecting bank and to the payor bank or other payor that the information is correctly encoded. If the customer of a depositary bank encodes, that bank also makes the warranty." 13 PA. CONS.STAT. § 4209(a). "A person to whom warranties are made . . . may recover from the warrantor . . . an amount equal to the loss suffered as a result of the breach, plus expenses and loss of interest incurred as a result of the breach." 13 PA. CONS.STAT. § 4209(c). The court noted in *France,* however, that "[section 4209] provides warranties to collecting banks and payors but not to a payee." *France,* 913 S.W.2d at 772. Such a warranty, if applicable, would not release the Zarras from their tax obligation because the government did not receive full payment.

Finally, the Zarras contend the government could have collected the missing funds from the bank. "If a drawer wrote a check for $25,000 and the depositary bank encoded $2,500, the payor bank becomes liable for the full amount of the check." 13 PA. CONS.STAT. § 4209 cmt. 2. "Since the payor bank can debit the drawer's account for $25,000, the payor bank has a loss only to the extent that the drawer's account is less than the full amount of the check." *Id.* As explained before, however, the government's ability to collect funds from an additional party does not discharge the taxpayer's obligation. Moreover, the government would likely be precluded from taking action against the bank at this point because the statute of limitations has elapsed. *See* 13 PA. CONS.STAT. § 3118(f) ("An action to enforce the obligation of a party to pay an accepted draft, other than a certified check, must be commenced . . . within six years after the date of the acceptance if the obligation of the acceptor is payable on demand.").

The Zarras argue they are unable to revoke the final settlement of the check, *see* 13 PA. CONS.STAT. § 4303, and they should not be forced to submit double payment. When the Zarras viewed their monthly statement in May 2000 and discovered the encoding error, they easily could have written another check or taken other action to cause the funds in their bank account to be used for payment of their obligation. Instead, the Zarras continued to write checks for other purposes and depleted the balance in their account.

The Zarras maintain that sending a second check would have potentially subjected them to double payment because the bank might yet debit their account to honor the original check. Interestingly, this theory does not squarely address the Zarras' continuing duty to satisfy their obligation to the government. The Zarras could have asked the government not to collect the remaining funds on the original check or requested reimbursement for losses if their account became overdrawn. Although the Zarras initially sought to satisfy their 1999 tax obligation, their payment by check was only conditional. Difficulties in making payment after May 2000 did not extinguish the Zarras' 1999 tax obligation to the government.

In sum, the Zarras did not adequately support their novel contention that an underencoded check discharges a tax obligation to the federal government to the full extent of the face amount of the check. A check does not release a tax liability until the government receives full payment. Although the Zarras were not responsible for the encoding error and although they contacted the IRS regarding the mistake, the Zarras clearly did not satisfy their tax obligation to the government for the 1999 tax year.

C. Laches, Waiver, and Equitable Estoppel

The Zarras assert the affirmative defenses of laches, waiver, and equitable estoppel to preclude the government from collecting the outstanding balance. The statute of limitations on IRS claims, however, has not run. *See* 26 U.S.C. § 6502(a)(1). The authority of the IRS to collect taxes owed within ten years after assessment overwhelms these common law doctrines, which are extraordinary remedies that are not warranted under the present circumstances.

First, "[i]t is well established that the United States is not subject to the defense of laches in enforcing its rights." United States v. St. John's Gen. Hosp., 875 F.2d 1064, 1071 (3d Cir.1989) (citing United States v. Summerlin, 310 U.S. 414, 416, 60 S.Ct. 1019, 84 L.Ed. 1283 (1940)). Thus, the Zarras cannot properly assert the affirmative defense of laches. Second, a waiver is "an intentional relinquishment or abandonment of a known right or privilege." Johnson v. Zerbst, 304 U.S. 458, 464, 58 S.Ct. 1019, 82 L.Ed. 1461 (1938). Equitable relief, such as waiver, is left to the discretion of the court. See, e.g., James v. Richman, 547 F.3d 214, 217 (3d Cir.2008). The Zarras did not demonstrate that the government voluntarily and intentionally abandoned or relinquished its known right to collect the remaining balance of taxes owed. On the contrary, less than one year after the encoding error, the government asserted its rights and demanded full payment. Thus, the Zarras cannot properly assert the affirmative defense of waiver.

Finally, "[i]n order to prevail on a traditional estoppel defense, a defendant must prove a misrepresentation upon which the defendant reasonably relied to his detriment." *St. John's,* 875 F.2d at 1069 (citations omitted). Moreover, "affirmative misconduct" must be shown before estoppel against the government can even be contemplated. *United States v. Pepperman,* 976 F.2d 123, 131 (3d Cir.1992). Estoppel is only appropriate in "rare and extreme circumstances" where the " 'interest of citizens in some minimum standard of decency, honor, and reliability in their dealings with their Government' " is imperiled. *Id.* (quoting *Heckler v. Community Health Servs.,* 467 U.S. 51, 61, 104 S.Ct. 2218, 81 L.Ed.2d 42 (1984)). "Estoppel claims have traditionally been put to especial rigor in the taxation context." *Bachner v. C.I.R.,* 81 F.3d 1274, 1282 (3d Cir.1996). Although an error occurred when the Zarras' check was processed, the government did not misrepresent material facts, and the Zarras could not have justifiably relied on the inaccurate encoding. Moreover, less than one year after the encoding error, the government asserted its rights and demanded full payment. Under these circumstances, the government never gave the Zarras any indication that they were relieved of their 1999 tax obligation. Thus, the Zarras cannot properly assert the affirmative defense of equitable estoppel.

D. Interest and Penalties

Because the Zarras have an outstanding tax liability, the Zarras, unless there is an applicable statutory exception, would owe interest on the unpaid balance dating back to the date the taxes were due. "If any amount of tax . . . is not paid on or before the last date prescribed for payment, interest . . . shall be paid for the period from such last date to the date paid." 26 U.S.C. § 6601(a). "Unless a statutory exception applies, neither the IRS nor the courts have discretion to excuse a taxpayer from payment of interest." *Anderson Columbia Co., Inc. v. United States,* 54 Fed.Cl. 756, 758 (Fed.Cl.2002) (citing *Johnson v. United States,* 602 F.2d 734, 738 (6th Cir.1979)). "In the absence of a clear legislative expression to the contrary, the question of who properly should possess the right of use of the money owed the Government for the period it is owed must be answered in favor of the Government." *Manning,* 338 U.S. at 566, 70 S.Ct. 386.

The Zarras failed to "pay the amount shown as tax" on their return. 26 U.S.C. § 6651(a)(2). They are, therefore, subject to mandatory penalties unless they demonstrate that this failure was due to "reasonable cause" and not due to "willful neglect." 26 U.S.C. § 6651(a). "[T]he Congressional purpose behind the penalty provision [is] to encourage the payment of taxes when due." *Industrial Indemnity v. Snyder,* 41 B.R. 882, 884 (Bankr.E.D.Wash.1984) (citation omitted). "To escape the penalty, the taxpayer bears the heavy burden of proving both (1) that the failure did not result from 'willful neglect,' and (2) that the failure was 'due to reasonable cause.' " *United States v. Boyle,* 469 U.S. 241, 245, 105 S.Ct. 687, 83 L.Ed.2d 622 (1985) (quoting 26 U.S.C. § 6651(a)(1)). "[T]he term 'willful neglect' may be read as meaning a conscious, intentional failure or reckless indifference." *Id.* (citations omitted). Regarding "reasonable cause" for failure to pay, a taxpayer must demonstrate that he "exercised ordinary business care and prudence in providing for payment of his tax liability and was nevertheless either unable to pay the tax or would suffer an undue hardship . . . if he paid on the due date." 26 C.F.R. § 301.6651–1(c)(1). "The principle underlying the IRS regulations and practices [is] that a taxpayer should not be penalized for circumstances beyond his control." *Boyle,* 469 U.S. at 249 n. 6, 105 S.Ct. 687.

Under the present circumstances, the Zarras' failure to pay their taxes was not due to "reasonable cause." There is no evidence of financial hardship or an inability to pay *at the time* the taxes were due. *See, e.g., East Wind Indus., Inc. v. United States,* 196 F.3d 499, 500–01 (3d Cir.1999). On the contrary, there were sufficient funds in the Zarras' account when they discovered that the check had been incorrectly processed and there is no evidence of illness or physical disability. *See, e.g., Erickson v. C.I.R.,* 172 B.R. 900 (Bankr.D.Minn.1994) (a quadriplegic debtor exercised care and prudence, relying on another due to his inability to perform the filings and make the payments himself). Although the Zarras argue that they failed to satisfy their obligation due to a mistake of law, *see, e.g., L.L. Morris Transp. Co. v. United States,* No. 76–47, 1980 WL 1580, at *4 (W.D.Ky. Feb. 25, 1980) (a transportation company was not unreasonable in concluding that a refining company had assumed responsibility for remitting the federal excise tax due), "ordinary business care and prudence," 26 C.F.R. § 301.6651–1(c)(1), would require that they make full payment once they discovered the error. Moreover, the IRS dispelled any notion that the Zarras were in compliance when it demanded full payment less than one year after the error occurred. The government never made any contrary representation upon which the Zarras could have relied. Stated concisely, ensuring full payment of their 1999 tax obligation was well within the Zarras' control.[12]

Additionally, after the Zarras became aware of the insufficient payment, their decision to spend their resources on other matters could be viewed as "reckless indifference" or even "intentional failure." The Zarras made the conscious decision not to submit a second check or find an alternative method to pay their outstanding tax obligation. Indeed, they eventually spent the funds in the account instead of paying their tax obligation. Under these circumstances, it would have been unreasonable for the Zarras to believe that their tax obligation to the government was satisfied. Thus, the Zarras failed to demonstrate that their failure was not due to "willful neglect."

In sum, the Zarras owe interest on their unpaid balance beginning on the date the taxes were due. In addition, the Zarras have not met their heavy burden to escape the mandatory penalties for failing to pay their taxes. If the Zarras had quickly corrected the mistake after they viewed their bank statement in May 2000, they would have had a compelling argument that an exception was warranted. Under the present circumstances, however, it would be disingenuous for the

---

[12] [fn 12] The Zarras' present financial condition is irrelevant in determining whether they would have suffered an undue hardship on the date the taxes were due.

Zarras to claim that satisfying their obligation to the government was outside their control.

IV. CONCLUSION

The Zarras did not pay their taxes in full for the 1999 tax year. They have not demonstrated any legitimate excuse, justification, or affirmative defense. No reasonable jury could conclude that there is any genuine issue of material fact for this case to proceed to trial. The government's motion for summary judgment must be granted and the Zarras' motion for summary judgment will be denied. An appropriate order shall follow.

NOTES AND QUESTIONS

1. Could the Zarras have sued the bank?
2. What could the Zarras have done after the IRS ignored their calls?

B. Sufficiency of Payment

The government makes it easy to pay taxes. Section 6311(a), which authorizes the government to accept payment, provides as follows:

> It shall be lawful for the Secretary to receive for internal revenue taxes (or in payment for internal revenue stamps) any commercially acceptable means that the Secretary deems appropriate to the extent and under the conditions provided in regulations prescribed by the Secretary.

The IRS accepts payments in many forms, including credit cards, checks, currency, and debit cards. The IRS also permits taxpayers to pay electronically when e-filing. Most of the revenue the IRS collects, however, comes from requiring employers to withhold from wages their employees' anticipated taxes. *See* IRC § 3402(a). If there is a sufficient gap between withholding and the amount due, a taxpayer may be required to pay quarterly estimated tax payments. *See* IRC § 6654.

Although the government makes it easy to pay taxes in many different forms, the government is not required to accept payment in forms that are worthless.

GOFF v. COMMISSIONER
135 T.C. 231 (2010)
United States Tax Court

HALPERN, Judge:

This case is before the Court to determine whether respondent may proceed with the collection of petitioner's unpaid Federal income tax for 1996 through 2006 and unpaid civil penalties for filing frivolous income tax returns for 1997, 1999, 2000, 2003, and 2004 (collectively, petitioner's liabilities or, simply, the liabilities). We review the determinations under section 6330(d)(1).

All section references are to the Internal Revenue Code of 1986, as amended and as applicable to this case, and all Rule references are to the Tax Court Rules of Practice and Procedure unless otherwise indicated.

The case presents two questions:

1. Whether a "Bonded Promissory Note" in the face amount of $5 million (the note) that petitioner submitted to the Internal Revenue Service (IRS) constitutes payment of the liabilities; and

2. whether we should impose an additional penalty on petitioner pursuant to section 6673 for instituting this proceeding primarily for delay or advancing a position that is frivolous or groundless.

FINDINGS OF FACT[13]

When she filed the petition, petitioner resided in Utah.

Respondent notified petitioner of his intent to collect petitioner's liabilities by levy, and, in response thereto, petitioner requested a pre-levy hearing with Appeals under section 6330.

During that hearing, petitioner argued that she had paid the liabilities by means of the note, which she had sent to the IRS. Respondent's Appeals Office (Appeals) team manager Sharon Patterson (Ms. Patterson) rejected petitioner's claim that the liabilities had been paid, and the determinations, signed by Ms. Patterson, followed.

Petitioner timely filed the petition, assigning error to the determinations primarily on the ground that "Payment for all liabilities alleged by IRS for LISA S GOFF, TIN * * * was tendered by Harvey Douglas Goff, Jr., hereinafter, 'Undersigned' on or about January 17, 2008." Petitioner added:

---

[13] [fn 1] At the conclusion of the trial, the Court set a schedule for opening and answering briefs and ordered the parties to file such briefs. The Court directed petitioner's attention to Rule 151, which addresses briefs, and, in particular, to Rule 151(e), which addresses the form and content of briefs. We have accepted from petitioner what appears to be her opening brief, although it does not contain proposed findings of fact, as Rule 151(e)(3) requires, or otherwise conform to the requirements of that Rule. Petitioner filed no answering brief. Respondent filed an opening brief with proposed findings of fact and otherwise conforming to Rule 151(e). Apparently seeing no need to answer petitioner's brief, respondent declined to file an answering brief. Pursuant to Rule 151(e)(3), each party, in its answering brief, must "set forth any objections, together with the reasons therefor, to any proposed findings of any other party". Petitioner did not file an answering brief and did not set forth objections to respondent's proposed findings of fact. Accordingly, we must conclude that petitioner has conceded that respondent's proposed findings of fact are correct except to the extent that those findings are clearly inconsistent with evidence in the record. See, e.g., Jonson v. Commissioner, 118 T.C. 106, 108 n. 4, 2002 WL 199830 (2002), affd. 353 F.3d 1181 (10th Cir.2003). Respondent, of course, is not similarly disadvantaged because petitioner's opening brief contained no proposed findings of fact.

Contrary to IRS' claim, Petitioner, at all relevant times prior to the * * * [section 6330] hearing and during the hearing itself, challenged the existence of a tax liability in that, the Undersigned tendered sufficient payment for the alleged liability and IRS failed to post the funds to the proper account.

Petitioner also assigned error on the ground that "The proposed levy, would trespass on a bona fide lien held by the Undersigned and thereby cause irreparable injury to the Undersigned."

The "Undersigned" referred to is petitioner's husband, Harvey D. Goff, Jr. (Mr. Goff). Both he and petitioner signed a document prepared by Mr. Goff, attached to the petition, which set forth petitioner's assignments of error and the facts on which she relies. Among the facts on which she relies are the following:

1. On or about March 20, 2007, the Undersigned deposits a bond with the Secretary of the Treasury upon which the Undersigned states his intention to draw against the proceeds of said bond in satisfaction of debts. The Undersigned, according to the terms of the bond order, grants the Secretary a thirty-day opportunity in which to return said bond to the Undersigned or, in the alternative accept the Undersigned's bond and terms.

2. Upon expiration of said 30–day opportunity, the Undersigned receives no communication from the Secretary, and said bond is not returned to the Undersigned. Accordingly, the Secretary accepts said bond pursuant to the terms of said bond.

3. On or about September 7, 2007, the Undersigned deposits, with the Secretary of the Treasury, a Private Discharging and Indemnity Bond No. RA819570054US–HDG subordinate to the March 20, 2007 bond which is issued pursuant to the Undersigned's full faith and credit. The stated purpose of said Private Discharging and Indemnity Bond is to indemnify, among others, the TIN assigned to Petitioner, the Petitioner, Internal Revenue Service and all subdivisions, agents and employees thereof. The terms of said Private Discharging and Indemnity Bond state that the Undersigned grants the Secretary the opportunity to return said bond within thirty days of receipt.

4. Upon expiration of said 30–day opportunity, the Undersigned receives no communication from the Secretary, and said Private Discharging and Indemnity Bond is not returned. Accordingly, the Secretary accepts said Private Discharging and Indemnity Bond pursuant to the terms of said bond.

5. At the Undersigned's instruction, during December 2007, Petitioner requests a consolidating billing from IRS that includes all amounts which IRS alleges were owed by Petitioner.

6. On or about January 11, 2008, Petitioner receives a letter identified as LTR 681C with reference # 0774035504 alleging a total amount due of $36,354.16.

7. On or about January 17, 2008, the Undersigned tenders payment for Petitioner's account through Notary Public Kevin P. Mahoney in the form of Bonded Promissory Note No. HDG–1005–PN in the amount of $5,000,000.00 using Certified Mail No. 7001 1140 0002 9580 3371.

8. Said promissory note is payable to Secretary of the United States Treasury * * *

The note tendered in alleged payment of petitioner's liabilities contains in part the following:

BONDED PROMISSORY NOTE

Registered via Utah Department of Commerce, Division of Corporations and UCC File No.* * * USPS CERTIFIED MAIL TRACKING NO.* * *

—— $5,000,000.00 ——

Five Million and 00/100 United States Dollars

To the Order of: Henry M Paulson, Jr. d/b/a Secretary of the United States Treasury, P.S. Lane d/b/a Operations Mgr., ACS Remote Ops. 1, Internal Revenue Service and Fiduciary Trustee

In the Amount of: Five Million and 00/100 United States Dollars ($5,000,000.00)

For Credit to: Internal Revenue Service Account * * * to the benefit of LISA STEPHENS GOFF A/K/A LISA GOFF * * * SS No. * * *

Routing Through: (Securitization Bond) Private Discharging and Indemnity Bond No. RA819570054US–HDG to Secretary of the Treasury Henry M. Paulson, Jr. * * *

This negotiable instrument, tendered lawfully by Harvey Douglas Goff Jr. ("Maker") in good faith shall evidence as a debt to the Payee pursuant to the following terms:

1. This Note shall be posted *in full* dollar for dollar pursuant to the above credit order and presented to the co-payee, Secretary of the Treasury Henry M. Paulson, Jr. by the Fiduciary(ies) in the attached preaddressed envelope by certified mail/RR (certificates completed and supplied) or electronic transfer.

2. Upon receipt of this instrument, Payee shall charge account * * * via Pass–Through Account H DOUGLAS GOFF * * * for the purpose of terminating any past, present, or future liabilities express or implied attached or attributed to Account No.* * * and/or Lisa Stephens Goff * * *

3. Payee shall ledger this Note for a period of thirty (30) days commencing the start of business on 16 January 2008 until close of business 14 February 2008 at an interest rate of seven percent (7%) per annum;

4. Upon maturity, this Note shall be due and payable in full with interest and any associated fees. Payment shall be posted in accordance with generally accepted accounting principles against *Private Discharging and Indemnity Bond No. RA819570054US–HDG* (Tracking Number RA 819 570 054 US) held and secured by Henry M. Paulsen, Jr., Secretary of the United States Treasury.

16 January 2008

Date

/s/ Harvey Douglas Goff, Jr.

Authorized Signature

At the bottom of the note, the names and addresses of five individuals were listed, presumably to show the person who issued the note (Mr. Goff), the persons who were to receive the note as payment (Henry M. Paulson, Jr., Secretary of the Treasury, and Linda E. Stiff, Acting Commissioner of the IRS), and those considered to be fiduciaries (P.S. Lane, Operations Manager, IRS, and Renee A. Mitchell, Director, Campus Compliance Operations, IRS).

Along with the note, petitioner sent processing instructions to the IRS on how the note was to be posted as payment of petitioner's liabilities. The note and processing instructions purported to place a legal duty on the IRS to apply up to $5 million toward the liabilities. The IRS ignored the note and processing instructions and did not on account thereof apply any amount in payment of petitioner's liabilities.

After filing the petition, petitioner attended a conference with respondent's counsel, who warned her that her position was frivolous.

Our notice setting this case for trial informed petitioner that, if the case could not be settled, then "the parties, before trial, must agree in writing to all facts and all documents about which there should be no disagreement." Our accompanying standing pretrial order required the parties to prepare and submit pretrial memoranda, setting forth basic information about the case.

Petitioner both refused to enter into a stipulation of facts and failed to submit a pretrial memorandum.

As discussed *supra* note 1, at the conclusion of the trial, we set a briefing schedule and directed the parties to submit briefs. When petitioner did not submit an opening brief on schedule, we extended the time for her to comply. In reply, we received documents from Mr. Goff, which we filed as petitioner's opening brief. Those documents in no way comply with Rule 151(e), addressing the form and content of briefs. In part, one of those documents states as follows:

> Thank you for your offer for my DEBTOR, LISA S GOFF, to file an opening brief by close of business April 28, 2010. Said offer is cast as a court order and a copy of said order is enclosed.

I accept your offer for value in behalf [sic] of myself and my debtor for sixty million four hundred thousand and 00/100 dollars ($60,400,000.00) and bill you and the court for my services in the matter.

A second document states:

It comes to my attention that the UNITED STATES TAX COURT is a for-profit corporation and is listed with Dunn & Bradstreet as such. * * *

Are you aware of and do you realize the liability you personally incur in acting as an agent for the incorporated UNITED STATES TAX COURT?

OPINION

I. Review of the Determinations

Section 6330(a) provides taxpayers with the opportunity to request an administrative review of the Commissioner's decision to take administrative action to collect by levy any tax owing. Appeals conducts that review, sec. 6330(b)(1), and, as stated, we review respondent's determinations under section 6330(d)(1). On the facts before us, we review those determinations de novo. *Boyd v. Commissioner,* 117 T.C. 127, 131, 2001 WL 1150032 (2001); *Landry v. Commissioner,* 116 T.C. 60, 62, 2001 WL 77050 (2001).

Respondent may proceed by levy to collect petitioner's liabilities. Simply put, neither the note nor anything in connection with the note constitutes payment of petitioner's liabilities. The United States Code provides that "coins and currency (including Federal reserve notes and circulating notes of Federal reserve' banks and national banks) are legal tender for all debts, public charges, taxes, and dues." 31 U.S.C. sec. 5103 (2006). Section 6311 addresses alternative methods of payment and authorizes the Secretary to receive for taxes any commercially acceptable means that he deems appropriate as prescribed by regulations. Sec. 6311(a), (d). No regulation issued by the Secretary allows private bonds or notes such as the note to be considered payment by commercially acceptable means. Other types of payment are not acceptable; e.g., the Commissioner has refused to accept real property in payment for tax liabilities. Rev. Rul. 76–350, 1976–2 C.B. 396. Similarly, the Commissioner is not obligated to accept an individual's personal property in satisfaction of her tax liabilities. E.g., *Calafut v. Commissioner,* 277 F.Supp. 266, 267 (M.D.Pa.1967).

At the conclusion of the trial, the Court asked petitioner to provide the Court with any argument as to why the note discharged her obligation to pay the liabilities. Petitioner answered only that her husband had tendered the note and she had not been advised by anyone of any defect in the note, nor had anyone returned it. Petitioner's brief adds nothing to that answer. Petitioner did not address at trial or on brief any other error that she had assigned to the determinations, including her claim that the proposed levy would trespass on a bona fide lien her husband held. We therefore consider that she has abandoned those assignments of error. See *Mendes v. Commissioner,* 121 T.C. 308, 312–313, 2003 WL 22927149 (2003) ("If an argument is not pursued on brief, we may consider that it has been abandoned."). We see no reason not to sustain the determinations, and we shall sustain them.

II. Section 6673(a)(1) Penalty

Under section 6673(a)(1), this Court may require a taxpayer to pay a penalty not in excess of $25,000 if (1) the taxpayer has instituted or maintained a proceeding primarily for delay, or (2) the taxpayer's position is "frivolous or groundless". A taxpayer's position is frivolous if it is contrary to established law and unsupported by a reasoned, colorable argument for change in the law. E.g., *Nis Family Trust v. Commissioner*, 115 T.C. 523, 544, 2000 WL 1772511 (2000). There is no support for petitioner's claim that the note discharged her obligation to pay the liabilities, and she has made no argument beyond her claim that the Government did not return the note or point out its defects. Moreover, she refused to enter into a stipulation of facts and disobeyed our order to submit a pretrial memorandum. She did not comply with the briefing schedule we set. When, in response to our order extending her time to file a brief, we received documents from her husband, they contained a ridiculous demand for money and a nonsensical claim that the Court is a for-profit corporation. Petitioner's principal position in this case is so weak as to be groundless, and her argument in support of that position is frivolous. Indeed, we can see no reason for this case other than delaying respondent's collection of tax liabilities and penalties for the 11 years in issue. Respondent's counsel warned petitioner that her position was frivolous. Petitioner has wasted both the Court's and respondent's limited resources and deserves a significant penalty. We shall, therefore require petitioner to pay a penalty under section 6673(a)(1) of $15,000.

An appropriate order and decision will be entered.

NOTES AND QUESTIONS

1. Why did the IRS not just cash the bond? Was the IRS being obstinate here?
2. Are there circumstances where the IRS would accept an IOU?

Not all remittances to the IRS constitute tax payments. Taxpayers may also submit deposits from which taxes will eventually be paid. Whether a remittance constitutes a payment or a deposit has surprisingly been the subject of a fair amount of litigation.

ROSENMAN v. UNITED STATES
323 U.S. 658 (1945)
Supreme Court of the United States

Mr. Justice FRANKFURTER delivered the opinion of the Court.

This is an action upon a claim for refund of a federal estate tax, and the specific question before us is whether the claim was asserted too late. The matter is governed by s 319(b) of the Revenue Act of 1926, 44 Stat. 9, 84, as amended by s 810(a) of the Revenue Act of 1932, 47 Stat. 169, 283, 26 U.S.C. s 910, 26 U.S.C.A. Int.Rev.Code, s 910, reading as follows:

'All claims for the refunding of the tax imposed by this title alleged to have been erroneously or illegally assessed or collected must be presented to the Commissioner within three years next after the payment of such tax. The amount of the refund shall not exceed the portion of the tax paid during the three years immediately preceding the filing of the claim, or if no claim was filed, then during the three years immediately preceding the allowance of the refund.'

Petitioners are executors of the will of Louis Rosenman, who died on December 25, 1933. Under appropriate statutory authority, the Commissioner of Internal Revenue extended the time for filing the estate tax return to February 25, 1935. But there was no extension of the time for payment of the tax which became due one year after the decedent's death, on December 25, 1934. The day before, petitioners delivered to the Collector of Internal Revenue a check for $120,000, the purpose of which was thus defined in a letter of transmittal: 'We are delivering to you herewith, by messenger, an Estate check payable to your order, for $120,000, as a payment on account of the Federal Estate tax. * * * This payment is made under protest and duress, and solely for the purpose of avoiding penalties and interest, since it is contended by the executors that not all of this sum is legally or lawfully due.' This amount was placed by the Collector in a suspense account to the credit of the estate. In the books of the Collector the suspense account concerns moneys received in connection with federal estate taxes and other miscellaneous taxes if, as here, no assessment for taxes is outstanding at the time. On February 25, 1935, petitioners filed their estate tax return according to which there was due from the estate $80,224.24. On March 28, 1935, the Collector advised petitioners that $80,224.24 of the $120,000 to their credit in the suspense account had been applied in satisfaction of the amount of the tax assessed under their return. On the basis of this notice, petitioners, on March 26, 1938, filed a claim for $39,775.76, the balance between the $120,000 paid by them under protest and the assessed tax of $80,224.24.

Upon completion, after nearly three years, of the audit of the return, the Commissioner determined that the total net tax due was $128,759.08. No appeal to the Board of Tax Appeals having been taken, a deficiency of $48,534.84 was assessed. The Collector thereupon applied the balance of $39,775.76 standing to the credit of petitioners in the suspense account in partial satisfaction of this deficiency, and on April 22, 1938, petitioners paid to the Collector the additional amount of $10,497.34, which covered the remainder of the deficiency plus interest. The Commissioner then rejected the petitioners' claim for refund filed in March of that year. On May 20, 1940, petitioners filed with the Collector a claim, based on additional deductions, for refund of $24,717.12. The claim was rejected on the ground, so far as now relevant, that the tax claimed to have been illegally exacted had been paid more than three years prior to the filing of the claim, except at to the amount of $10,497.34 paid by petitioners in 1938. Petitioners brought this suit in the Court of Claims which held that recovery for the amount here in dispute was barred by statute, 53 F.Supp. 722, 101 Ct.Cl. 437. To resolve an asserted conflict of decisions in the lower courts we brought the case here. 323 U.S. 691, 65 S.Ct. 52.

Claims for tax refunds must conform strictly to the requirements of Congress. A claim for refund of an estate tax 'alleged to have been erroneously or illegally assessed or collected must be presented to the Commissioner within three years next after the payment of such tax.' On the face of it, this requirement is couched in ordinary English, and since no extraneous relevant aids to construction have been called to our attention, Congress has evidently meant what these words ordinarily convey. The claim is for refund of a tax 'alleged to have been erroneously or illegally assessed or collected', and the claim must have been filed 'after the payment of such tax', that is, within three years after payment of a tax which according to the claim was erroneously or illegally collected. The crux of the matter is the alleged illegal assessment or collection, and 'payment of such tax' plainly presupposes challenged action by the taxing officials.

The action here complained of was the assessment of a deficiency by the Commissioner in April 1938. Before that time there were no taxes 'erroneously or illegally assessed or collected' for the collection of which petitioners could have filed a claim for refund. The amount then demanded as a deficiency by the Commissioner was, so the petitioners claimed, erroneously assessed. It is this erroneous assessment that gave rise to a claim for refund. Not until then was there such a claim as could start the time running for presenting the claim. In any responsible sense payment was then made by the application of the balance credited to the petitioners in the suspense account and by the additional payment of $10,497.34 on April 22, 1938. Both these events occurred within three years of May 20, 1940, when the petitioners' present claim was filed.

But the Government contends 'payment of such tax' was made on December 24, 1934, when petitioners transferred to the Collector a check for $120,000. This stopped the running of penalties and interest, says the Government, and therefore is to be treated as a payment by the parties. But on December 24, 1934, the taxpayer did not discharge what he deemed a liability nor pay one that was asserted. There was merely an interim arrangement to cover whatever contingencies the future might define. The tax obligation did not become defined until April 1938. And this is the practical construction which the Government has placed upon such arrangements. The Government does not consider such advances of estimated taxes as tax payments. They are, as it were, payments in escrow. They are set aside, as we have noted, in special suspense accounts established for depositing money received when no assessment is then outstanding against the taxpayer. The receipt by the Government of moneys under such an arrangement carries no more significance than would the giving of a surety bond. Money in these accounts is held not as taxes duly collected are held but as a deposit made in the nature of a cash bond for the payment of taxes thereafter found to be due. See Ruling of the Camptroller General, A48307, April 14, 1933, 1 (1935) Prentice-Hall Tax Service, Special Reports, paragraph 45. Accordingly, where taxpayers have sued for interest on the 'overpayment' of moneys received under similar conditions, the Government has insisted that the arrangement was merely a 'deposit' and not a 'payment' interest on which is due from the Government if there is an excess beyond the amount of the tax eventually assessed. See Busser v. United States, 3 Cir., 130 F.2d 537, 538; Atlantic Oil Producing Co. v. United States, 35 F.Supp. 766, 92 Ct.Cl. 441; Moses v. United States, D.C., 28 F.Supp. 817; Chicago Title & Trust Co. v. United States, D.C., 45 F.Supp. 323; Estate of Rogers v. Commissioner, 1942 Prentice-Hall B.T.A. Memoragraph Decisions, paragraph 42,275. If it is not payment in order to relieve the Government from paying interest on a subsequently determined excess, it cannot be payment to bar suit by the taxpayer for its illegal retention. It will not do to treat the same transaction as payment and not as payment, whichever favors the Government. See United States v. Wurts, 303 U.S. 414, 58 S.Ct. 637, 82 L.Ed. 932.

Exaction of interest from the Government requires statutory authority, and it merely carries out the true nature of an arrangement such as this to treat it as an estimated deposit and not as a payment which, if in excess of what should properly have been exacted, entitled the taxpayer to interest as the return on the use that the Government has had of moneys that should not have been exacted. (We need not here consider the effect of the Current Tax Payment Act of 1943, s 4(d), 57 Stat. 126, 140, 26 U.S.C.A. Int.Rev.Code, s 3770(c).) On the other hand, by allowing such a deposit arrangement, the Government safeguards collection of the assessment of whatever amount tax officials may eventually find owing from a taxpayer, while the taxpayer in turn is saved the danger of penalties on an assessment made, as in this case, years after a fairly estimated return has been filed. The construction which in our view the statute compels safeguards the interests of the Government, interprets a business transaction according to its tenor, and avoids gratuitous resentment in the relations between Treasury and taxpayer.

Reversed.

NOTES AND QUESTIONS

1. What difference did it make whether the remittance was a payment or a deposit?
2. The *Rosenman* case involved the pursuit of a refund of an estate tax. What would the result have been under the modern income tax? *See* IRC § 6513(b).

DEATON v. COMMISSIONER
440 F.3d 223 (2006)
United States Court of Appeals, Fifth Circuit

Before GARWOOD, DeMOSS and BENAVIDES, Circuit Judges.
Opinion
DeMOSS, Circuit Judge:

Barbara and Ronny Deaton (the "Deatons") appeal a decision of the United States Tax Court (the "Tax Court") sustaining a finding of the Internal Revenue Service Appeals Office (the "Appeals Office") that the Deatons' 1994 remittance of $125,000—which accompanied their Form 4868 application for an extension of time to file their 1993 tax return—was a "payment," not a "deposit," and that as such, it could not be credited against the Deatons' 1994-1996 tax liabilities because it fell outside the "look-back period" of I.R.C. § 6511(b)(2)(A).

I. FACTS AND PROCEEDINGS

On April 15, 1994, the deadline for filing a 1993 U.S. Individual Income Tax Return, the Deatons filed a Form 4868 with the Internal Revenue Service (IRS) to extend the time for filing their return. Form 4868, titled "Application for Automatic Extension of Time to File U.S. Individual Income Tax Return," automatically extends a taxpayer's time to file his return if the taxpayer meets certain conditions; however, it does not extend the time to pay tax. *See* Treas. Reg. § 1.6081-4(b) (1993) ("[A]ny automatic extension of time for filing an individual income tax return . . . shall not operate to extend the time for payment of any tax due on such return.").[14] To qualify for a Form 4868 automatic extension of time to file, the Deatons had to "[p]roperly estimate [their] 1993 tax liability using the information available to [them], [e]nter [their] tax liability on line 1 of Form 4868, [and] [f]ile Form 4868 by the due date of [their] return." I.R.S. Instructions for Form 4868 (Cat. No. 15385N) (1993); *see also* Treas. Reg. § 1.6081-4(a)(4) (1993) ("Such application for extension must show the full amount properly estimated as tax for such taxpayer for such taxable year . . . .."). Although the Deatons were not required to remit any amount to the IRS with their form, *see* I.R.S. Instructions for Form 4868 (Cat. No. 15385N) (1993) ("If you find you can't pay the full amount shown on line 3, you can still get the extension."),[15] the instructions to Form 4868 indicated that a taxpayer would be liable for interest and possibly a late payment penalty if he submitted less than the full amount of estimated taxes with his form, *id.*

To avoid incurring interest and any late payment penalty, the Deatons submitted to the IRS with their Form 4868 a check in the amount of $125,000, which they calculated as the line 3 "balance due" after deducting payments of $13,883 (in the form of withholdings) from their estimated tax liability of $138,883. Following receipt of the form, the IRS extended the Deatons' deadline for filing their 1993 return by six months; however, the Deatons missed the extended deadline and in fact did not file their 1993 return until January 2000,

---

[14] [fn 1] The 1993 version of Form 4868 clearly stated under its title, "This is not an extension of time to pay your tax." I.R.S. Form 4868 (OMB No. 1545-0188) (1993).

[15] [fn 2] Until 1992, full payment was a condition of receiving an extension; however, the IRS removed that condition in 1992 so that taxpayers who were unable to pay the full amount of estimated taxes could nevertheless obtain an automatic four-month filing extension and relief from late-filing penalties. *See* I.R.S. Notice 92-22, 1993-1 C.B. 305.

nearly six years after its due date. The Deatons also failed to file timely returns for the tax years 1994, 1995, and 1996.

On January 10, 2000, the Deatons filed delinquent returns for the tax years 1993 through 1996. On their 1993 return, they reported a tax liability of only $88,662, which indicated that they had overestimated their 1993 tax liability on Form 4868 by $50,221. The Deatons requested that this overpayment be carried forward and credited as a payment toward their tax liabilities for the years following 1993.

Shortly after the IRS received the Deatons' 1993-1996 tax returns, it formally assessed the amounts reported as tax on each of the returns. For 1993, the IRS applied the amount already paid by withholding ($13,883) and the April 1994 remittance ($125,000) to the reported tax liability of $88,662. The IRS then posted the resulting overpayment of $50,221 to an "excess collections" account and did not carry it forward on the Deatons' account as a credit for subsequent tax years as the Deatons requested. According to the IRS, the Deatons' credit request was barred by I.R.C. § 6511(b)(2)(A), which limits the amount of a credit or refund claimed by a taxpayer to the amount paid within the "look-back period" under that subsection, that is, the three years (plus the period of any extension of time for filing the return) immediately preceding the filing of the claim. I.R.C. § 6511(b)(2)(A). The Deatons had paid nothing to the IRS within the applicable look-back period, which dated back to July 10, 1996,[16] so their credit was limited to zero.

This litigation arose out of the IRS's attempt to levy the Deatons' property to satisfy their 1994-1996 tax liabilities, which remained unpaid because of the IRS's refusal to apply the 1993 overpayment as a credit in later years. After the IRS issued a Notice of Intent to Levy, the Deatons timely filed a request for a collection due process hearing with the IRS Appeals Office. In their request for a hearing, the Deatons asserted that the 1994 remittance of $125,000 was a "deposit" rather than a "payment," a status that would have protected the remittance from the look-back period for credits and refunds.[17] The Appeals Office rejected the Deatons' assertion, classified their 1994 remittance as a payment, subject to I.R.C. § 6511(b)(2)(A)'s look-back period, and sustained the IRS's proposed levy.

---

[16] [fn 3] Considering the six-month extension the IRS gave the Deatons to file their 1993 return, the look-back period was the three years and six months immediately preceding the date of their claim for a credit, January 10, 2000.

[17] [fn 4] *See* I.R.C. § 6511(b)(2)(A) ("[T]he amount of the credit or refund shall not exceed the portion of the tax *paid* within the period . . .." (emphasis added)). The distinct treatment of deposits and payments first arose in *Rosenman v. United States*, 323 U.S. 658, 65 S.Ct. 536, 89 L.Ed. 535 (1945), in which the Supreme Court recognized that § 6511's predecessor was not applicable to a deposit even though it would have been applicable to a payment. *Dantzler v. United States*, 183 F.3d 1247, 1249 (11th Cir.1999).

The Deatons were likewise unsuccessful before the Tax Court. Although the Tax Court acknowledged the judicially created distinction between a deposit and a payment, the court also recognized a three-way split of authority regarding the treatment of a Form 4868 remittance. Applying its own precedent in *Risman v. Commissioner,* 100 T.C. 191, 1993 WL 72856 (1993), which calls for an examination of the facts and circumstances of a case in order to determine whether the taxpayer intended his remittance as a deposit or a payment, the Tax Court reviewed the Deatons' tax records and a letter from their accountant asserting that the $125,000 was a deposit. Finding that the Deatons had failed to demonstrate their contemporaneous intent to treat the remittance as a deposit, the Tax Court sustained the Appeals Office's finding that the Deatons' remittance was a payment made outside the look-back period of § 6511(b)(2)(A) and upheld the Appeals Office's determination that the IRS's proposed levy could proceed. This appeal ensued. Because we agree with the Tax Court that the Deatons' 1994 remittance was a payment, rather than a deposit, we AFFIRM the Tax Court's decision.

II. DISCUSSION

A. Standard of Review

The sole issue on appeal is whether the Deatons' 1994 remittance of $125,000 was a payment or a deposit. This is a question of law that we review *de novo. San Antonio Sav. Ass'n v. Comm'r,* 887 F.2d 577, 581 (5th Cir.1989) ("This court has jurisdiction to review the decisions of the tax court 'in the same manner and to the same extent as decisions of the district courts in civil actions tried without a jury.' We therefore examine this decision as we do other summary judgment decisions. Because the dispute concerns findings of law, we review on a *de novo* standard." (quoting 26 U.S.C. § 7482 (1982))). The Tax Court's factual findings are reviewed for clear error. *Sandvall v. Comm'r,* 898 F.2d 455, 458 (5th Cir.1990).

B. Analysis

The Deaton's argue on appeal that the $125,000 remittance that accompanied their Form 4868 application for an extension of time to file was a deposit and that as such, it is not subject to the look-back period of I.R.C. § 6511(b)(2)(A). They ask this Court to reverse the Tax Court's decision and order the IRS to apply their 1993 overpayment as a credit to their 1994-1996 tax liabilities or refund the overpayment to them. The Deatons concede that if the 1994 remittance is properly classified as a payment, the IRS may keep their overpayment because of § 6511(b)(2)(A)'s look-back period.

In deciding this appeal, we must assess the impact of the Supreme Court's recent decision in Baral v. United States, 528 U.S. 431, 120 S.Ct. 1006, 145 L.Ed.2d 949 (2000), on this Circuit's longstanding rule that remittances made prior to assessment of a tax are deemed deposits rather than payments. See Harden v. United States, 74 F.3d 1237 (5th Cir.1995) (unpublished); Ford v. United States, 618 F.2d 357 (5th Cir.1980); Thomas v. Mercantile Nat'l Bank, 204 F.2d 943 (5th Cir.1953). The Deatons contend that *Baral* has no effect on their case or on our longstanding rule because it is limited to cases involving remittances governed by the "deemed paid" provision of I.R.C. § 6513(b)[18]—for example, wage withholdings and payments of estimated tax—and they argue that their remittance does not fall under that section. They urge that the proper characterization of their remittance depends on the facts and circumstances associated with it under *Rosenman*, which predates *Baral*. According to the Deatons, the facts and circumstances surrounding their 1994 remittance establish their contemporaneous intent to treat it as a deposit, and they assert that Fifth Circuit law at that time supports such a finding.[19] The Commissioner counters that after *Baral*, we should treat remittances accompanying Form 4868 applications as payments as a matter of law; alternatively, the Commissioner argues that the Tax Court correctly ruled under the facts-and-circumstances test that the Deatons' remittance was a payment, not a deposit. Because we have not previously explicitly addressed *Baral*'s impact on our law,[20] we do so here. And

---

[18] [fn 5] Section 6513(b) states,

Prepaid income tax.—For purposes of section 6511 or 6512—

(1) Any tax actually deducted and withheld at the source during any calendar year under chapter 24 shall, in respect of the recipient of the income, be *deemed to have been paid* by him on the 15th day of the fourth month following the close of his taxable year with respect to which such tax is allowable as a credit under section 31.

(2) Any amount paid as estimated income tax for any taxable year shall be *deemed to have been paid* on the last day prescribed for filing the return under section 6012 for such taxable year (determined without regard to any extension of time for filing such return).

(3) Any tax withheld at the source under chapter 3 shall, in respect of the recipient of the income, be *deemed to have been paid* by such recipient on the last day prescribed for filing the return under section 6012 for the taxable year (determined without regard to any extension of time for filing) with respect to which such tax is allowable as a credit under section 1462. For this purpose, any exemption granted under section 6012 from the requirement of filing a return shall be disregarded.

I.R.C. § 6513(b) (emphasis added).

[19] [fn 6] Because this Circuit treated pre-assessment remittances as deposits at the time the Deatons made their Form 4868 remittance, they argue that it was intended as a deposit under then-current law. This argument fails, as discussed in Part II.B.4.

[20] [fn 7] Although we have decided a deposit-payment case since *Baral*, see *Harrigill v. United States*, 410 F.3d 786 (5th Cir.2005), we did not discuss *Baral*'s impact on our law in that case because the parties conceded that the *Mercantile National Bank* line of authority, discussed below, was abrogated by *Baral*, see id. at 790 n. 6.

for the reasons stated below, we agree that the Deatons' remittance was a payment, not a deposit. However, we decline to adopt a per se rule to govern remittances accompanying Form 4868 applications as the Commissioner requests.

1. Origin of the Deposit-Payment Distinction

The distinction between deposits and payments was first established in *Rosenman*. In that case, the Supreme Court considered whether the predecessor to the current look-back provision barred a claim for refund of estimated estate taxes that the decedent's executors had remitted in response to an absolute deadline, but which they strenuously disputed as erroneous. *Rosenman*, 323 U.S. at 659-61, 65 S.Ct. 536, 89 L.Ed. 535 (1945). The executors had included a transmittal letter with the remittance, emphasizing that "[t]his payment is made under protest and duress, and solely for the purpose of avoiding penalties and interest, since it is contended by the executors that not all of this sum is legally or lawfully due." *Id.* at 660, 65 S.Ct. 536 (internal quotation marks omitted). The IRS credited the remittance to a special suspense account, which was created to hold the funds because no taxes had yet been formally assessed against the estate. *Id.* After completing an audit of the return nearly three years later, the IRS formally assessed a deficiency. *Id.* When the executors brought a claim for refund more than three years after the remittance—but within three years of the IRS's formal assessment—the claim was rejected as time barred. *Id.* at 660-61, 65 S.Ct. 536.

In deciding that the taxes were not "paid"—and that the limitations period therefore did not commence—until the tax was actually assessed by the IRS, the Supreme Court specifically considered all of the facts and circumstances surrounding the executors' original remittance, including the executors' intent as stated in the transmittal letter and the IRS's treatment of the remittance once received. *Id.* at 661-63, 65 S.Ct. 536. The Court determined that when the executors submitted the remittance, they "did not discharge what [they] deemed a liability nor pay one that was asserted. There was merely an interim arrangement to cover whatever contingencies the future might define." *Id.* at 662, 65 S.Ct. 536. Noting the IRS's deposit of the funds into a suspense account, the Court concluded that "[m]oney in these accounts is held not as taxes duly collected are held but as a deposit made in the nature of a cash bond for the payment of taxes thereafter found to be due." *Id.* The Court ruled that considering the specific facts and circumstances of the case, the remittance was a deposit and that the statute of limitations therefore did not bar the executors' claim for refund. Courts have since read *Rosenman* as creating a facts-and-circumstances test for distinguishing between deposits and payments. *See, e.g., VanCanagan v. United States,* 231 F.3d 1349, 1352-53 (Fed.Cir.2000); *Moran v. United States,* 63 F.3d 663, 667-68 (7th Cir.1995); *Blatt v. United States,* 34 F.3d 252, 255 (4th Cir.1994); *Ewing v. United States,* 914 F.2d 499, 503-04 (4th Cir.1990); *Fortugno v. Comm'r,* 353 F.2d 429, 435-36 (3d Cir.1965); *Risman,* 100 T.C. at 197-99. However, this Circuit did not join those courts in their reading of *Rosenman*.

2. Fifth Circuit Law Post-*Rosenman*

Our Circuit first applied *Rosenman* in Thomas v. Mercantile National Bank, 204 F.2d 943 (5th Cir.1953). The *Mercantile National Bank* panel read the *Rosenman* decision as establishing a rule that any amount remitted to the IRS prior to a formal assessment of tax is, as a matter of law, a deposit. Id. at 944. Citing *Rosenman*, the Court held a claim for refund timely because

> [u]ntil the Commissioner certified the assessment list . . . there was no deficiency assessment, and no liability on the part of the taxpayer, and consequently nothing to pay. The sum deposited with the Collector . . . was merely an advance deposit to cover additional tax liability expected to arise thereafter. Neither the estate's liability, nor the fact that there was an overpayment could be determined until the deficiency assessment was entered. It would be illogical to hold, as the United States contends, that the statute of limitation began to run against a claim for refund before the deficiency itself came into existence, and before the fact that there was an overpayment, and if so the amount thereof, became ascertainable.

Id. Mercantile National Bank thus took *Rosenman* beyond its narrow facts and circumstances, which the Supreme Court had specifically emphasized in reaching its decision, and adopted a per se rule that pre-assessment remittances are deposits.

Almost thirty years after *Mercantile National Bank* was decided, a panel of this Court begrudgingly applied its per se rule in Ford v. United States, 618 F.2d 357 (5th Cir.1980), but not without making clear its disagreement with *Mercantile National Bank*'s holding: "Despite our view of Supreme Court precedent, the course taken by our sister circuits, and appropriate tax policy, we are constrained . . . by the bonds of Thomas v. Mercantile National Bank at Dallas." Id. at 358. After thoroughly discussing the reasons for abandoning the rule and inviting the Court to reconsider it en banc, the panel nevertheless applied *Mercantile National Bank* as binding circuit precedent. Id. at 358-61. The motion for rehearing en banc was denied. Ford v. United States, 625 F.2d 1016 (5th Cir.1980).

Fifteen years later, the Fifth Circuit again addressed *Mercantile National Bank* in Harden v. United States, 74 F.3d 1237 (5th Cir.1995) (unpublished).[21] The facts of *Harden* are virtually identical to those of the instant case. The Hardens filed Form 4868 for both the 1984 and 1985 tax years, and they submitted remittances with each filing. *Harden*, 74 F.3d at 1237. Several years later, they filed their tax returns for those years, indicating substantially lower tax liabilities than the amounts previously remitted. Id. Like the Deatons, the Hardens sought to apply the overpayments as credits for subsequent tax years, but the IRS denied their request as time-barred. Id.

---

[21] [fn 8] Although *Harden* was unpublished, it is considered precedent because it was issued under our former rule concerning unpublished opinions. *See* 5TH CIR. R. 47.5.3 ("Unpublished opinions issued before January 1, 1996, are precedent." (footnote omitted)).

The government argued in *Harden* that *Mercantile National Bank* and *Ford* were distinguishable because they did not address taxpayer remittances accompanying Form 4868. According to the government, 26 U.S.C. § 6513 expressly defined such remittances as "payments" of tax for purposes of the statute of limitations, so the remittances were payments, not deposits, as a matter of law. Although the *Harden* panel appreciated the government's "rational and forceful argument," it concluded that it was "bound to the decisions of this court in [*Mercantile National Bank*] and *Ford*. In those cases we held that as a matter of law a remittance forwarded to the IRS before an assessment of tax is to be considered a deposit rather than a payment." *Id.*

3. Impact of Baral v. United States

We now hold that post-*Baral*, we are no longer bound by the *Mercantile National Bank* line of authority. In *Baral*, the Supreme Court explicitly rejected the taxpayer's argument that a tax cannot be "paid" until tax liability is assessed and thereby abrogated the *Mercantile National Bank* rule that a pre-assessment remittance is a deposit rather than a payment. *Baral*, 528 U.S. at 434, 437, 120 S.Ct. 1006 ("[T]he Code directly contradicts the notion that payment may not occur before assessment.").[22] The unanimous Court construed the plain language of 26 U.S.C. § 6513(b)(1) and (2) as providing unequivocally that two types of remittances, wage withholdings and payments of estimated income tax, are to be "deemed paid" on the due date of the tax return for the tax year in question, not when formal assessment occurs. *Baral*, 528 U.S. at 434-36, 120 S.Ct. 1006. This treatment necessarily precludes the argument that all pre-assessment remittances are deposits, the position that this Court took prior to *Baral* and that the Deatons argue still prevails.

According to the Deatons, *Baral* only applies to remittances that fall under 26 U.S.C. § 6513(b), not to transmittals made with Form 4868, and their position is bolstered by the Court's final statement in *Baral*:

> We need not address the proper treatment under § 6511 of remittances that, unlike withholding and estimated income tax, are not governed by a "deemed paid" provision akin to § 6513(b). Such remittances might include remittances of estimated estate tax, as in *Rosenman*, or remittances of any sort of tax by a taxpayer under audit in order to stop the running of interest and penalties. In the latter situation, the taxpayer will often desire treatment of the remittance as a deposit—even if this means forfeiting the right to interest on an overpayment—in order to preserve jurisdiction in the Tax Court, which depends on the existence of a deficiency, a deficiency that would be wiped out by treatment of the remittance as a payment. We note

---

[22] [fn 9] That the *Baral* Court was specifically addressing the Fifth Circuit's position as compared to those of various other circuits supports a finding of abrogation. *Id.* at 434, 120 S.Ct. 1006 ("In view of an apparent tension between [the Circuits], we granted certiorari."); *see also Harrigill v. United States*, 410 F.3d 786, 790 n. 6 (5th Cir.2005) (not refuting the parties' concession that *Baral* abrogated the Fifth Circuit rule).

that the Service has promulgated procedures to govern classification of a remittance as a deposit or payment in this context.

Id. at 439 n. 2, 120 S.Ct. 1006 (citations omitted). However, this statement does not answer either (1) whether the Deatons' remittance is one that is "governed by a 'deemed paid' provision akin to § 6513(b)" or (2) what the proper treatment is of remittances that are not "governed by a 'deemed paid' provision." The Deatons' position is that a remittance accompanying Form 4868 is not a remittance governed by a deemed paid provision and that remittances not governed by a deemed paid provision are subject to the facts-and-circumstances test established in *Rosenman*.[23] We take up this issue in subpart 4 below.

Post-*Baral*, ours is the only circuit to have addressed the deposit-payment distinction. In Harrigill v. United States, 410 F.3d 786 (5th Cir.2005), we addressed facts similar to the instant facts and held that the pre-assessment remittance at issue was a payment, not a deposit. Harrigill, like the Deatons, had filed a Form 4868 for the 1994 tax year and had submitted it with a remittance of the amount of tax she estimated to be due, which was later determined to be overstated. Id. at 787. Unlike the Deatons, however, Harrigill filed her tax return for 1994 within the limitations period, and the IRS duly credited her overpayment to her estimated taxes for the 1995 tax year, the return for which she had not yet filed. Id. at 787-88. When Harrigill later filed her 1995 return and found that she had again overestimated her tax liability, she sought to have the overpayment—which resulted from application of the first overpayment to her 1995 taxes—carried over as a credit for 1996. Id. at 788. The IRS denied Harrigill's request as time-barred, a decision we upheld. Id. at 788, 792.

In upholding the IRS's decision, we did not refute the parties' concession that *Baral* abrogated the *Mercantile National Bank* rule, id. at 790 n. 6, an abrogation we now expressly recognize, and we used a facts-and-circumstances

---

[23] [fn 10] The Deatons also complain that *Baral*'s application to their case should be limited because the *Mercantile National Bank* rule was the law at the time they made their $125,000 remittance. However, we are not free to disregard *Baral* just because it was not decided when the events leading to this appeal occurred:

> When [the Supreme] Court applies a rule of federal law to the parties before it, that rule is the controlling interpretation of federal law and must be given full retroactive effect in all cases still open on direct review and as to all events, regardless of whether such events predate or postdate [the] announcement of the rule.

Harper v. Va. Dep't of Taxation, 509 U.S. 86, 97, 113 S.Ct. 2510, 125 L.Ed.2d 74 (1993). This argument is also foreclosed by our panel decision in Harrigill v. United States, 410 F.3d 786 (5th Cir.2005), which declined to treat a pre-assessment remittance as a deposit even though that remittance would have been treated as a deposit at the time it was made under our pre-*Baral* precedent.

approach to determine whether the credit applied to Harrigill's estimated taxes for 1995 was an estimated payment of estimated income tax under § 6513(b)(2) subject to *Baral*'s rule that payments of estimated income tax are "deemed paid" on the due date of the return without extension, id. at 791-92. We did not address whether Harrigill's original remittance accompanying her Form 4868 application was a deposit or a payment as a matter of law because we determined that an application of credit, rather than a Form 4868 remittance, was at issue. The instant case, however, clearly involves a Form 4868 remittance, and we must now address the question left unanswered in *Harrigill*: Is a remittance submitted with a Form 4868 application for an extension of time to file a payment as a matter of law? Or is it subject to the facts-and-circumstances test of *Rosenman*? After *Baral*, this is essentially an issue of first impression in this Circuit; *Harden*, our prior Form 4868 case, which was based on *Mercantile National Bank*, no longer controls.

4. The Deatons' Remittance

The primary issue in this case is the impact of *Baral* and post-*Baral* law on the deposit-payment distinction. As discussed above, *Baral* abrogated the rule established in *Mercantile National Bank*. And the only post-*Baral* case to address the deposit-payment distinction used a facts-and-circumstances test to determine whether the remittance in question was a payment of estimated income tax under § 6513(b)(2) subject to *Baral*'s rule that payments of estimated income tax are deemed paid on the due date of the return without extension. *Harrigill*, 410 F.3d at 791-92. We have been called on here to decide what rule to apply post-*Baral* to characterize a remittance made in conjunction with a Form 4868 application for an extension of time to file. The alternatives offered are (1) a per se rule that all Form 4868 remittances are payments and (2) a facts-and-circumstances inquiry that would require a case-by-case analysis of any Form 4868 remittance made.

Like the *Harrigill* panel, we find it unnecessary to decide whether a Form 4868 remittance is a payment as a matter of law because we find that the Deatons' remittance of $125,000 in conjunction with their Form 4868 application for an extension of time to file constituted a payment of estimated income tax under § 6513(b)(2). We hesitate to adopt a per se rule in a case in which the record clearly indicates that the taxpayers' remittance was a payment, not a deposit, and we therefore decline to do so. We leave for another day the question of whether all Form 4868 remittances should be treated as payments of estimated tax, even though we recognize that several of our sister circuits have already answered this question in the affirmative. *See Dantzler v. United States*, 183 F.3d 1247, 1251 (11th Cir.1999); *Ertman v. United States*, 165 F.3d 204, 207 (2d Cir.1999); *Ott v. United States*, 141 F.3d 1306, 1308-09 (9th Cir.1998); *Gabelman v. Comm'r*, 86 F.3d 609, 611-12 (6th Cir.1996); *Weigand v. United States*, 760 F.2d 1072, 1074 (10th Cir.1985). We agree with the Tax Court that even under the facts-and-circumstances approach proposed by the Deatons, their $125,000 remittance must be considered a payment of estimated tax. *See VanCanagan v. United States*,

231 F.3d 1349, 1352-53 (Fed.Cir.2000). As such, their remittance is "governed by a 'deemed paid' provision" and controlled by *Baral*.

In their 1993 Form 4868, the Deatons indicated that "the amount [they] expect[ed]" to list as their 1993 tax liability was $138,883 and that they had a "balance due" of $125,000. The Deatons remitted that $125,000. The Deatons submitted no contemporaneous evidence supporting their contention that they intended this amount to be a deposit when remitted; there is nothing on the face of the document or on the check submitted with it indicating such an intent. There is no evidence that the Deatons made an attempt to use the IRS procedure for making a deposit. In addition, there is no evidence suggesting that the Deatons were disputing their tax liability as in *Rosenman*. The IRS has always treated their overpayment as an "excess collection." At best, the record suggests that the Deatons had difficulty estimating their tax liability and needed more time to file their 1993 tax return. That they had difficulty estimating their tax liability does not make their remittance of estimated tax a deposit of the kind recognized by *Baral* as retaining legal significance. *Baral*, 528 U.S. at 439 n. 2, 120 S.Ct. 1006.

We reject the Deatons' argument that in light of caselaw prevailing at the time of their remittance, we must presume that they intended to make a deposit. This argument requires that we find that they had actual or presumed knowledge of the prevailing law of this Circuit. They provide no factual evidence to support such a finding. Furthermore, the Deatons provide no legal authority to support their affirmative use of a presumption that a taxpayer knows the law. Such a presumption is normally reserved to the government in actions against taxpayers. *See, e.g., Cheek v. United States*, 498 U.S. 192, 199, 111 S.Ct. 604, 112 L.Ed.2d 617 (1991). The Deatons provide no principled reason for allowing the affirmative use of such a presumption against the government, and we refuse to invent such a reason here.

We hold that on the facts and circumstances of this case, the Deatons' remittance of $125,000 was an "amount paid as estimated income tax" under § 6513(b)(2), not a deposit.[24] Under that section, a remittance is deemed paid "on the last day prescribed for filing the return under section 6012 for such taxable year . . .." I.R.C. § 6513(b)(2). Because the $125,000 was thus paid outside the look-back period of § 6511(b)(2)(A), the Deatons cannot recover their overpayment. I.R.C. § 6511(b)(2)(A).

III. CONCLUSION

Accordingly, we AFFIRM the Tax Court's decision.

---

[24] [fn 11] Therefore, like the *Baral* Court, we need not address the treatment of remittances not governed by a deemed paid provision. *Baral*, 528 U.S. at 439 n. 2, 120 S.Ct. 1006.

NOTES AND QUESTIONS

1. What difference did it make whether the remittance was a payment or a deposit?
2. How is this case different from *Rosenman*?

C. Timeliness

A payment is timely if it is made with a timely filed return. *See* IRC § 6151(a). Like tax returns, a payment is deemed made when the IRS receives it. Just as with tax returns, there are exceptions. First, the mailbox rule applies to payments. *See* IRC § 7502(a)(1). Timely mailed is timely paid. Second, if the last day for payment falls on a weekend or legal holiday, the payment is still considered timely if paid on the next business day. *See* IRC § 7503.

Obtaining an extension for a payment of tax is more difficult than obtaining an extension for filing a tax return. The Code authorizes the IRS to grant an extension for payment for up to six months. *See* IRC § 6161(a)(1). The extension, however, is not automatic. A taxpayer must apply in advance and show undue hardship. *See* Reg. § 1.6161-1(b). Obtaining an extension does not stop the accrual of interest on the amount owed.

CHAPTER 10

COMPLIANCE LIMITATIONS PERIODS

A. Introduction

Once a taxpayer has reported and paid her liability, both she and the government generally have three years to consider changing the amount originally reported. In general, for the IRS to change the taxpayer's original amount reported, the IRS first reviews the return (see Chapter 11), tries to settle the liability (see Chapter 13), and issues a final determination notice regarding the change (see Chapter 14). As discussed earlier, the taxpayer may file an amended return to change the amount and file a claim for a refund. If the taxpayer discovers she underreported her tax liability and owes more money, the decision on whether to change the original amount reported is more complicated because the three-year period for claiming a refund is not relevant.

If the above three-year periods were simple, an entire chapter discussing them would be unnecessary. They are not simple. There are two sets of limitations periods in this context. First, the limitations period for a refund claim restricts a taxpayer from obtaining a refund on a claim made after the period has expired. There is also a look-back rule for refund claims that limits the refund amount. Second, the statute of limitations on assessment restricts the IRS from assessing a tax after the period has expired.

B. Limitations on Refund Claims

The limitations on claiming a tax refund are complex. The refund limitations turn on two compliance events, filing a tax return and paying the tax. Filing a return and paying tax are separate triggers because they are sometimes disconnected. Taxpayers generally file tax returns only once a year. Many payments are made prior to a return through withholding and estimated taxes, and the penalty for making a late payment is a fraction of the penalty for filing a late return.

Where a taxpayer has filed a return, the Code provides two periods in which a refund claim may be filed, one based on the return filing and one based on payment. Section 6511(a) provides as follows:

> Claim for credit or refund of an overpayment . . . shall be filed by the taxpayer within 3 years from the time the return was filed or 2 years from the time the tax was paid, whichever of such periods expires the later . . . .

Section 6511(a) also provides for a separate period permitting a refund claim where the taxpayer has filed no tax return. This period begins on the date of a payment. Section 6511(a) provides:

> Claim for credit or refund of an overpayment . . . shall be filed . . . if no return was filed by the taxpayer, within 2 years from the time the tax was paid.

For purposes of these limitations periods, returns filed before the due date are treated as though they were filed on the due date. *See* IRC § 6513(a).

If the taxpayer files the refund claim outside the three-year period following the tax return filing, there is a limitation on how much she can recover. This limitation is known as a look-back rule. Section 6511(b)(2) provides:

> If the [refund] claim was not filed within such 3-year period [following the tax return filing], the amount of the credit or refund shall not exceed the portion of the tax paid during the 2 years immediately preceding the filing of the claim.

Courts apply these periods rather strictly.

UNITED STATES v. BROCKAMP
519 U.S. 314 (1997)
Supreme Court of the United States

Justice BREYER delivered the opinion of the Court.

The two cases before us raise a single question. Can courts toll, for nonstatutory equitable reasons, the statutory time (and related amount) limitations for filing tax refund claims set forth in § 6511 of the Internal Revenue Code of 1986? We hold that they cannot.

These two cases present similar circumstances. In each case a taxpayer initially paid the Internal Revenue Service (IRS) several thousand dollars that he did not owe. In each case the taxpayer (or his representative) filed an administrative claim for refund several years after the relevant statutory time period for doing so had ended. In each case the taxpayer suffered a disability (senility or alcoholism), which, he said, explained why the delay was not his fault. And in each case he asked the court to extend the relevant statutory time period for an "equitable" reason, namely, the existence of a mental disability—a reason not mentioned in § 6511, but which, we assume, would permit a court to toll the statutory limitations period *if, but only if,* § 6511 contains an implied "equitable tolling" exception. See 4 C. Wright & A. Miller, Federal Practice and Procedure § 1056 (2d ed.1987 and Supp.1996); see also *Wolin v. Smith Barney, Inc.,* 83 F.3d 847, 852 (C.A.7 1996) (defining equitable tolling).

In both cases, the Ninth Circuit read § 6511 as if it did contain an implied exception that would permit "equitable tolling." It then applied principles of equity to each case. It found those principles justified tolling the statutory time period. And it permitted the actions to proceed. 67 F.3d 260 (1995); judgt. order reported at 70 F.3d 120 (1995). All other Circuits that have considered the matter, however, have taken the opposite view. They have held that § 6511 does not authorize equitable tolling. See *Amoco Production Co. v. Newton Sheep Co.,* 85 F.3d 1464 (C.A.10 1996); *Lovett v. United States,* 81 F.3d 143 (C.A.Fed.1996); *Webb v. United States,* 66 F.3d 691 (C.A.4 1995); *Oropallo v. United States,* 994 F.2d 25 (C.A.1 1993) *(per curiam);* and *Vintilla v. United States,* 931 F.2d 1444 (C.A.11 1991). We granted certiorari to resolve this conflict. And we conclude that the latter Circuits are correct.

The taxpayers rest their claim for equitable tolling upon Irwin v. Department of Veterans Affairs, 498 U.S. 89, 111 S.Ct. 453, 112 L.Ed.2d 435 (1990), a case in which this Court considered the timeliness of an employee's lawsuit charging his Government employer with discrimination, in violation of Title VII of the Civil Rights Act of 1964, 42 U.S.C. § 2000e et seq. The Court found the lawsuit untimely, but nevertheless tolled the limitations period. It held that the "rule of equitable tolling" applies "to suits against the Government, in the same way that it is applicable" to Title VII suits against private employers. 498 U.S., at 94–95, 111 S.Ct., at 456–457. The Court went on to say that the "same rebuttable presumption of equitable tolling applicable to suits against private defendants should also apply to suits against the United States." Id., at 95–96, 111 S.Ct., at 457.

The taxpayers, pointing to *Irwin*, argue that principles of equitable tolling would have applied had they sued private defendants, e.g., had they sought restitution from private defendants for "Money Had and Received." See C. Keigwin, Cases in Common Law Pleading 220 (2d ed. 1934). They add that given *Irwin*'s language, there must be a "presumption" that limitations periods in tax refund suits against the Government can be equitably tolled. And, they say, that "presumption," while "rebuttable," has not been rebutted. They conclude that, given *Irwin*, the Ninth Circuit correctly tolled the statutory period for "equitable" reasons.

In evaluating this argument, we are willing to assume, favorably to the taxpayers but only for argument's sake, that a tax refund suit and a private suit for restitution are sufficiently similar to warrant asking *Irwin*'s negatively phrased question: Is there good reason to believe that Congress did *not* want the equitable tolling doctrine to apply? But see *Flora v. United States,* 362 U.S. 145, 153–154, 80 S.Ct. 630, 634–635, 4 L.Ed.2d 623 (1960) (citing *Curtis's*

Administratrix v. Fiedler, 2 Black 461, 479, 17 L.Ed. 273 (1863)) (distinguishing common-law suit against the tax collector from action of assumpsit for money had and received); *George Moore Ice Cream Co. v. Rose,* 289 U.S. 373, 382–383, 53 S.Ct. 620, 623–624, 77 L.Ed. 1265 (1933); see also Plumb, Tax Refund Suits Against Collectors of Internal Revenue, 60 Harv.L.Rev. 685, 687 (1947) (describing collector suit as a fiction solely designed to bring the Government into court). We can travel no further, however, along *Irwin*'s road, for there are strong reasons for answering *Irwin*'s question in the Government's favor.

Section 6511 sets forth its time limitations in unusually emphatic form. Ordinarily limitations statutes use fairly simple language, which one can often plausibly read as containing an implied "equitable tolling" exception. See, *e.g.,* 42 U.S.C. § 2000e–16(c) (requiring suit for employment discrimination to be filed "[w]ithin 90 days of receipt of notice of final [EEOC] action . . ."). But § 6511 uses language that is not simple. It sets forth its limitations in a highly detailed technical manner, that, linguistically speaking, cannot easily be read as containing implicit exceptions. Moreover, § 6511 reiterates its limitations several times in several different ways. Section 6511 says, first, that a

"[c]laim for . . . refund . . . of any tax . . . shall be filed by the taxpayer within 3 years from the time the return was filed or 2 years from the time the tax was paid, whichever of such periods expires the later, or if no return was filed . . . within 2 years from the time the tax was paid." 26 U.S.C. § 6511(a).

It then says that

"[n]o credit or refund shall be allowed or made after the expiration of the period of limitation prescribed . . . unless a claim for . . . refund is filed . . . within such period." § 6511(b)(1).

It reiterates the point by imposing substantive limitations:

"If the claim was filed by the taxpayer during the 3–year period . . . the amount of the credit or refund shall not exceed the portion of the tax paid within the period, immediately preceding the filing of the claim, equal to 3 years plus the period of any extension of time for filing the return . . . ." § 6511(b)(2)(A).

And

"[i]f the claim was not filed within such 3–year period, the amount of the credit or refund shall not exceed the portion of the tax paid during the 2 years immediately preceding the filing of the claim." § 6511(b)(2)(B).

The Tax Code reemphasizes the point when it says that refunds that do not comply with these limitations "shall be considered erroneous," § 6514, and specifies procedures for the Government's recovery of any such "erroneous" refund payment. §§ 6532(b), 7405. In addition, § 6511 sets forth explicit exceptions to its basic time limits, and those very specific exceptions do not include "equitable tolling." See § 6511(d) (establishing special time limit rules for refunds related to operating losses, credit carrybacks, foreign taxes, self-employment taxes, worthless securities, and bad debts); see also *United States v. Dalm,* 494 U.S. 596, 610, 110 S.Ct. 1361, 1369, 108 L.Ed.2d 548 (1990) (discussing mitigation provisions set forth in 26 U.S.C. §§ 1311–1314); § 507 of the Revenue Act of 1942, 56 Stat. 961 (temporarily tolling limitations period during wartime).

To read an "equitable tolling" provision into these provisions, one would have to assume an implied exception for tolling virtually every time a number appears. To do so would work a kind of linguistic havoc. Moreover, such an interpretation would require tolling, not only procedural limitations, but also substantive limitations on the amount of recovery—a kind of tolling for which we have found no direct precedent. Section 6511's detail, its technical language, the iteration of the limitations in both procedural and substantive forms, and the explicit listing of exceptions, taken together, indicate to us that Congress did not intend courts to read other unmentioned, open-ended, "equitable" exceptions into the statute that it wrote. There are no counterindications. Tax law, after all, is not normally characterized by case-specific exceptions reflecting individualized equities.

The nature of the underlying subject matter—tax collection—underscores the linguistic point. The IRS processes more than 200 million tax returns each year. It issues more than 90 million refunds. See Dept. of Treasury, Internal Revenue Service, 1995 Data Book 8–9. To read an "equitable tolling" exception into § 6511 could create serious administrative problems by forcing the IRS to respond to, and perhaps litigate, large numbers of late claims, accompanied by requests for "equitable tolling" which, upon close inspection, might turn out to lack sufficient equitable justification. See H.R. Conf. Rep. No. 356, 69th Cong., 1st Sess., 41 (1926) (deleting provision excusing tax deficiencies in the estates of insane or deceased individuals because of difficulties involved in defining incompetence). The nature and potential magnitude of the administrative problem suggest that Congress decided to pay the price of occasional unfairness in individual cases (penalizing a taxpayer whose claim is unavoidably delayed) in order to maintain a more workable tax enforcement system. At the least it tells us that Congress would likely have wanted to decide explicitly whether, or just where and when, to expand the statute's limitations periods, rather than delegate to the courts a generalized power to do so wherever a court concludes that equity so requires.

The taxpayers' counterrebuttal consists primarily of an interesting historical analysis of the Internal Revenue Code's tax refund provisions. They try to show that § 6511's specific, detailed language reflects congressional concern about matters not related to equitable tolling. They explain some language, for example, in terms of a congressional effort to stop taxpayers from keeping the refund period open indefinitely through the device of making a series of small tax payments. See S.Rep. No. 398, 68th Cong., 1st Sess., 33 (1924). They explain other language as an effort to make the refund time period and the tax assessment period coextensive. See H.R.Rep. No. 2333, 77th Cong., 2d Sess., 52 (1942).

Assuming all that is so, however, such congressional efforts still seem but a smaller part of a larger congressional objective: providing the Government with strong statutory "protection against stale demands." Cf. *United States v. Garbutt Oil Co.*, 302 U.S. 528, 533, 58 S.Ct. 320, 323, 82 L.Ed. 405 (1938) (statute of limitations bars untimely amendment of claim for additional refund). Moreover, the history to which the taxpayers point reveals that § 6511's predecessor tax refund provisions, like § 6511, contained highly detailed language with clear time limits. See, *e.g.*, § 281(b) of the Revenue Act of 1924, ch. 234, 43 Stat. 301 (4–year limit on claims for overpayment of income, war-profits, or excess-profits tax and cap on refund amount); § 322(b) of the Revenue Act of 1932, ch. 209, 47 Stat. 242 (2–year limit for claim filing and corresponding limit on refund amount); Internal Revenue Code of 1954, 68A Stat. 808 (adopting current alternative time and amount limitations); see also § 810 of the Revenue Act of 1932, ch. 209, 47 Stat. 283 (imposing time and amount limits for estate tax refunds). And that history lacks any instance (but for the present cases) of equitable tolling. On balance, these historical considerations help the Government's argument.

For these reasons, we conclude that Congress did not intend the "equitable tolling" doctrine to apply to § 6511's time limitations. The Ninth Circuit's decisions are

Reversed.

NOTES AND QUESTIONS

1. Congress softened the result in *Brockamp* not long after the Supreme Court decided it. A taxpayer may have more time to claim a refund if she becomes "financially disabled." While a taxpayer is financially disabled, the limitations period for filing a refund claim is suspended. Under section 6511(h), financially disabled means that the taxpayer is

    > unable to manage his financial affairs by reason of a medically determinable physical or mental impairment . . . expected to result in death or . . . last[] not less than 12 months.

2. The IRS permits a taxpayer to claim financial disability only with a note from her doctor. *See* Rev. Proc. 99-21, 1999-1 C.B. 960.

3. Some describe lawmaking as a conversation between the three government branches. *Brockamp* is a great example. The executive branch through the IRS perhaps felt restricted from granting relief to these sympathetic taxpayers because Congress created a harsh rule. The judicial branch also felt the rule was harsh, but considered the rule to be definitive. The legislative branch might not have considered the issue prior to the *Brockamp*, but it appears to have listened.

C. Statute of Limitations on Assessment

The limitations period the IRS has to review a tax return and determine whether a deficiency in tax exists is simpler than the limitations on claiming a refund in that the assessment period has nothing analogous to the look-back period. On the other hand, the Code is more lenient on the IRS where the taxpayer behaves in certain ways. The return filing date starts the running of a three-year statute of limitations on assessment. Section 6501(a) provides as follows:

> Except as otherwise provided in this section, the amount of any tax imposed by this title shall be assessed within 3 years after the return was filed (whether or not such return was filed on or after the date prescribed) . . . and no proceeding in court without assessment for the collection of such tax shall be begun after the expiration of such period. . . .

Where a taxpayer has omitted a substantial amount of gross income—defined as 25% of the gross income reported on the tax return—the Code provides the IRS six years to assess tax instead of three. Section 6501(e)(1)(E) provides as follows:

> If the taxpayer omits from gross income an amount properly includible therein and . . . such amount is in excess of 25 percent of the amount of gross income stated in the return . . . the tax may be assessed, or a proceeding in court for collection of such tax may be begun without assessment, at any time within 6 years after the return was filed.

The assessment statute runs indefinitely for a false or fraudulent return. *See* IRC § 6501(c)(1). A taxpayer may not attempt to bypass the unending statute for a false return by filing an accurate return in hopes that the three-year statute will displace the open one.

BADARACCO v. COMMISSIONER
464 U.S. 386 (1984)
Supreme Court of the United States

Justice BLACKMUN delivered the opinion of the Court.

These cases focus upon § 6501 of the Internal Revenue Code of 1954, 26 U.S.C. § 6501. Subsection (a) of that statute establishes a general three-year period of limitations "after the return was filed" for the assessment of income and certain other federal taxes. Subsection (c)(1) of § 6501, however, provides an exception to the three-year period when there is "a false or fraudulent return with the intent to evade tax." The tax then may be assessed "at any time."[1]

---

[1] [fn 1] Section 6501(a) reads in full:

"Except as otherwise provided in this section, the amount of any tax imposed by this title shall be assessed within 3 years after the return was filed (whether or

The issue before us is the proper application of §§ 6501(a) and (c)(1) to the situation where a taxpayer files a false or fraudulent return but later files a nonfraudulent amended return. May a tax then be assessed more than three years after the filing of the amended return?

No. 82–1453. Petitioners Ernest Badaracco, Sr., and Ernest Badaracco, Jr., were partners in an electrical contracting business. They filed federal partnership and individual income tax returns for the calendar years 1965–1969, inclusive. "[F]or purposes of this case," these petitioners concede the "fraudulent nature of the original returns." App. 37a.

In 1970 and 1971, federal grand juries in New Jersey subpoenaed books and records of the partnership. On August 17, 1971, petitioners filed nonfraudulent amended returns for the tax years in question and paid the additional basic taxes shown thereon. Three months later, petitioners were indicted for filing false and fraudulent returns, in violation of § 7206(1) of the Code, 26 U.S.C. § 7206(1). Each pleaded guilty to the charge with respect to the 1967 returns, and judgments of conviction were entered. Crim. No. 766–71(DNJ). The remaining counts of the indictment were dismissed.

On November 21, 1977, the Commissioner of Internal Revenue mailed to petitioners notices of deficiency for each of the tax years in question. He asserted, however, only the liability under § 6653(b) of the Code, 26 U.S.C. § 6653(b), for the addition to tax on account of fraud (the so-called fraud "penalty") of 50% of the underpayment in the basic tax. See App. 5a.

Petitioners sought redetermination in the United States Tax Court of the asserted deficiencies, contending that the Commissioner's action was barred by § 6501(a). They claimed that § 6501(c)(1) did not apply because the 1971 filing of nonfraudulent amended returns caused the general three-year period of limitations specified in § 6501(a) to operate; the deficiency notices, having issued in November 1977, obviously were forthcoming only long after the expiration of three years from the date of filing of the nonfraudulent amended returns.

The Tax Court, in line with its then-recent decision in Klemp v. Commissioner, 77 T.C. 201 (1981), appeal pending, (CA9 No. 81–7744), agreed with petitioners. . . .

No. 82–1509. Petitioner Deleet Merchandising Corp. filed timely corporation income tax returns for the calendar years 1967 and 1968. The returns as so filed, however, did not report certain receipts derived by the taxpayer from its printing supply business. On August 9, 1973, Deleet filed amended returns for 1967 and 1968 disclosing the receipts that had not been reported. . . . Although the taxpayer corporation itself was not charged with criminal tax violations, and although no formal criminal investigation was initiated as to it, there were

---

not such return was filed on or after the date prescribed) or, if the tax is payable by stamp, at any time after such tax became due and before the expiration of 3 years after the date on which any part of such tax was paid, and no proceeding in court without assessment for the collection of such tax shall be begun after the expiration of such period."

criminal and civil investigations that centered on certain former officers of the taxpayer. After the completion of those investigations, the Commissioner, on December 14, 1979, issued a notice of deficiency to Deleet. App. 71a. The notice asserted deficiencies in tax and additions under § 6653(b) for 1967 and 1968.

Deleet paid the alleged deficiencies and brought suit for their refund in the United States District Court for the District of New Jersey. On its motion for summary judgment, Deleet contended that the Commissioner's action was barred by § 6501(a). It claimed that no deficiencies or additions could be assessed more than three years after the amended returns were filed, regardless of whether the original returns were fraudulent.

The District Court agreed and granted summary judgment for Deleet. 535 F.Supp. 402 (1981). It relied on the Tax Court's decision in *Klemp v. Commissioner, supra,* and on *Dowell v. Commissioner,* 614 F.2d 1263 (CA10 1980), cert. pending, No. 82–1873.

The Appeals. The Government appealed each case to the United States Court of Appeals for the Third Circuit. The cases were heard and decided together. That court, by a 2 to 1 vote, reversed the decision of the Tax Court in *Badaracco* and the judgment of the District Court in *Deleet. Badaracco v. Commissioner,* 693 F.2d 298 (1982). The Third Circuit's ruling is consistent with the Fifth Circuit's holding in *Nesmith v. Commissioner,* 699 F.2d 712 (1983), cert. pending, No. 82–2008. The Second Circuit has ruled otherwise. See *Britton v. United States,* 532 F.Supp. 275 (Vt.1981), aff'd mem., 697 F.2d 288 (CA2 1982). See also *Espinoza v. Commissioner,* 78 T.C. 412 (1982). . . . Because of the conflict, we granted certiorari, 461 U.S. 925, 103 S.Ct. 2084, 77 L.Ed.2d 296 (1983).

II

Our task here is to determine the proper construction of the statute of limitations Congress has written for tax assessments. This Court long ago pronounced the standard: "Statutes of limitation sought to be applied to bar rights of the Government, must receive a strict construction in favor of the Government." *E.I. Dupont de Nemours & Co. v. Davis,* 264 U.S. 456, 462, 44 S.Ct. 364, 366, 68 L.Ed. 788 (1924). See also *Lucas v. Pilliod Lumber Co.,* 281 U.S. 245, 249, 50 S.Ct. 297, 299, 74 L.Ed. 829 (1930). More recently, Judge Roney, in speaking for the former Fifth Circuit, has observed that "limitations statutes barring the collection of taxes otherwise due and unpaid are strictly construed in favor of the Government." *Lucia v. United States,* 474 F.2d 565, 570 (1973).

We naturally turn first to the language of the statute. Section 6501(a) sets forth the general rule: a three-year period of limitations on the assessment of tax. Section 6501(e)(1)(A) (first introduced as § 275(c) of the Revenue Act of 1934, 48 Stat. 745) provides an extended limitations period for the situation where the taxpayer's return nonfraudulently omits more than 25% of his gross income; in a situation of that kind, assessment now is permitted "at any time within 6 years after the return was filed."

Both the three-year rule and the six-year rule, however, explicitly are made inapplicable in circumstances covered by § 6501(c). This subsection identifies three situations in which the Commissioner is allowed an unlimited period within which to assess tax. Subsection (c)(1) relates to "a false or fraudulent return with the intent to evade tax" and provides that the tax then may be assessed "at any time." Subsection (c)(3) covers the case of a failure to file a return at all (whether or not due to fraud) and provides that an assessment then also may be made "at any time." Subsection (c)(2) sets forth a similar rule for the case of a "willful attempt in any manner to defeat or evade tax" other than income, estate, and gift taxes.

All these provisions appear to be unambiguous on their face, and it therefore would seem to follow that the present cases are squarely controlled by the clear language of § 6501(c)(1). Petitioners Badaracco concede that they filed initial returns that were "false or fraudulent with the intent to evade tax." Petitioner Deleet, for present purposes, upon this review of its motion for summary judgment, is deemed to have filed false or fraudulent returns with the intent to evade tax. Section 6501(c)(1), with its unqualified language, then allows the tax to be assessed "at any time." Nothing is present in the statute that can be construed to suspend its operation in the light of a fraudulent filer's subsequent repentant conduct. Neither is there anything in the wording of § 6501(a) that itself enables a taxpayer to reinstate the section's general three-year limitations period by filing an amended return. Indeed, as this Court recently has noted, *Hillsboro National Bank v. Commissioner,* 460 U.S. 370, ——, n. 10, 103 S.Ct. 1134, 1140, n. 10, 75 L.Ed.2d 130 (1983), the Internal Revenue Code does not explicitly provide either for a taxpayer's filing, or for the Commissioner's acceptance, of an amended return; instead, an amended return is a creature of administrative origin and grace. Thus, when Congress provided for assessment at any time in the case of a false or fraudulent "return," it plainly included by this language a false or fraudulent *original* return. In this connection, we note that until the decision of the Tenth Circuit in *Dowell v. Commissioner,* 614 F.2d 1263 (1980), cert. pending, No. 82–1873, courts consistently had held that the operation of § 6501 and its predecessors turned on the nature of the taxpayer's original, and not his amended, return.

The substantive operation of the fraud provisions of the Code itself confirms the conclusion that § 6501(c)(1) permits assessment at any time in fraud cases regardless of a taxpayer's later repentance. It is established that a taxpayer who submits a fraudulent return does not purge the fraud by subsequent voluntary disclosure; the fraud was committed, and the offense completed, when the original return was prepared and filed. See, *e.g., United States v. Habig,* 390 U.S. 222, 88 S.Ct. 926, 19 L.Ed.2d 1055 (1968); *Plunkett v. Commissioner,* 465 F.2d 299, 302–303 (CA7 1972). "Any other result would make sport of the so-called fraud penalty. A taxpayer who had filed a fraudulent return would merely take his chances that the fraud would not be investigated or discovered, and then, if an investigation were made, would simply pay the tax which he owed anyhow and thereby nullify the fraud penalty." *George M. Still, Inc. v. Commissioner,* 19 T.C. 1072, 1077 (1953), aff'd, 218 F.2d 639 (CA2 1955). In short, once a fraudulent return has been filed, the case remains one "of a false or fraudulent return," regardless of the taxpayer's later revised conduct, for purposes of criminal prosecution and civil fraud liability under § 6653(b). It likewise should remain such a case for purposes of the unlimited assessment period specified by § 6501(c)(1).

We are not persuaded by Deleet's suggestion, Brief for Petitioner in No. 82–1509, p. 15, that § 6501(c)(1) should be read merely to suspend the commencement of the limitations period while the fraud remains uncorrected. The Tenth Circuit, in *Dowell v. Commissioner, supra,* made an observation to that effect, stating that the three-year limitations period was "put in limbo" pending further taxpayer action. 614 F.2d, at 1266. The language of the statute, however, is contrary to this suggestion. Section 6501(c)(1) does not "suspend" the operation of § 6501(a) until a fraudulent filer makes a voluntary disclosure. Section 6501(c)(1) makes no reference at all to § 6501(a); it simply provides that the tax may be assessed "at any time." And § 6501(a) itself contains no mechanism for its operation when a fraudulent filer repents. By its very terms, it does not apply to a case, such as one of "a false or fraudulent return," that is "otherwise provided" for in § 6501. When Congress intends only a temporary suspension of the running of a limitations period, it knows how unambiguously to accomplish that result. See, *e.g.,* §§ 6503(a)(1), (a)(2), (b), (c), and (d).

The weakness of petitioners' proposed statutory construction is demonstrated further by its impact on § 6501(e)(1)(A), which provides an extended limitations period whenever a taxpayer's return nonfraudulently omits more than 25% of his gross income.

Under petitioners' reasoning, a taxpayer who *fraudulently* omits 25% of his gross income gains the benefit of the three-year limitations period by filing an amended return. Yet a taxpayer who *nonfraudulently* omits 25% of his gross income cannot gain that benefit by filing an amended return; instead, he must live with the six-year period specified in § 6501(e)(1)(A). We agree with the conclusion of the Court of Appeals in the instant cases that Congress could not have intended to "create a situation in which persons who committed willful, deliberate fraud would be in a better position" than those who understated their income inadvertently and without fraud. 693 F.2d, at 302.

We therefore conclude that the plain and unambiguous language of § 6501(c)(1) would permit the Commissioner to assess "at any time" the tax for a year in which the taxpayer has filed "a false or fraudulent return," despite any subsequent disclosure the taxpayer might make. Petitioners attempt to evade the consequences of this language by arguing that their original returns were "nullities." Alternatively, they urge a nonliteral construction of the statute based on considerations of policy and practicality. We now turn successively to those proposals.

III

Petitioners argue that their original returns, to the extent they were fraudulent, were "nullities" for statute of limitations purposes. See Brief for Petitioners in No. 82–1453, pp. 22–27; Brief for Petitioner in No. 82–1509, pp. 32–34. Inasmuch as the original return is a nullity, it is said, the amended return is necessarily "the return" referred to in § 6501(a). And if that return is nonfraudulent, § 6501(c)(1) is inoperative and the normal three-year limitations period applies. This nullity notion does not persuade us, for it is plain that "the return" referred to in § 6501(a) is the original, not the amended, return.

Petitioners do not contend that their fraudulent original returns were nullities for purposes of the Code generally. There are numerous provisions in the Code that relate to civil and criminal penalties for submitting or assisting in the preparation of false or fraudulent returns; their presence makes clear that a document which on its face plausibly purports to be in compliance, and which is signed by the taxpayer, is a return despite its inaccuracies. See, *e.g.*, §§ 7207, 6531(3), 6653(b). Neither do petitioners contend that their original returns were nullities for all purposes of § 6501. They contend, instead, that a fraudulent return is a nullity only for the limited purpose of applying § 6501(a). See Brief for Petitioners in No. 82–1453, p. 24; Brief for Petitioner in No. 82–1509, pp. 33–34. The word "return," however, appears no less than 64 times in § 6501. Surely, Congress cannot rationally be thought to have given that word one meaning in § 6501(a), and a totally different meaning in §§ 6501(b) through (q).

Zellerbach Paper Co. v. Helvering, 293 U.S. 172, 55 S.Ct. 127, 79 L.Ed. 264 (1934), which petitioners cite, affords no support for their argument. The Court in *Zellerbach* held that an original return, despite its inaccuracy, was a "return" for limitations purposes, so that the filing of an amended return did not start a new period of limitations running. In the instant cases, the original returns similarly purported to be returns, were sworn to as such, and appeared on their faces to constitute endeavors to satisfy the law. Although those returns, in fact, were not honest, the holding in *Zellerbach* does not render them nullities. To be sure, current Regulations, in several places, e.g., Treas.Reg. §§ 301.6211–1(a), 301.6402–3(a), 1.451–1(a) and 1.461–1(a)(3)(i) (1983), do refer to an amended return, as does § 6213(g)(1) of the Code itself, 26 U.S.C. § 6213(g)(1) (1976 ed., Supp. V). None of these provisions, however, requires the filing of such a return. It does not follow from all this that an amended return becomes "the return" for purposes of § 6501(a).

We conclude, therefore, that nothing in the statutory language, the structure of the Code, or the decided cases supports the contention that a fraudulent return is a nullity for statute of limitations purposes.

IV

Petitioners contend that a nonliteral reading should be accorded the statute on grounds of equity to the repentant taxpayer and tax policy. "Once a taxpayer has provided the information upon which the Government may make a knowledgeable assessment, the justification for suspending the limitations period is no longer viable and must yield to the favored policy of limiting the Government's time to proceed against the taxpayer." Brief for Petitioner in No. 82–1509, p. 12. See, also, Brief for Petitioners in No. 82–1453, p. 17.

The cases before us, however, concern the construction of existing statutes. The relevant question is not whether, as an abstract matter, the rule advocated by petitioners accords with good policy. The question we must consider is whether the policy petitioners favor is that which Congress effectuated by its enactment of § 6501. Courts are not authorized to rewrite a statute because they might deem its effects susceptible of improvement. See *TVA v. Hill,* 437 U.S. 153, 194–195, 98 S.Ct. 2279, 2301–2302, 57 L.Ed.2d 117 (1978). This is especially so when courts construe a statute of limitations, which "must receive a strict construction in favor of the Government." *E.I. Dupont de Nemours & Co. v. Davis,* 264 U.S., at 462, 44 S.Ct., at 366.

We conclude that, even were we free to do so, there is no need to twist § 6501(c)(1) beyond the contours of its plain and unambiguous language in order to comport with good policy, for substantial policy considerations support its literal language. First, fraud cases ordinarily are more difficult to investigate than cases marked for routine tax audits. Where fraud has been practiced, there is a distinct possibility that the taxpayer's underlying records will have been falsified or even destroyed. The filing of an amended return, then, may not diminish the amount of effort required to verify the correct tax liability. Even though the amended return proves to be an honest one, its filing does not necessarily "remov[e] the Commissioner from the disadvantageous position in which he was originally placed." Brief for Petitioners in No. 82–1453, p. 12.

Second, the filing of a document styled "amended return" does not fundamentally change the nature of a tax fraud investigation. An amended return, however accurate it ultimately may prove to be, comes with no greater guarantee of trustworthiness than any other submission. It comes carrying no special or significant imprimatur; instead, it comes from a taxpayer who already has made false statements under penalty of perjury. A responsible examiner cannot accept the information furnished on an amended return as a substitute for a thorough investigation into the existence of fraud. We see no "tax policy" justification for holding that an amended return has the singular effect of shortening the unlimited assessment period specified in § 6501(c)(1) to the usual three years. Fraud cases differ from other civil tax cases in that it is the Commissioner who has the burden of proof on the issue of fraud. See § 7454(a) of the Code, 26 U.S.C. § 7454(a). An amended return, of course, may constitute an admission of substantial underpayment, but it will not ordinarily constitute an admission of fraud. And the three years may not be enough time for the Commissioner to prove fraudulent intent.

Third, the difficulties that attend a civil fraud investigation are compounded where, as in No. 82–1453, the Commissioner's initial findings lead him to conclude that the case should be referred to the Department of Justice for criminal prosecution. The period of limitations for prosecuting criminal tax fraud is generally six years. See § 6531. Once a criminal referral has been made, the Commissioner is under well-known restraints on the civil side and often will find it difficult to complete his civil investigation within the normal three-year period; the taxpayer's filing of an amended return will not make any difference in this respect. See *United States v. LaSalle National Bank,* 437 U.S. 298, 311–313, 98 S.Ct. 2357, 2364–2365, 57 L.Ed.2d 221 (1978); see also Tax Equity and Fiscal Responsibility Act of 1982, Pub.L. 97–248, § 333(a), 96 Stat. 622. As a practical matter, therefore, the Commissioner frequently is forced to place a civil audit in abeyance when a criminal prosecution is recommended.

We do not find petitioners' complaint of "unfair treatment" persuasive. Petitioners claim that it is unfair "to forever suspend a Sword of Damocles over a taxpayer who at one time may have filed a fraudulent return, but who has subsequently recanted and filed an amended return providing the Government with all the information necessary to properly assess the tax." Brief for Petitioner in No. 82–1509, p. 26. See Brief for Petitioners in No. 82–1453, p. 16. But it seems to us that a taxpayer who has filed a fraudulent return with intent to evade tax hardly is in a position to complain of the fairness of a rule that facilitates the Commissioner's collection of the tax due. A taxpayer who has been the subject of a tax fraud investigation is not likely to be surprised when a notice of deficiency arrives, even if it does not arrive promptly after he files an amended return.

Neither are we persuaded by Deleet's argument that a literal reading of the statute "punishes" the taxpayer who repentantly files an amended return. See Brief for Petitioner in No. 82–1509, p. 44. The amended return does not change the status of the taxpayer; he is left in precisely the same position he was in before. It might be argued that Congress should provide incentives to taxpayers to disclose their fraud voluntarily. Congress, however, has not done so in § 6501. That legislative judgment is controlling here.

V

Petitioners contend, finally, that a literal reading of § 6501(c) produces a disparity in treatment between a taxpayer who in the first instance files a fraudulent return and one who fraudulently fails to file any return at all. This, it is said, would elevate one form of tax fraud over another.

The argument centers in § 6501(c)(3), which provides that in a case of failure to file a return, the tax may be assessed "at any time." It is settled that this section ceases to apply once a return has been filed for a particular year, regardless of whether that return is filed late and even though the failure to file a timely return in the first instance was due to fraud. See *Bennett v. Commissioner,* 30 T.C. 114 (1958), acq., 1958–2 Cum.Bull. 3. See also Rev.Rul. 79–178, 1979–1 Cum.Bull. 435. This, however, does not mean that § 6501 should be read to produce the same result in each of the two situations. From the language employed in the respective subsections of § 6501, we conclude that Congress intended different limitations results. Section 6501(c)(3) applies to a "failure to file a return." It makes no reference to a failure to file a timely return (cf. §§ 6651(a)(1) and 7203), nor does it speak of a fraudulent failure to file. The section literally becomes inapplicable once a return has been filed. Section 6501(c)(1), in contrast, applies in the case of "a false or fraudulent return." The fact that a fraudulent filer subsequently submits an amended return does not make the case any less one of a false or fraudulent return. Thus, although there may be some initial superficial plausibility to this argument on the part of petitioners, we conclude that the argument cannot prevail. If the result contended for by petitioners is to be the rule, Congress must make it so in clear and unmistakable language.

The judgment of the Court of Appeals in each of these cases is affirmed.

It is so ordered.

Justice STEVENS, dissenting.

The plain language of § 6501(c)(1) of the Internal Revenue Code conveys a different message to me than it does to the Court. That language is clear enough: "In the case of a false or fraudulent return with the intent to evade tax, the tax may be assessed, or a proceeding in court for collection of such tax may be begun without assessment, at any time." 26 U.S.C. § 6501(c)(1). What is not clear to me is why this is a case of "a false or fraudulent return."

In both cases before the Court, the Commissioner assessed deficiencies based on concededly nonfraudulent returns. The taxpayers' alleged prior fraud was not the basis for the Commissioner's action. Indeed, whether or not the Commissioner was obligated to accept petitioners' amended returns, he in fact elected to do so and to use them as the basis for his assessment. When the Commissioner initiates a deficiency proceeding on the basis of a nonfraudulent return, I do not believe that the resulting case is one "of a false or fraudulent return."

The purpose of the statute supports this reading. The original version of § 6501(c) was enacted in 1921. It was true in 1921, as it is today, that the fraudulent concealment of the facts giving rise to a claim tolled the controlling statute of limitations until full disclosure was made. Fraud did not entirely repeal the bar of limitations; rather the period of limitations simply did not begin to run until the fraud was discovered, or at least discoverable. See, *e.g., Exploration Co. v. United States,* 247 U.S. 435, 38 S.Ct. 571, 62 L.Ed.2d 1200 (1918). Moreover, this Court soon ruled that if a return constitutes an honest and genuine attempt to satisfy the law, it is sufficient to commence the running of the statute of limitations. . The Court has subsequently adhered to this position. See *Commissioner v. Lane-Wells Co.,* 321 U.S. 219, 64 S.Ct. 511, 88 L.Ed. 684 (1944); *Germantown Trust Co. v. Commissioner,* 309 U.S. 304, 60 S.Ct. 566, 84 L.Ed. 770 (1940). For example, the Court has construed another portion of the statute, dealing with underreporting of income, as inapplicable to returns which disclose the facts forming the basis for the deficiency.

> "We think that in enacting [the statute] Congress manifested no broader purpose than to give the Commissioner an additional two years to investigate tax returns in cases where, because of a taxpayer's omission to report some taxable item, the Commissioner is at a special disadvantage in detecting errors. In such instances the return on its face provides no clue as to the existence of the omitted item. On the other hand, when, as here, the understatement of a tax arises from an error in reporting an item disclosed on the face of the return the Commissioner is at no such disadvantage." .

In light of the purposes and common law background of the statute, as well as this Court's previous treatment of what a "return" sufficient to commence the running of the limitations period is, it seems apparent that an assessment based on a nonfraudulent amended return does not fall within § 6501(c)(1). Once the amended return is filed the rationale for disregarding the limitations period is absent. The period of concealment is over, and under general common law principles the limitations period should begin to run. The filing of the return means that the Commissioner is no longer under any disadvantage; full disclosure has been made and there is no reason why he cannot assess a deficiency within the statutory period.

The 1921 statute read as follows.

"That in the case of a false or fraudulent return with intent to evade tax, or of a failure to file a required return, the amount of tax due may be determined, assessed, and collected, and a suit or proceeding for the collection of such amount may be begun, at any time after it becomes due." Revenue Act of 1921, § 250(d), 42 Stat. 265.

Under this statute, the filing of a fraudulent return had no greater effect on the limitations period than the filing of no return at all. In either case, since the relevant facts had not been disclosed to the Commissioner, the proper tax could be assessed "at any time." In 1954 the statute was bifurcated; the provisions relating to a failure to file were placed into § 6501(c)(3). The legislative history of this revision indicates that the division was not intended to change the statute's meaning. This history supports petitioners' reading of the statute. Fraudulent returns were treated the same as no return at all since neither gives the Commissioner an adequate basis to attempt an assessment. Once that basis is provided, however, the statute is inapplicable; it is no longer a "case of a false or fraudulent return."

The Commissioner practically concedes as much since he agrees with the ruling in Bennett v. Commissioner, 30 T.C. 114 (1958), acq. 1958–2 Cum.Bull. 3, that if the taxpayer fraudulently fails to file a return, the limitations period nevertheless begins to run once a nonfraudulent return is filed. See also Rev.Rul. 79–178, 1979–1 Cum.Bull. 458. Yet there is nothing in the history of this statute indicating that Congress intended a bifurcated reading of a simple statutory command. There is certainly no logical reason supporting such a result; the Commissioner is if anything under a greater disadvantage when the taxpayer originally filed no return at all, since at least in the (c)(1) situation the Commissioner can compare the two returns. If the Commissioner can assess a deficiency within three years when no return was previously filed, he can do the same if the original return was fraudulent.

Whatever the correct standard for construing a statute of limitations when it operates against the government, see *ante,* at 761, surely the presumption ought to be that *some* limitations period is applicable.

"It probably would be all but intolerable, at least Congress has regarded it as ill-advised, to have an income tax system under which there never would come a day of final settlement and which required both the taxpayer and the Government to stand ready forever and a day to produce vouchers, prove events, establish values and recall details of all that goes into an income tax contest. Hence, a statute of limitation is an almost indispensible element of fairness as well as of practical administration of an income tax policy." *Rothensies v. Electric Battery Co.,* 329 U.S. 296, 301, 67 S.Ct. 271, 273, 91 L.Ed. 296 (1946).

However, under the Commissioner's position, adopted by the Court today, no limitations period will *ever* apply to the Commissioner's actions, despite petitioners' attempts to provide him with all the information necessary to make a timely assessment.

"Respondent would leave the statute open for that portion of eternity concurrent with the taxpayer's life, whether he lives three score and ten or as long as Methuselah. In most religions one can repent and be saved but in the peculiar tax theology of respondent no act of contrition will suffice to prevent the statute from running in perpetuity. Merely to state the proposition is to refute it, unless some very compelling reason of policy requires visiting this absurdity on the taxpayer." *Klemp v. Commissioner,* 77 T.C. 201, 207 (1981) (Wilbur, J., concurring).[2]

If anything, considerations of tax policy argue against the result reached by the Court today. In a system based on voluntary compliance, it is crucial that some incentive be given to persons to reveal and correct past fraud. Yet the rule announced by the Court today creates no such incentive; a taxpayer gets no advantage at all by filing an honest return. Not only does the taxpayer fail to gain the benefit of a limitations period, but at the same time he gives the Commissioner additional information which can be used against him at any time. Since the amended return will not give the taxpayer a defense in a criminal or civil fraud action, see *ante,* at 762, there is no reason at all for a taxpayer to correct a fraudulent return. Apparently the Court believes that taxpayers should be advised to remain silent, hoping the fraud will go undetected, rather than to make full disclosure in a proper return. I cannot believe that Congress intended such a result.

I respectfully dissent.

NOTES AND QUESTIONS

1. *Badaracco* held in part that a false return does not trigger a statutory period for the IRS to assess tax. A similar issue arises if no return is filed. Section 6501(c)(3) provides as follows:

    > In the case of failure to file a return, the tax may be assessed, or a proceeding in court for the collection of such tax may be begun without assessment, at any time.

---

[2] [fn 7] Even Judge Wilbur's estimation of the sweep of the Commissioner's position may be too modest, for under § 6901(c)(1) the Commissioner is entitled to assess deficiencies against a taxpayer's beneficiaries after his or her death for one year after the limitations period runs. Since the limitations period will never run, the Commissioner may presumably hound a taxpayer's beneficiaries and their descendants in perpetuity.

This means that no statutory period in which the IRS must assess tax begins because such an assessment may take place "at any time." In other words, a tax return must be filed to begin the running of the statute of limitations on assessment.

2. Which opinion is the most compelling, the majority or the dissent?
3. Does the holding discourage repentant filing?

The IRS also may take extra time to examine a return if it contains a substantial omission of income. *See* IRC § 6501(e)(1)(A). The meaning of "substantial omission of income" was not clarified until 2012 in the following case.

UNITED STATES v. HOME CONCRETE & SUPPLY, LLC
566 U.S. 478 (2012)
Supreme Court of the United States

Justice BREYER delivered the opinion of the Court, except as to Part IV–C.

Ordinarily, the Government must assess a deficiency against a taxpayer within "3 years after the return was filed." 26 U.S.C. § 6501(a) (2000 ed.). The 3–year period is extended to 6 years, however, when a taxpayer "*omits from gross income an amount properly includible therein* which is in excess of 25 percent of the amount of gross income stated in the return." § 6501(e)(1)(A) (emphasis added). The question before us is whether this latter provision applies (and extends the ordinary 3–year limitations period) when the taxpayer *overstates his basis* in property that he has sold, thereby *understating the gain* that he received from its sale. Following *Colony, Inc. v. Commissioner,* 357 U.S. 28, 78 S.Ct. 1033, 2 L.Ed.2d 1119 (1958), we hold that the provision does not apply to an overstatement of basis. Hence the 6–year period does not apply.

I

For present purposes the relevant underlying circumstances are not in dispute. We consequently assume that (1) the respondent taxpayers filed their relevant tax returns in April 2000; (2) the returns overstated the basis of certain property that the taxpayers had sold; (3) as a result the returns understated the gross income that the taxpayers received from the sale of the property; and (4) the understatement exceeded the statute's 25% threshold. We also take as undisputed that the Commissioner asserted the relevant deficiency within the extended 6–year limitations period, but outside the default 3–year period. Thus, unless the 6–year statute of limitations applies, the Government's efforts to assert a tax deficiency came too late. Our conclusion—that the extended limitations period does not apply—follows directly from this Court's earlier decision in *Colony*.

II

In *Colony* this Court interpreted a provision of the Internal Revenue Code of 1939, the operative language of which is identical to the language now before us. The Commissioner there had determined "that the taxpayer had understated the gross profits on the sales of certain lots of land for residential purposes as a result of having overstated the 'basis' of such lots by erroneously including in their cost certain unallowable items of development expense." *Id.,* at 30, 78 S.Ct. 1033.

The Commissioner's assessment came after the ordinary 3–year limitations period had run. And, it was consequently timely only if the taxpayer, in the words of the 1939 Code, had "omit[ted] from gross income an amount properly includible therein which is in excess of 25 per centum of the amount of gross income stated in the return. . .." 26 U.S.C. § 275(c) (1940 ed.). The Code provision applicable to this case, adopted in 1954, contains materially indistinguishable language. See § 6501(e)(1)(A) (2000 ed.) (same, but replacing "per centum" with "percent"). See also Appendix, *infra.*

In *Colony* this Court held that taxpayer misstatements, overstating the basis in property, do not fall within the scope of the statute. But the Court recognized the Commissioner's contrary argument for inclusion. 357 U.S., at 32, 78 S.Ct. 1033. Then as now, the Code itself defined "gross income" in this context as the difference between gross revenue (often the amount the taxpayer received upon selling the property) and basis (often the amount the taxpayer paid for the property). Compare 26 U.S.C. §§ 22, 111 (1940 ed.) with §§ 61(a)(3), 1001(a) (2000 ed.). And, the Commissioner pointed out, an overstatement of basis can diminish the "amount" of the gain just as leaving the item entirely off the return might do. 357 U.S., at 32, 78 S.Ct. 1033. Either way, the error wrongly understates the taxpayer's income.

But, the Court added, the Commissioner's argument did not fully account for the provision's language, in particular the word "omit." The key phrase says "*omits* . . . an amount." The word "omits" (unlike, say, "reduces" or "understates") means " '[t]o leave out or unmentioned; not to insert, include, or name.' " *Ibid.* (quoting Webster's New International Dictionary (2d ed. 1939)). Thus, taken literally, "omit" limits the statute's scope to situations in which specific receipts or accruals of income are *left out* of the computation of gross income; to inflate the basis, however, is not to "omit" a specific item, not even of profit.

While finding this latter interpretation of the language the "more plausibl[e]," the Court also noted that the language was not "unambiguous." *Colony,* 357 U.S., at 33, 78 S.Ct. 1033. It then examined various congressional Reports discussing the relevant statutory language. It found in those Reports

"persuasive indications that Congress merely had in mind failures to report particular income receipts and accruals, and did not intend the [extended] limitation to apply whenever gross income was understated. . .." *Id.,* at 35, 78 S.Ct. 1033.

This "history," the Court said, "shows . . . that the Congress intended an exception to the usual three-year statute of limitations only in the restricted type of situation already described," a situation that did not include overstatements of basis. *Id.,* at 36, 78 S.Ct. 1033.

The Court wrote that Congress, in enacting the provision,

"manifested no broader purpose than to give the Commissioner an additional two [now three] years to investigate tax returns in cases where, because of a taxpayer's omission to report some taxable item, the Commissioner is at a special disadvantage . . . [because] the return on its face provides no clue to the existence of the omitted item. . . . [W]hen, *as here* [*i.e.,* where the overstatement of basis is at issue], the understatement of a tax arises from an error in reporting an item disclosed on the face of the return the Commissioner is at no such disadvantage . . . whether the error be one affecting 'gross income' or one, such as overstated deductions, affecting other parts of the return." *Ibid.* (emphasis added).

Finally, the Court noted that Congress had recently enacted the Internal Revenue Code of 1954. And the Court observed that "the conclusion we reach is in harmony with the unambiguous language of § 6501(e)(1)(A)," *id.,* at 37, 78 S.Ct. 1033, *i.e.,* the provision relevant in this present case.

III

In our view, *Colony* determines the outcome in this case. The provision before us is a 1954 reenactment of the 1939 provision that *Colony* interpreted. The operative language is identical. It would be difficult, perhaps impossible, to give the same language here a different interpretation without effectively overruling *Colony*, a course of action that basic principles of *stare decisis* wisely counsel us not to take. *John R. Sand & Gravel Co. v. United States,* 552 U.S. 130, 139, 128 S.Ct. 750, 169 L.Ed.2d 591 (2008) ("*[S]tare decisis* in respect to statutory interpretation has special force, for Congress remains free to alter what we have done" (internal quotation marks omitted)); *Patterson v. McLean Credit Union,* 491 U.S. 164, 172–173, 109 S.Ct. 2363, 105 L.Ed.2d 132 (1989).

The Government, in an effort to convince us to interpret the operative language before us differently, points to differences in other nearby parts of the 1954 Code. It suggests that these differences counsel in favor of a different interpretation than the one adopted in *Colony*. For example, the Government points to a new provision, § 6501(e)(1)(A)(i), which says:

"In the case of a trade or business, the term 'gross income' means the total of the amounts received or accrued from the sale of goods or services (if such amounts are required to be shown on the return) prior to the diminution by the cost of such sales or services."

If the section's basic phrase "omi[ssion] from gross income" does not apply to overstatements of basis (which is what *Colony* held), then what need would there be for clause (i), which leads to the same result in a specific subset of cases?

And why, the Government adds, does a later paragraph, referring to gifts and estates, speak of a taxpayer who "omits . . . *items* includible in [the] gross estate"? See § 6501(e)(2) (emphasis added). By speaking of "items" there does it not imply that omission of an "amount" covers more than omission of individual items—indeed that it includes overstatements of basis, which, after all, diminish the *amount* of the profit that should have been reported as gross income?

In our view, these points are too fragile to bear the significant argumentative weight the Government seeks to place upon them. For example, at least one plausible reason why Congress might have added clause (i) has nothing to do with any desire to change the meaning of the general rule. Rather when Congress wrote the 1954 Code (prior to *Colony*), it did not yet know how the Court would interpret the provision's operative language. At least one lower court had decided that the provision did *not* apply to overstatements about the cost of goods that a business later sold. See *Uptegrove Lumber Co. v. Commissioner*, 204 F.2d 570 (C.A.3 1953). But see *Reis v. Commissioner*, 142 F.2d 900, 902–903 (C.A.6 1944). And Congress could well have wanted to ensure that, come what may in the Supreme Court, *Uptegrove*'s interpretation would remain the law where a "trade or business" was at issue.

Nor does our interpretation leave clause (i) without work to do. TRW Inc. v. Andrews, 534 U.S. 19, 31, 122 S.Ct. 441, 151 L.Ed.2d 339 (2001) (noting canon that statutes should be read to avoid making any provision "superfluous, void, or insignificant" (internal quotation marks omitted)). That provision also explains how to calculate the denominator for purposes of determining whether a conceded omission amounts to 25% of "gross income." For example, it tells us that a merchant who fails to include $10,000 of revenue from sold goods has not met the 25% test if total revenue is more than $40,000, regardless of the cost paid by the merchant to acquire those goods. But without clause (i), the general statutory definition of "gross income" requires subtracting the cost from the sales price. See 26 U.S.C. §§ 61(a)(3), 1012. Under such a definition of "gross income," the calculation would take (1) total revenue from sales, $40,000, minus (2) "the cost of such sales," say, $25,000. The $10,000 of revenue would thus amount to 67% of the "gross income" of $15,000. And the clause does this work in respect to omissions from gross income irrespective of our interpretation regarding overstatements of basis.

The Government's argument about subsection (e)(2)'s use of the word "item" instead of "amount" is yet weaker. The Court in *Colony* addressed a similar argument about the word "amount." It wrote:

> "The Commissioner states that the draftsman's use of the word 'amount' (instead of, for example, 'item') suggests a concentration on the quantitative aspect of the error—that is whether or not gross income was understated by as much as 25%." 357 U.S., at 32, 78 S.Ct. 1033.

But the Court, while recognizing the Commissioner's logic, rejected the argument (and the significance of the word "amount") as insufficient to prove the Commissioner's conclusion. And the addition of the word "item" in a different subsection similarly fails to exert an interpretive force sufficiently strong to affect our conclusion. The word's appearance in subsection (e)(2), we concede, is new. But to rely in the case before us on this solitary word change in a different subsection is like hoping that a new batboy will change the outcome of the World Series.

IV

A

Finally, the Government points to Treasury Regulation § 301.6501(e)–1, which was promulgated in final form in December 2010. See 26 CFR § 301.6501(e)–1 (2011). The regulation, as relevant here, departs from *Colony* and interprets the operative language of the statute in the Government's favor. The regulation says that "an understated amount of gross income resulting from an overstatement of unrecovered cost or other basis constitutes an omission from gross income." § 301.6501(e)–1(a)(1)(iii). In the Government's view this new regulation in effect overturns *Colony*'s interpretation of this statute.

The Government points out that the Treasury Regulation constitutes "an agency's construction of a statute which it administers." *Chevron, U.S.A. Inc. v. Natural Resources Defense Council, Inc.*, 467 U.S. 837, 842, 104 S.Ct. 2778, 81 L.Ed.2d 694 (1984). See also *Mayo Foundation for Medical Ed. and Research v. United States*, 562 U.S. ——, 131 S.Ct. 704, 178 L.Ed.2d 588 (2011) (applying *Chevron* in the tax context). The Court has written that a "court's prior judicial construction of a statute trumps an agency construction otherwise entitled to *Chevron* deference only if the prior court decision holds that its construction follows from the *unambiguous* terms of the statute. . . .." *National Cable & Telecommunications Assn. v. Brand X Internet Services*, 545 U.S. 967, 982, 125 S.Ct. 2688, 162 L.Ed.2d 820 (2005) (emphasis added). And, as the Government notes, in *Colony* itself the Court wrote that "it cannot be said that the language is unambiguous." 357 U.S., at 33, 78 S.Ct. 1033. Hence, the Government concludes, *Colony* cannot govern the outcome in this case. The question, rather, is whether the agency's construction is a "permissible construction of the statute." *Chevron, supra*, at 843, 104 S.Ct. 2778. And, since the Government argues that the regulation embodies a reasonable, hence permissible, construction of the statute, the Government believes it must win.

B

We do not accept this argument. In our view, *Colony* has already interpreted the statute, and there is no longer any different construction that is consistent with *Colony* and available for adoption by the agency.

C

The fatal flaw in the Government's contrary argument is that it overlooks the *reason why Brand X* held that a "prior judicial construction," unless reflecting an "unambiguous" statute, does not trump a different agency construction of that statute. 545 U.S., at 982, 125 S.Ct. 2688. The Court reveals that reason when it points out that "it is for agencies, not courts, to fill statutory gaps." *Ibid.* The fact that a statute is unambiguous means that there is "no gap for the agency to fill" and thus "no room for agency discretion." *Id.*, at 982–983, 125 S.Ct. 2688.

In so stating, the Court sought to encapsulate what earlier opinions, including *Chevron*, made clear. Those opinions identify the underlying interpretive problem as that of deciding whether, or when, a particular statute in effect delegates to an agency the power to fill a gap, thereby implicitly taking from a court the power to void a reasonable gap-filling interpretation. Thus, in *Chevron* the Court said that, when

> "Congress has explicitly left a gap for the agency to fill, there is an express delegation of authority to the agency to elucidate a specific provision of the statute by regulation. . . .. Sometimes the legislative delegation to an agency on a particular question is implicit rather than explicit. [But in either instance], a court may not substitute its own construction of a statutory provision for a reasonable interpretation made by the administrator of an agency." 467 U.S., at 843–844, 104 S.Ct. 2778.

See also United States v. Mead Corp., 533 U.S. 218, 229, 121 S.Ct. 2164, 150 L.Ed.2d 292 (2001); Smiley v. Citibank (South Dakota), N. A., 517 U.S. 735, 741, 116 S.Ct. 1730, 135 L.Ed.2d 25 (1996); INS v. Cardoza–Fonseca, 480 U.S. 421, 448, 107 S.Ct. 1207, 94 L.Ed.2d 434 (1987); Morton v. Ruiz, 415 U.S. 199, 231, 94 S.Ct. 1055, 39 L.Ed.2d 270 (1974).

Chevron and later cases find in unambiguous language a clear sign that Congress did *not* delegate gap-filling authority to an agency; and they find in ambiguous language at least a presumptive indication that Congress did delegate that gap-filling authority. Thus, in *Chevron* the Court wrote that a statute's silence or ambiguity as to a particular issue means that Congress has not "directly addressed the precise question at issue" (thus likely delegating gap-filling power to the agency). 467 U.S., at 843, 104 S.Ct. 2778. In *Mead* the Court, describing *Chevron*, explained:

> "Congress . . . may not have expressly delegated authority or responsibility to implement a particular provision or fill a particular gap. Yet it can still be apparent from the agency's generally conferred authority and other statutory circumstances that Congress would expect the agency to be able to speak with the force of law when it addresses ambiguity in the statute or fills a space in the enacted law, even one about which Congress did not actually have an intent as to a particular result." 533 U.S., at 229, 121 S.Ct. 2164 (internal quotation marks omitted).

Chevron added that "[i]f a court, *employing traditional tools of statutory construction,* ascertains that Congress had an intention on the precise question at issue, that intention is the law and must be given effect." 467 U.S., at 843, n. 9, 104 S.Ct. 2778 (emphasis added).

As the Government points out, the Court in *Colony* stated that the statutory language at issue is not "unambiguous." 357 U.S., at 33, 78 S.Ct. 1033. But the Court decided that case nearly 30 years before it decided *Chevron.* There is no reason to believe that the linguistic ambiguity noted by *Colony* reflects a post-*Chevron* conclusion that Congress had delegated gap-filling power to the agency. At the same time, there is every reason to believe that the Court thought that Congress had "directly spoken to the question at hand," and thus left "[no] gap for the agency to fill." *Chevron, supra,* at 842–843, 104 S.Ct. 2778.

For one thing, the Court said that the taxpayer had the better side of the textual argument. *Colony*, 357 U.S., at 33, 78 S.Ct. 1033. For another, its examination of legislative history led it to believe that Congress had decided the question definitively, leaving no room for the agency to reach a contrary result. It found in that history "persuasive indications" that Congress intended overstatements of basis to fall outside the statute's scope, and it said that it was satisfied that Congress "intended an exception . . . only in the restricted type of situation" it had already described. Id., at 35–36, 78 S.Ct. 1033. Further, it thought that the Commissioner's interpretation (the interpretation once again advanced here) would "create a patent incongruity in the tax law." Id., at 36–37, 78 S.Ct. 1033. And it reached this conclusion despite the fact that, in the years leading up to *Colony*, the Commissioner had consistently advocated the opposite in the circuit courts. See, e.g., *Uptegrove*, 204 F.2d 570; *Reis*, 142 F.2d 900; Goodenow v. Commisioner, 238 F.2d 20 (C.A.8 1956); American Liberty Oil Co. v. Commissioner, 1 T.C. 386 (1942). Cf. Slaff v. Commisioner, 220 F.2d 65 (C.A.9 1955); Davis v. Hightower, 230 F.2d 549 (C.A.5 1956). Thus, the Court was aware it was rejecting the expert opinion of the Commissioner of Internal Revenue. And finally, after completing its analysis, Colony found its interpretation of the 1939 Code "in harmony with the [now] unambiguous language" of the 1954 Code, which at a minimum suggests that the Court saw nothing in the 1954 Code as inconsistent with its conclusion. 357 U.S., at 37, 78 S.Ct. 1033.

It may be that judges today would use other methods to determine whether Congress left a gap to fill. But that is beside the point. The question is whether the Court in *Colony* concluded that the statute left such a gap. And, in our view, the opinion (written by Justice Harlan for the Court) makes clear that it did not.

Given principles of *stare decisis*, we must follow that interpretation. And there being no gap to fill, the Government's gap-filling regulation cannot change *Colony*'s interpretation of the statute. We agree with the taxpayer that overstatements of basis, and the resulting understatement of gross income, do not trigger the extended limitations period of § 6501(e)(1)(A). The Court of Appeals reached the same conclusion. See 634 F.3d 249 (C.A.4 2011). And its judgment is affirmed.

It is so ordered.

[Appendix omitted.]

Justice SCALIA, concurring in part and concurring in the judgment.

It would be reasonable, I think, to deny all precedential effect to Colony, Inc. v. Commissioner, 357 U.S. 28, 78 S.Ct. 1033, 2 L.Ed.2d 1119 (1958)—to overrule its holding as obviously contrary to our later law that agency resolutions of ambiguities are to be accorded deference. Because of justifiable taxpayer reliance I would not take that course—and neither does the Court's opinion, which says that "*Colony* determines the outcome in this case." Ante, at 1841. That should be the end of the matter.

The plurality, however, goes on to address the Government's argument that Treasury Regulation § 301.6501(e)–1 effectively overturned *Colony*. See 26 CFR § 301.6501(e)–1 (2011). In my view, that cannot be: "Once a court has decided upon its *de novo* construction of the statute, there no longer is a different construction that is consistent with the court's holding and available for adoption by the agency." *National Cable & Telecommunications Assn. v. Brand X Internet Services*, 545 U.S. 967, 1018, n. 12, 125 S.Ct. 2688, 162 L.Ed.2d 820 (2005) (SCALIA, J., dissenting) (citation and internal quotation marks omitted). That view, of course, did not carry the day in *Brand X*, and the Government quite reasonably relies on the *Brand X* majority's innovative pronouncement that a "court's prior judicial construction of a statute trumps an agency construction otherwise entitled to *Chevron* deference only if the prior court decision holds that its construction follows from the unambiguous terms of the statute." *Id.*, at 982, 125 S.Ct. 2688.

In cases decided pre-*Brand X*, the Court had no inkling that it *must* utter the magic words "ambiguous" or "unambiguous" in order to (poof!) expand or abridge executive power, and (poof!) enable or disable administrative contradiction of the Supreme Court. Indeed, the Court was unaware of even the utility (much less the necessity) of making the ambiguous/nonambiguous determination in cases decided pre-*Chevron*, before that opinion made the so-called "Step 1" determination of ambiguity *vel non* a customary (though hardly mandatory) part of judicial-review analysis. For many of those earlier cases, therefore, it will be incredibly difficult to determine whether the decision purported to be giving meaning to an ambiguous, or rather an unambiguous, statute.

Thus, one would have thought that the *Brand X* majority would breathe a sigh of relief in the present case, involving a pre-*Chevron* opinion that (*mirabile dictu*) makes it *inescapably clear* that the Court thought the statute ambiguous: "It *cannot* be said that the language is *unambiguous*." *Colony, supra*, at 33, 78 S.Ct. 1033 (emphasis added). As today's plurality opinion explains, *Colony* "said that the taxpayer had the *better* side of the textual argument," *ante*, at 1844 (emphasis added)—not what *Brand X* requires to foreclose administrative revision of our decisions: "the *only permissible* reading of the statute." 545 U.S., at 984, 125 S.Ct. 2688. Thus, having decided to stand by *Colony* and to stand by *Brand X* as well, the plurality should have found—in order to reach the decision it did—that the Treasury Department's current interpretation was unreasonable.

Instead of doing what *Brand X* would require, however, the plurality manages to sustain the justifiable reliance of taxpayers by revising *yet again* the meaning of *Chevron*—and revising it *yet again* in a direction that will create confusion and uncertainty. See *United States v. Mead Corp.*, 533 U.S. 218, 245– 246, 121 S.Ct. 2164, 150 L.Ed.2d 292 (2001) (SCALIA, J., dissenting); Bressman, How *Mead* Has Muddled Judicial Review of Agency Action, 58 Vand. L.Rev. 1443, 1457–1475 (2005). Of course there is no doubt that, with regard to the Internal Revenue Code, the Treasury Department satisfies the *Mead* requirement of some indication "that Congress delegated authority to the agency generally to make rules carrying the force of law." 533 U.S., at 226–227, 121 S.Ct. 2164. We have given *Chevron* deference to a Treasury Regulation before. See *Mayo Foundation for Medical Ed. and Research v. United States,* 562 U.S. – —, ——, 131 S.Ct. 704, 713–714, 178 L.Ed.2d 588 (2011). But in order to evade *Brand X* and yet reaffirm *Colony,* the plurality would add yet another lopsided story to the ugly and improbable structure that our law of administrative review has become: To trigger the *Brand X* power of an authorized "gap-filling" agency to give content to an ambiguous text, a pre-*Chevron* determination that language is ambiguous does not alone suffice; the pre-*Chevron* Court must in addition have found that Congress wanted *the particular ambiguity in question* to be resolved by the agency. And here, today's plurality opinion finds, "[t]here is no reason to believe that the linguistic ambiguity noted by *Colony* reflects a post-*Chevron* conclusion that Congress had delegated gap-filling power to the agency." *Ante,* at 1844. The notion, seemingly, is that post-*Chevron* a finding of ambiguity is accompanied by a finding of agency authority to resolve the ambiguity, but pre-*Chevron* that was not so. The premise is false. Post-*Chevron* cases do not "conclude" that Congress wanted the particular ambiguity resolved by the agency; that is simply the *legal effect* of ambiguity—a legal effect that should obtain whenever the language is in fact (as *Colony* found) ambiguous.

Does the plurality feel that it ought not give effect to *Colony*'s determination of ambiguity because the Court did not know, in that era, the importance of that determination—that it would empower the agency to (in effect) revise the Court's determination of statutory meaning? But as I suggested earlier, that was an ignorance which all of our cases shared not just pre-*Chevron,* but pre-*Brand X.* Before then it did not really matter whether the Court was resolving an ambiguity or setting forth the statute's clear meaning. The opinion might (or might not) advert to that point in the course of its analysis, but either way the Court's interpretation of the statute would be the law. So it is no small number of still-authoritative cases that today's plurality opinion would exile to the Land of Uncertainty.

Perhaps sensing the fragility of its new approach, the plurality opinion then pivots (as the *à la mode* vernacular has it)—from focusing on whether *Colony* concluded that there was gap-filling authority to focusing on whether *Colony* concluded that there was any gap to be filled: "The question is whether the Court in *Colony* concluded that the statute left such a gap. And, in our view, the opinion . . . makes clear that it did not." *Ante,* at 1844. How does the plurality know this? Because Justice Harlan's opinion "said that the taxpayer had the better side of the textual argument"; because it found that legislative history indicated "that Congress intended overstatements of basis to fall outside the statute's scope"; because it concluded that the Commissioner's interpretation would "create a patent incongruity in the tax law"; and because it found its interpretation "in harmony with the [now] unambiguous language" of the 1954 Code. *Ante,* at 1843–1844 (internal quotation marks omitted). But these are the sorts of arguments that courts *always* use in *resolving* ambiguities. They do not prove that no ambiguity existed, unless one believes that an ambiguity resolved is

CHAPTER 10—COMPLIANCE LIMITATIONS PERIODS | 345

an ambiguity that never existed in the first place. *Colony* said unambiguously that the text was ambiguous, and that should be an end of the matter—unless one wants simply to deny *stare decisis* effect to *Colony* as a pre-*Chevron* decision.

Rather than making our judicial-review jurisprudence curiouser and curiouser, the Court should abandon the opinion that produces these contortions, *Brand X*. I join the judgment announced by the Court because it is indisputable that *Colony* resolved the construction of the statutory language at issue here, and that construction must therefore control. And I join the Court's opinion except for Part IV–C.

* * *

I must add a word about the peroration of the dissent, which asserts that "[o]ur legal system presumes there will be continuing dialogue among the three branches of Government on questions of statutory interpretation and application," and that the "constructive discourse," " 'convers[ations],' " and "instructive exchanges" would be "foreclosed by an insistence on adhering to earlier interpretations of a statute even in light of new, relevant statutory amendments." *Post*, at 1852–1853 (opinion of KENNEDY, J.). This passage is reminiscent of Professor K.C. Davis's vision that administrative procedure is developed by "a partnership between legislators and judges," who "working [as] partners produce better law than legislators alone could possibly produce."[3] That romantic, judge-empowering image was obliterated by this Court in *Vermont Yankee Nuclear Power Corp. v. Natural Resources Defense Council, Inc.*, 435 U.S. 519, 98 S.Ct. 1197, 55 L.Ed.2d 460 (1978), which held that Congress prescribes and we obey, with no discretion to add to the administrative procedures that Congress has created. It seems to me that the dissent's vision of a troika partnership (legislative-executive-judicial) is a similar mirage. The discourse, conversation, and exchange that the dissent perceives is peculiarly one-sided. Congress prescribes; and where Congress's prescription is ambiguous the Executive can (within the scope of the ambiguity) clarify that prescription; and if the product is constitutional the courts obey. I hardly think it amounts to a "discourse" that Congress or (as this Court would allow in its *Brand X* decision) the Executive can change its prescription so as to render our prior holding irrelevant. What is needed for the system to work is that Congress, the Executive, and the private parties subject to their dispositions, be able to predict the meaning that the courts will give to their instructions. That goal would be obstructed if the judicially established meaning of a technical legal term used in a very specific context could be overturned on the basis of statutory indications as feeble as those asserted here.

Justice KENNEDY, with whom Justice GINSBURG, Justice SOTOMAYOR, and Justice KAGAN join, dissenting.

This case involves a provision of the Internal Revenue Code establishing an extended statute of limitations for tax assessment in cases where substantial income has been omitted from a tax return. See 26 U.S.C. § 6501(e)(1)(A) (2006

---

[3] [fn 2] 1 K. Davis, Administrative Law Treatise § 2.17, p. 138 (1978).

ed., Supp. IV). The Treasury Department has determined that taxpayers omit income under this section not only when they fail to report a sale of property but also when they overstate their basis in the property sold. See Treas. Reg. § 301.6501(e)–1, 26 CFR § 301.6501(e)–1 (2011). The question is whether this otherwise reasonable interpretation is foreclosed by the Court's contrary reading of an earlier version of the statute in *Colony, Inc. v. Commissioner,* 357 U.S. 28, 78 S.Ct. 1033, 2 L.Ed.2d 1119 (1958).

In *Colony* there was no need to decide whether the meaning of the provision changed when Congress reenacted it as part of the 1954 revision of the Tax Code. Although the main text of the statute remained the same, Congress added new provisions leading to the permissible conclusion that it would have a different meaning going forward. The *Colony* decision reserved judgment on this issue. In my view, the amended statute leaves room for the Department's reading. A summary of the reasons for concluding the Department's interpretation is permissible, and for this respectful dissent, now follows.

I

The statute at issue in *Colony,* 26 U.S.C. § 275(c) (1940 ed.), was enacted as part of the Internal Revenue Code of 1939. It provided for a longer period of limitations if the Government assessed income taxes against a taxpayer who had "omit[ted] from gross income an amount . . . in excess of 25 per centum of the amount of gross income stated in the return."

There was disagreement in the courts about the meaning of this provision in the statute as first enacted. The Tax Court of the United States, and the United States Court of Appeals for the Sixth Circuit, held that an overstatement of basis constituted an omission from gross income and could trigger the extended limitations period. See, *e.g., Reis v. Commissioner,* 142 F.2d 900, 902–903 (1944); *American Liberty Oil Co. v. Commissioner,* 1 T.C. 386 (1942). The United States Court of Appeals for the Third Circuit came to the opposite conclusion in a case where a corporation misreported its income after inflating the cost of goods it sold from inventory. See *Uptegrove Lumber Co. v. Commissioner,* 204 F.2d 570, 571–573 (1953). In the Third Circuit's view there could be an omission only where the taxpayer had left an entire "item of gain out of his computation of gross income." *Id.,* at 571. In the *Colony* decision, issued in 1958, this Court resolved that dispute against the Government. Acknowledging that "it cannot be said that the language is unambiguous," 357 U.S., at 33, 78 S.Ct. 1033, and relying in large part on the legislative history of the 1939 Code, the Court concluded that the mere overstatement of basis did not constitute an omission from gross income under § 275(c).

If the Government is to prevail in the instant case the regulation in question must be a proper implementation of the same language the Court considered in *Colony;* but the statutory interpretation issue here cannot be resolved, and the *Colony* decision cannot be deemed controlling, without first considering the inferences that should be drawn from added statutory text. The additional language was not part of the statute that governed the taxpayer's liability in *Colony,* and the Court did not consider it in that case. Congress revised the

Internal Revenue Code in 1954, several years before *Colony* was decided but after the tax years in question in that case. Although the interpretation adopted by the Court in *Colony* can be a proper beginning point for the interpretation of the revised statute, it ought not to be the end.

The central language of the new provision remained the same as the old, with the longer period of limitations still applicable where a taxpayer had "omit[ted] from gross income an amount . . . in excess of 25 per[cent] of the amount of gross income stated in the return." In *Colony,* however, the Court left open whether Congress had nonetheless "manifested an intention to clarify or to change the 1939 Code." *Id.,* at 37, 78 S.Ct. 1033. The 1954 revisions, of course, could not provide a direct response to *Colony,* which had not yet been decided. But there were indications that, whatever the earlier version of the statute had meant, Congress expected that the overstatement of basis would be considered an omission from gross income as a general rule going forward.

For example, the new law created a special exception for businesses by defining their gross income to be "the total of the amounts received or accrued from the sale of goods or services" without factoring in "the cost of such sales or services." 26 U.S.C. § 6501(e)(1)(A)(i) (1958 ed.) (currently § 6501(e)(1)(B)(i) (2006 ed., Supp. IV)). The principal purpose of this provision, perhaps motivated by the facts in the Third Circuit's *Uptegrove* decision, seems to have been to ensure that the extended statute of limitations would not be activated by a business's overstatement of the cost of goods sold. This did important work. There are, after all, unique complexities involved in calculating inventory costs. See, *e.g.,* O. Whittington & K. Pany, Principles of Auditing and Other Assurance Services 488 (15th ed. 2006) ("The audit of inventories presents the auditors with significant risk because: (*a*) they often represent a very substantial portion of current assets, (*b*) numerous valuation methods are used for inventories, (*c*) the valuation of inventories directly affects cost of goods sold, and (*d*) the determination of inventory quality, condition, and value is inherently complex"); see also Internal Revenue Service, Publication 538, Accounting Periods and Methods 17 (rev. Mar. 2008) (discussing methods for identifying the cost of items in inventory). Congress sought fit to make clear that errors in these kinds of calculations would not extend the limitations period.

Colony itself might be classified as a special "business inventory" case. Unlike the taxpayers here, the taxpayer in *Colony* claimed to be a business with income from the sale of goods, though the "goods" it held for sale were real estate lots. See *Intermountain Ins. Serv. of Vail v. Commissioner,* 650 F.3d 691, 703 (C.A.D.C.2011) (Tatel, J.) ("Colony described itself as a taxpayer in a trade or business with income from the sale of goods or services—i.e., as falling within [clause] (i)'s scope had the subsection applied pre–1954 . . ."). The Court, in turn, observed that its construction of the pre–1954 statute in favor of the taxpayer was "in harmony with the unambiguous language of [newly enacted] § 6501(e)(1)(A)." 357 U.S., at 37, 78 S.Ct. 1033. Clause (i) of the new provision, as just noted, ensured that the extended limitations period would not cover overstated costs of goods sold. The revised statute's special treatment of these costs suggests that overstatements of basis in other cases could have the effect of extending the limitations period.

It is also significant that, after 1954, the statute continued to address the omission of a substantial "amount" that should have been included in gross income. In the same round of revisions to the Tax Code, Congress established an extended limitations period in certain cases where "items" had been omitted from an estate or gift tax return. 26 U.S.C. § 6501(e)(2) (1958 ed.). There is at least some evidence that this term was used at that time to "mak[e] it clear" that the extended limitations period would not apply "merely because of differences between the taxpayer and the Government as to the valuation of property." Staff of the Joint Committee on Internal Revenue Taxation, Summary of the New Provisions of the Internal Revenue Code of 1954, 84th Cong., 1st Sess., 130 (Comm. Print 1955). Congress's decision not to use the term "items" to achieve the same result when it reenacted the statutory provision at issue is presumed to have been purposeful. See *Russello v. United States,* 464 U.S. 16, 23, 104 S.Ct. 296, 78 L.Ed.2d 17 (1983). This consideration casts further doubt on the premise that the new version of the statute, § 6501(e)(1)(A) (2006 ed., Supp. IV), necessarily has the same meaning as its predecessor.

II

In the instant case the Court concludes these statutory changes are "too fragile to bear the significant argumentative weight the Government seeks to place upon them." *Ante,* at 1841. But in this context, the changes are meaningful. *Colony* made clear that the text of the earlier version of the statute could not be described as unambiguous, although it ultimately concluded that an overstatement of basis was not an omission from gross income. See 357 U.S., at 33, 78 S.Ct. 1033. The statutory revisions, which were not considered in *Colony,* may not compel the opposite conclusion under the new statute; but they strongly favor it. As a result, there was room for the Treasury Department to interpret the new provision in that manner. See *Chevron U.S.A. Inc. v. Natural Resources Defense Council, Inc.,* 467 U.S. 837, 843–845, 104 S.Ct. 2778, 81 L.Ed.2d 694 (1984).

In an earlier case, and in an unrelated controversy not implicating the Internal Revenue Code, the Court held that a judicial construction of an ambiguous statute did not foreclose an agency's later, inconsistent interpretation of the same provision. *National Cable & Telecommunications Assn. v. Brand X Internet Services,* 545 U.S. 967, 982–983, 125 S.Ct. 2688, 162 L.Ed.2d 820 (2005) ("Only a judicial precedent holding that the statute unambiguously forecloses the agency's interpretation, and therefore contains no gap for the agency to fill, displaces a conflicting agency construction"). This general rule recognizes that filling gaps left by ambiguities in a statute "involves difficult policy choices that agencies are better equipped to make than courts." *Id.,* at 980, 125 S.Ct. 2688. There has been no opportunity to decide whether the analysis would be any different if an agency sought to interpret an ambiguous statute in a way that was inconsistent with this Court's own, earlier reading of the law. See *id.,* at 1003, 125 S.Ct. 2688 (STEVENS, J., concurring).

These issues are not implicated here. In *Colony* the Court did interpret the same phrase that must be interpreted in this case. The language was in a predecessor statute, however, and Congress has added new language that, in my view, controls the analysis and should instruct the Court to reach a different outcome today. The Treasury Department's regulations were promulgated in light of these statutory revisions, which were not at issue in *Colony*. There is a serious difficulty to insisting, as the Court does today, that an ambiguous provision must continue to be read the same way even after it has been reenacted with additional language suggesting Congress would permit a different interpretation. Agencies with the responsibility and expertise necessary to administer ongoing regulatory schemes should have the latitude and discretion to implement their interpretation of provisions reenacted in a new statutory framework. And this is especially so when the new language enacted by Congress seems to favor the very interpretation at issue. The approach taken by the Court instead forecloses later interpretations of a law that has changed in relevant ways. Cf. *United States v. Mead Corp.,* 533 U.S. 218, 247, 121 S.Ct. 2164, 150 L.Ed.2d 292 (2001) (SCALIA, J., dissenting) ("Worst of all, the majority's approach will lead to the ossification of large portions of our statutory law. Where *Chevron* applies, statutory ambiguities remain ambiguities subject to the agency's ongoing clarification"). The Court goes too far, in my respectful view, in constricting Congress's ability to leave agencies in charge of filling statutory gaps.

Our legal system presumes there will be continuing dialogue among the three branches of Government on questions of statutory interpretation and application. See *Blakely v. Washington,* 542 U.S. 296, 326, 124 S.Ct. 2531, 159 L.Ed.2d 403 (2004) (KENNEDY, J., dissenting) ("Constant, constructive discourse between our courts and our legislatures is an integral and admirable part of the constitutional design"); *Mistretta v. United States,* 488 U.S. 361, 408, 109 S.Ct. 647, 102 L.Ed.2d 714 (1989) ("Our principle of separation of powers anticipates that the coordinate Branches will converse with each other on matters of vital common interest"). In some cases Congress will set out a general principle, to be administered in more detail by an agency in the exercise of its discretion. The agency may be in a proper position to evaluate the best means of implementing the statute in its practical application. Where the agency exceeds its authority, of course, courts must invalidate the regulation. And agency interpretations that lead to unjust or unfair consequences can be corrected, much like disfavored judicial interpretations, by congressional action. These instructive exchanges would be foreclosed by an insistence on adhering to earlier interpretations of a statute even in light of new, relevant statutory amendments. Courts instead should be open to an agency's adoption of a different interpretation where, as here, Congress has given new instruction by an amended statute.

Under the circumstances, the Treasury Department had authority to adopt its reasonable interpretation of the new tax provision at issue. See *Mayo Foundation for Medical Ed. and Research v. United States,* 562 U.S. ——, ——, 131 S.Ct. 704, 713, 178 L.Ed.2d 588 (2011). This was also the conclusion reached in well-reasoned opinions issued in several cases before the Courts of Appeals. *E.g., Intermountain,* 650 F.3d, at 705–706 (reaching this conclusion "because the Court in *Colony* never purported to interpret [the new provision]; because [the new provision]'s 'omits from gross income' text is at least ambiguous, if not best read to include overstatements of basis; and because neither the section's structure nor its [history and context] removes this ambiguity").

The Department's clarification of an ambiguous statute, applicable to these taxpayers, did not upset legitimate settled expectations. Given the statutory changes described above, taxpayers had reason to question whether *Colony*'s holding extended to the revised § 6501(e)(1). See, *e.g., CC&F Western Operations L.P. v. Commissioner,* 273 F.3d 402, 406, n. 2 (C.A.1 2001) ("Whether *Colony*'s main holding carries over to section 6501(e)(1) is at least doubtful"). Having worked no change in the law, and instead having interpreted a statutory provision without an established meaning, the Department's regulation does not have an impermissible retroactive effect. Cf. *Smiley v. Citibank (South Dakota), N. A.,* 517 U.S. 735, 741, 744, n. 3, 116 S.Ct. 1730, 135 L.Ed.2d 25 (1996) (rejecting retroactivity argument); *Manhattan Gen. Equipment Co. v. Commissioner,* 297 U.S. 129, 135, 56 S.Ct. 397, 80 L.Ed. 528 (1936) (same). It controls in this case.

* * *

For these reasons, and with respect, I dissent.

NOTES AND QUESTIONS

1. What interpretive method is used in each opinion?
2. What administrative law case governs the level of deference to the IRS's interpretation in the majority opinion?
3. May the Court resolve an ambiguity left in a statute under *Chevron*? Is that what the Court did here?

When the IRS issues a statutory notice of deficiency regarding a taxpayer, the statute of limitations with respect to that tax year is suspended for the 90-day period the taxpayer has to petition the Tax Court plus 60 days. A taxpayer can waive a limitations period so the IRS can complete its audit. No collection action may begin after the expiration of the period.

The IRS and the taxpayer may agree to extend the statute of limitations on assessment, giving the IRS more time to complete an audit. Section 6501(c)(4) provides as follows:

Where, before the expiration of the time prescribed in this section for the assessment, . . . both the Secretary and the taxpayer have consented in writing to its assessment after such time, the tax may be assessed at any time prior to the expiration of the period agreed upon.

There are two types of extensions: (1) a limited time extension consent, or (2) an open-ended extension consent. A taxpayer may enter into restrictive consents, leaving the statute open only for certain issues. If the taxpayer does not consent to extend the assessment statute, and the IRS is near the end of the statute and has more work to do, it will likely not let the statute expire without any action. Rather, the IRS will more likely issue a statutory notice of deficiency on the basis of the information in hand. *See, e.g.,* Houlberg v. Commissioner, 50 T.C.M. (CCH) 1125, 1985 T.C.M. (RIA) ¶ 85,497, at 497 (1985). This action means that the IRS will issue the notice without the taxpayer's explanations that would have reduced the size of the IRS's asserted deficiency. Thus, in such a situation it is usually advantageous to the taxpayer to consent to an extended statute. A taxpayer may enter into an open-ended extension with the IRS, which gives the IRS an unlimited amount of time to audit the taxpayer. Either party may withdraw the consent with notice, in which case the IRS has 90 days to assess the tax. Both types of consents were at issue in the following case.

FREDERICKS v. COMMISSIONER
126 F.3d 433 (3d Cir. 1997)
United States Court of Appeals, Third Circuit

OPINION OF THE COURT
ALDISERT, Circuit Judge.

We must decide whether this is an appropriate case to apply the doctrine of estoppel against the Internal Revenue Service (IRS). Barry I. Fredericks appeals a decision of the United States Tax Court that approved a deficiency assessed by the Commissioner of Internal Revenue in July 1992 for Fredericks' 1977 income tax return. The IRS action requires the taxpayer to pay an additional tax of $28,361 and approximately $158,000 in interest on the basis of a disallowed tax-shelter deduction. The taxpayer filed a timely 1977 tax return, but the IRS took 14 years to decide if the tax-shelter deduction taken by the taxpayer was appropriate.

The IRS' assessment was filed long after the three-year statute of limitations had expired. However, at the request of the IRS Fredericks signed various consent agreements extending the time for the government to assess his 1977 tax return. The taxpayer's estoppel contention is based on alleged misrepresentations and misconduct by the IRS regarding its possession, solicitation and use of these consent forms. The appeal requires us to determine whether the IRS was estopped from making the assessment in 1992 because of its conduct regarding these consent agreements.

The taxpayer alleges the IRS committed the following misconduct in connection with the forms he and the IRS executed to extend the statute of limitations. First, the IRS misrepresented in 1981 that it never received a Form 872-A (Special Consent to Extend the Time to Assess Taxes), which Fredericks had signed to authorize an indefinite extension of the statute of limitations. Second, the IRS confirmed this misrepresentation in 1981, 1982 and 1983, by soliciting and executing three separate Forms 872, which extend the statute of limitations for one year. Third, the IRS discovered that it possessed the Form

872-A sometime before June 30, 1984, the date the last one-year extension expired, decided to rely on that form in continuing its investigation of Fredericks' tax return and failed to notify the taxpayer of its changed course of action. Fourth, the IRS used the Form 872-A to assess a deficiency in 1992, 11 years after informing the taxpayer that the Form 872-A did not exist, and eight years after the final one-year extension expired. Finally, the IRS imposed interest penalties totaling over five times the amount of the tax and covering the entire duration of its protracted investigation of the tax shelter.

The IRS rejected the taxpayer's statute-of-limitations defense, which was based on the third Form 872 executed by Fredericks and the government. The Commissioner argued that the Form 872-A remained in effect, even though the IRS had represented for the previous 11 years that no such form existed. The taxpayer contended that he relied on the IRS' affirmative misrepresentations over the years to his detriment and, thus, the Commissioner is estopped from using that Form 872-A.

We conclude that this taxpayer has met his burden of proving the traditional elements of equitable estoppel, and has mounted the high hurdle of establishing other special factors applicable to estoppel claims against the government. Accordingly, we will reverse the Tax Court's decision approving the assessment.

The Tax Court had jurisdiction pursuant to 26 U.S.C. §§ 6213(a), 6214 and 7442. We have jurisdiction under 26 U.S.C. § 7482(a)(1). The appeal was timely filed in accordance with Rule 13(a), Federal Rules of Appellate Procedure.

Tax Court decisions are reviewed in the same manner as district court decisions in non-jury civil cases. 26 U.S.C. § 7482(a); *Bachner v. Commissioner*, 81 F.3d 1274, 1277 (3d Cir.1996). Determinations that a party failed to establish its burden of proof are reviewed under the clearly erroneous standard. *In Re Brown*, 82 F.3d 801, 804 (8th Cir.1996); *Knop v. McMahan*, 872 F.2d 1132, 1140 (3d Cir.1989). We also review findings of fact for clear error, and we apply plenary review to the Tax Court's conclusions of law. *United States v. Asmar*, 827 F.2d 907, 913 n. 8 (3d Cir.1987).

I.

In 1978, Fredericks and his former wife filed a timely joint federal income tax return for 1977. In October 1980, the IRS sent Fredericks a Form 872-A, Special Consent to Extend the Time to Assess Taxes, requesting him to extend for the 1977 tax year the three-year statute of limitations within which the government must assess deficiencies. J.A. 22a. *See* 26 U.S.C. § 6501(a). On October 17, 1980, Fredericks signed and returned the Form 872-A, authorizing the government to assess deficiencies within 90 days of:

(a) the IRS' receipt of a Form 872-T, Notice of Termination of Special Consent to Extend the Time to Assess Tax, from the taxpayer; or

(b) the IRS' mailing of a Form 872-T to the taxpayer; or

(c) the IRS' mailing of a notice of deficiency for the relevant year.

None of these events occurred. According to the government's "received" date stamp on the Form 872-A, it was received by the Audit Division of the Manhattan District Director's Office on November 3, 1980, and signed and dated by the IRS on November 4, 1980.

In January 1981, an IRS agent telephoned Fredericks and requested him to sign a Form 872, Consent to Extend the Time to Assess Tax, for the 1977 tax year. According to Fredericks' trial testimony:

> [The] IRS agent . . . indicated that he was reviewing my tax return involved in the audit of my 1977 tax return, and . . . the statute of limitations was about to run and that the Government needed an extension of that statute. . . . I told the . . . agent that I had already executed and returned . . . an extension. . . . He told me he was in charge; he had my file and there was no extension in the file. He asked me did I receive . . . a copy of the extension back from the IRS signed. I said I did not. He indicated . . . that therefore the Government did not have it, it was probably lost in the mail, and that he needed me to execute another extension, otherwise the Government was going to assess the tax. But they didn't want to do that. They wanted time to review, and would I send them an 87-a new form. We did not mention numbers.

J.A. 81a-82a. The IRS did not contradict this testimony.

Consistent with Fredericks' testimony, the government sent a Form 872, which he signed and returned to the IRS. The Form 872 expressly extends the statute of limitations for only one year, whereas the Form 872-A authorizes an indefinite, although revocable, extension of the statute of limitations. The first Form 872 executed by the IRS and Fredericks extended the statute of limitations until December 31, 1982.

The agents telephoned Fredericks on two additional occasions and requested him to sign and return two additional Forms 872. On June 13, 1982, Fredericks signed and returned a consent to extend the statute of limitations to December 31, 1983; and on February 3, 1983, Fredericks signed and returned a Form 872 agreeing to extend the statute of limitations until June 30, 1984. Each of these Forms 872 was received and signed by an agent of the IRS Newark District Director's Office, and copies of these signed forms were subsequently forwarded to, and received by, Fredericks.

Throughout oral argument, counsel for the IRS made abundantly clear why the government requested these extensions of the statute of limitations:

> IRS COUNSEL: What really took so long in this case was the fact that it took a very long time for the IRS and the tax shelter which the IRS was investigating in which Mr. Fredericks had invested, to reach an agreement . . . .. [A] number of years went by . . . .. I believe that a couple of organizations were involved. It was a complicated settlement.

* * *

IRS COUNSEL: [I]t's very common when you have complicated tax shelters like this to ask for very long . . . extensions.

THE COURT: But you didn't ask for any additional extensions after the . . . expiration in 1984 did you?

IRS COUNSEL: No, we did not . . ..

Counsel for the IRS also made clear that the consent agreements extending the statute of limitations were repeatedly obtained for both the IRS' and the taxpayers' benefit:

IRS COUNSEL: Mr. Fredericks didn't want that tax assessed any more than the IRS agent did. And why was that? Because they were still in negotiation on the underlying tax shelter which was not resolved until 1988. That's why he didn't want the tax assessed and that's why the IRS agent didn't want the tax assessed . . ..

After February 1983, the IRS made no attempt to extend the statute of limitations, which pursuant to the third Form 872 expired on June 30, 1984. In light of the IRS' representations that it neither signed nor possessed a Form 872-A indefinite extension of the statute of limitations, the taxpayer concluded that the government lacked authority to assess a deficiency on his 1977 income tax return after that date.

On July 9, 1992—eight years and nine days after the June 30, 1984 expiration date—the IRS mailed a notice of deficiency to Fredericks and his former wife alleging they were liable for $28,361 in income tax, plus interest for the 1977 tax year. Fredericks filed a petition in the Tax Court challenging the deficiency assessment on grounds that it was barred by the June 30, 1984 statute of limitations agreed to in the third Form 872. Thus, Fredericks claimed the Commissioner was estopped from relying on the Form 872-A to avoid the statute-of-limitations defense, which completely bars the assessment of any deficiency.[4]

The Tax Court held a trial at which Fredericks testified and the Commissioner presented no witnesses. Significantly, the IRS presented no evidence as to the date it "discovered" its possession of the Form 872-A which it invoked to assess Fredericks' 1977 return in 1992. This is the same form the IRS affirmatively represented to the taxpayer as non-existent. Moreover, the IRS does not dispute that it waited until 1992 to notify the taxpayer that it had the Form 872-A and intended to rely on that form instead of the third Form 872 signed by the parties. At oral argument, counsel for the IRS stated that she did not know when the IRS discovered the Form 872-A or when it decided to rely on that form.

The Tax Court concluded that the government's action did not constitute an affirmative misrepresentation about any fact concerning the Form 872-A, and that Fredericks failed to prove the elements of estoppel. The court found that

---

[4] [fn 1] Petitioner's former wife did not join in the filing of the petition and is not a party in this case.

Fredericks did not establish that he relied to his detriment on the government's acts regarding the Forms 872 (one-year extensions) because he could have at any time filed a Form 872-T to terminate the previously executed Form 872-A (unlimited extension). The court decided that a deficiency of $28,361 was due. Fredericks now appeals that decision.

II.

The question is whether Fredericks sufficiently established the elements of an estoppel claim against the government such that it should be prevented from relying on the Form 872-A indefinite extension of the statute of limitations to pursue an otherwise time-barred assessment on Fredericks' 1977 tax return. Fredericks contends the government's July 9, 1992 assessment on his 1977 tax return was barred as of June 30, 1984, the date on which his and the IRS' agreement to extend the statute of limitations expired pursuant to the third Form 872 sought by the government. The Commissioner contends the Tax Court correctly concluded that estoppel is inappropriate here because Fredericks failed to demonstrate that the government's conduct constituted affirmative misconduct.

"Estoppel is an equitable doctrine invoked to avoid injustice in particular cases." Heckler v. Community Health Servs. of Crawford County, Inc., 467 U.S. 51, 59, 104 S.Ct. 2218, 2223, 81 L.Ed.2d 42 (1984). Parties attempting to estop another private party must establish that they relied to their detriment on their adversary's misrepresentation and that such reliance was reasonable because they neither knew nor should have known the adversary's conduct was misleading. Id.; U.S. v. Asmar, 827 F.2d 907, 912 (3d Cir.1987). The Tax Court has set forth the essential elements of estoppel:

> 1) a false representation or wrongful misleading silence; 2) an error in a statement of fact and not in an opinion or statement of law; 3) person claiming the benefits of estoppel must be ignorant of the true facts; and 4) person claiming estoppel must be adversely affected by the acts or statements of the person against whom estoppel is claimed.

Estate of Emerson v. Commissioner, 67 T.C. 612, 617-618, 1977 WL 3636 (1977).

This court is among the majority of circuits recognizing estoppel as an equitable defense against government claims, but in such a context we impose an additional burden on claimants to establish some "affirmative misconduct on the part of the government officials." *Asmar,* 827 F.2d at 911 n. 4, 912; *see also Kurz v. Philadelphia Elec. Co.,* 96 F.3d 1544 (3d Cir.1996). The additional element reflects the need to balance both the public interest in ensuring government can enforce the law without fearing estoppel and citizens' interests "in some minimum standard of decency, honor, and reliability in their relations with their Government." *Asmar,* 827 F.2d at 912 (citing *Community Health Servs. of Crawford County v. Califano,* 698 F.2d 615 (3d Cir.1983), *rev'd on other grounds sub nom. Heckler v. Community Health Servs. of Crawford County,* 467

U.S. 51, 104 S.Ct. 2218, 81 L.Ed.2d 42 (1984)). *See also United States v. St. John's Gen. Hosp.,* 875 F.2d 1064, 1069 (3d Cir.1989).

In Heckler v. Community Health Servs. of Crawford County, 467 U.S. 51, 104 S.Ct. 2218, 81 L.Ed.2d 42 (1984),[5] the Supreme Court reversed this court's holdings on the reliance and detriment elements, but left undisturbed our analysis and conclusions regarding the existence of affirmative misconduct. In finding affirmative misconduct, we stated:

> Not every form of official misinformation will be considered sufficient to estop the government. . . . Yet some forms of erroneous advice are so closely connected to the basic fairness of the administrative decision making process that the government may be estopped from disavowing the misstatement.

Califano, 698 F.2d at 622 (quoting Brandt v. Hickel, 427 F.2d 53, 56-57 (9th Cir.1970) (estoppel appropriate even though government's advice that contractor could resubmit bid without losing priority was erroneous and unauthorized)). We found that affirmative misconduct existed because the government "induced" the health care provider, "by the affirmative instructions of the [government agent]" to submit the cost reports without offsetting the grants at issue. "Not once, but on five separate occasions spanning over two years," the government advised the provider not to offset the grants. Id. 698 F.2d at 622. . . .

As the foregoing . . . instruct[s], we must determine whether Fredericks sufficiently met his burden of establishing the traditional elements of estoppel. This requires us to consider the elements of misrepresentation, reliance and detriment. We will discuss the affirmative-misconduct element in conjunction with our consideration of the IRS' misrepresentations, and then proceed to the reliance and detriment elements. Subsequently, we will address the special factors that must be present in an estoppel claim against the government.

III.

MISREPRESENTATIONS . . .

The Tax Court's findings on the traditional elements of estoppel focused on the absence of Fredericks' reliance on the government's acts. The court emphasized that he could have terminated the Form 872-A indefinite extension by filing a Form 872-T at any time. The court concentrated on Fredericks' conduct, rather than on that of the government, and in so doing committed reversible error. Beyond the statement of facts in its opinion, the court appears to have ignored the undisputed evidence that the IRS misrepresented to Fredericks that the Form 872-A was not on file and "probably lost in the mail." The IRS' request for three short-term extensions of the statute of limitations reinforced this misrepresentation and induced Fredericks to rely on the agreed-upon termination dates in those Forms 872. The Tax Court defied logic by suggesting that a taxpayer should file a form to terminate a document that according to the IRS

---

[5] [fn 2] Hereinafter, we refer to the Third Circuit Court of Appeals opinion in this case as *Califano,* and to the Supreme Court's opinion as *Crawford County.*

does not exist. Such a rule would require taxpayers to venture into an Alice in Wonderland of hypotheticals with the IRS. We reject in toto the Tax Court's reasoning and we decline to adopt a concept that suggests taxpayers should file Forms 872-T to terminate forms which the IRS insists do not exist. . . .

Here, the IRS did not refute evidence that it told Fredericks the Form 872-A "was probably lost in the mail." On three occasions over a period of two years the IRS induced Fredericks to sign Forms 872, establishing an agreement to three consecutive specific dates on which the statute of limitations would expire. The government's misrepresentation went beyond mere erroneous oral advice from an IRS agent; it consisted of affirmative, authorized acts inducing Fredericks to sign and rely on the terms of the Form 872 on three different occasions in three different years. Moreover, the IRS' misleading silence after finding and deciding to rely on the Form 872-A, coupled with its failure to notify Fredericks of its decision and its effective revocation of the third Form 872, constitute affirmative misconduct. . . .

In the case at bar, the agent who misrepresented that the IRS did not have a Form 872-A, and the agents who solicited and executed the subsequent Form 872 one-year extensions had authority to act as they did. . . . [B]ecause of the government's silence after its discovery of, and decision to rely on, the Form 872-A, the IRS agents induced Fredericks to continue to rely on the Forms 872. Had the taxpayer been informed of the IRS' discovery and its decision to adopt an alternative plan of action, he could have—and testified that he would have—exercised his right to terminate the Form 872-A.

When the IRS discovered its mistake in denying the existence of a previously executed Form 872-A, any number of agents presumably had authority to alert Fredericks to the prior misrepresentation that the form did not exist. We assume that these agents were also authorized to inform Fredericks that the IRS decided to disregard the third Form 872—which extended the statute until June 30, 1984—and decided to rely on this alternative form, which created an indefinite extension period. Instead, the IRS waited eight years before notifying Fredericks that it possessed the form, then filed an assessment and precluded him from exercising his right to terminate the Form 872-A. The IRS should be bound by the authorized acts and omissions of its agents and estopped from relying on the Form 872-A, and from denying the validity of the last Form 872 it executed with the taxpayer. . . .

In response to the question raised at oral argument whether the IRS had any obligation to notify the taxpayer when it discovered its possession of the Form 872-A, counsel for the IRS responded:

> I think that as a matter of fairness, and not as a matter of what is statutorily required in this case, that if there was someone at the IRS who realized that Mr. Fredericks had been misled, I do believe that they had an obligation to notify him. That is a different question than the question that we should be asking, which is: is it the proper case to apply equitable estoppel.

We disagree. We reject the notion that IRS agents examining Fredericks' file sometime in 1984 could have discovered a Form 872-A that was signed in 1980 and not known that the taxpayer had been misled as to its existence given that the three subsequently executed Forms 872 were also in Fredericks' file. It is exactly this combination of written agreements entered into by the IRS and Fredericks that prompted the IRS to forego soliciting additional one-year extensions.

The IRS was the only party with knowledge of all the facts in this case. The IRS' secreting of the reappearance of the Form 872-A, its failure to inform Fredericks of the form's reappearance, its decision to revoke without notice the third Form 872 agreement which limited the extension to June 30, 1984, and its filing of an assessment eight years later constitutes affirmative misconduct and gives rise to the most impressive case for estoppel against the IRS that our research has disclosed. . . .

Consider the following uncontroverted evidence: (1) the IRS' misrepresentation that it did not have the Form 872-A; (2) the IRS' three requests for, and execution of, annual extensions of the statute of limitations; (3) *the absence of any requests for annual extensions after June 30, 1984;* (4) the IRS' eight-year delay and production of the Form 872-A in 1992; and (5) the IRS' admission that the investigation of the tax shelter was actively ongoing until 1992. The only reasonable conclusion that can be drawn from the evidence is that the IRS had actual knowledge of the Form 872-A's existence at least prior to June 30, 1984. Otherwise, the government would have sought additional annual extensions because, as stated at oral argument, the investigation was ongoing.

The IRS confirmed its earlier misrepresentations by failing to notify the taxpayer that it possessed the Form 872-A and that the Commissioner intended to rely upon that form. The government's misleading silence was a perpetuation of its misrepresentation that the Form 872-A was never signed or received by the IRS. It was an affirmative decision to usurp the Form 872 agreement entered by the IRS setting June 30, 1984 as the expiration of the statute of limitations. The IRS' decision to lie doggo, and induce the taxpayer into thinking all was well, coupled with its additional eight-year delay in producing a document it previously represented as non-existent, compels us to conclude that the IRS was guilty of affirmative misconduct at least as of June 30, 1984. Fredericks has met his burden of establishing the misrepresentation and affirmative-misconduct elements of an estoppel claim against the government. We, therefore, proceed to an examination of the reliance and detriment elements of this doctrine.

IV.

RELIANCE

Parties claiming equitable estoppel must demonstrate not only that they relied on the alleged misrepresentations, but also that such reliance was reasonable "in that the party claiming the estoppel did not know nor should it have known that its adversary's conduct was misleading." *Crawford County,* 467 U.S. at 59, 104 S.Ct. at 2223. . . .

[C]ourts examining claims of estoppel against the government have looked beyond mere reasonableness to determine whether the alleged reliance was sufficient to invoke estoppel. Courts are more likely to find the reliance reasonable in governmental-estoppel claims if three additional factors exist: (1) if the government agents had authority to engage in the acts or omissions at issue; (2) if the agents' misrepresentation was one of fact, not law; and (3) if the government benefitted from its misrepresentation. We will address each of these in turn to illuminate the appropriateness of estoppel in this instance.

A.

Courts have held that a private party's reliance on governmental actions or omissions is not reasonable if such acts or omissions are contrary to the law or beyond the agents' authority. We stated the rule in *Ritter v. United States:*

The acts or omissions of the officers of the government, if they be authorized to bind the United States in a particular transaction, will work estoppel against the government, if the officers have acted within the scope of their authority. . . .

Here, the government does not dispute that the IRS had the authority to inform Fredericks that it did not have the Form 872-A, nor does the government dispute that the IRS had the authority to solicit or terminate agreements extending the statute of limitations. To the contrary, the government's counsel at oral argument suggested that IRS agents routinely enter such agreements. Moreover, the government has conceded that the IRS had an obligation—not merely the authority—to notify Fredericks that it had the Form 872-A when it realized its error and that Fredericks had been misled. The agents here acted within the scope of the law and their authority. Therefore, we conclude Fredericks' reliance on their acts and misleading silence was reasonable.

B.

Courts are more likely to apply estoppel when the government's conduct involves a misrepresentation of fact, rather than a misrepresentation of law. *See, e.g., Miller v. United States,* 500 F.2d 1007 (2d Cir.1974); *Estate of Emerson v. Commissioner,* 67 T.C. 612, 1977 WL 3636 (1977); *Exchange & Sav. Bank of Berlin v. United States,* 226 F.Supp. 56, 58 (D.Md.1964). However, some courts have gone further and invoked estoppel against the IRS even where the misrepresentation involved a question of law. *See Schuster v. Commissioner,* 312 F.2d 311 (9th Cir.1962) (IRS estopped from correcting prior mistake of law on which bank reasonably relied); *Stockstrom v. Commissioner,* 190 F.2d 283 (D.C.Cir.1951); *Joseph Eichelberger & Co. v. Commissioner,* 88 F.2d 874 (5th Cir.1937). We need not go that far because in this case the IRS misrepresented its possession of a Form 872-A consent agreement. This was a misrepresentation of fact, not of law; and we find Fredericks' reliance thereon to be reasonable.

C.

Courts are more willing to estop the government when the government itself benefited from the acts or omissions relied upon by the private party. *See, e.g., Walsonavich v. United States,* 335 F.2d 96 (3d Cir.1964) (IRS benefited from agreement to extend the statute of limitations for assessing deficiencies, and taxpayer was justified in relying on the same agreement to extend the period for filing a refund); *Joseph Eichelberger & Co. v. Commissioner,* 88 F.2d 874, 875 (5th Cir.1937) ("The United States got the benefit of [the Commissioner's] decision then and ought to abide by it now."); *Staten Island Hygeia Ice & Cold Storage Co. v. United States,* 85 F.2d 68 (2d Cir.1936) (IRS is bound by the burdens as well as the benefits of taxpayer's agreement to waive future claims).

One case focusing on the benefits obtained by the government has facts strikingly similar to those in the case at bar. In Stockstrom v. Commissioner, 190 F.2d 283 (D.C.Cir.1951), the taxpayer made gifts of less than $5,000 to several trusts in 1938. The IRS had ruled in 1937 that no gift tax was due on such transfers. An IRS officer affirmed this position in 1941, telling the taxpayer that no tax was due on his 1938 gifts. The taxpayer relied on the IRS' representations and, because no tax was due, did not file a gift tax return covering the 1938 transfers. In 1948, the IRS attempted to assess a deficiency based on the 1938 gifts, arguing that there was no statute of limitations on the assessment because the taxpayer never filed a return. The D.C. Circuit estopped the Commissioner from assessing the deficiency, finding that the taxpayer's failure to file a return was due entirely to the actions of the IRS. The court held: "[The Commissioner] induced the omission which he now relies upon as giving him unlimited time to assess a tax. The law as to such a situation has long since been established. . . . He who prevents a thing from being done may not avail himself of the non-performance which he has himself occasioned. . . ." Id. 190 F.2d at 288.

As in *Stockstrom,* the IRS induced the omission which it relies upon in assessing a deficiency against Fredericks. The IRS misrepresented that it did not have the Form 872-A, induced Fredericks to rely on three subsequently executed Forms 872 to aid the government in its investigation, and induced him to reasonably believe there was no Form 872-A to terminate. The government now attempts to benefit from Fredericks' failure to terminate this form many years after its initial misrepresentation and many years after its realization of—and silence regarding—its own error. As the D.C. Circuit stated in *Stockstrom,* "[w]e regard as unconscionable the Commissioner's claim of authority to assess a tax . . . when the Commissioner himself was responsible for that failure." *Id.* 190 F.2d at 289.

V.

DETRIMENT

"To analyze the nature of a private party's detrimental change in position, we must identify the manner in which reliance on the Government's misconduct has caused the private citizen to change his position for the worse." *Crawford County,* 467 U.S. at 61, 104 S.Ct. at 2224. Fredericks argues that he suffered a substantial economic detriment by relying on the IRS' misrepresentations. He reasonably relied on the third Form 872 and reasonably believed that the statute of limitations expired on June 30, 1984. He relied on the IRS' misrepresentations that there was no Form 872-A indefinite extension of the statute of limitations and, to his detriment, did not terminate that form. Fredericks permanently lost his right to terminate the Form 872-A and he lost the benefit of the statute of limitations in the third Form 872. Moreover, he was penalized by the IRS' application of an enhanced rate of interest that continues to be compounded daily.

This interest accrued while the IRS waited eight years after the June 30, 1984 statute of limitations expired to assess a deficiency. . . .

[Here,] Fredericks suffered a permanent loss of a legal right. He forever lost his right to terminate the Form 872-A, the only means through which the government could in 1992 assess his 1977 tax return. He was irreversibly deprived of the benefit of the three-year statute of limitations enacted by Congress, the benefit of the terms of the contracts he entered with the IRS to extend that period, and of any opportunity to terminate the revocable 872-A that the IRS misrepresented as lost. The loss of this right created a tangible economic detriment in the form of penalty-enhanced interest rates. Accordingly, we find that Fredericks has satisfied the detriment element of an equitable estoppel claim against the government.

VI.

ESTOPPEL AND THE GOVERNMENT

The Supreme Court has not directly met the issue whether estoppel against the IRS may be appropriate in certain circumstances. However, contrary to counsel for the Commissioner's emphatic statement at oral argument that in no case has estoppel been asserted successfully against the IRS, this court and others have applied the doctrine of estoppel to the IRS under various circumstances. . . .

The IRS is not the only federal agency against which courts have applied the doctrine of estoppel. Case law demonstrates that courts have invoked estoppel against the Post Office Department, the Department of Housing and Urban Development, the Land Management Office, the Postal Service, the Parole Commission, the Farmer's Home Administration, the War Department, the Department of Interior, the Department of Commerce and Labor and the General Land Office. . . . This plethora of precedent suggests that "[i]t is well settled that the doctrine of equitable estoppel, in proper circumstances, and with appropriate caution, may be invoked against the United States in cases involving internal revenue taxation," and in a variety of other contexts. *Simmons v. United States,* 308 F.2d 938, 945 (5th Cir.1962).

Although the Supreme Court has neither rejected outright nor articulated a specific test for estoppel claims against the government, the foregoing case law illuminates certain factors beyond the traditional elements of estoppel that we should consider before estopping the IRS. Those factors are: 1) the impact of the estoppel on the public fisc; 2) whether the government agent or agents who made the misrepresentation or error were authorized to act as they did; 3) whether the governmental misconduct involved a question of law or fact; 4) whether the government benefitted from its misrepresentation; and 5) the existence of irreversible detrimental reliance by the party claiming estoppel. We have addressed all but the first factor in conjunction with the traditional elements of estoppel, and we conclude that each of those factors cuts in favor of Fredericks. We now proceed to consider the impact on the public fisc in this case.

[VII.]

IMPACT ON THE PUBLIC FISC

Courts are more likely to estop the government when the public fisc—in particular, Congress' power to control public expenditures—is only minimally impacted, if at all. This consideration derives from *Schweiker v. Hansen,* 450 U.S. 785, 790-793, 101 S.Ct. 1468, 1471-74, 67 L.Ed.2d 685 (1981). The Court in *Schweiker* observed that future cases could be distinguished if the government entered written agreements that supported estoppel or if estoppel did not threaten the public fisc. Accordingly, in *Portmann v. United States,* 674 F.2d 1155 (7th Cir.1982), the court held that the U.S. Postal Service could be estopped from claiming certain packages were merchandise and from applying a lower insurable limit than that which would apply if the packages were deemed nonnegotiable documents. The court ruled that estoppel could be invoked if the plaintiff proved that the postal clerk assured her the packages could be insured as nonnegotiable documents. Important to the court's conclusion was that the public fisc would not be endangered if estoppel were permitted. The Seventh Circuit also articulated certain factors to be balanced in determining whether to grant estoppel. Among those factors was the potential danger of undermining important federal interests or risking severe depletion of the public fisc. *Id.* 674 F.2d at 1167.

We discussed Payne v. Block, 714 F.2d 1510, 1517-1518 (11th Cir.1983), in our analysis of the detriment element in Part IV. The court in *Payne* affirmed a district court order compelling the Farmers Home Administration to extend a loan application period, effectively estopping the government from adhering to its previously established application deadline. The court distinguished Schweiker v. Hansen on several grounds. Among these grounds was that in *Schweiker* estoppel would have threatened the public fisc with potential fraudulent claims by allowing any eligible claimants to obtain retroactive benefits by merely claiming that they visited the Social Security office and were told they were ineligible. In contrast, no threat of fraudulent claims existed in *Payne* because Congress had already authorized the funds for the loan program at issue and the money remained unallocated.

The public-fisc consideration cuts in favor of estopping the government in the case at bar. By enacting a three-year statute of limitations on the time within which the IRS must assess tax deficiencies, Congress clearly contemplated that in some instances taxpayers would retain funds—because the statute of limitations had run—to which they were not initially entitled. Therefore, invoking the statute of limitations to bar an IRS assessment cannot be deemed an intrusion into Congress' power to expend and allocate public funds. Neither Congress' power to control public expenditures nor its authority to enact statutes of limitations is impacted when a taxpayer invokes such a statute, either at the end of its original life or 11 years later pursuant to written agreements between the taxpayer and IRS.

Estoppel in this instance would not open the door to fraudulent claims. Therefore, the concerns about such claims raised in *Portmann* and *Schweiker* are inapplicable here. Unlike in *Schweiker* and *Portmann,* Fredericks' claim is based on more than mere oral assurances from government officials, although the government does not deny that its agent orally informed Fredericks that it did not have an extension on file and that the Form 872-A was probably lost. In this case, Fredericks proved, with documents authorized by Congress and signed by IRS agents, that the IRS executed three written agreements establishing specific dates on which the statute of limitations would expire. Thus, the *Schweiker* Court's concerns about a governmental estoppel that would open the door to potentially costly fraudulent claims based on mere oral misrepresentations from government officials are inapposite here.

The impact on the public fisc in this case would be nothing greater than that authorized by Congress in enacting a statute of limitations and authorizing the IRS to enter Form 872 written agreements extending the limitations period to specific dates. Congress certainly contemplated that taxpayers would rely on the dates fixed in those agreements to bar IRS assessments to which the government is no longer entitled because of the passage of time. *See Helvering v. Griffiths,* 318 U.S. 371, 403, 63 S.Ct. 636, 653, 87 L.Ed. 843 (1943) ("the statute of limitations bar[s] sometimes the Government and sometimes the taxpayer with capricious effects").

Estoppel here affects the public fisc by approximately $28,361, plus any interest that would have accrued before June 30, 1984—the day the statute of limitations in the last Form 872 signed by the IRS and Fredericks expired. We are satisfied that in the scope of the IRS' operations, this impact on the public fisc is not only minimal, but also a necessary result of Congress' enactment of enforceable statutes of limitations.

We conclude that Fredericks has met his burden of establishing the traditional elements of estoppel. The IRS misrepresented its possession of a Form 872-A indefinite extension of the statute of limitations and confirmed that misrepresentation by obtaining three Forms 872. The IRS' conduct constituted affirmative misconduct when it remained silent upon realizing its mistake and upon deciding to change its course of action to rely on the previously lost Form 872-A without notifying the taxpayer. Its decision to effectively revoke the third Form 872 without notice to the taxpayer also adds to the affirmative misconduct here. Fredericks relied upon the IRS' oral and written representations as to the relevant statute of limitations and lost his right to terminate the Form 872-A. His detriment is compounded by the IRS' assessment of an increased penalty rate of interest covering the entire duration of its protracted investigation.

We have addressed the special factors that must be considered in governmental-estoppel claims and we conclude that they favor estopping the IRS here. The impact on the public fisc is minimal and consistent with Congress' enactment of enforceable statutes of limitations. The acts and omissions of the IRS agents were authorized; the errors involved misrepresentations of fact, not law, and do not contravene any statutory or regulatory requirements. The government benefitted from its misrepresentations; and Fredericks relied on those misrepresentations to his detriment, irretrievably losing the benefit of the statute of limitations, the benefit of the contracts he entered with the IRS, and the right to terminate the Form 872-A that the government repeatedly and affirmatively represented as non-existent.

Having concluded that the IRS is estopped from relying on the Form 872-A to extend the statute of limitations, we hold that the Commissioner was time-barred from making any assessment, in full or in part, in 1992. The original three-year statute of limitations had run, as had the three one-year extensions agreed to by the parties. Any assessment by the IRS on Fredericks' 1977 tax return was time-barred by 1984. The taxpayer asserted the statute of limitations as a defense to a 1992 assessment, and the Commissioner is thus estopped from refusing to recognize that defense and from denying the effectiveness of the 1984 statute of limitations.

The dissent agrees that the IRS should be estopped, but argues that we should allow the government to assess a deficiency for the period before September 30, 1984—90 days after the last Form 872 one-year extension expired. This contention fails to recognize the precise nature of the estoppel here. The Commissioner is estopped from using the Form 872-A to deny that the statute of limitations had run in 1984. Thus, the entire 1992 assessment was time-barred. By operation of the estoppel doctrine, the Commissioner was stripped of authority to make any assessment whatsoever. The effect of the estoppel here does not raise a question of "equities"; it presents one of pure law—the operation of a statute that bars the Commissioner's action beyond a date certain.

Application of estoppel here does not merely limit the remedy available to the Commissioner; it negates the Commissioner's ability to trump an act of Congress, to wit, the statute of limitations. As stated above, by enacting a statute of limitations on the time for assessing tax deficiencies, Congress clearly contemplated that in some instances taxpayers would retain funds—because the limitations period had run—to which they were not initially entitled. That this may result in an "unnecessary windfall" to the party invoking the statute of limitations is totally irrelevant. Such is the nature of a congressionally enacted limitations period; it confers a benefit on any litigant asserting the defense. To be sure, "the statute of limitations bar[s] sometimes the Government and sometimes the taxpayer with capricious effects." *See, e.g., Helvering v. Griffiths*, 318 U.S. 371, 403, 63 S.Ct. 636, 653, 87 L.Ed. 843 (1943).

Estopping the government from capitalizing on Fredericks' failure to file an 872-T termination form, when the IRS itself procured both Fredericks' omission and his reliance on the alternative Forms 872, is not only consistent with more than a century of precedents, but also essential to maintaining fundamental notions of fair play. The Supreme Court has recognized such fundamental principles and applied them against both private parties and the government.

In R.H. Stearns Co. v. United States, 291 U.S. 54, 54 S.Ct. 325, 78 L.Ed. 647 (1934), the Court held that a taxpayer was estopped from asserting the statute of limitations as a bar to an assessment where the taxpayer himself had requested the Commissioner to delay the assessment. The Court stated:

The applicable principle is fundamental and unquestioned. He who prevents a thing from being done may not avail himself of the nonperformance which he has himself occasioned, for the law says to him, in effect: This is your own act, and therefore you are not damnified. . .. Sometimes the resulting disability has been characterized as an estoppel, sometimes as a waiver. The label counts for little. Enough for present purposes that the disability has its roots in a principle more nearly ultimate than either waiver or estoppel, the principle that no one shall be permitted to found any claim upon his own inequity or take advantage of his own wrong. A suit may not be built on an omission induced by him who sues.

Id. at 61-62, 54 S.Ct. at 328 (citations and internal quotations omitted). The taxpayer claimed that a waiver of the statute of limitations that he signed, but which the Commissioner did not sign until several years later, was invalid. The Court noted that all parties proceeded as though the waiver was on file and had been signed: "[t]he events that followed confirm this interpretation of the effect of the transaction." Therefore, the taxpayer was estopped from later claiming that the waiver was invalid. The facts in the case at bar are strikingly similar, and the same principles of law and equity should apply.

Here, all parties proceeded as though the IRS did not possess a Form 872-A. The events that followed, the IRS' three requests for Forms 872 and its silence upon finding the Form 872-A, confirmed this interpretation of the facts. We conclude that the same principle that the Court has applied against taxpayers— the principle that those who prevent a thing from being done may not avail themselves of the nonperformance which they themselves have occasioned— must apply to the Commissioner as well as the taxpayer in this instance. *See, e.g., United States v. Peck,* 102 U.S. (12 Otto) 64, 26 L.Ed. 46 (1880) (applying these fundamental principles of equity against the government as a party to a contract with a private individual).

* * *

Because we rule the Commissioner is estopped from asserting a deficiency in the 1977 tax return of Barry I. Fredericks, the decision of the Tax Court will be reversed.

[Appendices omitted.]

[Dissent of STAPELETON, J., omitted.]

NOTES AND QUESTIONS

1. How does this case compare to other cases where tax law requires strict adherence to rules?

2. For equitable estoppel to apply against the government, there is an additional requirement as compared to equitable estoppel against other parties. What is the additional requirement?

UNIT 3

IRS TAX DETERMINATION AUTHORITY

Even with severe negative consequences to cheating, a taxpayer has little incentive to comply with the tax laws if he believes the IRS will not catch him. To increase the probability the IRS will detect noncompliant activity, federal tax law grants the IRS the authority to investigate any taxpayer's return and determine whether the taxpayer owes more tax. To exercise this authority, the IRS reviews all taxpayer returns, examines on a deeper level the returns that appear the most questionable, provides (in general) an appeals process to taxpayers that disagree with the examination results, and issues a final determination.

CHAPTER 11

IRS RETURN REVIEW

A. Introduction

The first step, administrative review of all taxpayer returns, involves scoring the returns and matching them to information returns filed by third parties. The IRS scores returns by applying to each return an algorithm called the Discriminant Index Function (DIF). The higher the DIF score, the more likely a return will undergo further scrutiny. When the IRS receives a tax return that is inconsistent with third-party information returns, the IRS follows up with the automated underreporter program to resolve the discrepancy. Finally, the IRS contacts taxpayers in some cases to verify certain information. None of these administrative return reviews are considered an "examination" by the IRS's standards.

B. Administrative Review of Tax Returns

The IRS has broad authority to make determinations regarding tax liabilities. Indeed, section 6201 provides as follows:

The [IRS] is authorized and required to make the inquiries, determinations, and assessments of all taxes . . . imposed by this title . . . .[1]

---

[1] This provision actually refers to the "Secretary," but references in the Code to the Secretary are read as referring to the IRS. *See* IRC § 7701(11)(b) (defining the Secretary as the "Secretary of the Treasury or his delegate"); Delegation Order 150-10 (April 22, 1982) (delegating the Secretary's duties of "administration and enforcement of the Internal Revenue laws" to the IRS Commissioner).

This is no easy task. Taxpayers hold the information the IRS needs to carry out its duties. Possession of the information the IRS needs gives the taxpayer an advantage over the IRS. This disadvantage dissolves, however, when the IRS applies its institutional knowledge to its administrative review of taxpayer returns.[2] The IRS has enforcement mechanisms in place to review returns in short form—before initiating a full examination—that often make a full examination unnecessary.

1. Short-Form Return Reviews

It is understandable how a taxpayer may be lulled into thinking he has an advantage over the IRS based on the IRS's audit rate. Economics researchers have suggested that it could be rational for a taxpayer to cheat because of the low likelihood of getting caught. This research loosely assumes an audit rate of 1 percent. Relying on the 1% audit rate is a mistake, however, because doing so overlooks the fact that the IRS reviews all the tax returns it processes with an eye toward enforcement. All tax returns go through DIF scoring. In addition, the assumed audit rate does not include the IRS's audit-like procedure of reviewing returns using its error correction assessment authority or its automated underreporter program. With these two programs taken into account, the audit rate is closer to 7%. Neither the 1% audit rate nor the 7% audit-like rate accurately reflect the likelihood of getting caught cheating, however, because the rates assume random return selection, which is incorrect. Rather, the IRS selects returns for review and examination through scoring and other means.

2. DIF Scoring

While processing tax returns, the IRS reviews each one and scores it. *See* U.S. GOV'T ACCOUNTABILITY OFFICE, HOW THE INTERNAL REVENUE SERVICE SELECTS AND AUDITS INDIVIDUAL INCOME TAX RETURNS 9 (1976). The most firmly established score is a DIF score resulting from the application of an algorithm. Each return receives a DIF score. A sufficiently high DIF score triggers further review by an IRS "classifier," who weeds out unproductive returns. *See* TREASURY INSPECTOR GEN. FOR TAX ADMIN., No. 2010-30-096,

---

[2] On occasion, the IRS publicly disputes this point. A former commissioner of the IRS once lamented with respect to a particular enforcement program, "We were . . . taking a knife into a gunfight. . . . [W]e had . . . a couple of agents . . . here fighting against . . . well-staffed, well-organized corporations and tax advisers." Presumably the commissioner was aware this was a gross overstatement. There is always an information advantage to one side in any legal proceeding. In a legal proceeding with the IRS, however, the IRS makes the rules and has the resources of the most powerful nation in the world behind it. Thus, in any dispute with a taxpayer the IRS brings a weapon more on the magnitude of the Death Star to the gunfight rather than a knife.

CLASSIFIERS ARE ELIMINATING LESS PRODUCTIVE TAX RETURNS FROM THE AUDIT STREAM, BUT THEIR WORK NEEDS CLOSER MONITORING (2010). Once a classifier identifies a return for review, it is sent to an internal audit group, which makes a final determination as to whether to audit the return.

Although assigning a DIF score is not a full examination, the scoring process still should change the risk/reward calculus for a taxpayer considering the likelihood of getting caught. A 1% audit rate amounts to a 1% likelihood of getting caught only if the IRS chooses the returns for audit at random. The mere fact that the selection process is not random skews the likelihood of getting caught. A probable outcome becomes near completely unknown when taking into account that the DIF score algorithm undergoes frequent calibration.

The following case touches on the secretiveness of the DIF process and introduces many of the topics covered later in this unit.

AYYAD v. IRS
2018 WL 704849
United States District Court, District of Maryland

PAULA XINIS, United States District Judge

Pending before the Court in this Freedom of Information Act ("FOIA") case are cross-motions for summary judgment filed by Plaintiff Abdelrahman and Sara Ayyad ("Plaintiffs"), ECF No. 18, and Defendant Internal Revenue Service ("the IRS"), ECF No. 25. The issues are fully briefed and a hearing was held on February 1, 2018. For the reasons explained below, the Court GRANTS in part and DENIES in part Plaintiffs' motion, and GRANTS in part and DENIES in part the IRS's Motion.

I. BACKGROUND

The following facts are undisputed. Since 2006, Plaintiffs have been the subject of the Internal Revenue Service ("the IRS") examinations regarding their federal income tax returns for tax years 2006 through 2012. ECF No. 1. On March 9, 2016, Plaintiffs each filed FOIA requests, seeking the production of agency records including, but not limited to, the following:

- The full administrative file developed by Kenneth Feldman, an IRS Revenue Agent in Baltimore, Maryland office, from the date of his assignment through the date of the submission of the FOIA request;
- All records including, but not limited to, the examination, assessment, and appeals with respect to plaintiffs' income tax returns during the period of Mr. Feldman's assignment to plaintiffs' case;
- All written correspondence, electronic or otherwise, among Agent Feldman, Bisamber Misir, Quinton J. Ferguson, Larry Timms, and any other IRS employee relating to the examination of plaintiffs' account;
- Any records relating to any civil and/or criminal fraud investigation or assessments, including any correspondence from or to a fraud

technical advisor, any IRS employee engaged in a similar role as a fraud technical advisor, or any other IRS employees or agents engaged in the investigation and/or assessment of fraud. This request included, but was not limited to: Form 11661, Fraud Development Stats; Form 2797, Referral Report of Potential Criminal Fraud Cases; and/or any other forms prepared and/or filed in furtherance of a civil and/or criminal fraud investigation or assessment, and any records relating to the preparation and filing of those forms;

- The entire case history for all examinations for tax period 2006 through 2013;
- Any records relating to any accuracy-related penalty determinations or assessments;
- Any records relating to the preparation and filing of the statutory notice of deficiency dated November 30, 2012 issued by the IRS Richmond Office for tax period 2009;
- The identification of any official(s) having control of any records being requested; and
- The administrative appeals file for tax years 2006 through 2009 was specifically not requested.

ECF No. 1 at ¶ 7.

IRS Disclosure Specialist Jennifer J. Perez received and processed the requests on March 10, 2016. *See* Decl. of Jennifer J. Perez ("Perez Decl."), ECF No. 25–4 at ¶¶ 1, 4. Perez determined that the responsive records were likely located in Plaintiffs' IRS examination files which consists of relevant physical notes and records as well as an electronic file maintained in the agency's "Services' Information Management System" ("IMS"). Decl. of Kenneth N. Feldman ("Feldman Decl."), ECF No. 25–2 at ¶ 4.

On April 12, the IRS notified the Ayyads that it would process their FOIA requests as a single request because the Ayyads are married and their FOIA requests almost identical. ECF No. 1 at ¶ 25. Six days later, Perez informed Plaintiffs that the Service located 2,885 pages of responsive records and would provide them in "PDF" format. *Id.* at ¶ 12, Ex. B. Of these 2,885 responsive records, the agency redacted 21 pages and withheld 120 pages under claimed FOIA exemptions. *Id.* Plaintiffs requested that the IRS produce a *Vaughn* Index,[3] which the IRS did not do. *Id.* at ¶ 14. Plaintiffs filed an administrative appeal on

---

[3] [fn 1] Defendants in FOIA litigation often produce *Vaughn* Index to satisfy their evidentiary burden. A *Vaughn* Index is a "meticulous and specific documentation of its claimed justification for nondisclosure." *Spannaus v. U.S. Dep't of Justice*, 813 F.3d 1285, 1287 n.3 (4th Cir. 1987) (citing *Vaughn v. Rosen*, 484 F.2d 820 (D.C. Cir. 1973)), *cert. denied*, 415 U.S. 977 (1984). "The list must include sufficiently detailed information to enable a district court to rule whether the document falls within a FOIA exemption." *Rein v. U.S. Patent and Trademark Office*, 553 F.3d 353, 357 n.6 (4th Cir. 2009).

June 14, 2016, again requesting a *Vaughn* index from the IRS. The IRS denied the Ayyads' request on June 22, 2016. ECF No. 1 at ¶ 19; *see also* ECF No. 1–2 at 42–44.

On August 31, 2016, after exhausting all administrative remedies, Plaintiffs filed suit under 5 U.S.C. § 552, alleging that the IRS unlawfully withheld responsive agency records to which Plaintiffs are entitled. ECF No. 1. Plaintiffs again requested that the Court order the IRS to produce a *Vaughn* Index of all responsive records withheld under claim of exemption. *Id.* at 9.

On November 8, 2016, months after Plaintiffs' FOIA action was filed in this Court, IRS determined that they had not performed an adequate search in response to Plaintiffs' request for "all written correspondence, electronic or otherwise, among Agent Feldman, Mr. Bisamber Misir, Mr. Quinton J. Ferguson, Mr. Larry Timms, and any other IRS employee relating to the examination of plaintiffs' account." ECF No. 25–1 at ¶ 4; *see also* Decl. of William E. Rowe ("Rowe Decl."), ECF No. 28–1 at ¶¶ 18–19. IRS instructed Agent Feldman to provide all electronic correspondence related to Plaintiffs' examinations. *Id.* at ¶¶ 21–22; Feldman Decl., ECF No. 25–2 at ¶ 6. Agent Feldman located 872 additional pages of responsive electronic correspondence, of which the IRS redacted 176 pages and withheld 27 pages, claiming various FOIA exemptions. Rowe Decl., ECF No. 28–1 at ¶ 25. These emails were provided to Plaintiff's on March 2, 2017 with the Bates range IRS 000001–000872 ("March 2 release"). *See* 25–1 at 5. The IRS did not provide a *Vaughn* Index.

After reviewing the March 2 release, Plaintiffs' counsel noted that email correspondence between Agent Feldman and Bisamber Misir regarding Plaintiffs' tax returns, on which Plaintiff's counsel was originally copied, was missing from the IRS's disclosures. ECF No. 18–1. Plaintiff's counsel contacted the IRS regarding these missing emails on March 8, 2017. ECF No. 18–1 at 4. The IRS then conducted yet another search of Agent Feldman's Outlook inbox and enlisted several information technology specialists to determine why the emails were not produced by the initial search. Feldman Decl., ECF No. 25–2 at ¶¶ 10–17. After a month of investigation, the IRS was unable to ascertain why the referenced email was not included in Agent Feldman's search results and the investigation was closed. *Id.* The IRS released the missing emails to Plaintiff on May 31, 2017 with Bates range IRS001080–81. ECF No. 25–1 at 5–6. The IRS did not conduct further review of Agent Feldman's inbox or conduct searches of other email inboxes. ECF No. 25–1; Rowe Decl., ECF No. 28–1 at ¶ 45.

In addition to the missing electronic correspondence, Plaintiffs' counsel also informed the IRS that the March 2 release did not include the emails' respective attachments. ECF No. 18–1 at 3–4. On March 17, 2017, Plaintiff moved for summary judgment in their favor and renewed their request for a *Vaughn* Index. ECF No. 18.

On April 25, 2017, the Court issued an order requiring the IRS to release all remaining responsive, non-exempt records to Plaintiff by May 31, 2017. ECF No. 24. The IRS thereafter located *6,568 additional pages* of potentially responsive attachments not previously identified, more than a year after Plaintiffs' FOIA request and months of ongoing litigation. Within this newfound document trove, the IRS redacted 412 pages and withheld 3,474 pages. ECF No. 25-1 at 5; Feldman Decl., ECF No. 25-2 at ¶¶ 18–19; Rowe Decl., ECF No. 28-1 at ¶¶ 46–50. These responsive documents were provided—again without a *Vaughn* Index—to Plaintiffs on May 31, 2017, with the Bates range 000001–0006568. ECF No. 25-1 at 5–6. The IRS then filed its cross-motion for summary judgment, arguing that it has now fully complied with FOIA in releasing responsive documents and that the agency adequately claimed FOIA related exemptions for withheld and redacted documents. *Id.* at 7. In support, the IRS submitted affidavits with broad descriptions of the covered documents, but it did not submit a *Vaughn* Index. *See, e.g.,* ECF Nos. 18-1 at 11 & 25-1 at 6.

II. STANDARD OF REVIEW

Congress enacted FOIA to promote government transparency and "permit access to official information long shielded unnecessarily from public view." *Milner v. Dep't of Navy*, 562 U.S. 562, 565 (2011) (quoting *EPA v. Mink*, 410 U.S. 73, 79 (1973)); 5 U.S.C. § 552. FOIA is "a means for citizens to know 'what their Government is up to.' This phrase should not be dismissed as a convenient formalism. It defines a structural necessity in a real democracy." *Nat'l Archives & Records Admin. v. Favish*, 541 U.S. 157, 171–72 (2004) (internal quotations and citations omitted).

This strong interest in transparency, however, must be balanced against the "legitimate governmental and private interests [that] could be harmed by release of certain types of information." *United Techs. Corp. v. U.S. Dep't of Defense*, 601 F.3d 557, 559 (D.C. Cir. 2010). To that end, Congress established nine FOIA exemptions under which agencies may withhold information from disclosure. 5 U.S.C. § 552 (b). "These exemptions are explicitly made exclusive, and must be narrowly construed." *Milner*, 562 U.S. at 565 (internal quotations and citations omitted); *see also Jones v. Murphy*, 256 F.R.D. 510, 514 (D. Md. 2008) (noting that "[i]t is the responsibility of the Court to construe the privilege strictly and allow protection of documents only if specific requirements are met") (internal citations omitted).

An agency's decision to withhold records under a FOIA exemption is not entitled to deference, and the Court must conduct a *de novo* review of the administrative record with a strong presumption in favor of disclosure. 5 U.S.C. § 552(a)(4)(B); *Dep't of State v. Ray*, 502 U.S. 164, 173 (1991). FOIA's segregation requirement also requires the agency to provide "any reasonably segregable portion of a record" after it has redacted the exempt portions. 5 U.S.C. § 552(b). The Government bears the burden of providing that documents withheld in full are not "reasonably segregable." *Id.*; *see also Williamette Indus., Inc. v. United States*, 689 F.2d 865, 868 (9th Cir. 1982), *cert. denied*, 460 U.S. 1052 (1983).

Summary judgment is appropriate "if the pleadings, depositions, answers to interrogatories, and admissions on file, together with the affidavits, if any, show that there is no genuine issue as to any material fact and that the moving party is entitled to a judgment as a matter of law." *Hill v. Lockheed Martin Logistics*

Mgmt., Inc., 354 F.3d 277, 283 (4th Cir. 2004) (en banc) (internal quotation marks omitted). As a general rule, FOIA determinations should be resolved on summary judgment. *Hanson v. U.S. Agency for Intern. Dev.*, 372 F.3d 286, 290 (4th Cir. 2004).

III. ANALYSIS

The Ayyads, in short, argue that summary judgment should be granted in their favor because the IRS has failed to demonstrate that it performed a reasonable search and has not established that exemptions apply to withheld or redacted documents. The IRS, by contrast, argues that summary judgment is appropriate in its favor because the record evidence indisputably demonstrates adequate search and appropriate claimed exemptions. At summary judgment in a FOIA case, the Court reviews the record evidence to determine: (1) the reasonableness of its search for responsive records, and (2) that any redacted or withheld records fall under one of FOIA's disclosure exemptions. *Rein v. U.S. Patent & Trademark Office*, 553 F.3d 353, 362 (4th Cir. 2009). The Court addresses each element of this inquiry in turn.

1. Adequacy of the Government's Search

As to the claimed adequacy of the search, the agency must show that it has "conducted a search reasonably calculated to uncover all relevant documents." *Weisberg v. DOJ*, 705 F.2d 1344, 1451 (D.C. Cir. 1983). In deciding whether the government's search was reasonable, a court is to consider "not whether any further documents might conceivably exist but rather whether the government's search for responsive documents was adequate." *Perry v. Block*, 684 F.2d 121, 129 (D.C. Cir. 1982); *see also Ethyl Corp. v. U.S. EPA*, 25 F.3d 1241, 1246 (4th Cir. 1994). Thus, the adequacy of the search is determined "not by the fruits of the search, but by the appropriateness of the methods used to carry out the search." *Iturralde v. Comptroller of Currency*, 315 F.3d 311, 315 (D.C. Cir. 2003). "FOIA does not require a perfect search, only a reasonable one." *Rein v. U.S. Patent & Trademark Office*, 553 F.3d 353, 362 (4th Cir. 2009) (citing *Meeropol v. Meese*, 790 F.2d 942, 956 (D.C. Cir. 1986)).

Adequacy of a search does not require "meticulous documentation" of "an epic search for the requested records," but must be demonstrated through "affidavits that explain in reasonable detail the scope and method of the search conducted by the agency." *Perry*, 684 F.3d at 127; *see also Weisberg*, 627 F.2d at 371 (agency affidavits that "do not denote which files were searched, or by whom, do not reflect any systematic approach to document location, and do not provide information specific enough to enable [the requester] to challenge the procedures utilized" are insufficient to support summary judgment). An affidavit is "reasonably detailed" if it "set[s] forth the search items and the type of search performed . . . averring that all files likely to contain responsive materials (if such records exist) were searched." *Ethyl Corp*, 25 F.3d at 1247.

On summary judgment, for the plaintiffs to demonstrate the inadequacy of a FOIA search, they must "identify specific deficiencies in the agency's response" that contradict the adequacy of the search or suggest bad faith. *CareToLive v. FDA*, 631 F.3d 336, 341–42 (6th Cir. 2011); *see also Heily v. U.S. Dep't of*

Commerce, 69 Fed.Appx. 171, 173 (4th Cir. 2003). Here, Plaintiffs posit the following deficiencies: (1) Defendant's failure to search outside Agent Feldman's email for responsive electronic communications; (2) the absence of case history for tax years 2006–2009 and 2011–2013; (3) Plaintiff's unrebuttable evidence that at least five responsive emails were not included in the March 2 release; and (4) the disclosure's lack of Forms 11661 and 2727, which were explicitly requested by Plaintiffs. *See* ECF No. 18–1.

With respect to the IRS' focusing its search through Agent Feldman, this Court finds the search adequate, albeit troubling for different reasons. ECF No. 18–1 at 4. This Court is guided by the United States Court of Appeals for the Fourth Circuit's decision in *Rein v. U.S. Patent & Trademark Office*, 553 F.3d 353 (4th Cir. 2009). There, plaintiffs argued the inadequacy of an agency search for failing to search all requested employees for responsive material and the absence of several emails discovered in a parallel FOIA suit against a different agency. *See Rein*, 553 F.3d at 364–65. The Fourth Circuit determined that the agency's search was reasonable, noting that "FOIA does not require the Agenc[y] to search every employee so long as the searches are 'reasonably calculated to discover responsive materials,' " and that the plaintiffs "failed to raise substantial doubt as to the adequacy of the Agencies' searches, which were targeted to the specific individuals and units they believed would likely possess documents responsive to [plaintiffs'] request." *Id.* at 365 (citing *Ethyl Corp.*, 25 F.3d at 1246–47).

The IRS offers reasonably detailed affidavits as to the search conducted by the assigned government information specialist, Jennifer Perez, case agent Feldman, and the attorneys overseeing this case, Mark Cottrell and William Rowe. *See* Feldman Decl., ECF No. 25–2, Decl. of Mark E. Cottrell ("Cottrell Decl."), ECF No. 25–3, Perez Decl. at ECF No. 25–4, & Rowe Decl., at ECF No. 28–1; *see Wickwire Gavin, P.C. v. Defense Intelligence Agency*, 330 F. Supp. 2d 592, 597–98 (E.D. Va. 2004) (rejecting an affidavit that described the search in inappropriately vague and conclusory terms). Regarding the decision to only search Agent Feldman's email account, Mr. Rowe avers that because Agent Feldman is the "sole" revenue agent assigned to Plaintiffs' tax examination, Feldman would "typically" have been a sender, recipient, or copied on all Ayyad-related correspondence "due to the centrality of his role in relation to the examination." Rowe Decl., ECF No. 28–1 at ¶ 21; *see also* Feldman Decl., ECF No. 25–2 at ¶ 5 (Agent Feldman stating that he was "the recipient of, the sender of, or . . . copied on all correspondence between IRS employees regarding the examination."). Agent Feldman further describes in sufficient detail his search of his email account for responsive emails. *See* Feldman Decl., ECF No. 25–2 at ¶ 7. Feldman further establishes that he engaged in good-faith due diligence to ascertain why the missing emails were not included in the initial search. *Id.* at ¶¶ 9–17. Accordingly, the searches at this stage were reasonable. *Accord Rein v. U.S. Patent & Trademark Office*, 553 F.3d 353, 364 (4th Cir. 2009). Plaintiffs' accusations are insufficient to defeat this showing. *Id.*

Understandably, the Ayyads take issue with Agent Feldman's post-suit "discovery" of over 7,000 additional responsive documents not previously identified during the administrative searches. *See* Rowe Decl., ECF No. 28–1 at ¶¶ 23 & 50. The Court shares the Ayyads' concerns. It simply strains credulity that in this electronic age, a reasonably well-trained agent designated as the IRS' "disclosure" designee would somehow fail to request emails and attachments from the "sole" revenue agent assigned to the Ayyads' case. But that appears to be what happened here. *Compare* Perez Decl., ECF No. 25–4 at ¶¶ 11–13 *with* Rowe Decl., ECF No. 28–1 at ¶ 21; *see also* Rowe Decl., ECF No. 28–1 at ¶¶ 20. Nor does it make much sense that Agent Feldman, once consulted, would initially fail to turn over *thousands of pages* in email attachments. That said, the IRS has continued to search and disclose documents in an effort to comply with FOIA. *See Rein*, 553 F.3d at 364; *see also ViroPharma Inc. v. HHS*, Case No. PLF–08–2189, 2012 WL 892926 (D.D.C. Mar. 16, 2012) ("The continuing discovery and release of documents . . . shows good faith on the part of the agency.").

The Court also notes that on the IRS's proffered record, it is almost impossible to determine the significance of the remaining claimed deficiencies in the IRS production. This is because, as more fully explained below, the Court cannot ascertain whether any of the "missing" documents to which the Ayyads point are part of the withheld records under claimed exemptions. The Court suspects this may be the case. Accordingly, the Court will deny summary judgment on the claimed inadequacy of the IRS' search, subject to reconsideration upon *in camera* review of the withheld documents.

2. Government's Claim to FOIA Exemptions 3, 5, 6, 7A, and 7E

Although FOIA presumptively requires government agencies to disclose information to the public upon request, 5 U.S.C. § 552(a)(3), nine specific exemptions permit withholding for "categories of *information*, and are not defined so as to protect entire documents, *per se*." *Ethyl Corp. v. EPA*, 25 F.3d 1241, 1245 (4th Cir. 1994) (citing *City of Virginia Beach v. U.S. Dep't of Commerce*, 995 F.2d 1247, 1253 (4th Cir. 1993)) (emphasis in original). To claim an exemption, Defendant must "provide a reasonably detailed justification [for the non-disclosure] rather than conclusory statements to support its claim that the non-exempt material in a document is not reasonably segregable." *Schoenman v. FEBI*, 763 F. Supp. 2d 173, 202 (D.D.C. 2011). "An agency cannot meet its statutory burden of justification by conclusory allegations of possible harm. It must show by specific and detailed proof that disclosure would defeat, rather than further, the purposes of the FOIA." *Mea Data Cent., Inc. v. U.S. Dep't of the Air Force*, 566 F.2d 242, 258 (D.C. Cir. 1977). "Conclusory language in agency declarations that does not provide a specific basis for segregability findings by a district court may be found inadequate." *Judicial Watch v. Dep't of Treasury*, 796 F. Supp. 2d 13, 29 (D.D.C. 2011). United States District Courts have jurisdiction to enjoin agencies from "withholding Agency records and to order the production of any Agency records improperly withheld." 5 U.S.C. § 552(a)(4)(B). Moreover, when withholding a responsive record pursuant to enumerated exemptions, the Government must redact the portions that are exempt and "reasonably segregable," and disclose the remainder. 5 U.S.C. § 552(b). . . .

a. Exemption 5 Claims

Exemption 5 permits an agency to "withhold inter-agency or intra-agency memorandums or letters which would not be available by law to a party other than a party in litigation with the agency," and encompasses attorney work product doctrine and the deliberative process and attorney-client privileges. *Rein v. U.S. Patent & Trademark Office*, 553 F.3d 353, 365–66 (4th Cir. 2009) (citing § 552(b)(5)). "The Agencies bear the burden of providing sufficient factual information as to the document's nature or content from which the district court can independently assess the applicability of the claimed exemption." *Id.*, 553 F.3d at 370; *see also City of Virginia Beach, Va. v. U.S. Dep't of Commerce*, 995 F.2d 1247, 1253–54 (4th Cir. 1993) ("[T]he burden is on the agency to correlate, with reasonable specificity, materials within a document with applicable exemptions."); *Coastal States Gas Corp. v. Dep't of Energy*, 617 F.2d 854, 861 (D.C. Cir. 1980) ("[C]onclusory assertions of privilege will not suffice to carry the Government's burden of proof in defending FOIA cases."); *Mead Data Cent., Inc.*, 566 F.2d at 251 ("[W]hen an agency seeks to withhold information[,] it must provide a relatively detailed justification, specifically identifying the reasons why a particular exemption is relevant and correlating those claims with the particular part of a withheld document to which they apply."). The Government cannot meet its burden by " 'articulat[ing] the Exemption 5 privilege in general terms, using FOIA language, and coupl[ing] the statement of privilege for each document with a general description of each document.' " *Rein*, 553 F.3d at 368 (quoting *Ethyl Corp. v. U.S. EPA*, 25 F.3d 1241, 1249 (4th Cir. 1994)).

The IRS identifies scores of records for which it asserts Exemption 5 withholding, but provides few details on which this Court can assess the validity of the claimed exemption. For example, in the affidavits supporting the IRS' motion, it identifies records by Bates number followed by a vague and non-specific description that reads:

> "Emails between Revenue Agents and Counsel that discuss advice regarding: (1) the strategy and direction of plaintiffs' examination; (2) the scope of plaintiffs' examination; (3) the examinations or legal proceedings of third-part taxpayers; or (4) how the revenue laws should be applied to the facts in plaintiffs' examination. Also, some of the listed records are email messages between Revenue Agents that reveal legal advice from Counsel or otherwise reference the seeking of advice from Counsel."

ECF No. 28–1 at ¶ 35(a). The IRS also asserts attorney-client privilege over a number of documents broadly described as "Memorandums and other documents" in a similar chart. *See* Rowe Decl., ECF No. 28–1 at ¶ 54(a); *see also id.* at ¶ 17 (describing the documents as "intra-agency memorandum from Counsel to Revenue Agents that advises on the scope and direction of [p]laintiff's examination"); ECF Nos. 25–1 at 13–14 (broadly describing the content of the documents for which attorney-client privilege is claimed). By failing to identify the subject, recipient or sender, date, or otherwise include any detail as to each allegedly exempted document, the IRS denies the Court any meaningful opportunity to assess whether "attorney-client" privilege applies to the claimed documents. *Rein*, 553 F.3d at 369.

Similarly, the IRS offers a blanket description for a long list of documents or portions of documents claimed exempt under the deliberative process privilege. *See* ECF No. 28–1 at ¶¶ 33(a), 53(a). To be exempt under deliberative process, the Court must determine that the record is both "pre-decisional" and "deliberative." *Rein*, 553 F.3d at 370; *see also Ethyl Corp*, 25 F.2d at 1248–49. An agency's conclusory averments that "[a]ll of the withheld records listed in the table below are both deliberative and pre-decisional" are unhelpful. ECF No. 28–1 at ¶¶ 32–33 (stating that "[t]he withheld pages contain communications and memoranda" and "are deliberative because they discuss or propose options for reaching the proper enforcement determinations, or provide suggested revisions, legal analysis, and other comments on the language of the draft document requests, communications with the taxpayer, and various intra-agency communications involved in the examination."); *see also* ECF No. 28–1 at ¶ 53(a). As the Fourth Circuit in *Ethyl Corp* and *Rein* reasoned, an agency's "merely asserting their conclusion that the document is exempt, employing general language" handicaps the Court's ability to "independently assess the asserted privilege." *Rein v. U.S. Patent and Trademark Office*, 553 F.3d 353, 369 (4th Cir. 2009) (citing *Ethyl Corporation v. U.S. EPA*, 25 F.3d 1241, 1250 (4th Cir. 1994)). The Court is "entirely dependent upon [the agency's] assertions that the documents [a]re appropriately withheld." *Rein*, 553 F.3d at 369. This is not the oversight mandated by Congress under FOIA, and "to find such superficial entries to be sufficient would permit [the agency] to evade judicial review." *Id.*

The IRS fares somewhat better in establishing that work-product doctrine protects a number of documents from FOIA disclosure. "To be considered attorney work product, a document must have been 'prepared by an attorney in contemplation of litigation which sets forth the attorney's theory of his case and his litigation strategy.'" *Hanson v. U.S. Agency for Intern. Dev.*, 372 F.3d 286, 292–93 (4th Cir. 2004) (quoting *NLRB v. Sears, Roebuck & Co.*, 421 U.S. 132, 149 (1975)). The work product exemption includes factual information prepared by an attorney in anticipation of litigation. *Id.* The agency sufficiently pleads the applicability of Exemption 5 to memoranda and motions identified by the Rowe Declaration as drafts prepared in anticipation of litigation. ECF No. 28–1 at ¶ 55. The remaining documents withheld as "work-product" have once again been summarily described as "emails between Revenue Agents and Counsel regarding the legal proceedings of third-party taxpayers, such as discussions about the preparation of declarations, the status of the case, or case strategy, and emails between Revenue Agents and Counsel regarding litigation hold procedures." ECF No. 28–1 at ¶ 37(a). In sum, the IRS's affidavit is largely inadequate to support its request for summary judgment in its favor as to Exemption 5. . . .

4. Exemption 3 Claims

Exemption 3 allows an agency to withhold matters that are "specifically exempted from disclosure by statute . . ., provided that such statute (A) requires that the matters be withheld from the public in such a manner as to leave no discretion on the issue, or (B) establishes particular criteria for withholding or refers to particular types of matters to be withheld." § 552(b)(3). Here, the IRS claims withholding under 26 U.S.C.A. §§ 6103(a), 6103(b) and 6103(e)(7). Generally, 26 U.S.C.A. § 6103 limits the disclosure of "[r]eturns and return information . . . except as authorized by [Title 26]" to certain circumstances. The statute defines "return information" to include "a taxpayer's identity . . . [and] whether the taxpayer's return was, is being, or will be examined or subject to other investigation or processing." *Id.* at § 6103(b)(2). Section 6103 is "a statute contemplated by FOIA Exemption 3." *Solers, Inc. v. Internal Revenue Service*, 827 F.3d 323, 331 (4th Cir. 2016) (citing *Tax Analysts v. IRS*, 410 F.3d 715, 717 (D.C. Cir. 2005)).

Section 6103(b)(2) exempts from disclosure "standards used or to be used for the selection of returns for examination, or data used or to be used for determining such standards, if the Secretary determines that such disclosure will seriously impair assessment, collection, or enforcement under the internal revenue laws." 26 U.S.C.A. § 6103(b)(2). The IRS withheld, either in full or in part, all documents identifying Discriminant Index Function (DIF) scores. *See* Cottrell Decl., ECF No. 25–3 at ¶ 4–11. DIF methodology is used by the IRS to identify tax returns that "have a high probability of significant tax change if examined." *Id.* at ¶ 4. Disclosure of DIF scoring could "provide taxpayers with the opportunity to manipulate their DIF scores and possibly avoid examination by the Service." *Id.* at ¶ 6.

Plaintiffs do not contest the IRS' withholding of documents which include DIF scores. ECF No. 26–1 at 19. Therefore, summary judgment is granted as to those documents or portions of documents related to § 6103(b)(2). However, the IRS's claimed third-party taxpayer return information is woefully under supported. Although the Ayyads do not contest in principle that Exemption 3 would exclude third parties unrelated to Plaintiffs, *see* ECF No. 26–1 at 19, the IRS does not provide sufficient detail for the Court can determine whether the "third-parties" are in fact unrelated, or instead associated with Plaintiff's businesses and thus authorized for release. *See* ECF No. 26–1 at 19.

Finally, the IRS claims many documents under 26 U.S.C.A. § 6103(e)(7), which prohibits disclosure in circumstances where "the Secretary determines that such disclosure would not seriously impair Federal tax administration." 26 U.SC.A. § 6103(e)(7); Cottrell Decl., ECF No. 25–3 at ¶ 15. To meet its burden under FOIA, the IRS offers a list of responsive numbers, respectively described as "information recorded in the case activity notes," "transmittal forms and memorandum," "emails between Revenue Agents and/or attorneys," and "copies of forms and attachments." Cottrell Decl., ECF No. 25–3 at ¶ 15. Each category includes a broad swath of documents accompanied by a near-boilerplate recitation that disclosure would "reveal the nature, direction, scope and focus of the Revenue Agents' case." *Id.* No further detail is offered, and the Court cannot discern whether all documents are withheld in part or in full. *See id.* In short, the IRS support for the claimed assessments is once again insufficient. *See Rein v. U.S. Patent & Trademark Office*, 553 F.3d 363, 367–69 (4th Cir. 2009); *accord Pully v. IRS*, 939 F. Supp. 429, 435–36 (E.D. Va. 1996) (granting summary judgment under § 6103(e)(7) where the affidavit testimony grouped the documents into categories and described them as responses by financial institutions to summonses, public land records and federal bankruptcy files, third party interview notes, property transactions, and other agency's investigation notes); *Cujas v. IRS*, Case No. 97–741, 1998 WL 419999 at 3–*4 (M.D.N.C. Apr. 15, 1998) (granting summary judgment after reviewing the agency's *Vaughn* index and conducting *in camera* review). . . .

IV. *VAUGHN* INDEX AND *IN CAMERA* REVIEW

On the whole, the IRS has failed to sustain its burden of demonstrating the propriety of withholding documents under Exemptions 3, 5, 6, 7A, 7C, and 7E. Accordingly, the Court must conduct an *in camera* review of the withheld documents. [W]here government's evidence "is so vague as to leave the district court with an inability to rule, then some other means of review must be undertaken, such as *in camera* review." *See Rein v. U.S. Patent and Trademark Office*, 553 F.3d 353, 368 (4th Cir. 2009) (quoting *Ethyl Corporation v. U.S. EPA*, 25 F.3d 1241, 1250 (4th Cir. 1994)); *see also City of Virginia Beach, Va. v. U.S. Dep't of Commerce*, 995 F.2d 1247, 1251 (4th Cir. 1993).

This case has been pending for nearly eighteen months. The Ayyads' initial FOIA requests were propounded almost *two years* ago, and yet the conversation remains centered on the IRS' failure to fulfill its well-established obligation to describe *with particularity* the bases for claimed withholding so that the Court can properly assess the legal propriety of the claimed exemptions. This Court will not delay further review any longer.

Accordingly, the Court GRANTS Plaintiff's motion for summary judgment in part and DENIES the IRS' motion in part. The Court further ORDERS the IRS to produce to this Court a *Vaughn* index and underlying withheld documents for *in camera* review on or before March 2, 2018. The documents will be submitted electronically via disk and will be individually *hyperlinked* to their entries in the Vaughn index so as to expedite the Court's review. Although the Court is mindful that customarily a *Vaughn* index "functions as a surrogate for the production of documents for in camera review," *Solers*, 827 F.3d at 328, the Court orders dual production for several reasons. First, the IRS has claimed eight different categories of exemptions for thousands of pages spanning several tax years and multiple agency decisions. Second, the documents are pulled from multiple sources and in various formats, such as emails with attachments and hard document files, and simply producing the documents in hard copy will be unwieldy and nearly impossible to segregate by claimed privilege. Finally, the Court encourages the IRS to view its creation of a *Vaughn* index, in addition to disclosure, as its last opportunity to provide substantive and well-reasoned bases for disclosure in lieu of the boilerplate submissions currently before the Court.

A separate Order follows.

NOTES AND QUESTIONS

1. DIF scores and the algorithms used to arrive at the scores are kept secret by the IRS.
2. In 2011, the IRS created the Office of Compliance Analytics. This subdivision of the IRS likely mines public data to identify tax returns for review. The IRS, however, appears to avoid headlines on this topic to avoid political fallout.
3. The *Ayyad* case also highlights FOIA requests. A taxpayer under audit may use FOIA to find out what the IRS has reviewed prior to an internal appeal with the Appeals Office to confirm what is in the administrative record. A taxpayer's attorney may also want to use FOIA to find out what the IRS has looked at before the attorney began representing the taxpayer.

3. Math Error Correction

Another short-form tax return review takes place under the IRS's math error correction assessment authority. This procedure involves more scrutiny than DIF scoring, but not as much as a full examination. Under the IRS's math error correction authority, the IRS may assess computational errors without sending a notice of deficiency to the taxpayer. Section 6213(b)(1) provides as follows:

> If the taxpayer is notified that, on account of a mathematical or clerical error . . . an amount of tax in excess of that shown on the return is due, and [the IRS has assessed or will assess the amount], such notice shall not be [subject to the IRS's deficiency assessment restrictions] and the taxpayer shall have no right to file a petition with the Tax Court based on such notice, nor shall such assessment or collection be prohibited by the provisions of subsection (a) of this section. . . .

Thus, the IRS often will send a taxpayer a notice of a computational error that the taxpayer must either contest within 60 days or the IRS will assess the liability. IRS data shows the IRS contacted taxpayers with respect to 3 percent of individual tax returns filed in 2010.

The IRS's inquiry under the math error correction authority does not qualify as an examination, but it seems like one. In a sense, it is harsher than an examination because the taxpayer is not entitled to prepayment judicial review. In an examination, the IRS issues a statutory notice of deficiency, which gives the taxpayer 90 days to petition the U.S. Tax Court before the IRS may assess. *See* IRC § 6213(a). Pursuant to the IRS's error correction authority, a taxpayer must resolve the issues with the IRS during the 60-day period provided in the notice or the IRS may immediately assess the tax. Section 6213(b)(1) provides as follows:

If the taxpayer is notified that, on account of a mathematical or clerical error appearing on the return, an amount of tax in excess of that shown on the return is due, and that an assessment of the tax has been or will be made on the basis of what would have been the correct amount of tax but for the mathematical or clerical error, such notice shall not be considered as a notice of deficiency . . . and the taxpayer shall have no right to file a petition with the Tax Court based on such notice, nor shall such assessment or collection be prohibited . . . .

Also, the IRS does not invoke its summons authority with this type of administrative review. Either the taxpayer provides documents to substantiate his claims or the IRS assesses the tax and collects it. Once the IRS assesses the tax, the only option for a taxpayer to challenge the liability is to pay the tax, file a refund claim, and then sue to collect the refund.

The math error correction authority is not as innocuous as it sounds. As discussed above, the IRS may summarily assess any amounts after providing notice to the taxpayer. In addition, the term "math error" has become very broad. The Code provides 17 categories of math errors, including the omission of various types of information related to earned income and child-care credits. *See* § 6213(g)(2). These "math errors" are math errors in name only.

The heart of the following case is the math error correction authority.

SWIGGART v. COMMISSIONER
T.C. Memo. 2014-172
United States Tax Court

BUCH, Judge:

This case is before the Court on Mr. Swiggart's motion pursuant to Rule 231[4] for an award of reasonable administrative and litigation costs under section 7430. For the reasons discussed below, we conclude that Mr. Swiggart is entitled to administrative and litigation costs of $3,256.50.

BACKGROUND

On May 19, 2011, Mr. Swiggart filed a 2010 Form 1040, U.S. Individual Income Tax Return. Mr. Swiggart claimed head of household filing status, reported tax due of $15,766, and reported tax withheld of $13,617. Mr. Swiggart did not pay the remaining $2,149. Moreover, Mr. Swiggart did not report the name of the dependent who qualified him for the head of household filing status because he had agreed to allow the child's mother to claim the dependency exemption deduction for the child for 2010.

---

[4] [fn 1] Unless otherwise indicated, Rule references are to the Tax Court Rules of Practice and Procedure, and all section references are to the Internal Revenue Code in effect at all relevant times. All amounts are rounded to the nearest dollar.

On June 20, 2011, the IRS issued a math error notice to Mr. Swiggart, stating that the IRS had changed his filing status because the name of the dependent who qualified him for head of household filing status was not reported on his tax return. As a result, the IRS recalculated Mr. Swiggart's tax using a filing status of single and determined that Mr. Swiggart instead owed $4,354, an increase of $2,205 to the amount Mr. Swiggart had reported as due on his return.[5] In the notice, the IRS stated: "If you contact us in writing within 60 days of the date of this notice, we will reverse the change we made to your account."

Sixteen days later, on July 6, 2011, the IRS issued a Final Notice of Intent to Levy and Notice of Your Right to a Hearing, seeking to collect the amount from the math error notice plus penalties and interest.

On August 5, 2011, 46 days after the IRS issued the math error notice, Mr. Swiggart's counsel, Mr. Johnson, mailed a request for abatement by certified mail to the address listed on the math error notice. Also on August 5, 2011, Mr. Johnson mailed a Form 12153, Request for a Collection Due Process or Equivalent Hearing, by certified mail to the "person to contact" listed on the notice of intent to levy. Mr. Johnson attached a supporting statement to the request for a hearing listing the reasons he believed Mr. Swiggart was entitled to head of household filing status, stating why he believed the IRS' change in Mr. Swiggart's filing status was not a proper mathematical or clerical error under section 6213(g)(2), and stating that he had timely requested abatement under section 6213(b)(2)(A).

On September 15, 2011, respondent issued Mr. Swiggart a letter stating that the IRS was unable to process his claim for abatement because his supporting information was not complete and the additional information Mr. Swiggart provided did not give the IRS a basis to change the assessment.[6] On October 24, 2011, Mr. Johnson contacted the settlement officer assigned to the CDP hearing by letter informing him that the request for abatement had been denied despite his timely request and again requesting that the assessment be abated and that deficiency procedures be followed.

During the CDP hearing Mr. Swiggart provided a signed affidavit dated September 13, 2011, identifying his child by name and Social Security number and stating that his child spent the greater number of nights in 2010 with him but that he had an agreement with the child's mother to waive the dependency

---

[5] [fn 2] Of the $2,205, $2,142 is attributable solely to the change in filing status; the remainder consists of a section 6651(a)(2) addition to tax and interest.

[6] [fn 3] There are some inconsistencies in this letter. The letter states that Mr. Swiggart's claim was received on May 19, 2011 (the date of the return), but also states that there was a claim on August 16, 2011. The letter also states that Mr. Swiggart submitted an amended return, an allegation that neither party made to this Court and that is not supported by the record. Further, the letter states that the IRS has no record that Mr. Johnson was authorized to represent Mr. Swiggart in his request for abatement, but the letter was in fact sent in care of Mr. Johnson at Mr. Johnson's address.

exemption deduction for certain years, including 2010. The settlement officer agreed that claiming the child as a dependent was not required to qualify as a head of household, but the settlement officer also concluded that he could not abate the tax attributable to the change in filing status until Mr. Swiggart provided additional documents showing that the child had lived with him for more than half of the year. On February 8, 2012, IRS issued a notice of determination sustaining the proposed levy because Mr. Swiggart had not proven that he was entitled to head of household filing status and because he had not proposed a collection alternative or provided financial information showing whether he was eligible for a collection alternative.[7]

Mr. Swiggart, residing in Minnesota at the time, timely filed a petition disputing the notice of determination and asserting that the assessment respondent attempted to collect was invalid as to the portion relating to his filing status. Mr. Swiggart asserted that the change in filing status was not properly subject to a math error notice, that he had timely requested abatement, that the IRS had erroneously concluded that he was required to prove his entitlement to the filing status before abatement, and that respondent had erroneously determined the assessment was valid. Respondent's answer alleges that "the settlement officer provided the opportunity to contest liability which would cure any procedural issues" Mr. Swiggart raised.

On November 19, 2012, Mr. Swiggart filed a motion for summary judgment, requesting the Court to conclude that the portion of the assessment attributable to the change in filing status is void and that respondent may not levy to collect that portion.[8] Mr. Swiggart did not dispute the portion of the assessment attributable to the amount reported as due but unpaid with his return. On December 11, 2012, respondent filed an objection to Mr. Swiggart's motion for summary judgment, stating that he did not object to abating the portion of the assessment attributable to the change in filing status but did object to abating the portion Mr. Swiggart reported as due on his return, which he acknowledged Mr. Swiggart was not disputing. On March 8, 2013, respondent filed a supplement to his notice of objection, informing the Court that he agreed that Mr. Swiggart's motion for summary judgment should be granted only in part, as to the portion of the assessment attributable to the change in filing status. Respondent also stated in

---

[7] [fn 4] There are also inconsistencies in this letter. The notice of determination states that Mr. Swiggart raised and disputed the head of household filing status but also states that he made no challenges to the existence or the amount of the underlying liability. The notice of determination states both that the hearing occurred on January 11, 2012, with Mr. Johnson and that it occurred on January 17, 2012, with a representative named Nicole McGuire. It is clear portions of the notice of determination relate to another taxpayer's hearing with a different representative.

[8] [fn 5] The record is not clear as to whether there were two separate assessments or one assessment consisting of both the amount reported as due but unpaid with the return and the amount attributable to the change in filing status.

his supplement that the abatement had been approved but had not yet appeared on the certificate of assessment; respondent included a separate document showing that the abatement of $2,142 had been approved.

At trial on April 23, 2013, the parties filed a stipulation of settled issues. In the stipulation, the parties agreed that respondent had abated $2,142 of the assessment without prejudice to his right to reassess the amount using deficiency procedures and that the collection action is sustained as to the $2,149 that Mr. Swiggart reported as due but unpaid on his original return, plus penalties and interest. After trial Mr. Swiggart filed a motion for an award of costs and a memorandum in support of his motion. Respondent filed a response asserting that Mr. Swiggart was not the prevailing party and that he is not entitled to attorney's fees in excess of the statutory rate.

DISCUSSION

Section 7430(a) allows a taxpayer to recover reasonable administrative and litigation costs incurred in an administrative or court proceeding brought by or against the United States in connection with the determination, collection, or refund of any tax, interest, or penalty. Reasonable administrative costs are the reasonable and necessary costs incurred by the taxpayer in connection with the administrative proceeding. They include administrative fees imposed by the Commissioner, reasonable fees paid or incurred to retain the services of a representative who is licensed to practice before the IRS, reasonable expenses of expert witnesses, and reasonable costs for any study, analysis, or report that is necessary to the taxpayer's case.[9] Similarly, reasonable litigation costs include reasonable court costs, reasonable attorney's fees, reasonable expenses of expert witnesses, and reasonable costs of any study, analysis, or report necessary to the taxpayer's case.[10]

To recover administrative and litigation costs under section 7430(a), the taxpayer must satisfy each of the following requirements: (1) the taxpayer must not have unreasonably protracted the administrative or court proceedings and (2) the taxpayer must have been the "prevailing party".[11] In addition, with respect to a request for litigation costs, the taxpayer must also prove that he or she exhausted all administrative remedies available within the IRS.[12] Mr. Swiggart has the burden of establishing that he satisfied each requirement of section 7430.[13]

Respondent conceded that Mr. Swiggart exhausted the administrative remedies available to him within the IRS and that he did not unreasonably protract the proceedings. Respondent disputes that Mr. Swiggart was the prevailing party.

---

[9] [fn 6] Sec. 7430(c)(2); sec. 301.7430–4(b)(1), Proced. & Admin. Regs.
[10] [fn 7] Sec. 7430(c)(1).
[11] [fn 8] Sec. 7430(b)(2) and (3), (c)(4)(A).
[12] [fn 9] Sec. 7430(b)(1).
[13] [fn 10] *See* Rule 232(e).

PREVAILING PARTY

To be a prevailing party, a taxpayer must (1) substantially prevail with respect to the amount in controversy or the most significant issue or set of issues presented and (2) meet the timing and net worth requirements of 28 U.S.C. 2412(d)(1)(B) and (2)(B).[14] Respondent concedes Mr. Swiggart meets the net worth requirement, and we conclude he has met the timing and net worth requirements. Respondent asserts that Mr. Swiggart has not substantially prevailed with respect to the amount in controversy because he reported a tax due of $7 more than the portion of the assessment attributable to the change in filing status. Further, respondent asserts that Mr. Swiggart has not substantially prevailed as to the most important issue or set of issues because "[t]he most important issue in any CDP case is the validity of the Service's collection action."

Mr. Swiggart has consistently disputed the assessment of the amount attributable to the unilateral change in filing status, and the only issues presented to us were the validity of that portion of the assessment and the attempts to collect based on that assessment. Respondent has conceded that the portion of the assessment attributable to the change in filing status was invalid and that the collection action should not be sustained as to that portion of the assessment. Mr. Swiggart is the prevailing party.

SUBSTANTIALLY JUSTIFIED

A taxpayer will not be treated as the prevailing party if the Commissioner establishes that the position of the United States was substantially justified.[15] In his response to Mr. Swiggart's motion for award of costs, respondent did not assert that the position of the United States was substantially justified, and with good reason. A position is substantially justified if it has a reasonable basis in both fact and law and is justified to a degree that could satisfy a reasonable person.[16] A significant factor in determining whether the Commissioner's position is substantially justified as of a given date is whether on or before that date the taxpayer has presented all of the relevant information that is under the taxpayer's control and has presented relevant legal arguments supporting the taxpayer's position.[17]

Where a taxpayer seeks both administrative and litigation costs, we apply the "substantially justified" standard as of the two separate dates on which the Commissioner took a position, first in the administrative proceeding and later in the court proceeding.[18] For purposes of the administrative proceeding, the

---

[14] [fn 11] Sec. 7430(c)(4)(A).

[15] [fn 12] Sec. 7430(c)(4)(B)(i); Rule 232(e).

[16] [fn 13] See Pierce v. Underwood, 487 U.S. 552, 565, 108 S.Ct. 2541, 101 L.Ed.2d 490 (1988); see also Sher v. Commissioner, 89 T.C. 79, 84, 1987 WL 42457 (1987), aff'd, 861 F.2d 131 (5th Cir.1988).

[17] [fn 14] Corson v. Commissioner, 123 T.C. 202, 206–207, 2004 WL 1789898 (2004); sec. 301.7430–5(c)(1), Proced. & Admin. Regs.

[18] [fn 15] Sec. 7430(c)(7)(A) and (B); *Maggie Mgmt. Co. v. Commissioner,* 108 T.C. 430, 442, 1997 WL 311818 (1997).

Commissioner's position is that taken on the date of the notice of decision of the IRS Office of Appeals.[19] For purposes of the court proceeding, the Commissioner's position is the position set forth in the answer.[20] Where the Commissioner maintains the same position in both the administrative and court proceedings, we can consider his administrative and litigation positions together.[21] Under section 6213(b)(2)(A), if a taxpayer filed a request for abatement within 60 days of the issuance of the math error notice, "the Secretary *shall* abate the assessment." (Emphasis supplied.) Further, any reassessment "*shall* be subject to the deficiency procedures".[22] The parties agree and we find that Mr. Swiggart requested abatement within 60 days of the math error notice when he mailed his request to the Atlanta, Georgia, IRS address on the notice; therefore, respondent was required by statute to abate the assessment.[23] Further, Mr. Swiggart provided a copy of the request and relevant legal authority to the Office of Appeals during the CDP hearing. Mr. Swiggart's request for abatement was rejected by letter dated September 15, 2011, from an IRS office in Memphis, Tennessee.[24] That letter stated that the IRS would not abate the assessment because Mr. Swiggart had failed to prove he was entitled to head of household filing status. Further, the settlement officer also concluded that Mr. Swiggart was required to prove his entitlement to that status, despite Mr. Swiggart's citation of the statute requiring the assessment to be abated. The settlement officer concluded that the erroneous assessment was valid and that Mr. Swiggart's affidavit was insufficient to prove entitlement to head of household status and sustained the levy. By statute, the IRS was required to abate the assessment, and requiring Mr. Swiggart to prove entitlement to head of household status before abating the assessment was not substantially justified.

In the answer, respondent continued to maintain that the assessment was valid and that "the settlement officer provided the opportunity to contest liability which would cure any procedural issues". In *Freijie v. Commissioner,* 125 T.C. 14, 32–36, 2005 WL 1649142 (2005), the Court held that a taxpayer's opportunity in a section 6330 proceeding to dispute the underlying tax liability

---

[19] [fn 16] Sec. 301.7430–3(c)(2), Proced. & Admin. Regs.

[20] [fn 17] Maggie Mgmt. Co. v. Commissioner, 108 T.C. at 442.

[21] [fn 18] Maggie Mgmt. Co. v. Commissioner, 108 T.C. at 442–443; see also Cooley v. Commissioner, T.C. Memo.2012–164, slip op. at *18–*19.

[22] [fn 19] Sec. 6213(b)(2)(A) (emphasis supplied).

[23] [fn 20] Mr. Swiggart also asserted that respondent's issuance of the notice of levy was in violation of section 6213(b)(2)(B). That section provides that no levy or proceeding in court for the collection of an assessment arising out of a math error notice shall be made, begun, or prosecuted during the 60 days within which the assessment may be abated. However, a "notice of intent to levy is an action other than a levy". *See Eichler v. Commissioner,* 143 T.C. ——, —— (slip op. at 14) (July 23, 2014).

[24] [fn 21] It is not clear whether the September 15, 2011, letter was from an Office of Appeals.

does not cure an assessment made in derogation of his right to a deficiency proceeding. Respondent's position in the answer is not substantially justified.

Mr. Swiggart is the prevailing party; therefore, we must determine whether the attorney's fees and other costs that he seeks to recover are reasonable.

[The court then applied the cost calculations applicable at the time.]

CONCLUSION

Mr. Swiggart was the prevailing party in this case, and the IRS was not substantially justified in failing to abate the assessment attributable to the change in filing status. As a result, we will grant Mr. Swiggart's motion for an award of reasonable litigation and administrative costs under section 7430 in that he is awarded $3,256.50.

To reflect the foregoing,

An appropriate order and decision will be entered.

NOTES AND QUESTIONS

1. The court does not discuss the power behind the math error correction authority. It is like an invisible elephant in the room. Presumably, both the court and the parties are aware of the immense power behind the math error correction authority, but neither discuss it.

2. Although the heart of the case is about the math error correction authority, there is some other learning in this case on recovering costs from the IRS when the agency challenges a taxpayer without good reason. This topic is important in tax procedure, but it does not fit easily in a casebook and is rarely worth pursuing for a taxpayer. In *Swiggart*, however, the IRS wasted the court's and the taxpayer's time, and the taxpayer deserved to be compensated.

4. The Automated Underreporter Program (AUR)

The IRS's automated underreporter program is a program that matches third-party returns (such as Forms 1099) to the taxpayer's return. IRS I.R.M. § 4.19.3.1.1.1 (August 22, 2017) provides as follows:

> Potential [Automated Underreporter] cases are systemically identified through computer matching of tax returns with corresponding Information Returns Master File (IRMF) payer information documents. Cases are selected for inventory in a manner determined to provide overall compliance coverage. Selected cases undergo an in-depth review by a tax examiner to identify underreported and/or overdeducted issues which require further explanation to resolve the discrepancy.

This process detects apparent underreporting, which often leads the IRS to contact the taxpayer to obtain further information. The information acquisition process is similar to the math error correction procedures.

The IRS's automated underreporter program is more like an examination than the IRS's math error correction procedures. With both processes, the taxpayer receives notices that the IRS seeks substantiation of a specific tax return item. With respect to the automated underreporter program, however, if the taxpayer does not respond the IRS may not assess immediately. Rather, unlike the math error correction inquiries, when employing the automated underreporter program the IRS must send a statutory notice of deficiency—just as in a full examination—giving the taxpayer the opportunity to petition the Tax Court before the IRS may assess additional tax. Although the automated underreporter program is like a full audit with respect to the pre-assessment right to petition the Tax Court, the IRS does not abide by the statutory restriction on multiple examinations with respect to the program. *See* IRC § 7605(b); Rev. Proc. 2005-32, 2005-1 C.B. 1206.

C. Examination of Taxpayer Returns

The IRS's examination process, along with some examination-like procedures discussed above, fulfills the detection side of the deterrence equation. *See generally* Michael G. Allingham & Agnar Sandmo, *Income Tax Evasion: A Theoretical Analysis*, 1 J. PUB. ECON. 323 (1972). An examination in the tax context is the IRS's investigation of a tax return's accuracy. *See* IRC § 7602(a). The IRS gathers relevant information to evaluate the return and determine if the taxpayer who filed it owes more tax.

1. Types of Audits

There are three primary types of audits. The first type is the correspondence audit. A correspondence audit takes place by mail. As a general matter, this type of audit is rather narrow. The IRS sends a letter by mail requesting documentation for return items. According to the IRS's regulations, a taxpayer who receives a notice that the IRS has initiated a correspondence audit may request to meet an examiner in person. *See* Reg. § 601.105(b)(2)(i).

In a correspondence audit, a taxpayer has a limited amount of time to respond to the IRS's inquiries. If the taxpayer does not respond within the allotted time, the IRS—rather than resorting to its summons power—often disallows the item at issue and notifies the taxpayer that the disallowance may be appealed through the IRS's internal appeals process. If the case remains unresolved, the taxpayer receives a notice of deficiency giving the taxpayer 90 days to petition the Tax Court before the IRS begins collection if left unpaid. After a correspondence audit—as with other audit types—the Code restricts the IRS from re-auditing the taxpayer. *See* IRC § 7605(b).

Other than the opportunity to appeal and go to court after a correspondence audit, a correspondence audit is difficult to distinguish from the IRS invoking its math error correction authority. A taxpayer may not appeal or petition the Tax Court when the IRS exercises its math error correction assessment authority because it does so pursuant to summary assessment procedures rather than deficiency assessment procedures. If the IRS finds a math error that the taxpayer has not refuted, the IRS may collect without providing an appeal or issuing a statutory notice of deficiency.

An automated underreporter inquiry is also difficult to distinguish from a correspondence audit. The distinction between a correspondence audit and an automated underreporter inquiry is more subtle than the distinction between the math error correction authority and the correspondence audit. The automated underreporter program is subject to the same procedures as an audit. These procedures are the IRS's deficiency procedures. It appears that the only difference is that a correspondence audit goes beyond mere return matching, which is the sole review activity of the automated underreporter program.

The second type of audit is the field audit. *See* Reg. § 601.105(b)(3). A field audit takes place on the taxpayer's premises. This type of audit is often broad. The IRS seeks information about numerous issues and pursues new issues as they arise.

During a field audit, the IRS seeks information on an informal basis by issuing Information Document Requests (IDRs). If a taxpayer refuses or fails to respond to such a request, the process becomes formal, and the IRS turns to its summons authority. The IRS issues a summons to the taxpayer that describes the documents or records the IRS desires, which gives the taxpayer a second opportunity to respond to the IRS's request. If the taxpayer still refuses or fails to respond, the IRS may refer the summons to the Department of Justice for enforcement in federal district court.

A field audit can take a long time. The more complex the taxpayer's finances or operations, the longer the audit can take. Although the document request process itself can take a long time, the IRS has taken steps to shorten the process. When the IRS issues an IDR, the IRS's procedures require the field agents to issue a summons if the taxpayer does not respond within a certain amount of time. *See* Large Business and International Directive on Information Document Requests Enforcement Process LB&I-04-0214-004 (Feb. 28, 2014). The IRS uses this information to verify the taxpayer's return position.

The third type of audit is the office audit. *See* Reg. § 601.105(b)(2). An office audit takes place in the IRS's offices. An examiner requests a taxpayer to bring documents to the IRS's office to talk with an agent face to face. The typical office audit is broader than a correspondence audit but narrower than a field audit. In recent years, the IRS seems to have deemphasized this type of audit. Instead, the IRS usually conducts a correspondence audit or a field audit.

2. Specialized Audits

The IRS also conducts some specialized audits. Partnership audits are a salient example. Prior to specialized rules, the growth of large partnerships created untenable enforcement problems for the IRS. Although a partnership is a legal entity, it is not a taxpaying entity for federal tax purposes. Rather, each partner is responsible for reporting his share of income, deductions, and credits as allocated by the partnership. Prior to specialized rules, the IRS audited each partner in a partnership separately. None of the partners were bound by the tax treatment reported by other partners. Nor were partners bound by administrative and judicial determinations made with respect to other partners. As partnerships grew in size, the IRS had problems with "duplicative proceedings and the potential for inconsistent treatment of partners in the same partnership."

The first attempt to resolve these issues was a set of procedural rules enacted as part of the Tax Equity and Fiscal Responsibility Act of 1982 (TEFRA). *See* Tax Equity and Fiscal Responsibility Act of 1982, Pub. L. No. 97-248, §§ 401-06, 96 Stat. 324, 648-71 (1982). TEFRA addressed the above problems by imposing a consolidated partnership proceeding prior to the audit, assessment, and collection with respect to each partner. TEFRA imposes the following rules:

- Partnership items must be resolved in the partnership level proceeding prior to the resolution of affected items and nonpartnership items (which were still resolved at the partner level). *See* IRC § 6221 (2017).
- Each partner must report his taxes consistent with the partnership in most instances. *See* IRC § 6222(a) (2017).
- The partnership must assign a tax matters partner to handle the proceedings on behalf of the rest of the partners. *See* IRC § 6223(g) (2017).
- The statute of limitations for partners is extended to permit the resolution of the partnership level proceeding. *See* IRC § 6229(a) (2017).

Once partnership issues are resolved at the partnership level, the IRS may assess and collect tax from each partner. While alleviating some of the above problems, TEFRA created new ones in the process. The two most recognized problems are the following:

- Uncertainty with respect to whether the TEFRA regime applies. *See, e.g.,* Stone Canyon Partners v. Commissioner, 94 T.C.M. (CCH) 618, 2007 T.C.M. (RIA) ¶ 2007-377, *aff'd sub nom.* Bedrosian v. Commissioner, 358 Fed. Appx. 868 (9th Cir. 2009).
- (2) Ambiguity in the statute of limitations provisions under section 6229. *See* AD Global Fund, LLC v. United States, 67 Fed. Cl. 657, 675, 690-91 (2005), *aff'd*, 481 F.3d 1351 (Fed. Cir. 2007).

Enough frustration arose that Congress enacted new partnership audit rules that took effect in 2018 as part of the Bipartisan Budget Act of 2015 (BBA). Pub. L. No. 114-74, 129 Stat. 584 (2015) (amended by Protecting Americans from Tax Hikes Act of 2015, Pub. L. No. 114-113, 129 Stat. 3103). The BBA rules address the TEFRA problems in two ways. First, the BBA creates a centralized system. Under the centralized system, there is a partnership level proceeding similar to TEFRA. All partnership-related items, however, are resolved in the partnership proceeding. *See* IRC § 6221(a) (2018 (as amended by the BBA)). In other words, the BBA unraveled TEFRA's distinction between partnership items, affected items, and nonpartnership items. Second, the IRS may assess and collect the tax from the partnership. *See* IRC § 6225(a) (2018 (as amended by the BBA)). This means that there is no separate assessment and collection from the partners as under TEFRA.

The BBA refined some other rules as well, while retaining the general concepts from TEFRA. Partners are still required to report tax consistent with the partnership. *See* IRC § 6222(a). In addition, partners continue to be bound by the partnership's representative. *See* IRC § 6223(a).

It should be noted that the TEFRA partnership rules remain important. TEFRA will still apply to returns filed prior to January 1, 2018. It will take a number of years for all the TEFRA cases now in existence to work their way through the system to final resolution.

3. Return Selection

There are few limitations on how the IRS selects returns for audit. The IRS selects returns to examine in several different ways. As discussed above, the IRS scores returns while processing them. This scoring method permits the IRS to choose returns for examination based on tax return DIF scores.

The IRS has other ways of finding tax returns to examine as well. When a taxpayer files a refund claim or amended return, the IRS is likely to review the original return giving rise to the claim. Also, the IRS is likely to investigate a partner's tax return where the partnership's tax return has suspicious positions. And Mr. Irwin Schiff, an infamous tax protester, discovered there is nothing stopping the IRS from pursuing a taxpayer that has professed on television that he does not file or pay income tax. Mr. Schiff appeared as a guest on *The Tomorrow Show* with Tom Snyder and told the audience that they could get away with not paying income tax by filing incomplete returns (which is a misdemeanor under section 7203), which led to Mr. Schiff's prosecution. *See* United States v. Schiff, 612 F.2d 73, 78-81 (2d Cir. 1979).

Another important source for finding noncompliant taxpayers is paid informants. There are two statutory programs that authorize payments to informants in exchange for information leading to the recovery of unpaid taxes. First, the IRS has a discretionary payment program in which it may, at its discretion, award a portion of the money recovered to the informant. Section 7623(a) provides as follows:

> The [IRS] . . . is authorized to pay such sums as he deems necessary . . . from the proceeds of amounts collected by reason of the information provided, and any amount so collected shall be available for such payments.

The IRS has had this program since 1876. *See* Kneave Riggall, *Should Tax Informants Be Paid? The Law and Economics of a Government Monopsony*, 28 VA. TAX REV. 237, 239 (2008). An informant who receives an award under this program may not appeal. Under the current guidance on the IRS's web site, the IRS may pay an informant up to 15% of the amount the IRS recovers from the underreporting taxpayer. *See What Happens to a Claim for an Informant Award (Whistleblower)*, INTERNAL REVENUE SERV., Aug. 3, 2017, https://www.irs.gov/uac/what-happens-to-a-claim-for-an-informant-award-whistleblower.

The second program, the "whistleblower" program, is not discretionary. For information leading to a recovery of over $2 million and, if the IRS's action is against an individual, the individual had gross income over $200,000, the whistleblower receives between 15% and 30% of the recovery amount. The largest award to date occurred in 2012 when the IRS paid $104 million to a whistleblower whose information led to recovery of $400 million in taxes from taxpayers who had hidden assets in a Swiss bank.

Prior to this whistleblower case, Swiss bank secrecy laws prohibited banks there from disclosing any information about their clients and their clients' accounts. In 2013, the federal government negotiated with the Swiss government to permit Swiss banks to participate in investigating United States taxpayers. *See Joint Statement Between the U.S. Department of Justice and the Swiss Federal Department of Finance and Program for Non-Prosecution Agreements or Non-Target Letters for Swiss Banks*, U.S. DEP'T OF JUSTICE, August 29, 2013, https://www.justice.gov/tax/file/631356/download. Since 2009 when the original disclosure was made, the federal government has prosecuted numerous large Swiss banks for criminal violations and recovered billions more in taxes through various amnesty-like programs from individual taxpayers.

The above methods are all acceptable methods for the IRS to determine whether to examine a tax return. Generally, the IRS may select tax returns for examination in any manner it chooses. There is language in the Code providing a politically significant restriction, however. Section 7602(e) provides as follows:

> The [IRS] shall not use financial status or economic reality examination techniques to determine the existence of unreported income of any taxpayer unless the [IRS] has a reasonable indication that there is a likelihood of such unreported income.

Absent the "unless," this language would seem to restrict the IRS from selecting tax returns for audit by observing that a taxpayer owns a nice car, lives in a large house, or otherwise lives beyond his apparent means. The "unless," however, seems to swallow the whole prohibition. The IRS seems to agree. In its rulings, the IRS has not found a situation where the prohibition restricts its revenue agents.[25]

---

[25] *See* C.C.A. 2003-11-032 (Mar. 14, 2003) (advising that the prohibition does not apply to inquiries preliminary to an examination); *see also* F.S.A. 2002-06-055 (Feb. 8, 2002) (advising that the prohibition does not apply to direct audit methods); *see also* F.S.A. 2001-01-030 (Jan. 5, 2001) (advising that the prohibition does not prohibit revenue agents from driving by a taxpayer's house presumably to evaluate the taxpayer's economic status).

Another restriction, albeit implicit and rarely challenged, is discriminatory return selection, as in the following case.

GREENBERG'S EXPRESS, INC. v. COMMISSIONER
62 T.C. 324 (1974)
United States Tax Court

TANNENWALD, Judge:

These cases are before us on petitioners' motion for a protective order under Rule 103(a)(10), Tax Court Rules of Practice and Procedure. We deny the motion for the reasons stated below and append some additional comments which we hope will facilitate the further proceedings in these cases.

The substantive gravamen of petitioners' complaint is that the deficiency notices involved herein stem from second examinations of the books and records of the corporate petitioners under section 7605; . . . that such second examinations, although ultimately made in compliance with the formal requirements of section 7605(b), were not instituted or conducted in good faith and for a legitimate purpose; and that such second examinations and the deficiency notices which issued as a result thereof were based upon discriminatory selection of petitioners because two of their number are the sons of one Carlo Gambino, a purported target of a governmental investigation into organized crime. In support of this claim, petitioners allege that the revenue agent in charge of the second examinations, and a member of the Strike Force, stated, 'Your trouble is that "The Godfather" got so much publicity, everybody was breathing down everybody's neck and we were told that we had to do something to take the heat off, so we went out to get a Gambino.' Petitioners further allege that the deficiency determinations in themselves were arbitrary, unreasonable, and capricious because of respondent's failure to follow his established audit procedures and, in the case of certain of the corporate petitioners, his blanket disallowance of claimed business expense deductions and/or increases of round dollar amounts of taxable income.

On the basis of the foregoing, petitioners seek an order directing respondent to produce and deliver into the custody of the Court, and thereby make available for inspection by the petitioners prior to trial, all documents (whether in the custody of the Commissioner of Internal Revenue, the Secretary of the Treasury, the Attorney General of the United States, or any of their agents or designees) relating to the audit of petitioners' Federal income tax returns for 1966 through 1968 and any investigation of petitioners Thomas Gambino and Joseph Gambino by the Department of Justice, the Internal Revenue Service, or the Federal Strike Force Against Organized Crime operating in New York City. Petitioners assert that such an order is necessary to prevent the possible destruction or concealment of the documents involved and to enable the petitioners to prove, by such documents, the allegations of their amended petitions that respondent's determination of deficiencies in each of their Federal income tax liabilities for 1968 arose from official actions violating their constitutional rights.

Petitioners also ask us, in the event that their allegations are established, to declare respondent's determinations null and void and therefore decide that there is no deficiency due from any of them for 1968; alternatively, petitioners ask that we shift to respondent the burden of proof or the burden of going forward with the evidence.

In terms of petitioners' primary request herein—to wit, an impounding order under Rule 103(a)(10)—we are satisfied that they are not entitled to such relief. Initially, we note that Rule 103(a) contains the following prefatory language to the specification of the types of protective orders which the Court will consider issuing: 'for good cause shown, the Court may make any order which justice requires to protect a party or other person from annoyance, embarrassment, oppression, or undue burden or expense.'[26] We are unable to find that petitioners have made the necessary showing to justify the issuance of the requested order. Petitioners make the bare allegation that the Government officials who possess the documents they seek may be tempted to destroy or conceal them in order to cover up the alleged scheme of harassment directed against them. Petitioners, however, do nothing more than suggest the possibility of destruction or concealment of potential evidence. We are not prepared as a court to presume, on the strength of such mere speculation, that Government officials will in fact destroy or conceal potential evidence in pending litigation. The custodians of the documents which petitioners seek are already, by virtue of their offices, obligated to preserve any evidence which they know may be relevant to these cases and we, therefore, consider it unnecessary, at least at this point, to use our procedures in an attempt to assure compliance with their obligations. Cf. Harris v. Sunset Oil Co., 2 F.R.D. 93 (W.D. Wash. 1941).

Moreover, we note that impoundment is not customarily used to compel the production of documents before a court. Rather, it provides a means for retaining such documents in the court's custody after they have been properly produced by other means, such as pretrial discovery, subpoenas duces tecum, or voluntarily by a party or witness to the litigation. United States v. Birrell, 242 F.Supp. 191, 202-203 (S.D.N.Y. 1965). We will not exercise our power to impoundment as a means of providing petitioners with a device for obtaining access to documents which they might be able to obtain by some other available procedures for the production of documents. Cf. Rules 72 (production of documents) and 147 (subpoena duces tecum), Tax Court Rules of Practice and Procedure. Such procedures are to be 'preferred to a reflexive motion for a protective order.' See John W. Pearsall, 62 T.C. 94 (1974). Of course, these procedures are subject to the usual limitations on the scope of discovery, including resolution of the question (which we do not now decide) as to whether, under Rule 72, a notice to produce served upon respondent should be limited to documents or things directly 'in the possession, custody or control' of the Commissioner of Internal

---

[26] [fn 3] Rule 103(a)(10) permits the issuance of an order, 'That documents or records be impounded by the Court to insure their availability for purposes of review by the parties prior to trial and use at the trial.'

Revenue or may properly be extended so as to require respondent to produce documents or things 'in the possession, custody or control' of other departments and agencies of the United States Government. Cf. Kazuko S. Marsh, 62 T.C. 256 (1974). Finally, to the extent that such procedures may properly be utilized, they demand that petitioners give careful attention to developing a more precise description of the materials which they may seek; the blanket coverage of the motion herein is clearly beyond any reasonable bounds.[27] Cf. United States v. Roundtree, 420 F.2d 845, 851-852 (C.A. 5, 1969); United States v. National Steel Corporation, 26 F.R.D. 607 (S.D. Tex. 1960).

We come now to what we consider the crux of the matter before us: if petitioners were able to establish their allegations of discrimination in their selection as objects of an otherwise legitimate tax audit, would they be entitled to the benefit of any of the requested forms of relief? If not, such allegations would be immaterial to the resolution of the instant cases and petitioners would, therefore, not be warranted in their attempts to compel the production of any documents sought to establish those allegations. Cf. William O'Dwyer, 28 T.C. 698, 702-704 (1957), affd. 266 F.2d 575, 581 (C.A. 4, 1959).

As a general rule, this Court will not look behind a deficiency notice to examine the evidence used or the propriety of respondent's motives or of the administrative policy or procedure involved in making his determinations. Human Engineering Institute, 61 T.C. 61, 66 (1973), on appeal (C.A. 6, Jan. 2, 1974); Efrain T. Suarez, 58 T.C. 792, 813 (1972). Thus, we will not look into respondent's alleged failure to issue a 30-day letter to the petitioners or to afford them a conference before the Appellate Division. Cleveland Trust Co. v. United States, 421 F.2d 475, 480-482 (C.A. 6, 1970); Luhring v. Glotzbach, 304 F.2d 560 (C.A. 4, 1962); Crowther v. Commissioner, 269 F.2d 292, 293 (C.A. 9, 1959), affirming 28 T.C. 1293 (1957). The underlying rationale for the foregoing is the fact that a trial before the Tax Court is a proceeding de novo; our determination as to a petitioner's tax liability must be based on the merits of the case and not any previous record developed at the administrative level. William O'Dwyer, supra.

This Court has on occasion recognized an exception to the rule of not looking behind the deficiency notice when there is substantial evidence of unconstitutional conduct on respondent's part and the integrity of our judicial process would be impugned if we were to let respondent benefit from such conduct. Efrain T. Suarez, supra. But even in such limited situations, we have refused to declare the deficiency notice null and void, as petitioners would have us do. See Efrain T. Suarez, 58 T.C.at 814. See also Marx v. Commissioner, 179 F.2d 938, 942 (C.A. 1, 1950), affirming a Memorandum Opinion of this Court dated Jan. 24, 1949.

---

[27] [fn 4] We also note that, since only the taxable year 1968 is involved in the docketed cases with respect to which the motions herein have been made, it is at least open to question whether petitioners may reach documents, etc., pertaining to other taxable years.

In the area of the criminal law, 'mere selectivity in prosecution creates no constitutional problem.' See United States v. Steele, 461 F.2d 1148, 1151 (C.A. 9, 1972). On the other hand, 'While the Fifth Amendment contains no equal protection clause, it does forbid discrimination that is "so justifiable as to be violative of due process." ' (Citations omitted.) See Shapiro v. Thompson, 394 U.S. 618, 642 (1969). Even the conscious exercise of some selectivity is not in and of itself a Federal constitutional violation. See Oyler v. Boles, 368 U.S. 448, 456 (1962). Within these boundaries, the Federal courts have developed the test that before the complainant is entitled to relief, it must appear that the law has been 'applied and administered by public authority with an evil eye and an unequal hand' (see Yick Wo v. Hopkins, 118 U.S. 356, 373-374 (1886), or with 'questionable emphasis' (see United States v. Steele, 461 F.2d at 1152), through the use of an unjustifiable criterion such as race, religion, or expression of unpopular views. See also Two Guys v. McGinley, 366 U.S. 582, 588 (1961); United States v. Falk, 479 F.2d 616 (C.A. 7, 1973).

Assuming without deciding that a similar standard should be applied to civil tax litigation (cf. Hugo Romanelli, 54 T.C. 1448 (1970), reversed in part 466 F.2d 872 (C.A. 7, 1972), and John Harper, 54 T.C. 1121 (1970), it is conceivable that there may be situations where a taxpayer should be accorded some relief, if he were able to prove that he was selected for audit on a clearly unjustifiable criterion. But we think that such situations will be extremely rare and we are satisfied that petitioners' allegations, even if true, would not be sufficient. Petitioners do not deny—indeed, they assume for the purposes of their motions—that the audits involved herein stemmed from the Government's attempts to deal with organized crime. Nor do they at any point assert that the deficiency notices are without foundation, i.e., that they owe no tax. Cf. Enochs v. Williams Packing Co., 370 U.S. 1, 7 (1962); Miller v. Nut Margarine Co., 284 U.S. 498, 510 (1932). Compare Bob Jones University v. Simon, 416 U.S. 725 (1974).

What is more, petitioners are not faced with prejudicial action by a Government agency which will, absent protective intervention by this Court, result in a final determination of petitioners' tax liabilities or in the establishment of facts which will be deemed undisputed and inexorably lead to the imposition of such liabilities. Cf. Shapiro v. Thompson, supra; United States v. Falk, supra; United States v. Steele, supra. Indeed, their right to a trial de novo in this Court is the critical factor which distinguishes practically all of the cases relied upon by petitioners. Compare Bob Jones University v. Simon, supra; Robida v. Commissioner, 371 F.2d 518 (C.A. 9, 1967); Boyd v. United States, 345 F.Supp. 790 (E.D.N.Y. 1972). In this connection, we note that petitioners make no claim that they are presently or may be subjected to criminal prosecution as a consequence of respondent's actions. Compare Hinchcliff v. Clarke, 371 F.2d 697 (C.A. 6, 1967); see also Donaldson v. United States, 400 U.S. 517, 532-533 (1971).

The broad sweep of the power to enforce revenue laws has repeatedly been recognized. E.g., Donaldson v. United States, 400 U.S. at 534-536; United States v. Roundtree, 420 F.2d at 850-851; Human Engineering Institute, supra. When this power is evaluated against the commonly recognized pervasive influence of organized crime in this country, we cannot say that petitioners' allegations create an unjustifiable criterion. See S. Rept. No. 1097, 90th Cong., 2d Sess. (1968), 2 U.S. Cong. & Adm. News 2112, 2119-2120. Nor do we believe that the fact that petitioners' connection with the 'organized crime' frame of reference may turn out to be only because of a family or business relationship is sufficient to justify a contrary conclusion. Cf. United States v. Kahn, 415 U.S. 143 (1974). Clearly, the circumstances herein cannot be equated with the horrendous attempt to infer guilt by association in violation of a taxpayer's first amendment right of free speech which existed in Lenske v. United States, 383 F.2d 20 (C.A. 9, 1967), heavily relied upon by petitioners. Likewise, we do not believe that the selective process which may have been utilized herein meets the standard of 'harassment' or 'pressure' suggested, without any delineation, in United States v. Powell, 379 U.S. 48, 59 (1964). In short, we do not believe that petitioners' allegations, even if true, would be violative of the applicable requirements of due process. See Shapiro v. Thompson, supra. See also Bob Jones University v. Simon, supra.

The foregoing reasoning also disposes of petitioners' attempt to attack the validity of the second examinations under section 7605(b). In a prior proceeding, petitioners unsuccessfully attacked the summons issued in connection with such examinations. See United States v. Gambino, an unreported case (S.D.N.Y. 1971, 29 A.F.T.R.2d 72-1010, 72-1 U.S.T.C. par. 9439). Most, if not all, of the arguments made herein were considered and rejected by Judge Ryan in that proceeding. Assuming without deciding that the prior proceeding does not justify the application of collateral estoppel, we nevertheless reach the same conclusion independently. Cf. United States v. DeLuca, an unreported case (E.D.N.Y. 1972, 30 A.F.T.R.2d 72-5771, 72-2 U.S.T.C. par. 9738), affd. 474 F.2d 1336 (C.A. 2, 1973). Compare Arthur Meister, 60 T.C. 286, 294 (1973), on appeal (C.A. 3, Aug. 21, 1973). In so doing, we note that the procedural requirements of section 7605(b) and therefore the underlying purpose of the section were satisfied. See United States v. Powell, 379 U.S. at 54-56. We are also satisfied that the circumstances alleged herein do not constitute unconstitutional action on the part of the respondent which would justify, at least at this stage of the proceeding, shifting to respondent the burden of proof or of going forward with the evidence as we did in Efrain T. Suarez, supra. Nor do the allegations of blanket disallowances of deductions and/or increases of round dollar amounts of taxable income, in the case of the corporate petitioners, dictate any such action. To be sure, the evidence presented at the trial may be such that the Court will be required to determine the extent of petitioners' tax liabilities, if any, on the basis of the record before it and not merely on the basis that petitioners have failed to sustain their burden of proof. Helvering v. Taylor, 293 U.S. 507 (1935); Marx v. Commissioner, supra; Durkee v. Commissioner, 162 F.2d 184, 187 (C.A. 6, 1947), remanding 6 T.C. 773 (1946). Compare Human Engineering Institute, 61 T.C. at 66. But whether this situation will obtain will have to abide the event.

We conclude that petitioners' motion should be denied and that these cases should proceed to trial in due course.

An appropriate order will be entered.

NOTES AND QUESTIONS

1. What was the nature of the IRS's alleged discrimination, according to the taxpayers?
2. What types of IRS discrimination against a taxpayer might persuade the Tax Court to discipline or penalize the IRS in some way?

There is also somewhat of a restriction on an IRS revenue agent conducting a civil audit using the summons power for criminal investigation. A revenue agent should not conduct a criminal investigation because during a civil audit the taxpayer is not on notice that he or she is a suspect. Without the knowledge that one is a suspect, one cannot invoke Fifth Amendment protection from being compelled to be a witness against one's self. The following case digs deeper into these issues.

UNITED STATES v. CRESPO
281 F. Supp. 928 (D. Md. 1968)
United States District Court, District of Maryland

THOMSEN, Chief Judge.

This is a proceeding brought by the United States and a Special Agent of the Internal Revenue Service (IRS) under sections 7402(b) and 7604(a), IRC, 1954,[28] to compel compliance with two administrative summonses issued to Gustav J. Crespo, as president, and George J. Smith, Jr., as vice president, of Remington Sales Bureau, Incorporated, the taxpayer, demanding their testimony and the production of certain corporate books and records for the period April 1, 1963 through March 31, 1965, alleged to be necessary for a determination of its income tax liabilities for the years ending March 31, 1964 and March 31, 1965.

Crespo owns 60% of the stock of taxpayer, Smith the remaining 40%; there were no other stockholders during the years in question.

A hearing has been held to permit respondents to show cause why they should not be compelled to obey the summonses. During the hearing petitioners entered into a stipulation with Smith, which resulted in the dismissal of the action against him. Crespo has raised the following question[]: . . . Whether the IRS has already conducted 'one inspection' of the books and records of the corporate taxpayer for the tax years in question, as the quoted term is used in section 7605(b)? . . .

STATUTES

Section 7602, dealing with the examination of books and witnesses, provides:

---

[28] [fn 1] All section references herein, unless otherwise indicated, will be to sections of the Internal Revenue Code of 1954, 26 U.S.C.

'For the purpose of ascertaining the correctness of any return, making a return where none has been made, determining the liability of any person for any internal revenue tax or the liability at law or in equity of any transferee or fiduciary of any person in respect of any internal revenue tax, or collecting any such liability, the Secretary or his delegate is authorized—

'(1) To examine any books, papers, records, or other data which may be relevant or material to such inquiry;

'(2) To summon the person liable for tax or required to perform the act, or any officer or employee of such person, or any person having possession, custody, or care of books of account containing entries relating to the business of the person liable for tax or required to perform the act, or any other person the Secretary or his delegate may deem proper, to appear before the Secretary or his delegate at a time and place named in the summons and to produce such books, papers, records, or other data, and to give such testimony, under oath, as may be relevant or material to such inquiry; and

'(3) To take such testimony of the person concerned, under oath, as may be relevant or material to such inquiry.'

Section 7604(a) and section 7402(b) contain almost identical language. Section 7604(a), dealing with the enforcement of summons and the jurisdiction of district courts, provides:

'If any person is summoned under the internal revenue laws to appear, to testify, or to produce books, papers, records, or other data, the United States district court for the district in which such person resides or is found shall have jurisdiction by appropriate process to compel such attendance, testimony, or production of books, papers, records, or other data.'

Section 7605(b) provides:

'(b) Restrictions on examination of taxpayer.— No taxpayer shall be subjected to unnecessary examination or investigations, and only one inspection of a taxpayer's books of account shall be made for each taxable year unless the taxpayer requests otherwise or unless the Secretary or his delegate, after investigation, notifies the taxpayer in writing that an additional inspection is necessary.'

FINDINGS OF FACT FROM EVIDENCE

The tax returns of the corporate taxpayer for the fiscal years ending March 31, 1963, and March 31, 1964, were assigned in regular course to Henry Weider, a revenue agent, in September 1964. Between that time and March 1967, Weider examined the general ledger and adjusting accounts, cash receipts and disbursements books, bank statements, cancelled checks and check stubs, and the minute book of the corporation. He did not see the purchase invoices or correspondence between the corporation and M. C. Ramos, Commercial Envelope Co. or Standard Register Co., except the purchase invoices of M. C.

Ramos. The corporate return for the year ending March 31, 1965, was also assigned to Weider, as were the individual returns of Crespo, to which Weider gave some attention in February 1966, when he had several conversations with Crespo. Extensions of the statute of limitations were obtained from the corporation and from Crespo, so that Weider could complete his examination of the early years. In March 1967 Weider completed his examination for the year ending March 31, 1963, and wrote up reports on that year for the corporation and on the calendar years 1962 and 1963 for Crespo. On April 11, 1967, notices of deficiency were sent to the corporate taxpayer for the fiscal year ending March 31, 1963, and to Crespo et ux. for the calendar years 1962 and 1963. Petitions challenging those deficiencies were filed in the Tax Court by those taxpayers in July 1967; the cases are still pending in that Court.

While working on the aforesaid reports, in March 1967, Weider became aware of the possibility of fraud in connection with the returns of the corporate taxpayer and, in accordance with established practice, suspended his work and referred the matter to the Intelligence Division of the IRS.

A revenue agent, such as Weider, examines income tax returns and determines correct tax liabilities. He is not empowered to investigate criminal tax fraud, and when his examination reveals the possibility of fraud he must suspend his examination and refer the matter to the Intelligence Division for resolution of the fraud question.

When a referral is made to the Intelligence Division, a special agent is assigned to make a preliminary investigation. The primary duties of a special agent are the investigation of possible criminal violations of the income, estate, gift, employment and excise tax statutes, the development of information concerning possible criminal violations of those statutes, the evaluation of such information, and the recommendation of prosecution when warranted.[29]

---

[29] [fn 2] See statement of Organization and Functions promulgated by the Internal Revenue Service, 30 Fed.Reg. 9399-9400 (July 28, 1965), 1966 CCH Stand.Fed.Tax.Rep.Sec. 5988, which Special Agent Jackson agreed was applicable to him.

'1118.6 Intelligence Division.

'The Intelligence Division enforces the criminal statutes applicable to income, estate, gift, employment, and excise tax laws (except those relating to alcohol, tobacco, narcotics and certain firearms), by developing information concerning alleged criminal violations thereof, evaluating allegations and indications of such violations to determine investigations to be undertaken, investigating suspected criminal violations of such laws, recommending prosecution when warranted, and measuring effectiveness of the investigation and prosecution processes. The Division assists other Intelligence offices in special inquiries, drives and compliance programs and in the normal enforcement programs, including those combating organized wagering, racketeering and other illegal activity, by providing investigative resources upon regional or National

After a case is referred to a special agent, he may determine that further investigation by the Intelligence Division is not warranted. If, however, he believes that further investigation is warranted, the case becomes a joint investigation with the revenue agent. The special agent, however, is in charge of that investigation. If the investigation develops the probability of criminal fraud, the special agent submits a report recommending prosecution.[30]

The function of the revenue agent in such an investigation is to assist the special agent by advising him of what the revenue agent has previously learned, and by participating in such further examination of the books and records of the taxpayer and others as may be necessary to determine the correct tax liability. The determination of the correct tax liability is an essential part both of the determination by the special agent whether there has been any criminal fraud, and of the determination by the revenue agent of the tax deficiency, if any, and the propriety of assessing civil fraud penalties. The special agent's report of the results of his investigation are made available to the revenue agent to assist him in computing the civil tax liability of the taxpayer under investigation. This information is transmitted to the revenue agent whether or not fraud is found, whether or not prosecution is recommended, and whether or not a conviction is ever obtained. The results of the special agent's investigation will always affect the revenue agent's computation by raising, lowering or verifying the revenue agent's computation.

The Intelligence Division referred this corporate taxpayer's case to Special Agent William N. Jackson.[31] During the course of his investigation, Jackson determined that it was necessary to examine certain corporate books and records of corporate taxpayer pertaining to the tax years involved. On April 19, 1967, in accordance with sections 7602 and 7603, Jackson issued and personally served summonses upon respondent Crespo, as president of corporate taxpayer, and upon Smith, as vice president of the corporation,[32] calling on them to produce

---

Office request. It also assists U.S. Attorneys and Regional Counsel in the processing of Intelligence cases, including the preparation for and trial of cases.'

[30] [fn 3] If approved, the recommendation goes to the Assistant Regional Commissioner (Intelligence) for review and possible rejection. If approved by the Assistant Regional Commissioner, it goes to the Regional Counsel who can also reject or concur. From Regional Counsel the recommendation goes to the Chief Counsel of the Internal Revenue Service and also to the Department of Justice. If approved by the Department of Justice, the case goes to the United States Attorney for prosecution. The grand jury, of course, can decline prosecution.

[31] [fn 4] The investigation of a corporate taxpayer by the Intelligence Division would normally include any criminal fraud on the part of an individual corporate officer whether or not there were indications of such at the time of referral.

[32] [fn 5] A special agent is a delegate of the Secretary of the Treasury empowered to issue summonses under the authority of section 7602 and Treasury

certain books and records of corporate taxpayer. Crespo and Smith appeared before Special Agent Jackson pursuant to the summonses issued to them but refused to testify or produce the records demanded. None of the books, records or documents demanded by the summonses are in the possession of the United States or of Special Agent Jackson. Nor, with the exception of two or three cancelled checks, are any copies of the demanded documents in the possession of the government. Special Agent Jackson has not seen any of the books or records demanded.

DISCUSSION . . .

Respondents contend that the IRS has already conducted one inspection for the tax years in question, so that section 7605(b) prohibits another inspection in the absence of notice from the Secretary. Respondents argue that section 7605(b), quoted above, contains two separate restrictions: first, 'no taxpayer shall be subjected to unnecessary examination or investigations'; second, 'only one inspection of a taxpayer's books of account shall be made for each taxable year unless the taxpayer requests otherwise or unless the Secretary or his delegate, after investigation, notifies the taxpayer in writing that an additional inspection is necessary'.

Respondents do not contend that taxpayer is being subjected to 'unnecessary examinations or investigations'. Such an argument would be without merit.[33] Respondents rely only on the absence of a notice from the Secretary or his delegate.

The government argues that the intent and meaning of section 7605(b) is that such a notice is necessary only when the investigation, including a sufficient inspection of the taxpayer's books and records, has been completed and a determination of the tax liability for the year or years in question has been made. The government's position is given effect in Revenue Procedure 64-40, Cumulative Bulletin 1964-2, p. 971, 26 C.F.R. 601.105, the pertinent parts of which are set out in note 7[34] in the margin.

Regulation 301.7602-1 (TD 6421, October 23, 1959, and TD 6498, October 24, 1960).

[33] [fn 6] See Application of Magnus, 299 F.2d 335 (2 Cir. 1962) and cases cited in note 9.

[34] [fn 7] Revenue Procedure 64-40 reads in pertinent part:

'Section 1. Purpose. The purpose of this revenue procedure is to restate and supersede Revenue Procedure 63-9, C.B. 1963-1, 488, which sets forth the conditions under which cases closed by examination in the office of District Director of Internal Revenue may be reopened.

'Section 2. Scope.

'.01 For the purpose of this procedure, a case is considered closed when a taxpayer has been notified in writing of an adjustment to his tax liability or the acceptance of the return as filed.

Both sides cite portions of the legislative history to support their respective contentions.[35] However, neither the legislative history nor the few court decisions referring to section 7605(b) which have been cited or found are conclusive of the issue. Most of the cases involved factual situations quite different from that presented in the instant case.[36]

Respondents cited In re Paramount Jewelry Co., 80 F.Supp. 375 (S.D.N.Y.1948), in which the court held that an investigation that had involved an examination of the taxpayer's books three or four times during the past two years should not be halted as unnecessary by vacating a direction that books and records be produced but that, if the taxpayer insisted, it was entitled to receive a notice that an additional inspection was necessary before being required to produce the taxpayer's books for a fourth or fifth time. That case has apparently been cited only once, in Application of Magnus, 196 F.Supp. 127, 128 (S.D.N.Y.1961), where it was summarized substantially as set out above in an opinion dealing with a different question. On appeal in the *Magnus* case, the Second Circuit did not cite the *Paramount Jewelry* case, but noted that an investigation 'often requires a long period of time. There may be many ramifications which lead into many areas. Each new clue investigated is not a new investigation in a Section 7605(b) sense.' 299 F.2d 335, at 337 (2 Cir. 1962).

'.02 This procedure does not include any action pertaining to the reopening of cases or issues under the jurisdiction of the offices of the Appellate Division or the Regional Counsel.

'Section 3. Conditions for Reopening.

'.01 It is the administrative practice of the Internal Revenue Service not to reopen cases previously closed by the District Director, unless—

'1. There is evidence of fraud, malfeasance, collusion, concealment or the misrepresentation of material fact; or

'2. The prior closing involved a substantial error; or

'3. Other circumstances indicate that failure to reopen would be a serious administrative omission. * * *'

A Policy Statement contained in Internal Revenue Manual, section P-4020-2, approved September 14, 1962, adds: 'Reopenings resulting from post-review action must have the approval of the Assistant Regional Commissioner (Audit). Reopenings at the District level must have the approval of the District Director.'

[35] [fn 8] 61 Cong.Rec. 5202 (1921); Sen.Rep.No. 275, 67th Cong., 1st Sess., p. 31; H.Rep.No. 337, 67th Cong., 1st Sess., p. 16; 8A Mertens, Law of Federal Income Taxation, § 47.48, p. 140.

[36] [fn 9] United States v. Powell, 379 U.S. 48, 85 S.Ct. 248, 13 L.Ed.2d 112 (1964); United States v. Howard, 360 F.2d 373 (3 Cir. 1966); Reineman v. United States, 301 F.2d 267 (7 Cir. 1962); National Plate & Window Glass Company, Inc. v. United States, 254 F.2d 92 (2 Cir. 1958); Norda Essential Oil & Chemical Co., Inc. v. United States, 253 F.2d 700 (2 Cir. 1958); United States v. United Distillers Products Corporation, 156 F.2d 872, 873 (2 Cir. 1946).

Similarly, the fact that a revenue agent has seen a cash book, journal or ledger once does not mean that he may not need to see it again for a different purpose.

This Court does not accept the government's position that a notice from the Secretary is never needed unless the investigation, including a sufficient inspection of the taxpayer's books and records, has been completed and a determination made of the tax liability for the year or years in question.[37] When the investigation has not been completed, the question whether a further examination of the books and records would constitute a second 'inspection' within the meaning of section 7605(b) depends on the circumstances. If such examination of the books and records is part of a continuing investigation, made necessary by the discovery of invoices, correspondence, or other material which requires the agent to look at the books again, such examination is not a second 'inspection' within the meaning of section 7605(b).

The taxpayers and other people of the United States have an interest in seeing that income tax returns are carefully audited, and that revenue agents investigate leads which indicate that a taxpayer has understated his taxable income, intentionally or unintentionally. But taxpayers and other people also have an interest in requiring that the work be done as promptly as is practicable, and that they are not harassed by investigations which are prolonged beyond any reasonable need, or by repeated examinations of their books and records unless such further examinations are required by the discovery or development of new leads.

The Courts are not in a position to require that all agents operate with the same efficiency, or to pass on what individual books and records an agent may re-examine as the result of a new lead. But the Courts should intervene when taxpayers are able to show that agents have abused their discretion in wielding the extensive powers granted to them by the Internal Revenue Code.

In the present case respondents Crespo and Smith did not testify themselves, but rested on the testimony of the two agents. From the evidence the Court finds that by March 1967 Revenue Agent Weider had made a sufficient examination of the corporate taxpayer's books and records for the fiscal year ending March 31, 1963, to be able to complete his report for that year. On the other hand, Revenue Agent Weider has not yet completed his report for the years ending March 31, 1964 and March 31, 1965. He has examined some of taxpayer's records for those years, but has not seen other items, e.g., correspondence with M. C. Ramos, Commercial Envelope Co. and Standard Register Co., nor the purchase invoices of the latter two concerns. He desires, and the evidence shows that he needs, further information with respect to those items, because of various questions which have arisen as to the propriety of certain claimed deductions relating to those transactions.

---

[37] [fn 10] Certainly, such a notice is needed under those circumstances, and would be needed here if the government were seeking to examine the books and records for the year ending March 31, 1963.

This Court concludes that the original investigation of the corporation's tax liabilities for the years ending March 31, 1964, and March 31, 1965 is continuing and that the production of the books and records for those taxable years would not amount to a second inspection within the meaning of section 7605(b). Therefore, notice from the Secretary or his delegate to examine taxpayer's books and records for the taxable years ending March 31, 1964 and March 31, 1965 is not required. . . .

The petition for enforcement of the summons served on respondents is hereby granted. An appropriate order will be entered.

NOTES AND QUESTIONS

1. Most audits do not require a referral to the Criminal Investigation Division (CID, successor to the Intelligence Division referred to in *Crespo*). Without a referral to CID, there is a clearer beginning and end to an "inspection." In general, an audit ends with a proposed adjustment or a "no action" letter. The IRS rarely opens up an audit after such a resolution.

2. In what circumstances would a revenue agent refer a case to CID?

3. When the IRS makes inquiries with a taxpayer under its math error correction authority, the limit on multiple inspections does not apply because the IRS does not consider it an examination.

4. Audit Confidentiality

Many taxpayers file their returns and have no further contact with the IRS. Inevitably, however, some taxpayers must face off against one of the most powerful and feared administrative agencies in the world. Clashing with the IRS can give even the most rigidly compliant taxpayers some anxiety. To mitigate this anxiety, policy-makers created a statutory Taxpayer Bill of Rights. These rights are listed in section 7803(a)(3). The sources of these rights, however, are dispersed throughout the Code, Treasury Regulations, and various judicial opinions. The following is a table of taxpayer rights listed in section 7803(a)(3) and the source of those rights.

Section 7803(a)(3) Right	Source
(A) the right to be informed	IRC § 7521(b)(1) (requiring IRS to explain audit process and rights during the process); IRC § 7522 (requiring IRS to notify taxpayer of amounts owed and explain why amounts are owed)
(B) the right to quality IRS	IRC § 6212(a) (requiring the IRS to provide contact information about the Taxpayer Advocate Service in all Statutory Notices of Deficiency; IRC § 6304 (requiring the IRS to follow fair collection practices); Internal Revenue Service Restructuring Reform Act of 1998, Pub. L. No. 105-206, 112 Stat. 685 (RRA) § 3705(a)

	(requiring IRS employees to provide identifying information)
(C) the right to pay no more than the correct amount of tax	Superior Oil Co. v. Mississippi, 280 U.S. 390, 395-96 (1930) ("The only purpose of the [taxpayer] was to escape taxation. . . . The fact that it desired to evade the law, as it is called, is immaterial, because the very meaning of a line in the law is that you may intentionally go as close to it as you can if you do not pass it."); Helvering v. Gregory, 69 F.2d 809, 810 (2d Cir. 1934) ("Any one may so arrange his affairs that his taxes shall be as low as possible; he is not bound to choose that pattern which will best pay the Treasury; there is not even a patriotic duty to increase one's taxes.")
(D) the right to challenge the position of the Internal Revenue Service and be heard	IRC § 6212 (permitting a taxpayer to petition the Tax Court upon receipt of notice of deficiency from the IRS); IRC § 6320 (permitting a taxpayer to request a hearing when the IRS files a lien notice); IRC § 6330 (permitting a taxpayer to request a hearing when the IRS files a levy notice)
(E) the right to appeal a decision of the Internal Revenue Service in an independent forum	RRA § 1001(a)(4) (requiring the IRS to ensure an independent Appeals Office); Rev. Proc. 2012-18 (generally prohibiting ex parte communications between examiners from the IRS and Appeals Officers)
(F) the right to finality	IRC § 6501 (limiting the time the IRS has to assess tax to three years); IRC § 7481 (making a Tax Court decision final if not appealed); IRC § 7605(b) (generally limiting the IRS to one examination per tax period)
(G) the right to privacy	Reg. § 301.6330-1(e) (requiring Appeals Officer to consider the intrusiveness of the IRS's collection actions when the IRS places a lien on the taxpayer's property); IRC § 7602(e) (prohibiting the IRS from seeking intrusive lifestyle information during an audit unless there is a reasonable indication of unreported income)
(H) the right to confidentiality	IRC § 6103 (prohibiting the IRS's employees from disclosing tax information to third parties without consent); IRC § 7525 (providing a tax practitioner's privilege); Fed. R. Civ. Proc. 26(b)(3)(A) (protecting documents prepared in anticipation of litigation from disclosure to the government); IRC § 7602(c) (generally prohibiting the IRS from contacting third parties to obtain information during an examination without advance notice to the taxpayer)
(I) the right to retain representation	IRC § 7430 (providing for the recovery of attorney costs in certain instances); IRC § 7521(b)(2) (requiring the

	IRS to suspend an interview where the taxpayer requests a representative); IRC § 7526 (providing for Low Income Taxpayer Clinics to represent disadvantaged taxpayers)
(J) the right to a fair and just tax system	IRC § 6159 (providing for payment plans when unable to pay in full); IRC § 7803(c) (providing procedures to seek assistance from the Taxpayer Advocate Service)

Many of these rights are more like duties of IRS employees restated as taxpayer rights. Restating these duties as rights and listing them in one Code section makes them more accessible for taxpayers than they were before.

An important right that arises in the return review and examination process is confidentiality. Taxpayers have the right for their return information to remain confidential. Section 6103(a) provides as follows:

> Returns and return information shall be confidential, and except as authorized by this title . . . no officer or employee of the United States . . . shall disclose any return or return information obtained by him in any manner in connection with his service as such an officer or an employee or otherwise or under the provisions of this section.

Confidentiality is important in a system where taxpayers determine and report their own liabilities. Taxpayers might not be so forthright if their sensitive financial information were open to the public.

The IRS takes tax return information confidentiality seriously. They must. An employee who discloses tax return information can be charged with a felony punishable by imprisonment for up to five years. *See* IRC § 7213(a)(1). A taxpayer may also sue the federal government if an IRS employee discloses tax return information. *See* IRC § 7431(a)(1). In addition, an IRS employee commits a misdemeanor for "browsing" or looking up a taxpayer's return information on an IRS database while having no tax administration purpose to do so.

In this context, tax return information means nearly any information in the IRS's possession about a taxpayer. *See* IRC § 6103(b)(2). The right to confidentiality is intended to prevent disclosure to the public so that taxpayers will not become subject to harassment based on their financial status. This right is not intended, however, to prevent the IRS from sharing return information with law enforcement agencies or Congress. The IRS discloses immense amounts of tax return information to federal, state, and local law enforcement agencies every year.

In summary, the confidentiality requirements apply to the amount of income a taxpayer earns, whether a taxpayer owes money, etc. Thus, an IRS employee who is curious about whether a presidential candidate or a potential spouse is telling the truth regarding the extent of his or her wealth commits a misdemeanor by looking up the taxpayer's tax returns in an IRS database and commits a felony if he or she shares that information.

CHAPTER 12

IRS SUMMONSES

A. IRS Information Acquisition

In general, an audit is the invocation of the IRS's examination authority. Section 7602(a) authorizes the IRS to

> examine any books, papers, records, or other data which may be relevant or material . . . for the purpose of ascertaining the correctness of any return, making a return where none has been made, [or] determining the liability of any person for any internal revenue tax . . . .

The IRS invokes this authority to obtain more information necessary to determine if the taxpayer owes more tax. The IRS does not consider the short-form "examination" programs discussed in the previous chapter to be technical examinations. Rev. Proc. 2005-32, 2005-1 C.B. 1206, § 4. In neither the math error correction program nor the automated underreporter program does the IRS need to examine any books and records to make a determination. Rather, in both programs, there is a discrepancy between the amount the taxpayer reported and information already in the IRS's possession about the amount the taxpayer owed.

During an examination, the IRS may obtain information from taxpayers pursuant to its summons authority. In practice, however, the IRS obtains most of the information sought on an informal basis. The procedure is generally as follows. First, the IRS requests information informally. Second, if a taxpayer fails to provide the informally requested information in a timely fashion, the IRS might issue a summons, which is essentially a formal demand for information. Third, if the taxpayer fails to provide the demanded information, the IRS may refer the summons to the Department of Justice for enforcement in federal district court. The Code provides federal district courts the authority to compel a response to summonses through contempt orders. *See* IRC § 7604(a).

Aside from the Internal Revenue Manual, there are few formal references to IDRs. Cases referring to IDRs do so in passing rather than provide guidance on the scope, authority, or enforcement mechanisms related to these documents. The most authoritative document discussing IDRs is in the form of a Directive from the IRS's Large Business and International Division.

DIRECTIVE ON INFORMATION DOCUMENT REQUESTS
IRS Large Business and International Division (February 28, 2014)

The Large Business & International (LB&I) Division has issued two Directives relating to Information Document Requests (IDRs); Directive LB&I-04-0613-004 issued on June 18, 2013 and Directive LB&I-04-1113-009 issued on November 4, 2013 (the "Prior Directives"). These Directives reflect, in part, the best practices applicable to IDRs that are being utilized by LB&I examiners across the Division. This Directive incorporates and supersedes the Prior Directives and provides further clarification of the use of the new IDR processes.

This clarification is necessary to ensure that the procedures governing IDR issuance and enforcement are easily and clearly understood. In addition, it is important to continue to emphasize the importance of both the IRS and taxpayers engaging in robust discussions that include the issue that is the subject matter of an IDR, what information is necessary to evaluate that issue and why, what information the taxpayer has and how long it will take to provide it, and how long it will take the IRS to review the information for completeness and respond to the taxpayer.

Meaningful communication between the IRS and taxpayers in advance of an IDR being issued is essential to provide efficiencies for both parties. For example, the IRS will be better able to manage field specialists, determine reasonable estimated closing dates, and reduce unproductive time waiting for information. Similarly, taxpayers will be better able to manage their tax department resources with focused IDR requests that have reasonable time frames.

It is anticipated that when both the IRS and taxpayers engage in robust, good faith communication in advance of an IDR being issued, enforcement procedures will be needed only infrequently.

INTRODUCTION

Over the last several months, all LB&I examiners and specialists should have completed two mandatory training sessions on IDRs[;] one covers requirements for issuing IDRs and one covers new procedures for enforcing IDRs. This training and the IDR procedures set forth in this Directive are designed to make the IDR process as efficient and transparent as possible. These new procedures should improve our ability to gather information timely and reduce the need to enforce IDRs through summonses.

PLANNING AND EXAMINATION GUIDANCE

This Directive incorporates the guidance in the Directive dated June 18, 2013, given to LB&I examiners and specialists to follow when issuing an Information Document Request (IDR) during the information gathering phase of an examination. Attachment 1 to this Directive contains a summary of the

Requirements for Issuing IDRs. In addition, this Directive sets forth the enforcement process that must be used when a taxpayer does not timely and completely respond to an IDR that is issued in the manner described in this Directive; that is, an IDR that is issue focused, has been discussed with the taxpayer, and contains a response date that has been discussed with the taxpayer and, in most instances, has also been mutually agreed upon. Attachment 2 to this Directive describes the IDR Enforcement Process.

There is one exception to the requirement that an IDR state an issue. An IDR that is issued at the beginning of an examination that requests basic books and records and general information about a taxpayer's business is not subject to this requirement. All other IDRs must state an issue in compliance with the requirements in Attachment 1.

The new IDR Enforcement Process involves three graduated steps: (1) a Delinquency Notice; (2) a Pre-Summons Letter; and (3) a Summons. This process is mandatory and has no exceptions. It requires LB&I managers at all levels to be actively involved early in the process and ensures that Counsel is prepared to enforce IDRs through the issuance of a Summons when necessary.

If during the discussion of an IDR, a taxpayer indicates that the requested information will not be provided without a Summons, the IDR enforcement procedures do not apply and the IRS should move directly to the issuance of a Summons.

Pursuant to this Directive, the IDR Enforcement Process is effective beginning March 3, 2014. As of that date, the process applies only to IDRs that have been issued in accordance with the requirements contained in Attachment 1. If an IDR does not meet these requirements, it must be reissued to conform to the new requirements including a new response date, at which time the enforcement procedures described in Attachment 2 will apply to that IDR. In addition, to ensure a smooth transition to these new enforcement procedures, examiners and specialists should not issue Delinquency Notices prior to April 3, 2014.

This Directive is not an official pronouncement of law and cannot be used, cited or relied upon as such.

cc: Division Counsel, LB&I

Attachment 1
LB&I Directive on Information Document Requests (IDRs)
REQUIREMENTS FOR ISSUING IDRS

IDRs are an important part of the information gathering process during any examination. When issuing IDRs, LB&I examiners and specialists should follow the requirements listed below:

1. Discuss the issue related to the IDR with the taxpayer.
2. Discuss how the information requested is related to the issue under consideration and why it is necessary.
3. After this consultation with the taxpayer, determine what information will ultimately be requested in the IDR.

4. Ensure the IDR clearly states the issue that is being considered and that the IDR only requests information relevant to the stated issue. An IDR issued at the beginning of an examination that requests basic books and records and general information about a taxpayer's business is not subject to this requirement 4. Once this initial IDR has been issued, subsequent IDRs must state an issue in compliance with this requirement 4.

5. Prepare one IDR for each issue.

6. Utilize numbers or letters on the IDR for clarity.

7. Ensure that the IDR is written using clear and concise language.

8. Ensure that the IDR is customized to the taxpayer or industry.

9. Provide a draft of the IDR and discuss its contents with the taxpayer. Generally, this process should be completed within 10 business days.

10. After this discussion is complete, determine with the taxpayer a reasonable timeframe for a response to the IDR.

11. If agreement on a response date cannot be reached, the examiner or specialist will set a reasonable response date for the IDR.

12. When determining the response date, ensure that the examiner or specialist commits to a date by which the IDR will be reviewed and a response provided to the taxpayer on whether the information received satisfies the IDR. Note this date on the IDR.

Attachment 2

LB&I Directive on Information Document Requests (IDRs)

IDR ENFORCEMENT PROCESS

IDRs that are issued in compliance with the requirements of Attachment 1 are subject to the enforcement process set forth in this Attachment 2.

This process involves three graduated steps: (1) a Delinquency Notice; (2) a Pre-Summons Letter; and (3) a Summons. This process is mandatory and has no exceptions. The timing of the application of the Enforcement Process is set forth below in a separate section.

EXTENSION AUTHORITY

Before the Enforcement Process is triggered, an examiner or specialist has the authority to grant a taxpayer an extension of up to 15 business days before the Enforcement Process begins. This extension may be granted in the following two situations. An examiner or specialist may grant one extension with respect to the same IDR.

1. **Taxpayer Fails to Respond.** If a taxpayer fails to provide any response by the IDR due date, the examiner or specialist, should, within 5 business days of the IDR due date, discuss with the taxpayer the cause of the failure to respond and determine if an extension is warranted. If the examiner or specialist determines that the taxpayer's explanation warrants it, the examiner or specialist may grant the taxpayer an extension of up to 15 business days from the date the extension determination is made and communicated to the taxpayer.

2. **Taxpayer Provides Incomplete Response.** If a response is received but the examiner or specialist determines that it is not complete, the examiner or specialist should discuss with the taxpayer the reasons why the response is not complete and determine within 5 business days whether an extension is warranted. If the examiner or specialist determines that the taxpayer's explanation warrants it, the examiner or specialist may grant the taxpayer an extension of up to 15 business days from the time the extension determination is made and communicated to the taxpayers.

TIMING OF APPLICATION OF IDR ENFORCEMENT PROCESS

The timing of the application of the IDR Enforcement Process is set forth below.

No Response Received by Due Date

1. If no response is received by the IDR due date and no extension is granted, the IDR enforcement process begins on the date the extension determination is communicated to the taxpayer.
2. If an extension is granted and no response is received by the extended due date, the IDR enforcement process begins as of the extended due date.

Response Received by Due Date

If a response is received by the due date, the IRS must determine whether the response is complete. This determination should be made on or before the date the examiner or specialist stated in the IDR.

1. **If the IDR is considered complete upon review**, the examiner or specialist must notify the taxpayer that the IDR is complete and closed.
2. **If the IDR response is not complete**, the timing of the enforcement process is as follows:
   a. **If the IDR response is not complete, and no extension is granted**, the IDR enforcement process begins on the date the extension determination is communicated to the taxpayer.
   b. If the IDR response is not complete and an extension is granted
      i. If no additional information is received at the end of the extension period (may be up to 15 business days), the IDR enforcement process begins at the end of the extension period.
      ii. If additional information is received at the end of the extension period, this information must be reviewed for completeness. This review should be completed as soon as practical but in most cases not more than 15 business days from receipt of the response. If the IDR response is determined to be incomplete, the IDR enforcement process begins on the date the examiner or specialist notifies the taxpayer that the response remains incomplete. If the IDR is complete, the examiner or specialist should notify the taxpayer and close the IDR.

IDR ENFORCEMENT PROCESS

The process has three graduated steps: (1) a Delinquency Notice; (2) a Pre-Summons Letter; and (3) a Summons. This process is mandatory and has no exceptions. It requires LB&I managers at all levels to be actively involved early in the process and ensures that Counsel is prepared to enforce IDRs through the issuance of a Summons when necessary.

DELINQUENCY NOTICE (LETTER 5077)

Once the IDR Enforcement Process applies based on the timing described in section titled "Timing of Application of IDR Enforcement Process," the examiner or specialist along with their manager must complete the first phase of the enforcement process, the Delinquency Notice, by following the procedures described below:

1. Discuss the Delinquency Notice with the taxpayer. During this discussion, ensure that the taxpayer understands the next steps in the enforcement process if the information requested in the IDR is not provided by the response date established in the Delinquency Notice.

2. Issue the Delinquency Notice signed by the Team Manager to the taxpayer within 10 days of the application of the Enforcement Process.

3. The Delinquency Notice should include a response date that is generally no more than 10 business days from the date of the Delinquency Notice. A Territory Manager must approve any date beyond 10 business days.

4. Provide a copy of the Delinquency Notice and the IDR to your assigned Counsel.

PRE-SUMMONS LETTER (LETTER 5078)

If a taxpayer does not provide a complete response to an IDR by the Delinquency Notice response date, the examiner or specialist must complete the next phase of the enforcement process, the Pre-Summons Letter, by following the procedures described below:

1. Discuss the lack of a complete response to the Delinquency Notice with the Team Manager, Specialist Manager, the respective Territory Managers and Counsel and prepare the Pre-Summons Letter.

2. The appropriate Territory Manager must discuss the Pre-Summons Letter with the taxpayer. During this discussion, ensure that the taxpayer understands the next steps in the enforcement process if the information requested in the IDR is not provided by the response date established in the Pre-Summons Letter.

3. Issue a Pre-Summons Letter signed by the appropriate Territory Manager. This must be done as quickly as possible but generally no later than 10 business days after the due date of the Delinquency Notice. Address this letter to the taxpayer management official that is at a level equivalent to the LB&I Territory Manager. This should be a level of management above the taxpayer management official that received the Delinquency Notice.

4. Include a response date in the Pre-Summons Letter that is generally 10 business days from date of Pre-Summons letter.

5. A Director of Field Operations (DFO) must approve any date beyond the 10-business-days response period.

6. Discuss the Pre-Summons Letter with Counsel.

7. DFO(s) must be made aware of the Pre-Summons Letter prior to issuance.

SUMMONS

If a taxpayer does not provide a complete response to an IDR by the Pre-Summons Letter response date, the examiner or specialist must complete the next phase of the enforcement process, the Summons, by following the procedures described below:

1. Discuss the lack of response to the Pre-Summons Letter with the Team Manager, Specialist Manager, the respective Territory Managers and DFOs, and Counsel and prepare the Summons.

2. Coordinate the issuance of the Summons with assigned Counsel.

3. Summons procedures can be found in IRM Section 25.5.

NOTES AND QUESTIONS

1. In this directive, the IRS imposes strict requirements on IDR response timeframes. With these strict timeframes, can it still be said that IDRs are informal?

2. The IRS often asks for information that it is beyond its summons authority. If the taxpayer does not cooperate, the IRS issues a summons with language that is consistent with its authority. After this directive, will the IRS continue this strategy? Why or why not?

The IRS's summons authority is broad. In general, the IRS may "examine any books, papers, records, or other data" to "ascertain[] the correctness of any return." IRC § 7602(a). The Code gives teeth to this authority by providing that the IRS may enforce a summons in federal district court. *See* § 7604(a). Failure to comply with a court order compelling the production of summoned documents may result in an arrest and jail time.

UNITED STATES v. MELICK
959 F. Supp. 2d 193 (D.N.H. 2001)
United States District Court, District of New Hampshire

ORDER ON PETITION FOR CIVIL CONTEMPT

JOSEPH A. DiCLERICO, JR., District Judge.

The government has filed a petition for civil contempt (Doc. no. 20) alleging that C. Gregory Melick, a/k/a Charles Gregory Melick, has failed to comply with the court's August 6, 2010, order, (Doc. no. 16), requiring him to comply with the Internal Revenue Service ("IRS") summons that was the subject of the government's petition to enforce filed on May 11, 2010. (Doc. no. 1). Melick was ordered to appear at the Internal Revenue Office at 80 Daniel Street, Portsmouth, New Hampshire, on August 20, 2010, at 9:30 a.m., before Revenue Officer David Kalinowski or any other authorized Revenue Officer of the IRS, to give testimony and produce all books and records in his possession or control required and called for by the terms of the summons.[1] *See* Attachment A.

BACKGROUND

IRS Revenue Agent Sonia J. Cryan conducted an investigation of Melick's tax liability for 2003. The IRS seeks Melick's testimony and documents within his control in connection with the investigation. On February 26, 2010, Cryan issued an IRS summons ordering C. Gregory Melick to appear at the IRS's office in Laconia, New Hampshire, on March 16, 2010, to testify and produce all documents or records in his possession or control regarding "assets, liabilities, or accounts held in the taxpayer's name or for the taxpayer's benefit which the taxpayer wholly or partially owns, or in which the taxpayer has a security interest" for the period from September 1, 2009, to February 25, 2010. (Doc. no. 1, Ex. 2). Cryan served the summons on Melick on March 2, by taping it to his apartment door in a secured, confidential envelope. Melick failed to appear pursuant to the summons.

On May 11, 2010, the government filed a petition in this court to enforce the IRS summons. On May 17, this court issued an order for Melick to show cause why the petition should not be granted and scheduled a hearing for July 7, 2010, before the magistrate judge. The order gave Melick ten days to file a written response supported by affidavit and to file any motions. The order provided that the court would consider "[o]nly those issues raised by motion or brought into controversy by the responsive pleadings and supported by affidavit . . ." and that "any uncontested allegations in the petition [would] be considered as admitted." On May 24, a deputy sheriff with the Carroll County Sheriff's Office served Melick with the May 17 show cause order by handing it to him, along with the IRS petition and exhibits, at his Tamworth, New Hampshire, home.

In response to the order, on June 2 Melick filed a motion to dismiss under Rule 12(b), alleging, *inter alia,* lack of personal and subject matter jurisdiction. He also claimed that process and service of process were inadequate because the summons bore neither the signature of the Clerk of Court nor the court seal. The government objected.

On July 6, 2010, Melick returned the show cause order, petition, and exhibits to the court. On the first page of the order, he scrawled that the order was refused for insufficient process, lack of subject matter jurisdiction, lack of personal jurisdiction, and failure to state a claim.

Melick did not appear at the July 7, 2010, show cause hearing. On July 6, he filed a second motion to dismiss, again challenging the court's jurisdiction and asserting the same arguments he had made in his first motion to dismiss. The government again objected.

---

[1] [fn 1] The court has jurisdiction to compel a taxpayer to comply with an IRS summons under 26 U.S.C. § 7402(b) and 26 U.S.C. § 7604(a), and enforcement authority under 26 U.S.C. § 7604(b).

On July 8, 2010, the magistrate judge issued a report and recommendation addressing the IRS summons and Melick's June 2 motion to dismiss.[2] The magistrate judge found that the government had satisfied the factors set forth in *United States v. Powell,* 379 U.S. 48, 57–58, 85 S.Ct. 248, 13 L.Ed.2d 112 (1964), and that Melick had not met his burden of showing that the summons was invalid or that enforcement would be an abuse of the court's process. *See Powell,* 379 U.S. at 58, 85 S.Ct. 248. The magistrate judge recommended that Melick be ordered to obey the summons and that his June 2 motion to dismiss be denied for the reasons set forth in the government's objection. The magistrate judge also recommended that the government be awarded its costs. The court mailed the report and recommendation to Melick at his home address.

On July 12, 2010, Melick filed a notice of a change of address, informing the court that his mailing address was P.O. Box 422, Chocorua, New Hampshire. Melick stated that he might return mail addressed to the wrong party or sent to a different address. The court resent the magistrate judge's report and recommendation to the post office box address.

On July 22, 2010, Melick filed a second notice of change of address, stating that his correct mailing address was "Charles Gregory Melick, *Sui Juris,* c/o P.O. Box 422, Chocorua [03817–0422], New Hampshire, U.S.A." (Doc. no. 12). Melick again said that mail addressed to another name or to an address other than the one given would not be "received or accepted" by him. *Id.*[3] On July 30, the court sent Melick the report and recommendation for the third time. The court noted that Melick had returned mail sent to both his post office box and his street address and that the court had called the U.S. Post Office to confirm his address.[4]

On August 5, 2010, Melick filed a third notice of change of address, in which he provided a new mailing address, a post office box in North Conway, New Hampshire. (Doc. no. 15). The court sent the report and recommendation to the North Conway address.

On August 6, 2010, the court granted the government's petition to enforce its summons and denied both of Melick's motions to dismiss. The court observed that neither party had filed a timely objection to the magistrate judge's report and

---

[2] [fn 2] Melick's July 6 motion to dismiss was not docketed until July 9, 2010, one day after the magistrate judge's report and recommendation issued.

[3] [fn 3] Also on that date, the defendant sent a letter purporting to notify the court that the government had defaulted on its claims and thus that the court had "substantial grounds to dismiss the motion and vacate the order. . .." (Doc. no. 13). In his response on July 30, the Chief Deputy Clerk informed Melick that the court would not act upon his letter request because it was not in the form of a formal pleading, as required by the Federal Rules of Civil Procedure and local rules.

[4] [fn 4] Three days after the magistrate judge's report and recommendation was approved, the July 30 copy of the report and recommendation was returned to the court with the "Refused" notation checked.

recommendation, concerning Melick's June 2 motion to dismiss and the government's petition and, therefore, approved the recommended decision without further analysis. *See PowerShare, Inc. v. Syntel, Inc.,* 597 F.3d 10, 14 (1st Cir.2010). The court denied Melick's July 6, 2010, motion to dismiss, holding that the court had jurisdiction to enforce the IRS summons, awarded costs to the government, and ordered Melick to appear before an authorized Revenue Officer of the IRS at the IRS's Portsmouth, New Hampshire, office on August 20, 2010, at 9:30 a.m., to give testimony and produce the books and records called for by the February 26, 2 010, summons. The order directed the United States Marshal or his deputy to deliver service to Melick in hand and to file a return of service with the court. Melick was personally served on August 19, in accordance with the court's order.

Melick failed to appear at the IRS office on August 20, 2010, in response to the court's order. Three hours after his ordered appointment, Melick left a telephone message with the Taxpayer Walk-in Service that he would need to reschedule his appointment. On September 6, 2010, Melick wrote a letter to the IRS indicating that he had hired an "IRS Enrolled Agent Tax Preparer" to "compose a completed report of pertinent financial records for submission to the Internal Revenue Service" for the 2003 tax year. He estimated that he would be able to provide the 2003 information within 30 days. Revenue Officer David Kalinowski called Melick on September 13 to discuss his planned compliance with the summons. Melick told him that he had hired an accountant to prepare a substitute tax return for 2003. The IRS did not receive any responsive paperwork with regard to Melick's 2003 tax liability.

On November 17 and 23, 2010, Kalinowski attempted to contact Melick by telephone. On both occasions, he received no answer and left messages on Melick's answering machine asking him to return the call. In his November 23 message, Kalinowski indicated specifically that he was following up on Melick's promise to provide the information required by the summons, relative to his 2003 federal tax liability, and asked Melick to return his call by the close of business the next day. Melick did not return Kalinowski's calls.

On December 16, 2010, the government filed a motion to hold Melick in civil contempt of the August 6, 2010, order and served a copy of the motion and accompanying affidavit on Melick via first-class, postage-prepaid mail at his North Conway address. Melick did not object to the government's motion. On January 14, 2011, the court ordered Melick to appear for a show cause hearing on February 14, 2011. In its order, the court warned Melick that if he did not appear for the hearing, a warrant would issue for his arrest. Again, the order directed the United States Marshal to serve on Melick in hand a copy of the order and the government's petition and the accompanying exhibit and to file a return of service with the court.

Deputy United States Marshal Paul Schmieder personally served Melick on February 3, 2011, in the presence of Carroll County Sheriff Christopher Conley. Melick refused to take process when it was handed to him, so Schmieder dropped the process at Melick's feet. On the return of service filed with the court,

Schmieder noted that Melick had "stated it was not a lawful service because there was no court stamp on it and [it] did not address him by his legal name." (Doc. no. 23).

On February 11, 2011, Melick mailed a 14–page "warning notice" to the district court in which he claimed that the court and judge were "imposing provisions of a contract counter to public morals." He attached a copy of the court's January 14, 2011, show cause order, which is a clear indication that he was aware of the order. On February 14, Sheriff Conley wrote a letter to the court in which he stated that he had witnessed the "attempted service" of the January 14, 2011, show cause order. (Doc. no. 27). Sheriff Conley attached the show cause order and a number of affidavits to his letter, including an affidavit from Melick.

In the affidavit, Melick acknowledged that he had agreed to meet Schmieder at the Carroll County Sheriff's Office on February 3. Melick stated that when Schmieder arrived, Melick had directed him to hand the summons to Sheriff Conley for inspection. Melick stated that the sheriff had pointed out several "deficiencies" with the process.[5] Melick then told Schmieder that he declined to be served. Melick stated that he had watched Schmieder throw the process at his feet but "made no move towards [it]."

Melick failed to appear for the February 14, 2011, show cause hearing, as ordered. The court found and ruled that the February 3 service of process constituted valid personal service of the show cause order on Melick and that he had been duly notified to appear for the February 14 hearing. The court issued a bench warrant for Melick's arrest and detention and ordered that Melick be brought before a judge in this court for a show cause hearing on the government's petition for civil contempt.

Melick was arrested on October 6, 2011.

DISCUSSION

A. Service of Process

Melick claimed that the service of process of the January 14 order to show cause was insufficient because the document addressed Melick by the wrong name, did not bear a court seal or the clerk's signature, and had a return date of fewer than fourteen days. These arguments are unavailing.

1. Wrong Party

In his affidavit filed with Sheriff Conley's letter, Melick did not elaborate upon his claim that the process addressed him by the wrong name. The documents referred to Melick as "C. Gregory Melick." Although Melick's full name is Charles Gregory Melick, he was aware that "C. Gregory Melick" referred to him, as evidenced by the fact that he used the same name in his first motion to dismiss. (Doc. no. 4). To the extent that Melick would renew his argument, made in his first motion to dismiss, that the summons showed his

---

[5] [fn 5] These purported deficiencies were that the document addressed Melick by the wrong name, did not bear a court seal or clerk's signature, and had a return date of fewer than fourteen days.

name typed in all capital letters and thus referred to an unknown "C. GREGORY MELICK," such an argument is frivolous. *See, e.g., Ford v. Pryor,* 552 F.3d 1174, 1179 (10th Cir.2008).

2. Lack of Court Seal or Clerk's Signature

Melick argues that he did not receive adequate service of process because the show cause order lacked a court seal and the signature of the clerk of court. Although a court-issued summons would have the court seal and signature of the clerk of court, *see* Federal Rule of Civil Procedure 4(a)(1)(F) & (G), that was neither necessary nor required for purposes of the show cause order that was issued in this case.

The Federal Rules of Civil Procedure apply to IRS summons proceedings, but the court retains the flexibility to " 'limit the application of the rules in a summons proceeding . . . so long as the rights of the party summoned are protected and an adversary hearing, if requested is made available.' " *United States v. Elmes,* 532 F.3d 1138, 1142 (11th Cir.2008) (quoting *Donaldson v. United States,* 400 U.S. 517, 528–29, 91 S.Ct. 534, 27 L.Ed.2d 580 (1971)); *see also* Fed.R.Civ.P. 81(a)(3). Service of an IRS summons notifies the taxpayer "of the possibility that an action would later be initiated to enforce that summons." *Elmes,* 532 F.3d at 1144. "Under these circumstances, personal service of the district court's order to show cause and the petition to enforce [is] adequate to notify the [taxpayer] of the proceedings against him, and his rights [are] protected by the availability of an adversary hearing." *Id.* at 1144–45.

The same circumstances that existed in the *Elmes* case exist in this case. Melick was served with an IRS summons and then was served with the show cause order and the petition to enforce the IRS summons. A hearing was scheduled to give him an opportunity to contest the proceeding against him. Therefore, the "court was free to modify the required procedure under Rule 81(a)(3) by directing service upon [Melick] of only the show cause order and the petition." *Id.* at 1145. Melick was properly served, and he chose to ignore the order of the court and to forego the opportunity for a hearing.

3. Return Date

There is no requirement under the Federal Rules of Civil Procedure that a summons or show cause order be delivered at least fourteen days before the party is scheduled to appear at a show cause hearing.[6]

4. Method of Service

Melick appears to believe that he was not served with the show cause order because the Deputy United States Marshal Schmieder dropped it at his feet and Melick made no move to retrieve it. As the court previously stated in its February 15, 2011, procedural order, the delivery procedure constituted valid personal service of the show cause order. *See, e.g., Novak v. World Bank,* 703 F.2d 1305, 1310 n. 14 (D.C.Cir.1982) ("When a person refuses to accept service, service

---

[6] [fn 6] Melick may be referring to the state law requirement that writs be served fourteen days before the return day to which they are returnable. See N.H.R.S.A. 510:1. This procedural requirement does not apply in federal court.

may be effected by leaving the papers at a location, such as a table or on the floor, near that person.").

B. Civil Contempt

The government requests that Melick be held in civil contempt of court and incarcerated until such time as he complies with the court's August 6, 2010, enforcement order.

Civil contempt may be imposed to compel compliance with a court order. United States v. Saccoccia, 433 F.3d 19, 27 (1st Cir.2005). The moving party must prove civil contempt by clear and convincing evidence. AccuSoft Corp. v. Palo, 237 F.3d 31, 47 (1st Cir.2001) (citations and internal quotation marks omitted).[7] "In addition, contempt may only be established if the order allegedly violated is clear and unambiguous." Id. (citations and internal quotation marks omitted). "[A]ny ambiguities or uncertainties in such a court order must be read in a light favorable to the person charged with contempt." Islamic Inv. Co. of the Gulf (Bah.) Ltd. v. Harper (In re Grand Jury Investigation), 545 F.3d 21, 25 (1st Cir.2008). The validity of the underlying order is assumed, however; the legal or factual basis of the order is not open for reconsideration in a contempt proceeding. United States v. Lawn Builders of New Eng., Inc., 856 F.2d 388, 395 (1st Cir.1988). Where, as here, "the court's purpose is to coerce compliance, the available remedies include imprisonment of the contemner until he purges himself of contempt by complying with the order. . . ." G. & C. Merriam Co. v. Webster Dictionary Co., 639 F.2d 29, 41 n. 13 (1st Cir.1980) (citations omitted).

Both the IRS and the court have provided Melick with full due process and an opportunity to be heard.

C. Finding of Civil Contempt

The court, after a hearing held today, finds by clear and convincing evidence that Charles Gregory Melick has willfully refused, without just cause, to comply with the order of this court issued on August 6, 2010, requiring him to obey the IRS summons referred to hereinabove and attached hereto as "Attachment A."

Therefore, Charles Gregory Melick is found to be in civil contempt of the court's order issued on August 6, 2010.

At today's hearing Charles Gregory Melick agreed to comply with the August 6, 2010, order and produce the documents required by the February 26, 2010, IRS summons, without prejudice to raising specific issues of privilege with respect to specific documents individually.

---

[7] [fn 7] In many cases, civil contempt can be established without the need for an evidentiary hearing. In civil contempt proceedings, a party has a right to an evidentiary hearing only if, and to the extent that, genuine issues of material fact exist. Goya Foods, Inc. v. Wallack Mgmt. Co., 290 F.3d 63, 77 (1st Cir.2002); see also United States v. Winter, 70 F.3d 655, 661 (1st Cir.1995) ("Generally, a court may impose civil contempt sanctions pursuant to the minimal procedures of notice and an opportunity to be heard; the reason for this is that the civil contemnor may avoid the sanction by obeying the court's order.").

He shall report to this courthouse (Rudman Courthouse, 55 Pleasant Street, Concord, New Hampshire, Courtroom 1, Attorney Conference Room) on October 20, 2011, at 10:00 a.m., with the documents required by the IRS summons and to produce said documents to the IRS officer.

Failure to comply with this order will result in issuance of a bench warrant for the arrest of Charles Gregory Melick to be brought before this court to show cause why he did not appear in conformity with this order.

Failure to appear will also result in a charge of criminal contempt and issuance of an arrest warrant for Charles Gregory Melick for failure to comply with this order.

A copy of this order shall be served in hand on Melick by the United States Marshal and a return of service shall be filed with the court.

SO ORDERED.

[Attachment A omitted.]

NOTES AND QUESTIONS

1. How accurate must the government be in addressing a taxpayer by name in a summons?
2. If a taxpayer refuses to extend a hand to accept service of a summons, is the service invalid?
3. What are the potential consequences for failing to comply with an IRS summons?
4. Are such harsh consequences necessary?

In addition to obtaining information from the taxpayer, the IRS may summon books and records of third parties as well. Section 7602 is sufficiently broad in scope to include third parties, but the Code adds some burdens on the IRS. The IRS must notify the taxpayer about a summons issued to a third party, but not necessarily before the summons is served. Section 7609 provides as follows:

> [N]otice of the summons shall be given to any person so identified within three days of the day on which such service is made, but no later than the 23rd day before the day fixed in the summons as the day upon which such records are to be examined.

Although the taxpayer has the right to challenge the summons by initiating a proceeding to quash it, *see* section 7609(b)(2)(A), the taxpayer's challenge is limited to the served party's response to the summons rather than the IRS's service of the summons on the third party in the first place. *See* § 7609(a)(1).

HANSE v. UNITED STATES
2018 WL 1156201
United States District Court, Northern District of Illinois, Eastern Division

Judge ROBERT M. DOW, JR.

MEMORANDUM OPINION AND ORDER

Before the Court is Respondent the United States of America's ("Respondent's") motion [12] to dismiss Petitioner Franck Hanse ("Petitioner's") petition to quash IRS summons for failure to state a claim or, alternatively, for summary judgment. For the reasons explained below, Respondent's motion [12] is granted, and summary judgment is granted in favor of Respondent. The Court will enter a final judgment and close the case.

I. BACKGROUND

Petitioner is the subject of an investigation by the French tax authorities relating to his potential income tax and wealth tax liabilities for the tax years ending in 2013, 2014 and 2015. [12, Exhibit 2 (Palacheck Decl.), ¶ 4.] On September 7, 2016, pursuant to a treaty between the United States and France,[8] the French tax authorities sent the IRS an exchange-of-information request seeking information related to these investigations. [*Id.*, ¶ 3.] Specifically, the French tax authorities requested information relating to two transfers of funds totaling over 500,000 euros from Petitioner to a client trust account maintained by the law firm of Marc D. Sherman & Colleagues, P.C. ("Sherman"). [*Id.*, ¶¶ 6–7.]

The request stated that Petitioner was a French citizen domiciled in France; that the request was in conformity with the laws and practices of the French tax administration; and that the French tax authorities exhausted all means available in France to obtain the information that it was seeking. [*Id.*, ¶¶ 5, 11, 13.] The information sought in the request was not in the possession of the IRS, and there was a reasonable basis to believe that the summonsed records may contain information relevant to the French tax authorities' investigation into Petitioner's French tax liabilities. [*Id.*, ¶¶ 11, 14.] Deborah Palacheck, designated as the United States Competent Authority under tax treaties and tax information

---

[8] [fn 1] The United States and France are parties to the Convention Between the Government of the United States of America and the Government of the French Republic for the Avoidance of Double Taxation and the Prevention of Fiscal Evasion with Respect to Taxes on Income and Capital, Aug. 31, 1994, U.S.-Fr., (as amended by protocols signed on Dec. 8, 2004 and Jan. 13, 2009) (the "U.S.-France Treaty"). Article 27 of the U.S.-France Treaty provides that the competent authorities of the United States and France may exchange information "as may be relevant for carrying out the provisions of this Convention or to the administration or enforcement of the domestic laws concerning taxes of every kind and description imposed on behalf of the Contracting States." U.S.-France Treaty, art. 27, ¶ 1. The information exchanged "shall be treated as secret in the same manner as information obtained under the domestic laws of that State." Id., ¶ 2. The exchange of information provisions of the U.S.-France Treaty also provide that the provisions should not be construed to impose on a Contracting State the obligation "to supply information which is not obtainable under the laws or in the normal course of the administration" of either Contracting State. Id., ¶ 3(b).

exchange agreements, determined that this request from France was proper under the provisions of the U.S.-France Treaty and that it was appropriate to honor the request. [*Id.*, ¶¶ 1, 16.] Therefore, pursuant to the request and Respondent's obligations under the U.S.-France Treaty, an IRS agent personally served a summons on Sherman on June 1, 2017. [12, Exhibit 1 (Bjorvik Decl.), ¶ 2.] The summons requests nine categories of documents relating to the French income and wealth tax liabilities of Petitioner and, specifically, the euro transfers from Petitioner to Sherman. [1, Exhibit A (IRS Summons), at 5.] The summons names the time for production of the documents as July 5, 2017. [*Id.*, at 1.] Notice of the summons was also sent via certified mail on June 2, 2017 to those named in the summons (Petitioner and Byline Bank). [12, Exhibit 2 (Palacheck Decl.), at Exhibits B–C]. The notice was sent to Petitioner at the French address provided by the French authorities after the IRS searched its own records and did not find any additional addresses in its files for Petitioner. [*Id.*, ¶¶ 8–10.]

On June 19, 2017, Petitioner filed a timely petition to quash the IRS summons to Sherman pursuant to I.R.C. § 7609(b)(2). [See 1.] The petition raises three objections to the IRS summons. First, Petitioner contends that the IRS did not comply with the administrative steps required by the Internal Revenue Code. [*Id.*, ¶ 9.] Specifically, Petitioner states that the IRS (1) contacted third parties regarding his tax liabilities without providing advance notice to Petitioner as required by I.R.C. § 7602(c)(1) and 26 C.F.R. § 301.7602-2(d)(1), and (2) did not provide notice to petitioner of the summons as required by I.R.C. § 7609(a)(1). [*Id.*, ¶¶ 7–8.] Second, Petitioner contends that France may not be able to obtain, through its own laws, the information sought in the IRS summons because he is not a French resident, and the U.S.-France Treaty does not require the United States to supply information that is not obtainable under the laws of France. [*Id.*, ¶ 10.] Finally, Petitioner states that because Sherman is a law firm, some of the materials requested are protected from disclosure by attorney-client privilege. [*Id.*, ¶ 11.] Respondent thereafter filed a motion [12] to dismiss the petition or, alternatively, for summary judgment, which is currently before the Court.

II. LEGAL STANDARD

Respondent has moved to dismiss the petition under Federal Rule of Civil Procedure ("Rule") 12(b)(6) or, alternatively, for summary judgment under Rule 56 if the Court determines that the motion expands the scope of the pleadings. [See 12.] In ruling on a Rule 12(b)(6) motion, if "matters outside the pleadings are presented to and not excluded by the court, the motion must be treated as one for summary judgment under Rule 56." Fed. R. Civ. P. 12(d). Under such a scenario, "[a]ll parties must be given a reasonable opportunity to present all the material that is pertinent to the motion." *Id.* Here, both Petitioner and Respondent have had reasonable opportunity to present such material, given that Respondent titled its motion as a "Motion to Dismiss Petition to Quash or, Alternatively, for Summary Judgment." Respondent also supported its motion with two declarations and included a statement of material facts as required by Local Rule

56.1(a).[9] [See 12-1, at 1–3.] Petitioner clearly recognized that this Court might treat Respondent's motion as one for summary judgment, as he attached information outside of the pleadings to his opposition. [See 16, Exhibit A–B (Registration Cards from French Consulates in Geneva and Dubai).] Moreover, Petitioner did not move for additional discovery pursuant to Rule 56(d) or request an evidentiary hearing on his petition to quash the summons. See *2121 Arlington Heights Corp. v. I.R.S.*, 109 F.3d 1221, 1226 (7th Cir. 1997) (petitioner may request evidentiary hearing on a petition to quash IRS summons, and whether hearing is needed is left to the district court's discretion). The Court will thus proceed on the motion as one for summary judgment. See *Arns v. United States*, 39 F. App'x 442, 444 (7th Cir. 2002) (affirming judgment of district court in similar case where the district court treated motion to dismiss or for summary judgment as a Rule 56 motion for summary judgment).

Summary judgment is proper where "the movant shows that there is no genuine dispute as to any material fact and the movant is entitled to judgment as a matter of law." See Fed. R. Civ. P. 56(a). In determining whether summary judgment is appropriate, the Court must construe all facts in a light most favorable to the non-moving party and draw all reasonable inferences in that party's favor (here, Petitioner). *Majors v. Gen. Elec. Co.*, 714 F.3d 527, 532 (7th Cir. 2013) (citation omitted). Rule 56(a) "mandates the entry of summary judgment, after adequate time for discovery and upon motion, against any party who fails to make a showing sufficient to establish the existence of an element essential to that party's case, and on which that party would bear the burden of proof at trial." *Celotex Corp. v. Catrett*, 477 U.S. 317, 322 (1986). In other words, the moving party may meet its burden by pointing out to the court that "there is an absence of evidence to support the nonmoving party's case." *Id.* at 325. To avoid summary judgment, the nonmoving party must go beyond the pleadings and "set forth specific facts showing that there is a genuine issue for trial." *Anderson v. Liberty Lobby, Inc.*, 477 U.S. 242, 250 (1986) (internal quotation marks and citation omitted). "The mere existence of a scintilla of evidence in support of the plaintiff's position will be insufficient; there must be evidence on which the jury could reasonably find for the plaintiff." *Id.* at 252.

In the Northern District of Illinois, a party moving for summary judgment must file along with its motion a Local Rule 56.1(a) statement of undisputed facts,

---

[9] [fn 2] Respondent did not file its statement of material fact as a separate document, but instead included this statement in its memorandum in support of its motion. [See 12-1.] Because there is no explicit requirement that this statement be filed as a separate document, the Court considers Respondent's statement to be in compliance with the Local Rules. See *Del. Motel Assocs., Inc. v. Capital Crossing Serv. Co. LLC*, 2017 WL 4512709, at *2 (N.D. Ill. Oct. 10, 2017) (concluding it would be against "the spirit of the rules" to deny a motion for summary judgment merely because a statement of facts was not submitted in a separate document, where Local Rule 56.1 was otherwise complied with) (citation omitted).

consisting of short numbered paragraphs and citations to affidavits or other parts of the record relied on to support the facts set forth in each paragraph. N.D. Ill. L.R. 56.1(a). In response, the party opposing the motion must file its own statement of undisputed facts in the same manner. N.D. Ill. L.R. 56.1(b). If the party opposing summary judgment fails to file such a statement, "[a]ll material facts set forth in [the moving party's statement] will be deemed to be admitted." N.D. Ill. L.R. 56.1(b)(3)(C); see also *Raymond v. Ameritech Corp.*, 442 F.3d 600, 608 (7th Cir. 2006) (affirming district court's decision to admit the facts set forth in moving party's Local Rule 56.1 submission where nonmovant failed to timely respond). In this case, Respondent included a Local Rule 56.1(a) statement of material facts with its motion. [See 12-1, at 1–3.] Petitioner failed to file a Local Rule 56.1(b) statement of material facts with his response. Accordingly, the facts set forth in Respondent's statement are deemed admitted. See N.D. Ill. L.R. 56.1(b)(3)(C); see also *Parra v. Neal*, 614 F.3d 635, 636 (7th Cir. 2010).

III. ANALYSIS

Petitioner has moved to quash the IRS summons issued to Sherman pursuant to I.R.C. § 7609(b)(2). The Internal Revenue Code grants the IRS power to issue summonses "[f]or the purpose of * * * determining the liability of any person for any internal revenue tax." I.R.C. § 7602(a)(2). The IRS may also issue summonses to obtain information for a treaty partner. See *United States v. Stuart*, 489 U.S. 353, 357 (1989); *Lidas, Inc. v. United States*, 238 F.3d 1076, 1081 (9th Cir. 2001). As a person entitled to notice of the summons to Sherman under I.R.C. § 7609(a), Petitioner is entitled to move a district court to quash the summons. I.R.C. § 7609(b)(2) (any person identified in the summons is entitled to notice thereof, and those entitled to notice may move to quash that summons); *2121 Arlington Heights*, 109 F.3d at 1223.

In resolving a motion to quash an IRS summons, the government (Respondent) bears the initial burden to make a *prima facie* case that the IRS issued the summons in good faith. *2121 Arlington Heights*, 109 F.3d at 1224. To meet this burden, Respondent must satisfy the four factors articulated by the Supreme Court in *United States v. Powell*, 379 U.S. 48 (1964):

Respondent must show that the IRS summons (1) was issued for a legitimate purpose; (2) seeks information that may be relevant to that purpose; (3) seeks information not already within the possession of the IRS; and (4) was issued after the IRS satisfied all administrative steps required by the Internal Revenue Code. *2121 Arlington Heights*, 109 F.3d at 1224 (citing *Powell*, 379 U.S. at 57–58); see also *Khan v. United States*, 548 F.3d 549, 554 (7th Cir. 2008); *United States v. Bernhoft*, 666 F. Supp. 2d 943, 945 (E.D. Wis. 2009); *Good Karma, LLC v. United States*, 546 F. Supp. 2d 597, 602 (N.D. Ill. 2008).

Respondent's burden remains the same where the IRS summons is issued pursuant to a request from a treaty partner. See *Stuart*, 489 U.S. at 370 (IRS entitled to enforcement of summons issued pursuant to Canadian authorities' request "[s]o long as the IRS itself acts in good faith, as the term was explicated in [*Powell*], and complies with applicable statutes"). These requirements impose only a "minimal" burden on Respondent, and Respondent can usually satisfy it by submitting affidavits from the agents investigating the case. Miller v. United States, 150 F.3d 770, 772 (7th Cir. 1998); *2121 Arlington Heights*, 109 F.3d at 1224.

Once Respondent makes its *prima facie* case, the burden shifts to the Petitioner to come forward with specific facts that disprove any of the *Powell* factors or otherwise show that the IRS issued the summons in bad faith or in a manner that constitutes an abuse of process. *2121 Arlington Heights*, 109 F.3d at 1224. This is a heavy burden for the taxpayer to meet. *Id.*; see also *United States v. Kis*, 658 F.2d 526, 535 (7th Cir. 1981) ("[T]he burden on the taxpayer to prove Government wrongdoing is significantly greater than that on the Government to show its legitimate purposes.").[10]

A. Respondent's *Prima Facie* Case

To support its motion, Respondent has submitted declarations from Deborah Palacheck, the United States Competent Authority under tax treaties and tax information exchange agreements, and Alex Bjorvik, the IRS agent who personally served the summons on Sherman. [See 12, Exhibits 1–2.] With these declarations, Respondent has easily satisfied its minimal burden to establish a *prima facie* case that the summons to Sherman was issued in good faith. See *2121 Arlington Heights*, 109 F.3d at 1224 (the government's burden "isn't much of a hurdle"). First, Palacheck states that the summons was issued pursuant to a proper request from France under the provisions of the U.S.-France Treaty, and that the request stated that it is in conformity with the laws and administrative practices of the French tax administration. [12, Exhibit 2 (Palacheck Decl.), ¶¶ 13, 16.] Assisting a foreign tax authority is a legitimate purpose that satisfies the first *Powell* factor. See *Kalra v. United States*, 2014 WL 242763, at *2 (N.D. Ill. Jan. 21, 2014) (citing *Mazurek v. United States*, 271 F.3d 226, 230 (5th Cir. 2001)); *Lidas*, 238 F.3d at 1081; see also *Stuart*, 489 U.S. at 361 (IRS summons issued to assist Canadian tax investigation could be enforced). Second, Palacheck states that the records requested in the summons, if produced, may contain information relevant to the French tax authorities' determination of Petitioner's tax liabilities. [12, Exhibit 2 (Palacheck Decl.), ¶ 14.] This satisfies the second *Powell* factor.

---

[10] [fn 3] Respondent has not moved to enforce the summons served on Sherman. [See 12.] There is some authority in this district and elsewhere that the government does not need to initially establish a prima facie case when it moves only to dismiss a petition to quash an IRS summons (rather than moving for enforcement). Instead, the burden shifts immediately to the petitioner to establish a valid defense to the summons. See Kalra v. United States, 2014 WL 242763, at *1 n.2 (N.D. Ill. Jan. 21, 2014); Gonzalez v. United States, 2011 WL 4688721, at *2 n.2 (N.D. Ill. Oct. 4, 2011); O'Doherty v. United States, 2005 WL 3527271, at *5 (N.D. Ill. Dec. 20, 2005); see also Guglielmi v. United States, 2013 WL 1645718, at *1 (S.D.N.Y. Apr. 15, 2013); Peterson v. United States, 2012 WL 682346, at *2 (E.D. Pa. Mar. 2, 2012). Because the Court finds that Respondent has established a prima facie case, however, any issue of burden shifting is irrelevant.

See *2121 Arlington Heights*, 109 F.3d at 1224 (noting that *Powell* only requires that records sought in an IRS summons "may be" relevant) (citing *United States v. Arthur Young & Co.*, 465 U.S. 805, 814–15 (1984)). Regarding the third *Powell* factor, Palacheck states that the information is not in the possession of the IRS, and the French tax authorities indicated that they exhausted all means available in France to obtain the requested information. The French tax authorities also indicated a continuing need for this information after the petition to quash was filed. [12, Exhibit 2 (Palacheck Decl.), ¶¶ 11, 15.] Finally, the declarations submitted by both Palacheck and Bjorvik establish that the summons was properly served on Sherman and that notice was properly sent to Petitioner (as a third party referenced in the summons) pursuant to I.R.C. § 7609. Specifically, notice was sent to Petitioner via certified mail within three days of service of the summons on the summoned party. The notice was sent to Petitioner's French address after the IRS searched its records for any alternative addresses. [12, Exhibit 1 (Bjorvik Decl.), ¶¶ 1–2]; [12, Exhibit 2 (Palacheck Decl.), ¶¶ 8–10.] This satisfies the fourth *Powell* factor. See *Kis*, 658 F.2d at 536; *Kalra*, 2014 WL 242763, at *2. The government has therefore established its *prima facie* case that the IRS summons was valid. See *2121 Arlington Heights*, 109 F.3d at 1224; see also *Stuart*, 489 U.S. at 360–61 (affidavit from IRS agent established *prima facie* case that IRS summons issued to assist foreign tax investigation was issued in good faith); *Mazurek*, 271 F.3d at 230 (same); *Lidas*, 238 F.3d at 1082 (same).

B. Petitioner's Objections

Because Respondent has established a *prima facie* case that the IRS issued the summons to Sherman in good faith, the burden shifts to Petitioner to come forward with specific facts that disprove any of the *Powell* factors or otherwise challenge the good faith of the IRS summons. *2121 Arlington Heights*, 109 F.3d at 1224; see also *Kis*, 658 F.2d at 543 (noting that Petitioner's burden here "is significantly more stringent than that of a party opposing a motion for summary judgment").

1. The Good Faith of the French Tax Investigation

In his opposition to Respondent's motion, Petitioner argues that the French tax authorities are not entitled to the information sought by the summons to Sherman under French law. [16, at 1.] Specifically, Petitioner argues that he was a resident of Switzerland, not France, during the relevant tax years and, as a non-resident French citizen, he does not have to pay tax on income earned outside of France. [*Id.*] Petitioner also states that his wife still resides in France but their premarital arrangement does not affect his status as a French taxpayer. [*Id.*, at 2.] According to Petitioner, the French tax authorities should be required to resolve the question of his residency status before the IRS procures information to assist in the French investigation.

This appears to be a challenge to the first *Powell* factor requiring that the summons be issued for a legitimate purpose. Petitioner's arguments on this point fail, however, because the IRS was not required to assess the good faith of France's tax investigation into Petitioner before issuing the summons to Sherman.

While the Seventh Circuit has not spoken on this issue, other circuits have rejected arguments similar to those made here by Petitioner. In *Mazurek v. United States*, 271 F.3d 226 (5th Cir. 2001), the petitioner challenged an IRS summons issued pursuant to a French request under the U.S.-France Treaty by arguing that he was not a French resident during the periods implicated by the French tax investigation. *Mazurek*, 271 F.3d at 231–32. The Fifth Circuit rejected this argument because the petitioner improperly focused on the legitimacy of the French investigation rather than the legitimacy of the IRS's compliance with the *Powell* good faith requirements: "[t]o rebut the *Powell* requirement, [petitioner] must show that the *IRS* is acting in bad faith. As long as the IRS acts in good faith, it need not also attest to—much less prove—the good faith of the requesting nation." *Mazurek*, 271 F.3d at 231. Other courts have followed this reasoning and held that, in situations where the IRS issues a summons on behalf of a foreign country's tax investigation, the good faith of the requesting country is irrelevant as long as the IRS itself acted in good faith in issuing the summons. See, *e.g.*, *Villarreal v. United States*, 524 F. App'x 419, 423 (10th Cir. 2013) (rejecting allegations of a harassment campaign by the foreign tax authority because that entity's good faith "is irrelevant; what matters is the IRS's good faith in issuing the summons."); *Lidas*, 238 F.3d at 1082 ("[T]he IRS need not establish the good faith of the requesting nation."); *Kalra*, 2014 WL 242763, at *3 ("The *Powell* factors do not require the IRS to assess the adequacy of the [foreign tax authority's] tax practices or the scope of its tax investigation before issuing the summonses for the requested information."); *Guglielmi v. United States*, 2013 WL 1645718, at *2 (S.D.N.Y. Apr. 15, 2013) (the IRS is not required to assess adequacy of another country's tax law or practices, as such a requirement would "unwisely necessitate an inquiry into the propriety of the [foreign tax authority's] actions under [foreign] law") (quoting *Mazurek*, 271 F.3d at 231–32); *United States v. Hiley*, 2007 WL 2904056, at *3 (S.D. Cal. Oct. 2, 2007) ("The relevant question is not whether the [foreign tax authorities] can impose an income tax upon [petitioner], but whether the IRS issued its summonses in good faith.").

Thus, whether Petitioner is a resident of France, and whether the French tax authority has resolved or will resolve the issue of Petitioner's residency, is ultimately irrelevant to the issue that is currently before the Court—whether Petitioner has presented any specific facts to rebut Respondent's *prima facie* case that the IRS issued a summons to Sherman in good faith.[11] Petitioner has not

---

[11] [fn 4] Even if the good faith of the French tax investigation into Petitioner was relevant, Petitioner has not presented the Court with any statement of facts pursuant to Local Rule 56.1(a) to support his contentions regarding his French residency. And, because Respondent's facts have been deemed admitted, the fact that France's request to the IRS indicates that Petitioner is domiciled in France has been deemed admitted. [See 12-1, ¶ 6.] The factual assertions in Petitioner's opposition to Respondent's motion regarding his residency—including his explanation of his premarital agreement with his wife, his Swiss residency, and

challenged the good faith of the IRS in issuing the summons to Sherman, but instead merely argues that the "concerns animating the judiciary's deference to the IRS summons power * * * are at their nadir here" because there is no domestic tax investigation involved. [16, at 2.] Petitioner's assertions and arguments on this point do not satisfy his burden to rebut the IRS's good faith in issuing the summons, however, and thus are ultimately irrelevant. The Court will not inquire into the propriety of France's tax investigation into Petitioner's liabilities, and Petitioner has not met his burden to challenge the good faith of the IRS summons to Sherman by challenging the French investigation.[12] See *Net Promotion, Inc. v. United States*, 2012 WL 6015610, at *3 (D. Minn. Sept. 19. 2012) ("Whether Petitioner incurs French income tax liability has no effect on whether the IRS is acting in good faith to meet its obligations under the Treaty.").

2. Compliance with Internal Revenue Code

In his original Petition, Petitioner objects to the IRS summons to Sherman on the basis that the IRS did not comply with the notice requirements of I.R.C. § 7602(c)(1) and § 7609(a). [1, ¶¶ 7–9.] Petitioner did not raise these objections in his opposition to Respondent's motion or otherwise address Respondent's arguments that all required administrative steps were satisfied.

Petitioner's objections here fail to successfully rebut the IRS's good faith in issuing the summons to Sherman. First, Petitioner's argument regarding I.R.C. § 7602(c)(1) fails because he is not entitled to any advance notice of a third-party summons under this section of the Internal Revenue Code. This section provides that an IRS employee "may not contact any person other than the taxpayer with respect to the determination or collection of the tax liability of such taxpayer without providing reasonable notice in advance to the taxpayer that contacts with persons other than the taxpayer may be made." I.R.C. § 7602(c)(1); see also 26 C.F.R. § 301.7602-2(a). According to Petitioner, as the "taxpayer" he therefore should have been notified by the IRS that a third party would be contacted in

---

the tax treaty between France and Switzerland and its effects on his French tax liability—are almost entirely unsupported and do not help Petitioner meet his burden to rebut Respondent's prima facie case of good faith. Moreover, Petitioner does not even attempt to address Respondent's contention that the Euro transfers of interest to the French tax authorities may be subject to French taxation separate and apart from the issue of Petitioner's residency. [12-1, at 8.]

[12] [fn 5] Petitioner's argument that the United States is not required under the U.S.-France Treaty to provide any information to France that France could not obtain under its own laws is also of no help to Petitioner. [See 1, at 3.] The U.S.-France Treaty states that its provisions should not be construed to impose on a Contracting State the obligation "to supply information which is not obtainable under the laws or in the normal course of the administration" of either Contracting State. U.S.-France Treaty, art. 27, ¶ 3(b). But "even though it does not mandate the exchange of information at variance with French law, neither does the plain language of the Treaty forbid compliance with an otherwise proper treaty request." *Mazurek*, 271 F.3d at 233.

connection with an investigation into his tax liability. But, as Respondent points out, "tax liability" for purposes of this section "does not include the liability for any tax imposed by any other jurisdiction." 26 C.F.R. § 301.7602-2(c)(3)(C). The summons was issued to Sherman in relation to Petitioner's potential tax liability in France, not the United States, and therefore it does not fall into the relevant definition of "tax liability" for purposes of this section. Therefore, the IRS was not required to notify Petitioner in advance of a third party summons under I.R.C. § 7602(c)(1).

Second, Respondent has presented ample evidence of compliance with I.R.C. § 7609(a) that Petitioner has not challenged. I.R.C. § 7609(a) requires that any person identified in a third-party summons to be given notice of that summons "within 3 days of the day on which such service is made, but no later than the 23rd day before the day fixed in the summons as the day upon which such record are to be examined." I.R.C. § 7609(a)(1). Notice is sufficient if it is sent via certified or registered mail to the last known address of the person being given notice. *Id.* § 7609(a)(2). The summons at issue was served on Sherman on June 1, 2017. [12, Exhibit 1 (Bjorvik Decl.), ¶ 2.] Notice was sent to the two parties identified within the summons— Petitioner and Byline Bank—via certified mail on June 2, 2017. [12, Exhibit 2 (Palacheck Decl.), ¶¶ 9–10.] The notice to Petitioner was sent to the French address for Petitioner provided by the French government in its request, after the IRS searched its own databases for an alternative address and found none. [*Id.*, ¶ 8.] No more was required of the IRS to properly serve Petitioner under the relevant portion of the Internal Revenue Code. See *Lidas*, 238 F.3d at 1083–84 (IRS did not violate I.R.C. § 7609 when it sent notice of summons to the subject of a foreign tax investigation to the address for the subject provided by foreign authorities as well as to the subject's last known address in the IRS's own database).

3. Attorney-Client Privilege

Petitioner also raises a privilege objection in his petition: Petitioner states that Sherman is a law firm, and therefore some of the summoned materials are protected from disclosure by attorney-client privilege. [See 1, ¶ 11.] Again, Petitioner did not raise this objection in response to Respondent's motion, nor did he otherwise address Respondent's arguments on this point. Moreover, Petitioner's blanket assertion of privilege is insufficient to challenge the validity of the IRS summons to Sherman. See *United States v. First State Bank*, 691 F.2d 332, 335 (7th Cir. 1982) (rejecting blanket privilege challenge to IRS summons); see also *In re Grand Jury Proceedings*, 220 F.3d 568, 571 (7th Cir. 2000); *United States v. Lawless*, 709 F.2d 485, 487 (7th Cir. 1983) ("[A] blanket claim of privilege is unacceptable."). To properly assert a privilege, Petitioner has the burden to "on a document-by-document basis * * * at least identify the general nature of that document, the specific privilege he is claiming for that document, and facts which establish all the elements of the privilege he is claiming." *First State Bank*, 691 F.2d at 335; see also *United States v. BDO Seidman*, 337 F.3d 802, 811 (7th Cir. 2003) ("The mere assertion of a privilege is not enough; instead, a party that seeks to invoke the attorney-client privilege has the burden of establishing all of its essential elements."); *Holifield v. United States*, 909 F.2d 201, 204 (7th Cir. 1990) (rejecting claim of attorney-client privilege with respect to documents requested in IRS summons where petitioner made blanket privilege claim without setting forth specific facts to support that claim); *Bernhoft*, 666 F. Supp. 2d at 948 (petitioner's "assertions of blanket privilege, without any specific application to each document, are no more than brief conclusory summations that have been rejected by the [Seventh Circuit] in prior privilege determinations") (internal quotation marks and citation omitted). Petitioner has not supported his privilege claim with any facts from which the Court could find a privilege attaches to the documents that are requested in the summons. Petitioner does not even assert that Sherman was retained as his attorney; he merely states that Sherman is a law firm. [1, ¶ 11.] Petitioner also states that "some" of the materials are protected from disclosure by the privilege without identifying which materials he claims are privileged or why. [*Id.*] Therefore, he has not met his "heavy" burden of rebutting Respondent's *prima facie* case on this basis. *2121 Arlington Heights*, 109 F.3d at 1224; *Bernhoft*, 666 F. Supp. 2d at 949.

In sum, Petitioner has failed to rebut the IRS's good faith in issuing the summons to Sherman.

IV. CONCLUSION

For the foregoing reasons, Respondent's motion [12] is granted, and summary judgment is granted in favor of Respondent. The Court will enter a final judgment and close the case.

NOTES AND QUESTIONS

1. Is the standard for summary judgment different in the tax context?
2. Who bears the initial burden in a case to quash an IRS summons?

In some cases, the IRS might not know precisely what documents to ask for in a document request or summons. The IRS may, in such a case, issue a summons requiring that an employee provide testimony or answer questions. For example, if IRS personnel do not know what documents to ask for about a particular transaction because of the transaction's complexity, they may interview someone involved with the transaction to find out more about it before requesting documents. If the individual is unwilling to speak to the IRS informally, the IRS may issue a summons to compel the individual's testimony.

Similarly, where the IRS does not know all the participants in a transaction, the IRS may seek to determine the participants' identities by serving a John Doe summons on the promoter of the transaction. *See generally* IRC § 7609(f). To issue a John Doe summons, the IRS must go to federal district court first and show that the people the IRS seeks to identify are ascertainable, the IRS reasonably believes the people are not in compliance with the tax laws, and the identities are not otherwise available. The summons is a powerful and necessary tool. Recently, the IRS has issued John Doe summonses to find the names of clients with secret deposits in foreign banks that the IRS could not find any other way. Occasionally, however, the IRS casts its net wider than courts are comfortable with. For example, in December 2016, the IRS issued John Doe summonses to obtain transaction records for all U.S. users of Coinbase, a virtual currency.

B. Taxpayer Response to the IRS's Requests

Although the IRS may issue a summons to obtain documents without probable cause, the IRS's authority to obtain information with respect to a taxpayer is not boundless. The IRS may not compel a taxpayer to create new evidence or conduct more than one examination. *See* United States v. Davey, 543 F.2d 996, 1000 (2d Cir. 1976) (section "7602 does not require preparation or production of records not yet in existence"); United States v. Mobil Corp., 499 F. Supp. 479, 482 (N.D. Tex. 1980) (holding that the taxpayer "cannot be required to create new records or to alter the form of existing records to suit the government's convenience."). IRS personnel also must have a valid reason for invoking the summons power.[13] Finally, the IRS may not compel a taxpayer to disclose privileged communications and documents.

It is common for the IRS to informally request that a taxpayer provide a written summary of a transaction, set of transactions, or other information. The IRS does not, however, have the authority to *compel* the taxpayer to create such a summary.[14] Although the IRS may not compel the taxpayer to create the summary, there might be situations where it is advantageous for the taxpayer to provide such a summary. Summarizing a transaction might be advantageous where the transaction summary is likely to assist the IRS in completing the examination in a shorter timeframe. To accomplish this, the summary should be helpful to the IRS and not raise issues that will expand the examination. In an examination that is likely to last multiple years, it is important to resist the IRS's requests for summaries because once the taxpayer agrees to one summary, rejecting future requests might arouse suspicion.

Another restriction on the administrative summons authority, which turns out to be more like a low hurdle, is that the IRS may not issue a summons absent an

---

[13] *See* I.R.C. § 7605(b) (providing the IRS generally may not audit a taxpayer more than once); United States v. Powell, 379 U.S. 48, 57-58 (1964) (holding that there must be some factual basis for enforcement of a summons). Note that the point of the case is not that the IRS has a habit of harassing people. Rather, the IRS is held to a lower standard than probable cause.

[14] *See* United States v. Davey, 543 F.2d 996, 1000 (2d Cir. 1976) (section ""7602 does not require preparation or production of records not yet in existence"); United States v. Mobil Corp., 499 F. Supp. 479, 482 (N.D. Tex. 1980) (holding that the taxpayer "cannot be required to create new records or to alter the form of existing records to suit the government's convenience.").

administrative reason for doing so. In *United States v. Powell*, the taxpayer challenged an administrative summons for a year for which the three-year statute of limitations had closed.[15]

UNITED STATES v. POWELL
379 U.S. 48 (1964)
Supreme Court of the United States

Mr. Justice HARLAN delivered the opinion of the Court.

In March 1963, the Internal Revenue Service, pursuant to powers afforded the Commissioner by § 7602(2) of the Internal Revenue Code of 1954, summoned respondent Powell to appear before Special Agent Tiberino to give testimony and produce records relating to the 1958 and 1959 returns of the William Penn Laundry (the taxpayer), of which Powell was president. Powell appeared before the agent but refused to produce the records. Because the taxpayer's returns had been once previously examined, and because the three-year statute of limitations barred assessment of additional deficiencies for those years[16] except in cases of fraud (the asserted basis for this summons),[17] Powell contended that before he could be forced to produce the records the Service had to indicate some grounds for its belief that a fraud had been committed. The agent declined to give any such indication and the meeting terminated.

Thereafter the Service petitioned the District Court for the Eastern District of Pennsylvania for enforcement of the administrative summons. With this petition the agent filed an affidavit stating that he had been investigating the taxpayer's returns for 1958 and 1959; that based on this investigation the Regional Commissioner of the Service had determined an additional examination of the taxpayer's records for those years to be necessary and had sent Powell a letter to that effect; and that the agent had reason to suspect that the taxpayer had fraudulently falsified its 1958 and 1959 returns by overstating expenses. At the court hearing Powell again stated his objections to producing the records and asked the Service to show some basis for its suspicion of fraud. The Service chose to stand on the petition and the agent's affidavit, and, after argument, the District Court ruled that the agent be given one hour in which to re-examine the records.[18]

---

[15] *See Powell*, 379 U.S. at 49.

[16] [fn 1] I.R.C., § 6501(a).

[17] [fn 2] I.R.C., § 6501(c)(1), which in relevant part provides: 'In the case of a false or fraudulent return with the intent to evade tax, the tax may be assessed, or a proceeding in court for collection of such tax may be begun without assessment, at any time.'

[18] [fn 3] The parties subsequently agreed that if the Government was upheld in its claim of right to examine without showing probable cause, the one-hour time limitation would be removed.

The Court of Appeals reversed, 325 F.2d 914. It reasoned that since the returns in question could only be reopened for fraud, re-examination of the taxpayer's records must be barred by the prohibition of § 7605(b) of the Code[19] against 'unnecessary examination' unless the Service possessed information 'which might cause a reasonable man to suspect that there has been fraud in the return for the otherwise closed year';[20] and whether this standard has been met is to be decided 'on the basis of the showing made in the normal course of an adversary proceeding * * *.'[21] The court concluded that the affidavit in itself was not sufficient to satisfy its test of probable cause.[22] Consequently, enforcement of the summons was withheld.

Because of the differing views in the circuits on the standards the Internal Revenue Service must meet to obtain judicial enforcement of its orders,[23] we granted certiorari, 377 U.S. 929, 84 S.Ct. 1334, 12 L.Ed.2d 294.

We reverse, and hold that the Government need make no showing of probable cause to suspect fraud unless the taxpayer raises a substantial question that judicial enforcement of the administrative summons would be an abusive use of the court's process, predicated on more than the fact of re-examination and the running of the statute of limitations on ordinary tax liability.

I.

This enforcement proceeding was brought by the Government pursuant to § 7604(b) of the Code.[24] In Reisman v. Caplin, 375 U.S. 440, 84 S.Ct. 508, 11

---

[19] [fn 4] See page 252, infra.

[20] [fn 5] 325 F.2d 914, 915-916.

[21] [fn 6] Id., at 916.

[22] [fn 7] 'Probable cause' as used in this opinion is meant to include the full range of formulations offered by lower courts.

[23] [fn 8] Compare Foster v. United States, 265 F.2d 183 (C.A.2d Cir. 1959); United States v. Ryan, 320 F.2d 500 (C.A.6th Cir. 1963), affirmed today, 379 U.S. 61, 85 S.Ct. 232, with O'Connor v. O'Connell, 253 F.2d 365 (C.A.1st Cir. 1958), followed in Lash v. Nighosian, 273 F.2d 185 (C.A.1st Cir. 1959); Globe Construction Co. v. Humphrey, 229 F.2d 148 (C.A.5th Cir. 1956); De Masters v. Arend, 313 F.2d 79 (C.A.9th Cir. 1963).

[24] [fn 9] Section 7604(b) provides:

'Whenever any person summoned under section 6420(e)(2), 6421(f)(2), or 7602 neglects or refuses to obey such summons, or to produce books, papers, records, or other data, or to give testimony, as required, the Secretary or his delegate may apply to the judge of the district court or to a United States commissioner for the district within which the person so summoned resides or is found for an attachment against him as for a contempt. It shall be the duty of the judge or commissioner to hear the application, and, if satisfactory proof is made, to issue an attachment, directed to some proper officer, for the arrest of such person, and upon his being brought before him to proceed to a hearing of the case; and upon such hearing the judge or the United States commissioner shall have power to make such order as he shall deem proper, not inconsistent with the

L.Ed.2d 459, decided last Term subsequent to the rendering of the decision below, this Court stated that § 7604(b) 'was intended only to cover persons who were summoned and wholly made default or contumaciously refused to comply.' 375 U.S., at 448, 84 S.Ct., at 513. There was no contumacious refusal in this case. Thus the Government's conceded error in bringing its enforcement proceeding under § 7604(b) instead of § 7402(b) or § 7604(a),[25] each of which grants courts the general power to enforce the Commissioner's summonses 'by appropriate process,' raises a threshold question whether we must dismiss this case and force the Government to recommence enforcement proceedings under the appropriate sections. Since the Government did not apply for the prehearing sanctions of attachment and arrest peculiar to § 7604(b), and since these constitute the major substantive differences between the sections, we think it would be holding too strictly to the forms of pleading to require the suit to be recommenced, and therefore treat the enforcement proceeding as having been brought under §§ 7402(b) and 7604(a).

II.

Respondent primarily relies on § 7605(b) to show that the Government must establish probable cause for suspecting fraud, and that the existence of probable cause is subject to challenge by the taxpayer at the hearing.[26] That section provides:

> 'No taxpayer shall be subjected to unnecessary examination or investigations, and only one inspection of a taxpayer's books of account shall be made for each taxable year unless the taxpayer requests otherwise or unless the Secretary or his delegate, after investigation, notifies the taxpayer in writing that an additional inspection is necessary.'

We do not equate necessity as contemplated by this provision with probable cause or any like notion. If a taxpayer has filed fraudulent returns, a tax liability exists without regard to any period of limitations. Section 7602 authorizes the Commissioner to investigate any such liability.[27] If, in order to determine the

---

law for the punishment of contempts, to enforce obedience to the requirements of the summons and to punish such person for his default or disobedience.'

[25] [fn 10] The two sections are virtually identical. Section 7402(b) provides:

'If any person is summoned under the internal revenue laws to appear, to testify, or to produce books, papers, or other data, the district court of the United States for the district in which such person resides or may be found shall have jurisdiction by appropriate process to compel such attendance, testimony, or production of books, papers, or other data.'

[26] [fn 11] See n. 18, infra.

[27] [fn 12] Section 7602 provides:

'For the purpose of ascertaining the correctness of any return, making a return where none has been made, determining the liability of any person for any internal revenue tax or the liability at law or in equity of any transferee or

existence or nonexistence of fraud in the taxpayer's returns, information in the taxpayer's records is needed which is not already in the Commissioner's possession, we think the examination is not 'unnecessary' within the meaning of § 7605(b). Although a more stringent interpretation is possible, one which would require some showing of cause for suspecting fraud, we reject such an interpretation because it might seriously hamper the Commissioner in carrying out investigations he thinks warranted, forcing him to litigate and prosecute appeals on the very subject which he desires to investigate, and because the legislative history of § 7605(b) indicates that no severe restriction was intended.

Section 7605(b) first appeared as s 1309 of the Revenue Act of 1921, 42 Stat. 310. Its purpose and operation were explained by the manager of the bill, Senator Penrose, on the Senate floor:

> 'Mr. PENROSE. Mr. President, the provision is entirely in the interest of the taxpayer and for his relief from unnecessary annoyance. Since these income taxes and direct taxes have been in force very general complaint has been made, especially in the large centers of wealth and accumulation of money, at the repeated visits of tax examiners, who perhaps are overzealous or do not use the best of judgment in the exercise of their functions. I know that from many of the cities of the country very bitter complaints have reached me and have reached the department of unnecessary visits and inquisitions after a thorough examination is supposed to have been had. This section is purely in the interest of quieting all this trouble and in the interest of the peace of mind of the honest taxpayer.

> 'Mr. WALSH. * * * So that up to the present time an inspector could visit the office of an individual or corporation and inspect the books as many times as he chose?

> 'Mr. PENROSE. And he often did so.

---

fiduciary of any person in respect of any internal revenue tax, or collecting any such liability, the Secretary or his delegate is authorized—

'(1) To examine any books, papers, records, or other data which may be relevant or material to such inquiry;

'(2) To summon the person liable for tax or required to perform the act, or any officer or employee of such person, or any person having possession, custody, or care of books of account containing entries relating to the business of the person liable for tax or required to perform the act, or any other person the Secretary or his delegate may deem proper, to appear before the Secretary or his delegate at a time and place named in the summons and to produce such books, papers, records, or other data, and to give such testimony, under oath, as may be relevant or material to such inquiry; and

'(3) To take such testimony of the person concerned, under oath, as may be relevant or material to such inquiry.'

'Mr. WALSH. * * * And this provision of the Senate committee seeks to limit the inspection to one visit unless the commissioner indicates that there is necessity for further examination?

'Mr. PENROSE. That is the purpose of the amendment.

'Mr. WALSH. * * * I heartily agree with the beneficial results that the amendment will produce to the taxpayer.

'Mr. PENROSE. I knew the Senator would agree to the amendment, and it will go a long way toward relieving petty annoyances on the part of honest taxpayers.' 61 Cong.Rec. 5855 (Sept. 28, 1921).[28]

Congress recognized a need for a curb on the investigating powers of low-echelon revenue agents, and considered that it met this need simply and fully by requiring such agents to clear any repetitive examination with a superior. For us to import a probable cause standard to be enforced by the courts would substantially overshoot the goal which the legislators sought to attain. There is no intimation in the legislative history that Congress intended the courts to oversee

---

[28] [fn 13] Other relevant legislative history to like effect may be found in H.R.Rep. No. 350, 67th Cong., 1st Sess., 16 (1921); S.Rep. No. 275, 67th Cong., 1st Sess., 31 (1921); 61 Cong.Rec. 5202 (Aug. 18, 1921), remarks of Mr. Hawley. The provision was re-enacted in 1926. In the Senate, a substitute measure was adopted which would have limited the Commissioner to two examinations appertaining to returns of any one year. Senator Reed's objection to the original provision was: 'By merely claiming fraud the Government at any time can make examination after examination, subject only to one limitation, that it must give notice that it is going to make the examination. That, in ordinary course, is done by the mere writing of a letter,' 67 Cong.Rec. 3856 (Feb. 12, 1926). There is no indication in the discussion that the courts were thought to play any significant limiting role. The Senate substitute was ultimately deleted by the Conference Committee and the original provision resubstituted. H.R.Rep. No. 356, 69th Cong., 1st Sess., 55. The section was re-enacted in 1939 and 1954 without substantial change and without further elaboration of the congressional intent. Respondent contends that in re-enacting the provision, Congress must have been aware of, and acquiesced in, decisions of lower courts that a showing of probable cause is required. In re Andrews' Tax Liability, 18 F.Supp. 804 (1937); Zimmermann v. Wilson, 105 F.2d 583 (C.A.3d Cir. 1939); In re Brooklyn Pawnbrokers, 39 F.Supp. 304 (1941); Martin v. Chandis Securities Co., 128 F.2d 731 (C.A.9th Cir. 1942). These cases represent neither a settled judicial construction, see In re Keegan, 18 F.Supp. 746 (1937), nor one which we sould be justified in presuming Congress, by its silence, impliedly approved. Compare Shapiro v. United States, 335 U.S. 1, 68 S.Ct. 1375, 92 L.Ed. 1787.

the Commissioner's determinations to investigate. No mention was made of the statute of limitations[29] and the exception for fraud.

We are asked to read § 7605(b) together with the limitations sections in such a way as to impose a probable cause standard upon the Commissioner from the expiration date of the ordinary limitations period forward. Without some solid indication in the legislative history that such a gloss was intended, we find it unacceptable.[30] Our reading of the statute is said to render the first clause of § 7605(b) surplusage to a large extent, for, as interpreted, the clause adds little beyond the relevance and materiality requirements of § 7602. That clause does appear to require that the information sought is not already within the Commissioner's possession, but we think its primary purpose was no more than to emphasize the responsibility of agents to exercise prudent judgment in wielding the extensive powers granted to them by the Internal Revenue Code.[31]

This view of the statute is reinforced by the general rejection of probable cause requirements in like circumstances involving other agencies. In Oklahoma Press Pub. Co. v. Walling, 327 U.S. 186, 216, 66 S.Ct. 494, 509, 90 L.Ed. 614, in reference to the Administrator's subpoena power under the Fair Labor Standards Act, the Court said 'his investigative function, in searching out violations with a view to securing enforcement of the Act, is essentially the same as the grand jury's, or the court's in issuing other pretrial orders for the discovery of evidence, and is governed by the same limitations,' and accordingly applied the view that inquiry must not be "limited * * * by * * * forecasts of the probable result of the investigation." In United States v. Morton Salt Co., 338 U.S. 632, 642-643, 70 S.Ct. 357, 364, 94 L.Ed. 401, the Court said of the Federal Trade Commission, 'It has a power of inquisition, if one chooses to call it that, which is not derived from the judicial function. It is more analogous to the Grand Jury, which does not depend on a case or controversy for power to get evidence but can investigate merely on suspicion that the law is being violated, or even just because it wants assurance that it is not.' While the power of the Commissioner of Internal Revenue derives from a different body of statutes, we do not think the analogies to other agency situations are without force when the scope of the Commissioner's power is called in question.[32]

---

[29] [fn 14] Revenue Act of 1921, § 250(d), 42 Stat. 265, provided a four-year period of limitation on ordinary tax liability.

[30] [fn 15] The contrary view derives no support from the characterization of the limitations provision as a 'statute of response.' The present three-year limitation on assessment of ordinary deficiencies relieves the taxpayer of concern for further assessments of that type, but it by no means follows that it limits the right of the Government to investigate with respect to deficiencies for which no statute of limitations is imposed.

[31] [fn 16] The Court of Appeals appears to have been led astray by the fact that the Government argued its case on the premise that § 7604(b) was the governing statute.

[32] [fn 17] See 1 Davis, Administrative Law, § 3.12 (1958).

III.

Reading the statutes as we do, the Commissioner need not meet any standard of probable cause to obtain enforcement of his summons, either before or after the three-year statute of limitations on ordinary tax liabilities has expired. He must show that the investigation will be conducted pursuant to a legitimate purpose, that the inquiry may be relevant to the purpose, that the information sought is not already within the Commissioner's possession, and that the administrative steps required by the Code have been followed—in particular, that the 'Secretary or his delegate,' after investigation, has determined the further examination to be necessary and has notified the taxpayer in writing to that effect. This does not make meaningless the adversary hearing to which the taxpayer is entitled before enforcement is ordered.[33] At the hearing he 'may challenge the summons on any appropriate ground,' Reisman v. Caplin, 375 U.S. 440, at 449, 84 S.Ct. at 513.[34] Nor does our reading of the statutes mean that under no circumstances may the court inquire into the underlying reasons for the examination. It is the court's process which is invoked to enforce the administrative summons and a court may not permit its process to be abused.[35] Such an abuse would take place if the summons had been issued for an improper purpose, such as to harass the taxpayer or to put pressure on him to settle a collateral dispute, or for any other purpose reflecting on the good faith of the particular investigation. The burden of showing an abuse of the court's process is on the taxpayer, and it is not met by a mere showing, as was made in this case, that the statute of limitations for ordinary deficiencies has run or that the records in question have already been once examined.

The judgment of the Court of Appeals is reversed, and the case is remanded for further proceedings consistent with this opinion.

It is so ordered.

Reversed and remanded.

Mr. Justice DOUGLAS, with whom Mr. Justice STEWART and Mr. Justice GOLDBERG concur, dissenting.

Congress, by the three-year statute of limitations that bars assessments of tax deficiencies except (so far as relevant here) in case of fraud, 26 U.S.C. §§ 6501(a)

---

[33] [fn 18] Because § 7604(a) contains no provision specifying the procedure to be followed in invoking the court's jurisdiction, the Federal Rules of Civil Procedure apply, Martin v. Chandis Securities Co., 9 Cir., 128 F.2d 731. The proceedings are instituted by filing a complaint, followed by answer and hearing. If the taxpayer has contumaciously refused to comply with the administrative summons and the Service fears he may flee the jurisdiction, application for the sanctions available under § 7604(b) might be made simultaneously with the filing of the complaint.

[34] [fn 19] See 1 Davis, Administrative Law, § 3.12 (1958).

[35] [fn 20] See Jaffe, The Judicial Enforcement of Administrative Orders, 76 Harv.L.Rev. 865 (1963).

and (c), has brought into being a 'statute of repose'[36] that I would respect more highly than my Brethren. I would respect it by requiring the District Court to be satisfied that the Service is not acting capriciously in reopening the closed tax period. Since the agency must go to the court for process to compel the production of the records for the closed tax period, I would insist that the District Court act in a judicial capacity, free to disagree with the administrative decision unless that minimum standard is met.[37]

Oklahoma Press Pub. Co. v. Walling, 327 U.S. 186, 66 S.Ct. 494, 90 L.Ed. 614, does not seem to me to be relevant. It dealt with the usual investigative powers of administrative agencies; and as the Court said in that case, Congress set no standards for administrative action which the judiciary first had to weigh and appraise.[38] Id., 215-216, 66 S.Ct. 508-509. Here we have a congressional 'statute of repose' embodied in the three-year statute of limitations. I would make it meaningful by protecting it from invasion by mere administrative fiat. Where the limitations period has expired, an examination is presumptively 'unnecessary' within the meaning of § 7605(b)—a presumption the Service must overcome. That is to say, a re-examination of the taxpayer's records after the three-year period is 'unnecessary' within the meaning of § 7605(b), unless the District Court is shown something more than mere caprice for believing fraud was practiced on the revenue. Without that minimum safeguard the statutory status of repose becomes rather meaningless.

NOTES AND QUESTIONS

1. What are the *Powell* factors?
2. How difficult is it for the IRS to satisfy the burden imposed by *Powell*?

Although not a severe impediment, requiring satisfaction of the *Powell* factors restrains the IRS from abusing its summons authority.

The final restriction on the IRS's summons power is not so much a restriction but a concept. In general, the IRS does not use its summons authority to gather

---

[36] [fn 1] See the remarks of Senators Smith, Ashurst, and Reed in 67 Cong.Rec. 3852-3853.

[37] [fn 2] The First Circuit requires the Commissioner to show that 'a reasonable basis exists for a suspicion of fraud,' O'Connor v. O'Connell, 253 F.2d 365, 370; the Ninth Circuit requires that the decision to investigate for fraud appear as 'a matter of rational judgment based on the circumstances of the particulr case,' De Masters v. Arend, 313 F.2d 79, 90; the Third Circuit requires that the agent's suspicion of fraud be 'reasonable' in the eyes of the District Court. 325 F.2d 914, 916.

[38] [fn 3] The case is more like United States v. Morton Salt Co., 338 U.S. 632, 70 S.Ct. 357, where, as respects the power of the Federal Trade Commission to require issuance of 'special' reports, the Court reserved the right to prevent the 'arbitrary' exercise of that administrative power. Id., at 654, 70 S.Ct. at 369.

information for criminal investigations. In most cases, a revenue agent has referred the case to CID. It is also inappropriate for the summons power to be invoked with respect to a taxpayer whom the government is in the process of prosecuting.

UNITED STATES v. LaSALLE NATIONAL BANK
437 U.S. 298 (1978)
Supreme Court of the United States

Mr. Justice BLACKMUN delivered the opinion of the Court.

This case is a supplement to our decision in Donaldson v. United States, 400 U.S. 517, 91 S.Ct. 534, 27 L.Ed.2d 580 (1971). It presents the issue whether the District Court correctly refused to enforce Internal Revenue Service summonses when it specifically found that the special agent who issued them "was conducting his investigation solely for the purpose of unearthing evidence of criminal conduct." 76-1 USTC ¶ 9407, p. 84,073, 37 AFTR 2d ¶ 76-582, p. 76-1240 (ND Ill.1976).

I.

In May 1975, John F. Olivero, a special agent with the Intelligence Division of the Chicago District of the Internal Revenue Service (hereinafter IRS or Service), received an assignment to investigate the tax liability of John Gattuso for his taxable years 1970-1972. App. 26-27, 33. Olivero testified that he had requested the assignment because of information he had received from a confidential informant and from an unrelated investigation. Id., at 35. The case was not referred to the IRS from another law enforcement agency, but the nature of the assignment, Olivero testified, was "[t]o investigate the possibility of any criminal violations of the Internal Revenue Code." Id., at 33. Olivero pursued the case on his own, without the assistance of a revenue agent.[39] He received information about Gattuso from the Federal Bureau of Investigation as a result of the previous investigation. Id., at 36. He solicited and received additional data from the United States Attorney for the Northern District of Illinois, the Secret Service, the Department of Housing and Urban Development, the IRS Collection Division, and the Cosmopolitan National Bank of Chicago. Id., at 37-40.

---

[39] [fn 1] Frequently, a revenue agent of the IRS Audit Division will refer a case on which he is working to the Intelligence Division for investigation of possible fraud. After such a referral, and at other times, the special agent and the revenue agent work together. Because of the importance and sensitivity of the criminal aspects of the joint investigation, the special agent assumes control of the inquiry. See e.g., Internal Revenue Manual, ch. 4500, §§ 4563.431-4565.44 (CCH 1976 and 1978).

As part of a planned reorganization, the IRS has announced its intention to redesignate the Audit Division and the Intelligence Division as the Examinations Division and the Criminal Enforcement Division, respectively. IRS News Release, Feb. 6, 1978.

Mr. Gattuso's tax returns for the years in question disclosed rental income from real estate. That property was held in Illinois land trusts[40] by respondent LaSalle National Bank, as trustee, a fact revealed by land trust files collected by the IRS from banks. Id., at 27, 45. In order to determine the accuracy of Gattuso's income reports, Olivero proceeded to issue two summonses, under the authority of § 7602 of the Internal Revenue Code of 1954, 26 U.S.C. § 7602,[41] to respondent bank. Each summons related to a separate trust and requested, among other things, that the bank as trustee appear before Olivero at a designated time and place and produce its "files relating to Trust No. 31544 [or No. 35396] including the Trust Agreement" for the period 1970 through 1972 and also "all deeds, options, correspondence, closing statements and sellers statements, escrows, and tax bills pertaining to all property held in the trust at any time during" that period. App. 9-16. Respondent Joseph W. Lang, a vice president of the bank, appeared in response to the summonses but, on advice of counsel, refused to produce any of the materials requested. Brief for Respondents 2.

---

[40] [fn 2] Respondents describe an Illinois land trust as follows:

"An Illinois land trust is a contract by which a trustee is vested with both legal and equitable title to real property and the interest of the beneficiary is considered personal property. Under this trust the beneficiary or any person designated in writing by the beneficiary has the exclusive power to direct or control the trustee in dealing with the title and the exclusive control of the management, operation, renting and selling of the trust property together with the exclusive right to the earnings, avails and proceeds of said property. Ill.Rev.Stat. ch. 29, § 8.31 (1971)." Brief for Respondents 1-2, n. 1.

[41] [fn 3] Section 7602 reads:

"For the purpose of ascertaining the correctness of any return, making a return where none has been made, determining the liability of any person for any internal revenue tax or the liability at law or in equity of any transferee or fiduciary of any person in respect of any internal revenue tax, or collecting any such liability, the Secretary or his delegate is authorized—

"(1) To examine any books, papers, records, or other data which may be relevant or material to such inquiry;

"(2) To summon the person liable for tax or required to perform the act, or any officer or employee of such person, or any person having possession, custody, or care of books of account containing entries relating to the business of the person liable for tax or required to perform the act, or any other person the Secretary or his delegate may deem proper, to appear before the Secretary or his delegate at a time and place named in the summons and to produce such books, papers, records, or other data, and to give such testimony, under oath, as may be relevant or material to such inquiry; and

"(3) To take such testimony of the person concerned, under oath, as may be relevant or material to such inquiry."

The United States and Olivero, pursuant to §§ 7402(b) and 7604(a) of the Code, 26 U.S.C. §§ 7402(b) and 7604(a),[42] then petitioned the United States District Court for the Northern District of Illinois for enforcement of the summonses. App. 5. This was on November 11, 1975. Olivero testified that when the petition was filed he had not determined whether criminal charges were justified and had not made any report or recommendation about the case to his superiors. Id., at 30. It was alleged in the petition and in an incorporated exhibit that the requested materials were necessary for the determination of the tax liability of Gattuso for the years in question and that the information contained in the documents was not in the possession of the petitioners. Id., at 7, 17-18. The District Court entered an order to show cause, id., at 19, and respondents answered through counsel, who also represented Gattuso. Id., at 20-22.

At the ensuing hearing and in a post-hearing brief, respondents argued that Olivero's investigation was "purely criminal" in nature. Id., at 82. Gregory J. Perry, a lawyer specializing in federal taxation and employed by the same law firm that filed the answer, testified that in June 1975 Olivero told him that the Gattuso investigation "was strictly related to criminal violations of the Internal Revenue Code." Id., at 52. Respondents conceded that they bore the burden of proving that enforcement of the summonses would abuse the court's process, but they contended that they did not have to show "that there is no civil purpose to the Summons." Id., at 87. Instead, they urged that their burden was to show that the summonses were not issued in good faith because "the investigation is solely for the purpose of gathering evidence for use in a criminal prosecution." Id., at 77.

The District Court agreed with respondents' contentions. Although at the hearing the court seemed to recognize "that in any criminal investigation there's always a probability of civil tax liability," id., at 61, it focused its attention on the purpose of Special Agent Olivero:

"I'll say now that I heard nothing in Agent Olivero's testimony to suggest that the thought of a civil investigation ever crossed his mind.

"Now, unless I find something in the in camera inspection [of the IRS case file] that gives more support to the Government position than the Agent's

---

[42] [fn 4] Section 7402(b) states:

"If any person is summoned under the internal revenue laws to appear, to testify, or to produce books, papers, or other data, the district court of the United States for the district in which such person resides or may be found shall have jurisdiction by appropriate process to compel such attendance, testimony, or production of books, papers, or other data."

Section 7604(a) reads:

"If any person is summoned under the internal revenue laws to appear, to testify, or to produce books, papers, records, or other data, the United States district court for the district in which such person resides or is found shall have jurisdiction by appropriate process to compel such attendance, testimony, or production of books, papers, records, or other data."

testimony did, it would be my conclusion that he was at all times involved in a criminal investigation, at least in his own mind."[43] Id., at 62.

In its written memorandum, the District Court noted that *Donaldson* permitted the use of an IRS summons issued in good faith and prior to a recommendation for criminal prosecution. Relying on dictum in Reisman v. Caplin, 375 U.S. 440, 449, 84 S.Ct. 508, 11 L.Ed.2d 459 (1964), however, the court said that it was an improper use of the summons "to serve it solely for the purpose of obtaining evidence for use in a criminal prosecution." 76-1 USTC, at 84,072, 37 AFTR 2d, at 76-1240. If, at the time of its issuance, the summons served this proscribed purpose, the court concluded, the absence of a formal criminal recommendation was irrelevant, the summons was not issued in good faith, and enforcement was precluded. The court then held:

"It is apparent from the evidence that Special Agent John F. Olivero in his investigative activities had focused upon the possible criminal activities of John Gattuso, and was conducting his investigation solely for the purpose of unearthing evidence of criminal conduct by Mr. Gattuso." Id., at 84,073, 37 AFTR 2d, at 76-1240.

The United States Court of Appeals for the Seventh Circuit affirmed. 554 F.2d 302 (1977). It concluded that the District Court correctly had included the issue of criminal purpose within the good-faith inquiry:

"[T]he use of an administrative summons solely for criminal purposes is a quintessential example of bad faith. . . .

"We note that the district court formulated its factual finding by use of the expression 'sole criminal purpose' rather than by a label such as 'bad faith.' We find no basis for reversible error in that verbal formulation. The district court grasped the vital core of *Donaldson* and rendered its factual finding consistently therewith." Id., at 309.

The Court of Appeals further decided that the District Court had reached a factual, rather than a legal, conclusion when it found the summonses to have been issued solely for a criminal prosecution. Id., at 305. Appellate review, accordingly, was limited to application of the clearly-erroneous standard. Id., at 306. Although the Court of Appeals noted that Olivero had testified about the

---

[43] [fn 5] The District Court was aware of and recognized the Government's contention that the individual agent's motive in the investigation was not dispositive:

"The COURT: . . . [U]nder your theory any criminal investigation would not really be one until they closed it because there was always a possibility of a civil liability.

"If that's the law, you're in trouble, Mr. Cushner [counsel for respondents].

"I think it boils down to an issue of law so it's the cases really that I'm interested in plus any further clues I may find in the in camera inspection of the investigative file." App. 61-62.

The court agreed to inspect the IRS investigative file in camera after it refused to permit respondents to inspect the file. Id., at 50-51, 61-62.

existence of a civil purpose for the investigation, the court said that "the record establishes that the district court did not believe him." Id., at 309. The appellate court could not reverse the trial court's judgment, it said, because it was "not left with a firm and definite conviction that a mistake [had] been made." Id., at 306.

Because of the importance of the issue in the enforcement of the internal revenue laws, and because of conflict among the Courts of Appeals concerning the scope of IRS summons authority under § 7602,[44] we granted certiorari. 434 U.S. 996, 98 S.Ct. 632, 54 L.Ed.2d 489 (1977).

II.

In Donaldson v. United States, 400 U.S. 517, 91 S.Ct. 534, 27 L.Ed.2d 580 (1971), an IRS special agent issued summonses to a taxpayer's putative former employer and its accountant for the production of the employer's records of the taxpayer's employment and compensation. When the records were not forthcoming, the IRS petitioned for the enforcement of the summonses. The taxpayer intervened and eventually appealed the enforcement order. This Court addressed the taxpayer's contention that the summonses were unenforceable because they were issued in aid of an investigation that could have resulted in a criminal charge against the taxpayer. His argument there, see id., at 532, 91 S.Ct., at 543, was based on the following dictum in Reisman v. Caplin, 375 U.S., at 449, 84 S.Ct., at 513:

"[T]he witness may challenge the summons on any appropriate ground. This would include, as the circuits have held, the defenses that the material is sought for the improper purpose of obtaining evidence for use in a criminal prosecution, Boren v. Tucker, 239 F.2d 767, 772-773 . . . ."

---

[44] [fn 6] Compare United States v. Hodge & Zweig, 548 F.2d 1347, 1350-1351 (CA9 1977); United States v. Zack, 521 F.2d 1366, 1368 (CA9 1975); United States v. McCarthy, 514 F.2d 368, 374-375 (CA3 1975); United States v. Weingarden, 473 F.2d 454, 460 (CA6 1973); United States v. Wall Corp., 154 U.S.App.D.C. 309, 311, 475 F.2d 893, 895 (1972); and United States v. Billingsley, 469 F.2d 1208, 1210 (CA10 1972), with United States v. Morgan Guaranty Trust Co., 572 F.2d 36, 41-42 (CA2 1978); and United States v. Troupe, 438 F.2d 117, 119 (CA8 1971), regarding the conflict about whether the recommendation for criminal prosecution is dispositive of the so-called criminal purpose issue.

Compare United States v. Hodge & Zweig, 548 F.2d, at 1351; and United States v. Billingsley, 469 F.2d, at 1210, with United States v. Lafko, 520 F.2d 622, 625 (CA3 1975), regarding the conflict about whether the criminal recommendation from the IRS to the Department of Justice or the recommendation from the special agent to his superiors is important in the enforcement inquiry.

In the light of the citation to *Boren*,[45] the Court in *Donaldson* concluded that the dictum referred and was applicable to "the situation of a pending criminal charge or, at most, of an investigation solely for criminal purposes." 400 U.S., at 533, 91 S.Ct., at 544.

Discerning the meaning of the brief *Reisman* dictum, however, did not resolve for the Court the question posed by *Donaldson*. The validity of the summonses depended ultimately on whether they were among those authorized by Congress.[46] Having reviewed the statutory scheme, 400 U.S., at 523-525, 91 S.Ct., at 538-540, the Court concluded that Congress had authorized the use of summonses in investigating potentially criminal conduct. The statutory history, particularly the use of summonses under the Internal Revenue Code of 1939,[47] supported this conclusion, as did consistent IRS practice and decisions concerning effective enforcement of other comparable federal statutes.[48] The Court saw no reason to force the Service to choose either to forgo the use of congressionally authorized summonses or to abandon the option of recommending criminal prosecutions to the Department of Justice.[49] As long as the summonses were issued in good-faith pursuit of the congressionally authorized purposes, and prior to any recommendation to the Department for prosecution, they were enforceable. Id., at 536, 91 S.Ct., at 545.

III.

The present case requires us to examine the limits of the good-faith use of an Internal Revenue summons issued under § 7602. As the preceding discussion demonstrates, *Donaldson* does not control the facts now before us. There, the taxpayer had argued that the mere potentiality of criminal prosecution should have precluded enforcement of the summons. 400 U.S., at 532, 91 S.Ct., at 543. Here, on the other hand, the District Court found that Special Agent Olivero was investigating Gattuso "solely for the purpose of unearthing evidence of criminal conduct." 76-1 USTC, at 84,073, 37 AFTR 2d, at 76-1240. The question then becomes whether this finding necessarily leads to the conclusion that the

---

[45] [fn 7] In Boren v. Tucker, 239 F.2d 767, 772-773 (1956), the Ninth Circuit distinguished United States v. O'Connor, 118 F.Supp. 248 (Mass.1953), which involved an investigation of a taxpayer already under indictment.

[46] [fn 8] The Court had concluded earlier that the summoning of the employer's and the accountant's records for an investigation of the taxpayer did not violate the constitutional rights of any of them. 400 U.S., at 522, 91 S.Ct., at 538.

[47] [fn 9] See §§ 3614, 3615, 3616, and 3654 of the 1939 Code, 53 Stat. 438-440, 446.

[48] [fn 10] See United States v. Kordel, 397 U.S. 1, 11, 90 S.Ct. 763, 769, 25 L.Ed.2d 1 (1970) (Federal Food, Drug, and Cosmetic Act enforcement), citing Standard Sanitary Mfg. Co. v. United States, 226 U.S. 20, 51-52, 33 S.Ct. 9, 15-16, 57 L.Ed. 107 (1912) (Sherman Act enforcement).

[49] [fn 11] See Part III-B and n. 15, infra.

summonses were not issued in good-faith pursuit of the congressionally authorized purposes of § 7602.

A

The Secretary of the Treasury and the Commissioner of Internal Revenue are charged with the responsibility of administering and enforcing the Internal Revenue Code. 26 U.S.C. §§ 7801 and 7802. Congress, by § 7601(a), has required the Secretary to canvass revenue districts to "inquire after and concerning all persons therein who may be liable to pay any internal revenue tax." With regard to suspected fraud, these duties encompass enforcement of both civil and criminal statutes. The willful submission of a false or fraudulent tax return may subject a taxpayer not only to criminal penalties under §§ 7206 and 7207 of the Code, but, as well, to a civil penalty, under § 6653(b), of 50% of the underpayment. And § 6659(a) provides that the civil penalty shall be considered as part of the tax liability of the taxpayer. Hence, when § 7602 permits the use of a summons "[f]or the purpose of ascertaining the correctness of any return, . . . determining the liability of any person for any internal revenue tax . . . , or collecting any such liability," it necessarily permits the use of the summons for examination of suspected tax fraud and for the calculation of the 50% civil penalty. In *Donaldson*, 400 U.S., at 535, 91 S.Ct., at 544, we clearly noted that § 7602 drew no distinction between the civil and the criminal aspects; that it "contains no restriction"; that the corresponding regulations were "positive"; and that there was no significance, "for civil as compared with criminal purposes, at the point of a special agent's appearance." The Court then upheld the use of the summonses even though fraudulent conduct carried the potential of criminal liability. The Court repeated this emphasis in Couch v. United States, 409 U.S. 322, 326, 93 S.Ct. 611, 614, 34 L.Ed.2d 548 (1973):

"It is now undisputed that a special agent is authorized, pursuant to 26 U.S.C. § 7602, to issue an Internal Revenue summons in aid of a tax investigation with civil and possible criminal consequences."

This result is inevitable because Congress has created a law enforcement system in which criminal and civil elements are inherently intertwined. When an investigation examines the possibility of criminal misconduct, it also necessarily inquires about the appropriateness of assessing the 50% civil tax penalty.[50]

---

[50] [fn 12] The interrelated nature of the civil and criminal investigative functions is further demonstrated by the organization and functioning of the IRS. Pursuant to 26 CFR § 601.107 (1977), each revenue district has an Intelligence Division, "whose mission is to encourage and achieve the highest possible degree of voluntary compliance with the internal revenue laws." This purpose is implemented by "the investigation of possible criminal violations of such laws and the recommendation (when warranted) of prosecution and/or assertion of the 50 percent ad valorem addition to the tax." Ibid. See generally Internal Revenue Service Organization and Functions §§ 1113.563, 1114.8, and 1118.6, 39 Fed.Reg. 11572, 11581, 11601, and 11607 (1974).

The legislative history of the Code supports the conclusion that Congress intended to design a system with interrelated criminal and civil elements. Section 7602 derives assertedly without change in meaning,[51] from corresponding and similar provisions in §§ 3614, 3615, and 3654 of the 1939 Code. By § 3614(a) the Commissioner received the summons authority "for the purpose of ascertaining the correctness of any return or for the purpose of making a return where none has been made." Section 3615(b)(3) authorized the issuance of a summons "[w]henever any person who is required to deliver a monthly or other return of objects subject to tax delivers any return which, in the opinion of the collector, is erroneous, false, or fraudulent, or contains any undervaluation or understatement." Section 3654(a) stated the powers and duties of the collector:

"Every collector within his collection district shall see that all laws and regulations relating to the collection of internal revenue taxes are faithfully executed and complied with, and shall aid in the prevention, detection, and punishment of any frauds in relation thereto. For such purposes, he shall have power to examine all persons, books, papers, accounts, and premises . . . and to summon any person to produce books and papers . . . and to compel compliance with such summons in the same manner as provided in section 3615."

Under § 3616 punishment for any fraud included both fine and imprisonment. The 1939 Code, therefore, contemplated the use of the summons in an

---

In its Manual for employees, the IRS instructs that the jurisdiction of the Intelligence Division includes all civil penalties except those related to the estimated income tax. Internal Revenue Manual, ch. 4500, § 4561 (CCH 1976). The Manual adds:

"Intelligence features are those activities of developing and presenting admissible evidence required to prove criminal violations and the ad valorem penalties for civil fraud, negligence and delinquency (except those concerning tax estimations) for all years involved in cases jointly investigated to completion." Id., § 4565.31(4).

The Manual also contains detailed instructions for coordination between special agents and revenue agents during investigations of tax fraud. E.g., id., § 4563.431 (1978), and §§ 4565.22, 4565.32, 4565.41-4565.44 (1976).

Statistics for the fiscal year 1976 show that the Intelligence Division has a substantially greater involvement with civil fraud than with criminal fraud. Of 8,797 full-scale tax fraud investigations in that year, only 2,037 resulted in recommendations for prosecution. The 6,760 cases not recommended involved approximately $11 million in deficiencies and penalties. See 1976 Annual Report of the Commissioner of Internal Revenue 33, 61, 152.

[51] [fn 13] See H.R.Rep.No.1337, 83d Cong., 2d Sess., A436 (1954); S.Rep.No.1622, 83d Cong., 2d Sess., 617 (1954), U.S.Code Cong. & Admin.News 1954, p. 4025.

investigation involving suspected criminal conduct as well as behavior that could have been disciplined with a civil penalty.[52]

In short, Congress has not categorized tax fraud investigations into civil and criminal components. Any limitation on the good-faith use of an Internal Revenue summons must reflect this statutory premise.

B.

The preceding discussion suggests why the primary limitation on the use of a summons occurs upon the recommendation of criminal prosecution to the Department of Justice. Only at that point do the criminal and civil aspects of a tax fraud case begin to diverge. See United States v. Hodge & Zweig, 548 F.2d 1347, 1351 (CA9 1977); United States v. Billingsley, 469 F.2d 1208, 1210 (CA10 1972). We recognize, of course, that even upon recommendation to the Justice Department, the civil and criminal elements do not separate completely. The Government does not sacrifice its interest in unpaid taxes just because a criminal prosecution begins. Logically, then, the IRS could use its summons authority under § 7602 to uncover information about the tax liability created by a fraud regardless of the status of the criminal case. But the rule forbidding such is a prophylactic intended to safeguard the following policy interests.

A referral to the Justice Department permits criminal litigation to proceed. The IRS cannot try its own prosecutions. Such authority is reserved to the Department of Justice and, more particularly, to the United States Attorneys. 28 U.S.C. § 547(1). Nothing in § 7602 or its legislative history suggests that Congress intended the summons authority to broaden the Justice Department's right of criminal litigation discovery or to infringe on the role of the grand jury as a principal tool of criminal accusation. Accord, United States v. Morgan Guaranty Trust Co., 572 F.2d 36 (CA2 1978); United States v. Weingarden, 473

---

[52] [fn 14] Internal Revenue officials received similar summons authority in Revenue Acts prior to the 1939 Code. See, e.g., Revenue Act of 1918, § 1305, 40 Stat. 1142; Tariff Act of Oct. 3, 1913, § II ¶ I, 38 Stat. 178-179; Act of June 30, 1864, § 14, 13 Stat. 226.

The interrelated nature of fraud investigations thus was apparent as early as 1864. Section 14 of the 1864 Act permitted the issuance of a summons to investigate a suspected fraudulent return. It also prescribed a 100% increase in valuation as a civil penalty for falsehood. Section 15 established the criminal penalties for such conduct. Four years later, when Congress created the position of district supervisor, that official received similar summons authority. Act of July 20, 1868, § 49, 15 Stat. 144-145; see Cong.Globe, 40th Cong., 2d Sess., 3450 (1868). The federal courts enforced these summonses when they were issued in good faith and in compliance with instructions from the Commissioner. See In re Meador, 16 F.Cas. 1294, 1296 (No. 9,375) (ND Ga.1869); Stanwood v. Green, 22 F.Cas. 1077, 1079 (No. 13,301) (SD Miss.1870) ("it being understood that this right upon the part of the supervisor extends only to such books and papers as relate to their banking operations, and are connected with the internal revenue of the United States").

F.2d 454, 458-459 (CA6 1973); United States v. O'Connor, 118 F.Supp. 248, 250-251 (Mass.1953); see Donaldson v. United States, 400 U.S., at 536, 91 S.Ct., at 545; cf. Abel v. United States, 362 U.S. 217, 226, 80 S.Ct. 683, 690, 4 L.Ed.2d 668 (1960). The likelihood that discovery would be broadened or the role of the grand jury infringed is substantial if post-referral use of the summons authority were permitted. For example, the IRS, upon referral, loses its ability to compromise both the criminal and the civil aspects of a fraud case. 26 U.S.C. § 7122(a). After the referral, the authority to settle rests with the Department of Justice. Interagency cooperation on the calculation of the civil liability is then to be expected and probably encourages efficient settlement of the dispute. But such cooperation, when combined with the inherently intertwined nature of the criminal and civil elements of the case, suggests that it is unrealistic to attempt to build a partial information barrier between the two branches of the executive. Effective use of information to determine civil liability would inevitably result in criminal discovery. The prophylactic restraint on the use of the summons effectively safeguards the two policy interests while encouraging maximum interagency cooperation.[53]

C.

Prior to a recommendation for prosecution to the Department of Justice, the IRS must use its summons authority in good faith. Donaldson v. United States, 400 U.S., at 536, 91 S.Ct., at 545; United States v. Powell, 379 U.S. 48, 57-58, 85 S.Ct. 248, 254-255, 13 L.Ed.2d 112 (1964). In *Powell*, the Court announced several elements of a good-faith exercise:

---

[53] [fn 15] The Third Circuit has suggested that our reference in *Donaldson* to the recommendation for criminal prosecution ("We hold that under § 7602 an internal revenue summons may be issued in aid of an investigation if it is issued in good faith and prior to a recommendation for criminal prosecution," 400 U.S., at 536, 91 S.Ct., at 545) intended to draw a line at the recommendation to the Service's district office from the special agent, rather than at the recommendation from the Service to the Justice Department. United States v. Lafko, 520 F.2d, at 625. This misread our intent. Given the interrelated criminal/civil nature of tax fraud investigation whenever it remains within the jurisdiction of the Service, and given the utility of the summons to investigate civil tax liability, we decline to impose the prophylactic restraint on the summons authority any earlier than at the recommendation to the Department of Justice. We cannot deny that the potential for expanding the criminal discovery rights of the Justice Department or for usurping the role of the grand jury exists at the point of the recommendation by the special agent. But we think the possibilities for abuse of these policies are remote before the recommendation to Justice takes place and do not justify imposing an absolute ban on the use of the summons before that point. Earlier imposition of the ban, given the balance of policies and civil law enforcement interests, would unnecessarily hamstring the performance of the tax determination and collection functions by the Service.

"[The Service] must show that the investigation will be conducted pursuant to a legitimate purpose, that the inquiry may be relevant to the purpose, that the information sought is not already within the Commissioner's possession, and that the administrative steps required by the Code have been followed . . . . [A] court may not permit its process to be abused. Such an abuse would take place if the summons had been issued for an improper purpose, such as to harass the taxpayer or to put pressure on him to settle a collateral dispute, or for any other purpose reflecting on the good faith of the particular investigation." Ibid. (footnote omitted).

A number of the Courts of Appeals, including the Seventh Circuit in this case, 554 F.2d, at 309, have said that another improper purpose, which the Service may not pursue in good faith with a summons, is to gather evidence solely for a criminal investigation.[54] The courts have based their conclusions in part on *Donaldson*'s explanation of the *Reisman* dictum. The language of *Donaldson*, however, must be read in the light of the recognition of the interrelated criminal/civil nature of a tax fraud inquiry. For a fraud investigation to be solely criminal in nature would require an extraordinary departure from the normally inseparable goals of examining whether the basis exists for criminal charges and for the assessment of civil penalties.

In this case, respondents submit that such a departure did indeed occur because Special Agent Olivero was interested only in gathering evidence for a criminal prosecution. We disagree. The institutional responsibility of the Service to calculate and to collect civil fraud penalties and fraudulently reported or unreported taxes is not necessarily overturned by a single agent who attempts to build a criminal case. The review process over and above his conclusions is multilayered and thorough. Apart from the control of his immediate supervisor, the agent's final recommendation is reviewed by the district chief of the Intelligence Division, 26 CFR §§ 601.107(b) and (c) (1977); Internal Revenue Manual, ch. 9600, §§ 9621.1, 9622.1, 9623 (CCH 1977); see Donaldson v. United States, 400 U.S., at 534, 91 S.Ct., at 544. The Office of Regional Counsel also reviews the case before it is forwarded to the National Office of the Service or to the Justice Department. 26 CFR § 601.107(c) (1977); Internal Revenue Service Organization and Functions § 1116(3), 39 Fed.Reg. 11602 (1974); Internal Revenue Manual, ch. 9600, §§ 9624, 9631.2, 9631.4 (CCH 1977). If the Regional Counsel and the Assistant Regional Commissioner for Intelligence disagree about the disposition of a case, another complete review occurs at the national level centered in the Criminal Tax Division of the Office of General Counsel. Internal Revenue Service Organization and Functions § 1113(11) 22, 39 Fed.Reg. 11599 (1974); Internal Revenue Manual, ch. 9600, § 9651(1) (CCH

---

[54] [fn 16] See, e.g., United States v. Hodge & Zweig, 548 F.2d, at 1350, 1351; United States v. Zack, 521 F.2d, at 1368; United States v. Lafko, 520 F.2d, at 625; United States v. McCarthy, 514 F.2d, at 374-375; United States v. Theodore, 479 F.2d, at 753; United States v. Weingarden, 473 F.2d, at 459; United States v. Wall Corp., 154 U.S.App.D.C., at 311, 475 F.2d, at 895.

1977). Only after the officials of at least two layers of review have concurred in the conclusion of the special agent does the referral to the Department of Justice take place. At any of the various stages, the Service can abandon the criminal prosecution, can decide instead to assert a civil penalty, or can pursue both goals. While the special agent is an important actor in the process, his motivation is hardly dispositive.

It should also be noted that the layers of review provide the taxpayer with substantial protection against the hasty or overzealous judgment of the special agent. The taxpayer may obtain a conference with the district Intelligence Division officials upon request or whenever the chief of the Division determines that a conference would be in the best interests of the Government. 26 CFR § 601.107(b)(2) (1977); Internal Revenue Manual, ch. 9300, § 9356.1 (CCH 1977). If prosecution has been recommended, the chief notifies the taxpayer of the referral to the Regional Counsel. 26 CFR § 601.107(c) (1977); Internal Revenue Manual, ch. 9300, § 9355 (CCH 1977).

As in *Donaldson*, then, where we refused to draw the line between permissible civil and impermissible criminal purposes at the entrance of the special agent into the investigation, 400 U.S., at 536, 91 S.Ct., at 545, we cannot draw it on the basis of the agent's personal intent. To do so would unnecessarily frustrate the enforcement of the tax laws by restricting the use of the summons according to the motivation of a single agent without regard to the enforcement policy of the Service as an institution. Furthermore, the inquiry into the criminal enforcement objectives of the agent would delay summons enforcement proceedings while parties clash over, and judges grapple with, the thought processes of each investigator.[55] See United States v. Morgan Guaranty Trust Co., 572 F.2d 36 (CA2 1978). This obviously is undesirable and unrewarding. As a result, the question whether an investigation has solely criminal purposes must be answered only by an examination of the institutional posture of the IRS. Contrary to the assertion of respondents, this means that those opposing enforcement of a summons do bear the burden to disprove the actual existence of a valid civil tax determination or collection purpose by the Service. After all, the purpose of the good-faith inquiry is to determine whether the agency is honestly pursuing the goals of § 7602 by issuing the summons.

Without doubt, this burden is a heavy one. Because criminal and civil fraud liabilities are coterminous, the Service rarely will be found to have acted in bad faith by pursuing the former. On the other hand, we cannot abandon this aspect of the good-faith inquiry altogether.[56] We shall not countenance delay in submitting

---

[55] [fn 17] We recognize, of course, that examination of agent motive may be necessary to evaluate the good-faith factors of *Powell*, for example, to consider whether a summons was issued to harass a taxpayer.

[56] [fn 18] The dissent would abandon this aspect of the good-faith inquiry. It would permit the IRS to use the summons authority solely for criminal investigation. It reaches this conclusion because it says the Code contains no limitation to prevent such use. Its argument reveals a fundamental

a recommendation to the Justice Department when there is an institutional commitment to make the referral and the Service merely would like to gather additional evidence for the prosecution. Such a delay would be tantamount to the use of the summons authority after the recommendation and would permit the Government to expand its criminal discovery rights. Similarly, the good-faith standard will not permit the IRS to become an information-gathering agency for other departments, including the Department of Justice, regardless of the status of criminal cases.[57]

D.

In summary, then, several requirements emerge for the enforcement of an IRS summons.[58] First, the summons must be issued before the Service recommends to the Department of Justice that a criminal prosecution, which reasonably would relate to the subject matter of the summons, be undertaken.

---

misunderstanding about the authority of the IRS. The Service does not enjoy inherent authority to summon production of the private papers of citizens. It may exercise only that authority granted by Congress. In § 7602 Congress has bestowed upon the Service the authority to summon production for four purposes only: for "ascertaining the correctness of any return, making a return where none has been made, determining the liability of any person for any internal revenue tax . . . or collecting any such liability." Congress therefore intended the summons authority to be used to aid the determination and collection of taxes. These purposes do not include the goal of filing criminal charges against citizens. Consequently, summons authority does not exist to aid criminal investigations solely. The error of the dissent is that it seeks a limit on the face of the statute when it should seek an affirmative grant of summons authority for purely criminal investigations. We have made that search and could uncover nothing in the Code or its legislative history to suggest that Congress intended to permit exclusively criminal use of summonses. As a result, the IRS employs its authority in good faith when it pursues the four purposes of § 7602, which do not include aiding criminal investigations solely.

[57] [fn 19] To the limited extent that the institutional good faith of the Service with regard to criminal purpose may be questioned before any recommendation to the Department of Justice, our position on this issue necessarily rejects the Government's argument that prerecommendation enforcement of summonses must meet only the *Powell* elements of good faith. We have concluded that the Government's contention fails to recognize the essence of the good-faith inquiry. The *Powell* elements were not intended as an exclusive statement about the meaning of good faith. They were examples of agency action not in good-faith pursuit of the congressionally authorized purposes of § 7602. The dispositive question in each case, then, is whether the Service is pursuing the authorized purposes in good faith.

[58] [fn 20] These requirements are not intended to be exclusive. Future cases may well reveal the need to prevent other forms of agency abuse of congressional authority and judicial process.

Second, the Service at all times must use the summons authority in good-faith pursuit of the congressionally authorized purposes of § 7602. This second prerequisite requires the Service to meet the *Powell* standards of good faith. It also requires that the Service not abandon in an institutional sense, as explained in Parts III-A and III-C above, the pursuit of civil tax determination or collection.

IV.

On the record before us, respondents have not demonstrated sufficient justification to preclude enforcement of the IRS summonses. No recommendation to the Justice Department for criminal prosecution has been made. Of the *Powell* criteria, respondents challenge only one aspect of the Service's showing: They suggest that Olivero already may possess the evidence requested in the summonses. Brief for Respondents 16-19. Although the record shows that Olivero had uncovered the names and identities of the LaSalle National Bank land trusts, it does not show that the Service knows the value of the trusts or their income or the allocation of interests therein. Because production of the bank's complete records on the trusts reasonably could be expected to reveal part or all of this information, which would be material to the computation of Gattuso's tax liability, the *Powell* criteria do not preclude enforcement. Finally, the District Court refused enforcement because it found that Olivero's personal motivation was to gather evidence solely for a criminal prosecution. The court, however, failed to consider whether the Service in an institutional sense had abandoned its pursuit of Gattuso's civil tax liability.[59] The Court of Appeals did not require that inquiry. On the record presently developed, we cannot conclude that such an abandonment has occurred.

The judgment of the Court of Appeals is therefore reversed with instructions to that court to remand the case to the District Court for further proceedings consistent with this opinion.

It is so ordered.

---

[59] [fn 21] Respondents argue that the District Court made a factual finding when it concluded that the summonses were issued solely to gather evidence for a criminal prosecution. They then submit that the District Court's decision may be overturned only if this Court holds this finding to be clearly erroneous. Several Courts of Appeals have discussed the factual and legal issues that lurk in summons enforcement proceedings. Compare United States v. Zack, 521 F.2d, at 1367-1368; United States v. National State Bank, 454 F.2d 1249, 1252 (CA7 1972); Boren v. Tucker, 239 F.2d, at 773, with United States v. Weingarden, 473 F.2d, at 460. Whether the issue of the Service's good faith generally poses a factual question, or a legal and factual one, or a legal question, is not necessarily presented in the case now before the Court, and we do not reach it. The lower courts employed an incorrect legal standard to measure good faith when they limited their consideration to the personal motivation of Special Agent Olivero. In this case, then, a legal error compels reversal.

Mr. Justice STEWART, with whom The Chief Justice, Mr. Justice REHNQUIST, and Mr. Justice STEVENS join, dissenting.

This case is here only because of judicial misreadings of a passage in the Court's opinion in Donaldson v. United States, 400 U.S. 517, 533, 91 S.Ct. 534, 543, 27 L.Ed.2d 580. That passage has been read by the federal courts, in this case and in others, to mean that a summons under § 7602 of the Internal Revenue Code, 26 U.S.C. § 7602, is improper if issued in aid of an investigation solely for criminal purposes.[60] Yet the statute itself contains no such limitation, and the *Donaldson* opinion in fact clearly stated that there are but two limits upon enforcement of such a summons: It must be "issued in good faith and prior to a recommendation for criminal prosecution." 400 U.S., at 536, 91 S.Ct., at 545. I adhere to that view.

The Court concedes that the task of establishing the "purpose" of an individual agent is "undesirable and unrewarding." *Ante*, at 2367. Yet the burden it imposes today—to discover the "institutional good faith" of the entire Internal Revenue Service—is, in my view, even less desirable and less rewarding. The elusiveness of "institutional good faith" as described by the Court can produce little but endless discovery proceedings and ultimate frustration of the fair administration of the Internal Revenue Code. In short, I fear that the Court's new criteria will prove wholly unworkable.

Earlier this year the Court of Appeals for the Second Circuit had occasion to deal with the issue now before us in the case of United States v. Morgan Guaranty Trust Co., 572 F.2d 36. Judge Friendly's perceptive opinion for his court in that case read the *Donaldson* opinion correctly: This Court was there "laying down an objective test, 'prior to a recommendation for criminal prosecution,' that would avoid a need for determining the thought processes of special agents; and . . . the 'good faith' requirement of the holding related to such wholly different matters as those mentioned in" the case of United States v. Powell, 379 U.S. 48, 85 S.Ct. 248, 13 L.Ed.2d 112.[61] "Such a view would . . . be consistent with the only rationale that has ever been offered for preventing an otherwise legitimate use of an Internal Revenue Service third party summons, namely that Congress could not have intended the statute to trench on the power

---

[60] [fn 1] See ante, at 2362 n. 6.

[61] [fn 2] As Judge Friendly pointed out, this Court's *Powell* opinion simply declared that a court may not permit its process in enforcing a summons to be abused, and its examples of "abuse" were:

" 'Such an abuse would take place if the summons had been issued for an improper purpose, such as to harass the taxpayer or to put pressure on him to settle a collateral dispute, or for any other purpose reflecting on the good faith of the particular investigation.' [379 U.S., at 58, 85 S.Ct., at 254.]

"Nothing was said to indicate that an intention by the Commissioner to uncover criminal tax liability would reflect 'on the good faith' of the inquiry, and the rule of ejusdem generis would dictate the contrary." 572 F.2d, at 40.

of the grand jury or to broaden the Government's right to discovery in a criminal case . . . ." 572 F.2d, at 41-42.

Instead of standing by the objective and comparatively bright-line test of *Donaldson*, as now clarified, the Court today further muddies the waters. It does not even attempt to identify the source of the requirements it now adds to enforcement proceedings under §§ 7402(b) and 7604(a) of the Code. These requirements are not suggested by anything in the statutes themselves, and nobody suggests that they derive from the Constitution. They are simply imposed by the Court from out of nowhere, and they seem to me unjustified, unworkable, and unwise.

I would reverse the judgment, not for further hearings in the District Court, but with instructions to order enforcement of the summons.

NOTES AND QUESTIONS

1. In response to *LaSalle*, Congress amended section 7602 to authorize the IRS to utilize an administrative summons for investigating solely criminal charges.
2. Issuing a summons after a case has been referred to the Department of Justice for prosecution is still prohibited so that the IRS does not continue its investigation while in the process of prosecuting the taxpayer.

CHAPTER 13

TAXPAYER SUMMONS
DEFENSES

The last chapter discussed a few limitations on the IRS's summons authority. A major limitation that merits its own chapter is evidentiary privilege. The IRS's summons authority does not extend to privileged documents and records. There are four types of privileges that can apply to information the IRS seeks: (1) the attorney-client privilege, (2) the work product privilege, (3) the federal tax practitioner privilege, and (4) the Fifth Amendment Act of Production privilege. The IRS may compel a taxpayer to turn over information that is not subject to the limitations in the previous chapter and does not fall within one of these privileges.

A. Attorney-Client Privilege

In general, the attorney-client privilege protects from judicially compelled production an unwaived, confidential communication between an attorney and client about legal advice. Underlying the attorney-client privilege is the right to counsel under the Sixth Amendment. A defendant will not feel comfortable disclosing all material facts surrounding an alleged crime to an attorney if the government will have access to everything the defendant communicates. This is so especially if the defendant mistakenly believes he is guilty of the crime for which the government has charged him. There would be no one in the criminal prosecution context in whom the defendant could confide. The common criminal law example is the wife accused of killing her spouse. Without the attorney-client privilege, the accused wife might not be willing to disclose the events that occurred because the government could seize on any potential admission. The wife's description of the actual events might reveal to the attorney, however, that the accused merely engaged in self-defense and should be exonerated.

Similarly, without the attorney-client privilege, a taxpayer under audit would be unwilling to disclose material facts about his income if the IRS has access to everything the taxpayer communicates to his attorney. Suppose the taxpayer receives $100,000 in payment to her by a local business after she fell on their sidewalk and sprained her ankle. If the taxpayer fails to report the payment on her tax return and is later audited by the IRS, she might not want to disclose the payment to the IRS. If she explains the payment to her attorney and the circumstances, a competent tax attorney will recognize that it was unnecessary to report the payment because section 102(a) excludes from income payments made on account of personal injury.

It is important for a corporate client to know to whom the privilege attaches.

UPJOHN COMPANY v. UNITED STATES
449 U.S. 383 (1981)
Supreme Court of the United States

Justice REHNQUIST delivered the opinion of the Court.

We granted certiorari in this case to address important questions concerning the scope of the attorney–client privilege in the corporate context and the applicability of the work–product doctrine in proceedings to enforce tax summonses. 445 U.S. 925, 100 S.Ct. 1310, 63 L.Ed.2d 758. With respect to the privilege question the parties and various amici have described our task as one of choosing between two "tests" which have gained adherents in the courts of appeals. We are acutely aware, however, that we sit to decide concrete cases and not abstract propositions of law. We decline to lay down a broad rule or series of rules to govern all conceivable future questions in this area, even were we able to do so. We can and do, however, conclude that the attorney–client privilege protects the communications involved in this case from compelled disclosure and that the work–product doctrine does apply in tax summons enforcement proceedings.

I.

Petitioner Upjohn Co. manufactures and sells pharmaceuticals here and abroad. In January 1976 independent accountants conducting an audit of one of Upjohn's foreign subsidiaries discovered that the subsidiary made payments to or for the benefit of foreign government officials in order to secure government business. The accountants, so informed petitioner, Mr. Gerard Thomas, Upjohn's Vice President, Secretary, and General Counsel. Thomas is a member of the Michigan and New York Bars, and has been Upjohn's General Counsel for 20 years. He consulted with outside counsel and R. T. Parfet, Jr., Upjohn's Chairman of the Board. It was decided that the company would conduct an internal investigation of what were termed "questionable payments." As part of this investigation the attorneys prepared a letter containing a questionnaire which was sent to "All Foreign General and Area Managers" over the Chairman's signature. The letter began by noting recent disclosures that several American companies made "possibly illegal" payments to foreign government officials and emphasized that the management needed full information concerning any such payments made by Upjohn. The letter indicated that the Chairman had asked

Thomas, identified as "the company's General Counsel," "to conduct an investigation for the purpose of determining the nature and magnitude of any payments made by the Upjohn Company or any of its subsidiaries to any employee or official of a foreign government." The questionnaire sought detailed information concerning such payments. Managers were instructed to treat the investigation as "highly confidential" and not to discuss it with anyone other than Upjohn employees who might be helpful in providing the requested information. Responses were to be sent directly to Thomas. Thomas and outside counsel also interviewed the recipients of the questionnaire and some 33 other Upjohn officers or employees as part of the investigation.

On March 26, 1976, the company voluntarily submitted a preliminary report to the Securities and Exchange Commission on Form 8–K disclosing certain questionable payments.[1] A copy of the report was simultaneously submitted to the Internal Revenue Service, which immediately began an investigation to determine the tax consequences of the payments. Special agents conducting the investigation were given lists by Upjohn of all those interviewed and all who had responded to the questionnaire. On November 23, 1976, the Service issued a summons pursuant to 26 U.S.C. § 7602 demanding production of:

> All files relative to the investigation conducted under the supervision of Gerard Thomas to identify payments to employees of foreign governments and any political contributions made by the Upjohn Company or any of its affiliates since January 1, 1971 and to determine whether any funds of the Upjohn Company had been improperly accounted for on the corporate books during the same period.

> The records should include but not be limited to written questionnaires sent to managers of the Upjohn Company's foreign affiliates, and memorandums or notes of the interviews conducted in the United States and abroad with officers and employees of the Upjohn Company and its subsidiaries. App. 17a–18a.

The company declined to produce the documents specified in the second paragraph on the grounds that they were protected from disclosure by the attorney–client privilege and constituted the work product of attorneys prepared in anticipation of litigation. On August 31, 1977, the United States filed a petition seeking enforcement of the summons under 26 U.S.C. §§ 7402(b) and 7604(a) in the United States District Court for the Western District of Michigan. That court adopted the recommendation of a Magistrate who concluded that the summons should be enforced. Petitioners appealed to the Court of Appeals for the Sixth Circuit which rejected the Magistrate's finding of a waiver of the attorney–client privilege, 600 F.2d 1223, 1227, n. 12, but agreed that the privilege did not apply "[t]o the extent that the communications were made by officers and agents not responsible for directing Upjohn's actions in response to legal advice . . . for the

---

[1] [fn 1] On July 28, 1976, the company filed an amendment to this report disclosing further payments.

simple reason that the communications were not the 'client's.' " *Id.*, at 1225. The court reasoned that accepting petitioners' claim for a broader application of the privilege would encourage upper–echelon management to ignore unpleasant facts and create too broad a "zone of silence." Noting that Upjohn's counsel had interviewed officials such as the Chairman and President, the Court of Appeals remanded to the District Court so that a determination of who was within the "control group" could be made. In a concluding footnote the court stated that the work–product doctrine "is not applicable to administrative summonses issued under 26 U.S.C. § 7602." *Id.*, at 1228, n. 13.

II.

Federal Rule of Evidence 501 provides that "the privilege of a witness . . . shall be governed by the principles of the common law as they may be interpreted by the courts of the United States in light of reason and experience." The attorney–client privilege is the oldest of the privileges for confidential communications known to the common law. 8 J. Wigmore, Evidence § 2290 (McNaughton rev. 1961). Its purpose is to encourage full and frank communication between attorneys and their clients and thereby promote broader public interests in the observance of law and administration of justice. The privilege recognizes that sound legal advice or advocacy serves public ends and that such advice or advocacy depends upon the lawyer's being fully informed by the client. As we stated last Term in *Trammel v. United States*, 445 U.S. 40, 51, 100 S.Ct. 906, 913, 63 L.Ed.2d 186 (1980): "The lawyer–client privilege rests on the need for the advocate and counselor to know all that relates to the client's reasons for seeking representation if the professional mission is to be carried out." And in *Fisher v. United States*, 425 U.S. 391, 403, 96 S.Ct. 1569, 1577, 48 L.Ed.2d 39 (1976), we recognized the purpose of the privilege to be "to encourage clients to make full disclosure to their attorneys." This rationale for the privilege has long been recognized by the Court, see *Hunt v. Blackburn*, 128 U.S. 464, 470, 9 S.Ct. 125, 127, 32 L.Ed. 488 (1888) (privilege "is founded upon the necessity, in the interest and administration of justice, of the aid of persons having knowledge of the law and skilled in its practice, which assistance can only be safely and readily availed of when free from the consequences or the apprehension of disclosure"). Admittedly complications in the application of the privilege arise when the client is a corporation, which in theory is an artificial creature of the law, and not an individual; but this Court has assumed that the privilege applies when the client is a corporation. *United States v. Louisville & Nashville R. Co.*, 236 U.S. 318, 336, 35 S.Ct. 363, 369, 59 L.Ed. 598 (1915), and the Government does not contest the general proposition.

The Court of Appeals, however, considered the application of the privilege in the corporate context to present a "different problem," since the client was an inanimate entity and "only the senior management, guiding and integrating the several operations, . . . can be said to possess an identity analogous to the corporation as a whole." 600 F.2d at 1226. The first case to articulate the so-called "control group test" adopted by the court below, *Philadelphia v. Westinghouse Electric Corp.*, 210 F.Supp. 483, 485 (ED Pa.), petition for mandamus and prohibition denied *sub nom. General Electric Co. v. Kirkpatrick*, 312 F.2d 742 (CA3 1962), cert. denied, 372 U.S. 943, 83 S.Ct. 937, 9 L.Ed.2d 969 (1963), reflected a similar conceptual approach:

> Keeping in mind that the question is, Is it the corporation which is seeking the lawyer's advice when the asserted privileged communication is made?, the most satisfactory solution, I think, is that if the employee making the communication, of whatever rank he may be, is in a position to control or even to take a substantial part in a decision about any action which the corporation may take upon the advice of the attorney, . . . then, in effect, *he is (or personifies) the corporation* when he makes his disclosure to the lawyer and the privilege would apply. (Emphasis supplied.)

Such a view, we think, overlooks the fact that the privilege exists to protect not only the giving of professional advice to those who can act on it but also the giving of information to the lawyer to enable him to give sound and informed advice. See *Trammel, supra,* at 51, 100 S.Ct., at 913; *Fisher, supra,* at 403, 96 S.Ct., at 1577. The first step in the resolution of any legal problem is ascertaining the factual background and sifting through the facts with an eye to the legally relevant. See ABA Code of Professional Responsibility, Ethical Consideration 4–1:

> A lawyer should be fully informed of all the facts of the matter he is handling in order for his client to obtain the full advantage of our legal system. It is for the lawyer in the exercise of his independent professional judgment to separate the relevant and important from the irrelevant and unimportant. The observance of the ethical obligation of a lawyer to hold inviolate the confidences and secrets of his client not only facilitates the full development of facts essential to proper representation of the client but also encourages laymen to seek early legal assistance.

See also *Hickman v. Taylor*, 329 U.S. 495, 511, 67 S.Ct. 385, 393–394, 91 L.Ed. 451 (1947).

In the case of the individual client the provider of information and the person who acts on the lawyer's advice are one and the same. In the corporate context, however, it will frequently be employees beyond the control group as defined by the court below—"officers and agents . . . responsible for directing [the company's] actions in response to legal advice"—who will possess the information needed by the corporation's lawyers. Middle–level—and indeed lower–level—employees can, by actions within the scope of their employment, embroil the corporation in serious legal difficulties, and it is only natural that these employees would have the relevant information needed by corporate counsel if he is adequately to advise the client with respect to such actual or potential difficulties. This fact was noted in *Diversified Industries, Inc. v. Meredith*, 572 F.2d 596 (CA8 1978) (en banc):

> "In a corporation, it may be necessary to glean information relevant to a legal problem from middle management or non–management personnel as well as

from top executives. The attorney dealing with a complex legal problem 'is thus faced with a "Hobson's choice". If he interviews employees not having "the very highest authority", their communications to him will not be privileged. If, on the other hand, he interviews *only* those employees with the "very highest authority", he may find it extremely difficult, if not impossible, to determine what happened.' " *Id.*, at 608–609 (quoting Weinschel Corporate Employee Interviews and the Attorney–Client Privilege, 12 B.C.Ind. & Com. L.Rev. 873, 876 (1971)).

The control group test adopted by the court below thus frustrates the very purpose of the privilege by discouraging the communication of relevant information by employees of the client to attorneys seeking to render legal advice to the client corporation. The attorney's advice will also frequently be more significant to noncontrol group members than to those who officially sanction the advice, and the control group test makes it more difficult to convey full and frank legal advice to the employees who will put into effect the client corporation's policy. See, *e.g., Duplan Corp. v. Deering Milliken, Inc.*, 397 F.Supp. 1146, 1164 (DSC 1974) ("After the lawyer forms his or her opinion, it is of no immediate benefit to the Chairman of the Board or the President. It must be given to the corporate personnel who will apply it").

The narrow scope given the attorney–client privilege by the court below not only makes it difficult for corporate attorneys to formulate sound advice when their client is faced with a specific legal problem but also threatens to limit the valuable efforts of corporate counsel to ensure their client's compliance with the law. In light of the vast and complicated array of regulatory legislation confronting the modern corporation, corporations, unlike most individuals, "constantly go to lawyers to find out how to obey the law," Burnham, The Attorney–Client Privilege in the Corporate Arena, 24 Bus.Law. 901, 913 (1969), particularly since compliance with the law in this area is hardly an instinctive matter, see, *e.g., United States v. United States Gypsum Co.*, 438 U.S. 422, 440–441, 98 S.Ct. 2864, 2875–2876, 57 L.Ed.2d 854 (1978) ("the behavior proscribed by the [Sherman] Act is often difficult to distinguish from the gray zone of socially acceptable and economically justifiable business conduct").[2] The test adopted by the court below is difficult to apply in practice, though no abstractly formulated and unvarying "test" will necessarily enable courts to decide questions such as this with mathematical precision. But if the purpose of the attorney–client privilege is to be served, the attorney and client must be able to

---

[2] [fn 2] The Government argues that the risk of civil or criminal liability suffices to ensure that corporations will seek legal advice in the absence of the protection of the privilege. This response ignores the fact that the depth and quality of any investigations, to ensure compliance with the law would suffer, even were they undertaken. The response also proves too much, since it applies to all communications covered by the privilege: an individual trying to comply with the law or faced with a legal problem also has strong incentive to disclose information to his lawyer, yet the common law has recognized the value of the privilege in further facilitating communications.

predict with some degree of certainty whether particular discussions will be protected. An uncertain privilege, or one which purports to be certain but results in widely varying applications by the courts, is little better than no privilege at all. The very terms of the test adopted by the court below suggest the unpredictability of its application. The test restricts the availability of the privilege to those officers who play a "substantial role" in deciding and directing a corporation's legal response. Disparate decisions in cases applying this test illustrate its unpredictability. Compare, *e.g., Hogan v. Zletz*, 43 F.R.D. 308, 315–316 (ND Okl.1967), aff'd in part *sub nom. Natta v. Hogan*, 392 F.2d 686 (CA10 1968) (control group includes managers and assistant managers of patent division and research and development department), with *Congoleum Industries, Inc. v. GAF Corp.*, 49 F.R.D. 82, 83–85 (ED Pa.1969), aff'd, 478 F.2d 1398 (CA3 1973) (control group includes only division and corporate vice presidents, and not two directors of research and vice president for production and research).

The communications at issue were made by Upjohn employees[3] to counsel for Upjohn acting as such, at the direction of corporate superiors in order to secure legal advice from counsel. As the Magistrate found, "Mr. Thomas consulted with the Chairman of the Board and outside counsel and thereafter conducted a factual investigation to determine the nature and extent of the questionable payments *and to be in a position to give legal advice to the company with respect to the payments*." (Emphasis supplied.) 78–1 USTC ¶ 9277, pp. 83,598, 83,599. Information, not available from upper–echelon management, was needed to supply a basis for legal advice concerning compliance with securities and tax laws, foreign laws, currency regulations, duties to shareholders, and potential litigation in each of these areas.[4] The communications concerned matters within the scope of the employees' corporate duties, and the employees themselves were sufficiently aware that they were being questioned in order that the corporation could obtain legal advice. The questionnaire identified Thomas as "the company's General Counsel" and referred in its opening sentence to the possible illegality of payments such as the ones on which information was sought. App. 40a. A statement of policy accompanying the questionnaire clearly indicated the legal implications of the investigation. The policy statement was issued "in order that there be no uncertainty in the future as to the policy with respect to the practices which are the subject of this investigation." It began

---

[3] [fn 3] Seven of the eighty-six employees interviewed by counsel had terminated their employment with Upjohn at the time of the interview. App. 33a–38a. Petitioners argue that the privilege should nonetheless apply to communications by these former employees concerning activities during their period of employment. Neither the District Court nor the Court of Appeals had occasion to address this issue, and we decline to decide it without the benefit of treatment below.

[4] [fn 4] See id., at 26a–27a, 103a, 123a–124a. See also In re Grand Jury Investigation, 599 F.2d 1224, 1229 (CA3 1979); In re Grand Jury Subpoena, 599 F.2d 504, 511 (CA2 1979).

"Upjohn will comply with all laws and regulations," and stated that commissions or payments "will not be used as a subterfuge for bribes or illegal payments" and that all payments must be "proper and legal." Any future agreements with foreign distributors or agents were to be approved "by a company attorney" and any questions concerning the policy were to be referred "to the company's General Counsel." *Id.*, at 165a–166a. This statement was issued to Upjohn employees worldwide, so that even those interviewees not receiving a questionnaire were aware of the legal implications of the interviews. Pursuant to explicit instructions from the Chairman of the Board, the communications were considered "highly confidential" when made, *id.*, at 39a, 43a, and have been kept confidential by the company.[5] Consistent with the underlying purposes of the attorney–client privilege, these communications must be protected against compelled disclosure.

The Court of Appeals declined to extend the attorney–client privilege beyond the limits of the control group test for fear that doing so would entail severe burdens on discovery and create a broad "zone of silence" over corporate affairs. Application of the attorney–client privilege to communications such as those involved here, however, puts the adversary in no worse position than if the communications had never taken place. The privilege only protects disclosure of communications; it does not protect disclosure of the underlying facts by those who communicated with the attorney:

"[T]he protection of the privilege extends only to *communications* and not to facts. A fact is one thing and a communication concerning that fact is an entirely different thing. The client cannot be compelled to answer the question, 'What did you say or write to the attorney?' but may not refuse to disclose any relevant fact within his knowledge merely because he incorporated a statement of such fact into his communication to his attorney." *Philadelphia v. Westinghouse Electric Corp.*, 205 F.Supp. 830, 831 (q2.7).

See also *Diversified Industries*, 572 F.2d., at 611; *State ex rel. Dudek v. Circuit Court*, 34 Wis.2d 559, 580, 150 N.W.2d 387, 399 (1967) ("the courts have noted that a party cannot conceal a fact merely by revealing it to his lawyer"). Here the Government was free to question the employees who communicated with Thomas and outside counsel. Upjohn has provided the IRS with a list of such employees, and the IRS has already interviewed some 25 of them. While it would probably be more convenient for the Government to secure the results of petitioner's internal investigation by simply subpoenaing the questionnaires and notes taken by petitioner's attorneys, such considerations of convenience do not overcome the policies served by the attorney–client privilege. As Justice Jackson noted in his concurring opinion in *Hickman v. Taylor*, 329 U.S., at 516, 67 S.Ct., at 396: "Discovery was hardly intended to enable a learned profession to perform its functions . . . on wits borrowed from the adversary."

---

[5] [fn 5] See Magistrate's opinion, 78–1 USTC ¶ 9277, p. 83,599: "The responses to the questionnaires and the notes of the interviews have been treated as confidential material and have not been disclosed to anyone except Mr. Thomas and outside counsel."

Needless to say, we decide only the case before us, and do not undertake to draft a set of rules which should govern challenges to investigatory subpoenas. Any such approach would violate the spirit of Federal Rule of Evidence 501. See S.Rep. No. 93–1277, p. 13 (1974) ("the recognition of a privilege based on a confidential relationship . . . should be determined on a case–by–case basis"); *Trammel*, 445 U.S., at 47, 100 S.Ct., at 910–911; *United States v. Gillock*, 445 U.S. 360, 367, 100 S.Ct. 1185, 1190, 63 L.Ed.2d 454 (1980). While such a "case–by–case" basis may to some slight extent undermine desirable certainty in the boundaries of the attorney–client privilege, it obeys the spirit of the Rules. At the same time we conclude that the narrow "control group test" sanctioned by the Court of Appeals, in this case cannot, consistent with "the principles of the common law as . . . interpreted . . . in the light of reason and experience," Fed. Rule Evid. 501, govern the development of the law in this area.

III.

Our decision that the communications by Upjohn employees to counsel are covered by the attorney–client privilege disposes of the case so far as the responses to the questionnaires and any notes reflecting responses to interview questions are concerned. The summons reaches further, however, and Thomas has testified that his notes and memoranda of interviews go beyond recording responses to his questions. App. 27a–28a, 91a–93a. To the extent that the material subject to the summons is not protected by the attorney–client privilege as disclosing communications between an employee and counsel, we must reach the ruling by the Court of Appeals that the work–product doctrine does not apply to summonses issued under 26 U.S.C. § 7602.[6]

The Government concedes, wisely, that the Court of Appeals erred and that the work–product doctrine does apply to IRS summonses. Brief for Respondents 16, 48. This doctrine was announced by the Court over 30 years ago in *Hickman v. Taylor*, 329 U.S. 495, 67 S.Ct. 385, 91 L.Ed. 451 (1947). In that case the Court rejected "an attempt, without purported necessity or justification, to secure written statements, private memoranda and personal recollections prepared or formed by an adverse party's counsel in the course of his legal duties." *Id.*, at 510, 67 S.Ct., at 393. The Court noted that "it is essential that a lawyer work with a certain degree of privacy" and reasoned that if discovery of the material sought were permitted:

> much of what is now put down in writing would remain unwritten. An attorney's thoughts, heretofore inviolate, would not be his own. Inefficiency, unfairness and sharp practices would inevitably develop in the giving of legal advice and in the preparation of cases for trial. The effect on the legal profession would be demoralizing. And the interests of the clients and the cause of justice would be poorly served. *Id.*, at 511, 67 S.Ct., at 393–394.

---

[6] [fn 6] The following discussion will also be relevant to counsel's notes and memoranda of interviews with the seven former employees should it be determined that the attorney–client privilege does not apply to them. See n. 3, supra.

The "strong public policy" underlying the work–product doctrine was reaffirmed recently in *United States v. Nobles*, 422 U.S. 225, 236–240, 95 S.Ct. 2160, 2169–2171, 45 L.Ed.2d 141 (1975), and has been substantially incorporated in Federal Rule of Civil Procedure 26(b)(3).[7]

As we stated last Term, the obligation imposed by a tax summons remains "subject to the traditional privileges and limitations." *United States v. Euge*, 444 U.S. 707, 714, 100 S.Ct. 874, 879–880, 63 L.Ed.2d 741 (1980). Nothing in the language of the IRS summons provisions or their legislative history suggests an intent on the part of Congress to preclude application of the work–product doctrine. Rule 26(b)(3) codifies the work–product doctrine, and the Federal Rules of Civil Procedure are made applicable to summons enforcement proceedings by Rule 81(a)(3). See *Donaldson v. United States*, 400 U.S. 517, 528, 91 S.Ct. 534, 541, 27 L.Ed.2d 580 (1971). While conceding the applicability of the work–product doctrine, the Government asserts that it has made a sufficient showing of necessity to overcome its protections. The Magistrate apparently so found, 78–1 USTC ¶ 9277, p. 83,605. The Government relies on the following language in *Hickman*:

> We do not mean to say that all written materials obtained or prepared by an adversary's counsel with an eye toward litigation are necessarily free from discovery in all cases. Where relevant and nonprivileged facts remain hidden in an attorney's file and where production of those facts is essential to the preparation of one's case, discovery may properly be had. . . . And production might be justified where the witnesses are no longer available or can be reached only with difficulty. 329 U.S., at 511, 67 S.Ct., at 394.

The Government stresses that interviewees are scattered across the globe and that Upjohn has forbidden its employees to answer questions it considers irrelevant. The above–quoted language from *Hickman*, however, did not apply to "oral statements made by witnesses . . . whether presently in the form of [the attorney's] mental impressions or memoranda." *Id.*, at 512, 67 S.Ct., at 394. As to such material the Court did "not believe that any showing of necessity can be made under the circumstances of this case so as to justify production. . . . If there

---

[7] [fn 7] This provides, in pertinent part:

"[A] party may obtain discovery of documents and tangible things otherwise discoverable under subdivision (b)(1) of this rule and prepared in anticipation of litigation or for trial by or for another party or by or for that other party's representative (including his attorney, consultant, surety, indemnitor, insurer, or agent) only upon a showing that the party seeking discovery has substantial need of the materials in the preparation of his case and that he is unable without undue hardship to obtain the substantial equivalent of the materials by other means. In ordering discovery of such materials when the required showing has been made, the court shall protect against disclosure of the mental impressions, conclusions, opinions, or legal theories of an attorney or other representative of a party concerning the litigation."

should be a rare situation justifying production of these matters petitioner's case is not of that type." *Id.*, at 512–513, 67 S.Ct., at 394–395. See also *Nobles, supra*, 422 U.S., at 252–253, 95 S.Ct., at 2177 (WHITE, J., concurring). Forcing an attorney to disclose notes and memoranda of witnesses' oral statements is particularly disfavored because it tends to reveal the attorney's mental processes, 329 U.S., at 513, 67 S.Ct., at 394–395 ("what he saw fit to write down regarding witnesses' remarks"); *id*, at 516–517, 67 S.Ct., at 396 ("the statement would be his [the attorney's] language, permeated with his inferences") (Jackson, J., concurring).[8]

Rule 26 accords special protection to work product revealing the attorney's mental processes. The Rule permits disclosure of documents and tangible things constituting attorney work product upon a showing of substantial need and inability to obtain the equivalent without undue hardship. This was the standard applied by the Magistrate, 78–1 USTC ¶ 9277, p. 83,604. Rule 26 goes on, however, to state that "[i]n ordering discovery of such materials when the required showing has been made, the court shall protect against disclosure of the mental impressions, conclusions, opinions or legal theories of an attorney or other representative of a party concerning the litigation." Although this language does not specifically refer to memoranda based on oral statements of witnesses, the *Hickman* court stressed the danger that compelled disclosure of such memoranda would reveal the attorney's mental processes. It is clear that this is the sort of material the draftsmen of the Rule had in mind as deserving special protection. See Notes of Advisory Committee on 1970 Amendment to Rules, 28 U.S.C.App., p. 442 ("The subdivision . . . goes on to protect against disclosure the mental impressions, conclusions, opinions, or legal theories . . . of an attorney or other representative of a party. The *Hickman* opinion drew special attention to the need for protecting an attorney against discovery of memoranda prepared from recollection of oral interviews. The courts have steadfastly safeguarded against disclosure of lawyers' mental impressions and legal theories . . .").

Based on the foregoing, some courts have concluded that *no* showing of necessity can overcome protection of work product which is based on oral statements from witnesses. See, *e.g., In re Grand Jury Proceedings*, 473 F.2d 840, 848 (CA8 1973) (personal recollections, notes, and memoranda pertaining to conversation with witnesses); *In re Grand Jury Investigation*, 412 F.Supp. 943, 949 (ED Pa.1976) (notes of conversation with witness "are so much a product of the lawyer's thinking and so little probative of the witness's actual words that they are absolutely protected from disclosure"). Those courts declining to adopt an absolute rule have nonetheless recognized that such material is entitled to

---

[8] Thomas described his notes of the interviews as containing "what I considered to be the important questions, the substance of the responses to them, my beliefs as to the importance of these, my beliefs as to how they related to the inquiry, my thoughts as to how they related to other questions. In some instances they might even suggest other questions that I would have to ask or things that I needed to find elsewhere." 78–1 USTC ¶ 9277, p. 83,599.

special protection. See, *e.g., In re Grand Jury Investigation*, 599 F.2d 1224, 1231 (CA3 1979) ("special considerations . . . must shape any ruling on the discoverability of interview memoranda . . .; such documents will be discoverable only in a 'rare situation' "); Cf. *In re Grand Jury Subpoena*, 599 F.2d 504, 511–512 (CA2 1979).

We do not decide the issue at this time. It is clear that the Magistrate applied the wrong standard when he concluded that the Government had made a sufficient showing of necessity to overcome the protections of the work–product doctrine. The Magistrate applied the "substantial need" and "without undue hardship" standard articulated in the first part of Rule 26(b)(3). The notes and memoranda sought by the Government here, however, are work product based on oral statements. If they reveal communications, they are, in this case, protected by the attorney–client privilege. To the extent they do not reveal communications, they reveal the attorneys' mental processes in evaluating the communications. As Rule 26 and *Hickman* make clear, such work product cannot be disclosed simply on a showing of substantial need and inability to obtain the equivalent without undue hardship.

While we are not prepared at this juncture to say that such material is always protected by the work–product rule, we think a far stronger showing of necessity and unavailability by other means than was made by the Government or applied by the Magistrate in this case would be necessary to compel disclosure. Since the Court of Appeals thought that the work–product protection was never applicable in an enforcement proceeding such as this, and since the Magistrate whose recommendations the District Court adopted applied too lenient a standard of protection, we think the best procedure with respect to this aspect of the case would be to reverse the judgment of the Court of Appeals for the Sixth Circuit and remand the case to it for such further proceedings in connection with the work–product claim as are consistent with this opinion.

Accordingly, the judgment of the Court of Appeals is reversed, and the case remanded for further proceedings.

It is so ordered.

Chief Justice BURGER, concurring in part and concurring in the judgment.

I join in Parts I and III of the opinion of the Court and in the judgment. As to Part II, I agree fully with the Court's rejection of the so–called "control group" test, its reasons for doing so, and its ultimate holding that the communications at issue are privileged. As the Court states, however, "if the purpose of the attorney–client privilege is to be served, the attorney and client must be able to predict with some degree of certainty whether particular discussions will be protected." *Ante*, at 684. For this very reason, I believe that we should articulate a standard that will govern similar cases and afford guidance to corporations, counsel advising them, and federal courts.

The Court properly relies on a variety of factors in concluding that the communications now before us are privileged. See *ante*, at 685. Because of the great importance of the issue, in my view the Court should make clear now that, as a general rule, a communication is privileged at least when, as here, an employee or former employee speaks at the direction of the management with an attorney regarding conduct or proposed conduct within the scope of employment. The attorney must be one authorized by the management to inquire into the subject and must be seeking information to assist counsel in performing any of the following functions: (a) evaluating whether the employee's conduct has bound or would bind the corporation; (b) assessing the legal consequences, if any, of that conduct; or (c) formulating appropriate legal responses to actions that have been or may be taken by others with regard to that conduct. See, *e.g., Diversified Industries, Inc. v. Meredith*, 572 F.2d 596, 609 (CA8 1978) (en banc); *Harper & Row Publishers, Inc. v. Decker*, 423 F.2d 487, 491–492 (CA7 1970), aff'd by an equally divided Court, 400 U.S. 348, 91 S.Ct. 479, 27 L.Ed.2d 433 (1971); *Duplan Corp v. Deering Milliken, Inc.*, 397 F.Supp. 1146, 1163–1165 (DSC 1974). Other communications between employees and corporate counsel may indeed be privileged—as the petitioners and several *amici* have suggested in their proposed formulations—but the need for certainty does not compel us now to prescribe all the details of the privilege in this case.

Nevertheless, to say we should not reach all facets of the privilege does not mean that we should neglect our duty to provide guidance in a case that squarely presents the question in a traditional adversary context. Indeed, because Federal Rule of Evidence 501 provides that the law of privileges "shall be governed by the principles of the common law as they may be interpreted by the courts of the United States in the light of reason and experience," this Court has a special duty to clarify aspects of the law of privileges properly before us. Simply asserting that this failure "may to some slight extent undermine desirable certainty," *ante*, at 686, neither minimizes the consequences of continuing uncertainty and confusion nor harmonizes the inherent dissonance of acknowledging that uncertainty while declining to clarify it within the frame of issues presented.

NOTES AND QUESTIONS

1. Why does the Court dislike the lower court's control-group test?
2. How would corporate clients utilize the benefits the legal advice obtained if the control-group test had prevailed?

B. Work Product

Another important privilege is the work product privilege. It protects books and records created in anticipation of litigation from compelled disclosure. Rule 26(b)(3)(A) of the Federal Rules of Civil Procedure provides as follows:

> Ordinarily, a party may not discover documents and tangible things that are prepared in anticipation of litigation or for trial by or for another party or its representative . . . .

The rule overlaps with the work product protections provided in *Hickman v. Taylor*. Under both the Rules and *Hickman v. Taylor*, it is clear that the privilege's purpose is to permit a litigant to investigate and develop legal strategies for a client who might end up in litigation without being required to disclose his playbook to the opposing litigant. Accordingly, a taxpayer who is aware that the IRS has publicly taken a contrary view with respect to a transaction the taxpayer enters into ought to be able to draft a memorandum discussing his legal strategy regarding the transaction without the IRS obtaining access to the memorandum.

HICKMAN v. TAYLOR
329 U.S. 495 (1947)
Supreme Court of the United States

Mr. Justice MURPHY delivered the opinion of the Court.

This case presents an important problem under the Federal Rules of Civil Procedure, 28 U.S.C.A. following section 723c, as to the extent to which a party may inquire into oral and written statements of witnesses, or other information, secured by an adverse party's counsel in the course of preparation for possible litigation after a claim has arisen. Examination into a person's files and records, including those resulting from the professional activities of an attorney, must be judged with care. It is not without reason that various safeguards have been established to preclude unwarranted excursions into the privacy of a man's work. At the same time, public policy supports reasonable and necessary inquiries. Properly to balance these competing interests is a delicate and difficult task.

On February 7, 1943, the tug 'J. M. Taylor' sank while engaged in helping to tow a car float of the Baltimore & Ohio Railroad across the Delaware River at Philadelphia. The accident was apparently unusual in nature, the cause of it still being unknown. Five of the nine crew members were drowned. Three days later the tug owners and the underwriters employed a law firm, of which respondent Fortenbaugh is a member, to defend them against potential suits by representatives of the deceased crew members and to sue the railroad for damages to the tug.

A public hearing was held on March 4, 1943, before the United States Steamboat Inspectors, at which the four survivors were examined. This testimony was recorded and made available to all interested parties. Shortly thereafter, Fortenbaugh privately interviewed the survivors and took statements from them with an eye toward the anticipated litigation; the survivors signed these statements on March 29. Fortenbaugh also interviewed other persons believed to have some information relating to the accident and in some cases he made memoranda of what they told him. At the time when Fortenbaugh secured the statements of the survivors, representatives of two of the deceased crew members had been in communication with him. Ultimately claims were presented by representatives of all five of the deceased; four of the claims, however, were settled without litigation. The fifth claimant, petitioner herein, brought suit in a federal court under the Jones Act on November 26, 1943, naming as defendants the two tug owners, individually and as partners, and the railroad.

One year later, petitioner filed 39 interrogatories directed to the tug owners. The 38th interrogatory read: 'State whether any statements of the members of the crews of the Tugs "J. M. Taylor" and "Philadelphia" or of any other vessel were taken in connection with the towing of the car float and the sinking of the Tug "John M. Taylor".

Attach hereto exact copies of all such statements if in writing, and if oral, set forth in detail the exact provisions of any such oral statements or reports.'

Supplemental interrogatories asked whether any oral or written statements, records, reports or other memoranda had been made concerning any matter relative to the towing operation, the sinking of the tug, the salvaging and repair of the tug, and the death of the deceased. If the answer was in the affirmative, the tug owners were then requested to set forth the nature of all such records, reports, statements or other memoranda.

The tug owners, through Fortenbaugh, answered all of the interrogatories except No. 38 and the supplemental ones just described. While admitting that statements of the survivors had been taken, they declined to summarize or set forth the contents. They did so on the ground that such requests called 'for privileged matter obtained in preparation for litigation' and constituted 'an attempt to obtain indirectly counsel's private files.' It was claimed that answering these requests 'would involve practically turning over not only the complete files, but also the telephone records and, almost, the thoughts of counsel.'

In connection with the hearing on these objections, Fortenbaugh made a written statement and gave an informal oral deposition explaining the circumstances under which he had taken the statements. But he was not expressly asked in the deposition to produce the statements. The District Court for the Eastern District of Pennsylvania, sitting en banc, held that the requested matters were not privileged. 4 F.R.D. 479. The court then decreed that the tug owners and Fortenbaugh, as counsel and agent for the tug owners forthwith 'Answer Plaintiff's 38th interrogatory and supplemental interrogatories; produce all written statements of witnesses obtained by Mr. Fortenbaugh, as counsel and agent for Defendants; state in substance any fact concerning this case which Defendants learned through oral statements made by witnesses to Mr. Fortenbaugh whether or not included in his private memoranda and produce Mr. Fortenbaugh's memoranda containing statements of fact by witnesses or to submit these memoranda to the Court for determination of those portions which should be revealed to Plaintiff.' Upon their refusal, the court adjudged them in contempt and ordered them imprisoned until they complied.

The Third Circuit Court of Appeals, also sitting en banc, reversed the judgment of the District Court. 153 F.2d 212. It held that the information here sought was part of the 'work product of the lawyer' and hence privileged from discovery under the Federal Rules of Civil Procedure. The importance of the problem, which has engendered a great divergence of views among district courts,[9] led us to grant certiorari. 328 U.S. 876, 66 S.Ct. 1337.

The pre-trial deposition-discovery mechanism established by Rules 26 to 37 is one of the most significant innovations of the Federal Rules of Civil Procedure. Under the prior federal practice, the pre-trial functions of notice-giving issue-formulation and fact-revelation were performed primarily and inadequately by the pleadings.[10] Inquiry into the issues and the facts before trial was narrowly confined and was often cumbersome in method.[11] The new rules, however, restrict the pleadings to the task of general notice-giving and invest the deposition-discovery process with a vital role in the preparation for trial. The various instruments of discovery now serve (1) as a device, along with the pre-trial hearing under Rule 16, to narrow and clarify the basic issues between the parties, and (2) as a device for ascertaining the facts, or information as to the existence or whereabouts of facts, relative to those issues. Thus civil trials in the federal courts no longer need be carried on in the dark. The way is now clear, consistent with recognized privileges, for the parties to obtain the fullest possible knowledge of the issues and facts before trial.[12]

There is an initial question as to which of the deposition-discovery rules is involved in this case. Petitioner, in filing his interrogatories, thought that he was proceeding under Rule 33. That rule provides that a party may serve upon any adverse party written interrogatories to be answered by the party served.[13] The

---

[9] [fn 1] See cases collected by Advisory Committee on Rules for Civil Procedure in its Report of Proposed Amendments (June, 1946), pp. 40-47; 5 F.R.D. 433, 457-460. See also 2 Moore's Federal Practice (1945 Cum.Supp.), s 26.12, pp. 155-159; Holtzoff, 'Instruments of Discovery under Federal Rules of Civil Procedure,' 41 Mich.L.Rev. 205, 210-212; Pike and Willis, 'Federal Discovery in Operation,' 7 Univ. of Chicago L.Rev. 297, 301-307.

[10] [fn 2] 'The great weakness of pleading as a means for developing and presenting issues of fact for trial lay in its total lack of any means for testing the factual basis for the pleader's allegations and denials.' Sunderland, 'The Theory and Practice of Pre-Trial Procedure,' 36 Mich.L.Rev. 215, 216. See also Ragland, Discovery Before Trial (1932), ch. I.

[11] [fn 3] 2 Moore's Federal Proctice (1938), s 26.02, pp. 2445, 2455.

[12] [fn 4] Pike and Willis, 'The New Federal Deposition-Discovery Procedure,' 38 Col.L.Rev. 1179, 1436; Pike, 'The New Federal Deposition-Discovery Procedure and the Rules of Evidence,' 34 Ill.L.Rev. 1.

[13] [fn 5] Rule 33 reads: 'Any party may serve upon any adverse party written interrogatories to be answered by the party served or, if the party served is a public or private corporation or a partnership or association, by any officer thereof competent to testify in its behalf. The interrogatories shall be answered separately and fully in writing under oath. The answers shall be signed by the person making them; and the party upon whom the interrogatories have been served shall serve a copy of the answers on the party submitting the interrogatories within 15 days after the delivery of the interrogatories, unless the

District Court proceeded on the same assumption in its opinion, although its order to produce and its contempt order stated that both Rules 33 and 34 were involved. Rule 34 establishes a procedure whereby, upon motion of any party showing good cause therefor and upon notice to all other parties, the court may order any party to produce and permit the inspection and copying or photographing of any designated documents, etc., not privileged, which constitute or contain evidence material to any matter involved in the action and which are in his possession, custody or control.[14]

The Circuit Court of Appeals, however, felt that Rule 26 was the crucial one. Petitioner, it said, was proceeding by interrogatories and, in connection with those interrogatories, wanted copies of memoranda and statements secured from witnesses. While the court believed that Rule 33 was involved, at least as to the defending tug owners, it stated that this rule could not be used as the basis for condemning Fortenbaugh's failure to disclose or produce the memoranda and statements, since the rule applies only to interrogatories addressed to adverse parties, not to their agents or counsel. And Rule 34 was said to be inapplicable since petitioner was not trying to see an original document and to copy or photograph it, within the scope of that rule. The court then concluded that Rule 26 must be the one really involved. That provides that the testimony of any person, whether a party or not, may be taken by any party by deposition upon oral examination or written interrogatories for the purpose of discovery or for use as evidence; and that the deponent may be examined regarding any matter, not privileged, which is relevant to the subject matter involved in the pending action, whether relating to the claim or defense of the examining party or of any other

---

court, on motion and notice and for good cause shown, enlarges or shortens the time. Objections to any interrogatories may be presented to the court within 10 days after service thereof, with notice as in case of a motion; and answers shall be deferred until the objections are determined, which shall be at as early a time as is practicable. No party may, without leave of court, serve more than one set of interrogatories to be answered by the same party.'

[14] [fn 6] Rule 34 provides: 'Upon motion of any party showing good cause therefor and upon notice to all other parties, the court in which an action is pending may (1) order any party to produce and permit the inspection and copying or photographing, by or on behalf of the moving party, of any designated documents, papers, books, accounts, letters, photographs, objects, or tangible things, not privileged, which constitute or contain evidence material to any matter involved in the action and which are in his possession, custody, or control; or (2) order any party to permit entry upon designated land or other property in his possession or control for the purpose of inspecting, measuring, surveying, or photographing the property or any designated relevant object or operation thereon. The order shall specify the time, place, and manner of making the inspection and taking the copies and photographs and may prescribe such terms and conditions as are just.'

party, including the existence, description, nature, custody, condition and location of any books, documents or other tangible things.[15]

The matter is not without difficulty in light of the events that transpired below. We believe, however, that petitioner was proceeding primarily under Rule 33. He addressed simple interrogatories solely to the individual tug owners, the adverse parties, as contemplated by that rule. He did not, and could not under Rule 33, address such interrogatories to their counsel, Fortenbaugh. Nor did he direct these interrogatories either to the tug owners or to Fortenbaugh by way of deposition; Rule 26 thus could not come into operation. And it does not appear from the record that petitioner filed a motion under Rule 34 for a court order directing the producetion of the documents in question. Indeed, such an order could not have been entered as to Fortenbaugh since Rule 34, like Rule 33, is limited to parties to the proceeding, thereby excluding their counsel or agents.

Thus to the extent that petitioner was seeking the production of the memoranda and statements gathered by Fortenbaugh in the course of his activities as counsel, petitioner misconceived his remedy. Rule 33 did not permit him to obtain such memoranda and statements as dejuncts to the interrogatories addressed to the individual tug owners. A party clearly cannot refuse to answer interrogatories on the ground that the information sought is solely within the knowledge of his attorney. But that is not this case. Here production was sought of documents prepared by a party's attorney after the claim has arisen. Rule 33 does not make provision for such production, even when sought in connection with permissible interrogatories. Moreover, since petitioner was also foreclosed from securing them through an order under Rule 34, his only recourse was to take Fortenbaugh's deposition under Rule 26 and to attempt to force Fortenbaugh to produce the materials by use of a subpoena duces tecum in accordance with

---

[15] [fn 7] The relevant portions of Rule 26 provide as follows:

'(a) When Depositions May be Taken. By leave of court after jurisdiction has been obtained over any defendant or over property which is the subject of the action or without such leave after an answer has been served, the testimony of any person, whether a party or not, may be taken at the instance of any party by deposition upon oral examination or written interrogatories for the purpose of discovery or for use as evidence in the action or for both purposes. The attendance of witnesses may be compelled by the use of subpoena as provided in Rule 45. Depositions shall be taken only in accordance with these rules. The deposition of a person confined in prison may be taken only by leave of court on such terms as the court prescribes.

(b) Scope of Examination. Unless otherwise ordered by the court as provided by Rule 30(b) or (d), the deponent may be examined regarding any matter, not privileged, which is relevant to the subject matter involved in the pending action, whether relating to the claim or defense of the examining party or to the claim or defense of any other party, including the existence, description, nature, custody, condition and location of any books, documents, or other tangible things and the identity and location of persons having knowledge of relevant facts.'

Rule 45. Holtzoff, 'Instruments of Discovery under the Federal Rules of Civil Procedure,' 41 Mich.L.Rev. 205, 220. But despite petitioner's faulty choice of action, the District Court entered an order, apparently under Rule 34, commanding the tug owners and Fortenbaugh, as their agent and counsel, to produce the materials in question. Their refusal led to the anomalous result of holding the tug owners in contempt for failure to produce that which was in the possession of their counsel and of holding Fortenbaugh in contempt for failure to produce that which he could not be compelled to produce under either Rule 33 or Rule 34.

But under the circumstances we deem it unnecessary and unwise to rest our decision upon this procedural irregularity, an irregularity which is not strongly urged upon us and which was disregarded in the two courts below. It matters little at this later stage whether Fortenbaugh fails to answer interrogatories filed under Rule 26 or under Rule 33 or whether he refuses to produce the memoranda and statements pursuant to a subpoena under Rule 45 or a court order under Rule 34. The deposition-discovery rules create integrated procedural devices. And the basic question at stake is whether any of those devices may be used to inquire into materials collected by an adverse party's counsel in the course of preparation for possible litigation. The fact that the petitioner may have used the wrong method does not destroy the main thrust of his attempt. Nor does it relieve us of the responsibility of dealing with the problem raised by that attempt. It would be inconsistent with the liberal atmosphere surrounding these rules to insist that petitioner now go through the empty formality of pursuing the right procedural device only to reestablish precisely the same basic problem now confronting us. We do not mean to say, however, that there may not be situations in which the failure to proceed in accordance with a specific rule would be important or decisive. But in the present circumstances, for the purposes of this decision, the procedural irregularity is not material. Having noted the proper procedure, we may accordingly turn our attention to the substance of the underlying problem.

In urging that he has a right to inquire into the materials secured and prepared by Fortenbaugh, petitioner emphasizes that the deposition-discovery portions of the Federal Rules of Civil Procedure are designed to enable the parties to discover the true facts and to compel their disclosure wherever they may be found. It is said that inquiry may be made under these rules, epitomized by Rule 26, as to any relevant matter which is not privileged; and since the discovery provisions are to be applied as broadly and liberally as possible, the privilege limitation must be restricted to its narrowest bounds. On the premise that the attorney-client privilege is the one involved in this case, petitioner argues that it must be strictly confined to confidential communications made by a client to his attorney. And since the materials here in issue were secured by Fortenbaugh from third persons rather than from his clients, the tug owners, the conclusion is reached that these materials are proper subjects for discovery under Rule 26.

As additional support for this result, petitioner claims that to prohibit discovery under these circumstances would give a corporate defendant a tremendous advantage in a suit by an individual plaintiff. Thus in a suit by an injured employee against a railroad or in a suit by an insured person against an insurance company the corporate defendant could pull a dark veil of secrecy over all the pertinent facts it can collect after the claim arises merely on the assertion that such facts were gathered by its large staff of attorneys and claim agents. At the same time, the individual plaintiff, who often has direct knowledge of the matter in issue and has no counsel until some time after his claim arises could be compelled to disclose all the intimate details of his case. By endowing with immunity from disclosure all that a lawyer discovers in the course of his duties, it is said, the rights of individual litigants in such cases are drained of vitality and the lawsuit becomes more of a battle of deception than a search for truth.

But framing the problem in terms of assisting individual plaintiffs in their suits against corporate defendants is unsatisfactory. Discovery concededly may work to the disadvantage as well as to the advantage of individual plaintiffs. Discovery, in other words, is not a one-way proposition. It is available in all types of cases at the behest of any party, individual or corporate, plaintiff or defendant. The problem thus far transcends the situation confronting this petitioner. And we must view that problem in light of the limitless situations where the particular kind of discovery sought by petitioner might be used.

We agree, of course, that the deposition-discovery rules are to be accorded a broad and liberal treatment. No longer can the time-honored cry of 'fishing expedition' serve to preclude a party from inquiring into the facts underlying his opponent's case.[16] Mutual knowledge of all the relevant facts gathered by both parties is essential to proper litigation. To that end, either party may compel the other to disgorge whatever facts he has in his possession. The deposition-discovery procedure simply advances the stage at which the disclosure can be compelled from the time of trial to the period preceding it, thus reducing the possibility of surprise. But discovery, like all matters of procedure, has ultimate and necessary boundaries. As indicated by Rules 30(b) and (d) and 31(d), limitations inevitably arise when it can be shown that the examination is being conducted in bad faith or in such a manner as to annoy, embarrass or oppress the person subject to the inquiry. And as Rule 26(b) provides, further limitations come into existence when the inquiry touches upon the irrelevant or encroaches upon the recognized domains of privilege.

We also agree that the memoranda, statements and mental impressions in issue in this case fall outside the scope of the attorney-client privilege and hence are not protected from discovery on that basis. It is unnecessary here to delineate the content and scope of that privilege as recognized in the federal courts. For present purposes, it suffices to note that the protective cloak of this privilege does

---

[16] [fn 8] 'One of the chief arguments against the '"fishing expedition"' objection is the idea that discovery is mutual—that while a party may have to disclose his case, he can at the same time tie his opponent down to a definite position.' Pike and Willis, 'Federal Discovery in Operation,' 7 Univ. of Chicago L.Rev. 297, 303.

not extend to information which an attorney secures from a witness while acting for his client in anticipation of litigation. Nor does this privilege concern the memoranda, briefs, communications and other writings prepared by counsel for his own use in prosecuting his client's case; and it is equally unrelated to writings which reflect an attorney's mental impressions, conclusions, opinions or legal theories.

But the impropriety of invoking that privilege does not provide an answer to the problem before us. Petitioner has made more than an ordinary request for relevant, non-privileged facts in the possession of his adversaries or their counsel. He has sought discovery as of right of oral and written statements of witnesses whose identity is well known and whose availability to petitioner appears unimpaired. He has sought production of these matters after making the most searching inquiries of his opponents as to the circumstances surrounding the fatal accident, which inquiries were sworn to have been answered to the best of their information and belief. Interrogatories were directed toward all the events prior to, during and subsequent to the sinking of the tug. Full and honest answers to such broad inquiries would necessarily have included all pertinent information gleaned by Fortenbaugh through his interviews with the witnesses. Petitioner makes no suggestion, and we cannot assume, that the tug owners or Fortenbaugh were incomplete or dishonest in the framing of their answers. In addition, petitioner was free to examine the public testimony of the witnesses taken before the United States Steamboat Inspectors. We are thus dealing with an attempt to secure the production of written statements and mental impressions contained in the files and the mind of the attorney Fortenbaugh without any showing of necessity or any indication or claim that denial of such production would unduly prejudice the preparation of petitioner's case or cause him any hardship or injustice. For aught that appears, the essence of what petitioner seeks either has been revealed to him already through the interrogatories or is readily available to him direct from the witnesses for the asking.

The District Court, after hearing objections to petitioner's request, commanded Fortenbaugh to produce all written statements of witnesses and to state in substance any facts learned through oral statements of witnesses to him. Fortenbaugh was to submit any memoranda he had made of the oral statements so that the court might determine what portions should be revealed to petitioner. All of this was ordered without any showing by petitioner, or any requirement that he make a proper showing, of the necessity for the production of any of this material or any demonstration that denial of production would cause hardship or injustice. The court simply ordered production on the theory that the facts sought were material and were not privileged as constituting attorney-client communications.

In our opinion, neither Rule 26 nor any other rule dealing with discovery contemplates production under such circumstances. That is not because the subject matter is privileged or irrelevant, as those concepts are used in these rules.[17] Here is simply an attempt, without purported necessity or justification, to secure written statements, private memoranda and personal recollections prepared or formed by an adverse party's counsel in the course of his legal duties. As such, it falls outside the arena of discovery and contravenes the public policy underlying the orderly prosecution and defense of legal claims. Not even the most liberal of discovery theories can justify unwarranted inquiries into the files and the mental impressions of an attorney.

Historically, a lawyer is an officer of the court and is bound to work for the advancement of justice while faithfully protecting the rightful interests of his clients. In performing his various duties, however, it is essential that a lawyer work with a certain degree of privacy, free from unnecessary intrusion by opposing parties and their counsel. Proper preparation of a client's case demands that he assemble information, sift what he considers to be the relevant from the irrelevant facts, prepare his legal theories and plan his strategy without undue and needless interference. That is the historical and the necessary way in which lawyers act within the framework of our system of jurisprudence to promote justice and to protect their clients' interests. This work is reflected, of course, in interviews, statements, memoranda, correspondence, briefs, mental impressions, personal beliefs, and countless other tangible and intangible ways—aptly though roughly termed by the Circuit Court of Appeals in this case (153 F.2d 212, 223) as the 'Work product of the lawyer.' Were such materials open to opposing counsel on mere demand, much of what is now put down in writing would remain unwritten. An attorney's thoughts, heretofore inviolate, would not be his own. Inefficiency, unfairness and sharp practices would inevitably develop in the giving of legal advice and in the preparation of cases for trial. The effect on the

---

[17] [fn 9] The English courts have developed the concept of privilege to include all documents prepared by or for counsel with a view to litigation. 'All documents which are called into existence for the purpose—but not necessarily the sole purpose—of assisting the deponent or his legal advisers in any actual or anticipated litigation are privileged from production. * * * Thus all proofs, briefs, draft pleadings, etc., are privileged; but not counsel's indorsement on the outside of his brief * * *, nor any deposition or notes of evidence given publicly in open Court. * * * So are all papers prepared by any agent of the party bona fide for the use of his solicitor for the purposes of the action, whether in fact so used or not. * * * Reports by a company's servant, if made in the ordinary course of routine, are not privileged, even though it is desirable that the solicitor should have them and they are subsequently sent to him; but if the solicitor has requested that such documents shall always be prepared for his use and this was one of the reasons why they were prepared, they need not by disclosed.' Odgers on Pleading and Practice (12th ed., 1939), p. 264.

See Order 31, rule 1, of the Rules of the Supreme Court, 1883, set forth in The Annual Practice, 1945, p. 519, and the discussion following that rule. For a compilation of the English cases on the matter see 8 Wigmore on Evidence (3d ed., 1940), s 2319, pp. 618-622, notes.

legal profession would be demoralizing. And the interests of the clients and the cause of justice would be poorly served.

We do not mean to say that all written materials obtained or prepared by an adversary's counsel with an eye toward litigation are necessarily free from discovery in all cases. Where relevant and non-privileged facts remain hidden in an attorney's file and where production of those facts is essential to the preparation of one's case, discovery may properly be had. Such written statements and documents might, under certain circumstances, be admissible in evidence or give clues as to the existence or location of relevant facts. Or they might be useful for purposes of impeachment or corroboration. And production might be justified where the witnesses are no longer available or can be reached only with difficulty. Were production of written statements and documents to be precluded under such circumstances, the liberal ideals of the deposition-discovery portions of the Federal Rules of Civil Procedure would be stripped of much of their meaning. But the general policy against invading the privacy of an attorney's course of preparation is so well recognized and so essential to an orderly working of our system of legal procedure that a burden rests on the one who would invade that privacy to establish adequate reasons to justify production through a subpoena or court order. That burden, we believe, is necessarily implicit in the rules as now constituted.[18]

Rule 30(b), as presently written, gives the trial judge the requisite discretion to make a judgment as to whether discovery should be allowed as to written statements secured from witnesses. But in the instant case there was no room for that discretion to operate in favor of the petitioner. No attempt was made to establish any reason why Fortenbaugh should be forced to produce the written statements. There was only a naked, general demand for these materials as of right and a finding by the District Court that no recognizable privilege was involved. That was insufficient to justify discovery under these circumstances and the court should have sustained the refusal of the tug owners and Fortenbaugh to produce.

But as to oral statements made by witnesses to Fortenbaugh, whether presently in the form of his mental impressions or memoranda, we do not believe that any showing of necessity can be made under the circumstances of this case so as to justify production. Under ordinary conditions, forcing an attorney to repeat or write out all that witnesses have told him and to deliver the account to his adversary gives rise to grave dangers of inaccuracy and untrustworthiness. No legitimate purpose is served by such production. The practice forces the attorney to testify as to what he remembers or what he saw fit to write down regarding witnesses' remarks. Such testimony could not qualify as evidence; and to use it for impeachment or corroborative purposes would make the attorney much less

---

[18] [fn 10] Rule 34 is explicit in its requirements that a party show good cause before obtaining a court order directing another party to produce documents. See Report of Proposed Amendments by Advisory Committee on Rules for Civil Procedure (June, 1946); 5 F.R.D. 433.

an officer of the court and much more an ordinary witness. The standards of the profession would thereby suffer.

Denial of production of this nature does not mean that any material, non-privileged facts can be hidden from the petitioner in this case. He need not be unduly hindered in the preparation of his case, in the discovery of facts or in his anticipation of his opponents' position. Searching interrogatories directed to Fortenbaugh and the tug owners, production of written documents and statements upon a proper showing and direct interviews with the witnesses themselves all serve to reveal the facts in Fortenbaugh's possession to the fullest possible extent consistent with public policy. Petitioner's counsel frankly admits that he wants the oral statements only to help prepare himself to examine witnesses and to make sure that he has overlooked nothing. That is insufficient under the circumstances to permit him an exception to the policy underlying the privacy of Fortenbaugh's professional activities. If there should be a rare situation justifying production of these matters, petitioner's case is not of that type.

We fully appreciate the wide-spread controversy among the members of the legal profession over the problem raised by this case.[19] It is a problem that rests on what has been one of the most hazy frontiers of the discovery process. But until some rule or statute definitely prescribes otherwise, we are not justified in permitting discovery in a situation of this nature as a matter of unqualified right. When Rule 26 and the other discovery rules were adopted, this Court and the members of the bar in general certainly did not believe or contemplate that all the files and mental processes of lawyers were thereby opened to the free scrutiny of their adversaries. And we refuse to interpret the rules at this time so as to reach so harsh and unwarranted a result.

We therefore affirm the judgment of the Circuit Court of Appeals.

Affirmed.

Mr. Justice JACKSON, concurring.

The narrow question in this case concerns only one of thirty-nine interrogatories which defendants and their counsel refused to answer. As there was persistence in refusal after the court ordered them to answer it, counsel and clients were committed to jail by the district court until they should purge themselves of contempt.

The interrogatory asked whether statements were taken from the crews of the tugs involved in the accident, or of any other vessel, and demanded 'Attach hereto exact copies of all such statements if in writing, and if oral, set forth in detail the exact provisions of any such oral statements or reports.' The question is

---

[19] [fn 11] See Report of Proposed Amendments by Advisory Committee on Rules for Civil Procedure (June, 1946), pp. 44-47; 5 F.R.D. 433, 459, 460; Discovery Procedure Symposium before the 1946 Conference of the Third United States Circuit Court of Appeals, 5 F.R.D. 403; Armstrong, 'Report of the Advisory Committee on Federal Rules of Civil Procedure Recommending Amendments,' 5 F.R.D. 339, 353-357.

simply whether such a demand is authorized by the rules relating to various aspects of 'discovery'.

The primary effect of the practice advocated here would be on the legal profession itself. But it too often is overlooked that the lawyer and the law office are indispensable parts of our administration of justice. Law-abiding people can go nowhere else to learn the ever changing and constantly multiplying rules by which they must behave and to obtain redress for their wrongs. The welfare and tone of the legal profession is therefore of prime consequence to society, which would feel the consequences of such a practice as petitioner urges secondarily but certainly.

'Discovery' is one of the working tools of the legal profession. It traces back to the equity bill of discovery in English Chancery practice and seems to have had a forerunner in Continental practice. See Ragland, Discovery Before Trial (1932) 13-16. Since 1848 when the draftsmen of New York's Code of Procedure recognized the importance of a better system of discovery, the impetus to extend and expand discovery, as well as the opposition to it, has come from within the Bar itself. It happens in this case that it is the plaintiff's attorney who demands such unprecedented latitude of discovery and, strangely enough, amicus briefs in his support have been filed by several labor unions representing plaintiffs as a class. It is the history of the movement for broader discovery, however, that in actual experience the chief opposition to its extension has come from lawyers who specialize in representing plaintiffs because defendants have made liberal use of it to force plaintiffs to disclose their cases in advance. See Report of the Commission on the Administration of Justice in New York State (1934) 330, 331; Ragland, Discovery Before Trial (1932) 35, 36. Discovery is a two-edged sword and we cannot decide this problem on any doctrine of extending help to one class of litigants.

It seems clear and long has been recognized that discovery should provide a party access to anything that is evidence in his case. Cf. Report of Commission on the Administration of Justice in New York State (1934) 41, 42. It seems equally clear that discovery should not nullify the privilege of confidential communication between attorney and client. But those principles give us no real assistance here because what is being sought is neither evidence nor is it a privileged communication between attorney and client.

To consider first the most extreme aspect of the requirement in litigation here, we find it calls upon counsel, if he has had any conversations with any of the crews of the vessels in question or of any other, to 'set forth in detail the exact provision of any such oral statements or reports.' Thus the demand is not for the production of a transcript in existence but calls for the creation of a written statement not in being. But the statement by counsel of what a witness told him is not evidence when written plaintiff could not introduce it to prove his case. What, then, is the purpose sought to be served by demanding this of adverse counsel?

Counsel for the petitioner candidly said on argument that he wanted this information to help prepare himself to examine witnesses, to make sure he overlooked nothing. He bases his claim to it in his brief on the view that the

Rules were to do away with the old situation where a law suit developed into 'a battle of wits between counsel.' But a common law trial is and always should be an adversary proceeding. Discovery was hardly intended to enable a learned profession to perform its functions either without wits or on wits borrowed from the adversary.

The real purpose and the probable effect of the practice ordered by the district court would be to put trials on a level even lower than a 'battle of wits.' I can conceive of no practice more demoralizing to the Bar than to require a lawyer to write out and deliver to his adversary an account of what witnesses have told him. Even if his recollection were perfect, the statement would be his language permeated with his inferences. Every one who has tried it knows that it is almost impossible so fairly to record the expressions and emphasis of a witness that when he testifies in the environment of the court and under the influence of the leading question there will not be departures in some respects. Whenever the testimony of the witness would differ from the 'exact' statement the lawyer had delivered, the lawyer's statement would be whipped out to impeach the witness. Counsel producing his adversary's 'inexact' statement could lose nothing by saying, 'Here is a contradiction, gentlemen of the jury. I do not know whether it is my adversary or his witness who is not telling the truth, but one is not.' Of course, if this practice were adopted, that scene would be repeated over and over again. The lawyer who delivers such statements often would find himself branded a deceiver afraid to take the stand to support his own version of the witness's conversation with him, or else he will have to go on the stand to defend his own credibility—perhaps against that of his chief witness, or possibly even his client.

Every lawyer dislikes to take the witness stand and will do so only for grave reasons. This is partly because it is not his role; he is almost invariably a poor witness. But he steps out of professional character to do it. He regrets it; the profession discourages it. But the practice advocated here is one which would force him to be a witness, not as to what he has seen or done but as to other witnesses' stories, and not because he wants to do so but in self-defense.

And what is the lawyer to do who has interviewed one whom he believes to be a biased, lying or hostile witness to get his unfavorable statements and know what to meet? He must record and deliver such statements even though he would not vouch for the credibility of the witness by calling him. Perhaps the other side would not want to call him either, but the attorney is open to the charge of suppressing evidence at the trial if he fails to call such a hostile witness even though he never regarded him as reliable or truthful.

Having been supplied the names of the witnesses, petitioner's lawyer gives no reason why he cannot interview them himself. If an employee-witness refuses to tell his story, he, too, may be examined under the Rules. He may be compelled on discovery as fully as on the trial to disclose his version of the facts. But that is his own disclosure—it can be used to impeach him if he contradicts it and such a deposition is not useful to promote an unseemly disagreement between the witness and the counsel in the case.

It is true that the literal language of the Rules would admit of an interpretation that would sustain the district court's order. So the literal language of the Act of Congress which makes 'Any writing or record * * * made as a memorandum or record of any * * * occurrence, or event,' 28 U.S.C.A. § 695, admissible as evidence, would have allowed the railroad company to put its engineer's accident statements in evidence. Cf. Palmer v. Hoffman, 318 U.S. 109, 111, 63 S.Ct. 477, 479, 87 L.Ed. 645, 144 A.L.R. 719. But all such procedural measures have a background of custom and practice which was assumed by those who wrote and should be by those who apply them. We reviewed the background of the Act and the consequences on the trial of negligence cases of allowing railroads and others to put in their statements and thus to shield the crew from cross-examination. We said, 'Such a major change which opens wide the door to avoidance of cross-examination should not be left to implication.' 318 U.S. at page 114, 63 S.Ct. at page 481. We pointed out that there, as here, the 'several hundred years of history behind the Act * * * indicate the nature of the reforms which it was designed to effect.' 318 U.S. at page 115, 63 S.Ct. at page 481. We refused to apply it beyond that point. We should follow the same course of reasoning here. Certainly nothing in the tradition or practice of discovery up to the time of these Rules would have suggested that they would authorize such a practice as here proposed.

The question remains as to signed statements or those written by witnesses. Such statements are not evidence for the defendant. Palmer v. Hoffman, 318 U.S. 109, 63 S.Ct. 477. Nor should I think they ordinarily could be evidence for the plaintiff. But such a statement might be useful for impeachment of the witness who signed it, if he is called and if he departs from the statement. There might be circumstances, too, where impossibility or difficulty of access to the witness or his refusal to respond to requests for information or other facts would show that the interests of justice require that such statements be made available. Production of such statements are governed by Rule 34 and on 'Showing good cause therefor' the court may order their inspection, copying or photographing. No such application has here been made; the demand is made on the basis of right, not on showing of cause.

I agree to the affirmance of the judgment of the Circuit Court of Appeals which reversed the district court.

Mr. Justice FRANKFURTER joins in this opinion.

NOTES AND QUESTIONS

1. Does work product protection limit the search for the truth?
2. When will the court permit disclosure of work product materials?
3. Does the IRS sometimes seek documents that constitute work product, and, if so, why?

There are some limitations to claiming the work product privilege. One limitation is that the privilege can be waived where the litigant discloses the document in question to an adversary voluntarily. Unlike the attorney-client privilege, absolute confidentiality is not necessary. A claimant may disclose the documents to anyone who is not an adversary without waiving the protection. Assume a company is preparing multiple antitrust cases against other companies and the Federal Trade Commission. A waiver could occur in this situation if the company reveals a work product protected document to one of the opposing companies in the lawsuit. This issue arises in the tax context when a corporate taxpayer discloses documents to an auditor.

UNITED STATES v. DELOITTE LLP
610 F.3d 129 (2010)
United States Court of Appeals, District of Columbia Circuit

SENTELLE, Chief Judge:

The United States appeals from a district court order denying its motion to compel Dow Chemical Company's independent auditor, Deloitte & Touche USA, LLP,[20] to produce three documents in connection with ongoing tax litigation between Dow and the government. The district court ruled that all three documents were protected from discovery under the work-product doctrine. On appeal, the government contends that one of the documents is not work product because it was prepared by Deloitte during the audit process. In addition, while it concedes that the other two documents are work product, it argues that Dow waived work-product protection when it disclosed them to Deloitte. We vacate the district court's decision that the document prepared by Deloitte is work product and remand for in camera review to determine whether it is entirely work product. With respect to the other two documents, we affirm the district court's decision that Dow did not waive work-product protection when it disclosed them to Deloitte.

I. BACKGROUND

This discovery dispute arises from ongoing tax litigation in the U.S. District Court for the Middle District of Louisiana. The litigation concerns the tax treatment of two partnerships owned by Dow Chemical Company and two of its wholly-owned subsidiaries. The first of these partnerships was Chemtech Royalty Associates, L.P. (Chemtech I); it was succeeded by Chemtech II, L.P. (Chemtech II). In 2005, Dow filed a civil suit challenging IRS adjustments to partnership returns filed by Chemtech I and Chemtech II. *Chemtech Royalty Assocs., L.P. v. United States*, No. 05–944 (M.D. La. filed July 13, 2005). During discovery, the government subpoenaed documents from Dow's independent auditor, Deloitte & Touche USA, LLP. Since the subpoena sought production in Washington, D.C., it issued from the U.S. District Court for the District of Columbia. Deloitte produced a number of documents, but refused to produce three documents Dow identified as attorney work product. In response, the government filed a motion to compel production.

---

[20] [fn 1] Deloitte & Touche USA, LLP is now known as Deloitte LLP.

The three disputed documents are described in Dow's privilege log and in a declaration by William Curry, Dow's Director of Taxes. The first document is a 1993 draft memorandum prepared by Deloitte that summarizes a meeting between Dow employees, Dow's outside counsel, and Deloitte employees about the possibility of litigation over the Chemtech I partnership, and the necessity of accounting for such a possibility in an ongoing audit. This meeting took place after Dow informed Deloitte about the likelihood of litigation over the Chemtech I transaction. The second is a 1998 memorandum and flow chart prepared by two Dow employees—an accountant and an in-house attorney. The third is a 2005 tax opinion prepared by Dow's outside counsel. Curry's declaration explains that the second and third documents were disclosed to Deloitte so that it could "review the adequacy of Dow's contingency reserves for the Chemtech transactions." According to Curry, Deloitte "compelled Dow's production of these documents by informing the company that access to these documents was required in order to provide Dow with an unqualified audit opinion for its public financial statements." The privilege log describes the subject matter of these documents as "[t]ax issues related to the Chemtech partnership" and states that each one is a "[d]ocument prepared in anticipation of litigation." We will refer to the first document, which was prepared by Deloitte, as the "Deloitte Memorandum," and the second and third documents, which were created by Dow, as the "Dow Documents."

The district court denied the government's motion to compel without reviewing the disputed documents in camera. United States v. Deloitte & Touche USA LLP, 623 F.Supp.2d 39, 40–41 (D.D.C.2009). It concluded that the Deloitte Memorandum was work product because it was "prepared because of the prospect of litigation with the IRS over the tax treatment of Chemtech." Id. at 40 n. 1. The court further concluded that, although the document was created by Deloitte, it was nonetheless Dow's work product because "its contents record the thoughts of Dow's counsel regarding the prospect of litigation." Id. In addition, the court rejected the government's contention that Dow had waived work-product protection for the three documents. The court acknowledged that disclosing work product to a third party can waive protection if that disclosure is "inconsistent with the maintenance of secrecy from the disclosing party's adversary," id. at 41 (quoting Rockwell Int'l Corp. v. U.S. Dep't of Justice, 235 F.3d 598, 605 (D.C.Cir.2001)), but concluded that Dow's disclosure to Deloitte was not inconsistent with maintaining secrecy because (1) Deloitte was not a potential adversary and (2) nothing suggested that it was unreasonable for Dow to expect Deloitte to maintain confidentiality, id. The government appeals this ruling, and Dow has intervened to assert work-product protection. Since the government's motion to compel was the sole issue before the district court, its disposition of that motion was an appealable final judgment. In re Multi–Piece Rim Prods. Liab. Litig., 653 F.2d 671, 676 (D.C.Cir.1981).

II. ANALYSIS

The government contends that the Deloitte Memorandum is not attorney work product. Alternatively, it argues that even if the Deloitte Memorandum is work product, Dow waived work-product protection when it orally disclosed the information recorded therein to Deloitte. Turning to the Dow Documents, the government concedes they are attorney work product, but argues that Dow waived work-product protection when it gave them to Deloitte. We generally review the district court's discovery orders for abuse of discretion. *United States v. Williams Cos.*, 562 F.3d 387, 396 (D.C.Cir.2009). If the district court applied an incorrect legal standard, however, we review *de novo. In re Sealed Case,* 146 F.3d 881, 883–84 (D.C.Cir.1998).

A. The Work-Product Doctrine

The Supreme Court established the work-product doctrine in Hickman v. Taylor, 329 U.S. 495, 67 S.Ct. 385, 91 L.Ed. 451 (1947), which held that an attorney's notes recording his interviews with witnesses to the litigation-prompting incident were protected from discovery. Id. at 509–10, 67 S.Ct. 385. The Court recognized that to prepare for litigation, an attorney must "assemble information, sift what he considers to be the relevant from the irrelevant facts, prepare his legal theories and plan his strategy without undue and needless interference." Id. at 511, 67 S.Ct. 385. This preparation "is reflected . . . in interviews, statements, memoranda, correspondence, briefs, mental impressions, personal beliefs, and countless other tangible and intangible ways." Id. The Court reasoned that giving opposing counsel access to such work product would cause significant problems:

> [M]uch of what is now put down in writing would remain unwritten. An attorney's thoughts, heretofore inviolate, would not be his own. Inefficiency, unfairness and sharp practices would inevitably develop in the giving of legal advice and in the preparation of cases for trial. The effect on the legal profession would be demoralizing. And the interests of the clients and the cause of justice would be poorly served.

Id. Consequently, the Court concluded that attorney work product is protected from discovery unless "the one who would invade that privacy" carries the burden of "establish[ing] adequate reasons to justify production through a subpoena or court order." Id. at 512, 67 S.Ct. 385.

The work-product doctrine announced in *Hickman* was subsequently partially codified in Federal Rule of Civil Procedure 26(b)(3), which states:

> (A) *Documents and Tangible Things.* Ordinarily, a party may not discover documents and tangible things that are prepared in anticipation of litigation or for trial by or for another party or its representative (including the other party's attorney, consultant, surety, indemnitor, insurer, or agent).

FED.R.CIV.P. 26(b)(3)(A). Rule 26(b)(3) allows a court to order disclosure when the requesting party can show a "substantial need" for the material and an inability to procure equivalent information "without undue hardship." FED.R.CIV.P. 26(b)(3)(A)(ii). When a court orders disclosure under this exception, however, it must still "protect against disclosure of the mental impressions, conclusions, opinions, or legal theories of a party's attorney or other representative concerning the litigation." FED.R.CIV.P. 26(b)(3)(B). This type of work product, which is often described as opinion work product, "is virtually undiscoverable." *Dir., Office of Thrift Supervision v. Vinson & Elkins, LLP,* 124 F.3d 1304, 1307 (D.C.Cir.1997).

B. The Deloitte Memorandum

The government makes two categorical arguments that the Deloitte Memorandum cannot be work product. First, it argues that the Deloitte Memorandum cannot be work product because it was created by Deloitte, not Dow or its representative. Second, it argues that the Deloitte Memorandum cannot be work product because it was generated as part of the routine audit process, not in anticipation of litigation. If either argument is correct, the Deloitte Memorandum cannot be work product, regardless of its contents. We reject both arguments, but nevertheless conclude that the district court lacked sufficient information to determine that the entire Deloitte Memorandum is work product.

1.

The government first contends that Dow cannot claim work-product protection for the Deloitte Memorandum because it was prepared by Deloitte. Rule 26(b)(3) only protects "documents and tangible things that are prepared . . . by or for another party or its representative." FED.R.CIV.P. 26(b)(3)(A). Given this language, the government argues that the Deloitte Memorandum is not work product because Deloitte is not Dow's representative. It relies principally on *United States v. Arthur Young & Co.,* 465 U.S. 805, 104 S.Ct. 1495, 79 L.Ed.2d 826 (1984), in which the Supreme Court refused to recognize an accountant work-product privilege. In *Arthur Young,* the Court contrasted the role of an attorney with that of an accountant, explaining that an attorney is "a loyal representative whose duty it is to present the client's case in the most favorable possible light," whereas an independent certified public accountant has a "*public responsibility*" and "owes ultimate allegiance to the corporation's creditors and stockholders, as well as to the investing public." *Id.* at 817–18, 104 S.Ct. 1495. In the government's view, *Arthur Young* demonstrates that Deloitte cannot be Dow's representative, which in turn means that the Deloitte Memorandum cannot be work product under the plain language of Rule 26(b)(3). Dow counters that the "representative" for purposes of Rule 26(b)(3) is its counsel, whose thoughts and opinions are recorded in the document. In addition, it argues that the Deloitte Memorandum is work product because it contains the same type of opinion work product that is found in the Dow Documents, which the government concedes are work product.

Even if the government is correct in asserting that the Deloitte Memorandum falls outside the definition given by Rule 26(b)(3), this does not conclusively establish that it is not work product. The government mistakenly assumes that Rule 26(b)(3) provides an exhaustive definition of what constitutes work product. On the contrary, Rule 26(b)(3) only partially codifies the work-product doctrine announced in *Hickman.* Rule 26(b)(3) addresses only "documents and tangible things," but *Hickman*'s definition of work product extends to "intangible" things. 329 U.S. at 511, 67 S.Ct. 385. Moreover, in *Hickman,* the Court explained that the attorney's "mental impressions" were protected from discovery, so that he could not be forced to "repeat or write out" that information in discovery. *Id.* at 512–13, 67 S.Ct. 385. Thus *Hickman* provides work-product protection for intangible work product independent of Rule 26(b)(3). *Accord In re Seagate Tech., LLC,* 497 F.3d 1360, 1376 (Fed.Cir.2007); *In re Cendant Corp. Sec. Litig.,* 343 F.3d 658, 662 (3d Cir.2003); *United States v. 266 Tonawanda Trail,* 95 F.3d 422, 428 n. 10 (6th Cir.1996).

The government focuses on Deloitte's role in creating the document and on its relationship to Dow. Under Hickman, however, the question is not who created the document or how they are related to the party asserting work-product protection, but whether the document contains work product—the thoughts and opinions of counsel developed in anticipation of litigation. The district court found that the memorandum records those thoughts, even though Deloitte and not Dow or its attorney committed them to paper. The work product privilege does not depend on whether the thoughts and opinions were communicated orally or in writing, but on whether they were prepared in anticipation of litigation. Thus Deloitte's preparation of the document does not exclude the possibility that it contains Dow's work product.

2.

The government next contends that the Deloitte Memorandum cannot be work product because it was generated during an annual audit, not prepared in anticipation of litigation. The courts are not unanimous on the proper test for determining whether a document was prepared "in anticipation of litigation." Under the test adopted by most circuits, the question is whether the document was created "because of" the anticipated litigation. *See, e.g., Sandra T.E. v. S. Berwyn Sch. Dist. 100,* 600 F.3d 612, 622 (7th Cir.2010); *In re Prof'ls Direct Ins. Co.,* 578 F.3d 432, 439 (6th Cir.2009); *In re Grand Jury Subpoena,* 357 F.3d 900, 907 (9th Cir.2004); *PepsiCo, Inc. v. Baird, Kurtz & Dobson LLP,* 305 F.3d 813, 817 (8th Cir.2002); *Maine v. U.S. Dep't of the Interior,* 298 F.3d 60, 68 (1st Cir.2002); *Montgomery County v. Microvote Corp.,* 175 F.3d 296, 305 (3d Cir.1999); *United States v. Adlman,* 134 F.3d 1194, 1195 (2d Cir.1998); *Nat'l Union Fire Ins. Co. v. Murray Sheet Metal Co.,* 967 F.2d 980, 984 (4th Cir.1992). The Fifth Circuit, however, requires that anticipation of litigation be the "primary motivating purpose" behind the document's creation. *United States v. El Paso Co.,* 682 F.2d 530, 542 (5th Cir.1982).

Like most circuits, we apply the "because of" test, asking "whether, in light of the nature of the document and the factual situation in the particular case, the document can fairly be said to have been prepared or obtained because of the prospect of litigation." *In re Sealed Case,* 146 F.3d at 884 (quotation omitted). In addition, while this standard addresses a "document," it applies equally to work product in other forms. Thus for the Deloitte Memorandum, the question is whether it records information prepared by Dow or its representatives because of the prospect of litigation.

In the government's view, the Deloitte Memorandum was prepared not "because of the prospect of litigation," but as part of the routine audit process.

The government asserts that a document's *function*, not its *content*, determines whether it is work product. For this proposition the government relies on *Delaney, Migdail & Young, Chartered v. IRS*, 826 F.2d 124 (D.C.Cir.1987). In *Delaney*, a law firm sought to obtain under the Freedom of Information Act memoranda and supporting documents relating to the government's legal analysis of an Internal Revenue Service program concerning the use of statistical sampling in auditing large accounts. In that case it was the IRS that asserted work-product protection. The court held that the documents were work product because they "advise[d] the agency of the types of legal challenges likely to be mounted against a proposed program, potential defenses available to the agency, and the likely outcome." *Id.* at 127. In its reasoning, the court noted that a previous work-product decision had identified "the function of the documents as the critical issue." *Id.* at 127 (citing *Coastal States Gas Corp. v. Dep't of Energy*, 617 F.2d 854, 858 (D.C.Cir.1980)). The government seizes on this language, arguing that the Deloitte Memorandum is not work product because its function was to facilitate Deloitte's audit, not to prepare Dow for litigation.

We think the government misreads *Delaney*. While *Delaney* used the term "function," it was not considering any distinction between function and content in determining whether a document constituted work product. On the contrary, the court evaluated the function of the IRS documents at issue by examining their contents. It contrasted the documents at issue in the *Coastal States* case, which were like "an agency manual, fleshing out the meaning of the statute it was authorized to enforce," with the documents at issue in *Delaney*, which were memoranda describing potential legal challenges, possible defenses, and likely outcomes. Id. *Delaney* does not support the proposition that we should look solely to a document's function divorced from its contents in determining its status as work product.

The government also relies on two decisions holding that a corporation's tax accrual workpapers were not prepared in anticipation of litigation. In *El Paso*, the Fifth Circuit applied the "primary motivating purpose" standard and concluded that El Paso's tax accrual workpapers were not work product because the company's primary motivation in creating them was "to bring its financial books into conformity with generally accepted auditing principles" as required by federal securities laws. 682 F.2d at 543. The court reasoned that the "primary motivating force . . . [was] not to ready El Paso for litigation over its tax returns," but "to anticipate, for financial reporting purposes, what the impact of litigation might be on the company's tax liability." *Id.*

In United States v. Textron Inc., 577 F.3d 21 (1st Cir.2009) (en banc), the First Circuit likewise held that a corporation's tax accrual workpapers were not prepared in anticipation of litigation. Applying the "because of" test, the court concluded that the workpapers were "tax documents and not case preparation materials" that were "prepared in the ordinary course of business" and that their only purpose was "to support a financial statement and the independent audit of it." Id. at 28, 30. It found no evidence that the workpapers were prepared for "potential use in litigation" or that they "would in fact serve any useful purpose for Textron in conducting litigation if it arose." Id. at 30.

The government argues that *El Paso* and *Textron* demonstrate that when a document is created as part of an independent audit, as the Deloitte Memorandum was, its sole function is to facilitate that audit, which means it was not prepared in anticipation of litigation. Neither case convinces us. *El Paso* was decided under the "primary motivating purpose" test, which is more demanding than the "because of" test we employ. Under the more lenient "because of" test, material generated in anticipation of litigation may also be used for ordinary business purposes without losing its protected status. For example, in *Adlman*, the Second Circuit considered whether a document containing legal analysis about possible future litigation qualified as work product when it was procured to assist the parties in deciding whether to go through with a proposed merger. The court held that

> a document created because of anticipated litigation, which tends to reveal mental impressions, conclusions, opinions or theories concerning the litigation, does not lose work-product protection merely because it is intended to assist in the making of a business decision influenced by the likely outcome of the anticipated litigation. Where a document was created because of anticipated litigation, and would not have been prepared in substantially similar form but for the prospect of that litigation, it falls within Rule 26(b)(3).

134 F.3d at 1195. Under this same reasoning, material developed in anticipation of litigation can be incorporated into a document produced during an audit without ceasing to be work product. *Textron*, which did apply the "because of" standard, is distinguishable because it turned on the court's examination of the particular documents at issue. While the court concluded that those documents were not work product, it did not exclude the possibility that other documents prepared during the audit process might warrant work-product protection. Moreover, Judge Torruella's dissenting opinion in *Textron* makes a strong argument that while the court said it was applying the "because of" test, it actually asked whether the documents were "prepared for use in possible litigation," a much more exacting standard. 577 F.3d at 32.

In short, a document can contain protected work-product material even though it serves multiple purposes, so long as the protected material was prepared because of the prospect of litigation.

3.

Rejecting the government's categorical arguments establishes only that the Deloitte Memorandum may be protected work product under the law; we must now determine whether it is. On examination of the record, we conclude that the district court did not have a sufficient evidentiary foundation for its holding that the memorandum was purely work product. According to the record, the document was created during Deloitte's preparation of an audit report which in Deloitte's view required consideration of potential litigation. The meeting generating the document included both Deloitte and Dow employees, as well as Dow's outside counsel. The document itself was prepared by a third party. While none of this negates the possibility of work-product privilege, it could make it likely that the document includes other information that is not work product. According to Dow's privilege log and the Curry declaration, the memorandum does contain thoughts and analyses by legal counsel, but this does not rule out or even render unlikely the possibility that it also includes other facts, other thoughts, other analyses by non-attorneys which may not be so intertwined with the legal analysis as to warrant protection under the work-product doctrine. We will therefore remand this question to the district court for the purpose of independently assessing whether the document was entirely work product, or whether a partial or redacted version of the document could have been disclosed. Accordingly, we vacate the district court's decision that the Deloitte Memorandum was work product and remand so that the district court can examine the document *in camera* to determine whether it is entirely work product. *See In re Sealed Case,* 146 F.3d at 886–88 (remanding for *in camera* review to determine whether documents were prepared in anticipation of litigation); *In re Sealed Case,* 29 F.3d 715, 718 (D.C.Cir.1994) (same).

C. The Dow Documents

Although the government concedes that the Dow Documents are work product, it contends that Dow waived work-product protection by disclosing them to Deloitte. To the best of our knowledge, no circuit has addressed whether disclosing work product to an independent auditor constitutes waiver. Among the district courts that have addressed this issue, most have found no waiver. *E.g., Regions Fin. Corp. v. United States,* No. 2:06–CV–00895–RDP, 2008 WL 2139008, at *8 (N.D.Ala. May 8, 2008) (slip op.); *Lawrence E. Jaffe Pension Plan v. Household Int'l, Inc.,* 237 F.R.D. 176, 183 (N.D.Ill.2006); *In re JDS Uniphase Corp. Sec. Litig.,* No. C–02–1486 CW, 2006 WL 2850049, at *1 (N.D.Cal. Oct.5, 2006) (unpublished decision); *Am. S.S. Owners Mut. Prot. & Indem. Ass'n v. Alcoa S.S. Co.,* No. 04–Civ–4309, 2006 WL 278131, at *2 (S.D.N.Y. Feb.2, 2006) (unpublished decision); *Frank Betz Assocs., Inc. v. Jim Walter Homes, Inc.,* 226 F.R.D. 533, 535 (D.S.C.2005); *Merrill Lynch & Co., Inc. v. Allegheny Energy, Inc.,* 229 F.R.D. 441, 447–49 (S.D.N.Y.2004); *In re Honeywell Int'l, Inc. Sec. Litig.,* 230 F.R.D. 293, 300 (S.D.N.Y.2003); *Gutter v. E.I. Dupont de Nemours & Co.,* No. 95–CV–2152, 1998 WL 2017926, at *5 (S.D.Fla. May 18, 1998) (unpublished decision); *In re Pfizer Inc. Sec. Litig.,* No. 90 Civ. 1260, 1993 WL 561125, at *6 (S.D.N.Y. Dec.23, 1993) (unpublished decision). At least two courts have found waiver. *Medinol, Ltd. v. Boston Scientific Corp.,* 214 F.R.D. 113, 115–17 (S.D.N.Y.2002); *In re Diasonics Sec. Litig.,* No. C–83–4584–RFP, 1986 WL 53402, at *1 (N.D.Cal. June 15, 1986) (unpublished decision).

While voluntary disclosure waives the attorney-client privilege, it does not necessarily waive work-product protection. United States v. Am. Tel. & Tel. Co., 642 F.2d 1285, 1299 (D.C.Cir.1980) (*AT & T*). As we explained in *AT & T,* the attorney-client privilege and the work-product doctrine serve different purposes:

the former protects the attorney-client relationship by safeguarding confidential communications, whereas the latter promotes the adversary process by insulating an attorney's litigation preparation from discovery. Id. Voluntary disclosure waives the attorney-client privilege because it is inconsistent with the confidential attorney-client relationship. Id. Voluntary disclosure does not necessarily waive work-product protection, however, because it does not necessarily undercut the adversary process. Id. Nevertheless, disclosing work product to a third party can waive protection if "such disclosure, under the circumstances, is inconsistent with the maintenance of secrecy from the disclosing party's adversary." Rockwell Int'l Corp. v. U.S. Dep't of Justice, 235 F.3d 598, 605 (D.C.Cir.2001) (quoting AT & T, 642 F.2d at 1299). Under this standard, the voluntary disclosure of attorney work product to an adversary or a conduit to an adversary waives work-product protection for that material.

Applying this standard, the government contends that Dow has waived work-product protection for the Dow Documents because Deloitte is (1) a potential adversary and (2) a conduit to other adversaries. We reject both contentions and conclude that Dow has not waived the protection.

1.

The government contends that Deloitte is a potential adversary of Dow because disputes sometimes arise between independent auditors and their clients and because independent auditors have the power to issue opinions that adversely affect their clients. Neither argument demonstrates that Deloitte is a potential adversary for purposes of waiver analysis. First, as an independent auditor, Deloitte cannot be Dow's adversary. Even the threat of litigation between an independent auditor and its client can compromise the auditor's independence and necessitate withdrawal. See AMERICAN INSTITUTE OF CERTIFIED PUBLIC ACCOUNTANTS (AICPA), AICPA PROFESSIONAL STANDARDS, CODE OF PROFESSIONAL CONDUCT § 101.08 (2005) (hereinafter AICPA CODE OF PROFESSIONAL CONDUCT) (discussing the effect of actual and threatened litigation on auditor independence). Further, Deloitte's power to issue an adverse opinion, while significant, does not make it the sort of litigation adversary contemplated by the waiver standard. Similarly, "any tension between an auditor and a corporation that arises from an auditor's need to scrutinize and investigate a corporation's records and book-keeping practices simply is not the equivalent of an adversarial relationship contemplated by the work product doctrine." Merrill Lynch, 229 F.R.D. at 448. Second, the possibility of a future dispute between Deloitte and Dow does not render Deloitte a potential adversary for the present purpose. If it did, any voluntary disclosure would constitute waiver. Yet the work-product doctrine allows disclosures as long as they do not undercut the adversary process. See AT & T, 642 F.2d at 1299.

Here, the question is not whether Deloitte could be Dow's adversary in any conceivable future litigation, but whether Deloitte could be Dow's adversary in the sort of litigation the Dow Documents address. We conclude that the answer must be no. In preparing the Dow Documents, Dow anticipated a dispute with the IRS, not a dispute with Deloitte. The documents, which concern the tax implications of the Chemtech partnerships, would not likely be relevant in any dispute Dow might have with Deloitte. Thus Deloitte cannot be considered a potential adversary with respect to the Dow Documents.

The government argues that United States v. Massachusetts Institute of Technology, 129 F.3d 681 (1st Cir.1997), supports its argument that an independent auditor is a potential adversary. In that case, a defense contractor (MIT) under IRS investigation claimed work-product protection for expense reports it had disclosed to the Defense Contract Audit Agency, a branch of the Department of Defense. The First Circuit held that MIT had waived the protection by disclosing its expense reports to a potential adversary. Id. at 687. The court's reasoning is clear: MIT disclosed the expense reports to the auditing arm of the Defense Department, the most likely adversary in any dispute over expense reports. In doing so, it disclosed its work product not to an independent auditor, but to an auditor affiliated with a potential adversary. Dow's disclosure to its independent auditor, which is not a potential adversary in tax litigation over the Chemtech partnerships, is wholly different.

2.

The government also asserts that Deloitte is a conduit to Dow's adversaries. It claims the district court failed to address this question, but this ignores the district court's explicit statement that "no evidence suggests that it was unreasonable for Dow to expect Deloitte USA to maintain confidentiality." Deloitte, 623 F.Supp.2d at 41. Like the district court, we conclude that Deloitte is not a conduit to Dow's adversaries.

Our prior decisions applying the "maintenance of secrecy" standard, while fact-intensive, have generally made two discrete inquiries in assessing whether disclosure constitutes waiver. First, we have considered whether the disclosing party has engaged in self-interested selective disclosure by revealing its work product to some adversaries but not to others. Williams, 562 F.3d at 394; In re Subpoenas Duces Tecum, 738 F.2d 1367, 1372 (D.C.Cir.1984). Such conduct militates in favor of waiver, for it is "inconsistent and unfair to allow [parties] to select according to their own self-interest to which adversaries they will allow access to the materials." In re Subpoenas, 738 F.2d at 1372.

Second, we have examined whether the disclosing party had a reasonable basis for believing that the recipient would keep the disclosed material confidential. Williams, 562 F.3d at 394; In re Subpoenas, 738 F.2d at 1372–74. A reasonable expectation of confidentiality may derive from common litigation interests between the disclosing party and the recipient. In re Subpoenas, 738 F.2d at 1372. As we explained in AT & T, "[t]he existence of common interests between transferor and transferee is relevant to deciding whether the disclosure is consistent with the nature of the work product privilege." 642 F.2d at 1299. This is true because when common litigation interests are present, "the transferee is not at all likely to disclose the work product material to the adversary." Id. Alternately, a reasonable expectation of confidentiality may be rooted in a confidentiality agreement or similar arrangement between the disclosing party and the recipient. Nevertheless, a confidentiality agreement must be relatively strong and sufficiently unqualified to avoid waiver. In *Williams,* for example, we concluded that the government's assurance that it would maintain confidentiality "to the extent possible" was not sufficiently strong or sufficiently unqualified to prevent the government from disclosing the information to a criminal defendant under *Brady v. Maryland,* 373 U.S. 83, 83 S.Ct. 1194, 10 L.Ed.2d 215 (1963). 562 F.3d at 395–96. Likewise, we have determined that a mere promise to give the disclosing party notice before releasing documents does not support a reasonable expectation of confidentiality. *In re Subpoenas,* 738 F.2d at 1373.

The selective disclosure inquiry is straightforward. Selective disclosure involves disclosing work product to at least one adversary. As we have explained, Deloitte is not an adversary, so Dow's disclosure to Deloitte was not selective disclosure. The "reasonable expectation of confidentiality" inquiry is more complicated. As to common interests, Dow and Deloitte do not have common litigation interests in the Dow Documents—Dow has a litigation interest in the documents because of its interest in the Chemtech partnerships, but Deloitte has no similar interest in the documents. Absent common interests, the question is whether a confidentiality agreement or similar assurance gave Dow a reasonable expectation that Deloitte would keep its work product confidential.

We conclude that Dow had a reasonable expectation of confidentiality because Deloitte, as an independent auditor, has an obligation to refrain from disclosing confidential client information. Rule 301 of the American Institute of Certified Public Accountants (AICPA) Code of Professional Conduct provides: "A member in public practice shall not disclose any confidential client information without the specific consent of the client." AICPA CODE OF PROFESSIONAL CONDUCT § 301.01. William Curry's declaration explains that "Dow furnished these documents to D & T [Deloitte] with the expectation that D & T would retain the confidentiality of the two documents." Given the obligation imposed by Rule 301, we think this expectation was reasonable.

The government responds that this is a "qualified assurance" that does not suffice to prevent waiver because Rule 301 also explains that it "shall not be construed . . . to affect in any way the member's obligation to comply with a validly issued and enforceable subpoena or summons." *Id.* But an assertion of work-product protection challenges the enforceability of a subpoena with respect to those materials. Thus Deloitte could refuse to produce the documents, thereby allowing Dow to intervene and assert work-product protection, without violating its obligation to comply with enforceable subpoenas. Indeed, this is exactly what Deloitte did. Accordingly, this caveat does not significantly diminish the reasonableness of Dow's expectation of confidentiality.

The government also attempts to bolster its waiver argument by identifying instances in which an independent auditor might disclose information obtained from a company whose finances it audits. For example, it asserts that Deloitte could make Dow disclose its confidential tax analysis in footnotes to its public financial statements. Likewise, Deloitte could testify about confidential information obtained from Dow in proceedings brought by the SEC or private parties. Or Deloitte might report illegal acts it detects during its audit in accordance with § 10A of the Securities and Exchange Act, 15 U.S.C. § 78j–1. Finally, the government returns to *Arthur Young,* arguing that as an independent auditor, Deloitte is a "public watchdog" whose ultimate allegiance is to Dow's creditors, stockholders, and the investing public—all potential adversaries of Dow. In sum, the government contends that Dow could not reasonably expect confidentiality from Deloitte after giving it the Dow Documents, given the myriad ways Deloitte could reveal that information.

Of course Deloitte might disclose some information relevant to Dow's finances. But the government has neither pointed to any regulatory provision nor posited any specific circumstance under which Deloitte would be required to disclose attorney work product like that contained in the Dow Documents. An independent auditor can fulfill its duties and render an opinion concerning a company's public financial statements without revealing every piece of information it reviews during the audit process. In short, Deloitte's independent auditor obligations do not make it a conduit to Dow's adversaries.

Likewise, the government's reliance on *Arthur Young* is misplaced. In *Arthur Young,* the Court considered whether accountant work-product should be granted the same protection attorney work product receives. The government quotes the Court's statement that "[t]o insulate from disclosure a certified public accountant's interpretations of the client's financial statements would be to ignore the significance of the accountant's role as a disinterested analyst charged with public obligations." *Arthur Young,* 465 U.S. at 818, 104 S.Ct. 1495. All well and good. In this case, however, the government attempts to discover not an independent auditor's "interpretations of the client's financial statements," which *Arthur Young* would permit, but an attorney's thoughts and opinions developed in anticipation of litigation, which the work-product doctrine forbids.

Furthermore, we are mindful that independent auditors have significant leverage over the companies whose finances they audit. An auditor can essentially compel disclosure by refusing to provide an unqualified opinion otherwise. Finding waiver based on such disclosures could well encourage the sort of "[i]nefficiency, unfairness and sharp practices" that *Hickman* sought to avoid. For example, it might discourage companies from seeking legal advice and candidly disclosing that information to independent auditors. Moreover, the government has not proffered any good reason for wanting the Dow Documents other than its desire to know what Dow's counsel thought about the Chemtech partnerships. Granting discovery under these circumstances would undercut the adversary process and let the government litigate "on wits borrowed from the adversary," *Hickman,* 329 U.S. at 516, 67 S.Ct. 385 (Jackson, J., concurring). We conclude that the district court applied the correct legal standard and acted within its discretion in determining that Dow had not waived work-product protection. Consequently, we affirm the district court's decision denying the government's motion to compel with respect to the Dow Documents.

* * *

For the reasons set forth above, we vacate in part, affirm in part, and remand for further proceedings consistent with this opinion.

So ordered.

NOTES AND QUESTIONS

1. According to the court's reading of *Hickman*, what is required for work product protection?
2. Does the "because of" test really provide more protection than the "primary purpose" test?
3. What is the selective disclosure rule?

Another limitation is the qualified nature of the privilege. Work product is subject to disclosure where "the other party shows a substantial need for the materials to prepare its case and cannot, without undue hardship, obtain their substantial equivalent by other means."[21] This limitation rarely applies in tax cases, though the IRS has attempted to rely on it from time to time.

C. Federally Authorized Tax Practitioner Privilege

There is a statutory privilege that applies to tax practitioners, but it is problematic.[22] Under section 7525, a communication between a taxpayer and a federally authorized tax practitioner regarding tax advice receives "the same common law protections of confidentiality which apply to a communication between a taxpayer and an attorney."[23] This tax practitioner privilege is intended to be analogous to the attorney-client privilege. It does not, however, apply to criminal matters, tax shelters (with respect to written communications), or tax return preparation.[24] Courts have not been receptive to privilege claims under section 7525.[25]

---

[21] FED. R. CIV. P. 26(b)(3)(A)(ii).

[22] *See* I.R.C. § 7525(a)(1); Megan L. Brackney, *When a Client Says, "I Have Something to Tell You," Should You Listen?*, HANDLING A TAX CONTROVERSY: AUDIT, APPEALS, LITIGATION, & COLLECTIONS, SW015 ALI-CLE 17 ("Section 7525 may be the most useless provision in the Code, since it does not apply when the client actually needs it, such as during a criminal investigation.").

[23] *See* I.R.C § 7525(a)(1).

[24] *See* § 7525(a)(2)(A) (tax practitioner privilege not applicable to criminal matters); § 7525(b) (tax practitioner privilege not applicable to tax shelters); United States v. KPMG LLP, 237 F. Supp. 2d 35, 39 (D.D.C. 2002) (tax practitioner privilege not applicable to tax return preparation).

[25] *See, e.g.*, United States v. Frederick, 182 F.3d 496, 501 (7th Cir. 1999) ("[P]eople who are under investigation and represented by a lawyer have the same duty as anyone else to file tax returns. They should not be permitted, by using a lawyer in lieu of another form of tax preparer, to obtain greater confidentiality than other taxpayers."); Doe v. Wachovia Corp., 268 F. Supp. 2d

Although section 7525 provides weak protection for tax practitioners, there is a way that an accountant's communications can be cloaked by privilege. If an attorney hires an accountant to assist in representing a client, the attorney-client privilege applies to the communications between the accountant and either the attorney or client if they satisfy the other requirements for the privilege.[26] Unlike the tax practitioner privilege, the attorney-client privilege applies in criminal cases. Thus, under *Kovel*, it would be prudent for an accountant approached by a client with a criminal matter to refer the case to an attorney before proceeding.

There is also a crime-fraud exception to the attorney-client privilege. The attorney-client privilege does not apply to advice from an attorney in furtherance of a crime. This exception arises often in the summons context.

UNITED STATES v. BDO SEIDMAN, LLP
492 F.3d 806 (2007)
United States Court of Appeals, Seventh Circuit

Before RIPPLE, KANNE and WILLIAMS, Circuit Judges.
RIPPLE, Circuit Judge.

This is the third appeal arising out of an effort by the Internal Revenue Service ("IRS") to enforce administrative summonses against BDO Seidman, LLP ("BDO"), an accounting firm that allegedly failed to disclose potentially abusive tax shelters that it promoted. See United States v. BDO Seidman, 337 F.3d 802 (7th Cir.2003) (BDO II); United States v. BDO Seidman, Nos. 02–3914 & 02–3915, 2002 WL 32080709 (7th Cir. Dec.18, 2002) (BDO I). The IRS now appeals the district court's ruling that sustained BDO's claim of attorney-client privilege with respect to a memorandum written by one of BDO's employees. The IRS also appeals a separate ruling that sustained the tax practitioner and/or attorney-client privilege asserted by a number of BDO's clients ("Intervenors") with respect to 266 documents. The Intervenors cross-appeal the district court's ruling that one document, Document A–40, fell within the crime-fraud exception to the attorney-client and/or tax practitioner privilege. For the reasons set for forth in this opinion, we affirm in part and vacate and remand in part.

I.

BACKGROUND

A. The Enforcement Action

627, 636-37 (W.D.N.C. 2003) (holding that a John Doe summons seeking bank records from a bank rather than the taxpayer did not constitute a proceeding before the IRS, thus the section 7525 privilege did not apply).

[26] *See* United States v. Kovel, 296 F.2d 918 (2d Cir. 1961) ("[I]f the lawyer has directed the client, either in the specific case or generally, to tell his story in the first instance to an accountant engaged by the lawyer, who is then to interpret it so that the lawyer may better give legal advice, communications by the client reasonably related to that purpose ought fall within the privilege.").

In September 2000, the IRS received information suggesting that BDO was promoting potentially abusive tax shelters without complying with the Internal Revenue Code's ("IRC") listing requirements for such tax shelters. *See* 26 U.S.C. §§ 6111(a), 6112(a) (2000); *BDO II*, 337 F.3d at 806. Potentially abusive tax shelters included those transactions defined as "tax shelters" under § 6111(c) and arrangements identified by regulation as potentially abusive under § 6112(b).[27] Organizers of any potentially abusive tax shelter were required to maintain a list of persons to whom an interest in the shelter was sold. *See* 26 U.S.C. § 6112(a) (2000). Additionally, organizers and sellers of § 6111(c) tax shelters were required to register the tax shelter with the IRS. *See id.* § 6111(a). Failure to follow these registration and list-keeping requirements was sanctionable by penalties. *See id.* §§ 6707, 6708.[28]

The IRS commenced a compliance investigation into BDO's alleged violations. The IRS issued twenty summonses commanding production of documents, testimony relating to the transactions and information on the identity of the clients who had invested in the transactions. *BDO II*, 337 F.3d at 805–06. When BDO resisted these summonses, the IRS petitioned the United States District Court for the Northern District of Illinois for enforcement. *Id.* at 806. BDO contended that the summonses could not be enforced because the investigation had no legitimate purpose. It also contended that the summonses were overbroad, issued in bad faith and sought information already in the IRS' possession. Lastly, BDO submitted that the information sought was irrelevant to the investigation. *Id.* at 806. BDO further asserted that a number of the documents were protected by the attorney-client privilege, the tax practitioner privilege under 26 U.S.C. § 7525(a) or work product protection. *BDO II*, 337 F.3d at 806. The district court ruled that the IRS had issued the summonses in good faith and that enforcement would not constitute an abuse of process. It ordered BDO to produce all responsive documents except for those previously

---

[27] [fn 1] Sections 6111 and 6112 of the IRC were amended by the American Jobs Creation Act of 2004, Pub.L. No. 108–357, § 815, 118 Stat. 1418, 1581–83 (2004). The Act eliminated the distinction between § 6111(c) tax shelters and other arrangements identified by the Secretary under § 6112(b)(2) by replacing the terms "tax shelter" and "potentially abusive tax shelter" with "reportable transaction." Reportable transactions are "any transaction[s] with respect to which information is required to be included with a return or statement because . . . such transaction is of a type which the Secretary determines as having a potential for tax avoidance or evasion." 26 U.S.C. § 6707A. All reportable transactions must be reported to the IRS, see id. § 6111(a) (2000 & Supp. IV 2004), and must satisfy the IRC's list-keeping requirements, see id. § 6112(a).

[28] [fn 2] Sections 6707 and 6708 also were amended by the American Jobs Creation Act, see Pub.L. No. 108–357, §§ 816–817, 118 Stat. 1418, 1583–84 (2004), but they continue to provide penalties for failure to comply with the registration and list-keeping requirements of §§ 6111 and 6112. See 26 U.S.C. §§ 6707 & 6708 (2000 & Supp. IV 2004).

listed on privilege logs and submitted to the court by BDO for in camera inspection. *Id.* at 806–07.

BDO then notified its clients that it intended to produce documents that would reveal their identities to the IRS. In response, a number of clients sought to intervene as of right in order to assert the tax practitioner privilege under 26 U.S.C. § 7525(a).[29] The district court denied the motions to intervene, holding that the tax practitioner privilege would not prevent disclosure of the clients' names. *See BDO II,* 337 F.3d at 807. The clients appealed this denial to this court.

On December 18, 2002, we entered an order remanding the case to the district court to permit it to undertake an in camera inspection of the documents for which the would-be anonymous intervenors asserted a privilege. *See BDO I,* 2002 WL 32080709, at *1. We ordered the district court to make more extensive findings with respect to the claim of tax practitioner privilege for each document, taking into account the totality of the circumstances. *Id.* After conducting this in camera review, the district court determined that the tax practitioner privilege did not prevent disclosure of the clients' identities. R.73 at 7–31. The clients again appealed, and we affirmed the district court's ruling on the question of privilege and its denial of the motions to intervene. *BDO II,* 337 F.3d at 813.

After our decision affirming the district court's denial of the anonymous clients' motion to intervene, the Intervenors sought intervention as of right in order to assert a claim of privilege under the attorney-client privilege, tax practitioner privilege or work product doctrine with respect to 267 documents. The IRS filed a document titled "United States' Concurrence in Intervenors' Motions to Intervene and Challenge to Claims of Privilege" in which it argued that the district court should grant the motion, or, in the alternative, deny the claim of privilege. The IRS and the Intervenors also filed a joint motion in which the IRS consented to the intervention and the parties set forth a proposed briefing schedule. On July 15, 2004, the district court granted the Intervenors' motion.

B. Intervenors' Claims

The Intervenors asserted attorney-client privilege, tax practitioner privilege or work product protection with respect to 267 documents. The IRS submitted that the documents either were not covered by the tax practitioner privilege under the tax shelter exception found in 26 U.S.C. § 7525(b), as it existed at the time of the communications, or that the documents fell within the crime-fraud exception to both the attorney-client and tax practitioner privileges.

According to the IRS, BDO, in conjunction with other firms, had engaged in the practice of selling prepackaged tax shelters, the sole purpose of which was the unlawful attempt to evade tax liability. The district court determined that the IRS had failed to make a prima facie showing of crime or fraud that would justify a blanket determination that all of the documents fell within the crime-fraud exception. R.178 at 16. The court noted that, just because the IRS characterized the transactions "as abusive and unlawful cookie cutter tax shelters," such a

---

[29] [fn 3] See John and Jane Does Emergency Motion to Intervene, R.38; Richard and Mary Roes Emergency Motion to Intervene, R.42.

characterization did not make them so. *Id.* at 17. The court added that the question of whether BDO and the Intervenors had violated the IRC was the ultimate issue in the IRS' investigation and that a finding of fraud based solely on the IRS' allegations "would place the proverbial 'Cart before the Horse.' " *Id.* In a footnote, the district court added that, based on these same considerations, it could not hold that the Intervenors or BDO were engaged in tax shelters which would fall within the tax shelter exception to the tax practitioner privilege. *Id.* at n. 6.

Although the district court was unwilling to apply the crime-fraud exception in blanket fashion, it proceeded to review each document in camera to determine whether individual documents fell within the crime-fraud exception. *Id.* at 18. In conducting the review, the district court looked to the totality of the circumstances to determine whether there was sufficient evidence of crime or fraud to bring a document within this exception. *Id.* at 23. To guide this evaluation, the district court identified eight non-exclusive, non-determinative "potential indicators of fraud" which it drew from arguments made by the IRS, from two other cases involving allegedly fraudulent practices by BDO and from an unrelated IRS enforcement action against another accounting firm. R.178 at 23.[30] Based on these cases and other factors that the IRS had submitted were

---

[30] [fn 4] The first case to which the district court looked in deriving its potential indicators of fraud was Denney v. Jenkens & Gilchrist, 340 F.Supp.2d 338 (S.D.N.Y.2004). That case involved a civil RICO class action in which the plaintiffs alleged that Jenkens & Gilchrist had developed and BDO and others had marketed a tax shelter known as the Currency Options Bring Reward Alternatives ("COBRA"). BDO sought to enforce an arbitration clause in its consulting agreements. Based on what it deemed to be admissions by the parties, the court in *Denney* concluded that BDO and its clients had engaged in mutual fraud in connection with the consulting agreements to conceal the true purpose of the agreements: providing the clients with tax shelters advice. Id. at 346. Because the contracts were the product of mutual fraud between BDO and its clients, the arbitration clause was unenforceable. Id. at 347. The court based its conclusion that the contracts were mutually fraudulent on the vague language in the consulting agreements and its findings that BDO did not provide any of the consulting services described in the agreements. Id. at 346–47.

The next case the district court looked to in developing its potential indicators of fraud was Miron v. BDO Seidman, LLP, 342 F.Supp.2d 324 (E.D.Pa.2004). Like *Denney, Miron* involved the enforceability of an arbitration clause in one of BDO's consulting agreements and related to the COBRA transaction. See id. at 327. The district court in *Miron* noted the factors that led the court in *Denney* to find that the consulting agreements had been the product of mutual fraud, but concluded that the consulting agreements at issue were factually distinguishable. See id. at 329–30. In particular, the court found that BDO had provided the services described in its consulting agreements. Id. The court in *Miron* noted also that, unlike the consulting agreements in *Denney*, in

indicative of fraud, the district court arrived at the following eight factors to guide its in camera review of each of the 267 documents:

> (1) the marketing of pre-packaged transactions by BDO; (2) the communication by the Intervenors to BDO with the purpose of engaging in a pre-arranged transaction developed by BDO or [a] third party with the sole purpose of reducing taxable income; (3) BDO and/or the Intervenors attempting to conceal the true nature of the transaction; (4) knowledge by BDO, or a situation where BDO should have known, that the Intervenors lacked a legitimate business purpose for entering into the transaction; (5) vaguely worded consulting agreements; (6) failure by BDO to provide services under the consulting agreement yet receipt of payment; (7) mention of the COBRA transaction; and (8) use of boiler-plate documents.

R.178 at 23. The court further noted that the presence of these factors alone would not be sufficient to establish a prima facie case of fraud. *See id.* at 23–24. Rather, the potential indicators of fraud were intended to serve merely as guideposts. *See id.* at 24. The ultimate question of whether a prima facie showing of crime or fraud had been made with respect to a particular document was to be determined under the totality of circumstances.

Based on this review, the district court held that, with the exception of Document A–40, the IRS had failed to make a prima facie showing of a crime or fraud. *Id.* at 24. Thus, the district court upheld the Intervenors' claim of privilege with respect to 266 of the 267 documents, although it did not specify which privilege (attorney-client or tax practitioner) applied to each document. *See id.* at 13–14, 29.

After finding prima facie evidence that Document A–40 fell within the crime-fraud exception, the district court permitted the Intervenors to provide an

---

which the only identified goal was expanding business operations, the consulting agreements at issue were intended to limit also the clients' financial exposure on those expansions. Id. at 329. Based on these differences, the court concluded that the consulting agreements were not similarly suggestive of fraud. Id.

The third case to which the district court looked in arriving at its potential indicators of fraud was United States v. KPMG LLP, 316 F.Supp.2d 30 (D.D.C.2004). Unlike *Denney* and *Miron*, *KPMG* did not involve BDO. *KPMG* involved an action brought by the IRS to enforce summonses it issued to the accounting firm of KPMG as part of its investigation into KPMG's alleged promotion of, and participation in, tax shelters. Id. at 31–32. The court in *KPMG* held that boilerplate opinion letters provided to KPMG clients by the law firm of Brown & Wood were not protected by the attorney-client privilege because they had been provided as a part of "KPMG's marketing machine" rather than as reasoned legal advice. Id. at 40. The district court in the present action found the findings of the court in *KPMG* consistent with the IRS' allegation that BDO had engaged in the promotion of prepackaged tax shelters rather than individualized tax advice. See R.178 at 23.

explanation that would negate the evidence of crime or fraud. *Id.* at 24. The Intervenors provided their explanation to the court and the IRS responded. On May 17, 2005, after finding the Intervenors' explanation insufficient to rebut the prima facie evidence of crime or fraud, the district court ruled that Document A–40 fell within the crime-fraud exception to the tax practitioner or attorney-client privilege. R.190 at 10.

After the district court issued its final ruling with respect to Document A–40, the Court of Appeals for the Second Circuit reversed the decision of the United States District Court for the Southern District of New York in *Denney v. Jenkens & Gilchrist,* 340 F.Supp.2d 338 (S.D.N.Y.2004). *See Denney v. BDO Seidman, L.L.P.,* 412 F.3d 58, 66 (2d Cir.2005). The Intervenors moved for reconsideration under Rule 60(b) of the Federal Rules of Civil Procedure, arguing that, because the district court had relied on *Denney* when establishing the factors that would guide its in camera review of each document, the court should reexamine its earlier ruling. R.210 at 2–3. The district court denied the motion, holding that the Second Circuit's decision did not affect the controlling law in this case. *Id.* at 3. The court added that its finding of prima facie evidence of crime or fraud was based on the totality of the circumstances, an inquiry guided, but not controlled, by the eight factors it previously had identified. *Id.* at 6.

C. BDO's Privilege Claims

While its clients were seeking to intervene to protect their claims of privilege, BDO asserted its own claims of attorney-client privilege and work product protection with respect to 110 documents. The IRS responded that the documents were neither protected attorney-client communications nor work product, and, even if they were, the documents fell within the crime-fraud exception. R.127 at 2. After conducting an in camera inspection of each document, the district court determined that 103 of the documents were within the attorney-client privilege and that one other document, though not covered by the attorney-client privilege, fell within the work product doctrine. *Id.* at 3–9. However, the court concluded that six documents, as submitted to the court in redacted form, were not within the attorney-client privilege and ordered their disclosure as so redacted. *Id.* at 7. Based on the same in camera review, the district court found no evidence that the communications in 104 documents protected by the attorney-client privilege or work product doctrine were made to further a crime or fraud. *Id.* at 10.

One of the 104 documents that the district court had found to fall within the attorney-client privilege was a memorandum written by Michael Kerekes ("Kerekes Memorandum"). Kerekes was a lawyer and partner at BDO. In August 2000, he wrote a memorandum to BDO's outside counsel, David Dreier, a tax attorney with the law firm of White & Case LLP, requesting legal advice on pending IRS regulations. In January 2001, Donna Guerin, an attorney at the law firm of Jenkens & Gilchrist, received a copy of the memorandum under circumstances that remain the subject of dispute.[31] At the time attorney Guerin

---

[31] [fn 5] Guerin received the memorandum by fax. She asserts that the memorandum was sent to her by Robert Greisman, a partner with BDO.

received the Kerekes Memorandum, Jenkens & Gilchrist did not represent BDO, but these two entities, one an accounting firm and the other a law firm, serviced jointly clients on the same or related matters. According to attorney Guerin, she received the letter from BDO as input into an opinion letter regarding tax shelters that Jenkens & Gilchrist was preparing for both BDO and their common clients. Although BDO and Jenkens & Gilchrist subsequently were co-defendants in civil litigation, *see, e.g., Denney v. Jenkens & Gilchrist,* 340 F.Supp.2d 338, there was no litigation pending against BDO or Jenkens & Gilchrist at the time attorney Guerin received the Kerekes Memorandum.

After the district court's ruling on BDO's claim of privilege for the 110 documents, the IRS received the Kerekes Memorandum from Jenkens & Gilchrist in response to a subpoena. Upon viewing the memorandum, the IRS requested the court reconsider its privilege ruling with respect to the Kerekes Memorandum. The IRS asserted that the document fell within the crime-fraud exception to the attorney-client privilege or, alternatively, that the privilege had been waived. Based on its prior in camera review of the document, the district court rejected the IRS' claim that the Kerekes Memorandum fell within the crime-fraud exception. R.180 at 3–4. The court noted that, even though the contents of the Kerekes Memorandum were new to the IRS, they were not new to the court, and it had considered the arguments presented by the IRS in its prior in camera review of the Kerekes Memorandum. The district court further held that disclosure of the Kerekes Memorandum to attorney Guerin did not waive BDO's claim of privilege because the memorandum related to a common legal interest shared by BDO and Jenkens & Gilchrist and therefore fell within the common interest doctrine. *Id.* at 6. The district court added that it would reach the same conclusion even if the common interest doctrine did not apply because it had found ample precedent to sustain the privilege as an unintentional disclosure. *Id.*

Greisman contends that he does not remember faxing the memorandum to Guerin and that on the day it was faxed to her he was at a meeting at a hotel in Los Angeles. There is no record of a fax having been sent from the hotel to Jenkens & Gilchrist on that day and the document itself does not display the phone number of the origin of the fax. Further, the memorandum was not received in a single transmission. The last three pages of the memorandum were sent at around 3:20 p.m., with the balance of the memorandum, that is, the first portion of the memorandum, being sent in a separate transmission at around 4:00 p.m. In addition to the memorandum being sent out of order in two transmissions, the fax heading indicates that those portions of the memorandum sent at around 3:20 p.m. began at the second page of the transmission. The fax heading of the transmission sent around 4:00 p.m. indicates that the portion of the memorandum sent at that time began at the eighth page of the transmission. The balance of both transmissions does not appear in the record.

II.

DISCUSSION

The IRS timely appealed the district court's ruling with respect to the Kerekes Memorandum. The IRS contends that BDO waived any claim of privilege with respect to the memorandum when it disclosed the document to attorney Guerin. The IRS submits that the common interest doctrine does not apply because the communication was not made in anticipation of litigation. It further contends that the disclosure was voluntary, and, therefore, BDO cannot claim that the privilege is preserved because any disclosure was inadvertent. Alternatively, the IRS contends that the district court erred by not reconsidering its ruling that there was no evidence of crime or fraud in connection with the Kerekes Memorandum after it found such evidence with respect to Document A–40.

The IRS also appeals the district court's ruling that the tax shelter exception to the tax practitioner privilege, 26 U.S.C. § 7525(b) (2000), does not apply to the 267 documents for which the Intervenors claimed the privilege. The IRS contends that the burden was on the Intervenors to prove that the tax shelter exception did not apply, a burden the IRS claims the Intervenors did not meet.

The Intervenors cross-appeal the district court's finding of prima facie evidence of crime or fraud with respect to Document A–40. The Intervenors submit that the district court's finding was in error because the IRS failed to make a prima facie showing of each element of a particular crime or common law fraud.

A. The Kerekes Memorandum

We first shall address whether the district court erred in sustaining BDO's claim of attorney-client privilege under the common interest doctrine and in rejecting the IRS' position that the Kerekes Memorandum fell within the crime-fraud exception to the attorney-client privilege.

We review all necessary findings of fact and all applications of law to fact in connection with the district court's ruling on a privilege claim for clear error. *See United States v. Frederick,* 182 F.3d 496, 499 (7th Cir.1999) (application of law to fact); *United States v. Evans,* 113 F.3d 1457, 1461 (7th Cir.1997) (findings of fact). We shall reverse only if, on review of the entire evidence, we are "left with the definite and firm conviction that a mistake has been committed." *Malachinski v. Comm'r,* 268 F.3d 497, 505 (7th Cir.2001) (quoting *Coleman v. Comm'r,* 16 F.3d 821, 824 (7th Cir.1994)) (internal quotation marks omitted). On the other hand, the scope of a privilege is a question of law that we review de novo. *See BDO II,* 337 F.3d at 809. We review a district court's decision regarding the crime-fraud exception for an abuse of discretion. *United States v. Al–Shahin,* 474 F.3d 941, 946 (7th Cir.2007).

In federal courts, except when state law supplies the applicable rule of law, the attorney-client privilege is "governed by the principles of the common law as [it] may be interpreted by the courts of the United States in the light of reason and experience." Fed.R.Evid. 501. Although it ultimately was not adopted by Congress, the rule of attorney-client privilege promulgated by the Supreme Court in 1972 as part of the Proposed Federal Rules of Evidence has been recognized "as a source of general guidance regarding federal common law principles." *In re Grand Jury Investigation,* 399 F.3d 527, 532 (2d Cir.2005); *see also* 3 Jack B. Weinstein & Margaret A. Berger, Weinstein's Federal Evidence § 503.02 (Joseph M. McLaughlin, ed., 2d ed.2006). Proposed Rule 503 provided:

> A client has a privilege to refuse to disclose and to prevent any other person from disclosing confidential communications made for the purpose of facilitating the rendition of professional legal services to the client, (1) between himself or his representative and his lawyer or his lawyer's representative, or (2) between his lawyer and the lawyer's representative, or (3) by him or his lawyer to a lawyer representing another in a matter of common interest, or (4) between representatives of the client or between the client and a representative of the client, or (5) between lawyers representing the client.

See Proposed Fed.R.Evid. 503(b), 56 F.R.D. 183, 236 (1972). Put simply, in order for the attorney-client privilege to attach, the communication in question must be made: (1) in confidence; (2) in connection with the provision of legal services; (3) to an attorney; and (4) in the context of an attorney-client relationship.

The purpose of the privilege is to "encourage full disclosure and to facilitate open communication between attorneys and their clients." *BDO II,* 337 F.3d at 810. Open communication assists lawyers in rendering legal advice, not only to represent their clients in ongoing litigation, but also to prevent litigation by advising clients to conform their conduct to the law and by addressing legal concerns that may inhibit clients from engaging in otherwise lawful and socially beneficial activities. *See Frederick,* 182 F.3d at 500. The cost of these benefits is the withholding of relevant information from the courts. *BDO II,* 337 F.3d at 811.

Recognizing the inherent tension between the beneficial goals of the attorney-client privilege and the courts' right to every person's evidence, the courts have articulated the following principles to inform our analysis of the scope of the common interest doctrine:

> (1) "[C]ourts construe the privilege to apply only where necessary to achieve its purpose." *Id.*

> (2) Only those communications which "reflect the lawyer's thinking [or] are made for the purpose of eliciting the lawyer's professional advice or other legal assistance" fall within the privilege. *Frederick,* 182 F.3d at 500.

> (3) Because one of the objectives of the privilege is assisting clients in conforming their conduct to the law, litigation need not be pending for the communication to be made in connection to the provision of legal services. *See United States v. Schwimmer,* 892 F.2d 237, 243–44 (2d Cir.1989).

> (4) Because "the privilege is in derogation of the search for truth," any exceptions to the requirements of the attorney-client privilege "must be

strictly confined." *In re Grand Jury Proceedings (Thullen)*, 220 F.3d 568, 571 (7th Cir.2000).

Although occasionally termed a privilege itself, the common interest doctrine is really an exception to the rule that no privilege attaches to communications between a client and an attorney in the presence of a third person. *See Robinson v. Texas Auto. Dealers Ass'n,* 214 F.R.D. 432, 443 (E.D.Tex.2003). In effect, the common interest doctrine extends the attorney-client privilege to otherwise non-confidential communications in limited circumstances. For that reason, the common interest doctrine only will apply where the parties undertake a joint effort with respect to a common legal interest, and the doctrine is limited strictly to those communications made to further an ongoing enterprise. *See Evans,* 113 F.3d at 1467. Other than these limits, however, the common defense doctrine does not contract the attorney-client privilege. Thus, communications need not be made in anticipation of litigation to fall within the common interest doctrine.[32] Applying the common interest doctrine to the full range of communications otherwise protected by the attorney-client privilege encourages parties with a shared legal interest to seek legal "assistance in order to meet legal requirements and to plan their conduct" accordingly. *See In re Regents of the Univ. of California,* 101 F.3d 1386, 1390–91 (Fed.Cir.1996). This planning serves the public interest by advancing compliance with the law, "facilitating the administration of justice" and averting litigation. *Id.* at 1391. Reason and experience demonstrate that joint venturers, no less than individuals, benefit from planning their activities based on sound legal advice predicated upon open communication.

Having determined that BDO is not barred from asserting attorney-client privilege under the common interest doctrine simply because it was not shared under the threat of litigation, we next shall determine whether the district court's

---

[32] [fn 6] The weight of authority favors our conclusion that litigation need not be actual or imminent for communications to be within the common interest doctrine. At least five of our sister circuits have recognized that the threat of litigation is not a prerequisite to the common interest doctrine. See In re Grand Jury Subpoena (Custodian of Records, Newparent, Inc.), 274 F.3d 563, 572 (1st Cir.2001); In re Regents of the Univ. of California, 101 F.3d 1386, 1390–91 (Fed.Cir.1996); United States v. Aramony, 88 F.3d 1369, 1392 (4th Cir.1996); United States v. Schwimmer, 892 F.2d 237, 244 (2d Cir.1989); United States v. Zolin, 809 F.2d 1411, 1417 (9th Cir.1987), aff'd in part and vacated in part on other grounds, United States v. Zolin, 491 U.S. 554, 109 S.Ct. 2619, 105 L.Ed.2d 469 (1989). We have found only one circuit that requires a "palpable threat of litigation at the time of the communication." United States v. Newell, 315 F.3d 510, 525 (5th Cir.2002) (quoting In re Santa Fe Int'l Corp., 272 F.3d 705, 711 (5th Cir.2001)). This position runs contrary to the "established [rule] that the attorney-client privilege is not limited to actions taken and advice obtained in the shadow of litigation." In re Regents of the Univ. of California, 101 F.3d at 1390.

ruling on BDO's claim of privilege was clearly erroneous. The district court recognized that the scope of the common interest doctrine is limited to a common *legal* interest to which the parties formed a common strategy. *See* R.180 at 6. The district court concluded that BDO and Jenkens & Gilchrist, acting as joint venturers, shared a common legal interest "in ensuring compliance with the new regulation issued by the IRS," *id.,* and in making sure that they could defend their product against potential IRS enforcement actions.

There was, moreover, sufficient evidence to support the district court's determination in this regard. The Kerekes Memorandum originally was addressed to BDO's outside counsel, White & Case, and it sought advice on a legal question. At the time attorney Guerin received the Kerekes Memorandum, BDO and Jenkens & Gilchrist jointly serviced a number of common clients with respect to certain tax products. According to Guerin, Robert Greisman, a partner at BDO, sent her the memorandum as part of BDO's effort to coordinate with Jenkens & Gilchrist a common legal position that BDO and Jenkens & Gilchrist would communicate later to these common clients.[33]

Nonetheless, the IRS asserts that, because the purpose of the communication was to coordinate the content of the message to their common clients, the communication between BDO and Jenkens & Gilchrist was not made for the purpose of securing advice with respect to a common legal interest and, therefore, was not within the scope of the common interest doctrine. However, even if the ultimate reason for sharing the Kerekes Memorandum was to advance the joint interests of BDO and Jenkens & Gilchrist in their representations to their common clients, it does not follow that the communication itself was not made to secure legal advice with respect to a common legal interest. Communications do not cease to be for the purpose of receiving legal services just because the recipient intended to use the fruits of the legal services to guide its relations with customers. In essence, through the memorandum, two joint venturers, BDO and Jenkens & Gilchrist, undertook a consultation between their respective in-house counsel and BDO's outside counsel with respect to the legality of the proposed financial course of action they would recommend to their common clients. This effort, as the district court recognized, was clearly within the scope of the common interest doctrine.

The district court's findings do not leave us "with the definite and firm conviction that a mistake has been committed." *Malachinski,* 268 F.3d at 505 (quoting *Coleman,* 16 F.3d at 824) (internal quotation marks omitted). The district court's finding that the communication of the Kerekes Memorandum to attorney Guerin was within the common interest doctrine was not clearly erroneous. Further, because the privileged status of communications falling within the common interest doctrine cannot be waived without the consent of all of the parties, Jenkens & Gilchrist's subsequent voluntary disclosure of the Kerekes Memorandum in response to the IRS' subpoena did not waive BDO's

---

[33] [fn 7] There is no contention that the final communication from the joint venturers to their clients was privileged.

claim of privilege. See John Morrell & Co. v. Local Union 304A of the United Food & Commercial Workers, AFL–CIO, 913 F.2d 544, 556 (8th Cir.1990); In re Grand Jury Subpoenas (89–3 & 89–4, John Doe 89–129), 902 F.2d 244, 248 (4th Cir.1990); see also Advisory Committee's Note, Proposed Fed.R.Evid. 503(b), 56 F.R.D. 183, 239 (1972).[34][35]

---

[34] [fn 8] The district court held in the alternative that, even if the Kerekes Memorandum did not fall within the common interest doctrine, disclosure of the memorandum by BDO to attorney Guerin was inadvertent. The court concluded that, because the disclosure was inadvertent, BDO had not waived its claim of privilege for the memorandum. The IRS also challenges this alternative holding. Because the district court's application of the common interest doctrine was not clear error, we need not address this alternative ruling.

[35] [fn 9] The IRS contends that, after the court found that Document A40 fell within the crime-fraud exception, the district court should have revisited its conclusion that the crime-fraud exception to the attorney-client privilege did not vitiate the privilege with respect to the Kerekes Memorandum.

The IRS did challenge specifically the district court's earlier determination that the crime-fraud exception did not apply to the Kerekes Memorandum. See R.152 (sealed). This challenge pre-dated, however, the district court's determination with respect to Document A–40. Indeed, on the same day that the district court announced its initial conclusion that the IRS had made a prima facie showing that the communications in Document A–40 were made in furtherance of crime or fraud, the district court rejected the IRS' identical challenge to the Kerekes Memorandum. At no time after the district court stated that it had found prima facie evidence of crime or fraud with respect to Document A–40 did the IRS request the district court to re-evaluate its earlier ruling with respect to the Kerekes Memorandum. The IRS was not without opportunity to raise the issue. As discussed in greater detail in Part II.B, after concluding that there was prima facie evidence that Document A–40 fell within the crime-fraud exception, both the Intervenors and the IRS were permitted to submit additional arguments about the applicability of the crime-fraud exception to Document A–40. The IRS availed itself of this opportunity and filed additional memoranda with the court opposing the Intervenors' answer to the court's preliminary findings of crime or fraud with respect to Document A–40. Nowhere in these papers did the IRS request the district court revisit its earlier rulings on the Kerekes Memorandum.

Based on this record, we must conclude that the IRS has waived this issue. We have recognized that the waiver rule exists to provide the district court with the first opportunity to rule on a party's theories. Bailey v. Int'l Bhd. of Boilermakers, Iron Ship Builders, Blacksmiths, Forgers & Helpers, Local 374, 175 F.3d 526, 530 (7th Cir.1999). This requirement assures that we shall not usurp the role of the district court by engaging in initial fact finding. Id. It also assures an adequate record for review, id., a particularly important function in cases such as this one, where the fact-specific nature of the inquiry lies within the trial court's particular expertise, see *Frederick*, 182 F.3d at 499. Because the

B. Document A–40

We now address whether the district court erred when it held that the Intervenors could not assert a privilege with respect to Document A–40 because the document fell within the crime-fraud exception to the attorney-client and tax practitioner privileges. We review a district court's decision regarding the crime-fraud exception for an abuse of discretion. *Al–Shahin,* 474 F.3d at 946.

The crime-fraud exception places communications made in furtherance of a crime or fraud outside the attorney-client privilege. United States v. Zolin, 491 U.S. 554, 563, 109 S.Ct. 2619, 105 L.Ed.2d 469 (1989). The exception is based on the recognition that the privilege necessarily will "protect the confidences of wrongdoers." Id. at 562, 109 S.Ct. 2619. This cost is accepted as necessary to achieve the privilege's purpose of promoting the "broader public interests in the observance of law and the administration of justice." Id. (quoting Upjohn Co. v. United States, 449 U.S. 383, 389, 101 S.Ct. 677, 66 L.Ed.2d 584 (1981)) (internal quotation marks omitted). However, when the advice sought relates "*not to prior wrongdoing,* but to *future wrongdoing,*" the privilege goes beyond what is necessary to achieve its beneficial purposes. Id. at 562–63, 109 S.Ct. 2619 (quoting 8 John Henry Wigmore, Evidence In Trials At Common Law § 2298 (John T. McNaughton rev.1961)) (internal quotation marks omitted) (emphasis in original).

To invoke the crime-fraud exception, the party seeking to abrogate the attorney-client privilege must present prima facie evidence that "gives colour to the charge" by showing "some foundation in fact." *Al–Shahin,* 474 F.3d at 946 (quoting *Clark v. United States,* 289 U.S. 1, 15, 53 S.Ct. 465, 77 L.Ed. 993 (1933)) (internal quotation marks omitted). The party seeking to abrogate the privilege meets its burden by bringing forth sufficient evidence to justify the district court in requiring the proponent of the privilege to come forward with an explanation for the evidence offered against it. *See United States v. Davis,* 1 F.3d 606, 609 (7th Cir.1993). The privilege will remain "if the district court finds [the] explanation satisfactory." *Id.*

BDO and the Intervenors would require the party seeking to abrogate the attorney-client privilege to make out a prima facie case of each element of a particular crime or common law fraud to invoke the crime-fraud exception. Such a burden is inconsistent with our requirement that the party seeking to abrogate the privilege need only "give colour to the charge" by showing "some foundation in fact." *Al–Shahin,* 474 F.3d at 946 (quoting *Clark,* 289 U.S. at 15, 53 S.Ct. 465) (internal quotation marks omitted). The approach advocated by BDO and the Intervenors reflects the view of some circuits, which require enough evidence of crime or fraud to support a verdict in order to invoke the crime-fraud exception.

---

issue the IRS presents on appeal was never before the district court, we are left with no basis to evaluate the district court's ruling on a particularly fact-bound issue. The issue is waived.

See In re Feldberg, 862 F.2d 622, 625 (7th Cir.1988). We expressly have rejected that approach. *See id.*

We therefore must determine whether the district court abused its discretion in determining that the IRS had come forward with sufficient evidence to give color to its charge that Document A–40 was a communication in furtherance of a crime or fraud. The district court engaged in a document-by-document, in camera inspection of all 267 documents for which the Intervenors claimed a privilege to determine whether they fell within the crime-fraud exception. R.178 at 18. In determining whether there was prima facie evidence of criminal or fraudulent activity, the court looked at the totality of the circumstances, including the eight "potential indicators of fraud" discussed above.[36] *See id.* at 23. Based on the totality of circumstances, the district court found no prima facie evidence of crime or fraud with respect to 266 of the documents, a ruling that the IRS does not challenge.

Applying the same totality of the circumstance approach, the district court found prima facie evidence of crime or fraud with respect to Document A–40 and instructed the Intervenors to come forward with an explanation that would rebut the evidence. *Id.* at 24. The Intervenors responded and the IRS provided further evidence to rebut the Intervenors' response. After considering all of the evidence, the district court concluded that the Intervenors had failed to rebut the prima facie showing of crime or fraud. R.190 at 10.

The Intervenors now challenge the district court's ruling. First, the Intervenors point to the decision of the United States Court of Appeals for the Second Circuit in *Denney v. BDO Seidman, L.L.P.,* 412 F.3d 58 (2005), which reversed *Denney v. Jenkens & Gilchrist,* one of the cases from which the district court derived its potential indicators of fraud.[37] *See Denney v. BDO Seidman,* 412 F.3d at 66. The Second Circuit's decision in *Denney v. BDO Seidman* does not

---

[36] [fn 10] As noted above, the eight potential indicators of fraud identified by the district court were:

(1) the marketing of pre-packaged transactions by BDO; (2) the communication by the Intervenors to BDO with the purpose of engaging in a pre-arranged transaction developed by BDO or [a] third party with the sole purpose of reducing taxable income; (3) BDO and/or the Intervenors attempting to conceal the true nature of the transaction; (4) knowledge by BDO, or a situation where BDO should have known, that the Intervenors lacked a legitimate business purpose for entering into the transaction; (5) vaguely worded consulting agreements; (6) failure by BDO to provide services under the consulting agreement yet receipt of payment; (7) mention of the COBRA transaction; and (8) use of boiler-plate documents.

R.178 at 23.

[37] [fn 11] The potential indicators of fraud the district court drew from Denney v. Jenkens & Gilchrist were mention of the COBRA transaction, vaguely worded consulting agreements and failure to provide services under the consulting agreements.

draw into question the district court's totality of the circumstances analysis in this case.

In *Denney v. BDO Seidman,* the Second Circuit held that the District Court for the Southern District of New York had erred when it concluded, without factual support in the record, that the parties had agreed that their agreements were mutually fraudulent. *Denney v. BDO Seidman,* 412 F.3d at 66. The Second Circuit's decision did not address whether facts such as mention of the COBRA transaction, vaguely worded consulting agreements or failure to provide services under the consulting agreements, i.e., the factors that the district court in the present case derived from *Denney v. Jenkens & Gilchrist,* would be indicative of fraud. Moreover, the district court in the present case did not place dispositive weight on any one of the "potential indicators of fraud," nor did the court limit its analysis to the eight potential indicators. R.190 at 5.

The remainder of the Intervenors' challenge asserts that the IRS could not defeat the Intervenors' claim of privilege under the crime-fraud exception because the IRS had failed to allege a particular offense or the elements of common law fraud, and, in any event, the Intervenors had come forward with rebuttal evidence showing a legitimate purpose underlying the transactions in question. As we already have noted, our case law does not require a party seeking to invoke the crime-fraud exception to allege a particular offense or to make a prima facie showing with respect to each element of common law fraud. The IRS only was required to present sufficient evidence to "give colour to the charge" that the communication was made in furtherance of a crime or fraud by showing "some foundation in fact." *Al–Shahin,* 474 F.3d at 946 (quoting *Clark,* 289 U.S. at 15, 53 S.Ct. 465) (internal quotation marks omitted).

After concluding that there had been a prima facie showing that Document A–40 was a communication made in furtherance of a crime or fraud, the district court gave the Intervenors the opportunity to explain the communication. The Intervenors offered an explanation, but the district court did not find it satisfactory. Nor was the district court required to find the explanation satisfactory. Thus, the district court did not abuse its discretion when it concluded that the IRS had made a prima facie showing of crime or fraud which the Intervenors failed to explain satisfactorily.

C. Tax Practitioner Privilege

We now shall address whether the district court correctly applied the tax practitioner privilege found in § 7525 to the facts of this case. Prior to 2004, § 7525 provided:

§ 7525. Confidentiality privileges relating to taxpayer communications

(a) Uniform application to taxpayer communications with federally authorized practitioners.—

(1) General rule.—With respect to tax advice, the same common law protections of confidentiality which apply to a communication between a taxpayer and an attorney shall also apply to a communication between a taxpayer and any federally authorized tax practitioner to the extent the

communication would be considered a privileged communication if it were between a taxpayer and an attorney.

(2) Limitations. Paragraph (1) may only be asserted in—

(A) any noncriminal tax matter before the Internal Revenue Service; and

(B) any noncriminal tax proceeding in Federal court brought by or against the United States.

(3) Definitions. For purposes of this subsection—

(A) Federally authorized tax practitioner. The term "federally authorized tax practitioner" means any individual who is authorized under Federal law to practice before the Internal Revenue Service if such practice is subject to Federal regulation under section 330 of title 31, United States Code.

(B) Tax advice. The term "tax advice" means advice given by an individual with respect to a matter which is within the scope of the individual's authority to practice described in subparagraph (A).

(b) Section not to apply to communications regarding corporate tax shelters. The privilege under subsection (a) shall not apply to any written communication between a federally authorized tax practitioner and a director, shareholder, officer, or employee, agent, or representative of a corporation in connection with the promotion of the direct or indirect participation of such corporation in any tax shelter (as defined in section 6662(d)(2)(C)(iii)).

26 U.S.C. § 7525 (2000). To determine whether the district court correctly applied § 7525, we first must address: (1) the elements of the privilege and, specifically, whether the "exception" to the privilege for communications related to tax shelters is an element of the privilege or whether it is a true exception; and (2) the scope of the tax shelter exception.

1. Elements of the Tax Practitioner Privilege

As with all assertions of privilege, the proponent of the tax practitioner privilege must establish each element of the privilege. *See BDO II,* 337 F.3d at 811. On the other hand, with respect to exceptions to the privilege, the burden rests on the party seeking to overcome an otherwise valid claim of privilege to prove preliminary facts that would support a finding that the claimed privilege falls within an exception. *See* Charles Alan Wright & Kenneth W. Graham, Jr., 24 Federal Practice & Procedure § 5507, at 571 (1986).

The IRS submits that § 7525(b)'s ("subsection (b)") tax shelter "exception" to the tax practitioner privilege is not an exception to the privilege, but an element of the privilege itself. Thus, under the IRS' theory, the party asserting the privilege must establish that the communication was not made, in the words of the statute, "in connection with the promotion of the direct or indirect participation . . . in any tax shelter." 26 U.S.C. § 7525(b) (2000). The Intervenors, on the other hand, contend that the tax shelter "exception" is a true exception to the tax practitioner privilege, and, consequently, the opponent of the privilege bears the burden of establishing that the communication falls within the exception.

Prior to the American Jobs Creation Act of 2004, Pub.L. No. 108–357, 118 Stat. 1418 (2004),[38] subsection (b) read:

> The privilege under subsection (a) shall not apply to any written communication between a federally authorized tax practitioner and a director, shareholder, officer, or employee, agent, or representative of a corporation in connection with the promotion of the direct or indirect participation of such corporation in any tax shelter (as defined in section 6662(d)(2)(C)(iii)).

26 U.S.C. § 7525(b) (2000). The plain wording of this subsection evinces a clear intent to treat the rule embodied in subsection (b) as an exception to the tax practitioner privilege. The first sentence of subsection (b) refers to "the privilege under subsection (a)." *Id.* The fact that the privilege does not apply to the class of communications described in subsection (b) presupposes the existence of an otherwise applicable privilege.

This conclusion is supported further by the structure of § 7525 as a whole. Section 7525(a) ("subsection (a)") sets out a general rule, *id.* § 7525(a)(1), specific limitations on the situations in which that rule may be asserted, *id.* § 7525(a)(2), and defines key terms that further limit the scope of the rule, *id.* § 7525(a)(3). By placing some specific limitations on the general rule together with the general rule in subsection (a) while placing other limitations on the general rule in subsection (b), the structure of the statute suggests that not all limitations to the privilege are of the same character. The most natural reading of the section as a whole is to consider those limitations to the scope of the general rule found in subsection (a) to constitute elements of the privilege and those limitations found in subsection (b) as exceptions to the application of that privilege.

The rationale underlying the tax shelter exception further supports this conclusion. Subsection (b) originally was added in conference committee. The report of the conference committee explained that "[t]he Conferees [did] not

---

[38] [fn 12] The American Jobs Creation Act of 2004, Pub.L. No. 108–357, 118 Stat. 1418 (2004), amended subsection (b) to read:

The privilege under subsection (a) shall not apply to any written communication which is—

(1) between a federally authorized tax practitioner and

(A) any person,

(B) any director, officer, employee, agent, or representative of the person, or

(C) any other person holding a capital or profits interest in the person, and

(2) in connection with the promotion of the direct or indirect participation of the person in any tax shelter (as defined in section 6662(d)(2)(C)(ii)).

26 U.S.C. § 7525(b) (2000 & Supp. IV 2004). These changes applied only to communications made after October 24, 2004. See American Jobs Creation Act of 2004, Pub.L. No. 108–357, § 813(b), 118 Stat. 1418, 1581 (2004). The Act did not amend the elements of the tax practitioner privilege set forth in § 7525(a).

understand the promotion of tax shelters to be part of the routine relationship between a tax practitioner and a client." H.R.Rep. No. 105–599 at 269 (1998), U.S.Code Cong. & Admin.News 1998, p. 288 (Conf.Rep.). This rationale is analogous to the rationale underlying the crime-fraud exception, i.e., advice given to further future crime or fraud goes beyond what is necessary to achieve the beneficial aims of the privilege. *See Zolin,* 491 U.S. at 562, 109 S.Ct. 2619. Thus, in both situations, the rationale underlying the limitation on the claimed privilege goes to the necessity of the communications to achieve the beneficial aims of the privilege.

Thus, based on the text, structure and purpose of subsection (b), it is clear that the tax shelter "exception" is a true exception to the tax practitioner privilege. As with any other exception to a claimed privilege, the burden rests on the opponent of the privilege to prove preliminary facts that would support a finding that the claimed privilege falls within an exception. *Cf.* Wright & Graham, 24 Federal Practice & Procedure § 5507, at 571. As with the crime-fraud exception, the opponent meets this burden by bringing forth enough evidence to show "some foundation in fact" that the exception applies. *Cf. Al–Shahin,* 474 F.3d at 946 (quoting *Clark,* 289 U.S. at 15, 53 S.Ct. 465) (internal quotation marks omitted).

2. Scope of the Tax Shelter Exception

The Intervenors contend that the tax shelter exception found in subsection (b) applies only to tax shelters that shelter corporate taxes. The Intervenors rely on the subsection's heading and the legislative history of subsection (b) to support this contention. The IRS, on the other hand, submits that the tax shelter exception, as it existed in 2002, was not so limited. To support its position, the IRS relies on the text of the statute and the legislative history of subsection (b). The question thus becomes whether the tax shelter to which the communication relates must shelter corporate, as opposed to individual, taxes.

We begin with the text of the statute. "Only if the plain language of the statute is inconclusive or clearly contravenes expressed congressional intent do we look beyond the words themselves." *Oneida Tribe of Indians v. Wisconsin,* 951 F.2d 757, 761 (7th Cir.1991). To discern the scope of the tax shelter exception, we must look to the elements of the exception. To fall within subsection (b), a communication must be: (1) written; (2) "between a federally authorized tax practitioner and a director, shareholder, officer, or employee, agent, or representative of a corporation"; and (3) made "in connection with the promotion of the direct or indirect participation of such corporation in any tax shelter" as defined by 26 U.S.C. § 6662(d)(2)(C)(ii).[39] 26 U.S.C. § 7525(b) (2000). The plain text appears to apply to any tax shelter falling within the definition of a tax shelter found at 26 U.S.C. § 6662(d)(2)(C)(ii), and at least one

---

[39] [fn 13] Prior to 2004, subsection (b) referred to the definition of "tax shelter" found at 26 U.S.C. § 6662(d)(2)(C)(iii). As a result of amendments to § 6662, that definition is found now at 26 U.S.C. § 6662(d)(2)(C)(ii). For ease of analysis, we shall refer to the current code section.

district court has found that the tax shelter exception applies to individuals when the tax shelter required the participation of a corporation. *See Doe v. Wachovia Corp.*, 268 F.Supp.2d 627 (W.D.N.C.2003).

The Intervenors contend that subsection (b)'s heading, which, prior to the 2004 amendments, read "[s]ection not to apply to communications regarding corporate tax shelters," *see* 26 U.S.C. § 7525(b) (2000), demonstrated a clear congressional intent to limit subsection (b) to tax shelters for corporate income taxes. As a general rule, "[t]he title of a statute . . . cannot limit the plain meaning of the text." *Pennsylvania Dep't of Corr. v. Yeskey*, 524 U.S. 206, 212, 118 S.Ct. 1952, 141 L.Ed.2d 215 (1998) (quoting *Bhd. of R.R. Trainmen v. Baltimore & Ohio R.R. Co.*, 331 U.S. 519, 528–29, 67 S.Ct. 1387, 91 L.Ed. 1646 (1947)) (internal quotation marks omitted) (omissions in original). A statute's heading is "of use only when [it] shed[s] light on some ambiguous word or phrase." *Yeskey*, 524 U.S. at 212, 118 S.Ct. 1952 (quoting *Bhd. of R.R. Trainmen*, 331 U.S. at 529, 67 S.Ct. 1387) (internal quotation marks omitted) (alterations in original). As noted above, subsection (b) is not ambiguous. If anything, the heading adds ambiguity to subsection (b). Absent this heading, the subsection would not seem limited to corporate tax shelters at all.

Although the section heading suggests that Congress had corporate tax shelters in mind, "the fact that a statute can be applied in situations not expressly anticipated by Congress" demonstrates breadth, not ambiguity. *Yeskey*, 524 U.S. at 212, 118 S.Ct. 1952 (quoting *Sedima, S.P.L.R. v. Imrex Co.*, 473 U.S. 479, 499, 105 S.Ct. 3275, 87 L.Ed.2d 346 (1985)) (internal quotation marks omitted). The plain language of subsection (b) is certainly broad because it applies to "*any* written communication . . . in connection with the promotion of the direct or indirect participation of such corporation in *any* tax shelter," 26 U.S.C. § 7525(b) (2000) (emphasis added), but such breadth does not make the text ambiguous.

Further evidence of the intended breadth of the statute is found in its reference to the relatively broad "tax shelter" definition found in 26 U.S.C. § 6662(d)(2)(C)(ii) as opposed to the narrower definitions found in the pre–2004 version of 26 U.S.C. § 6111.[40] The definition of "tax shelter" found at 26 U.S.C. § 6662(d)(2)(C)(ii) defines a "tax shelter" as any partnership, entity, plan or arrangement, a significant purpose of which is the avoidance or evasion of Federal income tax. 26 U.S.C. § 6662(d)(2)(C)(ii).[41]

---

[40] [fn 14] See supra note 1. It is worth noting that the American Jobs Creation Act of 2004 left the definition of "tax shelter" found in § 6662(d)(2)(C)(ii) unchanged.

[41] [fn 15] Prior to the 2004 amendments to the section, 26 U.S.C. § 6111 contained two definitions of "tax shelter" applicable only to § 6111. One of these definitions defined a "tax shelter" as certain investments for which the representations made in connection with the sale of the investment would lead "any person" to believe that the investment would produce a "tax shelter ratio" over a threshold amount. 26 U.S.C. § 6111(c)(1) (2000). The other definition of "tax shelter" previously found in § 6111 defined "tax shelter" as any partnership,

Because subsection (b) is not ambiguous, we need not look to legislative history to determine its meaning. However, even if we were to consider legislative history, we would not find it useful because that history creates more ambiguity than it eliminates. Even the legislative history that the Intervenors cite in support of its argument that subsection (b) is limited to corporate taxes raises more questions than it answers. The Conference Report upon which the Intervenors rely states that the tax shelters to which subsection (b) applies "include, *but are not limited to,* those required to be registered as confidential corporate tax shelter arrangements under section 6111(d)." H.R.Rep. No. 105–599 at 269 (1998), U.S.Code Cong. & Admin.News 1998, p. 288 (Conf.Rep.) (emphasis added). All this statement tells us is that the tax shelters referenced in subsection (b) reach a broader class of arrangements than the confidential corporate tax shelters then defined in § 6111(d). It says nothing of how much broader the exception is intended to sweep.

The rest of the legislative history is equally unenlightening. Subsection (b) was added to the bill in conference committee and had not been part of the prior debate on the legislation. After subsection (b) was added, one of the key architects of the bill expressed concern that the privilege itself would lead to confusion and litigation. *See* 144 Cong. Rec. S7626 (daily ed. July 8, 1998) (statement of Sen. Moynihan). Confusion regarding the scope of the tax shelter exception was not limited to members of Congress; tax practitioners themselves expressed confusion as to the breadth of the tax shelter exception. *See* Sheryl Stratton, *Accountant–Client Privilege: Unclear from the Start,* 80 Tax Notes 7 (July 6, 1998).

Next, the Intervenors contend that the tax shelter exception applies only to communications "when the *corporation* is the *taxpayer.*" Intervenor's Br. at 20 (italics in original). According to the Intervenors, communication between a federally authorized tax practitioner and an S corporation's officers or agents in connection with the S corporation's participation in a tax shelter therefore would not fall within the tax shelter exception. The Intervenors assert that S corporations are not taxpayers and that "corporation" in this context means a C corporation.[42] *Id.* at 20–21.

---

entity, plan or arrangement, a significant purpose of which is the avoidance or evasion of Federal income tax for a direct or indirect participant which is a corporation, that is offered under conditions of confidentiality, and for which the promoters receive commissions exceeding $100,000. Id. § 6111(d)(1). In contrast, 26 U.S.C. § 6662(d)(2)(C)(ii) makes no reference to dollar or "tax shelter ratio" thresholds, nor does it require the tax shelter to benefit a corporation.

[42] [fn 16] A number of the Intervenors participated in BDO's programs through S corporations.

We cannot accept this argument. S corporations are both taxpayers and corporations under the IRC.[43] Although S corporations are not subject to taxes imposed by subtitle A, chapter 1 of the IRC, *see id.* § 1363(a), this exception merely means that they do not pay *directly* income taxes. Section 1363 does not exempt S corporations from other taxes imposed by the IRC, such as employment taxes (subtitle C) and excise taxes (subtitles D and E). Notably, the IRC defines "taxpayers" as "any person subject to *any* internal revenue tax." *Id.* § 7701(a)(14) (emphasis added).[44] This definition applies throughout the IRC, except when "otherwise distinctly expressed or manifestly incompatible" with the intent of the statute. *Id.* § 7701(a). Section 7525 does not express distinctly any intent to define "taxpayer" only to include income tax payers, nor would it be "manifestly incompatible" with § 7525 to extend the tax practitioner privilege to advice given in connection with taxes other than income taxes.

Additionally, S corporations must calculate their taxable income, *id.* § 1363(b), and file a return, *id.* § 6037(a). Further, the S corporation's taxable income is calculated in the same manner as an individual's, with certain exceptions which are not relevant here. *Id.* § 1363(b). Indeed, apart from non-separately computed income or losses, which are not relevant here, the S corporation calculates the income or losses passed through to its shareholders by calculating the S corporation's gross income and subtracting "the deductions allowed to *the corporation.*" *Id.* § 1366(a)(2) (emphasis added).

The Intervenors provide no support for their argument that the term "corporation," as used in § 7525(b) only means "C corporation." The IRC itself defines an S corporation as a "small business corporation for which an election under section 1362(a) is in effect," *id.* § 1361(a)(1); it defines a C corporation as "a corporation which is not an S corporation," *id.* § 1361(a)(2). This usage alone suggests that, when a particular section of the IRC is intended to apply only to C corporations, Congress will use that term, rather than the generic "corporation." Additionally, the IRC and implementing Treasury Regulations define "corporation" for federal tax purposes as "a business entity organized under a Federal or State statute . . . if the statute describes or refers to the entity as incorporated or as a corporation." 26 C.F.R. § 301.7701–2(b)(1).

The regulations relied upon by the Intervenors in support of their argument that "corporation," as used in subsection (b), means "C corporation" are inapposite. These regulations implement § 6111, which, as we have noted above,

---

[43] [fn 17] If S corporations were not taxpayers, then the tax shelter exception is irrelevant, as the tax practitioner privilege applies only to "communication[s] between a taxpayer and any federally authorized tax practitioner." 26 U.S.C. § 7525(a)(1). If the S corporation is not a taxpayer, the S corporation has no privilege to assert with respect to communications between the S corporation's director, shareholder, officer, employee, agent or representative and a federally authorized tax practitioner.

[44] [fn 18] A corporation is a person for purposes of the IRC. See 26 U.S.C. § 7701(a)(1).

applies to a much narrower definition of "tax shelter" than the one applied in subsection (b). Congress chose to define "tax shelter" for purposes of subsection (b) using a broader definition than that found in § 6111. However narrowly the cited regulations may confine the application of § 6111, they are of little relevance in defining the breadth of the definition found in 26 U.S.C. § 6662(d)(2)(C)(ii).[45]

---

[45] [fn 19] The regulation to which the Intervenors refer, 26 C.F.R. § 301.6111–2, was promulgated prior to the 2004 amendments to § 6111 (the Intervenors actually cite the temporary regulations, but those regulations have since become permanent; the definition of confidential corporate income tax shelter in the permanent regulations is the same as that in the temporary regulations). Section 6111 was and remains an anti-fraud statute, aimed at providing the IRS with records of financial products marketed for the purpose of reducing Federal income tax liability. The pre–2004 version of § 6111 identified two types of transactions for special scrutiny as "tax shelters." See 26 U.S.C. § 6111(c) & (d) (2000). The first sort of transaction defined tax shelters generally as investments offered for sale that, based on the representations in connection with the offering, would lead a reasonable person to infer that the investment would generate deductions and credits exceeding statutorily defined ratio of deductions and credits to the adjusted basis of the initial investment. See id. § 6111(c). Further, the investment had to be a registered security or "substantial." Id. The second definition of "tax shelter" deemed confidential transactions, a significant purpose of which was the avoidance or evasion of corporate income taxes and for which the tax shelter's promoter may receive at least $100,000 in fees, to be tax shelters. Id. § 6111(d). As is evident from the first definition of "tax shelter" found in the pre–2004 version of § 6111, the section as a whole is not limited in its consideration to corporate tax shelters. The regulations the Intervenors cite implement the pre–2004 version of § 6111 only with respect to the second definition of tax shelter, which was only one of the types of transactions identified by § 6111 as requiring special scrutiny. The current regulations continue to identify confidential corporate income tax shelters for purposes of implementing § 6111, even though § 6111 no longer uses the term "tax shelter."

Section 6662, on the other hand, is concerned with distinct issues. Section 6662 deals with penalties for underpayment of a taxpayer's tax liability. When an understatement of income is "substantial," § 6662 imposes a penalty of twenty percent of the amount of taxes underpaid. 26 U.S.C. § 6662(a)-(b). However, § 6662 provides that taxpayers may reduce the amount of an understatement, and hence the penalty imposed, by that portion of the understatement resulting from a position taken by the taxpayer for which there was substantial authority or, if the position is disclosed adequately on the tax return, for which there was a reasonable basis for such treatment. Id. § 6662(d)(2)(B). As an exception to this general rule, however, § 6662 provides that that portion of an understatement attributable to a tax shelter, i.e., a transaction into which the taxpayer enters, the

Finally, we address the Intervenors' contention that application of the tax shelter exception to tax shelters that do not involve corporate income taxes would "consume[ ] the general rule" by destroying the privilege any time a corporation participates in a tax shelter. Intervenors' Br. at 20. The Intervenors submit that, if the tax shelter exception extends to individual income taxes, any time a corporation, such as a banking corporation or investment corporation, is involved in the tax shelter, the general rule of tax practitioner privilege will be negated.

A close look at the tax shelter exception makes clear that the Intervenors' submission overstates significantly the scope of that exception. First, the exception applied only to written communications. Second, the written communication must have been between a federally authorized tax practitioner and a director, shareholder, officer, or employee, agent, or representative of a corporation. Third, the written communication must have been "in connection with the promotion of the direct or indirect participation of such corporation in any tax shelter," as defined in § 6662(d)(2)(C)(ii). 26 U.S.C. § 7525(b) (2000).

Because the exception is limited to written communications, oral communications between a tax practitioner and the corporate agent remain within the general rule of privilege. Further, because the tax shelter exception applies only when the written communication relates to the corporation's direct or indirect participation in a particular type of tax shelter, i.e., one meeting the definition found in § 6662(d)(2)(C)(ii), the tax shelter exception will not affect any otherwise privileged communication that does not relate to a transaction falling within that definition.

Most importantly, the tax shelter exception applies only to communications between the tax practitioner and the corporate agent. As noted earlier, the tax practitioner privilege is limited to communications that would be privileged if they had been made to an attorney.[46] The attorney-client privilege protects only

---

substantial purpose of which is to avoid or evade income taxes, cannot be used to reduce the amount of the taxpayer's understatement, and hence the penalty imposed. Id. § 6662(d)(2)(B)(i). Thus, § 6662 reflects a congressional policy decision that understatements above a particular threshold, i.e., substantial understatements, merit penalties. It also has made the policy choice that certain positions taken on tax returns, i.e., those supported by substantial authority or, when properly disclosed, a rational basis, should not result in the taxpayer incurring penalties unless the position taken is the result of a transaction into which the taxpayer entered for the purpose of evading or avoiding taxes.

[46] [fn 20] We have held previously that this limitation means that non-lawyer tax practitioners cannot claim the privilege when "doing other than lawyers' work." United States v. BDO Seidman, 337 F.3d 802, 810 (7th Cir.2003) (quoting United States v. Frederick, 182 F.3d 496, 502 (7th Cir.1999)) (internal quotation marks omitted). This statement cannot be taken to mean that the tax practitioner privilege authorizes non-attorneys to engage in the practice of law when representing others before the IRS. By limiting the availability of the privilege to those individuals authorized to practice before the IRS subject to

those statements made by the client to the attorney in confidence. *See Evans*, 113 F.3d at 1462. A communication is not made in confidence when the client intends that the communication shall be disclosed to unprivileged third parties. *See* 2 Christopher B. Mueller & Laird C. Kirkpatrick, Federal Evidence § 186, at 324 (2d ed.1994); *see also* Proposed Fed.R.Evid. § 503(a)(4), 56 F.R.D. 183, 236 (1972) ("A communication is 'confidential' if not intended to be disclosed to third persons other than those to whom disclosure is in furtherance of the rendition of professional legal services to the client or those reasonably necessary for the transmission of the communication."). However, an exception to this general rule permits disclosure of confidential communications by the attorney to an expert retained for the purpose of rendering legal services. 2 Mueller & Kirkpatrick, Federal Evidence § 186, at 324.

The tax practitioner privilege protects those communications which would be privileged if made to an attorney. *See* 26 U.S.C. § 7525(a). This protection is embodied both in the general rule regarding confidential communications and in the exception for disclosures to experts retained to assist the tax practitioner. With respect to individual income taxpayers, the tax shelter exception has the effect of taking communications intended to be passed along in written form to corporate agents in connection with the corporation's participation in a tax shelter out of the exception for communications to third party experts retained to assist the tax practitioner. Such communications are subject to the general rule that communications to third parties are not privileged. For all other confidential communications between the individual income tax payer and its tax practitioner, both the general rule and the exception for communications to a retained expert apply.

Thus, we cannot accept the Intervenors' prediction that application of the tax shelter exception to individual income tax payers, as it relates to communications made before October 21, 2004, would swallow the general rule of tax practitioner privilege any time a corporation was involved in the shelter.

3. The District Court's Decision

We turn now to the district court's ruling that the tax shelter exception did not apply to the Intervenors' documents. It is unclear what legal standard the district court applied in assessing the applicability of the tax shelter exception to

---

federal regulations and limiting the scope of the privilege to advice given within the individual's authority as a federally authorized tax practitioner, see 26 U.S.C. § 7525(a)(1), (3), § 7525 clearly is not intended to alter the scope of a federally authorized tax practitioner's authority to practice. Further, the regulations governing tax practitioners in activities before the IRS expressly state that nothing in the regulations shall "be construed as authorizing persons not members of the bar to practice law." 31 C.F.R. § 10.32. Taken in context, our prior observations on the scope of the privilege recognize nothing more than communications, though technically within the scope of practice before the IRS, that would fall outside of the attorney-client privilege are also outside of the tax practitioner privilege.

the communications at issue. The district court disposed of the matter in a footnote, in which it stated that, for the same reasons it found that the IRS' characterization of the Intervenors' conduct as falling within the crime-fraud exception, it did not find that the Intervenors engaged in tax shelters. *See* R.178 at 17 n. 6. However, the tax shelter exception requires no showing of crime or fraud. Further, the record is unclear regarding what evidence, if any, was produced by the IRS to support its contention that the documents fell within the tax shelter exception. The IRS did contend that a significant purpose of the financial products purchased by the Intervenors was to avoid or evade federal income tax and the record reflects that some of the Intervenors had purchased the financial product through a corporation. R.135 at 11. However, the district court's decision does not indicate how these allegations fell short of establishing the applicability of the tax shelter exception.

Additionally, the district court did not note which claims of privilege were sustained based on the attorney-client privilege and which were sustained based on the tax practitioner privilege. *See* R.178 at 13–14, 29. Because we cannot evaluate the legal standard employed by the district court, remand is necessary. *In re Grand Jury Proceedings (Thullen),* 220 F.3d at 572. Thus, we must vacate the district court's ruling with respect to the applicability of the tax shelter exception and remand for further consideration.

On remand, for each of the 266 documents that the district court concluded to fall within a valid claim of privilege, the court should first determine whether the document falls within the attorney-client privilege, the tax practitioner privilege or both privileges. For those documents that would fall within the attorney-client privilege or both the attorney-client and tax practitioner privilege, no further analysis is required, as the tax shelter exception applies only to the tax practitioner privilege. *See* 26 U.S.C. § 7525(b) (2000). For those documents falling solely within the tax practitioner privilege, the burden rests upon the IRS to come forward with sufficient evidence to demonstrate some foundation in fact that a particular document falls within the tax shelter exception. To meet this burden, the IRS must bring forward evidence that: (1) the communication relates to a tax shelter, as defined by § 6662(d)(2)(C)(ii); (2) the communication was made by a director, shareholder, officer, or employee, agent, or representative of the corporation; and (3) the communication was made in connection with the promotion of the direct or indirect participation of the corporation in such tax shelter.

CONCLUSION

For the forgoing reasons, the decision of the district court is affirmed in part and vacated and remanded in part.

AFFIRMED in part, VACATED and REMANDED in part

NOTES AND QUESTIONS

1. Why are organizers and sellers of tax shelters required to register with the IRS?

2.   How does the crime-fraud exception work?

D.   Fifth Amendment Act of Production Privilege

In addition to the above privilege claims, when there is potential criminal liability at issue, a taxpayer may claim the Fifth Amendment privilege.[47] This privilege may arise in two situations. The most obvious situation where a taxpayer may make a valid Fifth Amendment claim is where the IRS has summoned that taxpayer to provide testimony. In a summons proceeding, if the IRS attempts to compel an answer to a question that may incriminate the taxpayer, the taxpayer may refuse to answer.

There is a much less obvious situation where a taxpayer may claim the Fifth Amendment privilege. Where the IRS has requested documents, and the act of producing the documents could tend to incriminate the taxpayer, the taxpayer may refuse to turn over any documents. This is known as invoking the Fifth Amendment Act of Production privilege.[48] Although it does not seem like this situation would occur often, the IRS acknowledges this claim in its Internal Revenue Manual.[49] Section 25.5.4.1(2) of the Internal Revenue Manual provides as follows:

> IRC 7602 authorizes the IRS to summon taxpayers and third parties to testify and to produce books and records. However, if answering a question would tend to incriminate the summoned person, that person may assert his or her Fifth Amendment privilege and refuse to answer. In contrast, a summoned person has no Fifth Amendment privilege in the contents of voluntarily created, pre-existing documents because the Government did not compel that person to create the documents. However, the act of producing those documents may tend to incriminate a summoned person because the mere act of production compels that person to tacitly admit that the documents exist,

---

[47] U.S. CONST. amend. V.

[48] *See* United States v. Hubbell, 530 U.S. 27, 36 (2000); United States v. Ponds, 454 F.3d 313, 316 (2006).

[49] *See* I.R.M. § 25.5.5.4.1(2) ("IRC 7602 authorizes the IRS to summon taxpayers and third parties to testify and to produce books and records. However, if answering a question would tend to incriminate the summoned person, that person may assert his or her Fifth Amendment privilege and refuse to answer. In contrast, a summoned person has no Fifth Amendment privilege in the contents of voluntarily created, pre-existing documents because the Government did not compel that person to create the documents. However, the act of producing those documents may tend to incriminate a summoned person because the mere act of production compels that person to tacitly admit that the documents exist, they are in that person's possession, and he or she believes the documents produced are those required by the summons.").

they are in that person's possession, and he or she believes the documents produced are those required by the summons.

CHAPTER 14

IRS APPEALS OFFICE REVIEW

A. Concluding the Examination

At the conclusion of an audit, the examiner contacts the taxpayer with the results. There are three obvious potential results: (1) neither the taxpayer nor the IRS owes the other any money, (2) the IRS owes the taxpayer money, or (3) the taxpayer owes the IRS money. Where the examiner decides that neither the taxpayer nor the IRS owe each other anything, the IRS sends the taxpayer a "no change" letter. This indicates that the IRS does not propose any changes to the tax return under review.

In some instances, as in scenario (2), the examiner concludes the IRS owes the taxpayer money. This situation arises where the taxpayer has made an overpayment and is entitled to a refund. When the IRS makes a determination in an audit that the taxpayer has overpaid, it is not necessary for the taxpayer to request a refund. Rather, the IRS will send the taxpayer a check.

If, as in scenario (3), the examiner concludes that the taxpayer owes money, the next question is whether the taxpayer agrees with the examiner. Toward the conclusion of a face-to-face examination, the examiner will talk to the taxpayer to find out if he or she is in agreement. If the IRS and the taxpayer are in agreement, the examiner will have the taxpayer sign a form waiving restrictions on assessment. By signing the form, the taxpayer waives the right to contest the liability in Tax Court. This means that if the taxpayer has a change of heart and wants to challenge the IRS's determination, the taxpayer will have to pursue the case in federal district court or the Court of Federal Claims. The taxpayer has the option of reserving some issues to challenge and settling others.

If the taxpayer disagrees or partially disagrees with the examiner's conclusion, then the dispute continues. Generally, the IRS sends the taxpayer proposed adjustments and a report explaining them (the Revenue Agent Report (RAR)), and a letter providing the taxpayer with 30 days to appeal the proposed adjustments through the IRS's internal appeal process. This internal appeal, however, is not an appeal of right. If the IRS sends such a 30-day letter, the taxpayer may file a protest or, if the liability is low enough, request consideration by the Appeals Office.

Whether to provide a taxpayer an appeal from an examination is discretionary.[1] May taxpayers have, however, demanded appeal rights or otherwise misunderstand them. The following case discusses appeal rights in the context of extending the statute of limitations on assessment.

HOULBERG v. COMMISSIONER
T.C. Memo. 1985-497
United States Tax Court

GERBER, Judge:

By statutory notice, respondent determined . . . deficiencies in petitioners' Federal income tax. . . . The issues for decision are (1) whether the period of limitations on assessment for 1976 and 1977 was extended by valid consents or had expired prior to issuance of the notice of deficiency, and (2) whether the notice of deficiency was issued by a person lacking proper authority and, therefore, was invalid.

FINDINGS OF FACT

Some of the facts have been stipulated. The stipulation of facts and accompanying exhibits are so found and incorporated by this reference.

Petitioners are husband and wife and resided in Los Angeles, California, when they filed their petition. They timely filed joint Federal income tax returns for 1976, 1977, 1978, and 1979.

In November 1979, petitioners received a Form 872 (Consent to Extend the Time to Assess Tax) to extend the period of limitations on assessment for 1976 until September 30, 1981. The form provided in part: 'MAKING THIS CONSENT WILL NOT DEPRIVE THE TAXPAYER(S) OF ANY APPEAL RIGHTS TO WHICH THEY WOULD OTHERWISE BE ENTITLED.' The

---

[1] *See* Houlberg v. Commissioner, 50 T.C.M. (CCH) 1125, 1129, T.C.M. (P-H) ¶ 2224, at 85 (1985) (refusing to require the IRS to provide appeal rights to a taxpayer who refused to consent to an extension of the statute of limitations on assessment; "The Code imposes no general requirement on the IRS to confer with a taxpayer who has signed a waiver prior to issuing a notice of deficiency"); I.R.M. 33.3.6.1(3) ("If an issue in a case is designated, the taxpayer will not receive a 30-day letter with respect to remaining unresolved issues in the case. Rather, the taxpayer will be issued a statutory notice of deficiency."); INTERNAL REVENUE SERV., PUBLICATION 556, EXAMINATION OF RETURNS, APPEAL RIGHTS, AND CLAIMS FOR REFUND 8 (2013), https://www.irs.gov/publications/p556 ("[Y]our reasons for disagreeing must come within the scope of the tax laws. For example, you cannot appeal your case based only on moral, religious, political, constitutional, conscientious, or similar grounds.").

form was accompanied by a cover letter from the Internal Revenue Service (IRS) notifying petitioners that the return of K. T. Associates, a partnership with which they were involved, was under examination. The letter in part stated:

> We do not expect to receive the results of the entity(s) audit before the expiration of the normal statute of limitations. Generally, a delay in time is the result of the taxpayers exercising their right to appeal the IRS decision. In order to allow time for adequate consideration of your case in conjunction with the audit of the entity(s), we request that you sign the enclosed consent * * *.

After consulting with their accountant, Michael J. Ravin, petitioners signed the form and returned it to the IRS which accepted the consent.

In May 1981, petitioners received a Form 872A (Special Consent to Extend the Time to Assess Tax), which in part provided that any tax due for 1976 could be assessed on or before the 90th day after the IRS mailed a notice of deficiency. The form and its accompanying cover letter contained the same language regarding appeal rights as cited above. After consulting with Ravin, petitioners signed the form and returned it to the IRS which accepted the consent.

In October 1980, a Form 872A was sent to petitioners for 1977. Ravin advised petitioners to sign the consent and prepared a letter to be used by them in forwarding the consent to the IRS. The letter, dated December 5, 1980, provided in part:

> Our signing this extension of time is expressly contingent upon the fact that we are not waiving any of our rights to the normal administrative procedures afforded to us by the Internal Revenue Service in connection with audit of our 1977 income tax return.

The following language was added to the bottom of the last page of the Form 872A: 'SUBJECT TO THE ATTACHED LETTER DATED Dec. 5, 1980.'

On receipt of the letter and conditional extension, an IRS representative called Ravin and advised him that the IRS would accept only an unmodified consent. Ravin then suggested to petitioners that they sign an unaltered consent, which they did. The signed Form 872A and the cover letter sent with respect to 1977 contained the language regarding appeal rights previously cited.

In October 1981, a Form 872A was sent to petitioners with respect to 1978. Petitioners refused to sign it.

On April 15, 1982, petitioners were sent a notice of deficiency covering 1976, 1977, 1978, and 1979. The notice bore the District Director's name, and was initialed by Jerold M. Ching, a Quality Review Section Chief, Grade GS-13.

Petitioners did not have a conference with the IRS prior to issuance of the notice of deficiency. Subsequent to issuance of the notice, an administrative hearing was held between counsel for petitioners and a representative of respondent's appeals division, at which time the parties agreed [on] the deficiencies for the taxable years at issue. . . .

The parties agree that, if this Court rules for respondent with respect to the validity of the consents and the notice of deficiency, the deficiencies are as above.

OPINION

VALIDITY OF CONSENTS

Petitioners argue that the period of limitations on assessment for 1976 and 1977 expired prior to issuance of the notice of deficiency. They assert that they consented to extend the period of limitations in return for administrative review and the opportunity to present their views before issuance of a statutory notice, and that the consents are invalid because this condition was not met. Respondent maintains that the period of limitations was extended by valid consents. We agree with respondent.

Section 6501[2] states the general rule that a tax must be assessed within three years of the filing of a return. Section 6501(c)(4) permits the IRS and taxpayers to extend the period of limitations on assessment by written agreement. Since petitioners timely filed their tax returns for 1976 and 1977, the notice of deficiency, issued April 15, 1982, was barred unless the assessment period had been validly extended.

Petitioners maintain that they received both oral and written assurances that they would receive a hearing prior to issuance of a deficiency notice. At trial, petitioner Jens Houlberg (Houlberg) testified that towards the end of 1979, he was notified by mail that the IRS was conducting an audit of calendar years 1976 through 1979. Houlberg stated that he called Ravin, who told him that he would be afforded an opportunity to be heard before a notice of deficiency was issued. Houlberg further testified that other than his wife, Ravin, and counsel, he had not discussed the extensions with anyone. When asked the basis of his understanding, other than from his discussions with Ravin, that he would receive a pre-notice hearing, Houlberg described his experience with past audits. At no time did Houlberg testify that the IRS promised him a pre-notice hearing for the taxable years at issue.

Ravin, petitioner's accountant, also testified at the hearing. He stated that after receiving a copy of the first extension request, he called the IRS representative whose name appeared on the accompanying cover letter. Ravin related:

> I asked him at that point in time * * * (if) signing of the consent would preclude the Service from sending a notice of deficiency prior to Mr. Houlberg or myself * * * expressing our position before and during the normal administrative review procedure.

> And he told me that this would in no way preclude that.

Ravin further related that he had spoken with another IRS representative regarding the requested extension for 1978. Ravin stated:

---

[2] [fn 1] All statutory references are to the Internal Revenue Code of 1954, as amended and in effect for the taxable years at issue.

(I) reiterated the taxpayers' position with appeal rights being confirmed, that this in no way would jeopardize their ability to go through the normal administrative appeals prior to the notice of deficiency being issued.

Ravin continued that he had contacted still another IRS representative regarding the extension requested for 1977. He stated:

(I) again reiterated the same position, with respect to the administrative appeal rights. She agreed with me.

Ravin further testified that he was contacted by an IRS representative regarding the modified Form 872A petitioners had sent to the IRS. According to Ravin, the IRS representative

said that they could not accept a conditional extension, and that they would be sending out a normal extension of time requesting Mr. Houlberg to sign it. And at that point in time, I asked, well, did they understand that they were not waiving their appeal rights. And they said they certainly did, and it was very evident in the letter that I had sent — or Mr. Houlberg had sent.

At no time did Ravin testify that an IRS representative promised petitioners a hearing prior to issuance of a notice of deficiency. He essentially related that he was told that by signing the consents petitioners would not harm their appeal rights.

The final witness at the hearing was Glenn Marker. During 1981, Marker was chief of a unit involved with solicitation of consents to extend the period of limitations on assessments. Marker testified that he did not recall having had any conversations with petitioners or Ravin. He stated that he had never indicated to a taxpayer or a taxpayer's representative that by extending the statute of limitations they would be guaranteed an appeals conference prior to issuance of a deficiency notice. Marker further testified as to what taxpayers were told would occur if a taxpayer chose to extend the statute:

We would go on further to explain that if they chose to extend the statute, the case would then be retained in the Suspense Unit, awaiting the resolution of partnership adjustments, depend (sic) upon the outcome of the adjustments. If it was in the government's favor, we would try to solicit an agreement from the taxpayer, based upon the results of the partnership audit. And if the taxpayers then chose not to, the case would be moved forward for issuance of the 30-day letter.

The 30-day letter would then be issued, and they would have 30 days to file a protest to the government's position. And then, if they had not filed that letter, then it would go default to the 90-day section for against (sic) the issuance of the statutory notice of deficiency.

Marker was subsequently asked if

the process is the consent is signed, you finish up your audit, you then contact the taxpayer, the taxpayer is given an opportunity to settle it at that level, if he can't, then he is allowed to protest?

He responded affirmatively. He stated that he knew of no cases in which a consent was signed and a notice issued before an appeals conference was allowed. Later, however, he stated that although it was normal procedure to issue a 30-day letter, there were instances where statutory notices went out without such letters being sent. He described these instances as

> cases where we have determined them (the cases) to be litigating vehicles, that they cannot be resolved at the appellate level * * *. The manager looks at the case and makes a determination, and can actually recommend the issuance of a 90-day letter, because he doesn't feel that anything could be resolved at that level, the 30-day level.

Marker's testimony does not demonstrate that respondent promised petitioners pre-notice of deficiency appeal rights in return for petitioners' consent to extend the period of limitations, as petitioners assert. On the contrary, Marker stated that no such promises are made to taxpayers. Marker indicated that although pre-notice conferences are commonly held, taxpayers are not always afforded such meetings.

The waiver forms and accompanying cover letters similarly contain no explicit promise for a pre-notice conference.[3] Like the oral communications with IRS representatives that petitioners note, these written communications merely did not rule out the possibility of such a meeting.

The same contention petitioners make regarding the conditional nature of their consents was made previously by their accountant, Ravin, in his own case which was decided by this Court. Ravin v. Commissioner, T.C. Memo 1981-107, affd. without published opinion 755 F.2d 936 (9th Cir. 1985). In Ravin v. Commissioner, supra, we held that consents signed by Ravin were valid, even though an IRS agent had made, and a letter from the IRS contained, inaccurate statements concerning his appeal rights. With respect to the effect to be given statements of IRS agents to taxpayers, we stated:

> (t)he often stated general rule is that a revenue agent does not have the authority to bind the Commissioner. See United States v. Stewart, 311 U.S. 60 (1940); Bornstein v. United States, 170 Ct. Cl. 576, 345 F.2d 558 (1965);

---

[3] [fn 2] To the same effect are Rev. Proc. 79-22, 1979-1 C.B. 563, Rev. Proc. 57-6, 1957-1 C.B. 729, and IRS Publication 1035 (Extending the Tax Assessment Period), which petitioners cite. With respect to their citation to Publication 1035 as authority for their position, we point out to petitioners that the authoritative sources of Federal tax law are in the statutes, regulations, and judicial decisions and not in such informal publications. See Zimmerman v. Commissioner, 71 T.C. 367, 371 (1978), affd. without published opinion 614 F.2d 1294 (2d Cir. 1979).

Wilkinson v. United States, 157 Ct. Cl. 847, 304 F.2d 469 (1962). A claim of estoppel is usually rejected, although the taxpayer contends that he followed the erroneous advice of an agent and acted in reliance upon it. Cf. Montgomery v. Commissioner, 65 T.C. 511, 522 (1975); Boulez v. Commissioner, 76 T.C. 209 (1981). (41 T.C.M. at 1064, 1066, 50 P-H Memo T.C. par. 81, 107 at 81-381)

We further observed, with respect to the same language on the Forms 872 and 872A regarding appeal rights that we quote in this case, that

> (this language) does not state that any conferences will be automatically provided, but it merely states that by signing the Form 872 the taxpayer retains the same rights to an appellate conference prior to the issuance of the notice of deficiency as all other taxpayers. Put differently, it is nowhere indicated on the Form 872 that by signing it a taxpayer will improve his appeal rights. (41 T.C.M. at 1066, 50 P-H Memo T.C. at 382-81)

In Ravin v. Commissioner, supra, we additionally pointed out that procedural rules with respect to administrative appeals are merely directory, and compliance with them is not essential to the validity of a notice of deficiency. See also Luhring v. Glotzbach, 304 F.2d 560, 563 (4th Cir. 1962); Rosenberg v. Commissioner, 450 F.2d 529, 532 (10th Cir. 1971), affg. a Memorandum Opinion of this Court; Collins v. Commissioner, 61 T.C. 693, 701 (1974); Flynn v. Commissioner, 40 T.C. 770, 773 (1963). Accordingly, we find that the IRS did not violate its procedural rules by not conferring with petitioners prior to issuing a deficiency notice and, consequently, the requirements of section 6501(c)(4) have been met.

Petitioners further suggest that the consents are ineffective because petitioners signed them under the mistaken belief that a pre-notice hearing would be held.[4] As is implicit in our opinion in Ravin v. Commissioner, supra, a consent is valid where no hearing is held, even though a taxpayer expects such review. We know of no authority holding that a valid waiver of the period of limitations on assessment requires knowledge that a pre-notice administrative hearing may not be held. Petitioners note that they are not accountants. Petitioners were represented by an accountant (Ravin) and we are not persuaded that petitioners' backgrounds should dictate a different result than that reached in Ravin v. Commissioner, supra, with respect to the effectiveness of the waivers.

The Code imposes no general requirement on the IRS to confer with a taxpayer who has signed a waiver prior to issuing a notice of deficiency. For the reasons we have stated, we do not find that pre-notice administrative review was required in the specific circumstances of this case. Accordingly, we hold that the period for assessment for 1976 and 1977 was extended by valid consents.

---

[4] [fn 3] Petitioners were under no duress to sign the waivers. Compare Robertson v. Commissioner, T.C. Memo. 1973-205 (taxpayers, who had never previously dealt with the IRS, signed consents under threat of seizure of the their (sic) property and without the opportunity to consult with their attorney).

AUTHORITY TO ISSUE DEFICIENCY NOTICE

Petitioners argue that Jerold M. Ching, the Quality Review Section Chief (Grade GS-13), who issued the deficiency notice, lacked properly delegated authority to do so, and that the notice therefore is invalid. Respondent maintains that Jerold M. Ching had the delegated authority to issue the notice. We agree with respondent.

In Ravin v. Commissioner, supra, the taxpayers also argued that the IRS representative who issued the statutory notice did so without authority. The circumstances in which the statutory notice was issued are very similar in the two cases and, accordingly, Ravin v. Commissioner, supra, provides appropriate precedent for this case.

In Ravin v. Commissioner, supra, we pointed out the authority by which certain IRS representatives could issue deficiency notices:

Section 6212(a) provides that if the Secretary determines that there is an income tax deficiency, he is authorized to send a notice of deficiency to the taxpayer by certified mail or registered mail. The term 'Secretary' is defined in section 7701(a)(11)(B) as the 'Secretary of the Treasury or his delegate.' The phrase 'or his delegate' is defined in section 7701(a)(12)(A)(i) as 'any officer, employee, or agency of the Treasury Department duly authorized by the Secretary of the Treasury directly, or indirectly by one or more redelegations of authority, to perform the function mentioned or described in the context.' Under the provisions of section 301.7701-9(b), Proced. & Admin. Regs., when a function is vested by statute in the Secretary of the Treasury or his delegate, and the Treasury regulations provide that such function may be performed by a district director, then the provision in the regulations constitutes a delegation by the Secretary to the district director of the authority to perform such function. Section 301.6212-1(a) (Proced. & Admin. Regs.) provides that if a district director determines that there is an income tax deficiency, he is authorized to notify the taxpayer of the deficiency. Thus, the authority to issue notices of deficiency has been delegated by the Secretary to district directors. Under section 301.7701-9(c) (Proced. & Admin. Regs.) an officer authorized by regulations to perform a function has the authority to redelegate the performance of such function except to the extent that 'such power to do so redelegate is prohibited or restricted by proper order or directive.'

On July 27, 1980, the Los Angeles District Director issued Delegation of Authority No. LA-41 (Rev. 9), which redelegated his authority to issue notices of deficiency to Section Chiefs, Quality Review Staff. Delegation Order LA-41 (Rev. 9) cites as authority Delegation Order No. 77 (Rev. 14),[5] which was issued by the Commissioner of Internal Revenue. On March 21, 1982, the Commissioner issued Delegation Order No. 77 (Rev. 15),[6] which superseded Delegation Order No. 77 (Rev. 14). Delegation Order No. 77 (Rev. 15) was in

---

[5] [fn 4] Delegation Order No. 77 (Rev. 14) is found at 1980-1 C.B. 573.
[6] [fn 5] Delegation Order No. 77 (Rev. 15) is found at 1982-1 C.B. 335.

effect when the notice of deficiency was issued.[7] Since the authority of a District Director to delegate his authority to issue notices of deficiency is derived from sections 301.6212-1(a) and 301.7701-9, Proced. & Admin. Regs., the fact that Delegation Order LA-41 (Rev. 9) referred to Delegation Order 77 (Rev. 14), which had been superseded by Delegation Order 77 (Rev. 15) at the time the notice of deficiency was issued, is irrelevant to the validity of the notice. See Estate of Brimm v. Commissioner, 70 T.C. 15, 19-22 (1978), and Ravin v. Commissioner, supra. In both Estate of Brimm v. Commissioner, supra, and Ravin v. Commissioner, supra, although the District Director's delegation order in effect at the time the deficiency notice was issued cited as authority a superseded revision of Delegation Order No. 77, we found no jurisdictional defect.

Delegation Order No. 77 (Rev. 15) specifically reaffirms the District Director's power to redelegate his function of issuing statutory notices of deficiency and in no way prohibits the delegations found in Delegation Order LA-41 (Rev. 9). To the extent that the citation of Delegation Order No. 77 (Rev. 14) may constitute a defect in the chain of delegation of authority to issue notices of deficiency, the defect was extremely minor and did not prejudice petitioners' rights. See Estate of Brimm v. Commissioner, supra at 19-22; Perlmutter v. Commissioner, 44 T.C. 382, 400 (1965), affd. 373 F.2d 45 (10th Cir. 1967); Ravin v. Commissioner, supra.

Accordingly, we hold that the delegation to Jerold M. Ching was proper, and that he had authority to issue the notice of deficiency.

To reflect the foregoing,

Decision will be entered for respondent.

NOTES AND QUESTIONS

1. Is the IRS required to offer an Appeals Conference with taxpayers who have given written consent to extend the assessment statute?
2. To whom has the "Secretary" delegated the authority to issue deficiency notices?

Although administrative appeals are routine, there are situations where the IRS will decline to offer one. First, the IRS might not offer an appeal where the taxpayer refuses to let the IRS have more time to conduct its audit.[8] If the

---

[7] [fn 6] On April 19, 1982, Delegation Order LA-41 (Rev. 9) was superseded by Delegation Order LA-41 (Rev. 10), which cites Delegation Order 77 (Rev. 15) as authority for redelegation.

[8] See, e.g., Houlberg, 50 T.C.M. (CCH) at 1125, 1126, T.C.M. (P-H) ¶ 2221, at 85 (1985) (denying the taxpayer the opportunity for an Appeals Office proceeding because the taxpayer refused to sign a Form 872A to extend the statute of limitations on assessment).

examiner believes there is insufficient time to complete the audit, the examiner requests the taxpayer to extend the IRS's statute of limitations on assessment.

Second, the IRS might not permit a taxpayer to appeal where there is an overriding enforcement issue at stake. When there is an overriding enforcement issue, the IRS Chief Counsel "designates" a case for litigation.[9] The IRS might want to use a designated case to create precedent favorable to the IRS where there is an industry-wide issue.[10] Where the Chief Counsel has designated a case for litigation, the IRS does not settle for anything but a complete concession on the issue, does not permit an appeal, and sends an immediate statutory notice of deficiency to the taxpayer.[11]

Third, the IRS generally will not offer an appeal in a case where there is a criminal referral in place or under consideration. The purpose of the Appeals Office is to try to settle civil cases. Settlement of criminal cases occurs by plea bargaining with prosecutors rather than the civil enforcement arm of the IRS.

If there is still a live dispute between the IRS and taxpayer after the administrative appeal stage, the IRS sends the taxpayer a statutory notice of deficiency. This means that if the IRS offers no appeal, the IRS issues a statutory notice of deficiency as a matter of course. Also, the IRS issues a statutory notice of deficiency if the taxpayer declines the IRS's offer to consider an appeal.

B.   The IRS's Internal Appeals Procedures

After the conclusion of the examination, if there is still a live controversy then the IRS generally permits a taxpayer to appeal its proposed determination.[12] This appeal from an audit, however, is not a matter of right.[13] As discussed above, the IRS does not offer appeals consideration in every case.[14]

The administrative appeal, if offered, is the taxpayer's last chance to settle with the IRS before litigation.[15] That makes the administrative appeal one of the most important IRS functions.[16] Settlement with the IRS through an

---

[9] *See* Chief Counsel Notice CC-2004-017 (Apr. 14, 2004); I.R.M. 33.3.6.1(3); I.R.M. 1.2.47.9.

[10] *See* Chief Counsel Notice CC-2004-017 (Apr. 14, 2004).

[11] *See id.*

[12] *See* Reg. § 601.106(a)(1)(i).

[13] *See* Reg. § 601.106(b).

[14] *See also* Reg. § 601.106(b)(5)(a)-(b) (explaining that an organization has no right of appeal when a case concerning tax exemption or foundation classification is determined by the key district director or the national office).

[15] *See* Reg. § 601.106(d)(3)(ii).

[16] *See* INTERNAL REVENUE SERV., *Appeals*, last accessed Oct. 12, 2017, https://www.irs.gov/individuals/appeals-resolving-tax-disputes (stating the Office of Appeals resolves more than 100,000 disputes per year without going to Tax Court).

administrative appeal before trial is less expensive and more efficient than litigation.[17] An administrative appeal is also more private than litigation because the IRS is required to keep taxpayer return information confidential—including the existence or the outcome of a dispute in the Appeals Office—and lawsuits, including Tax Court proceedings, are public records. Despite its importance, an internal administrative appeal is not mandated by statute.

Because an internal IRS appeal is not mandated by statute, there is very little law on the appeal process. Appeals from audits are handled by the IRS's Appeals Office. The Appeals Office is a creature of the IRS's regulations.[18] It exists for the stated purpose of "resolv[ing] tax controversies, without litigation, on a basis [that] is fair and impartial to both the Government and the taxpayer and in a manner that will enhance voluntary compliance and public confidence in the integrity and efficiency of the IRS."[19]

On occasion, a taxpayer will believe the IRS should change its appeals procedures to suit the taxpayer's needs.

SALMAN v. SWANSON
1980 WL 1616
United States District Court, District of Nevada

REED, District Judge.
ORDER
The four defendants, although sued individually, are all employees of the Internal Revenue Service. The plaintiff has asked damages for deprivation of due process rights, in that he has been refused permission both to bring a tape recorder to an administrative appeal conference and to be represented at such conference by an individual who is not an attorney or certified public accountant or otherwise authorized to represent a taxpayer in Internal Revenue Service proceedings.

An examination by the IRS of the plaintiff's income tax returns for 1976 and 1977 gave rise to a 30-day letter advising the plaintiff of a possible deficiency by reason of his failure to report tip income and improper deduction for employee business expense. The letter offered an opportunity for a conference within the district wherein the areas of disagreement might be discussed informally.

The plaintiff asked for such a conference. In a letter dated August 21, 1979, he informed the IRS, among other things, that:

At this proposed hearing I will be represented by counsel of choice who is not an attorney, a certified public accountant or an individual enrolled to practice before the I.R.S. Our meeting will be attended by witnesses. I will also taperecord the meeting. At our proposed meeting I will not provide any

---

[17] *See id.*

[18] *See* Reg. § 601.106(a)(1)(i).

[19] I.R.M. 8.1.1.1(1).

papers that are private for according to Senate investigations of the I.R.S. taxpayers are not legally required to provide private papers.

The IRS advised the plaintiff of the rules governing authority to practice before it and informed him that tape recording of an administrative appeal conference is not permitted. Further, the IRS wrote to the plaintiff that his refusal to present any papers necessary to resolve tax controversies had led to a decision to process the case based on the information already in IRS's files.

The plaintiff then commenced this lawsuit. The defendants have moved to dismiss the complaint, with prejudice, because: (1) the Court lacks jurisdiction over the subject matter by reason of sovereign immunity; (2) the complaint fails to state a claim upon which relief can be granted, in that the allegations therein do not constitute a violation of constitutional rights; and (3) the Court lacks jurisdiction over the subject matter because the Anti-Injunction Act, 26 U.S.C. § 7421(a) prohibits a suit for damages against an official of the U.S. engaged in the assessment or collection of taxes.

It is now clear that a federal official may be sued for damages if he has violated the constitutional rights of the plaintiff. *Carlson v. Greene,* 48 U.S.L.W. 4425 (4/22/80); *Davis v. Passman,* 442 U.S. 228 (1979); *Bivens v. Six Unknown Named Agents of Federal Bureau of Narcotics,* 403 U.S. 388 (1971). Thus, if the plaintiff herein has alleged in his complaint facts constituting a denial of due process, the complaint will state a claim for relief.

Due process does not require a hearing at any particular time, but only before substantial rights are affected. Department & Specialty Store Emp. Union v. Brown, 284 F.2d 619 (9th Cir. 1961); cert. den. 366 U.S. 934 (1961). An administrative appeal conference provides the taxpayer with an opportunity to question the preliminary determinations made during an audit by the IRS. The taxpayer may not be compelled to attend such a conference. It is a voluntary, informal meeting. No order adverse to the taxpayer is entered by reason of the conference. It is an attempt to achieve agreement by virtue of the taxpayer explaining his view of the contested issues. Substantial rights of the plaintiff are not adversely affected thereby.

A governmental agency may extend to a disgruntled party a hearing, even though there is no legal entitlement to such a hearing. However, such an act of courtesy does not generate any duty to afford the party a full panoply of rights, as is due in a formal due process hearing involving a livelihood or a liberty interest. *Clark v. Whiting,* 607 F.2d 634 (4th Cir. 1979). In order to be entitled to a due process hearing, either a property or liberty interest of the party must be subject to loss as a result of the hearing. *Id.* A property interest is not created by the Constitution, but must stem from an independent source. *Board of Regents v. Roth,* 408 U.S. 564 (1972). The administrative appeal conference here involved would have afforded the plaintiff an opportunity to persuade the IRS that his tax returns were not erroneous. The conference could not have resulted in a greater tax liability or other loss of a property interest of the plaintiff.

The procedural protections specified in the Administrative procedures Act, such as are found in 5 U.S.C. § 554, are accorded only to adjudications required by statute to be determined on the record after opportunity for an agency hearing. *Yong v. Regional Manpower Admin., U.S. Dept. of Labor,* 509 F.2d 243 (9th Cir. 1975). No such statute is applicable herein.

The Internal Revenue Manual declares that, as a general rule, neither IRS representatives nor taxpayers shall be permitted to make their own tape or other verbatim recordings of meetings. The reasoning is that recordation would adversely affect the informal setting and inhibit the free exchange of information and opinions. Only where special circumstances exist so that both sides desire a recording is provision made for waiver of the rule.

The plaintiff has not specified any particular reason why he insisted upon making a recording of the conference. He merely claims that denial violated his Fifth Amendment due process rights. A few courts have considered this question and have found there is no such constitutional right. *Salman v. Frisch,* Civil No. R-79-59-BRT, in the United States District Court of Nevada, August 9, 1979; *McCarthy v. United States,* Civil No. C-78-0953-CFP in the United States District Court of the Northern District of California, May 4, 1978; *Allen v. Loury* [79-2 USTC P 9502], 44 A.F.T.R.2d 5241, in the United States District Court, Northern District of Ohio, October 2, 1978. Plaintiff cites *United States v. Duval,* Misc. 78-7 in United States District Court for the Eastern District of Washington in support of his position. However, in *Duval* the hearing was mandatory, resulting from an IRS summons. Here, appearance at the conference would have been voluntary. The IRS has no authority to summon the taxpayer to an administrative appeal conference.

The limitation of representation of a taxpayer to attorneys, certified public accountants and enrolled agents is supported by 5 U.S.C. § 500. Both sides have an interest in making sure only qualified individuals represent taxpayers in IRS proceedings. The enrolled agents have passed an examination which demonstrates their proficiency in tax matters. In the absence of federal law authorizing representation by qualified non-lawyers in proceedings before a government agency, such representation could well constitute an unauthorized practice of law. See *Sperry v. Florida,* 373 U.S. 379 (1963).

From the foregoing it can be seen that the plaintiff's complaint fails to state a claim upon which relief can be granted. First, the nature of the conference involved does not call for the type of due process formalities demanded by the plaintiff. Second, there is no constitutional right in the taxpayer at such a conference to make a tape recording. Third, the limitation on representation is reasonable and valid.

IT IS, THEREFORE, HEREBY ORDERED that the plaintiff's complaint be, and the same hereby is, dismissed with prejudice.

NOTES AND QUESTIONS

1. Why do the procedural rules limit representation to lawyers and CPAs?

2. Why are the Appeals Office conferences not bound by due process?
3. Tape recorders are now allowed in Appeals conferences. *See* IRS I.R.M. 8.1.6.5 (October 1, 2016).

One important function of the Appeals Office is to make tax disputes subject to settlement like other legal disputes.[20] In most legal disputes, an aggrieved party does not necessarily have to sue to obtain relief. The aggrieved party may ask for relief from a party whose acts created a cause of action. The mere threat of litigation facilitates settlement without the need to file a lawsuit. Employees at the IRS do not necessarily feel the same threat. They work for a large bureaucracy and get paid a salary. Thus, neither a settlement nor a lawsuit will have any financial effect on an employee's salary. Although some cases settle at the examination, examiners have very little discretion to settle cases.

In an artificial way, the regulations creating the Appeals Office make up for the fact that IRS employees have nothing to lose if a taxpayer sues. The Appeals Office takes into account litigation hazards when considering a settlement.[21] Allowing for litigation hazards artificially imposes the threat of litigation on settlement discussions in spite of the IRS's otherwise cold bureaucratic process. The Appeals Office settles about 100,000 cases every year.[22]

The Appeals Office has undergone heavy scrutiny despite the fact that Congress does not require the IRS to permit an internal appeal from an examination, which makes the Appeals Office essentially an administrative gift to taxpayers. The Appeals Office has struggled with accusations regarding its independence from examiners. In the latest effort to address taxpayer concerns, the Appeals Office has developed the Appeals Judicial Approach and Culture (AJAC) project. AJAC inspires Appeals Officers to operate more like judges than investigators, especially with respect to ex parte communications.[23]

---

[20] *See* Reg. § 601.106(b).

[21] *See* Reg. § 601.106(f)(2) ("Appeals will ordinarily give serious consideration to an offer to settle a tax controversy on a basis which fairly reflects the relative merits of the opposing views in light of the hazards which would exist if the case were litigated.").

[22] INTERNAL REVENUE SERV., *Appeals*, last accessed Oct. 12, 2017, https://www.irs.gov/individuals/appeals-resolving-tax-disputes ("Every year, the Office of Appeals helps more than 100,000 taxpayers resolve their tax disputes without going to Tax Court.").

[23] *See* SBSE-04-0714-0024 (July 9, 2014); AP-08-0714-0004 (July 2, 2014); AP-08-0713-03 (July 18, 2013).

IRS REVENUE PROCEDURE 2012-18
2012-10 I.R.B. 455
March 5, 2012

This procedure provides guidance regarding ex parte communications between Appeals and other Internal Revenue Service functions. Rev. Proc. 2000-43 amplified, modified and superseded.

SECTION 1. BACKGROUND

Section 1001(a) of the Internal Revenue Service Restructuring and Reform Act of 1998, Pub. L. No. 105-206, 112 Stat. 685 (RRA), required the Commissioner of Internal Revenue to develop and implement a plan to reorganize the Internal Revenue Service (IRS). In addition, the RRA specifically directed the Commissioner to "ensure an independent appeals function within the Internal Revenue Service, including the prohibition * * * of ex parte communications between appeals officers and other Internal Revenue Service employees to the extent that such communications appear to compromise the independence of the appeals officers." RRA section 1001(a)(4). In accordance with that directive, the Department of the Treasury and the IRS issued guidance in Rev. Proc. 2000-43, 2000-2 C.B. 404.

Since the issuance of Rev. Proc. 2000-43 in October 2000, the IRS has made changes to some of its business practices and adopted new ones that did not exist at the time that the revenue procedure was issued. Accordingly, Treasury and the IRS issued Notice 2011-62, 2011-32 I.R.B. 126 (Aug. 8, 2011), which set forth a proposed revenue procedure to revise Rev. Proc. 2000-43 by addressing these changed circumstances, as well as clarifying and modifying the rules in light of the IRS' experience working with that revenue procedure. . . .

Notice 2011-62 invited public comment regarding the proposed revenue procedure. Treasury and the IRS considered all comments received and the proposed revenue procedure has been modified to take into account the concerns raised. For example, the remedies section has been modified to provide that Appeals employees shall ask the taxpayer/representative for input regarding what is an appropriate remedy. The final agency decision maker regarding the appropriate remedy in each case will be a second-level manager. Also, the "opportunity to participate" section has been modified to clarify that if no agreement can be reached regarding a mutually acceptable date and time for the discussion or meeting, Appeals should notify the taxpayer/representative of the date and time that the discussion or meeting will take place. After having the discussion or meeting, Appeals should share with the taxpayer/representative the substance of the discussion or meeting, as appropriate, and give the taxpayer/representative a reasonable period of time within which to respond. Additionally, the discussion of the role of Appeals with respect to the development of settlement initiatives has been clarified. Lastly, consistent with the rule that the *ex parte* communication rules do not apply to communications between Appeals and Counsel with respect to cases docketed in the Tax Court, the section regarding remand memoranda in collection due process cases has been revised to remove the prohibition on including legal analysis or legal advice in remand memoranda. . . .

The procedures set forth in this revenue procedure are designed to accommodate the overall interests of tax administration, while preserving operational features that are vital to Appeals' case resolution processes within the structure of the IRS and ensuring open lines of communication between Appeals and the taxpayer/representative. Consistent with section 1001(a)(4), this revenue procedure does not adopt the formal *ex parte* procedures that would apply in a judicial proceeding. It is designed to ensure the independence of the Appeals organization, while preserving the role of Appeals as a flexible administrative settlement authority, operating within the IRS' overall framework of tax administration responsibilities.

.01 *Highlights*. As previously provided in Rev. Proc. 2000-43:

(1) Appeals will retain procedures for:

(a) Premature referrals.

(b) Raising certain new issues.

(c) Seeking review and comments from the originating function with respect to new information or evidence furnished by the taxpayer/representative.

(2) Appeals will continue to be able to obtain legal advice from the Office of Chief Counsel, subject to the limitations set forth in section 2.06(1), below.

(3) The Commissioner and other IRS officials responsible for overall IRS operations (including Appeals), as referenced in section 2.07(5), below, may continue to communicate *ex parte* with Appeals to fulfill their responsibilities.

.02 Notable Differences.

(1) Guiding principles have been added to aid in understanding the overall approach to applying the *ex parte* communication rules.

(2) Definitions for certain terms have been added or clarified.

(3) Transmittals and the permissible content of the administrative file have been clarified.

(4) The application of the *ex parte* communication rules to collection due process (CDP) cases, including those CDP cases that are remanded by the Tax Court, has been addressed.

(5) The discussion of Appeals' involvement in multifunctional meetings has been expanded.

(6) The application of the *ex parte* communication rules in the context of alternative dispute resolution proceedings has been addressed.

(7) The remedies available to taxpayers in the event of a breach of the *ex parte* communication rules have been clarified.

(8) A statement that the *ex parte* communication rules do not create substantive rights affecting a taxpayer's liability or the IRS' ability to determine, assess, or collect that tax liability has been added.

SECTION 2. GUIDANCE CONCERNING EX PARTE COMMUNICATIONS AND THE APPLICATION OF RRA SECTION 1001(a)(4)

.01 *Definitions*. For purposes of this revenue procedure and the application of RRA section 1001(a)(4), the terms set forth below are defined as follows:

(1) *Ex Parte Communication*. An "*ex parte* communication" is a communication that takes place between any Appeals employee (*e.g.*, Appeals Officers, Settlement Officers, Appeals Team Case Leaders, Appeals Tax Computation Specialists) and employees of other IRS functions, without the taxpayer/representative being given an opportunity to participate in the communication. The term includes all forms of communication, oral or written. Written communications include those that are manually or electronically generated. . . .

(3) Opportunity to Participate.

(a) *Oral communications*. The phrase "opportunity to participate" means that the taxpayer/representative will be given a reasonable opportunity to attend a meeting or be a participant in a conference call between Appeals and the originating function when the strengths and weaknesses of the facts, issues, or positions in the taxpayer's case are discussed. The taxpayer/representative will be notified of a scheduled meeting or conference call and invited to participate. If the taxpayer/representative is unable to participate in the meeting or conference call at the scheduled time, reasonable accommodations will be made to reschedule it. See also section 2.01(3)(d), below.

(b) *Written communications*. A taxpayer/representative is considered to have been given an "opportunity to participate" with respect to a written communication that is received by Appeals if the taxpayer/representative is furnished a copy of the written communication and given a chance to respond to it either orally or in writing.

(c) *Waiver*. If the taxpayer/representative is given an opportunity to participate in a discussion but declines to participate, Appeals should proceed with the discussion or meeting but should document the taxpayer's/representative's declination. A taxpayer/representative has the option of granting a waiver on a communication-by-communication basis or a waiver covering all communications that might occur during the course of Appeals' consideration of a specified case. If a taxpayer/representative provides a blanket waiver with respect to a particular case, the taxpayer/representative may revoke that waiver at any time, effective with respect to communications occurring subsequent to the revocation.

(d) *Unreasonable delay*. The IRS will not delay scheduling a meeting for a protracted period of time to accommodate the taxpayer/representative. Facts and circumstances will govern what constitutes a reasonable delay. If the taxpayer/representative seeks to unreasonably delay a meeting or conference call, Appeals should proceed with the discussion or meeting but should document the reason for proceeding without the taxpayer/representative. Additionally, if no agreement can be reached regarding a mutually acceptable date and time for the discussion or meeting, Appeals should notify the taxpayer/representative of the date and time that the discussion or meeting will take place. If the taxpayer/representative does not participate in the discussion or meeting, Appeals should share with the taxpayer/representative the substance of the discussion or meeting, as appropriate, and give the taxpayer/representative a reasonable period of time within which to respond.

.02 *Guiding Principles.* Except as specifically addressed in other provisions of this revenue procedure, the following guiding principles govern communications between Appeals and other IRS functions, including Counsel.

(1) *Principles of Tax Administration.* It is the role of the IRS, and those employees charged with the duty of interpreting the law, to determine the reasonable meaning of various Code provisions in light of the Congressional purpose in enacting them; to apply and administer the law in a reasonable and practical manner; and to perform this work in a fair and impartial manner, with neither a government nor a taxpayer point of view. See Rev. Proc. 64-22, 1964-1 C.B. 689.

(2) *Appeals' Independence.* Appeals serves as the administrative dispute resolution forum for any taxpayer contesting an IRS compliance action. It has long been Appeals' mission "to resolve tax controversies, without litigation, on a basis that is fair and impartial to both the Government and the taxpayer and in a manner that will enhance voluntary compliance and public confidence in the integrity and efficiency of the Service." IRM 8.1.1.1(1). RRA section 1001(a)(4) established a statutory basis for Appeals' independence by requiring that the Commissioner "ensure an independent appeals function within the Internal Revenue Service . . . ." Rather than establish an external appeals function (as suggested in some legislative proposals), RRA maintained Appeals within the IRS while seeking to significantly reinforce its independence. Consequently, despite their distinct roles within tax administration and required adherence to policies set by the Commissioner, Appeals and other IRS functions, including Counsel, share a responsibility to interact — in all circumstances — in a manner that preserves and promotes Appeals' independence. To further this independence, Appeals must continue its practice of impartial decision making while coordinating with other IRS functions to carry out the Commissioner's policies on tax administration.

Independence, therefore, is one of Appeals' most important core values, and the RRA statutory prohibition on *ex parte* communications "to the extent that such communications appear to compromise the independence of the appeals officers" is a significant component of Appeals' independence. The guidance set forth in this revenue procedure is designed to accommodate the overall interests of tax administration while ensuring that Appeals is adequately insulated from influence (or the appearance of influence) by other IRS functions, thereby providing Appeals with an unencumbered working environment within which to objectively and independently evaluate the facts and law that are relevant to each case and quantify the hazards of litigation based on that evaluation.

(3) Legal Advice.

(a) *In General*. The Chief Counsel is the legal adviser to the Commissioner and the IRS' officers and employees on all matters pertaining to the interpretation, administration, and enforcement of the internal revenue laws and related statutes. I.R.C. § 7803(b)(2)(A). As reflected in the Chief Counsel's mission statement, the IRS' mission statement, and section 2.02(1), above, attorneys in the Office of Chief Counsel are expected to provide legal advice based on an independent determination of the "correct and impartial interpretation of the internal revenue laws" and by applying "the [tax] law with integrity and fairness to all." The fact that various attorneys in the Office of Chief Counsel may be simultaneously engaged in multiple activities, including some activities involving an advocacy role, does not diminish the responsibility of each to exercise independent judgment in rendering legal advice.

(b) *Appeals*. Appeals employees generally are not bound by the legal advice that they receive from the Office of Chief Counsel with respect to their cases. Rather, the legal advice is but one factor that Appeals will take into account in its consideration of the case. Appeals employees remain ultimately responsible for independently evaluating the strengths and weaknesses of the issues in the cases assigned to them and making independent judgments concerning the overall strengths and weaknesses of the cases and the hazards of litigation. Accordingly, Appeals may obtain legal advice from the Office of Chief Counsel consistent with this revenue procedure without compromising Appeals' independence.

(4) *Opportunity to Participate*. As provided in section 2.01(1) and (3), above, by definition, if the taxpayer/representative is given an opportunity to participate with respect to a communication, that communication is not *ex parte*, and, thus, the communication is permissible under the *ex parte* communication rules. . . .

.03 Communications with Originating Function.

(1) *General Rule. Ex parte* communications between Appeals employees and employees of originating functions are prohibited to the extent the communications appear to compromise Appeals' independence. See RRA section 1001(a)(4). As discussed more fully below, not all *ex parte* communications are prohibited. . . .

(2) *Ministerial, Administrative, or Procedural Matters*. Communications between Appeals and an originating function regarding ministerial, administrative, or procedural matters during any stage of a case are permissible without involving the taxpayer/representative. If communications with the originating function extend beyond ministerial, administrative, or procedural matters in that the substance of the issues in the case is addressed, those communications are prohibited unless the taxpayer/representative is given an opportunity to participate. . . .

(3) *Prohibited Communications*. Examples of communications between Appeals and an originating function that are prohibited unless the

taxpayer/representative is given an opportunity to participate include, but are not limited to, the following:

(a) Discussions about the accuracy of the facts presented by the taxpayer and the relative importance of the facts to the determination.

(b) Discussions of the relative merits or alternative legal interpretations of authorities cited in a protest or in a report prepared by the originating function.

(c) Discussions of the originating function's perception of the demeanor or credibility of the taxpayer or taxpayer's representative.

(d) Discussions of the originating function's views concerning the level of cooperation (or lack thereof) of the taxpayer/representative during the originating function's consideration of the case.

(e) Discussions regarding the originating function's views concerning the strengths and weaknesses of the case or the parties' positions in the case.

(f) Communications from the originating function to advocate for a particular result or to object to a potential resolution of the case or an issue in the case.

(4) Administrative File.

(a) *In General.* The administrative file transmitted to Appeals by the originating function is not considered to be an *ex parte* communication within the context of this revenue procedure. The administrative file, which contains, among other things, the proposed determination and the taxpayer's protest or other approved means of communicating disagreement with the proposed determination, sets forth the boundaries of the dispute between the taxpayer and the IRS and forms the basis for Appeals to assume jurisdiction. . . .

(c) *Rebuttal to Protest.* If a rebuttal to the taxpayer's protest is prepared by the originating function, it must be shared with the taxpayer/representative by the originating function at the time that it is sent to Appeals.

(d) *Contents of Administrative File.* The administrative file shall be compiled and maintained by the originating function in accordance with the established procedures within that function or as otherwise directed by the reviewer(s) assigned to the case. The originating function, however, shall refrain from placing in the administrative file any notes, memoranda, or other documents that normally would not be included in the administrative file in the ordinary course of developing the case if the reason for including this material in the administrative file is to attempt to influence Appeals' decision-making process. For example, the originating function should not include gratuitous comments in the case history, a memo to the file, or a transmittal document, such as a T-Letter, if the substance of the comments would be prohibited if they were communicated to Appeals separate and apart from the administrative file. In contrast, it is permissible to contemporaneously include statements or documents that are pertinent to the originating function's consideration of the case in the administrative file even if the substance of those comments, statements, or documents would be prohibited if they were communicated to Appeals separate and apart from the administrative file.

(5) *Preconference Meetings.* Preconference meetings between Appeals and the originating function without providing the taxpayer/representative an opportunity to participate are an example of the type of communications that the *ex parte* communication rules were designed to prohibit. These meetings should not be held unless the taxpayer/representative is given an opportunity to participate.

(6) *Premature Referrals.* Appeals is the administrative settlement arm of the IRS. If a case is not ready for Appeals' consideration, Appeals may return it for further development or for other reasons described in IRM 8.2.1.6. Appeals may communicate with the originating function regarding the anticipated return of the case, including an explanation of the additional development that Appeals is requesting or other reasons why the case is being returned, but generally may not engage in a discussion of matters beyond the types of ministerial, administrative, or procedural matters set forth in section 2.03(2), above, as part of a discussion of whether the premature referral guidelines require further activity by the originating function. When the case is returned to the originating function, Appeals must timely notify the taxpayer/representative that the case has been returned to the originating function, in whole or in part, for further development. In addition, the supplemental report prepared by the originating function reflecting the additional development that was done must be shared with the taxpayer/representative.

(7) *Submission of New Information.* If new information or evidence is submitted to Appeals by the taxpayer/representative, the principles set forth in IRM 8.2.1.9.3 should be followed. In general, the originating function should be given the opportunity to timely review and comment on significant new information presented by the taxpayer. "Significant new information" is information of a nonroutine nature that, in the judgment of Appeals, may have had an impact on the originating function's findings or that may impact Appeals' independent evaluation of the strengths and weaknesses of the issues, including the litigating hazards relating to those issues. Normally, the review can be accomplished by sending the material to the originating function while Appeals retains jurisdiction of the case and proceeds with resolution of other issues. Alternatively, Appeals may return the entire case to the originating function and relinquish jurisdiction, in its sole discretion, in accordance with the IRM. The taxpayer/representative must be timely notified when a case is returned to the originating function or new material not available during initial consideration has been sent to the originating function. The results of the originating function's review of the new information must be communicated to the taxpayer/representative.

(8) *New Issues Raised in Appeals.* Appeals will continue to follow the principles of Policy Statement 8-2 and the "General Guidelines" outlined in IRM 8.6.1.6.2 in deciding whether to raise a new issue. Under Appeals' new issue policy, new issues must continue to meet the "material" and "substantial" tests

set forth in the IRM. Communications will be in accordance with the guiding principles in section 2.02(6), above.

(9) *Refund Claims Filed During the Appeals Process*. Refund claims filed during the Appeals process generally are referred to the originating function with a request for expedited review. Referrals of these refund claims to the originating function involves no discussion about the strengths and weaknesses of the issue, and thus, fall within the ministerial, administrative, or procedural matters exception set forth in section 2.03(2), above. The taxpayer/representative must be timely notified when the refund claim is referred to the originating function. The results of the originating function's review of the refund claim must be communicated to the taxpayer/representative.

(10) Collection Due Process.

(a) *Collection Cases In General*. The principles applicable to discussions between Appeals employees and officials in originating functions apply to cases that originate in the Collection function, such as CDP appeals, collection appeals program cases, offers in compromise, and trust fund recovery penalty cases. These discussions must be held in accordance with the guiding principles in section 2.02(6), above.

(b) *Ministerial, Administrative, or Procedural Matters*. Sections 6320 and 6330 of the Internal Revenue Code provide that, as part of a CDP hearing, the Appeals officer must obtain verification that the requirements of any applicable law or administrative procedure have been met. Communications seeking to verify compliance with legal and administrative requirements fall within the ministerial, administrative, or procedural matters exception set forth in section 2.03(2), above. Similarly, communications with respect to verification of assets/liabilities involving a collection alternative during a CDP hearing fall within the ministerial, administrative, or procedural matters exception. Therefore, those communications are permissible without providing the taxpayer/representative an opportunity to participate.

(c) *Remand By Tax Court*. As provided in section 2.06(2)(a), below, the *ex parte* communication rules do not apply to communications between Appeals and Counsel with respect to cases docketed in the Tax Court. CDP cases that are remanded by the Tax Court for further consideration (or reconsideration) by Appeals fall into a different category, however. Although remanded CDP cases remain under the Tax Court's jurisdiction, the Appeals employee assigned to the remanded CDP case must be impartial in the review of the remanded case within the meaning of section 6320(b)(3) or 6330(b)(3), as applicable, requiring the application of similar considerations to those underlying the *ex parte* communication rules. Therefore, the following guidelines apply to remanded CDP cases.

(i) Instructions Regarding the Remand

(A) The Counsel attorney who handled the CDP case in the Tax Court should prepare a written memorandum to Appeals explaining the reasons why the court remanded the case to Appeals, any special requirements in the court's Order (*e.g.*, whether and to what extent a new conference should be held; whether the case must be reassigned to a different Appeals employee than the Appeals employee who handled the original CDP case; and what material Appeals is prohibited from reviewing, if any), and what issues the court has ordered Appeals to address on remand. The memorandum should not discuss the credibility of the taxpayer or the accuracy of the facts presented by the taxpayer. A copy of the memorandum will be provided by the Counsel attorney to the taxpayer/representative.

(B) Communications to Appeals from the Counsel attorney handling the Tax Court case regarding deadlines relating to the remanded CDP case fall within the ministerial, administrative, or procedural matters exception, and thus, are permissible communications that may take place without providing the taxpayer/representative an opportunity to participate.

(ii) Legal Advice.

A request by Appeals for legal advice in connection with a remanded CDP case may be handled by the same Counsel attorney who is handling the Tax Court case.

(iii) *Review of Supplemental Notice By Counsel.* The Counsel attorney handling the Tax Court case should review the supplemental notice of determination before it is issued to the taxpayer. This review is for the limited purpose of ensuring compliance with the Tax Court's remand Order.

(11) *Post-Settlement Conference.* The post-settlement conference with Examination is held after the case has been closed by Appeals. The purpose of the conference is to inform Examination about the settlement of issues to ensure that Examination fully understands the settlement and the rationale for the resolution. The conference provides an opportunity for Appeals to discuss with Examination the application of Delegation Order 236, or subsequent delegation orders (*i.e.*, settlement by Examination consistent with a prior Appeals' settlement with the same or related taxpayer). The tax periods that are the subject of the post-settlement conference have been finalized and the participants are cautioned to limit discussion to the results in the closed cycle. Any discussion of the resolution of issues present in the closed periods does not compromise the independence of Appeals, and, thus, post-settlement conferences between Appeals and Examination are permissible without giving the taxpayer/representative an opportunity to participate. In contrast, any discussion that addresses open cycles in either Examination or Appeals with respect to the same or a related taxpayer is subject to the guidance provided in this revenue procedure relating to communications with the originating function contained in section 2.03, above. . . .

.05 Alternative Dispute Resolution.

(1) *Cases Not in Appeals' Jurisdiction.* Certain alternative dispute resolution (ADR) programs, such as fast track settlement, involve the use of Appeals

employees to facilitate settlement while the case is still in Examination's jurisdiction. See, *e.g.*, Rev. Proc. 2003-40, 2003-1 C.B. 1044 (Large and Mid-Size Business Fast Track Settlement Program); Announcement 2011-5, 2011-4 I.R.B. 430 (Small Business/Self Employed Fast Track Settlement Program); Announcement 2008-105, 2008-2 C.B. 1219 (Tax Exempt and Government Entities Fast Track Settlement Program); and subsequent published guidance regarding these or similar programs. Private caucuses between the mediator and individual parties are often a key element in the process. The prohibition against *ex parte* communications between Appeals employees and other IRS employees does not apply because Appeals employees are not acting in their traditional Appeals' settlement role. Consequently, Appeals employees may have *ex parte* communications with an originating function in connection with any Fast Track or similar ADR proceedings. For a discussion of communications between Appeals and Counsel, see section 2.06, below. In contrast, the *ex parte* communication rules apply in the context of Appeals' consideration of an issue under the Early Referral to Appeals process, Rev. Proc. 99-28, 1999-2 C.B. 109, or the Accelerated Issue Resolution program, Rev. Proc. 94-67, 1994-2 C.B. 800 (or subsequent published guidance regarding these programs). *Ex parte* communications are not an integral part of those types of ADR procedures because jurisdiction has shifted to Appeals in those cases.

(2) *Post-Appeals Mediation.* The *ex parte* communication rules do not apply to communications in connection with Post-Appeals Mediation proceedings. Revenue Procedure 2009-44, 2009-2 C.B. 462, describes an optional Appeals' mediation procedure that is available after Appeals' settlement discussions are unsuccessful and when all other issues are resolved except for the issue(s) for which mediation is being requested. See also Announcement 2011-6, 2011-4 I.R.B. 433. The Appeals employee who serves as the mediator in these proceedings to promote settlement negotiations between the parties, who are the taxpayer and Appeals, will not have been a member of the Appeals' team that considered the case. Section 6.02 of Rev. Proc. 2009-44 states that "the parties are encouraged to include, in addition to the required decision-makers, those persons with information and expertise that will be useful to the decision-makers and the mediator." 2009-2 C.B. at 463. Section 6.02 further provides that "Appeals has the discretion to communicate *ex parte* with the IRS Office of Chief Counsel, the originating function, *e.g.*, Compliance, or both, in preparation for or during the mediation session. Appeals also has the discretion to have Counsel, the originating function, or both, participate in the mediation proceeding." *Id.* . . .

.08 Communications with Other Governmental Entities.

(1) *Joint Committee on Taxation.* Section 6405 requires the IRS to submit a report to the Joint Committee on Taxation concerning any refund or credit in excess of the statutory amount, and the IRS must wait at least 30 days after submitting the report before making the refund or credit that is the subject of the report. The Joint Committee or its staff will occasionally question a settlement or raise a new issue. Communications between Appeals and the Joint Committee or

its staff are permissible without providing the taxpayer/representative an opportunity to participate. The *ex parte* communication rules only apply to communications between Appeals and other IRS employees. Since the Joint Committee is part of the Legislative Branch, not the IRS, the *ex parte* communication rules do not apply to communications with the Joint Committee or its staff.

(2) *Department of Justice.* Appeals may communicate with employees of the Department of Justice, including the U.S. Attorneys' offices, without giving the taxpayer/representative an opportunity to participate. The *ex parte* communication rules only apply to communications between Appeals and other IRS employees. Since the Department of Justice is not part of the IRS, the *ex parte* communication rules do not apply to communications with the Department of Justice.

.09 *Monitoring Compliance.* It is the responsibility of all IRS employees to ensure compliance with the *ex parte* communication rules. All IRS employees will make every effort to promptly terminate any communications not permitted by the *ex parte* communication rules. To improve understanding of the *ex parte* communication rules, Appeals and other impacted IRS employees, including Counsel, will receive training on the contents of this revenue procedure and will be encouraged to seek managerial guidance whenever they have questions about the propriety of an *ex parte* communication. Additionally, managers will consider feedback from other functions and will be responsible for monitoring compliance during their day-to-day interaction with employees, as well as during workload reviews and closed case reviews. Breaches will be addressed in accordance with existing administrative and personnel processes on a case-by-case basis.

.10 Remedies Available to Taxpayers.

(1) *General Rule.* The *ex parte* communication rules set forth in this revenue procedure do not create substantive rights affecting the taxpayer's tax liability or the IRS' ability to determine, assess, or collect that tax liability, including statutory interest and any penalties, if applicable. The IRS takes the *ex parte* communication rules seriously and will continue its efforts to ensure compliance through training and oversight. Most breaches of the *ex parte* communication rules may be cured by timely notifying the taxpayer/representative of the situation, sharing the communication or information in question, and affording the taxpayer/representative an opportunity to respond. Consequently, Appeals shall notify the taxpayer/representative of the breach and request input from the taxpayer/representative regarding the appropriate remedy for a breach of the *ex parte* communication rules. After considering the specific facts and discussing the matter with the taxpayer/representative, as appropriate, Appeals may determine that an additional remedy is warranted, including reassigning the case to a different Appeals/Settlement Officer who has had no prior involvement in the case. The specific administrative remedy, however, that may be made available in any particular case is within the sole discretion of Appeals. The deciding official for the determination of the appropriate remedy for a breach of the *ex parte* communication rules will be a second-level manager. For a

discussion of court directed cures for breaches of the *ex parte* communication rules, see section 2.10(2), below.

(2) *Collection Due Process Cases.* If the Tax Court determines that a breach of the *ex parte* communication rules occurred during the course of a CDP hearing in Appeals, the Tax Court may remand the case to Appeals for either a new or a supplemental hearing, depending upon what steps the court concludes are necessary to rectify the breach. See section 2.03(10)(c), above. . . .

1. Appeals from Examinations

If the Service grants the taxpayer an appeal from an examination, the taxpayer will receive a 30-day letter.[24] In general, a 30-day letter includes a notice of proposed adjustments to items on the taxpayer's return as well as an explanation of the adjustments.[25] The 30-day letter will also explain how to invoke the Appeals Office procedures. In the case of a taxpayer with more than $10,000 in dispute, the taxpayer invokes Appeals Office procedures by submitting a protest letter within 30 days.[26] Although no specific format is required, there are guidelines for submitting a protest in the first revenue procedure issued by the IRS each year. Generally, the protest letter identifies the taxpayer, identifies the points of contention between the taxpayer and the IRS, and analyzes the issues.

Once the taxpayer submits the protest letter, the Appeals Officer generally requests a conference with the taxpayer.[27] These conferences are informal.[28] The rules of evidence do not apply. A taxpayer may present direct evidence as to why he should prevail, or may present alternative proof.[29] An Appeals Officer is more likely to accept alternative proof than an examiner from the IRS. Although the conferences have traditionally been conducted in person where possible, the informality of the evidentiary requirements accommodates telephonic conferences as well.[30]

---

[24] *See* Reg. § 601.105(d).

[25] *Id.*

[26] Reg. § 601.106(a)(1)(iii)(c). A written protest letter is also required to obtain Appeals consideration for an all employee plan, exempt organizations, partnerships, and S corporation cases. Reg. § 601.106(a)(1)(iii)(d), (e).

[27] *See* Reg. § 601.106(b).

[28] *See* Reg. § 601.106(c).

[29] *Id.*

[30] The National Taxpayer Advocate has criticized the IRS's Appeals Office regarding its trend toward telephonic Appeals conferences rather than face-to-face conferences. *See* 1 NAT'L TAXPAYER ADVOCATE, 2014 ANNUAL REPORT TO CONGRESS 46-51 (noting the Appeals Office's trend toward withdrawing its presence from entire states, leading to fewer face-to-face conferences and more telephonic conferences; noting statistics showing that face-to-face Appeals

During the Appeals process, a taxpayer or an Appeals Officer may request a technical advice memorandum (TAM) from the IRS's Chief Counsel National Office.[31] The IRS's regulations provide this procedure in part to ensure that the Appeals Office resolves issues uniformly.[32] A taxpayer may also request a TAM where "the issue is so unusual or complex as to warrant consideration by the National Office."[33] A TAM request is like an appeal within an appeal. Although the IRS will consider a taxpayer's request where uniformity, uniqueness, or complexity are an issue, the Appeals Officer may request a TAM on any issue.[34] The Appeals Officer is bound by a TAM that favors the taxpayer.[35]

A taxpayer is not required to appeal to the Appeals Office directly from the examination. If the IRS has proposed an adjustment and the taxpayer fails to request Appeals consideration, the IRS issues a statutory notice of deficiency that gives the taxpayer 90 days to petition the Tax Court to review the IRS's determination.[36] Unless the taxpayer was not offered the opportunity to appeal before the deficiency notice, the IRS offers an appeal for cases for which the taxpayer has filed a Tax Court petition.[37] The IRS refers to these appeals as "docketed cases."

Some of the procedures in docketed cases are different from those arising directly from examination. Three procedures that are different are the protest letter requirement, the Appeals Officer's authority to settle a case, and the availability of TAM procedures. Unlike a pre-notice case, where the taxpayer generally must submit a protest letter to receive appeals consideration, there is no protest letter required for Appeals consideration in a docketed case. In addition, whereas in pre-notice cases the Appeals Officer has sole discretion to settle a case, once a case is docketed in Tax Court, the trial attorney for the case shares settlement authority with the Appeals Officer.

---

conferences lead to significantly higher taxpayer satisfaction than correspondence Appeals conference).

[31] *See* Reg. § 601.106(f)(9)(iii)(a) ("It is the responsibility of the Appeals Office to determine whether technical advice is to be requested on any issue being considered. However, while the case is under the jurisdiction of the Appeals Office, a taxpayer or his/her representative may request that an issue be referred to the National Office for technical advice . . . ."). The technical advice is usually provided in the form of a memorandum, which is referred to as a TAM.

[32] *See id.*

[33] *Id.*

[34] *See* Reg. § 601.106(f)(9)(ii)(a).

[35] Reg. § 601.106(f)(9)(viii)(c) ("The Appeals office is bound by technical advice favorable to the taxpayer. However, if the technical advice is unfavorable to the taxpayer, the Appeals office may settle the issue in the usual manner under existing authority.").

[36] *See* Reg. § 601.106(a)(1)(i).

[37] *Id.*

2. Appeals from Other Administrative Actions

The Appeals Office's traditional function has been to settle disputes arising from the IRS's examinations. Taxpayers and the IRS, however, rely on the Appeals Office for other administrative appeals as well. The two most significant areas involving the Appeals Office are collection appeals and penalty appeals.

i. Collection Appeals

The Appeals Office is integral to fairness in the IRS's collection process. Prior to 1998, once the IRS assessed a tax, the collection process proceeded without much consideration of the taxpayer's situation. Taxpayers perceived the IRS's practice as a very unforgiving exercise of power. Legislation enacted in 1998 requires the IRS to provide taxpayers the opportunity to request Collection Due Process (CDP) hearings during the collection process.[38] Personnel from the Appeals Office conduct these hearings. They are similar to the Appeals conferences, but the scope of issues the Appeals personnel may consider is limited to the ability to pay and method of payment.[39] In rare circumstances, a taxpayer may challenge the underlying liability. The taxpayer may challenge the underlying tax liability only where the taxpayer had no opportunity to do so prior to the CDP hearing.[40] By the time the taxpayer is in a CDP hearing, in general the taxpayer has already challenged the underlying liability in an audit, an appeal from the audit, and, potentially, in Tax Court.

ii. Penalty Appeals

The Appeals Office also hears penalty appeals that arise independent of underlying tax liability. In an audit result, a statutory notice of deficiency, or a refund disallowance, a penalty dispute and appeal can arise where a taxpayer agrees with the IRS's proposed or determined adjustments, but disagrees with the imposition of a penalty. Not all penalties, however, arise out of the IRS's deficiency or refund determination procedures. Some penalties are independently assessable. Because they are not part of the IRS's deficiency determination

---

[38] Internal Revenue Service Restructuring and Reform Act of 1998, Pub. L. No. 105-206, § 3401, 112 Stat. 685, 746.

[39] *See* Reg. § 301.6330-1(e)(1) ("The taxpayer may raise any relevant issue relating to the unpaid tax at the hearing, including appropriate spousal defenses, challenges to the appropriateness of the proposed levy, and offers of collection alternatives.").

[40] *See id.* ("The taxpayer also may raise challenges to the existence or amount of the underlying liability, including a liability reported on a self-filed return, for any tax period specified on the CDP Notice if the taxpayer did not receive a statutory notice of deficiency for that tax liability or did not otherwise have an opportunity to dispute the tax liability.").

procedures, the Tax Court has no way to assert jurisdiction over such a penalty. Accordingly, without a penalty appeal, the IRS's penalty imposition would not be subject to judicial review before payment. Generally, the IRS requires taxpayers to submit a protest for a penalty appeal, just as in a nondocketed appeal from an examination.

Although an internal appeal of an assessable penalty is not subject to review by the Tax Court directly, the Tax Court has jurisdiction to review a CDP determination where the underlying liability arose from an assessable penalty. As with other CDP proceedings, however, the taxpayer will not receive a second opportunity to dispute the merits of the penalty assessment if the taxpayer had the opportunity to dispute the merits of the penalty in the original penalty appeal.[41]

The examination results are not imposed as a punishment. Rather, the IRS has appeal procedures in place where Appeals Officers attempt to negotiate settlements with most taxpayers without going to court. The Appeals Office's success at settling cases with taxpayers shows that an examination is not in and of itself a punishment.

The IRS does not, however, settle all tax disputes. If the taxpayer and the IRS are too far apart, the IRS will issue a final determination. A taxpayer may dispute a final determination in court. If the IRS determined the taxpayer owes more tax than reported, the IRS issues a statutory notice of deficiency that gives the taxpayer the opportunity to petition the Tax Court. If the IRS denies a refund request, the IRS will issue a notice of disallowance. A taxpayer whose refund was disallowed may sue the IRS in the federal district court or the Court of Federal Claims.

C. Types of Settlements in Appeals

There are various methods to settle a case. Some have tried to take back a deal made with Appeals.

KRETCHMAR v. UNITED STATES
9 Cl. Ct. 191 (1985)
United States Claims Court

REGINALD W. GIBSON, Judge:

In this tax refund action, plaintiffs, Frank R. and Bertha M. Kretchmar, jointly seek a refund of federal income taxes, interest, and penalties in the amounts of $19,006.05, $27,404.64, and $24,250.02 for the taxable years 1976, 1977, and 1978, respectively. Plaintiffs claim that they were unlawfully assessed

---

[41] *See, e.g.,* Keller Tanks Servs. II, Inc. v. Commissioner, 854 F.3d 1178 (10th Cir. 2017); Iames v. Commissioner, 850 F.3d 160 (4th Cir. 2017); Bitter v. Commissioner, 113 T.C.M. (CCH) 1205, 2017 T.C.M. (RIA) ¶ 2017-046, at 296-97.

the foregoing additional amounts based upon an erroneous calculation of gross income for each of the years in question. Further, plaintiffs claim that the penalties assessed are without foundation in fact or in law.[42]

Without addressing the merits of these claims as to any of the foregoing years, defendant, in moving for summary judgment, avers that (1) plaintiffs' previous execution of IRS Form 870-AD,[43] Offer of Waiver of Restrictions on Assessment and Collection of Deficiency in Tax and of Acceptance of Overassessment, now estops plaintiffs from seeking a refund for each of said taxable years; (2) for the taxable year 1978, plaintiffs have failed to pay in full the totally assessed amount for such year thereby depriving this court of subject matter jurisdiction to award a refund for that year; and (3) plaintiffs' failure, in this action, to reply to defendant's answer averring fraud regarding the filing of plaintiffs' returns for the years in question was an admission entitling defendant to judgment on the fraud issue as a matter of law. Because we find that plaintiffs failed to pay the amount (tax and penalty) fully assessed for the taxable year 1978, this court is without jurisdiction to entertain a claim for such year. As for

---

[42] [fn 1] As to the penalties assessed pursuant to 26 U.S.C. § 6653(b) (1982), plaintiffs, in their response to defendant's motion for summary judgment, state merely that "[t]he Internal Revenue Service was wholly without grounds to assert penalties pursuant to Internal Revenue Code of 1954, § 6653(b)."

[43] [fn 2] IRS Form 870-AD (appellate division), entitled "Offer of Waiver of Restrictions on Assessment and Collection of Deficiency in Tax and of Acceptance of Overassessment," is the general purpose form which the IRS uses to register and memorialize settlement negotiations. The operative text embodying the substance of Form 870-AD is as follows:

> This offer is subject to acceptance for the Commissioner of Internal Revenue. It shall take effect as a waiver of restrictions on the date it is accepted. Unless and until it is accepted, it shall have no force or effect.

> If this offer is accepted for the Commissioner, *the case shall not be reopened* in the absence of fraud, malfeasance, concealment, or misrepresentation of material fact, an important mistake in mathematical calculation, or excessive tentative allowances of carrybacks provided by law; and *no claim for refund or credit shall be filed or prosecuted for the year(s) stated above other than for* amounts attributed to *carrybacks provided by law.*

> Note.—The execution and filing of this offer will expedite the above adjustment of tax liability. This offer, when executed and timely submitted, will be considered a claim for refund for the above overassessment, as provided in Revenue Ruling 68-65, C.B. 1968-I, 555. It will not, however, constitute a closing agreement under Section 7121 of the Internal Revenue Code.

Exhibit C, Appendix B to the Memorandum for the United States in Support of its Motion for Summary Judgment, January 22, 1985 (emphasis added).

the taxable years 1976 and 1977, we find that the plaintiffs are also barred from litigating the merits of their refund suit on the grounds that the doctrine of equitable estoppel, stemming from their previous execution of IRS Form 870-AD, is a complete impediment.[44]

FACTS

Plaintiffs, husband and wife residing in West Brookfield, Massachusetts, filed timely federal income tax returns for the taxable years in question, 1976, 1977, and 1978. Schedule C of each of said returns described plaintiffs' business, euphemistically, as "novelty sales," and reported gross receipts and net income in the identical amounts of $11,700, $19,140, and $30,000, for the taxable years 1976, 1977, and 1978, respectively.[45] No deductible expenses were claimed as having been incurred in connection with earning these amounts of income.

During the calendar year 1980, Internal Revenue Agent (IRA) Robert B. Puzzo conducted an audit of the plaintiffs' 1976, 1977, and 1978 returns. That audit report (December 12, 1980) resulted in plaintiffs being assessed income tax deficiencies of $12,156.76, $13,867.49, and $24,180.99, for the taxable years 1976, 1977, and 1978, respectively. In addition, plaintiffs were also assessed civil fraud penalties at the rate of 50% of the assessed tax deficiency plus deficiency interest ($6,078.39, $6,933.75, and $12,090.49 as to each respective tax year, pursuant to 26 U.S.C. § 6653(b)). In the aggregate, said audit generated a proposed assessment against plaintiffs in the amount of $75,307.89 in additional taxes and penalties. Said amounts were assessed within the periods prescribed by I.R.C. §§ 6501(a) and (c)(4), i.e., within three years from the date the returns were filed or within the period agreed to by voluntary extensions. Following the audit, a deficiency notice and offer of settlement, Form 870, was forwarded to the plaintiffs.

---

[44] [fn 3] We do not reach the question of fraud as averred by defendant and/or allegedly admitted by plaintiffs because that issue goes to the merits of the refund claim. This is so since here we will dispose of this case by the application of the doctrine of equitable estoppel and a jurisdictional bar as to the claim regarding the 1978 return, infra.

[45] [fn 4] "Euphemistically" is the appropriate adjective given subsequent revelations as to the real source of the understated income. From the documentation reflected in defendant's exhibits, it appears that on January 18, 1978, the Massachusetts State Police conducted a raid on plaintiffs' residence at which time $50,000 in cash was confiscated. A five-count indictment relating to illegal gambling activity followed therefrom, and plaintiff, Frank Kretchmar, pleaded guilty to each count. The Service, therefore, contends that given the fact that no income from the admitted gambling activities was listed on either of the 1976, 1977 or 1978 returns, the subsequently discovered unreported cash must have emanated from said illegal activity. See Exhibit F, Appendix to Reply Memorandum for the United States in Support of its Motion for Summary Judgment, March 7, 1985.

Plaintiffs rejected, *i.e.,* refused to execute, the Form 870 settlement offer and appealed the foregoing proposed deficiencies to the Appeals Office of the Internal Revenue Service (IRS). Upon further settlement negotiation, the IRS agreed in 1982 to *decrease* plaintiffs' assessed gross income by the amount of $6,000 for 1976, and $20,000 for 1978. No adjustment, however, was made for 1977 given the agreed diminution in 1976 and 1978. As a result of said readjustments by the Appeals Office, plaintiffs' reassessed taxes and penalties were reduced to $14,063.52, $20,801.24, and $20,104.15, for the three taxable years in question or an aggregate amount of $54,968.91. As evidence of the results of the compromise/settlement negotiations, and in order to preclude future assessments against such taxable years, plaintiffs executed Form 870-AD on January 29, 1982, which was accepted for the Commissioner of Internal Revenue on February 9, 1982. *See* Exhibits B and C, Appendix B, Memorandum for the United States dated January 22, 1985.

Shortly thereafter, *i.e.,* on or about March 15, 1982, plaintiffs received the IRS notice that the agreed to deficiency had been accepted by the defendant. That notice also contained an assessment issued in the total amounts of $18,163.20, $25,922.91, and $24,250.02 for the taxable years 1976, 1977, and 1978, respectively, which included taxes, penalties, and deficiency interest. Plaintiffs' complaint alleges that the total foregoing assessment was in fact paid in full for *all* of the foregoing years in question over the period June, 1982 through February, 1983. The facts, however, belie this averment and show that the *total* assessment for the taxable year 1978 was *not* paid in full as of February 3, 1984, *i.e.,* the date plaintiffs' petition was filed in this court. Plaintiffs have since conceded the fact that payment in full has *not* been made for the taxable year 1978.[46] As for the taxable years 1976 and 1977, the Service's records confirm the jurisdictional fact that plaintiffs have paid in full the agreed to amounts assessed on Form 870-AD for such years.

In spite of plaintiffs' promise in the Form 870-AD that "no [future] claim for refund or credit shall be filed . . . other than for amounts attributed to carrybacks" for the years in issue after the execution of the Form 870-AD, they nevertheless filed a timely claim for refund (Form 1040X), for each of the years in question, "other than for amounts attributed to carrybacks" with the Boston Appeals Office of the IRS on or about May 23, 1983. At that date, despite plaintiffs' previous execution of several forms extending *the general three-year limitations period* for deficiency assessment for 1976 and 1977 to December 31, 1982, defendant's right to assess any further deficiency as to *all* years under the general three-year period of limitations (§§ 6501(a) and (c)(4)) had then expired. On each such Forms 1040X, plaintiffs claimed, *inter alia,* that the originally reported income amounts on their returns for each year were correct; that the Form 870-AD was executed by a representative of plaintiffs who was acting outside the scope of his authority; that the Form 870-AD was itself illegal as it was executed beyond the

---

[46] [fn 5] See Plaintiffs' Response to Motion of the United States for Summary Judgment, February 8, 1985, at 11.

three year statute of limitations contained in 26 U.S.C. § 6501; and that no grounds existed to assess civil fraud penalties pursuant to 26 U.S.C. § 6653(b). The IRS rejected plaintiffs' contentions and disallowed all of plaintiffs' refund claims on December 12, 1983.

Plaintiffs, thereafter, commenced a refund action in this court on February 3, 1984. The petition here did not seek refunds "for amounts attributed to carrybacks," but rather requested refunds of the same amounts for each year which were sought in plaintiffs' earlier appeal to the Appeals Office dated May 23, 1983. In opposition, on January 22, 1985, defendant moved for summary judgment in which it invoked the doctrine of equitable estoppel for all years as a result of plaintiffs' execution of Form 870-AD, and also averred that this court lacks jurisdiction with regard to the claim respecting the taxable year 1978.

For reasons hereinafter delineated, we find that judgment should be granted in favor of defendant on its motion for summary judgment as to all taxable years in issue.

DISCUSSION

In passing on the operative issues for each taxable year, the court will address the claim regarding the taxable year 1978 first inasmuch as a jurisdictional bar is raised to the prosecution of that refund claim. Thereafter, we will discuss the impediment to the prosecution of the 1976 and 1977 refund claims because of the applicability of the doctrine of equitable estoppel.

A. Jurisdiction Re 1978 Claim for Refund

As a jurisdictional prerequisite, it has long been settled law that federal courts may *not* adjudicate tax refund suits for a given year until and *after* the deficiency assessed for that year has been paid *in full. Flora v. United States,* 357 U.S. 63, 78 S.Ct. 1079, 2 L.Ed.2d 1165 (1958), *aff'd on rehearing,* 362 U.S. 145, 80 S.Ct. 630, 4 L.Ed.2d 623 (1960). That holding has consistently obtained in both the Claims Court, and in the predecessor Court of Claims. *Tonasket v. United States,* 218 Ct.Cl. 709, 711-12, 590 F.2d 343 (1978); *Frise v. United States,* 5 Cl.Ct. 488, 490 (1984); *see also* 28 U.S.C. § 1491 (1982).

For the taxable years 1976 and 1977, defendant has made no challenge to this court's subject matter jurisdiction over plaintiffs' refund action. IRS records submitted by the defendant confirm that all taxes, interest, and penalties agreed to through the execution of settlement Form 870-AD have been paid in full for the taxable years 1976 and 1977.[47] Premised on the standards articulated in *Flora* and *Tonasket, supra,* since plaintiffs have paid in full all deficiencies assessed for the taxable years 1976 and 1977, tax refund jurisdiction in this court, as to those two years, is proper.

On the other hand, for the taxable year 1978, defendant has challenged this court's subject matter jurisdiction over plaintiffs' refund claim. Defendant alleges that for that taxable year, plaintiffs have made only two payments, aggregating

---

[47] [fn 6] See Exhibits D, E and F, Appendix B to the Memorandum for the United States in Support of its Motion for Summary Judgment, January 22, 1985.

$3,500, toward the total $24,250.02 deficiency agreed to on Form 870-AD.[48] Consequently, even after applying the modest overpayments from the 1976 and 1977 assessments to the outstanding 1978 balance, plaintiffs are left with a current unpaid balance of $18,425.44 in taxes, penalties, and interest for the taxable year 1978.[49] There is no question as to the fact of failure to pay in full, as contended by defendant, inasmuch as plaintiffs in their opposition to defendant's motion for summary judgment candidly concede as follows: "Plaintiffs reluctantly agree that the [d]efendant is correct on this issue."[50]

In addressing this identical issue, the predecessor Court of Claims stated in *Tonasket v. United States* that:

> . . . the jurisdictional basis for refund suits provides a second, independent ground for concluding that this court lacks jurisdiction. Section 1346(a)(1) gives the district courts concurrent jurisdiction with this court over actions to recover any internal-revenue tax, any penalty, or any sum erroneously or unlawfully collected. In *Flora v. United States,* 362 U.S. 145 [80 S.Ct. 630, 4 L.Ed.2d 623] (1960), the Supreme Court, after full consideration on reargument, affirmed its earlier construction of section 1346(a)(1) *as requiring full payment of all taxes or penalties before jurisdiction vested in the district courts.* 362 U.S. 146-47, 177 [80 S.Ct. 630, 631, 647, 4 L.Ed.2d 623]. Plaintiffs seek to avoid the full payment requirement by arguing that *Flora* does not apply to refund suits in the Court of Claims [now the U.S. Claims Court], or that *Flora* should be reconsidered on the basis of subsequent Supreme Court equal protection cases which plaintiffs interpret as making the *Flora* rule an unconstitutional discrimination against indigents. *We cannot construe Flora to preclude part-payment tax suits in district courts, but allowing such part-payment actions here.* Although the precise holding of *Flora* requires full payment before tax suits in district courts, the *ratio decidendi* of that ruling—that full payment before suit is necessary to preserve the harmony of a carefully structured tax litigation system, *id.* at 176-77—[80 S.Ct. at 646-47] *must extend to require full payment before suit in the Court of Claims.*

Tonasket, 218 Ct.Cl. at 711-12 (emphasis added). Given the foregoing, this court is constrained to conclude, and must hold, that it lacks subject matter jurisdiction over plaintiffs' 1978 refund claim.

B. Equitable Estoppel

1. Background

Defendant has next moved for summary judgment on plaintiffs' refund claims (the taxable years 1976-1977) on the ground that their previous execution of IRS Form 870-AD equitably estops plaintiffs from litigating these now

---

[48] [fn 7] See Exhibit F, Appendix B, supra note 6.

[49] [fn 8] See Id. The overpayment credits amounted to $2,324.58.

[50] [fn 9] See Plaintiff's Response to Motion of the United States for Summary Judgment, February 8, 1985, at 11.

compromised and settled claims. In short, defendant avers that it would be most inequitable and unjust, in the face of the bargained-for-concessions implicit in Form 870-AD signed by plaintiffs on January 29, 1982, and approved by defendant on February 9, 1982, to permit plaintiffs to file an efficacious claim for refund (May 23, 1983) long after the running of the general three-year statute of limitations (26 U.S.C. § 6501(a)) on additional assessments. Conversely, and in opposition, plaintiffs argue that (1) any estoppel of their claims would be "inequitable" given the fact that no compromise of their claims was made through the execution of Form 870-AD; (2) no prejudice would be visited on defendant should the agreement be revoked inasmuch as the statute had not run on additional assessments at the time plaintiffs filed their claims to the extent the defendant can prove either fraud or an omission in excess of 25 percent of the amount of gross income originally reported; (3) in fact the Form 870-AD was executed by an unauthorized person; and (4) the Form 870-AD is not valid because the statute of limitations (§ 6501(a)) expired *prior* to January 29, 1982.

Research discloses that the application of the doctrine of equitable estoppel, to bar the prosecution of tax refund claims settled and concluded by the execution of a Form 870-AD, has provoked not only controversy but outright inconsistency among various federal circuits. On the one hand, there are those courts which strictly hold, according to the Supreme Court in *Botany Worsted Mills v. United States,* 278 U.S. 282, 49 S.Ct. 129, 73 L.Ed. 379 (1929), that the only binding form of tax settlement is one which conforms to the finality prescribed through a settlement agreement pursuant to 26 U.S.C. § 7121 (1982).[51] The justification for this conclusion is apparently premised on the fact that Form 870-AD specifically states that it is not such an agreement.[52] Absent strict adherence to the formality envisioned in § 7121, these courts, therefore, reject the application of the doctrine of equitable estoppel relying instead on the Supreme

---

[51] [fn 10] 26 U.S.C. § 7121 (1982) states:

(a) Authorization.—The Secretary or his delegate is authorized to enter into an agreement in writing with any person relating to the liability of such person (or of the person or estate for whom he acts) in respect to any internal revenue tax for any taxable period.

(b) Finality.—If such agreement is approved by the Secretary or his delegate (within such time as may be stated in such agreement, or later agreed to) such agreement shall be final and conclusive, and, except upon a showing of fraud or malfeasance, or misrepresentation of a material fact—

(1) the case shall not be reopened as to the matters agreed upon or the agreement modified by any officer, employee, or agent of the United States, and

(2) in any suit, action, or proceeding, such agreement, or any determination, assessment, collection, payment, abatement, refund, or credit made in accordance therewith, shall not be annulled, modified, set aside, or disregarded.

[52] [fn 11] See supra note 2.

Court's admonishment that "[w]hen a statute limits a thing to be done in a particular mode, it includes the negative of any other mode." *Botany,* 278 U.S. at 289, 49 S.Ct. at 132. *Cf. Uinta Livestock Corp. v. United States,* 355 F.2d 761 (10th Cir.1966); *Associated Mutuals, Inc. v. Delaney,* 176 F.2d 179, 181 n. 1 (1st Cir.1949); and *Bank of New York v. United States,* 170 F.2d 20 (3d Cir.1948).

On the other hand, there are also those courts which have a tradition of affirmatively applying the doctrine of equitable estoppel to bar the litigation of claims previously concluded through the taxpayer's execution of a settlement Form 870-AD. These courts, *infra,* in essence, acknowledge the continued vitality of *Botany,* but they persuasively distinguish its holding by arguing that that case did not present the estoppel issue squarely to the Court. In support of this position, they refer to the following often cited *dicta* in *Botany,* to wit:

> It is plain that no compromise is authorized by this statute which is not assented to by the Secretary of the Treasury. For this reason, if for no other, the informal agreement made in this case did not constitute a settlement which in itself was binding upon the Government or the Mills. *And, without determining whether such an agreement, though not binding in itself, may when executed become, under some circumstances, binding on the parties by estoppel, it suffices to say that here the findings disclose no adequate ground for any claim of estoppel by the United States.*

Botany, 278 U.S. at 289, 49 S.Ct. at 132 (emphasis added, citations omitted). Since the Supreme Court has expressly reserved the issue of what circumstances might ultimately raise the execution of a Form 870-AD to a binding settlement, certain courts have consequently held that *Botany* does not estop the courts from developing their own law on the subject. Thus, it is on the foregoing premises that a properly executed Form 870-AD has become a recognized impediment, in certain circuits, to estop taxpayers from litigating the merits of tax refund claims settled therein. Cf. Stair v. United States, 516 F.2d 560 (2d Cir.1975); General Split Corp. v. United States, 500 F.2d 998 (7th Cir.1974); Quigley v. Internal Revenue Service, 289 F.2d 878 (D.C.Cir.1960); Cain v. United States, 255 F.2d 193 (8th Cir.1958); Daugette v. Patterson, 250 F.2d 753 (5th Cir.1957), cert. denied, 356 U.S. 902, 78 S.Ct. 561, 2 L.Ed.2d 580 (1958); Monge v. Smyth, 229 F.2d 361 (9th Cir.1956), appeal dismissed per curiam, 351 U.S. 976, 76 S.Ct. 1055, 100 L.Ed. 1493 (1956); Elbo Coals, Inc. v. United States, 763 F.2d 818 (6th Cir.1985).

2. Equitable Estoppel in the Predecessor Court of Claims

Research further discloses that the predecessor Court of Claims saw fit on a number of occasions to apply the doctrine of equitable estoppel on facts arising out of a taxpayer's previous execution of a Form 870-AD. *See Guggenheim v. United States,* 111 Ct.U. 165, 77 F.Supp. 186 (1948); *H.W. Nelson Co., Inc. v. United States,* 158 Ct.Cl. 629, 308 F.2d 950 (1962); *D.D.I., Inc. v. United States,* 199 Ct.Cl. 380, 467 F.2d 497 (1972); *McGraw-Hill, Inc. v. United States,* 224 Ct.Cl. 354, 623 F.2d 700 (1980) (doctrine affirmed but not applied on the specific facts of the case). In so doing, said Court of Claims made particular mention of the language cited from *Botany, supra.* For example, in the seminal case adopting the doctrine in the predecessor Court of Claims, *Guggenheim v. United States,* all of the formalities required for executing an efficacious Form 870-AD[53] were present. *Guggenheim,* 77 F.Supp. at 196. Both parties had signed, and the form was properly accepted by the Commissioner on the same day. *Id.* at 194. There, the court noted in contradistinction to *Botany* that:

> Many of the elements in the formal agreement involved in this case [*Guggenheim*] were lacking in that case [*Botany*]. Moreover, we do not understand that case to hold, as plaintiff contends, that under no circumstances will a closing agreement be held binding unless executed in accordance with Section [7121]. . . .

Guggenheim, 77 F.Supp. at 196. Having effectively distinguished *Botany,* the Court of Claims in *Guggenheim* went on to dismiss the tax refund action therein holding that cause of action to be equitably barred due solely to the plaintiff's previous execution of Form 870. *Id.* at 197.

Against the foregoing background, it is underscored that our research has uncovered no cases in the Claims Court or the Court of Appeals for the Federal Circuit (CAFC) since their inception in 1982, which have applied the doctrine of equitable estoppel premised on a taxpayer's prior execution of a Form 870-AD. That doctrine, however, has nevertheless been affirmed in other fact situations evidencing a similar detrimental reliance by defendant arising out of a previous agreement resolving an area of contention between the parties. Thus, although there is a factual dichotomy between the case at bar and the cases cited, *infra,* we view such fact variances to reflect a distinction without a significant difference. *See e.g., Alpena Savings Bank v. United States,* 8 Cl.Ct. 249 (1985) (bank loan guarantee); *Estate of Piper v. United States,* 8 Cl.Ct. 243 (1985) (estate and gift tax refund); *Estate of German v. United States,* 7 Cl.Ct. 641 (1985) (estate tax refund); *Pacific Gas & Electric Co. v. United States,* 3 Cl.Ct. 329 (1983) (implied-in-fact contract). While research has failed to unearth relevant Claims Court and CAFC precedent in which a Form 870-AD was involved, those decisions in the predecessor Court of Claims applying the doctrine of equitable estoppel are sufficient authority for this court to invoke this equitable defense in an appropriate case such as here. This is so because the Claims Court is compelled to follow, as binding precedent, applicable rulings in the predecessor Court of Claims. *See* RUSCC, General Order No. 1, October 7, 1982.[54]

---

[53] [fn 12] While in *Guggenheim,* the executed agreement was contained in a Form 870, that form had been modified to mirror, in all material particulars, the operative language contained in the Form 870-AD at issue here.

[54] [fn 13] RUSCC, General Order No. 1, October 7, 1982, states, inter alia:

> The United States Claims Court inherits substantially all of the jurisdiction, caseload and grand tradition of the United States Court of Claims. To assure continuity in carrying out the business of the court, and to

3. Application of the Doctrine—Equitable Estoppel

As outlined above, we apply the doctrine of equitable estoppel to preclude the litigation of plaintiffs' claims as to the taxable years 1976 and 1977. (While we may refer to the taxable year 1978, we deem it to be unnecessary to discuss the applicability of said doctrine to the taxable year 1978, inasmuch as plaintiffs concede that this court is without subject matter jurisdiction with respect to said year.) The discussion which follows demonstrates that in accordance with Court of Claims precedent, plaintiffs did, by executing the Form 870-AD, waive their right to further litigate the 1976 and 1977 claims, so that to reopen them at this juncture would significantly prejudice the defendant. On such facts, we find that equity favors the enforcement of plaintiffs' agreement.

In general terms, binding precedent teaches that the doctrine of equitable estoppel, arising out of the execution of a Form 870-AD, may be applied to hold a taxpayer to his bargain if the following three criteria are established: (1) the execution of the Form 870-AD was the result of mutual concession or compromise; (2) there was a meeting of the minds that the claims be extinguished; and (3) that to allow the plaintiff to reopen the case would be prejudicial given the defendant's reliance on the extinguishment thereof. *Guggenheim*, 77 F.Supp. at 196; *H.W. Nelson Co.*, 308 F.2d at 956-59; *D.D.I., Inc.*, 467 F.2d at 500-01; *McGraw-Hill, Inc.*, 623 F.2d at 706. As the pleading of the doctrine raises an affirmative defense, the burden is on the defendant to establish these criteria by the requisite quantum of proof.

a. Mutual Concession and Compromise

With respect to the first criterion, mutual concession or compromise, the defendant's documentary evidence clearly establishes this fact for all taxable years with striking similarity to the facts in *Guggenheim*. In *Guggenheim*, the court stated in that connection that:

> Plaintiff protested the proposed disallowance and thereafter conferences were held with plaintiff's representatives. A further investigation was made by a revenue agent. As a result of these discussions, the representatives of the Commissioner agreed to recommend for allowance a deduction . . . claimed by plaintiff. Plaintiff abandoned his contention that the other deductions claimed were allowable. The Commissioner's representative also agreed to make an adjustment in plaintiff's favor on account of certain dividends.

Guggenheim, 77 F.Supp. at 194. In the case at bar, plaintiffs similarly protested the audit report which initially assessed them some $75,307 in deficiencies (taxes

---

promote the interests of justice and service to the public, it is ordered as follows:

(1) *All published decisions of the United States Court of Claims are accepted as binding precedent for the United States Claims Court*, unless and until modified by decisions of the United States Court of Appeals for the Federal Circuit or the United States Supreme Court.

(emphasis added).

and penalties) in December 1980 for all of the years in issue. Likewise, as in *Guggenheim*, a further investigation was held in which an IRS report was issued containing the following revelations:

> *Taxpayers, in an effort to close this case, propose that the Government accept in the year 1976 a reduction of $6,000* as representing a repayment of the loan to Ray Heck as outlined above. *Taxpayers concede all adjustments in 1977. In 1978, it is proposed that the Government concede the inclusion of $13,661* deemed to have been for the purchase of JTC stock. *In the year 1978, taxpayers also propose that an amount of $6,339 be considered as cash on hand. It is recommended that this proposal of settlement be accepted as a reasonable conclusion to this case.*

Appeals Transmittal Memorandum and Supporting Statement, Feb. 12, 1982 (emphasis added).[55] This paraphrase of the ongoing dialogue between plaintiffs and defendant as contained in the referenced IRS report, evidencing the negotiations leading to the final adjustments which were then recorded on Form 870-AD, persuasively belies plaintiffs' assertion that "[t]he numbers placed on the Form 870-AD were not a compromise at all."[56] Indeed, as in *Guggenheim*, it is clear beyond cavil, and we so find, that plaintiffs' settlement, manifested by the execution of Form 870-AD in this case, was a bilateral process driven by mutual concession and compromise.

In support of our holding as to mutual concession and compromise, we also stress that plaintiffs' proof regarding their contrary assertion was thoroughly insufficient to raise, even by their contentions, a genuine issue of material fact. While we acknowledge plaintiffs' attempt to raise such genuine issues of material fact based on the holding in *Lignos v. United States*, 439 F.2d 1365 (2d Cir.1971), we find that case to be clearly distinguishable from the case at bar. In *Lignos*, the Second Circuit refused to affirm the district court's grant of summary judgment on the grounds of equitable estoppel because there *plaintiffs* had adduced sufficient proof to raise a *factual issue* regarding whether defendant had in truth "conceded" its position in arriving at the settlement recorded on the Form 870-AD. *Id.* The appellate court in *Lignos* reached this conclusion based upon plaintiff's *clear evidentiary* showing in the district court which included specific facts alleged through sworn affidavits. *Id.* In the case at bar, however, plaintiffs have neither apprised this court of any *specific facts* illustrating that there exists genuine issues for trial, nor have they proffered an affidavit averring such. Because of the foregoing, plaintiffs are entitled to no comfort from *Lignos*

---

[55] [fn 14] Exhibit F, Appendix to Reply Memorandum for the United States in Support of its Motion for Summary Judgment, March 7, 1985, page A20.

[56] [fn 15] See Plaintiff's Response to Motion of the United States for Summary Judgment, February 8, 1985, at 6. The court notes that plaintiffs failed to proffer any supporting documentary evidence to their bland self-serving denial of the existence of a mutual compromise.

particularly whereas here they have failed to comply with RUSCC 56(e). Rule 56(e) states that:

> When a motion for summary judgment is made . . ., an adverse party may not rest upon the *mere allegations* or denials of his pleading, but . . . *must set forth specific facts showing that there is a genuine issue for trial.* If he does not so respond, summary judgment, if appropriate, shall be entered against him.

RUSCC 56(e) (emphasis added). In essence, plaintiffs in the case at bar have done nothing more than rely on repeated, conclusory allegations that there was no compromise. Without more, such bland assertion(s) may not generate genuine issues of material fact, nor may they overcome the persuasive proof proffered by defendant.

b. Meeting of the Minds

The second criterion cited above requires that, concomitantly, there must also be a meeting of the minds to the effect that the right to raise any prospective claims or to otherwise reopen the case, for such years, be extinguished (save exceptions not here relevant). In *Guggenheim,* the court added substance to the evaluation of this concept by examining two additional factors: (1) the parties' course of conduct; and (2) the express language adopted by the parties on the Form 870-AD. *Guggenheim,* 77 F.Supp. at 195. As to course of conduct, the court stated:

> The conclusion is inescapable from the evidence that there was a meeting of minds as to the final disposition of the case. When that occurred, the Commissioner recomputed plaintiff's tax liability and transmitted to plaintiff the settlement document wherein was set out a deficiency for each of the years. In transmitting that document to plaintiff at that time, the Commissioner stated that he was accepting plaintiff's "proposal for settlement," and also referred to the document as an "agreement" when executed by plaintiff and approved on his behalf. In returning the document after execution, plaintiff likewise referred to it as an "agreement."

Id. at 195. In *Guggenheim,* at no time did either party objectively manifest a belief that what was being negotiated was anything less than a complete settlement for the taxable years in issue. While no correspondence similar to that in *Guggenheim* has been presented to the court in the case at bar, neither has any demonstrative evidence been submitted supporting plaintiffs' contention that a definitive settlement was *not* intended for all taxable years. In fact, on this issue the documentary evidence is thoroughly supportive of defendant's position, particularly when we examine defendant's Form 5278, Statement-Income Tax Changes, prepared by the Appeals Office of the IRS which contains a box plainly checked "settlement computation."[57] Similarly, in the Appeals Transmittal Memorandum and Supporting Statement, *supra,* the words "Proposal of

---

[57] [fn 16] Exhibit B, Appendix B, supra note 6.

Settlement" are used consistently throughout to characterize the nature of the procedural posture of plaintiffs' appeal.[58] While plaintiffs may, as an afterthought, *now* contend otherwise, the evidence is wanting and it strains credulity to contend that the lengthy and detailed negotiations, which led to the preparation and execution of Form 870-AD, were conducted with any purpose other than that they were aimed at a definitive settlement.

Moreover, in reviewing the undeniable language contained in the Form 870-AD together with other referenced evidence, *supra,* the ultimate intentions of the parties leave no room for doubt. This conclusion is compelled when one carefully reviews the Form 870-AD, wherein the following unambiguous statement appears directly above the plaintiffs' signatures:

> *If this offer is accepted for the Commissioner, the case shall not be reopened* in the absence of fraud, malfeasance, concealment or misrepresentation of material fact, an important mistake in mathematical calculation, or excessive tentative allowances of carrybacks provided by law; *and no claim for refund or credit shall be filed or prosecuted for the year(s) stated above other than for amounts attributed to carrybacks provided by law.*

Appendix B to the Memorandum for the United States in Support of Its Motion for Summary Judgment, January 22, 1985, Exhibit C (emphasis added). Thus, by signing the Form 870-AD containing the referenced language, plaintiffs, in essence, waived all further rights to contest the assessment for the stated taxable years, save for the specific exception not present in this case.[59] While the Form 870-AD was drafted by the defendant, no ambiguity exists as to the clear import of the intendment of the parties, *i.e.,* each side *expressly* waived its right (with exceptions not pertinent here) to subsequently litigate the settlement contained therein. For this court to find otherwise, at this posture, would contravene and directly ignore the clearly exhibited objective manifestations of the signatories.

Confronted with practically identical language on the Form 870 [60] in *Guggenheim,* the Court of Claims there equally underscored its opinion regarding the degree of mutuality between the parties by stating:

> In language which we think is too clear to be misunderstood and which would be rendered meaningless if plaintiff's interpretation were to prevail, the agreement states:
>
> > If this proposal is accepted by or on behalf of the Commissioner, the case shall not be reopened nor shall any claim for refund be filed or prosecuted respecting the taxes for the years above stated, in the absence

---

[58] [fn 17] Exhibit F, Appendix to Reply Memorandum, supra note 14.

[59] [fn 18] The specific exception is that a taxpayer may renounce a Form 870-AD and file a claim for refund or credit, for the stated year(s), "for amounts attributed to carrybacks provided by law."

[60] [fn 19] See supra note 12.

of fraud, malfeasance, concealment or misrepresentation of material fact, or of an important mistake in mathematical calculations.

There is no contention that there was any fraud, malfeasance, concealment, misrepresentation, or mistake in calculation. How this could be interpreted other than to preclude plaintiff from filing a claim for refund or prosecuting this suit is difficult to understand.

Guggenheim, 77 F.Supp. at 195 (emphasis added). Thus, on substantially identical facts as obtained in Guggenheim, we see no factual or legal basis to find other than that the parties manifested an unequivocal mutuality of intent to extinguish plaintiffs' claims.

c. Detrimental Reliance

The third, and final, criterion defendant must establish to effect the application of the doctrine of equitable estoppel is that of detrimental reliance. In the precise context of this case, to meet this burden, the proof must show that defendant detrimentally relied upon plaintiffs' execution of the Form 870-AD in question. The degree of detrimental reliance sufficient to support the application of the doctrine of equitable estoppel has been characterized by the courts in various ways. In *McGraw-Hill*, for example, the court stated that "equitable estoppel [is to be applied] whenever the IRS cannot be placed in the same position it was when the agreement was executed" []. *McGraw-Hill*, 623 F.2d at 706. More specifically, perhaps, is the definition given in *D.D.I.* wherein the court states that detrimental reliance is the result which obtains "where the statute of limitations has run on the collection of further deficiencies between the time an informal compromise agreement was executed and the time the refund claim was filed . . .." *D.D.I.*, 467 F.2d at 500.

Quite logically, the predecessor Court of Claims has also, by implication, suggested the necessity for the defendant's reliance to have been reasonable under the circumstances. In this regard, the key variable is the timing of the defendant's knowledge regarding the plaintiff's decision to change its position, *i.e.*, whether the repudiation of the Form 870-AD occurs at a time when the statute of limitations on assessment has expired. Or, on the other hand, the question is whether such knowledge preceded the running of the statute of limitations to the extent that the Service could be restored to the "same position," *i.e.*, by expeditiously effecting an additional assessment within the general three-year period of limitations (§ 6501(a)). The case of *Erickson v. United States,* 159 Ct.Cl. 202, 309 F.2d 760 (1962), is particularly instructive on this issue. In *Erickson,* the Court of Claims estopped the plaintiff from seeking a refund of deficiency interest made payable under a compromise agreement proposed by the taxpayer as a settlement of a claim being litigated in the Tax Court. The settlement agreement contained an award of interest, yet the Tax Court in ratifying the agreement, omitted the award of interest. In accordance with the written settlement agreement itself, the Commissioner collected the interest. In estopping plaintiff from suing for a refund of the interest, the Court of Claims commented on the reasonableness of the defendant's reliance as follows:

Taxpayer tells us that his counsel orally indicated to representatives of the defendant in October 1958, before the Tax Court orders had become final, that he intended to sue for most of the interest assessed and not refunded. This, he says, was sufficient warning to the Government that his position had changed. *But such informal oral statements, even if strongly asserted, would not change the reliance which the Government had already placed on the prior written agreement and could rightfully continue to place, at least until the agreement was formally repudiated in writing.*

Id. at 764-65 (emphasis added). Consistent with the foregoing statement by the court in *Erickson,* we construe the quoted language of *D.D.I.,* cited *supra,* to mean that the cut-off date for the defendant to claim detrimental reliance is certainly the date the Form 870-AD is "formally repudiated in writing." Thus, the prejudice to defendant emanating from detrimental reliance because of the running of the three-year limitations period, must have accrued at the date just prior to the time the claim for refund was filed with the IRS, or just prior to the date when any other written notice of repudiation was served on defendant, whichever occurs first. For defendant to proceed in allowing the three-year statute to run, after having received such written notice of repudiation, would clearly not be reasonable, nor indicative of the requisite prejudice required to be *caused* by the plaintiff. In other words, equity will only estop a plaintiff based on that prejudice which is traceable to its *own* action or inaction, not for that which is self-imposed by the defendant.

Plaintiffs insist that at the time they repudiated the Form 870-AD and filed their refund claims with the Service on May 23, 1983 (as well as at the date plaintiffs' petition was filed here (February 3, 1984)), the defendant was in no worse position to assess further deficiencies than it was in at the date the Form 870-AD became effective (February 9, 1982). That is to say plaintiffs argue that defendant was then "in the same position it was when the agreement was executed," as contemplated in *D.D.I., supra,* and it is, therefore, not barred from effecting additional assessments for taxable years 1976 and 1977 upon the proof of fraud (26 U.S.C. § 6501(c)(1)); nor would it be so barred upon proof of an omission of income in excess of 25 percent of reported gross income (26 U.S.C. § 6501(e)). Defendant, on the other hand, has strenuously insisted that due to the running of the general three-year statute of limitations on assessment on December 31, 1982 (26 U.S.C. § 6501(a)), and a concomitant shift in the burden of proof relative to the necessity of proving fraud as a basis for assessing a *deficiency* for the taxable years 1976 and 1977, defendant was *not* in the *same* position on May 23, 1983, as it was in at the time the Form 870-AD was executed (*i.e.,* January 29, 1982 and February 9, 1982). As discussed below, we find that at the date on which defendant received notice of plaintiffs' repudiation of the Form 870-AD (May 23, 1983), defendant had previously sufficiently relied to its detriment on the Form 870-AD so as to support the application of equitable estoppel to plaintiffs' refund claims. Therefore, regarding the existence of this final element—detrimental reliance, we agree with defendant as to both taxable years 1976 and 1977.

The detriment which we find sufficient to support defendant's claim of estoppel is both traditional, as contemplated under the standards articulated by *Guggenheim* and *D.D.I.*, and unique to the peculiar facts of this case. Starting with an examination of the facts as of the critical date of notice, May 23, 1983, we note that at that date, the three-year statutory period (inclusive of plaintiffs' extensions) had clearly run for both taxable years 1976 and 1977. For each of these two years, plaintiffs' consent to an extension of the three-year statutory period on assessment was effective up to December 31, 1982. The three-year period of limitations on assessments as extended for each year, therefore, expired approximately five months *before* plaintiffs filed their May 23, 1983 claims with the IRS. Consequently, on these facts, we find the precise prejudice which is cited to by the court in both *D.D.I.* and *McGraw-Hill*. Defendant cannot be put back in the "same position" today (or at any time after December 31, 1982) as it held before the Form 870-AD was signed simply because the *general statute* of limitations on additional assessments (§ 6501(a)), extended by § 6501(c)(4), which had *not* then run on February 9, 1982, had in fact expired at the date plaintiffs' claims for refund were filed.

On the foregoing, we are convinced that the *Guggenheim* case is, therefore, dispositive of this issue because substantially the same facts present here gave rise to a finding of prejudice there by the Court of Claims. Citing *cf.* to the case of *R.H. Stearns Co. v. United States,* 291 U.S. 54, 54 S.Ct. 325, 78 L.Ed. 647 (1934), the predecessor court stated:

> At the time the agreement in this case was executed the statute had not run on the collection of further deficiencies, but when the claims for refund were filed the statute had run. It would obviously be inequitable to allow the plaintiff to renounce the agreement when the Commissioner cannot be placed in the same position he was when the agreement was executed. A clear case for the application of the doctrine of equitable estoppel exists and should be applied.

Guggenheim, 77 F.Supp. at 196. For the reasons discussed infra, and contrary to plaintiffs' assertions in the case at bar, it is to the running of the general three-year statute of limitations (where extended, of course, by § 6501(c)(4)), and only to that statute, that we must look to determine the existence of the necessary prejudice to the defendant.[61]

We now turn to distinguish those factors which plaintiffs contend effectively mitigate any prejudice to defendant in spite of the running of the three-year statute as extended.

Plaintiffs' first argue that there would be no prejudice to defendant upon a reopening of the deficiency assessment and considering their claims for refund

---

[61] [fn 20] While the more substantive reasons for this conclusion are discussed infra, we think it important to note that in each of the cases cited throughout this opinion, only the three-year general statute was considered in relation to the finding of prejudice to the defendant.

because defendant continues to be free to assess additional income tax deficiencies upon proof of fraud (§ 6501(c)(1)). Section 6501(c)(1) provides, *inter alia,* that "[i]n the case of a false or fraudulent return with the intent to evade tax, the tax may be assessed . . . at any time." 26 U.S.C. § 6501(c) (1982). Plaintiffs therefore conclude that because of § 6501(c)(1), taken together with defendant's ultimate burden to prove fraud for purposes of sustaining the fraud penalty, there is no impediment on the defendant to now assess any deficiency it was able to establish back when the Form 870-AD became effective on February 9, 1982. Because of that perceived circumstance, plaintiffs reason that a consideration of their claims for refund would therefore visit no prejudice on defendant as to any year. Plaintiffs' averment is based on the premise that given the fact that defendant had the burden of proof on the fraud penalty issue, upon the initial assessment back in 1980, and that that same burden would obtain in this court in any proceeding on the merits relating to additional income taxes assessed, then defendant is in no more difficult a position to assess its deficiency *now* than it was in when the Form 870-AD was executed.

In its forceful argument to the contrary, the defendant states that while the burden of proof *as to only the fraud penalty* has been defendant's throughout, upon the running of the three-year statute of limitations on assessments, proof of fraud now becomes the *only* method (with one exception, *infra*) to assess an additional deficiency for each year in issue. In other words, *before* the three-year statute (as extended to December 31, 1982 for 1976 and 1977, and April 15, 1982 for 1978) had run, defendant's burden was only to prove fraud sufficient to entitle it to assess the fraud penalties but proof of fraud was not *then* an imperative in order to effect a timely income tax assessment. *After* the general statute of limitations had run, however, in order to make additional tax assessments, defendant would have to first prove that the understatement was due to fraud in order to effect a valid assessment. In essence, the power to assess a deficiency before the general three-year limitations period had expired, with the benefit of the presumptive correctness of the Commissioner's determination, would become *contingent* upon *defendant's* proof of fraud after the statutory three-year period had expired. Moreover, the benefit of the presumption would then be unavailable. This is the new burden which defendant claims is a resulting detriment.

Plaintiffs' attempt to rely on the § 6501(c)(1) fraud exception to claim that defendant is in as good a position *now* to assess a tax deficiency as it was in *prior* to the execution of the Form 870-AD, is clearly erroneous. Because the three-year statute has run as to all years, the power to make additional assessments for each year arises *only* upon an initial showing of fraud. This is obviously *not* the most favorable position defendant was in prior to the approval of the Form 870-AD early in 1982. At that time, defendant had *no* initial burden on the tax deficiency assessment (only on the fraud penalty). The initial burden to prove that the *tax* deficiency was in error was on the plaintiffs, *i.e.,* plaintiffs would have been required to overcome the presumptive correctness of the tax assessment although defendant would have the burden on the fraud *penalty*. In such case, if defendant failed in its burden on the fraud penalty, the fraud penalty *only* would fall. Now, upon proceeding to assess under § 6501(c)(1), defendant would have the burden as to *both* the tax deficiency as well as the fraud penalty. And upon a failure to prove fraud, it would lose both the tax and the penalty. Thus, the precise prejudice which *still* persists even under an application of § 6501(c)(1) is that defendant, contrary to the situation under the general statute of limitations, is now statutorily required to prove that the tax deficiency is due to *fraud* prior to making additional assessments.

Secondly, plaintiffs' reliance on § 6501(e), which permits a *six*-year limitations period[62] for assessment based upon a showing of a 25 percent understatement, relative to the taxpayer's originally reported gross income, is also ineffective to negate the prejudice to defendant based upon a running of the three-year statute. First, even assuming *arguendo* the six-year statute had not expired at the time plaintiffs' claims were filed with the IRS on May 23, 1983, prejudice to defendant would still exist based on defendant's burden to first establish the *applicability* of § 6501(e). In other words, defendant would have the affirmative burden to *prove* a 25 percent understatement in order to effect an assessment. We stress that *prior* to the running of the three-year statute, defendant would have had *no* such burden as was true on the date the 870-AD was executed. Thus, like the results under § 6501(c)(1) discussed *supra,* the power to assess a deficiency, after the three-year limitations period had expired, would become *contingent* upon defendant's initial proof of a 25 percent gross income understatement after the statutory three-year period had expired. We also view this added burden as the precise prejudice defendant would encounter, due to the running of the general three-year limitations period on assessments, if it proceeded under § 6501(e).

While it is clear that the six-year statute had *not* run for the taxable years 1977 and 1978 at the date plaintiffs filed their claims with the IRS (April 15, 1984/1985 vs. May 23, 1983), nevertheless, for the reasons expressed *infra,* we do not believe this fact in any way diminishes the *additional* prejudice which we find would be visited on defendant were such years reopened. This is due to the "package" nature of the particular settlement at bar which was derived from the *interdependent* concession and compromise of claims for *three* separate years. As discussed *supra,* for 1976 and 1978, defendant conceded significant amounts, previously charged as income, which were claimed to be otherwise by plaintiffs.

---

[62] [fn 21] The six-year limitations period provided by § 6501(e) runs from the due date of the return. For the taxable year 1976, the six-year period on assessments would run on April 15, 1983, and for 1977 it would run on April 15, 1984. Thus, additional tax assessments for taxable years 1976 under this statute could not be effected after April 15, 1983, because that statute ran prior to the date plaintiffs filed their claims for refund. Defendant was free to assess additional taxes for 1977 and 1978 after plaintiffs' claims were filed (May 23, 1983) because § 6501(e) limitations on assessment did not run until April 15, 1984 and 1985 respectively.

In return for settling 1977, as originally assessed, defendant conceded reductions in income for 1976 and 1978, and the resulting added burden of proof on defendant to affect an additional assessment, plaintiffs would have this court reopen this case for all years in order that plaintiffs might reverse their *own* concessions. Quite amazingly, plaintiffs assert this request based on a perception that to do so would result in *no* prejudice to defendant.

In response to plaintiffs' position, we believe that where the three-year limitation period has run as to even *one* year of a unified multi-year settlement, significant prejudice would result to defendant to allow a reopening of any included year whereas here said statute on assessment for that year has run. This is so because we do not view the "trade-offs" embodied in a multi-year Form 870-AD compromise to be reasonably and *unprejudicially* severable. Rather, such "trade-offs," in our view, are inextricably intertwined and contingent *across* all years in issue to the extent that, if the formula is involuntarily and/or unilaterally modified for any year, the benefit to one party may be transformed into a detriment to the other. For example, if the 1976 assessment were to stand—a year in which *defendant* conceded $6,000 in income—and 1977 were to be modified favorably to plaintiffs—a year in which *plaintiffs* conceded their position—the result would be that only defendant would be held to its Form 870-AD concession, while plaintiffs would have the benefit of renouncing their concession. Under such a scenario, plaintiffs would be guaranteed the benefit of their bargain, while the defendant would be deprived of its bargain.

This package concept, as applied to the facts of this case, finds sound support on somewhat different facts in the *D.D.I.* case cited *supra.* In *D.D.I.,* the Court of Claims applied equitable estoppel to bar a plaintiff's attempt to reopen several 870s entered into as part of a comprehensive package settlement which included the compromise of three pending lawsuits. After the Commissioner had agreed to dismiss the lawsuits, and had contingently agreed to execute 870s closing several other administrative claims on terms similar to those conceded in the lawsuits, the plaintiffs brought suit to reopen the aforementioned administrative settlements. Plaintiffs in *D.D.I.* relied, for reopening their Form 870s, on the doctrine of equitable recoupment claiming that in spite of the settlement on Form 870, and the running of the three-year statute, defendant still possessed a right to prove by offset and to recoup any amounts plaintiffs would be able to prove as refunds, and to that extent the reopening by plaintiff would not cause a detriment to defendant.

Plaintiffs cited for support the New York District Court case of Morris White Fashions, Inc. v. United States, 176 F.Supp. 760 (S.D.N.Y.1959), which had refused to apply equitable estoppel on summary judgment claiming it would first be necessary to determine whether equitable recoupment was available to the defendant. In distinguishing *Morris White*, the Court of Claims stated:

> However valid the reasoning of *Morris White* might be in a case concerning an informal compromise with a single taxpayer, *it is totally invalid when the compromise is a "package deal." Defendant, in this case, cannot open the cases of the litigating corporations even for use as set-offs.*

D.D.I., 467 F.2d at 500 (emphasis added). While we do note the case at bar concerns a "single taxpayer," i.e., married persons filing a single joint return, we nonetheless find the package concept, i.e., multiple years, relevant based upon our belief that like *D.D.I.*, equitable recoupment very well might not be available to make defendant whole in this case. In *D.D.I.*, equitable recoupment was found to be unavailable because set-offs could not be had at law or in equity among all of the different taxpayers involved in the unified package settlement. In the case at bar, we find equitable recoupment equally unavailable as the plaintiffs' unified package settlement represented compromises among different years which if disturbed will divest defendant of its bargain. Under the doctrine of equitable recoupment, such compromises, embracing different years, cannot, we believe, be involuntarily revisited and offset against one another without a detriment to one of the parties. Only those compromises and refunds within a single year can be offset for purposes of equitable recoupment. In other words, you cannot now unscramble the eggs without a detriment inuring to the defendant. Like *D.D.I.*, then, the same legal and equitable limits on the doctrine of equitable recoupment which precluded its application there, are also present here. In neither *D.D.I.* nor the case at bar would equitable recoupment be available to offset the contingencies which induced defendant's specific compromises. Therefore, barring the application of equitable recoupment, we find the package doctrine as expressed in *D.D.I.*, supra, fully supports our interpretation of that doctrine for purposes of finding prejudice to defendant in the case at bar.

According to long-standing precedent, "[a]n action for refund of taxes is essentially governed by equitable principles." *Erickson*, 309 F.2d at 763 (and case cited therein). To this we add that to get equity, a party must do equity. The package nature of plaintiffs' settlement on Form 870-AD precludes an equitable result from obtaining if plaintiffs were permitted to reopen this case and prevail once the three-year statute has expired.

4. Miscellaneous Claims

Finally, we note that in their futile attempt to overcome defendant's plea of equitable estoppel, plaintiffs also proffer the contention that the Form 870-AD, as executed, was not authorized by the taxpayers. Plaintiffs also have contended that the Form 870-AD is not a valid assessment because it was executed after the § 6501(a) statute of limitations had expired.

We think the foregoing contentions are frivolous afterthoughts and, thus, are entitled to short-shrift. With respect to the initial point, the court notes that the taxpayers' names are subscribed to the Form 870-AD and that plaintiffs failed to submit an affidavit of a handwriting expert in corroboration of their apparent position that they did not sign said Form 870-AD. And with respect to the second point, *i.e.,* the 870-AD is void because the statute of limitations on assessments had run prior to its execution, our review of the submissions discloses that the unimpeached documentary evidence is to the contrary. This is so because Exhibits B, C, and D, Consent To Extend The Time Of Assess Tax (Form 872), contained in defendant's Appendix to Reply Memorandum dated March 7, 1985, collectively extended the statute of limitations on assessments for the years 1976 and 1977 to December 31, 1982. It is patently clear that the statute, as extended for 1976 and 1977, had not expired as to either year upon the execution of Form 870-AD (nor had it expired for 1978 since that cut-off date was April 15, 1982, and the 870-AD was executed prior to that date).

In the face of the foregoing unimpeachable documentary evidence, we are troubled as to the motivation underlying plaintiffs' contentions. Whatever their reasons might be to make such an argument, in spite of Exhibits B, C, and D, *supra,* this circumstance makes balancing the equities of this case in favor of the defendant less troublesome.

CONCLUSION

The foregoing outlines the various forms of prejudice inuring to defendant which we have found based upon the detailed facts as presented in this case. Since we have also found the requisite concession or compromise, and a meeting of the minds with regard to extinguishing of the claim, we see no legal basis for denying defendant's motion for summary judgment. In short, the following language in *Guggenheim* thoroughly summarizes our position:

> A reasonable interpretation of the entire document is that what the parties sought to do was to close the case in such a manner that it could not be reopened either for a refund or for the assessment of deficiencies except in the case of fraud, malfeasance, etc. We see no reason for interpreting the document otherwise.

Guggenheim, 111 Ct. Cl. at 181, 77 F.Supp. 186. Defendant's motion for summary judgment is therefore granted (1) for the taxable year 1978 based on lack of subject matter jurisdiction and (2) for the taxable years 1976 and 1977 based on the doctrine of equitable estoppel. The Clerk shall dismiss the plaintiffs' petition.

IT IS SO ORDERED.

NOTES AND QUESTIONS

1. The first issue in this case provides a preview of the requirements for a refund suit to be discussed in Chapter 18. A taxpayer must pay the entire amount of any deficiency, along with some other procedural requirements, in order to sue the IRS for a refund.
2. When may a taxpayer re-open a case decided by the Appeals Office?

CHAPTER 15

IRS FINAL TAX DETERMINATIONS

A. Introduction

If the Appeals Office and the taxpayer do not reach a settlement, the last step in a tax dispute at the administrative level is for the IRS to issue a final determination. If the IRS is making a determination on a case that arose from an examination (*i.e.*, a deficiency), the IRS issues a statutory notice of deficiency. The deficiency notice gives the taxpayer the right to petition the Tax Court for review of the IRS's determination. If the IRS is making a determination on a case that arose from a refund request, the IRS issues a notice of refund disallowance. Once a refund request is disallowed, the taxpayer may sue in federal district court or the Court of Federal Claims to obtain the refund.

B. Final Administrative Determinations

Part of the administrative tax determination process involves documenting a final determination. Documenting a final determination facilitates tax dispute advancement to judicial review. Two types of final determinations made by the IRS that are subject to judicial review are the statutory notice of a deficiency in tax and the tax refund claim disallowance. Under the TEFRA partnership rules, the IRS issues a Final Partnership Administrative Adjustment, known as an FPAA, which is analogous to a statutory notice of deficiency.

1. The Notice of Deficiency

An important document in an ongoing tax dispute is the statutory notice of deficiency. After the IRS completes its examination and the taxpayer exhausts any administrative appeals or other remedies for an adverse determination, the IRS may not immediately begin collection of the tax deficiency. Section 6213(a) provides as follows:

> [N]o assessment of a deficiency in respect of [income and estate] tax . . . and no levy or proceeding in court for its collection shall be made, begun, or prosecuted until such notice has been mailed to the taxpayer, nor until the expiration of such 90-day . . . period, . . . nor, if a petition has been filed with the Tax Court, until the decision of the Tax Court has become final.

Prior to collection, the IRS must finalize its determination by sending a deficiency notice to the taxpayer. This deficiency notice notifies the taxpayer that the IRS has made a determination, the determination resulted in a finding that the taxpayer owes more tax (i.e., a deficiency, *see* section 6211(a)), and the IRS will assess and collect the tax owed unless the taxpayer petitions the United States Tax Court within a certain amount of time. Section 6212(a) provides as follows:

> If the Secretary determines that there is a deficiency in respect of any [income, estate, or excise on a nonprofit] tax . . . he is authorized to send notice of such deficiency to the taxpayer by certified mail or registered mail.

The IRS and practitioners have many names for the statutory notice of deficiency, which perhaps reflects the importance of the document as well as its various functions.

The IRS and practitioners often refer to the deficiency notice as the "90-day letter" because it provides the taxpayer 90 days to petition the U.S. Tax Court. *See* IRC § 6213(a). If a taxpayer fails to petition the Tax Court within 90 days (150 days if the notice is addressed to the taxpayer while residing in a foreign country), the IRS assesses the tax and begins collecting it. Petitioning the Tax Court suspends assessment until the Tax Court decision is final.

Another name for the deficiency notice is the "ticket to the Tax Court." This label reflects the jurisdictional nature of the notice. If the IRS determines a taxpayer owes more tax, a valid deficiency notice confers jurisdiction to the Tax Court. A taxpayer invokes the Tax Court's jurisdiction by petitioning the court after receiving the deficiency notice from the IRS.

The deficiency notice presumptively confers jurisdiction to the Tax Court if the IRS sends the notice to the taxpayer's last known address. Section 6212(b)(1) provides as follows:

> [N]otice of a deficiency in respect of [income] tax . . . if mailed to the taxpayer at his last known address, shall be sufficient . . . even if such taxpayer is deceased, or is under a legal disability, or, in the case of a corporation, has terminated its existence.

This rule acts as a safe harbor for the IRS. If the IRS sends the deficiency notice to the taxpayer's last known address, the taxpayer is deemed to have received sufficient notice. The IRS may benefit from the safe harbor only if it has fulfilled its duty to attempt to determine the taxpayer's actual address where the address on file turns out to be incorrect.

In addition, a deficiency notice that reaches the taxpayer can still be effective even if it was not sent to the taxpayer's last known address. *Mulvania v. Commissioner* illustrates this rule's operation.

MULVANIA v. COMMISSIONER
769 F.2d 1376
United States Court of Appeals, Ninth Circuit

GOODWIN, Circuit Judge.

The Commissioner of the Internal Revenue Service appeals a decision of the Tax Court that it lacked jurisdiction to assess a deficiency against taxpayer, Richard L. Mulvania, because he did not receive a valid notice of deficiency within the three-year statute of limitations on assessments. We affirm.

Mulvania timely filed an income tax return for 1977 showing his address as 57 Linda Isle Drive, Newport Beach, California. The return was prepared by Gerald F. Simonis Accountants, Inc. On June 13, 1979, the IRS sent a letter to Mulvania setting forth proposed adjustments to his 1974 and 1977 income tax. A copy of that letter was also forwarded to Simonis, who held a power of attorney requesting that copies of all documents sent to Mulvania also be sent to him. Mulvania received the letter.

On December 31, 1980, the IRS sent a letter to Mulvania requesting an extension of the limitations period for assessing Mulvania's 1977 tax liability, which was never executed. On April 15, 1981, the last day of the three-year statutory period in which the IRS could assess a tax deficiency, the IRS sent Mulvania a notice of deficiency with respect to the tax year 1977. The notice was sent by certified mail, addressed as "St. Linda Isle Drive," rather than "57 Linda Isle Drive," Mulvania's correct address. The postal service returned the notice to the IRS on April 21, 1981, marked "Not deliverable as addressed." The IRS placed the returned notice in Mulvania's file and, because the statutory period had expired, did not attempt to remail it.

On the same date that the misaddressed notice of deficiency was mailed to Mulvania, the IRS sent a copy of the notice by ordinary mail to Simonis, who received it on or about April 17, 1981. Expecting that Mulvania would soon call him about the notice, Simonis filed the notice and made a note to follow up. About June 1, 1981, when Simonis called Mulvania to discuss the notice of deficiency, he found out that Mulvania had never received the notice. There is no evidence in the record that Simonis discussed the contents of the notice with Mulvania.

On or about June 15, 1981, after Simonis (who is not a lawyer) advised Mulvania that Simonis' notice was not a valid notice of deficiency for 1977,

Mulvania decided not to file a petition in the Tax Court for a redetermination of assessment of deficiency. Mulvania changed his mind, however, and, on April 1, 1983, filed a petition in the Tax Court requesting a redetermination of the deficiency for 1977.

Both parties then filed cross-motions to dismiss for lack of jurisdiction. The Commissioner argued that Mulvania's petition, which was filed almost two years after the notice of deficiency was mailed, was untimely pursuant to 26 U.S.C. § 6123(a).[1] Mulvania claimed the Tax Court lacked jurisdiction to assess a deficiency for 1977 because the three-year statute of limitations had run, and Mulvania had never received a valid notice of deficiency which would have tolled the statute of limitations as provided in 26 U.S.C. § 6503(a).[2]

The Tax Court, granted Mulvania's motion to dismiss for lack of jurisdiction and denied the Commissioner's motion to dismiss. This appeal followed.

Section 6501(a)[3] provides that the amount of any deficiency in income tax shall be assessed within three years after the return is filed. Section 6503(a) provides, however, that the running of the three-year limitation period is suspended by "the mailing of a notice under section 6212(a)."[4] Section 6212(a)

---

[1] [fn 1] § 6213. Restrictions applicable to deficiencies; petition to Tax Court

(a) Time for filing petition and restriction on assessment.—Within 90 days, or 150 days if the notice is addressed to a person outside the United States, after the notice of deficiency authorized in section 6212 is mailed (not counting Saturday, Sunday, or a legal holiday in the District of Columbia as the last day), the taxpayer may file a petition with the Tax Court for a redetermination of the deficiency. . ..

[2] [fn 2] § 6503. Suspension of running of period of limitation

(a) Issuance of statutory notice of deficiency.—

(1) General rule.—The running of the period of limitations provided in section 6501 or 6502 on the making of assessments or the collection by levy or a proceeding in court, in respect of any deficiency . . ., shall (after the mailing of a notice under section 6212(a)) be suspended for the period during which the Secretary or his delegate is prohibited from making the assessment or from collecting by levy or a proceeding in court . . ., and for 60 days thereafter.

[3] [fn 3] § 6501. Limitations on assessment and collection

(a) General rule.—Except as otherwise provided in this section, the amount of any tax imposed by this title shall be assessed within 3 years after the return was filed (whether or not such return was filed on or after the date prescribed) or, if the tax is payable by stamp, at any time after such tax became due and before the expiration of 3 years after the date on which any part of such tax was paid, and no proceeding in court without assessment for the collection of such tax shall be begun after the expiration of such period.

[4] [fn 4] § 6212. Notice of deficiency

(a) In general.—If the Secretary determines that there is a deficiency in respect of any tax imposed by subtitles A or B or chapters 41, 42, 43, 44, or 45, authorizes the Commissioner, upon determining that there is a deficiency in income tax, to send a notice of deficiency to the taxpayer by certified mail or registered mail. Section 6212(b)(1)[5] provides that a notice of income tax deficiency shall be sufficient if it is mailed to the taxpayer at his last known address. Section 6213(a) permits a taxpayer to whom a notice of deficiency is mailed to file a petition in the Tax Court within 90 days after the notice is mailed.

Cases interpreting the interplay of these sections have fallen into three broad categories.

First, a notice of deficiency actually, physically received by a taxpayer is valid under § 6212(a) if it is received in sufficient time to permit the taxpayer, without prejudice, to file a petition in the Tax Court even though the notice is erroneously addressed. *Clodfelter v. Commissioner*, 527 F.2d 754, 757 (9th Cir.1975), *cert. denied*, 425 U.S. 979, 96 S.Ct. 2184, 48 L.Ed.2d 805 (1976); *Mulvania v. Commissioner*, 81 T.C. 65 (1983).

Second, a notice of deficiency mailed to a taxpayer's last known address is valid under § 6212(b)(1) regardless of when the taxpayer eventually receives it. *DeWelles v. United States*, 378 F.2d 37, 39-40 (9th Cir.), *cert. denied*, 389 U.S. 996, 88 S.Ct. 501, 19 L.Ed.2d 494 (1967).

Third, an erroneously addressed and undelivered registered notice of deficiency is not valid under either § 6212(a) or 6212(b)(1) even if the Commissioner also sends a copy of the notice by regular mail to the taxpayer's attorney. *D'Andrea v. Commissioner*, 263 F.2d 904, 907 (D.C.Cir.1959); *see Reddock v. Commissioner*, 72 T.C. 21 (1979).

In this case the actual notice of deficiency which was mailed to Mulvania became null and void when it was returned to the IRS; at that time, the IRS then knew that the notice had been misaddressed and had not been received. This is not a case in which the notice was improperly addressed, but the postal authorities nonetheless delivered the letter to the taxpayer. *Clodfelter*, 527 F.2d at 756. Mulvania has never physically received a notice of deficiency.

The Commissioner argues that because Mulvania's accountant received a courtesy copy of the notice and called Mulvania before the 90 days had expired, Mulvania therefore received valid notice and now lacks a basis for a petition in the Tax Court. Mulvania argues that a courtesy copy of a notice of deficiency

---

he is authorized to send notice of such deficiency to the taxpayer by certified mail or registered mail.

[5] [fn 5] § 6212. Notice of Deficiency

(b) Address for notice of deficiency.—

(1) Income and gift taxes and certain excise taxes.—In the absence of notice to the Secretary under section 6903 of the existence of a fiduciary relationship, notice of a deficiency in respect of a tax . . . if mailed to the taxpayer at his last known address, shall be sufficient . . . even if such taxpayer is deceased, or is under a legal disability, or, in the case of a corporation, has terminated its existence.

cannot be transformed into a valid notice of deficiency simply because the accountant called and told the taxpayer about the notice.

With a broad power of attorney, registered notice to the attorney or accountant may also serve as notice to the taxpayer under the law of principal and agent if the taxpayer himself received some notification in time to file a petition before the tax court. *Commissioner v. Stewart*, 186 F.2d 239, 242 (6th Cir.1951). *But see D'Andrea*, 263 F.2d at 907-08 (copy sent by ordinary mail insufficient where there was no evidence that taxpayer seasonably received the information contained in the notice to his attorney). A taxpayer may also designate the address of his representative as that to which any deficiency notice should be sent. *Expanding Envelope and Folder Corp. v. Shotz*, 385 F.2d 402, 404 (3rd Cir.1967); *see D'Andrea*, 263 F.2d at 907.

Because Simonis did not have a broad power of attorney, however, the law of principal and agent does not apply. Mulvania had only granted him a power of attorney which requests that courtesy copies of all communication be sent to his representative. The IRS clearly knew that Simonis was not to be the addressee of the official notice of deficiency; it sent him only a copy and only by ordinary, unregistered, uncertified mail. *See D'Andrea*, 263 F.2d at 905. *See also Keeton v. Commissioner*, 74 T.C. 377 (1980); *Houghton v. Commissioner*, 48 T.C. 656 (1967).

The Commissioner relies on two Tax Court cases for the proposition that the copy of the notice sent to Simonis sufficed to toll the three-year statute of limitations. In *Lifter v. Commissioner*, 59 T.C. 818 (1973), the notice of deficiency was sent to the taxpayers' last known address but was returned undelivered. The Commissioner then sent a copy of the notice to the taxpayers' attorney who had been appointed to handle their federal income tax matters. The taxpayers learned of the notice before the running of the statute of limitations and timely filed a petition with the Tax Court. The notice of deficiency was held valid.

Lifter may be distinguished from this case in three respects. First, the IRS sent the notice to what was reasonably believed to be petitioners' last known address, and a notice of deficiency mailed to a taxpayer's last known address is valid even if the taxpayer does not receive it. *DeWelles*, 378 F.2d at 39. Second, taxpayers invoked the jurisdiction of the Tax Court by filing a timely petition. By timely invoking Tax Court jurisdiction, taxpayers effectively waived any objection to the notice of deficiency. Finally, the attorney to whom a copy of the notice was sent apparently had a broad power of attorney, beyond mere receipt of copies of notices sent to taxpayers. The Commissioner in *Lifter* could have sent the original notice to the attorney alone. *See D'Andrea*, 263 F.2d at 905.

In Whiting v. Commissioner, T.C. Memo 1984-142 (1984), the notice was sent to taxpayers' previous address although the IRS had been informed of the change of address. The notice was returned undelivered. A copy of the notice was also sent to their attorney who eventually informed them of the notice. The taxpayers filed a timely petition with the Tax Court. They challenged the validity of the notice, but the Tax Court held it was valid because the petitioners became aware that the notice had been issued and timely filed a petition.

Whiting and this case differ in two critical respects. First, in *Whiting* the notice was sent to the wrong address, even after the IRS had been informed of the change of address. Here the notice was misaddressed because of a typographical error. Second, in *Whiting*, petitioners chose to invoke jurisdiction of the Tax Court after learning of the notice from their attorney. As in *Lifter*, by timely invoking Tax Court jurisdiction, taxpayers essentially acknowledged notice; the purpose of § 6212 had been satisfied. Here, Mulvania has never acknowledged notice by invoking Tax Court jurisdiction in a timely manner.

In *Whiting*, the Tax Court engaged in a cursory analysis of the validity of the notice, concluding that an error in the address to which the notice of deficiency is mailed does not render the notice invalid when the petition is timely filed, *citing Mulvania*, 81 T.C. at 68. In *Mulvania*, however, the taxpayer received the actual, physical notice of deficiency although it had been mailed to his former address and had later been hand delivered by his child.

The resolution of this issue is a "least-worse" result. Mulvania argues that he never received the actual written notice of deficiency because it was misaddressed. The IRS sent the notice on the last day of the statutory period, making it impossible for the Commissioner to remail the notice within the prescribed time once the error was discovered. To decide for the Commissioner would relieve the IRS of its cumulative errors, and create uncertainty in the law. The IRS argues, however, that this is a mobile society, clerical mistakes do happen, and the taxpayer had actual knowledge of the notice even if not its contents.

The Tax Court was understandably concerned that a decision in the Commissioner's favor would result in an uncertain rule depending upon whether the tax adviser happened to be a lawyer. As a lawyer, a tax adviser's call to Mulvania regarding the notice would have been privileged. The Tax Court correctly believed that a decision for the Commissioner would result in an uncertain rule, subject to manipulation by taxpayers who authorize copies to be sent to their accountant or lawyer, or by taxpayers with the most sophisticated tax advisers.

It is better for the government to lose some revenue as the result of its clerical error than to create uncertainty. If Simonis, either intentionally or unintentionally, had not informed Mulvania of the receipt of the copy of the notice of deficiency, then Mulvania would not have received any notification of the deficiency. Tax law requires more solid footings than the happenstance of a tax adviser telephoning a client to tell him of a letter from the IRS.

We conclude that, where a notice of deficiency has been misaddressed to the taxpayer or sent only to an adviser who is merely authorized to receive a copy of such a notice, actual notice is necessary but not sufficient to make the notice valid. The IRS is not forgiven for its clerical errors or for mailing notice to the wrong party unless the taxpayer, through his own actions, renders the Commissioner's errors harmless. In this case, the notice of deficiency became null and void when it was returned to the IRS undelivered. Regardless of the coincidence by which Mulvania later came to know of its existence, the taxpayer's actual knowledge did not transform the void notice into a valid one.

Had Mulvania timely petitioned the Tax Court for a redetermination of deficiency, the IRS error might have fallen into the line of harmless error cases where the taxpayer suffered no ill effects for the Commissioner's inadvertence. Such is not the case here.

NOTES AND QUESTIONS

1. How long does a taxpayer in a foreign country have to respond to a deficiency notice? *See* IRC § 6213(a).
2. Does knowledge that the IRS sent a deficiency notice make the notice valid for purposes of Tax Court jurisdiction?
3. Why is there a last-known-address rule?

There is no threshold for specificity to make a deficiency notice valid. The notice must be specific enough so that the taxpayer is on notice that the IRS has determined a deficiency in tax. This means that at a minimum the deficiency notice must contain some showing that the IRS actually made a determination that a deficiency in tax exists. *See* IRC § 6212(a). In such a case, the IRS does not need to "look behind the notice."

SCAR v. COMMISSIONER
814 F.2d 1363 (1987)
United States Court of Appeals, Ninth Circuit

FLETCHER, Circuit Judge:

Taxpayers Howard and Ethel Scar petition for review of the Tax Court's denial of their motion to dismiss for lack of jurisdiction and denial of their two summary judgment motions. Taxpayers argue that the Tax Court lacked jurisdiction because the Commissioner of the Internal Revenue Service (IRS) issued an invalid notice of deficiency. Alternatively, they argue that the Tax Court incorrectly denied their motions for summary judgment and should not have granted the Commissioner's request to amend his answer. We reverse.

BACKGROUND

On September 3, 1979, petitioners Howard and Ethel Scar filed a joint return for tax year 1978.[6] The Scars claimed business deductions totaling $26,966 in connection with a videotape tax shelter,[7] and reported total taxes due of $3,269.

---

[6] [fn 1] The return was timely, the Scars having received an extension of time to file.

[7] [fn 2] The Scars also claimed deductions and credits with regard to this tax shelter on their 1977 returns. They received a notice of deficiency in April of 1981 and petitioned the Tax Court for a redetermination in June of 1981. In

On June 14, 1982, the Commissioner mailed to the Scars a letter (Form 892); it listed taxpayers' names and address, the taxable year at issue (the year ending December 31, 1978), and specified a deficiency amount ($96,600). The body of the letter stated in part:

> We have determined that there is a deficiency (increase) in your income tax as shown above. This letter is a NOTICE OF DEFICIENCY sent to you as required by the law.

It informed the taxpayers that if they wished to contest the deficiency they must file a petition with the United States Tax Court within 90 days.

Attached to the letter was a Form 5278 ("Statement—Income Tax Changes") purporting to explain how the deficiency had been determined. It showed an adjustment to income in the amount of $138,000 designated as "Partnership—Nevada Mining Project." The Form 5278 had no information in the space on the form for taxable income as shown on petitioners' return as filed. It showed as the "total corrected income tax liability" the sum of $96,600 and indicated that this sum was arrived at by multiplying 70 percent times $138,000.

Another attached document, designated as "Statement Schedule 2," with the heading "Nevada Mining Project, Explanation of Adjustments," stated as follows:

> In order to protect the government's interest and since your original income tax return is unavailable at this time, the income tax is being assessed at the maximum tax rate of 70%.

> The tax assessment will be corrected when we receive the original return or when you send a copy of the return to us.

> The increase in tax may also reflect investment credit or new jobs credit which has been disallowed.

Also attached to the letter was a document, designated as "Statement Schedule 3," with the heading "Nevada Mining Project, Explanation of Adjustments." This document explained why the Nevada Mining Project deductions were being disallowed.

On July 7, 1982, the taxpayers filed a timely petition with the Tax Court to redetermine the deficiency asserted. In their petition, they alleged that they had never been associated with the "Nevada Mining Project Partnership" and had not claimed on their 1978 return any expenses or losses related to that venture. The Commissioner, on August 30, 1982, filed an answer denying the substantive allegations of the petition.

Sometime in September 1982, the Commissioner conceded in a telephone conversation with the taxpayers that the June 14 notice of deficiency was incorrect because it overstated the amount of disallowed deductions and wrongly connected taxpayers with a mining partnership. Nevertheless, the Commissioner

---

February of 1985 the Tax Court made a deficiency determination of $10,410 for the tax year 1977.

maintained that the notice of deficiency was valid. The Commissioner confirmed his position in a letter dated November 29, 1982, stating "the taxpayers should not be surprised by the fact that the Commissioner means to disallow the deductions claimed in 1978 for Executive Productions, Inc." because similar objections had been made to the deductions claimed for the same tax shelter on taxpayers' 1977 return. The Commissioner enclosed with this letter a revised Form 5278, which contained the appropriate shelter explanation and decreased the amount of tax due to $10,374, and notified the taxpayers that he intended to request leave from the Tax Court to amend his answer.

On December 6, 1982 the taxpayers filed a motion to dismiss for lack of jurisdiction, claiming that the June 14 notice of deficiency was invalid because the Commissioner failed to make a "determination" of additional tax owed before issuing the notice of deficiency. The Commissioner filed a response which conceded the inaccuracy of the notice of deficiency but maintained that it was sufficient to give the Tax Court jurisdiction. On March 21, 1983, the Tax Court held a hearing on the taxpayers' motion to dismiss. At the hearing, counsel for the Commissioner attempted to explain why the Form 5278 sent to the taxpayers contained a description of the wrong tax shelter. He stated that an IRS employee transposed a code number which caused the IRS to assert the deficiency on the basis of the Nevada mining project instead of the videotape tax shelter. No witness, however, testified to this fact at the hearing,[8] and no explanation was ever offered for the discrepancy of over $80,000 between the deficiency notice assessment and that later conceded to be the correct amount.

Following the March 21 hearing, the taxpayers filed a motion for summary judgment based on the Commissioner's concession that they had not been involved in any mining partnerships. The Commissioner shortly thereafter filed his motion to amend his answer to correct the error made in the notice of deficiency and accompanying documents. On November 17, 1983 the Tax Court, in an opinion reviewed by the full court, ruled on these various motions. The Tax Court majority upheld the validity of the June 14 notice of deficiency, finding that it satisfied section 6212(a),[9] which states the formal requirements for a deficiency notice. The Tax Court further ruled that the Commissioner could amend his answer as requested, and denied taxpayers' motion for summary judgment. The reviewed opinion contained several concurring and dissenting opinions. Five dissenting judges would have denied jurisdiction on the basis that the deficiency notice was invalid and four dissenting judges would not have permitted the Commissioner to amend his answer.

The Commissioner amended his answer and asserted in it, despite the patent incorrectness of the notice of deficiency and the acknowledgment of error by the

---

[8] [fn 3] The Commissioner argues that a witness was present at the hearing, but since taxpayers failed to object to counsel's explanation of the IRS's mistake, the witness was never called.

[9] [fn 4] All section references are to the Internal Revenue Code of 1954, Title 26 U.S.C., as amended and in effect for the years in issue.

Service, that the taxpayer had the burden of disproving the correctness of the Commissioner's revised determinations. The taxpayers renewed their motion for summary judgment. The Tax Court denied this second motion for summary judgment on the ground that triable issues of fact remained concerning whether the taxpayers' primary motivation for entering the videotape venture was the prospect of earning a profit or avoiding tax. On February 22, 1985, the Tax Court entered a decision, pursuant to a stipulation, that taxpayers owed $10,377 in additional tax.[10] The stipulation afforded the taxpayers the right to file a petition for review of the Tax Court's adverse rulings.

DISCUSSION

In order to decide whether the Tax Court had jurisdiction we review *de novo* the Tax Court's interpretation of section 6212(a). *Orvis v. Commissioner,* 788 F.2d 1406, 1407 (9th Cir.1986); *Ebben v. Commissioner,* 783 F.2d 906, 909 (9th Cir.1986).

Section 6212(a) states in part: "If the Secretary determines that there is a deficiency in respect of any tax imposed . . . he is authorized to send notice of such deficiency to the taxpayer by certified mail or registered mail." Section 6213(a) provides in part: "Within 90 days . . . after the notice of deficiency authorized in section 6212 is mailed . . . taxpayer may file a petition with the Tax Court for a redetermination of the deficiency." The Tax Court has jurisdiction only when the Commissioner issues a valid deficiency notice, and the taxpayer files a timely petition for redetermination. "A valid petition is the basis of the Tax Court's jurisdiction. To be valid, a petition must be filed from a valid statutory notice." *Stamm International Corp. v. Commissioner,* 84 T.C. 248, 252 (1985). *See Midland Mortgage Co. v. Commissioner,* 73 T.C. 902, 907 (1980).

The taxpayers correctly note that section 6212(a) authorizes the Commissioner to send a notice of deficiency only if he first "determines that there is a deficiency." Because the deficiency notice mailed to the taxpayers contained an explanation of a tax shelter completely unrelated to their return, contained no adjustments to tax based on their return as filed, and stated affirmatively that the taxpayers's return is "unavailable at this time," taxpayers maintain that the Commissioner could not have "determined" a deficiency with respect to them. The taxpayers assert that, in the absence of a determination, the deficiency notice was invalid and therefore the Tax Court lacked jurisdiction.

The Tax Court rejected this argument, finding that "[t]he requirements of section 6212(a) are met if the notice of deficiency sets forth the amount of the deficiency and the taxable year involved." *Scar v. Commissioner,* 81 T.C. 855, 860–61 (1983).

We agree with the Tax Court that no particular form is required for a valid notice of deficiency, Abrams v. Commissioner, 787 F.2d 939, 941 (4th Cir.), cert. denied, 479 U.S. 882, 107 S.Ct. 271, 93 L.Ed.2d 248 (1986); Benzvi v. Commissioner, 787 F.2d 1541, 1542 (11th Cir.), cert. denied, 479 U.S. 883, 107

---

[10] [fn 5] This amount is inexplicably $3.00 higher than the amount claimed by the Commissioner in his amended answer.

S.Ct. 273, 93 L.Ed.2d 250 (1986), and the Commissioner need not explain how the deficiencies were determined. Barnes v. Commissioner, 408 F.2d 65, 68 (7th Cir.) (citing Commissioner v. Stewart, 186 F.2d 239, 242 (6th Cir.1951)), cert. denied, 396 U.S. 836, 90 S.Ct. 94, 24 L.Ed.2d 86 (1969). The notice must, however, "meet certain substantial requirements." *Abrams*, 787 F.2d at 941. "The notice must at a minimum indicate that the IRS has determined the amount of the deficiency." *Benzvi*, 787 F.2d at 1542. The question confronting us is whether a form letter that asserts that a deficiency has been determined, which letter and its attachments make it patently obvious that no determination has in fact been made, satisfies the statutory mandate.[11]

In none of the cases on which the Tax Court relied was the notice challenged on the basis that there was no determination. See Abatti v. Commissioner, 644 F.2d 1385, 1389 (9th Cir.1981) (notice valid although it did not advise the taxpayer under which code section the IRS would proceed because fair warning was given before trial); Barnes, 408 F.2d at 68 (notice need not state the basis for the deficiency determination nor contain particulars of explanations concerning how alleged deficiencies were determined); Foster v. Commissioner, 80 T.C. 34, 229–30 (1983) (notice must advise taxpayer that Commissioner has, in fact, determined a deficiency, and must specify the year and amount), aff'd in part and vacated in part, 756 F.2d 1430 (9th Cir.1985), cert. denied, 474 U.S. 1055, 106 S.Ct. 793, 88 L.Ed.2d 770 (1986); Hannan v. Commissioner, 52 T.C. 787 (1969) (deficiency notice valid where record did not show that Commissioner had not assessed a deficiency even though Commissioner asserted that no deficiency

---

[11] [fn 6] The dissent misstates this case in complaining that the majority is requiring the Commissioner "to prove that he has reviewed specific data before making a determination." Dissent at 1371. Under normal circumstances it would be presumed that a determination had been made prior to notification. In this case, the taxpayers proved that a determination of their deficiency had not been made. Not only was there no relationship between the Scars and the tax shelter or the amount of the "deficiency," but also the attachment to the notice entitled "Nevada Mining Project, Explanation of Adjustments" stated: "In order to protect the government's interest and since your original income tax return is unavailable at this time, the income tax is being assessed at the maximum tax rate of 70%." Scar v. Commissioner, 81 T.C. 855, 856 (1983). The Scars demonstrated that the Commissioner had not, as the dissent argues at 1373–74, "clearly determined that the taxpayers had invested in a tax shelter" for the tax year 1978. Furthermore, even if the Commissioner had adduced proof through the "stand-by" witness, see supra note 3, that the Commissioner had examined the 1978 tax return of Executive Productions, Inc., a tax shelter, and that it reported an investment by the Scars, the Commissioner could not determine a deficiency for the Scars without examining their return for 1978 to see whether they had claimed a deduction for such an investment.

existed and that the notice had been issued in error).[12] The cases assume that the deficiency determination was made. With the exception of *Hannan*, they deal instead with the question of whether the notice imparted enough information to provide the taxpayer with fair notice.

The Tax Court asserts that it is following long-established policy not to look behind a deficiency notice to question the Commissioner's motives and procedures leading to a determination. *See, e.g., Riland v. Commissioner,* 79 T.C. 185, 201 (1982) (notice valid, even though IRS agents violated procedures set forth in internal manual and failed to forward relevant documents to agents handling the case); *Estate of Brimm v. Commissioner,* 70 T.C. 15, 23 (1978) (notice valid despite taxpayer's argument that procedures followed were not valid, the amount of time spent evaluating a case and the extent to which review functions were perfunctorily performed are irrelevant; even if Commissioner's procedures are flawed, the proper remedy would not be dismissal); *Greenberg's Express, Inc. v. Commissioner,* 62 T.C. 324, 327 (1974) (court will not look behind notice to examine whether Commissioner discriminatorily selected taxpayer for audit; even if his actions are discriminatory, notice not void).

We agree that courts should avoid oversight of the Commissioner's internal operations and the adequacy of procedures employed. This does not mean, however, that the courts cannot or should not decide the validity of a notice that can be determined solely by references to applicable statutes and review of the notice itself.

In this case, we need not look behind the notice sent to the taxpayers to determine its invalidity. The Commissioner acknowledges in the notice that the deficiency is not based on a determination of deficiency of tax reported on the

---

[12] [fn 7] In *Hannan*, the IRS attempted to avoid a Tax Court redetermination by asserting that the deficiency notice had been sent in error and that the taxpayers were liable for an addition in tax not attributable to a deficiency. Such additions can be assessed and collected immediately under § 6662 (formerly § 6659) without resort to the statutory deficiency procedures. The issue in *Hannan* was not whether a determination had occurred, but rather whether the Commissioner's contention that no deficiency actually existed deprived the Tax Court of jurisdiction.

In *Hannan*, the IRS clearly had made a determination of a deficiency in tax owed by taxpayers who were petitioning the tax court; the question was whether it was a determination of deficiency entitling the taxpayers to appeal before payment. The *Hannan* court found that the act of sending the notice constituted a determination of deficiency. 52 T.C. at 7981. That finding must, however, be read in the context of the case: The IRS had examined the taxpayers returns and made a determination that money was owing and the record did not show that the type of assessment requiring deficiency procedures had not been made. We do not read *Hannan* to stand for the proposition that the existence of a deficiency letter establishes the existence of a determination. To the extent that the *Hannan* court intended such a reading, we disagree with its interpretation of the tax code.

taxpayers' return and that it refers to a tax shelter the Commissioner concedes has no connection to the taxpayers or their return.

Section 6212(a) "authorize[s]" the sending of a deficiency notice "[i]f the Secretary *determines* that there is a deficiency." (emphasis added). We agree with Judge Goffe's statement in this case that "[e]ven a cursory review of this provision [section 6212(a)] discloses that Congress did not grant the Secretary unlimited and unfettered authority to issue notices of deficiency." *Scar,* 81 T.C. at 872 (Goffe, J., dissenting). In *Appeal of Terminal Wine Co.,* 1 B.T.A. 697, 701 (1925), the Board of Tax Appeals construed the meaning of the term "determine" as applied to deficiency determinations: "By its very definition and etymology the word 'determination' irresistibly connotes consideration, resolution, conclusion, and judgment."

The term "deficiency" is defined in section 6211(a) as the amount by which tax due exceeds "the amount shown as the tax by the taxpayer upon his return" (provided that a return showing an amount has been filed), plus previously assessed deficiencies over rebates made. A literal reading of relevant code sections, and the absence of evidence of contrary legislative intent, leads us to conclude that the Commissioner must consider information that relates to a particular taxpayer before it can be said that the Commissioner has "determined" a "deficiency" in respect to that taxpayer.[13] To hold otherwise would entail ignoring or judicially rewriting the plain language of the Internal Revenue Code.[14]

---

[13] [fn 8] In construing section 6212(a), we follow some basic, yet fundamental, rules:

As in all cases including statutory construction, "our starting point must be the language employed by Congress," Reiter v. Sonotone Corp., 442 U.S. 330, 337 [99 S.Ct. 2326, 2330, 60 L.Ed.2d 931] (1979), and we assume "that the legislative purpose is expressed by the ordinary meaning of the words used." Richards v. United States, 369 U.S. 1, 9 [82 S.Ct. 585, 591, 7 L.Ed.2d 492] (1962). Thus, "[a]bsent a clearly expressed legislative intention to the contrary, that language must ordinarily be regarded as conclusive." Consumer Product Safety Comm'n v. GTE Sylvania, Inc., 447 U.S. 102, 108 [100 S.Ct. 2051, 2056, 64 L.Ed.2d 766 (1980).
American Tobacco Co. v. Patterson, 456 U.S. 63, 68, 102 S.Ct. 1534, 1537, 71 L.Ed.2d 748 (1982).

The dissent complains that we are "overload[ing] the statutory requirement of a 'determination' of a deficiency with burdensome substantive content." Dissent at 1372. On the contrary, we work on the premise that Congress does not use words idly, and that "determination" is not devoid of content. If, in fact, that which is required by the unambiguous terms of the statute is more burdensome than Congress envisioned or intended, it is Congress, not the courts, that must remedy the problem.

[14] [fn 9] The dissent, characterizing the deficiency notice as a " 'ticket' to the tax court" suggests that the majority fails "to grasp the function of the deficiency

This reading of the Code is not a new one. Almost sixty years ago, the Board of Tax Appeals, while refusing to examine the intent, motive or reasoning of the Commissioner, emphasized that

> the statute clearly contemplates that before notifying a taxpayer of a deficiency and hence before the Board can be concerned, a determination must be made by the Commissioner. This must mean a thoughtful and considered determination that the United States is entitled to an amount not yet paid. If the notice of deficiency were other than the expression of a *bona fide* official determination, and were, say, a mere formal demand for an arbitrary amount as to which there were substantial doubt, the Board might easily become merely an expensive tribunal to determine moot questions and a burden might be imposed on taxpayers of litigating issues and disproving allegations for which there had never been any substantial foundation.

Couzens v. Commissioner, 11 B.T.A. 1040, 1159–60 (1928).

Recently, taxpayers who had invested in a "tax shelter" known as the "Liberty Financial 1983 Government Securities Trading Strategy" argued that so-called pre-filing notifications (PFNs) sent to them by the IRS were in fact deficiency notices entitling them to a Tax Court redetermination. The notices, which in most if not all cases were received after filing, informed the taxpayers that the IRS believed that deductions or credits claimed pursuant to Liberty Financial were not allowable; that the IRS would review the taxpayers' deductions and reduce returns or adjust the returns as required; that various penalties could be assessed; and that the taxpayers might wish to amend previously filed returns. *Abrams v. Commissioner,* 787 F.2d 939, 940–41 (4th Cir.), *cert. denied,* 479 U.S. 882, 107 S.Ct. 271, 93 L.Ed.2d 248 (1986). In agreeing with the IRS that the PFNs did not qualify as deficiency notices, the Fourth Circuit found the obvious lack of an actual determination of deficiency crucial:

> As the letter . . . made pellucidly clear, examination of the returns of each individual taxpayer had not as yet been made. The most important observation to be made about the letter is that it left no doubt that, as yet,

---

notice." Dissent at 1372. What the dissent fails to grasp, however, is that processes that may "serve their intended purposes" nonetheless may be legally insufficient. For example, notice by telephone would not suffice if written notice were required. Here, the statute requires that the Commissioner make a determination. None was made. The fact that the taxpayers received a deficiency notice does not cure the failure to make a determination.

The dissent in looking only to the fact that notice was sent skips over the Commissioner's failure to make the statutorily required determination. We readily agree with the dissent that in the usual case the sending of the notice of deficiency presumes a determination. See supra note 6. Where, however, the notice belies that presumption, it is both reasonable and necessary that the Commissioner demonstrate his compliance with the statute.

there had been no general review of any return, no computation of any deficiency nor reduction in refunds to which the taxpayers might otherwise be entitled. It was in essence only fair warning of what the taxpayers . . . might expect.

Abrams, 787 F.2d at 941. Similarly, the Eleventh Circuit found the lack of a determination dispositive: "We cannot conclude that a PFN is a notice of deficiency absent a clear indication that the IRS has reviewed the PFN recipient's return and determined that a deficiency of a stated amount exists." Benzvi v. Commissioner, 787 F.2d 1541, 1543 (11th Cir.), cert. denied, 479 U.S. 883, 107 S.Ct. 273, 93 L.Ed.2d 250 (1986).

These cases inform our judgment here. They support the view that the "determination" requirement of section 6212(a) has substantive content.[15] The Commissioner's and the dissent's contention that the issuance of a formally proper notice of deficiency[16] of itself establishes that the Commissioner has determined a deficiency must be rejected. To hold otherwise, would read the determination requirement out of section 6212(a).[17]

---

[15] [fn 10] It is, of course true, as the dissent points out, that Tax Court jurisdiction does not depend on the existence of an actual deficiency. Dissent at 1372 (quoting Stevens v. Commissioner, 709 F.2d 12, 13 (5th Cir.1983)). It is the purpose of the Tax Court to determine whether the Commissioner's determination is correct. *Stevens*, 709 F.2d at 13. We agree more fully, however, with the passage quoted in the dissent when that passage is quoted in full: " '[I]t is not the existence of a deficiency but the Commissioner's determination of a deficiency that provides a predicate for Tax Court jurisdiction.' " Id. (quoting *Hannan*, 52 T.C. at 791).

[16] [fn 11] In the case before us the Commissioner argues that, because the notice contained the Taxpayers' names, social security number, the tax year in question, and "the" amount of deficiency, it was "clearly sufficient." It is quite clear, however, that the notice did not contain the amount of deficiency, but rather contained an amount unrelated to any deficiency for which the Scars were responsible.

[17] [fn 12] Judge Sterrett, in dissenting, offered a sample of a valid deficiency letter under the statutory construction urged by the IRS and accepted by the Tax Court:

Dear Taxpayer:

There is a rumor afoot that you were a participant in the Amalgamated Hairpin Partnership during the year 1980. Due to the press of work we have been unable to investigate the accuracy of the rumor or to determine whether you filed a tax return for that year. However, we are concerned that the statute of limitations may be about to expire with respect to your tax liability for 1980.

Our experience has shown that, as a general matter, taxpayers tend to take, on the average, excessive (unallowable) deductions, arising out of investments in partnerships comparable to Amalgamated that aggregate some $10,000. Our

Finally, the Commissioner asserts that the proper remedy in this case is to eliminate the presumption of correctness that normally attaches to deficiency determinations, *see, e.g., Dix v. Commissioner,* 392 F.2d 313 (4th Cir.1968), not to dismiss for lack of jurisdiction. He relies, however, on cases that challenge the correctness of the determination, and not its existence. The Commissioner's belated willingness to assume the burden of proof before the Tax Court cannot cure his failure to determine a deficiency before imposing on taxpayers the obligation to defend themselves in potentially costly litigation in Tax Court. Jurisdiction is at issue here. Failure to comply with statutory requirements renders the deficiency notice null and void and leaves nothing on which Tax Court jurisdiction can rest. *See Sanderling Inc. v. Commissioner,* 571 F.2d 174, 176 (3d Cir.1978) ("The Tax Court has held that it has no jurisdiction where the deficiency notice does not cover a proper taxable period.") (citing *Columbia River Orchards, Inc. v. Commissioner,* 15 T.C. 253 (1950)); *McConkey v. Commissioner,* 199 F.2d 892 (4th Cir.1952), *cert. denied,* 345 U.S. 924, 73 S.Ct. 782, 97 L.Ed. 1355 (1953) (where taxpayer paid alleged deficiency before notice of deficiency was mailed, Tax Court lacked jurisdiction as there was no deficiency on which the court's jurisdiction could operate); *United States v. Lehigh,* 201 F.Supp. 224 (W.D.Ark.1961) (statement of "Income Tax Due" was invalid deficiency notice where it was not labeled as a deficiency notice, incorrectly stated the tax year involved, and was confusing in that it did not provide certain figures that the terms of the statement said were provided). *Cf. Mall v. Kelly,* 564 F.Supp. 371 (D.Wyo.1983) (deficiency assessments void where IRS had failed to meet requirement of reasonably and diligently determining and mailing sufficient notice to taxpayers' last known address).

Section 6212(a) of the Internal Revenue Code requires the Commissioner to determine that a deficiency exists before issuing a notice of deficiency. Because the Commissioner's purported notice of deficiency revealed on its face that no determination of tax deficiency had been made in respect to the Scars for the 1978 tax year, it did not meet the requirements of section 6212(a). Accordingly, the Tax Court should have dismissed the action for want of jurisdiction.[18]

---

experience has further shown that the average investor in such partnerships has substantial taxable income and consequently has attained the top marginal tax rate.

Accordingly, you are hereby notified that there is a deficiency in tax in the amount of $7,000 due from you for the year 1980 in addition to whatever amount, if any, you may have previously paid.

Sincerely yours,

Commissioner of Internal Revenue

Scar, 81 T.C. at 869 (Sterrett, J., dissenting).

[18] [fn 13] Cf. United States v. Lehigh, 201 F.Supp. 224, 234 (W.D.Ark.1961) ("The procedures set forth in the Internal Revenue Code were prescribed for the protection of both Government and taxpayer. Neglect to comply with those

Petition for review granted.

CYNTHIA HOLCOMB HALL, Circuit Judge, dissenting:

Today, the majority fortifies the impediments to tax collection on behalf of errant taxpayers seeking "no taxation without litigation." R. Jackson, *Struggle for Judicial Supremacy* 141 (1941). I believe the majority undermines the jurisdiction of the Tax Court by constructing a superfluous yet substantial hurdle to its jurisdiction. In reaching the conclusion that section 6212(a) of the Internal Revenue Code, 26 U.S.C. § 6212(a), imposes a substantive requirement on the Commissioner of the Internal Revenue Service to prove that he has reviewed specific data before making a determination, the majority eagerly expands jurisdictional requirements while discarding the carefully-honed and expedient jurisdictional rules that exist.

I.

The majority first turns a blind eye to reality when it finds that the incorrect explanation for the deficiency "[makes] it patently obvious that no determination has in fact been made." *See ante* at 1367. The 1978 tax return of taxpayers Howard and Ethel Scar was hardly an unlikely object of the Commissioner's suspicion. In 1977 the taxpayers participated in a videotape tax shelter, investing $6,500 in cash, signing a promissory note for $93,500, and then deducting over $15,000 in depreciation and other expenses from their 1977 tax return based on their "investment." The Commissioner audited this 1977 return and determined a deficiency of $15,875, finding that the taxpayers' "purchase of the film was lacking in profit motive and economic substance other than the avoidance of tax." The Commissioner mailed a notice of deficiency to the taxpayers, who responded by filing a petition for redetermination of the deficiency with the Tax Court on June 30, 1981.

The taxpayers' 1978 return included additional deductions totaling $27,040 based upon the now suspect videotape shelter. In all likelihood, the Commissioner's decision to issue a second deficiency notice regarding this 1978 return resulted from the continuation of the audit process which began with the previous year's tax return. This second deficiency notice, however, incorrectly explained the deficiency in terms of a Nevada mining venture in which the taxpayers had never participated. At the Tax Court hearing on March 21, 1983, counsel for the Commissioner explained that this misdescription resulted from a technical error: an IRS employee had transposed a code number, resulting in the incorrect identification of the basis of the deficiency as being the Nevada mining project instead of the videotape tax shelter. The Commissioner argues that a witness able to testify to this numerical error was present at the hearing, but was not called since the taxpayers did not object to this explanation of the IRS' mistake.

---

procedures may entail consequences which the neglecting party must be prepared to face, whether such party be the taxpayer or the Government.")

The procedural history of the taxpayers' efforts to challenge the 1978 deficiency consists largely of motions attempting to exploit this apparent mishap. These motions evince the tactics of delay employed by "every litigious man or every embarrassed man, to whom delay [is] more important than the payment of costs." *Tennessee v. Sneed,* 96 U.S. (6 Otto) 69, 75, 24 L.Ed. 610 (1877).

II.

The majority correctly recognizes that section 6212(a) authorizes the Commissioner to send a notice of deficiency only if he first determines that there is a deficiency. The taxpayers themselves concede that the notice of deficiency in this case satisfied section 6212(a)'s formal requirements of stating the amount of the deficiency and the taxable year involved. *See Stamm International Corp. v. Commissioner,* 84 T.C. 248, 253 (1985); *Foster v. Commissioner,* 80 T.C. 34, 229–30 (1983), *aff'd in part and vacated in part,* 756 F.2d 1430 (9th Cir.1985), *cert. denied,* 474 U.S. 1055, 106 S.Ct. 793, 88 L.Ed.2d 770 (1986); *Ziegler v. Commissioner,* 49 T.C.M. (CCH) 182, 189 (1984); *Stevenson v. Commissioner,* 43 T.C.M. (CCH) 289, 290–91 (1982) (citing *Commissioner v. Stewart,* 186 F.2d 239, 242 (6th Cir.1951)). *See also* Andrews, *The Use of the Injunction as a Remedy for an Invalid Federal Tax Assessment,* 40 Tax L. Rev. 653, 661 n. 39 (1985).

The majority then proceeds to overload the statutory requirement of a "determination" of a deficiency with burdensome substantive content. First, the majority ignores the rule that a deficiency notice need not contain any explanation whatsoever. *Abatti v. Commissioner,* 644 F.2d 1385, 1389 (9th Cir.1981); *Barnes v. Commissioner,* 408 F.2d 65, 69 (7th Cir.), *cert. denied,* 396 U.S. 836, 90 S.Ct. 94, 24 L.Ed.2d 86 (1969); *Stevenson,* 43 T.C.M. (CCH) at 290. *See also* B. Bittker, *Federal Taxation of Income, Estates and Gifts* ¶ 115.2.2 at 115–14 (1981) ("*Federal Taxation*").

Second, the majority fails to grasp the function of the deficiency notice. It is nothing more than "a jurisdictional prerequisite to a taxpayer's suit seeking the Tax Court's redetermination of [the Commissioner's] determination of the tax liability." *Stamm,* 84 T.C. at 252. "[T]he notice is only to advise the person who is to pay the deficiency that the Commissioner means to assess him; anything that does this unequivocally is good enough." *Olsen v. Helvering,* 88 F.2d 650, 651 (2nd Cir.1937). [19] Nothing more is required as a predicate to Tax Court

---

[19] [fn 1] The notice of deficiency mailed to the taxpayers included two forms: Form 892 and Form 5278. Form 892 is the basic deficiency notice. It includes the taxpayer's name, social security number, amount of the deficiency for the taxable year, and a short explanation of the taxpayer's options. Here, the Commissioner properly completed the Form 892. If the Commissioner had mailed only the Form 892, and nothing else, it is clear that this would have been a valid deficiency notice. *Abatti,* 644 F.2d at 1389; *Barnes,* 408 F.2d at 69; *Stevenson,* 43 T.C.M. (CCH) at 290. The Tax Court's jurisdiction would have been established, even though the Commissioner relied on the wrong tax shelter in making the determination.

598 | FEDERAL TAX PROCEDURE & ENFORCEMENT

jurisdiction.[20] In fact, this Circuit has recognized that " 'it is not the *existence* of a deficiency that provides a predicate for Tax Court jurisdiction.' " *Stevens v. Commissioner,* 709 F.2d 12, 13 (5th Cir.1983) (quoting *Hannan v. Commissioner,* 52 T.C. 787, 791 (1969) (emphasis in original)). The *Stevens* court lucidly commented:

> That seems obvious: the very purpose of the Tax Court is to adjudicate contests to deficiency notices. If the existence of an error in the determination giving rise to the notice deprived the Court of jurisdiction, the Court would lack power to perform its function.

709 F.2d at 13.

Therefore, the deficiency notice is effectively the taxpayer's "ticket" to the Tax Court. This "ticket" gives the taxpayer access to the only forum where he can litigate the relevant tax issue without first paying the tax assessed. If a properly-addressed deficiency notice states the amount of the deficiency, the taxable year involved, and notifies the taxpayer that he has 90 days from the date of mailing in which to file a petition for redetermination, then the notice is valid. The merits of the Commissioner's deficiency should not be litigated in the form of a motion to dismiss for lack of jurisdiction; once jurisdiction has been established, both sides will have the opportunity to press their views before the Tax Court.

The majority escapes from under the undesirable weight of authority requiring that the validity of a deficiency notice be determined primarily by its form by distinguishing these cases as not addressing the challenge that no determination was made by the Commissioner. In light of the emphasis of this authority on the *form* of the deficiency notice, I cannot agree with such a strained interpretation of these cases. *See* B. Bittker, *Federal Taxation* ¶ 115.2.2 at 115–12 ("[t]he requirement of an IRS *determination* coalesces with the requirement of

---

[20] [fn 2] "It may well be true that the [Commissioner] erred in his determination that a deficiency existed for this period. But when he once determined that there was a deficiency, that fact gives us jurisdiction to determine whether or not it was correctly arrived at." H. Milgrim & Bros. v. Commissioner, 24 B.T.A. 853, 854 (1931).

The key question is whether the inclusion of an erroneous Form 5278, which purports to explain the deficiency in terms of an unrelated tax shelter, invalidates the deficiency notice. I believe the inclusion of the wrong Form 5278 constitutes a preparation error which does not invalidate the deficiency notice. "An error in a notice of deficiency, which otherwise fulfills its purpose, will be ignored where the taxpayer is not misled thereby and is provided by it with information sufficient for the preparation of his case for trial." Meyers v. Commissioner, 81 T.C.M. (P–H) 276, 278 (1981). Here, the taxpayers were not misled by the stray Form 5278 because they had notice from the IRS that a mistake had been made before the Tax Court had set a trial date for either the 1977 or 1978 disputes concerning the videotape tax shelter.

a *notice* of deficiency, since the usual evidence that a deficiency has been 'determined' is the notice") (emphasis in original).

For example, in Hannan v. Commissioner, 52 T.C. 787 (1969), the Tax Court concluded that there was a valid notice of deficiency, despite the Commissioner's contentions that he neither determined a deficiency nor sought to collect one.[21] The Tax Court rejected the Commissioner's position and found it had jurisdiction:

> Here petitioners were sent a letter which admittedly meets all the formal requirements of a statutory notice of deficiency, notifying them that "We [respondent] have determined the income tax deficiencies shown above" and listing tax deficiencies and additions to tax under section 6651(a). This was a determination of a deficiency in tax, even though, as respondent argues, on trial it may develop that there is in fact no deficiency.

Id. at 791 (footnotes omitted).

The majority misreads *Hannan* in denying that *Hannan* stands for the proposition that deficiency notices are to be judged on their face, rather than on the substance of the Commissioner's determination. *See ante* at 1367 n. 7. It is true that the Tax Court partly explained its decision by stating that there was no proof that the Commissioner was not in fact asserting a deficiency and that the taxpayers could only protect their interests by filing a petition. Although one might read this statement as implying that the Tax Court based its decision on more than a facial examination of the deficiency notice, I understand the Tax Court to mean that because the notice was ambiguous, the taxpayers had no alternative but to file a petition. This concern does not detract from the court's emphasis on the *form* of the deficiency notice.

---

[21] [fn 3] In *Hannan*, the Commissioner assessed additions to tax for late filing. Under 26 U.S.C. § 6662 (formerly section 6659), if additions to tax are not attributable to a deficiency, the Commissioner can immediately assess and collect the additions. On the other hand, if the additions are attributable to a deficiency the Commissioner is required to follow statutory deficiency procedures. In *Hannan*, the Commissioner sent taxpayers a letter, on the form used for deficiency notices, setting forth amounts referred to as "deficiencies" in one column, together with the "additions to tax" in the next column.

The Commissioner argued in the Tax Court that no deficiency actually existed and therefore the Tax Court lacked jurisdiction. The Commissioner's attorney stated that the notice of deficiency was issued in error. The figures listed in the "deficiency" column correspond to the figures that the taxpayers had reported as tax due on their returns. The Commissioner presumably was contending that he had used the notice of deficiency form in order to collect additions to tax, and not to notify taxpayers of the existence of deficiencies. Because the Commissioner was not imposing taxes in excess of what taxpayers showed on their returns (i.e., he used the wrong form), he argued there was no deficiency.

Judging the deficiency notice in this case by the standards discussed above, I believe that the notice warned the taxpayers that the Commissioner had, rightly or wrongly, determined a deficiency and that the notice complied with the formal requirements of section 6212(a). The Commissioner clearly determined that the taxpayers had invested in a tax shelter without economic substance in order to avoid taxes. The inclusion of an erroneous explanation of the basis of the deficiency should not in itself deprive the Tax Court of jurisdiction to decide the question of whether the Commissioner can sustain the asserted deficiency.

The majority contends that here, it "need not look beyond the notice sent to the taxpayers to determine its invalidity." *See ante* at 1368. This, however, is exactly what the majority requires when it concludes that the "determination" requirement is only satisfied where the Commissioner shows he has determined a deficiency with respect to a particular taxpayer beyond the notice itself.[22]

---

[22] [fn 4] The majority in footnote 6 makes much of the government's statement that, "In order to protect the government's interest and since your original income tax return is unavailable at this time, the income tax is being assessed at the maximum rate of 70%." The majority points to this statement as evidence supporting their conclusion that the Commissioner did not make a determination. I disagree.

Although the "unavailability" of the Scars' return may indicate that the Scars' original paper return was not before the Commissioner, it does not show that specific data on that return or relating to the video-tape tax shelter was not considered. Due to the computerization of the IRS, the Commissioner no longer operates from original paper returns. See, e.g., Murphy, Glitches and Crashes at the IRS, TIME, Apr. 29, 1985, at 71; New Machines Helping IRS, Dun's Business Month, Jan. 1984, at 24; IRS, 1980 Annual Report, 9, 14, 42–43 (1981). With well over 100 million income tax returns plus an even larger number of information returns, such as Forms W–2's and 1099's, being filed annually, it is no wonder the Commissioner has turned to the computer. See Klott, Fewer IRS Workers to Process Tax Returns, N.Y. Times, Dec. 24, 1986, at 30, col. 3; IRS, 1981 Annual Report 5, 42–43 (Table 6) (1982). When a return is filed in a Service Center, pertinent summary data is entered into the computer system. 1980 Report at 14; Quaglietta, How IRS Service Centers Process Returns, 16 Prac.Acct. 63 (1983). Such summary data includes the fact that a return was filed, whether the tax was paid or a refund check was mailed, and other data needed to match information returns with the taxpayer's return. See 1980 Report at 4, 14; Cloonan, Compliance Programs, 16 Prac.Acct. 67 (1983). This matching is done by computer. 1980 Report at 4, 14; Walbert, A Net Too Wide, FORBES, Mar. 12, 1984, at 154. It is conceivable that the Commissioner had enough information on the computer to match information regarding both the tax shelter promoted by Executive Productions, Inc. and the Scars' suspect 1977 return to their 1978 income tax taxpayer's return, but not enough to determine the exact amount of a deficiency without calling up from storage the actual return. Thus, the Commissioner assessed the Scars at the 70% rate.

As a matter of tax policy, the rule against looking behind the deficiency notice appears to be well-grounded in the administrative necessities of the Commissioner's job. The Commissioner must administer tens of thousands of deficiency notices per year. A requirement that he prove the basis of his determination before the Tax Court can assert jurisdiction would unduly burden both the Commissioner and the Tax Court.

In addition, the majority's ruling that the inclusion of an erroneous explanation invalidates a deficiency notice creates an incentive for the Commissioner not to disclose his theory for asserting a deficiency when he sends the deficiency notice. If the Commissioner discloses his theory at this stage, the majority's rule invites every taxpayer to litigate whether the Commissioner has made a determination before litigating the merits.[23] Because it is to the taxpayer's advantage that the Commissioner disclose his theory when the notice is sent, I believe it is undesirable to establish a rule which would discourage him from doing so. *See Stewart v. Commissioner,* 714 F.2d 977, 986 (9th Cir.1983).

I view this case as presenting two related policy goals. One goal is to ensure that early in the assessment procedure each individual taxpayer receives fair notice as to the theory on which the Commissioner based his deficiency. The other goal is to encourage the Commissioner to disclose the theory on which he intends to rely in the deficiency notice whenever possible. However, because the Commissioner is not required to disclose his theory in the notice, the majority's rule that invalidates a deficiency notice accompanied with an erroneous description encourages the Commissioner to issue deficiency notices without *any* explanation. Such a rule detracts from the goal of early notice and taxpayers, on the whole, will suffer because the Commissioner is likely to use the deficiency notice solely for jurisdictional purposes and only thereafter reveal his reasons for issuing the notice. I believe that preserving the Tax Court tradition of not looking

---

As of 1980, the Commissioner had identified approximately 27,000 abusive tax shelters. 1980 Report at 3. In light of this number, the punching of the wrong computer key during an audit at the partnership level is a viable explanation for the unfortunate error of one of the 26,999 inapplicable tax shelters popping up and then being entered on the Scars' Form 5278.

So, as a result of the need to computerize information regarding the millions of filed returns and the huge number of tax shelters, we have a reasonable explanation for the two errors on the gratuitously prepared Form 5278 (the wrong shelter and the wrong tax rate of 70%). The taxpayer could have contested these errors and probably would have settled the amount of the tax due promptly. The importance of these errors is further undermined by the fact that they are found in Form 5278, which the Commissioner is not required to send with the basic deficiency notice, Form 892. See ante n. 1.

[23] [fn 5] This "invitation to litigation" represents a major step backward for those of us who believe that litigation should be streamlined, attorneys' fees should be kept within reasonable bounds, and courts should not be further over-burdened.

behind the deficiency notice promotes the goal of ensuring early notice to the taxpayer.

Finally, alternative remedies exist to protect the taxpayer's interests besides dismissal of the case for lack of jurisdiction. If the taxpayers are confused by the Commissioner's theory or explanation supporting the deficiency, they may seek clarification prior to trial. The Tax Court Rules "contemplate that after the case is at issue the parties will informally confer in order to exchange necessary facts, documents, and other data with a view towards defining and narrowing the areas of dispute. Rules 38, 70(a)(1), 91(a)."[24] *Foster,* 80 T.C. at 230. *See also Stevenson,* 43 T.C.M. (CCH) at 291. Here, the informal contacts between the parties resulted in the Commissioner's disclosure of his mistake within two months of when the taxpayers filed their petition for redetermination in the Tax Court.

Furthermore, the presumed correctness of the Commissioner's deficiency notice disappears if the deficiency is arbitrary or capricious, since the burden of proof then shifts to the Commissioner. *Helvering v. Taylor,* 293 U.S. 507, 513–16, 55 S.Ct. 287, 290–91, 79 L.Ed. 623 (1935); *Weimerskirch v. Commissioner,* 596 F.2d 358, 362 & n. 8 (9th Cir.1979); *Jackson v. Commissioner,* 73 T.C. 394, 401 (1979). *See also* Rule 142(a).

These measures are more than adequate to prevent the Commissioner from littering the country with baseless deficiency notices. *Scar,* 81 T.C. at 869 (Sterratt, J., dissenting). The precedent holding that the validity of the deficiency notice is to be determined on its face was effective in furthering policy goals which benefit the taxpayer and the public. The majority's opinion sabotages the machinery of tax collection, thereby portending injury to the taxpayer and to the public. I therefore dissent.

NOTES AND QUESTIONS

1. The Scars had entered into a videotape tax shelter. The Eighth Circuit described the classic videotape tax shelter as follows:

   > In a typical transaction, an investor leased a tape or tapes from a corporate or partnership lessor, and the lessor "passed through" investment tax credit pursuant to an IRC § 38 election, usually in an amount greater than the total lease payments. The investment tax credit passed through was sometimes based on the master recording's appraised value, as opposed to its cost or basis, since many were original creations. At other times, the investment tax credit was based on a sales price agreed to by a friendly or related buyer and seller, with payment made principally in the form of long-term, unsecured or undersecured promissory notes. The . . . tapes in question [are usually] greatly overvalued.

---

[24] [fn 6] Any citation to a Rule refers to the Tax Court Rules of Practice and Procedure (codified at 26 U.S.C. § 7453).

Mattingly v. United States, 924 F.2d 785, 786 (8th Cir. 1991).
2. If the IRS had not revealed that the taxpayers' return was unavailable, would the IRS have prevailed?
3. Is the dissent's argument that it should be difficult to invalidate a deficiency notice compelling? Does does it change your answer to learn that the dissenting judge, Judge Cynthia Holcomb Hall, is an expert on tax procedure because she is a former United States Tax Court Judge?

The IRS must have a factual predicate for the determination in a deficiency notice.[25] If this were not the case, the IRS could impose tax merely by fabricating income in the notice. Although the entire notice will not necessarily be invalidated, the determination with respect to unreported income that has no basis will be given no effect.

WEIMERSKIRCH v. COMMISSIONER
596 F.2d 358 (9th Cir. 1979)
United States Court of Appeals, Ninth Circuit

J. BLAINE ANDERSON, Circuit Judge:

The Commissioner issued a 90-day letter claiming that Weimerskirch had not reported income he allegedly received from selling heroin. Weimerskirch petitioned the Tax Court for redetermination of the deficiency. 26 U.S.C. § 7442, Et seq. After the Tax Court upheld the deficiency determination, Weimerskirch appealed to this court. 26 U.S.C. § 7482.

The Tax Court held that Weimerskirch had failed to rebut the Commissioner's presumption of correctness which attaches to a deficiency determination. Johnny Weimerskirch, 67 T.C. 672 (1977). We find that the Commissioner was not entitled to rely solely upon the presumption of correctness and reverse.

FACTS

Weimerskirch reported income of $5,762.00 on his income tax return for 1972. The Commissioner issued a statutory notice of deficiency claiming that Weimerskirch had $24,608.00 of additional income which he had failed to report. This resulted in a total tax liability of $8,994.00 plus a penalty of $1,453.75. Weimerskirch petitioned the Tax Court for a redetermination of the deficiency.

Little in the way of substantive evidence was introduced at trial to either prove or disprove what Weimerskirch's taxable income was for 1972. Weimerskirch called four witnesses and by stipulation introduced the tax return

---

[25] *See* Helvering v. Taylor, 293 U.S. 507, 514 (1935) ("We find nothing in the statutes, the rules of the Board [of Tax Appeals] or our decisions that gives any support to the idea that the Commissioner's determination shown to be without rational foundation and excessive will be enforced unless the taxpayer proves he owes nothing or, if liable at all, shows the correct amount.").

which he had filed for 1972. The Commissioner called no witnesses and introduced no evidence.

Weimerskirch's mother testified that she and her husband gave him at least $1,900.00, including $370.00 in wages, as well as gifts or groceries, during 1972. The tax return which Weimerskirch had filed showed his 1972 income as $5,762.00, with $370.00 from wages and $5,392.00 from other income. This was the only substantive evidence which tended to prove or disprove what Weimerskirch's income was for 1972.[26]

STANDARD OF REVIEW

On appeal, findings of fact made by the Tax Court are not overturned unless they are "clearly erroneous." Rockwell v. C.I.R., 512 F.2d 882, 884 (9th Cir. 1975), Cert. denied, 423 U.S. 1015, 96 S.Ct. 448, 46 L.Ed.2d 386; Caratan v. C.I.R., 442 F.2d 606, 609 (9th Cir. 1971). A finding is clearly erroneous when this court is "left with the definite and firm conviction that a mistake has been committed." C.I.R. v. Duberstein, 363 U.S. 278, 291, 80 S.Ct. 1190, 1200, 4 L.Ed.2d 1218 (1960). The determination by the Tax Court that Weimerskirch received income from the heroin sales was a finding of fact, and as such may only be overturned on review if it is clearly erroneous. See Gerardo v. C.I.R., 552 F.2d 549, 552 (3d Cir. 1977); Herbert v. C.I.R., 377 F.2d 65, 71 (9th Cir. 1967).

QUESTION PRESENTED

The only issue which we address is whether the Commissioner was entitled to rely upon the presumption of correctness on the facts of this particular case.[27]

---

[26] [fn 1] At the trial Weimerskirch called an Internal Revenue Service (IRS) agent who testified that he had reconstructed Weimerskirch's income by the following method: Weekly sales of 70 quarter spoons of heroin at $30.00 per quarter spoon, creating gross weekly sales revenue of $2,100.00. The cost of the heroin was figured at $900.00 per week, resulting in a $1,200.00 weekly net income. It was determined that Weimerskirch sold heroin for 25 weeks so that his income for the period was $30,000.00. The Tax Court held that this testimony was not admissible as substantive proof that Weimerskirch had unreported income from narcotics sales, but that it was admissible only to show the method by which the Commissioner made the deficiency determination. 67 T.C. at 674-675. The testimony was admissible for this limited purpose. See Avery v. C.I.R., 574 F.2d 467, 468 (9th Cir. 1978).

[27] [fn 2] Weimerskirch also challenges the Tax Court's refusal to disclose the names of two confidential informers who had furnished information to the IRS. Additionally, he challenges the court's refusal to allow examination of the IRS agent's notes and work papers which the agent had used to refresh his memory prior to testifying. An examination of these notes and papers would have revealed the identity of the two informants. The Tax Court examined the documents in camera before refusing to allow their disclosure.

In view of our decision, and after examining these notes and papers, we conclude that the denial of disclosure of the names and the documents was not an abuse of discretion in this case. See Roviaro v. United States, 353 U.S. 53, 77

The Tax Court upheld the Commissioner's deficiency determination on the basis that Weimerskirch had failed to overcome the presumption of correctness. On appeal, the Commissioner argues that "(i)t is elementary that in a Tax Court suit, the Commissioner's deficiency determination is presumptively correct. . . ."[28] Commissioner's brief at 13. However, before the Commissioner can rely on this presumption of correctness, the Commissioner must offer some substantive evidence showing that the taxpayer received income from the charged activity. United States v. Janis, 428 U.S. 433, 441-442, 96 S.Ct. 3021, 49 L.Ed.2d 1046 (1976); Suarez v. United States, 582 F.2d 1007, 1010 n. 3 (5th Cir. 1978); Carson v. United States, 560 F.2d 693, 696-698 (5th Cir. 1977); *Gerardo*, supra, 552 F.2d at 554-555. This was not done in the present case.

DISCUSSION

In *Janis*, supra, the Supreme Court decided that the exclusionary rule did not prevent the Internal Revenue Service (IRS) from using illegally-seized evidence as the basis from which to extrapolate a taxpayer's unreported income from wagering activities. Prior to addressing the exclusionary question, the Court stated that if the illegally-seized evidence could not be used, then the result would be:

> "a 'naked' assessment without any foundation whatsoever. . . . The determination of tax due then may be one 'without rational foundation and excessive,' and not properly subject to the usual rule with respect to the burden of proof in tax cases." (citations and footnotes omitted)

428 U.S. at 441, 96 S.Ct. at 3026. The Court noted that there was apparently some conflict between the Federal Courts of Appeals as to the burden of proof in tax cases, and then went on to make these observations:

> "However that may be, the debate does not extend to the situation where the assessment is shown to be naked and without any foundation.

. . . . .

S.Ct. 623, 1 L.Ed.2d 639 (1957); United States v. Anderson, 509 F.2d 724 (9th Cir. 1975), Cert. denied, 420 U.S. 910, 95 S.Ct. 831, 42 L.Ed.2d 840. Since there may have been some confusion about what the in camera evidence could be used for (see Clerk's Record at 62), we note that this court's examination was limited to the question of whether disclosure was required. Without disclosure, such evidence cannot be used as evidence to support the Commissioner's deficiency determination. See generally Commissioner v. Shapiro, 424 U.S. 614, 96 S.Ct. 1062, 47 L.Ed.2d 278 (1976) (discussed infra at n. 8).

[28] [fn 3] Because of our conclusion that the Commissioner was not entitled to rely upon the presumption at all, we do not reach the question as to who has the general burden of persuasion in this type of case. See Rockwell v. Commissioner, 512 F.2d 882 (9th Cir. 1975), Cert. denied, 423 U.S. 1015, 96 S.Ct. 448, 46 L.Ed.2d 386.

"Certainly, proof that an assessment is utterly without foundation is proof that it is arbitrary and erroneous."

428 U.S. at 442, 96 S.Ct. at 3026. While the quoted language may not have been dispositive of the issue decided in *Janis*, supra, it certainly is a strong indication that the Commissioner must offer some foundational support for the deficiency determination before the presumption of correctness attaches to it. After all, as the Court observed in Elkins v. United States, 364 U.S. 206, 80 S.Ct. 1437, 4 L.Ed.2d 1669 (1960), ". . . as a practical matter it is never easy to prove a negative . . . ." 364 U.S. at 218, 80 S.Ct. at 1444. See also Flores v. United States, 551 F.2d 1169, 1175 (9th Cir. 1977).

A Tax Court decision finding unreported income from gambling activities was reversed in *Gerardo*, supra, because of the lack of any evidence to support the Commissioner's presumption of correctness.[29] The court reasoned as follows:

". . . in order to give effect to the presumption on which the Commissioner relies, some evidence must appear which would support an inference of the taxpayer's involvement in gambling activity during the period covered by the assessment. Without that evidentiary foundation, minimal though if (sic) may be, an assessment may not be supported even where the taxpayer is silent. (citations omitted)

"While we realize the difficulties which the Commissioner encounters in assessing deficiencies in circumstances such as are presented here, we nevertheless must insist that the Commissioner provide some predicate evidence connecting the taxpayer to the charged activity if effect is to be given his presumption of correctness. Here, the record is barren of that underlying evidence . . . ."

552 F.2d at 554-555. Even though Weimerskirch did not testify in the present case, following the teachings of *Gerardo*, supra, the Commissioner still cannot rely on the presumption in the absence of a minimal evidentiary foundation.

In another case involving failure to report income from wagering activities, the Fifth Circuit was faced with a factual situation analogous to that presented here. *Carson*, supra. The court rejected the government's attempt to rely solely upon the presumption of correctness[30] and said:

"Such a position, which would support the most arbitrary of assessments so long as the taxpayer found himself unable to prove a negative, frequently

---

[29] [fn 4] The Commissioner's deficiency determination covering a later period of gambling activities was upheld. However, there was sufficient substantive evidence to support the Commissioner's determination for the subsequent period. *Gerardo*, supra, 552 F.2d at 553.

[30] [fn 5] In *Carson*, supra, the court found that the deficiency determination for another period of wagering activities was not clearly erroneous where there was sufficient substantive evidence to support the presumption. 560 F.2d at 698.

difficult in quite innocent circumstances, does not become the government's agents, and we readily reject it."

560 F.2d at 698. Even the most innocent of persons would have difficulty in disproving such a serious charge as selling heroin, when the party making the charge was not required to present any evidence.[31]

CONCLUSION

The Commissioner offered no evidence linking Weimerskirch to the sale of narcotics, or to the sale of heroin. There was no evidence from which it could even be inferred that he engaged in these activities, let alone for a 25-week period during 1972. No records were introduced to substantiate the computations made by the IRS agent. Additionally, the Commissioner did not attempt to substantiate the charge of unreported income by any other means, such as by showing Weimerskirch's net worth, bank deposits, cash expenditures, or source and application of funds. Instead, the Commissioner merely chose to rely upon the naked assertion that Weimerskirch made $30,000.00 from the sale of heroin during 1972. In view of the total absence of any substantive evidence in the record which could support the Commissioner's deficiency determination, we are left with the firm conviction that the Tax Court erred in finding that the presumption of correctness attached to the deficiency determination.[32] A deficiency determination which is not supported by the proper foundation of substantive evidence is clearly arbitrary and erroneous.[33]

---

[31] [fn 6] The court described the effect of the requirement that the Commissioner must provide some substantive evidence to support the deficiency determination as follows:

"Neither tax collection in general nor wagering activities in particular, however, have ever been thought wholly to excuse the government from providing some factual foundation for its assessments. The tax collector's presumption of correctness has a herculean muscularity of Goliathlike reach, but we strike an Achilles' heel when we find no muscles, no tendons, no ligaments of fact."

Carson, supra, 560 F.2d at 696.

[32] [fn 7] The present case is readily distinguishable from this court's recent decision in Avery v. C.I.R., 574 F.2d 467 (9th Cir. 1978). In *Avery*, the Commissioner was allowed to rely upon the presumption of correctness after making a deficiency determination which claimed that the taxpayer had failed to report income from the sale of heroin. The following evidence not only established the necessary foundation for the presumption but also rebutted the taxpayer's contrary testimony: (1) taxpayer had been convicted on charges stemming from her heroin sales during this period; (2) a DEA agent testified about actual purchases he had made from the taxpayer; (3) the taxpayer made statements about her heroin business to the DEA agent; and (4) the taxpayer had made several expensive purchases during the period in question.

[33] [fn 8] We also note that the requirement that the Commissioner make a sufficient showing of substantive evidence to support the deficiency

The reason for the requirement that there must be some evidentiary foundation linking the taxpayer to the alleged income-producing activity is especially acute where, as here, the government asserts that the taxpayer was engaged in an activity which is otherwise illegal. This is particularly true when the illegal activity is not only morally reprehensible, but also punishable by an extended prison sentence. By its allegation that a taxpayer has unreported income from the sale of narcotics, the government is affixing a label, a label which in this case reads "heroin pusher." To allow the government to do this without offering any probative evidence linking the taxpayer to the activity runs afoul of every notion of fairness in our system of law.

The decision of the Tax Court is REVERSED.

NOTES AND QUESTIONS

1. Is there really a presumption of correctness if the IRS has to offer substantive evidence to be entitled to it?
2. What is the burden of proof with respect to the showing of evidence the IRS must make to be entitled to the presumption?

If the taxpayer does not petition the Tax Court within the prescribed time period in the deficiency notice, the IRS will assess and collect the deficiency amount.

2. Refund Claim Disallowance

The final determination for a refund claim is different from a final determination for a deficiency determination. Although the deficiency notice is a prerequisite to the jurisdiction of the Tax Court in a deficiency case, the refund claim disallowance itself is not a prerequisite for the jurisdiction of a refund

---

determination before the presumption of correctness attaches to the determination is generally consistent with the approach which has been taken when a taxpayer seeks injunctive relief after the IRS has seized property pursuant to a jeopardy assessment for income taxes. Commissioner v. Shapiro, 424 U.S. 614, 96 S.Ct. 1062, 47 L.Ed.2d 278 (1976). In order to obtain an injunction against the collection of any tax, a taxpayer must show: (1) it is clear that under no circumstances could the government ultimately prevail, and (2) equity jurisdiction otherwise exists because the taxpayer will otherwise suffer irreparable injury. Enochs v. Williams Packing Co., 370 U.S. 1, 7, 82 S.Ct. 1125, 8 L.Ed.2d 292 (1962). In *Shapiro*, supra, the IRS had made a tax assessment based on the taxpayer's alleged sale of hashish. The Supreme Court agreed with the taxpayer that the government had an obligation to disclose the factual basis for the assessment. 424 U.S. at 626-627, 96 S.Ct. 1062. Otherwise, the taxpayer could never satisfy the requirement for injunctive relief that under no circumstances could the government prevail.

forum, either the federal district court or the U.S. Court of Federal Claims. A taxpayer may file suit in a refund forum, a federal district court, or the U.S. Court of Federal Claims, upon receiving a claim disallowance. A taxpayer may also file suit without a claim disallowance after the IRS has had six months to consider the claim. If the IRS does not issue a claim disallowance, the taxpayer has an unlimited amount of time to file suit. Once the IRS issues a claim disallowance, however, the taxpayer has two years to file suit.

HILL v. UNITED STATES
118 Fed. Cl. 373 (2014)
United States Court of Federal Claims

BRADEN, Judge.
I. RELEVANT FACTUAL BACKGROUND[34]
Mark A. Hill ("Plaintiff" or "Mr. Hill") is seeking payment of his misappropriated 2007 tax refund check for $1,182.46, as well as interest, punitive damages, and a ruling exempting this payment from the Treasury Offset Program, established by 31 U.S.C. § 3716. Compl. 4–5; *see also* Pl. Mot. 8–9.

On August 5, 2008, the Internal Revenue Service ("IRS") informed Mr. Hill that his tax return for 2007 "was received but could not be found." Compl. ¶ 2, Exs. 1, 13.

On January 19, 2009, the IRS sent a letter to Mr. Hill instructing him to send "a newly signed copy of the 2007 tax return." Compl. Ex. 2.

On February 27, 2009, Mr. Hill was sentenced to an eight-year prison term. Compl. Ex. 3 (containing the Judgment Entry re: December 2008 criminal prosecution). After sentencing, he was transported to the Corrections Reception Center ("CRC") in Orient, Ohio, where he executed a copy of his 2007 tax return sometime in March 2009. On April 2, 2009, he was transferred to the Chillicothe Correctional Institution in Chillicothe, Ohio. Compl. Ex. 13.

On April 6, 2009, the IRS Processing Center received Mr. Hill's 2007 tax return and processed it on June 5, 2009. Compl. Ex. 14. The IRS determined that Mr. Hill was entitled to a tax refund of $1,182.46, and, on June 5, 2009, mailed a check for that amount to the address provided on Plaintiff's 2007 Form 1040 tax return. Compl. Ex. 14; Gov't Resp. Ex. 1 at A–2.

On June 29, 2009, the refund check was returned by the United States Postal Office, marked undeliverable. Compl. Ex. 14. The IRS then issued a refund notice and requested Mr. Hill's current mailing address. Compl. Ex. 14. This notice was received by prison authorities who "erroneously delivered" it to

---

[34] [fn 1] The relevant facts discussed herein were derived from: Plaintiff's June 18, 2012 Complaint ("Compl.") and eighteen attached unnumbered exhibits ("Compl. Exs. 1–18"); Plaintiff's December 6, 2013 Motion For Summary Judgment ("Pl. Mot."), and the Government's May 1, 2014 Response ("Gov't Resp.").

another inmate also named Mark Hill ("Hill II"),[35] although it contained Mr. Hill's personal information, including his taxpayer identification number and social security number, which Hill II used to impersonate Mr. Hill and obtain the refund check. Gov't Resp. 2; Gov't Resp. Ex. 2 at A–5; Compl. Ex. 14. On July 9, 2009, the IRS was contacted via its toll-free phone number by an individual who claimed the refund and provided an address in Waverly, Ohio. Compl. Ex. 14; Gov't Resp. Ex. 2 at A–5. On July 24, 2009, the IRS issued the refund to the Waverly, Ohio address. Compl. Ex. 14. Hill II subsequently cashed the check at First Check Cash Advance, endorsing it as "Mark Hill" without the middle initial, even though it was addressed to "Mark A. Hill." Gov't Resp. Ex. 2 at A–5.

On October 21, 2009, the IRS informed Mr. Hill that his 2007 tax refund check $1,182.46 was issued on July 24, 2009. Mr. Hill promptly submitted an IRS Form 3911, Taxpayer Statement Regarding Refund. Compl. Ex. 5. On January 20, 2010, the IRS notified Mr. Hill that it would take four to six weeks to trace the refund check. Compl. Ex. 6. On August 2, 2010, the IRS informed Mr. Hill that an additional forty-five days was needed to complete the investigation. Compl. Ex. 8. Mr. Hill subsequently requested assistance from the Taxpayer Advocate Service, who, on May 10, 2011, provided him with a copy of the cancelled 2007 tax refund check and the location where it was cashed. Compl. Exs. 11, 12.

On May 19, 2011, Mr. Hill sent a letter to Secretary of the Treasury, requesting assistance in obtaining his refund. Compl. Ex. 13. On August 1, 2011, Mr. Hill received a response from the IRS Wage and Investment Division, explaining that his refund was misappropriated and providing information to resolve the matter. Compl. Ex. 14. Thereafter, Mr. Hill submitted an Affidavit of Accusation on September 21, 2011, to six separate organizations to obtain the 2007 tax refund, which led to an investigation of the Chillicothe Correctional Institution, the Institution Liaison, and Investigator from the Ohio State Highway Patrol ("OSHP"). Compl. Ex. 15; Gov't Resp. Ex. 2.

On October 12, 2011, Mr. Hill completed and submitted IRS forms for "Claims Against the United States For the Proceeds of a Government Check" (FMS Form 3858 and FMS form 1133), as directed by the Financial Management Service of the Department of the Treasury and the OSHP Investigator. Compl. ¶¶ 18–19 (citing OSHP Case # 11–036035–0900); id. Ex. 16. On November 30, 2011, Mr. Hill received correspondence from a Legal Administrative Specialist of the Check Resolution Division asking for additional information, which Plaintiff submitted on December 13, 2011. Compl. Exs. 17, 18.

II. PROCEDURAL HISTORY

On June 18, 2012, Mark Hill filed a Complaint in the United States Court of Federal Claims, pursuant to RCFC 9(m) and 28 U.S.C. § 1346, to obtain his 2007

---

[35] [fn 2] The identity of the individual who cashed Mark Hill's 2007 tax refund check is redacted in the OSHP Investigation Report, although the Government's Response, which was not filed under seal, states that his name is Mark Hill. See Gov't Resp. 2 & Ex. 2.

federal income tax refund, in the amount of $1,182.46, plus appropriate interest for each year beyond 2008, and $1,182.46 in punitive damages. Compl. at 4–5. The Complaint also demanded the costs of this action be paid and that the monetary judgment awarded not be subject to any offset, including court costs and student loan debt. Compl. at 4–5.

On December 18, 2012, the Government filed an Answer, stating, *inter alia,* that "[P]laintiff is not entitled to recover for a second time any amounts that have been already paid to him by any agency of the United States," and that "this [c]ourt has no jurisdiction to hear Plaintiff's claim for punitive damages . . . because the United States has not waived its sovereign immunity for such claims." Answer ¶¶ 25–26. The Government also stated that, pursuant to 26 U.S.C. § 6402, any recovery by Plaintiff may be credited against certain outstanding liabilities, including liability for any internal revenue tax. Answer ¶ 27.

On June 20, 2013, Plaintiff filed a Motion For Production Of Documents and requested a court order requiring Trooper S. Wells and Investigator P. Arledge "to produce, and provide Plaintiff, a report of facts and conclusions determined from the investigation of the misappropriated 2007 Federal Income Tax Refund Check in the amount of $1,182.46." On June 24, 2013, the court granted Plaintiff's June 20, 2013 Motion For Production Of Documents, construing the motion as "requesting a subpoena for production of documents in existence." Alternatively, in accordance with RCFC 31(a), the court stated that Plaintiff may depose the two individuals named in his Motion For Production Of Documents by written questions. In accordance with the court's June 24, 2013 Order, Trooper Sherri Wells produced the September 30, 2011 Ohio State Highway Patrol Report of Investigation, Constitutional Rights Waiver, and Statement Form ("OSHP Report"). *See* Gov't Resp. Ex. 2.

On December 6, 2013, Plaintiff filed a Motion For Summary Judgment ("Pl. Mot.").

On May 1, 2014, the Government filed an Opposition To Plaintiff's Motion For Summary Judgment ("Gov't Resp."). Plaintiff did not file a Reply.

III. DISCUSSION

A. Jurisdiction

The United States Court of Federal Claims has jurisdiction under the Tucker Act, 28 U.S.C. § 1491, "to render judgment upon any claim against the United States founded either upon the Constitution, or any Act of Congress or any regulation of an executive department, or upon any express or implied contract with the United States, or for liquidated or unliquidated damages in cases not sounding in tort." 28 U.S.C. § 1491(a)(1). The Tucker Act, however, is "a jurisdictional statute; it does not create any substantive right enforceable against the United States for money damages. . . .. [T]he Act merely confers jurisdiction upon [the United States Court of Federal Claims] whenever the substantive right exists." *United States v. Testan,* 424 U.S. 392, 398, 96 S.Ct. 948, 47 L.Ed.2d 114 (1976). Congress has authorized the United States Court of Federal Claims to adjudicate "[a]ny civil action against the United States for the recovery of any internal-revenue tax alleged to have been erroneously or illegally assessed or collected, or any penalty claimed to have been collected without authority or any sum alleged to have been excessive or in any manner wrongfully collected under the internal-revenue laws [.]" 28 U.S.C. § 1346(a)(1).

In tax refund suits, the "jurisdiction of the [United States] Court of Federal Claims is limited by the Internal Revenue Code." *Waltner v. United States,* 679 F.3d 1329, 1332–33 (Fed.Cir.2012); *see also United States v. Clintwood Elkhorn Mining Co.,* 553 U.S. 1, 4, 8–9, 128 S.Ct. 1511, 170 L.Ed.2d 392 (2008) (explaining that a taxpayer suing in the United States Court of Federal Claims to obtain a refund must "comply with the tax refund scheme established in the Code"). Jurisdiction is established if: (1) the taxpayer has paid his full federal tax liability for the year for which he claims a refund; (2) before filing suit, the taxpayer timely files an administrative claim for the refund with the IRS for the amount at issue; and (3) subsequently, the taxpayer timely files suit "provid[ing] the amount, date, and place of each payment to be refunded, as well as a copy of the refund claim" pursuant to RCFC 9(m). 2 CYC. OF FED. PROC. § 2:413 (3d ed.) (updated Aug. 2014); *see also* 26 U.S.C. § 7422(a) ("No suit or proceeding shall be maintained in any court for the recovery of any internal revenue tax alleged to have been erroneously or illegally assessed or collected, or of any penalty claimed to have been collected without authority, or of any sum alleged to have been excessive or in any manner wrongfully collected, until a claim for refund or credit has been duly filed with the Secretary[.]"); 26 U.S.C. § 6511(a) (setting the period of limitation on filing an administrative tax refund claim with the IRS); 26 U.S.C. § 6532(a) ("No suit or proceeding under section 7422(a) for the recovery of any internal revenue tax, penalty, or other sum, shall be begun before the expiration of 6 months from the date of filing the claim required under such section unless the Secretary renders a decision thereon within that time, nor after the expiration of 2 years from the date of mailing by certified mail or registered mail by the Secretary to the taxpayer of a notice of the disallowance of the part of the claim to which the suit or proceeding relates."); *Shore v. United States,* 9 F.3d 1524, 1526 (Fed.Cir.1993) (holding that a tax refund claim must be dismissed if the "principal tax deficiency has not been paid in full").

In addition, the United States Court of Federal Claims has jurisdiction under 31 U.S.C. § 3343 to determine whether a taxpayer is entitled to a replacement check from the Check Forgery Insurance Fund, since that statute is money-mandating. *See Curtin v. United States,* 91 Fed.Cl. 683, 687–88 (2010) (determining that Section 3343 is "a money-mandating statute"). To establish entitlement to relief under Section 3343, the taxpayer must establish that:

(1) the check was lost or stolen without the fault of the payee or a holder that is a special endorsee and whose endorsement is necessary for further negotiation;

(2) the check was negotiated later and paid by the Secretary or a depositary on a forged endorsement of the payee's or special endorsee's name; and

(3) the payee or special endorsee has not participated in any part of the proceeds of the negotiation or payment.

31 U.S.C. § 3343(b); *see also Curtin,* 91 Fed.Cl. at 688 (discussing the requirements of Section 3343).

In this case, the court has jurisdiction to adjudicate the claims alleged in the June 18, 2012 Complaint under both 28 U.S.C. § 1346 and 31 U.S.C. § 3343.

1. 28 U.S.C. § 1346

As to Section 1346, the evidence demonstrates that Plaintiff filed his 2007 Individual Federal Income Tax Return on April 15, 2008 and paid the federal tax liability due for 2007. Compl. Exs. 2, 14; Gov't Resp. Ex. 1 at A–2. The evidence also demonstrates that the IRS determined that Plaintiff overpaid his 2007 taxes by $1,176 and was entitled to a refund in the amount of $1,182.46 ($1,176 plus $6.46 in interest). Gov't Resp. Ex. 1 at A–2.

Plaintiff also has established that he timely filed an administrative claim for his 2007 refund check with the IRS. The Internal Revenue Code requires a taxpayer to file a claim for refund with the IRS filed within "3 years from the time the return was filed or 2 years from the time the tax was paid, whichever of such periods expires the later[.]" 26 U.S.C. § 6511(a); *see also Clintwood Elkwood Mining,* 553 U.S. at 5, 128 S.Ct. 1511 ("[U]nless a claim for refund of a tax has been filed within the time limits imposed by § 6511(a), a suit for refund . . . may not be maintained in any court." (quoting *United States v. Dalm,* 494 U.S. 596, 602, 110 S.Ct. 1361, 108 L.Ed.2d 548 (1990))). Therefore, in order to comply with the limitations set forth in 26 U.S.C. § 6511(a), Plaintiff must have filed a refund claim with the IRS no later than April, 15, 2011. *See* 26 U.S.C. § 6511(a). Plaintiff, however, did not submit the IRS formal claims documents—Form FMS–3858 (Claims Document) and Form FMS–1133 (Claim Against the United States for the Proceeds of a Government Check)—until October 12, 2011. Compl. Ex. 16; Program Operations Manual System (POMS) GN 02401.908, Social Security Administration (April 21, 2014).[36]

"Under the informal claims doctrine, a timely claim with purely formal defects is permissible if it fairly apprises the IRS of the basis for the claim within the limitations period." *Computervision Corp. v. United States,* 445 F.3d 1355, 1364 (Fed.Cir.2006); *see also Western Co. of N. Am. v. United States,* 323 F.3d 1024, 1035 (Fed.Cir.2003) (recognizing that the informal claim doctrine applies where the taxpayer repeatedly requested information from the IRS). The record in this case establishes that Plaintiff made several *informal* claims to the IRS within the three-year period. The United States Supreme Court has held that "a [timely] notice fairly advising the Commissioner of the nature of the taxpayer's claim . . . will nevertheless be treated as a[n effective] claim, where formal defects . . . have been remedied by amendment filed after the lapse of the statutory period." *United States v. Kales,* 314 U.S. 186, 194, 62 S.Ct. 214, 86 L.Ed. 132 (1941). In *Western,* the IRS erroneously assessed the taxpayer a "failure-to-file" penalty. *Western,* 323 F.3d at 1035. The taxpayer, in response,

---

[36] [fn 3] Available at http://policy.ssa.gov/poms.nsf/lnx/0202401908.

"repeatedly requested information about the basis for the penalty but did not file a formal claim." *Id.* These requests were documented in writing. *Id.* Under these circumstances, the taxpayer's refund claim was not barred, because, the plaintiff "made repeated requests for information that would have allowed filing of an informed claim . . . [and that served to] put the IRS on notice of [plaintiff's] challenges." *Id.* at 1034–35.

In this case, Plaintiff first inquired into the status of his refund on August 5, 2008, after which the IRS confirmed that his 2007 tax return was received, but could not be found. Compl. Ex. 1. On January 19, 2009, the IRS sent a letter to Plaintiff instructing him to send "a newly signed copy of the original 2007 tax return." Plaintiff did so in March of 2009. Compl. Ex. 2. The IRS Processing Center received the new 2007 tax return on April 6, 2009 and processed it on June 5, 2009. Compl. Ex. 14. The IRS determined that Plaintiff was entitled to a tax refund of $1,182.46, and, on June 5, 2009, mailed a check for that amount to the address provided on Plaintiff's 2007 Form 1040 tax return. Gov't Resp. Ex. 1 at A–2; Compl. Ex. 14. Plaintiff continued to correspond with the IRS and various other parties, within the period of limitations established by 26 U.S.C. § 6511, to obtain his refund check, including submitting Form 3911 (Taxpayer Statement Requiring Refund), providing the IRS with information to facilitate its effort to locate Plaintiff's refund check. Compl. ¶ 7, Ex. 5. Therefore, Plaintiff repeatedly requested information via written correspondence regarding the status of his refund throughout the limitations period and "put the IRS on notice" of the basis for his claim. *See Western,* 323 F.3d at 1035. Therefore, under the informal claims doctrine, Plaintiff's suit is not barred for failing to timely file an administrative refund claim with the IRS.

In addition, Plaintiff timely filed the June 18, 2012 Complaint in the United States Court of Federal Claims, complying with the requirements of RCFC 9(m). To timely file suit for a tax refund, Plaintiff must have filed not before "the expiration of 6 months from the date of filing the claim . . . unless the Secretary renders a decision thereon within that time, nor after the expiration of 2 years from the date of mailing by certified mail or registered mail by the Secretary to the taxpayer of a notice of the disallowance of the part of the claim to which the suit or proceeding relates." 26 U.S.C. § 6532(a). In this case, Plaintiff began submitting "informal claims" on August 5, 2008 and the IRS was "put on notice" of his refund claim on June 5, 2009 at the latest. Compl. Exs. 1, 14. Both of these dates are more than six months prior to the filing of Plaintiff s Complaint in the Court of Federal Claims. *See* 26 U.S.C. § 6532(a). Moreover, Plaintiff commenced this suit prior to "the expiration of 2 years from the date of mailing by certified mail or registered mail by the Secretary to the taxpayer of a notice of the disallowance of the part of the claim to which the suit or proceeding relates," because the Secretary never mailed to Plaintiff a "notice of disallowance of the part of the claim to which the suit . . . relates." 26 U.S.C. § 6532(a).

2. 31 U.S.C. § 3343.

The court also has jurisdiction under 31 U.S.C. § 3343, since that statute is a money-mandating source of substantive law and the facts alleged in the June 18,

2012 Complaint satisfy the requirements for relief. *See Curtin,* 91 Fed.Cl. at 687–88. Indeed, the Government does not contest that Plaintiff "meets the statutory criteria" for relief. Gov't Resp. 3 ("The [United States Court of Federal Claims] has found [Section 3343] is money-mandating and thus that jurisdiction properly exists over [P]laintiff's claims for a new check. Here, the facts indicate that [P]laintiff meets the statutory criteria." (citing *Curtin,* 91 Fed.Cl. at 687)).

For these reasons, the United States Court of Federal Claims has jurisdiction to adjudicate the claims alleged in the June 18, 2012 Complaint.

B. Standard of Review for *Pro Se* Litigants

The pleadings of a pro se plaintiff are held to a less stringent standard than those of litigants represented by counsel. See Haines v. Kerner, 404 U.S. 519, 520, 92 S.Ct. 594, 30 L.Ed.2d 652 (1972) (per curiam) (holding that pro se complaints, "however inartfully pleaded," are held to "less stringent standards than formal pleadings drafted by lawyers"). It has been the tradition of this court to examine the record "to see if [a pro se] plaintiff has a cause of action somewhere displayed." Manuel v. United States, 78 Fed.Cl. 31, 34 (2007) (quoting Ruderer v. United States, 188 Ct.Cl. 456, 468, 412 F.2d 1285 (1969)). Nevertheless, while the court may excuse ambiguities in a pro se plaintiff's complaint, the court "does not excuse [a complaint's] failures." Henke v. United States, 60 F.3d 795, 799 (Fed.Cir.1995); see also Wozniak v. United States, 219 Ct.Cl. 580, 581, 618 F.2d 119 (1979) (holding that even in a pro se tax suit a timely claim for refund must be filed to invoke the court's jurisdiction).

C. Standard of Review for a Motion for Summary Judgment Pursuant to RCFC 56

On a motion for summary judgment, the moving party must show that there is no genuine issue as to any material fact, and that he is entitled to judgment as a matter of law. *See Moden v. United States,* 404 F.3d 1335, 1342 (Fed.Cir.2005) ("Summary judgment is only appropriate if the record shows that there is no genuine issue as to any material fact and that the moving party is entitled to judgment as a matter of law."); *see also* RCFC 56(c). Only genuine disputes of material facts that might affect the outcome of the suit will preclude entry of summary judgment. *See Anderson v. Liberty Lobby, Inc.,* 477 U.S. 242, 248, 106 S.Ct. 2505, 91 L.Ed.2d 202 (1986) ("As to materiality, the substantive law will identify which facts are material. Only disputes over facts that might affect the outcome of the suit under the governing law will properly preclude the entry of summary judgment. Factual disputes that are irrelevant or unnecessary will not be counted."). The existence of "some alleged factual dispute between the parties will not defeat an otherwise properly supported motion for summary judgment." *Id.* at 247–48, 106 S.Ct. 2505. To avoid summary judgment, the nonmoving party must put forth evidence sufficient for a reasonable finder of fact to return a verdict for that party. *Id.* at 248–50, 106 S.Ct. 2505.

The moving party bears the initial burden of demonstrating the absence of any genuine issue of material fact. See Celotex Corp. v. Catrett, 477 U.S. 317, 325, 106 S.Ct. 2548, 91 L.Ed.2d 265 (1986) (holding the moving party must meet its burden "by 'showing'—that is, pointing out to the [trial court]—that there is an absence of evidence to support the nonmoving party's case."); see also Riley & Ephriam Constr. Co. v. United States, 408 F.3d 1369, 1371 (Fed.Cir.2005) ("The moving party bears the burden of demonstrating the absence of a genuine issue of material fact."). Once the moving party demonstrates the absence of a genuine issue of material fact, the burden shifts to the nonmoving party to show the existence of a genuine issue of material fact for trial. See Novartis Corp. v. Ben Venue Labs, Inc., 271 F.3d 1043, 1046 (Fed.Cir.2001) (explaining that, once a movant demonstrates the absence of a genuine issue of material fact, "the burden shifts to the nonmovant to designate specific facts showing that there is a genuine issue for trial").

On a motion for summary judgment, "the inferences to be drawn from the underlying facts . . . must be viewed in the light most favorable to the party opposing the motion." *United States v. Diebold, Inc.*, 369 U.S. 654, 655, 82 S.Ct. 993, 8 L.Ed.2d 176 (1962); *see also Anderson*, 477 U.S. at 255, 106 S.Ct. 2505 (holding that "all justifiable inferences be drawn in [the non-moving party's] favor."); *Casitas Mun. Water Dist. v. United States*, 543 F.3d 1276, 1283 (Fed.Cir.2008) ("[A]ll justifiable inferences [are drawn] in favor of the party opposing summary judgment.").

D. Plaintiff's May 20, 2014 Motion for Summary Judgment

1. Plaintiff's Argument

Plaintiff seeks summary judgment for "all relief sought in the complaint, including, but not limited to: (1) payment of $1,182.46 plus interest;" (2) an award of punitive damages that this court deems appropriate "for the undue delay caused by [the Government] in resolving this issue;" (3) an order that prohibits offsetting his 2007 refund with any debts owed to federal agencies not past due at the time when the 2007 tax refund was originally issued; and (4) an order compelling the Government "to pay the full cost of the action, including any reasonable amount determined to compensate Plaintiff's expenses in pursuing this case." Pl. Mot. 8–9.

To qualify for relief under 31 U.S.C. § 3343, *i.e.*, obtain the 2007 tax refund check, "it must be established that: (1) the check was lost or stolen without the fault of the payee, (2) the check was negotiated and paid by the Treasurer on a forged endorsement of Payee's name, and (3) the payee did not participate directly or indirectly in the proceeds of such negotiation or payment." Pl. Mot. 7 (citing 31 U.S.C. § 3343(b) and *Curtin*, 91 Fed.Cl. at 688). Plaintiff contends that the OSHP Report establishes undisputed facts that satisfy all three elements, which are not contested by the Government.

In addition, Plaintiff argues that the Government's defense against punitive damages is "a legal question requiring a *de novo* determination by this [court]." Pl. Mot. 7 (citing Gov't Answer ¶ 26 ("[T]his [c]ourt has no jurisdiction to hear [P]laintiff's claim for punitive damages . . . because the United States has not waived sovereign immunity for such claims.")). Plaintiff urges this court to consider the fact that the IRS's failure to redact Plaintiff's identification number on the notice it issued to the CRC facilitated the other individual's ability to appropriate Plaintiff's refund check. Plaintiff also contends that the IRS's loss of

Plaintiff's original tax return "contributed to the resulting misappropriation." Pl. Mot. 7. In addition, Plaintiff asserts that the IRS failed to take adequate action to resolve this issue after being informed by an Ohio law enforcement officer that Plaintiff's refund check had been cashed by a different individual, and that Plaintiff had not participated in the misappropriation, either directly or indirectly. Pl. Mot. 7.

Plaintiff also argues that his 2007 refund check is not subject to the United States Department of Treasury Offset Program, that "allows the Treasury to transfer a taxpayer's refund to another federal agency to pay a taxpayer's past due debt," because Plaintiff did not have any past due debts owed to any federal agency when his tax refund was due in 2008, or in 2009 after he resubmitted his 2007 tax return. Pl. Mot. 8 (citing 31 U.S.C. § 3720A(a)). Accordingly, if his 2007 refund was reduced, pursuant to 26 U.S.C. 6402(d), that reduction would amount to "an offset by illegal exaction." Pl. Mot. 8.

2. The Government's Response

The Government confirms that the "operative facts of the case" are not disputed. Gov't Resp. 2. Accordingly, the Government agrees that Plaintiff qualifies for reissuance of his 2007 tax refund check, in the amount of $1,182.46, under 31 U.S.C. § 3343.[37] Gov't Resp. 1. But, "summary judgment should be denied to the extent Plaintiff seeks interest [on that amount], punitive damages, or a ruling that payment [of that amount] is not subject to [the Treasury Offset Program]." Gov't Resp. 6.

First, Plaintiff cannot recover interest on his 2007 tax refund, because 31 U.S.C. § 3343, does not provide for recovery of interest. Gov't Resp. 4 (citing 31 U.S.C. § 3343(b) ("The Secretary of the Treasury shall pay from the Fund to a payee or special endorsee of a check drawn on the Treasury or a depositary designated by the Secretary the amount of the check without interest[.]")). A reissuance of a tax refund check under the Check Forgery Insurance Fund, established by 31 U.S.C. § 3343, is technically a new payment, not a tax refund. So, "[w]hile tax overpayments are refunded with interest," new payments pursuant 31 U.S.C. § 3343 are made in "the amount of the [original] check without interest." Gov't Resp. 4 (citing *Clark v. United States,* 206 F.Supp.2d 954 (N.D.Ind.2002), *aff'd* 326 F.3d 911 (7th Cir.2003)).

Second, the United States Court of Federal Claims does not have jurisdiction to adjudicate Plaintiff's claim for punitive damages. The Tucker Act is "only a jurisdiction statute; it does not create any substantive right enforceable against

---

[37] [fn 4] The facts establish that Plaintiff has met the conditions established by 31 U.S.C. § 3343. Gov't Resp. 3. First, the 2007 refund check was "deliberately redirected by another individual" "without Plaintiff's knowledge." Gov't Resp. 3 n.4. Second, that individual cashed the check, endorsing it under "Mark Hill." Gov't Resp. 3 n.4. Third, "according to the OSHP investigation," Plaintiff was not aware of the individual impersonating him, and therefore hadn't "participated in any part of the proceeds of the negotiation or payment." Gov't Resp. 3 n.4.

the United States for money damages." Gov't Resp. 4–5 (internal quotations omitted) (quoting *United States v. Mitchell*, 445 U.S. 535, 538, 100 S.Ct. 1349, 63 L.Ed.2d 607 (1980) and *Testan*, 424 U.S. at 398, 96 S.Ct. 948). Therefore, Plaintiff must "identify a substantive right for money damages against the United States separate from the Tucker Act." Gov't Resp. 5 (internal quotations omitted) (quoting *Todd v. United States*, 386 F.3d 1091, 1094 (Fed.Cir.2004)). Plaintiff's refund claim is made pursuant to 31 U.S.C. § 3343, but that Section does not contain a punitive damages provision. And, Plaintiff fails to identify an alternative source of law that would provide for recovery of punitive damages. As such, this court does not have jurisdiction to adjudicate Plaintiff's claim for punitive damages. Gov't Resp. 4.

Third, the reissuance of Plaintiff's 2007 tax refund check, under the Check Forgery Insurance Fund, is subject to the Treasury Offset Program, established by 31 U.S.C. § 3716, which "provides for offsets against any federal payments, except those specifically excepted, in the amount of any debt certified to the Secretary of the Treasury under the Debt Collection Act."[38] Pertinent case law indicates that a wide range of federal payments, including awards of attorney's fees and "repayment of improperly seized funds," are subject to offset. Gov't Resp. 6 (citing *United States v. Approximately $3,174.00 in U.S. Currency*, 928 F.Supp.2d 1040 (E.D.Wis.2013)). Payments made pursuant to 31 U.S.C. § 3343, however, are not exempt from operation of the Treasury Offset Program. As a result, payment of Plaintiff's 2007 tax refund check would be "subject to offset . . ., should [P]laintiff have a qualifying debt." Gov't Resp. 6 (citing 31 U.S.C. § 3716(c)).

3. The Court's Resolution
a. Plaintiff Is Entitled to $1,182.46
Section 3343(b) provides that

(b) The Secretary of the Treasury shall pay from the Fund to a payee or special endorsee of a check drawn on the Treasury or a depositary designated by the Secretary the amount of the check without interest if in the determination of the Secretary the payee or special endorse establishes that—

(1) the check was lost or stolen without the fault of the payee or a holder that is a special endorsee and whose endorsement is necessary for further negotiation;

(2) the check was negotiated later and paid by the Secretary or a depositary on a forged endorsement of the payee's or special endorsee's name; and

---

[38] [fn 5] Plaintiff's December 6, 2013 Motion For Summary Judgment cites 26 U.S.C. § 6402 in addressing the issue of offset. Gov't Resp. 5 n.5. Section § 6402 "permits offsets from overpayments of tax," but a reissuance of Plaintiff's 2007 tax refund check, pursuant to 31 U.S.C. § 3343, is a new payment, not a tax refund. Gov't Resp. 5 n.5. Thus, 26 U.S.C. § 6402 does not apply. Gov't Resp. 5 n.5.

(3) the payee or special endorsee has not participated in any part of the proceeds of the negotiation or payment.

31 U.S.C. § 3343(b).

The evidence adduced by both parties, discussed herein, demonstrates that Plaintiff's claim meets the requisite conditions for payment of $1,182.46, under the Check Forgery Insurance Fund, 31 U.S.C. § 3343. Compl. Ex. 4; Gov't Resp. 2, 3 n.4; Gov't Resp. Ex. 2.

b. Interest

Cognizant of Plaintiff's *pro se* status, the court considers the June 18, 2012 Complaint to allege two distinct claims: (1) a tax refund, pursuant to 28 U.S.C. § 1346; and (2) reissuance of his stolen June 5, 2009 refund check, pursuant to 31 U.S.C. § 3343. Compl. at 1 (citing 28 U.S.C. § 1346); Pl. Mot. 7 (arguing that Plaintiff qualifies for relief under 31 U.S.C. § 3343).

As discussed above, the United States Court of Federal Claims has jurisdiction to adjudicate a tax refund claim pursuant to 28 U.S.C. § 1346. The relevant governing statute concerning interest, 26 U.S.C. § 6611, provides: "Interest shall be allowed and paid upon any overpayment in respect of any internal revenue tax[.]" The IRS, in turn, has interpreted Section 6611 to allow, generally, the payment of interest "on any overpayment any tax . . . from the date of overpayment of the tax," with some exceptions. 26 C.F.R. § 301.6611–1;[39] *see also Marsh & McLennan Cos. v. United States,* 302 F.3d 1369, 1372–73 (Fed.Cir.2002) (describing the interaction between 26 U.S.C. § 6611 and 26 C.F.R. § 301.6611–1). Relevant to Plaintiffs situation is section (j) of that regulation that provides:

Refund of overpayment. No interest shall be allowed on any overpayment of tax imposed by subtitle A of the Code if such overpayment is refunded—

(1) In the case of a return filed on or before the last date prescribed for filing the return of such tax (determined without regard to any extension of time for filing such return), within 45 days after such last date, or

---

[39] [fn 6] Section (g) defines the interest period:

Period for which interest allowable in case of refunds. If an overpayment of tax is refunded, interest shall be allowed from the date of the overpayment to a date determined by the district director or the director of the regional service center, which shall be not more than 30 days prior to the date of the refund check. The acceptance of a refund check shall not deprive the taxpayer of the right to make a claim for any additional overpayment and interest thereon, provided the claim is made within the applicable period of limitation. However, if a taxpayer does not accept a refund check, no additional interest on the amount of the overpayment included in such check shall be allowed. 26 C.F.R. § 301.6611–1(g).

(2) After December 17, 1966, in the case of a return filed after the last day prescribed for filing the return, within 45 days after the date on which the return is filed.

However, in the case of any overpayment of tax by an individual (other than an estate or trust and other than a nonresident alien individual) for a taxable year beginning in 1974, "60 days" shall be substituted for "45 days" each place it appears in this paragraph.

26 C.F.R. § 301.6611–1(j).

Plaintiff timely filed his 2007 tax return on the "last date" for filing that return: April 15, 2008. Compl. ¶ 1; *see also* 26 C.F.R. § 301.6611–1(j)(1). Interest would be allowed, therefore, if the overpayment was not refunded within sixty days, *i.e.,* June 14, 2008. Since the IRS admitted to losing Plaintiff's 2007 tax return, the IRS unquestionably missed that sixty-day deadline. Compl. Ex. 1 (8/5/08 Letter from IRS to Mark Hill).

Instead, the IRS mailed the tax refund on June 5, 2009. Gov't Resp. Ex. 1 at A–2. Thus, pursuant to section 301.6611–1(g), Plaintiff is owed interest from the date of overpayment—April 15, 2008, through at least thirty days prior to the date of the refund check—May 6, 2009, which equals 386 days, excluding the end date. And, in fact, the June 5, 2009 tax refund included interest of $6.46 on the initial refund of $1,176.00, that seemingly reflects interest for this 386–day period. Gov't Resp. Ex. 1 at A–2. Therefore, Plaintiff has already received the interest to which he is entitled under the Internal Revenue Code, and reissuance of Plaintiff's refund check pursuant to 31 U.S.C. § 3343 will necessarily include the interest Plaintiff is due.

In arguing that Section 3343 specifically precludes the payment of interest for replacement checks, the Government fails to acknowledge that this is not the only statute at issue in this case. The Government is correct that, under Section 3343, a taxpayer is not entitled to interest on a reissued check. *See* 31 U.S.C. § 3343 ("The Secretary of the Treasury shall pay from the [Check Forgery Insurance] Fund . . . the amount of the check *without interest*[.]" (emphasis added)). Section 3343 generally applies to all lost or stolen checks, regardless of circumstance or originating agency. *Id.* (requiring only that the check be "drawn on the Treasury or a depositary designated by the Secretary). But, Section 3343 does not prohibit the IRS from awarding interest, pursuant to *other statutes or court orders,* and the Government cites to no authority to the contrary. Gov't Resp. 4.[40] And, the June 18, 2012 Complaint makes it clear that Plaintiff is pursuing a tax refund claim under 28 U.S.C. § 1346, in addition to relief pursuant

---

[40] [fn 7] The Government's citation to *Clark,* 206 F.Supp.2d 954, is irrelevant, because *Clark* did not involve a claim for interest, but only a request for a replacement check and related tort allegations. See *Clark,* 206 F.Supp.2d at 956 (discussing 31 U.S.C. § 3343); see also *Clark,* 326 F.3d at 912 n.1 (noting only that § 3343 allows "the Secretary of the Treasury to issue replacement checks, without interest").

to 31 U.S.C. § 3343. Nevertheless, for the reasons discussed above, when Plaintiff receives the reissued check, he will be receiving interest therein, pursuant to 26 C.F.R. § 301.6611–1. To the extent that Plaintiff believes he is entitled to interest subsequent to May 6, 2009, the court construes 26 C.F.R. § 301.6611–1(g) as precluding such relief. *See* 26 C.F.R. § 301.6611–1(g) ("If an overpayment of tax is refunded, interest shall be allowed from the date of the overpayment to a date determined by the district director or the director of the regional service center, *which shall be not more than 30 days prior to the date of the refund check.*" (emphasis added)).

In other words, since Plaintiff will receive the tax overpayment *with* interest, in the amount of $1,182.46, no additional interest is due.

c. Punitive Damages

In addition to reissuance of the 2007 tax refund check due him, Plaintiff seeks $1,182.46 in punitive damages pursuant to 31 U.S.C. § 3343. Compl. at 4–5. Section 3343, however, does not provide for punitive damages. See 31 U.S.C. § 3343(b) (allowing only for payment from the Check Forgery Insurance Fund to replace stolen Government-issued checks). And Plaintiff has identified no other independent basis to allow for the award of punitive damages. To the extent that the June 18, 2012 Complaint alleges tortious actions on the part of the Government in the misappropriation of Plaintiff's 2007 Federal income tax refund, the United States Court of Federal Claims does not have jurisdiction to hear claims under the Federal Tort Claims Act. See 28 U.S.C. § 1346(b)(1) (granting exclusive jurisdiction to federal district courts to hear tort claims against the United States). Moreover, the Federal Tort Claims Act does not waive sovereign immunity for "[a]ny claim arising in respect of the assessment or collection of any tax." 28 U.S.C. § 2680(c); see also Aetna Cas. & Sur. Co. v. United States, 71 F.3d 475, 477–78 (2d Cir.1995) (holding that payment of a refund falls within § 2680(c)). Therefore, Plaintiff's request for punitive damages is denied.

d. The Offset

The Government argues that, if Plaintiff has a qualifying debt, payment from the Check Forgery Insurance Fund or payment resulting from judgment of the United States Court of Federal Claims "must be subject to offset under the Treasury Offset Program." Gov't Resp. 6. The Government, however, did not file a counterclaim in this case. And to the court's knowledge, has not filed an action for an offset in another case. Therefore, Plaintiff's request for a declaratory judgment is not ripe and a declaratory judgment on this issue would constitute an impermissible advisory opinion because, at present, there is no "case or controversy" as to the offset. *See United Pub. Works of Am. (C.I.O.) v. Mitchell,* 330 U.S. 75, 116, 67 S.Ct. 556, 91 L.Ed. 754 (1947) ("It is clear that the declaratory judgment procedure is available in the federal courts only in cases involving actual controversies and may not be used to obtain an advisory opinion in a controversy not yet arisen."). If the Government withholds payment, pursuant to the Treasury Offset Program, Plaintiff may file a complaint in the *appropriate venue* at that time.

IV. CONCLUSION.

For these reasons, Plaintiffs December 6, 2013 Motion For Summary Judgment is granted-in-part and denied-in-part. The Government is ordered to issue a check in the amount of $1,182.46, pursuant to 31 U.S.C. § 3343.

IT IS SO ORDERED.

NOTES AND QUESTIONS

1. What duty does the IRS have to investigate a stolen identity?
2. How long does the IRS have to consider a refund claim?
3. How long does a taxpayer have to sue over a refund disallowance?
4. Under what conditions will the IRS pay interest on an overpayment?

Another difference between a deficiency case and a refund case is how stringent the requirements are for the final decision document. In the case of a deficiency, the IRS may lose the authority to assess and collect a tax if the deficiency notice is defective. In contrast, the requirements imposed on the IRS for a refund disallowance are not so stringent because, at the time the taxpayer files the refund claim, the IRS likely already has the tax in hand.

UNIT 4

JUDICIAL REVIEW OF TAX DISPUTES

The government's structure with separate sovereign functions keeps all three branches from resorting to tyranny. As a check on the executive branch, the tax laws permit a taxpayer in dispute with the IRS to challenge the IRS in court. In a prototypical case, by the time a court challenge occurs the taxpayer has decided to file a tax return, actually filed a tax return, and gone through the administrative review process where the IRS either determined the taxpayer has a tax deficiency or disallowed a refund claim. If the taxpayer received a deficiency determination, a forum choice remains. The taxpayer may sue in the U.S. Tax Court, the Court of Federal Claims, or a federal district court.

Among these three courts, there are two types of lawsuits, referred to as deficiency cases and refund cases depending on the underlying basis for the suit. A deficiency suit stems from an IRS deficiency determination. A refund suit arises from the IRS's refusal to grant the taxpayer a refund of an alleged overpayment. *See* 28 U.S.C. § 1346(a).

Many aspects of tax litigation are common to litigation outside the tax context. There are, however, some tax litigation features that are unique. Further, deficiency litigation and refund litigation share some procedures but have some unique aspects as well. This chapter and the next two chapters cover tax litigation generally, deficiency litigation in the U.S. Tax Court, and refund litigation, respectively. This chapter, on general tax litigation, discusses issues that are similar for both deficiency and refund cases. It also highlights some of the differences to be discussed in more detail either in the Tax Court chapter or in the refund litigation chapter.

Although a taxpayer may usually choose between deficiency and refund litigation, there is a third type of tax litigation. This type of tax litigation, however, is generally not a choice. Many tax disputes either arise while a taxpayer is in bankruptcy or cause a taxpayer to go into bankruptcy. The third type of tax litigation forum is the U.S. Bankruptcy Court.

CHAPTER 16

TAX LITIGATION OVERVIEW

A. Deficiency and Refund Litigation

There are many similarities between deficiency and refund litigation as well as a lot of differences. The similarities that are not common to all litigation tend to characterize tax litigation. Some differences are important to keep in mind once a taxpayer has decided on suing in a deficiency forum or a refund forum. The most important differences, however, are important for deciding which forum to choose. These differences must be considered prior to bringing the lawsuit.

1. Pre-Commencement Considerations

Prior to filing a typical tax lawsuit, a taxpayer usually must choose between deficiency litigation in Tax Court or refund litigation in the federal district court or Court of Federal Claims. These considerations include jurisdiction, cost, the applicable law, judicial tax expertise, elective streamlined treatment for small cases, jury trial availability, and equitable relief availability. There are myriad other differences between the typical tax forums, but these are the most important for choosing a judicial forum.

i.   *Jurisdiction*

Generally, a taxpayer may seek judicial review to challenge an IRS final determination against him or her. As discussed in the last chapter, there are two types of final determinations the IRS makes in civil tax disputes, deficiency determinations and refund disallowance determinations. Different courts have jurisdiction over the different types of determinations. The Tax Court has jurisdiction over suits arising from deficiency determinations, and the Court of Federal Claims and federal district courts have jurisdiction arising from refund disallowances. Before making a payment, a taxpayer may choose to petition the Tax Court to redetermine the IRS's deficiency determination. If the tax at issue does not fall under the Tax Court's jurisdiction, the taxpayer fails to petition the Tax Court, or the taxpayer decides not to sue in Tax Court, the taxpayer may pursue refund litigation by paying all the tax owed and requesting a refund with the expectation the IRS will disallow the refund request. The taxpayer may then sue in court to obtain the refund of money unlawfully held in the IRS's possession.

From the taxpayer's perspective, the first opportunity to file a lawsuit against the IRS is generally with the Tax Court following an audit and appeal. Next, the taxpayer may choose to sue in a refund forum, either the Court of Federal Claims or the federal district court following the IRS's refund review process. The chronological history of tax litigation reverses these two types of litigation. Originally, the only avenue for challenging a tax determination was to sue in a refund forum after having paid the assessment or tax. Later, Congress created the Bureau of Internal Revenue, the predecessor to the Tax Court, so taxpayers could challenge assessments or determinations prior to payment or assessment. A brief look at the history of tax litigation puts the current choices in context. After looking at the history of tax litigation, we will return to a chronological discussion of Tax Court litigation and then refund litigation.

At the dawn of time for tax litigation—long before Congress created a permanent tax collection agency—no right to challenge the government's tax determinations existed. The federal government generally has sovereign immunity against lawsuits. The government at the time, however, did not collect taxes through its own employees. Rather, collection agents collected federal taxes. Collection agents had no sovereign immunity because they were individuals.

The Supreme Court recognized that a taxpayer could obtain relief from an erroneous federal civil tax assessment in 1836 in Elliott v. Swartwout, 35 U.S. 137, 145-46 (1836). The action permitted was a suit in assumpsit against the collector for a refund of taxes paid, and the taxpayer was required to protest at the time of payment so that the collector would know not to transfer the funds collected to the government. The protest made it so that the collector could hold the money until resolution of the matter instead of passing to the federal government.

In 1855, Congress created the Court of Claims. The Court of Claims, the predecessor to the current Court of Federal Claims, permitted lawsuits against the United States, including tax cases. In 1887, Congress enacted the Tucker Act, which gave district courts and the Court of Claims explicit concurrent jurisdiction over tax challenges.

Between the Court of Claims' creation and the Tucker Act enactment, Congress created a Commissioner of Internal Revenue in 1862 to head the first permanent federal agency devoted to collecting federal taxes. This agency, the predecessor to the IRS, started out as the Office of the Commissioner of Internal Revenue and developed into the Bureau of Internal Revenue soon after.

The current income tax was enacted in 1913. During World War I, Congress also enacted an excess profits tax. These taxes were both more complex than excise taxes, head taxes, and tariffs. And the government needed money. One unfortunate practice the BIR engaged in around this time was to determine tax deficiencies for many taxpayers without a full review. *See* HAROLD DUBROFF & BRANT J. HELLWIG, THE UNITED STATES TAX COURT: AN HISTORICAL ANALYSIS 21 (2d ed. 2014). In order for a taxpayer to challenge such a deficiency determination, the taxpayer was required to pay the amount the BIR determined was owed, file a refund claim, and then sue in federal district court or Court of Claims. There was no way to challenge the deficiency prior to assessment or payment.

Congress remedied the absence of a pre-payment forum in 1924 by establishing the Board of Tax Appeals, the predecessor to the U.S. Tax Court. The Tax Court, however, does not have general jurisdiction over tax cases. Rather, it has very specific jurisdiction.[1] To the extent that a taxpayer desires to challenge a tax not covered by the Tax Court's jurisdiction, the suit may only occur in a refund forum.

A taxpayer may not sue in Tax Court and then file a concurrent suit in a refund forum. Section 6512 provides as follows:

> If the Secretary has mailed to the taxpayer a notice of deficiency [authorized by the Code] and if the taxpayer files a petition with the Tax Court within the time prescribed [by the Code], no credit or refund of income tax for the same taxable year . . . in respect of which the Secretary has determined the deficiency shall be allowed or made and no suit by the taxpayer for the recovery of any part of the tax shall be instituted in any court. . . .

This issue has arisen in various scenarios. The following case shows where this prohibition does not apply.

WAGNER v. COMMISSIONER
118 T.C. 330 (2002)
United States Tax Court

LARO, J.

Petitioners petitioned the Court under section 6320(c) to review a notice of a Federal tax lien placed upon their property. The lien arose from an assessment of Federal income taxes of $412,787.15 and $844.16 for 1991 and 1996, respectively. Petitioners now, after being served with respondent's answer and respondent's motion for summary judgment, move the Court to dismiss this case

---

[1] Many commenters characterize the Tax Court as having limited jurisdiction. Although this characterization is not untrue, it is meaningless because all federal courts have limited jurisdiction. *See* Kempe's Lessee v. Kennedy, 9 U.S. 173, 185 (1805) ("The courts of the United States are all of limited jurisdiction. . . .").

without prejudice to their right to seek in Federal District Court a determination that they incurred a net operating loss (NOL) in 1994 that may be carried back to 1991.[2] We shall grant petitioners' motion.[3] UNLESS OTHERWISE Noted, section references are to the internal revenue Code in effect for the relevant years, Rule references are to the Tax Court Rules of Practice and Procedure, and rule references are to the Federal Rules of Civil Procedure. Petitioners resided in Maitland, Florida, when their petition was filed.

The parties agree that the Court may dismiss this case pursuant to petitioners' request.[4] We distinguish this dismissal from our jurisprudence that holds that taxpayers may not withdraw a petition under section 6213 to redetermine a deficiency. That jurisprudence stems from the seminal case of *Estate of Ming v. Commissioner,* 62 T.C. 519, 1974 WL 2720 (1974).

In *Estate of Ming,* the taxpayers moved the Court to allow them to withdraw their petition for a redetermination of their 1964, 1965, and 1966 Federal income taxes. Presumably, they made their motion so that they could refile their lawsuit in District Court. We denied the motion. We noted that, whenever this Court dismisses a case on a ground other than lack of jurisdiction, we are generally required by section 7459(d)[5] to enter a decision finding that the deficiency in tax is the amount determined in the notice of deficiency. *Id.* at 522. We observed that entering such a decision would serve to preclude the taxpayers from litigating the case on its merits in District Court. *Id.* at 522–523. We noted that the Commissioner had been prejudiced by the taxpayers' filing of the petition by virtue of the fact that he was precluded from assessing and collecting the taxes which he had determined the taxpayers owed. *Id.* at 524.

In Estate of Ming v. Commissioner, supra at 521–522, we also relied on our opinion in Dorl v. Commissioner, 57 T.C. 720, 1972 WL 2407 (1972), affd. 507 F.2d 406 (2d Cir.1974), which held that a taxpayer may not remove a case from this Court in order to refile it in District Court. We observed in *Dorl* that the filing of a petition in this Court gives us exclusive jurisdiction under section

---

[2] [fn 1] Respondent argued in his motion for summary judgment that res judicata barred petitioners from establishing an NOL in 1994 that could be carried back to 1991. The Court determined petitioners' income tax liability for 1991 in *Estate of Wagner v. Commissioner,* T.C. Memo.1998–338.

[3] [fn 2] In so doing, we, of course, leave to the District Court to determine whether petitioners are entitled to any relief there, and, if so, what type of relief.

[4] [fn 3] Respondent does not object to dismissal without prejudice to petitioners' filing a refund suit in District Court but takes the position that the dismissal should be with prejudice to their refiling a petition under sec. 6320(c) in our own Court based on the same claim as their existing petition.

[5] [fn 4] Sec. 7459(d) provides in relevant part:

SEC. 7459(d). Effect of Decision Dismissing Petition.—If a petition for a redetermination of a deficiency has been filed by the taxpayer, a decision of the Tax Court dismissing the proceeding shall be considered as its decision that the deficiency is the amount determined by the Secretary. * * *

6512(a), which acts to bar a refund suit in the District Court for the same tax and the same year. We noted that this observation was supported by the legislative history accompanying the enactment of the predecessors of sections 6512(a) and 7459(d). That history states that, when a taxpayer petitions the Board of Tax Appeals, the Board's decision, once final, settles the taxpayer's tax liability for the year in question even if the decision resulted from a dismissal requested by the taxpayer. Estate of Ming v. Commissioner, supra at 522.

We believe that our holding in *Estate of Ming* is inapplicable to the setting at hand where petitioners have petitioned this Court under section 6320(c). Section 7459(d) applies specifically to a petition that is filed for a redetermination of a deficiency and makes no mention of a petition that is filed under section 6320(c) to review a collection action. Section 6320 was added to the Code as part of the Internal Revenue Service Restructuring and Reform Act of 1998, Pub.L. 105–206, sec. 3401, 112 Stat. 685, 746, and that act made no amendment to section 7459(d), which finds its roots in section 906(c) of the Revenue Act of 1926, ch. 27, 44 Stat. 107. Nor do we know of any provision in the Code that would require us, upon a dismissal of a collection action filed under section 6320(c), to enter a decision for the Commissioner consistent with the underlying notice of determination. Whereas the relevant legislative history supported our holding in *Dorl v. Commissioner, supra,* we are unaware of any legislative history that would support a holding contrary to that which we reach herein.

Our granting of petitioners' motion is supported by rule 41(a)(2),[6] which we

---

[6] [fn 5] In relevant part, rule 41 provides:

Rule 41. Dismissal of Actions

(a) Voluntary Dismissal: Effect Thereof.

(1) By Plaintiff; by Stipulation. * * * an action may be dismissed by the plaintiff without order of court (i) by filing a notice of dismissal at any time before service by the adverse party of an answer or of a motion for summary judgment, whichever first occurs, or (ii) by filing a stipulation of dismissal signed by all parties who have appeared in the action. Unless otherwise stated in the notice of dismissal or stipulation, the dismissal is without prejudice, except that a notice of dismissal operates as an adjudication upon the merits when filed by a plaintiff who has once dismissed in any court of the United States or of any state an action based on or including the same claim.

(2) By Order of Court. Except as provided in paragraph (1) of this subdivision of this rule, an action shall not be dismissed at the plaintiff's instance save upon order of the court and upon such terms and conditions as the court deems proper. * * * Unless otherwise specified in the order, a dismissal under this paragraph is without prejudice.

(d) Costs of Previously–Dismissed Action. If a plaintiff who has once dismissed an action in any court commences an action based upon or including the same claim against the same defendant, the court may make such order for the payment of costs of the action previously dismissed as it may deem proper * * *.

consult given the absence in our Rules of a specific provision as to this matter.[7] See Rule 1. Under rule 41(a)(2), a plaintiff is not entitled as a matter of right to a dismissal after the defendant has served a motion for summary judgment but is allowed such a dismissal in the sound discretion of the court. *Pontenberg v. Boston Scientific Corp.*, 252 F.3d 1253, 1255–1256 (11th Cir.2001); *LeCompte v. Mr. Chip, Inc.*, 528 F.2d 601 (5th Cir.1976). In general, a court "should" grant a dismissal under rule 41(a)(2) "unless the defendant will suffer clear legal prejudice, *other than the mere prospect of a subsequent lawsuit,* as a result." *McCants v. Ford Motor Co., Inc.*, 781 F.2d 855, 856–857 (11th Cir.1986). "The crucial question to be determined is, Would the defendant lose any substantial right by the dismissal." *Durham v. Fla. E. Coast Ry. Co.*, 385 F.2d 366, 368 (5th Cir.1967). In making this determination, a court must "weigh the relevant equities and do justice between the parties in each case, imposing such costs and attaching such conditions to the dismissal as are deemed appropriate." *McCants v. Ford Motor Co., Inc., supra* at 857.

The statutory period in which petitioners could refile their lawsuit in this Court appears to have expired. Section 6330(d)(1) requires that a petition to this Court be filed within 30 days of the determination that is the subject of section 6320. See also sec. 6320(c). The rule is deeply embedded in the jurisprudence of Federal law that the granting of a motion to dismiss without prejudice is treated as if the underlying lawsuit had never been filed. *Monterey Dev. Corp. v. Lawyer's Title Ins. Corp.*, 4 F.3d 605, 608 (8th Cir.1993); *Brown v. Hartshorne Pub. Sch. Dist.*, 926 F.2d 959, 961 (10th Cir.1991); *Robinson v. Willow Glen Acad.*, 895 F.2d 1168, 1169 (7th Cir.1990); *Long v. Board of Pardons and Paroles*, 725 F.2d 306 (5th Cir.1984); *Cabrera v. Municipality of Bayamon*, 622 F.2d 4, 6 (1st Cir.1980); *Humphreys v. United States*, 272 F.2d 411, 412 (9th Cir.1959); *A.B. Dick Co. v. Marr*, 197 F.2d 498, 502 (2d Cir.1952); *Md. Cas. Co. v. Latham*, 41 F.2d 312, 313 (5th Cir.1930). We conclude that respondent is not prejudiced in maintaining the subject collection action against petitioners as if the instant proceeding had never been commenced.

Accordingly, in the exercise of the Court's discretion, and after weighing the relevant equities including the lack of a clear legal prejudice to respondent, we shall grant petitioners' motion. In accordance with the foregoing,

An appropriate order of dismissal will be entered granting petitioners' motion to dismiss.

---

[7] [fn 6] Our Rule on dismissals, Rule 123(b), relates to dismissals "For failure of a petitioner properly to prosecute or to comply with these Rules or any order of the Court or for other cause which the Court deems sufficient". Pursuant to that Rule, "the Court may dismiss a case at any time and enter a decision against the petitioner." Id. Rule 123(b) does not apply to the setting at hand where petitioners voluntarily move the Court to dismiss their petition filed under sec. 6320(c) to review a notice of Federal tax lien.

NOTES AND QUESTIONS

1. Once the Tax Court dismissed the case in *Wagner*, could the taxpayer sue in federal district court? *See* 28 U.S.C. § 1346(a).
2. When "should" a court grant a taxpayer a dismissal without prejudice?
3. If the case had been a deficiency case rather than a collection case, would the court have granted the dismissal? *See* Estate of Ming v. Commissioner, 62 T.C. 519 (1974).

ii. Applicable Law

One fundamental and controversial feature of tax litigation is the opportunity to forum shop. The Tax Court's nationwide authority makes it so that the applicable law can vary depending on the court in which the taxpayer proceeds. As discussed in the next chapter, the Tax Court has the authority to decide cases nationwide. Although Tax Court cases and federal district court cases are appealed to the same regional courts, a district court will always be appealed to the same regional circuit court of appeals. If there is no precedent in the circuit that would have jurisdiction over the appeal, a district court might be able to reach a more favorable result than the Tax Court if the Tax Court has already developed precedent on the particular issue.

For example, consider a situation where the taxpayer has a captive bank regulated by the federal banking regulators. Assume that the Code provides a tax benefit to the taxpayer that depends on the captive bank being deemed a "person carrying on the banking business." In this hypothetical, there is no precedent in the circuit to which the case would be appealed. Assume further, however, that Tax Court precedent has held that the interpretation of what constitutes "a person carrying on the banking business" is narrow, and has held that an identical bank did not constitute "a person carrying on the banking business." *See* The Limited v. Commissioner, 113 T.C. 169 (1999), *rev'd*, 286 F.3d 324 (6th Cir. 2002). The taxpayer would likely prefer to take on the government in the district court where there is no controlling precedent than go to Tax Court and attempt to convince it to overturn its own precedent. Specifically, a district court decision is bound by its regional court of appeals but operates on a clean slate absent precedent in the circuit court. In contrast, a case in Tax Court creates a precedent applicable nationwide that binds the Tax Court in any circuit where no precedent on the issue exists. *See* Golsen v. Commissioner, 54 T.C. 742 (1970), *aff'd*, 445 F.2d 985 (10th Cir. 1971).

Another way that the applicable law can vary between tax forums is that the trial-level decisions are not all appealed to the same circuit courts of appeals. Appeals from cases in the Court of Federal Claims lie in the Federal Circuit rather than the regional circuit courts of appeals that review Tax Court and federal district court cases. In the example above, assume that the Federal Circuit has precedent that conflicts with the Tax Court, and has held that any captive bank constitutes "a person carrying on the banking business." In such a case, the taxpayer would want to sue in the Court of Federal Claims because it has favorable precedent.

iii.   Cost

Cost is a major factor in deciding the forum in which to sue the IRS. The least expensive forum in which to battle the IRS is the U.S. Tax Court due to some structural differences from refund forums. First, as discussed above, the Tax Court is a pre-payment forum. This means the taxpayer does not have to pay before filing suit. In refund forums, however, the taxpayer must pay the amount the IRS has asserted, request a refund, and then sue if the refund is not forthcoming.

This factor's importance becomes readily apparent when considering a case involving a timing issue such as when a taxpayer is entitled to a deduction. A taxpayer benefits from an earlier deduction rather than a later one due to the time value of money. If a deduction is claimed in one year and disallowed, the taxpayer will often still be entitled to a deduction, but in a later year. In such cases, the time value of money benefit can be meager as compared to the gross amount of the deduction. For example, in DaimlerChrysler v. Commissioner, 436 F.3d 644, 647 (6th Cir. 2005), the taxpayer had taken deductions in 1984 and 1985 amounting to over $865 million. At the time the taxpayer claimed each deduction, the taxpayer was suffering some financial distress. The taxpayer sued in the U.S. Tax Court, in which the Code permits a lawsuit prior to paying any tax. Even if there had been more beneficial precedent in the Court of Federal Claims, the taxpayer likely would not have had the money to pay the tax on $865 million in income before suing for a refund to take advantage of the Court of Federal Claims precedent. As discussed in the chapter on refund suits, a taxpayer must have paid the entire tax before suing.

Discovery costs are also less burdensome while litigating in Tax Court rather than a refund forum. Discovery in the Tax Court is less burdensome, as discussed in the next chapter, because of the informality requirements[8] and the stipulation process. In addition, depositions in Tax Court are limited as compared to litigation in other forums.

Another difference that can make litigation in Tax Court less expensive is the availability of small case procedures for low-income taxpayers. Low-income taxpayers may not be able to afford an attorney or have the time to brush up on the Federal Rules of Evidence. Congress has made it easier for a low-income taxpayer to challenge the IRS in court under section 7463. The procedures for such a case make it so that the cases can be heard more quickly than a regular case, as well as providing other advantages.

---

[8] Although this looks like an oxymoron, it is not.

iv.   Judicial Tax Expertise

Another factor to consider in deciding on a forum is the tax expertise of the judges. Tax Court judges are tax experts. The judges have various tax backgrounds, including government (all three branches) and private practice. In contrast, there are very few federal district court judges that are tax experts. In the Court of Federal Claims, there are occasionally tax experts appointed because it is not a court of general jurisdiction like federal district court. As will be discussed in Chapter 18, the Court of Federal Claims has jurisdiction over only a few subject matters.

v.   Jury Availability

For tax disputes, a jury trial is available only in federal district court. Neither the Tax Court nor the Court of Federal Claims has juries. A taxpayer who believes a jury is the only way to go will have only one choice. This topic is discussed in more detail in the following two chapters.

2. Commencement Process

As in most litigation, a party must commence the case by filing in court within a certain amount of time. As discussed in the previous chapter, in Tax Court, the taxpayer files a Tax Court petition within 90 days of receiving the notice of deficiency. To sue in a refund forum, the taxpayer must first request a refund from the IRS. The taxpayer, however, cannot sue immediately after filing the refund claim. Rather, the taxpayer must give the IRS some time to consider the refund claim, which is six months by statute. Once the IRS issues the notice of refund disallowance, the taxpayer has two years to sue the IRS in federal district court or the Court of Federal Claims.

The mailbox rule applies to filing a petition in Tax Court and filing a complaint in a refund forum. Section 7502(a) provides as follows:

> If any . . . document required to be filed . . . within a prescribed period or on or before a [statutorily] prescribed date . . . is, after such period or such date, delivered by United States mail . . . the date of the United States postmark stamped on the cover in which such . . . document . . . is mailed shall be deemed to be the date of delivery . . . .

This next case provides an example of how this issue plays out in court.

CORREIA v. COMMISSIONER
58 F.3d 468 (1995)
United States Court of Appeals, Ninth Circuit

Before: GOODWIN, FARRIS and KLEINFELD, Circuit Judges.
Opinion

PER CURIAM:

Taxpayers Vernon L. Correia and Charlotte M. Correia timely appeal the Tax Court's dismissal of their petition for redetermination of deficiency. The Tax Court dismissed the petition for lack of jurisdiction. We review de novo, *Billingsley v. Commissioner,* 868 F.2d 1081, 1084 (9th Cir.1989), and affirm.

I. BACKGROUND

The Commissioner of Internal Revenue issued a statutory notice of deficiency to Taxpayers on April 9, 1993. *See* 26 U.S.C. § 6211. Pursuant to 26 U.S.C. § 6213(a), Taxpayers had 90 days—until July 8, 1993—to file their petition for redetermination. On July 8 Taxpayers delivered their petition to Federal Express for delivery to the Tax Court. The petition was not delivered to the Tax Court until July 9. The Tax Court dismissed the petition as untimely.

II. DISCUSSION

The timely filing of a petition for redetermination is a jurisdictional requirement. *Shipley v. Commissioner,* 572 F.2d 212, 213 (9th Cir.1977). It is undisputed that Taxpayers' petition was not timely received by the Tax Court. However, Taxpayers contend that their otherwise untimely petition is saved by the timely-mailing-as-timely-filing provision of 26 U.S.C. § 7502. Under § 7502, for a document "delivered by United States mail . . . , the date of the United States postmark . . . shall be deemed to be the date of delivery." § 7502(a).

Section 7502 by its plain and unambiguous language applies to documents delivered by the United States Postal Service. It does not apply to documents delivered by private companies such as Federal Express. *Petrulis v. Commissioner,* 938 F.2d 78, 80 (7th Cir.1991); *Pugsley v. Commissioner,* 749 F.2d 691, 693 (11th Cir.1985); *see* Treas.Reg. § 301.7502-1(c). Nonetheless, Taxpayers contend that because § 7502 and its corresponding regulations reflect outdated notions of reliable delivery methods, we should "adopt a new rule" extending the scope of § 7502 to private delivery services. Although Taxpayers put forth what may be a legitimate policy rationale for extending the rule to private delivery services, it is for Congress, not the courts, to make such a change. *Petrulis,* 938 F.2d at 81.

Taxpayers also argue that the Tax Court violated their due process rights by sua sponte notifying the Commissioner of the late filing. Subject matter jurisdiction in the Tax Court cannot be conferred by the parties' consent or waiver. *Clapp v. Commissioner,* 875 F.2d 1396, 1398 (9th Cir.1989). The Tax Court properly examined its own jurisdiction. *See id.* at 1399 (jurisdiction of Tax Court reviewed in same manner as jurisdiction of Article III courts); *FW/PBS, Inc. v. Dallas,* 493 U.S. 215, 231, 110 S.Ct. 596, 607, 107 L.Ed.2d 603 (1990) ("federal courts are under an independent obligation to examine their own jurisdiction"). Its conduct did not violate due process.

AFFIRMED.

NOTES AND QUESTIONS

1. The point of this case is that the mailbox rule applies to documents filed in court in both deficiency litigation and refund litigation. At the time, the rule applied only to the United States mail. Since this case, the IRS has issued rules permitting other carriers. *See* Notice 2016-30, 2016-18 I.R.B. 676.
2. In what other contexts does the mailbox rule apply?
3. In what important context does the mailbox rule not apply?

3. Pre-Trial Procedures

i. Pre-Trial Settlement Efforts

Chapter 14 discussed the Appeals Office and its settlement efforts after an audit. If a taxpayer declines Appeals Office consideration after an audit and later petitions the Tax Court, the Appeals Office will generally attempt to settle a case after it is docketed. The Appeals Office is given a limited amount of time to obtain a settlement, after which settlement authority returns to the trial counsel attorney.

There is no corresponding process to settle immediately after the pleadings in a case in a refund forum. The Department of Justice attorneys who are litigating the case have authority to settle any case they are litigating. When a taxpayer sues in federal district court or the Court of Federal Claims, the IRS is no longer directly involved in the case. Accordingly, settlement discussions in these forums typically take place later in the process.

ii. Stipulations

Tax Court cases and refund cases are similar in that the parties are permitted to stipulate to facts. The stipulation process in Tax Court, however, goes beyond permission. In Tax Court, the parties are required to stipulate. *See* Rule 91, Tax Court Rules of Practice and Procedure. There are two important reasons for requiring the parties to stipulate. First, it encourages settlement. If the parties are able to agree on all the material facts, then no trial is necessary. Second, it makes litigation cheaper because the stipulation process serves as a trade-off for more invasive discovery. This issue is developed further in the Tax Court chapter.

iii. Discovery

Discovery is similar in all three forums. After all, litigation is litigation. In each forum, the parties may serve interrogatories on their adversaries, serve document production requests on their adversaries, and, if the discovery rules are not followed, either party may expect sanctions from the court.

There are differences in discovery, however, between the forums. Tax Court discovery is, by rule, informal. Rule 70(a)(1), Tax Court Rules of Practice and Procedure, provides as follows:

> [T]he Court expects the parties to attempt to attain the objectives of discovery through informal consultation or communication before utilizing the discovery procedures provided in these Rules.

This informality makes discovery less costly. The next chapter will delve into informality more deeply.

Depositions are also discouraged in Tax Court. Rule 70(a)(1), Tax Court Rules of Practice and Procedure, provides as follows:

> Discovery is not available under these Rules through depositions except to the limited extent provided in Rule 74. See Rules 91(a) and 100 regarding relationship of discovery to stipulations.

The next chapter will cover the rare circumstances where depositions are permitted in Tax Court.

4. Trial Proceedings

Trials are similar regardless of which forum a taxpayer chooses. The Federal Rules of Evidence (FRE) is used in deficiency and refund cases. In qualifying small cases in Tax Court, the application of the FRE is less formal. In jury trials, the parties argue over what evidence is admissible outside the jury's earshot. Courts must decide very carefully what evidence will come before the jury. In bench trials, in Tax Court and in refund forums, judges may admit evidence and assess its credibility later. It should be noted that the Tax Court has its own rules of procedure—the Federal Rules of Civil Procedure do not apply. The Tax Court Rules of Practice and Procedure are based on the Federal Rules of Civil Procedure so there are many similarities.

In general in tax cases, the taxpayer has the burden of proof because the taxpayer is essentially the plaintiff. The taxpayer sues to prevent assessment in Tax Court and to obtain a refund in federal district court and the Court of Federal Claims. Also, the taxpayer is suing over a government action. In Tax Court cases, the taxpayer sues over the IRS's deficiency determination, but the determination carries a presumption of correctness that the taxpayer must overcome with proof. *Welch v. Helvering* is the seminal case on the presumption of correctness.

WELCH v. HELVERING
290 U.S. 111 (1933)
Supreme Court of the United States

Mr. Justice CARDOZO delivered the opinion of the Court.

The question to be determined is whether payments by a taxpayer, who is in business as a commission agent, are allowable deductions in the computation of his income if made to the creditors of a bankrupt corporation in an endeavor to strengthen his own standing and credit.

In 1922 petitioner was the secretary of the E. L. Welch Company, a Minnesota corporation, engaged in the grain business. The company was adjudged an involuntary bankrupt, and had a discharge from its debts. Thereafter the petitioner made a contract with the Kellogg Company to purchase grain for it on a commission. In order to re-establish his relations with customers whom he had known when acting for the Welch Company and to solidify his credit and standing, he decided to pay the debts of the Welch business so far as he was able. In fulfillment of that resolve, he made payments of substantial amounts during five successive years. In 1924, the commissions were $18,028.20, the payments $3,975.97; in 1925, the commissions $31,377.07, the payments $11,968.20; in 1926, the commissions $20,925.25, the payments $12,815.72; in 1927, the commissions $22,119.61, the payments $7,379.72; and in 1928, the commissions $26,177.56, the payments $11,068.25. The Commissioner ruled that these payments were not deductible from income as ordinary and necessary expenses, but were rather in the nature of capital expenditures, an outlay for the development of reputation and good will. The Board of Tax Appeals sustained the action of the Commissioner (25 B.T.A. 117), and the Court of Appeals for the Eighth Circuit affirmed. 63 F.(2d) 976. The case is here on certiorari.

'In computing net income there shall be allowed as deductions * * * all the ordinary and necessary expenses paid or incurred during the taxable year in carrying on any trade or business.' Revenue Act of 1924, c. 234, 43 Stat. 253, 269, s 214, 26 U.S.C. s 955, 26 USCA s 955(a)(1); Revenue Act of 1926, c. 27, 44 Stat. 9, 26, s 214, 26 U.S.C. App. s 955, 26 USCA s 955(a)(1); Revenue Act of 1928, c. 852, 45 Stat. 791, 799, s 23(a), 26 USCA s 2023(a); cf. Treasury Regulations 65, Arts. 101, 292, under the Revenue Act of 1924, and similar regulations under the acts of 1926 and 1928.

We may assume that the payments to creditors of the Welch Company were necessary for the development of the petitioner's business, at least in the sense that they were appropriate and helpful. McCulloch v. Maryland, 4 Wheat. 316, 4 L.Ed. 579. He certainly thought they were, and we should be slow to override his judgment. But the problem is not solved when the payments are characterized as necessary. Many necessary payments are charges upon capital. There is need to determine whether they are both necessary and ordinary. Now, what is ordinary, though there must always be a strain of constancy within it, is none the less a variable affected by time and place and circumstance. Ordinary in this context does not mean that the payments must be habitual or normal in the sense that the same taxpayer will have to make them often. A lawsuit affecting the safety of a business may happen once in a lifetime. The counsel fees may be so heavy that repetition is unlikely. None the less, the expense is an ordinary one because we know from experience that payments for such a purpose, whether the amount is large or small, are the common and accepted means of defense against attack. Cf.

Kornhauser v. United States, 276 U.S. 145, 48 S.Ct. 219, 72 L.Ed. 505. The situation is unique in the life of the individual affected, but not in the life of the group, the community, of which he is a part. At such times there are norms of conduct that help to stabilize our judgment, and make it certain and objective. The instance is not erratic, but is brought within a known type.

The line of demarcation is now visible between the case that is here and the one supposed for illustration. We try to classify this act as ordinary or the opposite, and the norms of conduct fail us. No longer can we have recourse to any fund of business experience, to any known business practice. Men do at times pay the debts of others without legal obligation or the lighter obligation imposed by the usages of trade or by neighborly amenities, but they do not do so ordinarily, not even though the result might be to heighten their reputation for generosity and opulence. Indeed, if language is to be read in its natural and common meaning (Old Colony R. Co. v. Commissioner, 284 U.S. 552, 560, 52 S.Ct. 211, 76 L.Ed. 484; Woolford Realty Co. v. Rose, 286 U.S. 319, 327, 52 S.Ct. 568, 76 L.Ed. 1128), we should have to say that payment in such circumstances, instead of being ordinary is in a high degree extraordinary. There is nothing ordinary in the stimulus evoking it, and none in the response. Here, indeed, as so often in other branches of the law, the decisive distinctions are those of degree and not of kind. One struggles in vain for any verbal formula that will supply a ready touchstone. The standard set up by the statute is not a rule of law; it is rather a way of life. Life in all its fullness must supply the answer to the riddle.

The Commissioner of Internal Revenue resorted to that standard in assessing the petitioner's income, and found that the payments in controversy came closer to capital outlays than to ordinary and necessary expenses in the operation of a business. His ruling has the support of a presumption of correctness, and the petitioner has the burden of proving it to be wrong. Wickwire v. Reinecke, 275 U.S. 101, 48 S.Ct. 43, 72 L.Ed. 184; Jones v. Commissioner (C.C.A.) 38 F. (2d) 550, 552. Unless we can say from facts within our knowledge that these are ordinary and necessary expenses according to the ways of conduct and the forms of speech prevailing in the business world, the tax must be confirmed. But nothing told us by this record or within the sphere of our judicial notice permits us to give that extension to what is ordinary and necessary. Indeed, to do so would open the door to many bizarre analogies. One man has a family name that is clouded by thefts committed by an ancestor. To add to this own standing he repays the stolen money, wiping off, it may be, his income for the year. The payments figure in his tax return as ordinary expenses. Another man conceives the notion that he will be able to practice his vocation with greater ease and profit if he has an opportunity to enrich his culture. Forthwith the price of his education becomes an expense of the business, reducing the income subject to taxation. There is little difference between these expenses and those in controversy here. Reputation and learning are akin to capital assets, like the good will of an old partnership. Cf. Colony Coal & Coke Corp. v. Commissioner (C.C.A.) 52 F.(2d) 923. For many, they are the only tools with which to hew a pathway to success.

The money spent in acquiring them is well and wisely spent. It is not an ordinary expense of the operation of a business.

Many cases in the federal courts deal with phases of the problem presented in the case at bar. To attempt to harmonize them would be a futile task. They involve the appreciation of particular situations, at times with border-line conclusions. Typical illustrations are cited in the margin.[9]

The decree should be

Affirmed.

NOTES AND QUESTIONS

1. *Welch v. Helvering* is one of the most cited tax cases in history with over 12,000 cites at this writing. The reason the case has been cited so often is probably that it It is the seminal case for two different types of issues: for determining when an expense is ordinary and necessary, and for the presumption of correctness, which assigns the burden of proof to the taxpayer.

---

[9] [fn 1] Ordinary expenses: Commissioner v. People's Pittsburgh Trust Co. (C.C.A.) 60 F.(2d) 187, expenses incurred in the defense of a criminal charge growing out of the business of the taxpayer; American Rolling Mill Co. v. Commissioner (C.C.A.) 41 F.(2d) 314, contributions to a civic improvement fund by a corporation employing half of the wage earning population of the city, the payments being made, not for charity, but to add to the skill and productivity of the workmen (cf. the decisions collated in 30 Columbia Law Review 1211, 1212, and the distinctions there drawn); Corning Glass Works v. Lucas, 59 App.D.C. 168, 37 F.(2d) 798, 68 A.L.R. 736, donations to a hospital by a corporation whose employees with their dependents made up two-thirds of the population of the city; Harris & Co. v. Lucas (C.C.A.) 48 F.(2d) 187, payments of debts discharged in bankruptcy, but subject to be revived by force of a new promise. Cf. Lucas v. Ox Fibre Brush Co., 281 U.S. 115, 50 S.Ct. 273, 74 L.Ed. 733, where additional compensation, reasonable in amount, was allowed to the officers of a corporation for services previously rendered.

Not ordinary expenses: Hubinger v. Commissioner (C.C.A.) 36 F.(2d) 724, payments by the taxpayer for the repair of fire damage, such payments being distinguished from those for wear and tear; Lloyd v. Commissioner (C.C.A.) 55 F.(2d) 842, counsel fees incurred by the taxpayer, the president of a corporation, in prosecuting a slander suit to protect his reputation and that of his business; One Hundred Five West Fifty-Fifth Street v. Commissioner (C.C.A.) 42 F.(2d) 849, and Blackwell Oil & Gas Co. v. Commissioner (C.C.A.) 60 F.(2d) 257, gratuitous payments to stockholders in settlement of disputes between them, or to assume the expense of a lawsuit in which they had been made defendants; White v. Commissioner (C.C.A.) 61 F.(2d) 726, payments in settlement of a lawsuit against a member of a partnership, the effect being to enable him to devote his undivided efforts to the partnership business and also to protect its credit.

2. How high is the burden of proof to overcome the IRS's presumption of correctness?

There are some differences in trials among the three choices for judicial forums. One difference is government representation, *i.e.*, the agency for whom the government trial attorneys work. In Tax Court, IRS Chief Counsel attorneys represent the government, but in federal district court and the Court of Federal Claims Department of Justice attorneys represent the government. Regardless of who represents the government, it is unlikely to have an impact on the choice of forum unless a taxpayer has developed a bad reputation within the IRS that can be escaped by suing in a forum where IRS employees do not directly represent the IRS. Theoretically, the IRS Chief Counsel would have more access to the taxpayer's pre-litigation conduct.

Another difference is the use of estimates at trial. As discussed in the next two chapters, the Tax Court permits a taxpayer to provide estimates of tax items under a case called *Cohan v. Commissioner*, 39 F.2d 540 (2d Cir.1930). Courts have specifically rejected *Cohan* in refund forums. *See* Williams v. United States, 245 F.2d 559 (5th Cir. 1957).

5. Post-Trial Practice

There are some similarities in post-trial practice in deficiency and refund litigation. Post-trial briefs are required in bench trials in all three forums. Bench trials generally involve a longer process, which results from post-trial briefing. In jury trials, the jury reaches a verdict that becomes the judgment if neither party objects.

Another similarity after trial is the extent that a court of appeals defers to the trial court's findings. In both Tax Court and in refund forums, the courts of appeals defer to factual findings but review the law anew or *de novo*. In other words, unlike federal agencies, where courts defer to administrative legal findings, appellate courts give no deference to a trial court. This, however, was not always the case. Prior to 1948, appellate courts deferred to the Tax Court's legal holdings. There were many good reasons to do so, as set forth in the following case.

DOBSON v. COMMISSIONER
320 U.S. 489 (1943)
Supreme Court of the United States

Mr. Justice JACKSON delivered the opinion of the Court.

These four cases were consolidated in the Court of Appeals. The facts of one will define the issue present in all.

The taxpayer, Collins, in 1929 purchased 300 shares of stock of the National City Bank of New York which carried certain beneficial interests in stock of the

National City Company. The latter company was the seller and the transaction occurred in Minnesota. In 1930 Collins sold 100 shares, sustaining a deductible loss of $41,600.80, which was claimed on his return for that year and allowed. In 1931 he sold another 100 shares, sustaining a deductible loss of $28,163.78, which was claimed in his return and allowed. The remaining 100 shares he retained. He regarded the purchases and sales as closed and completed transactions.

In 1936 Collins learned that the stock had not been registered in compliance with the Minnesota Blue Sky Laws and learned of facts indicating that he had been induced to purchase by fraudulent representations. He filed suit against the seller alleging fraud and failure to register. He asked recission of the entire transaction and offered to return the proceeds of the stock, or an equivalent number of shares plus such interest and dividends as he had received. In 1939 the suit was settled, on a basis which gave him a net recovery of $45,150.63, of which $23,296.45 was allocable to the stock sold in 1930 and $6,454.18 allocable to that sold in 1931. In his return for 1939 he did not report as income any part of the recovery. Throughout that year adjustment of his 1930 and 1931 tax liability was barred by the statute of limitations.

The Commissioner adjusted Collins' 1939 gross income by adding as ordinary gain the recovery attributable to the shares sold, but not that portion of it attributable to the shares unsold. The recovery upon the shares sold was not, however, sufficient to make good the taxpayer's original investment in them. And if the amounts recovered had been added to the proceeds received in 1930 and 1931 they would not have altered Collins' income tax liability for those years, for even if the entire deductions claimed on account of these losses had been disallowed, the returns would still have shown net losses.

Collins sought a redetermination by the Board of Tax Appeals, now the Tax Court. He contended that the recovery of 1939 was in the nature of a return of capital from which he realized no gain and no income either actually or constructively, and that he had received no tax benefit from the loss deductions. In the alternative he argued that if the recovery could be called income at all it was taxable as capital gain. The Commissioner insisted that the entire recovery was taxable as ordinary gain and that it was immaterial whether the taxpayer had obtained any tax benefits from the loss deduction reported in prior years. The Tax Court sustained the taxpayer's contention that he had realized no taxable gain from the recovery.[10]

The Court of Appeals (133 F.2d 732, 735) concluded that the 'tax benefit theory' applied by the Tax Court 'seems to be an injunction into the law of an equitable principle, found neither in the statutes nor in the regulations.' Because the Tax Court's reasoning was not embodied in any statutory precept, the court held that the Tax Court was not authorized to resort to it in determining whether the recovery should be treated as income or return of capital. It held as matter of law that the recoveries were neither return of capital nor capital gain, but were

---

[10] [fn 1] Estate of James N. Collins v. Commissioner, 46 B.T.A. 765.

ordinary income in the year received.[11] Questions important to tax administration were involved, conflict was said to exist, and we granted certiorari.[12]

It is contended that the applicable statutes and regulations properly interpreted forbid the method of calculation followed by the Tax Court. If this were true, the Tax Court's decision would not be 'in accordance with law' and the Court would be empowered to modify or reverse it.[13] Whether it is true is a clear-cut question of law and is for decision by the courts.

The court below thought that the Tax Court's decision 'evaded or ignored' the statute of limitation, the provision of the Regulations that 'expenses, liabilities, or deficit of one year cannot be used to reduce the income of a subsequent year,'[14] and the principle that recognition of a capital loss presupposes some event of 'realization' which closes the transaction for good. We do not agree. The Tax Court has not attempted to revise liability for earlier years closed by the statute of limitation, nor used any expense, liability, or deficit of a prior year to reduce the income of a subsequent year. It went to prior years only to determine the nature of the recovery, whether return of capital or income. Nor has the Tax Court reopened any closed transaction; it was compelled to determine the very question whether such a recognition of loss had in fact taken place in the prior year as would necessitate calling the recovery in the taxable year income rather than return of capital.

The 1928 Act provides that 'the Board in redetermining a deficiency in respect of any taxable year shall consider such facts with relation to the taxes for other taxable years as may be necessary correctly to redetermine the amount of such deficiency * * *.'[15] The Tax Court's inquiry as to past years was authorized if 'necessary correctly to redetermine' the deficiency. The Tax Court thought in this case that it was necessary; the Court of Appeals apparently thought it was not. This precipitates a question not raised by either counsel as to whether the court is empowered to revise the Tax Court's decision as 'not in accordance with law' because of such a difference of opinion.

With the 1926 Revenue Act, Congress promulgated, and at all times since has maintained, a limitation on the power of courts to review Board of Tax Appeals (now the Tax Court) determinations. '* * * such courts shall have power to affirm or, if the decision of the Board is not in accordance with law, to modify or to reverse the decision of the Board * * *.'[16] However, even a casual survey of decisions in tax cases, now over 5,000 in number, will demonstrate that courts

[11] [fn 2] 133 F.2d 732.

[12] [fn 3] 319 U.S. 740, 63 S.Ct. 1434.

[13] [fn 4] Revenue Act of 1926, s 1003(b), 44 Stat. 9, 110, now Internal Revenue Code, s 1141(c)(1), 26 U.S.C.A. Int.Rev.Code, s 1141(c)(1).

[14] [fn 5] Treasury Regulations 103, s 19.43-2.

[15] [fn 6] Revenue Act of 1928, s 272(g), 45 Stat. 854, now Internal Revenue Code, s 272(g), 26 U.S.C.A. Int.Rev.Code, s 272(g).

[16] [fn 7] Revenue Act of 1926, s 1003(b), 44 Stat. 9, 110, now Internal Revenue Code, s 1141(c)(1), 26 U.S.C.A. Int.Rev.Code, s 1141(c)(1).

including this Court have not paid the scrupulous deference to the tax laws' admonitions of finality which they have to similar provisions in statutes relating to other tribunals.[17] After thirty years of income tax history the volume of tax litigation necessary merely for statutory interpretation would seem due to subside. That it shows no sign of diminution suggests that many decisions have no value as precedents because they determine only fact questions peculiar to particular cases. Of course frequent amendment of the statute causes continuing uncertainty and litigation, but all too often amendments are themselves made necessary by court decisions. Increase of potential tax litigation due to more taxpayers and higher rates lends new importance to observance of statutory limitations on review of tax decisions. No other branch of the law touches human activities at so many points. It can never be made simple, but we can try to avoid making it needlessly complex.

It is more difficult to maintain sharp separation of court and administrative functions in tax than in other fields. One reason is that tax cases reach circuit courts of appeals from different sources and do not always call for observance of any administrative sphere of decision. Questions which the Tax Court considers at the instance of one taxpayer may be considered by many district courts at the instance of others.

The Tucker Act authorizes district courts, sitting without jury as courts of claims, to hear suits for recovery of taxes alleged to have been 'erroneously or illegally assessed or collected.'[18] District courts also entertain common law actions against collectors to recover taxes erroneously demanded and paid under protest. Trial may be by jury, but waiver of jury is authorized[19] and in tax cases jury frequently is waived. In such cases the findings of the court may be either special or general. The scope of review on appeal may be affected by the nature of the proceeding, the kind of findings, and whether the jury was waived under a

---

[17] [fn 8] Compare Helvering v. Tex-Penn Oil Co., 300 U.S. 481, 57 S.Ct. 569, 81 L.Ed. 755, and Bogardus v. Commissioner, 302 U.S. 34, 58 S.Ct. 61, 82 L.Ed. 32, with Rochester Telephone Corp. v. United States, 307 U.S. 125, 59 S.Ct. 754, 83 L.Ed. 1147 (Federal Communications Commission); Shields v. Utah Idaho Central Railroad Co., 305 U.S. 177, 59 S.Ct. 160, 83 L.Ed. 111 (Interstate Commerce Commission); Sunshine Coal Co. v. Adkins, 310 U.S. 381, 399, 400, 60 S.Ct. 907, 915, 84 L.Ed. 1263; Gray v. Powell, 314 U.S. 402, 62 S.Ct. 326, 86 L.Ed. 301 (Bituminous Coal Commission); National Labor Relations Board v. Waterman S.S. Corp., 309 U.S. 206, 60 S.Ct. 493, 84 L.Ed. 704 (National Labor Relations Board).

[18] [fn 9] 28 U.S.C. s 41(20), 28 U.S.C.A. s 41(20).

[19] [fn 10] 28 U.S.C.A. s 773, 28 U.S.C. s 773, Act of May 29, 1930, c. 357, 46 Stat. 486, See Federal Rules of Civil Procedure, rules 38, 52, 28 U.S.C.A. following section 723c.

particular statutory authorization or independently of it.[20] The multiplicity and complexity of rules is such that often it is easier to review the whole case on the merits than to decide what part of it is reviewable and under what rule. The reports contain many cases in which the question is passed over without mention.

Another reason why courts have deferred less to the Tax Court than to other administrative tribunals is the manner in which the Tax Court finality was introduced into the law.

The courts have rather strictly observed limitations on their reviewing powers where the limitation came into existence simultaneously with their duty to review administrative action in new fields of regulation. But this was not the history of the tax law. Our modern income tax experience began with the Revenue Act of 1913. The World War soon brought high rates. The law was an innovation, its constitutional aspects were still being debated, interpretation was just beginning, and administrators were inexperienced. The Act provided no administrative review of the Commissioner's determinations. It did not alter the procedure followed under the Civil War income tax by which an aggrieved taxpayer could pay under protest and then sue the Collector to test the correctness of the tax.[21] The courts by force of this situation entertained all manner of tax questions, and precedents rapidly established a pattern of judicial thought and action whereby the assessments of income tax were reviewed without much restraint or limitation. Only after that practice became established did administrative review make its appearance in tax matters.

Administrative machinery to give consideration to the taxpayer's contentions existed in the Bureau of Internal Revenue from about 1918 but it was subordinate to the Commissioner.[22] In 1923, the situation was brought to the attention of Congress by the Secretary of the Treasury, who proposed creation of a Board of Tax Appeals, within the Treasury Department, whose decision was to conclude Government and taxpayer on the question of assessment and leave the taxpayer to pay the tax and then test its validity by suit against the collector.[23] Congress responded by creating the Board of Tax Appeals as 'an independent agency in the executive branch of the Government.'[24] The Board was to give hearings and notice thereof and 'make a report in writing of its findings of fact and decision in

---

[20] [fn 11] 28 U.S.C. s 875, 28 U.S.C.A. s 875. See Carloss, Monograph on Findings of Fact (Supt. of Documents, 1934) 4. Some 280 cases on the review of findings of fact are considered.

[21] [fn 12] See Cheatham v. United States, 92 U.S. 85, 89, 23 L.Ed. 561.

[22] [fn 13] For an account thereof, see opinion of Mr. Justice Brandeis in Williamsport Wire Rope Co. v. United States, 277 U.S. 551, 562, n. 7, 48 S.Ct. 587, 590, 72 L.Ed. 985.

[23] [fn 14] Annual Report of Secretary of Treasury, Finance 1 (1923) 10; Hamel, Practice and Evidence before the U.S. Board of Tax Appeals (1938) 5.

[24] [fn 15] Revenue Act of 1924, s 900(k), 43 Stat. 253, 336, 338, 26 U.S.C.A. Int.Rev.Acts, page 112.

each case.' [25] But Congress dealt cautiously with finality for the Board's conclusions, going only so far as to provide that in later proceedings the findings should be 'prima facie evidence of the facts therein stated.' [26] So the Board's decisions first came before the courts under a statute which left them free to go into both fact and law questions. Two years later Congress reviewed and commended the work of the new Board, [27] increased salaries and lengthened the tenure of its members, [28] provided for a direct appeal from the Board's decisions to the circuit courts of appeals or the Court of Appeals of the District of Columbia, [29] and enacted the present provision limiting review to questions of law. [30]

But this restriction upon judicial review of the Board's decisions came only after thirteen years of income tax experience had established a contrary habit. Precedents had accumulated in which courts had laid down many rules of taxation not based on statute but upon their ideas of right accounting or tax practice. It was difficult to shift to a new basis. This Court applied the limitation, but with less emphasis and less forceful resolution of borderline cases in favor of administrative finality than it has employed in reference to other administrative determinations. [31]

That neglect of the congressional instruction is a fortuitous consequence of this evolution of the Tax Court rather than a deliberate or purposeful judicial

---

[25] [fn 16] Id., s 900(h).

[26] [fn 17] Id., s 900(g).

[27] [fn 18] H.R.Rep. No. 1, 69th Cong., 1st Sess.; Sen.Rep.No. 52, 69th Cong., 1st Sess.

[28] [fn 19] Revenue Act of 1926, s 1000, 44 Stat. 9, 106, 105, amending Revenue Act 1924, ss 901(a), 900, 26 U.S.C.A. Int.Rev.Acts, page 305.

[29] [fn 20] Id., s 1001(a), 44 Stat. 9, 109, 26 U.S.C.A. Int.Rev.Acts, page 311.

[30] [fn 21] Id., s 1003(b), 44 Stat. 9, 110.

[31] [fn 22] E.g., Helvering v. Rankin, 295 U.S. 123, 131, 55 S.Ct. 732, 736, 79 L.Ed. 1343; Helvering v. Tax-Penn Oil Co., 300 U.S. 481, 491, 57 S.Ct. 569, 573, 81 L.Ed. 755; Bogardus v. Commissioner, 302 U.S. 34, 38, 39, 58 S.Ct. 61, 64, 82 L.Ed. 32. For a sample of the diverse treatment of Board decisions when reviewed by this Court, see Elmhurst Cemetery Co. v. Commissioner, 300 U.S. 37, 57 S.Ct. 324, 81 L.Ed. 491; Palmer v. Commissioner, 302 U.S. 63, 70, 58 S.Ct. 67, 70, 82 L.Ed. 50; Helvering v. National Grocery Co., 304 U.S. 282, 294, 58 S.Ct. 932, 938, 82 L.Ed. 1346; Colorado National Bank v. Commissioner, 305 U.S. 23, 59 S.Ct. 48, 83 L.Ed. 20; Helvering v. Lazarus & Co., 308 U.S. 252, 60 S.Ct. 209, 84 L.Ed. 226; Griffiths v. Commissioner, 308 U.S. 355, 60 S.Ct. 277, 84 L.Ed. 319; Helvering v. Kehoe, 309 U.S. 277, 60 S.Ct. 549, 84 L.Ed. 751; Higgins v. Commissioner, 312 U.S. 212, 61 S.Ct. 475, 85 L.Ed. 783; Powers v. Commissioner, 312 U.S. 259, 61 S.Ct. 509, 85 L.Ed. 817; Wilmington Trust Co. v. Helvering, 316 U.S. 164, 168, 62 S.Ct. 984, 986, 86 L.Ed. 1352; Merchants National Bank of Boston v. Commissioner, 320 U.S. 256, 64 S.Ct. 108. Compare the foregoing with the cases cited supra note 8.

policy is the more evident when we consider that every reason ever advanced in support of administrative finality applies to the Tax Court.

The court is independent, and its neutrality is not clouded by prosecuting duties. Its procedures assure fair hearings. Its deliberations are evidenced by careful opinions. All guides to judgment available to judges are habitually consulted and respected. It has established a tradition of freedom from bias and pressures.[32] It deals with a subject that is highly specialized and so complex as to be the despair of judges. It is relatively better staffed for its task than is the judiciary.[33] Its members not infrequently bring to their task long legislative or administrative experience in their subject. The volume of tax matters flowing through the Tax Court keeps its members abreast of changing statutes, regulations, and Bureau practices, informed as to the background of controversies and aware of the impact of their decisions on both Treasury and taxpayer. Individual cases are disposed of wholly on records publicly made, in adversary proceedings, and the court has no responsibility for previous handling. Tested by every theoretical and practical reason for administrative finality, no administrative decisions are entitled to higher credit in the courts. Consideration of uniform and expeditious tax administrations require that they be given all credit to which they are entitled under the law.

Tax Court decisions are characterized by substantial uniformity. Appeals fan out into courts of appeal of ten circuits and the District of Columbia. This diversification of appellate authority inevitably produces conflict of decision, even if review is limited to questions of law. But conflicts are multiplied by treating as questions of law what really are disputes over proper accounting. The mere number of such questions and the mass of decisions they call forth become a menace to the certainty and good administration of the law.[34]

---

[32] [fn 23] See reports of congressional committees on the Revenue Act of 1926, cited supra note 18.

[33] [fn 24] See Miller, Supporting Personnel of Federal Courts, 29 A.B.A.Journal 130, 131.

[34] [fn 25] 'Judge-made law is particularly prolific in connection with federal taxation, coming, as it does, from so many courts of coordinate jurisdiction. And the constant outpouring of decisions has steadily increased in volume. For the year 1920 a leading tax service catalogued only 300 decisions; (CCH Federal Tax Service (1921). * * * Today one must look to approximately 20,000 court and Board decisions, many pages of regulations, and about 5,000 rulings. Since 1924 the Board of Tax Appeals alone has published about 8,500 opinions, as well as approximately 4,000 unreported memorandum opinions. For the fiscal years 1935, 1936 and 1937, the number of Board dockets appealed to the Circuit Courts of Appeal has amounted, on the average, to 509 each year. The Supreme Court's balance sheet shows that federal taxation was the principal concern of that Court during the 1934 term, with 44 decisions being handed down in that field. During the three years, 1935, 1936, and 1937, the Supreme Court rendered

To achieve uniformity by resolving such conflicts in the Supreme Court is at best slow, expensive, and unsatisfactory. Students of federal taxation agree that the tax system suffers from delay in getting the final word in judicial review, from retroactivity of the decision when it is obtained, and from the lack of a roundly tax-informed viewpoint of judges.[35]

Perhaps the chief difficulty in consistent and uniform compliance with the congressional limitation upon court review lies in the want of a certain standard for distinguishing 'questions of law' from 'questions of fact.' This is the test Congress has directed, but its difficulties in practice are well known and have been subject of frequent comment. Its difficulty is reflected in our labeling some

---

decisions in 84 federal tax cases.' Paul, Selected Studies in Federal Taxation (1938) 2, n. 2.

'As of December 31, 1936, 4,700 decisions had been appealed to the Circuit Courts of Appeal (or the Court of Appeals of the District of Columbia) of which 3,996 had been disposed of. This left a pending Appellate docket of 704.' Id., 140, n. 133.

[35] [fn 26] Paul, Selected Studies in Federal Taxation (1938) 204, n. 18, comments on the number and variety of the sources contributing to tax law.

See Griswold, Book Review, 56 Harv.L.Rev. 1354.

Magill, The Impact of Federal Taxes (1943) 209, says: 'At the present time, it is impossible to obtain a really authoritative decision of general application upon important questions of law for many years after the close of any taxable year. The average period between the taxable year in dispute and a Supreme Court decision relating thereto is nine years. Meanwhile confusion reigns in the day-by-day settlement of the more debatable questions of the tax law. One circuit court holds that a certain situation gives rise to tax liability; another circuit holds the contrary. The Commissioner and the lower federal courts are both confronted with the problem of reconciling the irreconcilable. A great part of the criticism of changing interpretations of the law announced by the Commissioner of Internal Revenue is properly attributable to the multitude of tribunals with original jurisdiction in tax cases, and to the absence of provision for decisions with nationwide authority in the majority of cases. If we were seeking to secure a state of complete uncertainty in tax jurisprudence, we could hardly do better than to provide for 87 Courts with original jurisdiction, 11 appellate bodies of coordinate rank, and only a discretionary review of relatively few cases by the Supreme Court.'

questions as 'mixed questions of law and fact'[36] and in a great number of opinions distinguishing 'ultimate facts' from evidentiary facts.[37]

It is difficult to lay down rules as to what should or should not be reviewed in tax cases except in terms so general that their effectiveness in a particular case will depend largely upon the attitude with which the case is approached. However, all that we have said of the finality of administrative determination in other fields is applicable to determinations of the Tax Court. Its decision, of course, must have 'warrant in the record' and a reasonable basis in the law. But 'the judicial function is exhausted when there is found to be a rational basis for the conclusions approved by the administrative body.' Rochester Telephone Corp. v. United States, 307 U.S. 125, 146, 59 S.Ct. 754, 764, 83 L.Ed. 1147; Swayne & Hoyt v. United States, 300 U.S. 297, 304, 57 S.Ct. 478, 481, 81 L.Ed. 659; Mississippi Valley Barge Line Co. v. United States, 292 U.S. 282, 286, 287, 54 S.Ct. 692, 693, 694, 78 L.Ed. 1260; Gray v. Powell, 314 U.S. 402, 412, 62 S.Ct. 326, 332, 86 L.Ed. 301; Helvering v. Clifford, 309 U.S. 331, 336, 60 S.Ct. 554, 557, 84 L.Ed. 788; United States v. Louisville & N.R. Co., 235 U.S. 314, 320, 35 S.Ct. 113, 114, 59 L.Ed. 245; Wilmington Trust Co. v. Helvering, 316 U.S. 164, 168, 62 S.Ct. 984, 986, 86 L.Ed. 1352.

Congress has invested the Tax Court with primary authority for redetermining deficiencies, which constitutes the greater part of tax litigation. This requires it to consider both law and facts. Whatever latitude exists in resolving questions such as those of proper accounting, treating a series of transactions as one for tax purposes, or treating apparently separate ones as single in their tax consequences, exists in the Tax Court and not in the regular courts; when the court cannot separate the elements of a decision so as to identify a clear-cut mistake of law, the decision of the Tax Court must stand. In view of the division of functions between the Tax Court and reviewing courts it is of course the duty of the Tax Court to distinguish with clarity between what it finds as fact and what conclusion it reaches on the law. In deciding law questions courts may properly attach weight to the decision of points of law by an administrative body having special competence to deal with the subject matter. The Tax Court is informed by experience and kept current with tax evolution and needs by the volume and variety of its work. While its decisions may not be binding precedents for courts dealing with similar problems, uniform administration would be promoted by conforming to them where possible.

The Government says that 'the principal question in this case turns on the application of the settled principle that the single year is the unit of taxation.' But

---

[36] [fn 27] E.g., Helvering v. Rankin, 295 U.S. 123, 131, 55 S.Ct. 732, 736, 79 L.Ed. 1343; Helvering v. Tex-Penn Oil Co., 300 U.S. 481, 491, 57 S.Ct. 569, 573, 81 L.Ed. 755; Bogardus v. Commissioner, 302 U.S. 34, 39, 58 S.Ct. 61, 64, 82 L.Ed. 32.

[37] [fn 28] E.g., Anderson v. Commissioner, 9 Cir., 78 F.2d 636; Childers v. Commissioner, 9 Cir., 80 F.2d 27; Eaton v. Commissioner, 9 Cir., 81 F.2d 332; Rankin v. Commissioner, 3 Cir., 84 F.2d 551.

the Tax Court was aware of this principle and in no way denied it. Whether an apparently integrated transaction shall be broken up into several separate steps and whether what apparently are several steps shall be synthesized into one whole transaction is frequently a necessary determination in deciding tax consequences.[38] Where no statute or regulation controls, the Tax Court's selection of the course to follow is no more reviewable than any other question of fact. Of course we are not here considering the scope of review where constitutional questions are involved. The Tax Court analyzed the basis of the litigation which produced the recovery in this case and the obvious fact that 'regarding the series of transactions as a whole, it is apparent that no gain was actually realized.' It found that the taxpayer had realized no tax benefits from reporting the transaction in separate years. It said the question under these circumstances was whether the amount the taxpayer recovered in 1939 'constitutes taxable income, even though he realized no economic gain.' It concluded that the item should be treated as a return of capital rather than as taxable income. There is no statute law to the contrary, and the administrative rulings in effect at the time tended to support the conclusion.[39] It is true that the Board in a well considered opinion reviewed a number of court holdings, but it did so for the purpose of showing that they did not fetter its freedom to reach the decision it thought sound. With this we agree.

Viewing the problem from a different aspect, the Government urges in this Court that although the recovery is capital return, it is taxable in its entirety because taxpayer's basis for the property in question is zero. The argument relies upon s 113(b)(1)(A) of the Internal Revenue Code, 26 U.S.C.A. Int.Rev.Code, s 113(b)(1)(A), which provides for adjusting the basis of property for 'expenditures, receipts, losses, or other items, properly chargeable to capital account.' This provision, it is said, requires that the right to a deduction for a capital loss be treated as a return of capital. Consequently, by deducting in 1930 and 1931 the entire difference between the cost of his stock and the proceeds of the sales, taxpayer reduced his basis to zero. But the statute contains no such fixed rule as the Government would have us read into it. It does not specify the circumstances or manner in which adjustments of the basis are to be made, but merely provides that 'Proper adjustment * * * shall in all cases be made' for the items named if 'properly chargeable to capital account.' What, in the circumstances of this case, was a proper adjustment of the basis was thus purely an accounting problem and therefore a question of fact for the Tax Court to determine. Evidently the Tax Court thought that the previous deductions were not altogether 'properly chargeable to capital account' and that to treat them as an entire recoupment of the value of taxpayer's stock would not have been a 'proper

---

[38] [fn 29] See Paul, 'Step Transactions', Selected Studies in Federal Taxation (1938) 203.

[39] [fn 30] General Counsel's Memorandum 20854, 1939-1 Cum.Bull. 102, following G.C.M. 18525, 1937-1 Cum.Bull. 80; revoked by G.C.M. 22163, 1940-2, Cum.Bull. 76. This dealt with bad debt recoveries.

adjustment.' We think there was substantial evidence to support such a conclusion.

The Government relies upon Burnet v. Sanford & Brooks Co., 282 U.S. 359, 51 S.Ct. 150, 75 L.Ed. 383, for the proposition that losses of one year may not offset receipts of another year. But the case suggested its own distinction: 'While (the money received) equalled, and in a loose sense was a return of, expenditures made in performing the contract, still, as the Board of Tax Appeals found, the expenditures were made in defraying the expenses * * *. They were not capital investments, the cost of which, if converted, must first be restored from the proceeds before there is a capital gain taxable as income.' 282 U.S. at pages 363, 364, 51 S.Ct. at page 151, 75 L.Ed. 383. It is also worth noting that the Court affirmed the Board's decision, which had been upset by the circuit court of appeals, and answered, in part, the contention of the circuit court that certain regulations were applicable by saying, '* * * nor on this record do any facts appear tending to support the burden, resting on the taxpayer, of establishing that the Commissioner erred in failing to apply them.' 282 U.S. at pages 366, 367, 51 S.Ct. at page 152, 75 L.Ed. 383.

It is argued on behalf of the Commissioner that the Court should overrule the Board by applying to this question rules of law laid down in decisions on the analogous problem raised by recovery of bad debts charged off without tax benefit in prior years. The court below accepted the argument. However, instead of affording a reason for overruling the Tax Court, the history of the bad debt recovery question illustrates the mischief of overruling the Tax Court in matters of tax accounting. Courts were persuaded to rule as matter of law that bad debt recoveries constitute taxable income, regardless of tax benefit from the charge-off.[40] The Tax Court had first made a similar holding,[41] but had come to hold to the contrary.[42] Substitution of the courts' rule for that of the Tax Court led to such hardships and inequities that the Treasury appealed to Congress to extend relief.[43] It did so.[44] The Government now argues that by extending legislative

---

[40] [fn 31] Commissioner v. United States & International Securities Corp., 3 Cir., 130 F.2d 894; Helvering v. State-Planters Bank & Trust Co., 4 Cir., 130 F.2d 44, 143 A.L.R. 333.

[41] [fn 32] Lakeview Trust & Savings Bank v. Commissioner, 27 B.T.A. 290.

[42] [fn 33] Central Loan & Investment Co. v. Commissioner, 39 B.T.A. 981; Citizens State Bank v. Commissioner, 46 B.T.A. 964.

[43] [fn 34] Mr. Randolph Paul, Tax Adviser to the Secretary of the Treasury, in a statement to the House Committee on Ways and Means said: 'The Secretary has pointed out that wartime rates make it imperative to eliminate as far as possible existing inequities which distort the tax burden of certain taxpayers. I should like to discuss the inequities which the Secretary mentioned, as well as a few additional hardships. * * *

'(c) Recoveries of bad debts and taxes.—If a taxpayer who has taken a bad debt deduction later receives payment of such debt, such payment must be included in his income even though he obtained no tax benefit from the

relief in bad debt cases Congress recognized that in the absence of specific exemption recoveries are taxable as income. We do not find that significance in the amendment. A specific statutory exception was necessary in bad debt cases only because the courts reversed the Tax Court and established as matter of law a 'theoretically proper' rule which distorted the taxpayer's income. Congress would hardly expect the courts to repeat the same error in another class of cases, as we would do were we to affirm in this case.[45]

The Government also suggests that 'If the tax benefit rule were judicially adopted the question would then arise of how it should be determined,' and the difficulties of determining tax benefits, it says, create 'an objection in itself to an attempt to adopt such a rule by judicial action.' We are not adopting any rule of tax benefits. We only hold that no statute or regulation having the force of one and no principle of law compels the Tax Court to find taxable income in a transaction where as matter of fact it found no economic gain and no use of the transaction to gain tax benefit. The error of the court below consisted of treating as a rule of law what we think is only a question of proper tax accounting.

There is some difference in the facts of these cases. In two of them the Tax Court sustained deficiencies because it found that the deductions in prior years had offset gross income for those years and therefore concluded that the recoveries must to that extent be treated as taxable gain.[46] The taxpayers object

---

deduction in the prior year. While this result is theoretically proper under our annual system of taxation, it may produce severe hardships in certain cases through a distortion of the taxpayer's real income. At the same time, any departure from our annual system of taxation always produces administrative difficulties which serve to impede the collection of taxes.

'It is believed that the hardships can be removed and the administrative difficulties kept to a minimum by excluding from income amounts received in payment of the debt to the extent that the deduction on account of the debt in the prior year did not produce a tax benefit. The troublesome question whether a benefit resulted should be determined pursuant to regulations prescribed by the Commissioner with the approval of the Secretary. It is also suggested that this treatment be extended to refunds of taxes previously deducted.' Hearings before Committee on Ways and Means on Revenue Revision of 1942, 77th Cong., 2d Sess., Vol. I, 80, 87-88.

[44] [fn 35] Revenue Act of 1942, s 116, 56 Stat. 798, 812, 26 U.S.C.A. Int.Rev.Acts.

[45] [fn 36] The question of whether a recovery is properly accounted for as income in the year received or should be related to a previous reported deduction without tax benefit is one with a long history and much conflict. It arises not only in case of recoveries of previously charged off bad debts and recoveries of the type we have here. It is also present in case of refund of taxes or cancellation of expenses or interest previously reported as accrued, adjustments of depreciation and depletion or amortization, and other similar situations.

[46] [fn 37] John V. Dobson v. Commissioner, 46 B.T.A. 770.

that this conclusion disregards certain exemptions and credits which would have been available to offset the increased gross income in the prior years, so that the deductions resulted in no tax savings. In determining whether the recoveries were taxable gain, however, the Tax Court was free to decide for itself what significance it would attach to the previous reduction of taxable income as contrasted with reduction of tax. The statute gives no inkling as to the correctness or incorrectness of the Tax Court's view, and we can find no compelling reason to substitute our judgment. In No. 47 the decision of the Tax Court was upheld by the court below, and in that case the judgment is affirmed. In Nos. 44, 45, and 46, the Court of Appeals reversed the Tax Court, and for the reasons stated its judgments in those cases are reversed.

Reversed.

NOTES AND QUESTIONS

1. Section 7482(a) reversed the result in *Dobson* in 1948. The current law is that courts of appeals shall defer to the Tax Court to the same extent they would defer to a Disctrict Court. *See* IRC § 7482(a)(1). This language means that instead of deferring to the Tax Court's factual and legal findings as *Dobson* held, courts of appeals defer only to the Tax Court's factual findings. Holdings on legal issues are reviewed *de novo*.
2. Why did the Eighth Circuit Court of Appeals reverse the Tax Court in *Dobson*?
3. Why did the courts of appeals fail to give due deference to the Tax Court prior to *Dobson*?

A major difference in post-trial procedures is appellate review. Cases in federal district court are appealed to the regional circuit court of appeals for that region. Court of Federal cases, because the court has nationwide jurisdiction, are appealed to the Federal Circuit instead of a regional court of appeals. Conveniently, the Federal Circuit and the Court of Federal Claims are in the same building, the Howard T. Markey National Courts Building.

Although the Tax Court has nationwide jurisdiction like the Court of Federal Claims, cases originating in Tax Court are appealed to the regional court of appeals. The way it works is that a party may appeal to the regional court of appeals that has venue. Venue is determined by where the taxpayer resided when the petition was filed. Even more interesting than where the appeal lies is the implications for the applicable law in the case for Tax Court cases, which is discussed next chapter.

6. Post-Litigation Issues

With two different types of civil cases and three forums as well as enforcement overlap with criminal cases, one would expect the parties to tax disputes to try to game the system. The res judicata doctrines—claim preclusion and issue preclusion—minimize such gaming by mediating between the different forums. Claim preclusion, sometimes referred to as a more specific res judicata, bars a case that has already been decided from being tried again in the same or another court. Issue preclusion, also known as collateral estoppel, bars the relitigation of identical issue in different cases.

In Latin, res judicata refers to a "thing decided." Under claim preclusion, the thing that has been decided is a claim or cause of action. Neither party, nor their privies, may raise new matters after a claim has already been resolved. This rule encourages all parties involved in resolving a claim to raise all matters that can be raised prior to a final judgment because otherwise the matters will be forfeited. For example, if a taxpayer sues the IRS in Tax Court over the Earned Income Tax Credit for the 2018 tax year and loses, the taxpayer may not then petition the Tax Court again for the same tax year to sue over a casualty loss. The taxpayer had the opportunity to bring up any other matters in the original case but failed to do so. All other claims merge into the original suit and are considered resolved.

Under issue preclusion, the thing that has been decided is a subsidiary issue in a case. A party may be estopped from relitigating an issue that was resolved in collateral litigation. For example, if the a taxpayer is convicted of tax evasion under section 7201, in a subsequent civil case the court need not decide whether the elements of the fraud penalty under section 6663 have been satisfied because the elements of the two sanctions are nearly the same. *See* Wright v. Commissioner, 84 T.C. 636 (1985) (holding that the taxpayer was not collaterally estopped from raising a civil fraud defense when his tax conviction was for tax perjury under section 7206 rather than evasion under section 7201).

The next case is the seminal case on successive claims and issues in the tax context.

COMMISSIONER v. SUNNEN
333 U.S. 591 (1948)
Supreme Court of the United States

Opinion
Mr. Justice MURPHY delivered the opinion of the Court.

The problem of the federal income tax consequences of intra-family assignments of income is brought into focus again by this case.

The stipulated facts concern the taxable years 1937 to 1941, inclusive, and may be summarized as follows:

The respondent taxpayer was an inventor-patentee and the president of the Sunnen Products Company, a corporation engaged in the manufacture and sale of patented grinding machines and other tools. He held 89% or 1,780 out of a total of 2,000 shares of the outstanding stock of the corporation. His wife held 200 shares, the vice-president held 18 shares and two others connected with the corporation held one share each. The corporation's board of directors consisted of five members, including the taxpayer and his wife. This board was elected annually by the stockholders. A vote of three directors was required to take binding action.

The taxpayer had entered into several non-exclusive agreements whereby the corporation was licensed to manufacture and sell various devices on which he had applied for patents.[47] In return, the corporation agreed to pay to the taxpayer a royalty equal to 10% of the gross sales price of the devices. These agreements did not require the corporation to manufacture and sell any particular number of devices; nor did they specify a minimum amount of royalties. Each party had the right to cancel the licenses, without liability, by giving the other party written notice of either six months or a year.[48] In the absence of cancellation, the agreements were to continue in force for ten years. The board of directors authorized the corporation to execute each of these contracts. No notices of cancellation were given. Two of the agreements were in effect throughout the taxable years 1937—1941, while the other two were in existence at all pertinent times after June 20, 1939.

The taxpayer at various times assigned to his wife all his right, title and interest in the various license contracts.[49] She was given exclusive title and power

---

[47] [fn 1] The various devices involved were as follows:

(1) A cylinder grinder. The taxpayer applied for a patent on Nov. 17, 1927, and was issued one on Dec. 4, 1934. The royalty agreement to manufacture and sell this device was dated Jan. 10, 1928. This agreement expired on Jan. 10, 1938; a renewal agreement in substantially the same terms was then executed for the balance of the life of the patent, which ends on Dec. 4, 1951.

(2) A pinhole grinder. The taxpayer applied for a patent on Dec. 4, 1931, and was issued one on June 13, 1933. The royalty agreement to manufacture and sell this device was dated Dec. 5, 1931.

(3) A crankshaft grinder. The taxpayer applied for a patent on May 22, 1939, and was issued one on May 6, 1941. The royalty agreement to manufacture and sell this device was dated June 20, 1939.

(4) Another crankshaft grinder. The taxpayer applied for a patent on Dec. 29, 1939. He assigned this application to his wife on Dec. 29, 1942, and she was issued a patent on Jan. 26, 1943. The royalty agreement to manufacture and sell this device was dated June 20, 1939.

The taxpayer remained the owner of the first three patents throughout the year 1941, and he remained the owner of the patent application on the fourth device throughout that year.

[48] [fn 2] Six months' notice was provided in the agreement dated Jan. 10, 1928, covering the cylinder grinder. The other three agreements provided for one year's notice of cancellation.

[49] [fn 3] On Jan. 8, 1929, the taxpayer assigned to his wife 'all my rights, title and interest in and to the Royalty Which shall accrue hereafter to me' upon the royalty contract of Jan. 10, 1928, with respect to the cylinder grinder device. Since the Commissioner of Internal Revenue raised some question as to the sufficiency and completeness of this assignment, the taxpayer executed a further

over the royalties accruing under these contracts. All the assignments were without consideration and were made as gifts to the wife, those occurring after 1932 being reported by the taxpayer for gift tax purposes. The corporation was notified of each assignment.

In 1937 the corporation, pursuant to this arrangement, paid the wife royalties in the amount of $4,881.35 on the license contract made in 1928; no other royalties on that contract were paid during the taxable years in question. The wife received royalties from other contracts totaling $15,518,68 in 1937, $17,318.80 in 1938, $25,243.77 in 1939, $50,492,50 in 1940, and $149,002.78 in 1941. She included all these payments in her income tax returns for those years, and the taxes she paid thereon have not been refunded.

Relying upon its own prior decision in Estate of Dodson v. Commissioner, 1 T.C. 416,[50] the Tax Court held that, with one exception, all the royalties paid to the wife from 1937 to 1941 were part of the taxable income of the taxpayer. 6 T.C. 431. The one exception concerned the royalties of $4,881.35 paid in 1937 under the 1928 agreement. In an earlier proceeding in 1935, the Board of Tax Appeals dealt with the taxpayer's income tax liability for the years 1929—1931; it concluded that he was not taxable on the royalties paid to his wife during those years under the 1928 license agreement. This prior determination by the Board caused the Tax Court to apply the principle of res judicata to bar a different result as to the royalties paid pursuant to the same agreement during 1937.

The Tax Court's decision was affirmed in part and reversed in part by the Eighth Circuit Court of Appeals. 161 F.2d 171. Approval was given to the Tax Court's application of the res judicata doctrine to exclude from the taxpayer's

---

assignment on Dec. 21, 1931. This second assignment confirmed the first one and stated further that his wife was assigned 'all of my right, title and interest in and to said royalty contract of January 10, 1928 * * * And I hereby state that the royalties accruing under said royalty contract have heretofore been and are hereafter the sole and exclusive property of the said Cornelia Sunnen (his wife), and hereby declare that said royalties shall be paid to the said Cornelia Sunnen or to her order, and that she shall have the sole right to collect, receive, receipt for, retain or sue for said royalties.'

'Assignments similar in form and substance to the assignment of Dec. 21, 1931, were made as to the other three royalty contracts.

[50] [fn 4] In the *Dodson* case, Dodson owned 51% of the stock of a corporation and his wife owned the other 49%. He was the owner of a formula and trade mark. Pursuant to a contract which he made with the corporation, the corporation was given the exclusive use of the formula and trade mark for 5 years, renewable for a like period. Dodson was to receive in return a royalty measured by a certain percentage of the net sales. He then assigned a one-half interest in the contract to his wife, retaining his full interest in the formula and trade mark. The Tax Court held that his dominant stock position permitted him to cancel or modify the contract at any time, thus rendering him taxable on the income flowing from his wife's share in the contract.

income the $4,881.35 in royalties paid in 1937 under the 1928 agreement. But to the extent that the taxpayer had been held taxable on royalties paid to his wife during the taxable years of 1937-1941, the decision was reversed on the theory that such payments were not income to him. Because of that conclusion, the Circuit Court of Appeals found it unnecessary to decide the taxpayer's additional claim that the res judicata doctrine applied as well to the other royalties (those accruing apart from the 1928 agreement) paid in the taxable years. We then brought the case here on certiorari, the Commissioner alleging that the result below conflicts with prior decisions of this Court.

If the doctrine of res judicata is properly applicable so that all the royalty payments made during 1937-1941 are governed by the prior decision of the Board of Tax Appeals, the case may be disposed of without reaching the merits of the controversy. We accordingly cast our attention initially on that possibility, one that has been explored by the Tax Court and that has been fully argued by the parties before us.

It is first necessary to understand something of the recognized meaning and scope of res judicata, a doctrine judicial in origin. The general rule of res judicata applies to repetitious suits involving the same cause of action. It rests upon considerations of economy of judicial time and public policy favoring the establishment of certainty in legal relations. The rule provides that when a court of competent jurisdiction has entered a final judgment on the merits of a cause of action, the parties to the suit and their privies are thereafter bound 'not only as to every matter which was offered and received to sustain or defeat the claim or demand, but as to any other admissible matter which might have been offered for that purpose.' Cromwell v. County of Sac, 94 U.S. 351, 352, 24 L.Ed. 195. The judgment puts an end to the cause of action, which cannot again be brought into litigation between the parties upon any ground whatever, absent fraud or some other factor invalidating the judgment. See von Moschzisker, 'Res Judicata,' 38 Yale L.J. 299; Restatement of the Law of Judgments, ss 47, 48.

But where the second action between the same parties is upon a different cause or demand, the principle of res judicata is applied much more narrowly. In this situation, the judgment in the prior action operates as an estoppel, not as to matters which might have been litigated and determined, but 'only as to those matters in issue or points controverted, upon the determination of which the finding or verdict was rendered.' Cromwell v. County of Sac, supra, 353 of 94 U.S. And see Russell v. Place, 94 U.S. 606, 24 L.Ed. 214; Southern Pacific R. Co. v. United States, 168 U.S. 1, 48, 18 S.Ct. 18, 27, 42 L.Ed. 355; Mercoid Corp. v. Mid-Continent Co., 320 U.S. 661, 671, 64 S.Ct. 268, 273, 88 L.Ed. 376. Since the cause of action involved in the second proceeding is not swallowed by the judgment in the prior suit, the parties are free to litigate points which were not at issue in the first proceeding, even though such points might have been tendered and decided at that time. But matters which were actually litigated and determined in the first proceeding cannot later be relitigated. Once a party has fought out a matter in litigation with the other party, he cannot later renew that duel. In this sense, res judicata is usually and more accurately referred to as estoppel by judgment, or collateral estoppel. See Restatement of the Law of Judgments, ss 68, 69, 70; Scott, 'Collateral Estoppel by Judgment,' 56 Harv.L.Rev. 1.

These same concepts are applicable in the federal income tax field. Income taxes are levied on an annual basis. Each year is the origin of a new liability and of a separate cause of action. Thus if a claim of liability or non-liability relating to a particular tax year is litigated, a judgment on the merits is res judicata as to any subsequent proceeding involving the same claim and the same tax year. But if the later proceeding is concerned with a similar or unlike claim relating to a different tax year, the prior judgment acts as a collateral estoppel only as to those matters in the second proceeding which were actually presented and determined in the first suit. Collateral estoppel operates, in other words, to relieve the government and the taxpayer of 'redundant litigation of the identical question of the statute's application to the taxpayer's status.' Tait v. Western Md. R. Co., 289 U.S. 620, 624, 53 S.Ct. 706, 707, 77 L.Ed. 1405.

But collateral estoppel is a doctrine capable of being applied so as to avoid an undue disparity in the impact of income tax liability. A taxpayer may secure a judicial determination of a particular tax matter, a matter which may recur without substantial variation for some years thereafter. But a subsequent modification of the significant facts or a change or development in the controlling legal principles may make that determination obsolete or erroneous, at least for future purposes. If such a determination is then perpetuated each succeeding year as to the taxpayer involved in the original litigation, he is accorded a tax treatment different from that given to other taxpayers of the same class. As a result, there are inequalities in the administration of the revenue laws, discriminatory distinctions in tax liability, and a fertile basis for litigious confusion. Compare United States v. Stone & Downer Co., 274 U.S. 225, 235, 236, 47 S.Ct. 616, 71 L.Ed. 1013. Such consequences, however, are neither necessitated nor justified by the principle of collateral estoppel. That principle is designed to prevent repetitious lawsuits over matters which have once been decided and which have remained substantially static, factually and legally. It is not meant to create vested rights in decisions that have become obsolete or erroneous with time, thereby causing inequities among taxpayers.

And so where two cases involve income taxes in different taxable years, collateral estoppel must be used with its limitations carefully in mind so as to avoid injustice. It must be confined to situations where the matter raised in the second suit is identical in all respects with that decided in the first proceeding and where the controlling facts and applicable legal rules remain unchanged. Tait v. Western Md. R. Co., supra. If the legal matters determined in the earlier case differ from those raised in the second case, collateral estoppel has no bearing on the situation. See Travelers Ins. Co. v. Commissioner, 2 Cir., 161 F.2d 93. And where the situation is vitally altered between the time of the first judgment and the second, the prior determination is not conclusive. See State Farm Ins. Co. v. Duel, 324 U.S. 154, 162, 65 S.Ct. 573, 577, 89 L.Ed. 812; 2 Freeman on Judgments, 5th Ed. 1925, s 713. As demonstrated by Blair v. Commissioner, 300

U.S. 5, 9, 57 S.Ct. 330, 331, 81 L.Ed. 465, a judicial declaration intervening between the two proceedings may so change the legal atmosphere as to render the rule of collateral estoppel inapplicable.[51] But the intervening decision need not necessarily be that of a state court, as it was in the *Blair* case. While such a state court decision may be considered as having changed the facts for federal tax litigation purposes, a modification or growth in legal principles as enunciated in intervening decisions of this Court may also effect a significant change in the situation. Tax inequality can result as readily from neglecting legal modulations by this Court as from disregarding factual changes wrought by state courts. In either event, the supervening decision cannot justly be ignored by blind reliance upon the rule of collateral estoppel. Henricksen v. Seward, 9 Cir., 135 F.2d 986, 988, 989, 150 A.L.R. 1; Pelham Hall Co. v. Hassett, 1 Cir., 147 63, 68, 69; Commissioner v. Arundel-Brooks Concrete Corp., 4 Cir., 152 F.2d 225, 227, 162 A.L.R. 1200; Corrigan v. Commissioner, 6 Cir., 155 F.2d 164, 165; and see West Coast Life Ins. Co. v. Merced Irr. Dist., 9 Cir., 114 F.2d 654, 661, 662; contra: Commissioner v. Western Union Tel. Co., 2 Cir., 141 F.2d 774, 778. It naturally follows that an interposed alternation in the pertinent statutory provisions or Treasury regulations can make the use of that rule unwarranted. Tait v. Western Md. R. Co., supra, 625 of 289 U.S., 53 S.Ct. 706.[52]

Of course, where a question of fact essential to the judgment is actually litigated and determined in the first tax proceeding, the parties are bound by that determination in a subsequent proceeding even though the cause of action is different. See Evergreens v. Nunan, 2 Cir., 141 F.2d 927. And if the very same facts and no others are involved in the second case, a case relating to a different tax year, the prior judgment will be conclusive as to the same legal issues which appear, assuming no intervening doctrinal change. But if the relevant facts in the two cases are separable, even though they be similar or identical, collateral estoppel does not govern the legal issues which recur in the second case.[53] Thus the second proceeding may involve an instrument or transaction identical with, but in a form separable from, the one dealt with in the first proceeding. In that situation, a court is free in the second proceeding to make an independent examination of the legal matters at issue. It may then reach a different result or, if consistency in decision is considered just and desirable, reliance may be placed

---

[51] [fn 5] See also Henricksen v. Seward, 9 Cir., 135 F.2d 986; Monteith Bros. Co. v. United States, 7 Cir., 142 F.2d 139; Pelham Hall Co. v. Hassett, 1 Cir., 147 F.2d 63; Commissioner v. Arundel-Brooks Concrete Corp., 4 Cir., 152 F.2d 225; Corrigan v. Commissioner, 6 Cir., 155 F.2d 164. Compare Grandview Dairy v. Jones, 2 Cir., 157 F.2d 5.

[52] [fn 6] And see Commissioner v. Security-First Nat. Bank, 9 Cir., 148 F.2d 937.

[53] [fn 7] Stoddard v. Commissioner, 2 Cir., 141 F.2d 76, 80; Campana Corporation v. Harrison, 7 Cir., 135 F.2d 334; Engineer's Club of Philadelphia v. United States, 42 F.Supp. 182, 95 Ct.Cl. 92.

upon the ordinary rule of stare decisis. Before a party can invoke the collateral estoppel doctrine in these circumstances, the legal matter raised in the second proceeding must involve the same set of events or documents and the same bundle of legal principles that contributed to the rendering of the first judgment. Tait v. Western Maryland R. Co., supra. And see Griswold, 'Res Judicata in Federal Tax Cases,' 46 Yale L.J. 1320; Paul and Zimet, 'Res Judicata in Federal Taxation,' appearing in Paul, Selected Studies in Federal Taxation, 2d series, 1938, p. 104.

It is readily apparent in this case that the royalty payments growing out of the license contracts which were not involved in the earlier action before the Board of Tax Appeals and which concerned different tax years are free from the effects of the collateral estoppel doctrine. That is true even though those contracts are identical in all important respects with the 1928 contract, the only one that was before the Board, and even though the issue as to those contracts is the same as that raised by the 1928 contract. For income tax purposes, what is decided as to one contract is not conclusive as to any other contract which is not then in issue, however similar or identical it may be. In this respect, the instant case thus differs vitally from Tait v. Western Md. R. Co., supra, where the two proceedings involved the same instruments and the same surrounding facts.

A more difficult problem is posed as to the $4,881.35 in royalties paid to the taxpayer's wife in 1937 under the 1928 contract. Here there is complete identity of facts, issues and parties as between the earlier Board proceeding and the instant one. The Commissioner claims, however, that legal principles developed in various intervening decisions of this Court have made plain the error of the Board's conclusion in the earlier proceeding, thus creating a situation like that involved in Blair v. Commissioner, supra. This change in the legal picture is said to have been brought about by such cases as Helvering v. Clifford, 309 U.S. 331, 60 S.Ct. 554, 84 L.Ed. 788; Helvering v. Horst, 311 U.S. 112, 61 S.Ct. 144, 85 L.Ed. 75, 131 A.L.R. 655; Helvering v. Eubank, 311 U.S. 122, 61 S.Ct. 149, 85 L.Ed. 81; Harrison v. Schaffner, 312 U.S. 579, 61 S.Ct. 759, 85 L.Ed. 1055; Commissioner v. Tower, 327 U.S. 280, 66 S.Ct. 532, 90 L.Ed. 670; and Lusthaus v. Commissioner, 327 U.S. 293, 66 S.Ct. 539, 90 L.Ed. 679. These cases all imposed income tax liability on transferors who had assigned or transferred various forms of income to others within their family groups, although none specifically related to the assignment of patent license contracts between members of the same family. It must therefore be determined whether this *Clifford-Horst* line of cases represents an intervening legal development which is pertinent to the problem raised by the assignment of the 1928 agreement and which makes manifest the error of the result reached in 1935 by the Board. If that is the situation, the doctrine of collateral estoppel becomes inapplicable. A difference result is then permissible as to the royalties paid in 1937 under the agreement in question. But to determine whether the *Clifford-Horst* series of cases has such an effect on the instant proceeding necessarily requires inquiry into the merits of the controversy growing out of the various contract assignments from the taxpayer to his wife. To that controversy we now turn.[54]

Had the taxpayer retained the various license contracts and assigned to his wife the right to receive the royalty payments accruing thereunder, such payments would clearly have been taxable income to him. It has long been established that the mere assignment of the right to receive income is not enough to insulate the assignor from income tax liability. Lucas v. Earl, 281 U.S. 111, 50 S.Ct. 241, 74 L.Ed. 731; Burnet v. Leininger, 285 U.S. 136, 52 S.Ct. 345, 76 L.Ed. 665. As long as the assignor actually earns the income or is otherwise the source of the right to receive and enjoy the income, he remains taxable. The problem here is whether any different result follows because the taxpayer assigned the underlying contracts to his wife in addition to giving her the right to receive the royalty payments.

It is the taxpayer's contention that the license contracts rather than the patents and the patent applications were the ultimate source of the royalty payments and constituted income-producing property, the assignment of which freed the taxpayer from further income tax liability. We deem it unnecessary, however, to meet that contention in this case. It is not enough to trace income to the property which is its true source, a matter which may become more metaphysical than legal. Nor is the tax problem with which we are concerned necessarily answered by the fact that such property, if it can be properly identified, has been assigned. The crucial question remains whether the assignor retains sufficient power and control over the assigned property or over receipt of the income to make it reasonable to treat him as the recipient of the income for tax purposes. As was said in Corliss v. Bowers, 281 U.S. 376, 378, 50 S.Ct. 336, 74 L.Ed. 916; 'taxation is not so much concerned with the refinements of title as it is with actual command over the property taxed—the actual benefit for which the tax is paid.'

---

[54] [fn 8] The pertinent statutory provisions are of little help to the matter in issue. Section 22(a) of the Revenue Act of 1936, 49 Stat. 1648, and s 22(a) of the Revenue Act of 1938, 52 Stat. 447, cover the taxable years in question. Those sections, which are identical with the current s 22(a) of the Internal Revenue Code, 26 U.S.C.A.Int.Rev.Code, s 22(a), define 'gross income' to include 'gains, profits, and income derived from salaries, wages, or compensation for personal service * * *, of whatever kind and in whatever form paid, or from professions, vocations, trades, businesses, commerce, or sales, or dealings in property, whether real or personal, growing out of the ownership or use of or interest in such property; also from interest, rent, dividends, securities, or the transaction of any business carried on for gain or profit, or for gains or profits and income derived from any source whatever.' See also Art. 22(a)-1 of Treasury Regulations 94, promulgated under the 1936 Act; Art. 22(a)-1 of Treasury Regulations 101, promulgated under the 1938 Act; and s 19.22(a)-1 of Treasury Regulations 103, promulgated under the Internal Revenue Code.

It is in the realm of intra-family assignments and transfers that the *Clifford-Horst* line of cases has peculiar applicability. While specifically relating to short-term family trusts, the *Clifford* case makes clear that where the parties to a transfer are members of the same family group special scrutiny is necessary 'lest what is in reality but one economic unit be multiplied into two or more by devices which, though valid under state law, are not conclusive so far as s 22(a) is concerned.' 309 U.S. at page 335, 60 S.Ct. at page 556, 84 L.Ed. 788. That decision points out various kinds of documented and direct benefits which, if retained by the transferor of property, may cause him to remain taxable on the income therefrom. And it also recognizes that the fact that the parties are intimately related, causing the income to remain within the family group, may make the transfer give rise to informal and indirect benefits to the transferor so as to make it even more clear that it is just to tax him. Even more directly pertinent, however, is the *Horst* case, together with the accompanying *Eubank* case. See 2 Mertens, Law of Federal Income Taxation (1942), ss 18.02, 18.14. It was there held that the control of the receipt of income, which causes an assignor of property to remain taxable, is not limited to situations where the assignee's realization of income depends upon the future rendition of services by the assignor. See Lucas v. Earl, supra; Burnet v. Leininger, supra. Such may also be the case where the assignor controls the receipt of income through acts or services preceding the transfer. Or it may be evidenced by the possibility of some subsequent act by the assignor, or some failure to act, causing the income or property to revert to him. Moreover, the Horst case recognizes that the assignor may realize income if he controls the disposition of that which he could have received himself and diverts payment from himself to the assignee as a means of procuring the satisfaction of his wants, the receipt of income by the assignee merely being the fruition of the assignor's economic gain.

In Harrison v. Schaffner, supra, 312 U.S. at page 582, 61 S.Ct. at page 761, 85 L.Ed. 1055, it was again emphasized that 'one vested with the right to receive income did not escape the tax by any kind of anticipatory arrangement, however skillfully devised, by which he procures payment of it to another, since, by the exercise of his power to command the income, he enjoys the benefit of the income on which the tax is laid.' And it was also noted that 'Even though the gift of income be in form accomplished by the temporary disposition of the donor's property which produces the income, the donor retaining every other substantial interest in it, we have not allowed the form to obscure the reality.' 312 U.S. at page 583, 61 S.Ct. at page 762, 85 L.Ed. 1055. Commissioner v. Tower, supra, and its companion case, Lusthaus v. Commissioner, supra, reiterated the various principles laid down in the earlier decisions and applied them to income arising from family partnerships.

The principles which have thus been recognized and developed by the *Clifford* and *Horst* cases, and those following them, are directly applicable to the transfer of patent license contracts between members of the same family. They are guideposts for those who seek to determine in a particular instance whether such an assignor retains sufficient control over the assigned contracts or over the receipt of income by the assignee to make it fair to impose income tax liability on him.

Moreover, the clarification and growth of these principles through the *Clifford-Horst* line of cases constitute, in our opinion, a sufficient change in the legal climate to render inapplicable in the instant proceeding, the doctrine of collateral estoppel relative to the assignment of the 1928 contract. True, these cases did not originate the concept that an assignor is taxable if he retains control over the assigned property or power to defeat the receipt of income by the assignee. But they gave much added emphasis and substance to that concept, making it more suited to meet the 'attenuated subtleties' created by taxpayers. So substantial was the amplification of this concept as to justify a reconsideration of earlier Tax Court decisions reached without the benefit of the expanded notions, decisions which are now sought to be perpetuated regardless of their present correctness. Thus in the earlier litigation in 1935, the Board of Tax Appeals was unable to bring to bear on the assignment of the 1928 contract the full breadth of the ideas enunciated in the *Clifford-Horst* series of cases. And, as we shall see, a proper application of the principles as there developed might well have produced a different result, such as was reached by the Tax Court in this case in regard to the assignments of the other contracts. Under those circumstances collateral estoppel should not have been used by the Tax Court in the instant proceeding to perpetuate the 1935 viewpoint of the assignment.

The initial determination of whether the assignment of the various contracts rendered the taxpayer immune from income tax liability was one to be made by the Tax Court. That is the agency designated by law to find and examine the facts and to draw conclusions as to whether a particular assignment left the assignor with substantial control over the assigned property or the income which accrues to the assignee. And it is well established that its decision is to be respected on appeal if firmly grounded in the evidence and if consistent with the law. Commissioner v. Scottish American Co., 323 U.S. 119, 65 S.Ct. 169, 89 L.Ed. 113; Dobson v. Commissioner, 320 U.S. 489, 60 S.Ct. 239, 88 L.Ed. 248. That is the standard, therefore, for measuring the propriety of the Tax Court's decision on the merits of the controversy in this case.

The facts relative to the assignments of the contracts are undisputed. As to the legal foundation of the Tax Court's judgment on the tax consequences of the assignments, we are unable to say that its inferences and conclusions from those facts are unreasonable in the light of the pertinent statutory or administrative provisions or that they are inconsistent with any of the principles enunciated in the *Clifford-Horst* line of cases. Indeed, due regard for those principles leads one inescapably to the Tax Court's result. The taxpayer's purported assignment to his wife of the various license contracts may properly be said to have left him with something more than a memory. He retained very substantial interests in the contracts themselves, as well as power to control the payment of royalties to his wife, thereby satisfying the various criteria of taxability set forth in the *Clifford-Horst* group of cases. That fact is demonstrated by the following considerations:

(1) As president, director and owner of 89% of the stock of the corporation, the taxpayer remained in a position to exercise extensive control over the license contracts after assigning them to his wife. The contracts all provided that either party might cancel without liability upon giving the required notice. This gave the taxpayer, in his dominant position in the corporation, power to procure the cancellation of the contracts in their entirety. That power was nonetheless substantial because the taxpayer had but one of the three directors' votes necessary to sanction such action by the corporation. Should a majority of the directors prove unamenable to his desires, the frustration would last no longer than the date of the next annual election of directors by the stockholders, an election which the taxpayer could control by reason of his extensive stock holdings. The wife, as assignee and as a party to contracts expressly terminable by the corporation without liability, could not prevent cancellation provided that the necessary notice was given.

And it is not necessary to assume that such cancellation would amount to a fraud on the corporation, a fraud which could be enjoined or otherwise prevented. Cancellation conceivably could occur because the taxpayer and his corporation were ready to make new license contracts on terms more favorable to the corporation, in which case no fraud would necessarily be present. All that we are concerned with here is the power to procure cancellation, not with the possibility that such power might be abused. And once it is evident that such power exists, the conclusion is unavoidable that the taxpayer retained a substantial interest in the license contracts which he assigned.

(2) The taxpayer's controlling position in the corporation also permitted him to regulate the amount of royalties payable to his wife. The contracts specified no minimum royalties and did not bind the corporation to manufacture and sell any particular number of devices. Hence, by controlling the production and sales policies of the corporation, the taxpayer was able to increase or lower the royalties; or he could stop those royalties completely by eliminating the manufacture of the devices covered by the royalties without cancelling the contracts.

(3) The taxpayer remained the owner of the patents and the patent applications. Since the licenses which he gave the corporation were non-exclusive in nature, there was nothing to prevent him from licensing other firms to exploit his patents, thereby diverting some or all of the royalties from his wife.

(4) There is absent any indication that the transfer of the contracts effected any substantial change in the taxpayer's economic status. Despite the assignments, the license contracts and the royalty payments accruing thereunder remained within the taxpayer's intimate family group. He was able to enjoy, at least indirectly, the benefits received by his wife. And when that fact is added to the legal controls which he retained over the contracts and the royalties, it can fairly be said that the taxpayer retained the substance of all the rights which he had prior to the assignments. See Helvering v. Clifford, supra, 309 U.S. at pages 335, 336, 60 S.Ct. at pages 556, 557, 84 L.Ed. 788.

There factors make reasonable the Tax Court's conclusion that the assignments of the license contracts merely involved a transfer of the right to receive income rather than a complete disposition of all the taxpayer's interest in the contracts and the royalties. The existence of the taxpayer's power to terminate those contracts and to regulate the amount of the royalties rendered ineffective for tax purposes his attempt to dispose of the contracts and royalties. The transactions were simply a reallocation of income within the family group, a reallocation which did not shift the incidence of income tax liability.

The judgment below must therefore be reversed and the case remanded for such further proceedings as may be necessary in light of this opinion.

Reversed.

Mr. Justice FRANKFURTER and Mr. Justice JACKSON believe the judgment of the Tax Court is based on substantial evidence and is consistent with the law, and would affirm that judgment for reasons stated in Dobson v. Commissioner, 320 U.S. 489, 64 S.Ct. 239, 88 L.Ed. 248, and Commissioner v. Scottish American Co., 323 U.S. 119, 65 S.Ct. 169, 89 L.Ed. 113.

NOTES AND QUESTIONS

1. The relevant events of this case occurred before married couples could benefit by filing joint tax returns. Congress created the joint filing option in 1938, but they did not provide the beneficial rate structure for married couples until 1948. The holdings regarding res judicata, however, still apply.
2. What is the difference between collateral estoppel and res judicata?

There are some differences in the forums after the litigation has ended. Both differences exist because of the timing of the trial with respect to assessment and payment. A Tax Court case takes place before any payment has been made so interest accrues on the tax liability if the taxpayer owes any after the final decision has been reached. The taxpayer generally owes no interest after a refund suit because the liability has already been paid before the suit. If the government owes the taxpayer a refund, however, interest will likely be owed as well.

After a refund case, if the taxpayer loses, there is nothing to collect because the taxpayer has already paid. In Tax Court, however, if the Tax Court determines the taxpayer owes a deficiency in tax then the IRS may assess the tax and collect it if the taxpayer fails to pay the tax. The IRS's tax collection procedures are discussed in Chapters 5 and 6.

B. Bankruptcy Court

Another forum for tax litigation exists, but it is not one that is chosen. Taxpayers usually end up in a tax dispute in Bankruptcy Court involuntarily. Generally, financial problems other than taxes force the taxpayer into bankruptcy, but tax obligations can also push a taxpayer into bankruptcy.

Filing a petition in Bankruptcy Court has two effects. First, it creates a bankruptcy estate of the debtor's assets under the control of the bankruptcy court. *See* 11 U.S.C. §541(a). Second, it enjoins all further collection action by way of automatic stay. 11 U.S.C. §362(a)(6). It should be noted that statutes of limitations are suspended while under consideration of bankruptcy court.

The IRS may issue a statutory notice of deficiency even if a bankruptcy petition has been filed. If the IRS issues a deficiency notice, the Bankruptcy Court may let the taxpayer file a Tax Court petition or determine the liability itself. *See* 11 U.S.C. §362(d). The Bankruptcy Court is the only court other than the Tax Court that can hear deficiency cases.

The Bankruptcy Court also has jurisdiction over refund claims. If there is an overpayment, a trustee will succeed the debtor's claim. The trustee may request the refund from the IRS if a refund claim has not already been made. If the IRS fails to respond within 120 days, the Bankruptcy Court has jurisdiction to determine the claim. Bankruptcy Court cases are appealed to federal district court or a bankruptcy appellate panel.

CHAPTER 17

UNITED STATES TAX COURT LITIGATION

A. Tax Court Background

At any given time, approximately 98% of the tax cases in litigation are docketed in Tax Court. This high percentage makes the Tax Court the principal forum for judicial review of tax disputes with the IRS. The reasons the Tax Court is the primary choice for tax litigation were discussed in the previous chapter. First and foremost is cost. A taxpayer may sue in Tax Court prior to paying any amounts the IRS believes is due. Moreover, litigating in Tax Court is less burdensome on the taxpayer in terms of discovery.

The Tax Court's building sits in Washington, D.C.[1] Tax Court judges, however, travel to approximately 70 cities around the country to hear cases. Although judges travel to these locations for calendar calls on specific dates, the parties may request a special session for a trial on a different date or at the Tax Court building in Washington, D.C.

There are three categories of Tax Court judges. The first category is the member that has been appointed by the President, approved by the Senate, and has the authority to vote on conference cases before the Court. The Code provides positions for 19 such members that serve 15-year terms. The members elect a chief judge every two years. The second category is the Special Trial Judge. Special Trial Judges are appointed by the Tax Court's Chief Judge and serve at the pleasure of the Chief Judge. They have similar responsibilities as magistrate judges in federal district courts. The third category is Senior Judge. Senior judges are former voting members that have been recalled. These judges

---

[1] The Tax Court building's architecture is "breathtaking." Few have marveled at its beauty.

no longer vote on conference cases before the Court, but have similar responsibilities as members.

As discussed in the last chapter, all of the current judges have sufficient experience to be considered tax experts. In the Tax Court's history, the President has appointed judges to the Tax Court that were not tax experts. It is the author's understanding that these appointments did not work out well.

The Tax Court issues opinions with varying levels of precedential value. The opinion with the highest precedential value is an opinion reviewed by the members in conference. This is known as a conference opinion or reviewed opinion. Of slightly less precedential value is a division opinion. Both reviewed opinions and division opinions are officially reported in the U.S. Tax Court Reports (thus designated "T.C." in the title block). Tax Court judges also issue "Memorandum" opinions (designated "T.C. Memo." in the title block). Memorandum opinions are not officially reported but are easily accessible. They are not officially reported because they are of limited precedential value. In general, the Tax Court does not cite to memorandum opinions as precedent. *See* Dunaway v. Commissioner, 124 T.C. 80, 87 (2005). The Court does, however, often refer to memorandum opinions, and on occasion makes precedent-like references to them.[2] The least precedential opinion is the "Summary" opinion. The Tax Court issues summary opinions in "small" cases, a designation discussed later in this chapter. Under section 7463(b), an opinion issued under the small case provisions "shall not be reviewed in any other court and shall not be treated as a precedent for any other case." Thus, not only do they lack precedential value, summary opinions are also not subject to appeal.

To gain admission to practice before the Tax Court, an individual must either have a license to practice law in any state or have passed the four-hour examination the Tax Court conducts for non-attorneys. Few people pass the examination. In 2015, there were approximately 250 non-attorney members and 70,000 attorney members. *See* Nathan Richman, *A Peek Behind the Curtain at the Tax Court Exam for Non-Attorneys*, 148 TAX NOTES 1180 (2015).

None of the above information answers the question, what is the Tax Court? As discussed in the last chapter, the Tax Court's predecessor was the Board of Tax Appeals (BTA). The BTA was an independent administrative agency. In 1969, Congress designated the Tax Court an Article I court of record. Congress has not designated which government branch the Tax Court resides in. The Tax Court answers more of the question in the next case.

---

[2] Professor Andy Grewal argues that the Tax Court cites memorandum opinions as precedent, which creates problems because the Tax Court's position is that the opinions are not precedential. To resolve this issue, Professor Grewal argues the distinction between memorandum opinions and official opinions should be officially abandoned. *See* Amandeep S. Grewal, *The Un-Precedented Tax Court*, 101 IOWA L. REV. 2065, 2078 (2016) (describing the Tax Court's apparent approach as follows: "Memo opinions are nonprecedential, except when they are not.").

BATTAT v. COMMISSIONER
148 T.C. 32 (2017)
United States Tax Court

COLVIN, Judge:

This deficiency case[3] is before the Court on petitioners' motion to disqualify all Tax Court Judges (filed as a motion for recusal of Judge) and to declare section 7443(f)[4] unconstitutional. For reasons discussed below we will deny petitioners' motion.

In the Background section, we describe: (A) procedures for the removal of Tax Court Judges; (B) statutory provisions governing the Tax Court and the Supreme Court's opinion in Freytag v. Commissioner, 501 U.S. 868, 891 (1991); (C) caselaw relating to the jurisprudence and status of the Tax Court; and (D) Kuretski v. Commissioner, 755 F.3d 929, 943–945 (D.C. Cir. 2014), aff'g T.C. Memo. 2012–262, and the congressional response to *Kuretski*. In the Discussion section, we conclude that: (A) under the Rule of Necessity, it is proper for a Tax Court Judge to rule on petitioners' motion; (B) procedures for the removal of Tax Court Judges for cause do not violate separation of powers principles; and (C) petitioners are not entitled to a remedy on the basis of an appearance of bias. Finally, at Part D we provide a conclusion.

BACKGROUND

Petitioners resided in Florida when they filed the petition.

A. Procedures for the Removal of Tax Court Judges

Section 7443(f) authorizes the President to remove Judges of the Tax Court "after notice and opportunity for public hearing, for inefficiency, neglect of duty, or malfeasance in office, but for no other cause". The predecessor of section 7443(f) was first enacted as part of the Revenue Act of 1924 (1924 Act), ch. 234, sec. 900(b), 43 Stat. at 336–337.[5]

In 2015 Congress extended the judicial conduct and disability procedures of 28 U.S.C secs. 351–364 (2012), to Judges of the Tax Court. Consolidated Appropriations Act, 2016 (2015 Act), Pub. L. No. 114–113, sec. 431, 129 Stat. at 3125 (2015) (adding section 7466). Under section 7466 and 28 U.S.C. sec. 355, if the Judicial Conference of the United States (Judicial Conference)[6] determines

---

[3] [fn 1] Respondent determined a deficiency in petitioners' income tax for 2008 of $1,722,175 and an addition to tax under sec. 6651(a)(1) and an accuracy-related penalty under sec. 6662(a) of $82,337 and $344,435, respectively.

[4] [fn 2] Unless otherwise indicated, section references are to the Internal Revenue Code, as amended. Rule references are to the Tax Court Rules of Practice and Procedure.

[5] [fn 3] In 1926 the Presidential removal provision was amended to include the phrase "after notice and opportunity for public hearing". Revenue Act of 1926 (1926 Act), ch. 27, sec. 1000, 44 Stat. at 105–106.

[6] [fn 4] The Judicial Conference of the United States is the national policymaking body for the Federal courts. 28 U.S.C. sec. 331 (2012)

that there are grounds for removal of a Tax Court Judge under section 7443(f), then the Judicial Conference shall transmit the determination to the President. See Part B, infra p. 22.

B. Statutory Provisions Relating to the Establishment and Status of the Tax Court

1. 1924 to 1968

Congress created the Board of Tax Appeals in 1924 to permit taxpayers to challenge determinations made by the Internal Revenue Service (IRS) of their tax liabilities before payment.[7] The Revenue Act of 1924 provided that "[t]here is hereby established a board to be known as the Board of Tax Appeals" and "[t]he Board shall be *an independent agency in the executive branch of the Government.*" Revenue Act of 1924, ch. 234, sec. 900(a), (k), 43 Stat. at 336, 338 (emphasis added).

In 1926 Congress made various statutory changes with respect to the Board of Tax Appeals, but the statute continued to provide that the Board of Tax Appeals is *"an independent agency in the Executive Branch of the Government."* Revenue Act of 1926, ch. 27, sec. 900, 44 Stat. at 105–106 (emphasis added). In 1939 "[t]he Board of Tax Appeals * * * shall be continued as an *independent agency in the Executive Branch the of Government"* (emphasis added) was codified in the Internal Revenue Code of 1939, ch. 2, sec. 1100, 53 Stat. at 158. In 1942 Congress changed the name of the Board of Tax Appeals to the "Tax Court of the United States." After amendment by the Revenue Act of 1942, ch. 619, sec. 504(a), 56 Stat. at 957, section 1100 of the 1939 Code provided as follows:

> The Board of Tax Appeals * * * shall be continued *as an independent agency in the Executive Branch of the Government*. The Board shall be known as the Tax Court of the United States and the members thereof shall be known as the presiding judge and the judges of the Tax Court of the United States. [Revenue Act of 1942, ch. 619, sec. 504(a), 56 Stat. at 957; emphasis added.]

That provision was also included in section 7441 of the Internal Revenue Code of 1954, which provided as follows:

> The Board of Tax Appeals shall be continued as *an independent agency in the Executive Branch of the Government*, and shall be known as the Tax Court of the United States. The members thereof shall be known as the chief judge and the judges of the Tax Court." [Internal Revenue Code of 1954, ch. 76, sec. 7441, 68A Stat. at 879; emphasis added.]

In Dobson v. Commissioner, 320 U.S. 489 (1944), the Supreme Court held that, because the Tax Court was (at that time) an administrative body within the

---

[7] [fn 5] Before 1924 taxpayers who wished to contest a determination made by the Bureau of Internal Revenue (now the IRS) were required to pay the tax assessed and then file suit against the Government for a refund. See Flora v. United States, 362 U.S. 145, 151–152 (1960).

executive branch, decisions of the Tax Court on questions of fact were not reviewable if supported by any evidence in the record. *Dobson* was legislatively overturned in 1948 by an amendment to section 7482(a)(1) requiring the U.S. Courts of Appeals "to review * * * the Tax Court [decisions] * * * in the same manner and to the same extent as decisions of the district courts in civil actions tried without a jury". Act of June 25, 1948, ch. 646, sec. 36, 62 Stat. at 991.[8]

2. Tax Reform Act of 1969

In the Tax Reform Act of 1969 (1969 Act), Pub. L. No. 91–172, 83 Stat. 487, Congress "transformed" the Tax Court, Freytag v. Commissioner, 501 U.S. at 890–891, through two amendments to section 7441. First, Congress amended section 7441 to designate the Tax Court as an Article I court. As a result, section 7441 provided: "There is hereby established, under Article I of the Constitution of the United States, a court of record to be known as the United States Tax Court. The members of the Tax Court shall be the chief judge and the judges of the Tax Court." 1969 Act sec. 951, 83 Stat. at 730. Second, Congress amended section 7441 to delete the designation of the Tax Court as an "independent agency in the Executive Branch of the Government".[9]

In its report accompanying the 1969 Act,[10] the Senate Committee on Finance said:

---

[8] [fn 6] It is now well established that the Tax Court's findings of fact (like those of the U.S. District Courts) are accepted by the Courts of Appeals unless clearly erroneous. Dreicer v. Commissioner, 665 F.2d 1292, 1296 n.36 (D.C. Cir. 1981) (citing sec. 7482(a) and Commissioner v. Duberstein, 363 U.S. 278, 291 n.13 (1960)), rev'g T.C. Memo. 1979–395.

[9] The statute as it existed until 1969, providing that the Tax Court was part of the executive branch, was in keeping with the general understanding of the branch location of independent agencies. See, e.g., FMC v. S.C. State Ports Auth., 535 U.S. 743, 773 (2002) (Breyer, J., dissenting) (independent agencies are "appropriately considered to be part of the Executive Branch").

[10] [fn 8] Despite having observed that the meaning of a statute does not turn on the intent of individual lawmakers but "only on what intent has been enacted into law through the constitutionally defined channels of bicameralism and presentment", Teva Pharms. USA, Inc. v. Sandoz, Inc., 574 U.S. ——, ——, 135 S. Ct. 831, 845 (2015), the Supreme Court continues to refer to legislative history, see, e.g., Ariz.State Legislature v. Ariz. Indep. Redistricting Comm'n, 576 U.S. – ——, ——, 135 S. Ct. 2652, 2669 (2015); United States v. Kwai Fun Wong, 575 U.S. ——, ——, 135 S. Ct. 1625, 1632 (2015); Yates v. United States, 574 U.S. —— -, ——, 135 S. Ct. 1074, 1084 (2015); Warger v. Shauers, 574 U.S. ——, ——, 135 S. Ct. 521, 527 (2014); Samantar v. Yousef, 560 U.S. 305, 316 n.9 (2010) ("Our precedents demonstrate that the Court's practice of utilizing legislative history reaches well into its past. * * * 'We suspect that the practice will likewise reach well into the future'." (quoting Wis. Pub. Intervenor v. Mortier, 501 U.S. 597, 611–612 n.4 (1991))).

Since the Tax Court has only judicial duties, the committee believes it is anomalous to continue to classify it with quasi-judicial executive agencies that have rulemaking and investigatory functions. * * * [I]ts constitutional status as an executive agency, no matter how independent, raises questions in the minds of some as to whether it is appropriate for one executive agency [the pre–1969 tribunal] to be sitting in judgment on the determinations of another executive agency [the IRS].

* * *

The amendments are also concerned with making the Tax Court an Article I court rather than an executive agency and expanding its powers accordingly.
* * *

[S. Rept. No. 91–552, supra at 302–303, 1969–3 C.B. at 614–615; H.R. Conf. Rept. No. 91–782 (1969), 1969–3 C.B. 644, 645 ("The conference substitute * * * follows the Senate amendment.").]

Thus, the Senate Committee on Finance intended that the Tax Court no longer be classified "with" executive branch agencies. S. Rept. No. 91–552, supra at 302, 1969–3 C.B. at 614.[11]

In 1969 Congress also amended section 7456 to provide Tax Court Judges with the "quintessentially judicial" power, Freytag v. Commissioner, 501 U.S. at 891, to punish contempt of court by fine or imprisonment and provided that the Tax Court has "such assistance in the carrying out of its lawful writ, process, order, rule, decree, or command" as is available to Article III judges,[12] 1969 Act sec. 956, 83 Stat. at 732 (amending section 7456); see 18 U.S.C. sec. 401 (2012).

---

[11] [fn 9] The Tax Reform Act of 1969 (1969 Act), Pub. L. No. 91–172, sec. 961, 83 Stat. at 735–736, also provides:

The United States Tax Court established under the amendment made by section 951 is a continuation of the Tax Court of the United States as it existed prior to the date of enactment of this Act * * * no loss of rights or powers, interruption of jurisdiction, or prejudice to matters pending in the Tax Court of the United States before the date of enactment of this Act shall result from the enactment of this Act.

See also H.R. Conf. Rept. No. 91–782, at 341 (1969), 1969–3 C.B. 644, 682. This provision prevented inconvenience to the parties and the public by ensuring the continuity of cases pending before the Tax Court. It did not diminish the constitutional significance of the establishment of the Tax Court under Article I. Burns, Stix Friedman & Co. v. Commissioner, 57 T.C. 392, 395 (1971).

[12] [fn 10] U.S. Const. art. III, sec. 1 provides:

The judicial Power of the United States, shall be vested in one supreme Court, and in such inferior Courts as the Congress may from time to time ordain and establish. The Judges, both of the supreme and inferior Courts, shall hold their Offices during good Behaviour, and shall, at stated Times, receive for their

As stated supra pp. 7–8, in the 1969 Act Congress deleted the designation of the Tax Court as an "independent agency in the Executive Branch of the Government". The only amendment needed if Congress had intended to establish the Tax Court as an Article I court located in the executive branch would have been deletion of the words "as an independent agency". If only those words had been deleted, section 7441 would have said the Tax Court "shall be continued * * * in the Executive Branch of the Government". But that is not what Congress did. Congress also deleted from section 7441 the words "in the Executive Branch of the Government". That additional change would have been superfluous if Congress had intended for the Tax Court to remain within the executive branch. The deletion of words is properly considered in determining the meaning of statutes. See, e.g., United States v. Wells, 519 U.S. 482, 492–493 (1997).[13] Thus, the 1969 Act can fairly be read to mean that Congress intended to terminate the Tax Court's previously well-understood placement in the executive branch. Soon after the enactment of the 1969 Act, the Tax Court faced a challenge to the constitutionality of its exercise of judicial powers as an Article I court. In upholding the authority of the Tax Court as provided by the 1969 Act, we said:

> It is clear from the statutory language and the Senate Committee report * * * that Congress removed the Tax Court from the Executive Branch and established it as an article I court primarily for the purpose of recognizing its status as a judicial body and disposing of any problems that its status as an executive agency sitting in judgment on another executive agency might pose. [Burns, Stix Friedman & Co. v. Commissioner, 57 T.C. 392, 395 (1971); citation omitted.]

Thus, soon after the repeal by the 1969 Act of the statute designating the Tax Court as within the executive branch, we observed that, under the 1969 Act, the Tax Court was no longer within the executive branch.

3. Freytag v. Commissioner

In Freytag v. Commissioner, 501 U.S. at 887–888, the Supreme Court upheld the authority of the Chief Judge of the Tax Court under section 7443A(a) to appoint Special Trial Judges[14] because the Chief Judge of the Tax Court is the head of one of the "Courts of Law" and is not one of the "Heads of Departments" for purposes of the Appointments Clause under Article II.[15] In Freytag, the

---

Services, a Compensation, which shall not be diminished during their Continuance in Office.

[13] [fn 11] In United States v. Wells, 519 U.S. 482, 493 (1977), the Supreme Court gave effect to the deletion by Congress of the word "materiality" from the statute at issue, reasoning that "[t]he most likely inference in these circumstances is that Congress deliberately dropped the term 'materiality' " so as to no longer make materiality a required element of the statute at issue.

[14] [fn 12] The authority of Special Trial Judges in many respects resembles that of magistrate judges. Sec. 7443A.

[15] [fn 13] The Constitution provides:

Supreme Court observed that the Tax Court exercises a portion of the judicial power of the United States, does not exercise "executive, legislative, or administrative" power, "remains independent of the Executive and Legislative Branches", and closely resembles U.S. District Courts in its function and role in the Federal judicial scheme. Id. at 890–892. After concluding that the Tax Court can be a court of law under the Appointments Clause, id. at 888, the Supreme Court went on to "define the constitutional status of the Tax Court and its role in the constitutional scheme" by discussing in detail the statutes establishing the Tax Court:

> Having concluded that an Article I court, which exercises judicial power, can be a "Cour[t] of Law" within the meaning of the Appointments Clause, we now examine the Tax Court functions to define its constitutional status and its role in the constitutional scheme. See *Williams*, 289 U.S. at 563–567. The Tax Court exercises judicial, rather than executive, legislative, or administrative, power. It was established by Congress to interpret and apply the Internal Revenue Code in disputes between taxpayers and the Government. By resolving these disputes, the court exercises a portion of the judicial power of the United States.
>
> The Tax Court exercises judicial power to the exclusion of any other function. It is neither advocate nor rulemaker. As an adjudicative body, it construes statutes passed by Congress and regulations promulgated by the Internal Revenue Service. It does not make political decisions.
>
> The Tax Court's function and role in the federal judicial scheme closely resemble those of the federal district courts, which indisputably are "Courts of Law." Furthermore, the Tax Court exercises its judicial power in much the same way as the federal district courts exercise theirs. It has authority to punish contempts by fine or imprisonment, 26 U.S.C. § 7456(c); to grant certain injunctive relief, § 6213(a); to order the Secretary of the Treasury to refund an overpayment determined by the court, § 6512(b)(2); and to subpoena and examine witnesses, order production of documents, and administer oaths, § 7456(a). All these powers are quintessentially judicial in nature.
>
> The Tax Court remains independent of the Executive and Legislative Branches. Its decisions are not subject to review by either the Congress or the President. Nor has Congress made Tax Court decisions subject to review in

---

[The President] * * * shall nominate, and by and with the Advice and Consent of the Senate, shall appoint Ambassadors, other public Ministers and Consuls, Judges of the Supreme Court, and all other Officers of the United States, whose Appointments are not herein otherwise provided for, and which shall be established by Law: but the Congress may by Law vest the Appointment of such inferior Officers, as they think proper, in the President alone, in the Courts of Law, or in the Heads of Departments. [U.S. Const. art. II, sec. 2, cl. 2.]

the federal district courts. Rather, like the judgments of the district courts, the decisions of the Tax Court are appealable only to the regional United States courts of appeals, with ultimate review in this Court.[16] The courts of appeals, moreover, review those decisions "in the same manner and to the same extent as decisions of the district courts in civil actions tried without a jury. § 7482(a). This standard of review contrasts with the standard applied to agency rulemaking by the courts of appeals under § 10(e) of the Administrative Procedure Act, 5 U.S.C. § 706(2)(A). See Motor Vehicle Mfrs. Assn. v. State Farm Mut. Automobile Ins. Co., 463 U.S. 29, 43–44 (1983).

The Tax Court's exclusively judicial role distinguishes it from other non-Article III tribunals that perform multiple functions and provides the limit on the diffusion of appointment power that the Constitution demands. * * *

[Freytag v. Commissioner, 501 U.S. at 890–892.]

The Supreme Court rejected the Commissioner's characterization of the Tax Court as an entity other than a court. Id. at 887–888 ("Treating the Tax Court as * * * [an executive branch] 'Department' * * * would defy * * * the clear intent of Congress to transform the Tax Court into an Article I legislative court. The Tax Court is not * * * [an executive] 'Departmen[t].'").

The Supreme Court's analysis of the Tax Court in *Freytag* may be contrasted with its analysis of the Court of Appeals for the Armed Forces (until 1994 known as the U.S. Court of Military Appeals) in Edmond v. United States, 520 U.S. 651 (1997). Both the U.S. Court of Appeals for the Armed Forces and the Tax Court are courts of record established under Article I, sec. 7441, 10 U.S.C. sec. 941 (2012), and the judges of both of those courts are subject to removal for cause by the President, 10 U.S.C. sec. 942(c); sec. 7443(f). However, differences in the statutes governing those two Courts led the Supreme Court in *Edmond* to conclude that the Court of Military Appeals for the Armed Forces is within the executive branch and in *Freytag* to conclude that the Tax Court is independent of

---

[16] Congress has recently reaffirmed this point. Sec. 7482(b)(1)(F), enacted by the Consolidated Appropriations Act, 2016 (2015 Act), Pub. L. No. 114–113, div. Q, sec. 423, 129 Stat. at 3123 (2015), provides that spousal relief cases under sec. 6015 and collection cases under secs. 6320 and 6330 are appealable to the U.S. Court of Appeals for the circuit in which an individual resides. The enactment of sec. 7482(b)(1)(F) reaffirms application of the general rule that Tax Court cases are appealable to the various Courts of Appeals with respect to spousal relief and collection cases, which are relatively new areas of Tax Court jurisdiction enacted in 1998. Internal Revenue Service Restructuring and Reform Act of 1998 (RRA 1998), Pub. L. No. 105–206, secs. 3201 (spousal relief), 3401 (collection cases), 112 Stat. at 735–738, 746–749. This amendment prospectively changes the result in Byers v. Commissioner, 740 F.3d 668 (D.C. Cir. 2014), aff'g T.C. Memo. 2012–27, which had held that collection cases are appealable to the U.S. Court of Appeals for the District of Columbia Circuit.

the executive branch.[17] First, under 10 U.S.C. sec. 941, "for administrative purposes" the Court of Appeals for the Armed Forces is, by statute, in the executive branch, specifically, the Department of Defense.[18] *Edmond*, 520 U.S. at 664 n.2. In contrast, the Tax Court's statutory link to the executive branch was repealed by the 1969 Act.[19]

Second, 10 U.S.C. sec. 946 (2012) requires judges of the Court of Appeals for the Armed Forces to meet annually with the Judge Advocates General and two members of the public appointed by the Secretary of Defense to "survey the operation" of the military justice system. *Edmond*, 520 U.S. at 664 n.2. This contrasts with the Tax Court, which "exercises judicial power to the exclusion of any other function", Freytag v. Commissioner, 501 U.S. at 891, and which has no statutory mandate to survey the operation of the IRS or any of its offices.[20] These statutory differences led the Supreme Court to conclude that the Tax Court is

---

[17] [fn 15] Cf. Kuretski v. Commissioner, 755 F.3d 929, 944 (D.C. Cir. 2014) ("[T]he constitutional status of the Tax Court mirrors that of the Court of Appeals for the Armed Forces. The statutes establishing the status of the two courts precisely parallel one another").

[18] [fn 16] Congress made it clear that it did not intend for this phrase to undermine the judicial nature of the Court of Appeals for the Armed Forces. The House report accompanying the U.S. Court of Military Appeals Establishment Act states the following:

One of the purposes of this bill is to make it abundantly clear in the law that the Court of Military Appeals is a court, although it is a court under article I of the Constitution. There has been some claim that the court, having been put under the Department of Defense for administrative purposes, is in effect an administrative agency. If it had such status, it would not be able to question any of the provisions of the Manual for Courts–Martial since the manual had been promulgated by Presidential order. The bill makes it clear that the Court of Military Appeals is a court and does have the power to question any provision of the manual or any executive regulation or action as freely as though it were a court constituted under Article III of the Constitution. [H.R. Rept. No. 90–1480, at 2 (1968), 1968 U.S.C.C.A.N. 2053, 2054; in substantial accord S. Rept. No. 90–806, at 1–2 (1968).]

[19] [fn 17] We also note that sec. 7441 (as amended in 2015, after release of the opinion of the Court of Appeals in *Kuretski*) provides that the Tax Court is independent of the executive branch, and, in contrast to administration by the executive branch, sec. 7470 (also enacted in 2015) authorizes the Tax Court to exercise the managerial, administrative, and financial authorities provided for the Article III courts.

[20] [fn 18] Although not noted by the Supreme Court in *Edmond*, the statute establishing the Court of Appeals for the Armed Forces requires that not more than three judges of that court be from the same political party. See 10 U.S.C. sec. 942(b)(3) (2012). No similar provision applies to the appointment of Judges of the Tax Court.

independent of the executive branch and the Court of Military Appeals for the Armed Forces is within the executive branch.

4. Other Statutory Changes

The Ethics Reform Act of 1989, Pub. L. No. 101–194, sec. 601(a), 103 Stat. at 1760, 1761, provides that the Judicial Conference of the United States (Judicial Conference) is the supervising ethics authority for "officers and employees of the judicial branch". Tax Court Judges are included in the definitions of "judges" and "judicial officers". Id. sec. 202, 103 Stat. at 1724, 1742. The Judicial Conference is the supervising ethics authority for Tax Court Judges and employees.[21]

From 2006 to 2015 several provisions were enacted which further distance the Tax Court from any association with the executive branch and bolster the Tax Court's "quintessentially judicial" powers and design. Freytag v. Commissioner, 501 U.S. at 890. In 2006 section 6214 was amended to permit the Tax Court to apply the doctrine of equitable recoupment[22] to the same extent that it may be applied in Federal civil tax cases by the U.S. District Courts or the U.S. Court of Claims. Pension Protection Act of 2006, Pub. L. No. 109–280, sec. 858, 120 Stat. at 1020; S. Rept. No. 109–336, at 97 (2006).

Before 2006 section 1043 provided special rules for recognition of gain on the sale of property which would present a conflict of interest to "officer[s] or employee[s] of the executive branch of the Federal Government". In 2006 Congress amended section 1043 to apply to judicial officers, including Article III judges and "judges of the * * * Tax Court". Tax Relief and Health Care Act of 2006, Pub. L. No. 109–432, sec. 418(b), 120 Stat. at 2966. In 2008 Congress included Tax Court Judges in the definition of "Federal judges" in order to provide protection against false liens or encumbrances to Tax Court Judges. Court Security Improvement Act of 2007, Pub. L. No. 110–177, sec. 201(a), 121 Stat. at 2535–2536. Also in 2008 Congress expanded the duties of the U.S.

---

[21] [fn 19] In 1985 the Tax Court formally adopted the Code of Conduct for United States Judges, thus confirming the widely held understanding that the Code of Conduct applies to Tax Court Judges. See Harold Dubroff & Brant J. Hellwig, The United States Tax Court: An Historical Analysis 239 (2d ed., Government Publishing Office 2014) (1979), https://www.ustaxcourt.gov/book/Dubroff _Hellwig.pdf. The oath of office for Judges of this Court, by Tax Court practice, is identical to the oath for Article III judges, i.e., a combination of the constitutional oath, see 5 U.S.C. sec. 3331 (2012), and the oath for judges, see 28 U.S.C. sec. 453 (2012).

[22] [fn 20] Equitable recoupment is a judicially created doctrine that in certain circumstances allows a litigant to avoid the bar of an expired statutory limitations period. Bull v. United States, 295 U.S. 247 (1935). In the tax context the doctrine prevents the inconsistent tax treatment of a single transaction, item, or event affecting the same taxpayer or a sufficiently related taxpayer. Menard, Inc. v. Commissioner, 130 T.C. 54, 62 (2008).

Marshals Service to include providing security for and enforcing orders of the Tax Court. Id. secs. 101 and 102, 121 Stat. at 2534–2535.[23]

In 2011 section 7471(a) was amended to authorize the Tax Court to establish a personnel system similar to the personnel system for employees of Article III courts. Act of Jan. 4, 2011, Pub. L. No. 111–366, sec. 1(a), 124 Stat. at 4063. Section 7471(a)(4) provides in pertinent part that "[t]o the maximum extent feasible, the Tax Court shall compensate employees at rates consistent with those for employees holding comparable positions in courts established under Article III of the Constitution of the United States." Under the 2011 amendment, the Tax Court's personnel system shall provide that "any individual who would be a preference eligible in the executive branch" will be given preference "in a manner and to an extent consistent with preference accorded to preference eligibles in the executive branch." Sec. 7471(a)(10)(C). Section 7471(a)(10)(C) would be superfluous if the Tax Court were in the executive branch.

The 2015 Act[24] added several provisions applicable to the Tax Court and relevant here. First, section 7453 was amended to provide that "the proceedings of the Tax Court and its divisions shall be conducted in accordance with * * * the Federal Rules of Evidence." 2015 Act, div. Q, sec. 425, 129 Stat. at 3125. As a result of the 2015 Act, the Tax Court, which has applied the Federal Rules of Evidence since their enactment in 1975,[25] see, e.g., Conti v. Commissioner, 99 T.C. 370, 373 (1992), aff'd and remanded, 39 F.3d 658 (6th Cir. 1994), will follow the Federal Rules of Evidence as applied by the U.S. Court of Appeals to which a case is appealable, see Golsen v. Commissioner, 54 T.C. 742 (1970), aff'd, 445 F.2d 985 (10th Cir. 1971).[26]

---

[23] [fn 21] After the 2008 amendment, 28 U.S.C. sec. 566(a) (2012) provides: "It is the primary role and mission of the United States Marshals Service to provide for the security and to obey, execute, and enforce all orders of the United States District Courts, the United States Courts of Appeals, the Court of International Trade, and the United States Tax Court, as provided by law."

[24] [fn 22] The 2015 Act includes without change the provisions of S. 903, 114th Cong. (2015) ("Improve Access and Administration of the United States Tax Court"), reported by the Senate Finance Committee on April 14, 2015 (S. Rept. No. 114–14 (2015)). The provisions of S. 903 were introduced in the House of Representatives without change as tit. II, subtit. C, of the Tax Increase Prevention and Real Estate Investment Act of 2015, by Ways and Means Committee Chairman Brady on December 7, 2015, and were enacted with the 2015 Act.

[25] [fn 23] The Federal Rules of Evidence are considered to be enacted like any statute. Daubert v. Merrell Dow Pharm., Inc., 509 U.S. 579, 587 (1993).

[26] [fn 24] Before amendment in 2015, sec. 7453, first enacted in the 1926 Act, ch. 27, sec. 907, 44 Stat. at 107, required the Tax Court to apply the rules of evidence applicable in bench trials in the U.S. District Court for the District of Columbia.

Second, section 7470 provides that "the Tax Court may exercise, for purposes of management, administration and expenditure of funds of the Court, the authorities provided for such purposes by any provision of law * * * to a court of the United States" as defined in 28 U.S.C. sec. 451 (2012), i.e., the Supreme Court, the U.S. District Courts, the U.S. Courts of Appeals, and the Court of International Trade. 2015 Act, div. Q, sec. 432, 129 Stat. at 3126. Third, section 7470A authorizes the Tax Court to hold judicial conferences and to collect reasonable fees related to those conferences. Id. This authority parallels authorities provided to the U.S. Courts of Appeals by 28 U.S.C. sec. 333 (2012). Fourth, section 7473 extends to the Tax Court authority for handling fees similar to that provided to U.S. District Courts. 2015 Act, div. Q, sec. 432, 129 Stat. at 3126.[27]

Finally, section 7466[28] makes applicable to Tax Court Judges the judicial conduct and judicial disability procedures established by 28 U.S.C. secs. 351–364 (2012). As a part of these procedures, if the Judicial Conference of the United States (Judicial Conference) determines that there are grounds for removal of a Tax Court Judge under section 7443(f), then the Judicial Conference "shall so certify and transmit the determination and the record of proceedings" to the President. Sec. 7466(b); 28 U.S.C. sec. 355.[29]

Section 7466 provides several powers to the Tax Court identical to powers provided to Article III courts, including the powers to (1) issue subpoenas in connection with conduct hearings, see 28 U.S.C. sec. 356(a); (2) punish noncompliance with those subpoenas by contempt, see id. sec. 332(d)(2); (3) exercise the authority provided to Article III courts under 28 U.S.C. sec. 1821 (2012); (4) pay the fees and allowances described in that section, see sec. 7466(a)(1); and (5) award reimbursement for reasonable expenses, see 28 U.S.C. sec. 361.

---

[27] [fn 25] Certain fees paid to U.S. District Courts are deposited into a special fund of the Treasury to be available to offset funds appropriated for the operation and maintenance of those courts. 28 U.S.C. secs. 1914(a), 1931 (2012).

[28] [fn 26] Sec. 7466 was effective June 15, 2016. Rules implementing sec. 7466 by the Tax Court were adopted on June 14, 2016. U.S. Tax Court, Rules for Judicial Conduct and Disability Proceedings for the United States Tax Court, http://www.ustaxcourt.gov/rules/judicial_misconduct_or_disability/jcd_rules.pdf. Title 28 U.S.C. sec. 363 (2012) provides that those provisions are applicable to judges of the Courts of Appeals, the U.S. District Courts, the bankruptcy courts, the Court of Federal Claims, and to magistrate judges. The Court of Appeals for Veterans Claims is also subject to those provisions. 38 U.S.C. sec. 7253(g) (2012).

[29] [fn 27] Similarly, under 28 U.S.C. sec. 355, under certain circumstances the Judicial Conference shall certify and transmit to the House of Representatives the determination and the record of proceedings where impeachment may be warranted.

The trend in the evolution of the Tax Court's governing statutes from 1969 to 2015 is clear: Congress has continued to provide authority and design to the Tax Court more like those of other Federal courts and to distance the Tax Court from any operational or structural similarity to agencies within the executive branch.

C. Caselaw Relating to the Jurisprudence and Status of the Tax Court

The case or controversy requirement under Article III presumptively applies in the Tax Court. Antolick v. Commissioner, 422 Fed.Appx. 859, 860–861 (11th Cir. 2011); Charlotte's Office Boutique, Inc. v. Commissioner, 425 F.3d 1203, 1211 n.7 (9th Cir. 2005) ("[L]imitations imposed upon Article III courts, such as the existence of an actual case or controversy, have been presumptively applied to the Tax Court."), aff'g 121 T.C. 89 (2003); D'Andrea v. Commissioner, 263 F.2d 904, 906 (D.C. Cir. 1959); Anthony v. Commissioner, 66 T.C. 367, 368–370 (1976), aff'd without published opinion, 566 F.2d 1168 (3d Cir. 1977). Because the Tax Court is not an Article III court, application of case or controversy principles to the Tax Court results from caselaw, not from constitutional mandate. Baranowicz v. Commissioner, 432 F.3d 972, 975 (9th Cir. 2005) (stating that as an Article I court, the Tax Court is not fully constrained by the case or controversy limitation in Article III); Orum v. Commissioner, 412 F.3d 819, 821 (7th Cir. 2005), aff'g 123 T.C. 1 (2004).

The Tax Court has jurisdiction to decide constitutional disputes arising in cases over which it has jurisdiction. Estate of Brandon v. Commissioner, 828 F.2d 493, 499 (8th Cir. 1987) (remanding the case to the Tax Court to consider the constitutionality of an Arkansas dower statute), rev'g 86 T.C. 327 (1986), remanded to Estate of Brandon v. Commissioner, 91 T.C. 829, 835 (1988) (holding a gender-based Arkansas statute unconstitutional in the light of, for example, Frontiero v. Richardson, 411 U.S. 677 (1973)); Rager v. Commissioner, 775 F.2d 1081, 1083 (9th Cir. 1985) ("[W]e have often upheld Tax Court decisions which were based on a constitutional inquiry."), aff'g T.C. Memo. 1984–563; see also Crawford v. Commissioner, 266 F.3d 1120, 1122–1123 (9th Cir. 2001) (deciding a separation of powers issue relating to Special Trial Judges), aff'g T.C. Memo. 1999–361; Wiggins v. Commissioner, 904 F.2d 311, 314 (5th Cir. 1990) (holding retroactive application of a statute constitutional), aff'g 92 T.C. 869, 871–872 (1989).

Tax Court opinions are subject to stare decisis. Smith v. Commissioner, 926 F.2d 1470, 1479 (6th Cir. 1991) ("We are not unmindful of the heavy burden placed upon the tax court by the doctrine of stare decisis and that any decision to depart from the doctrine requires 'special justification.' "), aff'g 91 T.C. 1049 (1988); see also Estate of Maxwell v. Commissioner, 3 F.3d 591, 599 (2d Cir. 1993) (Walker, J., dissenting) ("It is well established that the Tax Court is governed by the doctrine of stare decisis. * * * Indeed, the doctrine applies with special force in the tax context, given the important reliance interests involved." (the majority in Estate of Maxwell did not dispute this point)), aff'g 98 T.C. 594 (1992); Sec. State Bank v. Commissioner, 111 T.C. 210, 213–214 (1998), aff'd, 214 F.3d 1254 (10th Cir. 2000); Hesselink v. Commissioner, 97 T.C. 94, 99–100 (1991). This well-established feature of American courts, see, e.g., Hilton v. S.C.

Pub. Rys. Comm'n, 502 U.S. 197, 202 (1991) ("Time and time again, this Court has recognized that 'the doctrine of stare decisis is of fundamental importance to the rule of law.' * * * [W]e will not depart from the doctrine of stare decisis without some compelling justification." (quoting Welch v. Tex. Dep't of Highways & Pub. Transp., 483 U.S. 468, 494 (1987))), contrasts with the less than certain state of the law applicable to administrative agencies. Courts of Appeals have differed on whether the doctrine of stare decisis applies to administrative decisions. See James E. Moliterno, "The Administrative Judiciary's Independence Myth", 41 Wake Forest L. Rev. 1191, 1198 (2006). Compare Butler Cty. Mem'l Hosp. v. Heckler, 780 F.2d 352, 355–356 n.3 (3d Cir. 1985) (recognizing agency's right to "change course"), and Courier Post Pub. Co. v. FCC, 104 F.2d 213, 218 (D.C. Cir. 1939) (holding the policy of the Commission expressed in decided cases "is not a controlling factor upon the Commission"), with Teamsters Local Union No. 455 v. NLRB, 765 F.3d 1198, 1204 (10th Cir. 2014) (holding an administrative agency "may not * * * depart from a prior policy sub silentio or simply disregard rules that are still on the books" (quoting FCC v. Fox Television Stations, Inc., 556 U.S. 502, 515 (2009))), and Mendez–Barrera v. Holder, 602 F.3d 21, 26 (1st Cir. 2010) ("An administrative agency must respect its own precedent, and cannot change it arbitrarily and without explanation, from case to case.").

The Tax Court is not subject to the Freedom of Information Act, which by its terms does not apply to "the courts of the United States".[30] 5 U.S.C. sec. 552(f)(1) (2012) (incorporating the definition of "agency" in 5 U.S.C. sec. 551(1) (2012)); Megibow v. Clerk of the U.S. Tax Court, 432 F.3d 387 (2d Cir. 2005); Byers v. U.S. Tax Court, No.15–1605 (RC) (D.D.C. Sept. 30, 2016); Ostheimer v. Chumbley, 498 F. Supp. 890, 892 (D. Mont. 1980) (same), aff'd without published opinion, 746 F.2d 1487 (9th Cir. 1984).

Tax Court Judges have immunity from liability for damages for acts committed within their judicial jurisdiction to the same extent as Article III judges and State court judges instead of the more narrow form of immunity provided for executive branch officials. Chisum v. Colvin, 276 F. Supp. 2d 1, 3 (D.D.C. 2003) (Tax Court Judges) (citing Mireles v. Waco, 502 U.S. 9, 9–10 (1991) (per curiam) (State court judges), and Pierson v. Ray, 386 U.S. 547, 553–554 (1967) (municipal judges)). In contrast, executive branch employees have limited immunity from lawsuits challenging actions taken in the course of their official duties, such as torts committed within the scope of their employment under the Federal Tort Claims Act, 28 U.S.C. sec. 2679 (2012).

D. Kuretski v. Commissioner and Section 7441 as Amended in 2015

---

[30] [fn 28] Tit. 5 U.S.C. sec. 551 (2012) provides in pertinent part as follows: "For the purpose of this subchapter—(1) 'agency' means each authority of the Government of the United States, whether or not it is within or subject to review by another agency, but does not include—(A) the Congress, (B) the courts of the United States".

In Kuretski v. Commissioner, 755 F.3d at 943–945, the taxpayer contended that the President's authority under section 7443(f) to remove Tax Court Judges for inefficiency, neglect of duty, or malfeasance in office is unconstitutional because it violates separation of powers principles.[31] The Court of Appeals held that the Tax Court is within the executive branch, making it unnecessary to decide whether authority for Presidential removal of Tax Court Judges violates separation of powers principles. Id. at 938–942. However, the following year Congress amended section 7441 by adding the sentence emphasized below:

> There is hereby established, under article I of the Constitution of the United States, a court of record to be known as the United States Tax Court. The Tax Court is not an agency of, and shall be independent of, the executive branch of the Government. The members thereof shall be known as the chief judge and the judges of the Tax Court. [2015 Act, div. Q, sec. 441, 129 Stat. at 3126; emphasis added.]

In the explanation of the change contained in the report of the Senate Finance Committee, the Committee said it was—

> concerned that statements in Kuretski v. Commissioner may lead the public to question the independence of the Tax Court, especially in relation to the Department of Treasury or the Internal Revenue Service. The Committee wishes to remove any uncertainty caused by Kuretski v. Commissioner, and to ensure that there is no appearance of institutional bias. [S. Rept. No. 114–14, at 10, accompanying S. 903.]

The Court of Appeals in Kuretski v. Commissioner, 755 F.3d at 932, said the Tax Court "exercises executive authority as part of the Executive Branch." In contrast, the Supreme Court in Freytag v. Commissioner, 501 U.S. at 891, said the Tax Court exercises exclusively judicial power and does not exercise executive, legislative, or administrative power.[32] The Court of Appeals in Kuretski v. Commissioner, 755 F.3d at 943–944, made no constitutional

---

[31] [fn 29] In Kuretski v. Commissioner, 755 F.3d at 938, the Court of Appeals said the taxpayer in that case contended that the Tax Court exercises judicial power under Article III. It is not apparent to us that the taxpayers in that case made that obviously incorrect argument. In fact, in their answering brief at p. 11 the Kuretskis state that they "do not challenge the Tax Court Judges' non-Article III status".

[32] [fn 30] The Court of Appeals in Kuretski v. Commissioner, 755 F.3d at 944, cited several examples of independent agencies which "sit in 'independent' judgment of other executive actors." For instance, the Merit Systems Protection Board sits in judgment of other agencies, 5 U.S.C. sec. 1204(a), as does the Federal Labor Relations Authority, 5 U.S.C. sec. 7105(g); the Occupational Safety and Health Review Commission sits in judgment of the Secretary of Labor, 29 U.S.C. sec. 659(c); and the Postal Regulatory Commission sits in judgment of Postal Service, 39 C.F.R. secs. 3001 to 3018.

distinction between the Tax Court and independent executive branch agencies even though, unlike the Tax Court, independent executive branch agencies exercise executive power under Article II of the Constitution. See also Humphrey's Ex'r v. United States, 295 U.S. 602, 629–630 (1935); PHH Corp. v. Consumer Fin. Prot. Bureau, No. 15–1177, slip op. at 4 (D.C. Cir. Oct. 11, 2016). In addition, independent executive branch agencies perform substantial nonadjudicatory functions, e.g., rulemaking, while the Tax Court "exercises judicial power to the exclusion of any other function." Freytag v. Commissioner, 501 U.S. at 891.[33]

In considering the relationship between independent executive branch agencies and other executive branch agencies, the Court of Appeals in Kuretski v. Commissioner, 755 F.3d at 944, said that Congress may allow independent executive branch agencies "a measure of independence from other executive actors". Presumably, "a measure of independence" means less than total independence. If the Tax Court were in the executive branch, the relevant "other executive actor" would be the IRS. Surely any taxpayer would find it repugnant if the Tax Court, which by congressional design is the Federal court which decides the most taxpayer disputes with the IRS, has only some nebulous "measure of independence" from the IRS.

According to the specific text added to section 7441 in 2015, particularly in contrast to the opinion of the Court of Appeals in *Kuretski*, it appears that in 2015 Congress emphasized the Supreme Court's characterization of the Tax Court in *Freytag* and Congress' own characterization of the Tax Court in the legislative history of the 1969 Act as independent of the executive branch. Specifically, by providing that the Tax Court is not an executive agency and is independent of the executive branch, the 2015 amendment to section 7441 in substance codifies the following language in the 1969 Finance Committee report, i.e.: "The committee believes it is anomalous to continue to classify * * * [the Tax Court] with quasi-judicial executive agencies". The 2015 amendment to section 7441 also codifies a clause from the Supreme Court's opinion in Freytag v. Commissioner, 501 U.S. at 891, i.e., "[t]he Tax Court remains independent of the Executive * * * Branch[es]".

---

[33] [fn 31] Unlike the statutes establishing the Tax Court, statutes establishing independent agencies in the executive branch typically require that appointments to their policymaking (i.e., quasi-legislative) governing bodies be balanced between the two major political parties. See, e.g., statutes establishing the Federal Trade Commission, 15 U.S.C. sec. 41 (2012); the Equal Employment Opportunity Commission, 42 U.S.C. sec. 2000e–4 (2012); the Federal Communications Commission, 47 U.S.C. sec. 154(b)(5) (2012); the Securities and Exchange Commission, 15 U.S.C. sec. 78d(a) (2012); and the Federal Election Commission, 52 U.S.C. sec. 30106 (2012); see also PHH Corp. v. Consumer Fin. Prot. Bureau, No. 15–1177 (D.C. Cir. Oct. 11, 2016).

DISCUSSION

Like the taxpayers in *Kuretski*, petitioners contend that the Tax Court is not within the executive branch and that the President's authority under section 7443(f)(1) violates separation of powers principles. For reasons discussed below, we will deny petitioners' motion.

A. Disqualification Is Not Required

Petitioners seek rulings that all Tax Court Judges must recuse themselves from deciding any further cases because, according to petitioners, section 7443(f) is unconstitutional. We disagree here that recusal is required and below at Part B that section 7443(f) is unconstitutional.

Courts have occasionally been presented with issues in which all judges of the court have a conflict of interest or are alleged to be biased, and, because it is necessary for the work of the court to proceed, have not recused themselves. See United States v. Will, 449 U.S. 200, 213–216 (1980) (judicial salaries) ("The Rule of Necessity has been consistently applied in this country in both state and federal courts."); Evans v. Gore, 253 U.S. 245 (1920) (taxation of judicial incomes), overruled by United States v. Hatter, 532 U.S. 557, 571 (2001); Guinn v. Finesilver, 48 F.3d 1232 (10th Cir. 1995); In re Complaint of Doe, 2 F.3d 308 (8th Cir. 1993) (recusal not required where a party sues judges who have heard that party's case); In re N.M. Nat. Gas Antitrust Litig., 620 F.2d 794, 795 (10th Cir. 1980); In re Va. Elec. Power Co., 539 F.2d 357, 360 (4th Cir. 1976) (utility rates); Cupp v. Commissioner, 65 T.C. 68, 86–87 (1975) (recusal not required in a Tax Court case brought by a taxpayer who previously sued all Tax Court Judges in other courts), aff'd without published opinion, 559 F.2d 1207 (3d Cir. 1977).

The Rule of Necessity has been expressed through a maxim of law that where all are disqualified, none are disqualified. *Evans*, 253 U.S. at 252–255. We conclude that under the Rule of Necessity we may properly act on petitioners' motion. There is indeed a necessity that we do so. Every case before us involves the issue that petitioners here present, and either we must suspend our activity in every case (thereby effectively granting petitioners' motion), or we must go about our business (thereby effectively denying it). We cannot avoid the question by the recusal of one Judge in the instant case.

B. Procedures for Removal of Tax Court Judges for Cause Do Not Violate Separation of Powers Principles

In this part we conclude that regardless of the branch location of the Tax Court, provisions authorizing removal of Tax Court Judges are constitutional.

1. Public Rights Doctrine

Although it is universally understood that our system has three branches of Government, the U.S. Constitution does not use "branch" in that context. Instead of identifying three branches of Government, the text of the Constitution identifies three "Power[s]"—i.e., it vests "[a]ll legislative Powers * * * in a Congress" (Article I), "[t]he executive Power * * * in a President" (Article II), and "[t]he judicial Power" in certain courts presided in by certain judges (Article III). The President is given only "the executive Power".[34]

Beyond what the Constitution expressly permits (such as appointment), Congress may not authorize the President to impede exercise by the Article III courts of "the judicial Power of the United States".

Article III, section 1, vests the power to adjudicate certain disputes solely in courts whose judges have lifetime appointments. The scope of this exclusive judicial power has been construed to be "matter[s] which, from * * * [their] nature, * * * [are] the subject of a suit at the common law, or in equity, or admiralty"; and outside that scope are matters that "congress may or may not bring within the cognizance of * * * [Article III courts], as it may deem proper." Murray's Lessee v. Hoboken Land & Improvement Co., 59 U.S. (18 How.) 272, 284 (1855).

The adjudication of public rights disputes may, for example, be assigned by Congress to Article I judges. N. Pipeline Constr. Co. v. Marathon Pipe Line Co., 458 U.S. 50, 73–74 (1982) (Brennan, J., plurality opinion). While the Tax Court exercises a portion of the judicial power of the United States, Freytag v. Commissioner, 501 U.S. at 890, it has jurisdiction to adjudicate only public rights disputes, see infra pp. 37–38, and thus does not exercise that portion of the judicial power that is reserved for Article III judges.

In considering the constitutionality of section 7443(f), the question that arises is: "Does providing to the President the authority to remove Tax Court Judges give the President any unconstitutional power to interfere with the Article III

---

[34] [fn 32] The only reference to "branch[es]" in the Constitution is to what are sometimes called the two "houses" of a legislature. See art. I, sec. 2 ("[T]he Electors in each State shall have the Qualifications requisite for Electors of the most numerous Branch of the State Legislature."); amend. XVII (to the same effect). Similarly, the Federalist Papers sometimes use "branch" to refer to one of the two legislative houses. See, e.g., The Federalist No. 37 (James Madison) ("the different legislative branches"), No. 47 (James Madison). The Federalist Papers sometimes refer to the legislative, the executive, and the judicial "departments", see, e.g., id. No. 45 (James Madison) ("the three great departments of the [governments of the] thirteen States"); id. No. 47 ("the legislative department" in the Massachusetts Constitution and "the judiciary department" in the New York Constitution); id. No. 48 (James Madison) ("the legislative, executive, and judiciary departments"), but also sometimes use "branch" to refer to the executive, legislative, or judicial branch as we now do, see, e.g., id. No. 41 (James Madison) No. 45, No. 49 (James Madison or Alexander Hamilton), No. 78 (Alexander Hamilton).

judicial power of the United States?" The answer is no; it gives the President no such unconstitutional power.

In Am. Ins. Co. v. 356 Bales of Cotton, 26 U.S. (1 Pet.) 511 (1828), the Supreme Court observed that Article IV bestowed upon Congress alone a complete power of government over territories not within the States and acknowledged Congress' authority to create courts for those territories that are not in conformity with Article III. N. Pipeline Constr. Co., 458 U.S. at 63–64. The Supreme Court followed similar reasoning when it reviewed Congress' creation of non-Article III courts in the District of Columbia. Kendall v. United States ex rel. Stokes, 37 U.S. (12 Pet.) 524, 618–619 (1938). Congress also may assign courts-martial authority other than to Article III courts. Dynes v. Hoover, 61 U.S. (20 How.) 65 (1857).

The Supreme Court has upheld the validity of statutes which authorize Article I courts and administrative agencies to decide public rights disputes. Id. at 67–68. In Murray's Lessee, 59 U.S. (18 How.) at 284, the Court stated: "[T]here are matters, involving public rights, which may be presented in such form that the judicial power is capable of acting on them, and which are susceptible of judicial determination, but which Congress may or may not bring within the cognizance of the courts of the United States, as it may deem proper." Because the sovereign could not be sued at common law (under which the sovereign was immune), "public rights" cases against the Government are not among the "suit[s] at the common law, or in equity, or admiralty" that constitute the exclusive sphere of the Article III courts. Id. The Court later expanded on this as follows:

> This [public rights] doctrine may be explained in part by reference to the traditional principle of sovereign immunity, which recognizes that the Government may attach conditions to its consent to be sued. * * * But the public-rights doctrine also draws upon the principle of separation of powers, and a historical understanding that certain prerogatives were reserved to the political Branches of Government. The doctrine extends only to matters arising "between the Government and persons subject to its authority in connection with the performance of the constitutional functions of the executive or legislative departments," * * * and only to matters that historically could have been determined exclusively by those departments * * *. The understanding of these cases is that the Framers expected that Congress would be free to commit such matters completely to nonjudicial executive determination, and that as a result there can be no constitutional objection to Congress' employing the less drastic expedient of committing their determination to a legislative court or an administrative agency. [N. Pipeline Constr. Co., 458 U.S. at 67–68 (quoting Crowell v. Benson, 258 U.S. 22, 50 (1932)).]

The Supreme Court has not definitely established in all respects the distinction between public rights and private rights, see, e.g., Stern v. Marshall, 564 U.S. 462, 490 (2011); however, generally speaking, controversies "between the government and others" involve public rights and thus may be removed from

Article III courts and delegated to Article I courts or administrative agencies for their determination, *N. Pipeline Constr. Co.*, 458 U.S. at 69–70 (quoting Ex Parte Bakelite Corp., 279 U.S. 438, 451 (1929)).

The Tax Court's jurisdiction is limited to the adjudication of public rights disputes.[35] The Tax Court decides only disputes between the sovereign and the subject which are neither suits at common law, nor in equity, nor admiralty. Under the Constitution, Congress had the option to grant no remedy at all as to these matters, and "as a result there can be no constitutional objection to Congress' * * * committing their determination to a legislative court or an administrative agency." Id. at 68.[36]

Separation of powers concerns may be implicated if Presidential removal power could interfere with "the constitutionally assigned mission of" the judicial branch. Mistretta v. United States, 488 U.S. 361, 411 n.35 (1989). But if the President sought to exercise the power to remove a Tax Court Judge, the President would not thereby be affecting any matter within the portion of the "judicial Power of the United States" that is necessarily exercised by Article III judges. The Tax Court handles no such matters, and the separation of powers is therefore not implicated.

2. Interbranch Authority

Interbranch removal is not necessarily constitutionally impermissible. In Bowsher v. Synar, 478 U.S. 714 (1986), the Supreme Court considered whether the assignment by Congress to the Comptroller General of the United States (a legislative branch official, removable for cause by Congress) of certain executive functions (e.g., reducing spending by each agency in implementing a sequester) under the Balanced Budget and Emergency Deficiency Control Act of 1985 violated the doctrine of separation of powers. The Supreme Court held that Congress had violated separation of powers principles in providing that executive authority to an official subject to removal by the Congress. Id. at 735–736. However, in discussing its holding in *Bowsher* in a later case, the Supreme Court said: "Nothing in *Bowsher*, however, suggests that one Branch may never exercise removal power, however limited, over members of another Branch. Indeed, we already have recognized that the President may remove a judge who

---

[35] [fn 33] Those disputes relate primarily to tax liability, tax payment obligations, and the tax status of various entities and transactions. See, e.g., secs. 6214(a) (deficiency), 6330(d)(1) (collection due process cases), 7623(b)(4) (whistleblower cases), 6015(e) (relief from joint and several liability), 6226 (final partnership administrative adjustments), 6404(i) (interest abatement claims), 6110(f)(3) (disclosure actions).

[36] [fn 34] Congress also could have assigned the adjudication of public law disputes to Article III courts. Art. III, sec. 2, of the Constitution provides in pertinent part: "The judicial Power shall extend to all Cases * * * arising under * * * the Laws of the United States, and * * * all * * * Controversies to which the United States shall be a Party".

688 | FEDERAL TAX PROCEDURE & ENFORCEMENT

serves on an Article I court." *Mistretta*, 488 U.S. at 411 n.35;[37] McAllister v. United States, 141 U.S. 174, 185 (1891).

In *McAllister*, the Supreme Court held it was not an unconstitutional violation of the separation of powers for the President to remove an individual appointed to a four-year term as a non-Article III District Judge for the District of Alaska (which was then a territory). In *Mistretta*, 488 U.S. at 409–411, the Supreme Court held that the President's authority to remove Article III judges from the Sentencing Commission, an independent body which the statute placed in the judicial branch, see 28 U.S.C. sec. 991 (2012), "for neglect of duty or malfeasance in office or for other good cause"[38] did not violate separation of powers principles. The Supreme Court also said its "paramount concern in *Bowsher* that Congress was accreting to itself the power to control the functions of another Branch is not implicated by a removal provision, like the one at issue * * * [in *Mistretta*], which provides no control in one Branch over *the constitutionally assigned mission* of another Branch." *Mistretta*, 488 U.S. at 411 n.35 (emphasis added). Such limited removal power gives the President no control over judicatory functions. Id.

The authority of the President to remove only for cause, like the removal provisions upheld in *Mistretta*, Morrison v. Olson, 487 U.S. 654, 688 (1988), and Humphrey's Ex'r v. United States, 295 U.S. 602, 630 (1935), is specifically crafted to prevent the President from exercising "coercive influence" over the public official who may be removed from office only for good cause. Mistretta, 488 U.S. at 411.

The removal statutes, section 7443(f) and 28 U.S.C. secs. 354(b) and 355, provide roles for both the President and the Judicial Conference of the United States, the later of which "shall" recommend removal in appropriate circumstances on the basis of "inefficiency", "neglect of duty", or "malfeasance" by a Tax Court Judge.[]

There is no statutory requirement that the President await action by or defer to action by the Judicial Conference in the removal of a Tax Court Judge. However, it appears reasonable to expect that, if the President were to consider a removal action under section 7443(f), there would at a minimum be interest in whether the Judicial Conference had found cause for removal. In any event, none of those issues arose before 2015 when the sole statutory provision relating to removal of Tax Court Judges referred to the President.

The Supreme Court has said that the terms "inefficiency", "neglect of duty", and "malfeasance" are very broad and could sustain removal for any number of actual or perceived transgressions. *Bowsher*, 478 U.S. at 728–730. However, even without considering the potential effect of the Judicial Conference on the

---

[37] [fn 35] This passage in Mistretta v. United States, 488 U.S. 361 (1989), shows that Article I judges need not be within the executive branch.

[38] [fn 36] That provision is similar to the President's authority to remove Tax Court Judges "after notice and opportunity for public hearing, for inefficiency, neglect of duty, or malfeasance in office, but for no other cause." Sec. 7443(f).

removal process, the President's authority to remove Tax Court Judges is more circumscribed than the removal authority at issue in *McAllister*, where the President was empowered to remove the judge of a territorial court for any reason whatever. Limiting removal power to "good cause" is a significant restriction of the President's discretion, Wiener v. United States, 357 U.S. 349 (1958), and is "an impediment to, not an effective grant of, Presidential control", *Morrison*, 487 U.S. at 706 (Scalia, J., dissenting) (citing *Humphrey's Ex'r*, 295 U.S. at 602).

C. Petitioners Request a Remedy Because of an Appearance of Bias.

In addition to voicing objections to section 7443(f), petitioners object to several features of Tax Court litigation, such as the burden of proof, sec. 7491; Welch v. Helvering, 290 U.S. 111 (1933); limitation of reimbursement of litigation costs, sec. 7430; the lack of jury trials, see Rule 74(c) (allowing the taking of depositions requested by one party without the consent of the other party only as an extraordinary procedure and when approved by the Court); Wickwire v. Reinecke, 275 U.S. 101, 105–106 (1929); Swanson v. Commissioner, 65 T.C. 1180, 1181, 1182 (1976). Petitioners contend that these features of Tax Court litigation are so flawed that the Tax Court should immediately suspend adjudication of all cases. Petitioners provide no legal justification (other than their constitutionality argument relating to the removal provision rejected above in Part C) for their request for relief. Absent a finding of unconstitutionality or other sufficient legal justification, we need not further consider petitioners' policy-related arguments.

D. Conclusion

The Court of Appeals in *Kuretski* had available at least two alternative routes for deciding the taxpayer's contentions. First, it could have decided (as it did) that the Tax Court is within the executive branch, thus mooting the separation of powers issue. Alternatively, without reaching the branch issue, it could have decided whether interbranch removal violates separation of powers principles irrespective of the Tax Court's branch status.

We have the same choice in acting on petitioners' motion. In contrast to the approach taken by the Court of Appeals in *Kuretski*, we hold in Part B, supra pp. 33–42, that Presidential authority to remove Tax Court Judges for cause does not violate separation of powers principles. We so conclude because, even though Congress has assigned to the Tax Court a portion of the judicial power of the United States, Freytag v. Commissioner, 501 U.S. at 890, the portion of that power assigned to the Tax Court includes only public law disputes and does not include matters which are reserved by the Constitution to Article III courts.

Courts are reluctant to overturn statutes on constitutional grounds. United States ex rel. Attorney Gen v. Del. & Hudson Co., 213 U.S. 366, 407–408 (1909). Petitioners have not met the heavy burden of showing the removal provision is unconstitutional or has the appearance of being a source of bias. Thus, whatever the merits of providing for Presidential authority to remove Tax Court Judges, that authority presents no concerns of constitutional magnitude. Thus we will deny petitioners' motion.

The 1969 Act sec. 951, 83 Stat. at 730, deleted from section 7441 the prior longstanding designation of the Tax Court as an "agency" and the provision that the Tax Court is "in the Executive Branch of Government". The deletion of words is properly considered in determining the meaning of statutes. See *Wells*, 519 U.S. at 492–493.[39] In *Freytag* the Supreme Court clearly stated the Tax Court's relationship to the three powers (executive, legislative, and judicial) identified in the Constitution. That is, in defining the Tax Court's "constitutional status and its role in the constitutional scheme", the Supreme Court said the Tax Court exercises only judicial power and does not exercise executive, legislative, or administrative power. Freytag v. Commissioner, 501 U.S. at 887–890. In our view, the public rights holding above resolves the removal issue without requiring that we address the tension with legislative intent that might be thought to arise under the opinion of the Court of Appeals in *Kuretski*. Having decided petitioners' motion on that basis, we will follow the lead of Congress and the Supreme Court in Freytag and not further address the branch placement of the Tax Court here.[40]

An appropriate order will be issued.

NOTES AND QUESTIONS

1. Were the taxpayer's arguments tax protester arguments? Why or why not?
2. Why is the Tax Court not subject to FOIA?
3. Why did the Tax Court set forth 12 different statutory enactments in the first two-thirds of the opinion?
4. Congress enacted a law providing that the Tax Court is not in the executive branch. Is Congress's enactment the final word on which branch the Tax Court is in?
5. Which government branch is the Tax Court in?

Although the focus in this chapter is deficiency litigation, it is notable that the Tax Court has jurisdiction over other matters as well. The most important matters over which the Tax Court has jurisdiction are the following:

- Declaratory judgment actions like tax exempt status
- Disclosure action for FOIA requests
- Relief from joint liability
- Certain collection actions
- Whistleblower cases

---

[39] [fn 37] The following year we opined that Congress intended in the 1969 Act to remove the Tax Court from the executive branch. Burns, Stix Friedman & Co. v. Commissioner, 57 T.C. at 395. We have not revisited that proposition herein or at any other time since 1971.

[40] [fn 38] For a discussion of the Tax Court's place in the branches of Government, see Brant J. Hellwig, "The Constitutional Nature of the United States Tax Court", 35 Va. Tax Rev. 269 (2015).

It should be noted that the default jurisdiction for a tax case lies in the refund forums even though the opportunity to invoke refund jurisdiction arises chronologically after deficiency jurisdiction. One major gap in the Tax Court's jurisdiction is over assessable penalties. Recall that assessable penalties are those that the IRS may assert without the limitations of deficiency procedures. Because such a penalty is independently assessable, no deficiency is ever asserted. The only way to challenge such penalties in court is to pay the penalty, request a refund, and sue upon disallowance of the refund. For example, in *Estate of Forgey* (Chapter 4), the IRS asserted a failure to file penalty under section 6651(a) both outside the deficiency proceedings and as part of a deficiency proceeding. The Tax Court held it had no jurisdiction over the penalty assessed prior to the return filing. That failure to file penalty was independently assessable and could be challenged only in a refund forum.

Where Congress has seen fit to provide jurisdiction to the Tax Court, the Code permits taxpayers to petition the Tax Court prior to paying any tax. Where the Tax Court lacks jurisdiction over an IRS action related to a taxpayer's taxes, the taxpayer may still challenge the IRS in a federal district court or the Court of Federal Claims.

B. Pre-Commencement

Prior to filing a petition in Tax Court, there are two unrelated characteristics of Tax Court litigation that a taxpayer should consider. First, the applicable law in Tax Court can be different than in the federal district court or the Court of Federal Claims. Second, small case procedures are available in Tax Court that are not available in either refund forum.

1. Applicable Law

As alluded to in the last chapter, the Tax Court has nationwide jurisdiction. Unlike the Court of Federal Claims, which also has nationwide jurisdiction, Tax Court appeals go to the regional circuit courts of appeals where the taxpayer resided when petitioning the Tax Court. Because Congress bestowed nationwide jurisdiction on the Tax Court, the Court has wrestled with whether it is bound by the regional circuit courts of appeals. Uniformity is better served by ignoring the nonuniform regional courts of appeals and following the Tax Court's own precedent. On the other hand, it seems inefficient to ignore a circuit's precedent only to be ordered to follow it on remand. The next two cases show the struggle.

LAWRENCE v. COMMISSIONER
27 T.C. 713 (1957)
United States Tax Court

MURDOCK, Judge:

The Commissioner determined a deficiency of $2,931.14 in the income tax of the petitioners for 1948. The facts have been stipulated. The stipulation is adopted as the findings of fact.

The petitioners, husband and wife, filed a joint Federal income tax return for 1948 with the collector of internal revenue, Los Angeles, California, on May 31, 1949, an extension to that date for filing having been granted. The notice of deficiency was not mailed until May 10, 1954, after the 3-year period, and after the 4-year period but before the 5-year period for assessment and collection had expired. The only question for decision is whether section 275(c) applies, giving the Commissioner 5 years from the filing of the return within which to assess and collect the deficiency now admitted to be due.

Section 275(c) is as follows:

> (c) OMISSION FROM GROSS INCOME.— If the taxpayer omits from gross income an amount properly includible therein which is in excess of 25 per centum of the amount of gross income stated in the return, the tax may be assessed, or a proceeding in court for the collection of such tax may be begun without assessment, at any time within 5 years after the return was filed.

The petitioners have admitted that the deficiency determined by the Commissioner is correct. The Commissioner, in determining that deficiency, included in income over $20,000 of capital gain which the petitioners had omitted from gross income on their return. It was not included in the computation of gross income on the return. Even the taxable one-half of that amount is substantially 'in excess of 25 per centum of the amount of gross income stated in the return.' The petitioners do not contend otherwise.

The petitioners contend that they disclosed the nature and amount of the now admitted additional income in a manner adequate to apprise the Commissioner in a statement made a part of the return. Arthur acquired a portion of the stock of Midway Peerless Oil Company in 1942 and that company was liquidated on December 15, 1948. The liquidation resulted in the capital gain now determined by the Commissioner and agreed to by the petitioners. The petitioners reported on their return a long-term capital gain of $8,567.38. . . .

It is obvious from the entire return that the taxpayers made a computation of their income and omitted 'from gross income an amount properly includible therein which is in excess of 25 per centum of the amount of gross income stated in the return.' The quoted words are from section 275(c) which first appeared in the Revenue Act of 1934. The House bill had eliminated the statute of limitations in such cases but the Senate insisted upon a 5-year period, saying:

> For instance, a case might arise where a taxpayer failed to report a dividend because he was erroneously advised by the officers of the corporation that it was paid out of capital or he might report as income for one year an item of income which properly belonged in another year. Accordingly, your committee has provided for a 5-year statute in such cases. * * * (1939-1 C.B. (Part 2) 619.)

The Tax Court can only apply the statute as Congress enacted it, and it has consistently held under similar circumstances that the 5-year period of limitations on assessment and collection applies rather than any shorter period, regardless of how honest the mistake and regardless of the possibility that from somewhere in the return or papers attached to it the information was given to the Commissioner of the transaction giving rise to the omitted income. Anna M. B. Foster, 45 B.T.A. 126, affd. 131 F.2d 405; Emma B. Maloy, 45 B.T.A. 1104; Estate of C. P. Hale, 1 T.C. 121; American Liberty Oil Co., 1 T.C. 386; William L. E. O'Bryan, 1 T.C. 1137; Katharine C. Ketcham, 2 T.C. 159, affd. (C.A. 2) 142 F.2d 996; Oleta A. Ewald, 2 T.C. 384, affd. 141 F.2d 750; M. C. Parrish & Co., 3 T.C. 119, affd. 147 F.2d 284; Leslie H. Green, 7 T.C. 263, 275; Peyton G. Nevitt, 20 T.C. 318; H. Leslie Leas, 23 T.C. 1058; Dean Babbitt, 23 T.C. 850; Colony, Inc., 26 T.C. 30.

The position taken by the petitioners in this case has now been enacted into law by section 6501(e)(1)(A)(ii) of the Internal Revenue Code of 1954, as follows:

> In determining the amount omitted from gross income, there shall not be taken into account any amount which is omitted from gross income stated in the return if such amount is disclosed in the return, or in a statement attached to the return, in a manner adequate to apprise the Secretary or his delegate of the nature and amount of such item.

This provision was not made retroactive and its legislative history states that it was a 'change from existing law,' thus supporting the view consistently taken by the Tax Court as to the previously existing law. H. Rept. No. 1337, 83d Cong., 2d Sess., p. A 414; S. Rept. No. 1622, 83d Cong., 2d Sess., P. 584. The court in Slaff v. Commissioner, 220 F.2d 65, 67, recognized that this legislation changed existing law.

This Court has also held that an omission within the meaning of section 275(c) could result from the overstatement of cost or a similar item, even though there was no omission of an income item from the computation of income shown on the return. Estate of J. W. Gibbs, Sr., 21 T.C. 443. The present situation is not such an omission and the fact that the Tax Court has been reversed in several cases of that type and affirmed in one does not help the present taxpayer. Uptegrove Lumber Co. v. Commissioner, 204 F.2d 570; Deakman-Wells Co. v. Commissioner, 213 F.2d 894, reversing 20 T.C. 610; Goodenow v. Commissioner, 238 F.2d 20, reversing 25 T.C. 1; Reis v. Commissioner, 142 F.2d 900, affirming 1 T.C. 9 and a Memorandum Opinion of this Court filed June 4, 1943. The Court of Appeals for the Third Circuit, in the Uptegrove case, considered section 275(c) ambiguous insofar as it applied to an omission resulting from the overstatement of cost, but it clearly differentiated that kind of an omission from one, such as is here present, where the taxpayer 'leaves some item of gain out of his computation of gross income.' It distinguished cases of the latter type 'because the applicability of the language of the statute, "omits from gross income", to the given facts was so clear.'

The only possible complication in the decision of the present case is whether it might be contrary to a fairly recent decision of the Court of Appeals for the Ninth Circuit, to which this case could go on appeal. The reference is to the *Slaff* case, supra. There, Slaff entered only one item, salary, on each of his returns. No computation of any kind was shown. After the one income item, reported in the place for income received, he wrote, 'exempt under Section 116 I.R.C.; therefore no taxable income.' The Tax Court held that there was a complete omission of 'gross taxable income' and section 275(c) applied. The Court of Appeals reversed but stated, '(w)e are in full accord with the rulings in' the *Uptegrove* and *Deakman-Wells* cases, supra, in which the opinions indicate agreement with the Tax Court in a case like the present one. See also *Goodenow*, supra. If the views of the Court of Appeals for the Ninth Circuit are the same as those of the Court of Appeals for the Third Circuit, there is no difficulty here, but if it does not distinguish this case from its *Slaff* case, then, even so, the Tax Court must respectfully adhere to its own views in this case.

One of the difficult problems which confronted the Tax Court, soon after it was created in 1926 as the Board of Tax Appeals, was what to do when an issue came before it again after a Court of Appeals had reversed its prior decision on that point. Clearly, it must thoroughly reconsider the problem in the light of the reasoning of the reversing appellate court and, if convinced thereby, the obvious procedure is to follow the higher court. But if still of the opinion that its original result was right,[41] a court of national jurisdiction to avoid confusion should follow its own honest beliefs until the Supreme Court decides the point.[42] The Tax Court early concluded that it should decide all cases as it thought right.

This was not too difficult if appeal in the later case would not lie to the reversing circuit. Missouri Pacific Railroad Co., 22 B.T.A. 267, 287, which followed Western Maryland Railway Co., 12 B.T.A. 889, after that case had been reversed, (C.A. 4) 33 F.2d 695. The difficulty increased when the Tax Court adhered to its own opinion when appeal would lie to the reversing circuit. Southern Railway Co., 27 B.T.A. 673, 688, affirmed on the bond discount issue (C.A. 4) 74 F.2d 887; Estate of Edward P. Hughes, 7 T.C. 1348, 1350; Harold Holt, 23 T.C. 469, 473. The pressure increased in situations where more than one Court of Appeals differed with the Tax Court, but was relieved if one or more agreed with the Tax Court. Robert L. Smith, 6 T.C. 255, 257. Cf. Putnam v. Commissioner, 352 U.S. 82. The Court of Appeals for the Eighth Circuit in that case affirmed a Memorandum Opinion of this Court (T.C. Memo. 1954-37), 224 F.2d 947. The Supreme Court affirmed, after granting certiorari, because of

---

[41] [fn 1] If the issue turned upon a rule of law peculiar to some State or States within that circuit, the practice of the Tax Court has been to follow the rule as laid down for that circuit.

[42] [fn 2] The United States Customs Court and the Court of Claims are other national courts operating on the trial court level, but they do not have similar problems since the appeals in each case go to an appellate court which also has a nationwide jurisdiction.

alleged conflict with Pollak v. Commissioner, (C.A. 3) 209 F.2d 57, reversing 20 T.C. 376; Edwards v. Allen, (C.A. 5) 216 F.2d 794; Cudlip v. Commissioner, (C.A. 6) 220 F.2d 565, reversing a Memorandum Opinion of this Court dated Nov. 10, 1953. See also Basalt Rock Co., 10 T.C. 600, revd. (C.A. 9) 180 F.2d 281, certiorari denied 339 U.S. 966, and Sokol Bros. Furniture Co. v. Commissioner, (C.A. 5) 185 F.2d 222, affirming a Memorandum Opinion of this Court dated Mar. 10, 1949, which had followed 10 T.C. 600, certiorari denied 340 U.S. 952. Several Courts of Appeals have affirmed the Tax Court on the point decided in the present case.

The Tax Court and its individual Judges have always had respect for the 11 Courts of Appeals, have had no desire to ignore or lightly regard any decisions of those courts, and have carefully considered all suggestions of those courts. The Tax Court not infrequently has been persuaded by the reasoning of opinions of those courts to change its views on various questions being litigated. Cf. Estate of William E. Edmonds, 16 T.C. 110; Albert L. Rowan, 22 T.C. 865; James M. McDonald, 23 T.C. 1091; Mills, Inc.,

This change of position sometimes backfires. The Tax Court, in Wm. J. Lemp Brewing Co., 18 T.C. 586, abandoned its decision on an issue in the face of reversals and disagreements on the part of Courts of Appeals for the Second and Eighth Circuits and the District of Columbia. It followed its new position on that point in De Soto Securities Co., 25 T.C. 175, but was reversed by the Court of Appeals for the Seventh Circuit, 235 F.2d 409. Again, the Tax Court, five Judges dissenting, in Burrus Mills, Inc., 22 T.C. 881, after being reversed on the point involved therein by the Courts of Appeals for the Second, Seventh, Third, and Sixth Circuits, concluded that it would have to follow those courts, but later, in a case coming from the Court of Claims, the Supreme Court of the United States decided the point as the Tax Court had originally decided it. United States v. Anderson, Clayton & Co., 350 U.S. 55. The Tax Court is not indifferent to the fact that a Court of Appeals has taken exception to its failure to follow a decision of that court. Cf. Stacey Mfg. Co. v. Commissioner, 237 F.2d 605. It repeatedly indicates in its opinions that it takes such action reluctantly and only because, after thorough re-examination, it cannot agree with the particular holding involved.

The Tax Court has always believed that Congress intended it to decide all cases uniformly, regardless of where, in its nationwide jurisdiction, they may arise, and that it could not perform its assigned functions properly were it to decide one case one way and another differently merely because appeals in such cases might go to different Courts of Appeals. Congress, in the case of the Tax Court, 'inverted the triangle' so that from a single national jurisdiction, the Tax Court appeals would spread out among 11 Courts of Appeals, each for a different circuit or portion of the United States. Congress faced the problem in the beginning as to whether the Tax Court jurisdiction and approach was to be local or nationwide and made it nationwide. Congress expected the Tax Court to set precedents for the uniform application of the tax laws, insofar as it would be able to do that. Hearings Before Ways and Means Committee, Revenue Act of 1926, pp. 10, 869, 878, 911, 926, 932; H. Rept. No. 1, 69th Cong., 1st Sess., pp. 17-19; 67 Cong.Rec. 1136-7, 3749 (1925).

The Tax Court feels that it is adequately supported in this belief not only by the creating legislation and legislative history but by other circumstances as well. The Tax Court never knows, when it decides a case, where any subsequent appeal from that decision may go, or whether there will be an appeal. It usually, but not always, knows where the return of a taxpayer was filed and, therefore, the circuit to which an appeal could go, but the law permits the parties in all cases to appeal by mutual agreement to any Court of Appeals. Sec. 7482(b)(2), I.R.C. 1954. Furthermore, it frequently happens that a decision of the Tax Court is appealable to two or even more Courts of Appeals. A few examples will illustrate. A corporation, having stockholders scattered over the United States, makes a distribution to all. The Commissioner holds it taxable as a dividend from accumulated earnings. The stockholders join in a trial before the Tax Court which decides the issue as to all petitioning stockholders, contrary to a decision of Court of Appeals A, which reversed a prior Tax Court decision, but perhaps in line with an affirming decision of Court of Appeals B. Cf. Edwin L. Wiegand, 14 T.C. 136, revd. (C.A. 7) 189 F.2d 167, affd. (C.A. 3, June 26, 1953, unreported), later reversed (C.A. 3) 194 F.2d 479. If it had rendered a separate different decision for those stockholders in Circuit A, what amount of accumulated earnings would remain for future distribution? Another situation was presented by the Richmond Hosiery Mills. That corporation filed its corporate returns for 3 years with the collector of internal revenue for the district of Georgia and for 1 intermediate year with the collector of internal revenue for the district of Tennessee. It received one notice of deficiency and filed a single petition in the Tax Court, each covering all 4 years. The Tax Court decided the case for all 4 years in a Memorandum Opinion and entered but one decision in the proceeding. The taxpayer took appeals to the Courts of Appeals for both the Fifth Circuit and the Sixth Circuit, in the former as to 3 of the years and in the latter as to a single year. The Sixth Circuit, in Richmond Hosiery Mills v. Commissioner, 237 F.2d 605, a companion case with Stacey Mfg. Co., supra, followed its own prior decision in Owensboro Wagon Co. v. Commissioner, 209 F.2d 617, reversing 18 T.C. 1107, while the Fifth Circuit, which had not previously passed on this question, in Richmond Hosiery Mills v. Commissioner, 233 F.2d 908, adopted the view of the Sixth Circuit as expressed in the *Owensboro* case. Or suppose partners live in different circuits. Are the decisions of the Tax Court as to them to vary accordingly? See Choate v. Commissioner, 324 U.S. 1, in which the appeal in the case of *Hogan* was taken to the Fifth Circuit which affirmed the Tax Court, Hogan v. Commissioner, 141 F.2d 92, and the appeal in the case of *Choate* was to the Tenth Circuit which reversed the Tax Court, Choate v. Commissioner, 141 F.2d 641, which was then reversed by the Supreme Court, thus affirming the Tax Court. Many more similar examples could be given. There is also the sometimes difficult problem of knowing from prior decisions of the appellate court precisely what its attitude is in relation to the current question before the Tax Court (cf. Estate of Catherine Cox Blackburn, 11 T.C. 623, modified 180 F.2d 952), particularly where it has more than one decision outstanding and each may seem to have a bearing but they are not too easily reconciled. The *Slaff* case already discussed is another example.

The Commissioner of Internal Revenue, who has the duty of administering the taxing statutes of the United States throughout the Nation, is required to apply these statutes uniformly, as he construes them. The Tax Court, being a tribunal with national jurisdiction over litigation involving the interpretation of Federal taxing statutes which may come to it from all parts of the country, has a similar obligation to apply with uniformity its interpretation of those statutes. That is the way it has always seen its statutory duty and, with all due respect to the Courts of Appeals, it cannot conscientiously change unless Congress or the Supreme Court so directs.

The taxpayers also argue that the Commissioner had only 4 years instead of 5 years within which to send out the notice of deficiency on which he could then assess and collect the tax. Section 275(e) on which they rely provides for a 4-year period of limitations '(i)f the taxpayer omits from gross income an amount properly includible therein under section 115(c) as an amount distributed in liquidation of a corporation, * * * .' Congress thereby gave an extra year to the Commissioner over the general 3-year period if the omission was of the kind described therein, but Congress gave the Commissioner 2 extra years if the omission was of the kind described in section 275(c). The two subsections overlap to some extent but since the omission here is of the kind described in section 275(c), it is immaterial whether or not it might also qualify for the lesser period allowed by section 275(e). There is nothing in the statute or its legislative history to indicate that if a particular omission was of the kind which came within both of these sections the Commissioner would be limited to the shorter period. See Estate of Arthur T. Marix, 15 T.C. 819, 825. The statute of limitations is not a bar to the assessment and collection of the deficiency in the present proceeding.

Reviewed by the Court.

Decision will be entered for the respondent.

NOTES AND QUESTIONS

1. Is the Tax Court's jurisdiction geographically limited?
2. What message did the Tax Court send to the Ninth Circuit in this case?
3. What was the basis of the Tax Court's holding in this case?
4. The Ninth Circuit reversed on other grounds. *See* Lawrence v. Commissioner, 258 F.2d 562 (9th Cir. 1958).

GOLSEN v. COMMISSIONER
54 T.C. 742 (1970)
United States Tax Court

The Commissioner determined a deficiency of $2,918.15 in petitioner's income tax for 1962. The only issue is whether a $12,441.40 payment made by petitioner Jack E. Golsen to the Western Security Life Insurance Co. is deductible as an interest payment pursuant to section 163, I.R.C. 1954.

FINDINGS OF FACT

The parties have stipulated certain facts, which, together with the attached exhibits, are incorporated herein by this reference.

Petitioners Jack E. and Sylvia H. Golsen are husband and wife. They filed a joint Federal income tax return for the calendar year 1962 with the district director of internal revenue, Oklahoma City, Okla., and resided in Oklahoma City at the time the petition was filed in this case.

During the latter part of 1961 and during 1962, Jack E. Golsen (Golsen) served as president of Hart Industrial Supply Co. and several affiliated corporations. The corporations were privately owned and did business in Texas and Oklahoma. By the end of 1961 the corporations had incurred indebtedness to banks in the aggregate amount of about $1.75 million, and Golsen had personally guaranteed all of it. Golsen was also personally indebted to a bank in the amount of $15,000. Moreover, during 1961 he had purchased 50 percent of the stock of the L & S Bearing Co. for approximately $625,000.

In December of 1961, Golsen carried about $230,000 in life insurance protection. In addition, several of the corporations whose loans he had guaranteed had taken out insurance on his life. However, in view of the size of his potential liabilities and his relatively illiquid financial position in late 1961, Golsen though that he ought to purchase additional life insurance to protect his family in the event of his unexpected death.

[The Court set forth a detailed factual discussion of a life insurance plan reflecting aggressive tax planning]

On their joint Federal income tax return for the calendar year 1962, the Golsens claimed a deduction for 'interest' paid to Western in the amount of $12,441.40. In his notice of deficiency the Commissioner disallowed the deduction.

OPINION

RAUM, Judge:

This case involves an ingenious device which, if successful, would result in petitioner's purchase of a substantial amount of life insurance for the protection of his family at little or no aftertax cost to himself, or possibly even with a net profit in some years. The device is based on an unusual type of insurance policy that appears to have been specially designed for this purpose in which the rates were set at an artificially high level with correspondingly high cash surrender and loan values to begin immediately during the very first year of the life of the policy. The plan contemplated the purchase of a large amount of such insurance, the 'payment' of the first year's premium, the simultaneous 'prepayment' of the next 4 years' premiums discounted at the annual rate of 3 percent, the immediate 'borrowing' of the first year's cash value at 4 percent 'interest,' and the immediate 'borrowing' back of the full reserve value generated by the 'prepayment,' also at 4-percent 'interest.' Each year thereafter, the plan called for the 'borrowing' of the annual increase in the loan or cash value of the policy at 4-

percent 'interest'; such increase, as a result of the artificially high premium, was more than sufficient to 'prepay' the discounted amount of the premium which would become due 4 years thereafter. The net result of these complicated maneuvers would be that the insured's net out-of-pocket (pretax) expenditures each year would be equal to the true actuarial cost of the insurance benefits that he was purchasing (i.e., net death benefits in substantial amounts even after the policies had been stripped of their cash surrender values)—although, in form, he appeared to be paying large amounts of 'interest.' At the heart of the device is the deduction allowed in section 163(a) of the 1954 Code with respect to 'interest paid * * * on indebtedness.' And if the device were successful, the deduction would reduce the aftertax cost of the insurance either to a small amount, or nothing at all, or there might even be a net profit, depending upon the tax bracket of the owner of the policy. Apart from a portion of the amount paid the first year as 'premiums' or 'advance premiums,' the remaining cash actually paid that year, and all other actual cash payments made by the insured throughout the life of the policy would be characterized as 'interest.'

The Government contends that the 'loan' features of such insurance contracts are devoid of economic substance, that taking these features as part of an integrated plan, no true 'indebtedness' was created nor was any bona fide 'interest' paid (regardless of whether any such feature might otherwise qualify under the statute if considered individually in isolation from the companion features),[43] that the substance of the transaction was that the 'interest' merely reflected the annual price which the insured paid for life insurance protection, and that such payment is nothing more than a nondeductible personal expense.

The nature of the problem is one that the Court is obviously ill-equipped to handle without expert actuarial assistance, and it was fortunate in this case to have the benefit of the testimony of an actuary who appeared to us to be highly qualified, and who presented a clear and convincing analysis of the transaction before us. That testimony established to our satisfaction that the receipt and prepayment agreement and the loan agreement and assignment of policy had no essential relationship whatever to the insurance benefits provided under the insurance contracts, that when, in accordance with the prearranged plan, the policy was stripped of its artificially high cash surrender values, such policy was merely the equivalent of renewable term insurance, and that actuarially the net

---

[43] [fn 6] Compare Gordon MacRae, 34 T.C. 20, 27, affirmed and remanded 294 F.2d 56 (C.A. 9), certiorari denied 368 U.S. 955:

'The steps taken, each in itself a legitimate commercial operation, were here each mirror images, and add up to zero. The various purchases and sales, each real without the other, neutralize one another and fairly shout to the world the essential nullity of what was done. No purchase and no sale is essentially identical with what was done here, i.e., identical and virtually simultaneous purchases and sales. The choice of the more complicated and involved method of doing nothing had no purpose, save the erection of the facade upon which petitioners now seek to rely.'

cash which the insured in fact paid to the insurance company, however described, merely represented the true cost of the insurance purchased. In the latter connection, the actuary testified as follows:

> The payments that are denominated as interest, when reduced by the cash that was returned from the insurance company, are the amounts that are left to support the insurance. In other words, they are the cost to the insured for which, in return, he gets the death benefit protection promised by the insurance company.

We are satisfied as to the soundness of this testimony and accept it as true. The purported loans herein were utterly devoid of economic substance and were simply the means whereby the true cost of the insurance—i.e., the true premiums in respect of the insurance really purchased—was reflected in the purported 'interest' allegedly 'paid' on such 'loans.' The 'interest' was thus not in fact compensation paid for the use of borrowed funds, the essential prerequisite for the deduction. See Old Colony R. Co. v. Commissioner, 284 U.S. 552, 560; Deputy v. DuPont, 308 U.S. 448, 497-498. As a consequence, if substance rather than form were to govern the result herein, we would conclude that the 'interest' deduction here claimed is not allowable.[44]

It has repeatedly been held that the substance of a transaction rather than the form in which it is cast is determinative of tax consequences unless it appears from an examination of the statute and its purpose that form was intended to govern. The following represent merely a random selection from a wide variety of such cases that are too numerous for comprehensive listing: Commissioner v. P. G. Lake, Inc., 356 U.S. 260, 265-267; Commission v. Court Holding Co., 324 U.S. 331, 334; Griffiths v. Helvering, 308 U.S. 355; Higgins v. Smith, 308 U.S.

---

[44] [fn 7] Moreover, even apart from the essential character of the transaction as reflecting the payment of premiums rather than interest, the payments under consideration do not in fact appear to represent compensation for the use of borrowed funds. Thus in 1962 Golsen purported simultaneously to pay premiums on each of his policies and then 'borrow' back nearly the entire amount which he had just paid out. At the same time, he also purported to pay 'interest' on the funds which he had just 'borrowed.' The net result of the transaction was that Golsen paid 'interest' (at the rate of 4 percent)to Western in order to obtain the use of funds which were originally his and which he had transferred to Western (where they would 'earn' 3 percent) for the very purpose of borrowing back—a transaction that was utterly lacking in economic substance. It is, of course, not unheard of for the owner of a policy to borrow the current cash value; one of the advantages of such a policy is that it provides a ready source of funds in the event of a need for cash for any purpose. But it is plain that from the outset Golsen intended to 'borrow back' funds immediately after 'paying' them over to Western. Unlike a lender, Western did not give up the use of funds from which it would have otherwise derived benefit. Unlike a borrower, Golsen did not obtain the use of funds which he would not otherwise have enjoyed.

473; Minnesota Tea Co. v. Helvering, 302 U.S. 609; Gregory v. Helvering, 293 U.S. 465; Weller v. Commissioner, 270 F.2d 294 (C.A. 3), affirming 31 T.C. 33 and W. Stuart Emmons, 31 T.C. 26; William R. Lovett, 37 T.C. 317. The thought was forcefully expressed in the now familiar language of Minnesota Tea Co. v. Helvering, 302 U.S.at 613, as follows: 'A given result at the end of a straight path is not made a different result because reached by following a devious path.' In terms of the present case, 'the given result at the end of (the) straight path' was the payment of the cost for insurance protection, and 'the different result by following a devious path' was reflected in the attempt to make such payments appear to be interest through the involved 'loan' transactions.

Insurance and annuity policies are peculiarly susceptible of manipulation so as to create illusion, and, in applying the substance-versus-form doctrine in such instances courts have at times referred to the transactions under review as 'shams,' or have characterized them as lacking in 'business purpose,' cf. Knetsch v. United States, 364 U.S. 361. Petitioners have seized upon such language, urging upon us that Golsen's transaction was not a 'sham,' that he was seriously buying life insurance for the protection of his family, and that there was thus no absence of 'business purpose.' The difficulty with that position is that, granted that there was a legitimate reason for the underlying acquisition of life insurance, there does not appear to be any such reason for the otherwise wholly meaningless superstructure of 'loans' erected on that base. The point was articulated with telling clarity in Ballagh v. United States, 331 F.2d 874 (Ct. Cl.), certiorari denied 379 U.S. 887, where the Court of Claims stated (p. 878): plaintiff is wide of the mark in supposing that his primary purpose of providing retirement income can make valid what would otherwise be a sham. For the transaction which we find to be a sham is not the initial insurance contract but the prepayment of all of the premiums and the loan agreement. We do not question that plaintiff's motive in buying the policy was a legitimate one. However, the subsequent prepayment of all premiums by borrowing from the insurance company itself was not necessary in so providing retirement income, and we find that such loan transaction did 'not appreciably affect his beneficial interest except to reduce his tax.'

See also Minchin v. Commissioner, 335 F.2d 30, 32 (C.A. 2).

Petitioners claim to find support for their position in this case by reason of the fact that Golsen's policies were issued in 1961 or early 1962. They rely upon section 264(a)(3) which was added to the 1954 Code in 1964[45] and which provides as follows:

SEC. 264. CERTAIN AMOUNTS PAID IN CONNECTION WITH INSURANCE CONTRACTS.

(a) GENERAL RULE—NO deduction shall be allowed for—

(3) Except as provided in subsection (c), any amount paid or accrued on indebtedness incurred or continued to purchase a carry a life insurance,

---

[45] [fn 8] See sec. 215, Revenue Act of 1964.

endowment, or annuity contract (other than a single premium contract or a contract treated as a single premium contract) pursuant to a plan of purchase all of the increases in the cash value of such contract (either from the insurer or otherwise).

* * * Paragraph (3) shall apply only in respect of contracts purchased after August 6, 1963.

The point is defective. Of course, section 264(a)(3) does not prohibit the deduction in respect of policies purchased before August 6, 1963, and there was no specific prohibition prior thereto in the Internal Revenue Code against such deduction.[46] But petitioners' right to the claimed deduction is based upon section 163, not section 264. The latter simply denies, or disallows, or prohibits deductions that might otherwise be allowable under some other provision of the statute. It does not confer the right to any deduction,[47] and the August 6, 1963, date represents merely the starting point for the operative effect of the specific disallowance provisions of section 264(a)(3). A closely parallel situation was considered in Knetsch v. United States, 364 U.S. at 367, where the Supreme Court held that a similar provision relating to deductions denied under section 264(a)(2) did not confer a right to deduction in respect of contracts purchased prior to the stated operative date of those provisions.[48] If the deduction sought by petitioners did not come within the provisions of section 163 prior to the 1964 amendment to the Code, nothing in that amendment retroactively created any such right. Cf. W. Lee McLane, Jr., 46 T.C. 140, affirmed 377 F.2d 557 (C.A. 9), certiorari denied 389 U.S. 1038.

The precise question relating to the deductibility of 'interest' like that involved herein has been adjudicated by two Courts of Appeals. In one case, Campbell v. Cen-Tex., Inc., 377 F.2d 688 (C.A. 5), decision went for the

---

[46] [fn 9] See H. Rept. No. 749, 88th Cong., 1st Sess., pp. 61, 62; S. Rept. No. 830, 88th Cong., 2d Sess., pp. 77-79.

[47] [fn 10] See Weller v. Commissioner, 270 F.2d 294, 298 (C.A. 3), where the Court of Appeals said:

'Section 24(a) (predecessor sec. 264) applies to specific items that are not deductible. The section does not even purport to indicate what items are deductible and, therefore, legislative history indicating that annuity contracts were specifically not included therein fails to conclude the issue. Regardless of Section 24(a)(6), the taxpayers' payments must still qualify as interest under Section 23(b) (predecessor sec. 163) to be deductible.' See also dissent of Wisdom, J., in United States v. Bond, 258 F.2d 577, 584 (C.A. 5), which was cited with apparent approval by the Supreme Court in Knetsch v. United States, 364 U.S. 361, 366 fn. 4.

[48] [fn 11] The committee reports with respect to those provisions, which the Supreme Court found not to be controlling in Knetsch, 364 U.S.at 369 fn. 7, bear a close resemblance to the committee reports relied upon by petitioners herein, fn. 9 supra.

taxpayer;[49] in the other, Goldman v. United States, 403 F.2d 776 (C.A. 10), affirming 273 F.Supp. 137 (W.D. Okla.), the Government prevailed. *Goldman* involved the same insurance company, the same type of policies, and the same financial arrangements as are before us in the present case. *Cen-Tex* involved a different insurance company but dealt with comparable financing arrangements. Despite some rather feeble attempts on the part of each side herein to distinguish the case adverse to it, we think that both cases are in point. It is our view that the Government's position is correct.

Moreover, we think that we are in any event bound by *Goldman* since it was decided by the Court of Appeals for the same circuit within which the present case arises. In thus concluding that we must follow Goldman, we recognize the contrary thrust of the oft-criticized[50] case of Arthur L. Lawrence, 27 T.C. 713. Notwithstanding a number of the considerations which originally led us to that decision, it is our best judgment that better judicial administration.[51] requires us to follow a Court of Appeals decision which is squarely in point where appeal from our decision lies to that Court of Appeals and to that court alone.[52]

---

[49] [fn 12] The same result was reached in two District Court cases. Priester Machinery Co. v. United States, 296 F.Supp. 604 (W.D. Tenn.); Wanvig v. United States, 295 F.Supp. 882 (E.D. Wis.), affirmed on another issue 423 F.2d 769 (C.A. 7, 1970).

[50] [fn 13] Norvel Jeff Mclellan, 51 T.C. 462, 465-467 (concurring opinion); Automobile Club of New York, Inc., 32 T.C. 906, 923-926 (dissenting opinion), affirmed 304 F.2d 781 (C.A. 2); Robert M. Dann, 30 T.C. 499, 510 (dissenting opinion); Del Cotto, 'The Need for a Court of Tax Appeals: An argument and a Study,' 12 Buffalo L.Rev. 5, 8-10 (1962); Vom Baur & Coburn, 'Tax Court Wrong in Denying Taxpayer the Rule Laid Down in His Circuit,' 8 J.Taxation 228 (1958); Orkin, 'The Finality of the Court of Appeals Decisions in the Tax Court: A Dichotomy of Opinion,' 43 A.B.A.J. 945 (1957); Note, 'Heresy in the Hierarchy: Tax Court Rejection of Court of Appeals Precedents,' 57 Colum.L.Rev. 717 (1957); Note, 'Controversy Between the Tax Court and Courts of Appeals: Is the Tax Court Bound by the Precedent of Its Reviewing Court?' 7 Duke L.J. 45 (1957); Note, 'The Tax Court, the Courts of Appeals, and Pyramiding Judicial Review,' 9 Stan.L.Rev. 827 (1957); Case note, 70 Harv.L.Rev. 1313 (1957). See also Sullivan v. Commissioner, 241 F.2d 46 (C.A. 7), affirmed 356 U.S. 27; Stern v. Commissioner, 242 F.2d 322 (C.A. 6), affirmed 357 U.S. 39; Stacey Mfg. Co. v. Commissioner, 237 F.2d 605 (C.A. 6).

[51] [fn 14] The importance of the *Lawrence* doctrine in respect of the functioning of this Court has been grossly exaggerated by some of the critics of that decision. That case was decided Jan. 25, 1957, and this is the first time during the intervening period of somewhat in excess of 13 years that the Court has ever deemed it appropriate to face the question whether or not to apply the *Lawrence* doctrine.

[52] [fn 15] Sec. 7482(b)(2), I.R.C. 1954, grants venue in any Court of Appeals designated by both the Government and the taxpayer by written stipulation.

Section 7482(a), I.R.C. 1954,[53] charges the Courts of Appeals with the primary responsibility for review of our decisions, and we think that where the Court of Appeals to which appeal lies has already passed upon the issue before us, efficient and harmonious judicial administration calls for us to follow the decision of that court. Moreover, the practice we are adopting does not jeopardize the Federal interest in uniform application of the internal revenue laws which we emphasized in *Lawrence*. We shall remain able to foster uniformity by giving effect to our own views in cases appealable to courts whose views have not yet been expressed, and, even where the relevant Court of Appeals has already made its views known, by explaining why we agree or disagree with the precedent that we feel constrained to follow. See Note, 57 Colum.L.Rev., supra at 723.

To the extent that *Lawrence* is inconsistent with the views expressed herein it is hereby overruled. We note, however, that some of our decisions, because they involve two or more taxpayers, may be appealable to more than one circuit. This case presents no such problem, and accordingly we need not decide now what course to take in the event that we are faced with it.

In view of the conclusion reached above we find it unnecessary to consider the Government's alternative contention that the claimed deduction is in any event forbidden by section 264(a)(2).

Reviewed by the Court.

Decision will be entered for the respondent.

WITHEY, J., dissenting: While I agree with the conclusion of the Court on the merits of this case, I dissent on the reversal of this Court's position on Arthur L. Lawrence, 27 T.C. 713, by the majority.

NOTES AND QUESTIONS

1. *Golsen* reversed *Lawrence* to the extent that the Tax Court in *Lawrence* held that it could ignore circuit court precedent in favor of its own.
2. Did the Tax Court hold that it was bound by circuit court precedent to which a case may be appealed?

However, if the Court of Appeals to which an appeal would otherwise lie has already passed upon the question in issue, it is hardly likely that the party prevailing before the Tax Court would join in such a stipulation.

[53] [fn 16] SEC. 7482. COURTS OF REVIEW.

(a) JURISDICTION.—The United States Courts of Appeals shall have exclusive jurisdiction to review the decisions of the Tax Court, except as provided in section 1254 of Title 28 of the United States Code, in the same manner and to the same extent as decisions of the district courts in civil actions tried without a jury; and the judgment of any such court shall be final, except that it shall be subject to review by the Supreme Court of the United States upon certiorari, in the manner provided in section 1254 of Title 28 of the United States Code.

3. Why did the Tax Court commit to following circuit court precedent to which a case may be appealed?

4. The Tax Court has followed *Golsen* in small cases even though such cases are not subject to appeal.

2. Small Cases

Where the amount at issue is less than $50,000, a taxpayer may elect to resolve the case with the Tax Court's small case procedures. Rule 170 of the Tax Court's Rules of Practice and Procedure provides as follows:

> The . . . "Small Tax Case Rules" set forth [herein] the special provisions which are to be applied to small tax cases. The term "small tax case" means a case in which the amount in dispute is $50,000 or less (within the meaning of the Internal Revenue Code) and the Court has concurred in the petitioner's election. . . . Except as otherwise provided in these Small Tax Case Rules, the other Rules of practice of the Court are applicable to such cases.

These cases comprise more than half of the Tax Court's docket. Procedures for small cases are an advantage the Tax Court has over other courts for taxpayers who qualify. The procedures are less formal, the trials take place in more convenient locations, and the trials occur more quickly than in a court with a full docket. The less strict adherence to formal rules makes it easier for taxpayers to represent themselves.

Taxpayers do not have a right to utilize the small case procedures. A taxpayer may request them in the Tax Court at any time during the proceedings before trial. *See* Rule 171(a) & (c), Tax Court Rules of Practice and Procedure. Requests for small case procedures are not always granted, especially if the IRS opposes the request on the grounds that the case will establish important precedent to apply to other cases.

The $50,000 limit works differently depending on whether the case is a deficiency case or a collection case. For small case procedures to resolve a deficiency, a taxpayer may concede an amount that would bring the amount at issue below $50,000. For small case procedures to resolve a collection case, the taxpayer may not concede an amount that would bring the amount at issue below $50,000.

The major differences between small cases and regular cases are that small cases by statute have no precedential value; small cases are conducted informally, the amount of time between the calendar call and the trial is likely to be smaller because the Tax Court goes to more cities for small cases; the Federal Rules of Evidence do not apply; in general Special Trial Judges hear the small cases rather than the member Tax Court judges; and there is no appeal from small cases.

The next case provides an example of an IRS challenge to a taxpayer's request for small case procedures.

DRESSLER v. COMMISSIONER
56 T.C. 210 (1971)
United States Tax Court

SCOTT, Judge:

On January 4, 1971, the petition in the above-entitled case was filed. The deficiency in dispute was stated to be for the year 1967 and in the amount of $498.20, the entire amount of deficiency for the year 1967 as shown by the notice of deficiency attached to the petition.

The petition was served on respondent on January 14, 1971, and on that same date there was served on petitioners, with a copy to respondent, a Notice to Petitioners Having a Small Tax Case, which stated in part as follows:

> In small tax cases such as yours, Rule 36 provides that you may make a request to have the proceedings conducted under the provisions of Section 7463, Code of 1954. A Request Form for this purpose is enclosed with this notice. Unless the Commissioner of Internal Revenue objects to your request—in which case you will be notified—your request will ordinarily be granted by the Court.

On February 5, 1971, petitioners filed a Request to Have Proceedings Conducted Under Section 7463.

Respondent on February 9, 1971, filed his answer, generally denying the allegations in the petition and on the same date, in accordance with the provisions of Rule 36(c)(2) of the Rules of Practice of this Court, filed his Motion to Deny Petitioners' Request for Conduct of Proceedings Under Section 7463. Respondent in support of his motion stated that he did not know of a case in which the precise issue involved in the instant case had been decided. Respondent stated that he had issued a revenue ruling, Rev. Rul. 59-270, 1959-2 C.B. 44, stating his position on the issue involved in this case.

Both parties state the issue involved in the above-entitled case to be whether petitioner John Dressler, a 'minister of music' in the Methodist Church, is a 'minister of the gospel' within the intendment of section 107, I.R.C. 1954, so as to be entitled under that section to exclude from his taxable income the amount of $2,599.92 which he received as a housing allowance during the year 1967.

The allegations contained in the petition state that petitioner John Dressler holds a degree in church and school music from the Academy of Music in Vienna and a master's degree in music from Birmingham Southern College in Birmingham, Ala.; that he has held the position of 'minister of music' in the Methodist Church for 26 years and from 1963 to the present time has held that position with the Peachtree Road Methodist Church in Atlanta, Ga.; that he has attended special leadership training courses which led to his being certified as a 'minister of music' in the Methodist Church; and that in January 1959 he was consecrated as a 'minister of music' by a bishop of the Methodist Church in a special laying on of hands ceremony. The petition further alleges that petitioner John Dressler as a 'minister of music' in the Methodist Church, performs duties of a sacerdotal nature and takes part in the conducting of the worship services of his congregation, including, but not by way of limitation, direction of the choir and congregational singing, selection of appropriate music for the choir and congregational signing, training of the choirs in the theology of hymns, as well as in vocal presentation, preparation, and conducting of the musical portion of the Lord's Supper services and baptismal services, counseling with congregation members about their personal problems, and visiting the sick at the local hospitals.

This Court held in Abraham A. Salkov, 46 T.C. 190 (1966), that a full-time cantor of the Jewish faith who was commissioned by the Cantors Assembly of America and installed by a congregation is a 'minister of the gospel' within the meaning of section 107 of the 1954 Code. In Robert D. Lawrence, 50 T.C. 494 (1968), we held that a 'minister of education' in the Baptist Church who was not an ordained minister but served a church that had a regular paster who was an ordained minister was not a 'minister of the gospel' within the meaning of section 107 and in W. Astor Kirk, 51 T.C. 66 (1968), affd. 425 F.2d 492 (C.A.D.C. 1970), held that a professional employee of the General Board of Christian Social Concerns of the Methodist Church who was not ordained, licensed, or commissioned as a minister and performed no functions of a sacerdotal character was not a 'minister of the gospel' within the meaning of section 107 even though 9 of the 11 professional employees of the Board of Christian Social Concerns of the Methodist Church who did work similar to that done by the taxpayer were ordained ministers of the Methodist Church.

Respondent's Rev. Rul. 59-270, supra, concludes that a 'minister of music' may not exclude from his gross income the rental value of a dwelling provided to him since he was not ordained, commissioned or licensed as a 'minister of the gospel.'

Respondent contends that the precise issue in the instant case has not been decided by this Court or other courts and states that he believes the issue is of sufficient legal importance to be tried as a regular case.

Petitioners in their memorandum in opposition to respondent's motion filed February 22, 1971, and through their counsel at the hearing on respondent's motion, argue that respondent has failed to present as a ground for his motion the only statutory basis for discontinuance of a case as a small tax case, which petitioners state is the basis provided in section 7463(d) that the Court concludes that there are reasonable grounds for believing that the amount of the deficiency placed in dispute exceeds or may exceed the applicable jurisdictional amount of $1,000 for any 1 year. Petitioners further argue that if they are incorrect in their interpretation of the only basis on which a request for the case to be heard in accordance with section 7463 may be denied, this case is not of sufficient legal or factual importance to warrant the amount which petitioners would be required to expend to try the case under other than the provisions of section 7463. Petitioners argue that section 7463 was intended to permit an economical trial for a taxpayer who contests a small amount of deficiency and that their request to try this case under the provisions of section 7463 should be granted since the issue here is primarily one of fact. Petitioners contend that previously decided cases have clarified the law with respect to the necessary requisites of a 'minister of the gospel' under section 107. Petitioners state that a decision in the instant case will not determine whether all 'ministers of music' in the Methodist Church or of all Protestant churches are entitled to the benefits of section 107, but rather will determine whether the petitioner John Dressler with his particular qualifications and the particular services he rendered to his church should be classed as a 'minister of the gospel.'

In our view respondent's motion is properly filed under the provisions of rule 36(c)(2) of the Rules of Practice of this Court. The provisions of section 7463(d) to which petitioners refer in their argument concern discontinuance of a case as a small tax case after this Court has concurred in the taxpayer's request as provided by section 7463(a) which generally would be when trial of the case commenced. This situation is covered by Rule 36(d) of the Rules of Practice of this Court. However, we agree with petitioners that a taxpayer should be entitled to have his case tried as a small tax case where the jurisdictional amount of the deficiency brings it within the provisions of section 7463 unless respondent shows that the issue involved is an issue of importance which will establish a principle of law applicable to other tax cases. In the instant case respondent has made no such showing. In previous cases this Court has concluded that in order to be a 'minister of the gospel' a taxpayer must be ordained, commissioned, or licensed as such or must perform sacerdotal duties.

From the allegations contained in the petition, the issue here appears to be primarily one of fact. Whether the certificate which petitioner John Dressler obtained and his consecration by the bishop amount in substance to his being commissioned, ordained, or licensed as a 'minister of the gospel' is a factual question. Whether the duties he performed are of a sacerdotal nature is also a factual question.

Respondent's counsel at the trial argued that because there are subsequent years in which the issue here involved will again arise with respect to this same petitioner, his motion should be granted. In our view this fact alone is not sufficient ground for refusing the request of a petitioner that his case be tried as a small tax case. It might be to a petitioner's advantage not to have a case involving a continuing issue heard under section 7463 so he could obtain a decision which would be a precedent for future years. However, in our view this is not a sufficient ground for the Court to grant a motion by respondent to deny a petitioner's request for a hearing under section 7463.

We therefore hold that respondent has not shown adequate reasons to support his Motion to Deny Petitioners' Request for Conduct of Proceedings under Section 7463, filed February 9, 1971. An order will be entered denying respondent's motion.

NOTES AND QUESTIONS

1. May a taxpayer appeal a case tried under the Tax Court's small case procedures?
2. Was the issue in this case one of fact or law?
3. Under what circumstances may the Tax Court deny a taxpayer the opportunity to proceed under the small case procedures?

C. Pre-Trial

Prior to trial, there are two types of procedures in Tax Court that are very different from federal district court and Court of Federal Claims procedures. First, stipulations are required in Tax Court as opposed to permitted in refund forums. Second, the parties are required to go about the discovery process informally before invoking the Tax Court's formal discovery procedures.

1. Stipulations

Stipulation is not only permitted in Tax Court, it is required. The parties must stipulate to everything they can reasonably stipulate to. Rule 91 of the Tax Court Rules of Practice and Procedures provides as follows:

> The parties are required to stipulate, to the fullest extent to which complete or qualified agreement can or fairly should be reached, all matters not privileged which are relevant to the pending case, regardless of whether such matters involve fact or opinion or the application of law to fact.

> Included in matters required to be stipulated are all facts, all documents and papers or contents or aspects thereof, and all evidence which fairly should not be in dispute.

Stipulations serve multiple functions in Tax Court. First, Tax Court cases are generally very document intensive. In a case with hundreds of documents, it would be unwieldy and wasteful to require the attorneys to establish through a witness the authenticity of each document. At trial, it might be necessary in the case of some documents to hand the document to a witness, ask the witness to identify it, and ask the witness if the document is what it purports to be. For example, to admit thousands of electronic mail messages, an attorney might have to ask an employer's local area network administrator whether each electronic message was from the employer's electronic mail system. It would take days to establish authenticity rather than the minutes to agree to their authenticity in a stipulation.

Second, both the IRS and taxpayers are aware that many documents in a tax case contain more information than is necessary. Narrowing down the information to items that can be set forth in a stipulation can make it so the judge deciding the case does not have to wade through boxes of documents.

Third, the stipulation process facilitates settlement. The parties must get together to talk about the facts of the case. They may find out they do not disagree about the facts, in which case they can either settle the case or, if there is a disagreement over a legal issue, submit a fully stipulated case.

The next case provides an example of the stipulation process at work.

BAKARE v. COMMISSIONER
T.C. Memo. 1994-72
United States Tax Court

NAMEROFF, Special Trial Judge:

This case, originally involving 34 petitioners, is before the Court on petitioner Norman Katz' motion to be relieved of his stipulation of settlement filed with the Court on June 26, 1987.

This case was part of a litigation project regarding a shelter entitled Midas International or "Uranium For Tax $". Petitioner, as well as many other investors, was represented by Attorney Gregory Alohawiwoole Altman (Altman). Nine docketed cases involving Midas International were selected by Altman and respondent as test cases and consolidated for trial. A stipulation of settlement was signed on petitioner's behalf by Altman and filed with the Court on June 26, 1987. In the stipulation of settlement, petitioner agreed to be bound by the results of the test case. By notice of deficiency dated January 30, 1986, respondent determined a deficiency in Federal income tax due from petitioner of $4,740, plus additions to tax under section 6653(a)(1) and (2).

In the test case, Howard v. Commissioner, T.C.Memo. 1988–531, affd. 931 F.2d 578 (9th Cir.1991), we held that the Midas International transactions were utterly devoid of economic substance and must be ignored for Federal income tax purposes. As a result, we determined that the taxpayers therein were not entitled to deductions for mining development expenditures under the provisions of section 616[54] or mining exploration costs under the provisions of section 617. We also sustained respondent's determinations as to the additions to tax under section 6653(a)(1) and (2) for negligence. Finally, we held that the taxpayers therein were liable for the increased interest under section 6621(c) with regard to underpayments attributable to disallowed deductions incurred in connection with the Midas International program for 1980 and 1981. The Court of Appeals for the Ninth Circuit affirmed our decision, stating:

> In a case such as this where the taxpayers have been found to have entered into sham transactions without primary profit motivation, they have failed to meet their burden of showing due care. No reasonably prudent person would have acted as they did. * * * [931 F.2d at 582.]

---

[54] [fn 1] All section references are to the Internal Revenue Code in effect for the years at issue. All Rule references are to the Tax Court Rules of Practice and Procedure.

In petitioner's motion to set aside the stipulation of settlement, petitioner alleges that Altman was unable to render competent legal representation as he had been diagnosed as a manic depressive and was taking lithium to control his medical condition, but the medication had become ineffective due to a kidney infection.

By order dated October 22, 1993, the Court, in considering petitioner's motion, ordered petitioner to file a supplement to his motion outlining (1) the issues which would be tried in the event his motion were granted, (2) the documents which he intended to offer in evidence, (3) the names and addresses of the witnesses which he intended to call, including a brief summary as to what they would testify to, and (4) a statement as to how his case differs from *Howard v. Commissioner, supra.* In petitioner's supplement to his motion, he stated that he would be the sole witness and that his testimony would prove that he had the requisite profit motive, used due care, and was reasonably prudent. No additional relevant documentation was attached to petitioner's supplement.

At the hearing on petitioner's motion, petitioner submitted a letter dated June 1, 1990, from Altman addressed to "Uranium For Tax $" clients indicating that he has an adverse health condition stemming from a brain disorder which is life threatening, and, is, therefore, terminating his law practice. No additional documentation as to Altman's health was offered by petitioner nor was any additional relevant documentation offered to support any of petitioner's allegations of Altman's incompetence prior to June 1, 1990. However, petitioner did state that while in attendance at the trial of the test cases, he observed some disturbing signs in Altman's behavior.[55]

As to the merits of the income tax case, petitioner urged the Court to trace the money invested in the program, and that such tracing would indicate that actual drilling was commenced, thereby proving that the project was not a sham. However, petitioner neither has any of the bank records nor has attempted to obtain them. At this late date, we believe that it is extremely unlikely that he would be able to obtain bank records dating back to 1980 and 1981.

Moreover, we note that in *Howard* we found that there was no evidence to establish that Power Resources, Inc., the New Mexico drilling company which was hired as a contractor, ever received any of the $23 million allegedly obtained from purported option sales. We further found that the evidence indicated that only a fraction of the initial cash payments made by investors was actually expended by Power Resources for drilling on the mining claims involved in the Uranium For Tax Dollars program. Thus, the Court has already considered the cash flow and the extent of the drilling in reaching its conclusion that the investment was a sham. Accordingly, we are not convinced of any need to revisit this issue.

---

[55] [fn 2] Petitioner, a certified public accountant who had advised many of his own clients to invest in the Uranium For Tax Dollars program, attended the trial as a consultant to Altman.

With regard to the additions to tax for negligence, petitioner contends that he relied upon the representations of Altman who allegedly visited the mining site, and that he, as a knowledgeable certified public accountant, had a bona fide profit-making objective. In *Howard v. Commissioner, supra,* we stated, as follows:

> With the exception of Mr. Bambeck and Mr. Grosvenor, all of the petitioners were college graduates actively pursuing careers in, inter alia, medicine, dentistry, financial planning, insurance and banking. Mr. Bambeck has been a general constructor for some 25 years and Mr. Grosvenor has been a mason contractor for some 20 years. The petitioners, for the most part, displayed a marked indifference to the economic plausibility of the Uranium For Tax Dollars programs upon which they embarked in 1980 and 1981. * * * We find it inconceivable that any prudent individual would really believe that their agent, chosen by the promoter, could assuredly and routinely sell a uranium option to acquire each and every mining claims lease in the Uranium For Tax Dollars programs within seven days for $20,000 (in 1980) or $15,000 (in 1981), with the assurance that the investor's check would be returned in the event a uranium option sale could not be arranged. Nor does it appear that any of the investors in the Uranium For Tax Dollars programs questioned the authenticity of the transaction which gave them a drilling expense deduction which included the full amount of their initial payment of $5,000 with no allowances whatever for fees or commissions normally paid to the seller of such packaged, tax-advantaged deals. In short, we deem it highly unlikely that any of the petitioners here involved actually believed that the transactions did in fact occur as heralded by the promoters. The commercial surrealism of these transactions should have alerted a reasonable person to the chimerical nature of the uranium mining venture in New Mexico. * * *

Rule 91(e) provides that a stipulation, to the extent of its terms, shall be treated as a conclusive admission by the parties to the stipulation. This Court will not permit a party to qualify, change, or contradict a stipulation, except where justice requires. We will enforce a settlement of stipulation, whether written or orally stipulated into the record, unless for reasons of justice a party should be relieved from the stipulation. *Cataldo v. Commissioner,* 476 F.2d 628 (2d Cir.1973), affg. per curiam T.C.Memo. 1971–219; *Sennett v. Commissioner,* 69 T.C. 694, 697 (1978); *Saigh v. Commissioner,* 26 T.C. 171, 177 (1956). We have also enforced stipulations to be bound where the parties have agreed to be bound by the outcome of a test case. *Hillman v. Commissioner,* 687 F.2d 164, 165 (6th Cir.1982), affg. T.C.Memo. 1982–468; *Sennett v. Commissioner, supra; Rakosi v. Commissioner,* T.C.Memo. 1991–630. Here the stipulation was entered into fairly and freely by both parties and was entirely in accordance with their intentions. There is nothing in the record to indicate that Altman, in 1987, was not a competent attorney of record for petitioner. The stipulation of settlement to be bound by the results of *Howard* was beneficial to petitioner in that his case was not scheduled for trial and he was not required to put on extensive proof of his case. It was not until several years had passed after the trial, the opinion of the Court was issued, and the Court's decision was affirmed on appeal and became final that petitioner decided to have the settlement set aside and to retry the entire case. We find no compelling circumstances that indicate an injustice is being done in upholding the stipulation of settlement, and, therefore, will not permit the stipulation of settlement to be set aside. Accordingly, we deny petitioner's motion to have the settlement stipulation set aside.

An appropriate order denying petitioner's motion will be issued.

NOTES AND QUESTIONS

1. May a party renege on a stipulation?
2. What similarity is there between a stipulation and a contract?

2. Discovery

i.   Informality

The United States Tax Court Rules of Procedure and Practice permit the parties to obtain discovery from each other. Discovery is available in most courts, such as federal district courts and the Court of Federal Claims. Where the Tax Court differs is the level of informality. The Tax Court's Rules require it. Rule 70(a)(1) provides as follows:

> In conformity with these Rules, a party may obtain discovery . . . . However, the Court expects the parties to attempt to attain the objectives of discovery through informal consultation or communication before utilizing the discovery procedures provided in these Rules.

Perhaps it would not be clear what this means today were it not for the following case.

BRANERTON CORP. v. COMMISSIONER
61 T.C. 691 (1974)
United States Tax Court

OPINION

DAWSON, Judge:

This matter is before the Court on respondent's motion for a protective order, pursuant to Rule 103(a)(2), Tax Court Rules of Practice and Procedure, that respondent at this time need not answer written interrogatories served upon him by petitioners in these cases. Oral arguments on the motion were heard on February 20, 1974, and, in addition, a written statement in opposition to respondent's motion was filed by the petitioners.

The sequence of events in these cases may be highlighted as follows: The statutory notices of deficiencies were mailed to the respective petitioners on April 20, 1973. As to the corporate petitioner, the adjustments relate to (1) additions to a reserve for bad debts, (2) travel, entertainment, and miscellaneous expenses, (3) taxes, and (4) depreciation. As to the individual petitioners, the adjustments relate to (1) charitable contributions, (2) entertainment expenses, (3) dividend income, and (4) medical expenses. Petitions in both cases were filed on July 2, 1973, and, after an extension of time for answering, respondent filed his answers on September 26, 1973. This Court's new Rules of Practice and Procedure became effective January 1, 1974. The next day petitioners' counsel served on respondent rather detailed and extensive written interrogatories pursuant to Rule 71. On January 11, 1974, respondent filed his motion for a protective order. The cases have not yet been scheduled for trial.

Petitioners' counsel has never requested an informal conference with respondent's counsel in these cases, although respondent's counsel states that he is willing to have such discussions at any mutually convenient time. Consequently, in seeking a protective order, respondent specifically cites the second sentence of Rule 70(a)(1) which provides: 'However, the Court expects the parties to attempt to attain the objectives of discovery through informal consultation or communication before utilizing the discovery procedures provided in these Rules.'

It is plain that this provision in Rule 70(a)(1) means exactly what it says. The discovery procedures should be used only after the parties have made reasonable informal efforts to obtain needed information voluntarily. For many years the bedrock of Tax Court practice has been the stipulation process, now embodied in Rule 91. Essential to that process is the voluntary exchange of necessary facts, documents, and other data between the parties as an aid to the more expeditious trial of cases as well as for settlement purposes.[56] The recently adopted discovery procedures were not intended in any way to weaken the stipulation process. See Rule 91(a)(2).

Contrary to petitioners' assertion that there is no 'practical and substantial reason' for granting a protective order in these circumstances, we find good cause for doing so. Petitioners have failed to comply with the letter and spirit of the discovery rules. The attempted use of written interrogatories at this stage of the proceedings sharply conflicts with the intent and purpose of Rule 70(a)(1) and constitutes an abuse of the Court's procedures.

Accordingly, we conclude that respondent's motion for a protective order should be granted and he is relieved from taking any action with respect to these written interrogatories. The parties will be directed to have informal conferences

---

[56] [fn1] Part of the explanatory note to Rule 91 (60 T.C. 1118) states that—

'The stipulation process is more flexible, based on conference and negotiation between parties, adaptable to statements on matters in varying degrees of dispute, susceptible of defining and narrowing areas of dispute, and offering an active medium for settlement.'

during the next 90 days for the purpose of making good faith efforts to exchange facts, documents, and other information. Since the cases have not been scheduled for trial, there is sufficient time for the parties to confer and try informally to secure the evidence before resorting to formal discovery procedures. If such process does not meet the needs of the parties, they may then proceed with discovery to the extent permitted by the rules.

An appropriate order will be entered.

NOTES AND QUESTIONS

1. The taxpayer did not appeal this case. Why?
2. Parties to a Tax Court case seeking discovery often draft discovery requests that are essentially ready to be submitted to the court, but first send them informally to opposing counsel as a *"Branerton* Letter." If the opposing counsel fails to fulfill the request, turning the *Branerton* Letter into a formal discovery document is a short step.
3. Why does the Tax Court require the parties to proceed informally before requesting the court's involvement?

ii. Depositions

The stipulation requirement is considered a trade-off. It is not necessary to engage in formal or intrusive discovery because the parties are able to accomplish their litigation objectives through the stipulation process. Accordingly, depositions are considered an extraordinary discovery request in Tax Court. Rule 70(a)(1) of the Tax Court Rules of Practice and Procedure, in addition to the language regarding informal discovery, provides as follows:

> Discovery is not available under these Rules through depositions except to the limited extent provided in Rule 74.

Depositions are only permitted if there is no other way to obtain the information or the witness is on his or her deathbed. *See* Rule 74. This next case exemplifies how the Tax Court handles requests to use depositions.

HOWE v. COMMISSIONER
T.C. Memo. 1985-213
United States Tax Court

MEMORANDUM OPINION
PETERSON, SPECIAL TRIAL JUDGE:

This case was assigned to Special Trial Judge Marvin F. Peterson for trial or other disposition pursuant to the provisions of section 7456[57] and Rule 180[58] et seq., Tax Court Rules of Practice and Procedure.

This case is presently before the Court on petitioners' motion to compel the taking of deposition under Rule 75(d) and Rule 83 filed on October 24, 1984. Respondent filed his objections to motion to compel the taking of deposition and a memorandum in support of his position on November 29, 1984.

The substantive issues of this case involve the deductibility of losses claimed by petitioners in connection with their ownership of interests in a coal mining venture. In particular, one issue concerns the fair market value and economic feasibility of the venture. In order to assist in the appraisal and evaluation of the venture, respondent retained the services of an independent expert, Mr. William F. Bates, whom petitioners seek to depose.

Initially on April 26, 1984, petitioners requested that respondent consent to the depositions of Bates and respondent's two other experts, Roland G. Soil and Walter Jones. Respondent refused to consent to these depositions. Subsequently, by notice of deposition pursuant to subpoena duces tecum, Bates was noticed for deposition on October 15, 1984. Petitioners argue that the deposition is necessary to the timely preparation of the case for trial and will reduce the time necessary to try the case by increasing the opportunity for stipulation of facts and documents.

Respondent objects to the taking of the deposition on the ground that Rule 75 does not permit deposition of an opposing party's expert witness. Respondent maintains that depositions of expert witnesses are available only through the consensual provisions of Rule 74.

In Estate of Van Loben Sels v. Commissioner, 82 T.C. 64 (1984) we considered the limited circumstances under which compulsory depositions will be ordered. Such depositions are available only as provided in Rule 75(b). Estate of Van Loben Sels v. Commissioner, supra at 68. Rule 75(b) requires that petitioner must first pass the threshold requirement that the information sought is discoverable within the meaning of Rule 70(b). Rule 70(b) does not provide specific rules regarding the permissible scope of discovery from opposing expert witnesses. However, in Estate of Van Loben Sels v. Commissioner, supra, we looked to Rule 71(d)(1) which specifies the information which can be discovered from an opposing party regarding the expected testimony of expert witnesses.[59]

---

[57] [fn 1] Statutory references are to the Internal Revenue Code of 1954, as amended, unless otherwise indicated.

[58] [fn 2] All rule references are to the Tax Court Rules of Practice and Procedure.

[59] [fn 3] Rule 71(d)(1) limits discovery to identifying each person whom the other party expects to call as an expert witness at the trial of the case, by giving his name, address, vocation or occupation, and a statement of his qualifications, and to state the subject matter and the substance of the facts and opinions to which the expert is expected to testify, and give a summary of the grounds for

In that case we concluded that Rule 75 cannot be interpreted to permit by the extraordinary means of compulsory depositions that which cannot be accomplished through the more lenient procedures for interrogatories, supra at 69. Under Rule 71(d)(l) the scope of discovery of information pertinent to expert witnesses only includes discovery from the opposing party and not directly from the expert, supra. Thus, we concluded that Rule 75 does not permit compulsory deposition of expert witnesses because the information sought cannot be elicited from them under Rule 71.

Petitioners argue that our holding in Estate of Van Loben Sels v. Commissioner is erroneous. They maintain that depositions under both Rules 74 and 75 are subject to the scope limitations of Rule 70(b). Therefore, they contend that there is no justification for allowing consensual deposition of experts while prohibiting compulsory depositions as outside the scope of Rule 70(b).

However, Rule 75 specifically states that a compulsory deposition is an extraordinary method of discovery. It may be used only where the NON-PARTY WITNESS can give testimony or possesses documents or things which are discoverable within the meaning of Rule 70(b). This restrictive language does not appear in Rule 74. Thus, there is ample reason to interpret the scope of discovery more narrowly in the case of depositions under Rule 75. Accordingly, petitioners may not take the deposition of respondent's expert witness.

Petitioners argue in the alternative that an order compelling the deposition is available under Rule 83. Rule 83 allows the taking of depositions upon approval or direction of the Court after trial has commenced. Petitioners urge us to calendar the case for trial, order the deposition pursuant to Rule 83 and then continue the case generally for further trial preparation.

Petitioners' request is a clear attempt to circumvent the discovery provisions of our rules. Rule 80 clearly states that depositions under Title VIII (Rules 80 through 85) may be taken only for the purpose of making testimony or any document or thing available as evidence. Depositions for discovery purposes may be taken only in accordance with Rules 74 and 75. Petitioners are clearly attempting to depose respondent's expert for discovery purposes. Therefore, Rule 83 is not applicable in the instant case. For the reasons set forth above, petitioners' motion to compel the taking of deposition under Rules 75(d) and 83 will be denied.

An appropriate order will be entered.

NOTES AND QUESTIONS

1. To what discovery method does the court compare its deposition procedures?

---

each such opinion. In lieu of such a statement, a copy of the expert's report may be furnished. Also see the note to this rule, 60 T.C. 1101 (1973), which states that the complex discovery provisions relating to experts in the Federal Rules are considered inappropriate for purposes of litigation in this Court.

2. May a party compel the deposition of the opposing party's expert witnesses?

D. Trial

A major difference between the deficiency and refund jurisdictions is that the Tax Court permits taxpayers to estimate the amount of an item if the taxpayer has established entitlement to utilize the item. This permission to use estimates is referred to as the *Cohan* rule. Coincidentally, *Cohan* is the title of the next case.

COHAN v. COMMISSIONER
39 F.2d 540 (2d Cir.1930)
United States Court of Appeals, Second Circuit

Before L. HAND, SWAN, and MACK, Circuit Judges.
L. HAND, Circuit Judge.

In the year 1918 Cohan was a theatrical manager and producer, doing business in partnership with one Harris. He had originally been an actor like his father and mother, with whom while a boy he had begun to act in vaudeville. After 1899 the parents with their two children, Cohan and his sister, divided their earnings, one quarter to each of the children and a half to the parents, the petitioner collecting for all and distributing. In that year they employed a manager and after his death another, who married the daughter in 1905 and with her left the group. The other three then employed Harris as their manager, and made a change in the distribution. Cohan had begun to write plays, on which he was getting royalties, which he first withdrew from the net earnings. The parents next took out five hundred dollars a week, and the four divided what was left, half to Harris, a quarter to Cohan, and the rest to the parents. Before 1914 Cohan and his father had left the stage and spent their time in directing their plays, until the father died on July 31, 1917.

On his father's birthday, in January, 1914, Cohan as an expression of affection wrote a letter to him, the only relevant parts of which declared that the two were, and had for years been, partners in all Cohan's enterprises. The mother had left the stage and was not engaged in helping her son when the father died. Shortly afterwards Cohan told her that his father's estate 'was to be hers, that he wanted her to remain interested in their business affairs and that these affairs would be conducted as they had been in the past.' Thereafter he always divided equally with her his profits from the firm of Cohan & Harris, as he had done with his father. On June thirtieth, 1920, he and Harris separated and Cohan continued alone, continuing to give her half his net profits.

The first question is whether upon the foregoing facts the Board was right in fixing Cohan's income as the whole of what he received from the firm of Cohan & Harris, while it lasted, and later as the whole of his own profits. He maintains that his mother was always his partner, and that he is entitled to deduct from his receipts the sums which he paid to her. If the father was a partner at the time of his death, that partnership ended and Cohan, the survivor, had to account to the legatees or next of kin. We do not know whether there was a will, but we may assume that there was none, as no mention is made of one. If so, the widow and each child took a third, but we are left in the dark as to what were the assets. They could not have included those of the firm of Cohan & Harris, of which the father was not a member, because although he helped Cohan in writing his plays, there is nothing in the findings to show that Harris was privy to this, or that he recognized him as an associate. The assets of the supposed firm of Cohan & Cohan were not therefore shown to have been more than such profits as might come to hand out of Cohan's share from Cohan & Harris, and of these the daughter had a third. Therefore, when Cohan told his mother that his father's estate 'was to be hers,' at most he did no more than increase her share of his undistributed profits from one to two thirds. There is no evidence that any part of these entered into his income for 1918, and the later years; or, if so, what that part was. The petitioner has therefore on any theory failed in his proof pro tanto.

Moreover, he did not create a new partnership between himself and his mother at the same interview. The relevant law of New York at the time was section two of the Partnership Law of 1909 (Laws N.Y. 1909, c. 44 (Consol. Laws N.Y. c. 39)), which defined a partnership as an 'association * * * of two or more persons who have agreed to combine their labor, property and skill, or some of them, for the purpose of engaging in any lawful trade or business, and sharing the profits and losses, as such, between them.' In October, 1919 (Laws 1919, c. 408), the Uniform Partnership Act became a law in New York, the definition in section ten of which is: 'An association of two or more persons to carry on as co-owners a business for profit.' 'Combine' in the first act is probably the equivalent of 'co-owners' in the second, and it is difficult to see any substantial difference between the two. At any rate it is clear that neither Cohan nor his mother intended to carry on a joint business, for it does not appear that she had the least direction of his affairs, or any part in the conduct of the business. What he apparently meant was to give her half his earnings in consideration of his filial affection for her, and for her assistance in his early unprosperous years. However this unusual gratitude may affect our estimate of his character, we have only to consider whether he had changed his legal rights. There can be no doubt that he remained always free to stop his payments, and that her share depended on the endurance of his feelings toward her.

The Uniform Partnership Act has been similarly understood in New York (Martin v. Peyton, 246 N.Y. 213, 158 N.E. 77), and elsewhere (Giles v. Vette, 263 U.S. 553, 44 S.Ct. 157, 68 L.Ed. 441; In re Hoyne, 277 F. 668, (C.C.A. 7); Petition of Williams, 297 F. 696 (C.C.A. 1)), though none of these decisions are in point upon the facts. It has much changed the common law, even if the equivocal decision of Cox v. Hickman, 8 H.L.C. 267, be accepted as controlling in this country. While it still remains true under section eleven (Laws 1919, c. 408) that profit sharing is prima facie evidence of the 'association' defined in section ten, we are not to understand that it is ever more. The later subdivisions of that section deny to it any probative effect in the situations defined, but do not under any circumstances make profitsharing ventures partnerships when it is otherwise apparent that the parties did not intend to 'carry on as co-owners' any business whatever. The law has no doubt been brought into accord with business usage, yet there is not, as there should not be, any standard other than that the parties shall enter upon a joint business venture, vague as that is.

While the point is not argued, it is theoretically possible to debate whether the transaction was a transfer of one half Cohan's rights in Cohan & Harris and later in his own business, though it did not create a partnership. In any such aspect it must be remembered that the attempt was not to give her any direct interest in the firm of Cohan & Harris, or, if it was, it was ineffectual, because of Harris's failure to assent. Cohan could have given her no present right in such profits as he might thereafter withdraw, and there could not be an immediate gift, even if present words of gift had been used. Whether such a gift would have inured to the benefit of the donee as soon as Cohan withdrew any profits, and before he paid them over, we need not say; the gift was revocable until then in any case, and the case falls within Mitchel v. Bowers, 15 F.(2d) 287 (C.C.A. 2), where the agreement contained an express power of revocation. Finally, the words were not those of present gift in any event, but at most only a promise in, and this is equally true after the firm of Cohan & Harris was dissolved as before.

The next question is as to certain royalties upon a play produced in 1910, called 'Get Rich Quick Wallingford.' Cohan had written this in collaboration with his father who contributed the fourth act. As joint authors, each had a share in the resulting property (Maurel v. Smith, 271 F. 211 (C.C.A. 2)), and we may assume that in the absence of any contract they would share alike. Cohan agreed, however, while the work was in preparation, that his father was to have all the profits, and this we take at least as a gratuitous contribution of his services. The father thus became the owner of the play, and it passed to his representatives upon his death. Since the widow and the children shared alike, Cohan's part in the royalties was only one-third, with which at most his income could be charged. Whether that part passed to his mother depends again upon the effect of the transaction we have been discussing, but which we have hitherto found it unnecessary to decide. Being a right of literary property incapable of delivery, we know of no way by which a valid gift could be made save by deed. Beaver v. Beaver, 117 N.Y. 421, 429, 432, 22 N.E. 940, 6 L.R.A. 403, 15 Am.St.Rep. 531; In re Van Alstyne, 207 N.Y. 298, 100 N.E. 802. While therefore we think that the income should have been reduced by two-thirds of the royalties for 1918—the only year in question—Cohan must bear his third. The Board's finding is modified pro tanto.

The next question arises over the royalties for the years 1919 and 1920 which came to Cohan for some songs which he wrote for a play called 'The Royal Vagabond.' All that the finds say, is that he 'agreed with his wife, Agnes M. Cohan, to give her the royalties from the sale of the songs.' Quite aside from anything else, this does not show even an effort to make a present gift.

Cohan and Harris were joint lessees of a theatre in Chicago, and had assigned the lease to a little company whose shares they held half and half. After the dissolution of the firm in 1920, for a while they tried to apportion their bookings by agreement, but this proved too troublesome, so that in November of that year they agreed that Cohan should have the entire rights in it, Harris to arrange elsewhere for his plays. He needed one hundred and fifty thousand dollars for this purpose, which Cohan lent him, but until August, 1922, they were to use the theatre in common, Harris' profits going to extinguish the loan which he did not personally promise to pay. In October, 1922, they made a second agreement by which Harris in final payment assigned his rights in the lease—though he had none—his shares in the company, and his interest in the security which the firm had put up with the lessor.

Cohan deducted the loan from his income in 1920 as an expense, and the Board refused to allow it. His theory is either that it was an expense of his business, or that it purchased certain wasting rights which should be annually amortized. Neither position is good in law. The loan was originally to be repaid out of Harris' earnings from the theatre, apparently on the supposition that these would discharge it within two years. We infer that they did not, else the second agreement would not have been necessary, under which the balance was discharged by the shares and the deposit. Neither the money received, nor the shares, were a wasting asset, unless possibly the shares; but as there is no evidence of any depreciation in the lease between the time of the assignment, October, 1922, and June thirtieth, 1923, the deduction cannot be computed.

In the production of his plays Cohan was obliged to be free-handed in entertaining actors, employees, and, as he naively adds, dramatic critics. He had also to travel much, at times with his attorney. These expenses amounted to substantial sums, but he kept no account and probably could not have done so. At the trial before the Board he estimated that he had spent eleven thousand dollars in this fashion during the first six months of 1921, twenty-two thousand dollars, between July first, 1921, and June thirtieth, 1922, and as much for his following fiscal year, fifty-five thousand dollars in all. The Board refused to allow him any part of this, on the ground that it was impossible to tell how much he had in fact spent, in the absence of any items or details. The question is how far this refusal is justified, in view of the finding that he had spent much and that the sums were allowable expenses. Absolute certainty in such matters is usually impossible and is not necessary; the Board should make as close an approximation as it can, bearing heavily if it chooses upon the taxpayer whose inexactitude is of his own making. But to allow nothing at all appears to us inconsistent with saying that something was spent. True, we do not know how many trips Cohan made, nor how large his entertainments were; yet there was obviously some basis for computation, if necessary by drawing upon the Board's personal estimates of the minimum of such expenses. The amount may be trivial and unsatisfactory, but there was basis for some allowance, and it was wrong to refuse any, even though it were the traveling expenses of a single trip. It is not fatal that the result will inevitably be speculative; many important decisions must be such. We think that the Board was in error as to this and must reconsider the evidence.

There remain two questions relating to the computation of the income, each arising under the statute. Cohan had filed his returns for 1918 and 1919 upon the basis of the calendar year. In December, 1920, he asked leave to change to a fiscal year, from July first to June thirtieth, that being the usual one in theatrical businesses. It was too late under the regulations to get leave for the year 1920, but the Commissioner granted it for the next year, requiring him to file a return for the first six months of 1921, under section 212(b) of that act (42 Stat. 237). This he did not do, but continued to file returns for the calendar years, ignoring the consent. The Board fixed his taxes on the basis of a fiscal year from July first to June thirtieth, beginning in 1921, and of a separate return for the six months between January first and June thirtieth, 1921. Upon the trial he swore a witness who had kept his books, but he did not introduce them, though the Board gave him ample opportunity; because of this failure the testimony was ruled out.

The ruling was plainly right, for, while it is customary to allow accountants and the like to prepare estimates drawn from documents in evidence, this can never be done without the originals themselves, and the argument shows some hardihood. Section 212(b) required the return to be made 'in accordance with the method of accounting regularly employed in keeping the books'; and in their absence it could not appear that the books were not kept on the basis of the fiscal year that he had been required to accept. Indeed we must assume that they were, because otherwise the statute would not have justified his demand in December, 1920. Had he chosen to dispute the admission so implied, his only course was to produce the books, and prove that he had in fact continued to keep them on the 'basis' of the calendar year.

The final question arises over the reassessment of the tax for the first six months of 1921. The Revenue Act of 1921 (42 Stat. 227) became a law on November twenty-third of that year, eleven months after Cohan had asked for leave to change his accounting period. Title 2 (the income tax) of the Act of 1918 (40 Stat. 1057) was repealed as of January first, 1921, the date on which the same title of the act of 1921 took effect (section 263). Section 226(c) of 1921 substituted a new method of computing the tax for a part of the year when the taxpayer changed his accounting period under section 226(a). Subdivisions (a) and (b) of that section were the same as the corresponding provisions of the Act of 1918 (40 Stat. 1075), but under these it was possible to file a return for a portion of the year as for the whole, thus escaping the heavy surtaxes upon a part of the income for the year in which the change was made. To correct this, subdivision (c) provided in substance that the part should be taken as a proportionate sample of a supposititious income for the whole year, that the tax should be assessed upon the sum so found, but that the taxpayer should pay only that fraction of it which the period of the partial return bore to the whole year.

This was obviously more onerous than what had gone before, and especially so in the case of any receipts which chanced to fall in the fractional period, and which were not recurrent during the remainder. For example, a man who wished to begin his fiscal year in February might make a large profit in January which was not repeated again; yet subdivision (c) required him to compute his tax as though he had got twelve such payments, one in every month, and, although he need pay only a twelfth of the total tax so found, he suffered severely in what he did pay. This is an extreme case and Cohan's period was only a half year, yet in that time he got several annual payments which did not recur in the second half of the year. This is his complaint.

The statute is explicit, and, if it applies and is valid, he must bear the exaction, for we cannot recast the law by apportioning the unique receipts ratably over a whole year. Had he chosen to change his books after the law was passed, nobody could doubt its applicability, but, as we have said, he got permission, and, as the proof stands, committed himself before January 1, 1921, the beginning of the period when by retroaction the Act of 1921 took effect, so that his tax is computed at a much higher rate than any which he could have anticipated. He argues that the statute was not retroactive as to section 326(c), and that, if it was, it was unconstitutional. At the outset we must remember that the question merely concerns the method of computation; the statute reaches nothing that it did not reach before; incomes had been taxed for eight years quite as completely as under the Act of 1921. Furthermore, the change was to correct an omission in the Act of 1918, which allowed taxpayers to escape the high surtaxes imposed as a consequence of the Great War.

Before the decision of Brushaber v. Union Pacific R.R., 240 U.S. 1, 24, 25, 36 S.Ct. 236, 60 L.Ed. 493, L.R.A. 1917D, 414, Ann.Cas. 1917B, 713, it had been supposed that the Fifth Amendment did not apply to taxing statutes at all, but the intimations in that case have since been followed by several decisions directly holding the contrary (Nichols v. Coolidge, 274 U.S. 531, 47 S.Ct. 710, 71 L.Ed. 1184, 52 A.L.R. 1081; Blodgett v. Holden, 275 U.S. 142, 48 S.Ct. 105, 72 L.Ed. 206; Untermyer v. Anderson, 276 U.S. 440, 48 S.Ct. 353, 72 L.Ed. 645), and it must now be considered that in extreme cases transactions, untaxed when they took place, cannot be reached by a later statute, certainly when not in contemplation at the time. It is true that Brushaber v. Union Pacific R.R. concerned the income tax, but the suggestion there made has as yet borne no fruit in such cases. It appears to us that there is a valid distinction between the taxation of incomes and of gifts or testamentary transfers (Lewellyn v. Frick, 268 U.S. 238, 45 S.Ct. 487, 60 L.Ed. 934; Shwab v. Doyle, 258 U.S. 529, 42 S.Ct. 391, 66 L.Ed. 747, 26 A.L.R. 1454). Nobody has a vested right in the rate of taxation, which may be retroactively changed at the will of Congress at least for periods of less than twelve months; Congress has done so from the outset. Brushaber v. Union Pac R.R. Co., 240 U.S. 1, 36 S.Ct. 236, 60 L.Ed. 493, L.R.A. 1917D, 414, Ann.Cas. 1917B, 713; Lynch v. Hornby, 247 U.S. 339, 38 S.Ct. 543, 62 L.Ed. 1149. The same rule applies to excises (Billings v. U.S. 596), even when imposed for the first time. There was here an evil to correct. Before the change, taxpayers had had the opportunity to escape a common burden, which the section ended by adopting a fair rule, taken by and large. True, a portion of a year is often not a fair sample of the whole, but it will work now for, and now against, the individual, as often one way as the other. It is notoriously impossible nicely to adjust the weight of taxes, and it is no objection that upon occasion the result may disappoint reasonable anticipations. The injustice is no greater than if a man chance to make a profitable sale in the months before the general rates are retroactively changed. Such a one may indeed complain that, could he have foreseen the increase, he would have kept the transaction unliquidated, but it will not avail him; he must be prepared for such possibilities, the system being already in operation. His is a different case from that of one who, when he takes action, has no reason to suppose that any transactions of the sort will be taxed at all.

No doubt the difference is one of degree, but constitutional matters are generally that; limitations like the Fifth Amendment are not like sailing rules, or traffic ordinances; they do not circumscribe the action of Congress by metes and bounds. Rather they are admonitions of fair dealing, whose disregard the courts will correct, if extreme and glaring. Custom counts for much in such matters, and consistency for little; men cannot hope to fit their doings in advance to a pattern which will be sure to endure. The most they can expect is that courts will intervene when the defeat of their expectations passes any measure that reasonable persons could think tolerable, and even then their grievance must be fairly outside the zone of possible debate.

So it does not seem to us that the situation here calls for so heroic a remedy as to declare the statute unconstitutional, nor indeed for the lesser one of wringing the words out of their natural meaning. Nobody can really think that section 263 in making title 2 of the Act of 1921 date as of January first of that year, excepted subdivision (c) of section 226. In most cases it would operate fairly enough; we could excise only those in which it did not, and that we certainly cannot do. In those cases like Shwab v. Doyle and Lewellyn v. Frick, the statute was not explicit as here, and, while colloquial language is a fumbling means of expression, there are limits to its elasticity; to deny the application of these words to the case at bar seems to us to pass the point of rupture. Cooper v. U.S., 280 U.S. 409, 50 S.Ct. 164, 74 L.Ed. ——— .

The decision is modified as to the royalties of 'Get Rich Quick Wallingford,' and the cause is remanded to make some allowance for the expenses of travel and the like; otherwise it is affirmed.

NOTES AND QUESTIONS

1. The *Cohan* rule no longer applies in the context in which the events at issue occurred. Section 274(d) requires substantiation to deduct the travelling expenses the taxpayer estimated in *Cohan*. The Tax Court, however, still applies the *Cohan* rule in contexts where section 274(d) does not apply. *See, e.g.,* Illinois Toolworks Inc. v. Commissioner, T.C. Memo. 2018-121 (applying *Cohan* to estimate a foreign corporation's basis).

2. Was there anything special about the taxpayer that convinced the Second Circuit that the Board of Tax Appeals should accept his estimates?

CHAPTER 18

TAX REFUND LITIGATION

A. Introduction

A taxpayer may sue the government for a refund of a tax overpayment. The simple case would be a taxpayer who timely filed her tax return with payment and then finds an error afterward that resulted in an overpayment. She would then request a refund and, if the IRS disallowed the refund request, file suit in the federal district court or the Court of Federal Claims. Not all decisions to file a refund claim, however, occur after the taxpayer has paid the tax. If the taxpayer has not paid yet, and desires to challenge an amount the IRS has proposed to assess, the taxpayer may be able to decide whether to petition the Tax Court rather than sue for a refund. If the decision is to sue for a refund, the taxpayer must pay the amount asserted or assessed first, request a refund, and then sue to claim the refund. At one time, a refund suit was the sole method of challenging a tax. It was an oppressive system. Fortunately, the Tax Court provides a forum for judicial review before any tax has to be paid.

Although the Tax Court is the primary forum for tax litigation, there are some general reasons a taxpayer may choose a refund suit rather than a suit in Tax Court. The most significant ones are discussed here. First, a refund forum might be the taxpayer's only option. Some IRS actions fall outside the Tax Court's jurisdiction. An example given in the last chapter is an assessable penalty. In addition, where the IRS has issued a notice of deficiency and the taxpayer paid the deficiency amount, the Tax Court no longer has deficiency jurisdiction. A taxpayer's only choice then is the refund route. Also, the IRS may have assessed or collected the tax from a taxpayer who has ignored all the IRS's notices discussed in this book. In such a case, the taxpayer's only option is pursuing a refund suit.

Second, a refund forum might have favorable precedent. As discussed in the last chapter, the Tax Court has nationwide jurisdiction. If the Tax Court has spoken on an issue, and the Federal Circuit has not, the taxpayer may have a better chance in the Court of Federal Claims where the Federal Circuit's precedent applies. Sometimes the Federal Circuit has different precedent than the 12 regional circuit courts of appeal.

Third, a refund forum might seem fairer to some taxpayers. Although the Tax Court handles 98% of the docketed cases, the amount of money at issue is not always as lopsided. Some large taxpaying entities believe that the Tax Court is biased against large businesses, so they choose to litigate in refund forums.

B. The Refund Forums

Federal district court and the Court of Federal Claims share concurrent jurisdiction over tax refund cases. *See* 28 U.S.C. § 1346(a)(1). Federal district courts are Article III courts that exercise "[t]he judicial power of the United States." *See* U.S. CONST. art. III, § 1. There is no question that federal district courts reside in the judicial branch of the federal government. The Court of Federal Claims is an Article I court, like the Tax Court. *See* 28 U.S.C. § 171(a). Unlike the Tax Court, the Court of Federal Claims resides in the judicial branch despite not being an Article III court. *See* Brant Hellwig, *The Constitutional Nature of the United States Tax Court*, 35 VA. TAX REV. 269, 316 (2016).

1. Federal District Court

Federal district courts have jurisdiction over refund claims. There are 94 federal judicial districts with a federal district court and over 350 federal court buildings where federal district court cases take place. Federal district courts have general jurisdiction over cases in law and equity. Article III of the Constitution protects district court judges from having their salary reduced and from being fired for political reasons. They come from diverse backgrounds, and there are very few with tax expertise.

The Federal Rules of Civil Procedure and the Federal Rules of Evidence apply to litigation in federal district court. Districts often have their own local rules, and judges often have their own standing pre-trial orders. District court judges tend to be less patient with pro se parties than the U.S. Tax Court.

The three advantages of litigating in district court are jury trial availability, convenience, and local bias. First, jury trials are available, and they are unavailable in any other tax judicial forum. If willfulness is at issue, perhaps a jury might look more favorably at the taxpayer than a judge. Or perhaps a jury might not understand an issue well enough to find for the government.

Second, a federal district court may be in a more convenient location than the location of Tax Court trials or Court of Federal Claims trials. The Tax Court travels to 70 cities to make trials convenient to taxpayers. In a rural area, however, these cities might be hours away from the most populated areas in a state. In South Dakota, for example, the Tax Court travels to Aberdeen. Aberdeen is approximately a three-hour drive from Sioux Falls, which is the most populated area of the state. Aberdeen is approximately a five-hour drive from Rapid City, the second most populated area of the state. In contrast, there are over 350 federal district court buildings in the country. In South Dakota, there is a federal court building in both of the two most populated areas, Sioux Falls and Rapid City.

Third, a taxpayer may be able to take advantage of local bias in a federal district court. One would not expect a court to ignore federal law in favor of a local taxpayer. But a federal district court judge will view with less skepticism a large employer with a good reputation in the area that litigates against the IRS than a Tax Court judge or Court of Federal Claims judge that visits from Washington, D.C.

2. The Court of Federal Claims

Another court that hears tax refund cases is the Court of Federal Claims. The Court is located in Washington, D.C. on Madison Place. The Federal Circuit, the appellate court that hears appeals from the Court of Federal Claims, is in the same building.

The Court of Federal Claims' constitutional status is more established than that of the Tax Court. Like the Tax Court, the Court of Federal Claims is an Article I court rather than an Article III court. Unlike the Tax Court, however, the Court of Federal Claims is considered in the judicial branch. The Tax Court's status is unclear.

Like the Tax Court, the Court of Federal Claims has nationwide jurisdiction. Judges travel to federal buildings with courtrooms around the country to hear cases. Unlike the Tax Court, however, only one court hears appeals from the court, the Federal Circuit.

The Court of Federal Claims has specific rather than general jurisdiction. It has jurisdiction over various types of cases against the government, including suits for tax refunds. Other subjects include government contracts, patent infringement, and copyright infringement.

Federal statute provides positions for 16 judges to serve on the Court of Federal Claims. Currently, there are no judges on the court appointed prior to 2005. Judges serve 15-year terms, much like Tax Court judges. Although the judges are not generalists, it is not common for any of the judges to be tax experts.

C. Refund Litigation

Although there are differences between litigating in federal district court and the Court of Federal Claims, there are some common characteristics to litigating in these courts because they both involve refund suits. The refund aspect of the litigation creates some major distinctions from deficiency litigation. Some major issues are (1) the period to bring a suit, (2) whether the grounds of a refund suit vary from the underlying administrative refund claim, (3) whether the taxpayer must pay the entire amount owed for a valid refund suit to take place, (4) the extent of stipulation practice, and (5) the use of estimates at trial.

1. Period to Bring Suit

Once a taxpayer submits a request for a refund from the IRS, the taxpayer may not sue immediately because the IRS needs time to review the request. Accordingly, before commencing a refund suit, the taxpayer must wait six months before filing suit. If the IRS denies the refund prior to six months, the taxpayer may also sue. Once the period to sue is triggered, the taxpayer has two years to file the suit.

Section 6532(a) provides as follows:

> No suit or proceeding . . . for the recovery of any internal revenue tax, penalty, or other sum, shall be begun before the expiration of 6 months from the date of filing the claim required under such section unless the [IRS] renders a decision thereon within that time, nor after the expiration of 2 years from the date of mailing by certified mail or registered mail by the [IRS] to the taxpayer of a notice of the disallowance . . . .

The taxpayer may also waive the right to a notice. This is common when the taxpayer has received a deficiency notice after an audit.

The IRS may waive the 2-year statute even after the statute has expired. In contrast, IRS may not waive the assessment statute under section 6501 after the period has expired. Section 6532 does not contain the same limitation.

Tax Court has no original jurisdiction over a disallowed refund claim. This does not, however, mean it may not determine that a refund exists. If a deficiency notice has been filed, the Tax Court has the authority to decide that an overpayment has been made and/or that a refund is due.

2. Substantial Variance

A refund suit is based on a refund claim that the IRS disallowed. Accordingly, the taxpayer cannot base the suit on grounds that substantially vary from the grounds raised in the refund claim the IRS considered and rejected. Otherwise, the government would not have sufficient notice to defend the suit. The government's substantial variance defense can be factual or legal, but it is more likely to succeed if the variance is factual. The IRS holds the government's institutional knowledge of the tax laws it administers, so it should be considered on notice for legal contentions. The following case involves a glaring factual variance.

OTTAWA SILICA CO. v. UNITED STATES
699 F.2d 1124 (1983)
United States Court of Appeals, Federal Circuit

Before DAVIS, NICHOLS and NIES, Circuit Judges.
OPINION
PER CURIAM.

This tax refund suit for tax years 1964, 1967, 1969-1971, comes before us on appeal from the United States Claims Court.[1] [The] issue[] involved: whether [taxpayer Ottawa Silica Company] may claim a charitable contribution for the transfer of land to a high school district. On [this] question[], Judge Colaianni ruled against taxpayer and therefore dismissed its petition. We fully agree with that opinion, which is appended hereto, and therefore affirm on the basis of that opinion.

Affirmed.

APPENDIX

The opinion of Judge Colaianni of the Claims Court follows:

In this action, plaintiff, Ottawa Silica Company, seeks to recover federal income taxes and assessed interest for its tax years 1964, 1967, 1969, 1970 and 1971, plus statutory interest. [The issue] to be resolved [is]: whether Ottawa Silica Company (Ottawa) is entitled to certain percentage depletion deductions for the years 1965-71 . . . .[2]

Ottawa is a family-owned corporation organized and existing under the laws of the State of Delaware and has its principal place of business in Ottawa, Illinois. Ottawa has been engaged in the mining, processing and marketing of industrial sand known as silica since 1900. Silica sand, also known as quartzite, as distinguished from common sand, is a highly refined industrial mineral. It is the basic raw material of the glass and ceramic industry. It is also used in the foundry industry as a core and molding sand. Its industrial uses in chemical markets include: paint, testing sand, and hydrofracing sand for the oil well industry. . . .

ARGUMENT . . .

The . . . issue raised by plaintiff concerns the degree to which the court will allow a taxpayer to vary the grounds of its suit from those raised in the claims for refund. Plaintiff has alleged that the IRS failed to allow it the full percentage depletion deduction that it was entitled to and, in so doing also failed to allow plaintiff the full consolidated net operating loss deduction it was entitled to for 1967. The parties have reached an agreement that is dispositive of the substantive aspects of both the percentage depletion and the net operating loss issues. The procedural issue which remains to be resolved is whether the grounds for relief

---

[1] [fn *] Pursuant to the order of this court dated October 4, 1982, the Claims Court entered a final judgment in accordance with Trial Judge Colaianni's recommended decision of April 7, 1982.

[2] [fn 2] The plaintiff raised several grounds for relief in its petition to this court. The parties have, by stipulation, agreed to dismiss the claim for interest paid or accrued on certain of plaintiff's indebtedness raised in paragraphs 6 and 7 of the petition and the issue of the rate of depletion raised in paragraph 8 of the petition. The latter stipulation does not include the issue of the computation of the proper gross income from mining nor defendant's variance argument raised in response to this claim. Further, the parties have reached an agreement that will dispose of the substantive aspects of the depletion deduction and the net operating loss deduction once this court resolves the so-called variance issue.

stated in plaintiff's claim for a refund are adequate to confer jurisdiction on this court over an aspect of the percentage depletion deduction not mentioned in the refund claim. It is my opinion that the jurisdiction of this court does not extend to those aspects of the percentage depletion deduction and the 1967 net operating loss that were not adequately raised on plaintiff's claims for refund.

During all times relevant to these proceedings, Ottawa and its subsidiaries sold a form of industrial sand, or quartzite, known as silica, which is a mineral described in section 613(b)(7) of the Internal Revenue Code. The code allows plaintiff a percentage depletion deduction for the silica it removes from each of its mining properties. The allowable deduction is the lesser of: (a) the gross income from the property multiplied by the appropriate percentage depletion rate specified in section 613(b)(7), or (b) 50 percent of the taxable income from the property. 26 U.S.C. § 613(a) (1976). The term "gross income from the property" means the gross income from mining, which is that amount of income "attributable to the processes of extraction of the ores or minerals from the ground and the application of mining processes." Treas.Reg. § 1.613-4(a). Packaging the ore or minerals is a non-mining process. *Id.*

On its federal income tax returns for the tax years 1964 through 1971, plaintiff took percentage depletion deductions for the silica it had mined from its properties. During this time plaintiff sold the silica both in bags and in bulk quantities. In computing the gross income from mining for each type of the silica products, plaintiff's accountants used a bulk sales price. They considered any extra income derived from the sale of bagged products as income attributable to a non-mining process. For that reason, they excluded the extra income from their calculations when determining the gross income from mining figure for the bagged products.

One of the items plaintiff sold was a bagged product known as Ottawa Testing Sand. Plaintiff sold the testing sand only in bags and for a price substantially higher than the bulk price of its other products. Plaintiff's accountants, however, computed the gross income from mining figure for the testing sand by using the bulk sales price. The accountants could have calculated the gross income by using the actual sales price of the testing sand less the costs attributable to the non-mining processes (bagging). Had they done so, the gross income from mining for the testing sand would have been greater than the figure obtained using the bulk price. Thus, the use of the bulk price produced a lower gross income from mining, which in turn yielded a lower percentage depletion deduction for the testing sand when multiplied by the applicable rate. Plaintiff first learned that it had understated the gross income from mining and the depletion deduction for the testing sand in July 1977, during an IRS audit of plaintiff's tax returns for 1972 through 1975.

On its tax returns for the years 1964 through 1972, plaintiff had used rates of 15 percent or 14 percent in calculating its percentage depletion deduction. After examining plaintiff's returns, the IRS reduced the depletion deduction by requiring plaintiff to use a 5 percent rate for some of its products. The reports prepared by the examining agents for the fiscal years ending on January 1, 1967,

December 31, 1967, and December 29, 1968, gave the following reasons for reducing the percentage depletion deductions:

A 15% rate of percentage depletion was claimed on all of the income from the sale of the silica sand and quartzite sold after the application of the ordinary mine treatment processes. A 5% rate of percentage depletion is recommended on the silica sand and quartzite sold for use as strecco stone, plaster, exposed aggregate, golf trap sand and like uses.

In a report dated May 31, 1973, the IRS made similar reductions of the depletion deduction for the fiscal years ending on December 28, 1969, January 3, 1971, and January 2, 1972. That report provided:

Taxpayer has computed depletion based on 15% in the first year and on 14% in the succeeding two years. Most of the products sold go into use in the glass or foundry industries. Some of the products are sold to construction industries and some small amounts are sold for such uses as golf trap sand or as playsand, which qualify only for a 5% depletion rate.

The IRS made no other adjustments to the percentage depletion deductions aside from the reduction of the depletion rate for some of plaintiff's products. . . .

Plaintiff subsequently paid the resulting tax deficiencies and filed timely refund claims on or about January 7, 1975, for the tax years 1967, 1969, 1970, and 1971. To each of these refund claims plaintiff attached a statement that provided:

This Statement is being attached to Refund Claims of Ottawa Silica Company and Subsidiary Companies for FYE 12/31/67, FYE 12/28/69, FYE 1/3/71 and FYE 1/2/72. The bases for these Refund Claims are as follows:

1. Pursuant to Revenue Agents Reports dated February 4, 1972, as supplemented by a Conference Report dated August 1, 1972, covering FYE 12/31/62, FYE 12/31/63, FYE 12/31/64, FYE 1/2/66, FYE 1/1/67, FYE 12/31/67 and FYE 12/29/68 and a Revenue Agents Report dated August 27, 1931 (presumably meaning 1973) covering FYE 12/28/69, FYE 1/3/71 and 1/2/72 Ottawa Silica Company and/or certain of its consolidated subsidiaries were erroneously denied deductions for the following items:

(a) * * *

(b) Percentage depletion as follows:

FYE	
1/2/66	$ 5,701.00
1/1/67	16,977.00
12/31/67	138,457.15
12/29/68	24,802.64
12/28/69	32,333.20
1/3/71	14,214.37
1/2/72	12,339.67

(c) * * *

(d) The consolidated net operating loss carryback properly deductible in FYE 12/31/67.

At this time plaintiff did not know that it had erred in calculating the depletion deduction for the Ottawa Testing Sand. It was only in July 1977 that plaintiff discovered that it could have taken a greater deduction for the testing sand, but by then the statute of limitations prevented the filing or amending of its refund claims for the tax years 1964 through 1971.

In June 1978 plaintiff petitioned this court for a refund of its income taxes, alleging *inter alia,* that the IRS had failed to allow it the full depletion deduction it was entitled to. Plaintiff now asks this court to grant it [certain] deductions for depletion. . . .

The conditions under which a taxpayer may sue the United States for the recovery of income taxes are defined by statute and by regulation. The Internal Revenue Code prohibits any taxpayer from maintaining an action to recover taxes from the Government unless a claim for a refund has first been filed with the Internal Revenue Service (IRS). 26 U.S.C. § 7422(a) (1976).[3] The regulations further provide that the claim for a refund "must set forth in detail each ground upon which a credit or a refund is claimed and facts sufficient to apprise the Commissioner of the exact basis thereof." Treas.Reg. § 301.6402-2(b)(1) (1955). Together, the statute and the regulation preclude a taxpayer-plaintiff from substantially varying at trial the factual bases of its arguments from those raised in the refund claims it presented to the IRS. *Union Carbide Corp. v. United States,* 222 Ct.Cl. 75, 90, 612 F.2d 558, 566 (1979); *Cook v. United States,* 220 Ct.Cl. 76, 86-87, 599 F.2d 400, 406 (1979).

This court has on many occasions considered the issue of variance and has adhered to the general rule that a ground for a refund that is neither specifically raised by a timely claim for a refund, nor comprised within the general language of the claim, cannot be considered by a court in a subsequent suit for a refund. *Union Pacific Railroad v. United States,* 182 Ct.Cl. 103, 108, 389 F.2d 437, 442 (1968); *see Forward Communications Corp. v. United States,* 221 Ct.Cl. 582, 623, 608 F.2d 485, 508 (1979); *John B. Lambert & Associates v. United States,*

---

[3] [fn 4] The statute provides:

"No suit or proceeding shall be maintained in any court for the recovery of any internal revenue tax alleged to have been erroneously or illegally assessed or collected, or of any penalty claimed to have been collected without authority, or of any sum alleged to have been excessive or in any manner wrongfully collected, until a claim for refund or credit has been duly filed with the Secretary, according to the provisions of law in that regard, and the regulations of the Secretary established in pursuance thereof."

26 U.S.C. § 7422(a).

212 Ct.Cl. 71, 86-87 (1976); *Fruehauf Corp. v. United States,* 201 Ct.Cl. 366, 378-79, 477 F.2d 568, 575 (1973). The reasons for this rule preventing substantial variance are:

> [T]o prevent surprise and to give adequate notice to the [Internal Revenue] Service of the nature of the claim and the specific facts upon which it is predicated, thereby permitting an administrative investigation and determination. * * * In addition, the Commissioner is provided with an opportunity to correct any errors, and if disagreement remains, to limit the scope of any ensuing litigation to those issues which have been examined and which he is willing to defend.

Union Pacific Railroad v. United States, 182 Ct.Cl. at 109, 389 F.2d at 442.

In the present case, plaintiff's refund claims contained no reference to the error it had made in computing the gross income from mining for the testing sand or to the effect of the error on the deductions for depletion and net operating loss.[4] This issue arose for the first time in the proceedings before this court. The defendant now argues that the court lacks jurisdiction over the testing sand aspect of plaintiff's depletion deduction because that issue is at substantial variance with the issues raised in the refund claims. Plaintiff contends, however, that our jurisdiction, having been properly invoked to consider the appropriate rate for part of the depletion deduction, extends as well to determining the appropriate depletion deduction for the testing sand. As part of this argument, plaintiff asserts that the timely refund claim for the rate issue established its right to sue for a refund on the whole depletion issue and that the testing sand error affects only the amount plaintiff is entitled to recover. This court cannot accept plaintiff's argument.

The statute and the regulations are quite clear. A taxpayer must specify the grounds and the factual bases from which they arise in its claim for a refund if it later wishes to litigate on those grounds. Plaintiff concedes that it failed to mention the testing sand error in its refund claims, but nonetheless relies on the above-stated argument to bring the testing sand error before this court.

Simply put, plaintiff's argument is without merit—the jurisdiction of this court to hear the dispute over the appropriate depletion rate to be used for some of plaintiff's products does not extend to the effect of the testing sand error on the depletion deduction and net operating loss. The errors plaintiff made in computing the depletion deduction for the Ottawa Testing Sand constitute a separate ground for relief, distinct from the issue of the appropriate rate asserted in the claims for refund. Each issue has a different factual basis and neither is a subsidiary of or integral to the other.[5] That being the case, the rule of substantial

---

[4] [fn 5] This is necessarily so because the error was not discovered by plaintiff or defendant until 1977, after the claims had been filed.

[5] [fn 6] This case does not present a situation in which the issue raised at the trial stage is derived from or is integral to the ground timely raised in the refund claim and thus may be considered as part of the initial ground. Cf. Union Pacific

variance precludes this court from exercising jurisdiction over the issues arising from the testing sand error because they were not first raised in the claim for a refund. *See L.E. Meyers Co. v. United States,* 673 F.2d 1366 (Ct.Cl., 1982); *Forward Communications Corp. v. United States,* 221 Ct.Cl. at 623, 608 F.2d at 508; *John B. Lambert & Associates v. United States,* 212 Ct.Cl. at 86-87.

Essentially, plaintiff is urging this court to embrace an expansive view of our jurisdiction over tax refund suits. To adopt plaintiff's view, however, would fly in the face of the statute and regulations that govern the grounds upon which a taxpayer may sue for a refund of taxes. One reason for requiring a taxpayer to specify the grounds for relief in its claim for a refund is to limit any subsequent litigation to those grounds that the IRS has already had an opportunity to consider and is willing to defend. *Union Pacific Railroad v. United States,* 182 Ct.Cl. at 109, 389 F.2d at 442; *see Forward Communications Corp. v. United States,* 221 Ct.Cl. at 623, 608 F.2d at 508. The case at bar presents precisely this sort of situation. To allow plaintiff to litigate the matter of the depletion deduction allowable for the testing sand would frustrate the purpose of the statute and regulations and would create an exception that would effectively nullify the substantial variance rule.

Plaintiff has attempted to escape the effect of the substantial variance rule by arguing that it established its right to recover on the depletion deduction by timely filing a refund claim in which it challenged the IRS's reduction of its rate of depletion. Plaintiff further asserts that the error made in computing the depletion deduction for the testing sand affects only the *amount* of recovery, not plaintiff's *right* to recover, and that the court may properly consider the testing sand error. In support of its position, plaintiff relies on *Red River Lumber Co. v. United States,* 134 Ct.Cl. 444, 446, 139 F.Supp. 148, 149-50 (1956). Although *Red River Lumber* does state that an error affecting only the amount of recovery may be raised at trial for the first time if the taxpayer has already established its right to recover by timely filing a refund claim, plaintiff's reliance on the case is misplaced.

The *Red River Lumber* case does not allow a taxpayer to introduce new factual bases of another ground for recovery for the first time at trial. This is essentially what plaintiff is attempting to use the case for. The computation of the gross income from mining figure for the testing sand is distinct from the issue concerning the appropriate rate of depletion raised in the refund claim. The erroneous gross income from mining figure constitutes a separate ground upon which plaintiff might have sought a refund had it been timely discovered. Certainly this error affected the amount of the depletion deduction and, in turn, the amount of plaintiff's potential recovery. But it does so only insofar as any separate ground for a refund necessarily affects the amount a litigant may be entitled to recover. The *Red River Lumber* case is distinguishable from the

---

Railroad v. United States, 182 Ct.Cl. at 109-10, 389 F.2d at 443 (citing instances in which subsidiary issues must necessarily have been considered as part of grounds in refund claim).

present one. There, the figure allowed to be changed was the sales price—a figure integral to determining gain, which was an issue properly before the court. Here, however, plaintiff wishes to raise the issue of the gross income from mining for the testing sand, which is not at all related to the issue of the rate of depletion that had been properly raised.

There are many distinct tax issues under the general heading of depletion. Plaintiff may not confer on itself the right to litigate on any one of them by the simple expedient of including one depletion issue in its claim for a refund. The purpose of the variance rule is to limit, not expand, the issues subject to litigation in a tax refund suit. *Union Pacific Railroad v. United States,* 182 Ct.Cl. at 108-09, 389 F.2d at 442. Unfortunately for plaintiff, it may not now raise the matter of the testing sand error and its effect on the depletion deduction or net operating loss deduction.

CONCLUSION

It is concluded that . . . the rule of variance precludes plaintiff from raising before this court any issues arising from its failure to properly compute the depletion deduction allowable for the Ottawa Testing Sand for the years here at issue. Accordingly, plaintiff's petition must be dismissed.

NOTES AND QUESTIONS

1. Would this case have come out differently if the statute of limitations had not expired?
2. Why does the IRS oppose substantial variance?
3. How closely must claims be related?

3. Full Payment Rule

Refund forums have jurisdiction over refunds. An issue that arises is whether a taxpayer can pay the part of the tax that is believed to be in dispute or whether the taxpayer must pay the entire liability for the tax year in issue. Courts have held that payment of only part of the tax liability and then requesting a refund is not sufficient to confer refund jurisdiction. It is a close call, but the issue is definitively decided in the following case.

FLORA v. UNITED STATES
362 U.S. 145 (1960)
Supreme Court of the United States

Mr. Chief Justice WARREN delivered the opinion of the Court.

The question presented is whether a Federal District Court has jurisdiction under 28 U.S.C. s 1346(a)(1), 28 U.S.C.A. s 1346(a)(1), of a suit by a taxpayer for the refund of income tax payments which did not discharge the entire amount of his assessment.

This is our second consideration of the case. In the 1957 Term, we decided that full payment of the assessment is a jurisdictional prerequisite to suit, 357 U.S. 63, 78 S.Ct. 1079, 2 L.Ed.2d 1165. Subsequently the Court granted a petition for rehearing. 360 U.S. 922, 79 S.Ct. 1430, 3 L.Ed.2d 1538. The case has been exhaustively briefed and ably argued. After giving the problem our most careful attention, we have concluded that our original disposition of the case was correct.

Under such circumstances, normally a brief epilogue to the prior opinion would be sufficient to account for our decision. However, because petitioner in reargument has placed somewhat greater emphasis upon certain contentions than he had previously, and because our dissenting colleagues have elaborated upon the reasons for their disagreement, we deem it advisable to set forth our reasoning in some detail, even though this necessitates repeating much of what we have already said.

THE FACTS

The relevant facts are undisputed and uncomplicated. This litigation had its source in a dispute between petitioner and the Commissioner of Internal Revenue concerning the proper characterization of certain losses which petitioner suffered during 1950. Petitioner reported them as ordinary losses, but the Commissioner treated them as capital losses and levied a deficiency assessment in the amount of $28,908.60, including interest. Petitioner paid $5,058.54 and then filed with the Commissioner a claim for refund of that amount. After the claim was disallowed, petitioner sued for refund in a District Court. The Government moved to dismiss, and the judge decided that the petitioner 'should not maintain' the action because he had not paid the full amount of the assessment. But since there was a conflict among the Courts of Appeals on this jurisdictional question, and since the Tenth Circuit had not yet passed upon it, the judge believed it desirable to determine the merits of the claim. He thereupon concluded that the losses were capital in nature and entered judgment in favor of the Government. 142 F.Supp. 602. The Court of Appeals for the Tenth Circuit agreed with the district judge upon the jurisdictional issue, and consequently remanded with directions to vacate the judgment and dismiss the complaint. 246 F.2d 929. We granted certiorari because the Courts of Appeals were in conflict with respect to a question which is of considerable importance in the administration of the tax laws.[6]

THE STATUTE

The question raised in this case has not only raised a conflict in the federal decisions, but has also in recent years provoked controversy among legal commentators.[7] In view of this divergence of expert opinion, it would be

---

[6] [fn 1] The decision of the Court of Appeals in *Flora* conflicted with Bushmiaer v. United States, 8 Cir., 230 F.2d 146. Cf. Coates v. United States, 2 Cir., 111 F.2d 609; Sirian Lamp Co. v. Manning, 3 Cir., 123 F.2d 776, 138 A.L.R. 1423; Suhr v. United States, 3 Cir., 18 F.2d 81, semble.

[7] [fn 2] As will appear later, prior to 1940 the general view was that full payment was a jurisdictional prerequisite. But a substantial difference of opinion arose after 1940, when the Court of Appeals for the Second Circuit decided

surprising if the words of the statute inexorably dictated but a single reasonable conclusion. Nevertheless, one of the arguments which has been most strenuously urged is that the plain language of the statute precludes, or at the very least strongly militates against, a decision that full payment of the income tax assessment is a jurisdictional condition precedent to maintenance of a refund suit in a District Court. If this were true, presumably we could but recite the statute and enter judgment for petitioner—though we might be pardoned some perplexity as to how such a simple matter could have caused so much confusion. Regrettably, this facile an approach will not serve.

Section 1346(a)(1) provides that the District Courts shall have jurisdiction, concurrent with the Court of Claims, of

'(1) Any civil action against the United States for the recovery of *any internal-revenue tax* alleged to have been erroneously or illegally assessed or collected, *or any penalty* claimed to have been collected without authority or *any sum* alleged to have been excessive or in any manner wrongfully collected under the internal-revenue laws * * *.' (Emphasis added.)

It is clear enough that the phrase 'any internal-revenue tax' can readily be construed to refer to payment of the entire amount of an assessment. Such an interpretation is suggested by the nature of the income tax, which is '*A tax* * * * imposed for each taxable year,' with the 'amount of *the* tax' determined in accordance with prescribed schedules.[8] (Emphasis added.) But it is argued that this reading of the statute is foreclosed by the presence in s 1346(a)(1) of the phrase 'any sum.' This contention appears to be based upon the notion that 'any sum' is a catchall which confers jurisdiction to adjudicate suits for refund of part of a tax. A catchall the phrase surely is; but to say this is not to define what it catches. The sweeping role which petitioner assigns these words is based upon a conjunctive reading of 'any internal-revenue tax,' 'any penalty,' and 'any sum.' But we believe that the statute more readily lends itself to the disjunctive reading which is suggested by the connective 'or.' That is, 'any sum,' instead of being related to 'any internal-revenue tax' and 'any penalty,' may refer to amounts which are neither taxes nor penalties. Under this interpretation, the function of the phrase is to permit suit for recovery of items which might not be designated as either 'taxes' or 'penalties' by Congress or the courts. One obvious example of such a 'sum' is interest. And it is significant that many old tax statutes described

---

Coates v. United States, 111 F.2d 609, against the Government. See Riordan, Must You Pay Full Tax Assessment Before Suing in the District Court? 8 J.Tax. 179; Beaman, When Not to Go to the Tax Court: Advantages and Procedures in Going to the District Court, 7 J.Tex. 356; Rudick and Wender, Federal Income Taxation, 32 N.Y.U.L.Rev. 751, 777-778; Note, 44 Calif.L.Rev. 956; Note, 2 How.L.J. 290.

[8] [fn 3] See I.R.C. (1954), ss 1(a), 1(b)(1), 68A Stat. 5, 6, 26 U.S.C.A. s 1(a), (b)(1). The same general pattern has existed for many years. See, e.g., ss 116, 117, of the Act of June 30, 1864, c. 173, 13 Stat. 281-282.

the amount which was to be assessed under certain circumstances as a 'sum' to be added to the tax, simply as a 'sum,' as a 'percentum,' or as 'costs.'[9] Such a rendition of the statute, which is supported by precedent,[10] frees the phrase 'any internal-revenue tax' from the qualifications imposed upon it by petitioner and permits it to be given what we regard as its more natural reading—the full tax. Moreover, this construction, under which each phrase is assigned a distinct meaning, imputes to Congress a surer grammatical touch than does the alternative interpretation, under which the 'any sum' phrase completely assimilates the other two. Surely a much clearer statute could have been written to authorize suits for refund of any part of a tax merely by use of the phrase 'a tax or any portion thereof,' or simply 'any sum paid under the internal revenue laws.' This Court naturally does not review congressional enactments as a panel of grammarians; but neither do we regard ordinary principles of English prose as irrelevant to a construction of those enactments. Cf. Commissioner of Internal Revenue v. Acker, 361 U.S. 87, 80 S.Ct. 144, 4 L.Ed.2d 127.

We conclude that the language of s 1346(a)(1) can be more readily construed to require payment of the full tax before suit than to permit suit for recovery of a part payment. But, as we recognized in the prior opinion, the statutory language is not absolutely controlling, and consequently resort must be had to whatever other materials might be relevant.[11]

---

[9] [fn 4] Revenue Act of 1924, c. 234, s 275(a), 43 Stat. 298, 26 U.S.C.A. s 293; Revenue Act of 1918, c. 18, s 250(e), 40 Stat. 1084; Act of June 6, 1872, c. 315, s 21, 17 Stat. 246; Act of June 30, 1864, c. 173, s 119, 13 Stat. 283. See also Helvering v. Mitchell, 303 U.S. 391, 405, 58 S.Ct. 630, 636, 82 L.Ed. 917.

[10] [fn 5] Lower courts have given this construction to the same three phrases in certain claim-for-refund and limitations provisions in prior tax statutes. United States v. Magoon, 9 Cir., 77 F.2d 804; Union Trust Co. of Rochester v. United States, D.C., 5 F.Supp. 259, 261 ('The natural definition of "tax" comprehends one "assessment" or one tax in the entire amount of liability'), affirmed 2 Cir., 70 F.2d 629, 630 ('We agree with the District Court that "tax," "penalty," and "sum" refer to distinct categories of illegal collections and "tax" includes the entire tax liability as assessed by the Commissioner'); United States v. Clarke, 3 Cir., 69 F.2d 748, 94 A.L.R. 975; Hills v. United States, 50 F.2d 302, 73 Ct.Cl. 128; 55 F.2d 1001, 73 Ct.Cl. 128; cf. Blair v. United States ex rel. Birkenstock, 271 U.S. 348, 46 S.Ct. 506, 70 L.Ed. 983.

[11] [fn 6] In the prior opinion we stated that, were it not for certain countervailing considerations, the statutory language 'might * * * be termed a clear authorization' to sue for the refund of part payment of an assessment. 357 U.S. at page 65, 78 S.Ct. at page 1081. It is quite obvious that we did not regard the language as clear enough to preclude deciding the case on other grounds. Moreover, it could at that time be assumed that the terms of the statute favored the taxpayer, because eight members of the Court considered the extrinsic evidence alone sufficient to decide the case against him. Although we are still of that opinion, we now state our views with regard to the bare words of the statute

LEGISLATIVE HISTORY AND HISTORICAL BACKGROUND

Although frequently the legislative history of a statute is the most fruitful source of instruction as to its proper interpretation, in this case that history is barren of any clue to congressional intent.

The precursor of s 1346(a)(1) was s 1310(c) of the Revenue Act of 1921,[12] in which the language with which we are here concerned appeared for the first time in a jurisdictional statute. Section 1310(c) had an overt purpose unrelated to the question whether full payment of an assessed tax was a jurisdictional prerequisite to a suit for refund. Prior to 1921, tax refund suits against the United States could be maintained in the District Courts under the authority of the Tucker Act, which had been passed in 1887.[13] Where the claim exceeded $10,000, however, such a suit could not be brought, and in such a situation the taxpayer's remedy in District Court was against the Collector. But because the Collector had to be sued personally, no District Court action was available if he was deceased.[14] The 1921 provision, which was an amendment to the Tucker Act, was explicitly designed to permit taxpayers to sue the United States in the District Courts for sums exceeding $10,000 where the Collector had died.[15]

The ancestry of the language of s 1346(a)(1) is no more enlightening than is the legislative history of the 1921 provision. This language, which, as we have stated, appeared in substantially its present form in the 1921 amendment, was apparently taken from R.S. s 3226 (1878). But s 3226 was not a jurisdictional statute at all; it simply specified that suits for recovery of taxes, penalties, or sums could not be maintained until after a claim for refund had been submitted to the Commissioner.[16]

Thus there is presented a vexing situation—statutory language which is inconclusive and legislative history which is irrelevant. This, of course, does not necessarily mean that s 1346(a)(1) expresses no congressional intent with respect

---

because the argument that these words are decisively against the Government has been urged so strenuously.

[12] [fn 7] 42 Stat. 311.

[13] [fn 8] 24 Stat. 505, as amended, 28 U.S.C. ss 1346, 1491, 28 U.S.C.A. ss 1346, 1491. See United States v. Emery, Bird, Thayer Realty Co., 237 U.S. 28, 35 S.Ct. 499, 59 L.Ed. 825.

[14] [fn 9] Smietanka v. Indiana Steel Co., 257 U.S. 1, 42 S.Ct. 1, 66 L.Ed. 99.

[15] [fn 10] See H.R.Conf.Rep. No. 486, 67th Cong., 1st Sess. 57; remarks of Senator Jones, 61 Cong.Rec. 7506-7507. Another amendment was added in 1925 giving the right to bring refund suits against the United States where the Collector was out of office. 43 Stat. 972. And in 1954, both the $10,000 limitation and the limitation with respect to the Collector being dead or out of office were eliminated. 68 Stat. 589.

[16] [fn 11] The text of R.S. s 3226 is set forth in note 16, infra, together with a more detailed account of the origin and development of the pertinent statutory language. The successor of R.S. s 3226 is I.R.C. (1954), s 7422(a), 68A Stat. 876, 26 U.S.C.A. s 7422(a).

to the issue before the Court; but it does make that intent uncommonly difficult to divine.

It is argued, however, that the puzzle may be solved through consideration of the historical basis of a suit to recover a tax illegally assessed. The argument proceeds as follows: A suit to recover taxes could, before the Tucker Act, be brought only against the Collector. Such a suit was based upon the common-law count of assumpsit for money had and received, and the nature of that count requires the inference that a suit for recovery of part payment of a tax could have been maintained. Neither the Tucker Act nor the 1921 amendment indicates an intent to change the nature of the refund action in any pertinent respect. Consequently, there is no warrant for importing into s 1346(a)(1) a full-payment requirement.

For reasons which will appear later, we believe that the conclusion would not follow even if the premises were clearly sound. But in addition we have substantial doubt about the validity of the premises. As we have already indicated, the language of the 1921 amendment does in fact tend to indicate a congressional purpose to require full payment as a jurisdictional prerequisite to suit for refund. Moreover, we are not satisfied that the suit against the collector was identical to the common-law action of assumpsit for money had and received. One difficulty is that, because of the Act of February 26, 1845, c. 22, 5 Stat. 727, which restored the right of action against the Collector after this Court had held that it had been implicitly eliminated by other legislation,[17] the Court no longer regarded the suit as a common-law action, but rather as a statutory remedy which 'in its nature (was) a remedy against the Government.' Curtis's Administratrix v. Fiedler, 2 Black 461, 479, 17 L.Ed. 273. On the other hand, it is true that none of the statutes relating to this type of suit clearly indicate a congressional intention to require full payment of the assessed tax before suit.[18] Nevertheless, the opinion of this Court in Cheatham v. United States, 92 U.S. 85, 23 L.Ed. 561, prevents us from accepting the analogy between the statutory action against the Collector and the common-law count. In this 1875 opinion, the Court described the remedies available to taxpayers as follows:

> 'So also, in the internal-revenue department, the statute which we have copied allows appeals from the assessor to the commissioner of internal revenue; and, if dissatisfied with his decision, on paying the tax the party can sue the collector; and, if the money was wrongfully exacted, the courts will give him relief by a judgment, which the United States pledges herself to pay.

> '* * * While a free course of remonstrance and appeal is allowed within the departments before the money is finally exacted, the general government has wisely made the payment of the tax claimed, whether of customs or of internal revenue, a condition precedent to a resort to the courts by the party

---

[17] [fn 12] See Cary v. Curtis, 3 How, 236, 11 L.Ed. 576.

[18] [fn 13] E.g., Act of Feb. 26, 1845, c. 22, 5 Stat. 727; Act of Mar. 3, 1863, c. 74, 12 Stat. 729; Act of June 30, 1864, c. 173, s 44, 13 Stat. 239-240.

against whom the tax is assessed. * * * If the compliance with this condition (that appeal must be made to the Commissioner and suit brought within six months of his decision) requires the party aggrieved to pay the money, he must do it. He cannot, after the decision is rendered against him, protract the time within which he can contest that decision in the courts by his own delay in paying the money. It is essential to the honor and orderly conduct of the government that its taxes should be promptly paid, and drawbacks speedily adjusted; and the rule prescribed in this class of cases is neither arbitrary nor unreasonable. * * *

'The objecting party can take his appeal. He can, if the decision is delayed beyond twelve months, rest his case on that decision; or he can *pay the amount claimed*, and commence his suit at any time within that period. So, after the decision, he can pay at once, and commence suit within the six months * * *.' 92 U.S. at pages 88-89, 23 L.Ed. 561. (Emphasis added.)

Reargument has not changed our view that this language reflects an understanding that full payment of the tax was a prerequisite to suit. Of course, as stated in our prior opinion, the *Cheatham* statement is dictum; but we reiterate that it appears to us to be 'carefully considered dictum.' 357 U.S. at page 68, 78 S.Ct. at page 1083. Equally important is the fact that the Court was construing the claim-for-refund statute from which, as amended, the language of s 1346(a)(1) was presumably taken.[19] Thus it seems that in *Cheatham* the Supreme Court interpreted this language not only to specify which claims for refund must first be presented for administrative reconsideration, but also to constitute an additional qualification upon the statutory right to sue the Collector. It is true that the version of the provision involved in *Cheatham* contained only the phrase 'any tax.' But the phrase 'any penalty' and 'any sum' were added well before the decision in *Cheatham*;[20] the history of these amendments makes it quite clear that they were not designed to effect any change relevant to the *Cheatham* rule;[21]

---

[19] [fn 14] See note 16, infra.

[20] [fn 15] *Cheatham* was decided in O.T.1875, while the phrases in question were added to the statute on June 6, 1872. See note 16, infra, for a discussion of the statute involved in *Cheatham* and its amendment.

[21] [fn 16] Section 19 of the Act of July 13, 1866, c. 184, 14 Stat. 152, was involved in *Cheatham*. That section provided:

'Sec. 19. * * * (N)o suit shall be maintained in any court for the recovery of any tax alleged to have been erroneously or illegally assessed or collected, until appeal shall have been duly made to the commissioner of internal revenue * * *.'

The phrases 'any penalty' and 'any sum' were first introduced into the statute in s 44 of the Act of June 6, 1872, c. 315, 17 Stat. 257-258, which read as follows:

'Sec. 44. That all suits and proceedings for the recovery of *any internal tax* alleged to have been erroneously assessed or collected, or *any penalty* claimed to have been collected without authority, *or for any sum* which it is alleged was

language in opinions of this Court after *Cheatham* is consistent with the *Cheatham* statement;[22] and in any event, as we have indicated, we can see nothing in these additional words which would negate the full-payment requirement.

If this were all the material relevant to a construction of s 1346(a)(1), determination of the issue at bar would be inordinately difficult. Favoring

---

excessive, or in any manner wrongfully collected, shall be brought within two years next after the cause of action accrued and not after; and all claims for the refunding of *any internal tax or penalty* shall be presented to the commissioner of internal revenue within two years next after the cause of action accrued and not after * * *.' (Emphasis added.)

A careful reading of this statute discloses the absurd result which would flow from construing the addition of the 'any sum' language to affect the full-payment rule, which, under this argument, would be based upon the 'any tax' phrase in the 1866 statute. That is, since the 'any sum' phrase occurs only in the statute of limitations portion of the 1872 statute, and not in the claim-for-refund provision, a person would be able to bring a suit for part payment without filing a claim for refund.

There were no material changes in R.S. s 3226, which provided:

'Sec. 3226. No suit shall be maintained in any court for the recovery of any internal tax alleged to have been erroneously or illegally assessed or collected, or of any penalty claimed to have been collected without authority, or of any sum alleged to have been excessive or in any manner wrongfully collected, until appeal shall have been duly made to the Commissioner of * * * Internal Revenue * * *.'

It is no doubt true, as petitioner says, that these various amendments were designed to require submission of all litigable claims to the Commissioner; but, as we have explained, this indicates no more than an intent to cover taxes, penalties, and sums which might, strictly speaking, be neither taxes nor penalties.

[22] [fn 17] Kings County Savings Institution v. Blair, 1886, 116 U.S. 200, 205, 6 S.Ct. 353, 356, 29 L.Ed. 657 ('No claim for the refunding of taxes can be made according to law and the regulations until after the taxes have been paid. * * * (N)o suit can be maintained for taxes illegally collected, unless a claim therefor has been made within the time prescribed by the law'); Pollock v. Farmers' Loan & Trust Co., 1895, 157 U.S. 429, 609, 15 S.Ct. 673, 700, 39 L.Ed. 759 (dissenting opinion) ('The same authorities (including the *Cheatham* case) have established the rule that the proper course, in a case of illegal taxation, is to pay the tax under protest or with notice of suit, and then bring an action against the officer who collected it'); Bailey v. George, 1922, 259 U.S. 16, 20, 42 S.Ct. 419, 66 L.Ed. 816 ('They might have paid the amount assessed under protest and then brought suit against the collector * * *.'). This view of *Cheatham* also corresponds to that of the Court of Appeals in this case. 246 F.2d at page 930. See also Bushmiaer v. United States, 8 Cir., 230 F.2d 146, 152-155 (dissenting opinion).

petitioner would be the theory that, in the early nineteenth century, a suit for recovery of part payment of an assessment could be maintained against the Collector, together with the absence of any conclusive evidence that Congress has ever intended to inaugurate a new rule; favoring respondent would be the *Cheatham* statement and the language of the 1921 statute. There are, however, additional factors which are dispositive.

We are not here concerned with a single sentence in an isolated statute, but rather with a jurisdictional provision which is a keystone in a carefully articulated and quite complicated structure of tax laws. From these related statutes, all of which were passed after 1921, it is apparent that Congress has several times acted upon the assumption that s 1346(a)(1) requires full payment before suit. Of course, if the clear purpose of Congress at any time had been to permit suit to recover a part payment, this subsequent legislation would have to be disregarded. But, as we have stated, the evidence pertaining to this intent is extremely weak, and we are convinced that it is entirely too insubstantial to justify destroying the existing harmony of the tax statutes. The laws which we consider especially pertinent are the statute establishing the Board of Tax Appeals (now the Tax Court), the Declaratory Judgment Act, 28 U.S.C.A. s 2201 et seq., and s 7422(e) of the Internal Revenue Code of 1954.

THE BOARD OF TAX APPEALS

The Board of Tax Appeals was established by Congress in 1924 to permit taxpayers to secure a determination of tax liability before payment of the deficiency.[23] The Government argues that the Congress which passed this 1924 legislation thought full payment of the tax assessed was a condition for bringing suit in a District Court; that Congress believed this sometimes caused hardship; and that Congress set up the Board to alleviate that hardship. Petitioner denies this, and contends that Congress' sole purpose was to enable taxpayers to prevent the Government from collecting taxes by exercise of its power of distraint.[24]

We believe that the legislative history surrounding both the creation of the Board and the subsequent revisions of the basic statute supports the Government. The House Committee Report, for example, explained the purpose of the bill as follows:

'The committee recommends the establishment of a Board of Tax Appeals to which a taxpayer may appeal *prior to the payment* of an additional assessment of income, excess-profits, war-profits, or estate taxes. *Although a taxpayer may, after payment of his tax, bring suit for the recovery thereof* and thus secure a judicial determination on the questions involved, he can not, in view of section 3224 of the Revised Statutes, which prohibits suits to enjoin the collection of taxes, secure such a determination prior to the payment of the tax. The right of appeal after payment of the tax is an

---

[23] [fn 18] 43 Stat. 336.

[24] [fn 19] I.R.C. (1954), s 6331, 68A Stat. 783, 26 U.S.C.A. s 6331. The Government has possessed the power of distraint for almost 170 years. See Act of Mar. 3, 1791, c. 15, s 23, 1 Stat. 204.

incomplete remedy, and does little to remove the hardship occasioned by an incorrect assessment. The payment of a large additional tax on income received several years previous and which may have, since its receipt, been either wiped out by subsequent losses, invested in nonliquid assets, or spent, sometimes forces taxpayers into bankruptcy, and often causes great financial hardship and sacrifice. These results are not remedied by permitting *the taxpayer to sue for the recovery of the tax after this payment.* He is entitled to an appeal and to a determination of his liability for the tax prior to its payment.'[25] (Emphasis added.)

Moreover, throughout the congressional debates are to be found frequent expressions of the principle that payment of the full tax was a precondition to suit: 'pay his tax * * * then * * * file a claim for refund'; 'pay the tax and then sue'; 'a review in the courts after payment of the tax'; 'he may still seek court review, but he must first pay the tax assessed'; 'in order to go to court he must pay his assessment'; 'he must pay it (his assessment) before he can have a trial in court'; 'pay the taxes adjudicated against him, and then commence a suit in a court'; 'pay the tax * * * (t)hen * * * sue to get it back'; 'paying his tax and bringing his suit'; 'first pay his tax and then sue to get it back'; 'take his case to the district court—conditioned, of course, upon his paying the assessment.'[26]

---

[25] [fn 20] H.R.Rep. No. 179, 68th Cong., 1st Sess. 7. The Senate Committee on Finance filed a similar report. S.Rep. No. 398, 68th Cong., 1st Sess. 8.

The reference to R.S. s 3224 in the House Report clearly was meant simply to demonstrate that a determination prior to payment be way of an injunction suit was not possible because of the statutory bar to such a suit. This anti-injunction provision has been law for many decades. See Act of Mar. 2, 1867, c. 169, s 10, 14 Stat. 475. It is now s 7421 of the Internal Revenue Code of 1954, 68A Stat. 876, 26 U.S.C.A. s 7421.

[26] [fn 21] See 65 Cong.Rec. 2621, 2684, 8110; 67 Cong.Rec. 525, 1144, 3529, 3755.

As we have indicated, some of these remarks were made during debates over proposed changes in the Board of Tax Appeals legislation during the middle of the 1920's, but they all reflect Congress' understanding of the pre-1924 procedure and of the changes which were made by establishment of the Board. For example, shortly after the Board legislation was passed, Congress considered and rejected a proposal to make appeal to the Board and then to a Circuit Court of Appeals the taxpayer's sole remedy. In the course of the debate, a number of Senators discussed at length the taxpayer's right to bring a refund action in court. Some of the cited quotations are taken from that debate. The following remark of Senator Fletcher is also illuminating:

'Mr. Fletcher. * * * *I think the most important right that is preserved here * * * is the right to go into the district court by the taxpayer upon the payment of the tax. I do not think that we ought to allow him to do that unless he does pay*

Petitioner's argument falls under the weight of this evidence. It is true, of course, that the Board of Tax Appeals procedure has the effect of staying collection,[27] and it may well be that Congress so provided in order to alleviate hardships caused by the long-standing bar against suits to enjoin the collection of taxes. But it is a considerable leap to the further conclusion that amelioration of the hardship of prelitigation payment as a jurisdictional requirement was not another important motivation for Congress' action.[28] To reconcile the legislative history with this conclusion seems to require the presumption that all the Congressmen who spoke of payment of the assessment before suit as a hardship understood—without saying—that suit could be brought for whatever part of the assessment had been paid, but believed that, as a practical matter, hardship would nonetheless arise because the Government would require payment of the balance of the tax by exercising its power of distraint. But if this was in fact the view of these legislators, it is indeed extraordinary that they did not say so.[29] Moreover, if

---

the tax; but when he pays the tax his right to go into the district court is preserved.' 67 Cong.Rec. 3529. (Emphasis added.)

See also the materials quoted in note 24, infra.

[27] [fn 22] See I.R.C. (1954), s 6213(a), 68A Stat. 771, 26 U.S.C.A. s 6213(a). For the pertinent 1924 legislation, see Revenue Act of 1924, c. 234, s 274, 43 Stat. 297.

[28] [fn 23] In Old Colony Trust Co. v. Commissioner, 279 U.S. 716, 721, 49 S.Ct. 499, 501, 73 L.Ed. 918, this Court expressed the view that the Board 'was created by Congress to provide taxpayers an opportunity to secure an independent review * * * in advance of their paying the tax found by the Commissioner to be due. Before the act of 1924, the taxpayer could only contest the Commissioner's determination of the amount of the tax after its payment.'

[29] [fn 24] There are a few interchanges among Senators which might be construed to indicate that they were thinking in terms of preventing distraint, but the same passages demonstrate even more clearly that these Senators also intended to eliminate the necessity of full payment as a prerequisite to suit. For example, the following debate occurred when Senator Reed, who was a member of the Committee on Finance, proposed an amendment which would have a permitted a taxpayer to refuse to pay the deficiency even after the Board had ruled against him and which would have required the Government to sue in a District Court.

'Mr. Reed of Missouri. * * *

'The practice, as I understand it, has been to require the taxpayer to pay in the amount of the increased assessment, and then to allow him to get it back if he can. In addition to this, distraints frequently have been issued seizing the property of the citizen * * *.

'Mr. Swanson. What are the processes by which a citizen who has overpaid can get back his money under the existing law?

'Mr. Reed of Missouri. As I understand it, he pays his tax. Then he makes an application for a return of it. That is heard through the long, troublesome processes which exist. * * * When the Treasury is satisfied * * * the taxpayer can go into court at that time. In the meantime, however, he has had to pay his money.

'Mr. Swanson. Does the Senator mean that if there is a dispute, the tax is not assessed permanently against him until the board reaches its final decision?

'Mr. Smoot. Until the board of appeals finally passes upon it, and after that if he wants to go to court he can do so, but in order to go to court he must pay his assessment.

'Mr. Reed of Missouri. He must pay it before he can have a trial in court.

'Mr. Walsh of Montana. Mr. President, the hardships * * * in connection with the collection of these taxes is a very real one. * * * At least two or three instances have come under my notice, and my assistance has been asked in cases where the assessing officers have * * * assessed against the (taxpayer) dilinquent taxes of such an amount that he found it impossible to pay in advance and secure redress through the ordinary proceeding in a court of law, simply because it would bankrupt him to endeavor to raise the money. He was therefore obliged to suffer a distraint. * * *

'* * * After the board of review determines the matter, it seems to me, that is as far as the Government ought to be interrupted in the matter of the collection of its revenues. Then the taxpayer would be obliged to pay the tax and take his ordinary action at law to recover whatever he claims was exacted of him illegally.' 65 Cong.Rec. 8109-8114.

A somewhat similar exchange occurred during the 1926 debate over a proposal to prohibit refund suits where an appeal had been taken to the Board.

'Mr. Reed of Missouri. * * * Now just one further question:

'Why is it that a taxpayer can not be given his day in court by direct action, without first requiring him to pay the tax that is assessed? I know I shall be met with the statement that it would mean interminable delay to the Government; but it frequently happens that the tax that is assessed is ruinous, and that the taxpayer can not raise the money. * * *

'In my own personal experience I have had two clients who were absolutely ruined by assessments that were unjust and that could not have stood up in a court of justice. * * * (A)nd it was no protection to them to say, 'Pay your taxes and then go into court,' because they did not have the money to pay the taxes and could not raise the money to pay the taxes and be out of the money two or three years.

'* * * I think the bill needs just one more amendment in this particular, and that is a provision that any citizen can go into court without paying any tax and resist the payment. In the meantime I agree that the Government for its own protection ought to be allowed, perhaps, in such a case as that to issue a distraint. But the idea that a man must first pay his money and then sue to get it back is anomaly in the law.' 67 Cong.Rec. 3530-3533.

Congress' only concern was to prevent distraint, it is somewhat difficult to understand why Congress did not simply authorize injunction suits. It is interesting to note in this connection that bills to permit the same type of prepayment litigation in the District Courts as is possible in the Tax Court have been introduced several times, but none has ever been adopted.[30]

In sum, even assuming that one purpose of Congress in establishing the Board was to permit taxpayers to avoid distraint, it seems evident that another purpose was to furnish a forum where full payment of the assessment would not be a condition precedent to suit. The result is a system in which there is one tribunal for prepayment litigation and another for post-payment litigation, with no room contemplated for a hybrid of the type proposed by petitioner.

THE DECLARATORY JUDGMENT ACT

The Federal Declaratory Judgment Act of 1934[31] was amended by s 405 of the Revenue Act of 1935 expressly to except disputes 'with respect to Federal taxes.'[32] The Senate Report explained the purpose of the amendment as follows:

> 'Your committee has added an amendment making it clear that the Federal Declaratory Judgments Act of June 14, 1934, has no application to Federal taxes. The application of the Declaratory Judgments Act to taxes would constitute a *radical departure* from the long-continued policy of Congress (as expressed in Rev.Stat. 3224 and other provisions) with respect to the determination, assessment, and collection of Federal taxes. Your committee believes that the orderly and prompt determination and collection of Federal taxes should not be interfered with by a procedure disigned to facilitate the settlement of private controversies, and that existing procedure both in the Board of Tax Appeals and the courts affords ample remedies for the correction of tax errors.'[33] (Emphasis added.)

It is clear enough that one 'radical departure' which was averted by the amendment was the potential circumvention of the 'pay first and litigate later' rule by way of suits for declaratory judgments in tax cases.[34] Petitioner would

---

Senator Reed later proposed that the appeal from the Board be to the District Court instead of to the Circuit Court of Appeals, and Senator Wadsworth, a member of the Finance Committee Asked:

'Does the Senator not think that other provision in the bill which permits the taxpayer to take his case to the district court—conditioned, of course, upon his paying the assessment—meets the situation?' 67 Cong.Rec. 3755.

[30] [fn 25] S. 1569, 81st Cong., 1st Sess.; S. 384, 82d Cong., 1st Sess.; H.R. 150 and H.R. 246, 83d Cong., 1st Sess.

[31] [fn 26] 48 Stat. 955, as amended, 28 U.S.C. ss 2201, 2202, 28 U.S.C.A. ss 2201, 2202.

[32] [fn 27] 49 Stat. 1027.

[33] [fn 28] S.Rep. No. 1240, 74th Cong., 1st Sess. 11

[34] [fn 29] 'Should the Declaratory Judgment Act be held to apply to tax cases it will mean a complete reversal of our present scheme of taxation. The principle

have us give this Court's imprimatur to precisely the same type of 'radical departure,' since a suit for recovery of but a part of an assessment would determine the legality of the balance by operation of the principle of collateral estoppel. With respect to this unpaid portion, the taxpayer would be securing what is in effect—even though not technically—a declaratory judgment. The frustration of congressional intent which petitioner asks us to endorse could hardly be more glaring, for he has conceded that his argument leads logically to the conclusion that payment of even $1 on a large assessment entitles the taxpayer to sue—a concession amply warranted by the obvious impracticality of any judicially created jurisdictional standard midway between full payment and any payment.

SECTION 7422(e) OF THE 1954 CODE

One distinct possibility which would emerge from a decision in favor of petitioner would be that a taxpayer might be able to split his cause of action, bringing suit for refund of part of the tax in a Federal District Court and litigating in the Tax Court with respect to the remainder. In such a situation the first decision would, of course, control. Thus if for any reason a litigant would prefer a District Court adjudication,[35] he might sue for a small portion of the tax in that tribunal while at the same time protecting the balance from distraint by invoking the protection of the Tax Court procedure. On the other hand, different questions would arise if this device were not employed. For example, would the Government be required to file a compulsory counterclaim for the unpaid balance in District Court under Rule 13 of the Federal Rules of Civil Procedure, 28 U.S.C.A.? If so, which party would have the burden of proof?[36]

Section 7422(e) of the 1954 Internal Revenue Code makes it apparent that Congress has assumed these problems are nonexistent except in the rare case where the taxpayer brings suit in a District Court and the Commissioner then notifies him of an additional deficiency. Under s 7422(e) such a claimant is given the option of pursuing his suit in the District Court or in the Tax Court, but he cannot litigate in both. Moreover, if he decides to remain in the District Court, the Government may—but seemingly is not required to—bring a counterclaim; and if it does, the taxpayer has the burden of proof.[37] If we were to overturn the

---

of "pay first and litigate later" will be changed to "litigate first and pay later." This principle has never before been departed from.' Wideman, Application of the Declaratory Judgment Act to Tax Suits, 13 Taxes 539, 540.

[35] [fn 30] For some practitioners' views on the desirability of litigating tax cases in Federal District Courts, see Dockery, Refund Suits in District Courts, 31 Taxes 523; Yeatman, Tax Controversies, 10 Tex.B.J. 9.

[36] [fn 31] These problems have already occurred to the bar. See Riordan, Must You Pay Full Tax Assessment Before Suing in the District Court? 8 J.Tax. 179, 181.

[37] [fn 32] 'Sec. 7422. Civil actions for refund.

'(e) Stay of Proceedings.—If the Secretary or his delegate prior to the hearing of a suit brought by a taxpayer in a district court or the Court of Claims

assumption upon which Congress has acted, we would generate upon a broad scale the very problems Congress believed it had solved.[38]

These, then, are the basic reasons for our decision, and our views would be unaffected by the constancy or inconstancy of administrative practice. However, because the petition for rehearing in this case focused almost exclusively upon a single clause in the prior opinion—'there does not appear to be a single case before 1940 in which a taxpayer attempted a suit for refund of income taxes without paying the full amount the Government alleged to be due,' 357 U.S. at page 69, 78 S.Ct. at page 1083—we feel obliged to comment upon the material introduced upon reargument. The reargument has, if anything, strengthened,

---

for the recovery of any income tax, estate tax, or gift tax (or any penalty relating to such taxes) mails to the taxpayer a notice that a deficiency has been determined in respect of the tax which is the subject matter of taxpayer's suit, the proceedings in taxpayer's suit shall be stayed during the period of time in which the taxpayer may file a petition with the Tax Court for a redetermination of the asserted deficiency, and for 60 days thereafter. If the taxpayer files a petition with the Tax Court, the district court or the Court of Claims, as the case may be, shall lose jurisdiction of taxpayer's suit to whatever extent jurisdiction is acquired by the Tax Court of the subject matter of taxpayer's suit for refund. If the taxpayer does not file a petition with the Tax Court for a redetermination of the asserted deficiency, the United States may counterclaim in the taxpayer's suit, or intervene in the event of a suit as described in subsection (c) (relating to suits against officers or employees of the United States), within the period of the stay of proceedings notwithstanding that the time for such pleading may have otherwise expired. The taxpayer shall have the burden of proof with respect to the issues raised by such counterclaim or intervention of the United States except as to the issue of whether the taxpayer has been guilty of fraud with intent to evade tax. This subsection shall not apply to a suit by a taxpayer which, prior to the date of enactment of this title, is commenced, instituted, or pending in a district court or the Court of Claims for the recovery of any income tax, estate tax, or gift tax (or any penalty relating to such taxes).' 68A Stat. 877.

The possibility of dual jurisdiction in this type of situation was confirmed by cases such as Camp v. United States, 4 Cir., 44 F.2d 126, and Ohio Steel Foundry Co. v. United States, 38 F.2d 144, 69 Ct.Cl. 158. See H.R.Rep. No. 1337, 83d Cong., 2d Sess. 109, A431; S.Rep. No. 1662, 83d Cong., 2d Sess. 148, 610.

[38] [fn 33] For additional evidence of recent congressional understanding of the jurisdictional requirement of s 1346(a)(1), see the House Report which explained the 1954 amendment abolishing the $10,000 limitation on tax suits against the United States, 68 Stat. 589. After explaining the taxpayer's right to contest a deficiency in the Tax Court, the report states: 'The taxpayer may, however, elect to pay his tax and thereafter bring suit to recover the amount claimed to have been illegally exacted.' H.R.Rep. No. 659, 83d Cong., 1st Sess. 2.

rather than weakened, the substance of this statement, which was directed to the question whether there has been a consistent understanding of the 'pay first and litigate later' principle by the interested government agencies and by the bar.

So far as appears, Suhr v. United States, 18 F.2d 81, decided by the Third Circuit in 1927, is the earliest case in which a taxpayer in a refund action sought to contest an assessment without having paid the full amount then due.[39] In holding that the District Court had no jurisdiction of the action, the Court of Appeals said:

> 'None of the various tax acts provide for recourse to the courts by a taxpayer until he has failed to get relief from the proper administrative body or has paid all the taxes assessed against him. The payment of a part does not confer jurisdiction upon the courts. * * * There is no provision for refund to the taxpayer of any excess payment of any installment or part of his tax, if the whole tax for the year has not been paid.' Id., at page 83.

Although the statement by the court might have been dictum,[40] it was in accord with substantially contemporaneous statements by Secretary of the Treasury A. W. Mellon, by Under Secretary of the Treasury Garrard B. Winston, by the first Chairman of the Board of Tax Appeals, Charles D. Hamel, and by legal commentators.[41]

---

[39] [fn 34] Petitioner cites two earlier cases in which the Government failed to raise the jurisdictional issue. Bowers v. Kerbaugh-Empire Co., 1926, 271 U.S. 170, 46 S.Ct. 449, 70 L.Ed. 886; Cook v. Tait, 1924, 265 U.S. 47, 44 S.Ct. 444, 68 L.Ed. 895. The Government distinguishes these cases on the ground that, although the total tax for the year had not been paid, the full amount due at the time of suit had been paid. This situation occurred because under s 250(a) of the Revenue Act of 1921, c. 136, 42 Stat. 264, the tax was paid in four installments, and the plaintiffs in *Cook* and *Bowers* apparently had paid the due installments. While we do not suggest that the statute will support this type of distinction, adoption of it by the Government or by the bar would not in any way impair the substantial consistency of the view that full payment has for many decades been a prerequisite to suit in District Court. An error as to the applicability of a principle to a unique factual situation does not mean that the principle itself has been rejected.

[40] [fn 35] The ground for the decision may have been that the District Court had no jurisdiction because the taxpayer was contesting the legality of the balance of the assessment before the Board of Tax Appeals.

[41] [fn 36] In welcoming the members of the Board of Tax Appeals on July 16, 1924, Under Secretary Winston described the difficulties which had arisen in the past.

'* * * Under the law a tax once assessed had to be paid by the taxpayer and then his remedy was to sue for its recovery. He must first find the cash for a liability for which he may not have provided. * * * The first interest of all of the people is, of course, that the Government continue to function, and to do this it must have the means of prompt collection of the necessary supplies to keep it going, that is, taxes. The method was, therefore, the determination by the Commissioner of the amount of tax due, its collection and suit to recover. * * * (T)he tax as assessed had to be paid and the taxpayer was left to his remedy in the courts. The payment of the tax was often a great hardship on the taxpayer, meaning in general that he had to raise the cash for an unexpected liability which might not be lawfully due.' Treas. Dept. Press Release, July 16, 1924. See also remarks by Under Secretary Winston in addressing the Seventeenth Annual Conference of the National Tax Association in September 1924, Proceedings of Seventeenth National Conference 271.

In commenting upon the Board of Tax Appeals legislation, which contemplated leaving the taxpayer to his District Court remedy if the decision of the Board was adverse, Secretary of the Treasury Mellon stated: 'The taxpayer, in the event that decision (of the Board) is against him, will have to pay the tax according to the assessment and have recourse to the courts * * *.' 67 Cong.Rec. 552.

On September 17, 1924, the first Chairman of the Board, Charles D. Hamel, read a paper before the Seventeenth Annual Conference of the National Tax Association on Taxation which contained the following remark: 'Prior to the enactment of the Act of 1924 * * * (i)f the decision on the appeal (to the Commissioner) was in favor of the government, the taxpayer, only after payment of the tax, had the right to protest the correctness of the decision in the courts * * *.' Proceedings 277-278.

One of the clearest statements of the rule by a commentator is to be found in Bickford, Court Procedure in Federal Tax Cases (Rev. ed. 1929) 3, 7-8, 9, 119.

'There are, however, certain other conditions which must be complied with before a suit is maintainable under this section. Briefly stated, these are as follows:

'1. The tax must have been paid.

'2. After payment, the taxpayer must have filed with the Commissioner * * * a sufficient claim for the refund of the taxes sued for.

'The first requirement is obvious. We have, in the preceding portions of this volume, found that a proceeding commenced in the Board of Tax Appeals is the only exception to the rule that no review by the courts is permissible at common law or under the statutes, until the tax has been paid and the Government assured of its revenue.' Id., at 119.

See also Hamel, The United States Board of Tax Appeals (1926), 10; Klein, Federal Income Taxation (1929), 1372, 1642, 1643; Mellon, Taxation: The People's Business (1924), 62—63; Ballantine, Federal Income Tax Procedure, Lectures on Taxation, Columbia University Symposium (1932), 179, 192—193; Caspers, Assessment of Additional Income Taxes for Prior Years, 1 Nat. Income Tax Mag. (Oct. 1923), 12; Graupner, The Operation of the Board of Tax Appeals, 3 Nat. Income Tax Mag. (1925), 295. But see Smith, National Taxes,

There is strong circumstantial evidence that this view of the jurisdiction of the courts was shared by the bar at least until 1940, when the Second Circuit Court of Appeals rejected the Government's position in Coates v. United States, 111 F.2d 609. Out of the many thousands of refund cases litigated in the pre-1940 period—the Government reports that there have been approximately 40,000 such suits in the past 40 years—exhaustive research has uncovered only nine suits in which the issue was present, in six of which the Government contested jurisdiction on part-payment grounds.[42] The Government's failure to raise the

---

Their Collection, and Rights and Remedies of the Taxpayer, 8 Geo.L.J. 1, 3 (Apr. 1920).

See also Beaman, When Not to Go to the Tax Court: Advantages and Procedures in Going to the District Court, 7 J.Tax. (1957), 356 ('(T)he Bushmiaer case (permitting suit for part of the tax) * * * runs counter to a long tradition of administrative practice and interpretation * * *.'); Rudick and Wender, Federal Income Taxation, 32 N.Y.U.L.Rev. (1957), 751, 777—778 ('It is generally said that a taxpayer has two remedies if he disagrees with a determination of the Commissioner. He may pay the deficiency, file a claim for refund, and sue for the tax in the district court * * *. Alternatively, the taxpayer may petition the Tax Court for review of a deficiency prior to payment. The recent Bushmiaer case is a third alternative. * * * (T)he Bushmiaer case conflicts with more than thirty years of experience in the administration and collection of taxes.'). (Footnote omitted.)

[42] [fn 37] Petitioner cites a number of cases in support of his argument that neither the bar nor the Government has ever assumed that full payment of the tax is a jurisdictional prerequisite to suit for recovery. The following factors rob these cases of the significance attributed to them by the petitioner:

(a) A number of them, although cited by petitioner in his petition for rehearing, were later conceded by him, after his examination of government files, not to be in point.

(b) A number of the cited cases involved excise taxes. The Government suggests—and we agree—that excise tax deficiencies may be divisible into a tax on each transaction or event, and therefore present an entirely different problem with respect to the full-payment rule.

(c) The cases arising after 1940 are insignificant. Once the Second Circuit Court of Appeals had ruled against the Government in Coates, taxpayers would naturally be much more inclined to sue before full payment, and the Government might well decide not to raise the objection in a particular case for reasons relating to litigation strategy.

(d) In some of the cases the only amount remaining unpaid at the time of suit was interest. As we have indicated, the statute lends itself to a construction which would permit suit for the tax after full payment thereof without payment of any part of the interest.

(e) In some of the cases the Government was not legally entitled to collect the unpaid tax at the time of suit, either because the tax system at the time permitted installment payment (see note 34, supra), because the unpaid portion had not yet been assessed, or for some other reason. Although the statute may not support any distinction based on facts of this nature, it is quite understandable that a taxpayer might have predicated a suit upon the theory that the distinction was meaningful and that the Government might not have contested it, whether because it agreed or for tactical reasons.

In the light of these considerations, we regard the following pre-1941 cases as immaterial: Baldwin v. Higgins, 2 Cir., 1938, 100 F.2d 405 (petitioner concedes); Sampson v. Welch, D.C.S.D.Cal.1938, 23 F.Supp. 271 (same); Charleston Lumber Co. v. United States, D.C.S.D.W.Va.1937, 20 F.Supp. 83 (same); Sterling v. Ham, D.C.Me.1933, 3 F.Supp. 386 (same); Farmers' Loan & Trust Co. v. Bowers, D.C.S.D.N.Y.1926, 15 F.2d 706, modified D.C.1927, 22 F.2d 464, reversed 2 Cir., 1928, 29 F.2d 14 (same); Heinemann Chemical Co. v. Heiner, 36-4 CCH Fed.Tax Serv. 9302 (D.C.W.D.Pa.1936), reversed 3 Cir., 1937, 92 F.2d 344 (only interest unpaid); Welch v. Hassett, D.C.Mass.1936, 15 F.Supp. 692, reversed 1 Cir., 1937, 90 F.2d 833, affirmed 1938, 303 U.S. 303 58 S.Ct. 559, 82 L.Ed. 858 (full assessment paid); Leavitt v. Hendricksen, 37-4 CCH Fed.Tax Serv. 9312 (D.C.W.D.Wash.1937) (no unpaid assessment); Bowers v. Kerbaugh-Empire Co., 1926, 271 U.S. 170, 46 S.Ct. 449, 70 L.Ed. 886 (all due installments paid); Cook v. Tait, 1924, 265 U.S. 47, 44 S.Ct. 444, 68 L.Ed. 895 (same).

Four pre-1941 cases remain. Of these, only two are clearly cases in which the jurisdictional issue was present and not raised by the Government. Tsivoglou v. United States, 1 Cir., 1929, 31 F.2d 706; Thomas v. United States, 1937, 18 F.Supp. 942, 85 Ct.Cl. 313; McFadden v. United States, D.C.E.D.Pa.1937, 20 F.Supp. 625, is in the 'doubtful' category. There the Commissioner had granted the taxpayer an extension of time for payment of 80% of his assessment and the suit was for the remaining 20%, which had been paid. The relevant facts of the last case, Peerless Paper Box Mfg. Co. v. Routzahn, D.C.N.D.Ohio 1927, 22 F.2d 459, are so unclear that the case means nothing. The Government had applied an admitted 1918 overpayment to a 1917 deficiency, but the deficiency was greater than the overpayment. The taxpayer sued to recover this overpayment, and whether there had been full payment at the time of suit depends upon whether the suit is regarded as one for refund of 1917 or 1918 taxes.

Nor can we agree entirely with petitioner's evaluation of a second group of pre-1941 cases—those in which the issue allegedly was present and the Government did raise it but lost. Five of these cases involved primarily the troublesome concurrent jurisdiction problem that arose before passage of s 7422(e) of the 1954 Code when a taxpayer both appealed to the Tax Court and brought suit in a Federal District Court. Brampton Woolen Co. v. Field, D.C.N.H.1931, 55 F.2d 325, reversed 1 Cir., 1932, 56 F.2d 23, certiorari denied 287 U.S. 608, 53 S.Ct. 12, 77 L.Ed. 529; Camp v. United States, 4 Cir., 1930, 44 F.2d 126; Emery v. United States, D.C.W.D.Pa.1928, 27 F.2d 992; Old Colony R. Co. v. United States, D.C.Mass.1928, 27 F.2d 994; Ohio Steel Foundry Co. v.

United States, 1930, 38 F.2d 144, 69 Ct.Cl. 158. In all of these cases except *Camp*, it appears that the Government did raise the part-payment question. It is true that the contention did not prevail, but this is not very meaningful. In the first place, this question was quite subordinate to the major issue, concurrent jurisdiction. In the second place, the Government won in *Brampton* on another jurisdictional ground. And finally, in contrast to *Flora*, in both *Camp* and *Ohio Steel Foundry* the full assessment had been paid at the time suit was brought; it was only later that an additional deficiency was asserted by the Commissioner.

To these cases should be added Riverside Hospital v. Larson, 38-4 CCH Fed.Tax Serv. 9542 (D.C.S.D.Fla.1938), where the Government raised the full-payment question and won, and Suhr v. United States, D.C.W.D.Pa.1926, 14 F.2d 227, affirmed 3 Cir., 1927, 18 F.2d 81, another concurrent jurisdiction case where the Government raised the issue and won, although the grounds for the decision are not entirely clear.

This, then, is how we see the pre-1941 situation: Of 14 cases originally cited as being cases in which the jurisdictional issue was present but not raised by the Government, five have been conceded by petitioner not to be in point; six, and possibly seven, are distinguishable for various reasons; and only two, or possibly three, remain. Of five cases cited as being cases in which the jurisdictional issue was raised by the Government, only one, Coates v. United States, 2 Cir., 1940, 111 F.2d 609, or at most three, really involved the *Flora* question. When to these are added *Riverside*, where the Government won, *Suhr*, where it may have won, and *Brampton Woolen Co.*, where it won in the Court of Appeals on another jurisdictional ground, the box score is as follows: two or three cases in which the Government failed to raise the issue; one, or possibly three, cases in which the Government argued the question and lost; one case in which it argued the question and won; one case in which it argued the question and may have won; and one case in which it raised the issue and prevailed on another jurisdictional defense—a total of nine cases at most in which the issue was presented, out of which the Government contested jurisdiction in six. Of course, this calculation may not be precise; but, in view of the many thousands of tax refund suits which have been brought during the decades in question, it is an accurate enough approximation to reflect a general understanding of the jurisdictional significance of 'pay first, litigate later.'

It would be bootless to consider each of the post-1940 cases cited by petitioner or to list the multitude of cases cited by the Government in which the jurisdictional issue has been raised. As we have stated, we believe these cases have no significance whatsoever. However, perhaps it is worth noting that all but a handful of the cases which petitioner, in the petition for rehearing, asserted to be ones in which the Government failed to raise the jurisdictional issue would be immaterial even if they were pre-*Coates*. Thus, for example, petitioner has conceded error with respect to three cases. Dickstein v. McDonald, D.C.M.D.Pa.1957, 149 F.Supp. 580, affirmed 3 Cir., 1958, 255 F.2d 640; O'Connor v. United States, D.C.S.D.N.Y.1948, 76 F.Supp. 962; Terrell v. United

issue in the other three is obviously entirely without significance. Considerations of litigation strategy may have been thought to militate against resting upon such a defense in those cases. Moreover, where only nine lawsuits involving a particular issue arise over a period of many decades, the policy of the Executive Department on that issue can hardly be expected to become familiar to every government attorney. But most important, the number of cases before 1940 in which the issue was present is simply so inconsequential that it reinforces the conclusion of the prior opinion with respect to the uniformity of the pre-1940 belief that full payment had to precede suit.

A word should also be said about the argument that requiring taxpayers to pay the full assessments before bringing suits will subject some of them to great hardship. This contention seems to ignore entirely the right of the taxpayer to appeal the deficiency to the Tax Court without paying a cent.[43] If he permits his time for filing such an appeal to expire, he can hardly complain that he has been unjustly treated, for he is in precisely the same position as any other person who is barred by a statute of limitations. On the other hand, the Government has a substantial interest in protecting the public purse, an interest which would be substantially impaired if a taxpayer could sue in a District Court without paying his tax in full. It is instructive to note that, as of June 30, 1959, tax cases pending in the Tax Court involved $920,046,748, and refund suits in other courts involved $446,673,640.[44] It is quite true that the filing of an appeal to the Tax

---

States, D.C.E.D.La.1946, 64 F.Supp. 418. A number of the cases involved excise taxes. E.g., Griffiths Dairy v. Squire, 9 Cir., 1943, 138 F.2d 758; Auricchio v. United States, D.C.E.D.N.Y.1943, 49 F.Supp. 184. In some of the cases only interest remained unpaid. Raymond v. United States, 58-1 U.S.T.C. 9397 (D.C.E.D.Mich.1958); Hogg v. Allen, D.C.M.D.Ga.1952, 105 F.Supp. 12. And some of the cases arose in the Third Circuit after a decision adverse to the Government in Sirian Lamp Co. v. Manning, 3 Cir., 1941, 123 F.2d 776, 138 A.L.R. 1423. Gallagher v. Smith, 3 Cir., 1955, 223 F.2d 218; Peters v. Smith, D.C.E.D.Pa.1954, 123 F.Supp. 711, reversed 3 Cir., 1955, 221 F.2d 721. It might be noted also that Jones v. Fox, D.C.Md.1957, 162 F.Supp. 449, cited as a case in which the Government argued the jurisdictional question and lost, was an excise tax case in which the court distinguished our prior decision in *Flora* because of the divisibility of the excise tax. Another such decision during the pre-1941 period was Friebele v. United States, D.C.N.J.1937, 20 F.Supp. 492.

[43] [fn 38] Petitioner points out that the Tax Court has no jurisdiction over excise tax cases. See 9 Mertens, Law of Federal Income Taxation (Zimet Rev.1958), s 50.08. But this fact provides no policy support for his position, since, as we have noted, excise tax assessments may be divisible into a tax on each transaction or event, so that the full-payment rule would probably require no more than payment of a small amount. See note 37, supra.

[44] [fn 39] Of this $446,673,640, District Court suits involved $222,177,920; Court of Claims suits, $220,247,436; and state court suits, $4,248,284.

Court normally precludes the Government from requiring payment of the tax,[45] but a decision in petitioner's favor could be expected to throw a great portion of the Tax Court litigation into the District Courts.[46] Of course, the Government can collect the tax from a District Court suitor by exercising its power of distraint—if he does not split his cause of action—but we cannot believe that compelling resort to this extraordinary procedure is either wise or in accord with congressional intent. Our system of taxation is based upon voluntary assessment and payment, not upon distraint.[47] A full-payment requirement will promote the smooth functioning of this system; a part-payment rule would work at cross-purposes with it.[48]

In sum, if we were to accept petitioner's argument, we would sacrifice the harmony of our carefully structured twentieth century system of tax litigation, and all that would be achieved would be a supposed harmony of s 1346(a)(1) with what might have been the nineteenth century law had the issue ever been raised. Reargument has but fortified our view that s 1346(a)(1), correctly

---

[45] [fn 40] See note 22, supra.

[46] [fn 41] The practical effects which might result from acceptance of petitioner's argument are sketched in Lowitz, Federal Tax Refund Suits and Partial Payments, 9 The Decalogue J. 9, 10:

'Permitting refund suits after partial payment of the tax assessment would benefit many taxpayers. Such a law would be open to wide abuse and would probably seriously impair the government's ability to collect taxes. Many taxpayers, without legitimate grounds for contesting an assessment, would make a token payment and sue for refund, hoping at least to reduce the amount they would ultimately have to pay. In jurisdictions where the District Court is considered to be a 'taxpayer's court' most taxpayers would use that forum instead of the Tax Court. Conceivably such legislation could cause the chaotic tax collection situations which exist in some European countries, since there would be strong impetus to a policy of paying a little and trying to settle the balance.'

[47] [fn 42] See Helvering v. Mitchell, 303 U.S. 391, 399, 58 S.Ct. 630, 633, 82 L.Ed. 917; Treas.Regs. on Procedural Rules (1954 Code) s 601.103(a).

[48] [fn 43] See Riordan, Must You Pay Full Tax Assessment Before Suing in the District Court? 8 J.Tax. 179, 181:

'1. If the Government is forced to use these remedies (distraint) on a large scale, it will affect adversely taxpayers' willingness to perform under our voluntary assessment system.

'2. It will put the burden on the Government to seek out for seizure the property of every taxpayer who chooses to sue for the refund of a partial payment. Often, the Government will not be able to do this without extraordinary and costly effort and in some cases it may not be able to do it at all.

'3. The use of the drastic-collection remedies would often cause inconvenience and perhaps hardship to the creditors, debtors, employers, employees, banks and other persons doing business with the taxpayer.'

construed, requires full payment of the assessment before an income tax refund suit can be maintained in a Federal District Court.

Affirmed.

[Dissenting opinion omitted.]

NOTES AND QUESTIONS

1. The issue of whether the full payment rule applies to penalties and interest as well as tax is treated inconsistently among the refund forums. In the Court of Federal Claims, the full payment rule applies to tax only. *See* Shore v. United States, 9 F.3d 1524 (Fed. Cir. 1993). Recent cases in federal district court have required full payment of an entire assessment, including any penalties and interest. *See, e.g.*, Magnone v. United States, 902 F.2d 192 (2d Cir. 1990).
2. What interpretive approach does the majority take?
3. Why impute a "surer grammatical touch" to Congress?
4. What would happen to Tax Court litigation if taxpayers were not required to make full payment before litigating in federal district court?

4. Exceptions to the Full Payment Rule

Although *Flora* definitively decided that a taxpayer must have paid the entire tax amount for jurisdiction to lie in a refund forum, the rule does not apply to every situation. In the case of a tax owed by many different taxpayers, it does not make sense to require each taxpayer to pay the full amount before suing when the amounts are divisible among the taxpayers. This is known as the divisible tax exception as discussed in the following case.

STEELE v. UNITED STATES
280 F.2d 89 (1960)
United States Court of Appeals Eighth Circuit

Before JOHNSEN, Chief Judge, and MATTHES, Circuit Judge.
OPINION
PER CURIAM.

Penalties were assessed administratively against the president and the secretary of Davidson-Steele, Inc., in the amount of $5,186.47 as to each officer for willfully failing to pay over to the Internal Revenue Service the withholdings of income taxes and social security taxes made by the corporation from the wages of its employees.

Each officer made a payment of $50 to the Internal Revenue Service on the amount of the assessment against him, and they thereafter brought suit in the District Court for refund of these payments, on the ground that the penalties were erroneously and illegally assessed against them.

The Government moved to dismiss the action, contending that, under the holding in Flora v. United States, 357 U.S. 63, 78 S.Ct. 1079, 2 L.Ed.2d 1165, no right to sue for refund could exist, because the entire penalty had not been paid.

The District Court dismissed the action on this basis, 172 F.Supp. 793, and the plaintiffs have appealed.

The Government now in effect concedes that it was in error in the position which it took in the District Court; that the withholdings involved constituted separate taxes as to the individual employees of the corporation; and that the penalties imposed similarly would be entitled to be regarded as divisible assessments made in relation to the individual withholdings.

A stipulation has been presented to us in which the parties agree that the situation is subject to the recognition made in footnotes 37 and 38 of the 171 and 175, 80 S.Ct. 630, at pages 644 and 646, 4 L.Ed.2d 623, that the full-payment rule is not applicable to an assessment of divisible taxes; and that on this basis the judgments herein should be reversed and the case remanded to the District Court for further proceedings on the merits.

We are in accord with and accept the view and implication of the stipulation that the penalties imposed amounted legally, under §§ 6671 and 6672 of the Internal Revenue Code of 1954, 26 U.S.C.A., to divisible assessments or taxes against the officers, in their relationship to and predication upon the separate taxes of the individual employees. Thus, the officers would be legally entitled to make payment of the amount of the penalty applicable to the withheld taxes of any individual employee, to make claim for refund, and to institute suit for recovery, as a means of settling the question of the right of the Government to have made penalty assessment against them personally in the circumstances of the situation.

The judgment as to each appellant is accordingly reversed, and the case is remanded for further proceedings on the merits.

Another exception follows from the full payment rule. It does not make sense to require payment of a tax liability to request a refund where the IRS has admitted it has already received an overpayment and owes the taxpayer that amount. This is a long-standing exception, known as the "account stated" exception, discussed in the following case.

BONWIT TELLER & CO. v. UNITED STATES
283 U.S. 258 (1931)
Supreme Court of the United States

Mr. Justice BUTLER delivered the opinion of the Court.

This action was brought to recover the amount of an overpayment of income tax for the year ended January 31, 1919, as determined by the Commissioner of Internal Revenue and shown in his certificate, No. 990,988, issued to plaintiff May 12, 1927. The government first filed a general traverse. But later, asserting lack of authority on the part of the Commissioner to make the determination and refund, it filed a counterclaim for the amount of a check sent plaintiff to pay the balance of the refund remaining after deducting a part to pay an additional tax assessed against it for the year ended January 31, 1917. That tax was then, as it is now conceded, barred by a statute of limitation. Bowers v. N.Y. & Albany Co., 273 U.S. 346, 47 S. Ct. 389, 71 L. Ed. 676. On special findings the court entered judgment dismissing plaintiff's complaint and the government's counterclaim, but gave the latter judgment for the cost of printing the record. 69 Ct. Cl. 638; (Ct. Cl.) 39 F. (2d) 730. On plaintiff's petition we granted a writ of certiorari. 282 U.S. 823, 51 S. Ct. 34, 75 L. Ed. ——.

The court found:

Plaintiff is a corporation engaged in the business of selling merchandise at retail. Its fiscal year begins February 1. July 14, 1919, it filed its return for the year ended January 31, 1919, reporting an income tax of $57,871.16 which was paid, one-half July 14 and the balance December 13 following. Pending audit of the return, the Commissioner fixed plaintiff's total tax liability for that year at $225,165.75 and in April, 1924, made a jeopardy assessment for $167,294.59, the excess over the amount returned and paid. The plaintiff promptly filed a claim for abatement of the full amount of the additional assessment.

November 19, 1924, the Bureau sent plaintiff a letter containing a schedule disclosing the computation of its tax for the year ended January 31, 1919, and showing a total overassessment of $178,161.02. From this amount there was deducted $10,866.43 found by the Commissioner to have been erroneously included in plaintiff's return and paid. The letter stated: 'Inasmuch as the provisions of section 281 of the Revenue Act of 1924[49] have not been complied with (in) regard to the full amount of the above overassessment, a portion in the amount of $10,866.43 cannot be allowed.' In accordance with that letter, the Commissioner allowed plaintiff's claim for abatement.

---

[49] [fn 1] Section 281, 43 Stat. 301 (26 USCA s 1065 note):

'(b) Except as provided in subdivision * * * (e) * * * no such credit or refund shall be allowed or made after four years from the time the tax was paid, unless before the expiration of such four years a claim therefor is filed by the taxpayer. * * *

'(e) If the taxpayer has, within five years from the time the return for the taxable year 1917 was due, filed a waiver of his right to have the taxes due for such taxable year determined and assessed within five years after the return was filed, or if he has, on or before June 15, 1924, filed such a waiver in respect of the taxes due for the taxable year 1918, then such credit or refund relating to the taxes for the year in respect of which the waiver was filed shall be allowed or made if claim therefor is filed either on or before April 1, 1925, or within four years from the time the tax was paid.

'(f) This section shall not * * * (2) bar from allowance a claim in respect of a tax for the taxable year 1919 or 1920 if such claim is filed before the expiration of five years after the date the return was due.'

May 16, 1925, the Bureau wrote plaintiff that an examination of its income tax return for the year ended January 31, 1919, disclosed an apparent overassessment, and that it could not then be allowed 'unless an income and profits tax waiver is filed on or before June 15, 1925, as provided by an Act of Congress dated March 3, 1925, amending section 281(e) of the Revenue Act of 1924.[50] Two waiver forms are therefore enclosed in order that you may, if you desire, execute and forward one of the forms to this office.' Plaintiff executed the waiver and May 22, 1925, returned it with a letter stating: 'In accordance with your request, we enclose you herewith waiver.' On the following day the waiver was received and accepted in writing by the Commissioner.

December 11, 1926, counsel for plaintiff sent the Bureau a letter which quoted the substance, as above given, of the letters of November 19, 1924, and May 16, 1925, and, in reference to the letter of May 22, 1925, said: 'Since that time we have heard nothing further from you and there has been no refund made to the taxpayer.' February 5, 1927, the head of the audit division approved and recommended for allowance the certificate of overassessment No. 990,988. The record of the case was checked to determine whether the plaintiff had filed a claim for refund prior to the expiration of the applicable period of limitation. And it was determined that the documents filed which included the audit letter of November 19, 1924, showing how the amount of the overpayment was ascertained, the letter of May 16, 1925, furnishing form of waiver, and the plaintiff's answer of May 22 following, inclosing the executed waiver, would be treated by the Bureau as an informal claim for refund filed May 23, 1925.

Plaintiff's letter of May 22, 1925, bears an undated indorsement: 'Inferential demand for the refund upon basis of the schedule sent taxpayer under date of November 19, 1924 * * * Rules and Regulations. Mulligan,' and another dated April 4, 1927: 'Approved by Mr. Mulligan and Mr. Sherwood for scheduling as is. O. Allen.'

February 9, 1927, the Bureau wrote plaintiff's counsel: '* * * In order that the allowance of the overassessment may be made, you are requested to file with this office a claim on the enclosed Form 843 setting forth the basis of the adjustment. * * *' Accordingly plaintiff executed the form and thereon stated that the application should be allowed for the reasons shown in the audit letter of November 19, 1924, a copy of which was attached. And February 17, 1927, plaintiff returned the form with a letter saying: '* * * We enclose herewith for filing, claim for refund in the sum of $10,866.43 * * * on Form 843.' The Claim was received and filed in the Bureau February 19; the Commissioner allowed the

---

[50] [fn 2] Act of March 3, 1925, 43 Stat. 1115 (26 USCA s 1065 note), added to section 281(e):

'If the taxpayer has, on or before June 15, 1925, filed such a waiver in respect of the taxes due for the taxable year 1919, then such credit or refund relating to the taxes for the taxable year 1919 shall be allowed or made if claim therefor is filed either on or before April 1, 1926, or within four years from the time the tax was paid.'

claim and on March 8 approved and scheduled to the collector the certificate of overassessment.

On the margin of the Bureau's record copy appear the following certifications: 'Waiver filed May 23, 1925. Informal claim for refund filed May 23, 1925, with waiver perfected by claim Form 843. (Signed) O. Allen, 3/4/27.' 'Claim for refund filed May 23, 1925, waiver filed May 23, 1925.' 'This C. of O. (certificate of overassessment) approved for scheduling as is by W. T. S. (Signed) O. Allen, 4/4/27.'

The collector credited $9,846.06 against the additional tax assessed for the year ending January 31, 1917. May 12, 1927, the Commissioner caused the certificate, showing the deduction made by the collector, to be delivered to plaintiff with a check for the balance of the overassessment and interest, $1,462.99. Plaintiff objected to the application of any part of the refund against such additional assessment on the ground that the 1917 tax was barred and declined to accept the check in full settlement, but offered to apply it in partial payment of the claim.

The government, in support of the judgment below, insists that no claim for refund was filed by plaintiff prior to April 1, 1926, the time permitted by the Act of March 3, 1925, 43 Stat. 1115, and that therefore the Commissioner was without authority to allow the claim.

The provision involved amends section 281(e) of the Revenue Act of 1924, 43 Stat. 302. It provides that, if the taxpayer has on or before June 15, 1925, filed a waiver of his right to have the tax due for the taxable year 1919 determined and assessed within five years after the return was filed, then refund relating to such tax shall be made if claim therefor is filed on or before April 1, 1926. The section is a part of a tax law giving to taxpayers opportunity to secure refund of overpayments that had become barred. Manifestly it is to be construed liberally in favor of the taxpayers to give the relief it was intended to provide. United States v. Merriam, 263 U.S. 179, 187, 44 S. Ct. 69, 68 L. Ed. 240, 29 A.L.R. 1547; Bowers v. N.Y. & Albany Co., supra, 273 U.S. 350, 47 S. Ct. 389, 71 L. Ed. 676; United States v. Updike, 281 U.S. 489, 496, 50 S. Ct. 367, 74 L. Ed. 984; United States v. Michel, 282 U.S. 656, 51 S. Ct. 284, 75 L. Ed. 598.

Plaintiff filed its waiver within time, and, in consideration of that, it admittedly secured the right to claim the refund. But it did not within the specified time formally make a claim for it. The government's point comes down to the question whether the waiver and the letter transmitting it together with what went before amounted to the filing of a claim within the meaning of the statute.

The Commissioner prior to that amendment had finally determined that in 1919 plaintiff had overpaid its tax by $10,866.43. That finding was made upon a consideration of the plaintiff's tax return, its claim for abatement of the jeopardy assessment, and presumably all material details of its business in the taxable year. The schedule contained in the audit letter of November 19, 1924, showed the manner in which the Bureau had computed the tax. And the refund of the ascertained overpayment was withheld by the Commissioner solely because of plaintiff's lack of compliance with section 281 as it then stood.

The letter of May 16, 1925, sent soon after section 281 was amended unmistakably referred to the overpayment that the Commissioner had found and reported. That an allowance of credit or refund was immediately intended is shown by the statement that it could not then be allowed unless waiver was filed as provided by the 1925 amendment. Plaintiff's prompt execution and return of the waiver and the Bureau's acceptance of it clearly show that both considered the facts already found and reported a sufficient basis for plaintiff's claim. That such was the view of the Commissioner is fully confirmed by the notations made on the letter transmitting the waiver and upon the office record of the certificate.

The question here is to be distinguished from that which would have arisen if, contrary to the taxpayer's insistence, the Commissioner had held that what was done did not constitute a filing of a claim. No statute provides for review of the Commissioner's determinations in favor of taxpayers when made within the scope of his authority. Such rulings are entitled to much weight. In this case he had already found that in 1919 plaintiff had overpaid its tax in the amount stated. He needed no additional information to enable him to determine whether credit or refund should then be made. There is no suggestion that the allowance was induced by or resulted from fraud or mistake. The facts found disclose that there was a reasonable or substantial compliance with the amendment. The Commissioner within the time allowed was advised of the grounds on which plaintiff's right to refund rested, and was not misled or deceived by plaintiff's failure to file formal claim and was fully warranted in holding that the waiver and earlier documents were sufficient. Tucker v. Alexander, 275 U.S. 228, 231, 48 S. Ct. 45, 72 L. Ed. 253.

The government further contends that, even if the Commissioner's allowance was authorized, this suit is barred by Rev. St. s 3226, as amended. 26 U.S.C., s 156 (26 USCA s 156).[51] It provides that no suit for the recovery of any internal revenue tax alleged to have been erroneously collected shall be begun after five years from the payment of such tax. The overpayment made was more than five years before the complaint was filed. This case is not within the clause giving two years after disallowance because here the claim was allowed. Plaintiff pleads its claim in two forms. The first is based upon the issue and delivery of the Commissioner's certificate showing plaintiff entitled to a refund in the amount specified. The second alleges an account stated showing that there is due plaintiff the amount claimed. The action is not for the overpayment of the tax in 1919, but is grounded upon the determination evidenced by the certificate issued by the Commissioner May 12, 1927. Upon delivery of the certificate to plaintiff, there

---

[51] [fn 3] 'No suit * * * for the recovery of any internal-revenue tax alleged to have been erroneously or illegally assessed or collected * * * shall be begun * * * after the expiration of five years from the date of the payment of such tax * * * unless such suit * * * is begun within two years after the disallowance of the part of such claim to which such suit * * * relates. * * *'

arose the cause of action on which this suit was brought. United States v. Kaufman, 96 U.S. 567, 570, 24 L. Ed. 792; United States v. Real Estate Savings Bank, 104 U.S. 728, 26 L. Ed. 908; Bank of Greencastle's Case, 15 Ct. Cl. 225. There is no merit in the contention that the suit is barred.

Judgment reversed.

NOTES AND QUESTIONS

1. Are *Steele* and *Bonwit Teller* actual exceptions to the *Flora* rule of full payment?
2. Why did the taxpayers in *Bonwit Teller* sue the government?

5. Stipulations Before Trial

As discussed in the last chapter, Tax Court rules require the parties to stipulate to everything they can reasonably stipulate to. Refund forums work differently. Procedure rules in the refund forums do not require stipulations. The parties are permitted to stipulate, and some district courts have local court rules that encourage stipulation. But this is not the same as requiring stipulation and providing a remedy for it. That said, a judge in a refund forum has the authority to require the parties to stipulate, as in the following case.

INTERNATIONAL PAPER CO. v. UNITED STATES
39 Fed. Cl. 478 (1997)
United States Court of Federal Claims

REGINALD W. GIBSON, Senior Judge.
INTRODUCTION
Currently pending before the court is plaintiff's motion for partial summary judgment, filed May 27, 1997, in the above-referenced federal income tax refund case. In said motion, plaintiff contends that, as a matter of law, each of its four (4) Alabama and Mississippi timber depletion blocks that were damaged or destroyed by Hurricane Frederic in September of 1979 is a "single, identifiable property" (i.e., the SIP), within the meaning of Treas. Reg. § 1.165–7(b)(2), for purposes of determining the limitation on the amount of its casualty loss deduction pursuant to 26 U.S.C. § 165(a) (hereinafter, the "Hurricane Frederic Casualty Loss SIP Issue").[52] Summary judgment is proper only where there is no

---

[52] [fn 1] Plaintiff's complaint, filed February 6, 1990, raised nine (9) separate substantive refund issues. On April 27, 1995, plaintiff was granted summary judgment on three issues. International Paper Co. v. United States, 33 Fed.Cl. 384 (1995). Thereafter, the parties settled an additional four issues in October of 1996. Joint Memorandum Re: Issues & Damages, filed October 11, 1996. Thereafter, an eighth issue was tentatively settled, pending approval by the Joint Committee On Taxation pursuant to 26 U.S.C. § 6405(a). Joint Status Report On

dispute as to any genuine issue of material fact and the moving party is entitled to judgment as a matter of law. RCFC 56(c); Lane Bryant, Inc. v. United States, 35 F.3d 1570, 1574 (Fed.Cir.1994).

At first blush, the Hurricane Frederic Casualty Loss SIP Issue seems ripe for summary disposition, inasmuch as defendant avers that it "does not oppose plaintiff's motion for partial summary judgment on the issue whether the single, identifiable properties damaged or destroyed are the four depletion blocks that were affected by Hurricane Frederic." *See* Defendant's Response To Plaintiff's Motion For Partial Summary Judgment, filed July 23, 1997. Moreover, at a status conference held on September 25, 1997, defendant unequivocally conceded, on the record, that no genuine issues of material fact exist with respect to the Hurricane Frederic Casualty Loss SIP Issue.[53] Pursuant to the aforesaid status conference, the court directed the parties to "file a joint stipulation as to *all* operative facts relating to the dispositive SIP issue." Order Dated September 25, 1997 (emphasis added). Thereafter, the parties filed a responsive joint stipulation, containing the following provisions *in haec verba*:

1. International Paper is an integrated, world-wide forest products company principally engaged in the production and sale of pulp, paper, packaging, lumber, and plywood products.

2. International Paper maintains substantial timberlands to help ensure an adequate source of raw material (merchantable timber) to its various manufacturing facilities.

3. International Paper separates its timber holdings into different timber depletion blocks, generally based on whether the timber is owned in fee or held pursuant to a long-term lease and also based on geographic or political boundaries.

4. In Alabama and Mississippi, International Paper's timber depletion blocks include Alabama Fee, Alabama U.S. Steel, Alabama Lease, and Mississippi Fee. In 1979 these blocks collectively contained approximately 1.4 million acres of timber. Each block has been maintained for many years.

5. In 1979, International Paper's timber depletion accounts were the original sources of all the historical cost basis of the timber within each block for both financial and accounting purposes, and were used for timber tax depletion and financial operational purposes.

6. On September 12, 1979, and continuing into the next day, Hurricane Frederic struck the coasts of Mississippi, Alabama, and Florida.

7. The storm moved along the Mississippi–Alabama state line and caused extensive damage to property in seven counties in Mississippi and four counties

---

Further Proceedings, filed February 21, 1997; Transcript Of Status Conference Held September 25, 1997, at 3–4, 17. Thus, only plaintiff's refund claim relating to Count IV, timber casualty losses caused by Hurricane Frederic, remains for the court's decision on the merits.

[53] [fn 2] Transcript Of Status Conference Held September 25, 1997, at 5–7. Moreover, defendant reiterated that it concedes said issue on the merits. Id. at 4.

in Alabama. Lighter damage occurred in an additional 10 counties in Mississippi, Alabama, and Florida.

8. International Paper had extensive timber holdings in the affected counties in Alabama and Mississippi. These timber holdings include the Alabama Fee, Alabama U.S. Steel, Alabama Lease, and Mississippi Fee timber depletion blocks.

9. In 1979, hurricane damage to IP's [International Paper's] timber was not covered by insurance. [And]

10. Two of IP's principal competitors in the Southeast United States are Westvaco and Weyerhaeuser.

Joint Stipulations Of Fact, filed October 6, 1997 ("Jt.Stip."). For the reasons stated hereinafter, it is not immediately apparent that the parties have fully complied with the court's directive to stipulate as to *all* the operative facts relating to the Hurricane Frederic Casualty Loss SIP Issue. Yet, upon thoughtful consideration of the legal principles governing the determination of the SIP in the context of timber casualty losses, we conclude that plaintiff is entitled to summary judgment on the Hurricane Frederic Casualty Loss SIP Issue.

DISCUSSION

In explicating the operative factual elements of the SIP determination in the case of timber casualty losses, the Court of Appeals for the Federal Circuit has declared that, as a matter of law, the SIP is the timber depletion block "when that property serves for *commercial, forest management, and depletion purposes.*" *Weyerhaeuser Co. v. United States,* 92 F.3d 1148, 1151 (Fed.Cir.1996) (emphasis added), *cert. denied,* 519 U.S. 1091, 117 S.Ct. 766, 136 L.Ed.2d 713 (1997), *aff'g in part and rev'g in part,* 32 Fed. Cl. 80 (1994).[54] Thus, a proffered timber property must serve three rather simplistic purposes in order to be deemed the SIP damaged or destroyed: (i) a commercial purpose; (ii) a forest management purpose; and (iii) a depletion purpose. This appears to be so, irrespective of the size of the block and whether the quantum thereof actually damaged or destroyed is substantial or *de minimis.* In the case at bar, the *stipulated facts* plainly and irrefutably establish that plaintiff's four timber depletion blocks served depletion purposes. Jt. Stip. at ¶ 5.

Less certain, on the facts as stipulated, is the extent to which commercial and forest management purposes influenced plaintiff's designation, maintenance, and use of its timber depletion blocks. Had the parties simply stipulated *in haec verba* that plaintiff's four timber depletion blocks serve "commercial [and] forest management . . . purposes," consistent with the Federal Circuit's pronouncement in *Weyerhaeuser, supra,* the conclusion would effortlessly follow that no genuine issue of material fact precludes summary judgment. However, rather than follow

---

[54] [fn 3] The depletion block is "the area into which the taxpayer aggregates its timber according to logical standards . . . such as geographical or political boundaries, management areas, or manufacturing points . . . [and is] that subdivision of a taxpayer's forest holdings selected as a means of tracking the adjusted basis in the timber." *Weyerhaeuser,* 92 F.3d at 1150. See generally Treas. Reg. § 1.611–3.

the straightforward, unconvoluted approach to drafting their stipulations of fact, the parties elected instead to aver vaguely that plaintiff's timber depletion accounts supplied the historical cost data of the timber within each depletion block for "both financial and accounting purposes" and, further, that said accounts were used for "financial operational purposes." Jt. Stip. at ¶ 5. In addition, the parties stipulated that plaintiff's division of its timber holdings into different depletion blocks is based on "whether the timber is owned in fee or held pursuant to a long-term lease," as well as on the basis of "geographic or political boundaries." Jt. Stip. at ¶ 3.[55] Consequently, the court must consider, on this record—whether the parties' choice of language presents or, more precisely, fails to negate a genuine issue of material fact pertinent to the Hurricane Frederic Casualty Loss SIP Issue.

It is axiomatic that the parties may not stipulate the court into error, for the court may disregard any stipulation that is inadvertent, contrary to law, contrary to fact, or made without proper authority. *Kaminer Constr. Corp. v. United States,* 203 Ct.Cl. 182, 197, 488 F.2d 980, 988 (1973).[56] The parties quite rightly declined to stipulate that each of plaintiff's four depletion blocks constitutes a SIP, for the Federal Circuit has unequivocally held that the SIP determination presents a question of law. *Weyerhaeuser,* 92 F.3d at 1151. That the litigants cannot bind the court with a stipulation of law has been long settled, and is clear beyond cavil. *Swift & Co. v. Hocking Valley Ry. Co.,* 243 U.S. 281, 289, 37 S.Ct. 287, 289–90, 61 L.Ed. 722 (1917).[57]

For precisely the same reason, it is an incomplete answer to say that defendant, by virtue of its written and oral statements, has conceded the Hurricane Frederic Casualty Loss SIP Issue by judicial admission. A judicial admission is a "formal act, done in the course of judicial proceedings, which waives or dispenses with *the production of evidence,* by conceding for purposes of litigation that *the proposition of fact* alleged by the opponent is true." *Hofer v. Bituminous Casualty Corp.,* 260 Iowa 81, 148 N.W.2d 485, 486 (1967), *quoted*

---

[55] [fn 4] Commercial and forest management purposes are no doubt evident in plaintiff's status as "an integrated, world-wide forest products company" which "maintains substantial timberlands to help ensure an adequate source of raw material (merchantable timber) to its various manufacturing facilities." Jt. Stip. at ¶¶ 1–2. However, merely regurgitating or parroting the truism that plaintiff is engaged in the timber business fails to ipso facto establish commercial and forest management rationales for plaintiff's designation of certain timberlands as depletion blocks.

[56] [fn 5] Decisions of the former Court of Claims are binding precedent for this Court, as well as for the Federal Circuit unless overruled by that Court en banc. South Corp. v. United States, 690 F.2d 1368 (Fed.Cir.1982) (en banc).

[57] [fn 6] Were it otherwise, the court would forsake that bedrock principle of American jurisprudence, announced many years ago by Mr. Chief Justice Marshall: "It is emphatically the province of the judicial department to say what the law is." Marbury v. Madison, 5 U.S. (1 Cranch) 137, 177, 2 L.Ed. 60 (1803).

with approval in Weyerhaeuser, 32 Fed.Cl. at 118 (emphasis added) (additional citations omitted). Thus, from an *evidentiary* viewpoint, "[j]udicial admissions are conclusively binding on the party asserting them." *Id.* (citing *Western World Ins. Co. v. Stack Oil, Inc.,* 922 F.2d 118, 122 (2d Cir.1990); *American Title Ins. Co. v. Lacelaw Corp.,* 861 F.2d 224, 226 (9th Cir.1988)). In the present case, the court finds that defendant's oral statements on the record in open court and its written submissions are the sort of "deliberate, clear and unequivocal" formal acts which constitute judicial admissions. *Anderson Bros. Corp. v. O'Meara,* 306 F.2d 672, 676 (5th Cir.1962). Yet defendant's judicial admissions are not dispositive of the controlling question of *law, i.e.,* the SIP determination. On the contrary, the sole function of defendant's judicial admissions, as with the parties' joint stipulations of fact, is to conclusively establish the uncontroverted character of the *facts* thereby averred, for purposes of deciding plaintiff's motion for partial summary judgment. Defendant's lack of opposition to the pending motion means only that the court *may,* in its discretion, enter summary judgment insofar as defendant, the nonmoving party, has elected not to "set forth specific facts showing that there is a genuine issue for trial." RCFC 56(e). *See Anderson v. Liberty Lobby, Inc.,* 477 U.S. 242, 249–50, 106 S.Ct. 2505, 2510–11, 91 L.Ed.2d 202 (1986). However, whether the court *must* enter summary judgment depends upon whether the parties' stipulations of fact meet plaintiff's initial burden of production under RCFC 56(c). *Id.* at 250 n. 4, 106 S.Ct. at 2511 n. 4; *Celotex Corp. v. Catrett,* 477 U.S. 317, 323, 106 S.Ct. 2548, 2552–53, 91 L.Ed.2d 265 (1986). To this question we now turn.

At the threshold, the operative question presented is—whether the parties' stipulations of fact obviate the need for a trial as to the Hurricane Frederic Casualty Loss SIP Issue, *i.e.,* "whether, in other words, there are any genuine factual issues that properly can be resolved only by a finder of fact because they may reasonably be resolved in favor of either party." *Anderson,* 477 U.S. at 250, 106 S.Ct. at 2511. Consistent with this principle, the court's inquiry in ruling on plaintiff's motion for partial summary judgment "necessarily implicates the substantive evidentiary standard of proof that would apply at the trial on the merits." *Id.* at 252, 106 S.Ct. at 2512. Therefore, entry of partial summary judgment for plaintiff is proper only if the court, sitting as the trier of fact, could reasonably conclude that the parties' stipulations of fact establish the three operative factual elements of the SIP determination by a preponderance of the evidence.[58]

As already noted herein, *supra,* the court regards the "depletion purpose" element as proven by virtue of the parties' stipulations. But the inquiry does not end there, for the parties' stipulations must also support a reasonable factual inference that plaintiff has created and used its four depletion blocks with commercial and forest management purposes in mind. *Weyerhaeuser,* 92 F.3d at

---

[58] [fn 7] Also relevant, but not materially so, are the affidavits submitted with plaintiff's motion for partial summary judgment. The parties' stipulations of fact reproduce in all significant respects the averments in said affidavits.

1151. While it is undeniable that the parties may freely stipulate to whatever facts they desire, *"the trial court has a duty to reject stipulations which are demonstrably false." Dillon, Read & Co., Inc. v. United States*, 875 F.2d 293, 300 (Fed.Cir.1989) (emphasis added). On the other hand, "at the summary judgment stage the judge's function is not to weigh the evidence and determine the truth of the matter but to determine whether there is a genuine issue for trial." *Anderson*, 477 U.S. at 249, 106 S.Ct. at 2511. Having applied these competing considerations to the stipulated facts at bar, the court is satisfied that plaintiff is entitled to judgment, as a matter of law, that each of its four timber depletion blocks constitutes a SIP.

On these stipulated facts, a reasonable trier of fact could logically conclude that commercial and forest management purposes motivate plaintiff's division of its timber holdings into different depletion blocks, since plaintiff makes these designations on the basis of "whether the timber is owned in fee or held pursuant to a long-term lease," as well as on the basis of "geographic or political boundaries." Jt. Stip. at ¶ 3. As an integrated forest products company, plaintiff undoubtedly has sound commercial and forest management reasons for keeping leased timberlands and owned timberlands separate and distinct. In the former case, but not the latter, it certainly seems plausible that commercial and forest management decisions would take contractual relations with a lessor into account. Likewise, political boundaries may very well affect how timberlands are managed from the standpoint of compliance with applicable state forestry laws, and geographic boundaries surely raise the implications of differing climatic and soil conditions upon the choice of silvicultural practices. The parties also stipulate that plaintiff used its timber depletion accounts relating to each depletion block for "financial operational purposes," and as the source of historical cost data of the timber within each depletion block for "both financial and accounting purposes." Jt. Stip. at ¶ 5. To infer commercial purposes from this language does not strain credulity. Moreover, where an integrated forest products company is concerned, the reference to "financial *operational* purposes" suggests a link to forest management decisions.

In sum, therefore, a reasonable trier of fact could find that the parties' stipulations of fact make out a *prima facie* case that the four timber properties designated by plaintiff as depletion blocks served "commercial, forest management, and depletion purposes," as a matter of law. *Weyerhaeuser*, 92 F.3d at 1151. As a consequence of defendant's unequivocal acquiescence to plaintiff's motion for partial summary judgment, there is no countervailing evidence. Accordingly, a reasonable trier of fact could rationally conclude, on the basis of this *prima facie* case, that the three operative factual elements of the SIP determination have been established by the necessary preponderance of the evidence. Plaintiff is, therefore, entitled to summary judgment on the Hurricane Frederic Casualty Loss SIP Issue.

Our conclusion finds independent support in the formulation of the rule laid down by the Federal Circuit in *Weyerhaeuser, id.* Although the Federal Circuit failed to expressly address the relative importance of the three operative factual elements of the SIP determination, it seems manifestly apparent that the "depletion purpose" element, so plainly demonstrated here at bar, is entitled to predominant weight.[59] In *Weyerhaeuser,* the findings, at trial, amply supported the conclusion that the "tree stand," a physical unit of timber much smaller in area than the depletion block, served many commercial and forest management purposes. *Weyerhaeuser,* 32 Fed.Cl. at 111–18. Notwithstanding its disagreement with the ultimate conclusion below that each tree stand constituted a SIP, the Federal Circuit declined to hold that *any* of the findings of fact at trial were clearly erroneous. *Weyerhaeuser,* 92 F.3d 1148 *passim.* Ergo, the fact that the taxpayer's proffered SIP designation—the depletion block—corresponded to its timber property designation for "depletion purposes" plainly tipped the evidentiary scales in the taxpayer's favor.

In short, *Weyerhaeuser* appears to instruct that a proffer of the depletion block as the SIP tends to foreclose somewhat the factual inquiry into the taxpayer's designation of its timber properties for "commercial" and "forest management" purposes.[60] Here at bar, each of the plaintiff's four timber depletion blocks is proffered as a SIP. Furthermore, in the posture of summary disposition pursuant to RCFC 56, there need not be an evidentiary record on which formal findings of fact might be based. *Anderson,* 477 U.S. at 250, 106 S.Ct. at 2511; *Celotex,* 477 U.S. at 323, 106 S.Ct. at 2552–53. Lacking a discernible mandate to engage in a searching factual inquiry as to how plaintiff's timber properties are designated for commercial and forest management purposes, the court is constrained to conclude that the parties' stipulations of fact comply in all material respects with the standard for timber SIP determinations set out in *Weyerhaeuser,* 92 F.3d at 1151. Thus, inasmuch as no genuine issue of *material* fact exists with respect to the Hurricane Frederic Casualty Loss SIP Issue, plaintiff is entitled to judgment as a matter of law.

CONCLUSION

Based upon the foregoing analysis, plaintiff's motion for partial summary judgment, filed on May 27, 1997, is hereby GRANTED. With respect to the amount of tax refund relating to the court's resolution of the Hurricane Frederic Casualty Loss SIP Issue in plaintiff's favor, the parties are hereby directed to file a joint status report with the court no later than December 15, 1997. Said joint status report shall explain the progress of the parties' efforts to reach agreement on the proper measure of the diminution in the fair market value of the four

---

[59] [fn 8] The Federal Circuit's *Weyerhaeuser* opinion cannot be faithfully read to imply that the "depletion purpose" element is entitled to dispositive weight, since the "commercial" and "forest management" purposes would thereby be rendered mere surplusage.

[60] [fn 9] Precisely how much this factual inquiry is constrained remains uncertain. The answer presumably awaits a timber casualty loss case in which the taxpayer's timber depletion blocks are constituted solely for tax depletion purposes, and serve no commercial or forest management purposes whatever. This difficult question is not squarely presented here.

timber depletion blocks damaged by Hurricane Frederic, in accordance with the court's order dated September 25, 1997.[61]

IT IS SO ORDERED.

NOTES AND QUESTIONS

1. Why would a judge require the parties to stipulate in a forum where stipulation is not usually required?
2. What is the difference between a judicial admission and a stipulation?
3. Who is bound by a judicial admission from an evidentiary standpoint?

6. Depositions

As discussed, depositions in Tax Court are an extraordinary discovery method. In refund forums, depositions are ordinary. Rule 30 of the Federal Rules of Civil Procedure provides as follows:

> A party may, by oral questions, depose any person, including a party, without leave of court except as provided in Rule 30(a)(2). The deponent's attendance may be compelled by subpoena under Rule 45.

Accordingly, if a taxpayer does not want to be bothered with providing oral testimony to the Department of Justice prior to trial, the Tax Court is a better choice.

---

[61] [fn 10] Having resolved the principal disputed issue of law presented by this claim, the court is confident that the parties can settle the few remaining issues of fact relating to the amount of the tax refund due to plaintiff, so as to bring this litigation to a close without a lengthy trial held solely on the issue of damages. For each of the four timber depletion blocks damaged by Hurricane Frederic, plaintiff's casualty loss deduction is limited to the lesser of (i) the diminution in the fair market value of the depletion block as a result of the casualty event; or (ii) the amount of the adjusted basis of the depletion block. Treas. Reg. § 1.165–7(b)(1). The adjusted basis of each of the four depletion blocks in question is undisputed, as defendant admitted in its response, dated April 15, 1992, to plaintiff's Request For Admission No. 284. See also Transcript Of Status Conference Held September 25, 1997, at 11 (defendant conceding same). As to the other element bearing upon the determination of plaintiff's deductible casualty loss, it is clear that plaintiff has the burden of proving that the damage and destruction wrought by Hurricane Frederic diminished the fair market value of the SIP. Westvaco Corp. v. United States, 225 Ct.Cl. 436, 445, 639 F.2d 700, 707 (1980). See also id. at 469–70, 639 F.2d at 720–21 (to same effect, remanding for determination of the diminution in the fair market value of the timber properties damaged or destroyed).

7. Estimates During Trial

In *Cohan v. Commissioner*, the Second Circuit required the Tax Court to accept estimates of items the taxpayer has established, such as an allowable deduction, of which the exact amount is unknown. Refund forums are less supportive of taxpayers who desire that the court accept estimates. The taxpayer in the next case learned this the hard way.

WILLIAMS v. UNITED STATES
245 F.2d 559 (1957)
United States Court of Appeals Fifth Circuit

Before RIVES, JONES and BROWN, Circuit Judges.
JOHN R. BROWN, Circuit Judge.

On a trial without a jury, the District Court held that Taxpayer, president, director and substantial stockholder (approximately 40%) of W. Horace Williams Company, Inc., had not brought forward '* * * sufficient evidence to establish with any reasonable certainty the amount of * * * entertainment and other expenses.' On that the court made a conclusion of law that 'The expense allowance to * * * (Taxpayer) * * * was not substantiated as an entertainment expense, and constitutes additional compensation to * * *' him.

The facts are amazingly simple: W. Horace Williams Company, Inc., incorporated in 1950, was established as a successor to the partnership of W. Horace Williams Company, which the evidence showed, and the Court found, was a large, highly successful and reputable engineering construction company operating principally in Louisiana. At the outset the Board of Directors, acting independently, by formal resolution fixed the president's salary at $3500 per month, and, in keeping with the previous years' practice while the business was operated as a partnership, granted an expense allowance of $500 per month ($6,000 per year) for which he would not have to account. Its purpose was to enable the president to engage in extensive entertainment of executives and responsible leaders of potential customers of the firm without subjecting him to the tedious responsibility of detailed accounting for such expenditures. There is no suggestion or finding, and none would be warranted,[62] that its purpose was tax evasion or avoidance.

---

[62] [fn 1] In companion litigation by the corporation, the Court held (no appeal was taken by the Government) that the salary of $42,000, considering the president's standing, ability and contribution to the gross business and profits of the corporation, was reasonable and that, while the $6,000 deducted by the corporation specifically as entertainment allowance paid to the president, was not adequately established as such by proof of entertainment expenses paid or incurred, it, added to the $42,000, was reasonable compensation for his services and hence deductible by the corporation as an ordinary and necessary business

But the Taxpayer made no effort to establish how much he spent or in any way identify any of its with respect to any particular entertainment, either of event, persons, or amounts. All he could say was that he was certain that he spent all or more than all of it in paying for food, liquor and travel in the entertainment of customers. The Court did not reject this as untrustworthy, suspicious or morally doubtful evidence. On the contrary, the Court held that Taxpayer '* * * doubtless did have certain entertainment and other expenses in 1950 in connection with the performance of his duties as president of * * *' the corporation.

What the Court held was that in a suit for refund, the burden is on the Taxpayer to show the tax wrongfully collected Reinecke v. Spalding, 280 U.S. 227, 50 S.Ct. 96, 74 L.Ed. 385; Helvering v. Taylor, 293 U.S. 507, 55 S.Ct. 287, 79 L.Ed. 623, and this carries a burden of demonstrating with some substantiality how much entertainment expense was actually paid or incurred.

That the trier, whether District Court of Tax Court, might have considerable latitude[63] in making estimates of amounts probably spent in the light of accepted practice amongst law-abiding businessmen of moral standing considering the nature and kind of records which might reasonably be kept for such expenditures, Cohan v. Commissioner, 2 Cir., 39 F.2d 540, 543, certainly does not require that such latitude be employed. The District Court may not be compelled to guess, or estimate. It may not be compelled to estimate even though such an estimate, if made, might have been affirmed. For the basic requirement is that there be sufficient evidence to satisfy the trier that at least the amount allowed in the estimate was in fact spent or incurred for the stated purpose. Until the trier has that assurance from the record, relief to the taxpayer would be unguided largesse.

Here the evidence did not offer that assurance to the District Court. His negative finding of insufficient evidence to afford a guide for the allowance of all claimed or, if not that, as a lesser amount a fair estimate, was not clearly

---

expense. Approximately $2500 in other entertainment expenses identified on the corporation's books and paid directly by it was also allowed.

[63] [fn 2] The Taxpayer points also to Heil Beauty Supplies, Inc. v. Commissioner, 1950 P.H. T.C. Mem. Dec. #50305, affirmed 8 Cir., 199 F.2d 193, and Revenue Ruling 54 195, C.B. 1954-1, p. 47: 'Due consideration should be given to the reasonableness of the taxpayer's stated expenditures for the claimed purposes in relation to his reported income, to the reliability and accuracy of his records in connection with other items more readily lending themselves to detailed recordkeeping, and to the general credibility of his statements in the light of the entire record of the case. Disallowing amounts claimed for such items merely because there is available no documentary evidence which will establish the precise amount beyond any reasonable doubt ignores commonly-recognized business practice as well as the fact that proof may be established by credible oral testimony.'

See also the recent case, The Home Sales Company v. Commissioner, CCH Dec. 22,379(M), T.C. Mem. 1957-78.

erroneous, Fed.Rules Civ.Proc. rule 52(a), 28 U.S.C.A. Certainly we could not compel the Court to allow the full $6,000 and between that figure and zero, the Taxpayer offered not a single guide, by illustration or otherwise upon which to exercise the asserted capacity to resolve by estimation. The Taxpayer failed reasonably to establish, § 22(n)(3), 26 U.S.C.A. 1952 Ed. 22(n)(3), the '* * * expenses paid or incurred by the taxpayer, in connection with the performance by him of services as an employee, under a reimbursement or other expense allowance arrangement with his employer * * *.'

Affirmed.

NOTES AND QUESTIONS

1. Although the *Cohan* rule has been followed in refund cases, such an occurrence is rare.
2. Why are estimates not normally accepted in refund cases?

Table of Authorities

CASES

All capitalized font indicates a principal case.

STATUTES

Index